Digest of Jurisprudence of the Special Court for Sierra Leone

Digest of Jurisprudence of the Special Court for Sierra Leone

2003-2005

CYRIL LAUCCI

MARTINUS NIJHOFF PUBLISHERS
LEIDEN / BOSTON

A C.I.P. record for this book is available from the Library of Congress.

Printed on acid-free paper.

ISBN-13: 978 90 04 15234 2
ISBN-10: 90 04 15234 2

© 2007 by Koninklijke Brill NV, Leiden, The Netherlands
Koninklijke Brill NV incorporates the imprints Brill, Hotei Publishers,
IDC Publishers, Martinus Nijhoff Publishers and VSP.

www.brill.nl

All rights reserved. No part of this publication may be reproduced, stored in a
retrieval system, or transmitted in any form or by any means, electronic, mechanical,
photocopying, microfilming, recording or otherwise, without written permission
from the Publisher.

Authorization to photocopy items for internal or personal use is granted by Brill
Academic Publishers provided that the appropriate fees are paid directly to The
Copyright Clearance Center, 222 Rosewood Drive, Suite 910, Danvers MA 01923, USA.
Fees are subject to change.

Printed and bound in The Netherlands.

*This book is dedicated to all the victims
of the armed conflict in Sierra Leone,
to orphans, to widows, to former child-soldiers
and to all those who are now condemned to an endless
hand-less begging.*

*This book is also dedicated to my father, who was an orphan of
another war,
And who had beautiful hands with which, as a potter,
he could make magic.*

CONTENTS

Foreword by Honorable Justice Raja Fernando xi
Foreword by Mr. Lovemore Munlo, SC xiii
Introduction xv

PART I

STATUTE OF THE SPECIAL COURT

Article 1 – Competence of the Special Court 1
Article 2 – Crimes against Humanity 26
Article 3 – Violations of Article 3 Common to the Geneva
  Conventions and of Additional Protocol II 33
Article 4 – Other Serious Violations of International
  Humanitarian Law 47
Article 6 – Individual Criminal Responsibility 63
Article 8 – Concurrent Jurisdiction 73
Article 9 – Non Bis in Idem 79
Article 10 – Amnesty 82
Article 13 – Qualification and Appointment of Judges 89
Article 14 – Rules of Procedure and Evidence 99
Article 15 – The Prosecutor 105
Article 17 – Rights of the Accused 111
Article 18 – Judgement 142
Article 19 – Penalties 145
Article 20 – Appellate Proceedings 149

PART II

RULES OF PROCEDURE AND EVIDENCE

Rule 3: Working Language 168
Rule 4: Sittings Away from the Seat of the Special Court 170
Rule 5: Non-Compliance with the Rules 171
Rule 6: Amendment of the Rules 175
Rule 7: Time Limits 178
Rule 7*bis*: Motions for Extension of Time 183
Rule 8: Requests and Orders 193
Rule 15: Disqualification of Judges 196

Rule 16: Absence and Resignation	204
Rule 17: Precedence	206
Rule 19: Functions of the President	207
Rule 21: Functions of the Vice-President	209
Rule 23: The Council of Judges	210
Rule 26*bis*: The Chambers	211
Rule 27: The Trial Chambers	216
Rule 28: Designated Judges	219
Rule 31: Appointment of the Deputy Registrar and Registry Staff	220
Rule 33: Functions of the Registrar	225
Rule 37: Functions of the Prosecutor	231
Rule 39: Conduct of Investigations	232
Rule 40*bis*: Transfer and Provisional Detention of Suspects	235
Rule 44: Appointment and Qualifications of Counsel	241
Rule 45: Defence Office	251
Rule 45*bis*: Declaration of Means by the Accused	281
Rule 46: Misconduct of Counsel	283
Rule 47: Review of Indictment	287
Rule 48: Joinder of Accused or Trials	311
Rule 50: Amendment of Indictment	326
Rule 51: Withdrawal of Indictment	345
Rule 52: Service of Indictment	347
Rule 53: Non-disclosure	352
Rule 54: General Provision	355
Rule 55: Execution of Arrest Warrants	361
Rule 56: Warrant of Arrest to Third States	364
Rule 57: Procedure after Arrest	367
Rule 58: Transfer to the Special Court from Third States	369
Rule 59: Failure to Execute a Warrant of Arrest or Transfer Order	371
Rule 60: Trial in the Absence of the Accused	372
Rule 61: Initial Appearance of Accused and Plea	377
Rule 62: Procedure upon Guilty Plea	384
Rule 64: Detention on Remand	386
Rule 65: Bail	397
Rule 65*bis*: Status Conferences	429
Rule 66: Disclosure of Materials by the Prosecutor	430
Rule 67: Reciprocal Disclosure of Evidence	456
Rule 68: Disclosure of Exculpatory Evidence	459
Rule 69: Protection of Victims and Witnesses	469
Rule 70: Matters Not Subject to Disclosure	500

Rule 72: Preliminary Motions	506
Rule 72*bis*: General Provisions on Applicable Law	539
Rule 73: Motions	542
Rule 73*bis*: Pre-Trial Conference	589
Rule 73 *ter*: Pre-Defence Conference	611
Rule 74: Amicus Curiae	614
Rule 74*bis*: Medical Examination of the Accused	621
Rule 75: Measures for the Protection of Victims and Witnesses	627
Rule 77: Contempt of the Special Court	636
Rule 78: Open Sessions	663
Rule 79: Closed Sessions	666
Rule 81: Records of Proceedings and Preservation of Evidence	678
Rule 82: Joint and Separate Trials	684
Rule 85: Presentation of Evidence	686
Rule 89: General Provisions	697
Rule 90: Testimony of Witnesses	717
Rule 92*bis*: Alternative Proof of Facts	734
Rule 94: Judicial Notice	742
Rule 94*bis*: Testimony of Expert Witnesses	752
Rule 95: Exclusion of Evidence	760
Rule 98: Motion for Judgment of Acquittal	761
Rule 104: Forfeiture of Property	768
Rule 108: Notice of Appeal	775
Rule 110: Record on Appeal	781
Rule 113: Submissions in Reply	782
Rule 115: Additional Evidence	784
Rule 116: Extension of Time Limits	785
Rule 117: Expedited Procedure	786
List of Reviewed Decisions	788
Complete Table of Contents	821
Index	869

FOREWORD BY HONORABLE JUSTICE RAJA FERNANDO, PRESIDENT OF THE SPECIAL COURT FOR SIERRA LEONE

I append my foreword to the present *Digest of Jurisprudence of the Special Court for Sierra Leone* with a non dissimulated pleasure. This book was most relevantly written by Mr. Cyril Laucci, Legal Adviser for the Appeals Chamber of the Special Court for Sierra Leone.

The history of this work may help to underline its relevance.

It was with an unsuspected ingenuousness that we, Judges of the Appeals Chamber, requested Mr. Cyril Laucci, in May 2005, to prepare a compendium of the decisions rendered by our Chamber so far. We could not expect, by the time, the impact of this request and of our Legal Adviser's response that he could, indeed, do "much more than a compendium".

Less than two months later, in early July 2005, we were served with a modestly called "Topical Index of Jurisprudence of the Appeals Chamber" containing references of the "most relevant paragraphs of [our] Decisions where legal findings of the Appeals Chamber can be read", as summarized by Mr. Laucci.

In early August 2005, following a much clever suggestion by Honourable Justice Emmanuel Ayoola, we received a new version of the "Index" containing seventy-two pages of most significant abstracts from the Appeals Chamber Decisions. Once again, we could barely expect the real meaning of Mr. Laucci's announcement that he would, on suggestion from Honourable Justice Renate Winter, "start to work on a new version including Trial Chambers Decisions, which may be used as a publication as part of the Special Court's Legacy Program".

I could barely describe my surprise when, during my visit to the Special Court in October 2005, Mr. Laucci announced me that he was about to finalize an about five hundred fifty pages *Digest* covering the whole jurisprudence of the Special Court, that is more than five hundred decisions. This last number alone was sufficient to feel dizzy: five hundred decisions in barely more than two years time . . . But on top of that, Mr. Laucci still announced that he would not stop there, but that this tome was only a first "mid-term" volume and that he intended to prepare a second volume covering the second period of life of the Court, from now until the final completion of its work.

This summarizes the first merit of Mr. Laucci's *Digest*: putting the work of the Special Court for Sierra Leone in perspective and realizing all the way covered since its creation. As such, this *Digest* is a gift that all Judges and Legal Officers of the Special Court should thank Mr. Laucci for: it gives the opportunity to realize the quantity and the quality of our work and is a timely encouragement for the completion of our task.

This *Digest* will also be a most useful tool, for those working in the Special Court for Sierra Leone, but also for jurists working in the field of International Criminal Law. It is an innovative, unprecedented way of discovering the jurisprudence of an international Court.

No need to say that the initiative of this *Digest* is fully consistent with the Legacy aspect of the Special Court's mandate, to leave behind a heritage that will help Sierra Leone, but also every countries in the world, to prevent the repetition of the dreadful horrors committed during the Sierra Leonean civil war.

I am convinced that this *Digest* will become the reference book as regards the jurisprudence of the Special Court for Sierra Leone.

For all this reasons, I am bent on congratulating Mr. Laucci for his performance and the quality of his *Digest*. I also act as the spokesman of each and every person working for the Special Court for Sierra Leone to give my most sincere thanks to Mr. Laucci for his major contribution to the recognition of our every-day, often challenging work.

Justice Raja Fernando
President of the Special Court for Sierra Leone

FOREWORD BY MR. LOVEMORE MUNLO, SC, REGISTRAR OF THE SPECIAL COURT FOR SIERRA LEONE

It gives me great pleasure to introduce the Digest of Jurisprudence of the Special Court for Sierra Leone, compiled by Mr. Cyril Laucci, Legal Adviser in the Appeals Chamber of the Court.

While the Special Court for Sierra Leone might be regarded as the youngest member in the family of International Criminal *ad hoc* Tribunals, it has, in its short existence, significantly contributed to the development of international criminal jurisprudence. In this regard, the Court's key rulings on the recruitment of child soldiers and forced marriage serve as examples of this contribution.

Due to its unique hybrid structure and location in the country where the conflict took place, the Court has, from its inception, sought to engage the public, on a national and international level, in education and information programmes. This process has now gained increased importance in view of the Court's Completion Strategy and its efforts to leave a tangible legacy for the people of Sierra Leone upon the completion of its operations.

In view of the above, publications such as the Digest of Jurisprudence of the Special Court for Sierra Leone play an important role in the institution's endeavours to promote an active dialogue with the national and international legal community. I trust that this compilation will assist academics and practitioners alike. In ending, I would like to take this opportunity to congratulate the author on his initiative.

Lovemore Green Munlo,
Freetown

INTRODUCTION

During my first month in Freetown, Sierra Leone, I met a journalist. He narrated to me the story of a young Sierra Leonean girl, who witnessed the killing of her parents and who, because she was crying, was poured melted plastic in her eyes. This girl will never read those lines; neither will the countless beggars whose both hands have been chopped turn the pages of this book. But this story, as well as the numerous testimonies of witnesses before the Special Court for Sierra Leone, persuaded me of the urgency of making sure that the main initiative undertaken by the international community to try to provide an answer to their claim for justice be known.

I am only a jurist, though, not an historian. This is not their story that is narrated in this book. The answer to a claim for justice is indictments, trials, convictions or acquittals, and potentially sentences, in the respect of the rights of the Defence, without which so-called justice becomes further injustice. But beyond that, as the thread making the fabric, the ultimate answer is law. This is what this Digest is devoted to. Its aim is to facilitate its discovery.

An Overview of the Special Court for Sierra Leone

The creation of the Special Court for Sierra Leone answers the specific request addressed, on 12 June 2000, by Sierra Leonean President Alhaji Ahmad Tejan Kabbah to the United Nations Secretary-General Kofi Annan to have those responsible for crimes "of concern to all persons in the world" brought before international justice.

By its Resolution 1315(2000) of 14 August 2000, the Security Council decided the creation of an independent special court on the basis of an Agreement to be concluded with the government of Sierra Leone: the resolution requested the Secretary-General to negotiate this Agreement with the authorities of Sierra Leone.

The Agreement was concluded on 16 January 2002.

It provides the establishment of a Special Court for Sierra Leone "to prosecute persons who bear the greatest responsibility for serious violations of international humanitarian law and Sierra Leonean law committed on the territory of Sierra Leone since 30 November 1996". The Statute of the Special Court is annexed to the Agreement.

The Agreement and the Statute describe an unprecedented international jurisdiction, which differs from its sister International Tribunals for the Former Yugoslavia and Rwanda on many aspects. It is composed of a mix of internationally and nationally appointed staff and Judges. Its sit is in Sierra Leone, in the very country where the crimes under its jurisdiction were committed. The crimes themselves are different from those under the jurisdiction of the ICTY and ICTR: Genocide does not appear in the list of crimes, which mentions crimes against humanity (Article 2 of the SCSL Statute), war crimes – namely Violations of Article 3 common to the Geneva Conventions and of Additional Protocol II (Article 3) and Other Serious Violations of International Humanitarian Law (Article 4) –, and crimes under Sierra Leonean Law (Article 5). On the procedural aspect, although Article 14(1) of the SCSL Statute provides that the Rules of Procedure and Evidence of the International Criminal Tribunal for Rwanda shall be applicable mutatis mutandis to the conduct of the legal proceedings before the Special Court, its article 14(2) permits amendments to it under the guidance of the Sierra Leonean Criminal Procedure Act, 1965. The main consequence of this reference to Sierra Leonean criminal procedure – but also of the respective nationalities of the Judges – is a much more Common Law oriented jurisprudence than before the other International tribunals. The Special Court does not rely on United Nations' budget, but is financed by voluntary contributions from States and other supporting institutions.

The first Prosecutor of the Special Court for Sierra Leone, Mr. David Crane, was appointed by the Secretary-General on 17 April 2002. The first Registrar, Mr. Robin Vincent, was appointed on 10 June 2002. The first Judges of the Special Court – five Judges appointed by the Secretary-General and three appointed by the Government of Sierra Leone – were sworn in on 2 December 2002 and composed the then only Trial Chamber and the Appeals Chamber. Chambers were completed in January 2005 by the addition of three additional Judges – two appointed by the Secretary-General, one by the Government of Sierra Leone – who formed the second Trial Chamber. Mr. Desmond De Silva, QC replaced Mr. David Crane as Prosecutor of the special Court in July 2005. Mr. Lovemore G. Munlo, SC replaced Mr. Robin Vincent as Registrar of the Special Court in October 2005.

The Special Court officially began its operations on 1 July 2002. The first Indictments were approved on 7 March 2003 and the first arrests followed. Among the thirteen publicly indicted persons, eleven were arrested. Charles Taylor (Case No. SCSL-03-01) and Johnny Paul Koroma (Case No. SCSL-03-03) still remain at large.[1] Two detainees, Foday Sankoh

---

[1] After the sending of the present Digest to the publisher, Accused Charles Ghankay Taylor has been arrested in Nigeria and transferred to the Special Court on 29 March 2006. His Initial Appearance was held on 3 April 2006 before Hon. Justice Lussick, Presiding Judge of Trial Chamber II. He entered a plea of not guilty on eacn count of the Amended Indictment filed on 17 March 2006.

(Case No. SCSL-03-02) and Sam Bockarie (Case No. SCSL-03-04) died in detention before the commencement of their trial. The cases of the nine remaining Accused were joined on 27 January 2004 in three trials:

- o Accused Sam Hinga Norman (Case No. SCSL-03-08), Moinina Fofana (Case No. SCSL-03-11) and Allieu Kondewa (Case No. SCSL-03-12) had their cases joined in the "Civil Defence Forces (CDF)" trial (Case No. SCSL-04-14), which started on 3 June 2004 before Trial Chamber I.
- o Accused Issa Hassan Sesay (Case No. SCSL-03-05), Morris Kallon (Case No. SCSL-03-07) and Augustine Gbao (Case No. SCSL-03-09) had their cases joined in the "Revolutionary United Front (RUF)" trial (Case No. SCSL-04-15), which started on 5 July 2004, also before Trial Chamber I.
- o Accused Alex Tamba Brima (Case No. SCSL-03-06), Brima Bazzy Kamara (Case No. SCSL-03-10) and Santigie Borbor Kanu (Case No. SCSL-03-13) had their cases joined in the "Armed Forces Revolutionary Council" (AFRC) trial (Case No. SCSL-04-16), which started on 7 March 2005 before Trial Chamber II.

These three cases reflect the main protagonists of the conflict in Sierra Leone:

- o The Civil Defence Forces (CDF) is an armed resistance group, mainly composed of traditional hunters, the *Kamajors*, which fought against the RUF and the AFRC;
- o The Revolutionary United Front (RUF) is the rebel group which started the war in March 1991, signed the Abidjan Peace Accord of 30 November 1996, joined the AFRC in June 1997, signed again the Lomé Peace Accord of 7 July 1999 and then the Abuja Cease-Fire Agreement of 10 November 2000 and the declaration putting an end to the conflict in January 2002;
- o The Armed Forces Revolutionary Council (AFRC) is the military junta which took the power in Sierra Leone after the *coup* of 25 May 1997, shared the power with the RUF, was chased from Freetown in February 1998 by the ECOMOG sent by the ECOWAS and continued to fight until the end of the war.

The CDF and AFRC Cases have now completed the presentation of the Prosecution cases and should start the presentation of the Defence cases by early 2006. The first judgments are expected by Autumn 2006.

Methodology of the Present Digest

The aim of this *Digest* is to present a collection of the most relevant abstracts of decisions, orders and judgments rendered by Chambers since the creation of the Court.

The author does not make any comment on the abstracts or decisions reviewed, but gives some references in footnotes as regards other decisions confirming the finding made in the abstracts. The choice to refrain from commenting the decisions is deliberate: this *Digest* is devised as a tool for practitioners and academics who will enjoy the full opportunity to comment on the legal findings presented to them. The author's only aim is to assist the readers in the discovery of the jurisprudence of the Special Court for Sierra Leone.

For the preparation of the present *Digest*, five hundred forty eight public decisions have been reviewed. These decisions have been rendered by the Trial Chambers, the Appeals Chamber and the President of the Special Court between the 7th of March 2003 and the 31st of December 2005. The author intends to publish a second volume after the completion of the Court's mandate, which will cover the second period of the Special Court's life.

These 548 decisions are not the totality of the decisions rendered by the Special Court over the period. First, confidential decisions are, for obvious reasons, not covered. Second, some orders which do not have much importance from a legal point of view – such as Orders fixing the dates of judicial recesses, Rule 4 Orders authorizing Judges to exercise their functions away from the seat of the Special Court, Rule 117 Orders appointing Appeal benches, – have been deliberately excluded. Third, administrative decisions rendered by the Registrar and the Principal Defender – as regards assignment and withdrawal of Counsel – have not been covered. Finally, other documents issued by Chambers which are not decisions *per se*, notably separate opinions appended by Judges to the majority decisions and practice directions, are also excluded. The complete list of the decisions reviewed is appended at the end of the *Digest*.

The decisions themselves are not reproduced. This *Digest* is a collection of the most relevant legal findings contained in the reviewed decisions. In selecting the abstracts, the criteria applied by the author are: 1/ abstracts which clarify a point of law, interpret a rule, 2/ abstracts which show how a specific rule is practically applied by a Chamber; 3/ abstracts which are otherwise meaningful as regards international justice, human rights, international humanitarian law,

The abstracts are presented with their full references (Chamber, Case, Title of the Decision, Date, Paragraphs). The format of the original decision (italics, bold, underlining spelling and/or grammatical mistakes) is respected. The footnotes contained in each abstract are reproduced in full as endnotes at the end of each abstract, so that they remain distinct from the actual footnotes made by the author – which appear as proper footnotes in the book –.

The abstracts are regrouped under the relevant articles of the Statute by the Rules of Procedure and Evidence of the Special Court, with a short – one line – description of the precise topic.

Examples:

- **Article 1: Competence of the SCSL – Nature of the Special Court**

This means that the abstract(s) presented below this title is (are) related to Article 1 of the Statute – which is entitled "Competence of the Special Court" – and address(es) the specific issue of the nature Special Court.

- **Rule 26*bis*: The Chambers – Role of the Judge**

Here, the abstract(s) below is (are) related to Rule 26*bis* – "The Chambers" – of the Rules of Procedure and Evidence and address(es) the role of the Judge.

Quick Reference Numbers ("QRN")

A Quick Reference System is used in order to help the readers to find the abstracts he/she is looking for. Every abstract contained in the *Digest* has a Quick Reference Number ("QRN"). These QRN contain four data:

- **"S" or "R"**: The QRN begins by a "S" – for Statute – or a "R" – for Rules. This data informs the reader on whether the abstract is reproduced in relation to an Article of the Statute or a Rule of the Rules of Procedure and Evidence. Abstracts related to Articles of the SCSL Statute are contained in the first Part of the *Digest*; those in relation to Rules are reproduced in the second Part.
- **"first number"**: The "S" or "R" is immediately followed by a number: this is the specific number of the Article Statute or of the Rule under which the abstract is presented.
- **"TC", "AC" or "P"**: This data indicates whether the quoted decision was rendered by a Trial Chamber (Trial Chamber I and Trial chamber II are not distinguished) – **"TC"** –, the Appeals Chamber – **"AC"** – or the President of the Special Court – **"P"** –. For each Article and Rule, decisions of the Trial Chambers are presented first, followed by Appeals Chamber's decisions and, where applicable, decisions issued by the President.

- **"last number":** The last data corresponds to the numbering of the abstracts under each of the above categories.

Examples:

- **S1-TC-1** is the QRN for the first decision presented in this *Digest* that has been rendered by a Trial Chamber in relation to Article 1 of the Statute.
- **R73-AC-9** is the QRN number for the ninth decision presented in this *Digest* that has been rendered by the Appeals Chamber in relation to Rule 73 of the Rules of Procedure and Evidence.
- **R77-P-1** refers to the first (and unique) decision quoted in this *Digest* that has been rendered by the President in relation to Rule 77 of the Rules of Procedure and Evidence.

The QRN are used, in the List of Reviewed Decisions appended at the end of this *Digest*, to identify the entries where the decisions are quoted. The QRN also appear in the Table of Contents.

PART I

STATUTE OF THE SPECIAL COURT

Article 1
Competence of the Special Court

1. The Special Court shall, except as provided in subparagraph (2), have the power to prosecute persons who bear the greatest responsibility for serious violations of international humanitarian law and Sierra Leonean law committed in the territory of Sierra Leone since 30 November 1996, including those leaders who, in committing such crimes, have threatened the establishment of and implementation of the peace process in Sierra Leone.

2. Any transgressions by peacekeepers and related personnel present in Sierra Leone pursuant to the Status of Mission Agreement in force between the United Nations and the Government of Sierra Leone or agreements between Sierra Leone and other Governments or regional organizations, or, in the absence of such agreement, provided that the peacekeeping operations were undertaken with the consent of the Government of Sierra Leone, shall be within the primary jurisdiction of the sending State.

3. In the event the sending State is unwilling or unable genuinely to carry out an investigation or prosecution, the Court may, if authorized by the Security Council on the proposal of any State, exercise jurisdiction over such persons.

TRIAL CHAMBERS DECISIONS

- **Article 1: Competence of the SCSL – Nature of the Special Court**

S1-TC-1
o *Prosecutor v. Kondewa*, Case No. SCSL-03-12-PT, Decision on the Urgent Defence Application for Release from Provisional Detention, 21 November 2003, para. 27:

27. The Chamber acknowledges that the Constitution of Sierra Leone is indeed the highest legal authoritative instrument within the judicial system of Sierra Leone, but nevertheless, takes issue with the Defence's contention. The Special Court was established by means of a bilateral agreement between the United Nations Organisation and the Government of Sierra

Leone, and, therefore, the Special Court is an independent institution, which is not governed by the Constitution of Sierra Leone. [...]

- **Article 1: Competence of the SCSL – "Persons Who Bear the Greatest Responsibility"**

S1-TC-2

o *Prosecutor v. Fofana*, Case No. SCSL-04-14-PT, Decision on the Preliminary Defence Motion on the Lack of Personal Jurisdiction Filed on Behalf of the Accused Fofana, 3 March 2004, para. 21-27:

21. The issue of the competence of the Special Court received significant attention during discussions on the establishment of the Special Court and the drafting of its Statute, as discussed by the Parties. The Chamber wishes to emphasise that the competence of the Special Court is different from that of other International Tribunals: both the International Criminal Tribunal for the former Yugoslavia ("ICTY") and the International Criminal Tribunal for Rwanda ("ICTR") have "the power to prosecute persons responsible for serious violations of international humanitarian law"[1] rather than "the power to prosecute persons who bear the greatest responsibility for serious violations of international humanitarian law and Sierra Leonean law". This was done on purpose. As a consequence of this particular terminology used to describe the Court's competence, the first question to be addressed is whether "persons bearing the greatest responsibility" is a jurisdictional requirement or merely an articulation of prosecutorial discretion.

22. The *travaux préparatoires* show that the issue was discussed between the Secretary-General and the Security Council. However, these discussions are not fully and completely reflected in the Parties' submissions. In his Report on the establishment of a Special Court for Sierra Leone,[2] the Secretary-General at paragraph 30 opined that:

> While those "most responsible" obviously include the political or military leadership, others in command authority down the chain of command may also be regarded "most responsible" judging by the severity of the crime or its massive scale. "Most responsible", therefore, denotes both a leadership or authority position of the accused, and a sense of the gravity, seriousness or massive scale of the crime. It must be seen, however, not as a test criterion or a distinct jurisdictional threshold, but as a guidance to the Prosecutor in the adoption of a prosecution strategy and in making decisions to prosecute in individual cases.

23. In the Letter dated 22 December 2000 from the President of the Security Council addressed to the Secretary-General, it was noted in paragraph 1, entitled Personal jurisdiction, that:

> The members of the Security Council continue to hold the view, as expressed in resolution 1315 (2000), that the Special Court for Sierra Leone should have personal jurisdiction over persons who bear the greatest responsibility for the commission of crimes, including crimes against humanity, war crimes and other serious violations of international humanitarian law, as well as crimes under relevant Sierra Leonean law committed within the territory of Sierra Leone. The members of the Security Council believe that, by thus limiting the focus of the Special Court to those who played a leadership role, the simpler and more general formulations suggested in the appended draft will be appropriate.[3]

24. In the Letter dated 12 January 2001 from the Secretary-General addressed to the President of the Security Council, at paragraph 2 it is stated:

> Members of the Council expressed preference for the language contained in Security Council resolution 1315 (2000), extending the personal jurisdiction of the Court to "persons who bear the greatest responsibility", thus limiting the focus of the Special Court to those who played a leadership role. However, the wording of sub-paragraph (a) of article 1 of the draft Statute, as proposed by the Security Council, does not mean that the personal jurisdiction is limited to the political and military leaders only. Therefore, the determination of the meaning of the term "persons who bear the greatest responsibility" in any given case falls initially to the prosecutor and ultimately to the Special Court itself. [. . .][4]

And in paragraph 3 it further states that:

> [. . .] It is my understanding that, following from paragraph 2 above, the words "those leaders who. . . . threaten the establishment of and implementation of the peace process" do not describe an element of the crime but rather provide guidance to the prosecutor in determining his or her prosecutorial strategy. Consequently, the commission of any of the statutory crimes without necessarily threatening the establishment and implementation of the peace process would not detract from the international criminal responsibility otherwise entailed for the accused.[5]

25. In a Letter dated 31 January 2001 from the President of the Security Council addressed to the Secretary-General, the President underscores the importance of that terminology as follows:

The members of the Council share your analysis of the importance and role of the phrase "persons who bear the greatest responsibility". The members of the Council, moreover, share your view that the words beginning with "those leaders who . . ." are intended as guidance to the Prosecutor in determining his or her prosecutorial strategy.[6]

26. The Chamber finds that these letters "led to modifications in the text of both the draft Agreement with the Government of Sierra Leone and the draft Statute of the Court. The Government of Sierra Leone was consulted on these changes and by letter of 9 February 2001 to the Legal Counsel expressed its willingness to accept the texts."[7] It is therefore the significant finding of the Chamber that the agreed text resulted in the adoption of the phrase "persons who bear the greatest responsibility" as articulated in Article 1(1) of the Special Court's Statute and that the Prosecutor's duties in this regard were prescribed by Article 15 of the Statute and by Rule 47 of the Rules, as set out above.

27. Based upon the foregoing findings, the Chamber therefore concludes that the issue of personal jurisdiction is a jurisdictional requirement, and while it does of course guide the prosecutorial strategy, it does not exclusively articulate prosecutorial discretion, as the Prosecution has submitted.

---

[1] See Article 1 of the ICTY Statue and Article 1 of the ICTR Statute. It should be noted that both the ICTY and the ICTR Statutes provide distinct geographical and temporal limitations.
[2] S/2000/915, 4 October 2000.
[3] S/2000/1234. The appended draft provided, in Article 1(1) of the Agreement: "There is hereby established a Special Court for Sierra Leone to prosecute persons who bear *the greatest responsibility* for serious violations of international humanitarian law and Sierra Leonean law committed in the territory of Sierra Leone since 30 November 1996. (Emphasis added).
[4] S/2001/40.
[5] S/2001/40.
[6] S/2001/95.
[7] Letter dated 12 July 2001 from the Secretary-General addressed to the President of the Security Council, S/2001/693.

- **Article 1: Competence of the SCSL – Principle of Legality**

S1-TC-3

o *Prosecutor v. Kanu*, Case No. SCSL-04-16-PT, Written Reasons for the Trial Chamber's Oral Decision on the Defence Motion on Abuse of Process Due to Infringement of Principles of *Nullum Crimen Sine Lege* and Non-Retroactivity as to Several Accounts, 31 March 2004, para. 33:

33. It is well established under customary international law that Crimes against Humanity, violations of Common Article 3 and of Additional Protocol II, and serious violations of international law entail individual criminal responsibility. Further, and as a matter of reference, Sierra Leone is a signatory to the four Geneva Conventions, Additional Protocol II to the Geneva Conventions and the Statute of the International Criminal Court. Therefore, there is no violation of the fundamental principle of legality in this case.

- **Article 1: Competence of the SCSL – Inherent Jurisdiction**

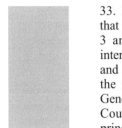

o *Prosecutor v. Brima*, Case No. SCSL-04-16-PT, Decision on Applicant's Motion Against Denial by the Acting Principal Defender to Enter a Legal Service Contract for the Assignment of Counsel, 6 May 2004, para. 39, 55-62:

39. [...] [T]he chamber is of the opinion that the motion, even though brought under the wrong Rule, can, and so do we decide, in the overall interests of justice and to prevent a violation of the rights of the Accused, be examined by invoking our inherent jurisdiction to entertain it and to adjudicate on it on the ground of a denial of request for assignment of Counsel within the context of Article 17(4)(d) of the Statute.

[...]

55. The Editors of Halsbury's Laws of England articulate the concept of inherent jurisdiction in these terms:

"... Unlike all other branches of law, except perhaps criminal procedure, there is a source of law which is peculiar to civil procedural law and is commonly called 'the inherent jurisdiction of the court'. In the ordinary way, the Supreme Court as a superior Court of record, exercises the full plenitude of judicial power in all matters concerning the general administration of justice within its territorial limits, and enjoys unrestricted and unlimited powers in all matters of substantive law, both civil and criminal, except in so far as that has been taken away in unequivocal terms by statutory enactment. The term 'inherent jurisdiction' is not used in contradistinction to the jurisdiction of the court exercisable at common law or conferred on it by statute or rules of court, for the Court may exercise its inherent jurisdiction even in respect of matters which are regulated by statute or Rule of court... In sum, it may be said that the inherent jurisdiction of the court is a virile and viable doctrine, and has been defined as being the reserve or fund of powers, a residual source of power, which the court may draw upon as necessary whenever it is just or equitable to do so, in particular to ensure the observance of the due process of law, to prevent improper vexation or oppression".

56. As to its juridical basis, the orthodox view is that the authority to exercise inherent jurisdiction derives not from any statute or rule of law, but from the very nature of the court as a Superior Court of law. LORD MORRIS in the case of CONNELLY V.S.D.P.P(1964)A.C. at p. 1301 had this to say on inherent jurisdiction:

> "There can be no doubt that a court which is endowed with a particular jurisdiction has powers which are necessary to enable it to act effectively within such jurisdiction. I would regard them as powers which are inherent in its jurisdiction. A court must enjoy some powers in order to enforce its rule of practice and to suppress any abuses of its process and to defeat any attempted thwarting of its process."

57. In essence, the juridical basis of this head of a Court's jurisdiction is the very authority of the Judiciary to uphold, to protect and to fulfil the judicial function of administering justice according to law in a regular, orderly and effective manner.[1]

58. The Chamber notes that the doctrine of inherent powers has recently been invoked by our Sister Tribunals – the ICTY and the ICTR. In PROSECUTOR V. TADIC,[2] the Appeals Chamber concluded that the Tribunal did have jurisdiction, to examine the plea against its own jurisdiction reasoning that such authority is "inherent in every judicial organ."[3]

59. Furthermore, in the case of THE PROSECUTOR V. BLASKIC,[4] the issue was that of the validity of a *subpoena* which Judge Macdonald in Trial Chamber II had issued both to the Republic of Croatia and to its Defence Minister personally. On the issue of inherent jurisdiction, the Appeals Chamber observed:

> "The power to make this judicial finding is an inherent power: the International Tribunal must possess the power to make all those judicial determinations that are necessary for the exercise of its primary jurisdiction. This inherent power inures to the benefit of the International tribunal in order that its basic judicial function may be fully discharged and its judicial role safeguarded."[5]

60. The BARAYAGWIZA (Abuse of Process) Decision of the ICTR,[6] also lends credit to the recourse to inherent jurisdiction principle by Tribunals. In that case, the central issue was that of abuse of process by the Prosecutor, for which the

Appeals Chamber found it necessary to invoke its inherent power to dismiss the indictment. The Trial Chamber had dismissed the Applicant's motion for orders to review or nullify his arrest and provisional detention. He appealed against the decision. Allowing the appeal, the Appeals Chamber alluded to the inherent jurisdiction or supervisory powers of a Court to curb an abuse of process or a travesty of justice.

61. We further note here that our Sister Tribunals have not hesitated to invoke their inherent jurisdiction and supervise Officials of the Court on the reasoning that such control and overseeing responsibility is fundamental to a Court's ability to regulate its own process and to ensure a fair trial.[7] In this regard and to make the point we are driving home, we refer to the ICTY decision in the case of THE PROSECUTOR Vs MOMCILO KRAJISNIK Case No IT-00-39-PT of 20th January 2004. In this case, the Registrar who, in ICTY, cumulates the functions of the Principal Defender, arbitrarily and unreasonably assessed the means of an indigent accused, MOMCILO KRAJISNIK, and declared him only partially indigent for legal aid purposes. Their Lordships, Judge Alphons Orie (Presiding), Judge Amin El Mahdi and Judge Joaquin Martin Carnivell, in the exercise of similar powers that we are invoking to assume jurisdiction in this Motion, concluded their judgement on an appeal against their Trial Chamber decision which quashed the Registrar's decision, in the following remarks:

> "It should be clear from the analysis in the previous section that the incidence of error and unreasonableness in the Registrar's decision is such as to justify an order quashing the Registrar's Decision". The Registrar, Their Lordship added, "should reconsider his position in the light of the Chamber decision".

62. This Chamber strongly adheres to the view that the Special Court for Sierra Leone, as an international judicial entity, in addition to its statutory jurisdiction as provided for in the Founding Instruments of the Court, is endowed with an inherent jurisdiction to enable it to act effectively in pursuance of its mandate. Indeed, we firmly hold so. Likewise, in principle, consistent with the aforementioned decisions of our Sister Tribunals, we rule that the Court's inherent jurisdiction does extend to the control and supervision of officers of the Court in the exercise of their statutory and related functions. [...]

---

[1] Jacob, *supra* note 2, p. 28.
[2] Decision on the Defence Motion for Interlocutory Appeal for Jurisdiction, Case IT-94-1, 2 October 1995, Appeals Chamber (Tadic (Jurisdiction)), referred to in an instructive article on the subject by Louise Symons entitled "The inherent power of the ICTY and ICTR", in *International Criminal Law review* 3: 369-404, 2003.

(3) Ibidem. p. 238.
(4) Judgement in the Request of the Republic of Croatia for Review of the Decision of Trial Chamber II of 18 July 1997, Case IT-95-4, 29 October 1997, Appeals Chamber.
(5) Ibidem. para. 33.
(6) Case ICTR-97-13, 3 November 1999, Appeals Chamber.
(7) See *Delalic and Ors* (Withdrawal of Counsel), Nyiramasuhuko and Ntahobali (Withdrawal of Counsel) and *Ntabakuze and Kabiligi* (Motion to Counter Indictment Void).

- **Article 1: Competence of the SCSL – The Special Court and the Truth and Reconciliation Commission (TRC)**

S1-TC-5

o *Prosecutor v. Norman*, SCSL-03-08-PT, Decision on the Request by the Truth and Reconciliation Commission of Sierra Leone to Conduct a Public Hearing with Samuel Hinga Norman, 29 October 2003, Preamble, para. 10, 12, 14:[1]

CONSIDERING ALSO that the Special Court is seized of an indictment charging the Accused with seven (7) counts of various offences within jurisdiction of the Special Court as herein before stated, but that the Court is, in law, obliged **NOT** to draw any conclusions about his role in the said conflict until the issue has been properly adjudicated before the said Court and therefore **CANNOT**, at this stage form any perception as that entertained by the **TRC and upon which the aforementioned Request is premised**;

EMPHASIZING that the jurisdiction to try the Accused for offences falling within the jurisdiction of the Court is exclusive to the Court and not shared concurrently with any other institution, national or international, and that the Court as, an International criminal Tribunal, cannot properly, in law, delegate this exclusive jurisdiction to any other entity or institution; and that any purported delegation of such authority would compromise its autonomy and the integrity of the trial of the Accused;

[...]

10. [...] [T]he Request of the Commission to conduct a public hearing with the Accused on, as the Request indicates, the centrality of his role in the conflict that took place in Sierra Leone a decade ago *clashes fundamentally with, and has*

---

[1] See also *Prosecutor v. Gbao*, Case No. SCSL-03-09-PT, Decision on the Request by the TRC of Sierra Leone to Conduct a Public Hearing with the Accused, 3 November 2003.

grave ramifications for, the cardinal principle of criminal law that a person accused of crime is presumed innocent until convicted. Even after conviction, he has the chance of proving that his conviction, barring a guilty plea, was a miscarriage of justice through the machinery of appeal. Almost every international convention, treaty or instrument on the subject of human rights and related themes has elevated this principle to the level of fundamental human rights, notably, the **Universal Declaration of Human Rights** (Article 11(1)). It is this principle that lies at the core of the adversarial procedure of the Special Court. In other words, the presumption of innocence (as it is succinctly or quaintly characterized) enjoys primacy within the Special Court's adversarial normative framework for the adjudication of crimes (Article 17(3) of the Court's Statute).

[. . .]

12. [T]he Accused is being invited to testify as a *'perpetrator of abuses and violations'*. This inference is supported by two assertions upon which the Request is predicated. The *first is that the accused did play a central role in the conflict in Sierra Leone; the second is that the Commission perceives that the Accused played a central role in the conflict as a 'victim' or is being invited to testify as an 'interested party'.* **Contrastingly, from the perspective of the Special Court, at this point in time, the issue of the alleged centrality of the Accused's role in the conflict is a highly contentious, and as yet, unsubstantiated issue as evidenced by the plea of not guilty to each count in the Indictment against the Accused.** I find, therefore, that the perception of the Commission that the Accused did play a central role in the conflict as a perpetrator of abuses and violations prior to his testimony before the Commission is inconsistent with the presumption of innocence, the key doctrine that undergirds the adversarial scheme of the Special Court. To reinforce this finding, it is important to note that on a contextual reading of the whole of the Truth and Reconciliation Commission Act, 2000, **the inference is irresistible that the word 'perpetrator' has a restrictive connotation with reference only to persons who committed abuses and violations during the conflict and are willing to confess their guilt**. The word, therefore, cannot properly be applied to an 'indictee' who has pleaded guilty to each of the seven (7) counts in the indictment in respect of which he is awaiting trial before the Special Court. The Truth and Reconciliation Commission Act, 2000 is predicated upon the notion of restorative justice which aims at the reconciliation of *self-confessed perpetrators, victims and the state as a whole*. Once a person has been indicted, he does not fall within the statutory ambit of the Act.

[. . .]

14. [...] [T]here are two competing and conflicting societal interests involved here. One is the widely accepted societal interest that all persons accused of criminal conduct are entitled to a fair and public trial *so that, in the ultimate analysis, the guilty may be punished and the innocent vindicated without moral blemish*. The other is the TRC's institutional role in developing and establishing the historical record of the decade-long conflict in Sierra Leone, *an equally valid and legitimate societal interest.* [...] *In the context of the instant Request, to yield to the institutional interest of the TRC would, in my considered judgement, certainly jeopardize the Accused' right to a fair and public trial and would constitute an unprincipled departure from a well-established and widely accepted judicial practice.* It is certainly not in the supreme interest of the Sierra Leone society for a person presumed innocent of crimes in respect of which he stands indicted (and not yet tried) to be given, as it were, a licence to incriminate himself elsewhere by the very forum to which he looks for protection of his due process rights and ultimate vindication.

[...]

S1-TC-6

o *Prosecutor v. Gbao*, Case No. SCSL-03-09-PT, Decision on the Request by the TRC of Sierra Leone to Conduct a Public Hearing with the Accused, 3 November 2003, para. 11-16, 18:

11. The first main reason is that the Request of the Commission to conduct a public hearing with the Accused on, as the Request indicates, the key role in the conflict that took place in Sierra Leone a decade ago *clashes fundamentally with, and has grave ramifications for, the cardinal principle that a person accused of crime is presumed innocent until convicted.*[1]

12. This fundamental tension is brought into sharp focus by the nature and effect of Condition (i) being sought by the Accused. By stipulating for this Condition the Accused is, (using a familiar legal metaphor) seeking a judicial shield to protect him from any injurious effects of the sword which, by his agreement, he would be placing in the hands of the Commission. In my considered judgment, such a stipulation will be devoid of legal efficacy for the reason that the Accused, by testifying, will be admitting that he was "*a perpetrator of abuses and violations*" during the conflict, and will be accepting the Commission's perception that he did play a key role in the conflict, despite the fact that he has pleaded not guilty to each of the 13 counts in the indictment against him. It is crystal-clear that the Commission's statutory mandate is to interview, among others, *perpetrators of abuses and viola-*

tions. Condition (i) is only meaningful and feasible within the context of the adversarial framework of the Special Court in that, at this point in time, *the alleged key role of the Accused in the conflict is a highly contentious, and as yet, unsubstantiated issue*[(2)] as evidenced by the pleas of not guilty to the indictment. Is the Accused, after **reprobating** in one forum, seeking a judicial license to **approbate** in another? Evidently, he is.

13. The second reason is that Condition (ii) is extremely problematical. Here, the Accused is seeking a fiat from the Court to be "*permitted to retain his right to silence at all times and that he be permitted to withdraw from the proceedings at anytime*" before the Commission. This is intriguing. A brief analysis will suffice to demonstrate what I mean. In one sense, it seems like it is an invitation to the Court ***to give approval with one hand and take it away with the other***. In a related sense, it is tantamount to the Accused asserting: "***I have come before you for permission to TESTIFY before the Commission but I am, simultaneously, seeking your leave to stand MUTE before the said Commission.***"

14. Another reason is that all of the other Conditions, taken individually and cumulatively, are hedged with qualifications and reservations antithetical to the notion of free-will, the essence of a consent voluntarily and knowingly given. These, like Conditions (i) and (ii), confirm strongly my doubts as to whether the interests of justice would be best served by granting the Accused approval to testify before the Commission based on the material on which I have had to apply my mind.

15. [. . .] I find that, as an "indictee", the Accused does not fall within the statutory ambit of the Act. He is also not a *self-confessed perpetrator*[(3)] as evidenced by his pleas to the thirteen (13) count indictment preferred against him.

16. Significant, too, for the purposes of the instant Request is that where there is a conflict between two legitimate and equally valid societal interests, one of them being the interest of society in ensuring that persons accused of crime be guaranteed their right to a fair and public trial, the consistent and accepted judicial trend, nationally and internationally, is to resolve the conflict in favour of the latter.[(4)] *In my considered judgement, therefore, to allow the institutional interest of the Commission to prevail in the face of the extremely entangled web of equivocations, qualifications and reservations exemplified by Conditions (i) – (xii) of the purported Agreement of the Accused and the elaborate and complicated set of restrictions sought to be placed on the nature and scope of the subject areas for questioning, would jeopardize the Accused's right to a fair and impartial public trial in due course and undermine the integrity of the proceedings in the Special Court.*

[...]

18. Finally based on the reasoning and the supporting judicial considerations in the foregoing paragraphs, it is my conclusive finding that the purported agreement of the Accused to testify before the Commission is heavily punctuated by an intricate web of qualifications and reservations, the cumulative effect of which is to deprive the said agreement of that core element upon which a consent voluntarily and knowingly given is predicated, namely, free-will. *This finding (as noted in paragraph 13) is buttressed by the request for the leave of the Court to testify before the Commission and at the same time, for the judicial indulgence to be able to stand mute before the Commission when he appears.* In these circumstances, it is the absolute duty of the Court, as custodian of the Accused's procedural and substantive due process rights, to refrain from endorsing what is, by any objective reckoning, an ill-conceived decision, on his part, to *reprobate* in a judicial forum by pleas of not guilty to a 13-count indictment and seek to *approbate* in another forum on the same cause. Judicially, therefore, I see no other reasonable approach but to preclude the Accused from embarking upon the intended course of action in the interests of justice and to preserve the integrity of the proceedings in the Special Court, thereby upholding firmly his right to a fair and impartial trial, the gravity of the *allegations* against him notwithstanding.

---

[1] *Prosecutor v. Norman*, SCSL-2003-08-PT, Decision on the Request by the Truth and Reconciliation Commission of Sierra Leone to Conduct a Public Hearing with Samuel Hinga Norman, 29 October 2003, para. 10.
[2] Id. para. 12.
[3] Id. para. 12.
[4] Id. para. 14.

- **Article 1: Competence of the SCSL – History**

S1-TC-7

o *Prosecutor v. Norman, Fofana, Kondewa*, Case No. SCSL-04-14-T, Majority Decision on the Prosecution's Application for Leave to File an Interlocutory Appeal Against the Decision on the Prosecution's Request for Leave to Amend the Indictment Against Samuel Hinga Norman, Moinina Fofana and Allieu Kondewa, 2 August 2004, para. 31:

31. Equally untenable, in the Chamber's considered judgement, is the Prosecution's contention that the Court is mandated to establish a complete and historical record of crimes committed during the armed conflict in Sierra Leone. This is a misconception. The Chamber's view is that the Court's role

is exclusively adversarial in terms of meting out justice to victims and persons found guilty of serious violations of humanitarian law and Sierra Leone law during the said conflict. The alleged mandate which the Prosecution attributes to the Court, of providing a complete and historical record of what happened in Sierra Leone during the said conflict is erroneous as it is neither borne out nor is it so stipulated in either the provisions of the Agreement setting up the Special Court or in its Statute.

APPEALS CHAMBER DECISIONS

* **Article 1: Competence of the SCSL – Nature of the SCSL – Application of International Law**

S1-AC-1

o *Prosecutor v. Kallon* (Case No. SCSL-04-15-AR72), *Norman* (Case No. SCSL-04-14-AR72), *Kamara* (Case No. SCSL-04-16-AR72), Decision on Constitutionality and Lack of Jurisdiction, 13 March 2004, para. 55:[2]

55. [. . .] [T]he Special Court Agreement is an international agreement governed by international law. The Special Court is accordingly an international tribunal and it is a norm of international law that for it to be "established by law", its establishment must accord with the rule of law. This means that it must be established according to proper international criteria; it must have the mechanisms and facilities to dispense even-handed justice, providing at the same time all the guarantees of fairness and it must be in tune with international human rights instruments.

S1-AC-2

o *Prosecutor v. Taylor*, Case No. SCSL-03-01-I, Decision on Immunity from Jurisdiction, 31 May 2004, para. 37-42:

37. Although the Special Court was established by treaty, unlike the ICTY and the ICTR which were each established by resolution of the Security Council in its exercise of powers by virtue of Chapter VII of the UN Charter, it was clear that

---

[2] See also *Prosecutor v. Gbao*, Case No. SCSL-04-15-AR72, Decision on Preliminary Motion on the Invalidity of the Agreement Between the United Nations and the Government of Sierra Leone on the Establishment of the Special Court, 25 May 2004.

the power of the Security Council to enter into an agreement for the establishment of the court was derived from the Charter of the United Nations both in regard to the general purposes of the United Nations as expressed in Article I of the Charter and the specific powers of the Security Council in Articles 39 and 41. These powers are wide enough to empower the Security Council to initiate, as it did by Resolution 1315, the establishment of the Special Court by Agreement with Sierra Leone. Article 39 empowers the Security Council to determine the existence of any threat to the peace. In Resolution 1315, the Security Council reiterated that the situation in Sierra Leone continued to constitute a threat to international peace and security in the region.

38. Much issue had been made of the absence of Chapter VII powers in the Special Court. A proper understanding of those powers shows that the absence of the so-called Chapter VII powers does not by itself define the legal status of the Special Court. It is manifest from the first sentence of Article 41, read disjunctively, that (i) The Security Council is empowered to 'decide what measures not involving the use of armed force are to be employed to give effect to its decision;' and (ii) it may (at its discretion) call upon the members of the United Nations to apply such measures. The decisions referred to are decisions pursuant to Article 39. Where the Security Council decides to establish a court as a measure to maintain or restore international peace and security it may or may not, at the same time, contemporaneously, call upon the members of the United Nations to lend their cooperation to such court as a matter of obligation. Its decision to do so in furtherance of Article 41 or Article 48, should subsequent events make that course prudent may be made subsequently to the establishment of the court. It is to be observed that in carrying out its duties under its responsibility for the maintenance of international peace and security, the Security Council acts on behalf of the members of the United Nations.[1] The Agreement between the United Nations and Sierra Leone is thus an agreement between *all* members of the United Nations and Sierra Leone. This fact makes the Agreement an expression of the will of the international community.[2] The Special Court established in such circumstances is truly international.

39. By reaffirming in the preamble to Resolution 1315 'that persons who commit or authorize serious violations of international humanitarian law are individually responsible and accountable for those violations and that *the international community will exert every effort to bring those responsible to justice in accordance with international standards of justice, fairness and due process of law*',[3] it has been made clear that the Special Court was established to fulfil an international mandate and is part of the machinery of international justice.

40. We reaffirm, as we decided in the Constitutionality Decision that the Special Court is not a national court of Sierra Leone and is not part of the judicial system of Sierra Leone exercising judicial powers of Sierra Leone. This conclusion disposes of the basis of the submissions of counsel for the Applicant on the nature of the Special Court.

41. For the reasons that have been given, it is not difficult to accept and gratefully adopt the conclusions reached by Professor Sands who assisted the court as *amicus curiae* as follows:[4]

  a) The Special Court is not part of the judiciary of Sierra Leone and is not a national court.
  b) The Special Court is established by treaty and has the characteristics associated with classical international organisations (including legal personality; the capacity to enter into agreements with other international persons governed by international law; privileges and immunities; and an autonomous will distinct from that of its members).
  c) The competence and jurisdiction *ratione materiae* and *ratione personae* are broadly similar to that of ICTY and the ICTR and the ICC, including in relation to the provisions confirming the absence of entitlement of any person to claim of immunity.
  d) Accordingly, there is no reason to conclude that the Special Court should be treated as anything other than an international tribunal or court, with all that implies for the question of immunity for a serving Head of State.

42. We come to the conclusion that the Special Court is an international criminal court. The constitutive instruments of the court contain indicia too numerous to enumerate to justify that conclusion. To enumerate those indicia will involve virtually quoting the entire provisions of those instruments. It suffices that having adverted to those provisions, the conclusion we have arrived at is inescapable.

---

[1] See Article 24(1) UN Charter.
[2] See the discussion by this Chamber in its earlier decision *Prosecutor v Moinina Fofana*, Case No. SCSL-2004-14-AR72(E), Decision On Preliminary Motion On Lack Of Jurisdiction Materiae: Illegal Delegation Of Powers By The United Nations, 25 May 2004.
[3] Resolution 1315 (2000), emphasis added.
[4] *Amicus Curiae* Submissions, para. 118(5)-(8).

S1-AC-3   o *Prosecutor v. Kanu*, Case No. SCSL-04-16-AR72, Decision on Motion Challenging Jurisdiction and Raising Objections Based on Abuse of Process, 25 May 2004, para. 2-5:

2. The Applicant labours under some misconception when he argues that the Agreement between the United Nations and the Sierra Leone Government had no 'direct effect within the domestic legal system of Sierra Leone'[1] and, therefore, the Special Court has no jurisdiction to try him. The Special Court is vested with its own specific jurisdiction and competence by the constitutive documents establishing it. As a treaty based institution it operates outside the legal system of Sierra Leone and does not derive its jurisdiction from or within that system.

3. It was argued that 'the entering of a bilateral agreement which established the Special court, may be [...] unconstitutional as it infringes the mentioned sovereign rights of the people of Sierra Leone.'[2] The said 'mentioned sovereign rights' were said to derive from the constitutional declaration that 'sovereignty belongs to the people of Sierra Leone from whom Government derives all its power, authority and legislative legitimacy'.[3] This, clearly, is a declaration of the basic norm of the Sierra Leone constitutional and legal order. Rather than having the consequence which the Applicant sought to attribute to it, it has the effect of enabling the Government validly to exercise those powers vested in it by the Constitution, of which the treating making power is one.

4. The further and fresh point was made by the Applicant that as a member of the Sierra Leone army he is entitled to be tried by fellow officers in a court-martial for any crime alleged to have been committed during his military service. This right is said to derive from Articles 169(3)(e) and 171(13) of the Constitution. As this Chamber had stated in the Decision on Constitutionality, the provisions of the national Constitution do not affect the jurisdiction of the Special Court. It is perhaps worth emphasizing that military personnel of any state may be subject to a system of internal discipline which may replace or oust the jurisdiction of national criminal courts in respect of serious crime. But the existence of such a domestic system of internal discipline cannot have the effect of ousting the jurisdiction of an international court which operates outside the national judicial system.

5. The arguments raised relating to constitutional validity of the provisions of the Agreement establishing the Special Court as regards transfer of a Sierra Leonean national to the custody of the Special Court does not raise a question relating to jurisdiction and can rightly be ignored.

---

[1] Preliminary Motion, para. 8.

(2) Preliminary Motion, para. 10.
(3) Article 5(2)(a) of Chapter XII of the Constitution of Sierra Leone, 1991.

- **Article 1: Competence of the SCSL – Principle of Legality**

S1-AC-4

o *Prosecutor v. Kallon* (Case No. SCSL-04-15-AR72), *Norman* (Case No. SCSL-04-14-AR72), *Kamara* (Case No. SCSL-04-16-AR72), Decision on Constitutionality and Lack of Jurisdiction, 13 March 2004, para. 81-82:

81. In relation to crimes against humanity, violations of Common Article 3 of the Geneva Conventions and Additional Protocol II and other serious violations of international law, as contained in Articles 2-4 of the Statute, the ICTY Appeals Chamber in *Prosecutor v. Delalic et al.*(1) gave their support to the Secretary-General's statement that violations of Common Article 3 had been criminalised for the first time with the establishment of the ICTR. This Chamber also endorses that statement of the Secretary-General.

82. Furthermore, we accept, as a correct statement of the law, the statement in Archbold's *International Criminal Courts*, that "[t]he fact that no court exists with jurisdiction to adjudicate crimes proscribed by international law at the time the offences were committed is not a bar to prosecution and not a violation of the principle *nullum crimen sine lege*."(2) We, therefore, reject the submission that the Special Court has no jurisdiction to hear such matters.

(1) *Prosecutor v Delalic et al.* ("Celebici Case"), ICTY Appeals Chamber Judgment, Case No. IT-96-21-A, 20 February 2001, para. 178.
(2) Archbold, *supra* note 48, para. 17-29.

S1-AC-5

o *Prosecutor v. Norman*, Case No. SCSL-04-14-AR72, Decision on Preliminary Motion Based on Lack of Jurisdiction (Child Recruitment), 31 May 2004, para. 25, 52-53:

25. It is the duty of this Chamber to ensure that the principle of non-retroactivity is not breached. As essential elements of all legal systems, the fundamental principle *nullum crimen sine lege* and the ancient principle *nullum crimen sine poena*, need to be considered. In the ICTY case of *Prosecutor v Hadžihasanović*, it was observed that "In interpreting the principle *nullum crimen sine lege*, it is critical to determine whether the underlying conduct at the time of its commission was punishable. The emphasis on conduct, rather than on the

specific description of the offence in substantive criminal law, is of primary relevance."[1] In other words it must be "foreseeable and accessible to a possible perpetrator that his concrete conduct was punishable".[2] As has been shown in the previous sections, child recruitment was a violation of conventional and customary international humanitarian law by 1996. But can it also be stated that the prohibited act was criminalised and punishable under international or national law to an extent which would show customary practice?

[...]

52. The rejection of the use of child soldiers by the international community was widespread by 1994. In addition, by the time of the 1996 Graça Machel Report, it was no longer possible to claim to be acting in good faith while recruiting child soldiers (contrary to the suggestion of the Defence during the oral hearing).[3] Specifically concerning Sierra Leone, the Government acknowledged in its 1996 Report to the Committee of the Rights of the Child that there was no minimum age for conscripting into armed forces "except the provision in the Geneva Convention that children below the age of 15 years should not be conscripted into the army."[4] This shows that the Government of Sierra Leone was well aware already in 1996 that children below the age of 15 should not be recruited. Citizens of Sierra Leone, and even less, persons in leadership roles, cannot possibly argue that they did not know that recruiting children was a criminal act in violation of international humanitarian law.[5]

53. Child recruitment was criminalized before it was explicitly set out as a criminal prohibition in treaty law and certainly by November 1996, the starting point of the time frame relevant to the indictments. As set out above, the principle of legality and the principle of specificity are both upheld.

---

[1] *Prosecutor v Hadžihasanović, Alagić and Kubura*, Case No. IT-01-47-PT, Decision on Joint Challenge to Jurisdiction, 12 November 2002, para. 62.
[2] Ibid.
[3] Counsel stated: "I would not say please do, but you can do it, it is not a crime under international law. As long as they [are] not members of warring factions you can do it...". See Transcript of 5-6 November 2003, para. 384.
[4] The Initial Report of States Parties: Sierra Leone 1996 CRC/C/3/Add.43 para. 28.
[5] Toronto Amicus Brief, para. 69.

- **Article 1: Competence of the SCSL – *Ratione Loci* Jurisdiction**

S1-AC-6

o *Prosecutor v. Kallon* (Case No. SCSL-04-15-AR72), *Norman* (Case No. SCSL-04-14-AR72), *Kamara* (Case No. SCSL-04-16-AR72), Decision on Constitutionality and Lack of Jurisdiction, 13 March 2004, para. 75, 78-79:

75. Even if, for the purpose of legal argument, the Chamber accepts that two-thirds of the territory of Sierra Leone was in the control of the RUF and the AFRC, it is a basic, fundamental and over-riding principle of International Law that "(t)he occupation and acquisition of territory through the use of force is illegal and territory gained in this manner does not belong to the conqueror."[(1)]

[...]

78. One vital conclusion that can be drawn from that decision is that whether or not an illegal regime is in effective control of a large part of a State's territory, it will not be recognised under International Law so long as the democratically elected Government exists and "so long as it is capable of controlling the affairs of the 'State' in the international community."[(2)] Accordingly, the Government of Sierra Leone did have authority to enter into an International Agreement, regardless of whether or not it was in 'effective control' of the majority of the territory of Sierra Leone.

79. It follows from all this that the submissions of the Defence on effective control are misconceived and without merit.

[(1)] Dixon, *Textbook on International Law*, 4th ed. 2000, para. 5.2.1.7.
[(2)] Dixon, *supra* note 77, para. 5.2.1.3.

- **Article 1: Competence of the SCSL – Inherent Jurisdiction – Absence of Express Statutory Provision**

S1-AC-7

o *Prosecutor v. Norman, Fofana, Kondewa*, Case No. SCSL-04-14-A, Decision on Prosecution Appeal Against the Trial Chamber's Decision of 2 August 2004 Refusing Leave to File an Interlocutory Appeal, 17 January 2005, para. 31-32:[3]

---

[3] See also *Prosecutor v. Brima, Kamara, Kanu*, Case No. SCSL-04-16-AR73, Decision on Brima-Kamara Defence Appeal Motion Against Trial Chamber II Majority Decision on Extremely Urgent Confidential Joint Motion for the Re-Appointment of Kevin Metzger and Wilbert Harris As Lead Counsel for Alex Tamba Brima and Brima Bazzy Kamara, 8 December 2005, para. 135.

31. [. . .] It is undoubted that courts have inherent powers to do what is necessary to fulfil their mandate, to carry out their judicial functions and to do that which is necessary to the fair administration of justice. A court also has the inherent power to control its proceedings to ensure that justice is done. On the other hand, an allegation of miscarriage of justice or the fact of being dissatisfied with a decision of the Trial Chamber does not, on its own, confer the right to appeal.

32. The Appeals Chamber may have recourse to its inherent jurisdiction, in respect of proceedings of which it is properly seized, when the Rules are silent and such recourse is necessary in order to do justice. The inherent jurisdiction cannot be invoked to circumvent an express Rule. When in the course of proceedings which the Appeals Chamber is already properly seized of, a situation arises which it has to deal with in order to further its jurisdiction and fulfil the purpose for which it is already vested with powers, the Appeals Chamber may have recourse to its inherent jurisdiction to exercise powers which will help to further and fulfil that purpose as justice demands, notwithstanding that the rules do not expressly confer such powers. Inherent powers of the court are powers which are inherent in a court by virtue of its nature. They are powers necessary for the administration of justice. They are not powers derived from the Rules or from statute but are powers which must be exercised in the interest of justice by reason of absence of express statutory provisions to cover a particular situation. It is an attribute of judicial power.

S1-AC-8

o *Prosecutor v. Brima, Kamara, Kanu*, Case No. SCSL-04-16-AR73, Decision on Brima-Kamara Defence Appeal Motion Against Trial Chamber II Majority Decision on Extremely Urgent Confidential Joint Motion for the Re-Appointment of Kevin Metzger and Wilbert Harris As Lead Counsel for Alex Tamba Brima and Brima Bazzy Kamara, 8 December 2005, para. 72-78, 135-139:

72. The requirement for a judicial review of administrative decisions where the Accused has an interest to protect was perfectly justified by Justice Pillay, the then President of the International Criminal Tribunal for Rwanda, in her decision of 13 November 2002:[1]

Modern systems of Administrative Law have built in review procedures to ensure fairness when individual rights and protected interests are in issue, or to preserve the interests of justice. In the context of the Tribunal, Rules 19 and 33(A) of the Rules ensure that such review is available in appropriate cases. While the Registrar has the responsibility of ensuring that all decisions are procedurally and substantially fair, not every decision by the Registrar can be the subject of review by the President. The Registrar must be free to conduct the business of the Registry without undue interference by Presidential review.

In all systems of administrative law, a threshold condition must be satisfied before an administrative decision may be impugned by supervisory review. There are various formulations of this threshold condition in national jurisdictions, but a common theme is that the decision sought to be challenged, must involve a substantive right that should be protected as a matter of human rights jurisprudence or public policy. An application for review of the Registrar's decision by the President on the basis that it is unfair procedurally or substantively, is admissible under Rules 19 and 33(A) of the Rules, if the accused has a protective right or interest, or if it is otherwise in the interests of justice.

73. The Appeals Chamber concurs with Justice Pillay's view on the need for a juridical review of administrative decisions affecting the rights of the Accused. However, the Appeals Chamber is not convinced that, in the specific situation of the Special Court, this judicial power should necessarily fall within the exclusive province of the President for the following reasons.

74. First, the Appeals Chamber notes that Article 24(E) and (F) of the Directive submits the Principal Defender's decision to withdraw Counsel to the judicial review of "the presiding Judge of the appropriate Chamber". This regulation is not problematic when, as in the current case, the trial is pending before a Trial Chamber, since the question is then submitted to the Presiding Judge of the Trial Chamber; but, once the case has reached the appeal phase, then the decision to withdraw Counsel would be submitted to the President of the Appeals Chamber, who is, pursuant to Article 12(3) of the Statute, the President of the Special Court. In that situation, would the decision to assign Counsel fall in the exclusive province of the President of the Special Court, he would be the only authority to judicially review the administrative decision to withdraw Counsel and then, once again, the decision denying the assignment of Counsel. That may put the President of the Special Court in a difficult situation.

75. Second, although the remedy provided by Article 12(A) of the Directive is not applicable in the current case, the Appeals Chamber notes that this Article gives jurisdiction to the Trial Chamber to review, by way of Preliminary Motion, the administrative decision on assignment of Counsel. The Appeals Chamber sees no reason to depart from that solution and considers that Article 12(A) should apply *mutatis mutandis* in the

present situation and allow to seize the Trial Chamber by way of an interlocutory Motion pursuant to Rule 73(A) of the judicial review of the administrative decision on assignment of counsel.

76. Third, the Appeals Chamber concurs with the finding made by Trial Chamber I in its decision of 6 May 2004 in the *Brima* Case, that such judicial review falls, due to the silence of the regulations applicable before the Special Court, within the inherent jurisdiction of the Trial Chamber:[2]

> [T]he chamber is of the opinion that the motion, even though brought under the wrong Rule, can, and so do we decide, in the overall interests of justice and to prevent a violation of the rights of the Accused, be examined by invoking our inherent jurisdiction to entertain it and to adjudicate on it on the ground of a denial of request for assignment of Counsel within the context of Article 17(4)(d) of the Statute.

77. The Appeals Chamber refers to the above quoted reasoning of President Pillay as regards the reasons for exercising such inherent jurisdiction.

78. For the foregoing reasons, the Appeals Chamber finds that the Trial Chamber had jurisdiction to judicially review the Registrar's Decision not to re-assign Counsel.

[. . .]

135. The Appeals Chamber refers to its above finding on the inherent jurisdiction of Chambers to judicially review administrative decisions affecting the rights of the Accused. The Appeals Chamber restates that such inherent jurisdiction may be exercised only in the silence of the regulations applicable to the matter.[3]

136. The Appeals Chamber notes that Article 13(F) of the Directive provides:

> Where the Principal Defender refuses to place the name of the applicant Counsel on the List of Qualified Counsel, or removes the name of Counsel from the List of Qualified Counsel, the concerned Counsel may seek review, by the President, of the Principal Defender's refusal. An application for review shall be in writing and the Principal Defender shall be given the opportunity to respond to it in writing.

137. For the reasons mentioned earlier as regards the Registrar's decision not to re-assign Counsel, the Appeals Chamber considers that where the Registrar uses the powers he keeps in concurrence with the Principal Defender, he shall do so in the same conditions as the Principal Defender would. In particular, where the regulations provide that the Principal Defender's

decision may be reviewed, the concurrent decision of the Registrar is submitted to the same condition.

138. Therefore, the Appeals Chamber considers that, pursuant to Article 13(F) of the Directive, the review of the decision to remove a Counsel from the List of Qualified Counsel, either taken by the Principal Defender or the Registrar, falls within the exclusive province of the President of the Special Court.

139. The Appeals Chamber therefore concludes that it has no jurisdiction to review the decision of the Registrar to remove Counsel from the List of Qualified Counsel and denies the ground and the related relief.

---

(1) ICTR, *Prosecutor v. Ntahobali*, ICTR-97-21-T, Decision on the Application by Arsène Shalom Ntahobali for Review of the Registrar's Decisions Pertaining to the Assignment of an Investigator" (President Pillay), 13 November 2002, para. 4-5.
(2) *Prosecutor v. Brima*, Case No. SCSL-2004-16-PT, Decision on Applicant's Motion Against Denial by the Acting Principal Defender to Enter a Legal Service Contract for the Assignment of Counsel, 6 May 2004, para. 39.
(3) *Prosecutor v. Norman, Fofana, Kondewa*, Case No. SCSL-2004-14-T, Decision on Prosecution Appeal Against the Trial Chamber's Decision of 2 August 2004 Refusing Leave to File an Interlocutory Appeal, 17 January 2005, para. 31-32.

- **Article 1: Competence of the SCSL – The Special Court and the TRC**

S1-AC-9

o *Prosecutor v. Norman*, Case No. SCSL-03-08-PT, Decision on Appeal by the Truth and Reconciliation Commission for Sierra Leone ("TRC" or "the Commission") and Chief Samuel Hinga Norman JP Against the Decision of His Lordship, Mr Justice Bankole Thompson Delivered on 30 October 2003 to Deny the TRC's Request to Hold a Public Hearing With Chief Samuel Hinga Norman JP, 28 November 2003, para. 33-34, 41, 44:[4]

33. [. . .] Truth Commissions and International Courts are both instruments for effectuating the promises made by states that victims of human rights violations shall have an effective remedy.(1) Criminal courts offer the most effective remedy – a trial, followed by punishment of those found guilty, in this

---

[4] See also *Prosecutor v. Gbao*, Case No. SCSL-04-15-A, Decision on Appeal by the Truth and Reconciliation Commission ("TRC") and Accused Against the Decision of Judge Bankole Thompson on 3 November 2003 to Deny the TRC's Request to Hold a Public Hearing with Augustine Gbao, 7 May 2004.

case of those who bear the greatest responsibility. TRC reports can assist society to move forward and beyond the hatreds that fuelled the war. Truth commissions offer two distinct prospects for victims – of truth, i.e. learning how and why they or their loved ones were murdered or maimed or mutilated, and of reconciliation, through understanding and forgiveness of those perpetrators who genuinely confess and regret. [...]

34. In what has been termed "transitional justice" periods, truth commissions may be the only way for weak governments. In this context they were common in South America in the 1980s – in Bolivia, Chile, El Salvador, Haiti, Argentina and so forth. They were usually accompanied by blanket amnesties and were not permitted to "name names" of those who might be identified as perpetrators of crimes against humanity, not to avoid prejudice to trials (which were not in prospect), but to avoid political embarrassment. The reports nonetheless shed light on abuses – in some cases, as with "*Nunca Mas*", very great light. They achieved a degree of truth, but without justice and in many cases without reconciliation – see the recent public demands in these countries to vacate amnesties and prosecute the perpetrators. The Lomé Accord of 1999 offered both a blanket amnesty and a TRC: only after that agreement was comprehensively violated did the international community deploy its muscle to insist on the prosecution of those bearing the greatest responsibility for the war.

[...]

41. In my judgement, Chief Hinga Norman is entitled to testify to the TRC upon condition that he has been fully apprised and advised of the dangers of so doing. I am satisfied that he has been expertly warned. His testimony must, however, be provided in a manner that reduces to an acceptable level any danger that it will influence witnesses (whether favourably or adversely) or affect the integrity of court proceedings or unreasonably affect co-defendants and other indictees. This in my judgement can be achieved by evidence prepared by him in writing (with the benefit of legal advice) and sworn in the form of an affidavit. I direct that if he wishes to take this course the Registrar should arrange for the swearing of the affidavit within the detention Unit in the presence of the TRC official, and permit the original affidavit to be handed over to the TRC, on condition that it gives an undertaking not to bring or assist any other person or agency to bring a prosecution for perjury under S9(2) of its Act. What public use, if any, is made thereafter of that affidavit will be a matter for the TRC and for the detainee and his lawyers. Should Counsel for the TRC have any further questions, these may be put to the indictee in writing and his answers may be sworn and

delivered in the same way. There shall be no public hearing of the kind requested or of any other kind prior to the conclusion of the trial. This is without prejudice to his right, if so advised, to make <u>unsworn</u> written statements to the TRC. It is without prejudice to his right to meet with commissioners in the Detention Unit, if they apply for that purpose, or to his right to meet them for confidential session, if a joint application is made for that purpose.

[...]

44. The work of the Special Court and the TRC is complementary and each must accommodate the existence of the other. The TRC is not in a position to suspend its work once trials begin in order to issue a final report when they are over, taking the evidence and verdicts into account. It would be seemly if the report that the TRC is [...] to issue in February refrains from passing concluded judgements on the criminal responsibility of any person who is detained to face trial in this Court. Should comment or conclusion be passer, it will of course have absolutely no effect on the minds of the judges of this Court who sit to provide a fair trial according to international standards. That said, the Special Court respects the TRC's work and will assist it so far as is possible and proper, subject only to our overriding duty to serve the interests of justice without which there may not be the whole truth and there is unlikely to be lasting reconciliation.

---

[1] Article 2(3) of the International Covenant on Civil and Political Rights, GA res. 2200A(XXI), 21 GAOR Suppl. No. 16 at 52.

> **Article 2**
> **Crimes Against Humanity**
>
> The Special Court shall have the power to prosecute persons who committed the following crimes as part of a widespread or systematic attack against any civilian population:
>
> a. Murder;
> b. Extermination;
> c. Enslavement;
> d. Deportation;
> e. Imprisonment;
> f. Torture;
> g. Rape, sexual slavery, enforced prostitution, forced pregnancy and any other form of sexual violence;
> h. Persecution on political, racial, ethnic or religious grounds;
> i. Other inhumane acts.

TRIAL CHAMBERS DECISIONS

- **Article 2: Crimes Against Humanity – Elements of Crimes**

S2-TC-1

o *Prosecutor v. Norman, Fofana, Kondewa*, Case No. SCSL-04-14-T, Decision on Motions for Judgment of acquittal Pursuant to Rule 98, 21 October 2005, para. 55-59, 66:

55. The common elements for Crimes Against Humanity include:

(a) there must be an attack;
(b) the acts of the accused must be part of the attack;
(c) the attack must be directed against any civilian population;
(d) the attack must be widespread or systematic;
(e) the accused must know that his acts constitute part of a pattern of widespread or systematic crimes directed against a civilian population.[1]

56. The Chamber endorses the view that an attack constitutes "a course of conduct involving the commission of acts", which need not constitute a military attack.[2] The Chamber, furthermore, agrees that "[t]he widespread characteristic refers to the scale of the acts perpetrated and to the number of victims",[3] and that "[t]he adjective 'systematic' signifies the organised nature of the acts of violence and the improbability of their random occurrence. Patterns of crimes – that is the

non-accidental repetition of similar criminal conduct on a regular basis – are a common expression of such systematic occurrence."[4]

57. The Chamber opines that the requirement for an attack to be "directed against" any "civilian population" requires that the civilian population "be the primary rather than an incidental target of the attack".[5] Accordingly, the Chamber adopts the interpretation of the ICTY Appeals Chamber in the *Kunarac* case which stated that:

> The expression 'directed against' is an expression which 'specifies that in the context of a crime against humanity the civilian population is the primary object of the attack'. In order to determine whether the attack may be said to have been so directed, the Trial Chamber will consider, *inter alia*, the means and method used in the course of the attack, the status of the victims, their number, the discriminatory nature of the attack, the nature of the crimes omitted in its course, the resistance to the assailants at the time and the extent to which the attacking force may be said to have complied or attempted to comply with the precautionary requirements of the laws of war.[6]

58. With respect to the term "civilian population", this Chamber adopts the broader interpretation as further described in the ICTY Trial Judgement in the *Blaskic* case:

> Crimes against humanity [...] do not mean only acts committed against civilians in the strict sense of the term but include also crimes against two categories of people: those who were members of a resistance movement and former combatants – regardless of whether they wore wear uniform or not – but who were not longer taking part in hostilities when the crimes were perpetrated because they had either left the army or were no longer bearing arms or, ultimately, had been placed *hors de combat*, in particular, due to their wounds or their being detained. The specific situation of the victim at the moment the crimes were committed, rather than his status, must be taken into account in determining his standing as a civilian.[7]

59. The Chamber also holds that the targeted population must be predominantly civilian in nature, although the presence of a number of non-civilians in their midst does not change the character of that population as civilian.[8]

[...]

66. The Chamber finds that the arguments raised by the Defence for Kondewa relating to the legitimacy and proportionality of an armed attack against the civilian population do

not apply to the offences charged as Crimes Against Humanity in the Indictment, nor do they apply to the other offences charged in the Indictment pursuant to Article 3 Common to the Geneva Conventions of 1949 and Additional Protocol II. Crimes Against Humanity may be committed in times of peace or times of armed conflict. The arguments raised by the Defence for Kondewa relate to charges pursuant to Grave Breaches of Additional Protocol I to the Geneva Conventions, namely Article 57, which proscribes making the civilian population or individual civilians the object of attacks, which this Chamber is not called upon to address because no Accused Person is being charged with any such violation in this trial.

---

(1) *Prosecutor v. Tadic*, Judgment, 15 July 1999, Appeals Chamber, paras 248 and 251; *Prosecutor v. Kunarac*, Judgment, 12 June 2002, Appeals Chamber, paras 85-100, 102-104 and 336; *Prosecutor v. Brdjanin*, Judgment, 1 September 2004, Trial Chamber, para 130.
(2) *Prosecutor v. Kunarac*, Judgment, 22 February 2001, Trial Chamber, para. 387.
(3) *Prosecutor v. Blaskic*, Judgment, 3 March 2000, Trial Chamber, para. 206. See also *Prosecutor v. Tadic*, Judgment, 7 May 1997, Trial Chamber, para. 648; *Prosecutor v. Naletilic*, Judgment, 31 March 2003, Trial Chamber, para. 236.
(4) *Prosecutor v. Kunarac*, Judgment, 22 February 2001, Trial Chamber, para. 429; *Prosecutor v. Kunarac*, Judgment, 12 June 2002, Appeals Chamber, para. 94. See also *Prosecutor v. Naletilic*, Judgment, 31 March 2003, Trial Chamber, para. 236; *Prosecutor v. Semanza*, Judgment, 15 May 2003, Trial Chamber, para. 329 ("'Systematic' describes the organized nature of the attack").
(5) *Prosecutor v. Kunarac*, Judgment, 12 June 2002, Appeals Chamber, para. 92. See also *Prosecutor v. Naletilic*, Judgment, 31 March 2003, Trial Chamber, para. 235; *Prosecutor v. Semanza*, Judgment, 15 May 2003, Trial Chamber, para. 330.
(6) *Prosecutor v. Kunarac*, Judgment, 12 June 2002, Appeals Chamber, para. 90.
(7) *Prosecutor v. Blaskic*, Judgment, 3 March 2000, Trial Chamber, para. 214.
(8) *Prosecutor v. Tadic*, Judgment, 7 May 1997, Trial Chamber, para. 638; *Prosecutor v. Kayishema and Ruzindana*, Judgment, 21 May 1999, Trial Chamber, para. 128.

- **Article 2(f): Crimes Against Humanity – "Torture" – Difference Between Torture and Inhumane and Degrading Treatment**

S2-TC-2

o *Prosecutor v. Sankoh*, Case No. SCSL-03-02-PT, Ruling on the Motion for a Stay of Proceedings Filed by the Applicant, 22 July 2003, page 9:

In fact, even though the provisions of Article 5 of the Universal Declaration of Human Rights enshrine the key elements of torture, degrading and inhuman treatment as does Article 5 of the African Charter of Human Rights and People's Liberty, it is observed that a treatment which amounts to inhuman and degrading treatment might not necessarily fulfil the ingredients of what constitutes the element of torture, but torture could encompass those acts that individually or collectively, constitute what is considered as being inhuman and degrading.

- **Article 2(i): Crimes Against Humanity – "Others Inhumane Acts" – Exclusion of Sexual Violence**

S2-TC-3

o *Prosecutor v. Norman, Fofana, Kondewa*, Case No. SCSL-04-14-T, Reasoned Majority decision on Prosecution Motion for a Ruling on the Admissibility of Evidence, 24 May 2005, para. 19:

19. [. . .] [T]he Chamber finds significantly as follows:

[. . .]

(iii)(a) that the particulars embodied in the Consolidated Indictment in respect of Counts 3 and 4 cannot be validly interpreted to be of an inclusive nature and as not excluding the broad range of unlawful acts which can lead to serious physical and mental harm, especially having proper regard to the formula, "and any other form of sexual violence" in Article 2(g) creating a separate specific residual category of sexual violence, of the same kind as rape, sexual slavery, enforced prostitution, and forced pregnancy;

(b) that in the light of the separate and distinct residual category of sexual offences under Article 2(g), it is impermissible to allege acts of sexual violence (other than rape, sexual slavery, enforced prostitution, forced pregnancy) under Article 2(i) since "other inhumane acts", even if residual, must logically be restrictively interpreted as covering only acts of a non-sexual nature amounting to an affront to human dignity;

(c) that the clear legislative intent behind the statutory formula "any other form of sexual violence" in Article 2(g) is the creation of a category of offences of sexual violence of a character that do not amount to any of the earlier enumerated sexual crimes, and that to permit such other forms of sexual violence to be charged under "other inhumane acts" offends the rule against multiplicity and uncertainty; [. . .]

- **Article 2(i): Crimes Against Humanity – "Others Inhumane Acts" – Forced Marriage**

S2-TC-4

o *Prosecutor v. Sesay, Kallon, Gbao*, Case No. SCSL-04-15-PT, Decision on Prosecution request for Leave to Amend the Indictment, 6 May 2004, para. 36, 50-51, 57:[5]

36. The Prosecution in its submissions in this case explains that the purpose of this motion to amend the indictment is to enable it to add to it, "a new charge" of crimes against humanity – Other Inhumane Act (forced marriages), as a new count in the Consolidated Indictment. This count, the Prosecution explains, will become the 8th [. . .].

[. . .]

50. Our immediate reflection on this issue that we have raised is that the count related to forced marriage which the prosecution is seeking our leave to add to the consolidated indictment is as much a sexual, indeed, a gender offence as those that were included in the initial individual indictments and that feature in the current consolidated indictment on which this application to amend is based.

51. We would like to say here that Forced Marriage is in fact what we would like to classify, as a 'kindred offence' to those that exist in the consolidated indictment in the view of the commonality of the ingredients needed to prove offences of this nature. Given this consideration and the fact that material related to those gender offences that feature on the consolidated indictment has long been disclosed to the Defence, we are of the opinion that the amendment sought is not a novelty that should necessitate fresh investigations as the defence contends. [. . .]

[. . .]

57. [. . .] We accordingly allow the Prosecution's motion to amend the Consolidated Indictment and order as follows:

(i) That the inclusion in the Consolidated Indictment of a new count 8 of "Other Inhumane Act, a crime against humanity, punishable under Article 2.i of the Statute", as well as the other amendments requested by the Prosecution, is hereby granted in the form contained in the Proposed Amended Indictment filed as Annex 1 to the Motion on 9 February 2004;

---

[5] See also *Prosecutor v. Brima, Kamara, Kanu*, Case No. SCSL-04-16-PT, Decision on Prosecution Request for Leave to Amend the Indictment, 6 May 2004, para. 36, 51-52, 58.

S2-TC-5   o *Prosecutor v. Brima, Kamara, Kanu*, Case No. SCSL-04-16-T, Decision on Prosecution request for Leave to Call an Additional Witness (Zainab Hawa Bangura) Pursuant to Rule 73bis(E), and on Joint Defence Notice to Inform the Trial Chamber of its Position vis-à-vis the Proposed Expert Witness (Mrs Bangura) Pursuant to Rule 94bis, 5 August 2005, para. 29:

> 29. [. . .] We further note the Prosecution submissions that the subject of forced marriages during the Sierra Leone conflict is an extremely sensitive topic, particularly given its distinct social and cultural consequences and its uniqueness to the Sierra Leone conflict and that the Trial Chamber would best be served to hear testimony from Mrs. Bangura, a Sierra Leonean expert on the matter. [. . .] We note and accept the fact that "forced marriage" is one of the forms or acts of the crime of "sexual violence" as charged in Counts 6-9 of the Further Amended Consolidated Indictment.[1] We further note and accept the Prosecution submission that Mrs Bangura's evidence is intended to include *(a)* the context within which forced marriage occurred during the conflict; *(b)* the socio-cultural meaning of forced marriage during the conflict; and *(c)* the long-term social, cultural, physical and psychological consequences of forced marriage during the conflict for its victims, all of which factors are relevant and material to the facts in issue in the trial. [. . .]

---

[1] *The Prosecutor v. Alex Tamba Brima* et al., Case No. SCSL-04-16-T, Further Amended Consolidated Indictment, 18 February 2005, paragraphs 51-57.

- **Article 2(i): Crimes Against Humanity – "Others Inhumane Acts" – Inhuman and Degrading Treatment**

S2-TC-6   o *Prosecutor v. Sankoh*, Case No. SCSL-03-02-PT, Ruling on the Motion for a Stay of Proceedings Filed by the Applicant, 22 July 2003, pages 9-11:

> As far as the first question is concerned, it is my considered opinion that for a treatment to be termed inhuman or degrading, it should be established that the said treatment, intended or not, and which at times could be spiced by a deprivation of liberty, be it lawful or otherwise, is such as causes or inflicts anguish, human suffering, hardship, and humiliation on the victim. In other words, it should amount to a violation of the human integrity of the individual subjected to it.

In fact, even though the provisions of Article 5 of the Universal Declaration of Human Rights enshrine the key elements of torture, degrading and inhuman treatment as does Article 5 of the African Charter of Human Rights and People's Liberty, it is observed that a treatment which amounts to inhuman and degrading treatment might not necessarily fulfil the ingredients of what constitutes the element of torture, but torture could encompass those acts that individually or collectively, constitute what is considered as being inhuman and degrading.

[...]

I am comforted in this view by an examination of certain judicial decisions whose facts savoured of acts of inhuman and degrading treatment such as that of Ireland vs. the U.K. (1978) 2 EHRR 25, where it were held that interrogation techniques such as sleep deprivation and a denial of adequate food was considered to be inhuman and degrading treatment just as treatment is considered inhuman if it causes intense physical or mental suffering. In the case of ***Cyprus vs. Turkey*** (1976) 4 EHRR 482, it was held that physical assault can amount to inhuman treatment, particularly where weapons or other instruments have been used, and so also are sexual assaults. In ***Ribitch vs Austria (1995) 21 EHRR 573*** it was considered an infringement of the protection of the individuals right against inhuman and degrading treatment where the person is deprived of his liberty and there is any recourse to physical force which has not been necessitated by his own conduct, and which act, diminishes human dignity.

Article 3
Violations of Article 3 common to the Geneva Conventions and of Additional Protocol II

The Special Court shall have the power to prosecute persons who committed or ordered the commission of serious violations of article 3 common to the Geneva Conventions of 12 August 1949 for the Protection of War Victims, and of Additional Protocol II thereto of 8 June 1977. These violations shall include:

a. Violence to life, health and physical or mental well-being of persons, in particular murder as well as cruel treatment such as torture, mutilation or any form of corporal punishment;
b. Collective punishments;
c. Taking of hostages;
d. Acts of terrorism;
e. Outrages upon personal dignity, in particular humiliating and degrading treatment, rape, enforced prostitution and any form of indecent assault;
f. Pillage;
g. The passing of sentences and the carrying out of executions without previous judgement pronounced by a regularly constituted court, affording all the judicial guarantees which are recognized as indispensable by civilized peoples;
h. Threats to commit any of the foregoing acts.

TRIAL CHAMBERS DECISIONS

- **Article 3: Violations of Article 3 Common to the Geneva and Protocol II – Elements of Crimes**

S3-TC-1

o *Prosecutor v. Norman, Fofana, Kondewa*, Case No. SCSL-04-14-T, Decision on Motions for Judgment of Acquittal Pursuant to Rule 98, 21 October 2005, para. 68-70:

68. In the Chamber's opinion the application of Article 3 of the Statute requires that the alleged acts of the Accused should have been committed in the course of an armed conflict. We are of the opinion that it is immaterial whether the conflict is internal or international in nature.[1] The Appeals Chamber of this Court and the Appeals Chamber of the ICTY and ICTR have recently restated this proposition. In *Prosecution v. Fofana*, the Appeals Chamber said:

It has been observed that "even thought he rules applicable in internal armed conflict still lag behind the law that applies in international conflict, the establishment and work of the ad hoc Tribunals has specifically contributed to diminishing the relevance of the distinction between the two types of conflict". The distinction is no longer of great relevance in relation to the crimes articulated in Article 3 of the Statute as these crimes are prohibited in all conflicts. Crimes during internal armed conflict form part of the broader category of crimes during international armed conflict. In respect of Article 3, therefore, the Court need only be satisfied that an armed conflict existed and that the alleged violations were related to the armed conflict.[2]

69. Relying on the ICTY Appeals Chamber in *Tadic* the Chamber rules that "an armed conflict exists whenever there is a resort to armed force between states or protracted armed violence between governmental author-ities and organized armed groups or between such groups within a state".[3]

70. Common Article 3 applies to "[p]ersons taking no active part in the hostilities, including members of armed forces who have laid down their arms and those placed *hors de combat* by sickness, wounds, detention, or any other cause", and Additional Protocol II similarly treats the class of non-combatants as "all persons who do not take a direct part or who have ceased to take part in hostilities".[4]

---

[1] *Prosecutor v. Kunarac*, Judgment, 12 June 2002, Appeals Chamber, paras 57 and 58; *Prosecutor v. Celebici*, Judgment, 16 November 1998, Trial Chamber, para. 303; *Prosecutor v. Celebici*, Judgment, 8 April 2003, Appeals Chamber, paras 140 and 150; *Prosecutor v. Anto Furundzija*, Judgment, 10 December 1998, Trial Chamber, para. 132; *Prosecutor v. Blaskic*, Judgment, 3 March 2000, Trial Chamber, para. 161; *Prosecutor v. Brdjanin*, Judgment, 1 September 2004, Trial Chamber, para. 127.
[2] Decision on Preliminary Motion on Lack of Jurisdiction Materiae: Nature of the Armed Conflict, 25 May 2004, para. 25.
[3] *Prosecutor v. Tadic*, Decision on Defence Motion for Interlocutory Appeal on Jurisdiction, 2 October 1995, Appeals Chamber, para. 70.
[4] Article 3(1) of Geneva Conventions of 1949. *See Akayesu* Trial Judgement, para. 629.

- **Article 3(a): Violations of Article 3 Common and Protocol II – "Murder"**

S3-TC-2   o *Prosecutor v. Norman, Fofana, Kondewa*, Case No. SCSL-04-14-T, Decision on Motions for Judgement of Acquittal Pursuant to Rule 98, 21 October 2005, para. 72-73:

72. This Chamber takes due cognisance of the fact that Murder as a Crime Against Humanity has consistently been defined as the death of the victim resulting from an act or omission of the accused committed with the intent either to kill or to cause serious bodily harm in the reasonable knowledge that it would likely result in death. It must also be shown that the victims were persons taking no active part in the hostilities.[1]

73. The Chamber is of the opinion, as it was held in the *Stakic* case, that to prove Murder, as a Violation of Article 3 Common to the Geneva Con-ventions and Additional Protocol II punishable under Article 3 of the Statute, it must be established that death resulted from an act or omission of the accused committed with the intent either to kill or to cause serious bodily harm in the reasonable knowledge that it would likely result in death. It must also be shown that the victims were persons taking no active part in the hostilities.[2]

---

[1] *Prosecutor v. Stakic*, Judgment, 31 July 2003, Trial Chamber, para. 584; *Prosecutor v. Strugar*, Decision on Defence Motion Requesting Judgement of Acquittal Pursuant to Rule 98 *bis*, 21 June 2004, Trial Chamber, para. 32; *Prosecuto v. Vasiljevic*, Judgment, 29 November 2002, Trial Chamber, para. 205; *Prosecutor v. Krnojelac*, Judgment, 15 March 2002, Trial Chamber, para. 324.
[2] *Prosecutor v. Stakic*, Judgment, 31 July 2003, Trial Chamber, para. 584; *Prosecutor v. Strugar*, Decision on Defence Motion Requesting Judgement of Acquittal Pursuant to Rule 98 *bis*, 21 June 2004, Trial Chamber, para. 32.

- **Article 3(a): Violations of Article 3 Common and Protocol II – "Cruel Treatment"**

S3-TC-3 o *Prosecutor v. Norman, Fofana, Kondewa*, Case No. SCSL-04-14-T, Decision on Motions for Judgment of Acquittal Pursuant to Rule 98, 21 October 2005, para. 93-95:

93. Consistent with the present state of international criminal law we are of the opinion that to sustain a conviction for Inhumane Acts, the Prosecution must prove "(i) the occurrence of an act or omission of similar seriousness to the other enumerated acts under the Article; (ii) the act or omission caused serious mental or physical suffering or injury or constituted a serious attack on human dignity" and (iii) the act or omission was performed deliberately by the accused or a person or persons for whose acts and omissions he bears criminal responsibility".[1] These ingredients together constitute the *actus reus*.

94. Furthermore, relying on established jurisprudence, the Chamber finds support for the proposition that the *mens rea* is satisfied "[w]here the principal offender, at the time of the

act or omission, had the intention to inflict serious physical or mental suffering or to commit a serious attack on the human dignity of the victim, or where he knew that his act or omission was likely to cause serious physical or mental suffering or a serious attack upon human dignity and was reckless as to whether such suffering or attack would result from his act or omission".[2]

95. Relying on the *Celebici* decision of the ICTY, The Chamber adopts the definition of Cruel Treatment as a Violation of Article 3 Common to the Geneva Conventions and of Additional Protocol II, as an intentional act or omission causing serious mental or physical suffering or injury or constituting a serious attack on human dignity. We take the view that such acts may include treatment that does not meet the purposive requirement for the offence of torture.[3] The law requires that it be shown that the victims were persons taking no active part in the hostilities.[4]

---

[1] *Prosecutor v. Vasiljevic*, Judgment, 29 November 2002, Trial Chamber, para. 234.
[2] *Prosecutor v. Krnojelac*, Judgment, 29 November 2002, Trial Chamber, para. 130; *Prosecutor v. Kayishema*, Judgment, 21 May 1999, Trial Chamber, paras 148-153; *Prosecutor v. Vasiljevic*, Judgment, 29 November 2002, Trial Chamber, para. 236.
[3] *Prosecutor v. Delalic et al.*, Judgement, 16 November 1998, Trial Chamber, paras 443 and 552 *cited in* Kriangsak Kittichaisaree, International Criminal Law, Oxford University Press, 2001.
[4] *Prosecutor v. Delalic et al.*, Judgment, 8 April 2003, Appeals Chamber, para. 424; *Prosecutor v. Vasilevic,* Judgment, 29 November 2002, Appeals Chamber, para. 234; *Prosecutor v. Naletilic*, Judgment, 31 March 2003, Trial Chamber, para. 246.

- **Article 3(b): Violations of Article 3 Common and Additional Protocoll II – "Collective Punishment"**

S3-TC-4

o *Prosecutor v. Norman, Fofana, Kondewa*, Case No. SCSL-04-14-T, Decision on Motions for Judgement of Acquittal Pursuant to Rule 98, 21 October 2005, para. 116-118:

116. This Chamber notes that Article 3 of the Statute of the Special Court Statute is a verbatim reproduction of Article 4 of Additional Protocol II to the Geneva Conventions and "collective punishments" in Article 3(b) of the Statute derives its origins from similar provisions in the Geneva Conventions and Additional Protocols.

117. The Chamber also further notes the ICRC commentaries on the prohibition of Collective Punishments in Article 4 which concluded that:

[Collective punishments] should be understood in its widest sense, and concerns not only penalties imposed in the normal judicial process, but also any other kind of sanction (such as confiscation of property) as the ICRC had originally intended. The prohibition of collective punishments was included in the article relating to fundamental guarantees by consensus. That decision was important because it is based on the intention to give the rule the widest possible scope, and to avoid any risk of a restrictive interpretation.[1]

118. Based on Article 4 of Additional Protocol II to the Geneva Conventions, Article 33 of the Fourth Geneva Convention and Commentaries on the aforesaid Article 33, the Chamber is of the view that the constitutive elements of the crime of collective punishments under Article 3(b) of the Statute are comprised of, in aggregation, the elements constitutive of Common Article 3 crimes and these two other specific elements, to wit, (i) a punishment imposed upon protected persons for acts that they have not committed and (ii) the intent, on the part of the offender, to punish the protected persons or group of protected persons for acts which form the subject of the punishment.

[1] Commentary on the Additional Protocols, at 1374.

- **Article 3(d): Violations of Article 3 Common and Protocol II – "Acts of Terrorism"**

S3-TC-5

o *Prosecutor v. Norman, Fofana, Kondewa*, Case No. SCSL-04-14-T, Decision on Motions for Judgement of Acquittal Pursuant to Rule 98, 21 October 2005, para. 109-112:

109. As regards this Count, the Chamber notes that in the case of *Galic*, the Trial Chamber of the ICTY provided the definition of the crime of terror as:

1. Acts of violence directed against the civilian population or individual civilians not taking direct part in hostilities causing death or serious injury to body or health within the civilian population.
2. The offender wilfully made the civilian population or individual civilians not taking direct part in hostilities the object of those acts of violence.
3. The above offence was committed with the primary purpose of spreading terror among the civilian population.[1]

110. However, this Chamber wishes to emphasise that while the charges in the *Galic* case related to violations of Article 15(2) of Additional Protocol I in the context of an international armed conflict, the Decision might be of assistance in interpreting Article 3(d) of the Special Court's Statute.

111. The Chamber notes that Protocol II does not define the term "acts of terrorism", and that whilst Article 4(d) of the aforesaid Protocol prohibits "acts of terrorism" generally and with respect to protected persons, Article 13(d) thereof refers only to a specific type of violence or threat, is one that is directed towards terrorizing the civilian population. In the Chambers opinion, Article 4(d) does encompass Article 13(d) and the latter provision is useful in interpreting the meaning of terrorism in the former provision. Relying on the ICRC Commentaries on Article 51 of the Protocol I, upon which Article 13(d) is based, the Chamber holds that the proscriptive ambit of Protocol II in respect of "acts of terrorism" does extend beyond acts of threats of violence committed against protected persons to "acts directed against installations which would cause victims terror as a side-effect."[2]

112. The Chamber concludes that the crime of Acts of Terrorism is comprised of the elements constitutive of Article 3 Common to the Geneva Conventions as well as the following specific elements:[3]

1. Acts or threats of violence directed against protected persons or their property.
2. The offender wilfully made protected persons or their property the object of those acts and threats of violence.
3. The acts or threats of violence were committed with the primary purpose of spreading terror among protected persons.

---

[1] *Prosecutor v. Galic*, Judgment, 5 December 2003, Trial Chamber, para. 133.
[2] ICRC, *Commentary on the Additional Protocols*, at 1375.
[3] *See Prosecutor v. Galic*, Judgment, 5 December 2003, Trial Chamber, para. 133. While the charges in the *Galic* case related to violations of Article 15(2) of Additional Protocol I in the context of an international armed conflict, it does serve as a useful precedent for interpreting Article 3(d) of the Special Court's Statute.

- **Article 3(e): Violations of Article 3 Common and Protocol II – "Outrages Upon Personal Dignity" – Inhuman and Degrading Treatment**

S3-TC-6

o *Prosecutor v. Sankoh*, Case No. SCSL-03-02-PT, Ruling on the Motion for a Stay of Proceedings Filed by the Applicant, 22 July 2003, pages 9-11:

As far as the first question is concerned, it is my considered opinion that for a treatment to be termed inhuman or degrading, it should be established that the said treatment, intended or not, and which at times could be spiced by a deprivation of liberty, be it lawful or otherwise, is such as causes or inflicts anguish, human suffering, hardship, and humiliation on the victim. In other words, it should amount to a violation of the human integrity of the individual subjected to it.

In fact, even though the provisions of Article 5 of the Universal Declaration of Human Rights enshrine the key elements of torture, degrading and inhuman treatment as does Article 5 of the African Charter of Human Rights and People's Liberty, it is observed that a treatment which amounts to inhuman and degrading treatment might not necessarily fulfil the ingredients of what constitutes the element of torture, but torture could encompass those acts that individually or collectively, constitute what is considered as being inhuman and degrading.

[...]

I am comforted in this view by an examination of certain judicial decisions whose facts savoured of acts of inhuman and degrading treatment such as that of Ireland vs. the U.K. (1978) 2 EHRR 25, where it were held that interrogation techniques such as sleep deprivation and a denial of adequate food was considered to be inhuman and degrading treatment just as treatment is considered inhuman if it causes intense physical or mental suffering. In the case of ***Cyprus vs. Turkey*** (1976) 4 EHRR 482, it was held that physical assault can amount to inhuman treatment, particularly where weapons or other instruments have been used, and so also are sexual assaults. In ***Ribitch vs Austria (1995) 21 EHRR 573*** it was considered an infringement of the protection of the individuals right against inhuman and degrading treatment where the person is deprived of his liberty and there is any recourse to physical force which has not been necessitated by his own conduct, and which act, diminishes human dignity.

- **Article 3(f): Violations of Article 3 Common and Protocol II – "Pillage"**

S3-TC-7
o *Prosecutor v. Norman, Fofana, Kondewa*, Case No. SCSL-04-14-T, Decision on Motions for Judgement of Acquittal Pursuant to Rule 98, 21 October 2005, para. 102:

> 102. The Chamber observes that the terms "pillage", "plunder" and 'spoliation' have been varyingly used to describe the unlawful appropriation of private and public property during armed conflict. For instance, The Trial Chamber of the ICTY in the case of *Celebici* noted that "plunder" should be understood as encompassing acts traditionally described as "pillage,"[1] and that pillage extends to cases of "organised" and "systematic" seizure of property from protected persons as well as to "acts of looting committed by individual soldiers for their private gain".[2] In the Chamber's opinion, the crime of Pillage includes the following constitutive elements:
>
> (1) The perpetrator appropriated private or public property;
> (2) The perpetrator intended to deprive the owner of the property and to appropriate it for private or personal use;
> (3) The appropriation was without the consent of the owner.

---

[1] *Prosecutor v. Delalic et al.*, Judgment, 16 November 1998, Trial Chamber, para. 590; *Prosecutor v. Simic et al.*, Judgment, 16 October 2003, Trial Chamber, para. 98.

[2] *Prosecutor v. Delalic et al.*, Judgment, 16 November 1998, Trial Chamber, para. 590; *Prosecutor v. Blaskic*, Judgment, 3 March 2000, Trial Chamber, para. 181; *Prosecutor v. Jelisic*, Judgment, 14 December 1999, Trial Chamber, para. 48.

APPEALS CHAMBER DECISIONS

- **Article 3: Violations of Article 3 Common and Protocol II – Applicability and Jurisdiction**

S3-AC-1
o *Prosecutor v. Fofana*, Case No. SCSL-04-14-AR72, Decision on Preliminary Motion on Lack of Jurisdiction *Materiae*: Nature of the Armed Conflict, 25 May 2004, para. 20-27:

> 20. Article 3 of the Statute is explicitly taken from Common Article 3 to the Geneva Conventions and Additional Protocol

II, both of which apply to internal armed conflicts.[1] The question is whether the reference to these two instruments imports a jurisdictional criterion relating to the nature of the conflict into Article 3 of the Statute. The Statute makes no specific reference to the nature of the conflict. However, given the express reference to Common Article 3 of the Geneva Conventions and Additional Protocol II, on its face it would seem that Article 3 must be construed as being applicable to internal armed conflicts. As argued by the Defence, the substantive norms cannot be divorced from the criteria essential to their applicability even if those criteria are not specifically incorporated into the Statute. The International Criminal Tribunal for Rwanda ("ICTR"), for example, in interpreting its own Statute, has found that the material requirements of applicability of Additional Protocol II must be satisfied where a specific reference has been made to Additional Protocol II in counts against an accused.[2] Notably, Article 3 of the Statute of the Special Court is taken verbatim from Article 4 of the ICTR Statute.

21. Any obstacle to the application of Article 3 to crimes committed during an international armed conflict is nevertheless overcome if the actual violations included in Article 3, sub-paragraphs (a) to (h), are found to be part of customary international law applicable in an identical fashion to both internal and international armed conflicts. Common Article 3 of the Geneva Conventions of 1949 was designed to reflect certain minimum mandatory rules applicable to internal armed conflicts that were already included within the broader framework of rules applicable to international armed conflicts. In the *Akayesu* case, the ICTR Trial Chamber summarized the position as follows:

> The four 1949 Geneva Conventions and the 1977 Additional Protocol I thereto generally apply to international armed conflicts only, whereas Article 3 common to the Geneva Conventions extends a *minimum threshold of humanitarian protection* as well to all persons affected by a non-international conflict, a protection which was further developed and enhanced in the 1977 Additional Protocol II. In the field of international humanitarian law, a clear distinction as to the thresholds of application has been made between situations of international armed conflicts, in which the law of armed conflicts is applicable as a whole, situations of non-international (internal) armed conflicts, where Common Article 3 and Additional Protocol II are applicable, and non-international armed conflicts where only Common Article 3 is applicable.[3]

The International Committee of the Red Cross Commentary to the Fourth Geneva Convention confirms that "th[e] minimum requirement in the case of non-international conflict, is *a fortiori* applicable in international armed conflicts. It proclaims the guiding principle common to all four Geneva Conventions, and from it each of them derives the essential provision around which it is built."[4]

22. In the 1986 *Nicaragua* case, the International Court of Justice ("ICJ") found that Common Article 3:

> defines certain rules to be applied in the armed conflicts of a non-international character. There is no doubt that, in the event of international armed conflicts, these rules also constitute a minimum yardstick, in addition to the more elaborate rules which are also to apply to international armed conflicts; and they are rules which, in the Court's opinion, reflect what the Court in 1949 called 'elementary considerations of humanity'.[5]

The ICJ went on to say that

> "[b]ecause the minimum rules applicable to international and non-international armed conflicts are identical, there is no need to address the question whether those actions must be looked at in the context of the rules which operate for the one or for the other category of conflict."[6]

The ICJ concluded that "general principles of humanitarian law include a particular prohibition, accepted by States, and extending to activities which occur in the context of armed conflicts, whether international in character or not".[7]

23. The Statute of the International Criminal Tribunal for the Former Yugoslavia ("ICTY") includes in its Article 3 "violations of the laws or customs of war" which have been found to include violations of Common Article 3.[8] Notably, no express mention is made of Common Article 3 or Additional Protocol II in the ICTY Statute. The Appeals Chamber of the ICTY held in the *Tadic* decision on jurisdiction that "with respect to the minimum rules in Common Article 3, the character of the conflict is largely irrelevant".[9] In that case the Appeals Chamber went on to conclude that:

> In the light of the intent of the Security Council and the logical and systematic interpretation of Article 3 [of the ICTY Statute], as well as customary international law, the Appeals Chamber concludes that, under Article 3, the International Tribunal has jurisdiction over the acts alleged in the indictment, regardless of whether they occurred within an internal or international armed conflict. Thus, to the extent that Appellant's challenge to jurisdiction under Article 3 is based on the nature of the underlying conflict, the motion must be denied.[10]

In the later case of *Prosecutor v Delalic*, the ICTY Appeals Chamber addressed directly the question whether Common

Article 3 is applicable to international armed conflicts. The Appeals Chamber explained:[11]

> Common Article 3 of the Geneva Conventions may be considered as the "minimum yardstick" of rules of international humanitarian law of similar substance applicable to both internal and international conflicts... It is both legally and morally untenable that the rules contained in common article 3, which constitute mandatory minimum rules applicable to internal conflicts, in which rules are less developed than in respect of international conflicts, would not be applicable to conflicts of an international character. The rules of common Article 3 are encompassed and further developed in the body of rules applicable to international conflicts. It is logical that this minimum be applicable to international conflicts as the substance of these core rules is identical.[12]

In the judgment of the Trial Chamber in the *Akayesu* case before the ICTR, it was held that the core protections in Protocol II which mirror the Common Article 3 protections (namely Articles 4(1) and 4(2) of Additional Protocol II) form part of customary international law.[13] It was also pointed out that the four Geneva Conventions and two Protocols were adopted primarily to protect the victims and potential victims of armed conflicts.[14]

24. Article 3, sub-paragraphs (a) to (f), and (h) of the Special Court Statute are taken directly from Article 4(2) of Protocol II, while Article 3(g) mirrors Article 3(1)(d) of Common Article 3. There can therefore be no doubt that the norms embodied in Article 3 of the Statute form part of customary international law. Any argument that these norms do not entail individual criminal responsibility has been put to rest in ICTY and ICTR jurisprudence.[15]

25. It has been observed that "even though the rules applicable in internal armed conflict still lag behind the law that applies in international conflict, the establishment and work of the ad hoc Tribunals has significantly contributed to diminishing the relevance of the distinction between the two types of conflict."[16] The distinction is no longer of great relevance in relation to the crimes articulated in Article 3 of the Statute as these crimes are prohibited in all conflicts. Crimes during internal armed conflict form part of the broader category of crimes during international armed conflict.[17] In respect of Article 3, therefore, the Court need only be satisfied that an armed conflict existed and that the alleged violations were related to the armed conflict.[18]

26. Where the rules are identical in respect of both internal and international armed conflict it cannot follow that because the provision in the Statute is framed in terms of the treaty

provision applicable to internal armed conflicts, the Court has no jurisdiction to apply the provision in the context of an international armed conflict.

27. Furthermore, although it cannot seriously be doubted that there is a distinction between international and internal armed conflict, sometimes it is a distinction without much practical significance since internal conflict can co-exist with international conflict. In the *Tadic* appeal judgment[19] it was held that "in case of an internal armed conflict breaking out on the territory of a State, it may become international (or, depending upon the circumstances, be international in character alongside an internal armed conflict) if (i) another State intervenes in that conflict through its troops, or alternatively if (ii) some of the participants in the internal armed conflict act on behalf of the other State."[20] Thus, the distinction between internal and international armed conflict may become blurred but the baseline protections in Common Article 3 and Additional Protocol II nevertheless apply.

---

[1] The chapeau of Common Article 3 reads: "In the case of armed conflict not of an international character occurring in the territory of one of the High Contracting Parties, each party to the conflict shall be bound to apply, as a minimum, the following provisions..." Article 1 of Additional Protocol II reads: "This Protocol, which develops and supplements Article 3 common to the Geneva Conventions of 12 August 1949 without modifying its existing conditions of application, shall apply to all armed conflicts which are not covered by Article 1 of the Protocol Additional to the Geneva Conventions of 12 August 1949, and relating to the Protection of Victims of International Armed Conflicts (Protocol I) and which take place in the territory of a High Contracting Party between its armed forces and dissident armed forces or other organized armed groups which, under responsible command, exercise such control over a part of its territory as to enable them to carry out sustained and concerted military operations and to implement this Protocol."
[2] See *Prosecutor v Akayesu*, Case No. ICTR-96-4-T, Judgement, 2 September 1998, para. 618.
[3] *Prosecutor v Jean-Paul Akayesu*, Case No. ICTR-96-4-T, Judgement, 2 September 1998, para. 601, emphasis added.
[4] Pictet, (ed), Commentary: IV Geneva Convention Relative to the Protection of Civilian Persons in Time of War, International Committee of the Red Cross, Geneva, 1958, p. 14.
[5] *Military and Paramilitary Activities (Nicaragua v United States)*, (1986) ICJ Reports 14, para. 218.
[6] Ibid., para. 219.
[7] Ibid., para. 255.
[8] *Prosecutor v Delalic et al.*, Case No. IT-96-21-T, Judgement, 16 November 1998, para. 298.
[9] *Prosecution v Tadic*, Case No. IT-94-1-AR72, Decision on the Defence Motion for Interlocutory Appeal on Jurisdiction, 20 October 1995, para. 102.
[10] Ibid., para. 137.
[11] The Appeals Chamber referred to the opinion of the International Committee of the Red Cross that the purpose of Common Article 3 was to "ensure respect for the few essential rules of humanity which all civilized nations consider as valid everywhere and under all circumstances and as being above and outside war itself". *Prosecutor v Delalic et al. (Celebici*

case), Case No. IT-96-21-A, Judgement, 20 February 2001, (*"Delalic* Appeal Judgment"), para. 143.
[12] *Delalic* Appeal Judgment, paras 147 and 150.
[13] *Prosecutor v Akayesu*, Case No. ICTR-96-4-T, Judgement, 2 September 1998, paras 601-17.
[14] Ibid., para. 603.
[15] *Prosecutor v Tadic*, Case No. IT-94-1-AR72, Decision on the Defence Motion for Interlocutory Appeal on Jurisdiction, 2 October 1995, 128-136, applied in *Prosecutor v Delalic et al. (Celebici case)*, Case No. IT-96-21-T, Judgement, 16 November 1998, para. 307 and *Delalic* Appeal Judgement, paras 159-174.
[16] F. Kalshoven; L. Zegveld, *Constraints on the Waging of War, An Introduction to International Humanitarian Law*, ICRC, 2001, 188.
[17] Archbold, *International Criminal Courts, Practice, Procedure and Evidence*, Sweet & Maxwell 2003, 337, 11-26.
[18] Ibid, 338, 11-27.
[19] *Prosecutor v Tadic*, Case No. IT-94-1-AR72, Judgement, 15 July 1999.
[20] Ibid., at para. 84.

- **Article 3: Violations of Article 3 Common and Protocol II – Nature of the Conflict**

S3-AC-2
o *Prosecutor v. Fofana*, Case No. SCSL-03-14-AR72, Decision on Preliminary Motion on Lack of Jurisdiction *Materiae*: Nature of the Armed Conflict, 25 May 2004, para. 31-32:

31. In the circumstances, the question whether the conflict in Sierra Leone was of an internal or international character and at which point, if any, it became internationalized, does not have any bearing on the applicability of Articles 3 and 4 of the Statute and therefore need not be considered by the Appeals Chamber.

32. In any event, the Appeals Chamber is not the proper venue for trial of issues of fact. In the light of the above, the legal points raised by the Applicant, such as the legal criteria for establishing the international character of an armed conflict are at this stage academic.

- **Article 3: Violations of Article 3 Common and Protocol II – Existence of an Armed Conflict Admitted by Way of Judicial Notice**

S2-AC-3
o *Prosecutor v. Fofana*, Case No. SCSL-04-14-AR73, Decision on Appeal Against "Decision on Prosecution's Motion for Judicial Notice and Admission of Evidence", 16 May 2005, para. 36-37, 39:

36. [...] The fact that there was an armed conflict in Sierra Leone is a 'notorious fact of history'. Furthermore, in the context of Sierra Leone these facts cannot be subject to *reasonable* dispute taking into consideration the general knowledge of the population. A multitude of victims with mutilations which cannot stem from anything other than an armed conflict allows for an accurate and ready determination of this fact by immediately obtainable evidence. To contest the fact that there was an armed conflict is frivolous. The armed conflict even provided the context in which the Special Court was created to try those who bear the greatest responsibility for crimes committed.

37. Furthermore, the fact that an armed conflict existed is capable of accurate and ready determination by a wide range of other authoritative sources, as for example, the existence of the United Nations peacekeeping mission established by Security Council resolution.

[...]

39. This Chamber now turns to the question of whether the factual finding that an armed conflict existed amounts to a legal finding. Even if the existence of an armed conflict is a general prerequisite or precondition for the crimes under Articles 3 and 4 of the Statute, acknowledging that such a conflict exists does not of itself draw any legal conclusion regarding the individual criminal responsibility of the Accused, not even of him taking part in that conflict. In the case of *Simic*, conclusions about the nature of the armed conflict (a prerequisite for the competence of the court) were not judicially noticed. The fact that an armed conflict had occurred was judicially noticed.

Article 4
Other Serious Violations of International Humanitarian Law

The Special Court shall have the power to prosecute persons who committed the following serious violations of international humanitarian law:

a. Intentionally directing attacks against the civilian population as such or against individual civilians not taking direct part in hostilities;
b. Intentionally directing attacks against personnel, installations, material, units or vehicles involved in a humanitarian assistance or peacekeeping mission in accordance with the Charter of the United Nations, as long as they are entitled to the protection given to civilians or civilian objects under the international law of armed conflict;
c. Conscripting or enlisting children under the age of 15 years into armed forces or groups or using them to participate actively in hostilities.

TRIAL CHAMBERS DECISIONS

- **Article 4(c): Other Serious Violations – "Enlisting Children Under the Age of 15 Years into Armed Forces"**

S4-TC-1

o *Prosecutor v. Norman, Fofana, Kondewa*, Case No. SCSL-04-14-T, Decision on Motions for Judgment of acquittal Pursuant to Rule 98, 21 October 2005, para. 123-124:

123. Article 4(c) of the Statute prohibits:

Conscripting or enlisting children under the age of 15 years into armed forces or groups or using them to participate actively in hostilities.

124. Based on Article 4(c) of the Statute, Article 77(2) of Additional Protocol I, Article 4(3)(c) of Additional Protocol II, Articles 8(2)(b)(xxvi), 8(2)(e)(vii) of the Rome Statute, and relevant interpretations of the foregoing international instruments by the Preparatory Committees on the Establishment of an International Criminal Court specifically in respect of the offences of conscripting, enlisting, and using children under the age of 15 years in military operations, the Chamber holds that the elements common to the aforementioned offences are as follows:

(i) The perpetrator conscripted or enlisted one or more persons into an armed force or group or used one or more persons to participate actively in hostilities;

(ii) Such person or persons were under the age of 15 years;
(iii) The perpetrator knew or had reason to know that such person or persons were under the age of 15 years;
(iv) The conduct took place in the context of and was associated with an armed conflict;
(v) The perpetrator was aware of factual circumstances that established the existence of an armed conflict.

APPEALS CHAMBER DECISIONS

- **Article 4: Other Serious Violations – Applicability and Jurisdiction – Not Limited to Internal Armed Conflicts**

S4-AC-1

o *Prosecutor v. Fofana*, Case No. SCSL-04-14-AR72, Decision on Preliminary Motion on Lack of Jurisdiction *Materiae*: Nature of the Armed Conflict, 25 May 2004, para. 28-30:

28. As observed by the Defence, Article 4 'lacks a specific reference to the nature of the underlying conflict',[1] and it is not linked to a specific conventional provision. The Defence traces Article 4 to Article 8(2)(e) of the Statute of the International Criminal Court (ICC) and it is true that the wording of Article 4(a) to (c) is identical to sub-paragraphs (i), (iii) and (vii) of Article 8(2)(e). However, the fact that the Statute of the Special Court pragmatically borrows wording from a Statute that has been painstakingly formulated to define in the most precise terms the crimes embodied in it does not mean that the entire context of applicability of Article 8(2)(e) has also been incorporated.

29. The Special Court Statute does not include the preface to Article 8(2)(e) of the ICC Statute which refers to "other serious violations of the laws and customs applicable in armed conflicts not of an international character, within the established framework of international law". Furthermore, as the Prosecution points out, the wording in Article 4 also reflects that of Article 8(b), sub-paragraphs (i), (iii) and (xxvi) of the ICC Statute concerning "serious violations of the laws and customs applicable in international armed conflict". Although Article 4(c) refers to enlisting children under the age of 15 "into armed forces or groups", as in Article 8(2)(e) of the ICC Statute, as opposed to "into the national armed forces", as in Article 8(2)(b), the chosen wording may simply have been designed to reflect most accurately the circumstances of the acts of child recruitment alleged to have occurred in Sierra Leone.

30. The Appeals Chamber finds that there is no merit to the argument that because the Statute may have been drafted with

reference to an internal armed conflict and because Article 4 most likely was borrowed from Article 8(2)(e) of the ICC Statute dealing with internal conflicts, the Court's jurisdiction to apply Article 4 is restricted to internal armed conflicts.

⁽¹⁾ Preliminary Motion, para. 7.

- **Article 4: Other Serious Violations – Additional Protocol II and Convention on the Rights of Children Form Part of Customary International Law**

S4-AC-2   o *Prosecutor v. Norman*, Case No. SCSL-04-14-AR72, Decision on Preliminary Motion Based on Lack of Jurisdiction (Child Recruitment), 31 May 2004, para. 18-20:

18. As regards State practice, the list of States having legislation⁽¹⁾ concerning recruitment or voluntary enlistment clearly shows that almost all States prohibit (and have done so for a long time) the recruitment of children under the age of 15. Since 185 States, including Sierra Leone, were parties to the Geneva Conventions prior to 1996, it follows that the provisions of those conventions were widely recognised as customary international law. Similarly, 133 States, including Sierra Leone, ratified Additional Protocol II before 1995. Due to the high number of States Parties one can conclude that many of the provisions of Additional Protocol II, including the fundamental guarantees, were widely accepted as customary international law by 1996. Even though Additional Protocol II addresses internal conflicts, the ICTY Appeals Chamber held in *Prosecutor v Tadić* that "it does not matter whether the 'serious violation' has occurred within the context of an international or an internal armed conflict".⁽²⁾ This means that children are protected by the fundamental guarantees, regardless of whether there is an international or internal conflict taking place.

19. Furthermore, as already mentioned, all but six States had ratified the Convention on the Rights of the Child by 1996. This huge acceptance, the highest acceptance of all international conventions, clearly shows that the provisions of the CRC became international customary law almost at the time of the entry into force of the Convention.

20. The widespread recognition and acceptance of the norm prohibiting child recruitment in Additional Protocol II and the CRC provides compelling evidence that the conventional norm entered customary international law well before 1996. The fact that there was not a single reservation to lower the legal obligation under Article 38 of the CRC underlines this,

especially if one takes into consideration the fact that Article 38 is one of the very few conventional provisions which can claim universal acceptance.

---

(1) Available at www.child-soldiers.org and annexed to the UNICEF Amicus Brief.
(2) *Prosecutor v. Dusko Tadić*, Case No. IT-94-1-AR72, Decision on the Defence Motion for Interlocutory Appeal on Jurisdiction, 2 October 1995, ("*Tadić* Jurisdiction Decision"), para. 94.

• **Article 4: Other Serious Violations – All Parties Bound by International Humanitarian Law**

S4-AC-3

o *Prosecutor v. Norman*, Case No. SCSL-04-14-AR72, Decision on Preliminary Motion Based on Lack of Jurisdiction (Child Recruitment), 31 May 2004, para. 22-23:

22. As stated in the Toronto Amicus Brief, and indicated in the 1996 Machel Report, it is well-settled that all parties to an armed conflict, whether States or non-State actors, are bound by international humanitarian law, even though only States may become parties to international treaties.(1) Customary international law represents the common standard of behaviour within the international community, thus even armed groups hostile to a particular government have to abide by these laws.(2) It has also been pointed out that non-State entities are bound by necessity by the rules embodied in international humanitarian law instruments, that they are "responsible for the conduct of their members"(3) and may be "held so responsible by opposing parties or by the outside world".(4) Therefore all parties to the conflict in Sierra Leone were bound by the prohibition of child recruitment that exists in international humanitarian law(5)

23. Furthermore, it should be mentioned that since the mid-1980s, States as well as non-State entities started to commit themselves to preventing the use of child soldiers and to ending the use of already recruited soldiers.(6)

---

(1) Toronto Amicus Brief, para. 13.
(2) Jean-Marie Henckaerts, *Binding Armed Opposition Groups through Humanitarian Treaty Law and Customary Law* in Relevance of International Humanitarian Law to Non-State Actors, Proceedings of the Brugge Colloquium, 25-26 October 2002.
(3) See F. Kalsoven and L. Zegveld, *Constraints on the Waging of War, An Introduction to International Humanitatian Law*, (International Committee of the Red Cross, March 2001), p. 75.
(4) Ibid.
(5) Toronto Amicus Brief, para. 13.
(6) UNICEF Amicus Brief, para. 49.

S4-AC-4

o *Prosecutor v. Kallon, Kamara*, Cases No. SCSL-04-15-AR72, SCSL-04-16-AR72, Decision on Challenge to Jurisdiction: Lomé Accord Amnesty, 13 March 2004, para. 45-48:

45. Notwithstanding the absence of unanimity among international lawyers as to the basis of the obligation of insurgents to observe the provisions of Common Article 3 to the Geneva Conventions,[1] there is now no doubt that this article is binding on States and insurgents alike and that insurgents are subject to international humanitarian law. That fact, however, does not by itself invest the RUF with international personality under international law.

46. Common Article 3 of the Geneva Conventions recognises the existence of "Parties to the conflict". The penultimate sentence of Common Article 3 provides that: "The parties to the conflict should further endeavour to bring into force, by means of special agreements, all or part of the other provisions of the present Convention". But the final clause of Common Article 3 also provides that "[t]he application of the preceding provisions shall not affect the legal status of the Parties to the conflict." It has been explained that the penultimate sentence "underlines the fact that parties to an internal conflict are bound only to observe Article 3, remaining free to disregard the entirety of the remaining provisions in each of the Convention"[2] and that the final clause indicates that the insurgents may still be made subject to the State's municipal criminal jurisdiction. In an authoritative book on international law the view was expressed that:

> a range of factors needs to be carefully examined before it can be determined whether an entity has international personality and, if so, what right, duties and competences apply in the particular case. Personality is a relative phenomenon varying with the circumstances.[3]

47. It suffices to say, for the purpose of the present case, that no one has suggested that insurgents are bound because they have been vested with personality in international law of such a nature as to make it possible for them to be a party to the Geneva Conventions. Rather, a convincing theory is that they are bound as a matter of international customary law to observe the obligations declared by Common Article 3 which is aimed at the protection of humanity. No doubt, the Sierra Leone Government regarded the RUF as an entity with which it could enter into an agreement. However, there is nothing to show that any other State had granted the RUF recognition as an entity with which it could enter into legal relations or that the Government of Sierra Leone regarded it as an entity other than a faction within Sierra Leone.

48. Although a degree of organisation of the insurgents may be a factor in determining whether the factual situation of internal armed conflict existed, the distinction must be borne in mind between the factual question whether the insurgents are sufficiently organised and the question of law, with which the issue in these proceedings is concerned, whether as between them and the legitimate government international law regarded them as having treaty-making capacity. International law does not seem to have vested them with such capacity. The RUF had no treaty-making capacity so as to make the Lomé Agreement an international agreement.

---

[1] *See e.g.* Convention Relative to the Treatment of Prisoners of War, Geneva, 12 August 1949, 75 UNTS 135.
[2] L. Moir, *The Law of Internal Armed Conflict*, (Cambridge 2002), pp. 63-64. The author at p. 65 was of the view that the application of Article 3 does not constitute a recognition by the government that the insurgents have any authority, and certainly does not amount to a recognition of belligerency. He noted that "scholars have since argued that, despite the obvious intention of the framers of the Conventions, Article 3 must confer a measure of international legal personality upon the insurgents, at least they become the holders of rights and obligations under the Article."
[3] Shaw, *International Law*, p. 176.

- **Article 4: Other Serious Violations – Individual Responsibility for Child Recruitment**

S4-AC-5

o *Prosecutor v. Norman*, Case No. SCSL-04-14-AR72, Decision on Preliminary Motion Based on Lack of Jurisdiction (Child Recruitment), 31 May 2004, para. 26-51:

26. In the ICTY case of *Prosecutor v. Tadić*, the test for determining whether a violation of humanitarian law is subject to prosecution and punishment is set out thus:

The following requirements must be met for an offence to be subject to prosecution before the International Tribunal under Article 3 [of the ICTY Statute]:

(i) the violation must constitute an infringement of a rule of international humanitarian law;
(ii) the rule must be customary in nature or, if it belongs to treaty law, the required conditions must be met;
(iii) the violation must be "serious", that is to say, it must constitute a breach of a rule protecting important values, and the breach must involve grave consequences for the victim [. . .];
(iv) the violation of the rule must entail, under customary or conventional law, the individual criminal responsibility of the person breaching the rule.[1]

1. International Humanitarian Law

27. With respect to points i) and ii), it follows from the discussion above, where the requirements have been addressed exhaustively, that in this regard the test is satisfied.

2. Rule Protecting Important Values

28. Regarding point iii), all the conventions listed above deal with the protection of children and it has been shown that this is one of the fundamental guarantees articulated in Additional Protocol II. The Special Court Statute, just like the ICTR Statute before it, draws on Part II of Additional Protocol II entitled "Humane Treatment" and its fundamental guarantees, as well as Common Article 3 to the Geneva Conventions in specifying the crimes falling within its jurisdiction.[2] "All the fundamental guarantees share a similar character. In recognising them as fundamental, the international community set a benchmark for the minimum standards for the conduct of armed conflict."[3] Common Article 3 requires humane treatment and specifically addresses humiliating and degrading treatment. This includes the treatment of child soldiers in the course of their recruitment. Article 3(2) specifies further that the parties "should further endeavour to bring into force [...] all or part of the other provisions of the present convention", thus including the specific protection for children under the Geneva Conventions as stated above.[4]

29. Furthermore, the UN Security Council condemned as early as 1996 the "inhumane and abhorrent practice"[5] of recruiting, training and deploying children for combat. It follows that the protection of children is regarded as an important value. As can be verified in numerous reports of various human rights organizations, the practice of child recruitment bears the most atrocious consequences for the children.[6]

3. Individual Criminal Responsibility

30. Regarding point iv), the Defence refers to the Secretary-General's statement that "while the prohibition on child recruitment has by now acquired a customary international law status, it is far less clear whether it is customarily recognised as a war crime entailing the individual criminal responsibility of the accused."[7] The ICTY Appeals Chamber upheld the legality of prosecuting violations of the laws and customs of war, including violations of Common Article 3 and the Additional Protocols in the *Tadić* case in 1995.[8] In creating the ICTR Statute, the Security Council explicitly recognized for the first time that serious violations of fundamental guarantees lead to individual criminal liability[9] and this was confirmed later on by decisions and judgments of the ICTR. In its Judgment in the *Akayesu* case, the ICTR Trial Chamber, relying on the *Tadić* test, confirmed that a breach of a rule protecting important values was a "serious violation" entailing criminal responsibility.[10] The Trial Chamber noted that

Article 4 of the ICTR Statute was derived from Common Article 3 (containing fundamental prohibitions as a humanitarian minimum of protection for war victims) and Additional Protocol II, "which equally outlines 'Fundamental Guarantees'".[11] The Chamber concluded that "it is clear that the authors of such egregious violations must incur individual criminal responsibility for their deeds".[12] Similarly, under the ICTY Statute adopted in 1993, a person acting in breach of Additional Protocol I to the Geneva Conventions may face criminal sanctions, and this has been confirmed in ICTY jurisprudence.[13]

31. The Committee on the Rights of the Child, the international monitoring body for the implementation of the CRC, showed exactly this understanding while issuing its recommendations to Uganda in 1997.[14] The Committee recommended that: "awareness of the duty to fully respect the rules of international humanitarian law, in the spirit of article 38 of the Convention, *inter alia* with regard to children, should be made known to the parties to the armed conflict in the northern part of the State Party's territory, and that **violations of the rules of international humanitarian law entail responsibility being attributed to the perpetrators.**"[15]

32. In 1998 the Rome Statute for the International Criminal Court was adopted. It entered into force on 1 July 2002. Article 8 includes the crime of child recruitment in international armed conflict[16] and internal armed conflict,[17] the elements of which are elaborated in the Elements of Crimes adopted in 2000:[18]

> Article 8
> War crimes
>
> 1. The Court shall have jurisdiction in respect of war crimes in particular when committed as part of a plan or policy or as part of a large-scale commission of such crimes.
>
> 2. For the purpose of this Statute, "war crimes" means:
>
> [...]
>
> (b) Other serious violations of the laws and customs applicable in international armed conflict, within the established framework of international law, namely, any of the following acts: [...]
>
> xxvi) Conscripting or enlisting children under the age of fifteen years into the national armed forces or using them to participate actively in hostilities.

33. The Defence, noting the concerns of the United States, argues that the Rome Statute created new legislation.[19] This argument fails for the following reasons: first, the first draft of the Rome Statute was produced as early as 1994 referring

generally to war crimes;[20] second, in the first session of the Preparatory Committee it was proposed that the ICC should have the power to prosecute serious violations of Common Article 3 and Additional Protocol II;[21] third, discussion continued during 1996 and 1997 when Germany proposed the inclusion of child recruitment under the age of fifteen as a crime "within the established framework of international law";[22] and finally, it was the German proposal to include "conscripting or enlisting children under the age of fifteen years [. . .]" that was accepted in the final draft of the Statute. With regard to the United States, an authoritative report of the proceedings of the Rome Conference states "the United States in particular took the view that [child recruitment] did not reflect international customary law, and was more a human rights provision than a criminal law provision. However, the majority felt strongly that the inclusion was justified by the near-universal acceptance of the norm, the violation of which warranted the most fundamental disapprobation."[23] The question whether or not the United States could be said to have persistently objected to the formation of the customary norm is irrelevant to its status as such a norm.[24] The discussion during the preparation of the Rome Statute focused on the codification and effective implementation of the existing customary norm rather than the formation of a new one.

34. Building on the principles set out in the earlier Conventions, the 1999 ILO Convention 182 Concerning the Prohibition and Immediate Action for the Elimination of the Worst Forms of Child Labour, provided:

Article 1

Each Member which ratifies this Convention shall take **immediate and effective measures** to secure the prohibition and elimination of the worst forms of child labour as a matter of urgency.

Article 2

For the purposes of this Convention, **the term "child" shall apply to all persons under the age of 18**.

Article 3

For the purposes of this Convention, the term "the worst forms of child labour" comprises:

(a) all forms of slavery or practices similar to slavery, such as the sale and trafficking of children, debt bondage and serfdom and forced or compulsory labour, **including forced or compulsory recruitment of children for use in armed conflict.**

It is clear that by the time Article 2 of this Convention was formulated, the debate had moved on from the question whether the recruitment of children under the age of 15 was prohibited or indeed criminalized, and the focus had shifted to the next step in the development of international law, namely the raising of the standard to include all children under the age of 18. This led finally to the wording of Article 4 of the Optional Protocol II to the Convention on the Rights of the Child on the Involvement of Children in Armed Conflict.[25]

35. The CRC Optional Protocol II was signed on 25 May 2000 and came into force on 12 February 2002. It has 115 signatories and has been ratified by 70 states. The relevant Article for our purposes is Article 4 which states:

> 1. Armed groups that are distinct from the armed forces of a State should not, under any circumstances, recruit or use in hostilities persons **under the age of 18 years**.
>
> 2. States Parties shall take all feasible measures to prevent such recruitment and use, including the adoption of legal measures necessary **to prohibit and criminalize such practices**.

36. The Defence argues that the first mention of the criminalization of child recruitment occurs in Article 4(2) of the CRC Optional Protocol II.[26] Contrary to this argument, the Article in fact demonstrates that the aim at this stage was to raise the standard of the prohibition of child recruitment from age 15 to 18, proceeding from the assumption that the conduct was already criminalized at the time in question.

37. The Appeals Chamber in *Prosecutor v. Dusko Tadić*, making reference to the Nuremberg Tribunal, outlined the following factors establishing individual criminal responsibility under international law:

> the clear and unequivocal recognition of the rules of warfare in international law and State practice indicating an intention to criminalize the prohibition, including statements by government officials and international organizations, as well as punishment of violations by national courts and military tribunals.[27]

The Appeals Chamber in *Tadić* went on to state that where these conditions are met, individuals must be held criminally responsible, because, as the Nuremberg Tribunal concluded:

> [c]rimes against international law are committed by men, not by abstract entities, and only by punishing individuals who commit such crimes can the provisions of international law be enforced.[28]

38. A norm need not be expressly stated in an international convention for it to crystallize as a crime under customary international law. What, indeed, would be the meaning of a customary rule if it only became applicable upon its incorpo-

ration into an international instrument such as the Rome Treaty? Furthermore, it is not necessary for the *individual criminal responsibility* of the accused to be explicitly stated in a convention for the provisions of the convention to entail individual criminal responsibility under customary international law.[29] As Judge Meron in his capacity as professor has pointed out, "it has not been seriously questioned that some acts of individuals that are prohibited by international law constitute criminal offences, even when there is no accompanying provision for the establishment of the jurisdiction of particular courts or scale of penalties".[30]

39. The prohibition of child recruitment constitutes a fundamental guarantee and although it is not enumerated in the ICTR and ICTY Statutes, it shares the same character and is of the same gravity as the violations that are explicitly listed in those Statutes. The fact that the ICTY and ICTR have prosecuted violations of Additional Protocol II provides further evidence of the criminality of child recruitment before 1996.

40. The criminal law principle of specificity provides that criminal rules must detail specifically both the objective elements of the crime and the requisite *mens rea* with the aim of ensuring that all those who may fall under the prohibitions of the law know in advance precisely which behaviour is allowed and which conduct is instead proscribed.[31] Both the Elements of Crimes[32] formulated in connection with the Rome Statute and the legislation of a large proportion of the world community specified the elements of the crime.

41. Article 38 of the CRC states that States Parties have to take "all feasible measures" to ensure that children under 15 do not take part in hostilities and Article 4 urges them to "undertake all appropriate legislative [...] measures" for the implementation of the CRC. As all "feasible measures" and "appropriate legislation" are at the disposal of states to prevent child recruitment, it would seem that these also include criminal sanctions as measures of enforcement. As it has aptly been stated: "Words on paper cannot save children in peril."[33]

42. In the instant case, further support for the finding that the *nullum crimen* principle has not been breached is found in the national legislation of states which includes criminal sanctions as a measure of enforcement.

43. The Defence submitted during the oral hearing that there is not a single country in the world that has criminalized the practice of recruiting child soldiers and that child recruitment was not only not a war crime but it was doubtful whether the provisions of the CRC protected child soldiers.[34] A simple reading of Article 38 of the CRC disposes of the latter argument. Concerning the former argument, it is clearly wrong. An abundance of states criminalized child recruitment in the

aftermath of the Rome Statute, as for example Australia. In response to its ratification of the Rome Statute, Australia passed the *International Criminal Court (Consequential Amendments) Act*.[35] Its purpose was to make the offences in the Rome Statute offences under Commonwealth law. Section 268.68(1) creates the offence of using, conscripting and enlisting children in the course of an international armed conflict and sets out the elements of the crime and the applicable terms of imprisonment. Section 268.88 contains similar provisions relating to conflict that is not an international armed conflict.

44. By 2001, and in most cases prior to the Rome Statute, 108 states explicitly prohibited child recruitment, one example dating back to 1902,[36] and a further 15 states that do not have specific legislation did not show any indication of using child soldiers.[37] The list of states in the 2001 Child Soldiers Global Report[38] clearly shows that states with quite different legal systems – civil law, common law, Islamic law – share the same view on the topic.

45. It is sufficient to mention a few examples of national legislation criminalizing child recruitment prior to 1996 in order to further demonstrate that the *nullum crimen* principle is upheld. As set out in the UNICEF Amicus Brief,[39] Ireland's Geneva Convention Act provides that any "minor breach" of the Geneva conventions [...], as well as any "contravention" of Additional Protocol II, are punishable offences.[40] The operative Code of Military justice of Argentina states that breaches of treaty provisions providing for special protection of children are war crimes.[41] Norway's Military Penal Code states that [...] anyone who contravenes or is accessory to the contravention of provisions relating to the protection of persons or property laid down in [...] the Geneva Conventions [...] [and in] the two additional protocols to these Conventions [...] is liable to imprisonment.[42]

46. More specifically in relation to the principle *nullum crimen sine poena*, before 1996 three different approaches by states to the issue of punishment of child recruitment under national law can be distinguished.

47. First, as already described, certain states from various legal systems have criminalized the recruitment of children under 15 in their national legislation. Second, the vast majority of states lay down the prohibition of child recruitment in military law. However, sanctions can be found in the provisions of criminal law as for example in Austria[43] and Germany[44] or in administrative legislation, criminalizing any breaches of law by civil servants. Examples of the latter include Afghanistan[45] and Turkey.[46] Legislation of the third group of states simply makes it impossible for an individual to recruit children, as the military administration imposes strict controls through an obligatory cadet schooling, as for example in England,[47]

Mauritania[48] and Switzerland.[49] In these states, provisions for punishment are unnecessary as it is impossible for the crime to be committed.

48. Even though a punishment is not prescribed, individual criminal responsibility may follow.[50] Professor Cassese has stated that:

> It is common knowledge that in many States, particularly in those of civil law tradition, it is considered necessary to lay down in law a tariff relating to sentences for each crime [...] This principle is not applicable at the international level, where these tariffs do not exist. Indeed States have not yet agreed upon a scale of penalties, due to widely differing views about the gravity of the various crimes, the seriousness of guilt for each criminal offence and the consequent harsh- ness of punishment. It follows that courts enjoy much greater judicial discretion in punishing persons found guilty of international crimes.[51]

However, Article 24 of the ICTY Statute provides some guidance in the matter as it refers to the general practice regarding prison sentences. The point of reference is thus not a concrete tariff but quite generally the practice of prison sentences.[52] The penalties foreseen in national legislation specify prison sentences for breaching the prohibition on the recruitment of children under the age of fifteen.

49. When considering the formation of customary international law, "the number of states taking part in a practice is a more important criterion [...] than the duration of the practice."[53] It should further be noted that "the number of states needed to create a rule of customary law varies according to the amount of practice which conflicts with the rule and that [even] a practice followed by a very small number of states can create a rule of customary law if there is no practice which conflicts with the rule."[54]

50. Customary law, as its name indicates, derives from custom. Custom takes time to develop. It is thus impossible and even contrary to the concept of customary law to determine a given event, day or date upon which it can be stated with certainty that a norm has crystallised.[55] One can nevertheless say that during a certain period the conscience of leaders and populations started to note a given problem. In the case of recruiting child soldiers this happened during the mid-1980s. One can further determine a period where customary law begins to develop, which in the current case began with the acceptance of key international instruments between 1990 and 1994. Finally, one can determine the period during which the majority of States criminalized the prohibited behaviour, which in this case, as demonstrated, was the period between 1994 and

1996. It took a further six years for the recruitment of children between the ages of 15 and 18 to be included in treaty law as individually punishable behaviour. The development process concerning the recruitment of child soldiers, taking into account the definition of children as persons under the age of 18, culminated in the codification of the matter in the CRC Optional Protocol II.

51. The overwhelming majority of states, as shown above, did not practise recruitment of children under 15 according to their national laws and many had, whether through criminal or administrative law, criminalized such behaviour prior to 1996. The fact that child recruitment still occurs and is thus illegally practised does not detract from the validity of the customary norm. It cannot be said that there is a contrary practice with a corresponding *opinio iuris* as States clearly consider themselves to be under a legal obligation not to practise child recruitment.

---

[1] *Tadić* Jurisdiction Decision, para. 94.
[2] UNICEF Amicus Brief, para. 64.
[3] UNICEF Amicus Brief, para. 65.
[4] Toronto Amicus Brief, paras 20 and 21.
[5] Security Council Resolution S/RES/1071 (1996), 30 August 1996 para. 9.
[6] This is true both at the stage of recruitment and at the time of release, and also for the remainder of the child's life.
[7] Fofana – Reply to the Prosecution Response to the Motion, para. 19, referring to the Report of the Secretary-General on the Establishment of a Special Court for Sierra Leone, 4 October 2000, S/2000/ 915, para. 17.
[8] *Tadić* Jurisdiction Decision, paras 86-93.
[9] Statute of the International Criminal Tribunal for Rwanda, S/RES/ 935 (1994), 1 July 1994 (as amended), Article 4.
[10] *Prosecutor v. Akayesu*, Case No. ICTR-96-4-T, Judgment, 2 September 1998, paras 616-17.
[11] Ibid., para. 616.
[12] Ibid.
[13] See *Tadić* Jurisdiction Decision.
[14] See UNICEF Amicus Brief, para. 34.
[15] Concluding observations of the Committee on the Rights of the Child: Uganda, 21 October 1997 upon submission of the Report in 1996, CRC/C/15/Add.80.
[16] Article 8(2)(b)(xxvi).
[17] Article 8(2)(e)(vii).
[18] UN Doc. PCNICC/2000/1/Add.2(2000). Elements of Article 8(2)(e)(vii) War crime of using, conscripting and enlisting children:
  1. The perpetrator conscripted or enlisted one or more persons into an armed force or group or used one or more persons to participate actively in hostilities.
  2. Such person or persons were under the age of 15 years.
  3. The perpetrator knew or should have known that such person or persons were under the age of 15 years.
  4. The conduct took place in the context of and was associated with an armed conflict not of an international character.
  5. The perpetrator was aware of factual circumstances that established the existence of an armed conflict.
[19] Preliminary Motion, para. 9.

(20) Report of the International Law Commission on the work of its forty-sixth session, UN General Assembly Doc. A/49/355, 1 September 1994. Summary of the Proceedings of the Preparatory Committee during the period 25 March-12 April 1996, Annex I: Definition of Crimes.
(21) UNICEF Amicus Brief, para. 86.
(22) Working Group on Definitions and elements of Crimes, *Reference Paper on War Crimes submitted by Germany*, 12 December 1997.
(23) Herman Von Hebel and Darryl Robinson, *Crimes within the Jurisdiction of the Court*, in R. Lee (ed), *The International Criminal Court: The Making of the Rome Statute*, chapter 2, pp. 117-118.
(24) Notably, the United States, despite not having ratified the CRC, has recognized the Convention as a codification of customary international law. See Toronto Amicus Brief para. 24 and note 41.
(25) UN Doc. A/54/RES/263, 25 May 2000, entered into force 12 February 2002 ("CRC Optional Protocol II").
(26) Preliminary Motion, para. 7.
(27) *Tadić* Jurisdiction Decision, para. 128.
(28) The Trial of Major War Criminals: Proceedings of the International Military Tribunal Sitting at Nuremberg Germany, Part 22, (1950) at 447.
(29) See *Prosecutor v. Tadić*, Case No. IT-94-1, Decision on Defence Motion on Jurisdiction, 10 August 1995, para. 70.
(30) Theodor Meron, *International Criminalization of Internal Atrocities*, (1995) 89 AJIL 554, p. 562.
(31) Antonio Cassese, *International Criminal Law* (Oxford University Press, 2003), p. 145.
(32) UN Doc. PCNICC/2000/1/Add.2(2000).
(33) During the 57th session of the Commission of Human Rights, The Special Representative of the Secretary General, Mr. Olara A. Otunnu addressed the Assembly with regard to the Graça Machel Report. He said: "Over the past 50 years, the nations of the world have developed and ratified an impressive series of international human rights and humanitarian instruments. [. . .] However, the value of these provisions is limited to the extent to which they are applied." *Rights of the Child, Children in Armed Conflict*, Interim Report of the Special Representative of the Secretary-General, Mr. Olara A. Otunnu, submitted to the Economic and Social Council pursuant to General Assembly Resolution 52/107, E/CN.4/1998/119, 12 March 1998, paras 14-15.
(34) The Defence asserted that "the offence does not appear in the criminal calendar of any national state, there is not a single country in the world that makes this a crime". See Transcript of 5-6 November 2003, paras 284 and 338 (referring to G. Goodwin-Gill and I. Cohen, *Child Soldiers* (Oxford University Press, 1994).
(35) *International Criminal Court (Consequential Amendments) Act*, 2002 No. 42 (Cth).
(36) Norway, Military Penal Code as amended (1902), para. 108.
(37) See Child Soldiers Global Report 2001, published by the coalition to stop the Use of Child Soldiers. Available at www.child-soldiers.org and annexed to the UNICEF Amicus Brief.
(38) Ibid.
(39) UNICEF Amicus Brief, para. 47.
(40) Ireland,*Geneva Conventions Act* as amended (1962), Section 4(1) and (4).
(41) Argentina, *Draft Code of Military Justice* (1998), Article 292, introducing a new article 876(4) in *the Code of Military Justice*, as amended (1951).
(42) Norway, *Military Penal code* as amended (1902), para. 108.
(43) Austrian legislation sets the minimum age for recruitment at 18 in *Wehrgesetz 2001*, BGBl. I Nr. 146/2001 as amended in BGBl. I Nr. 137/2003 and provides for criminal sanctions in *Strafgesetzbuch*, BGBl. Nr. 60/1974 in Articles 27 and 302.
(44) German legislation sets the minimum age for compulsory recruitment at

18 in *Wehrpflichtgesetz*, 15 December 1995 (as amended), para. 1 and provides for a sanction in *Wehrstrafgesetz*, 24 May 1974, para. 32.

(45) *Decree S. No* 20, Article 1, states that "The Afghan citizen volunteer to join the National Army should [...] be aged between 22-28 years." Art. 110 *Penal Law for Crimes of Civil Servants and Crimes against Public Welfare and Security*, 1976 states that "An official who deliberately registers a minor as an adult or vice-versa on his nationality card, court records or similar documents shall be punishable [...]"

(46) Article 2 of the *The Military Service Law* (Amended 20 November 1935-2248/Article 1) states that "The military age shall be according to the age of every male as recorded in his main civil registration [...] starting on the first day of January in the year in which he becomes twenty [...]. The *Turkish Penal Code* (Amended 12 June 1979-2248/Article 19) states in Article 240 that "a civil servant who has abused his/her office for any reason whatsoever other than the circumstances specified in the law shall be imprisoned for one year to three years [...] He/she shall also be disqualified from the civil service temporarily or permanently."

(47) According to the *Education (School Leaving Date) Order* 1997, made under the *Education Act 1996*, section 8(4), a child may not legally leave school until the last Friday in June of the school year during which they reach the age 16. According to *HM Armed forces Enquiry Questionnaire*, AFCO Form 2, January 2000, Armed forces do not recruit those under the age of 16 and the recruitment process, including selection, medical examination and obtaining parental consent may only begin at 15 years and nine months. Rachel Harvey, *Child soldiers in the UK: Analysis of recruitment and deployment practices of under-18s and the CRC* (June 2002), p. 13, note 73.

(48) *Loi No. 62 132 sur le recrutement de l'armée.* Articles 7 and 9, 29 June 1962.

(49) Loi fédérale sur l'armée et l'administration militaire, Article 131, 3 February 1995.

(50) *Prosecutor v. Tadić*, Case No. IT-94-1, Decision on Defence Motion on Jurisdiction, 10 August 1995, para. 70.

(51) Antonio Cassese, *International Criminal Law*, (Oxford University Press, 2003), p. 157.

(52) Daniel Augenstein, Ethnische Saüberungen in ehemaligen Jugoslawien – Rechtliche Aspekte, Seminar "Zwangsumsiedlungen, Deportationen und "ethische Saüberungen" im 20. Jahrhundert", Sommersemester 1997, p. 18.

(53) Michael Akehurst, *Custom As a Source of International Law*, The British Year Book of International Law 1974-1975 (Oxford at the Clarendon Press, 1977), p. 16.

(54) Ibid., p. 18.

(55) Contrary to the Defence Reply, para. 13.

Article 6
Individual Criminal Responsibility

1. A person who planned, instigated, ordered, committed or otherwise aided and abetted in the planning, preparation or execution of a crime referred to in articles 2 to 4 of the present Statute shall be individually responsible for the crime.

2. The official position of any accused persons, whether as Head of State or Government or as a responsible government official, shall not relieve such person of criminal responsibility nor mitigate punishment.

3. The fact that any of the acts referred to in articles 2 to 4 of the present Statute was committed by a subordinate does not relieve his or her superior of criminal responsibility if he or she knew or had reason to know that the subordinate was about to commit such acts or had done so and the superior had failed to take the necessary and reasonable measures to prevent such acts or to punish the perpetrators thereof.

4. The fact that an accused person acted pursuant to an order of a Government or of a superior shall not relieve him or her of criminal responsibility, but may be considered in mitigation of punishment if the Special Court determines that justice so requires.

5. Individual criminal responsibility for the crimes referred to in article 5 shall be determined in accordance with the respective laws of Sierra Leone.

TRIAL CHAMBERS DECISIONS

- **Article 6(1): Individual Criminal Responsibility – Generalities**

S6-TC-1
o *Prosecutor v. Kondewa*, SCSL-03-12-PT, Decision and Order on Defence Preliminary Motion for Defects in the Form of the Indictment, 27 November 2003, para. 9:[6]

9. [. . .] In the Chamber's opinion, as a matter of statutory interpretation, Article 6(1) 'sets out the parameters of personal criminal responsibility under the Statute. Any act falling under

---

[6] See also *Prosecutor v. Kamara*, SCSL-04-16-PT, Decision and Order on Defence Preliminary Motion on Defects in the Form of the Indictment, 1 April 2004, para. 49.

one of the five categories contained in the provision may entail the criminal responsibility of the perpetrator or whoever has participated in the crime in one of the ways specified in the same provision of the Statute.'[1] [...]

---

[1] *The Prosecutor v. Dusko Tadic*, Judgement of Appeals Chamber, Case No. IT-94-1-A, 15 July 1999, para. 186.

S6-TC-2

o *Prosecutor v. Issa Hassan Sesay* (Case No. SCSL-2003-05-PT), *Alex Tamba Brima* (Case No. SCSL-2003-06-PT), *Morris Kallon* (Case No. SCSL-2003-07-PT), *Augustine Gbao* (Case No. SCSL-2003-09-PT), *Brima Bazzy Kamara* (Case No. SCSL-2003-10-PT), *Santigie Borbor Kanu* (Case No. SCSL-2003-13-PT), Decision and Order on Prosecution Motions for Joinder, 27 January 2004, para. 22-24:[7]

22. [...] [T]he Chamber deems it imperative to restate that it is a cardinal principle of international criminal law that criminal responsibility is based on the notion of personal culpability.[1] Jurisprudentially, the doctrine of personal culpability has its origins in, and is a transplant from, national criminal law systems,[2] providing some theoretical support for the monist school of thought that international law and municipal law are constituent elements of a single, integrated universal normative order. In the specific context of the Special Court's evolving jurisprudence, as an international criminal tribunal, the doctrine of personal culpability is replicated in Article 6(1) of its Statute [...].

23. The statutory ambit of Article 6(1) of the Statute is sufficiently broad to encompass individual criminal responsibility for any of the five enumerated categories for any person who 'planned', 'instigated', 'ordered', 'committed' or 'aided and abetted in the planning, preparation or execution of a crime' specified in Articles 2-4 of the statute. The clear statutory effect of Article 6(1) is that criminal liability *on an individual basis* by an offender or any other person who has been involved in the crime can be incurred in any one of the enumerated modes prescribed by the said Statute. Hence, the need for persons accused of crimes to be tried separately and individually, as a logical emanation of the principle of individual criminal culpability.

---

[7] See also, *Prosecutor v. Sam Hinga Norman* (Case No. SCSL-2003-08-PT), *Moinina Fofana* (Case No. SCSL-2003-11-PT), *Allieu Kondewa* (Case No. SCSL-2003-12-PT), Decision and Order on Prosecution Motions for Joinder, 27 January 2004, para. 11.

24. This fundamental principle notwithstanding, the Chamber wishes to observe that Article 6(1) also encompasses and recognises *the doctrine of collective criminal responsibility* in the sense that in the penal setting of war crimes, the most egregious offences of the criminal law are 'perpetrated by a collectivity of persons in furtherance of a common criminal design'.[3][...]

---

[1] See *Prosecutor v. Dusko Tadic*, Case No. IT-94-1-A, Appeal Judgement, Appeals Chamber, 15 July 1999, para. 186.
[2] Id. Para. 186.
[3] *Prosecutor v. Dusko Tadic, supra* note 9, para. 193.

S6-TC-3

o *Prosecutor v. Norman, Fofana, Kondewa*, Case No. SCSL-04-14-T, Decision on Motions for Judgment of acquittal Pursuant to Rule 98, 21 October 2005, para. 130:

130. The Chamber recognizes, as a matter of law, generally, that Article 6(1) of the Statute of the Special Court does not, in its proscriptive reach, limit criminal liability to only those persons who plan, instigate, order, physically commit a crime or otherwise, aid and abet in its planning, preparation or execution. Its proscriptive ambit extends beyond that to prohibit the commission of offences through a joint criminal enterprise, in pursuit of the common plan to commit crimes punishable under the Statute. Furthermore, Article 6(3) of the Statute holds superiors criminally responsible for the offences committed by their subordinates, where a superior has knowledge or reason to know that subordinate(s) are about to or have committed an offence and that superior fails to take the necessary and reasonable measures to prevent or to punish the perpetrators thereof.[1]

---

[1] Kriangsak Kittichaisaree, International Criminal Law, Oxford University Press (2001), p. 251.

- **Article 6(1)/6(3): Individual Criminal Responsibility – Charges Under 6(1) and 6(3) Are Cumulative**

S6-TC-4

o *Prosecutor v. Sesay*, SCSL-03-05-PT, Decision and Order on Defence Preliminary Motion for Defects in the Form of the Indictment, 13 October 2003, para. 7, 12-14:

7. [...] Individual criminal responsibility under Article 6(1) and criminal responsibility as a superior under Article 6(3) of

the Statute are not mutually exclusive and can be properly charged both cumulatively and alternatively based on the same facts.[1]

[...]

12. [...] [R]elying *persuasively* on the decisions of the ICTY in *Prosecutor v. Kvocka et al.*,[2] and *Prosecutor v. Mile Mrksic*[3] and that of the ICTR in *Prosecutor v. Musema*[4] and a considered analysis of Article 6(1) and 6(3), it is the view of the Chamber that depending on the circumstances of the case, it may be required that with respect to Article 6(1) case against an accused, the Prosecution is under an obligation to 'indicate in relation to each individual count precisely and expressly the particular nature of the responsibility alleged', in other words, that the particular head or heads of liability should be indicated.[5] For example, it may be necessary to indicate disjunctively whether the accused 'planned, instigated, ordered, committed or otherwise aided and abetted in the planning, preparation, or execution' of the particular crime against humanity, or violations of Article 3 common to the Geneva Conventions and Additional Protocol II, or other serious violation of international humanitarian law, as alleged. This may be required to ensure clarity and precision as regards the exact nature and cause of the charges against the accused and to enable him to adequately and effectively prepare his defence. Such a methodology would also have the advantage of showing that each count is neither duplicitous nor multiplicitous. However, the Chamber must emphasize that the material facts to be pleaded in an indictment may vary with the specific head of Article 6(1) responsibility, and the specificity with which they must be pleaded will necessarily depend upon any or some or all of the factors articulated in paragraph 8 herein especially where the crimes in question are of an international character and dimension. For example, the material facts relating to 'planning' the particular crime may be different from those supporting an allegation that the accused 'ordered' the commission of the crime depending on the factors set out in paragraph 8.

13. Further, in a case based on superior responsibility pursuant to Article 6(3), minimum material facts to be pleaded in the indictment are as follows:

a) (i) that the accused held a superior position;
   (ii) in relation to subordinates, sufficiently identified;
   (iii) that the accused had effective control over the said subordinates;
   (iv) that he allegedly bears responsibility for their criminal acts;
b) (i) that the accused knew or had reason to know that the crimes were about to be or had been committed by his subordinates;
   (ii) the related conduct of those subordinates for whom he is alleged to be responsible;

(iii) the accused failed to take the necessary and reasonable means to prevent such crimes or to punish the persons who committed them.

14. With regard to the nature of the material facts to be pleaded in a case under Article 6(3) it follows, in the Chamber's view, that certain facts will necessarily be pleaded with a far lesser degree of specificity than in one under Article 6(1). It would seem, therefore, that in some situations under Article 6(3), given the peculiar features and circumstances of the case and the extraordinary nature of the crimes, it may be sufficient merely to plead as material facts the legal prerequisites to the offences charged as noted in Paragraph 13 herein. Further, [. . .] the Chamber finds the Defence submission that the Prosecution must clearly distinguish the acts for which the Accused incurs criminal responsibility under Article 6(1) of the Statute from those for which he incurs criminal responsibility under Article 6(3) to be legally unsustainable. The Chamber also finds that it may be sufficient to plead the legal prerequisites embodied in the statutory provisions. The Defence contention that the same facts cannot give rise to both heads of liability is, likewise, meretricious. The implication that they are mutually exclusive flies in the face of the law.[6]

---

[1] *Kvocka, supra* 9 para. 50; see also *Prosecutor v. Musema*, ICTR-96-13-T, Judgement, TCI, 27 January 2001, para. 884-974, para. 891-895, and *Prosecutor v. Delalic et al.*, Judgement, IT-96-21-T, 16 November 1998.
[2] *Supra* 11.
[3] Case No ICTY-95-13-PT. Decision on the Form of the Indictment, 19 June 2003.
[4] *Supra* 11.
[5] *The Prosecutor v. Delalic and Others*, Case ICTY-96-21-A, Judgement, 20 February 2001.
[6] See *Kvocka, supra* 12.

- **Article 6(3): Individual Criminal Responsibility – Command Responsibility – Guidance from Other International Tribunals**

S6-TC-5

o *Prosecutor v. Norman*, Case No. SCSL-03-08-PT, Decision on the Defence Preliminary Motion on Lack of Jurisdiction: Command Responsibility, 15 October 2003, para. 20:

20. The Chamber concurs with the relevance cast by the Defence on the outcome of the decision of the Appeals Chamber of the ICTY for the furtherance of the doctrine of command responsibility with respect to an internal armed conflict. In addition, the Chamber accepts that relevant jurisprudence such as decisions and judgements from the common Appeals Chamber of the ICTY and the ICTR can provide important guidance,

mutatis mutandis, to the implementation of the mandate of the Special Court.[...]

APPEALS CHAMBER DECISIONS

- **Article 6(2): Individual Criminal Responsibility – Immunity of Jurisdiction Before the Special Court**

S6-AC-1

o *Prosecutor v. Taylor*, Case No. SCSL-03-01-I, Decision on Immunity from Jurisdiction, 31 May 2004, para. 45-53:

45. Article 6(2) is substantially in the same terms as Article 7(2) of the Statute of the ICTY and Article 6(2) of the Statute of the ICTR. Article 27(2) of the Statute of the International Criminal Court (ICC) which entered into force on 1 July 2002 provides that:

> The Statute shall apply equally to all persons without any distinction based on official capacity. In particular, official capacity as a Head of State or Government, a member of a Government or parliament, an elected representative or a government official shall in no case exempt a person from criminal responsibility under this Statute, nor shall it, in and of itself, constitute a ground for reduction of sentence.

> Immunities or special procedural rules which may attach to the official capacity of a person, whether under national or international law, shall not bar the court from exercising its jurisdiction over such a person.

46. A forerunner of Article 6(2) of the Statute and of similar provisions in the Statutes of the ICTY, ICTR and ICC is Article 7 of the Charter of the International Military Tribunal[1] ("the Nuremberg Charter") which provides that:

> The official position of defendants, whether as Heads of State or responsible officials in Government Departments, shall not be considered as freeing them from responsibility or mitigating punishment.

47. The General Assembly by resolution 177(II) directed the International Law Commission to "formulate the principles of international law recognized in the Charter of the Nuremberg Tribunal and in the judgment of the Tribunal."[2] The International Law Commission proceeded in carrying out the directive on the footing that the General Assembly had already affirmed the principles recognized in the Nuremberg Charter and in the Judgment of the Tribunal and that what it was required to do was merely to formulate them. On that basis it formulated a provision from Article 7 of the Nuremberg Charter, Principle III as follows:

> The fact that a person who committed an act which constituted a crime under international law acted as Head of State or responsible official does not relieve him from responsibility under international law.[3]

As long ago as 12 December 1950 when the General Assembly accepted this formulation of the principle of international law by the International Law Commission, that principle became firmly established.[4]

48. Mitigation of punishment mentioned in Article 7 was not mentioned in the formulation of principles because the Commission was of the opinion that the question of mitigation of punishment was a matter for the competent court to decide.[5] It should go without saying that mention of punishment implies a trial. This point is here emphasized to show that the omission of mention of sentence was not intended to support any argument that would separate responsibility from punishment.

49. The nature of the offences for which jurisdiction was vested in these various tribunals is instructive as to the circumstances in which immunity is withheld. The nature of the Tribunals has always been a relevant consideration in the question whether there is an exception to the principle of immunity.

50. More recently in the *Yerodia* case, the International Court of Justice upheld immunities in national courts even in respect of war crimes and crimes against humanity relying on customary international law. That court, after carefully examining "state practice, including national legislation and those few decisions of national higher courts such as the House of Lords or the French Court of Cassation",[6] stated that it "has been unable to deduce from this practice that there exists under customary international law any form of exception to the rule according immunity from criminal jurisdiction and inviolability to incumbent Ministers of Foreign affairs, where they are suspected of having committed war crimes or crimes against humanity."[7] It held:

> ... although various international conventions on the prevention and punishment of certain serious crimes impose on states obligations of prosecution or extradition, thereby requiring them to extend their criminal jurisdiction, such extension of jurisdiction in no way affects immunities under customary international law, including those of Ministers for Foreign Affairs. These remain opposable before the courts of a foreign state, even where those courts exercise such a jurisdiction under these conventions.[8]

But in regard to criminal proceedings before "certain international criminal courts" it held:

an incumbent or former Minister for Foreign Affairs may be subject to criminal proceedings before *certain international criminal courts*, where they have jurisdiction. Examples include the International Criminal tribunal for the former Yugoslavia, and the International Criminal tribunal for Rwanda, established pursuant to Security Council resolutions under Chapter VII of the United Nations Charter, and the future International Criminal Court created by the 1998 Rome Convention. The latter's statute expressly provides, in Article 27, paragraph 2, that '[I]mmunities or special procedural rules which may attach to the official capacity of a person, whether under national or international law, shall not bar the Court from exercising its jurisdiction over such person'.[9]

51. A reason for the distinction, in this regard, between national courts and international courts, though not immediately evident, would appear due to the fact that the principle that one sovereign state does not adjudicate on the conduct of another state; the principle of state immunity derives from the equality of sovereign states and therefore has no relevance to international criminal tribunals which are not organs of a state but derive their mandate from the international community. Another reason is as put by Professor Orentlicher in her *amicus* brief that:

> states have considered the collective judgment of the international community to provide a vital safeguard against the potential destabilizing effect of unilateral judgment in this area.[10]

52. Be that as it may, the principle seems now established that the sovereign equality of states does not prevent a Head of State from being prosecuted before an international criminal tribunal or court. We accept the view expressed by Lord Slynn of Hadley that

> "there is . . . no doubt that states have been moving towards the recognition of some crimes as those which should not be covered by claims of state or Head of State or other official or diplomatic immunity when charges are brought before international tribunals."[11]

53. In this result the Appeals Chamber finds that Article 6(2) of the Statute is not in conflict with any peremptory norm of general international law and its provisions must be given effect by this court. We hold that the official position of the Applicant as an incumbent Head of State at the time when these criminal proceedings were initiated against him is not a bar to his prosecution by this court. The Applicant was and is subject to criminal proceedings before the Special Court for Sierra Leone.

(1) London, 8 August 1945, United Nations Treaty Series, vol. 82, 279.
(2) General Assembly, Resolution 177(II), Formulation of the principles recognized in the Charter of the Nürnberg Tribunal and in the judgment of the Tribunal, 21 November 1947.
(3) International Law Commission, Principles of International Law Recognized in the Charter of the Nürnberg Tribunal and in the Judgment of the Tribunal, submitted to the General Assembly as part of the Commission's report which appears in *Yearbook of the International Law Commission*, 1950, vol. II.
(4) Ibid., pp. 374-75.
(5) Ibid.
(6) *Yerodia* case, para. 58.
(7) Ibid.
(8) Ibid., para. 59.
(9) Ibid., para. 61 (emphasis added).
(10) Brief, above note at p. 15.
(11) See *R v. Bartle and the Commissioner of Police for the Metropolis and others, Ex parte Pinochet*, House of Lords, 25 November 1998.

- **Article 6(2): Individual Criminal Responsibility – Immunity of Jurisdiction (Cessation)**

S6-AC-2

o *Prosecutor v. Taylor*, Case No. SCSL-03-01-I, Decision on Immunity from Jurisdiction, 31 May 2004, para. 59:

59. [. . .] [I]t is apt to observe that the Applicant had at the time the Preliminary Motion was heard ceased to be a Head of State. The immunity *ratione personae* which he claimed had ceased to attach to him. Even if he had succeeded in his application the consequence would have been to compel the Prosecutor to issue a fresh warrant.

- **Article 6(2): Individual Criminal Responsibility – Immunity of Arrest**

S6-AC-3

o *Prosecutor v. Taylor*, Case No. SCSL-03-01-I, Decision on Immunity from Jurisdiction, 31 May 2004, para. 26-30:

26. [. . .] For an ordinary accused the workability of [Rules 61, 66(A)(i), 72(A) and 73(A)] is not in doubt and occasions no problem. It is because the Accused in this case was at the time a warrant was issued for his arrest a Head of State that the application of the Rules becomes controversial, in that it may sound incongruous that a Head of State in strict compliance with the provisions of the Rules submits himself to the Court before he can raise the question of his immunity.

27. The question of sovereign immunity is a procedural question. Shaw is of the opinion that it is one to be taken as a preliminary issue.(1) It may with some plausibility be argued that

the fact that it could be taken as a preliminary issue does not contradict the requirement that it should be taken after initial appearance if 'preliminary' means 'before trial'.

28. On a combined reading of Article 1 and Article 6 of the Statute of the Special Court in which it is clear that the court has competence to prosecute persons who bear the greatest responsibility for serious violations of international humanitarian law and Sierra Leonean law (Article 1) and the official position (including as Head of State) of such persons shall not relieve them of criminal responsibility nor mitigate punishment (Article 6(2)). In the *Yerodia* case similar provisions in the ICTY Statute and the Statute of the International Criminal Court ("ICC") were interpreted as making persons holding high office, including Heads of State, subject to criminal proceedings for certain offences "before certain criminal courts". But, then, to begin to apply that interpretation of the law as contained in the *Yerodia* case may indeed be tantamount to applying an interpretation that is challenged without first deciding the substance and merit of the application.

29. In the *Yerodia* case, the ICJ held that the mere issuance of a warrant of arrest by Belgium against the then incumbent Minister for Foreign Affairs of the Democratic Republic of Congo constituted a violation of an obligation of Belgium towards the DRC and ordered Belgium to cancel the warrant. The matter was not raised as a jurisdictional issue in a Belgian court.

30. Technically, an accused who has not made an initial appearance before this court cannot bring a preliminary motion in terms of Rule 72(A), nor a motion under Rule 73 of the Rules and in a normal case such application may be held premature and accordingly struck out. However, this case is not in the normal course. To insist that an incumbent Head of State must first submit himself to incarceration before he can raise the question of his immunity not only runs counter, in a substantial manner, to the whole purpose of the concept of sovereign immunity, but would also assume, without considering the merits, issues of exceptions to the concept that properly fall to be determined after delving into the merits of the claim to immunity. Although the present Applicant is no longer an incumbent Head of State, a statement of general principles must embrace situations in which an Applicant remains an incumbent Head of State. The application with which this decision is concerned was made when the Applicant was a Head of State. The Appeals Chamber exercises its inherent power and discretion to permit the Applicant to make this application notwithstanding the fact that he has not made an initial appearance. [...]

---

[1] M. Shaw, *International Law* (5th ed, Cambridge University Press, 2003), p. 623.

> **Article 8**
> **Concurrent Jurisdiction**
>
> 1. The Special Court and the national courts of Sierra Leone shall have concurrent jurisdiction.
>
> 2. The Special Court shall have primacy over the national courts of Sierra Leone. At any stage of the procedure, the Special Court may formally request a national court to defer to its competence in accordance with the present Statute and the Rules of Procedure and Evidence.

TRIAL CHAMBERS DECISIONS

- **Article 8(2): Concurrent Jurisdiction – Primacy on Sierra Leonean Tribunals**

S8-TC-1

○ *Prosecutor v. Brima*, Case No. SCSL-03-06-PT, Ruling on the Application for the Issue of a Writ of *Habeas Corpus* Filed by the Applicant, 22 July 2003:[8]

It should be recalled here that the Special Court was created by Resolution No. 1315, 2000 of the Security Council dated the 14th of August, 2000, and an Agreement dated the 16th of January, 2002, signed between the United Nations and the Government of Sierra Leone to which is annexed, the Statute that forms an integral part of the said Agreement. The Special Court was so created because of the deep concern expressed by the Security Council at the very serious crimes committed within the territory of Sierra Leone, against the People of Sierra Leone and the United Nations and Associated Personnel, and the need to create an independent Special Court to prosecute persons who bear the greatest responsibility for the commission of serious violations of international humanitarian law and crimes committed under the Sierra Leonean law.

[. . .]

[Article 14(2) of the Statute] underscores the fact that the Sierra Leonean Criminal Procedure Act, 1965 which is an emanation of the sierra Leonean Parliament, the Municipal

---

[8] See also *Prosecutor v. Kanu*, Case No. SCSL-04-16-PT, Written Reasons for the Trial Chamber's Oral Decision on the Defence Motion on Abuse of Process Due to Infringement of Principles of *Nullum Crimen Sine Lege* and Non-Retroactivity as to Several Accounts, 31 March 2004, para. 37-38.

Legislative Organ of this Country and which regulates the procedure and conduct of proceedings in all Courts vested with criminal jurisdiction by the 1991 Constitution of the Republic of Sierra Leone, is not applicable to the proceedings in the Special Court, even though it equally, like the Sierra Leonean Criminal Courts, is vested with an essentially criminal jurisdiction, albeit, of an international character.

Pursuant to the provisions of Article 14 sub 1 and sub 2 of the Statute, all Judges of the Special Court of Sierra Leone at a Plenary Meeting held in London, adopted, on the 8th of March, 2003, Rules of Procedure and Evidence which today are applicable in the functioning of the Special Court and very independently of any other Rules of Procedure and Evidence and least still, of those contained in the Sierra Leonean 1965 Criminal Procedure Act, or any other which are an emanation of the municipal legislative mechanisms of the Republic of Sierra Leone.

Viewed from another perceptive, the Special Court of Sierra Leone holds its existence, not to the Constitution or to the Parliament of the Republic of Sierra Leone, but solely to the Security Council resolution No: 1315 2000, of the 14th August 2000 and the International Agreement between the United Nations and the Government of Sierra Leone which set it up. This Resolution and Agreement are both international instruments which had to come into force as required by international law and practice, following a ratification instrument of the Government of Sierra Leone. It is this formality that warranted the enactment by the sierra Leonean Parliament, of the Special Court Agreement Ratification Act 2000, and this, very long after the coming into force of the 1991 Constitution of the Republic of Sierra Leone.

From these dates, it can be deduced that the Sovereign People and the equally Sovereign Parliament of the Republic of Sierra Leone, in enacting the 1991 Constitution in time of peace, never could have enacted or even envisaged constitutional provisions for structures which were supposed to regulate a post civil war stabilizing institution which is what the Special Court of Sierra Leone represents today.

[...]

The natural meaning, the matural interpretation of Section 125 and other provisons of the Sierra Leonean Constitution is that these provisions are only meant to apply to the Courts of Sierra Leone and the Courts which come within the judicial hierarchy of the Constitution of the Republic of Sierra Leone.

I therefore hold that application of Section 125 and other sections of the Constitution which had been referred to by Learned Counsel for the Applicant, is only limited to the Courts created by the 1991 Constitution of Sierra Leone and not to a post 1991 International creation that owes it existence to an international instrument of the Security Council and equally International Agreement between the United Nations and the Government of Sierra Leone.

To crown it all, Section 10 of the Special Court Agreement Ratification Act provides, and I quote:

> 'The Special Court shall exercise its jurisdiction and powers conferred upon it by the Agreement.'

Section 11(2) of the same Ratification Act provides:

> "The Special Court shall not form part of the Judiciary of Sierra Leone."

In the course of arguments in Court, Learned Counsel for the Applicant, Mr Terence Terry, urged me to state a case to the Supreme Court of Sierra Leone on the constitutionality of the provisions of Article 11(2) of the Ratification Act 2002 which he submitted, are unconstitutional in so far as they are inconsistent with the provisions of the 1991 Constitution of the republic of Sierra Leone.

It is my considered opinion in this regard that the jurisdiction of the Special court is limited only to matters that fall under the provisions of the Statute and the Agreement. Indeed, nowhere in these instruments is the Special Court of Sierra Leone subjected to the jurisdiction of the Supreme Court of Sierra Leone, nor is it empowered or authorised to state cases to that Court or even to get into examining issues relating to constitutionality or even arrogating itself with the competence of declaring unconstitutional, a sovereign enactment of the Sovereign Legislature of the Republic of Sierra Leone or Acts of its Executive Organs.

I therefore hold, from the foregoing analysis, that the Special Court, even though created by a special International Agreement between the United Nations and the Government of Sierra Leone, and even though, by that same International Agreement, Distinguished Judges, Counsels and Jurists of Sierra Leonean origin are appointed to serve on it, is not, should not, and cannot be considered as forming an integral part of Courts of the Republic of Sierra Leone. Rather, it is, to all intents and purposes, a Special International Criminal Jurisdiction whose mandate is defined by Security Council Resolution Number 1315, 2000 of the 14th of August, 2000, and further that all appeals from the Trial Chamber of the Special Court lie, in the last resort, not to the Supreme Court of the Republic of Sierra Leone, but before its Appeal Chamber which is the highest and final jurisdiction in its judicial hierarchy. It therefore has no connection with the Supreme Court of Sierra Leone nor is it subjected to its jurisdiction, supervisory or otherwise.

APPEALS CHAMBER DECISIONS

- **Article 8(2): Concurrent Jurisdiction – Primacy on Sierra Leonean Tribunals**

S8-AC-1

o *Prosecutor v. Kallon, Norman, Kamara*, Cases No. SCSL-04-15-AR72, SCSL-04-14-AR72, SCSL-04-14-AR72, Decision on Constitutionality and Lack of Jurisdiction, 13 March 2004, para. 66-71:[9]

66. It is obvious that the Special Court could not have been mentioned in Chapter VII of the Constitution for the simple reason that the Special Court did not exist when the Constitution was promulgated.

67. As we have already held, the Special Court is not part of the Judiciary of Sierra Leone. It is the product of a treaty agreement between the Government and the UN. The Statute of the Court is annexed to the Special Court Agreement and forms an "integral part" of it.[(1)] Concurrent jurisdiction with the Sierra Leone national courts and primacy over them emanate from that Agreement of which Article 8 of the Statute of the Court is a part. The Special Court Agreement has been ratified according to law thereby incorporating it into the Laws of Sierra Leone.

68. Although Article 8 may appear repugnant when viewed in light of sections 122 and 125 of the Constitution, it does not, in our judgment, amend the judicial framework or court structure of Sierra Leone because the Special Court is not part of the Sierra Leone Judiciary and is outside the structure of the national courts.

69. It is instructive to note that the Statutes of the ICTY and the ICTR have similar provisions.[(2)] Each of those International Tribunals has concurrent jurisdiction with national courts to prosecute persons for serious violations of international humanitarian law and each has primacy over national courts. Each of those Tribunals, at any stage of the procedure may formally request national courts to defer to the competence of the Tribunal in accordance with their respective Statutes and Rules of procedure. While acknowledging that the ICTY and ICTR have Chapter VII powers of the UN Charter ensuring that there is an obligation on all UN mem-

---

[9] See also *Prosecutor v. Kanu*, Case No. SCSL-04-16-PT, Written Reasons for the Trial Chamber's Oral Decision on the Defence Motion on Abuse of Process Due to Infringement of Principles of *Nullum Crimen Sine Lege* and Non-Retroactivity as to Several Accounts, 31 March 2004, para. 40; *Prosecutor v. Kondewa*, Case No. SCSL-04-14-PT, Decision on Preliminary Motion on Lack of Jurisdiction: Establishment of Special Court Violates Constitution of Sierra Leone, 25 May 2004, para. 2.

bers to co-operate, in the case of the Special Court, as the Agreement is between the UN and Sierra Leone, its primacy is limited to Sierra Leone alone, as also the obligation to co-operate with the Special Court.

70. Article 8 is intended to ensure that for offences other than those committed by "peacekeepers and related personnel",[3] the Special Court will have primacy over the national courts of Sierra Leone. This is consistent with the Special Court's mandate to prosecute "those who bear the greatest responsibility for serious violations of international humanitarian law and Sierra Leonean law committed in the territory of Sierra Leone since 30 November 1996 . . ."[4]

71. In our judgement, Article 8 does not contravene the Constitution as alleged or at all particularly having regard to our finding that the Special Court is an international tribunal.

---

[1] See Article 1(2) of the Special Court Agreement.
[2] See Article 9 of the Statute of the ICTY and 8 of the Statute of the ICTR.
[3] Article 1(2) of the Statute of the Special Court.
[4] Article 1(1) of the Statute of the Special Court.

S8-AC-2

o *Prosecutor v. Kallon, Kamara*, Case No. SCSL-04-15-AR72, SCSL-04-16-AR72, Decision on Challenge to Jurisdiction: Lomé Accord Amnesty, 13 March 2004, para. 85, 90:

85. Upon its establishment the Special Court assumed an independent existence and is not an agency of either of the parties which executed the Agreement establishing the Court. It is described as 'hybrid' or of 'mixed jurisdiction' because of the nature of the laws it is empowered to apply. Its description as hybrid should not be understood as denoting that it is part of two or more legal systems. Prosecutions are not made in the name of Sierra Leone which plays no part in initiating or terminating prosecution and has no control whatsoever over the Prosecutor who exercises an independent judgement in his prosecutorial decision. The understanding of the United Nations in signing the Lomé Agreement is that the amnesty granted therein will not extend to such crimes covered by Articles 2 to 4 of the Statute of the Court. The understanding of Sierra Leone from the statement made on the inauguration of the Truth Commission was that the amnesty affected only prosecutions before national courts. All these are consistent with the provisions of Article 10 of the Statute and the universal jurisdiction of other states by virtue of the nature of the crime to prosecute the offenders.

[. . .]

90. The prosecution of the accused by an independent autonomous court, initiated by an independent prosecutor and not brought in the name of Sierra Leone, is not tainted by whatever undertaking any accused claiming the benefit of the amnesty may have believed he had from the Government of Sierra Leone. Such undertaking could not affect the independent judgment of the Prosecutor who is not responsible to the Sierra Leonean Government.

Article 9
Non Bis in Idem

1. No person shall be tried before a national court of Sierra Leone for acts for which he or she has already been tried by the Special Court.

2. A person who has been tried by a national court for the acts referred to in articles 2 to 4 of the present Statute may be subsequently tried by the Special Court if:

   a. The act for which he or she was tried was characterized as an ordinary crime; or
   b. The national court proceedings were not impartial or independent, were designed to shield the accused from international criminal responsibility or the case was not diligently prosecuted.

3. In considering the penalty to be imposed on a person convicted of a crime under the present Statute, the Special Court shall take into account the extent to which any penalty imposed by a national court on the same person for the same act has already been served.

TRIAL CHAMBER DECISIONS

- **Article 9:** *Non Bis In Idem* – Attempt to Relitigate Matters Determined in Another Case – *State Decisis*

S9-TC-1   o *Prosecutor v. Kanu*, Case No. SCSL-04-16-PT, Written Reasons for the Trial Chamber's Oral Decision on the Defence Motion on Abuse of Process Due to Infringement of Principles of *Nullum Crimen Sine Lege* and Non-Retroactivity as to Several Accounts, 31 March 2004, para. 37-40:

37. In the Decision dated 22 July 2003, which considered the *habeas corpus* application by Alex Tamba Brima, it was held that [. . .]

38. It was further held in the *Brima* case that [. . .]

39. In bringing this argument as a Motion raising abuse of process, Counsel for the Accused seems to be trying to re-litigate, this time by a devious route, the same issue as one of an abuse of process, having already raised it as a serious matter of jurisdiction. The Trial Chamber wishes to observe emphatically that, although it does not intend to discourage creative and imaginative legal argument, Counsel should make

every effort to bring motions before the Chamber under the correct rules of procedure.

40. The Trial Chamber also recalls the decision by the Appeals Chamber "Decision on Constitutionality and Lack of Jurisdiction" which affirms that the Special Court operates in the sphere of international law and is not subject to the Constitution of Sierra Leone.[1] Considering the principal of judicial hierarchy and the doctrine of *stare decisis* and in light of the other reasons hereinbefore advanced, we consider this argument by Counsel as frivolous and accordingly dismiss it.

---

[1] See, e.g., *Prosecutor v. Brima Bazzy Kamara*, Case No. SCSL-2004-16-AR72(E), Decision on Constitutionality and Lack of Jurisdiction, dated 13 March 2004 and filed 15 March 2004.

- **Article 9(1):** *Non Bis In Idem* – **Initial and Consolidated Indictments**

S9-TC-2

o *Prosecutor v. Norman*, Case No. SCSL-04-14-T, Decision on the First Accused's Motion for Service and Arraignment on the Consolidated Indictment, 29 November 2004, para. 33-35:

33. The common law prohibition of double jeopardy prevents an Accused person from being subject to a further trial in which he or she has been charged with an offence and either acquitted or convicted on these charges. The prohibition prevents an Accused from being convicted twice for the same offence.[1] The Civil law principle of *ne bis in idem* also entitles the Accused not to be tried twice for the same offence. Unlike double jeopardy, however, the principle of *ne bis in idem* prevents repeated prosecutions for the same conduct in the same or different legal systems, whereas the notion of double jeopardy "is a double exposure to sentencing which is applicable to all the different stages of the criminal justice process in the *same* legal system: prosecution, conviction, and punishment".[2]

34. The principle that an Accused may not be subject to subsequent proceedings in respect of the same offence for which he or she has already been convicted or acquitted is expressed in the context of international human rights law, which is respected by the Trial Chamber of the Special Court. Article 14(7) of the *International Covenant on Civil and Political Rights* provides that:

No one shall be liable to be tried or punished again for an offence for which he has already been finally convicted or acquitted in accordance with the law and penal procedure of each country.

35. Article 9(1) of the Statute enshrines the principle of *non bis in idem* [. . .].

---

(1) See *Abney v. United States* 431 US 651 (1977), at 660-662.
(2) Kriangsak Kittichaisaree, INTERNATIONAL CRIMINAL LAW, Oxford University Press (2001) p. 289.

Article 10
Amnesty

An amnesty granted to any person falling within the jurisdiction of the Special Court in respect of the crimes referred to in articles 2 to 4 of the present Statute shall not be a bar to prosecution.

APPEALS CHAMBER DECISIONS

- **Article 10: Amnesty – Status of the Lomé Agreement**

S10-AC-1
o *Prosecutor v. Kallon, Kamara*, Cases No. SCSL-04-15-AR72, SCSL-04-16-AR72, Decision on Challenge to Jurisdiction: Lomé Accord Amnesty, 13 March 2004, para. 39-42, 44, 49-50:[10]

39. [. . .] The role of the UN as a mediator of peace, the presence of a peace-keeping force which generally is by consent of the State and the mediation efforts of the Secretary-General cannot add up to a source of obligation to the international community to perform an agreement to which the UN is not a party. As will be seen, action taken by the Security Council upon failure of a party to implement the peace agreement derives from Chapter VII of the UN Charter and not from the peace agreement.

40. Almost every conflict resolution will involve the parties to the conflict and the mediator or facilitator of the settlement, or persons or bodies under whose auspices the settlement took place but who are not at all parties to the conflict, are not contracting parties and who do not claim any obligation from the contracting parties or incur any obligation from the settlement.

41. In this case, the parties to the conflict are the lawful authority of the State and the RUF which has no status of statehood and is to all intents and purposes a faction within the State. The non-contracting signatories of the Lomé Agreement were moral guarantors of the principle that, in the terms of Article XXXIV of the Agreement, "this peace agreement is implemented with integrity and in good faith by both parties".

---

[10] See also *Prosecutor v. Gbao*, Case No. SCSL-04-14-AR72, Decision on Preliminary Motion on the Invalidity of the Agreement Between the United Nations and the Government of Sierra Leone on the Establishment of the Special Court, 25 May 2004.

The moral guarantors assumed no legal obligation. It is recalled that the UN by its representative appended, presumably for avoidance of doubt, an understanding of the extent of the agreement to be implemented as not including certain international crimes.

42. An international agreement in the nature of a treaty must create rights and obligations regulated by international law so that a breach of its terms will be a breach determined under international law which will also provide principle means of enforcement. The Lomé Agreement created neither rights nor obligations capable of being regulated by international law. An agreement such as the Lomé Agreement which brings to an end an internal armed conflict no doubt creates a factual situation of restoration of peace that the international community acting through the Security Council may take note of. That, however, will not convert it to an international agreement which creates an obligation enforceable in international, as distinguished from municipal, law. A breach of the terms of such a peace agreement resulting in resumption of internal armed conflict or creating a threat to peace in the determination of the Security Council may indicate a reversal of the factual situation of peace to be visited with possible legal consequences arising from the new situation of conflict created. Such consequences such as action by the Security Council pursuant to Chapter VII arise from the situation and not from the agreement, nor from the obligation imposed by it. Such action cannot be regarded as a remedy for the breach. A peace agreement which settles an internal armed conflict cannot be ascribed the same status as one which settles an international armed conflict which, essentially, must be between two or more warring States. The Lomé Agreement cannot be characterised as an international instrument. That it does not have that character does not, however, answer the further question whether, as far as grave crimes such as are stated in Articles 2 to 4 of the Statute of the Court are concerned, it offers any promise that is permissible or enforceable in international law.

[...]

44. [...] [W]hat is a treaty or an international agreement is not determined by the classification of a transaction by a State, but by whether the agreement is regarded as such under international law and regulated by international law.

[...]

49. The conclusion seems to follow clearly that the Lomé Agreement is neither a treaty nor an agreement in the nature of a treaty. However, it does not need to have that character for it to be capable of creating binding obligations and rights between the parties to the agreement in municipal law. The consequence of its not being a treaty or an agreement in the

nature of a treaty is that it does not create an obligation in international law.

50. The validity of Article IX of the Lomé Agreement in the municipal law of Sierra Leone is not of prime importance in these proceedings since the challenge to its validity had not been based on municipal law. It is expedient for this Court to confine itself to the limited questions that arise in regard to Article IX of the Lomé Agreement. These are, ultimately, whether in international law it bars this Court from exercising jurisdiction over the defendants in regard to crimes against humanity allegedly committed by them before the date of the Lomé Agreement, and whether it provides materials that are grounds for this Court to exercise a discretion to stay the proceedings as being an abuse of process.

- **Article 10: Amnesty – Effects of the Amnesty**

S10-AC-2

o *Prosecutor v. Kallon, Kamara*, Cases No. SCSL-04-15-AR72, SCSL-04-16-AR72, Decision on Challenge to Jurisdiction: Lomé Accord Amnesty, 13 March 2004, para. 67-73, 80-84, 88:

67. The grant of amnesty or pardon is undoubtedly an exercise of sovereign power which, essentially, is closely linked, as far as crime is concerned, to the criminal jurisdiction of the State exercising such sovereign power. Where jurisdiction is universal,[1] a State cannot deprive another State of its jurisdiction to prosecute the offender by the grant of amnesty. It is for this reason unrealistic to regard as universally effective the grant of amnesty by a State in regard to grave international crimes in which there exists universal jurisdiction. A State cannot bring into oblivion and forgetfulness a crime, such as a crime against international law, which other States are entitled to keep alive and remember.

68. A crime against international law has been defined as "an act committed with intent to violate a fundamental interest protected by international law or with knowledge that the act would probably violate such an interest, and which may not be adequately punished by the exercise of the normal criminal jurisdiction of any state."[2] In *re List and Others*, the US Military Tribunal at Nuremberg defined an international crime as: "such act universally recognized as criminal, which is considered a grave matter of international concern and for some valid reason cannot be left within the exclusive jurisdiction of the State that would have control over it under ordinary circumstances."[3] However, not every activity that is seen as an international crime is susceptible to universal jurisdiction.[4]

69. The question is whether the crimes within the competence of the Court are crimes susceptible to universal jurisdiction. The crimes mentioned in Articles 2-4 of the Statute are international crimes and crimes against humanity. Indeed, no suggestion to the contrary has been made by counsel. One of the most recent decisions confirming the character of such crimes is the *Tadić* Jurisdiction Decision.[5] The crimes under Sierra Leonean law mentioned in Article 5 do not fall into the category of such crimes and are not mentioned in Article 10.

70. One consequence of the nature of grave international crimes against humanity is that States can, under international law, exercise universal jurisdiction over such crimes. In *Attorney General of the Government of Israel v. Eichmann* the Supreme Court of Israel declared:

> The abhorrent crimes defined in this Law are not crimes under Israeli law alone. These crimes which struck at the whole of mankind and shocked the conscience of nations, are grave offences against the law of nations itself (*delicta juris gentium*). Therefore, so far from international law negating or limiting the jurisdiction of countries with respect to such crimes, international law is, in the absence of an International Court, in need of the judicial and legislative organs of every country to give effect to its criminal interdictions and to bring the criminals to trial. The jurisdiction to try crimes under international law is universal.[6]

Also, in *Congo v. Belgium*[7] it was held by the International Court of Justice that certain international tribunals have jurisdiction over crimes under international law. This viewpoint was similarly held by the ICTY in *Furundzija*.[8]

71. After reviewing international practice in regard to the effectiveness or otherwise of amnesty granted by a State and the inconsistencies in state practice as regards the prohibition of amnesty for crimes against humanity, Cassese conceptualised the status of international practice thus:

> There is not yet any general obligation for States to refrain from amnesty laws on these crimes. Consequently, if a State passes any such law, it does not breach a customary rule. Nonetheless if a court of another State having in custody persons accused of international crimes decide to prosecute them although in their national State they would benefit from an amnesty law, such court would not thereby act contrary to general international law, in particular to the principle of respect for the sovereignty of other States.[9]

The opinion stated above is gratefully adopted. It is, therefore, not difficult to agree with the submission made on behalf of Redress that the amnesty granted by Sierra Leone cannot cover crimes under international law that are the subject of universal jurisdiction. In the first place, it stands to reason that a state cannot sweep such crimes into oblivion and forgetfulness which other states have jurisdiction to prosecute by reason of the fact that the obligation to protect human dignity is a peremptory norm and has assumed the nature of obligation *erga omnes*.[10]

72. In view of the conclusions that have been arrived at in paragraph 69, it is clear that the question whether amnesty is unlawful under international law becomes relevant only in considering the question whether Article IX of the Lomé Agreement can constitute a legal bar to prosecution of the defendants by another State or by an international tribunal. There being no such bar, the remaining question is whether the undertaking contained in Article IX is good ground for holding that the prosecution of the defendants is an abuse of process of the Court.

73. It is not difficult to agree with the submissions made by the *amici curiae*, Professor Orentlicher and Redress that, given the existence of a treaty obligation to prosecute or extradite an offender, the grant of amnesty in respect of such crimes as are specified in Articles 2 to 4 of the Statute of the Court is not only incompatible with, but is in breach of an obligation of a State towards the international community as a whole.[11] Nothing in the submissions made by the Defence and the interveners detracts from that conclusion. The case of *Azapo v. President of the Republic of South Africa*[12] is purely one dealt with under the domestic laws of South Africa. It was not a case in which the jurisdiction of another State or of an international court to prosecute the offenders is denied. The decisive issues which have arisen in the case before us did not arise in that case.

[. . .]

80. [. . .] Article 10 of the Statute which provides that amnesty granted to any person falling within the jurisdiction of the Special Court in respect of the crimes referred to in articles 2 to 4 of the present Statute shall not be a bar to prosecution is an express limitation on an exercise of the discretion of the Court to bar proceedings solely on the strength of such amnesty.

81. It must be stated, though no one has so suggested, that there was no bad faith in the inclusion of Article 10 in the Statute. There was the clear statement in the preamble to Resolution 1315 (2000) of the Security Council that "[t]he Special representative of the Secretary-General appended to his signature of the Lomé Agreement a statement that the United Nations holds the understanding that the amnesty provisions of the Agreement shall not apply to international crimes of genocide, crimes against humanity, war crimes and other seri-

ous violations of international humanitarian law". There was also the statement earlier referred to by the President of Sierra Leone that the amnesty was intended to be effective only in regard to the national courts.

82. The submission by the Prosecution that there is a "crystallising international norm that a government cannot grant amnesty for serious violations of crimes under international law" is amply supported by materials placed before this Court. The opinion of both *amici curiae* that it has crystallised may not be entirely correct, but that is no reason why this court in forming its own opinion should ignore the strength of their argument and the weight of materials they place before the Court. It is accepted that such a norm is developing under international law. Counsel for Kallon submitted that there is, as yet, no universal acceptance that amnesties are unlawful under international law, but, as amply pointed out by Professor Orentlicher, there are several treaties requiring prosecution for such crimes. These include the 1948 Convention on the Prevention and Punishment of the Crime of Genocide,[13] the Convention against Torture and Other Cruel, Inhuman or Degrading Treatment or Punishment,[14] and the four Geneva conventions.[15] There are also quite a number of resolutions of the UN General Assembly and the Security Council reaffirming a state obligation to prosecute or bring to justice. Redress has appended to its written submissions materials which include relevant conclusions of the Committee against torture, findings of the Human Rights Commission, and relevant judgments of the Inter-American Court.

83. Professor Orentlicher cautiously concluded that "to the extent that the amnesty encompasses crimes against humanity, serious war crimes, torture and other gross violations of human rights its validity is highly doubtful".[16] She was, however, emphatic in her opinion that the amnesty contravenes the United Nation's commitment to combating impunity for atrocious international crimes.

84. Even if the opinion is held that Sierra Leone may not have breached customary law in granting an amnesty, this court is entitled in the exercise of its discretionary power, to attribute little or no weight to the grant of such amnesty which is contrary to the direction in which customary international law is developing and which is contrary to the obligations in certain treaties and conventions the purpose of which is to protect humanity.

[...]

88. Whatever effect the amnesty granted in the Lomé Agreement may have on a prosecution for such crimes as are contained in Articles 2 to 4 in the national courts of Sierra Leone, it is ineffective in removing the universal jurisdiction to

prosecute persons accused of such crimes that other states have by reason of the nature of the crimes. It is also ineffective in depriving an international court such as the Special Court of jurisdiction.

---

(1) Under the universality principle, each and every state has jurisdiction to try particular offences. See Shaw, *International Law*, p. 592 (note above).
(2) International Law in the Twentieth Century: Essay by Quincy Wright, pp. 623, 641.
(3) See Kittichaisare, *International Criminal Law*, (Oxford, 2001), p. 3.
(4) "The fact that a particular activity may be seen as an international crime does not itself establish universal jurisdiction and state practice does not appear to have moved beyond war crime, crimes against peace and crimes against humanity in terms of permitting the exercise of such jurisdiction." See Shaw, *International Law*, p. 597.
(5) See *supra*.
(6) *Attorney-General of the Government of Israel v. Eichman* (1961) 36 ILR 5, 12.
(7) *Case concerning Arrest Warrant of 11 April 2000 (Democratic Republic of the Congo v. Belgium)* (2002) ICJ Reports, 14 February 2002, para. 61.
(8) *Furundzija* Trial Judgement, para. 14.
(9) A. Cassese, *International Criminal Law* (Oxford, 2003), 315.
(10) See *Barcelona Traction, Light and Power Co Case (Belgium v. Spain)* [1970] ICJ Reports 3; See also Moir, *The Law of Internal Armed Conflict*, 57, "It has been suggested that three groups of [peremptory] norms exist: those protecting the foundations of law, peace and humanity; those rules of co-operation protecting fundamental common interests; and those protecting humanity to the extent of human dignity, personal and racial equality, life and personal freedom." See also I. Brownlie, *Principles of International Law*, (6th Ed., 2003) where prohibition of crimes against humanity is included as an example of a *ius cogens* norm, p. 489.
(11) Indeed in 1999, the UN Commission on Human Rights made what can be regarded as a statement of universal jurisdiction in the following terms: "[I]n any armed conflict, including an armed conflict not of an international character, the taking of hostages, wilful killing and torture or inhuman treatment of persons taking no active part in hostilities constitutes a grave breach of international humanitarian law, and that all countries are under obligation to search for persons alleged to have committed or to have ordered to be committed, such grave breaches and bring such persons regardless of their nationality, before their own courts." See *Situation of Human Rights in Sierra Leone*, U.N. Commission on Human Rights, 54th Session, U.N. Doc. E/CN.4/RES/1999/1 (1999). See also, Babafemi Akinrinade, 'International Humanitarian Law and the Conflict in Sierra Leone', 15 *Notre Dame Journal of Law, Ethics and Public Policy*, 391-454 (Fall 2001) at pp. 442-443.
(12) *Azapo v. President of the Republic of South Africa* (4) SA 653 (1996).
(13) Convention on the Prevention and Punishment of the Crime of Genocide, adopted by UN General Assembly on 9 December 1948, 78 UNTS 277.
(14) Convention against Torture and other Cruel, Inhuman or Degrading Treatment or Punishment, 4 February 1985, (1984) ILM 1027.
(15) Convention for the Amelioration of the Condition of the Wounded and Sick in Armed Forces in the Field; Convention for the Amelioration of the Condition of Wounded, Sick and Shipwrecked Members of Armed Forces at Sea; Convention Relative to the Treatment of Prisoners of War; Convention Relative to the Protection of Civilians in Time of War. Geneva, 12 August 1949.
(16) Orentlicher *amicus* brief, p. 24.

Article 13
Qualification and Appointment of Judges

1. The judges shall be persons of high moral character, impartiality and integrity who possess the qualifications required in their respective countries for appointment to the highest judicial offices. They shall be independent in the performance of their functions, and shall not accept or seek instructions from any Government or any other source.

2. In the overall composition of the Chambers, due account shall be taken of the experience of the judges in international law, including international humanitarian law and human rights law, criminal law and juvenile justice.

3. The judges shall be appointed for a three-year period and shall be eligible for reappointment.

TRIAL CHAMBERS DECISIONS

- **Article 13(1): Qualification and Appointment of Judges – Impartiality – Assertions of Partiality to Be Supported by Evidence**

S13-TC-1

o *Prosecutor v. Kondewa*, Case No. SCSL-03-12-PT, Order Pursuant to Rule 72(E) – Defence Motion Based on Lack of Jurisdiction / Abuse of Process: Amnesty Provided by Lomé Accord, 8 December 2003:[11]

NOTING that the Defence states in paragraph 16 of the Motion that: "It is recognised that there may be pressure on the Trial Chamber, as a constituent element of the Special Court, in part established by the United Nations, to follow the opinion of the Secretary-General of the United Nations as expressed in his report and find that the amnesty granted at Lomé has no application before the Special Court" and that "the Trial Chamber must conduct an impartial and fair assessment of the law and facts presented and determine the extent of application of the Lomé Accord and the amnesty contained therein in its own right and independently of the opinion already expressed by the Secretary-General and the United Nations." Unless there is evidence offered to support such an

---

[11] See also *Prosecutor v. Kallon*, Case No. SCSL-03-07-PT, Order Pursuant to Rule 72(E) – Defence Motion Based on Lack of Jurisdiction – Abuse of Process: Amnesty Provided by Lomé Accord, 30 September 2003.

assertion the Trial Chamber would like to state unequivocally that assertions or comments of that nature are highly objectionable and unacceptable and are not conducive to proper conduct of a trial.

APPEALS CHAMBER DECISIONS

- **Article 13(1): Qualification and Appointment of Judges – Judicial Independence – Funding of the Special Court for Sierra Leone**

S13-AC-1

o *Prosecutor v. Norman*, Case No. SCSL-04-14-AR72, Decision on Preliminary Motion on Lack of Jurisdiction (Judicial Independence), 13 March 2004, para. 15-17, 20-43:

Provisions relating to Funding and Management of the Court

15. Article 6 of the Agreement provides for the funds of the Court in the following terms:

> The expenses of the Special Court shall be borne by voluntary contributions from the international community. It is understood that the Secretary-General will commence the process of establishing the Court when he has sufficient contributions in hand to finance the establishment of the Court and 12 months of its operation plus pledges equal to the anticipated expenses of the following 24 months of the Court's operation. It is further understood that the Secretary-General will continue to seek contributions equal to the anticipated expenses of the Court beyond its first three years of operation. Should voluntary contributions be insufficient for the Court to implement its mandate, the Secretary-general and the Security Council shall explore alternate means of financing the Special Court.

16. Article 7 of the Agreement provides for the establishment by "interested States" of a Management Committee "to assist the Secretary-General in obtaining adequate funding, and provide advice and policy direction on all non-judicial aspects of the operation of the Court, including questions of efficiency, and to perform other functions as agreed by interested States." The Management Committee is composed of important contributors to the Special Court.

Provision regarding the Termination of the Agreement

17. By virtue of Article 23 of the Agreement, the Agreement shall be terminated by agreement of the Parties upon completion of the judicial activities of the Special Court.

[…]

V. SAFEGUARD OF JUDICIAL INDEPENDENCE

20. Safeguard of judicial independence takes several forms. However, since the question raised by the motion falls within a narrow compass it is unnecessary to enter into any lengthy discourse of the concept of judicial independence or of the various mechanisms usually put in place to safeguard judicial independence.

21. One prominent safeguard of judicial independence in a democratic State is the doctrine of separation of powers which, in regard to the independence of the judiciary, operates to reserve to the judiciary the exercise of judicial powers of the State and protects the judiciary from being so dependent on other arms of Government as to raise a reasonable apprehension of a real likelihood that judicial functions of the judiciary are performed under the influence of another arm of Government or body.

22. In practice, in regard to the judiciary, there are various models of separation of powers. However, in hardly any is the judiciary required or expected to raise revenue by itself to fund its operations so that it could maintain judicial independence. Indeed, as will be seen shortly, were the judiciary to run its operations and pay its judges from moneys generated from its judicial activities the apprehension of likelihood of bias would become more real and reasonable.

23. In some models the executive deals with staffing and administration of the judiciary, sometimes under the umbrella of a Ministry of Justice. In others the executive is excluded from participation in such process. In some models the judiciary is self-accounting, in others the budget of the judiciary is part of the budget of a Ministry of Justice in which the judiciary is treated, at least for budgetary purposes, as a department of the Ministry of Justice.

VI. FUNDING ARRANGEMENT AND INDEPENDENCE

24. Where the allegation is that the funding arrangement of a judiciary raises a real likelihood of bias so that an accused entertains a reasonable apprehension that he cannot have a fair trial, much more is required than merely showing that the court derives its funding from a source which may be displeased by its decisions. There are other considerations, the principal of which is whether such funding arrangement leads to a real likelihood that the court will be influenced by such arrangement to give decisions, not on the merits of the case, but to please the funding body or agency. Such factors as the obligation, moral or legal, of the funding body or agency and the guarantee of payment of judicial remuneration, however the judiciary is funded, are relevant factors.

25. Denial of adequate funding of the judiciary which would emasculate its performance while the payment of judicial remuneration remained protected must be distinguished from denial of funding where judicial remuneration is unprotected and would therefore affect the payment of judicial remuneration. The former is a shirking of responsibility by the state to provide an efficient or any machinery of justice, while the latter may raise a concern of real likelihood of judicial bias. The conclusion seems clear that it is not every inadequacy in funding arrangement that leads to an inability of courts to dispense justice without bias.

26. It has long been acknowledged that judicial independence rests on the twin pillars of security of tenure of the judge and guarantee of judicial remuneration and its protection from the whims and caprices of governments or bodies charged with the responsibility of funding the judiciary.

27. As early as 1701 it was provided by the Act of Settlement that:

> Judges Commission be made Quamdiu se bene gesserint [that is, during good behaviour] and their salaries ascertained and established.[1]

Commenting on that English statute, Chief Justice Burgher, delivering the lead opinion of the US Supreme Court in *United States v. Will*,[2] said:

> The English statute is the earliest legislative acknowledgment that control over the tenure and compensation of judges is incompatible with a truly independent judiciary, free of improper influence from other forces within government.[3]

In the same vein as in the Act of Settlement, several modern Constitutions make provision for the security of tenure of judges and for protection of judicial remuneration. Thus, by section 138(1) of the Constitution of Sierra Leone of 1991,[4] it is provided that:

> The salaries, allowances, gratuities and pensions of Judges of the Superior Court of judicature shall be charged upon the Consolidated Fund.

Section 138(3) of the same Constitution provided that:

> The salary, allowances, privileges, right in respect of leave of absence, gratuity or pension and other conditions of service of a Judge of the Superior Court of Judicature shall not be varied to his disadvantage.

A similar but shorter provision to the same effect is contained in section 1 of Article III of the Constitution of the United States[5] which provides that:

... The Judges, both of the supreme and inferior courts, shall hold their offices during good behavior, and shall, at stated times, receive for their services, a compensation, which shall not be diminished during their continuance of office.

28. Some would reason that a safeguard of judicial independence is the payment of handsome remuneration to judges. Another view, and this would appear to be the better view, is that the level of remuneration of a judge is an acknowledgment of the high skill he possesses and which he is expected to bring to the discharge of his judicial function in order to enhance the quality of justice. Be that as it may, of more value in securing judicial independence are the assurance and guarantee of security of tenure and guarantee and protection of the level and payment of judicial remuneration.

VII. THE MAIN QUESTION

29. Notwithstanding what would appear to be a digression to the wider area of the concept of judicial independence relevant, perhaps, as a backdrop to a consideration of the main issue raised by the Preliminary Motion, the question in these proceedings, in the final analysis, falls within a narrow compass. The question relates to the funding of the Court and it is whether funding of the Court by voluntary contribution of interested States coupled with the structure of the Management Committee deprives the Court of the necessary guarantees of independence and impartiality.

30. As earlier stated, mere complaint about funding arrangements of a Court cannot by itself be a ground for imputing a real likelihood of bias to a judge. What is material and has to be established is that such funding arrangements are capable of creating a real and reasonable apprehension in the mind of an average person that the judge is not likely to be able to decide fairly. A rough and ready test which seems apt can be fashioned out of a passage in the lead opinion of Chief Justice Taft in the U.S. Supreme Court case of *Tumey v. Ohio*[6] where he said:

> ... the requirement of due process of law in judicial procedure is not satisfied by the argument that men of the highest honour and the greatest self-sacrifice could carry it on without danger of injustice. Every procedure which would offer a possible temptation to the average man as a judge to forget the burden of proof required to convict the defendant, or which might lead him not to hold the balance nice, clear, and true between the State and the accused denies the latter due process of law.[7]

In the U.S. case of *Ward v. Village of Monroeville*,[8] the U.S. Supreme Court formulated a test thus:

whether the mayor's situation is one which 'would offer a possible temptation to the average man as a judge to forget the burden of proof required to convict the defendant, or which might lead him not to hold the balance nice, clear and true between the State and the accused...'[9]

31. The test in these two cases, adapted by substituting 'Court's' for 'mayor's' in the first line in the passage above, seems apt for the purpose of this case, having regard to the suggestion which is the pith and substance of the argument advanced by counsel for the applicant that the funding arrangement of the Court is such as would reasonably be seen as likely to put pressure on the judges of the Court to convict the accused so that they may thereby please the donor States to prevent them from withholding their contributions to the funds of the Court. Astonishing as the suggestion may seem, and, indeed is, it is one that evokes the need to apply the test stated above and to examine whether it has any foundation in fact.

32. Before reverting to the present case, it is of interest to note, albeit very briefly, one case in which the above test has been applied to the advantage of the accused and another in which it has been held inapplicable. All are cases decided by the U.S. Supreme Court which appears to have developed a rich jurisprudence in this area of law.

33. In *Tumey v Ohio*[10] the facts, taken from the syllabus, are as follows: Under statutes of Ohio, offences against stay prohibition, involving a wide range of fines enforceable by imprisonment may be tried without a jury before the mayor of any rural village situated in the county (however populous) in which offences occur. His judgment upon the facts is final and conclusive unless so clearly unsupported as to indicate mistake, bias, or wilful disregard of duty. The fines are divided between the State and the village. The village, by means of the fines collected, hires attorneys and detectives to arrest alleged offenders anywhere in the county and prosecute them before the mayor. In addition to his salary, the mayor, when he convicts, but not otherwise, receives his fees and costs amounting to a substantial income. The fine offers means of adding materially to the financial prosperity of the village, for which the mayor, in his executive capacity, is responsible. It was held that the due process of law was denied the defendant in the case. The court held that the mayor had a pecuniary interest as a result of his judgment such as to disqualify him. The court said:

> It appears from the evidence in this case, and would be plain if the evidence did not show it, that the law is calculated to awaken the interest of all those in the village charged with the responsibility of raising the public money and expending it, in the pecuniarily successful

conduct of such a court. The mayor represents the village, and cannot escape his representative capacity. [. . .] With his interest as mayor in the financial condition of the village, and his responsibility therefore, might not a defendant with reason say that he feared he could not get a fair trial or a fair sentence from one who would have so strong a motive to help his village by conviction and a heavy fine?[11]

As a statement of principle the court said:

But it certainly violates the Fourteenth Amendment, and deprives a defendant in a criminal case of due process of law, to subject his liberty or property to the judgment of a court the judge of which has a direct, personal, substantial, pecuniary interest in reaching a conclusion against him in his case.[12]

34. On the other hand, in *Dugan v. Ohio*[13] the petitioner was convicted and fined by the mayor of a city for a violation of the Ohio liquor law committed within the city limits. The legislative powers of the city were exercised by a commission of five, of whom the mayor was one, and its executive powers by the commission and a manager, who was the active executive. The functions of the mayor, as such, were judicial only. His sole compensation was a salary fixed by the vote of the other commissioners, and payable out of a general fund to which the fines accumulated in his court under all laws contributed, the salary being the same whether the trial before him resulted in convictions or acquittals. It was held that the mayor's relation to the fund and to the financial policy of the city were too remote to warrant a presumption of bias towards conviction in prosecutions before him as a judge.[14]

35. In this case direct pecuniary interest in the result of a trial is not suggested by the applicant's case. Nonetheless, it was suggested that apprehension that the funding of the Court may be so severely diminished were the court to render decisions which displease major donors to the funds of the court, to the detriment of the ability of the Court to pay remunerations to judges, would have the same prejudicial consequences for the ability of the judges to dispense justice fairly as if they had direct pecuniary interest in the proceedings.

36. The position is sufficiently clear to enable it to be stated in the following propositions:

    a. A judge is disqualified from adjudication where he has a direct, personal or pecuniary interest in the litigation and, particularly, in criminal trials where pecuniary benefit accrues to him by his convicting.[15]

    b. A judge is not disqualified from adjudicating where there is no objective reason to infer on any showing that failure to convict (or acquit) in any case or cases would deprive him of or affect his fixed remuneration.[16]

c. A judge should disqualify himself if a reasonable and informed person would believe that there is a real danger of bias.

d. A reasonable person will not rush to an assumption that a judge will violate his oath and the duties of his office on a remote and speculative belief that his remuneration may be affected in any way by the decision he gives.

VIII. ABSENCE OF FACTUAL BASIS FOR ALLEGATION

37. On the true facts, it is manifest that the assumptions on which the applicant based his challenge to the jurisdiction of the Court are far-fetched and have no factual basis that can support the contention that the funding arrangement of the Court could reasonably occasion the denial of a fair hearing. The judges of the Court are on fixed term contracts of three years, though subject to re-appointment. The remuneration payable to each judge is certain and fixed by the contract of appointment. The liability of the Court to pay such remuneration is not in any way conditional upon whether the parties to the Agreement establishing the Court are able to raise voluntary contributions to fund the court, since, indeed, by Article 6 of the Agreement it is provided that:

> "Should voluntary contributions be insufficient for the Court to implement its mandate, the Secretary-General and the Security Council shall explore alternate means of financing the Special Court." Finally, the Agreement establishing the Court can only be terminated by virtue of Article 23 of the Agreement "upon completion of the judicial activities of the Special Court."

38. It is clear from these indisputable facts that there is no way in which the remuneration of the judges of the Court is tied to the funding of the court by voluntary contribution of donor States or can be subject to manipulation.

39. The concerns which engender the applicant's motion are of limited scope and relate only to the funding of the Court by voluntary contribution. Reference by counsel to the Canadian Supreme Court case *Reference Re Remuneration of Judges*[17] seems unnecessary beyond a mention of the now uncontroversial principle, which applicant's counsel stated the decision stood for, that judicial salaries must be protected from executive, legislative or managerial manipulation. The issues discussed in that case of circumstances in which reduction of judicial salary may be permissible or whether judges may negotiate their salaries are really not material to the determination of

the main issue in this case. The Canadian Supreme Court ruled that the way the reduction of salaries was carried out was unconstitutional. In our case, the question is whether the judges would feel pressured to produce results in the form of convictions in order to attract sufficient funds for the Special Court, lest their salaries be reduced. Special Court judges' salaries are certain and fixed by the contract of appointment. The reduction of judges' salaries is in itself unrealistic. Similarly, although in the final analysis the ground on which an objection is raised in this case boils down to likelihood of bias, the bias alleged is not of the same type as was discussed in the case of *ex parte Pinochet* (No. 2)[18] where the bias alleged was not as to pecuniary interest of the judges in the result of the proceedings, but one likely to be occasioned by the close relationship of one of the judges to a cause promoted by an intervener (Amnesty International) who was in the rather unusual circumstances of the case deemed to have been a party.

40. It may well be stated, if only in an attempt at relative exhaustiveness, that if the voluntary contributor States to the funds may be said to have a 'cause' it is not a cause that is in issue in the case or that can be said to be of controversy in democratic societies. That 'cause' is that a man will not be condemned without a fair and public trial and that there must be an end to impunity of serious violations of international humanitarian law. It is in furtherance of the 'cause' that the Court in its Rules established a Defence Office for the purpose of ensuring the rights of suspects and accused.[19]

41. Undoubtedly, states which have contributed to the funds of the Court must have done so because they believe in due process of law and the rule of law. It is far-fetched, preposterous and, almost, bad taste to suggest that donor states, which in their national practice promote and respect human rights and the rule of law and promote such values internationally, would be committed to funding and sustaining a court in the expectation that it will operate contrary to those same values.

42. Although the objection of the applicant has been couched in terms of judicial independence and bias, it is expedient and sufficient to limit the determination of the objection to the limited question that has been identified. The Court is not one functioning as an arm of a state in a particular legal order or system. Its jurisdiction is of an extremely limited nature and the lifespan of the Court itself is predictably limited. It is for this reason that it is unnecessary to examine at any length the functions of the Management Committee, which in no way approximates either to the executive or the legislature in a State nor wields powers of such organs which may be subject to review by the Special Court. The Committee has no cause to influence and cannot, in performance of its role, influence the Court in the determination of cases before it.

43. It suffices for the determination of the Preliminary Motion to hold that the funding arrangements of the Court cannot be reasonably seen in any way to lead to any real likelihood of bias in the Court in the determination of matters before it.

---

[1] Act of Settlement, 12 & 13 Will. III, ch. 2, § III, cl. 7 (1701).
[2] *United States v. Will* 449 U.S. 200 (1980).
[3] Ibid. at p. 218.
[4] The Constitution of Sierra Leone 1991, 24 September 1991.
[5] U.S. Const. art. III, § 1 (2004).
[6] *Tumey v. Ohio*, 273 U.S. 510 (1927).
[7] Ibid. at p. 532.
[8] *Ward v. Village of Monroeville*, 409 U.S. 57 (1972), citing *Tumey*, ibid.
[9] Ibid. 60.
[10] *Supra* (6).
[11] *Tumey v. Ohio, supra* note (6), at p. 533.
[12] *Tumey v. Ohio, supra* note (6), at p. 523.
[13] *Dugan v. Ohio*, 277 U.S. 61 (1928).
[14] Ibid., at p. 65.
[15] See *Ward v. Village of Monroeville supra* note (8); See *Tumey v. Ohio, supra* note *(6)*.
[16] *Dugan v. Ohio, supra* note *(6)*.
[17] *Reference Re Remuneration of Judges of the Provincial Court of Prince Edward Island* [1997] 3 S.C.R. 3.
[18] *R. v. Metropolitan Stipendiary Magistrate ex parte Pinochet Ugarte (No. 2)* [2000] 1 A.C. 119.
[19] Rule 45 of the Rules.

Article 14
Rules of Procedure and Evidence

1. The Rules of Procedure and Evidence of the International Criminal Tribunal for Rwanda obtaining at the time of the establishment of the Special Court shall be applicable *mutatis mutandis* to the conduct of the legal proceedings before the Special Court.

2. The judges of the Special Court as a whole may amend the Rules of Procedure and Evidence or adopt additional rules where the applicable Rules do not, or do not adequately, provide for a specific situation. In so doing, they may be guided, as appropriate, by the Criminal Procedure Act, 1965, of Sierra Leone.

TRIAL CHAMBERS DECISIONS

- **Article 14: Rules of Procedure and Evidence – Interpretation of Statutory Instruments – Ordinary and Natural Meaning**

S14-TC-1
o *Prosecutor v. Brima*, Case No. SCSL-04-16-PT, Decision on Applicant's Motion Against Denial by the Acting Principal Defender to Enter a Legal Service Contract for the Assignment of Counsel, 6 May 2004, para. 43-45, 89-91:[12]

[. . .] In this regard, we would like to recall in order to emphasize, that in interpreting statutory or regulatory instruments, due regard should primarily be paid to their ordinary and natural meaning so as to avoid, like the [Principal Defender] is urging us to accept, importing extraneous interpretations to statutory provisions or regulations which are as clear as those we have just reproduce for purposes of scrutinous examination.

90. To underscore the importance of this approach, the Chamber would like to refer to and adopt the dictum of LORD HERSCHEL in the case of THE BANK OF ENGLAND VS. VAGLIANO BROTHERS [1891] AC 107 at 144, where His Lordship had this to say:

"I think the proper cause is in the first instance, to examine the language of the Statute and to ask what its natural meaning is."

---

[12] See also *Prosecutor v. Sesay*, Case No. SCSL-04-15-T, Decision on Sesay Motion Seeking Disclosure of the Relationship Between Governmental Agencies of the United States of America and the Office of the Prosecutor, 2 May 2005, para. 33.

91. This dictum of Lord Herschell which was relied on by this Chamber in interpreting Section 125 of the Constitution of Sierra Leone when adjudicating on the Habeas Corpus Application of this same Applicant in Case No. SCSL-03-06-PT of 22nd July 2003, has stood the test of time because it limits the prevalent temptation to import into a clearly enacted Statute or Regulation, extraneous meanings and interpretation which, in the long run, not only enable the authority to assume legislative functions which is *ultra vires*, but also produces a result that is directly contradictory or even contrary to the necessary intendment of the legislative or regulatory instrument."

- **Article 14: Rules of Procedure and Evidence – Purposive Interpretation**

S14-TC-2

o *Prosecutor v. Kondewa*, No. SCSL-04-14-T, Decision on Motion to Compel the Production of Exculpatory Witness Statement, Witness Summaries and Materials Pursuant to Rule 68, 8 July 2004, para. 19:[13]

19. [. . .] [T]he Chamber wishes to observe, by way of first principles, that no rule, however formulated, should be applied in a way that contradicts its purpose. A kindred notion here is that a statute or rule must not be interpreted so as to produce an absurdity. In effect, it is rudimentary law that a statute or rule must be interpreted in the light of its purpose. Another basic canon of statutory interpretation is that a statute is to be interpreted in accordance with the legislative intent. Restating the law on statutory interpretation, the Trial Chamber of the ICTY in the case of Prosecutor v. Delalic had this to say:

> "The fundamental rule for the construction of the provision of a statute, to which all others are subordinate, is that a statute is to be expounded according to the intent of the law maker. In an effort to discover the intention of the law maker many rules to aid interpretation have been formulated. Of the many rules, one of the most familiar and commonly used is the literal or golden rule of construction. By this rule, the interpreter is expected to rely on the words in the statute, and to give such words their plain natural import in the order in

---

[13] See also *Prosecutor v. Sesay*, Case No. SCSL-04-15-T, Decision on Defence Motion for Disclosure Pursuant to Rule 66 and 68 of the Rules, 9 July 2004, paras 16-17; *Prosecutor v. Sesay*, Case No. SCSL-04-15-T, Decision on Sesay Motion Seeking Disclosure of the Relationship Between Governmental Agencies of the United States of America and the Office of the Prosecutor, 2 May 2005, para. 34.

which they are placed. The rationale is that the law maker should be taken to mean what is plainly expressed. The underlying principle which is also consistent with common sense is that the meaning and intention of a statutory provision shall be discerned from the plain and unambiguous expression used therein rather than from any notions which may be entertained as just and expedient."[1]

---

[1] *Prosecutor v. Delacic et al.*, IT-96-21, Decision on the Motion on Presentation of Evidence by the Accused, Esad Landzo, ICTY, 1 May 1999, para. 17.

S14-TC-3

o *Prosecutor v. Norman, Fofana, Kondewa*, Case No. SCSL-04-14-T, Order on an Application by the Prosecution to Hold a Closed Session Hearing of Witnesses TF2-082 and TF2-032, 13 September 2004:[14]

CONSIDERING that the Rules must be consistent with the purpose and object of the Statute and provide appropriate means to give effect to the Statute; and that a proper application of the Statute and Rules of the Special Court requires that purposive and contextual principles of interpretation be applied by the Trial Chamber;

APPEALS CHAMBER DECISIONS

- **Article 14: Rules of Procedure and Evidence – Amendment**

S14-AC-1

o *Prosecutor v. Norman, Kallon, Gbao*, Cases No. SCSL-03-08-PT, SCSL-03-07-PT, SCSL-03-09-PT, Decision on the Applications for a Stay of Proceedings and Denial of Right to Appeal, 4 November 2003, para. 9:

9. We are urged by the Defence to follow precisely in the footsteps of the ICTR and ICTY, and to revert to Rule 72 as it exists in the former, there being – it is asserted – no reason to change it. But these courts are significantly different insti-

---

[14] See also *Prosecutor v. Norman, Fofana, Kondewa*, Case No. SCSL-04-14-T, Order on an Application by the Prosecution to Hold a Closed Session Hearing of Witness TF2-151, 24 September 2004; *Prosecutor v. Norman, Fofana, Kondewa*, Case No. SCSL-04-14-T, Order on an Application by the Prosecution to Hold a Closed Session Hearing of Witness TF2-223, 27 October 2004.

tutions and have personnel and budgets very greatly in excess of ours. At the time of our second plenary – July 2003 – the average length of time at the ICTR that detainees have had to spend awaiting trial was 43 months. Nine detainees of that court had been awaiting trial for more than 5 years. At the ICTY, the average length of pre-trial detention was 20 months. That is, of course, before the trials themselves, which have also taken a long time to complete – on average, 21.5 months at the ICTR from Prosecution opening statement to delivery of the Trial Chamber verdict. Some of these delays are attributable in part to preliminary procedural motions being decided first by the Trial Chamber, often after extensive argument, before being processed for final determination by the Appeals Chamber. It is against this background that the changes to Rule 72 must be understood. So too must the intentions of the United Nations and the Government of Sierra Leone in establishing the Special Court.

- **Article 14: Rules of Procedure and Evidence – Amendment – Sierra Leonean Law Guidance**

S14-AC-2

o *Prosecutor v. Norman, Kallon, Gbao*, Cases No. SCSL-03-08-PT, SCSL-03-07-PT, SCSL-03-09-PT, Decision on the Applications for a Stay of Proceedings and Denial of Right to Appeal, 4 November 2003, para. 3, 28-29:

3. [...] The Court operates pursuant to a statute, Article 14 of which adopts the ICTR rules of procedure and evidence extant at the time of the Agreement, subject to the power of the Special Court judges to amend or add to them if they "do not, or do not adequately, provide for a specific situation". The exercise of this broadly permissive power may be guided by the Criminal Procedure Act 1965 of Sierra Leone.

[...]

28. [...] [I]t was the unanimous opinion of the judges in plenary session, that the Rules we inherited did not adequately provide for the disposal of important preliminary motions in a manner that was consonant with the principle of fair and expeditious justice, having regard to the time frame of the Special Court and the *Magna Carta* promise which is entrenched in the common law of Sierra Leone and in Article 14(3) of the ICCPR.

29. Furthermore, Article 14 of the Statute specifically directs the Court's attention to the law of Sierra Leone in deciding whether the ICTR rules contain adequate provisions for situations that may arise. We have directed attention to the force

of *Magna Carta*. Under Sierra Leone law there is no right of appeal against interlocutory decisions in criminal proceedings – quite obviously to avoid disruption and delay to those proceedings. Moreover, as we explain in paragraph 24 above, constitutional issues requiring a stay of criminal proceedings are determined by the Supreme Court of Sierra Leone without appeal. This is a further indication of the inadequacy, from common law and Sierra Leone perspective, of an ICTR rule which permits what may well be a pre-trial delay of many months while a case is rehearsed in the Trial Chamber before coming to the Appeals Chamber for authoritative determination.

S14-AC-3

o *Prosecutor v. Norman*, Case No. SCSL-04-14-AR73, Decision on Amendment of the Consolidated Indictment, 16 May 2005, para. 46:

46. [. . .] This court has been permitted by Article 14(2) of its Statute to draw upon the Criminal Procedure Act, 1965 of Sierra Leone precisely because that Act lays down the basic procedures of adversary criminal trials that are followed in Sierra Leone, which may be appropriate for our circumstances. [. . .]

- **Article 14: Rules of Procedure and Evidence – Purposive Interpretation of the Rules of Procedure and Evidence**

S14-AC-4

o *Prosecutor v. Norman, Fofana, Kondewa*, Case No. SCSL-04-14-AR73, Decision on Amendment of the Consolidated Indictment, 16 May 2005, para. 45:[15]

45. [. . .] This court is strictly bound in all its proceedings by its constitutive documents: the Statute and the Agreement, by which it was established by a treaty between the United Nations and the Government of Sierra Leone. Under that constitution, its judges in plenary session have adopted and from time to time will amend, the Rules of Evidence and Procedure which apply to proceedings in the Chambers. The purpose of these rules is to enable trials to proceed fairly, expeditiously and effectively and they are to be interpreted according to that

---

[15] See also *Prosecutor v. Samura* (Case No. SCSL-05-01), *Brima (Margaret), Jalloh, Kamara (Anifa), Kamara (Ester)* (Case No. SCSL-05-02), Written Reasons for the Decision on the standing of Independent Counsel and on Disclosure Obligations, 23 June 2005, para. 14.

purpose. In common law countries this "purposive interpretation" approach is now generally applied in respect of subsidiary legislation and rules of court, in preference to canons of construction used by courts for determining the meaning of Acts of Parliament – "the literal rule"; "the mischief rule"; "the golden rule"; and so on. [...] There is no need for Trial Chambers to perform this kind of exegesis when applying the Special Court Rules: their language should be given its ordinary meaning but they must be applied in their context and according to their purpose in progressing the relevant stage of the trial process fairly and effectively.

S14-AC-5

o *Prosecutor v. Brima, Kamara, Kanu*, Case No. SCSL-04-16-AR77, Decision on Defence Appeal Motion Pursuant to Rule 77(J) on Both the Imposition of Interim Measures and an Order Pursuant to Rule 77(C)(iii), 23 June 2005, para. 28:

28. The defence seek to appeal these decisions taken under Rule 77(C) in reliance upon a literal reading of Rule 77(J) divorced from its context. "Any decision" they argue, whether interlocutory or indeed utterly procedural – a decision to adjourn, for example – can provide the trigger for summoning three international Judges to consider the Appeal. This would cause unjustifiable expense and intolerable delay to a process which demands speedy resolution, especially when it involves members of a defence team or relatives of defendants. A literal interpretation which leads to such absurdity should if possible be avoided. As Judge David Hunt pointed out in Prosecutor v Milutinovic and ors, "The Rules of procedure and Evidence were intended to be the servants and not the masters of the Tribunal's Procedures".[1] Older common law decisions use a more dated analogy ("the relation of rules of practice to the work of justice is intended to be that of handmaid rather than mistress"[2] but the principle is the same: literal interpretation of Rules of Court which would lead to counter-productive or bizarre results or lack of public confidence should be avoided by purposive interpretation.

---

[1] Prosecutor v Milutinovic and ors, ICTY, 8 November 2002, IT-99-37-1, Decision on disclosure of *ex parte* submissions, para. 29.
[2] In the matter of an Arbitration 1907 1KB1, at p. 4 (per Henn-Collins MR).

Article 15
The Prosecutor

1. The Prosecutor shall be responsible for the investigation and prosecution of persons who bear the greatest responsibility for serious violations of international humanitarian law and crimes under Sierra Leonean law committed in the territory of Sierra Leone since 30 November 1996. The Prosecutor shall act independently as a separate organ of the Special Court. He or she shall not seek or receive instructions from any Government or from any other source.

2. The Office of the Prosecutor shall have the power to question suspects, victims and witnesses, to collect evidence and to conduct on-site investigations. In carrying out these tasks, the Prosecutor shall, as appropriate, be assisted by the Sierra Leonean authorities concerned.

3. The Prosecutor shall be appointed by the Secretary-General for a three-year term and shall be eligible for re-appointment. He or she shall be of high moral character and possess the highest level of professional competence, and have extensive experience in the conduct of investigations and prosecutions of criminal cases.

4. The Prosecutor shall be assisted by a Sierra Leonean Deputy Prosecutor, and by such other Sierra Leonean and international staff as may be required to perform the functions assigned to him or her effectively and efficiently. Given the nature of the crimes committed and the particular sensitivities of girls, young women and children victims of rape, sexual assault, abduction and slavery of all kinds, due consideration should be given in the appointment of staff to the employment of prosecutors and investigators experienced in gender-related crimes and juvenile justice.

5. In the prosecution of juvenile offenders, the Prosecutor shall ensure that the child-rehabilitation programme is not placed at risk and that, where appropriate, resort should be had to alternative truth and reconciliation mechanisms, to the extent of their availability.

TRIAL CHAMBERS DECISIONS

- **Article 15(1): The Prosecutor – Discretionary Power to Prosecute**

S15-TC-1 o *Prosecutor v. Sesay, Kallon, Gbao*, Case No. SCSL-04-15-PT, Decision on Prosecution Request for Leave to Amend the Indictment, 6 May 2004, para. 25-26, 32-34:[16]

> 25. We would like to observe here that what at times justifies applications to amend charges as in this case, stems from drafting imperatives of criminal law, where for every offence alleged and supported by the available evidence, there must be a separate and distinct count.
>
> 26. Following this practice, it is the traditional role and practice of the prosecution to bring as many counts in an indictment as possible and although it does impose on him the obligation to bring all the charges that are borne out by the evidence, nothing prevents or prohibits him either from preferring and bringing all the charges which he thinks are supported by the evidence at his disposal, not only with a view to a proper determination of the case, but also and above all, to serve the overall interests of justice.
>
> [...]
>
> 32. The Statute of the Special Court in its Article 15(1) stipulates *inter alia* that the Prosecutor shall act independently as a separate organ of the Special Court: "He or she shall not seek or receive instructions from any government or from any other source.
>
> 33. Article 15(4), still of the Statute, inter alia, stipulates as follows:
>
>> "... Given the nature of the crimes committed and the particular sensitivities of girls, young women and children victims of rape and sexual assault, abductions and slavery of all kinds, due consideration should be given in the appointment of staff to the employment of the prosecutors and investigators experienced in gender-related crimes and juvenile justice."
>
> 34. These provisions underscore the necessity for international criminal justice to highlight the high profile nature of the emerging domain of gender offences with a view to bringing the alleged perpetrators to justice. In the light of the above, it is expected, and we hold the view, that the Prosecutor who is

---

[16] See also *Prosecutor v. Brima, Kamara, Kanu*, Case No. SCSL-04-16-PT, Decision on Prosecution Request for Leave to Amend the Indictment, 6 May 2004, paras. 25-26, 32-34.

at the helm of the investigation process, should exercise vigilance, diligence and attention, bring before justice for trial, all those accused of having committed gender and other categories of offences within the competence of the Court without any "undue delay", as stipulated in Article 17(4)(c) of the Statute of the Court.

S15-TC-2

o *Prosecutor v. Norman, Fofana, Kondewa,* Case No. SCSL-04-14-T, Majority Decision on the Prosecution's Application for Leave to File an Interlocutory Appeal Against the Decision on the Prosecution's Request for Leave to Amend the Indictment Against Samuel Hinga Norman, Moinina Fofana and Allieu Kondewa, 2 August 2004, para. 29-30:

29. [. . .] In the Chamber's view, [. . .] the recognition of a prosecutorial statutory obligation to prosecute "to the full extent of the law" [does not] become the paramount consideration in any such equation, given the widespread recognition nationally and internationally, of the discretionary power enjoyed by the prosecutor not to prosecute even where there is evidence to justify the institution of criminal proceedings that could, under the Agreement and the Statute, possibly be included in the indictment.

30. By contending that the Office of the Prosecutor is obliged to prosecute "to the full extent of the law" is the Prosecution implying that it is obliged to prosecute all crimes for which there may be supporting evidence? By analogy, such an argument loses any legal cogency, if any, it may claim when applied to the exercise of the broad prosecutorial discretion in determining whether, in the context of prosecuting "persons who bear the greatest responsibility for serious violations of international humanitarian law and Sierra Leonean law committed in the territory of Sierra Leone since 30 November 1996", the indictments preferred on the one hand reflect the totality of all offences and on the other hand, all the perpetrators alleged to have committed such grave crimes against humanity. It may be pertinent, in this regard, to ask the following question: *On what grounds or principle, should the prosecutorial duty to prosecute to "the full extent of the law" be limited in application to the range of alleged criminality involved but not the range of the alleged perpetrators?* In our opinion, the overall interests of justice are not served by such limitations or differentiation in the exercise of the prosecutorial discretion.

- **Article 15(1): The Prosecutor – Independence of the Prosecutor**

S15-TC-3

o *Prosecutor v. Sesay*, Case No. SCSL-04-15-T, Decision on Sesay Motion Seeking Disclosure of the Relationship Between Governmental Agencies of the United States of America and the Office of the Prosecutor, 2 May 2005, para. 22, 40-43, 50-52:

22. In the Chamber's opinion, it is absolutely clear that Article 15(1) reinforces, in unambiguous terms, an internationally accepted norm governing the exercise of prosecutorial authority, in International Criminal Tribunals namely, autonomy and independence. To this end, the Chamber acknowledges that it is imperative not only in preserving the integrity of the administration of criminal justice in international law but also to ensure the confidence of the international community in mechanisms set up to ensure accountability for war crimes against humanity, that the Office of the Prosecutor enjoys an unfettered functional and investigative discretion, subject only to recognised and accepted judicial controls in respect of the functions conferred on it by the Statute of the Special Court.

[...]

40. The Chamber notes that both the Defence and the Prosecution agree that within the proper context and interpretation of the Statute and the Rules, Article 15(1) does vest on the Prosecution, the autonomy and independence in the discharge of its functions, and that the Office of the Prosecutor must act as an independent body that does not take instructions from any other entity.

41. It seems clear to the Chamber that the arguments and submissions of the Defence as regards the alleged breach of Article 15(1) are predicated upon the assumption that the Office of the Prosecutor has taken instructions from another entity. The Prosecution submits that it has not. The crux of the matter, from the Chamber's perspective, is whether there is, at this point in time, any evidentiary basis or factual foundation for the allegation put forward by the Defence, to warrant a conclusive finding of fact that there has in law been a breach of Article 15(1). The Defence assert that the evidence from which such inference should be drawn is that of General Tarnue that Dr. White's actions were, according to Dr. White, to be based upon a decision of the State Department of the Government of the United States.

42. Does this piece of evidence irresistibly sustain the Defence contentions, even if given a liberal evaluation? In other words, does it necessarily follow that because General Tarnue stated that Dr. White told him that the latter's actions were to

be based on a decision of the State Department of the U.S. Government, the Office of the Prosecutor was acting on the instructions 'received' from the U.S. Government? In the Chamber's opinion, an inference of this nature cannot lightly be drawn from such evidence, given its grave implications for the justice process.

43. The Chamber, likewise, emphasises that the suggestion of the Defence that General Tarnue's testimony revealed a relationship between the Office of the Prosecutor and the United States of America, even if it were true, could not in law justify, without more, the inference that the Prosecution was receiving instructions from the U.S Government in breach of Article 15(1). This is so even if the Office of the Prosecutor sought assistance from the U.S. Government as envisaged by Rule 8(C) of the Rules of Procedure and Evidence. Certainly, in the Chamber's view, it would do violence to the plain meaning and context of the Statute and the Rules if conceptually the words "instructions" and "assistance" were construed as being synonymous and interchangeable. The contentions of the Defence on this issue, therefore, are legally unsustainable in that, on the whole, the Defence has failed to substantiate, by *prima facie* proof, the allegation of breach of Article 15(1), on the part of the Office of the Prosecutor. This Chamber does not find any, as the Defence contends, "master-servant" relationship between Dr. White, as FBI agent and the Prosecution which would occasion a breach of Article 15(1).

[...]

50. In seeking to establish a breach of Article 15(1) of the Statute, there has been a total lack of specificity on instructions received which the Defence alleges amounts to a breach by the Prosecution of its statutory obligations under Article 15(1). These same comments apply to the application where the Defence seeks to compel the Prosecution to disclose exculpatory evidence under Rule 68 as to the assistance offered by Dr. White to General Tarnue to obtain asylum and a relocation of himself and his family in the U.S.A.

51. In this regard, the Chamber would like to state here that for the Defence to succeed in this Motion, it is not enough to premise its application either on presumptions, on speculations, or on probabilities. If it does, as it seems, seek to establish the subservience of the Prosecutor to a foreign Government or Agency, it must provide concrete proof of those instructions and their contents and not just invite this Chamber, merely on the basis of speculation and without any legal or factual proof, to draw such a conclusion or even such an inference.

52. We are strongly of the opinion that mere evidence of the cooperation between the Prosecution and the FBI or the US Government, without proof that the former received

instructions from the latter, including the nature and contents of such instructions, does not, per se, fulfill the test to establish a violation of Article 15(1) of the Statute.

- **Article 15(1): The Prosecutor – Prosecutorial Latitude to Call Witnesses of His Choice**

o *Prosecutor v. Brima, Kamara, Kanu*, Case No. SCSL-04-16-T, Decision on Prosecution request for Leave to Call an Additional Witness (Zainab Hawa Bangura) Pursuant to Rule 73*bis*(E), and on Joint Defence Notice to Inform the Trial Chamber of its Position vis-à-vis the Proposed Expert Witness (Mrs Bangura) Pursuant to Rule 94*bis*, 5 August 2005, para. 33:

> 33. [. . .] More importantly, we are of the view that the Prosecution enjoys a prosecutorial latitude in the domain of the strategies it puts into place to establish its case particularly in light of the provisions of Article 15 (1) of the Statute which confers on the Prosecutor the competence to act independently as a separate organ of the Special Court (within the limits and confines of the law and the doctrine of equality of arms). Accordingly we do not consider it to be in the interests of justice at this stage to curtail that independence by compelling the Prosecution to call Ms. Christina Solomon as their witness, at the behest of the Defence.

Article 17
Rights of the Accused

1. All accused shall be equal before the Special Court.

2. The accused shall be entitled to a fair and public hearing, subject to measures ordered by the Special Court for the protection of victims and witnesses.

3. The accused shall be presumed innocent until proved guilty according to the provisions of the present Statute.

4. In the determination of any charge against the accused pursuant to the present Statute, he or she shall be entitled to the following minimum guarantees, in full equality:

   a. To be informed promptly and in detail in a language which he or she understands of the nature and cause of the charge against him or her;
   b. To have adequate time and facilities for the preparation of his or her defence and to communicate with counsel of his or her own choosing;
   c. To be tried without undue delay;
   d. To be tried in his or her presence, and to defend himself or herself in person or through legal assistance of his or her own choosing; to be informed, if he or she does not have legal assistance, of this right; and to have legal assistance assigned to him or her, in any case where the interests of justice so require, and without payment by him or her in any such case if he or she does not have sufficient means to pay for it;
   e. To examine, or have examined, the witnesses against him or her and to obtain the attendance and examination of witnesses on his or her behalf under the same conditions as witnesses against him or her;
   f. To have the free assistance of an interpreter if he or she cannot understand or speak the language used in the Special Court;
   g. Not to be compelled to testify against himself or herself or to confess guilt.

TRIAL CHAMBERS DECISIONS

- **Article 17: Rights of the Accused – Generalities**

S17-TC-1
o *Prosecutor v. Norman*, SCSL-03-08-PT, Decision on the Request by the Truth and Reconciliation Commission of Sierra Leone to Conduct a Public Hearing with Samuel Hinga Norman, 29 October 2003, para. 15:

> 15. [...] In the overarching scheme of things, it is the duty of International Judges to safeguard the interest of the International Community that persons charged with international crimes are accorded what may properly be characterized as 'super due process rights' in vindicating themselves regardless of national considerations, however compelling. On the issue of 'super due process rights' for persons accused of international crimes, it should be observed that one perception of international criminal justice is that it does not afford indictees adequate procedural justice due largely to the horrendous nature and enormity of the crimes in respect of which they are indicted.

- **Article 17(2): Rights of the Accused – Right to a Fair Trial**

S17-TC-2
o *Prosecutor v. Gbao*, SCSL-03-09-PT, Decision on the Prosecution Motion for Immediate Protective Measures for Witnesses and Victims and for Non-Public Disclosure, 10 October 2003, para. 33-41:

> 33. The Defence asserts that the right to a fair trial consists of three fundamental components "of relevance for present purposes". The Special Court would like to highlight the fact that no human rights instrument defines the right to a fair trial as being composed of three fundamental components. Given Article 14 of the International Covenant on Civil and Political Rights (ICCPR) or Article 6 of the European Convention on Human Rights and Fundamental Freedoms (ECHR), it is quite clear that the right to a fair trial is much more comprehensive and is composed of many other fundamental rights. Therefore, in the Special Court's opinion, the Defence cannot simply state, as it does, that the right to a fair trial comprises three so-called fundamental components without providing any evidentiary or authoritative support for such a proposal. In this respect, it is the Special Court's view that the Defence cannot simply extract the three components that it deems are relevant for his contention and exclude the others, as such could lead to perverse conclusions.

34. Furthermore, the Special Court takes issue with the Defence's view that the three so-called minimum guarantees are intangible rights and notes that the Defence has not submitted any evidence or authorities to support this contention. The Defence appears to have failed to appreciate the contents of Article 17 (2) of the Statute. The Special Court deems that it is clearly stated in the Statute that protective measures in favour of witnesses and victims do constitute a valid reason to limit the right of the Accused to a fair trial. The Special Court would like to observe that this does not entail that the trial of the Accused will not be respectful of all due requirements of fairness. It should all the more be remembered, as it is detailed in the Aleksovski case[1] before the ICTY, that the concept of fair trial must be understood as fairness to both parties and not just to the Accused.

– *The minimum guarantees of a fair trial being a principle of customary international law*

35. The Special Court has considered the Defence contention that the above-mentioned minimum guarantees of a fair trial have become an established principle of customary international law. It should be noted again that the Defence does not refer to any authority, and has not produced any evidence to support its assertion.

36. In asserting this contention, the Defence refers only to these three components of what it claims is of relevance for present purposes and does not mention, nor consider any of the remaining rights. The Special Court is of the view that the right to a fair trial must be understood as a whole, not as a flexible right which can be interpreted by the Defence as it deems best serves its purpose.

37. The rights of the Accused as set out in Article 17 of the Statute reproduce *in extenso* Article 21 of the ICTY Statute and Article 20 of the ICTR Statute, which themselves are directly inspired by Article 14 of the International Covenant on Civil and Political Rights (ICCPR) and by Article 6 of the European Convention on Human Rights and Fundamental Freedoms (ECHR). Moreover, it should also be stated that Article 61 of the Rome Statute of the International Criminal Court (ICC) has relied upon the standards set by other international human rights instruments in dealing with the rights of the Accused.

38. The repetition of the same guarantees in all major international human rights instruments could be viewed as creating a strong presumption that the right of the Accused to a fair trial has acceded to the status of international custom. However, in making such an allegation, it is the Special Court's view that the Defence did not fully consider the criteria that must be fulfilled for a practice to be viewed as an

international custom. According to Article 38 (1) (b) of the Statute of the International Court of Justice (ICJ), an international custom is "a general practice accepted as law". Therefore, the States must have a common practice of what they believe they are legally compelled to do. It is likely that all democratic States respect the right of the Accused to a fair trial, as it is commonly understood by the said States, not only because it is embodied in their national legislation and in international human rights conventions, but also because, were it not law, they would still believe it to be so.

39. However, the Special Court is of the view that the answer to this question is not well established: the various international law instruments do not provide any such indication and there is no doctrinal consensus. Indeed, several learned authors have opposite views on this matter. Christoph J. M. Safferling[2] points out that in American literature, there is "a strong inclination to include fair trial among customary norms". He refers to Richard B. Lillich, who considers the whole Universal Declaration of Human Rights as customary,[3] and to Theodor Meron, who "[b]elieve[s] that at least a core number of the due process guarantees stated in Article 14 of the ICCPR have a strong claim to customary law status. Such rights include the right to be tried by a competent, independent and impartial tribunal established by law, the right to presumption of innocence, the right of everyone not to be compelled to testify against himself or to confess guilt, the right of everyone to be tried in his or her presence and to defend himself or herself in person or through legal assistance of his or her own choosing, the right of everyone to examine witnesses against him or her and the right to have one's conviction and sentence reviewed by a higher tribunal according to law."[4] Safferling, however, underlines the fact that these assertions are not supported by any further explanation and that the authors do not examine the elements which constitute custom, i.e. State practice and *opinio juris*. Safferling further cites and agrees with Phillip Alston and Bruno Simma, who have criticized this view and have a different approach to human rights. Human rights would belong to the third category of sources of international law according to Article 38 of the ICJ Statute, namely principles of international law. This view is shared by many European authors, in order not to blur the concept of customary law.[5]

40. Moreover, even if there were absolute certainty as to whether the right of the Accused to a fair trial were indeed part of customary international law, this would still not entail that such a right constitute a *jus cogens* norm, i.e. a peremptory norm which cannot receive derogation. The Special Court finds it useful to stress the fact that, in this respect, there is a difference between *jus cogens* and customary norms. Peremptory norms are defined in Article 53 of the Vienna Convention

on the Law of Treaties (1969) as norms "accepted and recognised by the international community of States as a whole as a norm from which no derogation is permitted and which can be modified only by a subsequent norm of general international law having the same character". It is well recognised that not all customary norms are intangible.[6]

41. Based upon the foregoing, the Special Court is of the considered view that it has not been established that the right of the Accused to a fair trial has become part of customary international law.

---

[1] ICTY, *The Prosecutor v. Aleksovski*, Appeals Chamber Decision on Admissibility of Evidence, 16 February 1999, para. 25.
[2] Christoph J.M. Safferling, *Towards An International Criminal Procedure*, Oxford Monographs in International Law, Oxford University Press, 2001, p. 25.
[3] See Lillich in Meron, *Human Rights in International Law*, Oxford University Press, 1984, pp. 116-117.
[4] Meron, *Human Rights and Humanitarian Norms as Customary Law*, Oxford University Press, 1989, pp. 96-97.
[5] Christoph J.M. Safferling, *Towards An International Criminal Procedure*, Oxford Monographs in International Law, Oxford University Press, 2001, pp. 25-26.
[6] On the issue of international customary law and *jus cogens* norms, see *Nicaragua v. USA* ICJ Rep 1986 14; and ICTY, *The Prosecutor v. Anto Furundzija*, Judgment, 10 December 1998, para. 153, in which the Trial Chamber held, as regards torture, that "*because of the importance of the values [the principle of prohibition of torture] protects, this principle has evolved into a peremptory norm or* jus cogens, *that is a norm that enjoys a higher rank in the international hierarchy than treaty law and even 'ordinary' customary rules*".

S17-TC-3

o *Prosecutor v. Norman*, Case No. SCSL-04-14-T, Consequential Order on the Withdrawal of Ms. Quincy Whitaker as Court Appointed Counsel for the First Accused, 19 November 2004:

NOTING that the right to a fair trial enshrined in Article 17(2) of the Statute of the Special Court ("Statute") concerns not only the interests of the Accused but also the institutional interests of the judicial system;[1]

---

[1] See *Farhad v. United States*, 190 F.3d 1097 (9th Cir, 1999), 1107-08.

- **Article 17(2): Rights of the Accused – Equality of Arms**

S17-TC-4
o *Prosecutor v. Gbao*, SCSL-03-09-PT, Decision on the Prosecution Motion for Immediate Protective Measures for Witnesses and Victims and for Non-Public Disclosure, 10 October 2003, para. 43-50:

43. The Special Court finds it useful to look into the jurisprudence of the European Court of Human Rights (ECHR), according to which disclosure is based on: (a) the requirement that there be equality of arms between the prosecution and the defence (*Jespers v. Belgium* (1981), 27DR61, ECmHR); (b) the defendant's right to adequate time and facilities to prepare a defence under Article 6(3) (b) of the ECHR (*Edwards v. The United Kingdom* (1992) 15 EHRR 417, ECtHR); and (c) the requirement in Article 6(3) (d) that there be parity of conditions for the examination of witnesses (*Edwards v. The United Kingdom*, Commission Report).

44. In *Kaufman v. Belgium* ((1986) 50 DR 98 ECmHR, p.115), the European Commission held that the principle that there should be equality of arms between the parties before a court is fundamental to the notion of a fair trial under Article 6 of the ECHR. The Commission has repeatedly held that the right to a fair hearing in both civil and criminal proceedings entails that everyone who is party to such proceedings shall have a reasonable opportunity of presenting his case to the court under conditions that do not place him at substantial disadvantage vis-à-vis his opponent. In particular, each party must know the case being made against him, have an effective opportunity to challenge it and an effective opportunity to advance his own case.

45. The jurisprudence of the European Court of Human Rights can provide guidance as to the possibility of limiting the right of the Accused to a fair trial. In *Rowe and Davies v. the United Kingdom* ((2000) 30 EHRR 1, ECHR, para. 61), the Court states that there may be circumstances in which materials need not be disclosed to the defence on grounds of public interest immunity, but they must be subject to strict scrutiny by the courts. This would be the case when protective measures in favour of witnesses are required by the Prosecution.

46. Having recalled what is meant by equality of arms in the jurisprudence of the European Court of Human Rights, the Special Court deems it appropriate, at the present stage, to stress the difference that exists between international human rights law and international criminal law. While international human rights law can provide guidance to judges sitting within international criminal courts, it should be borne in mind that the

specificities of international criminal law sometimes require a different approach. As Judge Richard May and Marieke Wierda explain in their authoritative work on international criminal evidence,[1] international trials constitute a continuous balancing of interests and rights, and this is why they are so challenging.

47. As regards international criminal law, the Special Court does not view the situation to which the Accused is confronted when protective measures are ordered by the Special Court for Prosecution witnesses as constituting a violation of the principle of equality of arms, as is contended by the Defence, in relation to the system in which the departure date of the deadline for disclosure is the date of testimony. The process of granting witness protection entails a balance between *"full respect"* for the rights of the Accused and *"due regard"* for the protection of victims and witnesses.[2] In trying to achieve such a balance, the Special Court finds the rolling disclosure system to be fair; the restriction imposed on the right of the Accused to a fair trial in this respect is both necessary and proportionate to the aim of the restriction, i.e. witness and victim protection. The system of rolling disclosure does limit the right of the Accused to a fair trial at the preliminary stage of the proceedings, but, in the Special Court's opinion, only within the boundaries of reasonableness and to the least extent possible in the prevailing circumstances. Furthermore, the contention, according to which it would be unfair to impose disclosure on the Defence at a stage when it is already fully absorbed in advocacy and in the conduct of the trial itself, cannot be accepted by the Special Court: indeed, at the pre-trial stage, this cannot be the case. Moreover, it should also be borne in mind that although the Defence may not have access to materials which could lead to identification of the witnesses, it nevertheless has access to all other materials, thereby enabling it to prepare adequately for the trial. Moreover, should the Defence lack enough time for preparation, it must be recalled that it is always entitled to apply to the Trial Chamber, in due course, for appropriate remedies.

48. The principle of equality of arms has been frequently referred to in the jurisprudence of the *ad hoc* Tribunals.[3] In several cases before these Tribunals, the Defence has argued that there was not a complete equality of arms between the Prosecution and the Defence. In the *Tadic* case before the ICTY,[4] the Appeals Chamber held that a fair trial must entitle the accused to adequate time and facilities to prepare his defence. Therefore, while the European jurisprudence views equality of arms as being a procedural equality between the parties, the Appeals Chamber decided that, given the nature of international tribunals, the approach had to be different and that *"under the Statute of the International Tribunal the principle of equality of arms must be given a more liberal*

interpretation than that normally upheld with regard to proceedings before domestic courts. This principle means that the Prosecution and the Defence must be equal before the Trial Chamber. It follows that the Chamber shall provide every practicable facility it is capable of granting under the Rules and Statute when faced with a request by a party for assistance in presenting its case".[5] This case dealt with evidence which was difficult for the Defence to obtain, due to the lack of cooperation on the part of the States having custody of the said evidence. This decision nonetheless clearly states that the facilities that are to be afforded to the parties include the adoption of protective measures.[6]

49. The Special Court has considered the *Tadic* jurisprudence in perspective with the *Kayishema and Ruzindana* case before the ICTR, where Counsel for Kayishema were requesting from the Trial Chamber to be afforded the same resources as the Prosecution. In the latter case, the Chamber held that "the rights of the accused and equality between the parties should not be confused with the equality of means and resources" and that "*the rights of the accused as laid down in Article 20 and in particular (2) and (4) (b) of the Statute shall in no way be interpreted to mean that the Defence is entitled to the same means and resources as available to the Prosecution*".[7] The Special Court is of the opinion that equality of arms before international criminal tribunals is more than a mere procedural equality, like it is for international human rights law, but does not necessarily entail a strict equality in terms of means and resources.

50. In reaching such a conclusion, the Special Court has acknowledged the fact that the Accused is entitled, before international criminal tribunals, to such fundamental rights as the presumption of innocence, the right to remain silent and to not have any negative inference drawn from his choice to exercise this right, and consequently, the Prosecution has the burden of proving that the Accused is guilty beyond reasonable doubt, in compliance with Rule 87(A), and the Defence does not have to prove the Accused's innocence.

---

[1] Judge Richard May and Marieke Wierda, *International Criminal Evidence*, Transnational Publishers, 2002, p. 298.
[2] See Separate Opinion of Judge Stephen in ICTY, *Tadic*, Protective Measures for Victims and Witnesses, 10 August 1995.
[3] On the issue of equality of arms before international criminal tribunals, see: Judge Richard May and Marieke Werda, *International Criminal Evidence*, Transnational Publishers, 2002, pp. 266-273.
[4] ICTY, *Tadic*, Appeals Chamber Judgment, 15th July 1999, para. 30.
[5] *Id.*, para. 52.
[6] *Id.*

(7) ICTR, *Kayishema and Ruzindana*, Order on the Motion by the Defence Counsel for Application of Article 20 (2) and (4) (b) of the Statute of the ICTR, 5th May 1997.

S17-TC5

o *Prosecutor v. Sesay, Kallon, Gbao*, Case No. SCSL-04-15-PT, Decision on Prosecution Request for Leave to Amend the Indictment, 6 May 2004, para. 28:[17]

"28. We recall here that in the *Tadic* case, the Appeals Chamber of the International Criminal Tribunal for the former Yugoslavia (ICTY) took the view that "Equality of arms" obligates a judicial body to ensure that neither party is put to a disadvantage when presenting its case. This Chamber in the *Gbao* case disposed of by His Lordship Judge Pierre Boutet took the same position."

- **Article 17(2): Rights of the Accused – Measures for Protection of Victims and Witnesses**

S17-TC-6

o *Prosecutor v. Kallon*, Case No. SCSL-03-07-PT, Decision on the Defence Application for Leave to Appeal 'Decision on the Prosecution's Motion for Immediate Protective Measures for Witnesses and Victims and for Non-Public Disclosure, 10 December 2003, para. 25, 29:

25. Against the background of these rights of the Accused, justice in International Criminal tribunals and the Statutes and Rules of Procedure and Evidence which govern them, equally recognise the rights of witnesses and victims of those crimes against international humanitarian law allegedly committed to some protective measures. This is amply demonstrated in the provisions of Article 17(2) of the Statute, which whilst guaranteeing the rights of the Accused on the one hand, subjects him or her on the other to measures ordered by the Special Court for the protection of victims and witnesses. [. . .]

[. . .]

29. The Chamber would like to observe that what is guaranteed to the Accused is a fair and public hearing which should be conducted without undue delay as provided under Article 17(2) and 17(4)(C) of the Statute. This right is limited to

---

[17] See also *Prosecutor v. Brima, Kamara, Kanu*, Case No. SCSL-04-16-PT, Decision on Prosecution Request for Leave to Amend the Indictment, 6 May 2004, para. 28.

fairness. It is neither unlimited nor all-embracing for, as we observe, it has to be read and interpreted subject to the equally entrenched statutory rights of victims and witnesses to protective measures as expressly provided for under Article 17(2) of the Statute.

- **Article 17(3): Rights of the Accused – Presumption of Innocence**

S17-TC-7   o *Prosecutor v. Norman*, Case No. SCSL-03-08-PT, Decision on the Request by the Truth and Reconciliation Commission of Sierra Leone to Conduct a Public Hearing with Samuel Hinga Norman, 29 October 2003, para. 13:

13. [. . .] [T]here are two key applications of the presumption of innocence, as a doctrine in direct contraposition to the presumption of guilt. Firstly, it refers to the treatment of suspects and accused persons before and during the trail that, in the expectation of society, such persons be accorded respect for their innocence and human dignity. Secondly, it refers to the logistics of proof in criminal cases as to which party bears the persuasive burden of proof. The general operative principle in domestic and international criminal tribunals alike is that the Prosecution bears the burden of proving the guilt of the accused 'beyond reasonable doubt'. *By contrast, an institution before which an accused appears to testify that already characterizes the accused as a 'perpetrator' logically places the burden of disproving his guilt or proving his innocence on the accused and deprives him of a fundamental right guaranteed by the Universal Declaration of Human Rights.* This may endanger the rights of any such accused to a fair and impartial trial in due course.

- **Article 17(3): Rights of the Accused – Presumption of Innocence – Burden of Proof**

S17-TC-8   o *Prosecutor v. Sesay, Kallon, Gbao*, Case No. SCSL-04-15-PT, Decision on Prosecution Request for Leave to Amend the Indictment, 6 May 2004, para. 29-31:[18]

29. We appreciate that the burden of proof that the Prosecution bears in every criminal trial is understandably very

---

[18] See also *Prosecutor v. Brima, Kamara, Kanu*, Case No. SCSL-2004-16-PT, Decision on Prosecution Request for Leave to Amend the Indictment, 6 May 2004, para. 29-31.

heavy. It commences with the detection and production of solid and convincing evidence to establish the guilt of the accused beyond all reasonable doubts. The other important component of the burden of proof is the charge or charges which the Prosecution files in order to reflect the evidence it has at its disposal and can adduce in order to discharge the obligation of "proof beyond all reasonable doubt".

30. We would like to acknowledge here, the fact that this burden of proof is even more demanding in matters before the international criminal tribunals than it is in the municipal systems. The reason is that the protection of the rights of suspects and accused persons is not only often more clearly spelt out and entrenched in the statutes of those tribunals, but is also, in addition, reinforced by other international conventions and instruments that are conspicuously absent in municipal legislations.

31. To attain these objectives, we think that the Prosecution must and indeed, should be given the latitude, to resort to all means that the law permits to enable it to fully exercise its authority under the Statute and under the general and accepted principles of law and practice in the domain under review, and this, with a view to giving it the opportunity to fully assume and discharge those prosecutorial functions.

- **Article 17(4)(b): Rights of the Accused – Adequate Time and Facilities to Prepare His Defence**

S17-TC-9
o *Prosecutor v. Norman*, SCSL-2004-14-T, Decision on Request by Samuel Hinga Norman for Additional Resources to Prepare His Defence, 23 June 2004, para. 12-19:

Request for Computer

12. The Trial Chamber grants the request of the Accused for a computer set. The Accused shall be provided with a desktop computer and printer in his cell for use at anytime. On the basis of security concerns, however, expressed by the Registrar, including the Acting Chief of the Detention Facility and the Chief of Security for the Special Court, the computer will not be connected to the internet or Special Court Network. Should any materials be required by the Accused from these resources, he may make a request to the Defence Office and/or his Standby Counsel to provide such necessary materials.

Request for Telephone

13. Currently the Accused is provided with a wireless "DECT" phone, which he can use from any location within

the detention facility between the hours of 7.00 a.m. to 9.00 p.m. In accordance with Rule 44(A) of the Rules Governing the Detention of Persons Awaiting Trial or Appeal Before the Special Court for Sierra Leone or Otherwise Detained on the Authority of the Special Court for Sierra Leone ("Rules of Detention"), adopted on the 7th of March, 2003, and amended on the 25th of September, 2003 and the 4th of May, 2004, telephone calls between Accused and Counsel are privileged unless otherwise ordered by a Judge or a Chamber.

14. The Trial Chamber considers that the Accused may be further assisted by placing a stationary desk telephone in his cell which he can use at any time for the purpose of being in contact with his Standby Counsel. The phone will be programmed with the telephone numbers of his Standby Counsel, both inside and outside Sierra Leone.

15. As telephone costs are borne by the Court, usage will be reviewed to ensure that the number and duration of telephone calls is reasonable.

Request for Stationery

16. The Detention Facility provides stationery to detainees and should continue to provide the Accused with stationery requests which are reasonable and proportionate to the requirements of representing himself on the understanding that the Chamber has assigned Standby Counsel to assist him in the process.

Request for Assistant

17. The Trial Chamber considers that the provision of four Standby Counsel to the Accused to assist him in the defence of his case is adequate, and it is not necessary to appoint an additional assistant.

Request for Investigator

18. The Trial Chamber considers that any investigations required by the Accused for his defence at trial is a matter within the competence of the Defence Office who shall make the necessary arrangements that are required.

Request for Modification of "Lock-Up" Hours

19. The Trial Chamber considers that the lockup hours for the detention facility, from 10.00 p.m. to 7.00 a.m. each day are reasonable. Furthermore, upon being provided with a computer and a stationary phone in his cell, the Accused may continue to prepare his case after lock-up time. Where exceptional circumstances would exist, and on a case-by-case basis, he may also apply to the Detention Facility to be outside his cell beyond the regular "lock-up" hours.

S17-TC-10 o *Prosecutor v. Norman*, Case No. SCSL-04-14-T, Order Revoking Additional resources Provided to Sam Hinga Norman for the Preparation of His Self Defence, 27 October 2004:

RECALLING that in this Ruling the Registrar was ordered to review the requirement for the additional resources for the First Accused and to provide a report to the Chamber with a view to assist the Chamber in determining whether these measures should be maintained;

HAVING CONSIDERED the Memoranda submitted to the Chamber by the Registrar pursuant to the Chamber's Ruling,[1] whereby the Registrar stated that, in his opinion, there is no need to continue providing the First Accused with additional resources, given that he is no longer representing himself, and that continuing to provide such facilities would result in unequal treatment as none of the other detainees have such facilities;

PURSUANT TO Rule 54 of the Rules of Procedure and Evidence of the Special Court;

ORDERS AS FOLLOWS:

ORDERS the Chief of Detention Facility to withdraw from the exclusive use of the First Accused the following resources, provided to him for the purpose of representing himself, that include:

   a. a desktop computer;
   b. a printer;
   c. a stationery desk telephone;
   d. computer desk and chair; and
   e. filing cabinet.

ORDERS the Chief of Detention Facility to ensure that the First Accused is provided with all those resources and facilities generally available and accorded to other detainees of the Detention Facility of the Special Court, such as stationery and access to telephone.

---

[1] Review of Additional Facilities Provided to Samuel Hinga Norman for Preparation of Defence, dated 8 October 2004 and Review of Additional Facilities Provided to Samuel Hinga Norman for Preparation of Defence, dated 15 October 2004.

- **Article 17(4)(c): Rights of the Accused – Right to Be Tried Without Undue Delay**

S17-TC-11
o *Prosecutor v. Kallon*, Case No. SCSL-03-07-PT, Decision on the Defence Application for Leave to Appeal 'Decision on the Prosecution's Motion for Immediate Protective Measures for Witnesses and Victims and for Non-Public Disclosure, 10 December 2003, para. 34:

> 34. While it is conceded that a definition of this term can hardly be formulated with a universally legally accepted precision, it can at least be generally accepted that the term an "expeditious trial" is one which is conducted within time limits that are, in the circumstances, considered reasonable. These must include the hurdles to be surmounted in relation to various procedural intricacies and technicalities inherent in a trial of that nature and taking into account factors related to the respect of the rights of the Accused, those of the Prosecution, and nonetheless, those of the witnesses and victims, coupled with the imperative necessity of ensuring that the trial, as much as possible, and as much as the law would permit, is fair and public.

- **Article 17(4)(d): Rights of the Accused – Right to Self-Representation**

S17-TC-12
o *Prosecutor v. Norman*, SCSL-04-14-T, Decision on the Application of Samuel Hinga Norman for Self-Representation Under Article 17(4)(d) of the Statute of the Special Court, 8 June 2004, para. 8-9, 17-22, 25-32:[19]

> 8. Clearly, as a matter of statutory construction, Article 17(4)(d) does guarantee to an accused person, first and foremost, the right to self-representation. This is clear from the plain and literal meaning of that provision. But the critical question to focus on is whether this guaranteed right of self-representation is absolute having regard to the statutory purport and intendment of Article 17(4)(d). In the judgment of this Trial Chamber, the answer is that the said right is not absolute but rather, a qualified right. This interpretation of the statutory provision is amply corroborated by the qualifying clause of Article 17(4)(d), which provides as follows:

---

[19] See also *Prosecutor v. Norman*, Case No. SCSL-04-14-T, Consequential Order on Assignment and Role of Standby Counsel, 14 June 2004.

"and to have legal assistance assigned to him or her, in any case where the interests of justice so require."

9. In the light of these provisions, it is clear and The Chamber so holds, that the right to self representation by an accused person is a qualified and not an absolute right and particularly so because Article 17(4)(d) provides that legal assistance could be assigned to him or her in "any case where the interests of justice so require."

[...]

17. In deliberating on this issue, the Chamber has addressed this same issue that was at stake in the case of the *Prosecutor v. Slobodan Milosevic*,[1] in the International Criminal Tribunal for former Yugoslavia (ICTY). In this case, Milosevic asserted the right to self representation form the outset. Samuel Hinga Norman, the 1st Accused, on the contrary, is asserting this same right as lately as on the first day of his trial after over a year in pre-trial detention during which time he has been defended by a legal team composed of Learned Lead Counsel, Mr. Jenkins Johnston, and subsequently, Mr. Sulaiman Tejan-Sie, who, at his request, has represented him from the 17th of March 2003, in Bonthe Island up to the 3rd of June, 2004 when Exhibit 1 surfaced in the proceedings.

18. In fact, the Trial Chamber of the ICTY stated that it was satisfied that Milosevic, who had clearly and unequivocally informed the Chamber from the outset that he did not want to be represented by Defence Counsel, was competent to exercise the right to defend himself in person even though The Chamber held that the right is not absolute.

19. The key distinctions, between these two cases for our purposes, are that whilst Milosevic is being tried alone, Hinga Norman is being tried with 2 co-accused persons. In addition to this, whilst Milosevic indicated his option for self-representation from the outset as soon as he was transferred to the custody of ICTY, Hinga Norman did this only on the 3rd of June, 2004, the very date which had, with his approbation, been fixed for the commencement of his trial, to invoke and exercise this same statutory right.

20. The task therefore, of properly assuming the mantle of conducting his defence could turn out to be difficult, onerous and exacting if not impossible and would necessarily result in unnecessarily prolonging the proceedings. In the Milosevic case, the Chamber, in addition to holding that the right to self-representation is not absolute, also held that there may be circumstances where it is in the interests of justice, as is, in our opinion the case here, to appoint Counsel. The Court then proceeded to appoint 3 *amici curiae* to cater for Milosevic's interests and his procedural links with the Tribunal.

21. In the case of the *Prosecutor v. Vojislav Seselj*,[2] the Accused, a Professor of Law at the University of Belgrade, surrendered himself to the ICTY. When legal assistance was offered him, he turned it down and stated from the outset that he would defend himself. The Prosecution filed a Motion requesting an Order from the Trial Chamber that Defence Counsel be assigned to him. The Chamber dismissed the Motion, recognized the accused's right to self-representation, but at the same time, decided to appoint a "stand-by counsel" to cater for his eventual legal needs and to coordinate these needs with the institutional obligation of the Court to ensure that the overall interests of justice prevail, thereby confirming once again, the thesis that the statutory right of self representation is not absolute.

22. In that context, it is useful to consider the established procedure adopted in the United States of appointing stand-by counsel, by the Court. The Supreme Court in this regard, approved the appointment of Stand-by Counsel and discussed the role of such Counsel in its Decision in McKaskle v. Wiggins[3] where the accused was permitted to proceed pro se, but the trial court appointed a stand-by counsel to assist him. The Supreme Court had this to say:

> "Accordingly, we make explicit today what is already explicit in Feretta: A defendant's Sixth Amendment rights [to self-representation] are not violated when a trial judge appoints a stand-by counsel – even over the defendant's objection – to relieve the judge the need to explain and enforce basic rules of courtroom protocol or to assist the defendant in overcoming routine obstacles that stand in the way of the defendant's achievement of his own clearly indicated goals. Participation by counsel to steer a defendant through the basic procedures of trial is per-missible even in the unlikely event that it somewhat undermines the pro se defendant's appearance of control over his own defence."

[...]

25. In arriving at this conclusion, we are guided by the opinion of Hon. Judge Reinhardt's in the case of *Farhad v. United States*,[4] where The Learned Judge said that the permitting of self representation regardless of the consequences, threatens to divert criminal trials from their clearly defined purpose of providing a fair and reliable determination of guilt or innocence. He observed that a defendant could not waive his right to a fair trial and that this right implicates not only the interests of the accused but also the institutional interests of the judicial system.

26. The philosophy of the Chamber on this crucial issue compels us to factor into the equation, certain critical issues

namely: (i) that the right of counsel which is statutorily guaranteed by Article 17(4)(d) of our Statute is predicated upon the notion that representation by Counsel is an essential and necessary component of a fair trial. (ii) The right to counsel relieves trial Judges of the burden to explain and enforce basic rules of courtroom protocol and to assist the accused in overcoming routine and regular legal obstacles which the accused may encounter if he represents himself, for, the Court, to our mind, is supposed, in the adversarial context, to remain the arbiter and not a pro-active participant in the proceedings. (iii) Given the complexity of the trial in the present case, it cannot be denied that a joint trial of such magnitude, having regard to the gravity of the offences charged, and considering the number of witnesses to be called by the Prosecution and the Defence, make for a trial fraught with a high potential of complexities and intricacies typical of evolving international criminal law. (iv) There is also the public interest, national and international, in the expeditious completion of the trial. (v) Furthermore, there is the high potential for further disruption to the Court's timetable and calendar which we are already witnessing in this case. In fact, 2 Prosecution witnesses who the Chamber insisted should testify on the 3rd of June, after the opening statements and ceremonies, were taken back without achieving this objective. Given the time limited mandate of the Court, this creates a serious cause for concern. (vi) The tension between giving effect to the 1st Accused's right to self representation and that of his co-accused, to a fair and expeditious trial as required by law.

27. When all these factors are taken into consideration and weighed individually and cumulatively for purposes of determining the present application, the Chamber is of the opinion, and without in any way seeking to contest the existence of the said right of self-representation which to us is qualified and not absolute, that this is certainly not a proper case where the accused person's request to exercise this right to self-representation should be granted without qualifications or preconditions. We take this stand because we foresee that granting the request in Exhibit 1 unconditionally could lead to certain procedural difficulties in the conduct of his trial which could occasion an injustice.

28. In this regard, we would like to affirm here that The Trial Chamber cannot allow the integrity of its proceedings to be tarnished or to be conducted in a manner that is not in conformity with the aspirations, of the norms of the judicial process. As a matter of law, it is our duty as a Chamber at all times, to protect the integrity of the proceedings before us and to ensure that the administration of justice is not brought into disrepute. This we can achieve by ensuring, amongst other measures, that persons who are accused and indicted for serious offences such as these, are properly represented by

Counsel because this safeguard is very vital in ensuring that the overall interests of justice are served and of the Rule of Law, upheld.

29. On this institutional judicial policy consideration, The European Court of Human Rights, in the case of *Croissant v. Germany*,[5] whose judgment was rendered on the 25th of September, 1992, had this to say:

> "It is for the Courts to decide whether the interests of justice require that the accused be defended by Counsel appointed by them. When appointing Counsel, the national courts must certainly have regard to the defendants wishes – However, they can override those wishes when there are relevant and sufficient grounds for holding that this is necessary in the interest of justice"

30. We hold that the 1st Accused has a right to self-representation, but that such a right, being qualified and not absolute, could, in the light of certain circumstances, be derogated should the interests of justice so dictate.

31. To this end, and having regard to all the preceding factors articulated for the purposes of determining this application, We rule and Order as follows:

32. **THAT** the right to self-representation solicited in this case by the 1st Accused, Samuel Hinga Norman, can only be exercised with the assistance of Counsel to be assigned to the trial and in whatever capacity they are assigned or designated, stand-by or otherwise, without prejudice to the Registrar's discretion to designate, if the 1st Accused so expresses this desire, Members of his former Defence Team, and this, in accordance with the provisions of Article 17(4)(d) of the Statute of the Special Court The Rules of Procedure and Evidence, and of the provisions of the Directive for the Assignment of Counsel promulgated by the Registrar of the Special Court on the 3rd of October, 2003.

---

[1] *Prosecutor v. Slobodan Milosevic*, Case No. IT-02-54-T, Reasons for Decision on the Prosecution Motion Concerning Assignment of Counsel, 4 April 2003.
[2] *Prosecutor v. Vojislav Seselj*, Case No. IT-03-67-PT, Decision on Prosecution's Motion for Order Appointing Counsel to Assist Vojislav Seselj with his Defence, 9 May 2003.
[3] McKaskle v. Wiggins, 465 US 168 (1984).
[4] *Farhad v. United States*, Case No. 19 F.3d 1097 (9th Cir. 1999).
[5] *Croissant v. Germany*, European Court of Human Rights, Case No. 62/1001/314/385, Judgment, 25 September 1992.

- **Article 17(4)(d): Rights of the Accused – Right to Self-Representation – "Interests of Justice"**

S17-TC-13

o *Prosecutor v. Norman*, SCSL-04-14-T, Decision on the Application of Samuel Hinga Norman for Self-Representation Under Article 17(4)(d) of the Statute of the Special Court, 8 June 2004, para. 10-14:[20]

10. The interests of justice, we observe, is a multi faceted legal concept which is all encompassing and a vital component of the principle of the Rule of law. In this case for instance, where the 1st Accused, Hinga Norman, has been in detention since the month of March 2003, the interests of justice require, as is provided for in Article 17(4)(c) of the Statute, that he be tried "without undue delay".

11. This, as provided for under Rule 26*bis* of the Rules of Procedure and Evidence, connotes the necessity and the obligation imposed on the Chamber to ensure that a trial is fair and expeditious and that even though this right is conditioned on a "full respect of the rights of the accused", we consider and so hold, that these rights would not include an absolute right of self-representation.

12. The question to put here is whether the attendant consequences that would flow from our granting the request in Exhibit 1 would, in the overall interests of justice, be consistent with the statutory guarantees to a fair and expeditious trial to be reserved by the Court to the accused particularly where, as in this case, his detention has been as long as over one year. [. . .]

13. The 1st Accused is jointly indicted with 2 others who our records show, neither understand nor speak the English language. For this reason, they require a permanent translator from English to Mende and vice versa of course, for the Chamber. Each of these 2 accused persons has a legal team to represent them. If the application in Exhibit 1 were granted, this would have the potential to negatively impact on the fairness and expeditiousness of the trial of these co-accused persons given the complexities and intricacies of the judicial process and considering the gravity of the alleged crimes.

14. We are of the opinion and do state here that the 1st Accused cannot, and indeed, should not be allowed to exercise this qualified right to self-representation, to the detriment of the rights of his two co-accused to a fair and expeditious trial.

---

[20] *Prosecutor v. Gbao*, Case No. SCSL-04-15-T, Decision on Application for Leave to Appeal Decision on Application to Withdraw Counsel, 4 August 2004, para. 51.

- **Article 17(4)(d): Rights of the Accused – Right to Self-Representation and Refusal to Attend Proceedings**

S17-TC-14
o *Prosecutor v. Norman, Fofana, Kondewa*, No. SCSL-04-14-T, Ruling on the Issue of Non-Appearance of the First Accused Samuel Hinga Norman, the Second Accused Moinina Fofana, and the Third Accused, Allieu Kondewa at the Trial Proceedings, 1 October 2004, para. 23:

23. The Trial Chamber considers that the exercise of the right to self-representation should not become an obstacle to the achievement of a fair trial. As stated by the Trial Chamber of the ICTY in the *Milosevic*[1] case, "the right to represent oneself must therefore yield when it is necessary to ensure that the trial is fair". The Trial Chamber therefore concludes that on account of the Accused's deliberate absence from Court, his right to self-representation is revoked, and in accordance with Rule 60 of the Rules, the CDF trial will be continued in the absence of the First Accused and that he will be represented by Court Appointed Counsel.[2]

---

[1] *Prosecutor v. Milosevic,* Reasons for Decision on Assignment of Defence Counsel, 22nd September 2004, para. 34.
[2] Rule 60, Rules of Procedure and Evidence of the Special Court for Sierra Leone.

- **Article 17(4)(d): Rights of the Accused – Right to Self-Representation – Standby Counsel**

S17-TC-15
o *Prosecutor v. Norman*, Case No. SCSL-04-14-T, Consequential Order on Assignment and Role of Standby Counsel, 14 June 2004:

CONSIDERING that the right to self-representation is not absolute and that the interests of justice may require the assignment of legal assistance;

CONSIDERING that the right to counsel and the right to self-representation do not exclude each other;

CONSIDERING that the CDF trial involves multiple defendants and that the rights of each accused person must be fully respected at all times throughout the trial process;

CONSIDERING that the right of the Accused to self-representation must be balanced against the right to a fair and expeditious trial;

CONSIDERING that it is in the overall interests of justice to assign a Standby Counsel to assist the Accused, in the exercise of his right to self-representation;

- **Article 17(4)(d): Rights of the Accused – Right to Representation of the Accused Choosing**

S17-TC-16

o *Prosecutor v. Brima*, Case No. SCSL-04-16-PT, Decision on Applicant's Motion Against Denial by the Acting Principal Defender to Enter a Legal Service Contract for the Assignment of Counsel, 6 May 2004, para. 40-41:

40. [...] The Chamber observes that Article 17(4)(d) of the Statute guarantees to the Applicant, as an indigent, the right to be represented by a Counsel 'of his or her own choosing'.

41. It should be noted that this provision is mandatory and even though jurisprudential and interpretational evolutions have significantly whittled down this right which is now more qualified than it is absolute, the Chamber will not, given the particular circumstances of this and of each case, particularly those involving allegations of serious breaches of the rule of law and the due process, lose sight of the pre-eminently mandatory and defence protective character of the provisions of Article 17(4)(d) of the Statute.

S17-TC-17

o *Prosecutor v. Brima, Kamara*, Case No. SCSL-04-16-T, Decision on the Extremely Urgent Confidential Joint Motion for the Re-Appointment of Kevin Metzger and Wilbert Harris as Lead Counsel for Alex Tamba Brima and Brima Bazzy Kamara and Decision on Cross-Motion by Deputy Principal Defender to Trial Chamber II for Clarification of its Oral Order of 12 May 2005, 9 June 2005, para. 41-46:

41. The applicants have stressed the right of the accused to Counsel of their "own choosing" as provided by Article 17(4)(d) and have argued this allows them to have the Counsel they previously refused to instruct and co-operate with re-assigned to them. They submit the Trial Chamber must "ensure that the right [...] is not arbitrarily interfered with [...]"

42. This provision has been considered by various courts, both the International Tribunals and, as stated in the brief by Mr. Knoops, by the European Courts when interpreting Article 6 of the European Convention on Human Rights.

43. The accused in this case have declared themselves indigent and have, in accordance with Article 17(E)(d), a right to have legal assistance assigned.

44. However, the right to have legal assistance does not carry with it an absolute right to any Counsel.

45. As was held in the *Prosecutor v. Martic* by ICTY:

> "the jurisprudence of the International Tribunal and of the International Criminal Tribunal for Rwanda indicates that the right of the indigent accused to counsel of his own choosing may not be unlimited but that, in general, the choice of any accused regarding this Defence Counsel in proceedings before the Tribunals shall be respected; that, in the view of the Chamber, the choice of all accused should be respected unless there exist well-founded reasons not to assign Counsel of choice".[1]

And in ICTY Prosecutor v. Knežević:

> "Contrary to the submission of the Accused and Mr. Drasko Zec, the right of indigent accused to counsel of his own choosing is not without limits; that the decision for the assignment of counsel rests with the Registrar, having to take into consideration the wishes of the accused, unless the Registrar has reasonable and valid grounds not to grant the request."[2]

46. And as stated by Ms. Knoops in paragraph 2 of his brief, the right of an accused to counsel "can be subject to certain restrictions, such restrictions should of course be interpreted in the perspective of the overall right of the accused to have a fair trial."

---

[1] *The Prosecutor v. Martic*, Case No. IT-95-11-PT, Decision on Appeal against Decision of the Registry, 2 August 2002.
[2] *The Prosecutor v. Knežević*, Case No. IT-95-4-PT, IT-95-8/1-PT, Decision on Accused's request for Review of Registrar's Decision as to Assignment of Counsel, 6 September 2002.

- **Article 17(4)(g): Rights of the Accused – Right Not to Be Compelled to Testify Against Himself or to Confess Guilt**

S17-TC-18

o *Prosecutor v. Gbao*, Case No. SCSL-03-09-PT, Decision on the Request by the TRC of Sierra Leone to Conduct a Public Hearing with the Accused, 3 November 2003, para. 17:

17. A further reason is that it does not seem right, from a judicial as distinct from a non-judicial perspective, for a

tribunal. Before which an accused stands indicted for international crimes to which he has pleaded not guilty to afford him easy recourse to another tribunal or institution for the purpose of incriminating himself as to the general subject areas forming the substrata of the charges for which he is indicted. To facilitate such recourse especially in the light of the accused's own doubts, equivocations and reservations will unquestionably, in my considered judgment, jeopardize not only his right to be presumed innocent but more so his right "not to be compelled to testify against himself or not to confess his guilt" guaranteed by Article 14 (3) of the International Covenant of Civil and Political Rights, 1966.

APPEALS CHAMBER DECISIONS

- **Article 17: Rights of the Accused – Shared Responsibility for the Implementation of the Rights of the Accused**

S17-AC-1

o *Prosecutor v. Brima, Kamara, Kanu*, Case No. SCSL-04-16-AR73, Decision on Brima-Kamara Defence Appeal Motion Against Trial Chamber II Majority Decision on Extremely Urgent Confidential Joint Motion for the Re-Appointment of Kevin Metzger and Wilbert Harris As Lead Counsel for Alex Tamba Brima and Brima Bazzy Kamara, 8 December 2005, para. 84:

84. It may be inferred from the creation of the Defence Office by the Registrar pursuant to Rule 45 that the Registrar bore the primary responsibility for ensuring the rights of the Accused pursuant to Article 17 of the Statute and that, by establishing the Defence Office, he delegated this responsibility to it. But this interpretation would be contrary to the Statute of the Special Court according to which the responsibility for ensuring the rights of the Accused does not fall on any organ in particular but rather appears, in the silence of Article 17, as a common duty shared by the three organs. The Rules cannot vary the responsibilities of the organs of the Court under the Statute. Moreover, other Rules provide the responsibility of the other organs of the Special Court, notably Chambers,[(1)] for other aspects of ensuring the rights of the accused. The delegation given by the Registrar to the Defence Office is therefore limited to certain aspects of the Registrar's responsibility for ensuring the rights of the accused under the Statute, namely the administrative aspect of the task, which includes notably, assignment, payment, withdrawal and replacement of Counsel. On his part, the Registrar still keeps the responsibility for ensuring certain aspects of the rights of

the Accused, notably as regards their rights in detention pursuant to Rule 33(C).

---

(1) E.g. Rule 26 *bis*.

- **Article 17: Rights of the Accused – Abuse of Process**

S17-AC-2

o *Prosecutor v. Kallon, Kamara*, Cases No. SCSL-04-15-AR72, SCSL-04-16-AR72, Decision on Challenge to Jurisdiction: Lomé Accord Amnesty, 13 March 2004, para. 79-80:

> 79. At the root of the doctrine of abuse of process is fairness. The fairness that is involved is not fairness in the process of adjudication itself but fairness in the use of the machinery of justice. The consideration is not only about unfairness to the party complaining but also whether to permit such use of the machinery of justice will bring the administration of justice into disrepute. In *A. G. of Trinidad and Tobago v Phillip*(1) the Privy Council said, rightly:
>
>> The common law has now developed a formidable safeguard to protect persons from being prosecuted in circumstances where it would be seriously unjust to do so. It could well be an abuse of process to seek to prosecute those who have relied on an offer of promise of a pardon and complied with the conditions subject to which that offer or promise was made. If there were not circumstances justifying the state in not fulfilling the terms of its offer or promise, then the courts could well intervene to prevent injustices: see *Reg. v. Mines and Green* [1983] 33 S.A.S.R. 211.
>
> 80. Where there is an express provision of a statute that a tribunal shall not take into consideration a fact or an event as ground for declining to exercise its jurisdiction (other than a fact or event that affects the fairness of the trial itself as to constitute a violation of the right to fair hearing), such tribunal will be acting unlawfully if it circumvents the express provision of the statute under the guise of an inherent discretionary power. [. . .]

---

(1) G. of Trinidad and Tobago v Phillip 1 A.C.396 at 417 (1995).

- **Article 17: Rights of the Accused – Freedom of Speech**

S17-AC-3

o *Prosecutor v. Norman*, Case No. SCSL-03-08-A, Decision on Appeal by the Truth and Reconciliation Commission for Sierra Leone ("TRC" or "the Commission") and Chief Samuel Hinga Norman JP Against the Decision of His Lordship, Mr Justice Bankole Thompson Delivered on 30 October 2003 to Deny the TRC's Request to Hold a Public Hearing With Chief Samuel Hinga Norman JP, 28 November 2003, para. 18, 21, 39-40:

18. [Chief Hinga Norman] expected a speedy trial but after six months in custody there was not yet a trial date. He is himself a Minister of Government and political leader. He heard broadcast testimony from the President and he too wanted to make his appeal to 'the people'. He thinks that it is discriminatory not to permit him to do so. He possesses, even as an indictee remanded in custody, a qualified right to freedom of speech. That right must be capable of assertion, in some meaningful way, to answer, if he wishes, any allegations that have been made against him in another forum: particular resonance attaches to free speech when it is sought as a "right to reply". He is entitled to set out his own account for posterity. The practical question concerns only the method by which this should be done whilst he awaits his trial.

[. . .]

21. It must be understood that these were protections laid down not to obstruct the TRC but to provide fundamental protection for men facing charges alleging heinous crimes which if proved could lead to long years of imprisonment. That protection was essential where they were facing impromptu questioning by a skilled counsel for the TRC and by the commissioners themselves. There was not, indeed never has been, any inhibition against an indictee volunteering or communicating information to the TRC in writing, either directly or through his lawyers. The indictee retains freedom of speech to this very considerable extent, that he can write a book, if he wishes, about 'his role in the conflict and his insights and views into its causes, course and character' and have it sent to the TRC by his lawyers, who will sensibly vet it first. It is surprising that the TRC does not appear to have requested information in <u>written</u> form from the indictee. It is also surprising that it has shifted its request from a two day private interview with investigators to a full-scale public hearing broadcast 'live' to the nation.

[. . .]

39. It would clearly not be right that the TRC apply its 'reconciliation' processes of public hearing, confrontation with victims, live broadcast and so on to Special Court indictees who have not pleaded guilty. This would, for the reasons given above, be wholly inappropriate. It might conceivably be permitted for an indictee whose guilty plea had been entered and accepted by the Court and by the Prosecution, but that is not the case. I have to decide how to effectuate the wish to testify of an indictee who, his counsel tell me, intends to plead 'not guilty' and to vigorously defend the legality of his actions in putting down an insurrection by use of what he will contend was reasonable force. His free speech entitlement may only be restricted – like his freedom of movement – to the extent that is consonant with his present status as an indictee.

40. That status does not only restrict his speech in the interests of security. It carries with it a host of considerations about ensuring the fairness of his trial (and 'fairness' includes fairness to the Prosecutor and its witnesses) and fairness to other indictees who face trial. At common law, a prisoner retains all the rights other than those taken away expressly or by necessary implication: *Raymond v Honey*;[1] *Ex parte Simms*.[2] These cases were pressed by counsel for the indictee, although they establish that <u>convicted</u> prisoners retain rights to urge wrongfulness of their convictions (but not to engage a political debate).[3] Although the indictee here may well wish to discuss political issues, the important distinction is that he is unconvicted and may to that extent be accorded more freedom. But that freedom is bounded, nonetheless, by the requirements to exercise it compatibly with his status as an indictee, which for present purposes means in a manner that gives rise to no real apprehension that it will disturb the fair trial process which he and others are obliged to go through. The argument, whether viewed as a free expression claim by an indictee or a concomitant claim to receive that expression by the TRC, cannot permit the applicants to dictate the <u>manner</u> in which the Special Court must effectuate it."

---

[1] [1983] 1AC 6.
[2] [1999] 3 WLR 328.
[3] Ibid., p. 337.

- **Article 17(2): Rights of the Accused – Right to a Fair and Public Hearing – Difference Between Publicity and Oral Character of the Proceedings**

S17-AC-4   o *Prosecutor v. Brima, Kamara, Kanu*, Case No. SCSL-04-16-AR73, Decision on Brima-Kamara Defence Appeal Motion Against Trial Chamber II Majority Decision on Extremely

Urgent Confidential Joint Motion for the Re-Appointment of Kevin Metzger and Wilbert Harris As Lead Counsel for Alex Tamba Brima and Brima Bazzy Kamara, 8 December 2005, para. 101-105:

101. As Third Ground of Appeal, the Defence challenges the denial of an order for a public hearing on its application. The Defence submits that the right of the Accused to a fair and public trial is guaranteed by Article 17(2) of the Statute and that the only statutory restriction upon that right is that of measures imposed by the Trial chamber for the protection of victims and witnesses. The Defence submits that Rule 73(A) gives the Trial Chamber the power and discretion to hear motions in open court and that the Trial Chamber misinterpreted this Rule in a way which erodes the rights of the Accused under Article 17 of the Statute.

102. Article 17(2) of the Statue provides that the accused shall be given a fair and public hearing the purpose of which is to "protect litigants from the administration of justice in secret with no public scrutiny".[1] This right can be restricted as provided for in Article 17(2) of the Statute in order to protect victims and witnesses. This right is implemented in the Rules of Procedure and Evidence, in particular Rule 78 which provides that "[a]ll proceedings before a Trial Chamber, other than deliberations of the Chamber, shall be held in public, unless otherwise provided".

103. The issue of publicity of the proceedings shall however be distinguished from the issue of their written or oral character. Written submissions are, unless otherwise specifically provided, public. Article 4(B) of the Practice Direction on Filing Documents provides:

> "Where a Party, State, organization or person seeks to file all or part of a document on a confidential basis, the party shall mark the document as 'CONFIDENTIAL' and indicate, on the relevant Court Management Section form, the reasons for the confidentiality. The Judge or Chamber shall thereafter review the document and determine whether confidentiality is necessary. Documents that are not filed confidentially may be used in press releases and be posted on the official website of the Special Court."

104. The publicity of written submissions and decisions implies, as mentioned in Article 4(B) of the Practice Direction on Filing of Documents, their potential use in press releases and their accessibility through the Special Court's Website. In these circumstances there is no question of justice being administered secretly.

105. The Appeals Chamber therefore finds no merits in the assertion that Rule 73(A) provision according to which interlocutory motions may be ruled "based solely on the written submissions of the parties, unless it is decided to hear the parties in open Court", is, or may be interpreted, in contradiction with the Accused right to a fair and public hearing pursuant to Article 17(2) of the Statute. In the current case, all the submissions filed in relation to the Motion to re-assign before the Trial Chamber were filed publicly and are freely accessible on the Special Court's Website, as well as the Impugned Decision.

---

(1) *Pretto v. Italy* (A/71): (1984) 6 E.H.R.R. p. 182.

- **Article 17(3): Rights of the Accused – Presumption of Innocence**

S17-AC-5   o *Prosecutor v. Norman*, Decision on Appeal by the Truth and Reconciliation Commission for Sierra Leone ("TRC" or "the Commission") and Chief Samuel Hinga Norman JP Against the Decision of His Lordship, Mr Justice Bankole Thompson Delivered on 30 October 2003 to Deny the TRC's Request to Hold a Public Hearing With Chief Samuel Hinga Norman JP, 28 November 2003, para. 10, 15:

10. [. . .] The presumption of innocence, to which the Judge attached much weight, is really a rule which places the burden of proof on the Prosecution at trial; it is not a straitjacket which insulates an indictee, against his wishes, from all forms of questioning prior to his trial. [. . .]

[. . .]

15. [. . .] I was told at the hearing by the TRC representatives that the Commissioners are preparing to make some assessments of responsibility, and I have been given no assurance that indictees awaiting or undergoing trial will not be 'judged' guilty or innocent by the Commissioners (who are not qualified judges), whether or not they testify to the TRC. The TRC has made no 'self-denying ordinance' in this or any other respect that is comparable to the decision of the Special Court Prosecutor to refrain from using evidence presented to the TRC. If its report carries any conclusion about criminal responsibility of an indictee, then the professional judges of the Special court will have to ignore that premature judgement, as indeed they are trained to do. But its publication may create expectations and anxieties among prospective witnesses or other defendants and prove indirectly damaging to either Prosecution or Defence. For the very reason that it would necessarily be a premature judgement, it might be shaken or reversed

after all the evidence is heard and exposed to the test of cross-examination at the trial. Any such result might discredit TRC report, but the Court must take no account of this: its judges remain committed by oath to reach their verdicts according to the evidence before them.

- **Article 17(4)(c): Rights of the Accused – Expeditious Trial**

S17-AC-6

o *Prosecutor v. Norman, Kallon, Gbao*, Cases No. SCSL-03-08-PT, SCSL-03-07-PT, SCSL-03-09-PT, Decision on the Applications for a Stay of Proceedings and Denial of Right to Appeal, 4 November 2003, para. 7-8, 10-11:

The right to Expeditious Trial

7. This right has a particular resonance in Sierra Leone, which on British occupation and thereafter was vouchsafed the great guarantee of Magna Carta: "To no one will we sell, to no one will we refuse or delay, right or justice". That is a central component of the common law of the Commonwealth as reflected today in criminal proceedings by the availability of the motion for abuse of process to secure the release of defendants oppressed by delays caused by prosecutors or courts. It would be indulgent to cite all the historical and literary examples of criminal justice systems which have in the public perception failed or succeeded according to whether their processes have been completed within a reasonable time. The right is now firmly entrenched in international law, through the force of Article 14(3)(c) of the ICCPR and decisions of courts such as the European Court of Human Rights and the Privy Council.

8. It appears in the ICCPR as a right guaranteed to a defendant, but for international human rights law it offers a vital and concomitant guarantee to victims of war crimes and crimes against humanity. If there can be no peace without justice, there can be no peace until justice is done. Victims and relatives of victims are entitled to have those accused of hideous offences which have caused them so much grief to be tried expeditiously: they may not achieve personal closure until the process concludes. Similarly, the international community which establishes special courts expects them to work expeditiously as well as fairly. That justice delayed is justice denied is no less true for being a truism.

[...]

10. The UN deliberately chose to establish a Special Court on a different model to existing tribunals. That it was concerned to avoid undue delay in holding and conducting trials is plain from Security Council resolution 1315 itself, the preamble to

which recites the need to establish "a strong and credible court [...] to expedite the process of bringing justice and reconciliation to Sierra Leone and the region". References to expedition are found in paragraph 1, and in paragraph 8(b) to the necessity for "the efficient, independent and impartial functioning of the special court". The consequent report of the Secretary-General seeks "to assure the population that while a credible special court cannot be established overnight, everything possible will be done to expedite its functioning" (paragraph 7), and paragraph 42 argues for the establishment of an appeals chamber separate from that of the ICTR precisely because the alternative "might delay beyond acceptable human rights standards the detention of the accused pending the hearing of appeals." The report concludes (paragraph 74) by urging the Security Council to "bear in mind the expectations that have been created and the state of urgency that permeates all discussions of the problem of impunity in Sierra Leone".

11. These concerns are reflected in the Court's Statute and Agreement, most notably in the provision for three year terms for its Prosecutor, Registrar and all its judges- an implication that this is an appropriate time frame in which to deal at least with the initial indictees. Of course, there may be later indictments and the three year terms of office are renewable. However, it is clear that the judges must give full force and effect to the need for expeditious trial. Ms. Whitaker conceded that this value must be 'balanced' against the right of preliminary appeal for which she was contending although if the latter right, on examination, turns out either to the non-existent or to have no real value for defendants, there is nothing to be weighed in the balance. We remind ourselves that there are indictees arrested in March 2003 who have been in prison now for over eight months. They are entitled to a trial process which will result either in their liberty or their punishment and which will have that result just as soon as is compatible with their fair trial rights. The international community, the people of Sierra Leone and their alleged victims all have a concomitant interest in expeditious determination of guilt or innocence.

- **Article 17(4)(d): Rights of the Accused – Legal Assistance of the Accused Choosing**

S17-AC-7
o *Prosecutor v. Brima, Kamara, Kanu*, Case No. SCSL-04-16-AR73, Decision on Brima-Kamara Defence Appeal Motion Against Trial Chamber II Majority Decision on Extremely Urgent Confidential Joint Motion for the Re-Appointment of Kevin Metzger and Wilbert Harris As Lead Counsel for Alex Tamba Brima and Brima Bazzy Kamara, 8 December 2005, para. 89-90:

89. The Appeals Chamber does not see any merits in the Defence allegation that the exclusion of the withdrawn Counsel from re-assignment violates the accused's right to a Counsel of their own choosing. On this aspect, the Appeals Chamber concurs with the Trial Chamber's finding in the Impugned Decision,[1] agreed upon by both Respondents,[2] that the right to counsel of the Accused's own choosing is not absolute, especially in the case of indigent accused, and observes that the conditions of exercise of this right are set up by the Directive. In particular, the indigent Accused shall be consulted on the choice of his counsel pursuant to article 9(A)(i) of the Directive and he may only elect one Counsel from the list of qualified counsel set up by the Principal Defender in accordance with Rule 45(C) and Article 13 of the Directive. The Appeals Chamber notes that this consultation process goes substantially further in the protection of the indigent accused right to a counsel of their own choosing than the regulations applicable before other sister Tribunals, which provide that the Registrar chooses and appoints Counsel but does not mention any consultation with the Accused.[3] The SCSL regulations are also fully consistent with the jurisprudence of the European Court for Human Rights, in particular its Decision in the *Mayzit v. Russia* Case relied upon by the Applicants:[4]

> Notwithstanding the importance of a relationship of confidence between lawyer and client, the right to choose one's own counsel cannot be considered to be absolute. It is necessarily subject to certain limitations where free legal aid is concerned and also where it is for the courts to decide whether the interests of justice require that the accused be defended by counsel appointed by them. When appointing defence counsel the national courts must certainly have regard to the defendant's wishes. However, they can override those wishes when there are relevant and sufficient grounds for holding that this is necessary in the interests of justice (see *Croissant v. Germany*, judgment of 25 September 1992, Series A no. 237-B, § 29).

90. It is therefore the view of the Appeals Chamber that the aforementioned regulations applicable before the Special Court are fully consistent with Article 17(4)(d) right of the Accused to a counsel of his own choosing.

---

[1] Impugned Decision, para. 44.
[2] Defence Office's Response, pp. 6-7; Registrar's Response, para. 2, 15.
[3] Article 10(A)(i) of the ICTR Directive on Assignment of Counsel; Article 11(A)(i) of the ICTY Directive on Assignment of Counsel. See also the jurisprudence referred to at para. 45 of the Impugned Decision.
[4] *Mayzit v. Russia*, ECHR (2005), 20 January 2005, para. 66.

> **Article 18**
> **Judgement**
>
> The judgement shall be rendered by a majority of the judges of the Trial Chamber or of the Appeals Chamber, and shall be delivered in public. It shall be accompanied by a reasoned opinion in writing, to which separate or dissenting opinions may be appended.

APPEALS CHAMBER DECISIONS

- **Article 18: Judgement – Separate Opinions Shall Be Filed Together With the Majority Decision**

S18-AC-1

o *Prosecutor v. Brima, Kamara, Kanu*, Case No. SCSL-04-16-AR73, Decision on Brima-Kamara Defence Appeal Motion Against Trial Chamber II Majority Decision on Extremely Urgent Confidential Joint Motion for the Re-Appointment of Kevin Metzger and Wilbert Harris As Lead Counsel for Alex Tamba Brima and Brima Bazzy Kamara (AC), 8 December 2005, para. 20-24:

20. The Appeals Chamber takes this opportunity to emphasise that Article 18 of the Statute provides that judgements – or decisions – shall be accompanied by a reasoned opinion, which in practice embodies the reasoning of the decision, to which separate or dissenting opinions may be appended. Article 18 does not provide a time difference between the filing of the Decision and the filing of any concurring/dissenting opinion and the word "appended" clearly means that, in the spirit of the Statute, those opinions shall be filed at the very same time as the majority decision.

21. This interpretation is consistent with this Appeals Chamber's jurisprudence that the Statute and Rules of the Special Court should be interpreted according to the purpose of enabling "trials to proceed fairly, expeditiously and effectively".[1] An expeditious determination of interlocutory motions would be favoured by a time-limit running from the date of the appealed decision itself. At the same time, to compel the parties to decide whether or not they should request leave to appeal without knowing the entire considerations having led to the decision and the reason why a judge of the bench may dissent from the majority decision, would be unfair and would jeopardise the effective right of the parties to appeal interlocutory decisions. Although the applicant is not supposed to submit

his/her grounds of appeal in his/her application for leave to appeal, concurring/dissenting opinions may bear on his/her decision to appeal the majority decision. The Appeals Chamber therefore finds that those concurring/dissenting opinions shall be filed together with the majority decision, in order to put the parties in a position to decide whether or not to apply for leave to appeal.

22. This interpretation is also confirmed by the common practice before other International Tribunals, which is to file, at the same time, the decision and its concurring/dissenting opinions, without any delay. This Appeals Chamber has always followed this practice of other International Tribunals on the filing of concurring/dissenting opinions.

23. Both Trial Chambers of the Special Court for Sierra Leone have on occasions departed from this common practice and have filed concurring/dissenting opinions after the related decision is rendered. A review of the Trial Chambers practice shows that the time difference between the filing of the decisions and the concurring/dissenting opinions has sometimes reached several months, thereby delaying substantially the proceedings and casting uncertainty on the opinion of Judges on important legal issues. The Appeals Chamber notes that this practice does not occur in every case and that some opinions are filed on the same day as the related decisions.

24. The Appeals Chamber deems it necessary to put an end to the regrettable practice that has developed in the Trial Chambers and clearly finds that, pursuant to article 18 of the Statute, the concurring/dissenting opinions that are not properly "appended" to the decision they relate to, and filed together with it, are not admissible and shall be disregarded.

---

[1] *Prosecutor v. Norman, Fofana, Kondewa*, Case No. SCSL-2004-14-A, Decision on Amendment of the Consolidated Indictment, 16 May 2005, para. 45; *Prosecutor v. Brima, Kamara, Kanu*, Case No. SCSL-2004-16-A, Decision on Defence Appeal Motion Pursuant to Rule 77 (J) on Both the Imposition of Interim Measures and an Order Pursuant to Rule 77(C)(iii), 23 June 2005, para. 28.

DECISIONS OF THE PRESIDENT

- **Article 18: Judgement – Reasons of Decisions**

S18-P-1

o *Prosecutor v. Norman*, Case No. SCSL-04-14-RD47, Decision on Request to Reverse the Order of the Acting Registrar Under Rule 47(A) of the Rules of Detention of 6 June 2005, 29 June 2005, para. 9, 17:

9. I have noted the typographical error which appears in the Decision, which refers to "Rule 47(v) of the Detention Rules" instead of "Rule 47(A)(v)". This error is confirmed by the Registrar in his letter of 15 June 2005. It is my view that such a typographical error does not affect the legality of the Decision which clearly relies in the same paragraph on the Registrar's powers to regulate communication, provided by Rule 47 of the Rules of Detention. The power to prohibit communications and visits does appear in the very title of Rule 47 of the Rules of Detention and is clearly granted by this Rule. In the same way, the power to suspend visits and/or communications is undeniably included in the power to "prohibit, regulate or set conditions" provided by the Rule. The reference that is made to Rule 47 of the Rules of Detention in the Decision therefore gives a sufficient legal basis for the Registrar to exercise that power.

[. . .]

17. [. . .] [S]uch "reasonable grounds" should have been explained in the Decision in order to make sure that the reasons of the sanction were clearly understood by the Applicant and to provide the President with sufficient information for his determination on a potential request to reverse pursuant to Rule 47(G) of the Rules of Detention. It is therefore my conclusion that the Acting Registrar erred in law by failing to specify the "reasonable grounds for believing" that the sanction was necessary, but that this error does not invalidate the Decision.

Article 19
Penalties

1. The Trial Chamber shall impose upon a convicted person, other than a juvenile offender, imprisonment for a specified number of years. In determining the terms of imprisonment, the Trial Chamber shall, as appropriate, have recourse to the practice regarding prison sentences in the International Criminal Tribunal for Rwanda and the national courts of Sierra Leone.

2. In imposing the sentences, the Trial Chamber should take into account such factors as the gravity of the offence and the individual circumstances of the convicted person.

3. In addition to imprisonment, the Trial Chamber may order the forfeiture of the property, proceeds and any assets acquired unlawfully or by criminal conduct, and their return to their rightful owner or to the State of Sierra Leone.

TRIAL CHAMBERS DECISIONS

- **Article 19(2): Penalties – Determination of Sentence – Applicable Factors – Gravity of the Offence – Contempt Proceedings**

S19-TC-1

o *Prosecutor v. Brima (Margaret), Jalloh, Kamara (Ester)* (Case No. SCSL-05-02), *and Kamara (Anifa)* (Case No. SCSL-05-03), Sentencing Judgement in Contempt Proceedings, 21 September 2005, para. 21-24, 26, 29:

21. In determining the appropriate sentence to be imposed against the four Contemnors, I must first consider the gravity of the offence.

22. The Contemnors are the wives and friend of the three Accused in the case of the *Prosecutor v. Brima, Kamara and Kanu.*,[1] referred to as the AFRC trial, which is currently ongoing before Trial Chamber II of the Special Court. On the 9th of March 2005, a witness known by the pseudonym TF1-023 testified for the first time in the case of the *Prosecutor v. Brima et al.*

23. The Contemnors have admitted that on the 9th of March 2005 after having attended trial proceedings, they saw a vehicle with tinted windows and, knowing that it was transporting a protected witness, called out the first name of the witness

and told her in Krio that they knew she was testifying. They also uttered words in Krio whose effect was to threaten and intimidate the witness for testifying.

24. In that trial, Witness TF1-023 was categorised as a Group 1 (witness of fact), Category A (victim of sexual assault and gender crimes) witness. By virtue of that category, Witness TF1-023 enjoyed certain protective measures ordered by the Special Court [...].

[...]

26. The actions of the Contemnors on the 9th of March 2005 did constitute contempt of court in that they revealed the identity and threatened the security of a protected witness and this has been clearly acknowledged by the guilty pleas of all the Contemnors, pleas that have been accepted by this Court.

[...]

29. Any breach or violation of these measures, either by revealing the identification of witnesses or in any other way, is considered and seen as very serious. It is important, therefore, that you Contemnors, and the public at large, understand the absolute necessity of respecting this Court's orders on protective measures.

(1) *Prosecutor v. Brima et al.*, SCSL-04-16-T.

- **Article 19(2): Penalties – Determination of Sentence – Applicable Factors – Individual Circumstances – No Forethought – No Criminal Record – Contempt Proceedings**

S19-TC-2

o *Prosecutor v. Brima (Margaret), Jalloh, Kamara (Ester)* (Case No. SCSL-05-02), *and Kamara (Anifa)* (Case No. SCSL-05-03), Sentencing Judgement in Contempt Proceedings, 21 September 2005, para. 30-31:

30. This being said, it would appear from the facts of this case that there was no forethought in the actions of the Contemnors. As their Counsel have emphasized, the Contemnors are the wives and friend of the three Accused in the case of the *Prosecutor v. Brima et al.* and they are obviously very emotionally involved in the trial process. Their actions, however, clearly had the effect of making witness TF1-023 feel concerned and threatened.

31. According to the information available and as stated by Counsel for these Contemnors, none of the Contemnors have any previous criminal convictions in Sierra Leone nor in the

Special Court. For all of them, this is their first brush with the law and none of them has even appeared in Court before this incident.

- **Article 19(2): Penalties – Determination of Sentence – Applicable Factors – Individual Circumstances – Guilty Plea – Contempt Proceedings**

S19-TC-3

o *Prosecutor v. Brima (Margaret), Jalloh, Kamara (Ester)* (Case No. SCSL-05-02), *and Kamara (Anifa)* (Case No. SCSL-05-03), Sentencing Judgement in Contempt Proceedings, 21 September 2005, para. 32-33:

32. All of the Contemnors have entered pleas of guilty thereby avoiding the necessity of a trial. This facilitated and expedited the proceedings as was suggested by the Principal Defender in his submissions. I also note that the Contemnors Ester Kamara and Anifa Kamara appeared voluntarily before the Special Court even without having been previously served with the *Order in Lieu of Indictment* against them.

33. Rule 101(B) provides that I am to consider all mitigating factors upon determining the appropriate sentence. I accept the general principle in sentencing for criminal offences that a guilty plea is to be considered a mitigating factor. Indeed, this has also been reflected in the established jurisprudence of other international criminal tribunals.[1]

---

[1] See, for instance, *Prosecutor v. Blaskic*, IT-95-14, Judgment, TC, 3 March 2000, para. 777; *Prosecutor v. Simic*, IT-95-9/2, Judgment, TC, 17 October 2002, paras 84-85; and *Prosecutor v. Plavsic*, IT-00-39 & 40/1, Judgment, TC, 27 February 2003, paras 66-81. In particular, in *Blaskic*, cited above, the Trial Chamber held that a guilty plea "may it itself constitute a factor substantially mitigating the sentence".

- **Article 19(2): Penalties – Determination of Sentence – Applicable Factors – Individual Circumstances – Remorse – Contempt Proceedings**

S19-TC-4

o *Prosecutor v. Brima (Margaret), Jalloh, Kamara (Ester)* (Case No. SCSL-05-02), *and Kamara (Anifa)* (Case No. SCSL-05-03), Sentencing Judgement in Contempt Proceedings, 21 September 2005, para. 34:

34. I am satisfied that the Contemnors have demonstrated remorse for their actions that have been found to constitute contempt of court by pleading guilty. All of the Contemnors, both personally and through their Counsel, have expressed their apologies to the Court and the Witness that was threatened and have assured the Court that they would not commit such an act again in the future.

- **Article 19(2): Penalties – Determination of Sentence – Applicable Factors – Mitigating Factors – Participation in the Peace Process**

S19-TC-5   o *Prosecutor v. Sesay*, Case No. SCSL-04-15-PT, Decision on Application of Issa Sesay for Provisional Release, 31 March 2004, para. 51:

51. Although the evidence indicates that the Accused participated in the peace process that followed the end of the hostilities, I do consider that this issue in these circumstances could be rather regarded as a possible mitigating factor, should he be convicted, than as evidence that he will appear for trial.

Article 20
Appellate Proceedings

1. The Appeals Chamber shall hear appeals from persons convicted by the Trial Chamber or from the Prosecutor on the following grounds:

   a. A procedural error;
   b. An error on a question of law invalidating the decision;
   c. An error of fact which has occasioned a miscarriage of justice.

2. The Appeals Chamber may affirm, reverse or revise the decisions taken by the Trial Chamber.

3. The judges of the Appeals Chamber of the Special Court shall be guided by the decisions of the Appeals Chamber of the International Tribunals for the former Yugoslavia and for Rwanda. In the interpretation and application of the laws of Sierra Leone, they shall be guided by the decisions of the Supreme Court of Sierra Leone.

TRIAL CHAMBERS DECISIONS

- **Article 20(3): Appellate Proceedings – Guidance by other International Tribunals Decisions**

S20-TC-1

o *Prosecutor v. Norman*, Case No. SCSL-03-08-PT, Decision on the Prosecutor's Motion for Immediate Protective Measures for Witnesses and Victims and for Non-Public Disclosure, 23 May 2003, para. 11:

11. Concerning the need for the protection of witnesses' identities, at the pre-trial phase as distinct from the trial phase, I have sufficiently advised myself on the applicable body of jurisprudence. Without meaning to detract from the precedential or persuasive utility of decisions of the ICTR and the ICTY, it must be emphasized, that the use of the formula "shall be guided by" in Article 20 of the Statute does not mandate a slavish and uncritical emulation, either precedentially or persuasively, of the principles and doctrines enunciated by our sister tribunals. Such an approach would inhibit the evolutionary jurisprudential growth of the Special Court consistent with its own distinctive origins and features. On the contrary, the Special Court is empowered to develop its own jurisprudence having regard to some of the unique and different socio-cultural and juridical dynamics prevailing in the locus of the Court. This is not to contend that sound and

logically correct principles of law enunciated by ICTR and ICTY cannot, with necessary adaptations and modifications, be applied to similar factual situations that come before the Special Court in the course of adjudication so as to maintain logical consistency and uniformity in judicial rulings on interpretation and application of the procedural and evidentiary rules of international criminal tribunals.

S20-TC-2

o *Prosecutor v. Gbao*, Case No. SCSL-03-09-PT, Decision on Prosecution Motion for Immediate Protective Measures for Witnesses and Victims and for Non-Public Disclosure, 10 October 2003, para. 31-32:

31. From a plain reading of Article 20 (3) of the Statute, it is clear, to the Special Court's understanding, that the jurisprudence from the two ad hoc Tribunals is not binding upon the Special Court, but can be used as guidance in so far as it is adapted to the specificities of the Special Court.

32. Furthermore, need it be said that international criminal justice is at a developing stage and that there is a constant need for referral to the International Criminal Tribunals' jurisprudence, bearing in mind the necessity of judicial coherence of rulings on interpretation and application of the law.

S20-TC-3

o *Prosecutor v. Norman*, Case No. SCSL-03-08-PT, Decision on the Defence Preliminary Motion on Lack of Jurisdiction: Command Responsibility, 15 October 2003, para. 20:

20. The Chamber concurs with the relevance cast by the Defence on the outcome of the decision of the Appeals Chamber of the ICTY for the furtherance of the doctrine of command responsibility with respect to an internal armed conflict. In addition, the Chamber accepts that relevant jurisprudence such as decisions and judgements from the common Appeals Chamber of the ICTY and the ICTR can provide important guidance, *mutatis mutandis*, to the implementation of the mandate of the Special Court. [. . .]

S20-TC-4

o *Prosecutor v. Kamara,* Case No. SCSL-03-10-PT, Decision on the Prosecution Motion for Immediate Protective Measures for Witnesses and Victims and for Non-Public Disclosure, 23 October 2003, para. 16:

16. [...] Without meaning to detract from the precedential or persuasive utility of decisions of the ICTR and the ICTY and to diminish the general thrust of the Prosecution's submissions on this point at paragraphs 17 and 19 of the Motion it must be emphasized that the use of the formula "shall be guided by" in Article 20 of the Statute does not mandate a slavish and uncritical emulation, either precedentially or persuasively, of the principles and doctrines enunciated by our sister tribunals. Such an approach would inhibit the evolutionary jurisprudential growth of the Special Court consistent with its own distinctive origins and features. On the contrary, the Special Court is empowered to develop its own jurisprudence having regard to some of the unique and different socio-cultural and juridical dynamics prevailing in the *locus* of the Court. *This is not to contend that sound and logically correct principles of the law enunciated by ICTR and ICTY cannot, with necessary adaptations and modifications, be applied to similar factual situations that come before the Special Court in the course of adjudication so as to maintain logical consistency and uniformity in judicial rulings on interpretation and application of the procedural and evidentiary rules of the international criminal tribunals.*

S20-TC-5

o *Prosecutor v. Kanu*, Case No. SCSL-03-13-PT, Decision on the Prosecution Motion for Immediate Protective Measures for Witnesses and Victims, 24 November 2003, para. 24:

24. Having so far considered the submissions of both parties, I would like to refer to and to recognise the extent of the application of the provisions of Article 20(3) of the Statute of the Special Court which stipulates as follows:

'the Judges of the Appeals Chamber of the Special Court shall be guided by decisions of the Appeals Chamber of the International Tribunals for the former Yugoslavia and for Rwanda'

and to observe that although not expressly stated, this provision, by a necessary intendment, is also ordinarily applicable to the Trial Chamber of the Special Court where the Judges, without of course losing sight of some legal and factual variables and the environmental realities of Sierra Leone as against or in contrast to the situations in Rwanda and Yugoslavia and their realities, have been inspired by those decisions.

S20-TC-6

o *Prosecutor v. Sesay, Brima, Kallon, Gbao, Kamara*, and *Kanu*, Cases No. SCSL-03-05-PT, SCSL-03-06-PT, SCSL-03-07-PT, SCSL-03-09-PT, SCSL-03-10-PT, and SCSL-2003-13-PT, Decision and Order on Prosecution Motions for Joinder, 27 January 2004, para. 26:[21]

26. Although generally mindful of the desirability for the Special Court, as was stated in some of its prior Decisions on the Prosecutor's Motions for Immediate Protective Measures for Witnesses and Victims and for Non-Public Disclosure,[(1)] to develop its own case law, it will, as a matter of principle adhere to persuasive jurisprudential enunciations of its sister Tribunals, the ICTY and ICTR, with necessary adaptations of course, to fit into its own jurisprudence based on its Rules and local realities on the one hand, and the need to ensure uniformity in judicial rulings on interpretation of the procedural, evidentiary and substantive rules and principles of International Criminal Tribunals, on the other.[(2)]

[(1)] See the Decisions of 23 May 2003 in *Prosecutor v. Issa Hassan Sesay*, SCSL-03-05-PT at para 11, *Prosecutor v. Alex Tamba Brima*, SCSL-03-06-PT at para 11, *Prosecutor v. Morris Kallon*, SCSL-03-07-PT at para 12, *Prosecutor v. Samuel Hinga Norman*, SCSL-03-08-PT at para 11; and *Prosecutor v. Moinina Fofana*, SCSL-03-11-PT, Decision of 16 October 2003 at para 13; *Prosecutor v. Brima Bazzy Kamara*, SCSL-03-10-PT, Decision of 23 October 2003 at para. 16, in each case par Judge Thompson as follows:
"... it must be emphasized that the use of the formula "shall be guided by" in Article 20 of the Statute does not mandate a slavish and uncritical emulation either precedentally or persuasively, of the principles and doctrines enunciated by our sister tribunals."
[(2)] See Decision of 23 May 2003 in *Prosecutor v. Issa Hassan Sesay*, SCSL-2003-05-PT, at para 11, note 13 above.

S20-TC-7

o *Prosecutor v. Kamara*, SCSL-04-16-PT, Decision and Order on Defence Preliminary Motion on Defects in the Form of the Indictment, 1 April 2004, para. 22-25:[22]

22. In this connection, the Trial Chamber emphasises that application of the ICTY and ICTR jurisprudence is not due to a statutory imperative predicated upon a binding relationship

---

[21] See also *Prosecutor v. Norman, Fofana, Kondewa*, Cases No. SCSL-03-08-PT, SCSL-03-11-PT and SCSL-2003-12-PT, Decision and Order on Prosecution Motions for Joinder, 27 January 2004, para. 16; *Prosecutor v. Kallon*, Case No. SCSL-200415-PT, Decision on the Motion by Morris Kallon for Bail, 24 Febraury 2004, para. 32.
[22] See also *Prosecutor v. Kanu*, Case No. SCSL-03-16-PT, Decision on Motion for Exclusion of Prosecution Witness Statements and Stay of Filing of Prosecution Statements, 30 July 2004, para. 19.

of these UN Security Council-established International Criminal Tribunals on the Special Court; indeed, the Statute of the Special Court specifies that the Appeals Chamber of the Special Court shall be "guided" by, and not bound by, decisions of the Appeals Chamber of the two International Tribunals.[1] There is, however, a special relationship envisioned between the Special Court and the International Tribunals, as each institution is established to permit prosecutions for *inter alia* "serious violations of international humanitarian law". As such, the International Tribunals, the Special Court and the International Criminal Court belong to a unique, and still emerging, system of international criminal justice.

23. This special relationship is reflected not only in Article 20 of the Statute but also through the fact that, under the Statute of the Special court, the Rules of Procedure and Evidence of the ICTR applied *mutatis mutandis* to the conduct of legal proceedings before this Court.[2] It can therefore be concluded that the drafters of the Statute of the Special Court not only envisioned that this Court would follow the procedures established by the ICTR – with necessary modifications – but furthermore, that the Rules of Procedure and Evidence of the ICTR can be construed as reflective of the general principles of law applicable to criminal proceedings in which the principles of international criminal law and international humanitarian law are applied.

24. Like the Special Court,[3] the ICTY and the ICTR are bound to apply customary international law,[4] and their decisions do, as a matter of principle, apply customary international law. It is for this reason that this Court applies persuasively decisions taken at the ICTY and ICTR. While noting that the obligations upon the ICTY and ICTR, as well as the Special Court, in relation to the application of customary international law and respect for the principle of *nullum crimen sine lege* are specifically related to the subject-matter of these institutions, the Trial Chamber finds that the two Tribunals also apply general principles of law on matters related to evidence and procedure.[5] The Trial Chamber observes that decisions of both Tribunals are based on recognised sources of law consistent with Article 38 of the Statute of the International Court of Justice.[6]

25. Accordingly, as stated in some major decisions so far,[7] the Special Court will apply the decisions of the ICTY and ICTR for their persuasive value, with necessary modifications and adaptations, taking into account the particular circumstances of the Special Court.[8] The Trial Chamber will, however, where it finds it necessary or particularly instructive, conduct its own independent analysis of the state of customary law or a general principle of law on matters related to *inter alia* evidence or procedure. Additionally, in cases where the Trial

Chamber finds that its analysis of a certain point or prin-ciples of law may differ from that of either the ICTY or ICTR, it shall base its decisions on its own reasoned analysis."

---

(1) Article 20(3) of the statute of the Special Court. See also, report of the Secretary-General on the establishment of a Special Court for Sierra Leone, S/2000/915, 4 October 2000 ("Report of the Secretary-General on Special Court"), paras. 40-46 (on the proposal of sharing one Appeals Chamber between the International Tribunals and the Special Court). Paragraph 41 is particularly instructive: "While in theory the establishment of an overarching Appeals Chamber as the ultimate judicial authority in matters of interpreta-tion and application of international humanitarian law offers a guarantee of developing a coherent body of law, in practice, the same result may be achieved by linking the jurisprudence of the Special Court to that of the International Tribunals, without imposing on the shared Appeals Chamber the financial and administrative constraints of formal institutional link."

(2) See, Article 14 of the Statute of the special Court.

(3) See Report of the Secretary-General on special Court, para. 12: "In recog-nition of the principle of legality, in particular *nullum crimen sine lege*, and the prohibition on retroactive legislation, the international crimes enumerated, are crimes considered to have the character of customary international law at the time of the alleged commission of the crime."

(4) See, Report of the Secretary-General pursuant to paragraph 2 of the Security Council Resolution 808(1993). S/25704, 3 May 1993 (on the Statute of the ICTY), para. 34 (on subject-matter jurisdiction): In the view of the Secretary-General, the application of the principle *nullum crimen sine lege* requires that the international tribunal should apply rules of international humanitarian law which are beyond any doubt part of customary law so that the problem of adherence of some but not all States to specific conventions does not arise. This would appear to be particularly important in the context of an international tribunal prosecuting persons responsible for serious viola-tions of international humanitarian law; and Report of the Secretary-General pursuant to Paragraph 5 of Security Council Resolution 955(1994), S/1994/134, 13 February 1995 (on the Statute of the ICTR), para. 12 (on subject-matter jurisdiction): "... the Security Council has elected to take a more expansive approach to the choice of the applicable ;aw that than the one underlying the statute of the Yugoslav Tribunal, and included within the subject-matter juris-diction of the Rwanda Tribunal international instruments regardless of whether they are considered part of customary international law or whether they have customarily entailed the individual criminal responsibility of the perpetrator of the crime. [...]"

(5) The Trial Chamber notes that rule 89 of the Rules of Procedure and Evidence of both the ICTR and the ICTY provides, in relevant part: "(A) A Chamber shall apply the rules of procedure and evidence set forth in this Section, and shall not be bound by national rules of evidence. (B) In cases not otherwise provided for in this Section, a Chamber shall apply rules of evidence which will best favour a fair determination of the matter before it and are consonant with the spirit of the Statute and the general principles of law."

(6) Article 38(1) of the Statute of the International Court of Justice states: "1. The Court, whose function is to decide in accordance with international law such disputes as are submitted to it, shall apply: a. international conventions, whether general or particular, establishing rules expressly recognized by the contesting states; b. international custom, as evidence of a general practice accepted as law; c. the general principles of law recognized by civilized nations; d. subject to the provisions of Article 59, judicial decisions and the teachings of the most highly qualified publicists of the various nations, as subsidiary means for the determination of rules of law."

(7) See, e.g., *Prosecutor v. Issa Hassan Sesay*, Case No. SCSL-03-05-PT, Decision on the Prosecutor's Motion for Immediate Protective Measures for Witnesses and Victims and for Non-Public Disclosure, 23 May 2003, paras. 11-12. See also, Joinder Decision, paras. 26-28.

(8) The Trial Chamber is cognisant of the fact that the temporal jurisdiction of each of the International Criminal Tribunals may impact upon the applicability of certain of their findings of the state of customary international law at the time relevant to those Tribunals, as opposed to the temporal jurisdiction of the Special Court.

S20-TC-8

o *Prosecutor v. Norman, Fofana, Kondewa*, Case No. SCSL-04-14-T, Decision on Motions for Judgment of acquittal Pursuant to Rule 98, 21 October 2005, para. 27-28:

27. A corollary of Article 14 of the Statute which we would, in these circumstances, like to highlight, is Article 20(3) of the Statute which stipulates that the Judges of the Appeals Chamber of the Special Court shall be guided by the decisions of the Appeals Chamber of the International Tribunals for the former Yugoslavia and for Rwanda.

28. We would like to observe in this regard, that even though this Article alludes only to the Appeals Chamber of the Special Court, this Trial Chamber considers that it has the latitude, in the spirit of mutual judicial guidance that exists amongst International Criminal Tribunals, and even in the absence of the provisions of Article 20(3) of the Statute, to be guided by the decisions of Our Sister Trial Chambers of the ICTY and of the ICTR, and to those rendered by their Appeals Chamber, particularly where the facts, the law, or the statutory instruments on which their decisions, at the time they were delivered, were based, are in *pari materia* with the cases that we are called to adjudicate upon.

APPEALS CHAMBER DECISIONS

• **Article 20: Appellate Proceedings – Need for an Oral Hearing**

S20-AC-1

o *Prosecutor v. Fofana*, Case No. SCSL-04-14-AR72, Decision on Preliminary Motion on Lack of Jurisdiction *Materiae*: Nature of the Armed Conflict, 25 May 2004, para. 33:

33. [. . .] The Appeals Chamber has not found it necessary to hear oral arguments on issues that have been addressed exhaustively during two rounds of written argument. Oral argument would have been necessary had the Chamber felt

compelled to determine the actual nature of the conflict as a question of fact, however, this question does not arise.

- **Article 20: Appellate Proceedings – Right to Appeal**

S20-AC-2

o *Prosecutor v. Norman, Kallon, Gbao*, Cases No. SCSL-03-08-PT, SCSL-03-07-PT, SCSL-03-09-PT, Decision on the Applications for a Stay of Proceedings and Denial of Right to Appeal, 4 November 2003, para. 18-25:

8. The Applicants argue that the consequence of Rule 72 is that all preliminary motions relating to jurisdiction "are not subject to review of any kind contrary to basic human rights norms". They are in fact subject to determination by an Appeals Chamber which is the highest court in the Special Court system and the issue is whether that contravenes "basic human rights norms". The only such "norm" cited by the applicants is Article 14(5) of the ICCPR which provides that "everyone convicted of crime shall have the right to have his conviction and sentence reviewed by a higher tribunal according to law". It is obvious that this right applies only to those who have been convicted and sentenced and not to those in the position of the applicants who have yet to be tried. Moreover, Article 14(5) of the ICCPR is effectuated in terms by Article 20 of the Statute which requires the Appeals Chamber to hear appeals from convicted persons about alleged errors of procedure, law or fact made by the Trial Chamber. Our inherent jurisdiction to dispose of pre-trial motions referred by the Trial Chamber is in no way, shape or form a contravention of Article 14(5).

19. It is not necessary, in order to dispose of this ground, to consider whether Article 14(5) has crystallised as a rule of customary international law, other than to remark that the very agreement by the UN to the terms of Article 20 of the Special Court Statute affords some evidence that it has indeed reached the status termed by international lawyers "jus cogens" – i.e. a rule binding on all states through their acknowledgement of its imperative force. It did not have that status in 1946 – see the Nuremberg Charter – and there are reservations, by countries as important as Italy, Germany, Belgium and Norway to the extension of this Rule to convictions rendered by higher courts.[1] Certainly, there is a right in international law to appeal against a death sentence and to review any substantial prison sentence or any conviction for a serious offence, although it is doubtful whether "review" implies an automatic right to argue that the conviction was wrong, as distinct from an opportunity to seek leave to make such an argument. There

is no treaty authority and no significant precedent to which our attention has been drawn which elevates and extends the right to have a conviction or sentence reviewed to a general right to have every issue, particularly an issue determined by the highest court, capable of or subject to a review procedure.

20. There is, in short, no "human rights norm" – basic or not – of the kind for which the applicants contend. This is unsurprising since any such "right" would undermine and tend to demolish what is a basic human rights rule, namely the right in criminal cases to expeditious justice. We have detailed that right in paragraphs 7-11 above, and explained why it is binding upon us. There being no competing international law right, the question of 'weighing competing values' urged by Ms. Whitaker, does not arise.

21. It is true that some preliminary motions may have a dramatic effect on trials – they may preclude convictions altogether. That does not alter the fact that the Article 14(5) right relied on is bestowed only on persons who have been convicted. No decision or evidence has been advanced to suggest that higher courts would decide pure issues of law differently were there to have been a preliminary determination in a lower court. The International Court of Justice itself – the World Court – has no first tier, and the European Court of Human Rights now sits without a preliminary determination by a Commission – a body removed largely because of the fact that the first tier was productive of delays. (The ECHR often has the benefit of decisions by national courts, although not in cases where there have been no domestic remedies to exhaust.) In the common law system, the rule that jurisdictional points may be taken at any time means that the highest court in a two or three tier system may have to decide them for the first time. The US Supreme Court, too, has an original jurisdiction. European countries have made reservations to Article 14(5) of the Covenant to preserve the right of their highest courts to enter convictions in criminal cases without appeal – a frequent occurrence where the prosecution is given the right of appeal against an acquittal, and the highest appeal court decides to convict. This exception to Article 14(5) is reflected in Article 2(2) of the Seventh Protocol to the European Convention of Human Rights where the right of convicts to appeal is excluded "in cases in which the person concerned may be tried in the first instance by the highest tribunal, or was convicted following an appeal against acquittal."

22. This position obtains in the ICTY and ICTR, the Appeals Chamber of which has the power to convict following a trial chamber acquittal and from this conviction there is no appeal. The Special Court Appeals Chamber has a similar power.

23. That the Article 14(5) principle is applicable only to convicts was plainly stated by the ICTY Appeals Chamber in

Prosecutor v. Delic where the unconvicted accused argued that the Article included a right to appeal against a detention order. At paragraph 19 the bench stated "it is clear from the plain words of this article that the right to review in question applies only to *conviction and sentence*, not to provisional release or other interlocutory matters".[2] This authority is directly against the applicants. The only case they cite is that concerning Milan Vujin, who was found guilty of contempt of court by one Appeals Chamber and where right to appeal had to be effectuated by setting up another appeals chamber to hear his appeal.[3] This case relevantly serves as an example of the exercise of an inherent power by an Appeals Chamber in order to function effectively (there being no power to punish contempt provided by the statute). But it certainly cannot support the applicants' argument: it was a straightforward and correct application of Article 14(5) because Vujin had been convicted of an offence carrying professional dishonour and up to seven years in prison. As a convict, he was entitled to an appeal, and the appeals chamber accepted that it should have referred the matter first to the trial chamber, rather than have convicted Vujin itself.

24. The position in Sierra Leone is of some importance, given our power to rely on its procedural law in amending our own rules. There is no right of appeal against an interlocutory decision in criminal proceedings, but these may be stayed while a constitutional question – including human rights issues – are referred without trial court determination to the Supreme Court of Sierra Leone under sections 124 and 127 of the Constitution. From such decisions, binding of course on the court of criminal trial, there is no appeal. We note in passing that Chief Hinga Norman's counsel threatens to submit a complaint against Sierra Leone to the Human Rights Committee under the Optional Protocol for determination of the legality of the amended Rule 72.[4] We say nothing about the legitimacy of such a course but mention the matter only to make plain that any complaint, petition or other communication, to any body other than a Chamber of this Court, will not be permitted to serve as the basis for an application to stay the proceedings.

25. International law comprises a set of binding rules which crystallise through a process of treaty ratification, state practice, court decisions and juristic writings. The Nuremberg Tribunal to which we owe the legacy of international criminal law, comprised four international judges from whose legendary decision on 30 September 1946 there was no appeal – a fact that has not detracted from its authority and persuasiveness. It completed all processes within twelve months. By the time its legacy began to be appreciated, in 1993-4, with the establishment of the ICTR and the ICTY, international law had moved on at least to the extent that it can now be stated that every

conviction and every sentence for a war crime or a crime against humanity must be capable of review, by way of right in the defendant to seek leave to argue before an independent and impartial court that there were errors of fact or law which occasioned a wrongful conviction or sentence. Our aim is scrupulously to adhere to <u>established</u> fair trial guarantees, by procedures which avoid crippling delays and exorbitant expense. No system of human justice is infallible, however many protections are offered to defendants: we can only do justice that is expeditious, fair and efficient. It may not be exquisite, but it will not be rough.

---

[1] See Separate Opinion of Judge Shahabuddeen in *Prosecutor v. Rutaganda*, Case No. ICTR-96-3-A, Judgment (Appeals Chamber), 26 May 2003.
[2] *Prosecutor v. Delic*, Case No. IT-96-21-T, Decision on Application for Leave to Appeal (Provisional Release) by Hazim Delic, 22 November 1996.
[3] *Prosecutor v. Tadic*, Case No. IT-94-1-A-R77, Judgment on Allegations of Contempt against Prior Counsel, Mila Vujin, 31 January 2000.
[4] Defence Reply para. 13.

- **Article 20: Appellate Proceedings – Scope of Appeal**

S20-AC-3

o *Prosecutor v. Norman, Kallon, Gbao*, Cases No. SCSL-03-08-PT, SCSL-03-07-PT, SCSL-03-09-PT, Decision on the Applications for a Stay of Proceedings and Denial of Right to Appeal, 4 November 2003, para. 4, 26-27:

4. Every criminal legal system must provide a process for trying and sentencing defendants and for hearing appeals from the trial verdict. Thus Article 20 of the Statute requires the Appeals Chamber to hear appeals by convicted persons and from the Prosecutor in relation to alleged errors in law, procedure or fact made by the Trial Chamber. But Article 20 does not purport to be an exhaustive or limiting definition of the powers of the Appeals Chamber, which may function in many other respects that are important to the working of the Special Court. And that Court, like all other court systems, must provide for the disposal of issues which do not concern either the conviction or sentence of any particular defendant – general issues which may be raised, for example, by a defendant or by the Prosecution prior to any conviction. Such issues will include challenges to the lawfulness to the Court itself; matters which the common law describes as "pleas in bar" such as pardon or amnesty; questions as to the existence in international criminal law of the crime charged; the jurisdiction of the Court to try an offence or alleged offender. Such issues must be determined, and the way in which they are determined will be settled, where the constitutive documents are silent, by Rules of Procedure agreed by the judges in plenary sessions.

[...]

26. The applicants further urge that Article 20 of the Statute is a defining or limiting provision which confines the Appeals Chamber to a second instance role and such a role only in respect of appeals from persons convicted by the Trial Chamber or else by the Prosecutor. This is untenable: Article 20 is a statutory guarantee of the Covenant promise in Article 14(5), but it does not serve, expressly or impliedly, to strip the Appeals Chamber of all other function or of its inherent powers. Indeed, on such a reading, the Appeals Chamber would not be able to consider jurisdictional issues at all until after a conviction – an interpretation which would fly in the face of the ICTY appeal decision in *Tadic*[1] which held that 'such a fundamental matter as the jurisdiction of the International Tribunal should not be kept for decision at the end of a potentially lengthy, emotional and expensive trial'. The point of the fast-track mechanism in Rule 72 is to serve the interests of defendants by permitting them to make challenges which might set them at liberty sooner rather than later and it is ironic that they, through their counsel, should challenge it.

27. In any event, the Special Court has an inherent power to organise itself, through its procedural rules, in a way that its judges agree will best assist its work so long as such rules do not contravene any express provision of the Agreement and Statute. Such power in common law courts has been upheld by the House of Lords (*Jones* 1964) and by the ICTR Appeals Chamber in *Tadic* which explains that inherent jurisdiction 'is a necessary component of the judicial function'[2] and does not need to be expressly provided for in the constitutive documents of the tribunal."

---

[1] Decision on the Defence Motion for Interlocutory Appeal on Jurisdiction, para. 4.
[2] Decision on the Defence Motion for Interlocutory Appeal on Jurisdiction, para. 18.

- **Article 20: Appellate Proceedings – No Interference With Trial Chamber's Discretion**

S20-AC-4

o *Prosecutor v. Sesay*, Case No. SCSL-04-15-AR65, Decision on Appeal Against Refusal of Bail, 14 December 2004, para. 26:

26. It should be observed from the outset that the Appeals Chamber will not interfere with the valid exercise of discretion by a Judge of the Trial Chamber unless it is clear that the Judge erred.

- **Article 20(1): Appellate Proceedings – "Grounds" – "Requests" – Submissions in Response or Reply**

S20-AC-5

o *Prosecutor v. Brima, Kamara, Kanu*, Case No. SCSL-04-16-AR73, Decision on Brima-Kamara Defence Appeal Motion Against Trial Chamber II Majority Decision on Extremely Urgent Confidential Joint Motion for the Re-Appointment of Kevin Metzger and Wilbert Harris As Lead Counsel for Alex Tamba Brima and Brima Bazzy Kamara, 8 December 2005, para. 43-52:

43. On the issue of new grounds developed by a respondent in response to a motion filed before the Trial Chamber, Trial Chamber I of the Special Court for Sierra Leone already ruled in another case:

The Chamber wishes to express its strong disfavour of the practice of expanding the nature of submissions in response to a motion to the extent of introducing specific, new and separate arguments amounting to, as it has been identified by the Defence in its Response, a "counter motion". The proper course of action in order to avoid confusion with reference to the nature and time limits for subsequent responses and replies is for the Defence to identify and distinguish the new legal issue, and then file a separate and distinct motion.[1]

44. In the *AFRC* Case, on the issue of new requests sought for the first time in Reply, Trial Chamber II already held:

The Trial Chamber notes that, in its Reply, the Defence sought to substantially modify the relief sought. This is a practice that must be discouraged. A Reply is meant to answer matters raised by the other party in its Response, not to claim additional relief to that sought in the Motion. Obviously the other party, having already filed a Response to the Motion, has no way under the Rules to answer the new prayer, except to apply to the Trial Chamber for leave to do so. In future, the Trial Chamber will not hear claims for additional relief contained in a Reply.[2]

This same finding was made in the Impugned Decision.[3]

45. Trial Chamber II also stressed that such practice casts confusion with reference to the nature and time limits for subsequent responses and replies:

The Trial Chamber wishes to express its strong disfavour for the practice of combining pleadings or submissions for which the Rules prescribe different filing time limits. As the Defence has rightly observed, Rule 7 (C) of the Rules provides that "unless otherwise ordered by the Trial Chamber, a response to a motion shall be filed within ten days while a reply to response shall be filed within five days." We note that in this case the Prosecution's Combined Reply comprises two pleadings, namely the Prosecution Response to the Defence Reply (for which a filing time limit of five days is applicable), and the Prosecution's Reply to the Defence Notice and Request (for which a filing time limit of ten days is applicable). The proper and preferred course of action is for the parties to file the various responses and replies in separate documents in order to avoid confusion over issues as well as time frames. In the present case we observe that the irregularity by the Prosecution has not occasioned a miscarriage of justice as their "Combined Reply" was filed on the 18 May 2005, five days after the filing of the Defence Reply. The Prosecution therefore appears to have complied with both time limits prescribed by Rule 7(C). The preliminary objection is accordingly overruled. [4]

46. As regards new grounds made in a response before the Appeals Chamber, it must first and foremost be reminded that the requirement for leave to submit grounds to the Appeals Chamber prevents a party which did not apply for leave to appeal from submitting new grounds of appeal. The Appeals Chamber already ruled that:

> for the need to deal with the issue raised in these proceedings once and for all in order to clear any doubt as to the limits of the Court's inherent jurisdiction, it would have been in order to refuse to entertain the proceedings on the ground that there is no procedural foundation for approaching the Appeals Chamber in matters such as this, touching on a decision of the Trial Chamber rendered in a motion under Rule 73(A), without prior leave of the Trial Chamber.[5]

Consequently, a party who has not applied for a leave to appeal cannot take advantage of the leave granted to another party to raise grounds of appeal in its response to the appeal motion.

47. As regards new grounds or requests made by the appellant in its reply, Paragraph 10 of the Practice Direction for Certain Appeals provides that, where leave to appeal is granted, the appellant shall, in accordance with the Rules, file and serve on the other parties a notice of appeal containing, notably, (c) the grounds of appeal and (d) the relief sought. A new ground or request made by the appellant in its reply cannot, by that very fact, comply with Paragraph 10 of the Practice Direction since it was not mentioned in the notice of appeal. Moreover, the

above comments made by Trial Chambers about "confusion with reference to the nature and time limits for subsequent responses and replies" cast on the trial proceedings are equally applicable in appeal. For these reasons, the Appeals Chamber finds that such new grounds or requests are inadmissible.

48. This finding, however, shall not apply to new submissions made in response or reply by the Parties in connection with the grounds and requests properly submitted in the appeal. The confusion met in the current Appeal between, on the one hand, grounds and requests, and, on the other hand, submissions, requires some urgent clarification by the Appeals Chamber.

49. "Grounds" are defined in Paragraph 10(c) of the Practice Direction for Certain Appeals which provides that they consist of "clear concise statements of the *errors* complained of".[6] Although Article 20(1) of the Statute and Rule 106 apply to appeals from convicted persons, the list of errors referred to in these provisions may provide some guidance, albeit limited, to interlocutory appeals under Rule 73(B). These errors are "(a) A procedural *error*; (b) An *error* on a question of law invalidating the decision; (c) An *error* of fact which has occasioned a miscarriage of justice."[7] To that list, a decision of Trial Chamber I in the *RUF* Case added appeals based on a legal issue that is of "general significance to the Tribunal's jurisprudence",[8] but that extension of the standard grounds of appeal relied on a prior version of the International Criminal Tribunal for the Former Yugoslavia ("ICTY") Rule 73(B)[9] and goes against the otherwise established jurisprudence of the Special Court for Sierra Leone on the matter.

50. As regards "requests", Paragraph 10(d) of the Practice Direction provides that the notice of appeal shall mention "the relief sought". On the nature of that relief, Article 20(2) of the Statute and Rule 106(B) may also be of some guidance in reaching the finding that it may consist in the reversal or revision of the decision taken by the Trial Chamber.[10]

51. When new grounds or requests not mentioned in the notice of appeal are, for the above reasons, inadmissible, new arguments, that are related to, either supporting or challenging, the appellant's admissible grounds and requests may be considered admissible in a response to the appeal motion. Submission of these new arguments is the main purpose of a response to an appeal motion and does not cast any "confusion with reference to the nature and time limits for subsequent responses and replies" in the proceedings: indeed, they can only be replied by the appellant in the normal way provided by the Rules and do not create a new right to respond for the other Parties.

52. New arguments in reply may also be deemed admissible, with the limitation that they should be strictly limited to the

purpose of replying to the arguments developed in response to the appeal motion. New arguments supporting the appeal motion which do not reply to the Respondent's arguments challenging it shall accordingly not be admitted. To rule otherwise would jeopardize the Respondent's right to challenge the appeal motion.

---

[1] *Prosecutor v. Sesay, Kallon, Gbao*, Case No. SCSL-2004-15-T, Decision on Prosecution Request for Leave to Call Additional Witnesses and Disclose Additional Witness Statements, 11 February 2005, para. 28.

[2] *Prosecutor v. Brima, Kamara, Kanu*, Case No. SCSL-2004-16-T, Decision on Joint defence Motion on Disclosure of All Original Witness Statements, Interview Notes and Investigator's Notes Pursuant to Rule 66 and/or 68, 4 May 2005, para. 20. See also *Prosecutor v. Brima, Kamara, Kanu*, Case No. SCSL-2004-16-T, Decision on Objection to Question Put by Defence in Cross-Examination of Witness TF1-227, 15 June 2005, para. 43.

[3] *Prosecutor v. Brima, Kamara*, Case No. SCSL-2004-16-T, Decision on the Extremely Urgent Confidential Joint Motion for the Re-Appointment of Kevin Metzger and Wilbert Harris as Lead Counsel for Alex Tamba Brima and Brima Bazzy Kamara and Decision on Cross-Motion by Deputy Principal Defender to Trial Chamber II for Clarification of its Oral Order of 12 May 2005, 9 June 2005, para. 20.

[4] *Prosecutor v. Brima, Kamara, Kanu*, Case No. SCSL-2004-16-T, Decision on Prosecution request for Leave to Call an Additional Witness (Zainab Hawa Bangura) Pursuant to Rule 73*bis*(E), and on Joint Defence Notice to Inform the Trial Chamber of its Position vis-à-vis the Proposed Expert Witness (Mrs Bangura) Pursuant to Rule 94*bis*, 5 August 2005, para. 27.

[5] *Prosecutor v. Norman, Fofana, Kondewa*, Case No. SCSL-2004-14-A, Decision on Prosecution Appeal Against the Trial Chamber's Decision of 2 August 2004 Refusing Leave to File an Interlocutory Appeal, 17 January 2005, para. 24.

[6] Paragraph 10(C) of the Practice Direction on Certain Appeals (Emphasis added)

[7] Article 20(1) of the Statute; Rule 106 of the Rules of Procedure and Evidence (Emphasis added).

[8] *Prosecutor v. Gbao*, Case No. SCSL-2004-15-T, Decision on Application for Leave to Appeal Decision on Application to Withdraw Counsel, 4 August 2004, para. 54-55, 57.

[9] For an application of that old Rule by the ICTY Appeals Chamber, see *Prosecutor v. Tadic*, Case No. IT-94-1-A, Appeal Judgement, 15 July 1999, para. 247; *Prosecutor v. Kupreskic*, Case No. IT-95-16-A, Appeal Judgement, 23 October 2001, para. 22. Rule 73(B) of the ICTY currently provides: "Decisions on all motions are without interlocutory appeal save with certification by the Trial Chamber, which may grant such certification if the decision involves an issue that would significantly affect the fair and expeditious conduct of the proceedings or the outcome of the trial, and for which, in the opinion of the Trial Chamber, an immediate resolution by the Appeals Chamber may materially advance the proceedings. (Amended 12 Apr 2001, amended 23 Apr 2002).

[10] *See* also *Prosecutor v. Sesay*, Case No. SCSL-2004-15-T, Decision on Defence Motion, 15 July 2004, para. 13 and *Prosecutor v. Kallon*, Case No. SCSL-2004-15-T, Decision on Confidential Motion, 11 October 2004, para. 21, on the nature of "requests" before the Trial Chambers.

- **Article 20(1)(c): Appellate Proceedings – Error of Fact**

S20-AC-6

o *Prosecutor v. Brima, Kamara, Kanu*, Case No. SCSL-04-16-AR73, Decision on Brima-Kamara Defence Appeal Motion Against Trial Chamber II Majority Decision on Extremely Urgent Confidential Joint Motion for the Re-Appointment of Kevin Metzger and Wilbert Harris As Lead Counsel for Alex Tamba Brima and Brima Bazzy Kamara, 8 December 2005, para. 111-113:

111. As regards findings of fact made by the Trial Chamber, the Appeals Chamber recalls that, pursuant to Article 20(1)(c) of the Statute of the Special Court, it can only be seized of "an error of fact which has occasioned a miscarriage of justice" and that, pursuant to Article 20(2), the "Appeals Chamber may affirm, reverse or revise the decisions taken by the Trial Chamber". This Appeals Chamber has already held that these dispositions were also applicable to interlocutory appeals.[1]

112. These dispositions are the same as before other sister International Tribunals.[2] They have been interpreted by the Appeals Chamber of both sister International Tribunals as implying a limited control of the Trial Chamber's assessment of facts, which may be overturned by the Appeals Chamber only where no reasonable trier of fact could have reached the same finding or where the finding is wholly erroneous. This Appeals Chamber concurs with the finding made in *The Prosecutor v. Semanza*, which relies on several judgements of both ICTR and ICTY Appeals Chamber:[3]

> As regards errors of fact, as has been previously underscored by the Appeals Chamber of both this Tribunal and of the International Criminal Tribunal for the former Yugoslavia ("ICTY"), the Appeals Chamber will not lightly overturn findings of fact made by a trial chamber. Where an erroneous finding of fact is alleged, the Appeals Chamber will give deference to the trial chamber that heard the evidence at trial as it is best placed to assess the evidence, including the demeanour of witnesses. The Appeals Chamber will only interfere in those findings where no reasonable trier of fact could have reached the same finding or where the finding is wholly erroneous. If the finding of fact is erroneous, it will be quashed or revised only if the error occasioned a miscarriage of justice.[4]
>
> The Appeals Chamber emphasises that, on appeal, a party cannot merely repeat arguments that did not succeed at trial in the hope that the Appeals Chamber will consider them afresh. The appeals process is not a trial

de novo and the Appeals Chamber is not a second trier of fact. The burden is on the moving party to demonstrate that the trial chamber's findings or decisions constituted such an error as to warrant the intervention of the Appeals Chamber. Thus, arguments of a party which do not have the potential to cause the impugned decision to be reversed or revised may be immediately dismissed by the Appeals Chamber and need not be considered on the merits. [5]

113. The Appeals Chamber of the Special Court sees no reason to depart from this common jurisprudence of both sister International Criminal Tribunals' Appeals Chamber and will apply it in the current case.

---

[1] *Prosecutor v. Norman, Fofana, Kondewa*, Case No. SCSL-2004-14-AR73, Decision on Amendment of the Consolidated Indictment, 16 May 2005, para. 76.
[2] *See* Articles 24(1)(b) and 24(2) of the ICTR Statute; Articles 25(1)(b) and 25(2) of the ICTY Statute.
[3] *Prosecutor v. Semanza*, ICTR-97-20-A, Judgement, 20 May 2005, para. 8.
[4] *Niyitegeka* Appeal Judgement, para. 8; *Krstic* Appeal Judgement, para. 40; *Krnojelac* Appeal Judgement, para. 11-13, 39; *Tadic* Appeal Judgement, para. 64; *Celebici* Appeal Judgement, para. 434; *Aleksovski* Appeal Judgement, para. 63; *Vasiljevic* Appeal Judgement, para. 8.
[5] See in particular *Rutaganda* Appeal Judgement, para. 18.

- **Article 20(2): Appellate Proceedings – Power of the AC to Affirm, Reverse or Revise**

S20-AC-7

o *Prosecutor v. Norman, Fofana, Kondewa*, Case No. SCSL-04-14-AR73, Decision on Amendment of the Consolidated Indictment, 16 May 2005, para. 76:

76. [...] The Defence has argued that the Appeals Chamber does not have authority to alter a Trial Chamber decision but must merely remit it to the Trial Chamber when it finds an error of fact or law. This is plainly wrong and the Prosecution correctly points out that this Chamber has clear authority under the Rules to revise decisions of the Trial Chamber. Article 20(2) of the Statute puts the matter beyond doubt by providing that the Appeals Chamber may "affirm, reverse or revise" the decision taken by the Trial Chamber (and see Rule 106(B)). By initiating this appeal, the Prosecution shoulders the risk that this Chamber may decide finally whether it should have the permission to amend that the Trial Chamber order left open.

- **Article 20(3): Appellate Proceedings – Guidance by other International Tribunals Decisions**

S20-AC-8

o *Prosecutor v. Kallon*, Case No. SCSL-04-15-PT, Decision on Application for Leave to Appeal Against Refusal of Bail, 23 June 2004, para. 10:[23]

10. I take cognisance of the fact that "the Judges of the Appeals Chamber of the Special Court shall be guided by the decisions of the Appeals Chamber of the International Tribunals for the former Yugoslavia and for Rwanda."[1] This provision, however, does not deter the newly constituted Special Court for Sierra Leone from developing its own jurisprudence and case law, being guided, of course, by the relevant decisions of the two international tribunals to which I have hereinbefore referred.

[1] Article 20(3) of the Special Court Statute.

S20-AC-9

o *Prosecutor v. Norman*, Case No. SCSL-04-14-AR73, Decision on Amendment of the Consolidated Indictment, 16 May 2005, para. 46:

46. It must also be remembered, both when applying the Rules and when making procedural decisions on matters about which the Rules are silent (as they often are) that this court is unique – as the UN Secretary General in his Report put it, *sui generis* –. It was provided at its outset with the Rules of Procedure and Evidence of the International Criminal Tribunal for Rwanda ("ICTR") as they existed in 2002, but its judges were expressly given the plenary power to amend and adapt them to the special circumstances of the Special Court. It follows that procedures and practices that have grown up in the ICTR and International Criminal Tribunal for the former Yugoslavia ("ICTY") should not be slavishly followed – they often reflect the different or difficult circumstances in which these courts have to operate – bilingually; sitting far from the scene of the crimes, and so on. [...]

---

[23] See also *Prosecutor v. Sesay*, Case No. SCSL-04-14-AR65, Decision on Application for Leave to Appeal Against Refusal of Bail, 28 July 2004, para. 11.

PART II

RULES OF PROCEDURE AND EVIDENCE

Rule 3: Working Language
(amended 7 March 2003)

(A) The working language of the Special Court shall be English.
(B) The accused or suspect shall have the right to use his own language.
(C) Any person appearing before or giving evidence to the Special Court, who does not have sufficient knowledge of English, may ask for permission to use his own language.
(D) The Registrar shall make any necessary arrangements for interpretation and translation.

TRIAL CHAMBERS DECISIONS

- **Rule 3(A): Working Language – Comprehensibility**

R3-TC-1   o *Prosecutor v. Norman*, Case No. SCSL-04-14-T, Decision on Request by the First Accused for Leave to Appeal Against the Trial Chamber's Decision on First Accused's Motion on Abuse of Process, 24 May 2005:

CONSIDERING that the language used by the Court Appointed Counsel in his Motion in many instances is not "comprehensible and considered"[1] and mindful in this regard of the admonishment not to use "exaggerated language", already given by the Appeals Chamber of the Special Court to the Court Appointed Counsel;[2]

---

[1] *See, inter alia*, Motion, para. 10; *see* also Appeals Indictment Decision, para. 48.
[2] Appeals Indictment Decision, para. 48.

APPEALS CHAMBER DECISIONS

- **Rule 3(A): Working Language – Comprehensibility**

R3-AC-1
o *Prosecutor v. Norman, Fofana, Kondewa*, Case No. SCSL-04-14-AR73, Decision on Amendment of the Consolidated Indictment, 16 May 2005, para. 48:

48. We finally note that while submissions to this Court may contain robust criticism of the impugned Decision, they ought not use exaggerated language which could imply deceit rather than error. Rule 3(A) provides that "the working language of the Special Court shall be English". For the English language to work, it must be comprehensible and considered. Part of the Defence Reply dated 14 January 2005 is neither. [...]

> **Rule 4: Sittings Away from the Seat of the Special Court**
> *(amended 7 March 2003)*
>
> A Chamber or a Judge may exercise their functions away from the Seat of the Special Court, if so authorized by the President. In so doing, audio or video-link technology, email or other available electronic instruments may be used if authorised by the President or Presiding Judge.

TRIAL CHAMBERS DECISIONS

- **Rule 4: Sittings Away from the Seat of the Special Court – Decisions Rendered Away from the Seat of the Special Court**

R4-TC-1

o *Prosecutor v. Brima*, Case No. SCSL-04-16-T, Decision on Renewed Defence Motion for Defects in the Form of the Indictment and Application for Extension of Time, 24 May 2005, para. 10-11:

> 10. Further, the Defence questions the validity of the first Decision by contending that the President's Order pursuant to Rule 4 granting Justice Sebutinde authority to exercise her functions away form the seat of the Special Court postdates the first Decision. This very serious allegation impugns the integrity of the Judges and has no factual basis.
>
> 11. The record of filing with the Court Management shows that the Order of the President was filed at 17.00 hours on the 2 March 2005 and that the Decision of the Trial Chamber was filed next day at 10.31 hours which facts were made known to Defence Counsel by way of electronic notification specifying the filing times and dates prior to the filing of the instant motion. To impugn the integrity of the Judges when contrary facts were within the knowledge of Defence Counsel verges on the scandalous.

Rule 5: Non-Compliance with the Rules
(amended 29 May 2004)

Where an objection on the ground of non-compliance with the Rules or Regulations is raised by a party at the earliest opportunity, the Trial Chamber or the Designated Judge may grant relief if the non-compliance has caused material prejudice to the objecting party.

TRIAL CHAMBERS DECISIONS

Rule 5: Non-Compliance with the Rules – Objections to Be Raised "at the Earliest Opportunity"

R5-TC-1

o *Prosecutor v. Brima, Kamara, Kanu*, Case No. SCSL-04-16-T, Decision on the Confidential Joint Defence Motion to Declare Null and Void Testimony-in-Chief of Witness TF1-023, 25 May 2005, para. 8-9, 13:

> 8. The Trial Chamber notes that no exception was taken by Defence Counsel at the time the Trial Chamber ordered a closed session. In fact, Defence Counsel permitted the witness to be examined in chief without objection. At the end of examination in chief, all Defence Counsel evinced an intention to cross-examine but not at that time. They indicated that leave of the Court would be sought at a later date to recall the witness. This Trial Chamber considers and holds that the clear decision on the part of Defence Counsel to permit examination-in-chief to continue and indicate that they would seek leave to cross-examine at a later date knowing they would later apply to have the evidence adduced in closed session declared null and void is not in keeping with the professional standards this Court expects of Counsel in their duty to the Court.
>
> 9. The Trial Chamber adopts the words of the ICTR in the *Prosecutor v. Casimir Bizimungu* that "parties should act diligently and expeditiously whenever there is an alleged violation of the Rules".[1] [. . .]
>
> [. . .]
>
> 13. Rule 5 obliges an objecting party to:
>
> (1) raise the objection at the earliest opportunity and
> (2) show that the non-compliance has caused material prejudice before relief may be granted.

The Defence has not complied with either of these pre-conditions nor have they explained their non-compliance."

⁽¹⁾ *The Prosecutor v. Casimir Bizimungu et al.*, Case No. ICTR-99-50-T, Decision on Prosper Mugiraneza's Motion for Appropriate Relief for Violation of Rule 66(TC), 4 Fenruary 2005, para. 10.

R5-TC-2

o *Prosecutor v. Norman, Fofana, Kondewa*, Case No. SCSL-04-14-T, Decision on Urgent Motion for Reconsideration of the Orders for Compliance with the Order Concerning the Preparation and Presentation of the Defence Case, 7 December 2005, para. 18-19:

18. In addition, the Chamber wishes to stress that when an Order is issued and, in particular, when specific time limits are provided for, a party must comply with such Order. Should any party wish to raise any unexpected issues concerning the non-compliance with an Order, it must do so within the overall purview of the Rules. An objection cannot be considered to constitute a compliance with a clear and specific order of the Chamber.

19. Indeed, a cursory reading of Rule 5 requires a party to raise an objection on the ground of non-compliance at the earliest opportunity.[1] The Defence waited nearly one month before putting forward its objections to the Order of the 21st of October, 2005. Considering the current phase of preparation for the imminent commencement of the Defence case, the Defence is called to exercise diligence in the discharge of its obligations, to act scrupulously and to respect and comply with Orders issued by the Chamber in relation thereto. The Defence position in this regards is manifestly untenable from the perspective of two grounds analogous to the context of the exercise of an equitable jurisdiction, namely (i) that delay defeats equity and (ii) that he who seeks equity must do equity.

⁽¹⁾ See also, more specifically referring to objections on the ground of non-compliance with disclosure obligations, *Prosecutor against Sesay, Kallon and Gbao*, Case No. SCSL-04-15-T, Ruling on an Application for Exclusion of Certain Supplemental Statements of Witness TF1-316 and Witness TF1-122, 1 June 2005, paras 31-32.

APPEALS CHAMBER DECISIONS

Rule 5: Non-Compliance with the Rules – Failure to Raise an Objection "At the Earliest Opportunity"

R5-AC-1

o *Prosecutor v. Norman, Fofana, Kondewa*, Case No. SCSL-04-14-AR73, Decision on Amendment of the Consolidated Indictment, 16 May 2005, para. 65-68:

66. This specific Rule – indexed and headed **Non Compliance with the Rules** – indicates that a party's failure to raise a timely objection to non-compliance may stop it from taking any advantage from a rule breach at a later stage.

67. Courts have inherent powers which they regularly use to excuse failures to comply with their orders and this failure, more technical than most, should have been excused after the tender of a suitable apology, once it was belatedly raised by the Defence. That was the approach of the Trial Chamber majority. In its decisions of 29 November 2004 (Norman) and 8 December 2004 (Fofana and Kondewa) it expressed itself as satisfied after reviewing the entire pre-trial process, that no unfair (or any) prejudice was caused to the Accused by the Prosecution's failure to comply with the terms of the Court Order as to personal service pursuant to Rule 52. Judge Itoe strongly dissented. He thought Rule 52 applied literally and compliance was mandatory. He explained his dissent in these terms:

"It is my considered opinion, and I do so hold, that what law and justice is all about, for us judges, is to uphold and to prevent a breach of the law and to provide a remedy for such a breach if any, and in so doing, to boldly tick right what is right, and when it comes to it, to equally and boldly tick wrong, what is really and in the process, to disabuse our minds of any influence that could misdirect us to tick right, what is ostensibly wrong, or wrong, what is ostensibly right because it would indeed be unfortunate for justice and the due process if, by whatever enticing or justifying rhetoric, or by any means whatsoever, however ostensibly credible or plausible it may seem, we reverse this age-long legal norm and philosophy as this would amount to rocking the very foundation on which our Law and our Justice stand and have, indeed, held onto, and so firmly stood the test of times."[1]

68. We do not think that the breach of a machinery provision in a court order, even if predicated upon a Rule, can be regarded in such hyperbolic terms. Rule 52 was not intended to apply to the situation that had arisen and the object of the court order requiring personal service was achieved by substituted service on Counsel. The clear provision of Rule 5 makes

relief for non-compliance contingent upon the default being raised "at the earliest opportunity" – not six months after it must have become apparent. Insofar as the Defence appeal turns on complaints about the service of the Indictment to Counsel rather than client, they must be rejected."

---

[1] Para. 41 of the Dissenting Opinion

Rule 6: Amendment of the Rules
(amended 29 May 2004)

(A) Proposals for amendment of the Rules may be made by a Judge, the Prosecutor, the Registrar, the Principal Defender and by the Sierra Leone Bar Association or any other entity invited by the President to make proposals for amendments.

(B) Proposals for amendment may be adopted at a Plenary Meeting of the Special Court.

(C) An amendment of the Rules may be adopted otherwise than as stipulated in Sub-Rule (B) above, provided it is approved unanimously by any appropriate means either done in writing or confirmed in writing.

(D) An amendment shall, unless otherwise indicated, enter into force immediately. The Registrar shall publish the amendment by appropriate means.

TRIAL CHAMBERS DECISIONS

- **Rule 6: Amendment of the Rules – Rights of the Accused**

R6-TC-1   o *Prosecutor v. Norman, Fofana, Kondewa*, Case No. SCSL-04-14-PT, Order to the Prosecution to File Disclosure Materials and Other Materials in Preparation of the Commencement of Trial, 1st April 2004:[24]

CONSIDERING that the Trial Chamber seeks to ensure that the rights of the Accused are not infringed, but rather are enhanced, by the amendment of Rule 66 of the Rules;

---

[24] See also *Prosecutor v. Sesay, Kallon, Gbao*, Case No. SCSL-04-15-PT, Order to the Prosecution to File Disclosure Materials and Other Materials in Preparation of the Commencement of Trial, 1st April 2004; *Prosecutor v. Brima, Kamara, Kanu*, Case No. SCSL-04-16-PT, Order to the Prosecution to File Disclosure Materials and Other Materials in Preparation of the Commencement of Trial, 1st April 2004.

- **Rule 6(D): Amendment of the Rules – Entry on Force - Opposability**

R6-TC-2
o *Prosecutor v. Kallon*, Case No. SCSL-03-07-PT, Decision on the Motion for Leave to Appeal Order on the Defence Application for Extension of Time to File Reply to Prosecution Response to the First Preliminary Motion (Lomé Agreement), 29 September 2003, para. 17:

17. In accordance with Rule 6(D) of the Rules, these amendments entered into force immediately. The Chamber, however, finds that, at the time of filing its Motion, the Defence was unaware of these changes in the procedure for both the determination of preliminary motions and for an application for leave to appeal decisions rendered before this Chamber and could not foresee them. However, in fairness for the Accused, the Chamber is of the opinion that in the present case the less stringent test that existed at the time of filing the Motion for the granting of leave to appeal a Chamber decision shall apply to the instant application.

R6-TC-3
o *Prosecutor v. Kallon*, Case No. SCSL-03-07-PT, Decision on the Defence Application for Leave to Appeal 'Decision on the Prosecution's Motion for Immediate Protective Measures for Witnesses and Victims and for Non-Public Disclosure, 10 December 2003, para. 22:

22. In view of the fact that the Application was filed before the new amendment came into force, the Trial Chamber has opted to decide this application on the basis of Rule 73(B) as it was before the above amendment, because it is at this stage, less onerous and more advantageous to the Applicant.

R6-TC-4
o *Prosecutor v. Kanu*, Case No. SCSL-04-16-PT, Decision on Motion for Exclusion of Prosecution Witness Statements and Stay of Filing of Prosecution Statements, 30 July 2004, para. 15:[25]

15. Both Motions were filed shortly after the adoption of the aforementioned amendments, respectively on 18 and 19

---

[25] See also *Prosecutor v. Brima*, Case No. SCSL-04-16-PT, Decision on Motion for Exclusion of Prosecution Witness Statements and Stay of Filing of Prosecution Statements, 2 August 2004, para. 15.

March 2004. Rule 6 of the Rules in this respect provides that an amendment of the Rules becomes effective from the date of its approval.[1] Therefore, the New Rule 66 as amended rather than the Old Rule 66 of the Rules became effective as of 14 March 2004 and was immediately applicable to the Motions pursuant to Rule 6 of the Rules as of that date.

---

[1] In addition, the record of that Plenary Meeting reveals that the Acting Principal Defender was present at the discussion on the proposed amendment to Rule 66 of the Rules.

Rule 7: Time Limits
(amended 1 August 2003)

(A) Unless otherwise ordered by a Chamber or by a Designated Judge, or otherwise provided by the Rules, where the time prescribed by or under the Rules for the doing of any act shall run from the day after the notice of the occurrence of the event has been received in the normal course of transmission by the Registry, counsel for the Accused or the Prosecutor as the case may be.

(B) Where a time limit is expressed in days, only ordinary calendar days shall be counted. Weekdays, Saturdays, Sundays and Public Holiday shall be counted as days. However, should the time limit expire on a Saturday, Sunday or Public Holiday, the time limit shall automatically be extended to the subsequent working day.

(C) Unless otherwise ordered by a Chamber or a Designated Judge, any response to a motion shall be filed within ten days. Any reply to the response shall be filed within five days.

TRIAL CHAMBERS DECISIONS

Rule 7: Time Limits – Notification – Duty to Ensure Ability to Receive Documents

R7-TC-1

o *Prosecutor v. Kamara*, SCSL-03-10-PT, Decision on the Defence Motion for Extension of Time to File Response to Prosecution Motion for Joinder and for Adjournment of Hearing, 1 December 2003, para. 18-21:

18. The Court notes that according to Rule 7(A) of the Rules, "... the time prescribed by or under the Rules for the doing of any act shall run from the day after the notice of the occurrence of the event has been received in the normal course of transmission ...." It is important in the interests of expediency and fairness that the same rules apply to the serving of a document via electronic transmission and in hard copy format. In the opinion of the Chamber, the ordinary rules guiding the reception of documents during office hours are also applicable to the transmission of materials by email. Therefore the time at which a document is deemed to have been received is the time at which it is received in the party's inbox, or equivalent, rather than either the time at which it is sent by the Court Management Section, or the time at which Counsel actually checks that inbox.

19. However, in addition to the existing procedure, it is understood that the Defence Office will now ensure that two members of every defence team are made aware of the existence of a served document if electronic filing is the chosen method of service for Lead Counsel. Assigned Counsel will now be contacted by telephone by a Legal Officer of the Defence Team each day that a document is filed, to ensure that the parties are notified. Thus the time at which Defence teams will be deemed to have received documents is the time at which one of the Defence teams' offices first receives notification. In addition, all Associate Counsel with an email account will be served copies of any documents issued relating to their client's cases.

20. At the time of the serving of the Motion for Joinder in the instant case the Defence Office policy of notifying two members of the Defence team had not been adopted, and thus only one person, Lead Counsel, was served with the Motion for Joinder. The Chamber also considers the fact that the Special Court had not up until this time considered this matter and issued guidance as to the meaning of the term "received" in relation to electronic service. [...]

21. Now that the Special Court has given guidance on the correct procedure, motions brought in the future which raise the same issues will likely be denied. There should be no reason for such matters to arise again given that Associate Counsel will now be contacted. Nevertheless parties will also be expected to make every effort to ensure that they are able to receive documents by email, whether this is done by changing services or by appointing another person to check their accounts.

Rule 7(C): Time Limits – Filing a Response – Inadmissibility of Further "Objections"

R7-TC-2

o *Prosecutor v. Kondewa*, Case No. SCSL-04-14-PT, Order Rejecting the Filing of the Defence Objection to Prosecution's Motion for Judicial Notice and Admission of Facts, 05 May 2004:

HAVING RECEIVED the Objection to Prosecution's Motion for Judicial Notice and Admission of Evidence ("Objection"), filed on 4 May 2004 on behalf of Allieu Kondewa ("Accused");

[...]

CONSIDERING that any response to the Judicial Notice Motion was due on 28 April 2004;

TAKING INTO ACCOUNT the Decision on the Defence Motion requesting an Extension of Time within which to Respond to Prosecution's Motion for Judicial Notice and Admission of Evidence ("Decision") of 30 April 2004, denying an application for extension of time for Counsel for the Accused to prepare a response to the Judicial Notice Motion due to lack of good and sufficient cause or exceptional circumstances;

[...]

FINDING, however, that the Objection contravenes the peremptory disposition of the Decision and should therefore be considered as filed outside the time limits prescribed in Rule 7(C) of the Rules;

HEREBY REJECTS the filing of the Objection;

INVITES Counsel for the Accused to adhere to the principle of *res judicata* in connection with his right to file any response to the Judicial Notice; and

INSTRUCTS the Court Management Section of the Registry to remove the Objection from the official court record of this case.

- **Rule 7(C): Time Limits – Expeditious Consideration of Motion**

R7-TC-3

o *Prosecutor v. Sesay, Kallon, Gbao*, Case No. SCSL-04-15-PT, Order for Expedited Filing, 4 February 2004:[26]

NOTING the request of the Prosecution for the Motion to be dealt with expeditiously;

CONSIDERING that a fair and expeditious consideration of the Motion necessitates the imposition of an expedited timetable for the filing of any remaining written submissions;

PURSUANT to rule 7(C) of the Rules;

HEREBY ORDERS as follows:

1. Any Defence response to the Motion shall be filed within 5 days from the service of the present Order;
2. Any Prosecution reply to a response shall be filed within 3 days from the service thereof;

---

[26] See also *Prosecutor v. Brima, Kamara, Kanu*, Case No. SCSL-04-16-PT, Order for Expedited Filing, 4 February 2004; *Prosecutor v. Sesay, Kallon, Gbao*, Case No. SCSL-04-15-PT, Order for Expedited Filing, 17 May 2004; *Prosecution v. Gbao*, Case No. SCSL-04-15-T, Order for Expedited Filing, 13 July 2004.

DIGEST OF JURISPRUDENCE OF THE SPECIAL COURT FOR SIERRA LEONE 181

R7-TC-4

o *Prosecutor v. Norman*, Case No. SCSL-04-14-PT, Interim Order and Scheduling Order, 2 April 2004:[27]

RECOGNIZING the urgency of the matter;

CONSIDERING that I am seized of the Motion and a decision thereon is still pending;

CONSIDERING that the right of the Accused to a fair and expeditious consideration of the Motion requires the imposition of an expedited timetable for the filing of any remaining written submissions;

PURSUANT TO Rule 7(C) and Rule 54 of the Rules;

[...]

FURTHER ORDER that the Motion will be determined on an *inter partes* basis, limited to the Prosecution and the Accused; and, for this purpose

ALSO ORDER that:

1. Any response from the Defence Counsel for the Accused to the Motion shall be filed by 04.00 pm on Monday, 5 April 2004, if any;
2. Any Prosecution reply to a response shall be filed by 04.00 pm on Wednesday, 7 April 2004, if any; and
3. Oral representations in support of the parties written submissions will be heard at an in camera hearing to be held in Chambers before me on Thursday, 8 April 2004 at 10.00 am.

CONSEQUENTLY INSTRUCT the Registry and, in particular, the Court Management Section, to facilitate the execution of the Orders above.

R7-TC-5

o *Prosecutor v. Norman, Fofana, Kondewa*, Case No. SCSL-04-14-PT, Order for Filing of a Consolidated Reply, 13 May 2004:[28]

CONSIDERING the need for the Motion to be dealt with expeditiously;

---

[27] See also *Prosecutor v. Kallon*, Case No. SCSL-04-15-PT, Scheduling Order for *In Camera* Hearing, 23 April 2004; *Prosecutor v. Sesay, Kallon, Gbao*, Case No. SCSL-04-15-PT, Order for Expedited Filing, 30 April 2004.

[28] See also *Prosecutor v. Sesay, Kallon, Gbao*, Case No. SCSL-04-15-PT, Order for the Filing of a Consolidated Reply, 13 May 2004.

PURSUANT to Rule 7(C) and Rule 54 of the Rules of Procedure and Evidence;

ORDER that any Prosecution reply shall be filed in a single and consolidated form, of no more than 15 pages in length, on or before Tuesday, 18 May 2004 and such reply, if any, shall be filed before 4.00 p.m.

> **Rule 7*bis*: Motions for Extension of Time**
> *(adopted 14 May 2005)*
>
> Any response to a motion for extension of time shall be filed within three days of the receipt of the motion. Any reply to the response shall be filed within two days of the receipt of the response. However, a motion for an extension of time may be disposed of without giving the other party the opportunity to respond if a Judge or Chamber is of the opinion that no prejudice will be caused to the other party.

TRIAL CHAMBERS DECISIONS

- **Rule 7*bis*: Motions for Extension of Time – Applicable Criteria**

R7*bis*-TC-1
  o *Prosecutor v. Kallon*, Case No. SCSL-03-07-PT, Decision on the Defence Motion for Extension of Time to File Preliminary Motions, 14 June 2003, para. 8-9:[29]

  8. [...] It is clear from a plain reading of Rule 7 that it is descriptive only as to time limits and does not provide authority for time extension.

  9. [...] Although not specifically stated under this Rule, the Chamber is disposed to adopt the "good cause" criteria for determining the merits of such motions [for extension of time] under Rule 73 while maintaining and ensuring that the proceedings would be fair and expeditious.

R7*bis*-TC-2
  o *Prosecutor v. Kamara*, Case No. SCSL-03-10-PT, Order on the Request by the Defence Office for Suspension of Consideration of Prosecution's Motion for Protective Measures Until Counsel Is Assigned, 26 June 2003, para. 7:

  7. Pursuant to Rule 7(C) of the Rules, the time limit for a response to a motion expires seven days from the moment of receipt of

---

[29] See also *Prosecutor v. Kallon*, Case No. SCSL-03-07-PT, Order on the Defence Application for Extension of Time to File Reply to Prosecution Response to Preliminary Motion, 24 June 2003; *Prosecutor v. Norman*, Case No. SCSL-03-08-PT, Order on the Prosecution Application for an Extension of Time to Respond to Four Defence Motions as to Jurisdiction, 03 July 2003; *Prosecutor v. Sesay*, SCSL-03-05-PT, Decision no the Defence Motion Requesting the Suspension of delays for Filing Preliminary Motions or New Request for an Extension of Delays, 7 November 2003, para. 22.

the motion. The Trial Chamber may order for an extension or abbreviation of time. Such an extension of time may however only be granted in exceptional circumstances or due to good cause being shown.

R7*bis*-TC-3
o *Prosecutor v. Kallon*, Case No. SCSL-03-07-PT, Decision on the Defence Application for Extension of Time to File Reply to Prosecution Response to the First Defence Preliminary Motion (Lomé Agreement), 16 July 2003, para. 11:

11. Pursuant to Rule 7 of the Rules it remains at the discretion of the Chamber to modify the time limits for responses and replies without particular requirements. The Trial Chamber, however, previously decided that such modification, namely an extension or an abbreviation, should be granted in exceptional circumstances and for good cause.

R7*bis*-TC-4
o *Prosecutor v. Kondewa*, SCSL-04-14-PT, Decision on Defence Motion Requesting an Extension of Time Within Which to Respond to Prosecution's Motion for Judicial Notice and Admission of Evidence, 30 April 2004:

FINDING, however, that in the present circumstances there does not exist good and sufficient cause or exceptional circumstances to grant an extension of time to prepare a response to the Judicial Notice Motion;

HEREBY DENY the request and dismiss the Motion.

- **Rule *7bis*: Motions for Extension of Time – "Good Cause" Criterion**

R7*bis*-TC-5
o *Prosecutor v. Kamara*, Case No. SCSL-03-10-PT, Order on the Request by the Defence Office for Suspension of Consideration of Prosecution's Motion for Protective Measures Until Counsel Is Assigned, 26 June 2003, para. 8:

8. In the current case the newly assigned Defence Counsel has not yet been served with the Prosecutions Motion on Protective Measures due to technical difficulties. This situation may be considered as exceptional circumstances and consequently in order to ensure that the Accused is able to properly prepare his defence and more specifically respond to the current motion, it is in the interest of justice that an extension of time be granted.

R7bis-TC-6

o *Prosecutor v. Sesay,* Case No. SCSL-03-05-PT, Order on the Defence Motion Requesting that the Time Limit to Respond to the Motion Filed by the Prosecution for a Joinder to Commence Upon Receipt of the Modified or Particularised Indictment(s) or on a Date Set by the Trial Chamber, 12 November 2003:

CONSIDERING the Defence Request that the deadline for a response to the Joinder Motion be set for 10 days after the Prosecution comply with the Decision, on the basis that the Defence is otherwise unable to consider properly whether or not a joinder is in the interests of justice;

CONSIDERING the Prosecution Response that it is not necessary for Defence Counsel to see the Bill of Particulars or the amended indictment in order to respond to the Joinder Motion, and thus that the Defence have not shown "good cause or exceptional circumstances" as is necessary to be granted an extension of time;

[. . .]

CONSCIOUS of the importance of the Joinder Motion and the fact that it would have considerable impact and consequences on the conduct of the Prosecution and the Defence in the matters;

IN THE INTERESTS OF fairness, equity and an expeditious determination of the Joinder Motion;

CONSIDERING that the Defence has, in the light of the above, demonstrated and shown good cause to justify the granting of the application for extension of time;

R7bis-TC-7

o *Prosecutor v. Kallon,* SCSL-04-15-PT, Decision on the Defence Motion for Extension of Time to File Response to the Prosecution Motion for Judicial Notice and Admission of Evidence, 26 April 2004:

NOTING, in particular, that the Motion seeks extension of time to file a response to the Judicial Notice Motion on the basis that neither Counsel for the Accused nor the Defence Office are currently in possession of relevant materials ("Materials") pertaining to the case against the Accused, such Materials being still in possession of the Previous Counsel;[1]

[. . .]

HAVING ALSO HEARD the submissions of the Principal Defender as to the reasons for the questionable delay in the transfer of the Materials from the Previous Counsel to the Defence Office;

WHEREAS the Principal Defender submitted that the Previous Counsel has now specifically undertaken to send the Materials by means of express courier and said Materials will be at the disposal of the new Counsel on Saturday 1 May 2004;

[...]

MINDFUL of the rights of the Accused, and in particular of the provisions of Article 17 of the Statute of the Special Court on the right to have adequate time and facilities for the preparation of his defence;

CONCERNED with the conduct of the Previous Counsel with respect to the prompt fulfilment of his duty to return the Materials in compliance with the Directive following the Withdrawal Decision and the compliance with this Court's orders about protective measures;[2]

FINDING that in the present circumstances there exists good and sufficient cause and exceptional circum-stances to grant, in the interest of justice, an extension of time to prepare a response, if any, to the Judicial Notice Motion;

---

[1] Motion, paras 8 and 32.
[2] *Prosecutor v. Morris Kallon*, SCSL-03-07-PT, Decision on the Prosecutor's Motion for Immediate Protective Measures for Witnesses and Victims and for Non-Public Disclosure, 23 May 2003; *id.*, Annex to the Decision on the Prosecutor's Motion for Immediate Protective Measures for Witnesses and Victims and for Non-Public Disclosure: Orders for Immediate Protective Measures for Witnesses and Victims and for Non-Public Disclosure.

R7bis-TC-8

o *Prosecutor v. Gbao*, Case No. SCSL-04-15-PT, Decision on Defence Urgent Request for Extension of Time to Respond the Prosecution's Motion to Hear Evidence Concurrently, 5 May 2004:

CONSIDERING that the Motion requests an extension of time to respond to the Motion for Concurrent Evidence on the basis of the absence of members of the defence team for the Accused;[1]

MINDFUL of the rights of the Accused, and in particular of the provisions of Article 17 of the Statute of the Special Court on the right to have adequate time and facilities for the preparation of his defence;

CONSIDERING that the Motion, filed on 4 May 2004, requests extension of time to respond to the Motion for Concurrent Evidence until 10 April 2004;[2]

FINDING that such extension of time renders the Motion ambiguous and impossible to accede to, and therefore requires its dismissal as inadmissible there being no clear indication of the precise time extension sought;

FINDING FURTHER that in the present circumstances there does not exist good and sufficient cause or exceptional circumstances to grant such an extension of time to prepare a response to the Motion for Concurring Evidence;

---

[1] Motion, paras 4-5.
[2] *Id.*, para. 1. In addition, the Motion contains other ambiguous references to April 2004. See *id.*, paras 5-6.

- **Rule *7bis*: Motions for Extension of Time – Time of the Application**

R7*bis*-TC-9   o *Prosecutor v. Norman*, Case No. SCSL-03-08-PT, Order on Defence Request for Extension of Time Within Which to File Reply to the Prosecution Response to Defence Preliminary Motion, 17 September 2003:

CONSIDERING that, in its Request, the Defence, having however already filed its replies to the Prosecution Responses to the Four Preliminary Motions outside the prescribed time limits, applied for an extension of time to file such replies on the grounds that the Defence Counsel was ill;

CONSIDERING that the Chamber is of the opinion that such application should be interpreted as an application to grant leave to the late filing of the same Replies rather than a request of extension of time, having the Replies already been filed at the time the Defence Request has been filed;

[...]

CONSIDERING that the Chamber finds that the Defence Request is supported by good cause and, furthermore, **CONSIDERING** that the Chamber is satisfied of the parties' agreement on the extension of time to file such Replies;

[...]

ALLOWS the late filing of the Replies [...].

R7bis-TC-10

o *Prosecutor v. Kondewa*, SCSL-03-12-PT, Decision on the Urgent Defence Application for Release from Provisional Detention, 21 November 2003, para. 19-20:[30]

19. The Chamber takes notice of the Office of the Prosecutor's letter to the Trial Chamber, dated the 26th day of June 2003, whereby Luc Côté, Chief of Prosecutions, explained why the Response was only served to the Defence on the 20th day of June 2003, instead of the 19th day of June, according to the deadline requirements provided for in Rule 7 of the Rules.

20. The Chamber finds this explanation acceptable.

- **Rule *7bis*: Motions for Extension of Time – Lack of Legal Basis**

R7bis-TC-11

o *Prosecutor v. Brima*, Case No. SCSL-04-16-T, Decision on Renewed Defence Motion for Defects in the Form of the Indictment and Application for Extension of Time, 24 May 2005, para. 5-9:

5. Counsel for the Accused Brima filed a Defence Motion for Defects in the Form of the Indictment on 1 March 2005. The Motion was a preliminary motion and therefore should have been filed at the very latest, by the 27 May 2004, which was the last day of the ten-day period allowed by Rule 50 (B) (iii). Notwithstanding this, the Motion did not seek an extension of time.

6. The Trial Chamber, in its decision of the 2 March 2005, found that the Motion was clearly out of time and dismissed it.

7. The present Renewed Defence Motion for Defects in the Form of the Indictment and Application for Extension of Time (if Applicable), seeks exactly the same relief as the previous motion. Counsel for the Accused Brima has not referred us to any statutory provision, nor to any jurisprudence, which would support the view that we have jurisdiction to review our own previous decision.

8. A motion such as the present one is not provided for in the Rules of Procedure and Evidence and does not form part of the procedures of the Trial Chamber.

9. Accordingly, we find that the Trial Chamber does not

---

[30] See also *Prosecutor v. Fofana*, SCSL-03-11-PT, Decision on the Urgent Defence Application for Release from Provisional detention, 21 November 2003.

have jurisdiction to entertain the Motion. In the result, there is no need for us to consider the merits of the Motion.

- **Rule *7bis*: Motions for Extension of Time – Appeal – "Exceptional Circumstances or Good Cause"**

R7*bis*-TC-12
  o *Prosecutor v. Brima*, Case No. SCSL-03-06-PT, Decision on the Application for Extension of Time for Leave to Be Granted to File Defence Motion to Appeal Against the Decision Refusing an Application for the Issue of the Writ of *Habeas Corpus*, 16 October 2003, para. 16-17:

  16. The Rules do not specify a test that should be applied when considering the granting of extensions of time. Nevertheless, jurisprudence from the Special Court has already indicated guidance on this matter. In *Prosecutor v. Kallon*, SCSL-2003-07[1], the Trial Chamber noted that extensions of time should only be granted upon the showing of "exceptional circumstances or good cause." Although the present case involves an extension of time for leave to appeal rather than extension of time to file reply, the test seems to offer appropriate and helpful guidance. The Chamber will use this test in order to rule on the current Request.

  17. The Chamber notes that in the above case, the Trial Chamber held that "exceptional circumstances may exist when the circumstances rest outside of the parties' power or control". This gives helpful direction on the way in which the test should be interpreted, and will be considered in assessing whether or not the Request fulfils the test."

  [1] 'Order on the Defence Application for Extention of Time to file Reply to Prosecution Response to Preliminary Motions', of the 24th day of June 2003

- **Rule *7bis*: Motions for Extension of Time – Materiality of the Subject**

R7*bis*-TC-13
  o *Prosecutor v. Gbao*, Case No. SCSL-03-09-I, Order on the Urgent Request for Direction on the Time to Respond to and/or an Extension of Time for the Filing of a Response to the Prosecution Motions and the Suspension of Any Ruling on the Issue of Protective Measures That May Be Pending Before Other Proceedings Before the Special Court as a Result of Similar Motions Filed to Those that Have Been Filed by the Prosecution in this Case, 16 May 2003:

NOTING that pursuant to Rule 7 of the Rules the time-limits for filing a response to the Prosecution Motions has expired;

CONSIDERING that the subject of the Prosecution Motions, and with particular reference to the protective measures for witnesses and victims, albeit of extreme importance, is a common and accepted procedure in international criminal law;

DUE to the materiality of this subject of the Motions to future trial proceedings, the Special Court pursuant to its authority under Rule 7(A) of the Rules may order an extension of a time limit;

CAUTIONING that the Special Court will not allow any further delays in the future and that, in particular, an extension of a time limit remains exceptional;

- **Rule 7*bis*: Motions for Extension of Time – Repetitive Applications**

R7*bis*-TC-14   o *Prosecutor v. Brima*, Case No. SCSL-03-06-PT, Decision on the application for Extension of Time for Leave to Be Granted to File Defence Motion to Appeal Against the Decision Refusing an Application for the Issue of the Writ of *Habeas Corpus*, 16 October 2003, para. 21:[31]

21. Counsel for the Accused contends in the Reply that although he has submitted other applications for extension of time in the past, this should have no bearing upon the current Request, and that it is a question to be decided before the Appeals Chamber on another occasion. In the Chamber's opinion this is not the case. The Chamber considers that it is indeed relevant that Counsel for the Defence has requested extensions of time before and that it is a pertinent factor for the Chamber to take into consideration at the present time.

- **Rule 7*bis*: Motions for Extension of Time – Time Limit to Raise Objections under Rule 92*bis***

R7*bis*-TC-15   o *Prosecutor v. Sesay, Kallon, Gbao*, Case No. SCSL-04-15-T, Order for Extension of Time to Respond the Prosecution Confidential Notice Under 92*bis* to Admit Transcripts of

---

[31] See also *Prosecutor v. Kallon*, Case No. SCSL-03-07-PT, Order on the Defence Further Application for Extension of Time to File Preliminary Motions, 8 July 2003.

Testimony of TF1-023, TF1-104 and TF1-169, 27 October 2005:

CONSIDERING that the Application requests an extension of time to respond to the Prosecution Notice on the basis that the Defence Counsel will be travelling to Freetown during this period, the volume of material in question, the lack of notice prior to the start of the trial session and the fundamental nature of the issues raised;[1]

MINDFUL of the rights of the Accused, and in particular of the provisions of article 17 of the Statute of the Special Court for Sierra Leone on the right to have adequate time and facilities for the preparation of his defence;

CONSIDERING that the Application requests an extension of time for an additional seven days until the 7th of November 2005 or until the Trial Chambers considers appropriate;[2]

CONSIDERING that the Prosecution does not object to such extension of time;

FINDING that the request for an extension of time is reasonable given the particular circumstances of this Notice;

SATISFIED that an extension of time for the Defence to file its objection until Thursday, the 3rd of November 2005 will provide the Defence with adequate time to properly respond to the Prosecution Notice and be in the interests of justice.

APPEALS CHAMBER DECISIONS

- **Rule 7*bis*: Motions for Extension of Time – Time Limits for Filing – Reasons of Delay**

R7*bis*-AC-1   o *Prosecutor v. Norman, Fofana, Kondewa*, Case No. SCSL-04-14-A, Decision and Order on Prosecution Request for an Extension of Time, 12 November 2004:

EMPHASISING that ordinarily applications for variation of time limits should be filed before the expiration of the time limit sought to be extended and that all Parties have an obligation to comply with the requirements laid down in the Practice Direction;

DECIDE that, acting pursuant to paragraph 20 of the Practice Direction, the Prosecution Request is granted. The one day delay in filing the Prosecution Response has been satisfactorily explained, the reasons for the delay being miscalculation of time and application of a wrong rule. This not being a case

in which a party simply ignored the Rules and went to sleep, and the delay being for just one day, it is proper in the interest of justice to exercise a discretion to extend time to file the Prosecution Response. No prejudice will thereby be occasioned to the Defence. In the result, the time within which the Prosecution Response should have been filed is extended until the date of the filing of the Prosecution Response on 5 November 2004 [. . .]

Rule 8: Requests and Orders
(amended 1 August 2003)

(A) The Government of Sierra Leone shall cooperate with all organs of the Special Court at all stages of the proceedings. Requests by any organ of the Special Court shall be complied with in accordance with Article 17 of the Agreement. An order issued by a Chamber or by a Judge shall have the same force or effect as if issued by a Judge, Magistrate or Justice of the Peace of a Sierra Leone court.

(B) Except in cases to which Rule 11, 13, 59 or 60 applies, where a Chamber or a Judge is satisfied that the Government of Sierra Leone has failed to comply with a request made in relation to any proceedings before that Chamber or Judge, the Chamber or Judge may refer the matter to the President to take appropriate action.

(C) The Special Court may invite third States not party to the Agreement to provide assistance on the basis of an ad hoc arrangement, an agreement with such State or any other appropriate basis.

(D) Where a third State, which has entered into an ad hoc arrangement or an agreement with the Special Court, fails to cooperate with requests pursuant to any such arrangement or agreement, the President may take appropriate action.

(E) Where it appears to the Prosecutor that a crime within the jurisdiction of the Special Court is or has been the subject of investigations or criminal proceedings instituted in the courts of any State, he may request the State to forward to him all relevant information in that respect. The Government of Sierra Leone shall transmit to him such information forthwith in accordance with Article 17 of the Agreement.

TRIAL CHAMBERS DECISIONS

- **Rule 8(A): Requests and Orders – Assistance Between the Government of Sierra Leone and the Special Court**

  R8-TC-1 o *Prosecutor v. Norman*, Case No. SCSL-04-14-PT, Decision on Inter Partes Motion by Prosecution to Freeze the Account of the Accused Sam Hinga Norman at Union Trust Bank (SL) Limited or at Any Other Bank in Sierra Leone, 19 April 2004:

NOTING that Part IV of The Special Court Agreement 2002, (Ratification) Act, 2002 provides for mutual assistance between Sierra Leone and the Special Court, and that Section 15(3)(a) of the said Act enacts that "nothing in this Act shall limit the type of assistance the Special Court may request under the Agreement" signed between the Government of Sierra Leone and the United Nations on 16 January 2002;

NOTING FURTHER that Section 20 of the aforesaid Act provides that "for the purpose of execution, an Order of the Special Court shall have the same force or effect as if it had been issued by a Judge, Magistrate, or Justice of the Peace of a Sierra Leonean Court";

PRE-EMINENTLY RECOGNISING that such framework for mutual assistance between the Government of Sierra Leone and the Special Court is predicated upon the paramount need to ensure that the justice process at all times adheres to the principle of *legality* and not the principle of *diplomacy*; and that no Order made pursuant thereto should infringe the said principle of *legality* in the context of the applicable jurisprudence;

R8-TC-2

o *Prosecutor v. Kanu*, Case No. SCSL-04-16-PT, Decision on Defence Motion in Respect of Santigie Borbor Kanu for an Order under Rule 54 with Respect to release of Exculpatory Evidence, 1st June 2004, para. 27-30:

27. First, the Special Court lacks legal authority to apply any enforcement measures against the State of Sierra Leone, there being no express statutory authority in the founding instruments of the Court for that purpose, nor can it be asserted that the Court's inherent jurisdiction includes such power. Any other view of the law on this theme would amount to a disregard for or encroachment upon, the entrenched doctrine of state sovereignty.

28. Second, predicated upon its founding instruments, the Special Court, not being endowed with enforcement agents of its own, must depend and rely upon the co-operation of the sovereign State of Sierra Leone in order to prosecute persons alleged to bear the greatest responsibility for serious violations of international humanitarian law during the hostilities which took place during the rebel war. In essence, under the statutory co-operation scheme, there devolves upon the State of Sierra Leone an international contractual obligation, which is treaty-based, to assist the Special Court effectively investigate crimes, collect evidence, summon witnesses and have indictees arrested and delivered to the Special Court.

29. Third, as emphasized in *Blaskic* in respect of Article 29 of the ICTY Statute, the power granted to the ICTY to issue orders to sovereign States is exceptional and novel, one not hitherto recognised under customary international law. To the same extent, analogically, does Article 17 of the Special Court's Statute create the unique power authorising the Special Court to issue orders to the sovereign State of Sierra Leone. It follows, therefore, that the contractual obligation created under the bilateral arrangement between the United Nations and the Government of sierra Leone specifically applies to cases where the State of Sierra Leone is required to produce documents in possession of its officials.

30. In addition to the above key principles undergirding the statutory framework for co-operation between the Court and the State of Sierra Leone articulated in paragraphs 25-29, it is now necessary to stipulate for the purposes of applications of this nature seeking orders for the implementation of article 17, that for such applications to succeed, the applicant must fulfil the criteria laid down in the *Blaskic* Judgement.

Rule 15: Disqualification of Judges
(amended 29 May 2004)

(A) A Judge may not sit at a trial or appeal in any case in which his impartiality might reasonably be doubted on any substantial ground.

(B) Any party may apply to the Chamber of which the Judge is a member for the disqualification of the said Judge on the above ground.

C) Where the Judge voluntarily withdraws from the Trial Chamber, the President may assign the alternate judge, in accordance with Article 12(4) of the Statute, or another Trial Chamber Judge to sit in his place. Where a judge voluntarily withdraws from the Appeals Chamber, the Alternate Judge may sit in his place.

(D) Where it is alleged that a Judge is not fit to sit as member of the Special Court, the matter shall be referred from the Chamber to the Council of Judges.

(E) Should the Council of Judges determine that:

(i) the allegations contained in the application appear to be of a serious nature, and

(ii) there appears to be a *prima facie* basis for such application, it shall refer the matter to the Plenary Meeting which will consider it and make a recommendation to the body which appointed the Judge, if required.

(F) At each stage, the challenged Judge shall be entitled to present his comments on the matter, but shall not take part in the deliberations and in the decision thereof.

(G) The Judge who approves an indictment or who is involved with any pre-trial or interlocutory matter against a suspect or accused, shall not for that reason be disqualified from sitting as a member of a Chamber for the trial or appeal of that accused.

APPEALS CHAMBER DECISIONS

- **Rule 15(B): Disqualification of Judges – Apprehension of Bias**

R15-AC-1

o *Prosecutor v. Sesay*, Case No. SCSL-04-15-A, Decision on Defence Motion Seeking the Disqualification of Justice Robertson from the Appeals Chamber, 13 March 2004, para. 2, 15-18:

2. The Defence submits that the matters which constitute the core of the Motion for disqualification are contained within a book entitled *Crimes Against Humanity – The Struggle for Global Justice* that he published in 2002.[1] The Defence contention is that Justice Robertson's opinions, comments and statements are expressed in terms that demonstrate the clearest and most grave bias, or in the alternative, the same objectively give rise to the appearance of bias. The Defence submits that the Judge pursuant to Rule 15(A) of the Rules of Procedure and Evidence of the Special Court ("the Rules") must withdraw from the Appeals Chamber forthwith and permanently. If Justice Robertson does not withdraw, then pursuant to Rule 15(B) of the Rules the remaining members of the Appeals Chamber must submit, disqualify him from the Appeals Chamber. The Motion quotes the following extracts from the book:

(i) Chapter – "An End to Impunity"

"Those who order atrocities believe at the time that their power will always enable them to bargain with any new government to let bygones be bygones, and history since Nuremburg has tended to prove them correct – *most bizarrely in Sierra Leone, when by the Lome agreement in July 1999 the UN not only amnestied Foday Sankoh, the nation's butcher, but rewarded his pathological brutality by making him deputy leader of the government and giving him control of the diamond mines*".[2]

(ii) Chapter – "Slouching Towards Nemesis"

"... *so amnesties given to perpetrators of such deeds (genocide and torture by frightened or blackmailed government) cannot be upheld by international law, even when agreed by international diplomats. For this reason, the UN was justified in reinterpreting the amnesty given to the despicable Foday Sankoh: it pardoned him only for crimes committed under Sierra Leone law, not international law*".[3]

(iii) Chapter – "Lessons from Sierra Leone"

"The Lome Peace Agreement, brokered by the UN, with UK and US support, purchased peace at a most extraordinary price. The democratically elected government was forced to share power with rebels who were pardoned for the most grotesque crimes against humanity, and their leader, liberated from prison, was made Deputy Prime Minister in charge of the nation's diamond resources, the very object of his ruthless campaign. As it happened, not even his capitulation could satisfy Foday Sankoh: his renewed attacks on a ragtag army of UN peacekeepers obliged the former colonial power, Great Britain to return in force, much to the relief of the populace. The case of Sierra Leone provides object lessons in (inter alia) ... The impossibility of UN peacekeepers maintaining neutrality in a civil war where one side is given to committing such crimes ... "[4]

"Styled the Revolutionary United Front (RUF) it recruited gangs of violent, dispossessed youths and armed them with AK47s for their missions of pillage, rape and diamond – heisting. The RUF had no political agenda: its sponsor was Charles Taylor, Liberia's vicious warlord. But when, in 1995, the RUF threatened to attack Sierra Leone's capital Freetown, the military government paid a South African mercenary force, Executive Outcomes, to protect the city and re-train the government army. They did well enough for elections to be held again in 1996, which returned Ahmed Kabbah, a former UN official. By this time, the RUF had perfected its special contribution to the chambers of horrors: the practice of 'chopping' the limbs of inccoent civilians. It was a means of spreading terror, especially slogan, "Don't vote or don't write", came true for thousands of citizens, forced to lay their right hand on RUF chopping – blocks after they had chosen to vote. Mutilation worked, as a means of terrifying the population, and so the RUF devised more devilish tortures, such as lopping off a leg as well as an arm, sewing up vaginas with fishing lines, and padlocking mouths. Given their level of barbarism, how could Sankoh and the RUF leadership ever have been invited by Western diplomats to share power"[5]

"Jackson chummed up with Charles Taylor and expressed admiration for the imprisoned Foday Sankoh, likening him to Nelson Mandela (who was not a psychopath given to mutilating civilians). Jackson's ignorance and moral blindness does not excuse the Western and UN diplomats who agreed to release Sankoh from prison, bestow upon him an apparently valid amnesty, and hand him the only prize in Sierra Leone worth having – control of the diamond mines.[6]

> *"The RUF, programmed to kill and pillage and mutilate, continue, continued to do so after Lome, so the UN sent in another 'peacekeeping' mission..."*[7]
>
> *"So much for hindsight: a warring faction... [referring to the RUF]... guilty of atrocities on a scale that amounts to a crime against humanity must never again be forgiven sufficiently to be accorded a slice of power: on the contrary, its leaders deserve to be captured and put on trial".*[8]

15. [...] The crucial and decisive question is whether an independent bystander so to speak, or the reasonable man, reading those passages will have a legitimate reason to fear that Justice Robertson lacks impartiality. In other words, whether one can apprehend bias. I have no doubt that a reasonable man will apprehend bias, let alone an accused person and I so hold.

16. As Lord Hewart C.J. said in *R v. Sussex Justices, Ex parte McCarthy*: "Justice must not only be done, but should manifestly and undoubtedly be seen to be done".[9] On this sacred and overriding principle I accept the submission that Judges must be above suspicion of bias and the presumption of innocence must be respected at all times until guilt is proved.

17. It only now remains for me to deal with Rule 15(E) and I say without hesitation that it does not apply in this case. In this context I agree with Justice Robertson when he says in effect that Rule 15(E) applies only to those cases where a judge is "palpably unfit – e.g. through ill health or criminal conviction". In that circumstance the other Judges of the Chamber may not force his resignation, but may only refer the matter to the Council of Judges which in the words of the Rule "will consider the matter and make a recommendation to the body which appointed the Judge, if required".

18. It follows from all I have said that I find some merit in the application to this extent: that Justice Robertson ought to be disqualified from adjudicating on the following matters:

(i) those motions involving alleged members of the RUF for which decisions are pending, in this Chamber; and
(ii) Cases involving the RUF if and when they come before the Appeals Chamber.

AND SO I ORDER.

---

[1] Geoffrey Robertson, Crimes Against Humanity – the Struggle for Global Justice (The New Press, 2002) ("Crimes Against Humanity").
[2] Crimes Against Humanity, page 220.
[3] Ibid., page 277.
[4] Ibid., pages 465-466
[5] Ibid., page 466.
[6] Ibid., page 467.

⁽⁷⁾ Ibid., pages 467-468.
⁽⁸⁾ Ibid., page 469.
⁽⁹⁾ Rev v. Sussex Justices, Ex parte McCarthy (1923) 1 K.B. 256 at page 259.

o *Prosecutor v. Norman*, Decision on the Motion to Recuse Judge Winter from the Deliberation in the Preliminary Motion on the Recruitment of Child Soldiers, 28 May 2004, para. 22-23, 25-31:

> 22. [...] In its Decision on the Disqualification of Justice Robertson in the case of *Sesay*,[1] this Chamber held that the applicable test for determining applications made under Rule 15(B) is whether an independent bystander or reasonable person will have a legitimate reason to fear that the judge in question lacks impartiality, "in other words, whether one can apprehend bias".[2]
>
> 23. This is consistent with the ICTY jurisprudence, in particular the test derived from the Judgement in the case of *Furundzija* as set out as follows:
>
>> [t]he Appeals Chamber finds that there is a general rule that a Judge should not only be subjectively free from bias, but also that there should be nothing in the surrounding circumstances which objectively gives rise to an appearance of bias. On this basis, the Appeals Chamber considers that the following principles should direct it in interpreting and applying the impartiality requirement of the Statute:
>>
>> A. A Judge is not impartial if it is shown that actual bias exists.
>>
>> B. There is an unacceptable appearance of bias if:
>>
>> i) a Judge is a party to the case, or has a financial or proprietary interest in the outcome of a case, or if the Judge's decision will lead to the promotion of a cause in which he or she is involved, together with one of the parties. Under these circumstances, a Judge's disqualification from the case is automatic; or
>>
>> ii) the circumstances would lead a reasonable observer, properly informed, to reasonably apprehend bias."[3]
>
> The focus is therefore on "an unacceptable appearance of bias". While the first category leads to automatic disqualification, the more difficult area is where the Judge is neither a party to the case nor has an improper interest in the outcome of the decision. In this case, we come back to the objective test of whether there is a reasonable appre-

hension of bias. This test has since been widely applied, in such cases as *Celebici*,[4] *Krajisnik*[5] and *Seselj*.[6] Most recently, the Bureau of the ICTR confirmed this Chamber's characterization of this standard in its decision in the case of *Karemera*.[7]

[...]

25. [...] [T]here is a general rule that judges should not only be subjectively free from bias but that there should be nothing in the surrounding circumstances which objectively gives rise to an appearance of bias. However, it should be emphasised that the starting point for any determination of such claim – as noted by the Prosecution – is that "there is a presumption of impartiality which attaches to a Judge."[8] This presumption derives from their oath of office and the qualifications for their appointment in Article 13 of the Statute, and places a high burden on the party moving for the disqualification to displace that presumption.[9]

26. As observed by the Prosecution, while it is not uncommon for authors of publications to submit their drafts for experts for their comments and suggestions and to acknowledge their assistance, the views expressed in the publication remains those of the author and cannot be attributed to the person who reviewed the draft. There is no material to suggest that Judge Winter *approved* the draft. She was one of over 50 persons who reviewed the draft and who supported the drafting process.

27. The "hypothetical fair-minded observer", as articulated in the *Krajisnik* decision, is by implication someone from the outside, who, as an *observer* (and not a party) recognises and understands the circumstances well enough to tell whether or not the public sense of Justice would be challenged by the presence of a particular Judge on the bench in the case.[10] Applying this standard, in relation to (a), I am therefore unable to agree with the Defence suggestion that on the above facts a reasonable observer properly informed of the professional practice of reviewing publications would reasonably apprehend bias.

28. In relation to (b), as the Prosecution points out, the February 2002 publication relates to a project undertaken by the Iran Country Office of UNICEF that involved a study tour to Austria where Justice Winter is a Judge. A party challenging the judge's impartiality must demonstrate that the judge entertains a personal interest in, or a particular concern for, any other parties. While it is not necessary that such an interest be of a financial or pecuniary nature, it must be that the judge in question "is so closely associated [...] that he can properly be said to have an interest in the out-come of the proceedings".[11] Such a personal interest or particular

concern is different from a professional interest in the subject matter of the case.[12] The fact that there may be some history of professional association, however limited, is not alone sufficient to meet the required threshold.

29. Similarly, in relation to (c), teaching in an international Masters programme – as with reviewing a report – does not in and of itself show or even suggest an appearance of bias. On the material before the Chamber, there are no details provided of the nature of Justice Winter's involvement in the Freiburg Masters Programme, and to consider this point further would be purely speculative.

30. On the contrary, we find that each of the grounds relied upon by the Defence Motion, rather than proving any actual or perceived bias on the part of Justice Winter with regard to the question of if and when the recruitment of child soldiers became a crime under international law, are evidence of the internationally recognised qualifications of Justice Winter in the general field of juvenile justice. The ICTY Appeals Chamber has pointed out that "it would be an odd result if the fulfilment of the qualification requirements of Article 13 were to operate as a disqualifying factor on the basis that it gives rise to an inference of bias."[13] As required by Article 13(2) of the Statute of the Special Court, taking account of such expertise in juvenile justice in the composition of the Chambers is entirely appropriate and a distinction must be drawn between the requirements for a person to serve as a Judge of the Tribunal and the issues relating to the grounds of disqualification of a Judge from sitting in a particular case.[14]

31. As a final matter, we note that the Defence claims that it was clear from Justice Winter's interventions in the Appeal hearing that she remained firmly committed to the view expressed in the report. First, whether or not Justice Winter expressed a view similar to the one in the publications does not create the link between Justice Winter and the publications the Defence is trying to establish. Furthermore, the fact that Justice Winter may have expressed an opinion which is unfavourable to the Defence is not a sufficient ground for bias."

---

[1] *Sesay* decision, above note 17.
[2] Ibid. para. 15.
[3] *Furundzija*, above note 16, at para. 189.
[4] *Prosecutor v Zejnil Delalic, Zdravko Mucic, Hazim Delic, Esad Landzo (Celebici case)* Appeals Chamber Judgement, 20 February 2001.
[5] *Prosecutor v Momcilo Krajisnik* – Case No. IT-00-39-PT, Decision by a single Judge on the Defence Application for Withdrawal of a Judge from the Trial, 22 January 2003.
[6] *Prosecutor v Vojislav Seselj*, Decision on Motion for Disqualification, IT-03-67-PT, 10 June 2003 ("*Seselj* decision").
[7] *The Prosecutor v Karemera, Rwamajuba, Ngirumpatse, Nzirorera*, Case No ICTR-98-44-T, Decision on Motion by Karemera for Disqualification of Trial Judges, 17 May 2004 at para. 9.

(8) *Furundzija*, above note 16 at para. 196.
(9) *Prosecutor v. Karemera, Rwamajuba, Ngirumpatse, Nzirorera*, Case No ICTR-98-44-T, Decision on Motion by Karemera for Disqualification of Trial Judges, 17 May 2004 at para. 10.
(10) *Krajisnik*, above note 37.
(11) *Pinochet No 2*, above note 15, per Lord Goff.
(12) *Krajisnik*, above note 37.
(13) *Celebici* Appeals Chamber Judgment, above note 36 at para. 702 (citing *Furundzija*).
(14) *Prosecutor v. Zejnil Delalic, Zdravko Mucic, Hazim Delic, Esad Landzo (Celebici case)*, Decision Of The Bureau On Motion To Disqualify Judges Pursuant To Rule 15 Or In The Alternative That Certain Judges Recuse Themselves, 25 October 1999.

Rule 16: Absence and Resignation
(amended 29 May 2004)

(A) If a Judge is unable to continue sitting in a proceeding, trial or appeal which has partly been heard for a short duration and the remaining Judges are satisfied that it is in the interests of justice to do so, those remaining Judges may order that the proceeding, trial or appeal continue in the absence of that Judge for a period of not more than five working days.

(B) If a Judge is, for any reason, unable to continue sitting in a proceeding, trial or appeal which has partly been heard for a period which is or is likely to be longer than five days, the President may designate an alternate Judge as provided in Article 12(4) of the Statute.

  (i) If an alternate Judge is not available as provided in Article 12(4) of the Statute, and the remaining Judges are satisfied that it would not affect the decision either way, the remaining Judges may continue in the absence of that Judge.
  (ii) Where a trial or appeal chamber proceeds in the absence of one Judge, in the event that the decision is split evenly a new proceeding, trial or appeal shall be ordered.

(C) If a Judge is, for any reason, unable to sit in a proceeding, trial or appeal which has not yet been heard but has been scheduled, the President may designate an alternate Judge as provided in Article 12 (4) of the Statute.

(D) A Judge who decides to resign shall give notice of his resignation in writing to the President, who shall transmit it to the Secretary-General of the United Nations and the Government of Sierra Leone.

TRIAL CHAMBERS DECISIONS

- **Rule 16(A): Absence and Resignation – Inability to Sit for a Short Duration**

R16-TC-1   o *Prosecutor v. Brima, Kamara, Kanu*, Case No. SCSL-04-16-T, Order Under Rule 16 to Continue Trial in Absence of a Judge, 5 July 2005:[32]

---

[32] See also *Prosecutor v. Brima, Kamara, Kanu*, Case No. SCSL-04-16-T, Order Under Rule 16 to Continue Trial in Absence of a Judge, 11 October 2005.

NOTING that Justice Sebutinde is unable to continue to sit in the trial for a short duration;

BEING SATISFIED that it would be in the interests of justice to continue in the absence of Justice Sebutinde, in accordance with the Rule 16(A) of the Rules of Procedure and Evidence of the Special Court for Sierra Leone ("Rules");

Rule 17: Precedence
(amended 7 March 2003)

(A) All Judges are equal in the exercise of their judicial functions, regardless of dates of election, appointment, age or period of service.

(B) Judges elected or appointed on different dates shall take precedence according to the dates of their election or appointment; Judges elected or appointed on the same date shall take precedence according to age.

(C) In case of re-election, the total period of service as a Judge of the Special Court shall be taken into account.

TRIAL CHAMBERS DECISIONS

- **Rule 17(A): Precedence – Temporary Replacement of Presiding Judge**

R17-TC-1
  o *Prosecutor v. Brima, Kamara, Kanu*, Case No. SCSL-04-16-T, Order Under Rule 16 to Continue Trial in Absence of a Judge, 11 October 2005:

   NOTING the provision of Rule 27(D) of the Rules, which state:

   The provisions of Rule 17 will apply in the event of the Presiding Judge being unable to carry out his functions.

   NOTING the provisions of Rule 17(B) of the Rules, which state:

   Judges elected on different dates shall take precedence according to the dates of their election or appointment; Judges elected or appointed on the same date shall take precedence according to age.

   NOTING that pursuant to the said Rule 17(B), Justice Lussick will act as Presiding Judge in the absence of Justice Doherty;

Rule 19: Functions of the President
(amended 7 March 2003)

(A) The President shall preside at all plenary meetings of the Special Court, co-ordinate the work of the Chambers and supervise the activities of the Registry as well as exercise all the other functions conferred on him by the Agreement, the Statute and the Rules.

(B) The President may after appropriate consultation issue Practice Directions, consistent with the Agreement, the Statute and the Rules, addressing detailed aspects of the conduct of proceedings before the Special Court.

TRIAL CHAMBERS DECISIONS

- **Rule 19(A): Functions of the President – Authority on the Registrar**

R19-TC-1
o *Prosecutor v. Brima, Kamara, Kanu*, Case No. SCSL-04-16-T, Decision on Defence Submission Providing Evidentiary Proof of Registry's Repeated Dissemination of Confidential Documents to the Press and Public Affairs Office, 18 October 2005, para. 10-11:

10. There is no doubt the Registrar has been charged with the responsibility for the "administration and servicing of the Special Court" and that he does so under the authority of the President. In turn Rule 19 charges the President with supervision of the activities of the Registry. It is the Registrar and not the Trial Chamber who has the responsibility and power to instruct Court Management under Rule 33(A).

11. As shown by decisions of other International Tribunals if a party is aggrieved by a decision of the Registrar, the Party may submit his complaint to the President[1]. [. . .]

---

[1] See *Prosecutor v. Ndindiliyimana*, Case No. ICTR-00-56-I, Decision on Augustin Ndindiliyimana's Motion for an Order that the Registrar Hold a Hearing on the Suspension of the Contract of His Investigator Pierre-Claver Karangwa, 12 November 2002; *Prosecutor v. Gatete*, Case No. ICTR-2000-61-I, Decision on the Defence Request for Necessary Resources for Investigations, 2 November 2004.

DECISIONS OF THE PRESIDENT

- **Rule 19(A): Functions of the President – Coordination of the Work of Chambers**

R19-P-1

o *Prosecutor v. Brima, Kamara, Kanu*, Case No. SCSL-04-16-PT, Order Assigning a Case to a Trial Chamber, 17 January 2005:

CONSIDERING Rule 19(A) of the Rules of Procedure and Evidence of the Special Court ("Rules"), which authorizes the President to coordinate the work of the Chambers;

CONSIDERING the need to ensure expeditious proceedings before the Special Court;

NOTING the Decision and Order of the Prosecution Motions for Joinder by Trial Chamber I of 28 January 2004;

HAVING CONSULTED the Presiding Judges of Trial Chamber I and Trial Chamber II;

HEREBY transfer and assign Case No. SCSL-04-16-PT, *The Prosecutor v. Alex Tamba Brima, Brima Bazzy Kamara and Santigie Kanu* to Trial Chamber II [. . .]

- **Rule 19(A): Functions of the President – Coordination of the Work of Chambers – Contempt Proceedings**

R19-P-2

o *Prosecutor v. Samura* (Case No. SCSL-05-01), *Brima (Margaret), Jalloh and Kamara (Ester)* (Case No. SCSL-05-02), and *Kamara (Anifa)* (Case No. SCSL-05-03), Order Assigning Cases to a Trial Chamber, 2 May 2005:

I, JUSTICE EMMANUEL AYOOLA, President of the Special Court for Sierra Leone ("Special Court");

CONSIDERING Rule 19(A) of the Rules of Procedure and Evidence of the Special Court ("Rules"), which authorizes the President to coordinate the work of the Chambers;

[. . .]

HEREBY confirm the assignment of Case No. SCSL-05-1, *Prosecutor v. Brima Samura* and Case No SCSL-05-2, *Prosecutor v. Margaret Fomba Brima, Neneh Binta Bah Jalloh, Anifa Kamara, Ester Kamara* to Trial Chamber I or a single judge thereof.

Rule 21: Functions of the Vice-President
(amended 29 May 2004)

The Vice-President, who's term of office shall be four months, shall exercise the functions of the President in case the latter is absent from Sierra Leone or is unable to act.

DECISIONS OF THE PRESIDENT

- **Rule 21: Functions of the Vice-President – Absence of the President**

R21-P-1
- *Prosecutor v. Sankoh*, Case No. SCSL-03-02-I, Order Modifying Condition of Detention, 29 March 2003:

    SITTING AS Justice George Gelaga King, Vice-President of the Special Court, presiding pursuant to the provisions of Rule 21 of the Rules of Procedure and Evidence ("the Rules");

Rule 23: The Council of Judges
(amended 29 May 2004)

(A) There shall be a Council of Judges which shall be composed of the President, the Vice-President and the Presiding Judge of the Trial Chamber or Chambers.

(B) The President shall consult the Council of Judges on all major questions or matters relating to the functioning of the Special Court.

(C) In order to ensure the coordination of the activities of all organs of the Special Court, the Council of Judges, or its representative, shall meet with the Registrar, the Prosecutor and the Principal Defender, or their representatives.

(D) The President shall consult the Council of Judges with respect to the functions set forth in Rules 19 and 33, and particularly all the Registry activities relating to the administrative support provided to the Chambers.

APPEALS CHAMBER DECISIONS

- **Rule 23(B): Council of Judges – Major Questions Relating to the Functioning of the Special Court – Disqualification of Judges**

R23-AC-1
    o *Prosecutor v. Sesay*, Case No. SCSL-04-15-A, Decision on Defence Motion Seeking the Disqualification of Justice Robertson from the Appeals Chamber, 13 March 2004, para. 17:

> 17. It only now remains for me to deal with Rule 15(E) and I say without hesitation that it does not apply in this case. In this context I agree with Justice Robertson when he says in effect that Rule 15(E) applies only to those cases where a judge is "palpably unfit – e.g. through ill health or criminal conviction". In that circumstance the other Judges of the Chamber may not force his resignation, but may only refer the matter to the Council of Judges which in the words of the Rule "will consider the matter and make a recommendation to the body which appointed the Judge, if required".

Rule 26*bis*: The Chambers
(adopted 29 May 2004)

The Trial Chamber and the Appeals Chamber shall ensure that a trial is fair and expeditious and that proceedings before the Special Court are conducted in accordance with the Agreement, the Statute and the Rules, with full respect for the rights of the accused and due regard for the protection of victims and witnesses.

TRIAL CHAMBERS DECISIONS

- **Rule 26*bis*: The Chambers - Role of the Judge**

R26*bis*-TC-1
o *Prosecutor v. Gbao*, Case No. SCSL-03-09-I, Order on the Urgent Request for Direction on the Time to Respond to and/or an Extension of Time for the Filing of a Response to the Prosecution Motions and the Suspension of Any Ruling on the Issue of Protective Measures That May Be Pending Before Other Proceedings Before the Special Court as a Result of Similar Motions Filed to Those that Have Been Filed by the Prosecution in this Case, 16 May 2003:

CONSIDERING that issues before the Special Court are conducted before professional Judges, who by virtue of their education and experience are able to ponder independently without prejudice to each and every case which will be brought before them;

CONSIDERING that a request that no rulings on protective measures will be made on other proceedings would halt the continuance of the pre-trial stage for the other Accused and that the Trial Chamber has an obligation to all Accused to be tried within a reasonable time;

R26*bis*-TC-2
o *Prosecutor v. Gbao*, Case No. SCSL-03-09-PT, Decision on the Prosecution Motion for Immediate Protective Measures for Witnesses and Victims and for Non-Public Disclosure, 10 October 2003, para. 60:

60. The Special Court would like to recall that the role of every judge is to scrutinize the proceedings and make sure that, at all moments, every ordered measure is still appropriate.

As the French Constitution nicely puts it, in its Article 66, one should always remember that every judge is the protector of individual freedoms.

R26bis-TC-3

o *Prosecution v. Sesay, Kallon, Gbao*, Case No. SCSL-04-15-PT, Decision on the Prosecution Motion for Concurrent Hearing of Evidence Common to Cases SCSL-04-15-PT and SCSL-04-16-PT, 11 May 2004, para. 38:[33]

"38. The Prosecution further submits that hearing the same witness twice, in two separate trials, on essentially the same evidence by the same panel of judges will jeopardise the principle of a fair trial in that the appearance that the judges would have already assessed the credibility of the evidence when conducting the second hearing would undermine the credibility of the judicial process and would be contrary to the interest of justice. This submission, in the Chamber's opinion, is specious and speculative from two perspectives: namely (i) that the judges have sworn to discharge their judicial functions faithfully, conscientiously, and impartially; (ii) that it is the accepted norm implicit in the Bangalore Principles of Judicial Conduct,[(1)] that profession-ally trained and qualified judges are able to assess the credibility of witnesses with a remarkable degree of dispassionateness as opposed to trial juries. Accordingly, this Court already held that:

"Issues before the Special Court are conducted before professional Judges, who by virtue of their education and experience are able to ponder independently without prejudice to each and every case which will be brought before them."[(2)]

It may be inquired – Why would they suddenly lose their disciplined focus and objectivity when confronted with separate joint trials?"

[(1)] Adopted by the Judicial Group on Strengthening Judicial Integrity, as revised at the Round Table Meeting of Chief Justices held at the Peace Palace, The Hague, 25-26 November 2002.
[(2)] *Prosecutor v. Gbao*, SCSL-2003-09-I, Order on the Urgent Request for Direction on the Time to Respond to and/or an Extension of Time for the Filing of a Response to the Prosecution Motions, 16 May 2003, page 2 per Judge Boutet. See also *Prosecutor v. Delalic et al.*, IT-96-21-T, decision on the Motion of the Prosecution for the Admissibility of Evidence, 19 January 1998, para. 20 and *Prosecutor v. Ntakirutimana et al.*, ICTR-96-10-I and ICTR-96-17-T, Decision on the Prosecutor's Motion to Join the Indictments ICTR-96-10-I and ICTR-96-17-T, 22 February 2001, para. 26.

[33] See also *Prosecutor v. Brima, Kamara, Kanu*, Case No. SCSL-04-16-PT, Decision on the Prosecution Motion for Concurring Hearing of Evidence Common to Cases SCSL-04-15-PT and SCSL-04-16-PT, 11 May 2004, para. 38.

- **Rule 26*bis*: The Chambers – "Judicial Economy", "Consistency in Jurisprudence", "Credibility of Judicial Process"**

R26*bis*-TC-4

o *Prosecution v. Sesay, Kallon, Gbao*, Case No. SCSL-04-15-PT, Decision on the Prosecution Motion for Concurrent Hearing of Evidence Common to Cases SCSL-04-15-PT and SCSL-04-16-PT, 11 May 2004, para. 33, 35, 45, 47:

33. In terms of substance and as to their main focus, all of the Prosecution's submissions can be grouped into two (2) main categories. The first category is that the Motion will serve the interest of justice in the sense that it will advance judicial economy, consistency in jurisprudence and the credibility of the judicial process. Noting that judicial economy, consistency in jurisprudence and credibility of the judicial process are not universally acknowledged factors of criminal adjudication, the key question for the Chamber is whether the conclusion that the interest of justice will be served by granting the Order sought logically follows from the premise that the Order, if granted, will promote these presumed values of international criminal justice. We think not; nor would an empirical inquiry testing the validity of such a hypothesis convince us otherwise because of all the possible intervening variables that could be at play; for example, the possibility of two accused persons from one group or their counsel becoming suddenly indisposed for a protracted period of time during the common hearing involving both groups. This submission is clearly without merit. Implicit in it are three (3) unproven assumptions:

(i) that judicial economy is a necessary function of the accused's right to a fair trial;
(ii) that consistency in jurisprudence is an issue free from juristic controversy; and
(iii) that credibility of the judicial process is a well-recognised concept within the province of law and can easily be evaluated.

[...]

35. [...] [I]t is the Chamber's view that the legal rationalisation about judicial economy that has come to feature prominently in the evolving jurisprudence of sister international tribunals, to wit, the need to strike a balance between such a factor in the context of international criminal adjudication and the right of the accused to a fair trial, has generally been formulated in a manner that attaches greater primacy to judicial economy over the accused's right to a fair and expeditious trial. As was noted in the Decision of *Prosecutor v. Krajisnik*, "judicial economy should never outweigh the right of the Accused to a fair trial."[(1)] *In our opinion, a tribunal's*

reputation and credibility must be measured not in terms of judicial economy but its capability to deliver superior quality justice fairly and dispassionately, and with reasonable expedition.

[...]

45. Noting that the thrust of the Prosecution's argument in support of the Motion rested on three notions, chief among which is judicial economy, the Chamber deems it worthwhile to recall that this Court has constantly been reminded by the Prosecution during various submissions before it and by the Court's Administration, including the Management Committee, of its limited judicial life-span, fiscal and budgetary constraints on its operations, and the need for judicial economy in the conduct of trials. In response, this Chamber can do no better than adopt the words of his Honour Judge David Hunt in the case of *Prosecutor v. Slobodan Milosevic*.[2] In that case, the learned Judge had this to say:

> The international community has entrusted the Tribunal with the task of trying persons charged with serious violations of international humanitarian law. It expects the Tribunal to do so in accordance with those rights of the accused to which reference is made in the previous paragraph. If the Tribunal is not given sufficient time and money to do so by the international community, then it should not attempt to try those persons in a way which does not accord with those rights. In my opinion, it is improper to take the Completion Strategy into account in departing from interpretations which had earlier been accepted by the Appeals Chamber where this at the expense of those rights.

[...]

47. Finally, the Chamber wishes to observe that, as a sovereign entity within its jurisdictional competence, a court must not recoil from its supreme responsibility of maintaining the integrity of its proceedings both in the interests of the Prosecution and the Defence, and more so in protecting the procedural and substantive due process rights of persons accused of crime until proven guilty. To sacrifice those rights in favour of political or economic expediency is tantamount to abdicating its sovereign attributes of independence. Hence, it must be emphasised that the limited judicial life-span of a Court cannot provide justification in law for abridging or curtailing the right of an accused person to a fair trial.

---

[1] *Prosecutor v. Krajisnik*, IT-00-39 and 40, Decision on Prosecution's Motion for Judicial Notice of Adjudicated Facts and Admission of Written Statements of Witnesses Pursuant to Rule 92*bis*, 28 February 2003, para. 20.
[2] *Prosecutor v. Slobodan Milosevic*, IT-02-54-AR73.4, Dissenting Opinion

of Judge David Hunt on Admissibility of Evidence in Chief in the Form of Written Statement, Appeals Chamber, 21 October 2003, para. 21.

- **Rule 26*bis*: The Chambers – Correspondences to the Trial Chamber to Be Filed Inter Partes**

R26*bis*-TC-5

o *Prosecutor v. Sesay, Kallon, Gbao*, Case No. SCSL-04-14-PT, Order to Extend the Time for Filing of the Prosecution Supplemental Pre-Trial Brief, 2 April 2004:

CONSIDERING the oral request by the Prosecution through the Registrar for an extension of time to file its supplemental pre-trial brief in light of the judicial recess;[1]

---

[1] See, Letter from David Crane to Judge Bankole Thompson, 31 March 2004, attached hereto and thereby made available to the Defence. The Trial Chamber takes this opportunity to remind the Parties that any correspondence to the Trial Chamber shall be filed *inter partes*, save those matters which require consideration *ex parte*.

Rule 27: The Trial Chambers
(amended 14 May 2005)

(A) The Presiding Judge of each Trial Chamber shall be elected for a renewable term of one year.

(B) The Presiding Judge shall coordinate the work of the Chamber and liaise with the Registrar on matters affecting the Trial Chamber and will exercise such other functions as may be conferred on him by the Agreement, the Statute, and the Rules.

(C) The Presiding Judge may issue, after appropriate consultations, Practice Directions in relation to the Trial Chamber.

(D) The provisions of Rule 17 will apply in the event of the Presiding Judge being unable to carry out his functions.

TRIAL CHAMBERS DECISIONS

- **Rule 27(B): Trial Chambers – Functions of the Presiding Judge – Competitive Authority with the President on Registrar's Decisions**

R27-TC-1

o *Prosecutor v. Brima, Kamara, Kanu*, Case No. SCSL-04-16-T, Decision on Defence Submission Providing Evidentiary Proof of Registry's Repeated Dissemination of Confidential Documents to the Press and Public Affairs Office, 18 October 2005, para. 10-11:

10. There is no doubt the Registrar has been charged with the responsibility for the "administration and servicing of the Special Court" and that he does so under the authority of the President. In turn Rule 19 charges the President with supervision of the activities of the Registry. It is the Registrar and not the Trial Chamber who has the responsibility and power to instruct Court Management under Rule 33(A).

11. As shown by decisions of other International Tribunals if a party is aggrieved by a decision of the Registrar, the Party may submit his complaint to the President.[1] However, the instant case relates not only to an administrative decision of the Registrar but to the filing of documents in the Trial Chamber which, in turn, is governed by the Practice Direction on Filing of Documents before the Special Court of Sierra Leone (The "Practice Direction"). Article 4(B) of the Practice Direction provides:

Where a Party, State, organization or person seeks to file all or part of a document on a confidential basis, the party shall mark the document as 'CONFIDENTIAL' and indicate, on the relevant Court Management section form, the reasons for the confidentiality. The Judge or Chamber shall thereafter review the document and determine whether confidentiality is necessary. Documents that are not filed confidentially may be used in press releases and be posted on the official website of the Special Court.

Article 4(B) imposes an obligation on the Judge or the Trial Chamber to decide if the document needs to retain its confidentiality. We note that Article 4(B) provides that documents that are not filed confidentially may be used in press releases.

12. In this regard, we note the Registrar's submission that the confidential documents are sent to the Head of Press and Public Affairs Office, not for purposes of publication, but to avoid or prevent such publication by others. We further note that Counsel, in his submission, has not alleged any dissemination of confidential documents by the Press and Public Affairs Office. We accept and find that this practice by the Registrar is to prevent the leaking of confidential material. However, we are of the opinion that the spirit and letter of Article 4(B) of the Practice Direction is to give the Judge or Trial Chamber the primary duty to review all confidential documents.

FOR THE ABOVE REASONS WE ORDER THAT

1) documents filed confidentially shall only be transmitted to the parties on which the filing party intends to serve them; and
2) documents filed as confidential shall not be disseminated to other persons except with the express leave of the Trial Chamber.

---

(1) See *Prosecutor v. Ndindiliyimana*, Case No. ICTR-00-56-I, Decision on Augustin Ndindiliyimana's Motion for an Order that the Registrar Hold a Hearing on the Suspension of the Contract of His Investigator Pierre-Claver Karangwa, 12 November 2002; *Prosecutor v. Gatete*, Case No. ICTR-2000-61-I, Decision on the Defence Request for Necessary Resources for Investigations, 2 November 2004.

R27-TC-2

o *Prosecutor v. Kanu*, Case No. SCSL-04-16-T, Decision on the Defence Motion for the Temporary Provisional Release to Allow the Accused Santigie Borbor Kanu to Visit His Mother's Grave, 18 October 2005, para. 12-13:

12. [...] In reality Mr. Kanu's application is one for an order for special measures of detention outside the Detention

Facility under Rule 64 of the Rules. In that regard we also agree that the proper functionary to make such an order is the Registrar with the approval of the President of the Special Court.

13. Furthermore, since the Motion does not call upon the Trial Chamber to review a decision or order of the Registrar in this regard, the Trial Chamber finds no valid reason to usurp or interfere with the Registrar's powers under Rule 64 of the Rules.

- **Rule 27(B): Trial Chambers – Functions of the Presiding Judge – Contempt Proceedings**

R27-TC-3

o *Prosecutor v. Samura* (Case No. SCSL-05-01), *Brima (Margaret), Jalloh and Kamara (Ester)* (Case No. SCSL-05-02), and *Kamara (Anifa)* (Case No. SCSL-05-03), Order Designating a judge for Contempt Proceedings, 2 May 2005:

I, HON. JUSTICE BENJAMIN MUTANGA ITOE, Presiding Judge of Trial Chamber I;

[...]

NOTING the *Order Assigning Cases to a Trial Chamber* filed by the President of the Special Court on the 2nd of May, 2005 ("Order of the President");

[...]

NOTING that the Order of the President confirms the assignment of the Contempt Proceeding to Trial Chamber I or to a single Judge thereof;

PURSUANT to Rules 27 and 77 of the Rules;

DO HEREBY

DESIGNATE Hon. Justice Pierre Boutet to deal as necessary with the contempt proceedings against Brima Samura, Case No. SCSL-05-01, and Margaret Fomba Brima, Neneh Binta Bah Jalloh, Anifa Kamara and Ester Kamara, Case No. SCSL-05-02;

Rule 28: Designated Judges
(amended 1 August 2003)

After consultation with the Judges concerned, the Presiding Judge of the Trial Chamber shall designate for a given period such Judges as necessary to whom indictments, warrants, and all other pre-trial matters not pertaining to a case already assigned to a Chamber, shall be transmitted for review. The Registrar shall publish the information by appropriate means and as soon as possible.

TRIAL CHAMBERS DECISIONS

- **Rule 28: Designated Judges – Limit of Competence**

R28-TC-1

o *Prosecutor v. Brima*, Case No. SCSL-03-06-PT, Ruling on the Application for the Issue of a Writ of *Habeas Corpus* Filed by the Applicant, 22 July 2003:

[...] Counsel for the Applicant alleges that the indictment contains erroneous information in that it alleges that his client had joined the Sierra Leonean Army in 1985 and rose to the rank of a Staff Sergeant.

[...]

[...] Even if a doubt is created in respect of his having served in the Sierra Leonean Army, I cannot at this stage, as a designated Pre-trial Judge, resolve this issue which I consider properly within the competence and jurisdiction of the Trial Chamber and which, in my judgement, is the rightful venue to examine evidence on those facts which touch on the indictment and on the warrant of arrest in the course of the trial of the Applicant.

Rule 31: Appointment of the Deputy Registrar and Registry Staff
(amended 7 March 2003)

The Registrar shall appoint such other staff as may be required for the efficient functioning of the Registry, including a Deputy Registrar, if necessary.

TRIAL CHAMBERS DECISIONS

- **Rule 31: Appointment of the Deputy Registrar and Registry Staff – Acting Officials**

R31-TC-1   o *Prosecutor v. Brima*, Case No. SCSL-04-16-PT, Decision on Applicant's Motion Against Denial by the Acting Principal Defender to Enter a Legal Service Contract for the Assignment of Counsel, 6 May 2004, para. 78-81, 106, 110-112, 117-119:

> 78. [...] In fact, in view of the very nature and functioning of public or private services, it is, and should always be envisaged, that the substantive holder of the position is not expected to be there at all times. In order to ensure a proper functioning and a continuity of services with a view to avoiding a disruption in the administrative machinery, the Administration envisages and recognizes the concept of "Acting Officials" in the absence of their substantive holders.
>
> 79. The Chamber, contrary to the Applicant's submission on this issue, is of the opinion that where an official is properly appointed or designated to act in a position during the absence of the substantive holder of that position, the Acting Official enjoys the same privileges and prerogatives as those of the substantive official and in that capacity, can take the decisions inherent in that position. [...]
>
> 80. This said however, the Chamber would like to observe that to perform such functions which could give rise to far reaching and contentious confrontations as has happened in the instant case where the Official, like the 1st Respondent in this case, should be, and should indeed have been regularly, clearly, and expressly appointed or designated by the [Registrar] as the Acting Principal Defender whilst waiting for the recruitment of the substantive holder of the position.
>
> 81. We say this because the exercise of administrative duties, functions or discretions, is founded on the notion of empowerment

to exercise the duties that go with that office or the discretions that relate to it. This empowerment is conferred on the official purporting to so act, by a legislative, statutory, regulatory or administrative instrument which clearly defines his competence, and on which the substantive holder of the position functions and takes decisions.

[. . .]

106. In arriving at these conclusions on the issues raised so far, the Chamber has taken cognizance of an Administrative Law Treatise on this subject which succinctly sums up the law as follows:

> "An element which is essential to the lawful exercise of power is that it should be exercised by the authority upon whom it is conferred, and by no one else. The principle is strictly applied, even where it causes administrative inconvenience except in cases where it may reasonably be inferred that the power was intended to be delegable. Normally the courts are rigorous in requiring the power to be exercised by the precise person or body stated in the Statute, and in condemning as *ultra vires*, action taken by agents, sub committees or delegation however expressly authorized by the authority endowed with the power." See H.W.R. Wade and C.F. Forsyth – Administrative Law, 7th Edition: P-347.

107. In the Motion under examination, we have noted that the [Registrar], in a document dated 7th July 2003, only gave limited express delegation of powers to the 1st Respondent on Financial and Budgetary matters. It is expressly silent on whether he was made the Acting Principal Defender or whether those powers were delegated to him in that capacity.

108. We further note that the [Registrar] who affirmed during the oral hearing in Chambers that he enjoys a very wide discretion from the Management Committee in the exercise of his powers under the Statute and the Rules, did not expressly designate the 1st Respondent as Acting Principal Defender so as to enable the latter to lawfully exercise the prerogatives that are conferred on, and exercisable only by the Principal Defender under the provisions of Rule 45 of the rules of Procedure and Evidence and under the Directive on the Assignment of Counsel. This was and is still, in our opinion, necessary particularly within the present context of a decision as grave in nature and in its consequences as that provided for in Article 16(C) of the said Directive which confers on the Principal Defender, a power coupled with a discretion, to exercise that power or not.

[. . .]

110. It is the absence of this regular designation or appointment of the 1st respondent to so act for the Principal Defender,

as he was in fact doing, and the manner in which he interpreted and applied the instruments under which he so acted to arrive at the decisions which are contested by the Applicant, coupled with the content of the said decisions, that have contributed to this dispute in which the Applicant and his Counsel, Mr. Terence Michael Terry, are contesting and questioning the regularity and validity of these decisions, and do invite the Chamber to quash and set them aside.

111. It is the finding of the Chamber therefore, in the light of the above analysis, that Mr. Sylvain Roy, a Defence Advisor in the Office of the Principal Defender, in the absence of an express appointment to the position of Acting Principal Defender, could not perform the duties that he purported to be performing nor could he take decisions in relation thereto and that if he did, as he indeed did, it was *ultra vires* his powers and that consequently the said decisions were null and void.

112. It is our view and conviction as a Chamber, that the legal doctrine of *ultra vires* on which the dispensation of administrative law is principally founded, is a very vital component of the principle of the Rule of Law and of the Due Process. It constitutes an important substratum in the edifice of judicial administration without which it can easily crumble. Indeed, what accounts for and justifies the perenity of this vital doctrine is the role it has played and continues to play in the protection of rights of all sorts, individual and collective, against the formidable armada of the privileged and the ruling class, to which any body or group, particularly the less privileged, and including of course, even erstwhile omnipotent who at times end up in stormy waters, could fall a victim. It is that vital weapon in the armoury of the judicial machinery that checks, controls, mitigates and combats administrative despotism, illegalities and arbitrariness which could otherwise become the order of the day even in the most advanced democracies, and nip in the bud, the implantation of the doctrine of good governance that is rapidly perfecting its grip on the judicial, administrative and political cultures of emerging societies around the world.

[...]

117. In these circumstances, the public and litigants including the Applicant and Mr. Terry, had already accepted and familiarized themselves with the fact that the 1st Respondent was in fact, the "*de facto*" Acting Principal Defender even though he was not, but could regularly have been, so as to legalise and legitimize at least the form as opposed to the merits of the contentious decisions which he has taken, as emanating from an authority vested with those powers.

118. The Chamber accordingly accepts the legitimacy of all the decision which Mr. Sylvain Roy, defence Advisor, had

taken purportedly acting as the Principal Defender, and which have so far, not been contested excepting of course, the decisions taken in the matter that is now before us which has been contested by the Applicant.

119. In taking this stand, the Chamber is again comforted in this view by a statement of law in HWR. Wade and Forsyth – Administrative Law 7th Edition: Page 326 where the Learned Authors opine:

> The acts of the Officer or a Judge may be held to be valid in Law even though his own appointment is involved and in truth he has no legal power at all. The logic of annulling all his acts has to yield to the desirability of upholding them where he has acted in the office under a general supposition of his competence to do so. In such a case he is called an officer or Judge "*de facto*" as opposed to an officer or Judge "*de jure*".

APPEALS CHAMBER DECISIONS

- **Rule 31: Appointment of the Deputy Registrar and Registry Staff – Acting Officials**

R31-AC-1

o *Prosecutor v. Brima, Kamara, Kanu*, Case No. SCSL-04-16-AR73, Decision on Brima-Kamara Defence Appeal Motion Against Trial Chamber II Majority Decision on Extremely Urgent Confidential Joint Motion for the Re-Appointment of Kevin Metzger and Wilbert Harris As Lead Counsel for Alex Tamba Brima and Brima Bazzy Kamara (AC), 8 December 2005, para. 94:

> 94. To deny the Applicants' request to declare the Registrar's decision not to re-assign Counsel null and void, the Trial Chamber first justifies the intervention of the Registrar in that matter on the ground that, "in the absence of the actual Principal Defender, certain obligations to carry out duties fall out upon the Registrar".[1] The Appeals Chamber disagrees with that opinion of the Trial Chamber. As held by Trial Chamber I in its decision of 6 May 2004 in the same case:[2]
>
>> In fact, in view of the very nature and functioning of public or private services, it is, and should always be envisaged, that the substantive holder of the position is not expected to be there at all times. In order to ensure a proper functioning and a continuity of services with a view to avoiding a disruption in the administrative machinery, the Administration envisages and recognizes the

concept of "Acting Officials" in the absence of their substantive holders.

The Chamber, contrary to the Applicant's submission on this issue, is of the opinion that where an official is properly appointed or designated to act in a position during the absence of the substantive holder of that position, the Acting Official enjoys the same privileges and prerogatives as those of the substantive official and in that capacity, can take the decisions inherent in that position.

The Appeals Chamber concurs with this opinion of Trial Chamber I and considers that, in the absence of the actual Principal Defender, the duty to decide on the reassignment of the withdrawn Counsel automatically fell on the Deputy Principal Defender in her acting capacity.

---

(1) Para. 38 of the Impugned Decision.
(2) *Prosecutor v. Brima*, Case No. SCSL-2004-16-PT, Decision on Applicant's Motion Against Denial by the Acting Principal Defender to Enter a Legal Service Contract for the Assignment of Counsel, 6 May 2004, para. 78-79.

Rule 33: Functions of the Registrar
(amended 29 May 2004)

(A) The Registrar shall assist the Chambers, the Plenary Meetings of the Special Court, the Council of Judges, the Judges and the Prosecutor, the Principal Defender and the Defence in the performance of their functions. Under the authority of the President, he shall be responsible for the administration and servicing of the Special Court and shall serve as its channel of communication.

(B) The Registrar, in the execution of his functions, may make oral or written representations to Chambers on any issue arising in the context of a specific case which affects or may affect the discharge of such functions, including that of implementing judicial decisions, with notice to the parties where necessary.

(C) The Registrar, mindful of the need to ensure respect for human rights and fundamental freedoms and particularly the presumption of innocence, shall, with the approval of the Council of Judges, adopt and amend rules governing the detention of persons awaiting Trial or Appeal or otherwise detained by the Special Court and ensure conditions of detention.

(D) The Registrar may, with the approval of the Council of Judges, issue Practice Directions addressing particular aspects of the practice and procedure in the Registry of the Special Court and in respect of other matters within the powers of the Registrar.

TRIAL CHAMBERS DECISIONS

- **Rule 33: Functions of the Registrar – Discretionary Powers**

R33-TC-1
o *Prosecutor v. Brima*, Case No. SCSL-04-16-PT, Decision on Applicant's Motion Against Denial by the Acting Principal Defender to Enter a Legal Service Contract for the Assignment of Counsel, 6 May 2004, para. 97-99, 114:

97. As a matter of law, and so we hold, a discretion cannot be exercised when the issue in respect of which it is purported to be exercised, is not provided for by law, or where the exercise of such discretion is either contrary to the law or manifestly unreasonable.

98. This view is supported by the decision in the case of LAW SOCIETY OF NEW BRUNSWICK VS. RYAN [2003] 1SCR 247 where JUSTICE LACOBUCCI characterized a patently unreasonable decision as one that is "so flawed that no amount of curial deference can justify letting it stand." In yet another Canadian case of THE CANADIAN UNION OF PUBLIC EMPLOYEES LOCAL 963 VS NEW BRUNSWICK LIQUOR CORPORATION, "CUPE" [1979] 2 SCR, 227, LORD JUSTICE DICKSON stated that a 'decision is unreasonable if it cannot be rationally supported by the relevant legislation'.

99. [...] Indeed, as was held in the case of PUBLIC SERVICE OF NEW SOUTH WALES VS OSMOND (1986) 60 ALJ 209, for a discretion to be exercised validly, it must be seen to have been exercised reasonably, fairly, and justly. [...]

[...]

114. In this regard, we again refer to the Legal Treatise, WADE & FORYTH: ADMINISTRATIVE LAW, 7th Edition, P.41, where the Learned Authors have this to say:

> "A public authority may not act outside its powers (*ultra vires*). Any administrative act or order which is *ultra vires* or outside jurisdiction is void in law, i.e. deprived of legal effect. This is because in order to be valid, it needs statutory authorization and if it is not within the powers given by the Act, it has no leg to stand on. The Court will then quash it or declare it to be unlawful or prohibit any action to enforce it."

It follows from the above legal statement that for the decision to be valid, it must first be authorized by Statute and secondly, it must conform with the power given by the Statute. In this regard Lord MACNAUGHTEN in the case of WESTMINSTER CORPORATION V. L. & NW RAILWAY [1905] AC 426 and 430 made the following observations:

> "It is well settled that a public body invested with statutory powers such as those conferred upon the corporation must take care not to exceed or abuse its powers. It must keep within the limits of the authority committed to it. It must act in good faith. And it must act reasonably. The last proposition is involved in the second, if not the first."

- **Rule 33(A): Functions of the Registrar – Authority of the President**

R33-TC-2   o *Prosecutor v. Brima, Kamara, Kanu*, Case No. SCSL-04-16-T, Decision on Defence Submission Providing Evidentiary Proof of Registry's Repeated Dissemination of Confidential Documents to the Press and Public Affairs Office, 18 October 2005, para. 10-11:

10. There is no doubt the Registrar has been charged with the responsibility for the "administration and servicing of the Special Court" and that he does so under the authority of the President. In turn Rule 19 charges the President with supervision of the activities of the Registry. It is the Registrar and not the Trial Chamber who has the responsibility and power to instruct Court Management under Rule 33(A).

11. As shown by decisions of other International Tribunals if a party is aggrieved by a decision of the Registrar, the Party may submit his complaint to the President[1]. [...]

---

[1] See *Prosecutor v. Ndindiliyimana*, Case No. ICTR-00-56-I, Decision on Augustin Ndindiliyimana's Motion for an Order that the Registrar Hold a Hearing on the Suspension of the Contract of His Investigator Pierre-Claver Karangwa, 12 November 2002; *Prosecutor v. Gatete*, Case No. ICTR-2000-61-I, Decision on the Defence Request for Necessary Resources for Investigations, 2 November 2004.

- **Rule 33(B): Functions of the Registrar – Representations to Chambers**

R33-TC-3   o *Prosecutor v. Brima, Kamara, Kanu*, Case No. SCSL-04-16-T, Order for a Written Representation from the Registrar Pursuant to Rule 33, 21 June 2005:[34]

FINDING nevertheless that it would be helpful to have a written representation of the Registrar in response in order to determine this matter;

---

[34] See also *Prosecutor v. Brima, Kamara, Kanu*, Case No. SCSL-04-16-T, Order for a Written Representation of the Registrar Pursuant to Rule 33 on Security Measures for a Potential Temporary release of the Accused Kanu, 22 September 2005; *Prosecutor v. Brima, Kamara, Kanu*, Case No. SCSL-04-16-T, Order for a Written Representation from the Registrar Pursuant to Rule 33 on Security Measures for a Site Visit to Karina Town in the Bombali District of Sierra Leone, 10 October 2005.

RECALLING Rule 33 and Rule 27(B) of the Rules;

HEREBY instructs the Registrar to file a written representation in response to the Defence Submission not later than 30 June 2005.

- **Rule 33(D): Functions of the Registrar – Practice Directions – Binding Authority**

R33-TC-4
o *Prosecutor v. Gbao*, Case No. SCSL-03-09-PT, Decision on the Prosecution Motion for Immediate Protective Measures for Witnesses and Victims and for Non-Public Disclosure, 10 October 2003, para. 26-27:

26. The Special Court acknowledges the fact that the Defence exceeded the page limit when filing its Response, which according to the terms of the Practice Direction on Filing Documents before the Special Court for Sierra Leone of the 27th day of February 2003, should not exceed ten (10) pages (Article 9 (3) (C)).

27. Leave is hereby granted to exceed the page limit prescribed. However, the Special Court wishes to recall to the Defence, and for that matter to all parties, that, unless specifically authorized by the Special Court, they are compelled to respect the terms of all Practice Directions, in so far as they are an emanation of the Rules (Rule 19 (B), Rule 27 (C) or Rule 33 (D)), and can only be deviated from with leave to that effect.

R33-TC-5
o *Prosecutor v. Norman*, Case No. SCSL-04-14-T, Order on Filing, 7 February 2005:

NOTING that the Motion fails to comply with Article 4(G) of the Practice Direction on Filing Documents Before the Special Courts for Sierra Leone ("Practice Direction"), adopted on the 27th of February, 2003 and Amended on the 1st of June, 2004, where Article 4(G) states:

The typeface shall be 12 points, "Times New Roman" font, with 1.5 line spacing. An average page shall contain a maximum of 300 words.

CONSIDERING that the Motion is a clear breach of Article 4(G) of the Practice Direction;

PURSUANT to Rule 54 of the Rules;

THE TRIAL CHAMBER THEREFORE

R33-TC-6

o *Prosecutor v. Brima, Kamara, Kanu*, Case No. SCSL-04-16-T, Decision on Objection to Question Put by Defence in Cross-Examination of Witness TF1-227, 15 June 2005, para. 1-2:

1. As a preliminary matter, the Defence notes that it has filed pages and documents in excess of the limits provided by the Practice Direction for Filing Documents before the Special Court for Sierra Leone ("Practice Direction") and seeks leave pursuant to Article(6) of the Practice Direction.

2. Leave is granted in this Decision, but the parties are hereby warned not, in future, to present the Trial Chamber with a fait accompli. Application for leave, with reasons, shall be made orally or in writing prior to filing.

APPEALS CHAMBER DECISIONS

* **Rule 33(B): Functions of the Registrar – Representations to Chambers – Notice to the Parties**

R33-AC-1

o *Prosecutor v. Brima, Kamara, Kanu*, Case No. SCSL-04-16-AR73, Decision on Brima-Kamara Defence Appeal Motion Against Trial Chamber II Majority Decision on Extremely Urgent Confidential Joint Motion for the Re-Appointment of Kevin Metzger and Wilbert Harris As Lead Counsel for Alex Tamba Brima and Brima Bazzy Kamara, 8 December 2005, para. 142-145:

142. As regards the oral consultation that was admittedly made by the Registrar to the Trial Chamber, the Appeals Chamber observes that the Registrar justifies its oral consultation of the Trial Chamber on the ground of Rule 33(B).[(1)] Rule 33(B) provides:

> The Registrar, in the execution of his functions, may make oral or written representations to Chambers on any issue arising in the context of a specific case which affects or may affect the discharge of such functions, including that of implementing judicial decisions, with notice to the parties where necessary.

143. The Appeals Chamber recognizes that in the exercise of its administrative functions and servicing of the Special Court pursuant to Article 16(1) of the Statute, the Registrar may need to confer with the Chambers from time to time. These consultations do not necessarily need to be made *inter partes*, namely in the presence of the Parties to the case. Rule 33(B)

specifically provides that such notice to the Parties shall be made only "where necessary". Such necessity may arise, in particular, where the interests of the Accused are concerned.

144. The Appeals Chamber notes the Defence Office's submission that "contrary to Rule 33, the [Registrar] did not notify the Accused nor their Counsel about his consultation with the Trial Chamber yet the matter at hand was very crucial to their rights".[2] The Appeals Chamber agrees that, would this consultation have been crucial to the rights of the Accused, the Registrar should have notified the Parties pursuant to Rule 33(B).

145. But the Appeals Chamber finds that the oral consultation between the Registrar and the Trial Chamber was apparently limited to the re-confirmation of the Oral Decision to withdraw Counsel, which was rendered on 12 May 2005 and confirmed on 16 May 2005 and, in particular, the meaning of the consequential order to appoint *another* Counsel to each Accused pursuant to Rule 45(E). In those circumstances, the Appeals Chamber does not agree that this consultation, which appears to have been only motivated by the Defence Office's insistence to re-appoint the *same* Counsel in contravention with the Trial Chamber's express and repeated order to appoint *another* Counsel, was crucial to the rights of the Accused. The Appeals Chamber therefore concludes that there was no necessity to notify this consultation to the Parties pursuant to Rule 33(B).

---

[1] Para. 59 of the Registrar's Response.
[2] Page 20 of the Defence Office's Response.

Rule 37: Functions of the Prosecutor
(amended 7 March 2003)

(A) The Prosecutor shall perform all the functions provided by the Statute in accordance with the Rules and with such Regulations, consistent with the Agreement and the Statute and the Rules, as may be framed by him.

(B) The Prosecutor's powers under Parts IV to VIII of the Rules may be exercised by staff members of the Office of the Prosecutor authorized by him, or by any person acting under his direction.

TRIAL CHAMBERS DECISIONS

- **Rule 37: Functions of the Prosecutor – Qualifications**

R37-TC-1
o *Prosecutor v. Brima, Kamara, Kanu*, Case No. SCSL-04-16-T, Decision on Objection to Question Put by Defence in Cross-Examination of Witness TF1-227, 15 June 2005, para. 22-24:

22. The Rules define "Prosecutor" as "The Prosecutor appointed pursuant to Art. 3 of the Agreement between the United Nations and the Government of Sierra Leone".

23. Article 3 (3) of the Agreement between the United Nations and the Government of Sierra Leone on the Establishment of the Special Court provides *inter alia*:

> The Prosecutor and the Deputy Prosecutor shall be of high moral character and possess the highest level of professional competence and extensive experience in the conduct of investigations and prosecutions of criminal cases.

24. The highest level of professional competence and experience brings with it an awareness that those under their control must act in a professional, competent and ethical manner. It carries a duty to supervise and ensure conformity with such standards.

Rule 39: Conduct of Investigations
(amended 7 March 2003)

In the conduct of an investigation, the Prosecutor may:

(i) Summon and question suspects, interview victims and witnesses and record their statements, collect evidence and conduct on-site investigations;

(ii) Take all measures deemed necessary for the purpose of the investigation, including the taking of any special measures to provide for the safety, the support and the assistance of potential witnesses and sources;

(iii) Seek, to that end, the assistance of any State authority concerned, as well as of any relevant international body including the International Criminal Police Organization (INTERPOL); and

(iv) Request such orders as may be necessary from a Trial Chamber or a Judge.

TRIAL CHAMBERS DECISIONS

- **Rule 39(iii): Conduct of Investigations – Cooperation of States**

R39-TC-1

o *Prosecutor v. Sesay*, Case No. SCSL-04-15-T, Decision on Sesay Motion Seeking Disclosure of the Relationship Between Governmental Agencies of the United States of America and the Office of the Prosecutor, 2 May 2005, para. 23, 25-29, 44-47:

23. The Chamber acknowledges that it was in recognition of the need for co-operation between the Court, the relevant Sierra Leone authorities and other states to fulfil the Court's mandate that Article 15(1) of the Statute, Section 15 of the Special Court Agreement and Rule 39 of the Court's Rules, were enacted. The provisions of Article 15(1) of the Statute are already set out in paragraph 21 above. Section 15(1) of the Act enables the Court to request assistance from the State of Sierra Leone through the office of the Attorney-General. Rule 39 expressly vests the Prosecutor with certain clearly – defined powers, for the purpose of conducting an investigation [...].

[...]

25. The Chamber opines that [the provisions of Rules 39 and 8(C)] are quite explicit in their intent to ensure that the prosecuting arm of the Court is guaranteed the necessary investigative and prosecutorial logistics and support to enable the Court to function effectively and efficiently in the discharge of its duties within the mandate that has been conferred on it.

26. In addition to these provisions, this is clearly a case that comprises crimes with international components and connections in foreign countries like Liberia, where Prosecution Witness General Tarnue, who has already testified, hails from.

27. This being the case, it is within the discretion of the Prosecution, in the conduct of its investigations, to transcend, should this become necessary, the national frontiers of Sierra Leone with a view to co-operating and working with and alongside willing foreign bodies or agencies.

28. In this context, it is, in our view, legitimate for the Prosecution to seek the assistance of any State, Authority, or any relevant international body as stipulated in Rule 39 of the Rules of Procedure and Evidence of the Court, in order not only to properly fulfill the mandate conferred on it by Statute but also to discharge the heavy burden of proof it bears to establish the guilt of the accused beyond reasonable doubt.

29. Indeed and as was pertinently pointed out by the Appeals Chamber of the ICTY in the *Blaskic* case:

> "... It is self evident that the International Tribunal, in order to bring to trial persons living under the jurisdiction of Sovereign States not being endowed with enforcement agents of its own, must rely upon the cooperation of the States. The International Tribunal must turn to States if it is effectively to investigate crimes, collect evidence, summon witnesses and have indictees arrested and surrendered to the International Tribunal."[1]

[...]

44. The Chamber recalls that both the Defence and Prosecution agree that within the framework of the Court's Statute and Rules, the Office of the Prosecutor is vested with some measure of discretionary latitude in seeking assistance from internal and external agencies for the purpose of the conduct of its investigations. We observe that, unlike Article 15(1) of the Statute which is an exclusionary clause designed to protect and preserve prosecutorial independence, there is no similar statutory prohibition for the Prosecution, in the exercise of its prosecutorial discretion, to seek, within the confines of the law, any assistance from other bodies and Institutions in fulfilling the duties conferred on it by the Statute. Clearly, Article 15(2) of the Statute is explicit in its purport and intendment that:

"The Office of the Prosecutor shall have power to question suspects, victims, and witnesses, to collect evidence and evident on – site investigations. In carrying out these tasks, the Prosecutor shall, as appropriate, be assisted by the Sierra Leone authorities concerned."

45. By parity of reasoning, Rules 8(C), (D) and (E), 39, and 40 of the Court's Rules of Procedure and Evidence cumulatively establish a machinery for co-operation between the Office of the Prosecutor and external agencies or entities, be they States, Governments, Organisations, Bureaus, or related bodies.

46. In this regard, the Defence submissions do not really challenge the authority of the Office of the Prosecutor to seek assistance in the conduct of its investigations. Accordingly, the Chamber concludes that there is clear statutory authority for the Prosecution to seek assistance from both internal and external sources for the purposes of the conduct of its investigations in the course of fulfilling its mandate to bring to justice those who bear the greatest responsibility for crimes against humanity, war crimes and related offences during the hostilities that took place in Sierra Leone at the material times.

47. The complexity, roles, and functions of any such agencies or bodies cannot legally operate as limiting or restricting such authority in the absence of any express statutory provision to that effect."

---

[1] Prosecutor v. Blaskic, *supra*.

Rule 40*bis*: Transfer and Provisional Detention of Suspects
(amended 29 May 2004)

(A) In the conduct of an investigation, the Prosecutor may transmit to the Registrar, for an order by the Designated Judge, a request for the transfer and/or provisional detention of a suspect in the premises of the Detention Facility. This request shall indicate the grounds upon which the request is made and, unless the Prosecutor wishes only to question the suspect, shall include a provisional charge and a brief summary of the material upon which the Prosecutor relies.

(B) The Designated Judge shall order the transfer and provisional detention of the suspect if the following conditions are met:

(i) The Prosecutor has requested a State to arrest the suspect and to place him in custody, in accordance with Rule 40, or the suspect is otherwise detained by a State;

(ii) Where there are provisional charges, and where there is reason to believe that the suspect may have committed a crime or crimes specified in those provisional charges over which the Special Court has jurisdiction; and

(iii) The Designated Judge considers provisional detention to be a necessary measure to prevent the escape of the suspect, physical or mental injury to or intimidation of a victim or witness or the destruction of evidence, or to be otherwise necessary for the conduct of the investigation.

(C) The provisional detention of the suspect may be ordered for a period not exceeding 30 days from the day after the transfer of the suspect to the Detention Facility.

(D) The order for the transfer and provisional detention of the suspect shall be signed by the Designated Judge and bear the seal of the Special Court. The order shall set forth the basis of the request made by the Prosecutor under Sub-Rule (A), including the provisional charge, and shall state the Designated Judge's grounds for making the order, having regard to Sub-Rule (B). The order, shall also specify the initial time limit for the provisional detention of the suspect and when served on the suspect be accompanied by a statement of his rights, as specified in this Rule and in Rules 42 and 43.

(E) As soon as possible, copies of the order and of the request by the Prosecutor shall be served upon the suspect and his counsel by the Registrar.

(F) At the Prosecutor's request indicating the grounds upon which it is made and if warranted by the needs of the investigation, the Designated Judge who made the initial order, or another Designated Judge, may decide, subsequent to an *inter partes* hearing and before the end of the period of detention, to extend the provisional detention for a period not exceeding 30 days.

(G) At the Prosecutor's request indicating the grounds upon which it is made and if warranted by special circumstances, the Designated Judge who made the initial order, or another Designated Judge, may decide, subsequent to an *inter partes* hearing and before the end of the period of detention, to extend the detention for a further period not exceeding 30 days.

(H) The total period of provisional detention shall in no case exceed 90 days after the day of transfer of the suspect to the Special Court, at the end of which, in the event the indictment has not been approved and an arrest warrant signed, the suspect shall be released or, if appropriate, be delivered to the authorities of the State to which the request was initially made.

(I) The provisions in Rules 55(B) to 59 shall apply to the execution of the order for the transfer and provisional detention of the suspect.

(J) After his transfer to the seat of the Special Court, the suspect, assisted by his counsel, shall be brought, without delay, before the Designated Judge who made the initial order, or another Designated Judge, who shall ensure that his rights are respected.

(K) During detention, the Prosecutor, the suspect or his counsel may submit to the Trial Chamber all applications relative to the propriety of provisional detention or to the suspect's release.

(L) Without prejudice to Sub-Rules (C) to (H), the Rules of Detention shall apply to the provisional detention of persons under this Rule.

TRIAL CHAMBERS DECISIONS

- **Rule 40*bis*(B): Transfer and Provisional Detention of Suspects – Decision of the Designated Judge**

R40*bis*-TC-1 o *Prosecutor v. Gbao*, Case No. SCSL-03-09-PD, Order for Transfer and Provisional Detention Pursuant to Rule 40*bis*, 18 March 2003:

WHEREAS the Prosecutor reports that he is investigating crimes allegedly committed by Augustine Gbao in the territory of Sierra Leone since 30 November 1996, crimes which fall within the jurisdiction of the Special Court;

WHEREAS, according to the Prosecutor, AUGUSTINE GBAO participated in widespread attacks against UNAMSIL peacekeepers and personnel, including the unlawful killing and abduction of UNAMSIL peacekeepers;

WHEREAS the Special Court considers, on the basis of the request submitted by the Prosecutor, and on the evidence brought to its attention in the affidavit attached to the request, that there is a reason to believe that AUGUSTINE GBAO may, in the light of the above have committed SERIOUS VIOLATIONS OF INTERNATIONAL HUMANITARIAN LAW, CRIMES AGAINST HUMANITY, VIOLATIONS OF ARTICLE 3 COMMON TO THE GENEVA CONVENTIONS AND OF ADDITIONAL PROTOCOL II, punishable respectively under Article 4.b., Article 2.a., Article 3.a. and 3.c. of the Statute of the Special Court ("the Statute");

WHEREAS, furthermore, the Prosecutor contends that the provisional detention of AUGUSTINE GBAO is a necessary measure to prevent his escape and also prevent the suspect from seeking to intimidate or to cause bodily harm to victims or witnesses or to destroy evidence, or to be otherwise necessary for the conduct of the investigation in the matter concerning him;

WHEREAS, the Judge, in the light of the above, is convinced that the provisional detention of AUGUSTINE GBAO is necessary;

R40*bis*-TC-2

o *Prosecutor v Kondewa*, Case No. SCSL-03-12-PD, Decision on the Urgent Defence Application for Release from Provisional Detention, 21 November 2003, para. 34-36:[35]

34. [...] Rule 40 *bis* (A) provides that when requesting an order for transfer and provisional detention, such a request shall indicate the grounds upon which it is made and shall include provisional charge and a *brief summary* of the material upon which the Prosecution is relying. According to the language of Rule 40 *bis* (B), once the requirements in paragraphs (i), (ii) and (iii) are met, the Designated Judge has to comply with the

---

[35] See also *Prosecutor v Fofana*, SCSL-03-11-PD, Decision on the Urgent Defence Application for Release from Provisional Detention, 21 November 2003.

request and order the transfer and provisional detention of the suspect.

35. In making his ruling pursuant to Rule 40 *bis* (B) (iii), the Designated Judge relied on the statements submitted to him by the Prosecution. The issue was to determine whether such statements were sufficient to satisfy the requirements of Rule 40 *bis* (iii). The Designated Judge found that the information provided was indeed sufficient and could only have dismissed the Prosecution's Request for Transfer and Provisional Detention if there had been valid reasons not to accept, believe or to disregard such information. Although it might have been preferable for the Prosecution to provide more detailed statements, were it possible, it still remains that such is not a requirement under Rule 40 *bis* (A) of the Rules, nor is there any requirement that there be specified factual basis in support of the request.

36. Hence, the Defence having not shown that the information provided by the Prosecution was insufficient, the Chamber declares itself satisfied with such information and would also like to mention that it is certainly not sufficient for the Defence to simply state that the Designated Judge could not have exercised appropriate judicial control without providing any evidence to support the allegation that the disclosure by the Prosecution might not have been 'full and frank'.

- **Rule 40*bis*(B): Transfer and Provisional Detention of Suspects – Necessity of the Detention – Proportionality Test**

R40*bis*-TC-3   o *Prosecutor v. Kondewa*, Case No. SCSL-03-12-PD, Decision on the Urgent Defence Application for Release from Provisional Detention, 21 November 2003, para. 38-40, 42-43:[36]

38. [. . .] [T]he requirement of 'necessity' of the detention deserves a particular understanding as far as international criminal tribunals and courts are concerned. In the case of *The Prosecutor v. Krajisnik and Plavsic*, the Trial Chamber held in its Decision on Momcilo Krajisnik's Notice of Motion for Provisional Release that 'provisional release continues to be the exception and not the rule'.[(1)] Moreover, in the case of *The Prosecutor v. Hadzihasanovic et al.* before the ICTY,[(2)] the Trial Chamber held that the application of the principles embodied in the International Covenant on Civil and Political

---

[36] See also *Prosecutor v Fofana*, SCSL-2003-11-PD, Decision on the Urgent Defence Application for Release from Provisional detention, 21 November 2003.

Rights (ICCPR) and in the European Convention for the Protection of Human Rights and Fundamental Freedoms (ECHR) 'stipulates that *de jure* pre-trial detention should be the exception and not the rule as regards prosecution before an international court'. However, it also stated that, since, unlike national courts, the ICTY does not have its own coercive powers to enforce its decisions, 'pre-trial detention de facto seems to be rather the rule'. Therefore, the ICTY Trial Chamber concluded that judicial control of the respect of the fundamental rights of suspects should be made *in concreto*, not *in abstracto*, as regards international criminal courts.

39. The Chamber concurs with the above findings and, as regards the Special Court, wishes to insist on the fact that it is indispensably necessary to bear in mind its specificity as opposed to any other domestic tribunal or court; indeed, given the very serious nature of the crimes which fall under its jurisdiction, certain procedural guarantees may require to be applied differently before it. It is the Chamber's view that this would certainly be the case with regard to provisional release.

- *The proportionality test*

40. The Chamber finds that the issue of the necessity of the transfer and detention of the Suspect is closely related to that of the proportionality test applicable to provisional release.

[...]

42. The Defence refers to the aforementioned case of *The Prosecutor v. Hadzihasanovic et al.* before the ICTY,[3] where the Trial Chamber applied the principle of proportionality according to which, when interpreting Rule 65 of the ICTY Rules of Procedure and Evidence,[4] the Judges had to consider whether the measure was 'suitable, necessary and if its degree of and scope remain in a reasonable relationship to the envisaged target'. The Trial Chamber found that 'it was no longer necessary to execute the order for the execution on remand pending trial', because the guarantees offered by each of the three Co-Accused and by the Government of Bosnia and Herzegovina reasonably safeguarded the proper conduct of the proceedings.

43. However, as regards the Suspect before the Special Court, the Chamber takes notice of the fact that no such guarantees have been secured, neither by the Suspect himself, nor by the Government of Sierra Leone. Moreover, in the aforementioned case, the ICTY Trial Chamber took into account the fact that the Accused had surrendered voluntarily to the Tribunal. There is no indication that this was the case of the Suspect before this Court.

---

[1] *The Prosecutor v. Krajisnik and Plavsic*, Decision on Momcilo Krajisnik's Notice of Motion for Provisional Release, IT-00-39, 8 October 2001, para. 12.

⁽²⁾ *The Prosecutor v. Hadzihasanovic et al.*, Decision Granting Provisional Release, IT-01-47-AR72, 19 December 2001, para. 8.
⁽³⁾ Ib.
⁽⁴⁾ On provisional release.

- **Rule 40*bis*(K): Transfer and Provisional Detention of Suspects – Applications – Procedure**

R40*bis*-TC-4 o *Prosecutor v. Kondewa*, SCSL-03-12-PD, Decision on the Urgent Defence Application for Release from Provisional Detention, 21 November 2003, para. 29-30:[37]

> 29. The Chamber finds that the language of Rule 40 *bis* (K) is unambiguous and clearly provides that the *Trial Chamber* is competent to hear all applications relative to the propriety of provisional detention or to the release of suspects. Moreover, the Chamber finds that it should also be taken into account that Rule 40 *bis* (K) provides additional protection of the rights of suspects: the fact that the decision on arbitrary arrest and detention is to be made by all three Judges of the Chamber is a reinforced guarantee of fairness of the ruling.
>
> 30. Furthermore, Rule 40 *bis* (K) provides that applications on the propriety of provisional detention or to the suspect's release may be made 'during detention' and such applications can indeed then be made at any time during that period. Nothing in the Rules allows for such applications to also be made to the Designated Judge during the hearing under Rule 40 *bis* (J).

---

[37] See also *Prosecutor v. Fofana*, SCSL-03-11-PD, Decision on the Urgent Defence Application for Release from Provisional Detention, 21 November 2003.

Rule 44: Appointment and Qualifications of Counsel
(amended 29 May 2004)

(A) Counsel engaged by a suspect or an accused shall file his power of attorney with the Registrar at the earliest opportunity. Subject to verification by the Registrar, a counsel shall be considered qualified to represent a suspect or accused, provided that he has been admitted to the practice of law in a State and practiced criminal law for a minimum of five years.

(B) In the performance of their duties counsel shall be subject to the relevant provisions of the Agreement, the Statute, the Rules, the Rules of Detention and any other rules or regulations adopted by the Special Court, the Headquarters Agreement, the Code of Professional Conduct and the codes of practice and ethics governing their profession and, if applicable, the Directive on the Assignment of Defence Counsel.

TRIAL CHAMBERS DECISIONS

- **Rule 44(B): Appointment and Qualifications of Counsel – Role of the Defence Counsel**

R44-TC-1

o *Prosecutor v. Norman*, Case No. SCSL-04-14-T, Decision on the Application of Samuel Hinga Norman for Self-Representation Under Article 17(4)(d) of the Statute of the Special Court, 8 June 2004, para. 23-24:

23. The role of the Defence Counsel, it has been stated, is institutional and is meant to serve, not only the interests of his client, but also those of the Court and the overall interests of justice. This is why we are strongly of the opinion that the action by the Accused to relieve his Counsel of their judicial duty of defending him and on the date of his trial and certainly on the grounds of a right which he enjoys under Statute should be viewed or endorsed with a lot of caution.

24. In the case of the *Prosecutor v. Barayagwiza*,[1] the Trial Chamber of the ICTR held that Counsel is assigned not appointed and in the view of the Chamber, this does not only entail obligations towards the client but also implies that he represents the interests of the Tribunal to ensure that the Accused receives a fair trial.

(1) *Prosecutor v. Barayagwiza*, Case No. ICTR-97-19-T, Decision on Defence Counsel Motion to Withdraw, 2 November 2000.

R44-TC-2

o *Prosecutor v. Gbao*, Case No. SCSL-04-15-T, Decision on application to Withdraw Counsel, 7 July 2004, para. 17:

17. We also note that all counsel before the Special Court has an obligation to act as an officer to the Court, in addition to acting in the interests of the Accused person.

R44-TC-3

o *Prosecutor v. Norman, Fofana, Kondewa*, Case No. SCSL-04-14-T, Consequential Order on the Role of Court Appointed Counsel, 1 October 2004:

ORDERS that the duty of Court Appointed Counsel will be to represent the case of the First, Second and Third Accused, and in particular, shall:

a. represent the Accused by investigating and preparing for the testimony of Prosecution witnesses and cross-examining them;
b. prepare for and examine those witnesses Court Assigned Counsel deem it appropriate to call for his defence;
c. make all submissions on fact and law that they deem it appropriate to make in the form of oral and written motions before the court;
d. seek from the Trial Chamber such orders as they consider necessary to enable them to present the Accused's case properly, including the issuance of subpoenas;
e. discuss with the Accused the conduct of the case, endeavour to obtain his instructions thereon and take account of views expressed by the Accused, while retaining the right to determine what course to follow; and
f. act throughout in the best interests of the Accused;

STATES that this Order may be modified at any time should necessity arise.

R44-TC-4

o *Prosecutor v. Brima, Kamara, Kanu*, Case No. SCSL-04-16-T, Consequential Order on the Role of Court Appointed Counsel, 13 May 2005:

RECALLING the oral majority order delivered by the Trial Chamber on 12 May 2005 on the "Confidential Joint Defence Submission on the Withdrawal of Counsel in the AFRC Case" and the Accused Kanu's "Defence Motion to Inform the Trial Chamber on the Legal Position of the Defence in View of Contempt of Court Developments;

[...]

ORDERS that the duty of Glenna Thompson and Kojo Graham as Counsel for Alex Tamba Brima and Mohamed Pa-Momo Fofanah as Counsel for Brima Bazzy Kamara shall be to represent their clients until Lead Counsel will be assigned to these two Accused, and in particular, shall:

1. represent the Accused by investigating and preparing for the testimony of Prosecution witnesses and cross-examining them;
2. prepare for and examine those witnesses Counsel deem appropriate to call for their defence;
3. make all submissions on fact and law that Counsel deem appropriate to make in the form of oral and written motions before the court;
4. seek from the Trial Chamber such orders as they consider necessary to enable them to present the Accused's case properly, including the issuance of subpoenas;
5. discuss with the Accused the conduct of the case, endeavour to obtain his instructions thereon and take account of views expressed by the Accused, while retaining the right to determine what course to follow;
6. draw to the attention of the Trial Chamber any exculpatory or mitigating evidence;
7. act throughout in the best interests of the Accused and in any other way which Counsel considers appropriate in order to secure a fair and expeditious trial;

- **Rule 44(B): Appointment and Qualifications of Counsel – Role of the Standby Counsel**

R44-TC-5

o *Prosecutor v. Norman*, SCSL-04-14-T, Consequential Order on Assignment and Role of Standby Counsel, 14 June 2004:

CONSIDERING that it is in the overall interests of justice to assign a Standby Counsel to assist the Accused, in the exercise of his right to self-representation;

CONSIDERING that Standby Counsel will provide legal

assistance to the Accused and ensure the safeguard to his right to a fair and expeditious trial;[38]

CONSIDERING that a counsel-client privilege applies to any communications and correspondence between the Accused and Standby Counsel;

CONSIDERING that Standby Counsel, in providing assistance to the Accused, shall be subject to "the relevant provisions of the Agreement, the Statute, the Rules, the Rules of Detention and any other rules or regulations adopted by the Special Court, the Headquarters agreement, the Code of Professional Conduct and the codes of practice and ethics governing their profession and, if applicable, the Directive on the Assignment of Defence Counsel", as provided in Rule 44(B) of the Rules;

[...]

FOR THE FOREGOING REASONS;

PURSUANT TO Rule 54 of the Rules, the Trial Chamber;

HEREBY ORDERS that Standby Counsel are to be assigned to the Accused to assist him in the exercise of his right to self-representation and for the purposes of these proceedings;

FURTHER ORDERS that the role of Standby Counsel, be strictly defined as follows:

1. To assist the Accused in the exercise of his right to self-representation;
2. To assist the Accused in the preparation and presentation of his case during the trial phase, whenever requested to do so by the Accused;
3. To actively guide the Accused through the procedures of the trial in accordance with the Statute and the Rules;
4. To investigate relevant facts and law, identify possible defences and suggest steps to be taken by the Accused;
5. To receive all Court documents, filings and disclosed materials that are received by or sent to the Accused;
6. To be present in the courtroom during the proceedings;
7. To offer legal advice to the Accused;
8. To address the Court whenever requested to do so by the Accused or by the Trial Chamber;
9. To put questions to witnesses on behalf of the Accused if called upon to do so by the Trial Chamber,

---

[38] *Prosecutor v. Vojislav Seselj*, Decision on Prosecution's Motion for Order Appointing Counsel to Assist Vojislav Seselj With His Defence, 9 May 2003, para. 28.

in particular to sensitive or protected witnesses, or in the event of abusive conduct by the Accused, without depriving the Accused of his right to control the content of the examination;
10. To be actively engaged in the substantive preparation of the case and to participate in the proceedings, and to be prepared to take over representation of the Accused should the Accused engage in disruptive conduct or conduct requiring his removal from the courtroom as outlined in Rule 80(B) in the Rules of Procedure and Evidence;
11. To assemble and present information relevant to all the stages of the proceedings;
12. To refrain from conduct that may directly or indirectly impact adversely on the exercise of the Accused's right of self representation;

- **Rule 44(B): Appointment and Qualifications of Counsel – Composition of the Defence Team – Information to the Registry**

R44-TC-6

o *Prosecutor v. Gbao*, Case No. SCSL-03-09-PT, Decision on the Prosecution Motion for Immediate Protective Measures for Witnesses and Victims and for Non-Public Disclosure, 10 October 2003, para. 59:[39]

59. Regarding order (h) requested by the Prosecution in its Motion, the Special Court acknowledges that there is no dispute as to the necessity, in the interest of justice, of controlling the identities of all persons working for each Defence team. However, the Special Court does not consider it appropriate, nor justified, that the Defence be compelled to provide to the Trial Chamber and to the Prosecution a designation of such persons and to advise the Trial Chamber and the Prosecution in writing of any changes in the composition of the Defence team. The Defence argues that such a designation should rather be made available to the Registrar. The Special Court agrees with the Defence and holds that it is a highly necessary step to take. However, as the organisation of the Special Court for Sierra Leone also includes a Defence Office, such a designation, in the opinion of the Special Court, should more appropriately also be made available to the said Defence Office. Therefore, requested order (h) of the Motion shall be modified and is granted in the following form: the Special

---

[39] See also *Prosecutor v. Sesay, Kallon, Gbao*, Case No. SCSL-04-15-PT, Decision on Prosecution Motion for Modification of Protective Measures for Witnesses, 5 July 2004, para. 22.

Court orders the Defence to provide to the Registrar and to the Defence Office a designation of all persons working on the Defence team who have access to any information referred to in paragraphs 20 (a) through 20 (e) of the Motion, and orders the Defence to advise the Registrar and the Defence Office in writing of any changes in the composition of the Defence team.

- **Rule 44(B): Appointment and Qualifications of Counsel – Authority of the Directive on the Assignment of Defence Counsel**

R44-TC-7

o *Prosecutor v. Brima*, Case No. SCSL-04-16-PT, Decision on Applicant's Motion Against Denial by the Acting Principal Defender to Enter a Legal Service Contract for the Assignment of Counsel, 6 May 2004, para. 35:

35. [. . .] [T]he provisions of the Directive on the Assignment of Counsel promulgated by the Registrar on the 3rd October, 2003, cannot operate to either replace or to amend the Rules of Procedure and Evidence adopted by the Plenary of Judges of the Special Court.

- **Rule 44(B): Appointment and Qualifications of Counsel – Contradiction Between the Code of Conduct of Counsel and the Bar Code of Counsel**

R44-TC-8

o *Prosecutor v. Brima, Kamara, Kanu*, Case No. SCSL-04-16-T, Decision on the Confidential Application for Withdrawal by Counsel for Brima and Kamara and on the Request for Further Representation by Counsel for Kanu, 20 May 2005, para. 44, 47-50:

44. Under Rule 44(B), Counsel is subject, amongst other things, to the Statute, the Rules, and the codes of practice and ethics governing their profession. Rules 44(B) states:

> In the performance of their duties counsel shall be subject to the relevant provisions of the Agreement, the Statute, the Rules, the Rules of Detention and any other rules or regulations adopted by the Special Court, the Headquarters Agreement, **the Code** of Professional Conduct and the codes of practice and ethics governing their profession and, if applicable, the Directive on the Assignment of Defence Counsel.

[. . .]

47. In our opinion, a counsel could not possibly be in breach of his Bar Code by continuing to act for a client where the Trial Chamber, in the interests of justice and to protect the rights of the accused, makes an order under laws to which the counsel is subject in the performance of his duties, compelling him to remain assigned to the accused, or directing him to represent the accused.

48. We find that Lead Counsels' subjective concerns that they may be in breach of their Bar Code are not such exceptional circumstances as to allow them to withdraw from the case.

49. It follows from what has been said that there can be no doubt that Lead Counsel have experienced some serious difficulties in their relationship with their clients. In such circumstances, we approve the statement by the ICTY's President in *Milosevic*, that:

> "Representing criminal defendants is not an easy task. Assigned Counsel would do well to recognize that fact, to realize the breadth of activities that they can carry out even in the absence of [their client's] cooperation, and to continue making the best professional efforts on [their client's] behalf that are possible under the circumstances."[1]

50. Although the lawyer/client relationship is far from satisfactory, it has not completely broken down, since there are still some communications between them, and Lead Counsel pass on information to the Court on behalf of the Accused. Given the complex nature of the relationship between Lead Counsel and their clients, we find that the difficulties discussed above, although serious, are not, by themselves, so exceptional as to warrant the withdrawal of Counsel.

---

[1] *The Prosecutor v. Slobodan Milošević*, The President's Decision Affirming the Registrar's Denial of Assigned Counsel's Application to Withdraw, 7 February 2005, para. 13.

- **Rule 44(B): Appointment and Qualifications of Counsel – Appointed Counsel – Applicable Rules – Withdrawal**

R44-TC-9

o *Prosecutor v. Norman*, Case No. SCSL-04-14-T, Consequential Order on the Withdrawal of Ms. Quincy Whitaker as Court Appointed Counsel for the First Accused, 19 November 2004:

CONSIDERING that the act of assignment of Counsel by the Registrar or by the Principal Defender, pursuant to Rules 44 and 45 of the Rules of Procedure and Evidence of the Special Court ("Rules") and the Directive on the Assignment of

Counsel, and the act of appointment of Counsel by the Trial Chamber, in the interests of justice, and pursuant to Rule 60 of the Rules, are different means of designating Counsel to represent an Accused person, who upon assignment or appointment are subjected to the same obligations to act both in the interests of the Accused and in the overall interests of justice;

CONSIDERING that in the performance of their duties, Court Appointed Counsel shall be subject to the relevant provisions of the Statute, of the Agreement, of the Rules, of any other rules, regulations or Codes of Conduct adopted by the Special Court, of the host Country Agreement, of the Directive on the Assignement of Counsel, and of the codes of practice and ethics governing their profession, and that these provisons, as they explicitly apply to Assigned Counsel, apply *mutatis mutandis* to Court Appointed Counsel;

CONSIDERING therefore, that the relevant provisions as outlined above, that govern the withdrawal of Assigned Counsel, apply *mutatis mutandis* to Court Appointed Counsel;

R44-TC-10

o *Prosecutor v. Norman*, Case No. SCSL-04-14-T, Ruling on request for Withdrawal of Mr. Tim Owen QC, as Court Appointed Counsel for the First Accused, 1 March 2005:

NOTING Articles 23, 24 and 25 of the Directive on the Assignment of Counsel;

CONSIDERING that the decision of the Trial Chamber to appoint Counsel for the First Accused was made to ensure the fairness of the trial and that it follows that an application that fundamentally challenges that decision is subject to the jurisdiction of the Trial Chamber;[1]

CONSIDERING the professional and practical difficulties that Mr. Tim Owen, Q.C., has advanced as grounds for his unwillingness to represent the First Accused as Court Appointed Counsel;

CONSIDERING that the reasons advanced by Mr. Tim Owen, Q.C. for his requested withdrawal as Court Appointed Counsel demonstrate good cause and that this request for withdrawal is in the interests of justice;

THE TRIAL CHAMBER THEREFORE:

DETERMINES that the Request of Mr. Tim Owen, Q.C. to withdraw as Court Appointed Counsel for the First Accused should be granted; and

INSTRUCTS the Registrar, in consultation with the Principal Defender, pursuant to Article 24 of the Practice Directive, to grant the request for withdrawal of Mr. Tim Owen, Q.C. as Court Appointed Counsel for the First Accused and to take the necessary measures to give effect to this Decision.

[1] *Prosecutor v. Milosevic*, Decision on Interlocutory Appeal of the Trial Chamber's Decision on the Assignment of Defence Counsel, 1 November 2004, para. 15; *Prosecutor v. Milosevic*, Reasons for Decision on Assignment of Defence Counsel, 22 September 2004, para. 34.

- **Rule 44(B): Appointment and Qualifications of Counsel – Defence Team – Investigators**

R44-TC-11
o *Prosecutor v. Samura*, Case No. SCSL-05-01, Judgment in Contempt Proceedings, 26 October 2005, para. 66-67:

66. It is generally accepted that defence investigators, due to the specific nature of their work, could be considered as an integral part of a Defence Team and, therefore, bound as such by any order of a Chamber directed to a particular Defence Team. In particular, as recently held in the *Karemera et al.* trial at the ICTR:

Defence Investigators are not members of the public but part of the Defence team. They are responsible for obtaining the factual information relevant for the Defence to defend the accusations against them. They spend a considerable amount of time in the field and therefore usually possess first-hand-experience of the locations in question and of the facts adduced at trial. They have interviewed witnesses who will appear during the proceedings. The contribution of the Investigators is therefore an integral part of the work of the Defence.[1]

67. Trial Chamber I recognized this in allowing certain Defence investigators who, by the very nature of their work, provide immediate and invaluable information to assist in the preparation and conduct of the defence of the Accused to be present in the well of the Courtroom during closed session hearings.[2] In particular, the Trial Chamber held that Defence Counsel will be held accountable "for ensuring the Defence Investigators that comprise members of the Defence Team and who may be present during closed session hearings, do not disclose the identity of protected witnesses or the evidence given during those closed sessions to anybody outside the Defence Team".[3]

(1) *Prosecutor v. Karemera at al.*, Case No. ICTR-98-44-PT, Decision on the Defence Motion to Permit Investigators to Attend Closed Sessions, 18 August 2005, para. 8.
(2) *Prosecutor v. Norman et al.*, Case No. SCSL-04-14-T, Decision on Joint Motion by Sam Hinga Norman, Moinina Fofana and Allieu Kondewa Seeking Permission for Defence Investigators to Sit in Court During Closed Sessions, 28 February 2005, paras 11ff.
(3) *Id.*, para. 18.

Rule 45: Defence Office
(amended 14 May 2005)

The Registrar shall establish, maintain and develop a Defence Office, for the purpose of ensuring the rights of suspects and accused. The Defence Office shall be headed by the Special Court Principal Defender.

(A) The Defence Office shall, in accordance with the Statute and Rules, provide advice, assistance and representation to:

  (i) suspects being questioned by the Special Court or its agents under Rule 42, including non-custodial questioning;
  (ii) accused persons before the Special Court.

(B) The Defence Office shall fulfil its functions by providing, *inter alia*:

  (i) initial legal advice and assistance by duty counsel who shall be situated within a reasonable proximity to the Detention Facility and the seat of the Special Court and shall be available as far as practicable to attend the Detention Facility in the event of being summoned;
  (ii) legal assistance as ordered by the Special Court in accordance with Rule 61, if the accused does not have sufficient means to pay for it, as the interests of justice may so require;
  (iii) adequate facilities for counsel in the preparation of the defence.

(C) The Principal Defender shall, in providing an effective defence, maintain a list of highly qualified criminal defence counsel whom he believes are appropriate to act as duty counsel or to lead the defence or appeal of an accused. Such counsel, who may include members of the Defence Office, shall:

  (i) speak fluent English;
  (ii) be admitted to practice law in any State;
  (iii) have at least 7 years' relevant experience; and
  (iv) have indicated their willingness and full-time availability to be assigned by the Special Court to suspects or accused.

(D) Any request for replacement of an assigned counsel shall be made to the Principal Defender. Under exceptional circumstances, the request may be made to a Chamber upon good cause being shown and after having been satisfied that the request is not designed to delay the proceedings.

(E) Subject to any order of a Chamber, Counsel will represent the accused and conduct the case to finality. Failure to do so, absent just cause approved by the Chamber, may result in forfeiture of fees in whole or in part. In such circumstances the Chamber may make an order accordingly. Counsel shall only be permitted to withdraw from the case to which he has been assigned in the most exceptional circumstances. In the event of such withdrawal the Principal Defender shall assign another Counsel who may be a member of the Defence Office, to the indigent accused.

(F) Notwithstanding Rules 44(A) and 45(C)(iii), the Principal Defender may, in exceptional circumstances, assign as co-counsel, individuals with less than five years admission to the bar of a State.

TRIAL CHAMBERS DECISIONS

- **Rule 45: Defence Office – Role of the Defence Office**

R45-TC-1
o *Prosecutor v. Kamara*, Case No. SCSL-03-10-PT, Order on the Request by the Defence Office for Suspension of Consideration of Prosecution's Motion for Protective Measures Until Counsel Is Assigned, 26 June 2003, para. 3-6:

3. The Defence Office is an innovative and unique appearance in international criminal law. Neither the International Tribunals for Rwanda and the Former Yugoslavia, nor the newly established International Criminal Court provide for such an institution. Even though the Defence Office is established and maintained by the Registrar, it is and remains an independent organ in the administration of justice, essential for the proper functioning of the Court and whose duties are to ensure that the Rights of Accused and Suspects are respected and that they are afforded an effective defence at the Special Court.

4. This implies as well that the Defence Office has obligations and duties, albeit of a different nature toward the Court to ensure that the Accused receives a fair trial. Therefore as long as a Suspect or Accused has not chosen or has not been assigned a Defence Counsel it is the responsibility of the Defence Office to ensure that his rights are properly and adequately respected. The performance of such duties entails the right and obligation of the Defence Office to actively file motions on behalf of a Suspect or Accused, until he has chosen or has been assigned a permanent Defence Counsel.

5. The current application of the Defence Office accomplishes precisely this function, as during the administration of an assignment of a Defence Counsel the time limit for the Prosecution Motion on Protective Measures was underway. In this administrative process of assignment of counsel and due to strict time limitations it became apparent that there could be a conflict as to who should legally represent and best act for the Accused in the said circumstances. It should be noted that the Defence Counsel was finally assigned a day prior to the expiration of the time limit prescribed to file a response to the motion. From the foregoing it becomes apparent that the issue to be dealt with is therefore not a question of the suspension of the Prosecution Motion for Protective Measures but more appropriately one of extension of time limits.

6. Although the Special Court concludes that the Defence Office would have had the capacity and authority to act for the Accused it would appear preferable and would provide for more expeditious proceedings, given that the Defence Counsel has now been assigned, to consider, in the interest of all parties, such Counsel as the Counsel of record for this Accused.

R45-TC-2

o *Prosecutor v. Kallon*, Case No. SCSL-03-07-PT, Decision on the application for Leave to Submit *Amicus Curiae* Briefs, 17 July 2003, para. 10-12:

10. [. . .] In the context of the instant Motion, however, the Chamber recalls that the Defence Office seeks leave to make *amicus curiae* submissions on the three main grounds: (a) that, as in *Milosevic* case, "it retains the right and duty to make submissions to assist the proper determination of the case," (b) that it is "desirable for the proper determination of the case that the Chamber should have benefit" of such submissions; and (c) that because of its "historical significance as the first "public defender's office" to be established in an international court or tribunal, that it is in the interests of justice" for leave to be granted.

11. First, the Chamber wishes to observe that the analogy between the role of the *amicus curiae* in the *Milosevic* case and that of the Defence Office, as alleged, is inapposite and uninstructive. In the *Milosevic* case, the accused refused legal representation and insisted on self-representation. Furthermore, it was at the Chamber's initiative that the Registrar was instructed to appoint an *amicus curiae* not in response to an application. Second, as regards the instant Motion, all the accused in respect of whom preliminary motions based on lack of jurisdiction have been filed are fully represented by permanent

counsel. Significantly, in this connection, the Chamber wishes to emphasize that once a defence counsel has been appointed, the Defence Office of the Special Court, as presently organized and structured is, and in terms of its future evolution, will remain, a legal resource support unit for the permanent pool of defence counsel representing suspects and accused persons, essentially researching common legal issues such as jurisdiction in conjunction with the latter. It would, therefore, be highly undesirable for the proper determination of the cases of these accused for the Defence Office to perform the role of a third party intervener or *amicus curiae* though, in the view of the Chamber, it is not disputed that the Defence Office does, as it claims, retain "the right and duty to make submissions to assist in the proper determination of the case" involving Morris Kallon. Thirdly, the Chamber holds that it is extremely doubtful whether the Defence Office can properly be characterized as "an organisation or person" within the meaning of Rule 74.

12. Based on the foregoing analysis, the Chamber considers that the Motion brought by the Defence Office is misconceived and meretricious.

- **Rule 45: Defence Office – Duty of the Registrar to Maintain a Defence Office – Powers of the Registrar**

R45-TC-3

o *Prosecutor v. Brima, Kamara*, Case No. SCSL-04-16-T, Decision on the Extremely Urgent Confidential Joint Motion for the Re-Appointment of Kevin Metzger and Wilbert Harris as Lead Counsel for Alex Tamba Brima and Brima Bazzy Kamara and Decision on Cross-Motion by Deputy Principal Defender to Trial Chamber II for Clarification of its Oral Order of 12 May 2005, 9 June 2005, para. 31, 38-40, 61:

31. If Counsel seek to base their submission on the reference to the Registrar consulting with the Trial Chamber, then the submission fails to take account of the powers to the Registrar, pursuant to Rule 33B, to make oral or written representations to the Chamber on any issue arising in the context of a specific case which may affect the discharge of his functions. These functions, as the Deputy Principal Defender and the Registrar submit, include the duty to maintain a Defence office pursuant to Rule 45.

[...]

38. [...] As the Deputy Principal Defender has conceded in the absence of the Principal Defender, certain obligations to carry out duties fall upon the Registrar. He has a further overall duty to act as principal administrator of the Court.

39. In exercising his duty, the Registrar sought to uphold an order of the Trial Chamber allowing Counsel's application to withdraw and ordering that another Counsel be assigned in accordance with Rule 45(E).

40. To argue that upholding and implementing a Court Order, made on the application of the parties concerned, is "without legal or just cause" is fallacious.

[...]

61. Looking at the history of this case since we made our order on the 12 May 2005, it seems to us as though the Deputy Principal Defender has gone out of her way to undermine our decision. Almost a month has gone by and she has not made any attempt to appoint new lead counsel. It appears she is unwilling to do her job, and unwilling to follow the directions of the Registrar, who has overall authority over the administration of the Special Court and, in particular, over the assignment of counsel, which is an administrative matter.

- **Rule 45: Defence Office – Decisions of the Principal Defender – Power of the Trial Chamber to Judicially Review**

R45-TC-4

o *Prosecutor v. Brima*, Case No. SCSL-04-16-PT, Decision on Applicant's Motion Against Denial by the Acting Principal Defender to Enter a Legal Service Contract for the Assignment of Counsel, 6 May 2004, para. 51-52, 63-71:

51. We understand by this submission that the [Registrar] is claiming immunity from judicial review by this Chamber, a legally constituted International Tribunal, in exercise of its inherent jurisdiction, of the decisions which are subject of the litigation, made by an Official of the Registry of the Chamber. In the same vein, we observe that the [Registrar] contests the Chamber's inherent jurisdiction.

52. In this regard, we are of the opinion that an arbitrary and illegal withdrawal, as we find in this case, of the Applicant's 'chosen' Counsel by the [Principal Defender], is tantamount to a denial of his statutory right to a Counsel 'of his own choosing', and hold more importantly that this Motion, brought and even entertained under Rule 17(4)(d) of the statute, is properly before us within the context of the exercise of our inherent jurisdiction.

[...]

63. We note in the case of the CHIEF CONSTABLE OF NORTH WALES POLICE VS EVANS (1982) 1 WLR 1155 at 1174, that Lord Birngham defined a Judicial review as a "review of the manner in which the decision was made", requiring that statutory powers be exercised reasonably, in good faith, and on correct grounds,[1] evidently implicating the parameters of the doctrine of *ultra vires*.

64. In the Chamber's view, the subject-matter of the application before the Court is essentially one that goes to the issue of the legality or the reasonableness of the exercise of the statutory power by the [Principal Defender] in refusing to conclude a Legal Services Contract for the assignment of Counsel to the Accused, the Applicant herein, and in fact, withdrawing, by his letter dated 12th of December, 2003, the Provisional Assignment of Counsel to the Applicant.

65. On these jurisdictional objections, it is our considered opinion, from the foregoing analysis, that the Trial Chamber, in view of the mandatory provisions of Article 17(4)(d) of the Statute can, as it does now, invoke its judicial prerogative based on the concept of our inherent jurisdiction, to entertain and adjudicate on a motion of the nature of the one under consideration.

66. We would like to say here that dismissing this Motion either on the merits or on the jurisdictional grounds as the Respondents urge to do, would amount to conceding to the merits of the objections of both the [Principal Defender and the Registrar] to our jurisdiction and competence to entertain it and in particular, would be approving a judicial endorsement of the [Registrar]'s submissions, claiming immunity from a Judicial review of [the Principal Defender]'s acts which are palpably arbitrary, *ultra vires* and offensive to law.

67. This, in our opinion, would further amount to a total abdication on our part, of our sovereign obligation and judicial responsibility as a Court and as Judges, to subject questionable administrative acts to Judicial scrutiny and review in order to check and curb arbitrary acts, conduct, or decisions taken by our Administrative Officials in particular, and by the Executive Organs in general.

68. In this regard, we cite the remarks of LORD REID in the case of PADFIELD VS. MINISTRY OF AGRICULTURE, FISHERIES AND FOOD [1968] AC 997 which we consider and analogous to the Brima/Terry situation now in our hands and where His Lordship had this to say:

> "... In a matter of this kind it is not possible to draw a hard and fast line, but if the Minister, by reason of his having misconstrued the Act for any reason, so uses his

discretion as to thwart or run counter the policy and objects of the Act, then our Law would be defective if persons aggrieved were not entitled to the protection of the Court."

69. The Applicant and his Counsel, in the situation in which they find themselves, and given the dictum of LORD MORRIS in CONNELLY VS THE D.P.P., certainly deserve the relief envisaged in LORD REID's dictum, notwithstanding the jurisdictional objections by both the [Principal Defender and the Registrar] which we dismiss as frivolous, unfounded and bereft of any merits.

70. The stand we have taken in this regard is consonant with the justification the Learned Editors of Halsbury's Laws of England advance to justify the utility of the inherent jurisdiction of the court in terms of a residual source of power to enable the court... "in particular to ensure the observance of the due process of the law, to prevent improper vexation or oppression" such as the Applicant and his Counsel were indeed subjected to by the [Principal Defender] in the instant case.

71. The further justification for our stand is based on the dictum of Lord Morris in the case of CONNELLY VS. D.P.P. (already cited), where the Lord Justice said, and I quote:

"A court must enjoy some powers in order to enforce its rule of practice and to suppress any abuses of its process and to defeat any attempted thwarting of its process". This tendency, we observe, is clearly manifested by both Respondents in their submissions which we are reviewing."

---

[1] Wade, H.W.R. and C.F. Forsyth, *administrative Law*, 7th Edition Oxford: Clarendon Press, 1994 at 380-381; see also de Smith, S.A. *Judicial Review of Administrative Action*, 3rd Edition, London: Stevens, 1973.

- **Rule 45(C): Defence Office – Choice of Counsel**

R45-TC-5
o *Prosecutor v. Brima*, Case No. SCSL-04-16-PT, Decision on Applicant's Motion Against Denial by the Acting Principal Defender to Enter a Legal Service Contract for the Assignment of Counsel, 6 May 2004, para. 5-8:

5. The choice of and the criteria for qualifying to be appointed as assigned Counsel are governed by the provisions of Rule 45(C) of the Rules of Procedure and Evidence as well as by Article 13 of the Directive on the Assignment of Counsel.

6. It should be noted that in the event of listed Counsel being retained by the Principal defender to assume and ensure the defence of the accused, the Principal Defender is supposed to enter into a Legal Services Contract with the retained Counsel and this, in accordance with the provisions of Articles 14(A) and 16 of the Directive on the Assignment of Counsel.

7. One of the criteria to be fulfilled by the Assigned Counsel seeking to enter into a Legal Services Contract, according to Rule 45(C)(iv) of the rules of Procedure and Evidence as restated in by Article 13(B)(v) of the Directives, is that he or she must "have indicated their willingness and fulltime availability to be assigned by the Special Court to suspects or accused".

8. Article 14(C) of the Directive provides as follows:

> "No Counsel shall be assigned to more than one Suspect or Accused unless the concerned Suspects or Accused have received independent legal advice and have waived their right to be represented by separate Counsel. Any application by Counsel to be assigned to more than one suspect or Accused must be made through the Principal Defender, to the Presiding Judge of the appropriate Chamber."

- **Rule 45(C)(iv): Defence Office – Criteria of Eligibility of Counsel – Full Time Availability – Illness**

R45-TC-6

o *Prosecutor v. Brima*, Case No. SCSL-04-16-PT, Decision on Applicant's Motion Against Denial by the Acting Principal Defender to Enter a Legal Service Contract for the Assignment of Counsel, 6 May 2004, para. 43-45, 86-89, 92-93:

43. There is no suggestion that Mr. Terry at any time did not assume this role diligently. [. . .] This was what gave the [Principal Defender] cause to suspect his health status and his readiness to be available at all times to defend his client's interests within the meaning, according to him, the [Principal Defender], of the provisions of Rule 45(C) of the Rules of Procedure and Evidence.

44. The Applicant's Counsel rejected that suggestion because he maintains and even reiterated this fact during the oral hearing of this Motion, that his indisposition on these occasions is a bygone and that he has fully been living up to his obligations to his client, the Applicant. We note that this assertion is neither contradicted by the Respondents nor by the Applicant.

45. Given the above facts, the Chamber is of the opinion that the withdrawal by the [Principal Defender] for the reasons he

has advanced, of the provisional assignment of Applicant's 'chosen Counsel' within the meaning of Article 17(4)(d) of the Statute, tantamounts to a violation by the [Principal Defender] of the rights of the Accused as guaranteed under Article 17(4)(d) of the Statute, particularly so because the withdrawal itself was premised on an illegality and a misconception in the interpretation and in the application of the provisions of Rule 45(C) of the Rules under which he purports to have acted.

[. . .]

86. The issue which the Chamber considers crucial to examine in this matter is not whether the [Principal Defender] is a Medical Officer or not, but whether he could, under Rule 45(C) of the Rules of Procedure and Evidence, or even under any of the provisions of the Directive on the Assignment of Counsel, impose on the Applicant's Counsel, the obligation to produce a medical certificate of fitness or in the alternative, subject him to undergoing a medical examination as he did in his letter to him dated the 10th of November, 2003, albeit at the expense of the "Defence Office but from a budget other than that for the defence of Brima" to quote the [Principal Defender]'s letter to Counsel for the Applicant. [. . .]

87. The Chamber observes that based on the ordinary traditional canons of statutory interpretation, nowhere, in an ordinary reading and meaning of [Rule 45(C) and Article 13(B) of the Directive on the Assignment of Counsel], is the presentation of a medical certificate or even undergoing a medical examination made one of the conditions precedent for Counsel's qualification either to enter into a Legal Services Contract with the Principal Defender, or to be included on the list of assignable Counsel.

88. The only reason the [Principal Defender] has put across to justify the presentation of a medical certificate or undergoing medical examination is that it is a means to ensure the fitness of the Counsel to conduct a proper defence for the Accused pursuant to the provisions of Rule 45 of the rules and those of Articles 13(B) and 13(D) of the Directive, and that this exigency is more in the interest of protecting the rights of the Accused under Article 17 of the Statute and Rule 45(C) of the Rules.

89. We neither share this interpretation nor the submission of the [Principal Defender] in relation to the provisions of Rule 45(C) of the Rules and of Articles 13(B) and 13(D) of the Directive. [. . .]

[. . .]

92. We observe, contrary to the [Principal defender]'s submissions to this effect, that the provisions of Article 13(A) of the Directive did not intend to, nor do they justify his insistence,

on a medical verification of the Applicant's Counsel. Indeed, holding otherwise would be attributing to a very clear regulatory instrument, a strange and extraneous interpretation and meaning which was never envisaged especially so because the Applicant contends that his Counsel is the only one of all others on the list of Defence Counsel, who has been subjected to a medical scrutiny, a fact which he contends, is discriminatory.

93. We accordingly hold that the decision by the [Principal Defender] to withdraw the Applicant's Counsel's Provisional Assignment on the grounds of his refusal to undergo a medical examination, having been made without any statutory or regulatory authority to do so, is *ultra vires*, and deserves to be quashed as being both arbitrary and unlawful.

- **Rule 45(C): Defence Office – Criteria of Eligibility of Counsel – Full Time Availability – Counsel Representing More Than One Accused – Article 14(C) of the Directive**

R45-TC-7

o *Prosecutor v. Brima*, Case No. SCSL-04-16-PT, Decision on Applicant's Motion Against Denial by the Acting Principal Defender to Enter a Legal Service Contract for the Assignment of Counsel, 6 May 2004, para. 103-104:

103. On this issue, the Chamber observes that although the Taylor Indictment is approved and a warrant of arrest issued, he has not yet made his initial appearance to take a plea as he is yet to be arrested and physically brought within the jurisdiction of the Special Court. It is only at that stage that his status will be verified vis à vis the Applicant's situation with a view to determining whether the Applicant's Counsel is in breach of the provisions of Rule 14(C) of the Directives on the Assignment of Counsel or not.

104. Consequently, we find and accordingly so hold, that the decision to refuse to enter into a Legal Services Contract with the Applicant's Counsel and to withdraw and cancel the Provisional Assignment of the Applicant's Counsel on the grounds of a violation of Article 14(C) of the Directive, a fact which is yet to be verified and determined, is premature and illegal as such a ground cannot be invoked at this early stage when the alleged conflict of interest is yet to be established by the [Principal Defender].

- **Rule 45(D): Defence Office – Replacement of Counsel – Exceptional Circumstances – Attempt to Delay the Proceedings**

R45-TC-8
  o *Prosecutor v. Brima, Kamara*, Case No. SCSL-04-16-T, Decision on the Extremely Urgent Confidential Joint Motion for the Re-Appointment of Kevin Metzger and Wilbert Harris as Lead Counsel for Alex Tamba Brima and Brima Bazzy Kamara and Decision on Cross-Motion by Deputy Principal Defender to Trial Chamber II for Clarification of its Oral Order of 12 May 2005, 9 June 2005, para. 48-52:

  48. We note the Defence reply that the "circumstances where Counsel previously withdrew his services for stated reasons and circumstances, some of which have changed" (paragraph 8). We have no direct evidence from Counsel that their circumstances have changed, and given that this application emanates from a letter from the accused purportedly written on the same day as the Trial Chamber's order, we question the bona fides of that statement.

  The only change since our decision is that the accused are apparently now willing to give instructions to counsel, but all the other factors we considered in arriving at our decision are still in existence. We cannot escape the conclusion that the two lead counsel were not sincere in their reasons for bringing their motion to withdraw from the case and that they never expected it to succeed.

  49. Further, it is unclear on what legal grounds this application is made. The application does not say it is founded on Rule 45(D) and makes no submission that there are exceptional circumstances that would allow the Trial Chamber to exercise its jurisdiction under Rule 45(D).

  50. It appears that this application in reality is simply an application to reverse a majority decision given by the Trial Chamber on 12 May 2005 because in that decision all relief prayed for was granted to Counsel. A decision upholding the submissions made and granting the relief prayed for could hardly be appealed. Given the alacrity with which the accused and their Counsel and the Deputy Principal Defender sought to go behind that order and seek to reverse it, causes us to doubt the sincerity of the application to withdraw. By not giving instruction to their Counsel leading to withdrawal of counsel from the case, coupled with an immediate application to reinstate the same Counsel, the accused have seriously delayed and obstructed this trial.

  51. Moreover, since the Accused had not been coming to court and were not giving instructions to their counsel

(although those were not the only reasons why counsel sought to withdraw from the case), we directed under Rule 60(B) that the Accused be represented by Court-appointed counsel (who were already part of the Defence team) and that the Principal Defender assign another lead counsel to each of the Accused. We were satisfied that these were the proper measures to protect the rights of the Accused, in particular their right to be tried without undue delay as enshrined in Article 17(4)(c). We do not have the jurisdiction to revisit that decision, nor do we see any good reason to re-appoint the counsel concerned. In any event, it appears that the said Counsel are not eligible to be reappointed since they are no longer on the list of qualified counsel required to be kept under Rule 45(C).

52. Having held that this Motion is not founded on bona fide motives and seeks to reverse an order granting relief which the Defence itself sought, we consider this Motion to be frivolous and vexatious and for this and the foregoing reasons, we dismiss the motion and refuse the relief prayed for therein.

- **Rule 45(E): Defence Office – Term of Representation**

R45-TC-9

o *Prosecutor v. Kallon*, Case No. SCSL-04-15-PT, Decision on the Defence Motion for Extension of Time to File Reply to "Prosecution Response to Defence Motion for Quashing Consolidated Indictment", 19 March 2004:

COGNISANT of the Rules and, in particular, of Rule 45(E), providing that "Counsel will represent the accused and conduct the case to finality" and that such conduct should apply until either the termination of the case or the termination of the provision of legal representation;

- **Rule 45(E): Defence Office – Withdrawal of Counsel – Withdrawal by the Defence Office**

R45-TC-10

o *Prosecutor v. Brima*, Case No. SCSL-04-16-PT, Decision on Applicant's Motion Against Denial by the Acting Principal Defender to Enter a Legal Service Contract for the Assignment of Counsel, 6 May 2004, para. 46-48, 95, 99:

46. We have taken note of the [Principal Defender]'s argument that withdrawing the provisional assignment of Mr. Terry or refusing at this stage of the proceedings which we consider advanced, to enter into Legal services Contract with him in order to ensure the defence of the Applicant, does not violate

the latter's rights under Article 17(4)(d) of the Statute because according to him, some other Counsel can and will indeed be assigned to him.

47. This argument, in our opinion, is superficial, cosmetic, unimpressive and unconvincing for the following reasons:

(i) The new Counsel to be assigned to the Applicant may not be of his real "choosing" as required by the Statute, particularly having regard to the manner in which the [Principal Defender] has terminated the otherwise apparently healthy and confidence-inspiring statutory Counsel/Client relationship that so far exists between the Applicants and his Counsel, Mr. Terence Michael Terry.

(ii) More importantly, we observe that at his stage of the proceedings when we are at the door steps of the trial procedures, a newly assigned Counsel, having regard to the bulk and intricacies of the work involved in the preparatory stages for trial that started since March, 2003, will not be able to provide to the Applicant, the same services that will properly, convincingly, effectively, and adequately ensure his defence and protect his equally important and vital statutory entitlement to a fair and expeditious trial.

48. We in fact therefore find that the [Principal Defender]'s impugned decision, viewed from this perspective, a fortiori, violated, for no legal or just cause, the mandatory statutory provisions of Article 17(4)(d) of the statute of the special Court particularly so because we note from the records that the Applicant has hitherto been happy with and has never expressed any dissatisfaction against his 'chosen' and assigned Counsel nor did he ask or have any reason to request his withdrawal in preference of another assigned Counsel who the [Principal Defender] volunteers to provide for him in replacement of Mr. Terry.

[. . .]

95. The Chamber has observed that Article 16(C) under which the [Principal Defender] purportedly acted to withdraw the Provisional Assignment of the Applicant's Counsel, confers a discretion on the Principal Defender to withdraw or not to. We also observe that Article 13(D), which the [Principal Defender] has invoked as giving him a leeway to probing into the medical history or fitness of the Applicant's Counsel, also confers on him, a discretion into what is enumerated in D(i), D(ii), D(iii) and D(iv).

[. . .]

99. [. . .] Indeed, as was held in the case of PUBLIC SERVICE OF NEW SOUTH WALES VS OSMOND (1986) 60

ALJ 209, for a discretion to be exercised validly, it must be seen to have been exercised reasonably, fairly, and justly. This, we find, was not the case with the decision of the [Principal Defender], in the case under examination where we hold that he could not exercise any powers or discretion whatsoever because he lacked the statutory authority to take the decision he took.

- **Rule 45(E): Defence Office – Withdrawal of Counsel – Application to Withdraw – Exceptional Circumstances**

o *Prosecutor v. Gbao*, Case No. SCSL-04-15-T, Decision on application to Withdraw Counsel, 7 July 2004, para. 11, 13-16:

11. According to Rule 45(E) of the Rules, "most exceptional circumstances" would need to be established in order to allow Defence Counsel for Mr. Gbao to withdraw from the case at this stage of the process. No such exceptional circumstances have been advanced in this case. Instead, Mr. Gbao has stated only that he wants his counsel to withdraw since he does not recognize the legitimacy of the Special Court. We consider that this assertion is patently misconceived.

[...]

13. It is, therefore, our considered opinion that the ground that Mr. Gbao has advanced, that is, the non-recognition of the legitimacy of the Special Court, cannot constitute "exceptional circumstances" under Rule 45(E) that are required for allowing Counsel to withdraw. Counsel has the obligation to conduct this case to its finality and must continue to do so. We therefore do so hold and direct.

14. In making this finding, the Trial Chamber would like to refer to the decision of the International Criminal Tribunal for Rwanda ("ICTR") in the case of the *Prosecutor* v. *Barayagwiza* of the 2nd November 2000.[1] In that decision, the Court found that Mr. Barayagwiza's assertion that he did not want to be represented since he did not believe that the ICTR was an independent and impartial tribunal, could not constitute "exceptional circumstances" warranting the withdrawal of defence Counsel.

15. It is clear from examining all of the circumstances of this case that the interests of justice would not be served by allowing Mr. Gbao to be unrepresented before this Court. The Trial Chamber accordingly takes the position that it must safeguard the rights of the accused and the integrity of the proceedings before the Court by insisting that Mr. Gbao should continue

to be represented by the Counsel that have represented him throughout these proceedings. We hold in this regard that an accused person cannot waive his right to a fair and expeditious trial whatever the circumstances.

16. In the *Barayagwiza* decision, the ICTR remarked:

> In the present case, Mr Barayagwiza is actually boycotting the United Nations Tribunal. He has chosen both to be absent in the trial and to give no instructions as to how his legal representation should proceed in the trial or as to the specifics of his strategy. In such a situation, his lawyers cannot simply abide with his "instruction" not to defend him. Such instructions, in the opinion of the Chamber, should rather be seen as an attempt to obstruct judicial proceedings. In such a situation, it cannot reasonably be argued that Counsel is under an obligation to follow them, and that not do[ing] so would constitute grounds for withdrawal.

---

(1) *Prosecutor v. Barayagwiza*, Case No. ICTR-97-19-T, Decision on Defence Counsel Motion to Withdraw, 2 November 2000.

o *Prosecutor v. Brima, Kamara, Kanu*, Case No. SCSL-04-16-T, Decision on the Confidential Application for Withdrawal by Counsel for Brima and Kamara and on the Request for Further Representation by Counsel for Kanu, 20 May 2005, para. 34-39, 42, 52-62:

34. [. . .] [I]t is well settled in the jurisprudence of the ad hoc Tribunals, that lack of instructions does not constitute "most exceptional circumstances" under Rule 45 (E) warranting the withdrawal of Counsel.

35. In the case of *The Prosecutor v. Barayagwiza* the ICTR found as follows:

> *As the Chamber observed in its decision of 25 October 2000, Mr Barayagwiza does not lack confidence in his two lawyers. Neither does he argue that they are incompetent. The core of his argument is that he will not be given a fair trial. [. . .]This allegation is without foundation. [. . .]*
>
> *The Chamber finds it obvious that Mr Barayagwiza's arguments do not constitute exceptional circumstances as required under Rule 45 (I). Rather, Mr Barayagwiza is merely boycotting the trial and obstructing the course of justice. As such, the Chamber shall not entertain the request of the accused for the withdrawal of his counsel, on this basis.*

> *In the present case, Mr Barayagwiza is actually boycotting the United Nations Tribunal. He has chosen both to be absent in the trial and to give no instructions as to how his legal representation should proceed in the trial or as to the specifics of his strategy. In such a situation, his lawyers cannot simply abide with his "instruction" not to defend him. Such instructions, in the opinion of the Chamber, should rather be seen as an attempt to obstruct judicial proceedings. In such a situation, it cannot reasonably be argued that Counsel is under an obligation to follow them, and that not do so would constitute grounds for withdrawal.*[(1)]

36. The ICTR, in the case of *The Prosecutor v. Bagosora*, observed that:

> *Appeals Chamber case law has emphasised that an accused does not have the right to unilaterally destroy the trust between himself and his counsel in the hope that such actions will result in the withdrawal of his counsel.*[(2)]

37. We also approve the statement of the ICTY in the case of *The Prosecutor v. Slobodan Milošević* that:

> *[. . .] an accused cannot manufacture a reason for an Article 19(A) withdrawal by refusing to cooperate with his attorney.*[(3)]

38. The jurisprudence of the international criminal tribunals is in compliance with international human rights standards as confirmed by *Croissant v. Germany*:

> *It is for the Courts to decide whether the interests of justice require that the accused be defended by Counsel appointed by them. When appointing Counsel, the national courts must certainly have regard to the defendant's wishes – However, they can override those wishes when there are relevant and sufficient grounds for holding that this is necessary in the interest of justice.*[(4)]

39. In line with *Barayagwiza*, we find in the present case that, by withdrawing instructions from their counsel, the Accused are merely boycotting the trial and obstructing the course of justice. It is well established law that the inability of Counsel to obtain instructions from his client does not constitute "the most exceptional circumstances" within the meaning of Rule 45(E).

[. . .]

42. We can understand Lead Counsels' concerns that the anticipated testimony has affected their relationship with their clients. However, they have not established any reason why the anticipated testimony would affect their capacity to act as Counsel in the present trial. In the circumstances, we find that

the anticipated testimony of Lead Counsel in contempt proceedings before Trial Chamber I do not constitute "the most exceptional circumstances" under Rule 45(E).

[. . .]

52. The threats referred to are detailed in Lead Counsels' submissions in paragraph 6 above. We are not aware of any guidelines from other international courts on the appropriate measures a Trial Chamber ought to adopt in such a situation.

53. One of the consequences of the Report on Intimidation of Defense Lawyers in Northern Ireland by the U.N. Special Rapporteur Param Cumaraswamy, which recommended an independent judicial inquiry into the 1989 murder of a prominent defence lawyer, was that Human Rights Organisations stressed the need for lawyers to be able to practice "unhindered in their duties by abusive treatment."[5]

54. The United Nations Basic Principles on the Role of Lawyers recommends measures that Governments can take to protect lawyers.[6] Article 16 provides that "Governments shall ensure that lawyers are able to perform all of their professional functions without intimidation, hindrance, harassment or improper interference." Article 17 states: "Where the security of lawyers is threatened as a result of discharging their functions, they shall be adequately safeguarded by the authorities".

55. In the present case we do not think that close protection – as suggested by the Prosecution – will allay the fears of Lead Counsel and we do not think it is the answer. We presume that since Lead Counsel did not want to reveal their said sources, they therefore did not apply for investigations into these allegations by the Security Section of the Special Court or other possible measures to ensure their safety in Sierra Leone.

56. We are not alone in our grave concerns for the safety of Lead Counsel and their families. The Defence submitted that there is "a significant threat of danger to their persons or family";[7] the Principal Defender accepted "wholeheartedly [. . .] that [secu-rity concerns] may be an exceptional circumstance for withdrawal"[8]; and the Prosecution conceded that "[t]hreats made to any Counsel appearing before the Special Court are a matter to be taken extremely seriously"[9]

57. As can be seen from their submissions, Lead Counsel are sufficiently worried by the threats to move the Trial Chamber for orders allowing them to withdraw from the case. We do not think that they have made that application lightly. They are experienced barristers fully aware of their professional obligations to their clients and to the Court. They perceive a danger to their families or themselves if they continue to act for the Accused. We are unable to say that their perception is wrong.

58. We must bear in mind that, unlike the ICTY, ICTR and ICC, this trial is taking place in the country where the alleged offences are said to have occurred, and this gives rise to substantial security concerns. We are therefore of the view that the fears of Lead Counsel are justified.

59. Taken individually, we find that the arguments put forward by Lead Counsel regarding their difficulties, i.e. that their clients won't come to court, that their clients will not give them instructions, that there is a deteriorating relationship, not helped by the possibility that they may be called to give evidence in contempt proceedings against the clients' wives, that they see themselves acting, in the circumstances, against the principles of their own Bar Code, do not constitute "the most exceptional circumstances" warranting the withdrawal of Counsel. However, when all of these problems are considered together with the threats hanging over their heads, the cumulative result, in our view, creates an intolerable situation which places Lead Counsel under an impossible burden.

60. The Accused are charged with crimes of a most serious nature. They are entitled to the best Counsel available, Counsel who can fully dedicate themselves to their demanding task. We are of the view that Lead Counsel, with their present difficulties, would not be capable of acting in the best interests of their clients. We doubt that they would be able to represent their clients to the best of their ability when, apart from everything else, they are concerned for their own safety and that of their families. Although we are loath to come to a decision which possibly may adversely affect an expeditious trial, we are of the view that the rights of the Accused to be represented by counsel would best be served by appointing counsel able to carry out their duties free of the constraints inhibiting present Lead Counsel.

61. Accordingly, we find that the cumulative effect of all of these factors constitutes "the most exceptional circumstances" under Rule 45(E), warranting Lead Counsel to withdraw from the case.

62. Because the present case is peculiar in that there are a number of elements that go toward establishing the most exceptional circumstances, there is probably no reasonable likelihood of similar situations arising in the future. In any event, we do not go so far as to say that threats made to counsel would, in every case, satisfy the test of "the most exceptional circumstances" required by Rule 45(E). Each case would need to be decided on its individual merits."

---

[1] *The Prosecutor v. Jean-Bosco Barayagwiza*, Case No. ICTR-97-19-T, Decision on Defence Counsel Motion to Withdraw, 2 November 2000, para. 14 ff.
[2] *The Prosecutor v. Théoneste Bagosora et al.*, Case No. ICTR-98-41-T, Decision on Maitre Paul Skolnik's Application for Reconsideration of the

Chamber's Decision to Instruct the Registrar to Assign him as Lead Counsel for Gratien Kabiligi, 24 March 2005, para. 21.
(3) *The Prosecutor v. Slobodan Milošević*, Decision Affirming the Registrar's Denial of Assigned Counsel's Application to Withdraw, 7 February 2005, para. 10.
(4) *Croissant v. Germany,* European Court of Human Rights, Case No. 62/1001/314/385, Judgment, 25 September 1992.
(5) Report of the Special Rapporteur on the independence of judges and lawyers, Mr. Param Cumaraswamy, submitted pursuant to Commission on Human Rights resolution 1997/23, E/CN.4/1998/ 39/Add.4, 5 March 1998. The Report was endorsed by five of the world's leading international human rights organizations: Amnesty International, the International Commission of Jurists, Human Rights Watch, the International Federation of Human Rights, and the Lawyers Committee for Human Rights, see E/CN.4/Sub.2/1998/NGO/2.
(6) Adopted by the Eighth United Nations Congress on the Prevention of Crime and the Treatment of Offenders, Havana, Cuba, 27 August to 7 September 1990
(7) Brima and Kamara Defence Motion, 5 May 2005, para. 15.
(8) Principle Defender's Submission, 5 May 2005, para. 9. ii.
(9) Prosecutions Submission, 9 May 2005, para. 12.

- **Rule 45(E): Defence Office – Withdrawal of Counsel – Appointment of "Another Counsel"**

R45-TC-13

o *Prosecutor v. Brima, Kamara*, Case No. SCSL-04-16-T, Decision on the Extremely Urgent Confidential Joint Motion for the Re-Appointment of Kevin Metzger and Wilbert Harris as Lead Counsel for Alex Tamba Brima and Brima Bazzy Kamara and Decision on Cross-Motion by Deputy Principal Defender to Trial Chamber II for Clarification of its Oral Order of 12 May 2005, 9 June 2005, para. 36:

36. As the Deputy Principal Defender has correctly stated, the duty to assign Counsel in the event of a withdrawal rests in the Principal Defender. However, we do not consider this entirely relevant as Rule 45(E) provides the appointment must be of "another" Counsel. There is no provision for re-assignment of former Counsel in the event that they or their clients, or both, have changed their mind.

- **Rule 45(F): Defence Office – Withdrawal of Counsel – Interim Representation by Co-Counsel**

R45-TC-14

o *Prosecutor v. Brima, Kamara, Kanu*, Case No. SCSL-04-16-T, Decision on the Confidential Application for Withdrawal by Counsel for Brima and Kamara and on the Request for Further Representation by Counsel for Kanu, 20 May 2005, para. 64-65, 68-69:

64. Pursuant to Rule 45 (E), we grant Lead Counsel permission to withdraw from the case. This does not leave the Accused Brima and Kamara without representation. They would still have Co-Counsel who are part of the Defence team to represent them pending appointment of new Lead Counsel. In fact, in the absence of Lead Counsel, the Accused Brima and Kamara have repeatedly been represented by Co-Counsel.[1] On one of these occasions, Co-Counsel told the Trial Chamber that they were sufficiently able and competent to carry on with the trial in the absence of Lead Counsel.[2] Indeed, we have no doubts as to their competence. Furthermore, the Defence has stated in Court that it has a unified Defence strategy, and it has often been the case so far that oral Motions and submissions in court have been made by one counsel on behalf of all Accused. In this regard, we note that Lead Counsel for the Accused Kanu and his Defence team are still in the case.

65. We therefore conclude that the Accused Brima and Kamara would suffer no prejudice if they were to be temporarily represented by their respective co-counsel.

[...]

68. We note that Rule 45(E) provides that "*[i]n the event of such withdrawal the Principal Defender* **shall assign another Counsel**..." This may or may not cause regrettable delays. Nevertheless, we note that this Court has established a Defence Office for exactly these situations. It is the duty of the Defence Office to support new Counsel and to introduce them to the case.

69. We are of the view that the rights of the Accused – in particular their right to be tried without undue delay as enshrined in Article 17 (4) (c) of the Statute – would best be served by directing Co-Counsel pursuant to Rule 60 (B) to represent the Accused on an interim basis until the respective Defence teams are complete again through the assignment of new Lead Counsel.

---

[1] Lead Counsel for Brima and Kamara were absent with the consent of their clients on the following trial days: 7 to 11 March 2005, 5 to 11 April 2005; Additional absence of Lead Counsel for Kamara: 12 to 14 April 2005.
[2] Transcripts, 5 April 2005, page 9.

APPEALS CHAMBER DECISIONS

- **Rule 45: Defence Office – Distribution of Powers Between the Defence Office and the Registry**

R45-AC-1

o *Prosecutor v. Brima, Kamara, Kanu*, Case No. SCSL-04-16-AR73, Decision on Brima-Kamara Defence Appeal Motion Against Trial Chamber II Majority Decision on Extremely Urgent Confidential Joint Motion for the Re-Appointment of Kevin Metzger and Wilbert Harris As Lead Counsel for Alex Tamba Brima and Brima Bazzy Kamara, 8 December 2005, para. 79-83, 85-87, 95:

79. It is the view of the Appeals Chamber that the Statute, the Rules of Procedure and Evidence and the Directive on the Assignment of Counsel describe a coherent system in which the main responsibility for assigning Counsel to the Accused is given to the Defence Office set up by the Registrar pursuant to Rule 45.

80. The Defence Office and, at his head, the Principal Defender are notably responsible for:
- Ensuring the rights of suspects and accused;[1]
- Providing *representation* to the suspects and accused;[2]
- Maintaining a list of highly qualified criminal defence counsel who are appropriate to act as duty counsel or to lead the defence or appeal of an accused;[3]
- Determining the suspect or accused requests for assignment of Counsel;[4]
- Assigning Counsel;[5]
- Assigning Counsel in the interests of justice;[6]
- Notifying *his* Decision to assign Counsel to the suspect or accused and his Counsel;[7]
- Negotiating and Entering Legal Services Contracts with the Assigned Counsel;[8]
- Determining requests for replacement of assigned Counsel;[9]
- Withdrawing Counsel when the Suspect or Accused is no longer indigent;[10]
- Withdrawing Counsel in other situations;[11]
- In the event of the withdrawal of a Counsel, *assigning another Counsel* to the Accused.[12]

81. On the other hand, the Registrar is given the responsibility:
- for the administration and servicing of the Special Court;[13]
- for establishing, maintaining and developing a Defence Office, for the purpose of ensuring the rights of suspects and accused;[14]

- for assisting the Principal Defender in the performance of his functions;[15]
- for maintaining and developing a Defence Office, for the purpose of ensuring the rights of suspects and accused.[16]

82. The Appeals Chamber notes that the Statute itself does not mention the Defence Office, or the Principal Defender, and is mute on which organ is given the responsibility for ensuring the rights of the Accused provided in Article 17 of the statute. Article 16(1) of the Statute provides that the Registry is responsible for the administration and servicing of the Special Court, which duty may include some aspects of protection of the rights of the Accused, but is nevertheless quite distinct. On the other hand, Rule 45 does provide for the establishment of a Defence Office by the Registrar and that this Defence Office is given the main responsibility for ensuring the rights of suspects and accused.

83. It results from the Statute and Rules that the Defence Office is not an independent organ of the Special Court, as Chambers, the Office of the Prosecutor and the Registry are pursuant to Articles 11, 12, 15 and 16 of the Statute. As a creation of the Registrar, the Defence Office and at its head, the Principal Defender, remain under the administrative authority of the Registrar. Although the Defence Office is given the main responsibility for ensuring the rights of the accused by accomplishing the functions mentioned above, it is supposed to exercise its duty under the administrative authority of the Registrar who, notably, is in charge of recruiting its staff, including the Principal Defender, in accordance with his general responsibility on administration pursuant to Article 16(1) of the Statute.

[. . .]

85. Having clarified the repartition of responsibilities between the Registrar and the Defence Office, it appears that the responsibility to reassign the withdrawn Counsel, or to assign other Counsel in compliance with Trial Chamber II's express order, fell in the province of the Defence Office pursuant to Rule 45(E) and Article 23(D) of the Directive.

86. Does that mean that the Registrar could not interfere in the matter? The Appeals Chamber does not find so for two reasons. First, the above mentioned correspondences of the Deputy Principal Defender to the Registrar show that she expected and requested his *written instructions* on the matter, thereby putting him in a position of administrative authority under which the Deputy Principal Defender intended to act. Second, having found that, by creating the Defence Office, the Registrar delegated part of his power and responsibility in the enforcement of the rights of the Defence to it, it results from English administrative law,[17] that the Registrar did not divest

himself of his power and can therefore act concurrently with the Principal Defender, in particular when she requires him to do so as in the current case.

87. The Appeals Chamber therefore finds that the Registrar had the power to decide on the issue of the re-assignment of the withdrawn Counsel, especially when he had expressly been seized of the matter by the Deputy Principal Defender, thereby deferring to his administrative authority on the Defence Office. The Appeals Chamber observes that the Registrar was extremely cautious in not interfering in the Principal Defender's province by limiting his intervention to instructions, when he may have decided to appoint by himself new Counsels to the Accused. The Appeals Chamber now turns to the question of whether the Registrar did take the right decision.

[...]

95. However, the Appeals Chamber agrees with the Trial Chamber's next finding that the Registrar "has a further overall duty to act as principal administrator of the Court". The Appeals Chamber finds that the Registrar's capacity to decide not to re-assign Counsel derived from his administrative authority on the Defence Office and, as explained above, from the delegation of his statutory prerogatives as regards the enforcement of the rights of the Defence pursuant to Articles 16(1) and 17 of the SCSL Statute, which did not divest him from his powers in the matter.

---

[1] Rule 45 (*Chapeau*) and Article 1(A) of the Directive.
[2] Rule 45(A) (Emphasis added).
[3] Rule 45(C) and Articles 13 and 23(B)(iii) of the Directive.
[4] Article 9(A) and 12(B) of the Directive.
[5] Article 9(A)(i) of the Directive.
[6] Article 10 of the Directive.
[7] Article 11 of the Directive (Emphasis added).
[8] Article 1(A), 14 and 16(C) to(F).
[9] Rule 45(D).
[10] Article 23(A) of the Directive.
[11] Article 24(A) and (B) of the Directive.
[12] Rule 45(E) and Article 23(D) of the Directive. (Emphasis added).
[13] Article 16(1) of the Statute and Rule 33(A);
[14] Rule 45 (*Chapeau*).
[15] Rule 33(A).
[16] Rule 45 and Article 1(A) of the Directive.
[17] *Huth v. Clarke* (1890) 25 QBD 391. *See also* the Local Government Act 1972 s 101(4); and *Halsbury's Laws of England*, Administrative Law, 2. Administrative Powers.

- **Rule 45(C): Defence Office – List of Qualified Counsel – Jurisdiction to Review Decision to Withdraw Counsel from the List**

R45-AC-2
o *Prosecutor v. Brima, Kamara, Kanu*, Case No. SCSL-04-16-AR73, Decision on Brima-Kamara Defence Appeal Motion Against Trial Chamber II Majority Decision on Extremely Urgent Confidential Joint Motion for the Re-Appointment of Kevin Metzger and Wilbert Harris As Lead Counsel for Alex Tamba Brima and Brima Bazzy Kamara, 8 December 2005, para. 135-139:

> 135. The Appeals Chamber refers to its above finding on the inherent jurisdiction of Chambers to judicially review administrative decisions affecting the rights of the Accused. The Appeals Chamber restates that such inherent jurisdiction may be exercised only in the silence of the regulations applicable to the matter.[1]
>
> 136. The Appeals Chamber notes that Article 13(F) of the Directive provides:
>
>> Where the Principal Defender refuses to place the name of the applicant Counsel on the List of Qualified Counsel, or removes the name of Counsel from the List of Qualified Counsel, the concerned Counsel may seek review, by the President, of the Principal Defender's refusal. An application for review shall be in writing and the Principal Defender shall be given the opportunity to respond to it in writing.
>
> 137. For the reasons mentioned earlier as regards the Registrar's decision not to re-assign Counsel, the Appeals Chamber considers that where the Registrar uses the powers he keeps in concurrence with the Principal Defender, he shall do so in the same conditions as the Principal Defender would. In particular, where the regulations provide that the Principal Defender's decision may be reviewed, the concurrent decision of the Registrar is submitted to the same condition.
>
> 138. Therefore, the Appeals Chamber considers that, pursuant to Article 13(F) of the Directive, the review of the decision to remove a Counsel from the List of Qualified Counsel, either taken by the Principal Defender or the Registrar, falls within the exclusive province of the President of the Special Court.
>
> 139. The Appeals Chamber therefore concludes that it has no jurisdiction to review the decision of the Registrar to remove Counsel from the List of Qualified Counsel and denies the ground and the related relief.

---

[1] *Prosecutor v. Norman, Fofana, Kondewa*, Case No. SCSL-2004-14-T, Decision

on Prosecution Appeal Against the Trial Chamber's Decision of 2 August 2004 Refusing Leave to File an Interlocutory Appeal, 17 January 2005, para. 31-32.

- **Rule 45(E): Defence Office – Withdrawal of Counsel – Exceptional Circumstances – Accused Refusal to Be Represented**

R45-AC-3

o *Prosecutor v. Gbao*, Case No. SCSL-04-15-AR73, Decision on Appeal Against Decision on Withdrawal of Counsel, 23 November 2004, para. 44-45:

"44. The Trial Chamber may appear, at first blush, to have erred in relying on Rule 45(E) and thereby treating the matter as if it had before it an application by counsel to withdraw his representation. However, reference to exceptional circumstances can be understood as emphasizing that the Accused was not in a position to request or instruct that his counsel withdraw from the case without showing good cause. The Trial Chamber was correct in reaching the conclusion that refusal to recognize the Court did not constitute good cause.

45. Reference to Rule 45(E) seems to be supported by the ICTR Trial Chamber decision in *Prosecutor v. Barayagwiza* of 2 November 2000[1] which our Trial Chamber referred to. It is to be noted, though glossed over by the Defence and the Prosecution, that in the *Barayagwiza* case both the accused and the lawyers asked for withdrawal of the lawyers' mandate. With regard to the request of the accused that Chamber had this to say in response to Mr. Barayagwiza's arguments in which he challenged the ability of the ICTR to render independent and impartial justice and that that was good reason for his instruction that his lawyers ceased to represent him at the trial:

> The Chamber finds it obvious that Mr. Barayagwiza's arguments do not constitute exceptional circumstances as required under Rule 45(I). Rather, Mr. Barayagwiza is merely boycotting the trial and obstructing the course of justice. As such the Chamber shall not entertain the request of the accused for withdrawal of his counsel, on this basis."[2]

---

[1] Decision on Defence Counsel Motion to Withdraw.
[2] Ibid., para. 16, emphasis added.

- **Rule 45(E): Defence Office – Withdrawal of Counsel – Re-Assignment of Withdrawn Counsel Is Not Permissible**

R45-AC-4

o *Prosecutor v. Brima, Kamara, Kanu*, Case No. SCSL-04-16-AR73, Decision on Brima-Kamara Defence Appeal Motion Against Trial Chamber II Majority Decision on Extremely Urgent Confidential Joint Motion for the Re-Appointment of Kevin Metzger and Wilbert Harris As Lead Counsel for Alex Tamba Brima and Brima Bazzy Kamara, 8 December 2005, para. 88:

> 88. Rule 45(E) of the Rules of Procedure and Evidence provides that in the event of the withdrawal of a Counsel, "the Principal Defender shall assign another Counsel who may be a member of the Defence Office, to the indigent accused". Article 24 – Withdrawal of Assignment in Other Situations – of the Directive, applicable in the current case, provides in Paragraph (D) that "[t]he Principal Defender shall immediately assign a new Counsel to the Suspect or Accused". Neither Rule 45(E) nor Article 24(D) does provide, in the circumstances of the withdrawal of Counsel, discretion of the Principal Defender to reassign the same Counsel as withdrawn. The choice of the new Counsel to be assigned belongs to the Principal Defender, in consultation with the suspect or accused, pursuant to Article 9(A)(i) of the Directive, but Rule 45(E) and Article 24(D) make it clear that the assigned Counsel shall be different from the withdrawn one.

- **Rule 45(E): Defence Office – Assignment of Counsel – Power to Review Decision Refusing Assignment of Counsel**

R45-AC-5

o *Prosecutor v. Brima, Kamara, Kanu*, Case No. SCSL-04-16-AR73, Decision on Brima-Kamara Defence Appeal Motion Against Trial Chamber II Majority Decision on Extremely Urgent Confidential Joint Motion for the Re-Appointment of Kevin Metzger and Wilbert Harris As Lead Counsel for Alex Tamba Brima and Brima Bazzy Kamara, 8 December 2005, para. 69-78:

> 69. Rule 45 is mute on the remedy against a decision refusing the assignment of Counsel. This issue is specifically addressed in the Directive, which provides:[1]
>
>> The Suspect or Accused whose request for assignment of counsel has been denied or who is subject to a

demand under Article 9(A)(ii) of this Directive may bring a Preliminary Motion before the appropriate Chamber objecting to the Principal Defender's decision in accordance with Rule 72(B)(iv) of the Rules.

70. It is obvious that the disposition of Article 12(A) of the Directive do apply only in the case of the initial assignment of Counsel, at a stage where Preliminary Motions can be filed pursuant to Rule 72(A), namely "within 21 days following disclosure by the Prosecutor to the Defence of all the material envisaged by Rule 66(A)(i)". The possibility that Article 12(A) of the Directive may derogate Rule 72(A) of the Rules of Procedure and Evidence by allowing the filing of Preliminary Motions at other stages of the procedure, especially once the trial has started, cannot be contemplated since the Directive was precisely issued by the Registrar acting upon the authority given to him by the Rules. The Appeals Chamber concurs on this point with the finding of Trial Chamber in its decision of 6 May 2004 in the *Brima* Case, that "the provisions of the Directive on the Assignment of Counsel promulgated by the Registrar on the 3rd October, 2003, cannot operate to either replace or to amend the Rules of Procedure and Evidence adopted by the Plenary of Judges of the Special Court".[2] The remedy contemplated in Article 12(A) is therefore not applicable in the current case, since the stage of Preliminary Motions is far overstayed.

71. The Appeals Chamber notes that the jurisprudence of other sister Tribunals has admitted, in the silence of the Rules and Directive applicable before those Tribunals, that the Registrar's administrative decision denying the assignment of Counsel could be reviewed by the President, when the Accused had an interest to protect.[3] However, such power to judicially review an administrative decision of the Registrar is denied to the Trial Chamber.[4]

72. The requirement for a judicial review of administrative decisions where the Accused has an interest to protect was perfectly justified by Justice Pillay, the then President of the International Criminal Tribunal for Rwanda, in her decision of 13 November 2002:[5]

> Modern systems of Administrative Law have built in review procedures to ensure fairness when individual rights and protected interests are in issue, or to preserve the interests of justice. In the context of the Tribunal, Rules 19 and 33(A) of the Rules ensure that such review is available in appropriate cases. While the Registrar has the responsibility of ensuring that all decisions are procedurally and substantially fair, not every decision by the Registrar can be the subject of review by the President. The Registrar must be free to conduct the business of the Registry without undue interference by Presidential review.

In all systems of administrative law, a threshold condition must be satisfied before an administrative decision may be impugned by supervisory review. There are various formulations of this threshold condition in national jurisdictions, but a common theme is that the decision sought to be challenged, must involve a substantive right that should be protected as a matter of human rights jurisprudence or public policy. An application for review of the Registrar's decision by the President on the basis that it is unfair procedurally or substantively, is admissible under Rules 19 and 33(A) of the Rules, if the accused has a protective right or interest, or if it is otherwise in the interests of justice.

73. The Appeals Chamber concurs with Justice Pillay's view on the need for a juridical review of administrative decisions affecting the rights of the Accused. However, the Appeals Chamber is not convinced that, in the specific situation of the Special Court, this judicial power should necessarily fall within the exclusive province of the President for the following reasons.

74. First, the Appeals Chamber notes that Article 24 (E) and (F) of the Directive submits the Principal Defender's decision to withdraw Counsel to the judicial review of "the presiding Judge of the appropriate Chamber". This regulation is not problematic when, as in the current case, the trial is pending before a Trial Chamber, since the question is then submitted to the Presiding Judge of the Trial Chamber; but, once the case has reached the appeal phase, then the decision to withdraw Counsel would be submitted to the President of the Appeals Chamber, who is, pursuant to Article 12(3) of the Statute, the President of the Special Court. In that situation, would the decision to assign Counsel fall in the exclusive province of the President of the Special Court, he would be the only authority to judicially review the administrative decision to withdraw Counsel and then, once again, the decision denying the assignment of Counsel. That may put the President of the Special Court in a difficult situation.

75. Second, although the remedy provided by Article 12(A) of the Directive is not applicable in the current case, the Appeals Chamber notes that this Article gives jurisdiction to the Trial Chamber to review, by way of Preliminary Motion, the administrative decision on assignment of Counsel. The Appeals Chamber sees no reason to depart from that solution and considers that Article 12(A) should apply *mutatis mutandis* in the present situation and allow to seize the Trial Chamber by way of an interlocutory Motion pursuant to Rule 73(A) of the judicial review of the administrative decision on assignment of counsel.

76. Third, the Appeals Chamber concurs with the finding made by Trial Chamber I in its decision of 6 May 2004 in the *Brima* Case, that such judicial review falls, due to the silence of the regulations applicable before the Special Court, within the inherent jurisdiction of the Trial Chamber:[6]

> [T]he chamber is of the opinion that the motion, even though brought under the wrong Rule, can, and so do we decide, in the overall interests of justice and to prevent a violation of the rights of the Accused, be examined by invoking our inherent jurisdiction to entertain it and to adjudicate on it on the ground of a denial of request for assignment of Counsel within the context of Article 17(4)(d) of the Statute.

77. The Appeals Chamber refers to the above quoted reasoning of President Pillay as regards the reasons for exercising such inherent jurisdiction.

78. For the foregoing reasons, the Appeals Chamber finds that the Trial Chamber had jurisdiction to judicially review the Registrar's Decision not to re-assign Counsel.

---

[1] Article 12(A) of the Directive.
[2] *Prosecutor v. Brima*, Case No. SCSL-2004-16-PT, Decision on Applicant's Motion Against Denial by the Acting Principal Defender to Enter a Legal Service Contract for the Assignment of Counsel, 6 May 2004, para. 35.
[3] *See* ICTR, *Prosecutor v. Nzirorera*, ICTR-98-44-T, President's Decision on Review of the Decision of the Registrar Withdrawing Mr. Andrew McCartan as Lead Counsel of the Accused Joseph Nzirorera (President Pillay), 13 May 2002, p. 3, sect. (xi); ICTY, *Prosecutor v. Hadzihasanovic et al.*, IT-01-47-PT, Decision on the Prosecution's Motion for Review of the Decision of the Registrar to Assign Mr. Rodney Dixon as Co-Counsel to the Accused Kubura (TC), 26 March 2002, para. 12-13; ICTY, *Prosecutor v. Delalic et al.*, IT-96-21-PT, Decision of the President on the Prosecutor's Motion for the Production of Notes Exchanged Between Zejnil Delalic and Zdravko Mucic (President Cassese), 11 November 1996.
[4] ICTR, *Prosecutor v. Ntahobali*, ICTR-97-21-T, Decision on Ntahobali's Extremely Urgent Motion for the Re-instatement of Suspended Investigator, Mr Thaddée Kwitonda (TC), 14 December 2001, para. 17.
[5] ICTR, *Prosecutor v. Ntahobali*, ICTR-97-21-T, Decision on the Application by Arsène Shalom Ntahobali for Review of the Registrar's Decisions Pertaining to the Assignment of an Investigator" (President Pillay), 13 November 2002, para. 4-5.
[6] *Prosecutor v. Brima*, Case No. SCSL-2004-16-PT, Decision on Applicant's Motion Against Denial by the Acting Principal Defender to Enter a Legal Service Contract for the Assignment of Counsel, 6 May 2004, para. 39.

- **Rule 45(E): Defence Office – Assignment of Counsel – Legal Services Contracts**

R45-AC-6

o *Prosecutor v. Brima, Kamara, Kanu*, Case No. SCSL-04-16-AR73, Decision on Brima-Kamara Defence Appeal Motion Against Trial Chamber II Majority Decision on Extremely Urgent Confidential Joint Motion for the Re-Appointment of Kevin Metzger and Wilbert Harris As Lead Counsel for Alex Tamba Brima and Brima Bazzy Kamara, 8 December 2005, para. 99:

99. Without need to enter the details of privity of contract and of the way Legal Services Contracts are concluded, the Appeals Chamber observes that, pursuant to Article 1(A) of the Directive, the Legal Services Contract is defined as an "agreement between Contracting Counsel and the Principal Defender for the representation of a Suspect or Accused before the Special Court for Sierra Leone outlined in Article 16 of this Directive". As confirmed by Article 16(C) of the Directive, which provides that it is entered "as soon as practicable after assignment", the Legal Services Contract is passed between the assigned Counsel and the Principal Defender. Since Mssrs. Metzger and Harris were no more assigned after their voluntary withdrawal on 12 May 2005, and could not be reassigned pursuant to Rule 45(E), Article 24(D) of the Directive and the Trial chamber's express order, there was no way a Legal Services Contract could be concluded between them and the Principal Defender.

Rule 45*bis*: Declaration of Means by the Accused
(amended 1 August 2003)

(A) If, after his transfer to the Special Court, the suspect or accused wishes to request legal assistance, he shall make a declaration of his means to the Registrar.

(B) If a suspect or an accused elects to conduct his own defence, he shall so notify the Registrar in writing at the first opportunity.

TRIAL CHAMBERS DECISIONS

- **Rule 45*bis*(A): Declaration of Means by the Accused – Request for Legal Assistance**

R45*bis*-TC-1
o *Prosecutor v. Kallon*, Case No. SCSL-03-07-I, Order for Legal Assistance, 19 March 2003:

CONSIDERING the Declaration of Means and the Request for Legal Assistance presented by the Accused pursuant to Rule 45*bis* of the Rules;

[...]

HEREBY INSTRUCT the Registrar to provide legal assistance to the Accused as necessary, pending further investigation by the Registrar into his means;

ENJOIN the Accused to select Counsel who satisfies the requirements of Rule 45(C) of the Rules from the short list provided by the Registry.

APPEALS CHAMBER DECISIONS

- **Rule 45*bis*(B): Declaration of Means by the Accused – Request for Self-Representation**

R45*bis*-AC-1
o *Prosecutor v. Gbao*, Case No. SCSL-04-15-AR73, Decision on Appeal Against Decision on Withdrawal of Counsel, 23 November 2004, para. 49:

49. Judicial proceedings are not undertaken in a world of speculation or make-believe, nor would a court create an imaginary ambiguity where none exists. There is no room for

doubt that the Accused had on 6 July 2004 made clear his refusal to recognize the Court and had on 7 July 2004 confirmed this refusal and his non-participation in the trial. In the light of these facts, to regard the issue before the Trial Chamber as one of the right to legal representation is to create an imaginary scenario totally divorced from the circumstances and from the plain and express intention of the Accused. A claim to a right to legal representation or self-representation before a tribunal cannot be implied from a persistent posture of non-recognition of the tribunal.

- **Rule 45*bis*(B): Declaration of Means by the Accused – Self-Defence Creating Estoppel**

R45*bis*-AC-2

o *Prosecutor v. Norman, Fofana, Kondewa*, Case No. SCSL-04-14-AR73, Decision on Amendment of the Consolidated Indictment, 16 May 2005, para. 74:

74. [...] The Defence had been provided in February 2004 with the consolidated Indictment and took no point on the additions to it until 20 September, when it filed a motion seeking further appearance pursuant to Rule 61 on the consolidated Indictment and a formal quashing of the previous Indictment upon which he initially appeared. Norman was defending himself for part of this period, but that fact cannot avoid the consequence of his conduct if his own self-defence has created an estoppel: those who choose to defend themselves cannot then plead layman's oversight, or ignorance of legal rules.

Rule 46: Misconduct of Counsel
(amended 29 May 2004)

(A) A Chamber may, after a warning, impose sanctions against or refuse audience to a counsel if, in its opinion, his conduct remains offensive or abusive, obstructs the proceedings, or is otherwise contrary to the interests of justice. This provision is applicable to counsel for the prosecution.

(B) A Chamber may determine that counsel is no longer eligible to represent a suspect or accused before the Special Court, pursuant to Rule 45. If declared ineligible, removed counsel shall transmit to replacement counsel all materials relevant to the representation.

(C) Counsel who bring motions, or conduct other activities, that in the opinion of a Chamber are either frivolous or constitute abuse of process may be sanctioned for those actions as the Chamber may direct. Sanctions may include fines upon counsel; non-payment, in whole or in part, of fees associated with the motion or its costs, or such other sanctions as the Chamber may direct.

(D) A Judge or a Chamber may also, with the approval of the President, communicate any misconduct of counsel to the professional body regulating the conduct of counsel in his State of admission.

(E) If a counsel assigned pursuant to Rule 45 is sanctioned by being refused audience, the Chamber shall instruct the Registrar to replace the counsel.

(F) This Rule is applicable to counsel for the Prosecution as well as counsel appearing for the Defence and to any counsel appearing as *amicus curiae*.

(G) The Registrar may set up a Code of Professional Conduct enunciating the principles of professional ethics to be observed by counsel having right of audience before the Special Court, subject to adoption by the Plenary Meeting. Amendments to the Code shall be made in consultation with representatives of the Prosecutor and Defence counsel, and subject to adoption by the Plenary Meeting. If the Registrar has strong grounds for believing that counsel has committed a serious violation of the Code of Professional Conduct so adopted, he may report the matter to the President for appropriate action under this rule.

(H) Decisions made by a Trial Chamber under Sub-Rules (A) to (C) above may be appealed with leave from that Chamber. Where such leave is refused, the Party may apply to a bench of at least three Appeals Chamber Judges for leave.

TRIAL CHAMBERS DECISIONS

- **Rule 46(C): Misconduct of Counsel – Frivolous Motions and Abuse of Process – Sanction (Or Not)**

R46-TC-1

o *Prosecutor v. Norman*, Case No. SCSL-04-14-T, Decision on First Accused's Motion on Abuse of Process, 28 April 2005, para. 20:

> 20. We would like to observe here that the language used by Learned Counsel for the Applicant is unprofessional and borders on contempt. In this regard, The Chamber would like to draw Learned Counsel's attention to the provisions of Rule 46(C) of the Rules [...].
>
> [...]
>
> **FOR THE ABOVE REASONS, THE TRIAL CHAMBER FINDS AS FOLLOWS:**
>
> **THAT THIS** Motion which in itself, is misconceived and without any merits constitutes an abuse of process.
>
> **IT IS THEREFORE DENIED AND ACCORDINGLY DISMISSED.**

R46-TC-2

o *Prosecutor v. Norman*, Case No. SCSL-04-14-T, Decision on request by the First Accused for Leave to Appeal Against the Trial Chamber's Decision on First Accused's Motion on Abuse of Process, 24 May 2005:

> **NOTING** Rule 46(C) of the Rules [...]
>
> **CONSIDERING** that this Motion constitutes an abuse of the process;
>
> **THE TRIAL CHAMBER HEREBY DENIES** the Application for leave to appeal and **ORDERS** the Principal Defender to withhold from Court Appointed Counsel for the First Accused all costs and fees associated with the Motion.

R46-TC-3

o *Prosecutor v. Norman*, Case No. SCSL-04-14-T, Decision on Norman Counsel's Request for Leave to Appeal under Rule 46(H), 25 July 2005:

NOTING the finding of the ICTR Trial Chamber in *Prosecutor v. Nzirorera*, in respect of the power of the Chamber to impose sanctions, which provided that:

The Chamber is of the view that such a Rule, which grants a court or a tribunal an effective power to regulate its own proceedings, including the conduct of the parties, is reasonably required in any judicial system. The power to impose sanctions should, however, be exercised cautiously, bearing in mind the interests of justice and the right to a fair trial.[1]

NOTING further the conclusion of the ICTR Trial Chamber in the same case that:

The sanctions orders are not substantive. They are merely ancillary or consequential to the substantive motions. They reflect the conclusion by the Trial Chamber that bringing those motions was frivolous or was an abuse of process.[2]

CONSIDERING that the sanction for bringing an abuse of process motion is not a criminal sanction[3] and therefore the First Accused will suffer no irreparable prejudice for sanctioning his Counsel;

---

[1] *Prosecutor v. Nzirorera*, ICTR-98-44-PT, Decision on Motion to Vacate Sanctions Rules 73(F) and 120 of the Rules of Procedure and Evidence, 23 February, 2005, para. 6.
[2] *Prosecutor v. Nzirorera*, ICTR-98-44-PT, Decision on Joseph Nzirorera's Motion for Order Finding Prior Decisions to Be of "No Effect", Rules 46(A) and 73 of the Rules of Procedure and Evidence, 24 May, 2005, para. 12.
[3] *Prosecutor v. Nzirorera*, ICTR-98-44-AR73(F), Decision on Counsel's Appeal From Rule 73(F) Decisions, 9 June 2004, p. 3.

- **Rule 46(H): Misconduct of Counsel – Frivolous Motions and Abuse of Process – Leave to Appeal Sanctions**

R46-TC-4

o *Prosecutor v. Norman*, Case No. SCSL-04-14-T, Decision on Norman Counsel's Request for Leave to Appeal under Rule 46(H), 25 July 2005:

CONSIDERING that although Rule 46(H) of the Rules provides for the possibility to appeal decisions made pursuant to Rule 46(A) or Rule 46(C) of the Rules, it does not articulate the standard for granting or refusing leave for such an appeal;

CONSIDERING that neither Rules of the International Criminal Tribunal for Rwanda ("ICTR") nor Rules of the International Criminal Tribunal for the former Yugoslavia ("ICTY") provide for the right to appeal a decision of the Trial Chamber that imposes sanctions against Counsel for bringing a frivolous motion or a motion, which constitutes an abuse of process;[1]

CONSIDERING that the standard for granting an interlocutory appeal against the Chamber's decision made under Rule 45(A) or Rule 46(C) of the Rules, is the standard prescribed by Rule 73(B) of the Rules;

---

[1] Rule 73(F) of the ICTR Rules provides that "In addition to the sanctions envisaged by Rule 46, a Chamber may impose sanctions against Counsel if Counsel brings a motion, including a preliminary motion, that, in the opinion of the Chamber, is frivolous or is an abuse of process. Such sanctions may include non-payment, in whole or in part, of fees associated with the motion and/or costs thereof." Rule 73(D) of the ICTY Rules provides that "Irrespective of any sanctions which may be imposed under Rule 46 (A), when a Chamber finds that a motion is frivolous or is an abuse of process, the Registrar shall withhold payment of fees associated with the production of that motion and/ or costs thereof."

Rule 47: Review of Indictment
(amended 1 August 2003)

(A) An indictment submitted in accordance with the following procedure shall be approved by the Designated Judge.

(B) The Prosecutor, if satisfied in the course of an investigation that a suspect has committed a crime or crimes within the jurisdiction of the Special Court, shall prepare and submit to the Registrar an indictment for approval by the aforementioned Judge.

(C) The indictment shall contain, and be sufficient if it contains, the name and particulars of the suspect, a statement of each specific offence of which the named suspect is charged and a short description of the particulars of the offence. It shall be accompanied by a Prosecutor's case summary briefly setting out the allegations he proposes to prove in making his case.

(D) The Registrar shall submit the indictment and accompanying material to the Designated Judge for review.

(E) The designated Judge shall review the indictment and the accompanying material to determine whether the indictment should be approved. The Judge shall approve the indictment if he is satisfied that:

  (i) the indictment charges the suspect with a crime or crimes within the jurisdiction of the Special Court; and
  (ii) that the allegations in the Prosecution's case summary would, if proven, amount to the crime or crimes as particularised in the indictment.

(F) The Designated Judge may approve or dismiss each count.

(G) If at least one count is approved, the indictment shall go forward. If no count is approved, the indictment shall be returned to the Prosecutor.

(H) Upon approval of the indictment:
  (i) The Judge may, at the request of the Prosecutor, issue such orders and warrants for the arrest, detention, surrender or transfer of persons, and any other orders as may be required for the proceedings in accordance with these Rules.; and
  (ii) The suspect shall have the status of an accused.

(I) The dismissal of a count in an indictment shall not preclude the Prosecutor from subsequently submitting an amended indictment including that count.

TRIAL CHAMBERS DECISIONS

- **Rule 47(C): Review of Indictment – Formal Validity of the Indictment**

R47-TC-1

o *Prosecutor v. Sesay*, SCSL-03-05-PT, Decision and Order on Defence Preliminary Motion for Defects in the Form of the Indictment, 13 October 2003, para. 5-8:[40]

> 5. The fundamental requirement of an indictment in international law as a basis for criminal responsibility underscores its importance and nexus with the principle *nullum crimen sine lege* as a *sine qua non* of international criminal responsibility. Therefore, as the foundational instrument of criminal adjudication, the requirements of due process demand adherence, within the limits of reasonable practicability, to the regime of rules governing the framing of indictments. [...]
>
> 6. The cumulative effect of [Article 17(4)(a) of the Statute and Rule 47(C) of the Rules of Procedure and Evidence] is to ensure the integrity of the proceedings against an accused person and to guarantee that there are no undue procedural constraints or burdens on his liability to adequately and effectively prepare his defence. Predicated upon these statutory provisions, the Chamber deems it necessary, at this stage, to articulate briefly the general applicable principles from the evolving jurisprudence on the framing of indictments in the sphere of international criminality. One cardinal principle is that an indictment must embody a concise statement of the facts specifying the crime or crimes preferred against the accused. A second basic principle is that to enable the accused to adequately and effectively prepare his defence, the indictment must plead with sufficient specificity or particularity the facts underpinning the specific crimes. Judicial reports for these principles abound in both national legal systems and the international legal system.
>
> 7. As to the specific principles on the framing of indictments deductible from the evolving jurisprudence of sister international criminal tribunals, the Chamber finds that the following propositions seem to represent the main body of the law:

---

[40] See also *Prosecutor v. Kanu*, Case No. SCSL-03-13-PT, Decision and Order on the Defence Preliminary Motion for Defects in the Form of the Indictment, 19 November 2003, para. 5-6, 21; *Prosecutor v. Kondewa*, SCSL-03-12-PT, Decision and Order on Defence Preliminary Motion for Defects in the Form of the Indictment, 27 November 2003, para. 6; *Prosecutor v. Kamara*, Case No. SCSL-04-16-PT, Decision and Order on Defence Preliminary Motion of Defects in the Form of the Indictment, 1 April 2004, para. 32-33.

(i) Allegations in an indictment are defective in form if they are not sufficiently clear and precise so as to enable the accused to fully understand the nature of the charges brought against him.[1]

(ii) The fundamental question in determining whether an indictment was pleaded with sufficient particularity is whether an accused had enough detail to prepare his defence.[2]

(iii) The indictment must state the material facts underpinning the charges, but need not elaborate on the evidence by which such material facts are to be proved.[3]

(iv) The degree of specificity required in an indictment is dependent upon whether it sets out material facts of the Prosecution's case with enough detail to inform the accused clearly of the charges against him so he may prepare his defence.[4]

(v) The nature of the alleged criminal conduct with which the accused is charged, including the proximity of the accused to the relevant events is a decisive factor in determining the degree of specificity in the indictment.[5]

(vi) The indictment must be construed as a whole and not as isolated and separate individual paragraphs.[6]

(vii) The practice of identifying perpetrators of alleged crimes by reference to their category or group is permissible in law.[7]

(viii) Where an indictment charges the commission of crimes on the part of the accused with "other superiors", the Prosecutor is not obliged to provide an exhaustive list of such "other superiors".[8]

(ix) In cases of mass criminality the sheer scale of the offences makes it impossible to give identity of the victims.[9]

(x) Identification of victims in indictments by reference to their group or category is permissible in law.[10]

(xi) The sheer scale of the alleged crimes make it 'impracticable' to require a high degree of specificity in such matters as the identity of the victims and the time and place of the events.[11]

(xii) Individual criminal responsibility under Article 6(1) and criminal responsibility as a superior under Article 6(3) of the Statute are not mutually exclusive and can be properly charged both cumulatively and alternatively based on the same facts.[12]

8. Based generally on the evolving jurisprudence of sister international tribunals, and having particular regard to the object and purpose of Rule 47(C) of the Special Court Rules of Procedure and Evidence which, *in its plain and ordinary meaning*, does not require an unduly burdensome or exacting

degree of specificity in pleading an indictment, but is logically consistent with the foregoing propositions of law, the Chamber considers it necessary to state that in framing an indictment, the degree of specificity required must necessarily depend upon such variables as (i) the nature of the allegations, (ii) the nature of the specific crimes charged, (iii) the scale or magnitude on which the acts or events allegedly took place, (iv) the circumstances under which the crimes were allegedly committed, (v) the duration of time over which the said acts or events constituting the crimes occurred, (vi) the time span between the occurrence of the events and the filing of the indictment, (vii) the totality of the circumstances surrounding the commission of the alleged crimes.

---

[1] *The Prosecutor v. Karemera*, ICTR-98-44-T, Decision on the Defence Motion Pursuant to Rule 72 of the Rules of Procedure and Evidence, pertaining to, *inter alia*, lack of jurisdiction and defects in the form of the Indictment, ICTR, Trial Chamber, April 25, 2001, para. 16. See also *Prosecutor v. Kanyabashi*, ICTR-96-15-I, Decision on Defence Preliminary Motion for Defects in the Form of the Indictment, 31 May 2000, para. 5.1.
[2] *Kupreskic*, Judgement AC, para 88, see also *The Prosecutor v. Laurent Semanza*, Case No. ICTR-97-20-T, 15 May, 2003.
[3] *Kupreskic*, Judgement AC, para. 88.
[4] *Prosecutor v. Elizaphan and Gerald Ntakirutimana*, Judgement and Sentence, Case No. ICTR-96-10 and ICTR-96-17-T, TCI, 2 February, 2003.
[5] *Prosecutor v. Meakic, Gruban, Fustar, Banovic, Knezevic*, "Decision on Dusan Fustar's Preliminary Motion on the Form of the Indictment", IT-02-65-PT, 4 April, 2003.
[6] *Prosecutor v. Krnojelac*, "Decision on the Defence Preliminary Motion on the Form of the Indictment", IT-97-25, 24 February, 1999, para 7.
[7] *Prosecutor v. Kvocka et al.*, IT-98-30-PT, "Decision on defence Preliminary Motion on Form of Indictment" TC III, 12 April 1999, para 22.
[8] *Prosecutor v. Nahimana*, ICTR-96-11-T, "Decision on the Defence Motion on Defects in the Form of the Amended Indictment, 17 November, 1998, paras 3-4.
[9] *Kvocka et al,* supra 6, paras 16-17.
[10] *Krnojelac, supra* 6.
[11] *Ntakirutimana, supra* 4.
[12] *Kvocka, supra* 9 para 50; see also *Prosecutor v. Musema*, ICTR-96-13T, Judgement, TCI, 27 January 2001, para. 884974, para. 891895, and *Prosecutor v. Delalic et al.*, Judgement, IT-96-21T, 16 November 1998.

R47-TC-2

o *Prosecutor v. Norman, Fofana, Kondewa*, Case No. SCSL-04-14-T, Reasoned Majority decision on Prosecution Motion for a Ruling on the Admissibility of Evidence, 24 May 2005, para. 18:

18. It is trite law that an indictment as the fundamental accusatory instrument which sets in motion the criminal adjudicatory process, must be framed in such a manner as not to offend the rule against multiplicity, duplicity, uncertainty or vagueness, and that where specific factual allegations are intended to be relied

upon or proven in support of specific counts in the indictment they ought to be pleaded with reasonable particularity.[1]

---

[1] In the Sierra Leone jurisdiction, the Court of Appeal deplored the idea of an indictment framed in such a way as to create duplicity, multiplicity or uncertainty in a count or counts both as to the offences or supporting factual allegations – See *Lansana and Eleven Others v. Reginam*, ALR. SL. 186 (1970-71) discussed in *The Criminal Law of Sierra Leone* by Bankole Thompson, published by the University Press of America Inc., Maryland, 1999 at pages 177-207.

- **Rule 47(C): Review of Indictment – Vagueness of Indictment – Generalities**

R47-TC-3   o *Prosecutor v. Sesay*, SCSL-03-05-PT, Decision and Order on Defence Preliminary Motion for Defects in the Form of the Indictment, 13 October 2003, para. 9, 20-23, 33:[41]

9. In this regard, it must be emphasized that where the allegations relate to ordinary or conventional crimes within the setting of domestic or national criminality, the degree of specificity required for pleading the indictment may be much grater than it would be where the allegations relate to unconventional or extraordinary crimes for example, mass killings, mass rapes and wanton and widespread destruction of property (in the context of crimes against humanity and grave violations of international humanitarian law) within the setting of international criminality. This distinction, recently clearly articulated in the jurisprudence,[1] follows as a matter of logical necessity, common sense, and due regard to the practical realities. To apply different but logically sound rules and criteria for framing indictments based on the peculiarities of the crimogenic setting in which the crimes charged in an indictment allegedly took place is nit tantamount to applying less than minimum judicial guarantees for accused persons appearing before the Special Court. [...]

[...]

20. [...] [I]n cases where the Prosecution alleges that an accused personally committed the criminal acts, an indictment generally must plead with particularity the identity of the victims and the time and place of the events. Exceptionally, however, the law is that in cases of mass criminality (as can be

---

[41] See also *Prosecutor v. Kanu*, Case No. SCSL-03-13-PT, Decision and Order on the Defence Preliminary Motion for Defects in the Form of the Indictment, 19 November 2003, para. 17-19; *Prosecutor v. Kamara*, SCSL-04-16-PT, Decision and Order on Defence Preliminary Motion on Defects in the Form of the Indictment, 1 April 2004, para. 19, 39-42.

gathered from the whole of the Indictment herein) the sheer scale of the offences may make it impossible to identify the victims.[2] Further, the Chamber wishes to emphasize that even where mass criminality is not being alleged, the specificity required to plead these kinds of facts is not necessarily as high where criminal responsibility is predicated upon superior or command responsibility[3] [...].

21. [...] The Chamber does not find the formulation '*at all times relevant to the this Indictment*' problematic in terms of adequate notice of the alleged abductions and forced labour thereby making it difficult for the Accused to prepare his defence. It is, likewise, not vague.

22. The Chamber agrees with the Prosecution that the use of the said formulation is with reference to a determinable time-frame. It presupposes that the alleged criminal activities took place over that time frame and with much regularity, a presupposition that can only be refuted by evidence. Given the brutal nature of the specific crimes alleged, the alleged massive and widespread nature of the criminality involved, and the peculiar circumstances in which they allegedly took place, the date range specified in the Indictment is not too broad or inconsistent with the latitude of prosecutorial discretion allowed to the Prosecution in such matters. In addition, the Chamber notes that the said paragraph is specific as to the victims of the alleged forced labour and that the place of events is patently restrictive, to wit, '*at various locations in the District*' in contrast, for example, '*at various locations in Sierra Leone*', or '*at various places in West Africa*'. [...]

23. [...] [I]t is inaccurate to suggest that the phrases '*various locations*' and '*various areas including*' in the relevant counts are completely devoid of details as to what is being alleged. Whether they are permissible or not depends primarily upon the context. For example, paragraphs 41, 44, 45 and 51 allege that the acts took place in various locations within those districts, a much narrower geographical unit than, for example, '*within the Southern or Eastern Province*' or '*within Sierra Leone*'. This is clearly permissible in situations where the alleged criminality was of what seems to be cataclysmic dimensions. By parity of reasoning, the phrases '*such as*' and '*including but not limited to*' would, in similar situations, be acceptable if the reference is, likewise, to locations but not otherwise. It is, therefore, the Chamber's thinking that taking the Indictment in its entirety, it is difficult to fathom how the Accused is unfairly prejudiced by the use of the said phrases in the context herein. In the ultimate analysis, having regard to the cardinal principle of the criminal law that the Prosecution must prove the case against an accused beyond reasonable doubt, the onus is on the Prosecution to adduce evidence at the trial to support the charges, however formulated. The Chamber

finds that even though, as a general rule, phrases of the kind should be avoided in framing indictments, yet in the specific context of paragraphs 23 and 24 they do not unfairly prejudice the Accused or burden the preparation of his defence. [. . .]

[. . .]

33. [. . .] [T]he Chamber is satisfied that the phrase '*but not limited to those events*' is impermissibly broad and also objectionable in not specifying the precise allegations against the Accused. It creates a potential for ambiguity. Where there is such potential, the Chamber is entitled to speculate that may be the omission of the additional material facts was done with the aim of moulding the case against the accused in the course of the trial depending on how the evidence unfolds.[4] It is trite law that the Prosecutor should not plead what he does not intend to prove. In the chamber's considered view, the use of such a formulation is tantamount to pleading by ambush. The doctrine of fundamental fairness precludes judicial endorsement of such a practice. [. . .]

---

[1] See *Archbold International Criminal Courts, Practice, Procedure and Evidence*, Sweer & Maxwell Ltd, London, 2003, at para 6-45 where it stated: In examining the position of indictments in national law and the degree of specificity required, the Trial Chamber in *Prosecutor v. Kvocka*, Decision on defence Preliminary Motion on the Form of Indictment, April 12, 1999, paras 14-18, recognized that although a minimum amount of information must be provided in an indictment for it to be valid in form, the 'degree of particularity required in indictments before the International Tribunal is different from, and perhaps not as high as, the particularity required in domestic criminal law jurisdictions. The Trial Chamber at para 17, stipulated that this difference is partly due to the massive scale of the crimes falling within the Tribunal's jurisdiction, which might make it impossible to identify all the victims, the perpetrators and the means employed to carry out the crimes.
[2] *The Prosecutor v. Laurent Semanza*, supra 2.
[3] Id.
[4] *Kupreskic*, supra 2.

o *Prosecutor v. Kanu*, Case No. SCSL-03–13–PT, Decision and Order on the Defence Preliminary Motion for Defects in the Form of the Indictment, 19 November 2003, para. 24-25:

24. Evidently, as a proposition deducible from the ICTY caselaw on the subject, learned Counsel is correct in referencing the point. But he himself rightly notes, at the same page, that the ICTY held in *Kvocka* case[1] that "the massive scale of crimes (. . . . .) make it impractical to require a high degree of specificity in such matters as the identity of the victims and the dates for the commission of crimes." The citation also

references the *Krnojelac*⁽²⁾ decision as authority for the proposition that "albeit... the indictment must enable the accused and the defence to finally and adequately prepare the defence so that it must provide (some) information as to the identity of victims, place, date of the alleged crimes and means by which the offence was committed". The clear effect, in the Chamber's view, of *Kvocka* is to postulate, as learned Counsel himself acknowledges, *that specificity in cases of such extraordinary crimes, as alleged, is not absolute*. This view of the law is consistent with the principles developed by this Court in Sesay, relying persuasively upon logically coherent and consistent decisions of ICTY and ICTR on the subject.

25. Based upon those principles and consistent with the decision in *Sesay*, the Chamber finds that the Indictment, as a whole, *except in relation to the use of the formulations "but not limited to these events" "including, but not limited to," "included but were not limited to"*, contains sufficient information to put the Accused on notice as to the charges against him. The Chamber also finds that, in the context of the extraordinary character of the crimes alleged, the dates, locations and offences charged are sufficiently clear to notify the Accused of the charges against him as one of those who allegedly "bear the greatest responsibility" for the said crimes, and to enable him to put forward the defence of alibi. Further, the Chamber does not find legally compelling and cogent the contention that specificity is required to enable an accused person to engage in cross-examination of witnesses. Of course, the Chamber agrees with learned Counsel that the requirement of specificity is part and parcel of the notion of a fair trial. *However, the Chamber wishes to emphasize that it remains true (as noted in paragraph 23) that, in the ultimate analysis, the crux of the matter is whether the Prosecution have proved their case beyond a reasonable doubt predicated upon the charges as formulated.*

⁽¹⁾ Supra note 11.
⁽²⁾ "Decision on the Defence Preliminary Motion on the Form of the Indictment", IT-99-25, 24 February 1999.

o *Prosecutor v. Kondewa*, Case No. SCSL-03-12-PT, Decision and Order on Defence Preliminary Motion for Defects in the Form of the Indictment, 27 November 2003, para. 10:[42]

---

[42] See also *Prosecutor v. Kamara*, SCSL-04-16-PT, Decision and Order on Defence Preliminary Motion on Defects in the Form of the Indictment, 1 April 2004, para. 49.

10. [. . .] Moreover, the Chamber notes that, despite the fact that the law governing the framing of indictments bristles with technicalities, yet it must be emphasized 'that the materiality of a particular fact cannot be decided in the abstract. It is dependent on the nature of the Prosecution's case. A decisive factor in determining the degree of specificity with which the Prosecution is required to particularise the facts of its case in the indictment is the nature of the alleged criminal conduct charged to the accused.'[1] [. . .] Whether the Accused, for example *'planned'*, or *'instigated'*, or *'ordered'*, the commission of any of the crimes specified in Articles 2 to 4 of the Statute is, in the Chamber's view, pre-eminently an evidentiary matter,[2] the key determinant of the success or failure of the Prosecution's case.

---

[1] *Kupreskic et al.* Appeals Judgement, para. 89.
[2] See *The Prosecutor v. Santigie Borbor Kanu, supra*, note 2, para. 21 where the Chamber observed that "the Prosecution must stand or fall by their own charges", *per* Judge Thompson.

R47-TC-6 o *Prosecutor v. Norman*, Case No. SCSL-04-14-T, Decision on the First Accused's Motion for Service and Arraignment on the Consolidated Indictment, 29 November 2004, para. 22-29:[43]

22. An Indictment, as the primary accusatory instrument against an Accused person, must plead the essential aspects of the Prosecution case with sufficient detail. In accordance with Rule 47(c) of the Rules:

> The indictment shall contain, and be sufficient if it contains, the name and particulars of the suspect, a statement of each specific offence of which the named suspect is charged and a short description of the particulars of the offence. It shall be accompanied by a Prosecutor's case summary briefly setting out the allegations he proposes to prove in making his case.

23. If the Prosecution fails to plead the essential aspects of the Prosecution Case in the Indictment, it will suffer from a material defect.[1] As stated by the Appeals Chamber of the International Criminal Tribunal for the Former Yugoslavia ("ICTY") in the *Kupreskic* case:

---

[43] See also *Prosecutor v. Fofana*, Case No. SCSL-04-14-T, Decision on the Second Accused's Motion for Service and Arraignment on the Consolidated Indictment, 6 December 2004, para. 25-30, 32.

It is not acceptable for the Prosecution to omit the material aspects of its main allegations in the Indictment with the aim of moulding the case against the accused in the course of the trial depending on how the evidence unfolds.[2]

24. Pursuant to Article 17(4) of the Statute, the Accused must be informed of the "nature and cause of the charge against him". There is a distinction between the material facts upon which the prosecution relies, and which must be pleaded in the Indictment, and the evidence by which those material facts will be proved, which do not need to be pleaded.[3] The materiality of the facts to be pleaded depends on the nature of the Prosecution case and the alleged proximity of the Accused to those events. As stated by the Trial Chamber of the International Criminal Tribunal for the former Yugoslavia in the *Brdanin* case, in a trial based upon, for example, superior responsibility:

> [W]hat is most material is the relationship between the accused and the others who did the acts for which he is alleged to be responsible, and the conduct of the accused by which he may be found to have known or had reason to know that the acts were about to be done, or had been done, by those others, and to have failed to take the necessary and reasonable measures to prevent such acts or to punish the persons who did them. However, so far as those acts of the other persons are concerned, although the prosecution remains under an obligation to give all the particulars which it is able to give, the relevant facts will usually be stated with less precision, and that is because the detail of those acts (by whom and against whom they are done) is often unknown – and because the acts themselves often cannot be greatly in issue.[4]

25. The Trial Chamber in the *Brdanin* case further considered that in a case based upon individual responsibility where the Accused is alleged to have personally committed the acts pleaded in the Indictment:

> [T]he material facts must be pleaded with precision – the information pleaded as material facts must, so far as it is possible to do so, include the identity of the victim, the places and the approximate date of those acts and the means by which the offence was committed. Where the prosecution is unable to specify any of these matters, it cannot be obliged to perform the impossible. Where the precise date cannot be specified, a reasonable range of dates may be sufficient. Where a precise identification of the victim or victims cannot be specified, a reference to their category or position as a group may be sufficient. Where the prosecution is unable to specify

matters such as these, it must make it clear in the indictment that it is unable to do so and that it has provided the best information it can.[5]

26. An Indictment may be amended, however, at trial, where the evidence turns out differently than expected. The Trial Chamber may grant an adjournment for this purpose, or certain evidence may be excluded as not being within the scope of the Indictment.[6] In cases where an Indictment provides insufficient details as to the essential elements of the Prosecution case, the jurisprudence of the Tribunal accepts that a defendant may not be unfairly prejudiced where the defence is put on reasonable notice of the Prosecution case before trial, for example, in the Prosecution Pre-Trial Brief, or at the latest, in the Prosecution opening statement.

27. In the *Kupreskic* case, the Appeals Chamber of the ICTY held that "the question whether an Indictment is pleaded with sufficient particularity is dependent upon whether it sets out the material facts of the Prosecution case with enough detail to inform a defendant clearly of the charges against him so that he may prepare his defence."[7] Trial Chambers of the ICTY have held that:

[a]ll legal prerequisites to the application of the offences charged constitute material facts, and must be pleaded in the indictment. The materiality of other facts (facts not directly going to legal prerequisites), which also have to be pleaded in the Indictment, cannot be determined in the abstract. Each of the material facts must usually be pleaded expressly, although it may be sufficient in some circumstances if it is expressed by necessary implication. This fundamental rule of pleading, however, is not complied with if the pleading merely assumes the existence of a pre-requisite.[8]

28. This Trial Chamber, in its Decision in the case of *Sesay*, held that when framing an Indictment, the degree of specificity required:

[m]ust necessarily depend upon such variables as (i) the nature of the allegations; (ii) the nature of the specific crimes charged; (iii) the scale or magnitude on which the acts or events allegedly took place (iv) the circumstances under which the crimes were allegedly committed; (v) the duration of time over which the said acts or events constituting the crimes occurred; (vi) the time span between the occurrence of the events and the filing of the indictment; (vii) the totality of the circumstances surrounding the commission of the alleged crimes.[9]

29. Applying the foregoing principle to the instant situation, the Trial Chamber considers that given the alleged nature and scale of the offences charged, and the alleged mode of

partiipation of the Accused in a position of command responsibility, and as part of a joint criminal enterprise with a common plan to commit such offences, it would not be realistic to expect for these offences to be plead with "pin-point particularity".[10] At the same time, however, greater specificity will be required for other modes of participation in offences pursuant to Article 6(1) of the Statute, and the alleged offences and material facts must be plead with enough precision to inform the Accused clearly of the charges against him so that he may prepare his defence.

---

[1] *Prosecutor v. Kupreskic*, Appeals Judgement, para. 114.
[2] Supra, para. 92.
[3] See *Prosecutor v. Brdanin*, Decision on Objections by Momir Talic to the Form of the Amended Indictment, 20 February 2001, para. 18.
[4] *Id*, para. 19.
[5] *Id*, para. 22.
[6] Supra, para. 92.
[7] *Prosecutor v. Kupreskic,* Appeal Judgement, para. 88.
[8] *Prosecutor v. Enver Hadzihasanovic et al.*, Case No. IT-01-47-PT, Decision on Form of Indictment, 7 December 2001 ("*Hadzihasanovic* Decision on Form of the Indictment"), para. 10; see also *Prosecutor v. Mile Mrksic*, Case No. IT-95-13/1-PT, Decision on Form of the Indictment, 19 June 2003, para. 11.
[9] *Prosecutor v. Issa Hassan Sesay*, Decision and Order on defence Preliminary Motion for Defects in the Form of the Indictment, 13 October 2003, para. 8.
[10] *Prosecutor v. Kanu*, Decision and Order on Defence Preliminary Motion for Defects in the Form of the Indictment, 19 November 2003, Para. 21.

R47-TC-7

o *Prosecutor v. Kamara*, Case No. SCSL-04-16-PT, Decision and Order on Defence Preliminary Motion on Defects in the Form of the Indictment, 1 April 2004, para. 38-39, 46:

38. [...] The Trial Chamber further states that there is clear persuasive authority that the words "*between about*" and "*about*" to denote a time frame of the commission of the alleged crimes are permissible in the context of alleged widespread and mass criminality especially where dates or times are not material elements of the alleged offences.[1]

39. In the Trial Chamber's view, such time frames, as alleged in the Indictment, do not legally impede the Accused from properly preparing his defence particularly regarding establishing an *alibi*, as the Defence asserts. [...]

[...]

46. The next Defence challenge under this category, found in (d), relates to alleged vagueness and lack of specificity as to the names and number of victims. The Trial Chamber [...] finds no merit in the allegations for the following reasons.

Firstly, that, as an exception to the general rule, that were it is alleged that an accused personally committed criminal acts, the indictment must plead with particularity the identity of the victims, in case of mass criminality the sheer scale of the offences may make it impossible to identify the victims.[2] Secondly, that there is no applicable magical formula as to the degree of specificity required for the purposes of pleading "an indictment alleging criminality in the international domain as distinct from criminality in the domestic sphere".[3] It is precisely a matter of common sense and what is reasonable, having regard to "the scale or magnitude on which the acts or events allegedly took place" and "the totality of the circumstances surrounding the commission of the alleged crimes".[4] Thirdly, that whether the phrases complained of, for example, *"an unknown number"*, are permissible or not "depends primarily upon the context," and that they would be "'clearly permissible in situations where the alleged criminality was of what seems to be cataclysmic dimensions' and where statistics are hard to come by."[5]

[1] *Prosecutor v. Kayishema*, Case No. ICTR-95-1-T-21, Judgement, 21 May, 1999, paras 81 and 85-86.
[2] See, *The Prosecutor v. Laurent Semanza*, Case No. ICTR-97-20-T, 15 May 2003 and also *Sesay* Decision, para. 20.
[3] See, *Kanu* decision, para. 19. The Trial Chamber recalls that guideline, however, do exist. See fn. 18 *supra*. See also, *Prosecutor v. Zoran Kupreskic et al.*, Case No. IT-95-16-A, Judgement, 23 October 2001, para. 89: "the materiality of a particular fact cannot be decided in the abstract. It is dependent on the nature of the Prosecution case. A decisive factor in determining the degree of specificity with which the Prosecution is required to particularise the facts of its case in the indictment is the nature of the alleged criminal conduct charged to the accused. For example, in a case where the Prosecution alleges that an accused personally committed the criminal acts, the material facts, such as the identity of the victim, the time and place of the events and the means by which the acts were committed, have to be pleaded in detail."
[4] Id.
[5] Id., citing *Sesay* Decision, para. 23.

- **Rule 47(C): Review of Indictment – Vagueness of Indictment – Article 6(3) Charges**

R47-TC-8   o *Prosecutor v. Sesay*, Case No. SCSL-03-05-PT, Decision and Order on Defence Preliminary Motion for Defects in the Form of the Indictment, 13 October 2003, para. 13-14:[44]

---

[44] See also *Prosecutor v. Kamara*, SCSL-04-16-PT, Decision and Order on Defence Preliminary Motion on Defects in the Form of the Indictment, 1 April 2004, para. 55.

13. Further, in a case based on superior responsibility pursuant to Article 6(3), minimum material facts to be pleaded in the indictment are as follows:

a) (i) that the accused held a superior position;
 (ii) in relation to subordinates, sufficiently identified;
 (iii) that the accused had effective control over the said subordinates;
 (iv) that he allegedly bears responsibility for their criminal acts;
b) (i) that the accused knew or had reason to know that the crimes were about to be or had been committed by his subordinates;
 (ii) the related conduct of those subordinates for whom he is alleged to be responsible;
 (iii) the accused failed to take the necessary and reasonable means to prevent such crimes or to punish the persons who committed them.

14. With regard to the nature of the material facts to be pleaded in a case under Article 6(3) it follows, in the Chamber's view, that certain facts will necessarily be pleaded with a far lesser degree of specificity than in one under Article 6(1). It would seem, therefore, that in some situations under Article 6(3), given the peculiar features and circumstances of the case and the extraordinary nature of the crimes, it may be sufficient merely to plead as material facts the legal prerequisites to the offences charged as noted in Paragraph 13 herein. Further, [...] the Chamber finds the Defence submission that the Prosecution must clearly distinguish the acts for which the Accused incurs criminal responsibility under Article 6(1) of the Statute from those for which he incurs criminal responsibility under Article 6(3) to be legally unsustainable. The Chamber also finds that it may be sufficient to plead the legal prerequisites embodied in the statutory provisions. The Defence contention that the same facts cannot give rise to both heads of liability is, likewise, meretricious. The implication that they are mutually exclusive flies in the face of the law.[1]

---

[1] See Kvocka, supra 12.

- **Rule 47(C): Review of Indictment – Vagueness of Indictment – Joint Criminal Enterprise**

R47-TC-9   o *Prosecutor v. Sesay*, Case No. SCSL-03-05-PT, Decision and Order on Defence Preliminary Motion for Defects in the Form of the Indictment, 13 October 2003, para. 26-27, 30:

26. Another specific Defence challenge revolves around the description of a common plan. [...] The law on this issue where it is alleged (as in the instant Indictment) that the specific international crimes with which an accused is charged involved numerous perpetrators acting in concert, is that the degree of particularity required in pleading the underlying facts is not as high as in case of domestic criminal courts.[1]

[...]

27. It is evident from paragraph 23 that the Indictment sets out with much particularity the nature of the alleged joint criminal enterprise, namely '*to take actions necessary to gain and exercise political power and control over the territory of Sierra Leone in particular the diamond areas*'. [...]

[...]

30. [...] *Archbold*, para 6–57 sets out the criteria for charging joint criminal enterprise in these terms:

> An indictment charging joint criminal enterprise is required to include the nature of the enterprise, the time periods involved, and the nature of the accused's participation in the criminal enterprise (*Krnojelac, Decision on Form of Amended Indictment*, May 11, 2000) [...]"

---

[1] See *Archbold*, supra 12 at para. 6–45.

R47-TC-10 o *Prosecutor v. Kanu,* Case No. SCSL-03-13-PT, Decision and Order on the Defence Preliminary Motion for Defects in the Form of the Indictment, 19 November 2003, para. 14-15:

14. The Defence contention that the Indictment does not adequately specify the category of joint criminal enterprise alleged, in the opinion of the Chamber, lacks substance for the reasons hereinafter articulated. In this connection, the Chamber disagrees with the Defence submission that there is an obligation on the Prosecutor to elect between the basic joint criminal enterprise concept of liability and the extended one. The Chamber finds nothing in the case-law authorities requiring the Prosecution to elect between the basic category of joint criminal enterprise theory of liability and the extended category theory. The Appeals Judgment in *Prosecutor v Tadic*[1] imposes no such obligation. On this issue, all the Court did in that case was recall that a close scrutiny of the relevant case-law on the subject "shows that broadly speaking, the notion of common purpose encompasses three distinct categories of collective criminality", and then articulate in paragraphs 196 – 206 the different categories of joint criminal

enterprise, and the extent to which the second category is a variant of the first. The Chamber also wishes to emphasize that the *Prosecutor v Krnojelac*[2] is no authority for the proposition that there is an obligation on the Prosecution to elect in an indictment between the two categories of joint criminal enterprise liability. Clearly, in that case the Trial Chamber held that where "only a basic joint criminal enterprise had been pleaded, it would not be fair to the Accused to allow the Prosecutor to rely upon the extended form of joint criminal enterprise liability in the absence of such an amendment to the Indictment to plead it expressly".[3] For the foregoing reasons, the Chamber cannot sustain the Defence challenge.

15. As regards the issue that the Indictment fails to establish a nexus between the joint criminal enterprise and the specific crimes alleged, the Chamber's response is that such nexus seems clear from a careful reading of paragraph 24 of the Indictment, the scope of which is of general applicability to the whole Indictment, to wit:

> "The crimes alleged in this Indictment, including unlawful killings, abductions, forced labour, physical and sexual violence, use of child soldiers, looting and burning of civilian structures, were either actions within the joint criminal enterprise or were a reasonably foreseeable consequence of the joint criminal enterprise".

---

[1] Case No. IT-94-IA, July 15, 1999.
[2] IT-95-25 "Decision on the Defence Preliminary Motion on the Form of the Indictment", 24 February 1999.
[3] Id. *supra* note 4. Judgment 15 March 2002 para. 86.

o *Prosecutor v. Kamara*, Case No. SCSL-04-16-PT, Decision and Order on Defence Preliminary Motion on Defects in the Form of the Indictment, 1 April 2004, para. 53:

53. As to the Defence contention that the Prosecution must disclose the names of persons outside Sierra Leone to whom diamonds were to be provided in return for assistance in carrying out the joint criminal enterprise, the Trial Chamber reiterates that this is an evidentiary matter. Equally pertinent to dispelling this Defence misconception, is that the time frame of the joint criminal enterprise is sufficiently pleaded as "*All times relevant to this Indictment*". By parity of reasoning, the Trial Chamber notes that the nature of the Accused's participation is pleaded in paragraphs 18–23, and that the identity of those involved in the joint criminal enterprise is sufficiently pleaded in paragraphs 8, 19, 21, and 22. In respect of the related contentions that the Prosecution must plead the Accused's state of mind in relation to the joint criminal enterprise, that

the voluntariness of the Accused must also be pleaded, and that there is no definition of the "unlawful means" in the context of joint criminal enterprise, the Trial Chamber makes shortshrift of these contentions with two brief observations. Firstly, that they are essentially evidentiary matters and secondly, that there is some degree of specificity in respect of these allegations in so far as the factual context of the case, as alleged, admits. The Trial Chamber, accordingly, rejects these challenges as ill-conceived.

- **Rule 47(C): Review of Indictment – Form of Indictment – Cumulative Charging**

R47-TC-12 o *Prosecutor v. Kanu*, Case No. SCSL-03-13-PT, Decision and Order on the Defence Preliminary Motion for Defects in the Form of the Indictment, 19 November 2003, para. 23:

23. [...] The Chamber's interpretation of the above extracts is that the same crimes which were committed to terrorize the civilian population, and those set forth in paragraphs 32 through 52 and also charged in Counts 3-13 were the same crimes that were committed to punish the civilian population. The Chamber is strongly of the view that any other interpretation is tantamount to doing violence to the language of the Indictment. From the Chamber's perspective, the phrase "collective punishments" is not problematic; what acts constitute "collective punishments" is a function of evidence that will be determined at the trial. The Defence contention, therefore, fails.

- **Rule 47(E): Review of Indictment – Discretion of the Reviewing Judge**

R47-TC-13 o *Prosecutor v. Fofana*, Case No. SCSL-04-14-PT, Decision on the Preliminary Defence Motion on the Lack of Personal Jurisdiction Filed on Behalf of the Accused Fofana, 3 March 2004, para. 31:

31. As a matter of statutory interpretation, it is clear, therefore, from the provisions of Rule 47 that the Designated Judge has the discretion to accept or reject an indictment, in whole or in part. [...]

- **Rule 47(E): Review of Indictment – Scope of Review**

R47-TC-14 o *Prosecutor v. Fofana*, Case No. SCSL-04-14-PT, Decision on the Preliminary Defence Motion on the Lack of Personal Jurisdiction Filed on Behalf of the Accused Fofana, 3 March 2004, para. 31-38:

31. [...] It is the Chamber's considered view that this review procedure of an indictment must take into account the personal jurisdictional requirements, the temporal jurisdictional requirements and the subject-matter requirements of the Special Court, as set out in the Statute.

32. The review of an indictment is not simply a "rubber stamp" procedure; rather, it is a process during which the Designated Judge carefully reviews the contents of the proposed indictment and the Prosecutor's case summary to determine whether there is sufficient information to establish reasonable grounds to believe that the person committed the crime charged.

33. The Chamber recalls that Rule 47 of the Rules was amended at the Plenary in March 2003: Rule 47(B) had been identical to that of the ICTR Rules.[1] This amendment does not mean, however, that the Chamber abandoned the general principle of criminal law that there must be a sufficient basis for each crime charged.[2] The Chamber notes that the decision on the first nine indictments issued by the Special Court – including one which followed the March 2003 Plenary – explicitly found that the Designated Judge was satisfied "from the material tendered by the Prosecution that there is sufficient evidence to provide reasonable grounds for believing" that the named accused "has committed crimes within the jurisdiction of the Court and that the allegations would, if proven, amount to the crimes specified and particularized in the said indictment."[3]

34. While the decision approving the indictment for the Accused Fofana does not contain this language, but rather reflects the language of the current Rule 47(B),[4] the Chamber recalls the right enshrined in the Statute, as well as international human rights instruments, that all accused shall be equal before the Special Court.[5] As has been found by Judge Alphons Orie at the ICTY, while the screening mechanisms of Prosecutors' cases and indictments vary, the purpose remains the same: "to protect the accused against oppressive unfounded charges."[6]

35. Accordingly, the Designated Judge who approved the Indictment brought against Fofana satisfied himself that sufficient information to provide reasonable grounds for believing that

the Accused committed the crimes charged in the Indictment and that the allegations would, if proven, amount to the crimes specified therein.

36. Furthermore, the Designated Judge satisfied himself that the temporal and personal jurisdictional requirements were satisfied. It is noted that there is no challenge to the temporal jurisdictional requirement having been properly pleaded.

37. The third issue, therefore, which must be addressed, is what test should be satisfied or standard employed at the time of the review of an indictment in determining whether the necessary personal jurisdiction requirements are fulfilled in this case.

38. The Trial Chamber finds that the standard employed to satisfy the personal jurisdiction requirement should be no different than the standard to satisfy the subject-matter jurisdictional requirement. The Designated Judge must therefore be satisfied that sufficient information to provide reasonable grounds for believing that the Accused is a person who bears the greatest responsibility for serious violations of international humanitarian law and Sierra Leonean law, including those leaders who, in committing such crimes, have threatened the establishment of and implementation of the peace process in Sierra Leone.

---

[1] The former Rule 47(B) of the Rules provided: "The Prosecutor, if satisfied in the course of an investigation that there is sufficient evidence to provide reasonable grounds for believing that a suspect has committed a crime within the jurisdiction of the [Special Court], shall prepare and forward to the Registrar an indictment for confirmation by a Judge, together with supporting material."

[2] See, e.g., Article 65(5) and (7) of the Statute of the International Criminal Court ("sufficient evidence to establish substantial grounds to believe that the person committed the crime charged"); Article 5(1)(c) of the European Convention for the Protection of Human Rights and Fundamental Freedoms ("ECHR") ("the lawful arrest or detention of a person effected for the purpose of bringing him before the competent legal authority of reasonable suspicion of having committed and offence or when it is reasonably considered necessary to prevent his committing an offence or fleeing after having done so"). See also, The Code for Crown Prosecutors, Article 5(1) ("enough evidence to provide a 'realistic prospect for conviction' against each defendant on each charge") and Article 5(2) ("a realistic prospect for conviction . . . means that a jury or bench of magistrates, properly directed in accordance with the law, is more likely than not to convict the defendant of the charge alleged").

[3] See, e.g., *The Prosecutor against Charles Taylor*, Case No. SCSL-03-01-I, Decision Approving the Indictment and Order for Non-Disclosure, 7 March 2003; *The Prosecutor against Augustine Gbao*, Case No. SCSL-03-09-I, Decision Approving the Indictment, 16 April 2003.

[4] *The Prosecutor against Moinina Fofana*, Case No. SCSL-03-11 I, Decision Approving the Indictment and Order for the Continued Detention of the Accused, 26 June 2003, page 2: "Being Satisfied from the material tendered by the Prosecutor that the indictment charges the suspect with crimes against the jurisdiction of the Special Court, and that the allegations in the

Prosecutor's case summary would, if proven, amount to crimes as specified and particularized in the indictment".

(5) See, Article 17(1) of the Statute of the Special Court. See also, International Covenant on Civil and Political Rights, Article 14(1); ECHR, Article 14.

(6) *Prosecutor v. Ratko Mladić*, Case No. IT-95-5/18-I, Order Granting Leave to File an Amended Indictment and Confirming the Amended Indictment, 8 November 2002, para. 22. See also, paras 23-26.

- **Rule 47(E): Review of Indictment – Criteria of Review**

R47-TC-15

o *Prosecutor v. Taylor*, Case No. SCSL-03-01-I, Decision Approving the Indictment and Order for Non-Disclosure, 7 March 2003:[45]

BEING SATISFIED from the material tendered by the Prosecutor that there is sufficient evidence to provide reasonable grounds for believing that the suspect has committed crimes within the jurisdiction of the Court and that the allegations would, if proven, amount to the crimes specified and particularised in the said Indictment [...]

R47-TC-16

o *Prosecutor v. Kondewa*, Case No. SCSL-03-12-I, Decision Approving the Indictment and Order for the Continued Detention of the Accused, 26 June 2003:[46]

BEING SATISFIED from the material tendered by the Prosecutor that the indictment charges the suspect with crimes within the jurisdiction of the Special Court, and that the alle-

---

[45] See also *Prosecutor v. Sankoh*, Case No. SCSL-03-02-I, Decision Approving the Indictment and Order for Non-Disclosure, 7 March 2003; *Prosecutor v. Koroma*, Case No. SCSL-03-03-I, Decision Approving the Indictment and Order for Non-Disclosure, 7 March 2003; *Prosecutor v. Bockarie*, Case No. SCSL-03-04-I, Decision Approving the Indictment and Order for Non-Disclosure, 7 March 2003; *Prosecutor v. Sesay*, Case No. SCSL-03-05-I, Decision Approving Indictment and Order for Non-Disclosure, 7 March 2003; *Prosecutor v. Brima*, Case No. SCSL-03-06-I, Decision Approving Indictment and Order for Non-Disclosure, 7 March 2003; *Prosecutor v. Kallon*, Case No. SCSL-03-07-I, Decision Approving Indictment and Order for Non-Disclosure, 7 March 2003; *Prosecutor v Norman*, Case No. SCSL-03-08-I, Decision Approving the Indictment and Order for Non-Disclosure, 7 March 2003; *Prosecutor v. Gbao*, Case No. SCSL-03-09-I, Decision Approving the Indictment, 16 April 2003.

[46] See also *Prosecutor v. Kamara*, Case No. SCSL-03-03-I, Decision Approving the Indictment, the warrant of arrest and Order for Non-Public Disclosure, 28 May 2003; *Prosecutor v. Fofana*, Case No. SCSL-03-11-I, Decision Approving the Indictment and Order for the Continued Detention of the Accused, 26 June 2003; *Prosecutor v. Kanu*, Case No. SCSL-03-13-I, Decision Approving the Indictment, the Warrant of Arrest, and Order for Transfer and Detention, and Order for Non-Public Disclosure, 16 September 2003.

gations in the Prosecutor's case summary would, of proven, amount to crimes as specified and particularised in the indictment [...]

R47-TC-17 o *Prosecutor v. Brima*, Case No. SCSL-03-06-PT, Ruling on the Application for the Issue of a Writ of *Habeas Corpus* Filed by the Applicant, 22 July 2003:

From the foregoing analysis, it is clear that the Application by the Prosecutor for the approval of the indictment is made to the Judge *ex-parte* and that the Judge, in my opinion, either applying the objective or subjective test, approves it as such. The Prosecutor cannot indeed at that stage, without having called evidence in Court, be expected to establish a *prima facie* case nor can the Judge, in such circumstances, without evidence having been so adduced, so find. Indeed, all the indictment needs to satisfy for it to be approved is what is contained in Rule 47(E) and not that the documents so submitted should establish a *prima facie* case against the accused.

Once the Judge at this stage is satisfied that the indictment and the facts accompanying it, if proven, amounts to the crime or crimes particularized in the indictment, he should, without more, like His Lordship, Judge Bankole Thompson did, sign the indictment so submitted by the Prosecutor.

APPEALS CHAMBER DECISIONS

- **Rule 47: Review of Indictment – No Requirement for a *Prima Facie* Case**

R47-AC-1 o *Prosecutor v. Norman, Fofana, Kondewa*, Case No. SCSL-04-14-AR73, Decision on Amendment of the Consolidated Indictment, 16 May 2005, para. 49:

49. [...] The Indictment was reviewed under Rule 47(E) by a designated judge for the purpose of ensuring that the crimes it charged were within the jurisdiction of the court and that allegations made by the Prosecution "would if proven, amount to the crime or crimes as particularised in the Indictment". This exercise does not, as in certain other courts, require a judicial finding of a *prima facie* case: the judge is concerned only to ensure that the particulars which the Prosecution claims it can prove would amount to a triable offence.

- **Rule 47(C): Review of Indictment – Information to Be Included in the Indictment**

R47-AC-2

o *Prosecutor v. Norman, Fofana, Kondewa*, Case No. SCSL-04-14-AR73, Decision on Amendment of the Consolidated Indictment, 16 May 2005, para. 51–54:

> 51. The Norman Indictment, like the other Indictments laid by the Prosecution, may have been influenced by precedents from the ICTY and ICTR, but it is regrettable that they did not follow more accurately the style prescribed by Rule 47(C). This rule envisages that after particulars of personal identification there should be "a statement of each specific offence of which the named subject is charged". Each such statement is what is commonly known as a *count* of the Indictment, which encapsulates the offence with which the subject is charged – i.e. the law which he is alleged to have broken. The count should then be followed by a "short description" of the *particulars* of the offence – the time, place, reference to co-offenders and so on. Then, as a *separate document*, albeit appended to or served with the Indictment, a "prosecutor's case summary" briefly setting out the allegations he proposes to prove – a *précis*, as it were, of his opening speech.
>
> 52. Rule 47(C) is clear. The "Indictment" should comprise only a list of counts, with each count followed by brief particulars. The case summary which should accompany the Indictment forms no part of it. The significance of this practice is that once a defendant is *arraigned* – i.e. required to plead to the counts of an Indictment, which under international criminal procedure reflected in our Rule 61 is referred to as an "initial appearance and plea" – no word or phrase of any count or any particular of a count may be changed without the permission of the court, by an application to amend the Indictment which is made in the presence of the Defence. The Prosecutor's case summary, however, is not a document susceptible to amendment by the court. It accompanies the Indictment in order to give the Accused better details of the charges against him and to enable the designated judge to decide whether to approve the Indictment under Rule 47(E). It does not bind the Prosecutor in the sense that he is obliged to apply to amend it if his evidence changes. The Prosecutor is obliged to give full disclosure of any such evidence and is obliged to alert the Defence to any significant change in the way the case will be put at trial, but the "Prosecutor's case summary" is not part of the Indictment, which is the formal document which triggers the trial.
>
> 53. It appears to us that some of the difficulties in this case originated with the Prosecutor's failure to appreciate the clear

distinction between what should go in the Indictment and what should be left to the case summary. He produced, as the Indictment, a document that put the counts at the end instead of at the beginning, as if they were conclusions to be inferred from detailed allegations, both "general" and "individual" and from "charges" which took the form of further general allegations, many details of which could have been left for the case summary. In the result, of course, the Defence was not prejudiced: on the contrary, the Indictment included many more "particulars" than the Prosecution was obliged to give. The Prosecutor, by his own choice, therefore shouldered a heavier burden of applying for amendments than was strictly necessary. The Defence understandably never complained that its Indictment was overloaded with particulars. The designated judge did not take the point, and did not need to: the Indictment was more than "sufficient" for the purpose of Rule 47.

54. The Prosecution inflicted this form of Indictment on the court and on itself, without prejudice to the defendants. An Indictment in this form is not invalid although it may be ill-advised. It was the form in which both Kondewa (SCSL-2003-12-I) and Fofana (SCSL-2003-2-I) were individually indicted on 24 June 2003, some three months after Hinga Norman. The counts in their two Indictments are identical, as are the sections headed "General Allegations" and "Charges". There are only minor changes to reflect their different alleged positions in the Civil Defence Forces ("CDF"), in the sections headed "Individual Criminal Responsibility". Their Indictments were similar to the Norman Indictment, although there were a number of minor changes which made the allegations against the CDF leadership more precise. There were two important additions, however: the "charges" in para 19(d) and (e) of the Fofana and Kondewa Indictments, reflected in counts 1 and 2 (para 20(e) and (f)), find no counterpart in the Norman Indictment. These "new" allegations against the CDF leadership – although the Prosecution says they are really details of the general allegation of unlawful conduct in the original Norman Indictment – were made public in June 2003, and it must have been obvious to Norman's very experienced lawyers that there was every likelihood that the Prosecution would in due course seek to level these charges against their client. The Prosecution alleged that he was the CDF leader, and the "new" charges, in the Indictments of his alleged lieutenants, would evidently apply to him as well. Obvious as this must have been, it remains the fact that the Prosecution made no application to amend so as to include them in the Norman Indictment.

- **Rule 47(C): Review of Indictment – Vagueness of Indictment**

R47-AC-3

o *Prosecutor v. Norman, Fofana, Kondewa*, Case No. SCSL-04-14-AR73, Decision on Amendment of the Consolidated Indictment, 16 May 2005, para. 55, 83:

55. It is unexplained as to why Fofana and Kondewa were not jointly indicted from the outset, since the evidence against them would certainly involve the same witnesses and legal arguments. Instead, the cases against the three CDF defendants proceeded separately for a time, and some made preliminary motions objecting to the lack of clarity in the particulars of their individual Indictments although no objection was ever raised to their form. On 27 November 2003, for example, the Trial Chamber gave a decision on a motion to delete certain words and phrases which were vague and imprecise: the Trial Chamber understandably ruled that the expressions "but not limited to these events" and "included but not limited to" were impermissibly open-ended. The Prosecution was ordered either to delete them or to provide details by way of a bill of particulars.[1]

[...]

83. In paragraph 19 of its decision of 29 November 2004 the Trial Chamber correctly identified all the changes that had been made by the Prosecution in the consolidated Indictment. In some cases, the additions plainly fell into the second category we have identified above – they provide greater precision in respect of existing charges. For example, the objectively vague phrase "but not limited to, . . .", which appeared in the original Norman Indictment has been excised and replaced by identifications of specific towns and places where crimes are alleged to have been committed or by specific descriptions of unlawful behaviour. There can be no objection to permitting amendments of this kind. [...]

---

[1] *Prosecutor v. Kondewa*, SCSL-03-12, Decision and Order on Defence Preliminary Motion For Defects in the Form of the Indictment, 27 November 2003.

> **Rule 48: Joinder of Accused or Trials**
> *(amended 14 March 2004)*
>
> (A) Persons accused of the same or different crimes committed in the course of the same transaction may be jointly indicted and tried.
>
> (B) Persons who are separately indicted, accused of the same or different crimes committed in the course of the same transaction, may be tried together, with leave granted by a Trial Chamber pursuant to Rule 73.
>
> (C) A Trial Chamber may order the concurrent hearing of evidence common to the trials of persons separately indicted or joined in separate trials and who are accused of the same or different crimes committed in the course of the same transaction. Such a hearing may be granted with leave of a Trial Chamber pursuant to Rule 73.

TRIAL CHAMBERS DECISIONS

- **Rule 48: Joinder – Purpose of the Joinder – "Collective Criminal Responsibility"**

R48-TC-1

o *Prosecutor v. Sesay* (Case No. SCSL-03-05-PT), *Brima* (Case No. SCSL-03-06-PT), *Kallon* (Case No. SCSL-03-07-PT), *Gbao* (Case No. SCSL-03-09-PT), *Kamara* (Case No. SCSL-03-10-PT), *Kanu* (Case No. SCSL-03-13-PT), Decision and Order on Prosecution Motions for Joinder, 27 January 2004, para. 24:

24. [...] [T]he Chamber wishes to observe that Article 6(1) also encompasses and recognises *the doctrine of collective criminal responsibility* in the sense that in the penal setting of war crimes, the most egregious offences of the criminal law are 'perpetrated by a collectivity of persons in furtherance of a common criminal design'.[1] *It is this principle of collective criminal responsibility that forms the doctrinal basis of the Prosecution's Motions for joint trial in respect of the Accused persons herein who were separately indicted on diverse dates in the year 2003.* The Motions [seek leave that the Accused] be jointly tried pursuant to the aforesaid Rule 48(B) on the grounds that, using the exact language of the Rule, they are '*accused of the same or different crimes committed in the course of the same transaction*'. [...]

---

[1] Prosecutor v. Dusko Tadic, supra note 9, para. 193.

- **Rule 48: Joinder – Chamber's Discretion**

R48-TC-2
o *Prosecutor v. Sesay* (Case No. SCSL-03-05-PT), *Brima* (Case No. SCSL-03-06-PT), *Kallon* (Case No. SCSL-03-07-PT), *Gbao* (Case No. SCSL-03-09-PT), *Kamara* (Case No. SCSL-03-10-PT), *Kanu* (Case No. SCSL-03-13-PT), Decision and Order on Prosecution Motions for Joinder, 27 January 2004, para. 25:

25. [...] In the Chamber's judgement, the cumulative effect of [Articles 17(2) and 17(4)(c) of the Statute and Rule 48(B)] provisions is the vesting of a discretionary jurisdiction in the Special Court to grant the joinder of indictments, weighing the overall interests of justice and the rights of the accused person. In fact, the founding instruments of both the ICTY and ICTR are to the same effect.

- **Rule 48: Joinder – Applicable Principles**

R48-TC-3
o *Prosecutor v. Sesay* (Case No. SCSL-03-05-PT), *Brima* (Case No. SCSL-03-06-PT), *Kallon* (Case No. SCSL-03-07-PT), *Gbao* (Case No. SCSL-03-09-PT), *Kamara* (Case No. SCSL-03-10-PT), *Kanu* (Case No. SCSL-03-13-PT), Decision and Order on Prosecution Motions for Joinder, 27 January 2004, para. 27-29:[47]

27. [...] [I]t is necessary for the Chamber, in this first set of Motions for joinder of accused persons brought before it, to articulate briefly the relevant general principles in this area of law. *A key principle in this regard is that regardless of whether the Accused were indicted together or not, where the factual allegations in the indictment support the Prosecution's theory of the existence of a common transaction smong the Accused and there is no resulting material prejudice to the Accused, joinder may be granted.*[(1)] *Another key principle is that even if the Accused were charged separately, joinder may still be granted where the Prosecution's theory of the existence of a common transaction is supported by the allegations within the factual parameters of the Indictments.*[(2)]

---

[47] See also *Prosecutor v. Norman* (SCSL-03-08-PT), *Fofana* (SCSL-03-11-PT), *Kondewa* (SCSL-03-12-PT), Decision and Order on Prosecution Motions for Joinder, 27 January 2004, para. 17-19.

28. Predicated upon the foregoing reasoning, the Chamber deems it quite instructive to ascertain the state of the evolving jurisprudence of ICTY and ICTR by summarising below the *specific principles* on the question of joinder. These are the main propositions deducible from case-law authorities in those two jurisdictions:

(a) Under Rule 48, a joinder of Accused persons charged with the same or different crimes committed in the course of the same transaction is permissible in law;[3]

(b) The term 'transaction' in Rule 2 of the Rules implies that an Accused can be jointly tried with others if their acts fall within the scope of Rule 48;[4]

(c) In a joinder case, Rule 48 must be read in light of the definition of 'transaction' in Rule 2 and Rule 82(B);[5]

(d) The plain and ordinary meaning of 'transaction' is 'a number of acts or omissions whether occurring as one event, at the same time or different transactions being part of a common scheme, strategy or plan';[6]

(e) In determining the permissibility under Rule 48 of joinder of Accused persons who have been indicted separately, the Court must be satisfied that:

  i. The acts of the Accused must be connected to material elements of a criminal act. For example, the acts of the Accused may be non-criminal/legal acts in furtherance of future criminal acts;
  ii. The criminal acts to which the acts of the Accused are connected must be capable of specific determination in time and in space;
  iii. The criminal acts to which the acts of the Accused are connected must illustrate the existence of a common scheme, strategy or plan.[7]

(f) Factors to be taken into consideration in determining whether the interests of justice will be served by a joinder include:

  i. the public interest in savings and expenses and time;
  ii. the interest of transparent justice that there be consistency and fairness with respect to the verdicts of persons jointly tried pursuant to Rule 48;
  iii. the public interest in avoiding discrepancies and inconsistencies inevitable from separate trials of joint offenders;[8] and
  iv. whether joinder would allow for a more consistent and detailed presentation of evidence, and for a better protection of the victims' and witnesses' physical and mental safety by eliminating the need for them to make several journeys;[9]

(g) The need for a consistent and detailed presentation of evidence and that of protecting victims and witnesses must be balanced, in a joinder equation, against the rights of the Accused to a trial without undue delay and any other possible resultant prejudice to the Accused;[10]

(h) The Chamber, in an application for joinder, must confine itself to the parameters of the factual allegations embodied in the Indictment;[11]

(i) An application for joinder is not to be treated as a trial;[12]

(j) Concurrent presentation of evidence pertaining to one Accused with that pertaining to another Accused does not *per se* constitute a conflict of interests, nor does calling a co-Accused to testify during the joint trial constitute a conflict of interests between them;[13]

(k) The fact that there is evidence which may, in law, be admissible against one Accused and not others, is not necessarily a ground for severance in an international tribunal where trial is by judges without a jury, since it is generally assumed that judges can rise above such risk of prejudice and apply their professional judicial minds to the assessment of evidence;[14]

(l) Rule 82 vests in an Accused in a joint trial all the rights of a single Accused on trial before a Trial Chamber; accordingly the Accused jointly tried does not lose any protection under Articles 20 and 21 of the ICTY and Articles 19 and 20 of the ICTR Statute;[15]

(m) The interpretation of the phrase 'the same transaction' in Rule 48 is a question of law;[16]

(n) The acts of the Accused for the purpose of joinder may form part of the same transaction notwithstanding that they were carried out in different areas and over different periods, provided that there is a sufficient nexus between the acts committed in the two areas;[17]

(o) Joinder is permissible under Rule 48 where possible public interest and the concern for judicial economy would require joint offences to be tried together;[18]

(p) It is impermissible in law for the purposes of joinder to join unconnected acts on the ground that they are part of the same plan;[19]

(q) In determining whether to grant joinder Rule 48 should be construed in the light of the Statute as a whole especially in the light of the entitlement of the Accused to a fair hearing;[20]

(r) Joinder should not be granted where the interests of justice would be prejudiced – those interests relate not only to the Accused but also to the interests of the Prosecution and the international community in the trial of any accused charged with serious violations of international humanitarian law;[21]

(s) To justify joinder what must be proved is that:
  i. there was a common scheme or plan; and
  ii. that the Accused committed crimes during the course of it.

It does not matter what part the particular Accused played provided that he participated in a common plan. It is not necessary to prove a conspiracy between the Accused in the sense of direct coordination or agreement.[22]

29. This Chamber endorses generally the specific principles and propositions developed by the ICTY and ICTR on the question of joinder as enumerated in the preceding paragraph as legally sound and logical.

---

[1] See Archbold, International Criminal Courts, Practice, Procedure and Evidence, Sweet & Maxwell Ltd., London, 2003 at pages 204-207.
[2] Id.
[3] See *Prosecutor v. Ntabakuze and Kabiligi*, Case No. ICTR-97-34-I, Decision on the Defence Motion Requesting an Order for Separate Trials, 30 September 1998.
[4] See *Nyiramasuhuko* Decision, *supra* note 1, para 7.
[5] See *Prosecutor v. Ntabakuze and Kabiligi*, *supra*, note 17.
[6] Id.
[7] Id.
[8] See *Prosecutor v. Delalic et al.*, IT-96-21-T, Decision on the Motion by the Defendant Delalic Requesting Procedures for Final determination of the Charges Against Him, 1 July 1998, para 35, cited in *Archbold*, *supra* note 15 at page 206.
[9] See *Prosecutor v. Kayishema*, ICTR-95-1-T, Decision on the Joinder of the Accused and Setting the Date for Trial, 6 November 1996 at page 3.
[10] See *Prosecutor v. Bagosora et al.*, ICTR-96-7, Decision on the Prosecutor's Motion for Joinder, 29 June 2000, paras 145-146.
[11] Id. Paras 119-122.
[12] Id.
[13] See *Prosecutor v. Kovacevic et al.*, IT-97-24-AR73, Decision on the Motion for Joinder of Accused and Concurrent Presentation of Evidence, 14 May 1998.
[14] *Prosecutor v. Barayagwiza*, ICTR-97-19-I, Decision on the request of the Defence for Severance and Separate Trial, 26 September 2000.
[15] *The Prosecutor v. Delalic et al., supra*, note 22.
[16] See *Prosecutor v. Milosevic*, IT-99-37-AR73, IT-01-50-AR73, IT-01-51-AR73, Decision on Prosecutor's Interlocutory Appeal from Refusal to Order Joinder, 1 February 2002, at para 19.
[17] See *Prosecutor v. Ntakirutimana et al.*, ICTR-96-10-I, ICTR-96-17-I, Decision on the Prosecution's Motion to Join the Indictments, 22 February 2001.
[18] *Prosecutor v. Kanyabashi*, ICTR-95-15-A, Decision on the Defence Motion for Interlocutory Appeal on Jurisdiction of the Trial chamber, 3 June 1999, para. 31.
[19] *Prosecutor v. Kovacevic et al.*, IT-97-24-AR73, Decision Stating Reasons for Appeals Chamber's Order of 29 May 1998, 2 July 1998.
[20] See *Prosecutor v. Bagosora*, *supra*, note 24.

(21) Id.
(22) *Prosecutor v. Kordic and Cerkez*, IT-95-14/2-PT, Decision on Accused Mario Cerkez's Application for Separate Trial, 7 December 1998, para 10.

- **Rule 48: Joinder – The Test for Joinder**

R48-TC-4

o *Prosecutor v. Sesay* (Case No. SCSL-03-05-PT), *Brima* (Case No. SCSL-03-06-PT), *Kallon* (Case No. SCSL-03-07-PT), *Gbao* (Case No. SCSL-03-09-PT), *Kamara* (Case No. SCSL-03-10-PT), *Kanu* (Case No. SCSL-03-13-PT), Decision and Order on Prosecution Motions for Joinder, 27 January 2004, para. 30-32:[48]

30. It is evident from the foregoing that prominent among the approaches to the question of joinder in the ICTY and ICTR is the three-pronged test propounded in the case of *Prosecutor v. Ntabakuze and Kabiligi*.[(1)] Cognisant of the value of this test, the Chamber, however, taking its judicial cue from Lord Morris's speech in *director of Public Prosecutions v. Doot & Others*,[(2)] cited by the ICTR Trial Chamber in *Bagosora*, wishes to re-emphasize the words of the learned Law Lord that:

'questions of joinder, whether of offence or of offenders, are considerably matters of judicial practice which this court unless restrained by statute has inherent power both to formulate its own rules and to vary them in the light of current experience and the needs of justice. Here is essentially s field in which rules of fairness and convenience should be evolved and where there should be no fetter to the fashioning of such rules.'

31. Consistent with this approach, the Chamber's preference is for a test based on a plain and literal interpretation of the object and purpose of Rule 48(B). convinced that the legislative intent behind Rule 48(B) is to render joinder permissible only in cases where the acts and omissions of accused persons (who have been separately indicted) amount to the same or different crimes committed in the course *of the same transaction simpliciter*, we are of the opinion that to succeed on a joinder motion pursuant to Rule 48(B) of the Rules of the Special Court for Sierra Leone, the Prosecution must show:

(a) that the Accused persons sought to be joined and tried together were separately charged with the same or differ-

---

[48] See also *Prosecutor v. Norman* (SCSL-03-08-PT), *Fofana* (SCSL-03-11-PT), *Kondewa* (SCSL-03-12-PT), Decision and Order on Prosecution Motions for Joinder, 27 January 2004, para. 20-22.

ent crimes committed in the course of the same 'transaction' as defined in Rule 2;

(b) that the factual allegations in the Indictments will, if proven, show a consistency between the said crimes as alleged in the Indictments and the Prosecution's theory that they were committed in furtherance, or were the product, of a common criminal design, and

(c) that it will be in the interests of justice to try the Accused jointly, due regard being given to their rights as guaranteed by Article 17(2) and 17(4)(c) of the Statute of the Court.

32. We also wish to emphasise that in applying 'the consistency or product test', there is no presumption of automaticity in favour of the Prosecution. Further, there is no obligation on the Accused to show material prejudice or its likelihood. The question of whether the factual allegations will, if proven, show a consistency between the specified crimes and the Prosecution's theory of consistency with a common criminal design is essentially a judicial exercise, involving a determination 'whether, on the basis of legal and factual assessment, there exists a justification for holding',[3] within the limits of reasonableness a joint trial of the Accused in question.

---

[1] *Supra* note 17.
[2] (1973) A.C. 807 (House of Lords).
[3] *Nyiramasuhuko* decision, *supra* note 1, at para. 4.

- **Rule 48: Joinder – Interest of Justice**

R48-TC-5

o *Prosecutor v. Sesay* (Case No. SCSL-03-05-PT), *Brima* (Case No. SCSL-03-06-PT), *Kallon* (Case No. SCSL-03-07-PT), *Gbao* (Case No. SCSL-03-09-PT), *Kamara* (Case No. SCSL-03-10-PT), *Kanu* (Case No. SCSL-03-13-PT), Decision and Order on Prosecution Motions for Joinder, 27 January 2004, para. 42-44:[49]

42. In resolving the question of whether the joinder will be in the interests of justice, the Chamber recalls, by way of persuasive guidance, some of the key factors articulated in the jurisprudence of both the ICTY and ICTR to be taken into account when determining whether the interests of justice will be served by a joinder. These include:

---

[49] See also *Prosecutor v. Norman* (SCSL-03-08-PT), *Fofana* (SCSL-03-11-PT), *Kondewa* (SCSL-03-12-PT), Decision and Order on Prosecution Motions for Joinder, 27 January 2004, para. 28-31.

(a) the public interest in savings and expenses and time;
(b) the interest of transparent justice that there be consistency and fairness with respect to the verdicts of persons jointly tried pursuant to Rule 48;
(c) the public interest in avoiding discrepancies and inconsistencies inevitable from separate trials of joint offenders;
(d) the need for consistent and detailed presentation of evidence;
(e) better protection of the victims' and witnesses' physical and mental safety by eliminating the need for them to make several journeys; and
(f) due regard fro judicial economy.

43. The evolving jurisprudence of the ICTY and ICTR also highlights these additional factors:

(a) the interests of the Prosecution;
(b) the interests of the international community in the trial of persons charged with serious violations of international humanitarian law; and
(c) pre-eminently, whether joinder will infringe the rights of the Accused to a fair and expeditious trial.

44. In the specific and peculiar context of the Special Court, this Chamber now articulates the key factors to be borne in mind in the final determination of whether a joinder of the Indictments herein will serve the interests of justice. These include:

(a) the Special Court's limited mandate as to persons who are prosecutable, meaning all those 'who bear the greatest responsibility for serious violations of international humanitarian law and Sierra Leonean law committed in the territory of Sierra Leone since 30 November 1996';
(b) that the majority of the Accused herein were indicted on average nine (9) months ago and are still awaiting trial;
(c) that the said Accused persons have been in custody ever since their Indictments, despite application for bail by some of them;
(d) that there is currently only one Trial Chamber (with a mere possibility of a second) to undertake the judicial workload of conducting nine (9) separate trials;
(e) that many of the witnesses to be called by the Prosecution are common to all the Accused;
(f) the practical, emotional and mental hardships likely to be experienced by Prosecution witnesses if they were to testify in six (6) separate trials;
(g) the need for protection of Prosecution witnesses;
(h) the possibility, if a second Trial chamber is established, of the two Trial Chambers reaching different decisions in separate trials on the same issues of law;
(i) the possibility of overlapping testimonies in separate trials;
(j) that separate trials of the Accused do have a high potential of being very protracted thereby prolonging the ordeal

and emotional suffering of the Accused while they await the outcome of their respective cases;

(k) that a joint trial (rather than separate trial) would be more in keeping with and would effectively protect and enforce, the pre-eminent due process right of each of the Accused to a fair and expeditious public trial;

(l) the need to guarantee the Accused persons to the greatest possible extent a fair and expeditious trial free from unnecessary legal technicalities; and

(m) the paramount interest of international community in the expeditious but fair trial of persons accused of egregious offences of international humanitarian law as a definitive response to the culture of impunity.

- **Rule 48: Joinder – Procedure – No Requirement for Expected Consolidated Indictment at the Stage of the Motion for Joinder**

R48-TC-6

o *Prosecutor v. Sesay* (Case No. SCSL-03-05-PT), *Brima* (Case No. SCSL-03-06-PT), *Kallon* (Case No. SCSL-03-07-PT), *Gbao* (Case No. SCSL-03-09-PT), *Kamara* (Case No. SCSL-03-10-PT), *Kanu* (Case No. SCSL-03-13-PT), Decision and Order on Prosecution Motions for Joinder, 27 January 2004, para. 21:[50]

21. [. . .] In so far as the Special Court is concerned, the chamber is of the opinion that, due to the need for expeditiousness and flexibility in its processes and proceedings, recourse to procedural technicalities of this nature will unquestionably impede the Special Court in the expeditious dispatch of its judicial business. Therefore, [. . .] the Chamber does not think, in the context of the judicial peculiarities of the Special Court, that it is necessary for the Prosecution to exhibit both the original and anticipated consolidated indictments to establish a basis for joinder.

---

[50] See also *Prosecutor v. Norman* (Case No. SCSL-03-08-PT), *Fofana* (Case No. SCSL-03-11-PT), *Kondewa* (Case No. SCSL-03-12-PT), Decision and Order on Prosecution Motions for Joinder, 27 January 2004, para. 11.

- **Rule 48: Joinder – Procedure – Requirement for Complete Disclosure of Supporting Materials Attached to the Initial Indictments at the Stage of the Motion for Joinder**

R48-TC-7

o *Prosecutor v. Fofana*, Case No. SCSL-03-11-PT, Order on the Defence request for an Extension of Time for the Filing of a Response to the Prosecution Motion for Joinder, 12 November 2003:

ACCEPTING AND RECOGNISING that in order for the Defence to make an appropriate and adequate assessment with respect to this Joinder Motion it required having had reasonable access to the Supporting Materials;

IN THE INTERESTS OF maintaining the fairness of the process and in order to proceed to an expeditious determination of the Joinder Motion;

CONSIDERING that in these circumstances it would constitute good cause;

GRANTS the application for extension of time to file a Response.

R48-TC-8

o *Prosecutor v. Sesay*, Case No. SCSL-03-05-PT, Order on the Defence Motion Requesting that the Time Limit to Respond to the Motion Filed by the Prosecution for a Joinder to Commence Upon Receipt of the Modified or Particularised Indict-ment(s) or on a Date Set by the Trial Chamber, 12 November 2003:

CONSIDERING the Defence Request that the deadline for a response to the Joinder Motion be set for 10 days after the Prosecution comply with the Decision, on the basis that the Defence is otherwise unable to consider properly whether or not a joinder is in the interests of justice;

CONSIDERING the Prosecution Response that it is not necessary for Defence Counsel to see the Bill of Particulars or the amended indictment in order to respond to the Joinder Motion, and thus that the Defence have not shown "good cause or exceptional circumstances" as is necessary to be granted an extension of time;

[...]

CONSCIOUS of the importance of the Joinder Motion and the fact that it would have considerable impact and consequences on the conduct of the Prosecution and the Defence in the matters;

IN THE INTERESTS OF fairness, equity and an expeditious determination of the Joinder Motion;

CONSIDERING that the Defence has, in the light of the above, demonstrated and shown good cause to justify the granting of the application for extension of time;

- **Rule 48(C): Joinder – Concurrent Hearing of Evidence**

R48-TC-9

o *Prosecution v. Sesay, Kallon, Gbao*, Case No. SCSL-04-15-PT, Decision on the Prosecution Motion for Concurrent Hearing of Evidence Common to Cases SCSL-2004-15-PT and SCSL-2004-16-PT, 11 May 2004, para. 29-31, 36, 38, 40, 42-44:[51]

29. In ascertaining the applicable principles in respect of motions of this type, it is instructive to note, firstly, that Rule 48(C) does not specify the relevant criteria for granting such motions. However, the Chamber takes the view that the applicable criteria are logically, with necessary adaptations and modifications, of the same generic type as those contained in sub-rules (A) and (B) of the aforesaid Rule 48 and Rule 49. We are reinforced in this observation by the finding that, on a plain and literal interpretation of Rule 48(C), there are two (2) conditions that must be fulfilled before the Court can properly entertain the application. They are:

o that the Accused persons in question were either separately indicted or joined in separate trials in respect of the same or different crimes; and
o that the crimes alleged must have been committed in the course of the same transaction.

Procedurally, the Chamber wishes to observe that it is abundantly clear that the Prosecution is within its right to file the instant application, having satisfied the conditions precedent for such a Motion.

30. Secondly, as a matter of statutory instruction, it is clear that Rule 48(C) does not imply or import any notion of automaticity in respect of the Order sought once the Prosecution has satisfied the conditions precedent. The Rule confers on the Trial Chamber a discretion in the matter. It is trite law that where a discretion is vested in an authority or a body, such discretion is to be exercised reasonably and judiciously, and,

---

[51] See also *Prosecutor v. Brima, Kamara, Kanu*, Case No. SCSL-04-16-PT, Decision on the Prosecution Motion for Concurring Hearing of Evidence Common to Cases SCSL-2004-15-PT and SCSL-2004-16-PT, 11 May 2004, para. 29-31, 36, 38, 40, 42-44.

we should add, in the case of an application of such dimension and complexity, '*with great circumspection*' due to the extraordinary nature of the procedure which is the subject-matter of the application whilst at the same time keeping an open judicial mind to the issue.

31. Furthermore, it is the Chamber's view that the primary focus of the exercise of a discretion under Rule 48(C) should be on how the extraordinary procedure applied for would impact upon the rights of the Accused in question, and not how it would or would not enhance the Prosecution's capability in presenting its case in an efficient manner. It is important for the Court to preserve such a focus especially where it has ordered separate joint trials for each category of accused persons. Unless the Court is satisfied that the Prosecution has established that the exceptional procedure sought would not impact adversely, or be prejudicial to, the right of the accused to be tried fairly and expeditiously, and that the integrity of the proceedings would not be compromised, the presumption should be against granting the Order.

[...]

36. [...] [T]he Chamber wishes to observe that it is one of the harsh realities of the functioning of the criminal law, as a social control mechanism, that witnesses called to testify as to the commission of crimes of international gravity and dimension will experience some measure of inconvenience and hardship. *In the instant situation, such inconvenience and hardship could be reduced by prosecutorial creativity and foresight, given the provision of 'back-up witnesses' as was stated by learned Counsel for the Prosecution during the Pre-Trial Conferences.* Furthermore, the interests of victims and witnesses will remain protected in accordance with Article 16 of the Statute of the Special Court through the Victims and Witnesses Unit and by the judicious use of Rule 92*bis* of the Rules.

[...]

38. The Prosecution further submits that hearing the same witness twice, in two separate trials, on essentially the same evidence by the same panel of judges will jeopardise the principle of a fair trial in that the appearance that the judges would have already assessed the credibility of the evidence when conducting the second hearing would undermine the credibility of the judicial process and would be contrary to the interest of justice. This submission, in the Chamber's opinion, is specious and speculative from two perspectives: namely (i) that the judges have sworn to discharge their judicial functions faithfully, conscientiously, and impartially; (ii) that it is the accepted norm implicit in the Bangalore Principles of Judicial Conduct,[1] that professionally trained and qualified judges are able to assess the credibility of witnesses with a remarkable degree of dispassionateness as opposed to trial juries. [...]

[...]

40. It may be recalled that it was submitted by the Prosecution that the concurrent presentation of evidence common to both cases (a) does not constitute a conflict of interests, (b) would only apply to Prosecution witnesses and (c) would not directly implicate the Accused individuals in the commission of crimes, but rather, would only relate to acts of others than the Accused individuals. The Chamber's short response to these kindred submissions is that in the light of the Responses from the Defence, these issues remain highly contentious, based on how the Witness List and the summaries of evidence are interpreted. It is likewise noteworthy, from the Chamber's viewpoint, that the Prosecution's submission that risks of possible mutual recriminations or possible conflicts in defence strategies can be dealt with by application of the doctrine of severance is not convincing from a practical perspective given all the unknown variables.

[...]

42. The Chamber's evaluation of the merits of the Motion thus far leads, compellingly, to only one conclusion. It is that the 'concurrent hearing of evidence' or 'common trunk' order sought by the Prosecution is an attempt, on its art, to re-litigate an issue already decided by the Court. It is trite law that there must be finality to litigation. In this regard, the Prosecution is perilously caught within the web of the common law doctrine of issue estoppel.

43. [...] **Hence we hold and accordingly rule, that the notion of 'common trunk' or 'concurrent hearing of evidence', particularly in light of the amount of evidence sought to be introduced through such a process and in the context of the Chamber's Joinder Decision, is conceptually irreconcilable with the notion of 'joint separate trials'.**

44. However, we do observe that our ruling as to the conceptual irreconcilability between a 'concurrent hearing of evidence' and 'joint separate trials', in the context of this case, does not, in any way, detract from the theoretical attractiveness of the notion of a 'common trunk hearing'. *In practical terms, all the Chamber wishes to convey is that given its Joinder Decision, it would be imprudent for the Court to become, as it were, an empirical testing-ground of the theory of 'concurrent hearing of evidence' where, based on the Chamber's appreciation of the evolving jurisprudence of sister tribunals, it has not been successfully applied for in any international criminal jurisdiction.*[2]

---

[1] Adopted by the Judicial Group on Strengthening Judicial Integrity, as revised at the Round Table Meeting of Chief Justices held at the Peace Palace, The Hague, 25-26 November 2002.

(2) See *Prosecutor v. Kovacevic et al.*, IT-97-24-AR73, Decision on Motion for Joinder of Accused and Concurrent Presentation of Evidence, 14 May 1998 and *Prosecutor v. Brdanin, Tadic and Stakic*, IT-99-36-PT and IT-99-24-PT, Decision on Prosecution's Motions for a Joint Hearing, 11 January 2002.

R48-TC-10

o *Prosecution v. Sesay, Kallon, Gbao*, SCSL-2004-15-T, Order Permitting the Temporary Transfer of Certain Exhibits, 31 May 2005:

COGNIZANT that the trial against the RUF Accused and the trial before Trial Chamber II against the Accused Alex Tamba Brima, Brima Bazzy Kamara and Santigie Borbor Kanu ("AFRC Accused") share some factual connections and a number of common witnesses;

NOTING that the Prosecution has asserted that the Prosecution has and will continue to tender exhibits in the RUF trial that it will also be seeking to tender in the AFRC trial before Trial Chamber II;

CONSIDERING that it is in the interests of justice to facilitate the temporary transfer of original exhibits between the RUF and AFRC trials in a secure manner;

RELYING on its general power pursuant to Rule 54 of the Rules of Procedure and Evidence of the Special Court;

THE CHAMBER HEREBY ORDERS:

1. The Prosecution shall provide 24 hours notice to the Chambers Legal Officer of the RUF trial and Court Management Services in advance of the date on which the Prosecution requires the temporary transfer of the exhibit;

2. Court Management Services shall produce two copies of the exhibit in question and certify them to be true copies of the original;

3. Court Management Services shall retain one true copy of the exhibit in the RUF trial materials while the original exhibit and the second true copy shall be made available in the AFRC trial proceedings before Trial Chamber II;

4. As soon as practicable, Court Management Services shall return the original exhibit to the RUF trial materials and notify the Chambers Legal Officer of the RUF trial of such return;

5. Court Management Services shall maintain a log that records the temporary transfer and return of all exhibits tendered in the RUF trial proceedings.

APPEALS CHAMBER DECISIONS

- **Rule 48: Joinder – No Requirement for Consolidation of Individual Indictments**

R48-AC-1   o *Prosecutor v. Norman, Fofana, Kondewa*, Case No. SCSL-04-14-AR73, Decision on Amendment of the Consolidated Indictment, 16 May 2005, para. 58:

58. Rule 48(A) permits the Prosecution, without leave of the court, to jointly indict persons accused of committing crimes in the course of the same transaction. This course it could have adopted when indicting Fofana and Kondewa. Instead, it sought leave to have them, and Norman, tried together. Rule 48(B) anticipates that such a joint trial will proceed on the individual Indictments on which the defendants have already appeared and pleaded pursuant to Rule 61. It does not provide for consolidation of individual Indictments, a step which is unnecessary and can make no sensible difference that we can see to the proceeding or the outcome. The Prosecution in its appeal submissions still cannot explain why it sought consolidation, other than that this is the "normal practice in other criminal tribunals". So it may be, but in this court it still requires to be justified.

Rule 50: Amendment of Indictment
(amended 14 March 2004)

(A) The Prosecutor may amend an indictment, without prior leave, at any time before its approval, but thereafter, until the initial appearance of the accused pursuant to Rule 61, only with leave of the Designated Judge who reviewed it but, in exceptional circumstances, by leave of another Judge. At or after such initial appearance, an amendment of an indictment may only be made by leave granted by a Trial Chamber pursuant to Rule 73. If leave to amend is granted, Rule 47(G) and Rule 52 apply to the amended indictment.

(B) If the amended indictment includes new charges and the accused has already made his initial appearance in accordance with Rule 61:

   (i) A further appearance shall be held as soon as practicable to enable the accused to enter a plea on the new charges;
   (ii) Within seven days from such appearance, the Prosecutor shall disclose all materials envisaged in Rule 66(A)(i) pertaining to the new charges;
   (iii) The accused shall have a further period of ten days from the date of such disclosure by the Prosecutor in which to file preliminary motions pursuant to Rule 72 and relating to the new charges.

TRIAL CHAMBERS DECISIONS

- **Rule 50: Amendment of Indictment – Procedure – Order to Submit Indication of Specific Changes**

R50-TC-1

o *Prosecutor v. Norman, Fofana, Kondewa*, Case No. SCSL-04-14-PT, Order to Submit Indication of Specific Changes to Indictments, 26 February 2004:[52]

SEIZED of the Request for Leave to File an Amended Indictment filed by the Office of the Prosecutor ("Prosecution") on 9 February 2004 pursuant to Rule 50(A) and 73(A) of the Rules of Procedure and Evidence of the Special Court ("Rules");

---

[52] See also *Prosecutor v. Sesay, Kallon, Gbao*, Case No. SCSL-04-15-PT, Order to Submit Indication of Specific Changes to Indictments, 26 February 2004; *Prosecutor v. Brima, Kamara, Kanu*, Case No. SCSL-04-16-PT, Order to Submit Indication of Specific Changes to Indictments, 26 February 2004.

[...]

CONSIDERING that the fair and expeditious consideration of the Motion will be advanced by a precise indi-cation of the changes made to the former indictments;

HEREBY ORDERS the Prosecution to file by 1 March 2004:

1. In narrative or chart-form, a paragraph-by-paragraph comparison of the Consolidated Indictment with the Original Indictments, indicating the specific source of each paragraph in the Consolidated Indictment and any deletions, modifications or additions of text thereto; and

2. A track-change version of the proposed Amended Indictment as compared to the Consolidated Indictment, thereby indicating deletions, modifications or additions of text.

- **Rule 50(A): Amendment of Indictment – Discretion of the Trial Chamber**

R50-TC-2

o *Prosecutor v. Sesay, Kallon, Gbao*, Case No. SCSL-04-15-PT, Decision on Prosecution Request for Leave to Amend the Indictment, 6 May 2004, para. 24:[53]

24. It is important to note here that the power conferred on the Court to grant an amendment is discretionary and that it should be exercised judiciously and in the overall interests of justice.

R50-TC-3

o *Prosecutor v. Norman, Fofana, Kondewa*, Case No. SCSL-04-14-PT, Decision on Prosecution Request for Leave to Amend the Indictment, 20 May 2004, para. 81:

81. Again, granting this amendment at this stage reposes on the inherent jurisdiction of the Chamber to exercise a discretion provided it does not amount to an abuse of process and as was observed in the case of THE HOUSE OF SPRING GARDENS LTD VS. WAITE [1990] 3 WLR 347, [1990] 2AER 990 (CA), the Court, "in invoking and exercising its inherent jurisdiction in this regard, prevents the misuse of its procedure in a way that would be manifestly unfair to a party to a litigation before it or would in some other way, bring the administration of justice into disrepute".

---

[53] See also *Prosecutor v. Brima, Kamara, Kanu*, Case No. SCSL-04-16-PT, Decision on Prosecution Request for Leave to Amend the Indictment, 6 May 2004, para. 24.

R50-TC-4 o *Prosecutor v. Brima, Kamara, Kanu*, Case No. SCSL-04-16-PT, Decision on the Prosecution Application to Further Amend the Amended Consolidated Indictment by Withdrawing Counts 15-18, 15 February 2005:

CONSIDERING that the Trial Chamber will normally exercise its discretion to permit the amendment, provided that the amendment does not cause any injustice to the accused, or does not otherwise prejudice the accused unfairly in the conduct of his defence;

- **Rule 50(A): Amendment of Indictment – Time of the Application for Leave to Amend**

R50-TC-5 o *Prosecutor v. Sesay, Kallon, Gbao*, Case No. SCSL-04-15-PT, Decision on Prosecution request for Leave to Amend the Indictment, 6 May 2004, para. 27, 43-57:[54]

27. The crucial consideration in this process, in our opinion, is one of timing. The question to be asked, is whether application for the amendment is brought at a stage in the proceedings where it would not prejudice the rights of the Defence to a fair and expeditious trial and furthermore, whether it is made in the overall interest of justice rather than its having the effect of giving an undue advantage to the pro-secution, thereby putting in jeopardy, the doctrine of equality of arms between the Prosecution and the Defence.

[...]

43. We would like in this regard, to refer to the case of the PROSECUTION VS KAREMERA ICTR-98-44-AR73 in which the Appeals Chamber of the ICTR held that in assessing whether a delay resulting from an amendment to an indictment will be "undue", the tribunal must consider factors such as the diligence of the Prosecution in advancing the case and the timeliness of the request. In that case, the Appeals Chamber had this to say:

> "Although amending an indictment frequently causes delay in a short term, the Appeals Chamber takes the view that this procedure can also have the overall effect of simplifying proceedings, by narrowing the scope of the allegations, by improving the Accused's and the

---

[54] See also *Prosecutor v. Brima, Kamara, Kanu*, Case No. SCSL-04-16-PT, Decision on Prosecution Request for Leave to Amend the Indictment, 6 May 2004, para. 27, 44-58.

Tribunals understanding of the Prosecution's case, or by averting possible challenges to the indictment or the evidence presented at the trial."

44. In the case of THE PROSECUTION VS CASIMIR BIZIMUNGU & OTHERS CASE NO ICTR-99-50-AR50, 12 February 2004, the Appeals Chamber of the ICTR had this comment to make in disallowing the Prosecutions Appeal against a refusal by the Trial Chamber to grant a motion for an amendment of the indictment and I quote:

"... amendments that narrow the indictment and thereby increase the fairness and efficiency of proceedings should be encouraged and usually accepted... Had the Prosecution solely attempted to add particulars to its general allegations, such amendments might well have been allowable because of their positive impact on the fairness of the trial..." (at paragraphs 19-20)

45. The crucial consideration in this process, in our opinion, is one of timing and whether the application for the amendment is brought at the stage in the proceedings where it would not prejudice the rights of the accused to a fair an expeditious trial and furthermore, whether it is made in the overall interests of justice rather than having the effect of giving an undue advantage to the prosecution, thereby putting in jeopardy, the doctrine of 'equality of arms' between the Prosecution and the Defence.

46. What, however, is desirable and should be ensured is for the Prosecution, in the exercise of its duties as a separate organ under the Statute, to enjoy at certain acceptable stages of the proceedings, a free hand in executing its duties and obligations to the Court and this, before the heavy hammer of justice comes down to decide on whether it is still enduring with the weight of the irksome burden of proof that it carries all along, or whether it has discharged it and indeed, beyond any reasonable doubt. In making this observ-ation however, we do not lose sight of the fact that the Prosecution in so acting, must do so within the confines of the law and by respecting, not only the legal protection accorded to the accused by the Statute, but also, the principle of a fair and expeditious trial within the context of course, of the doctrine of equality of arms between the Prosecution and the Defence.

47. In this Motion, we find that the Prosecution, during the investigations that preceded the initial appearances of the accused persons, properly addressed their minds to gender offences and the necessity to gather the required evidence to have their perpetrators prosecuted. To ensure that this happens the Prosecution, during the investigations that preceded initial appearances, detected gender offences. In drawing up hereafter the initial individual indictments of the accused which were approved

on the 7th of March, 2003, and on which initial appearances were based, the Prosecution ensured that these individual indictments contained a number of counts related to gender offences such as rape, sexual slavery and other forms of sexual violence and finally outrages against personal dignity.

48. Furthermore, in the consolidated indictment which was approved by the Trial Chamber following a motion filed to this effect, the Prosecution again included all these enumerated gender offences which featured in the initial individual indictments.

49. In the present motion, the Prosecution is seeking our leave to amend the already existing consolidated indictment on which the proceedings are now based, in order to add one count, and one count only, based on Forced Marriage. The question to be addressed in these circumstances is whether this additional count or offence as the case is, is new in terms of its being a complete novelty in the arsenal of all the counts that constitute the entire consolidated indictment.

50. Our immediate reflection on this issue that we have raised is that the count related to forced marriage which the prosecution is seeking our leave to add to the consolidated indictment is as much a sexual, indeed, a gender offence as those that were included in the initial individual indictments and that feature in the current consolidated indictment on which this application to amend is based.

51. We would like to say here that Forced Marriage is in fact what we would like to classify, as a 'kindred offence' to those that exist in the consolidated indictment in the view of the commonality of the ingredients needed to prove offences of this nature. Given this consideration and the fact that material related to those gender offences that feature on the consolidated indictment has long been disclosed to the Defence, we are of the opinion that the amendment sought is not a novelty that should necessitate fresh investigations as the defence contends. This is only logical because granting it would neither occasion an "undue delay" of the trial of the accused, nor a breach of the statutory rights of the accused as provided for under the provisions of Article 17(4)(a) of the Statute and also because it would not consequently as well, either place the prosecution in an unduly advantageous position to the detriment of the defence, nor would it violate the principle of "equality of arms".

52. In the particular context of this case, we accept the Prosecution's argument that this application to amend, for the reasons that the offences sought to be added were disclosed to the accused and the Defence promptly, fulfils the criterion of timeliness having been filed even before the trial proceedings take off although we know that some applications for amendments

could, and have in fact been accepted, at the depth of the trial for considerations based on the overall interest of justice.

53. In this regard, and to underscore the fulfilment of the criterion of timeliness, an examination of some municipal decisions which are in line with the philosophy of the evolving jurisprudence in international criminal justice as far as the amendment of charges is concerned and at what stage such applications could be entertained, are quite instructive and illuminating.

54. In the case of *AYANSHINA VS. POLICE* (1951), 12 WACA 260, the then West African Court of Appeal held that it was permissible to add a fresh count after a submission had been made that there was no case to answer on the original charge and before a ruling in favour of the submission had been given. In another case, *R. V KANO & ARISAH* (1951) 20 NLR, 32, a decision of the Supreme Court of Nigeria which was upheld, still by the then West African Court of Appeal, it was held permissible to amend a charge after the final addresses and before judgment was delivered provided, as the Court observed, the "alteration could be made at that stage without injustice to the accused". Indeed this decision is very reflective of the provisions of Section 148(1) of the Criminal Procedure Act of Sierra Leone which provides in effect that such applications for amendments of charges 'unless having regard to the merits of the case, the requested amendments cannot be made without injustice'.

55. It might be difficult today to accept the applicability of the scope of these decisions in International Criminal Tribunals but they serve to emphasise the variables of the concept of timeliness in introducing an amendment and the ideal timeliness and promptitude that characterized the Prosecution's action in this matter, and to underscore the flexibility of the exercise of the judicial discretion in granting or refusing a motion to amend while emphasising that the same essential ingredients would necessarily include an examination on a case to case basis and the respect at all times, for the overall interests of justice.

56. In light of the above, we would like in our reasoning in this matter, to refer to the case of *THE PROSECUTOR V ALFRED MUSEMA*, ICTR-96-13-T, 6 May 1999, where, like in the instant case, the application to amend consisted of adding only one count and to expand on the facts in the existing indictment. In the *Musema* case, the amendment was granted on the grounds that it was a mere technicality which the Trial Chamber considered would not, if granted, be prejudicial to the statutory rights of the Accused.

57. We are therefore of the opinion that the Prosecution has satisfied these criteria.

R50-TC-6

o *Prosecutor v. Norman, Fofana, Kondewa*, Case No. SCSL-04-14-PT, Decision on Prosecution Request for Leave to Amend the Indictment, 20 May 2004, para. 35-36, 67-78:

35. The crucial consideration in this process, in our opinion, is one of timing and whether the application for the amendment is brought at a stage in the proceedings where it would not prejudice the rights of the accused to a fair and expeditious trial and furthermore, whether it is made in the overall interests of justice rather than its having the effect of giving an undue advantage to the prosecution, thereby putting in jeopardy, the doctrine of equality of arms between the Prosecution and the Defence.

36. We recall here that in the TADIC CASE, the Appeals Chamber of the ICTY took the view that "Equality of arms" obligates a judicial body to ensure that neither party is put to a disadvantage when presenting its case.

[...]

67. It was mainly the interest of the accused which principally preoccupied the Trial and the Appeals Chamber of the ICTR in refusing an amendment sought by the Prosecution in the case of THE PROSECUTION VS CASIMIR BIZIMUNGU, JUSTIN MUGENZI, JEROME BACUMUM PAKA AND PROSPORE MUGARASEZA, CASE NO ICTR-99-50-I of 6th October 2003. [...]

68. The Court of Appeal in upholding the Trial Chamber's refusal to grant the motion by the prosecution to amend the indictment on the grounds hereinbefore enunciated had this to say:

> "... Although the Prosecution may seek leave to expand its theory of the accused's liability after the confirmation of the original indictment, the risk of prejudice from such expansions is high and must be carefully weighed. On the other hand, amendments that narrow the indictment and thereby increase the fairness and efficiency of proceedings, should be encouraged and usually accepted ... However, the Prosecution chose to combine changes that narrowed the indictment with changes that expanded its scope in a manner prejudicial to the Accused ...".

The Appeal of the accused was accordingly dismissed.

69. In our opinion, the procedure for the amendment of the indictments provided for under Rule 50 (new) which we are applying in this case since the matter is being adjudicated upon after its coming into force on the 11th of May, 2004, is, as we have noted, a judicial discretion and a vital regulatory weapon at the disposal of the interests of justice in the con-

duct of criminal prosecutions and that Judges should exercise this discretion judiciously.

70. Without seeking to be enumerative in order not to be limitative on the broadly based criteria for exercising this discretion one way or the other, we are of the opinion that it is intended to enable the Court, on a case to case basis, either of its own motion on the basis of the evidence, or at the instance of the Prosecution, to effect amendments which are timely; which are made principally in the overall interests of justice with a view to enhancing the fairness and the integrity of the proceedings; and which neither occasion an undue delay of the proceedings against the accused, nor prejudice or pervert the course of justice, or have the effect of violating the statutory rights of the accused.

71. In fact, the outcome of an application to amend an indictment should, and does necessarily, hang on an some elastic device which, in the exercise of that judicial discretion by the Court, can either be distended or constricted, depending on all the circumstances which determine the applicable criteria in a particular case, and which, in any event, must take into consideration, the rights of the Parties and the overall interests of justice.

72. The prosecution in the motion before us, canvasses the argument that the application to amend is timely and that it would not occasion an undue delay in commencing the trial of the accused because the application is made even before the trial commences.

73. Plausible as this argument sounds, we would like to say that it is not convincing in that what preoccupies us is as much the granting of the amendment as the consequences that such an amendment would generate and how it would impact on the subsequent hearing of this case which is scheduled to commence in the very near future.

74. The Defence, as we have observed, argues that if the amendment to include 4 new counts and new geographical locations were granted, it would have to file new preliminary motions under Rules 50 and 72 of the Rules of Procedure and Evidence and also conduct detailed investigations before being ready for the trial. This certainly as we have already observed, will take time and would occasion a disruption and a postpone-ment of our schedule to commence the trials, a situation which, to our mind, could have been avoided if the prosecution had acted diligently and brought this application as early as in June, 2003, or soon thereafter, when it accepts and concedes, that evidence for gender offences against these accused was already available to it.

75. Let us say here that we indeed have come a very long way to arriving at this stage when we are about to commence

the trial of the accused, a process which has been impaired and delayed principally by the flood of pre-trial motions filed by both the Prosecution and the Defence and also by other statutory pre-trial procedures which we had to, and did in fact dispose of in preparation for and before commencing the trials.

76. These included more importantly, those filed by the Prosecution which, with a view to easing and fast tracking the process, were filed just when status conferences were supposed to commence, for a consolidation of the 9 individual indictments to 2 only and a joinder of the accused persons into 2 groups namely, the RUF and the AFRC group on the one hand, and the CDF group on the other. This we granted in the manner that appeared to us to be more in conformity with legal realities and the protection of the rights of the accused. It is again the Prosecution that has filed yet another motion to amend the indictment, an application which, if granted, will in our opinion, put the trial on hold, to the detriment of the Article 17 rights guaranteed to the accused by the Statute.

77. There must, at a certain stage, as we traditionally are compelled to observe, be an end to litigation which, as we know, is often engendered, at times on purpose, by a multiplicity of judicial processes. In this regard, we are of the opinion that exercising our discretion at this stage and in these circumstances in favour of granting the amendment sought by the Prosecution after obvious prosecutorial lapses that cannot be redeemed without violating the statutory rights of the accused, would not only manifestly amount to an abuse of the exercise of this inherent judicial power conferred on us, but would also be tantamount to an abuse of process.

78. The argument by the Prosecution that the application is timely because it is brought before the commencement of the trial, as opposed to those amendments which are granted even at an advanced stage of the trial, is strategic and sounds very attractive and plausible. However, given the context of this particular case, this valid argument easily collapses in the light of the preceding analysis and because of the prosecutorial inattention to appreciate the particularity of the cases and the Court which is supposed to hear and determine them, and to have acted diligently and indeed, more expeditiously, in introducing the motion to amend much earlier."

R50-TC-7 o *Prosecutor v. Norman, Fofana, Kondewa*, Case No. SCSL-04-14-T, Majority Decision on the Prosecution's Application for Leave to File an Interlocutory Appeal Against the Decision on the Prosecution's Request for Leave to Amend the Indictment Against Samuel Hinga Norman, Moinina Fofana and Allieu Kondewa, 2 August 2004, para. 36-38:

36. In this regard, it is our conviction and finding, that the Prosecution, because of its neglect in respecting the statutory obligation of timeliness, both in instituting criminal proceedings or seeking leave for an amendment to the indictment at the appropriate time, particularly in the peculiar circumstances of the limited mandate of the Special Court, was solely responsible for the refusal by the majority decision of the Chamber, of the Application for leave to amend the indictment.

37. Indeed, our analyses in our majority judgement of the 29th of May, 2004, as illustrated by the following excerpts clearly demonstrate the aforementioned lapses on the part of the prosecution. [. . .]

38. In these circumstances, therefore, the Prosecution is now estopped from raising the issue of irreparable prejudice as this was occasioned the lack of diligence and promptitude on its part in carrying out investigations for the gender crimes, which it rather belatedly wanted to incorporate into the consolidated indictment, coupled with the lack of respect for the principle of timeliness in seeking the amendment for a trial whose commencement was very imminent and which actually started on the 3 June 2004, after we rendered our decision which the Prosecution is contesting, on the 29 May 2004.

- **Rule 50(A): Amendment of the Indictment – Initial and Amended Indictments**

R50-TC-8 o *Prosecutor v. Norman*, Case No. SCSL-04-14-T, Decision on the First Accused's Motion for Service and Arraignment on the Consolidated Indictment, 29 November 2004, para. 36-37:

36. A consolidated indictment which covers the same charges and accused as the initial indictments does not constitute a new indictment. The initial indictments are essentially subsumed into the consolidated indictment. Official withdrawal of the initial indictment is not necessary. In the United States, for example, indictments that are consolidated become, in legal

effect, separate counts of one indictment.[1] Under English law, where an 'amended' indictment adds no new allegations or offences such that it represents a change in form but not in substance, it is not a fresh indictment. There is only one indictment.[2]

37. There is clearly only one indictment in existence against the Accused person, as reflected in the Joinder Decision and Consolidated Indictment. No official withdrawal of the Initial Indictment is necessary.

---

[1] See *Pankratz Lumber Co. V. U.S.*, 50 F.2d 174, C.A. 9 1931 (9th Circ.); *Dunaway v. United States* (1953) 92 US App DC 299, 205 F3d 23.
[2] *R v. Fyffe*, (1991) Crim. L.R. 1992, Jun, 442-444, CA.

R50-TC-9

o *Prosecutor v. Kallon*, Case no. SCSL-04-15-T, Decision on Motion on Issues of Urgent Concern to the Accused Morris Kallon, 9 December 2004, para. 26:

26. In the Chamber's view, the issue of staying the Original Indictment raised by the Second Accused is meretricious for the reason that, as a matter of law, the veiled suggestion of double jeopardy is misconceived. It is trite law that the Amended Consolidated Indictment merely "consolidated and superseded the Original individual separate indictments" including that of the Second Accused, "thus, as it were, extinguishing and relegating them into a state of legal oblivion."[1]

---

[1] *Prosecutor v. Norman, Fofana and Kondewa*, Case No. SCSL-04-14-T, Separate Concurring Opinion of Judge Bankole Thompson on Decision on First Accused's Motion for Service and Arraignment on the Consolidated Indictment, 29 November 2004, para. 23.

- **Rule 50(B): Amendment of Indictment – Need for a Further Appearance**

R50-TC-10

o *Prosecutor v. Norman*, Case No. SCSL-04-14-T, Decision on the First Accused's Motion for Service and Arraignment on the Consolidated Indictment, 29 November 2004, para. 30-32:

30. Upon close analysis of the Consolidated Indictment, there are clearly new factual allegations adduced in support of existing confirmed counts, as well as new substantive elements of the charges that were not in the Initial Indictment of the First Accused. In the opinion of the Trial Chamber these

changes do not appear to be simply "semantic", as alleged by the Prosecution in their Motion for Joinder, but rather are material to the Indictment. While some of the differences between the two Indictments simply provide greater specificity, and provide background facts, many of the changes are, however, material to the Indictment. [...] In addition, there are new substantive elements of charges, in paragraphs 24 to 27 and 29 of the Consolidated Indictment, that are material, and include the charges of unlawful arrest and detention, "conscription" of children, personal injury and extorting of money from civilians. We consider that all these additions to the Consolidated Indictment, without any amendment to the counts against the Accused and personal service on the Accused, in accordance with the prescribed procedure, could prejudice the Accused's right to a fair trial if the trial proceeds on this basis.

[...]

31. With respect to arraignment on the Indictment, it is clear in the Rules and the practice of the International Tribunals, that a consolidated or amended indictment need not be confirmed by a Trial Chamber or Judge if the initial indictments that were subject to joinder were already confirmed, and the charges in the amended indictment are essentially the same or similar to the original ones. This position is also clear in national systems. In the United Kingdom case of *R v. Fyffe*, it was recognised that the general rule that "[r]e-arraignment is unnecessary where the amended indictment merely reproduces the original allegations in a different form, albeit including a number of new counts".[1]

32. In the case at hand, the Accused entered a plea to the charges against him at his initial appearance in March, 2003. These charges remained in force against him, however, as we have found, there were material changes made to the Consolidated Indictment. The Trial Chamber finds that the Accused has not been afforded the opportunity to make a plea to these material changes to the Indictment, and that unfair prejudice may result if the Indictment is not amended and the Accused served with the Indictment and arraigned on the material changes to the Indictment.

---

[1] *R v. Fyffe* [1992] Crim. L.R. 442, C.A.

R50-TC-11

o *Prosecutor v. Fofana*, Case No. SCSL-04-14-T, Decision on the Second Accused's Motion for Service and Arraignment on the Consolidated Indictment, 6 December 2004, para. 16-17, 33-35:[55]

16. With respect to arraignment on the Indictment, it is clear in the practice of the International Tribunals,[(1)] that a consolidated indictment need not be confirmed by a Trial Chamber or Judge if the initial indictments that were subject to joinder were already confirmed, and the charges in the consolidated indictment are essentially the same or similar to the original ones. This position is also clear in national systems. In the United Kingdom case of *R v. Fyffe*, it was recognised that the general rule that "[r]e-arraignment is unnecessary where the amended indictment merely reproduces the original allegations in a different form, albeit including a number of new counts".[(2)]

17. When dealing with an amended indictment containing new charges, Rule 50(B) of the Rules provides in this respect that a further appearance may be held to enable the Accused to enter a plea on the new charges. This particular Rule provides for a further appearance in relation to the new charges only. This provision would find application only when there have been new charges.

[. . .]

33. The Trial Chamber has carefully considered the added locations in the Consolidated Indictment against the Second Accused and finds that these involve towns in the regions of Kenema, Bo and Moyamba. [. . .] The Trial Chamber takes note that no new regions have been added to the Consolidated Indictment that were not included in the Initial Indictment against the Accused, nor has there been any extension of timeframes for the commission of the offences in the Consolidated Indictment. The only additions to the Indictment include the towns set forth in paragraph 21 of this Decision, which are towns within the Districts of Kenema, Bo, and Moyamba.

34. Upon close analysis of the Consolidated Indictment in comparison to the Initial Indictment, the Trial Chamber concludes that the additions made to the Consolidated Indictment are of no materiality as they simply provide details for greater specificity to the factual allegations included in the Initial Indictment against the Accused. There are no new crimes or charges against the Accused.

---

[55] See also *Prosecutor v. Kondewa*, Case No. SCSL-04-14-T, Decision on the Third Accused's Motion for Service and Arraignment on the Consolidated Indictment, 8 December 2004, para. 25-27.

35. In the case at hand, the Accused entered a plea to the charges against him at his initial appearance on the 1st of July, 2003. These charges remained in force against him, and there have been no material changes made to the Consolidated Indictment. The Trial Chamber, therefore, finds that there are no requirements or obligations in the Rules or in the interests of justice to afford the Accused the opportunity to make a plea on the Consolidated Indictment. Consequently, it cannot be said that any unfair prejudice would result from him not being arraigned on the Consolidated Indictment.

---

(1) See for example, case of *Prosecutor v. Kvocka*, IT-98-30/T; *Prosecutor v. Kvocka*, Decision on Prosecution Request for Leave to File a Consolidated Indictment and to Correct Confidential Schedules, 13 October 2000; *Prosecutor v. Ademi*, IT-04-74, *Prosecutor v. Ademi*, Decision on Motion for Joinder of Accused, 30 July 2004; *Prosecutor v. Krajisnik*, IT-00-39; These cases are distinguishable, for example, from the case of *Prosecutor v. Blagojevic*, IT-02-60-PT, where the Indictment was consolidated before the initial appearances; and the case of *Prosecutor v. Limaj*, IT-03-66, where a further appearance was held on 27 February 2004, following new charges being added to the Second Amended Indictment; and in the case of *Prosecutor v. Mrksic*, IT-95-13/1, where a further plea was entered on 16 February 2004, to added counts in the Consolidated Indictment. For Rules governing the arraignment of the Accused on an amended Indictment, see Rule 50 of the Rules of Procedure and Evidence of the Special Court and Rule 50 of the Rules of the ICTR and ICTY, which provide that a further arraignment will be held where an amended indictment contains new charges.
(2) *R v. Fyffe* [1992] Crim. L.R. 442, C.A.

- **Rule 50(B): Amendment of Indictment – *Proprio Motu* Review of the Amended Indictment**

R50-TC-12

o *Prosecutor v. Norman*, Case No. SCSL-04-14-T, Decision on the First Accused's Motion for Service and Arraignment on the Consolidated Indictment, 29 November 2004, para. 16, 20-21:[56]

16. The Trial Chamber is aware that it is not its function to ascertain for itself whether the form of an Indictment complies with the pleading principles as outlined in the Rules, as this is normally a function for the parties, although a Court is entitled *proprio motu* to raise issues as to the form of an Indictment, particularly when such matters may affect the fairness of the process. In accordance with the principle of a fair trial, and the obligation to consider any unfair prejudice that

---

[56] See also *Prosecutor v. Kondewa*, Case No. SCSL-04-14-T, Decision on the Third Accused's Motion for Service and Arraignment on the Consolidated Indictment, 8 December 2004, para. 18.

may ensue from non-service and arraignment on the Consolidated Indictment, the Trial Chamber will consider whether there are any new charges to the Consolidated Indictment by comparison to the Initial Indictment.

[...]

20. Upon a detailed comparative analysis of the differences between the Initial Indictment for the First Accused and the Consolidated Indictment, the Trial Chamber comes to the conclusion that [...] some substantive elements of the charges have been added.

21. The Trial Chamber turns now to consider *proprio motu* whether these additions and changes to the Consolidated Indictment are material to the Indictment, in which case an unfair prejudice might ensure to the Accused on account of him facing these changes, having not been personally served and arraigned on the Consolidated Indictment, or alternatively, whether the additions simply provide greater specificity to general allegations, that are not material.

APPEALS CHAMBER DECISIONS

- **Rule 50: Amendment of Indictment – Criteria – Late Amendment**

R50-AC-1

o *Prosecutor v. Norman, Fofana, Kondewa*, Case No. SCSL-04-14-AR73, Decision on Amendment of the Consolidated Indictment, 16 May 2005, para. 77-82, 88:

77. That order forced the Prosecution to choose whether to make the amendment application that it should have made before the trial started, or else to abandon its new particulars. Its appeal submissions seek to excuse their addition to the consolidated Indictment on the basis that they are not "new" particulars, or at least do not amount to material changes. We reject these submissions. The Prosecution has made a number of significant changes, contrary to the expectation its representation had fostered in obtaining approval for the consolidated Indictment, and was in consequence under a duty to apply for leave to amend. In deciding whether to cut the Gordian knot and now grant leave, we must first determine the test upon which such leave is granted. The matter is complicated by the fact that the application to add these details must be treated as an amendment application made in the middle of the trial and not as an application made in pre-trial proceedings back in February 2004, when the Defence was first notified of them through substituted service of the consolidated Indictment. The significance of this distinction is

that the test for permitting late amendments is much more rigorous than a test of "interests of justice" and "lack of prejudice to the defence" that applies at the pre-trial stage. Had the Prosecution applied for leave at the correct time, namely February 2004, we have no doubt that the Trial Chamber would have permitted all these amendments. The more difficult question is whether we should permit them now.

78. In principle, the Indictment may be amended at any stage of the proceedings, up to the conclusion of the trial, if the court is satisfied that the defence will not be prejudiced by the amendment and that making it will be in the interests of justice. The Special Court Rules do not preclude late amendments. By "Indictment" we mean the counts stating the charges and the short particulars which should accompany them.

79. Amendments to an Indictment, broadly speaking, fall into three categories:

(i) Formal or semantic changes, which should not be opposed.
(ii) Changes which give greater precision to the charge or its particulars, either by narrowing the allegation or identifying times, dates or places with greater particularity or detail. Such amendments will normally be allowed, even during the trial.
(iii) Substantive changes, which seek to add fresh alleagations amounting either to separate charges or to a new allegation in respect of an existing charge.

80. Amendments in the third category will be carefully scrutinised and call for clear justification if they are to be allowed once the trial is underway. The Prosecution at this stage must satisfy the court not only that the substantial amendments cause no prejudice to the defence but that they will not delay or interrupt the trial. Once a criminal trial has begun it should proceed with as little distraction as possible to its conclusion on the Indictment as opened by the Prosecution. In inquisitorial systems and civil trials there is more flexibility, but it is fundamental to the adversarial system of criminal justice that once a trial is underway with live witnesses it should proceed straight-forwardly without change of goal-posts.

81. At a pre-trial stage, the position is very different although obviously more justification is required the closer to the date fixed for trial. But so long as the Defence can adequately prepare, amendments will normally be allowed. There are many reasons why justice requires the court to give the Prosecution pre-trial flexibility: the initial Indictment will not reflect the evidence it has gathered since, often as potential witnesses muster the courage to come forward as peace takes hold or as the court earns respect or as its outreach programmes take effect. It can only serve the interests of justice to permit the Prosecution to reconsider and refine its case in the pre-trial period.

82. That is not to say that the Trial Chamber should in this period allow the Prosecution its head. It is not concerned to "supervise" the Prosecutor but it is concerned to ensure that the trial which is in preparation is manageable and will work fairly and expeditiously. It is a notorious fact that Prosecutors sometimes overload their Indictments, and the Trial Chamber must be alert to prevent "overcharging" which can lengthen trials beyond endurance. The Prosecutor has no duty to indict a defendant for every offence in respect of which there exists *prima facie* evidence against him. We emphasise this, because the Prosecution submissions verge on asserting such a duty. In fact, the overriding duty of a Prosecutor – what determines, in fact, his or her professional ability – is to shape a trial by selecting just so many charges that can most readily be proved and which carry a penalty appropriate to the overall criminality of the Accused. In national systems, this is reflected in Prosecution practices of selecting specimen charges or proceeding only on certain counts of a long Indictment. In international courts, where defendants may be accused of command responsibility for hundreds if not thousands of war crimes at the end of a war that has lasted for years, the need to be selective in deciding which charges to include in a trial Indictment is a test of Prosecution professionalism. In this respect, the Trial Chamber must oversee the Indictment, in the interests of producing a trial which is manageable.

88. Amendments that do not amount to new counts should generally be admitted, even at a late stage, if they will not prejudice the defence or delay the trial process. The submissions before us indicate that they will not have either effect. The Norman Defence has known that the amendments were "on the cards" since June 2003 and, since February 2004, that the Prosecution was proceeding upon them. It did not invoke Rule 5, or make any complaint about their inclusion in the consolidated Indictment, until September 2004. It acquiesced in their inclusion for two trial sessions, and have prepared the case on the basis that they could be included. We are satisfied that the amendment will not involve an undue lengthening of the time of trial.

- **Rule 50: Amendment of Indictment – Criteria – Less Serious Allegation**

R50-AC-2   o *Prosecutor v. Norman, Fofana, Kondewa*, Case No. SCSL-04-14-AR73, Decision on Amendment of the Consolidated Indictment, 16 May 2005, para. 83:

83. [. . .] In count 8, the allegation of "conscripting" children under 15 is watered down to the allegation of "initiating" them into armed forces – a less serious allegation. This

amendment too must be allowed. Whatever "initiate" may mean, the change in wording, by lessening the seriousness of the original charge, cannot possibly prejudice the defendant.

- **Rule 50: Amendment of Indictment – Reference to Rule 47(G) and Rule 52**

R50-AC-3

o *Prosecutor v. Norman, Fofana, Kondewa*, Case No. SCSL-04-14-AR73, Decision on Amendment of the Consolidated Indictment, 16 May 2005, para. 62-63:

62. The reference to Rule 52 is doubtless explained by the final sentence in Rule 50: 'If leave to amend is granted, Rule 47(G) and Rule 52 apply to the amended Indictment.' However, purposive interpretation of this provision means that it applies only to the extent that it can *sensibly* apply. Rule 47(G), for example, will have no application if leave to amend a particular is granted: it states 'If at least one count is approved, the Indictment shall go forward. If no count is approved, the Indictment shall be returned to the Prosecutor.' So far as Rule 52, set out below, is concerned, Rule 52(A) and Rule 52(C) are obviously inapplicable to the stage at which original Indictments are consolidated, although the requirements of personal service (Rule 52(B)) and publicity (Rule 52(D)) are sensibly applicable to the consolidated Indictment if it has been amended.

63. The reference to service in accordance with Rule 52 does not appear to have been the subject of any argument, although Rule 52 is plainly concerned principally with ensuring that the Accused is personally presented with the charges against him as soon as possible after his arrest, a fundamental defence right guaranteed by the Special Court Statute and all international human rights instruments. [...]

- **Rule 50: Amendment of Indictment – Previous Indictment(s) "Not to Be Proceeded With"**

R50-AC-4

o *Prosecutor v. Norman, Fofana, Kondewa*, Case No. SCSL-04-14-AR73, Decision on Amendment of the Consolidated Indictment, 16 May 2005, para. 70:

70. [...] It is a somewhat metaphysical approach to say that each of three individual Indictments are "essentially subsumed" in a consolidated Indictment. The existential position is that the fourth Indictment is certainly different, and "new"

in the sense that it is a separate document entered in the Registry with a different number – in this case, SCSL-2004-14-PT. However much it may replicate, in language and content, the three original Indictments, they at present remain on file in the Registry, essentially unsubsumed. What is their status? Might they revive in the event that the trial is abandoned or stopped for abuse of process? The defendants are understandably anxious on this score, while the Prosecution has been unhelpful and complacent. It informs us that it sees no reason to do anything about the initial Indictments. It makes no application to have them left on the file, marked "not to be proceeded with" which is a procedure sometimes adopted. Although we do not think that the fears expressed by the defendants about double jeopardy – i.e. that they might be tried on the counts of the old Indictments if acquitted on the consolidated Indictment – would ever be allowed to come to pass, we agree with them that the Prosecution should not be permitted to have it both ways. If the Prosecution de-clines to withdraw the old Indictments, then we must remove all apprehension from the Defence by ordering them to be marked "not to be proceeded with". This trial has proceeded and will continue to proceed on a consolidated Indictment that was approved by the Trial Chamber in its decisions of 29 November and 8 December 2004. That approval was based, however, upon the Prosecution representation that there would be no material change in the statements of offence or the particulars provided in the consolidated Indictment.

- **Rule 50(B): Amendment of Indictment – Requirement for Further Appearance**

R50-AC-5   o *Prosecutor v. Norman, Fofana, Kondewa*, Case No. SCSL-04-14-AR73, Decision on Amendment of the Consolidated Indictment, 16 May 2005, para. 72:

72. We must point out that whatever the commonsense of the general approach taken in *Fyffe*, under our Rule 50(B), "if the amended Indictment includes new charges" the Accused must make a further appearance in order to enter a plea to them pursuant to Rule 61. A count of an Indictment is the formal encapsulation of the legal basis of the charge. So, if the consolidated Indictment includes new counts, even though the particulars remain the same, Rule 50(B) applies and pleas must be taken. However, in the cases of Kondewa and Fofana, the consolidated Indictment produced no significant changes, let alone any additional charge or count. A further appearance was therefore not required by the rule. The Trial Chamber was correct to reject that argument on the finding, in the cases of Kondewa and Fofana, that there had been no new count levelled against them by the consolidated Indictment.

Rule 51: Withdrawal of Indictment
(amended 1 August 2003)

(A) The Prosecutor may withdraw an indictment at any time before its approval pursuant to Rule 47.

(B) After the approval of an indictment pursuant to Rule 47, but prior to the commencement of the trial, the Prosecutor may withdraw an indictment upon providing to the Trial Chamber in open court a statement of the reasons for the withdrawal.

(C) Once the trial of an accused has commenced, the Prosecutor may withdraw an indictment only by leave granted by the Trial Chamber.

(D) The withdrawal of the indictment shall be promptly notified to the accused and to counsel for the accused.

TRIAL CHAMBERS DECISIONS

- **Rule 51: Withdrawal of Indictment – Death of the Accused**

R51-TC-1

o *Prosecutor v. Sankoh*, Case No. SCSL-03-02-PT, Withdrawal of Indictment, 8 December 2003:[57]

CONSIDERING the certified copy of the Death Certificate issued for Foday Saybana Sankoh of the 2nd day of August 2003;

CONSIDERING Rule 51(B) of the Rules of Procedure and Evidence of the Special Court for Sierra Leone;

CONSIDERING ALSO the appearance of the Prosecutor before the Trial Chamber on the 5th day of December 2003;

NOTING the statement of reasons presented by the Prosecutor to the Trial Chamber on the 5th day of December 2003, in which the Prosecutor submitted that the evidence available has indicated to his satisfaction that Sam Bockarie is deceased;

NOTING that the Defence has no objection to the withdrawal;

---

[57] See also *Prosecutor v. Bockarie*, Case No. SCSL-03-04-PT, Withdrawal of Indictment, 8 December 2003.

NOW THEREFORE

THE CHAMBER ACCEPTS the Prosecutor's statement of reasons;

and **ENDORSES** the withdrawal of the Indictment.

Rule 52: Service of Indictment
(amended 29 May 2004)

(A) Service of the indictment shall be effected personally on the accused at the time the accused is taken into the custody of the Special Court or as soon as possible thereafter.

(B) Personal service of an indictment on the accused is effected by giving the accused a copy of the indictment approved in accordance with Rule 47.

(C) An indictment that has been permitted to proceed by the Designated Judge shall be retained by the Registrar, who shall prepare certified copies bearing the seal of the Special Court. If the accused does not understand English and if the language understood is a written language known to the Registrar, a translation of the indictment in that language shall also be prepared. In the case that the accused is illiterate or his language is an oral language, the Registrar will ensure that the indictment is read to the accused by an interpreter, and that he is served with a recording of the interpretation.

(D) Subject to Rule 53, upon approval by the Designated Judge the indictment shall be made public.

TRIAL CHAMBERS DECISIONS

- **Rule 52: Service of Indictment – Order to Serve the Indictment**

R52-TC-1 o *Prosecutor v. Taylor*, Case No. SCSL-03-01-I, Warrant of Arrest and Order for Transfer and Detention, 7 March 2003:[58]

---

[58] See also *Prosecutor v. Sankoh*, Case No. SCSL-03-02-I, Warrant of Arrest and Order for Transfer and Detention, 7 March 2003; *Prosecutor v. Koroma*, Case No. SCSL-03-03-I, Warrant of Arrest and Order for Transfer and Detention, 7 March 2003; *Prosecutor v. Bockarie*, Case no. SCSL-03-04-I, Warrant of Arrest and Order for Transfer and Detention, 7 March 2003; *Prosecutor v. Sesay*, Case No. 03-05-I, Warrant of Arrest and Order for Transfer and Detention, 7 March 2003; *Prosecutor v. Brima*, Case No. 03-06-I, Warrant of Arrest and Order for Transfer and Detention, 7 March 2003; *Prosecutor v. Kallon*, Case No. 03-07-I, Warrant of Arrest and Order for Transfer and Detention, 7 March 2003; *Prosecutor v. Norman*, Case No. 03-08-I, Warrant of Arrest and Order for Transfer and Detention, 7 March 2003; *Prosecutor v. Koroma*, Case No. SCSL-03-03-I, Warrant of Arrest and Order for Transfer and Detention, 25 November 2003.

HEREBY ORDERS THE REGISTRAR OF THE SPECIAL COURT

(C) to cause to be served on the Accused, at the time of his arrest, or as soon as practicable immediately following his arrest, in English or have read to him in a language he understands, a certified copy of the Warrant of Arrest, a certified copy of the Indictment, a statement of the rights of the Accused and to caution the Accused that any statement made by him shall be recorded and may be used as evidence against him in coordination with the National Authorities of the State concerned;

- **Rule 52: Service of Indictment – Service on Counsel**

R52-TC-2

o *Prosecutor v. Norman*, Case No. SCSL-04-14-T, Decision on the First Accused's Motion for Service and Arraignment on the Consolidated Indictment, 29 November 2004, para. 11-13:[59]

11. The Chief of Court Management has informed the Trial Chamber that the Accused was not personally served with the Consolidated Indictment. According to this report, the said Indictment was only served on Counsel for the Accused, as the Prosecution had not asked for *personal service* on the Accused.

12. In accordance with Rule 52 of the Rules, the Trial Chamber had ordered in its Decision on Joinder, for the Consolidated Indictment to be served on each Accused person. This order was as follows:

> That a single consolidated indictment be prepared as the Indictment on which the joint trial shall proceed [. . .];
>
> [. . .]
>
> That the said Indictment be served on each Accused in accordance with Rule 52 of the Rules.

13. Based upon the foregoing, the Trial Chamber finds that the service of the Indictment on Counsel for the Accused does not comply with Rule 52 of the Rules, or the Order of the Trial Chamber. While such a failure to serve the Consolidated

---

[59] See also *Prosecutor v. Fofana*, Case No. SCSL-04-14-T, Decision on the Second Accused's Motion for Service and Arraignment on the Consolidated Indictment, 6 December 2004, para. 13-15; *Prosecutor v. Kondewa*, Case No. SCSL-04-14-T, Decision on the Third Accused's Motion for Service and Arraignment on the Consolidated Indictment, 8 December 2004, para. 13-15.

Indictment personally on the Accused constitutes a procedural error, this alone would not, however, in and of itself, unfairly prejudice the Accused's right to a fair trial.

R52-TC-3
o *Prosecutor v. Kallon*, Case No. SCSL-04-15-T, Decision on Motion on Issues of Urgent Concern to the Accused Morris Kallon, 9 December 2004, para. 20-22:

20. In a Separate Concurring Opinion to a recent Decision of this Chamber on this issue, it was observed that:

"... as a matter of statutory interpretation, Rule 52(B) governing the service of indictments within the jurisdiction of the Special Court for Sierra Leone departs from the acknowledged and recognized body of jurisprudence on the subject, both nationally and internationally. Under national criminal law systems and from international criminal law practice, the notion of "personal service" of legal process bears the extended legal meaning of service of the process in question on Counsel for the accused as the duly authorised legal representation, on record, for the said accused. In effect, based on the foregoing reasoning, it would be sufficient in law, for the purposes of "personal service", if the Consolidated Indictment in question were served upon Counsel for the First Accused. By contrast, however, the legislative intent behind our Rule 52(B) was to adopt a restrictive rather than an extended legal connotation of "personal service" of indictments within the Special Court adversarial scheme. It does not fall within the judicial domain of the Trial Chamber to question the legislative wisdom behind the formulation of Rule 52(B) in its present form. Therefore, applying the golden rule of statutory interpretation, Rule 52(B) must be given its plain and literal meaning."[1]

21. Guided by the foregoing proposition as to the legal effect of Rule 52 of the Rules, it is the considered view of this Chamber, following two recent Decisions[2] on the issue, that the law of this tribunal makes it clearly mandatory for an accused person to be served a copy of the indictment personally at the time he or she is taken into the custody of the Court or as soon as possible thereafter. Rule 52(B) is quite explicit in its terms that "personal service" is to be effected by giving the accused a copy of the indictment approved in accordance with the aforesaid Rule. Consistent with this reasoning, and noting that in the context of this Motion the records of Court Management Section disclosed that the Second Accused was not personally served with the Consolidated Indictment as prescribed

by Rule 52(B) but that service was effected on his counsel, the Chamber finds that there has been, in fact and in law, non-compliance with Rule 52(B) of the Rules in relation to the Second Accused's entitlement to be personally served with a copy of the Consolidated Indictment in conformity with the Order of the Trial Chamber made pursuant to its Joinder Decision.

22. The Chamber further holds that such non-compliance does not procedurally invalidate the trial proceeding or any subsequent proceeding on two main grounds. The first is that such an omission or defect does not, without more, prejudice the right of the Second Accused to a fair trial based on the state of the official records and the fact that he has subsequently appeared to take his trial and that his Counsel have cross-examined extensively prosecution witnesses on his behalf. The second ground upon which we base the foregoing reasoning that infringement of Rule 52(B) does not invalidate the trial proceeding or any subsequent proceedings is that where an accused person has pleaded "not guilty" to a charge or charges in an indictment he shall, "without further form, be deemed to have put himself upon his trial, and after such a plea, it shall not be open to the accused, except with the leave of the Court, to object that he is not properly upon his trial, by reason of some defect, omission or irregularity relating to the depositions, or preliminary investigation, or any other matter arising out of the preliminary investigation."[3] The Second Accused is therefore estopped from contending that he is not properly upon his trial having pleaded "not guilty" to the Original Indictment and its additional count in the Amended Consolidated Indictment.

---

[1] *Prosecutor v. Norman, Fofana and Kondewa*, Case No. SCSL-04-14-T, Separate Concurring Opinion of Judge Bankole Thompson on Decision of First Accused's Motion For Service and Arraignment on the Consolidated Indictment, 29 November 2004, para. 3.

[2] *Prosecutor v. Norman, Fofana and Kondewa*, Case No. SCSL-04-14-T, Decision on First Accused's Motion for Service and Arraignment on the Consolidated Indictment, 29 November 2004; and *id.*, Decision on Second Accused's Motion for Service and Arraignment on the Consolidated Indictment, 6 December 2004.

[3] See Section 133(1) and (2) of the Sierra Leone Criminal Procedure Act 1965. Article 14(2) of the Statute of the Court authorizes recourse to the jurisprudence of Sierra Leone for guidance, albeit as a matter of discretion, whenever the Rules and Evidence of the Court "do not, or adequately provide for a specific situation." It is crystal-clear that there is, at present, no rule of the Special Court on the legal effect or consequence of a plea of "not guilty" by an accused to an indictment as a matter of procedure. For instance, does non-compliance with a rule of procedure necessarily result in a nullity? Evidently, the Sierra Leone law does not adopt this approach. See also Article 20(3) of the Statute for recourse to the jurisprudence of the Supreme Court of Sierra Leone.

APPEALS CHAMBER DECISIONS

- **Rule 52: Service of Indictment – Service on Counsel**

R52-AC-1
o *Prosecutor v. Norman, Fofana, Kondewa*, Case No. SCSL-04-14-AR73, Decision on Amendment of the Consolidated Indictment, 16 May 2005, para. 65:

65. [. . .] Service on Counsel, the agent for the defendant, normally constitutes service on the defendant, and in this case there is no doubt that Counsel quickly apprised all three defendants of the contents of the consolidated Indictment and advised them about it. In the geography of the Special Court, the Defence Counsel offices are situated in the court precincts a few hundred yards from the detention centre where the Accused are held in custody: it is not as if the Indictment was served on Counsel in another country or even in another part of town. No prejudice could conceivably have been caused by the error and this is emphasised by the fact that the Defence took no point on the incorrectness of the service for over six months, being content in the meantime for the case to continue on the consolidated Indictment as served on Counsel. The Defence, by this delay, is precluded from reliance upon Rule 5, which provides that *"Where an objection on the ground of non-compliance with the Rules or Regulations is raised by a party at the earliest opportunity, the Trial Chamber or the Designated Judge may grant relief."*

> **Rule 53: Non-disclosure**
> *(amended 1 August 2003)*
>
> (A) In exceptional circumstances, the Designated Judge may, in the interests of justice, order the non-disclosure to the public of any documents or information until further order.
>
> (B) When approving an indictment the Designated Judge may, on the application of the Prosecutor, order that there be no public disclosure of the indictment until it is served on the accused, or, in the case of joint accused, on all the accused.
>
> (C) The Designated Judge or the Trial Chamber may, on the application of the Prosecutor, also order that there be no disclosure of an indictment, or part thereof, or of all or any part of any particular document or information, if satisfied that the making of such an order is required to give effect to a provision of the Rules, to protect confidential information obtained by the Prosecutor, or is otherwise in the interests of justice.

TRIAL CHAMBERS DECISIONS

- **Rule 53: Non-Disclosure – Order to the Authorities of Sierra Leone**

R53-TC-1

o *Prosecutor v. Sesay*, Case No. SCSL-03-05-I, Warrant of Arrest and Order for Transfer and Detention, 7 March 2003:[60]

HEREBY ORDERS THE RELEVANT AUTHORITIES OF THE GOVERNMENT OF SIERRA LEONE

(E) not disclose to the public, including media or any public record, the existence of the Indictment and this Warrant of Arrest, or any part thereof or information pertaining to the Indictment and this Warrant for Arrest until further order of the Court or at the direction of the Prosecutor;

---

[60] See also *Prosecutor v. Brima*, Case No. SCSL-03-06-I, Warrant of Arrest and Order for Transfer and Detention, 7 March 2003; *Prosecutor v. Kallon*, Case No. SCSL-03-07-I, Warrant of Arrest and Order for Transfer and Detention, 7 March 2003; *Prosecutor v. Norman*, Case No. SCSL-03-08-I, Warrant of Arrest and Order for Transfer and Detention, 7 March 2003.

- **Rule 53: Non-Disclosure – Request to Third States**

R53-TC-2
o *Prosecutor v. Taylor*, Case No. SCSL-03-01-I, Warrant of Arrest and Order for Transfer and Detention, 7 March 2003:[61]

HEREBY REQUESTS ALL STATES CONCERNED

(D) not disclose to the public, including media or any public record, the existence of the Indictment and this Warrant of Arrest, or any part thereof or information pertaining to the Indictment and this Warrant for Arrest until further order of the Court or at the direction of the Prosecutor;

- **Rule 53: Non-Disclosure – Order for Disclosure**

R53-TC-3
o *Prosecutor v. Sankoh*, Case No. SCSL-03-02-I, Order for Disclosure of Indictment, Warrant of Arrest and Order for Transfer and Detention, 14 March 2003:

CONSIDERING the arrest of the Accused on 10 March 2003 and his transfer to the custody of the Special Court on the same date;

CONSIDERING that the initial appearance of the Accused under Rule 61 of the Rules of Procedure will take place on 15 March 2003;

HAVING HEARD the Prosecutor's favourable opinion on the disclosure to the public of the Indictment and the Warrant of Arrest and Order for Transfer and Detention;

PURSUANT to Rule 28 and Rule 53 of the Rules,

HEREBY ORDERS, starting from 15 March 2003, the public disclosure of the Indictment and the Warrant of Arrest and Order for Transfer and Detention of the Accused.

---

[61] See also *Prosecutor v. Sankoh*, Case No. SCSL-03-02-I, Warrant of Arrest and Order for Transfer and Detention, 7 March 2003; *Prosecutor v. Koroma*, Case No. SCSL-03-03-I, Warrant of Arrest and Order for Transfer and Detention, 7 March 2003; *Prosecutor v. Bockarie*, Case no. SCSL-03-04-I, Warrant of Arrest and Order for Transfer and Detention, 7 March 2003.

R53-TC-4

o *Prosecutor v. Koroma*, Case No. SCSL-03-03-I, Order for the Disclosure of the Indictment, 28 March 2003:

NOTING the Prosecutor's favourable opinion on the disclosure to the public of the Indictment against the Accused;

PURSUANT to Rule 28 and Rule 53 of the Rules,

HEREBY ORDERS, starting from 28th of March, 2003, the public disclosure of the Indictment against the Accused.

R53-TC-5

o *Prosecutor v. Taylor*, Case No. SCSL-03-01-I, Order for the Disclosure of the Indictment, the Warrant of Arrest and Order for Transfer and Detention and the Decision Approving the Indictment and Order for Non-Disclosure, 12 June 2003:

CONSIDERING that it would be in the public interest to now proceed with such disclosure;

NOW THEREFORE

PURSUANT to Rules 53 and 54 of the Rules,

HEREBY ORDERS the public disclosure of the Indictment against the Accused, the Warrant of Arrest and Order for Transfer and Detention and the Decision Approving the Indictment and Order for Non-Disclosure;

The additional material supporting the Indictment shall not be disclosed to the public until further order of the Special Court.

> **Rule 54: General Provision**
>
> At the request of either party or of its own motion, a Judge or a Trial Chamber may issue such orders, summonses, subpoenas, warrants and transfer orders as may be necessary for the purposes of an investigation or for the preparation or conduct of the trial.

TRIAL CHAMBERS DECISIONS

- **Rule 54: Orders – Necessity of the Order**

R54-TC-2
- *Prosecutor v. Brima, Kamara, Kanu*, Case No. SCSL-04-16-T, Decision on Joint Defence Motion for General Orders Pursuant to Rule 54, 28 July 2005, para. 20, 42:

    20. The Rule is a general rule in unambiguous language. Clearly, the test for whether the Trial Chamber ought to issue the orders sought by the Defence, is whether to do so is necessary (not simply useful or helpful) for the purposes of an investigation or for the preparation or conduct of the trial.[1]

    [...]

    42. We find that the test for the application of Rule 54 mentioned earlier has not been met in this case. The relief sought by the Defence is in respect of situations which have not been conclusively proved to exist, and hence cannot be regarded as being necessary for the purposes prescribed in Rule 54. Accordingly, we find that no grounds have been established for orders under Rule 54.

---

[1] See *Prosecutor v. Delalic et al.*, Case No. No. IT-96-21-T, Decision of the President on the Prosecutor's Motion for the Production of Notes Exchanged between Zejnil Delalic and Zdravko Mucic, 11 November 1996; see also Jones & Powles, International Criminal Practice 3rd. Edition, at para. 8.4.3.

- **Rule 54: Order – *Subpoena Duces Tecum* – State Cooperation**

R54-TC-2
- *Prosecutor v. Kanu*, Case No. SCSL-04-16-PT, Decision on Defence Motion in Respect of Santigie Borbor Kanu for an Order under Rule 54 with Respect to Release of Exculpatory Evidence, 1st June 2004, para. 19-30:

19. Consistent with the Court's general philosophy of drawing, persuasively from the judicial experiences of sister international criminal tribunals,[1] as to their approaches in determining complex and delicate legal issues of international criminal law importance with necessary adaptations, it is instructive, to explore and expound the law governing states' cooperation with international criminal tribunals. In this regard, it must be noted that, at the level of the International Criminal Tribunal for the former Yugoslavia ("ICTY") some judicial light has been shed on this rather esoteric area of the law in the case of the *Prosecutor v. Blaskic*.[2] In that case, the Appeals Chamber insightfully addressed certain central issues germane to the subject of the instant application. These are:

(a) whether the international tribunal can issue subpoenas to states and state officials;

(b) whether the international tribunal can issue binding orders to states;

(c) the nature and scope of such binding orders;

(d) whether the international tribunal can direct binding orders to states officials.

20. The following extract from the *Blaskic* Judgement serves to put that decision in its factual and legal context:

"The Appeals Chamber of the International Criminal Tribunal for the former Yugoslavie ("International Tribunal") is seized of the question of the validity of a *subpoena duces tecum* issued by Judge Gabrielle Kirk McDonald to the Republic of Croatia ('Croatia') and its Defence Minister, Mr. Gojko Susak, on 15 January 1997. This matter arises by way of a challenge by Croatia to the Decision of Trial Chamber II on 18 July 1997 ("Subpoena Decision") upholding the issuance of the said *subpoena duces tecum* by Judge McDonald, and ordering compliance therewith by Croatia within 30 days. Croatia has challenged the legal power and authority of the International Tribunal to issue compulsory order to States and high government officials. The legal issues that have been argued before this Chamber address the power of a Judge in a Trial Chamber of the International Tribunal to issue *subpoena duces tecum* in general and, in particular, to a state, the power of a Judge or Trial Chamber of the International tribunal to issue *subpoena duces tecum* to high government officials of a State and other individuals; the appropriate remedies to be taken if there is non-compliance with such *subpoena duces tecum*, and other issues including the question of the national necessity interests of sovereign states."

21. In addressing the first question, namely, *whether the international tribunal can issue subpoenas to states and states officials*, the Appeal Chamber's approach was twofold. Firstly, the Chamber reasoned thus:

"... the International Tribunal does not possess any power to take enforcement measures against States. Had the drafters of the Statute intended to vest the International Tribunal with such a power, they would have expressly provided for it. In the case of an international judicial body, this is not a power that can be regarded as inherent in its functions. Under current international law States can only be the subject of countermeasures taken by other States or of sanctions visited upon them by the organized international community, i.e. the United Nations or other intergovernmental organisations."

Secondly, the Chamber emphasised that:

"Under present international law, it is clear that states, by definition, cannot be the subject of criminal sanctions akin to those provided for in national criminal systems."[3]

22. *On the issue of the international tribunal's power or lack thereof to issue binding orders to states*, the Appeals Chamber had this to say:

"However, it is self-evident that the International Tribunal, in order to bring to trial persons living under the jurisdiction of sovereign states, not being endowed with enforcement agents of its own, must rely upon the cooperation of States. The International Tribunal must turn to states if it is effectively to investigate crimes, collect evidence, summon witnesses and have indictees arrested and surrendered to the International Tribunal. The drafters of the Statute realistically took account of this in imposing upon all states the obligation to lend cooperation and judicial assistance to the International Tribunal. The obligation is laid down in Article 29... The exceptional legal basis of Article 29 accounts for the novel and indeed unique power granted to the International Tribunals to issue orders to sovereign states (under customary international law, states, as a matter of principle, cannot be "ordered" either by other states or international bodies."[4]

23. On the question of *the obligation of states under Article 29*, the Appeals Chamber noted that it

"concerns both action that states may take only and exclusively through their organs (this, for instance, happens in case of an order enjoining a state produce documents in the possession of ones of its officials)."[5]

24. *As to the nature and scope of binding orders that can be issued by the International Tribunal*, the Chamber laid down certain criteria which a request for an order for production of documents issued under Article 29(2) of the Statute, whether before or after commencement of a trial, must satisfy. These are:

(i) it must identify specific documents and not broad categories;
(ii) it must set out succinctly the reasons why such documents are deemed relevant to the trial, except if giving reasons might jeopardize prosecutorial or defence strategy;
(iii) it must not be unduly onerous;
(iv) it must give the requested state sufficient time for compliance.[6]

All these conditions must be met.

25. Guided persuasively by the principles enunciated by the ICTY in the *Blaskic* Judgement, as Designated Judge, I now proceed to adopt with modifications, if necessary, the test laid down in that case, for the purpose of applications of this type brought before the Special Court. In my considered opinion, Article 17 of the Agreement between the United Nations and the Government of Sierra Leone on the establishment of a Special Court for Sierra Leone and section 21 of the Ratification Act together form the doctrinal bedrock of the machinery for co-operation between the Government of Sierra Leone and the Court in the execution of its statutory mandate.

26. On a level of specificity, articulated in paragraphs 27-29 are the three key principles for future guidance of the Court in determining the merits of applications of this nature.

27. First, the Special Court lacks legal authority to apply any enforcement measures against the State of Sierra Leone, there being no express statutory authority in the founding instruments of the Court for that purpose, nor can it be asserted that the Court's inherent jurisdiction includes such power. Any other view of the law on this theme would amount to a disregard for or encroachment upon, the entrenched doctrine of state sovereignty.

28. Second, predicated upon its founding instruments, the Special Court, not being endowed with enforcement agents of its own, must depend and rely upon the co-operation of the sovereign State of Sierra Leone in order to prosecute persons alleged to bear the greatest responsibility for serious violations of international humanitarian law during the hostilities which took place during the rebel war. In essence, under the statutory co-operation scheme, there devolves upon the State of Sierra Leone an international contractual obligation, which is treaty-based, to assist the Special Court effectively investigate crimes,

collect evidence, summon witnesses and have indictees arrested and delivered to the Special Court.

29. Third, as emphasized in *Blaskic* in respect of Article 29 of the ICTY Statute, the power granted to the ICTY to issue orders to sovereign States is exceptional and novel, one not hitherto recognised under customary international law. To the same extent, analogically, does Article 17 of the Special Court's Statute create the unique power authorising the Special Court to issue orders to the sovereign State of Sierra Leone. It follows, therefore, that the contractual obligation created under the bilateral arrangement between the United Nations and the Government of sierra Leone specifically applies to cases where the State of Sierra Leone is required to produce documents in possession of its officials.

30. In addition to the above key principles undergirding the statutory framework for co-operation between the Court and the State of Sierra Leone articulated in paragraphs 25-29, it is now necessary to stipulate for the purposes of applications of this nature seeking orders for the implementation of article 17, that for such applications to succeed, the applicant must fulfil the criteria laid down in the *Blaskic* Judgement.

[...]

HEREBY GRANT THE SAID MOTION AND REQUEST THE CO-OPERATION and assistance of the competent authorities of the State of Sierra Leone as follows:

1. That the Governement and/or military authorities at the Ministry of Finance and/or Cockerill Army Headquarters in the Republic of Sierra Leone, and more particularly, Lieutenant Colonel Sheku Mohamed Koroma, Captain Sylvanus of the Military Police and Colonel S.O. Williams, **DO PROVIDE** th the Defence herein an official statement confirming the correctness of the information embodied in Exhibit 1 of the Motion with verifications of the Accused's detention period at Cockerill Army Headquarters as evident from Folios A and N attached to the Motion.

2. That the appropriate authorities of the Ministry of Finance and/or Cockerill Army Headquarters in the Republic of Sierra Leone **DO PROVIDE** to the Defence herein the CCP salary vouchers as specified in the Motion (enhancing the period April-June and/or any other documents which may establish the presence of the Accused during the period of April-June 2000 at the location of CCP in Freetown.

3. That the applicant is granted liberty to apply for the subsidiary order at a later appropriate stage.

AND EXPRESS APPRECIATION to the Government of Sierra Leone for its co-operation and assistance in this matter.

[1] See *Prosecutor v. Issa Hassan Sesay*, Case No. SCSL-03-05-PT, Decision on the Prosecutor's Motion for Immediate Protective Measures for Witnesses and Victims and for Non-Public Disclosure, 23 May 2003, para. 11; see also *Prosecutor v. Issa Hassan Sesay, Alex Tamba Brima, Morris Kallon, Augustine Gbao, Brima Bazzy Kamara, Santigie Borbor Kanu*, Decision and Order on Prosecution's Motion for Joinder, 27 January 2004, para. 26.
[2] *Prosecutor v. Tihomir Blaskic*, Judgement on the Request of the Republic of Croatia for review of the Decision of Trial Chamber II, 18 July 1997; 29 October, 1997 ("*Blaskic* Judgement").
[3] *Id.* para. 25.
[4] *Id.* para. 26.
[5] *Id.* para. 27.
[6] *Id.* para. 32.

> **Rule 55: Execution of Arrest Warrants**
> *(amended 29 May 2004)*
>
> (A) A warrant of arrest shall be signed by the Designated Judge and shall bear the seal of the Special Court. It shall be accompanied by a copy of the indictment, and a statement of the rights of the accused.
>
> (B) The Registrar shall transmit to the relevant authorities of Sierra Leone in whose territory or under whose jurisdiction or control the accused resides, or was last known to be, three sets of certified copies of:
>
> (i) The warrant for arrest of the accused and an order for his transfer to the Special Court;
> (ii) The approved indictment;
> (iii) A statement of the rights of the accused; and if necessary a translation thereof in a language understood by the accused.
>
> (C) The Registrar shall request the said authorities to:
>
> (i) Cause the arrest of the accused and his transfer to the Special Court;
> (ii) Serve a set of the aforementioned documents upon the accused;
> (iii) Cause the documents to be read to the accused in a language understood by him and to caution him as to his rights in that language; and
> (iv) Return one set of the documents together with proof of service, to the Special Court.
>
> (D) When an arrest warrant issued by the Special Court is executed, a member of the Prosecutor's Office may be present as from the time of arrest.

TRIAL CHAMBERS DECISIONS

- **Rule 55: Execution of Arrest Warrants – Transmission to the Authority of Sierra Leone**

R55-TC-1   o *Prosecutor v. Sesay*, Case No. SCSL-03-05-I, Warrant of Arrest and Order for Transfer and Detention, 7 March 2003:[62]

---

[62] See also *Prosecutor v. Brima*, Case No. SCSL-03-06-I, Warrant of Arrest and Order

HEREBY ORDERS THE REGISTRAR OF THE SPECIAL COURT

(A) to address this Warrant of Arrest, Decision Approving the Indictment, the Approved Indictment of the accused and a Statement of the Rights of the Accused to the national authorities of Sierra Leone in accordance with Rule 55;

- **Rule 55: Execution of Arrest Warrants – Format**

R55-TC-2   o *Prosecutor v. Brima*, Case No. SCSL-03-06-PT, Ruling on the Application for the Issue of a Writ of *Habeas Corpus* Filed by the Applicant, 22 July 2003:

[...] I observe that the relevant provisions of Rules 47(H) and 55 do not consecrate a format for a warrant of arrest. It would appear to me sufficient, if, as the instant warrant does, the name of the person to be arrested is specified and the said person is identified and arrested accordingly. In any event, having been taken into custody, a mere technical flaw in the warrant of arrest neither renders the said arrest nor the detention based on that arrest illegal.

- **Rule 55(C): Execution of Arrest Warrants – Obligation to Serve the Accused with a Case Summary**

R55-TC-3   o *Prosecutor v. Kamara*, SCSL-04-16-PT, Decision and Order on Defence Preliminary Motion on Defects in the Form of the Indictment, 1 April 2004, para. 36:

36. [...]

iii. On the execution of the Warrant of Arrest, the Accused was served, in conformity with the established practice of the Special Court and pursuant to the provisions of Rules 52 and 55 of the Rules, with the Indictment, the Warrant, the Decision Approving the Indictment and a set of basic legal instruments pertain- ing to the Special Court, *but was not served, either directly or through his Counsel, with the Case Summary accompanying the Indictment.*

---

for Transfer and Detention, 7 March 2003; *Prosecutor v. Kallon*, Case No. SCSL-03-07-I, Warrant of Arrest and Order for Transfer and Detention, 7 March 2003; *Prosecutor v. Norman*, Case No. SCSL-03-08-I, Warrant of Arrest and Order for Transfer and Detention, 7 March 2003.

 Accordingly, the Trial Chamber upholds the first arm of the Defence objection and hereby orders the Prosecution to serve on the Defence, a certified true copy of the Case Summary accompanying the Indictment when it was submitted for approval, within three days of the date of service of this Decision. In granting this request, the Trial Chamber notes that the filing of the Case Summary does not *per se* have an impact on alleged defects in the form of the Indictment.

Rule 56: Warrant of Arrest to Third States
(amended 7 March 2003)

(A) Upon the request of the Prosecutor, and if satisfied that to do so would facilitate the arrest of an accused who may move from State to State, or whose whereabouts are unknown, a Judge may address a warrant of arrest to any third State, as well as any relevant international body including the International Criminal Police Organisation (INTERPOL).

(B) The Registrar shall transmit such a warrant to the national authorities of such States, or to the relevant international body, as may be indicated by the Prosecutor.

TRIAL CHAMBERS DECISIONS

- **Rule 56: Warrant of Arrest to Third States – Cooperation of Third States – Ad Hoc Arrangements**

R56-TC-1
o *Prosecutor v. Taylor*, Case No. SCSL-03-01-I, Warrant of Arrest and Order for Transfer and Detention, 7 March 2003:[63]

To: The Governments of all States.

[...]

HEREBY ORDERS THE REGISTRAR OF THE SPECIAL COURT

(A) to invite such States to enter into Agreements or ad hoc arrangements which may facilitate the **SEARCH, ARREST AND TRANSFER** to the Special Court of the Accused in accordance with Rule 58;

HEREBY REQUESTS ALL STATES CONCERNED

(A) to assist and facilitate the Office of the Prosecutor of the Special Court, at any location, in the search for and seizure of all evidence related to the crimes alleged to have been committed by the Accused;

---

[63] See also *Prosecutor v. Sankoh*, Case No. SCSL-03-02-I, Warrant of Arrest and Order for Transfer and Detention, 7 March 2003; *Prosecutor v. Koroma*, Case No. SCSL-03-03-I, Warrant of Arrest and Order for Transfer and Detention, 7 March 2003; *Prosecutor v. Bockarie*, Case no. SCSL-03-04-I, Warrant of Arrest and Order for Transfer and Detention, 7 March 2003.

[...]

A Member of the Office of the Prosecutor may be present from the time of arrest.

- **Rule 56: Warrant of Arrest to Third States – All States and INTERPOL**

R56-TC-2
o *Prosecutor v. Taylor*, Case No. SCSL-03-01-I, Warrant of Arrest and Order for Transfer and Detention, 7 March 2003:[64]

To: The Governments of all States.

[...]

HEREBY ORDERS THE REGISTRAR OF THE SPECIAL COURT

to address this Warrant of Arrest, Decision Approving the Indictment, the Approved Indictment of the accused and a Statement of the Rights of the Accused to the national authorities of such States, or to the relevant international body, including the International Criminal Police Organisation (INTERPOL), as may be indicated by the Prosecutor in accordance with Rule 56;

R56-TC-3
o *Prosecutor v. Koroma*, Case No. SCSL-03-03-I, Warrant of Arrest and Order for Transfer and Detention, 25 November 2003:

CONSIDERING ALSO the Co-Operation Agreement between the International Criminal Police Organisation – INTERPOL and the Special Court for Sierra Leone dated 3rd day of November 2003 (hereinafter "the Agreement");

CONSIDERING Rule 56 of the Rules;

HEREBY ORDERS:

1. That JOHNNY PAUL KOROMA, also known as JPK, be arrested immediately;

---

[64] See also *Prosecutor v. Sankoh*, Case No. SCSL-03-02-I, Warrant of Arrest and Order for Transfer and Detention, 7 March 2003; *Prosecutor v. Koroma*, Case No. SCSL-03-03-I, Warrant of Arrest and Order for Transfer and Detention, 7 March 2003; *Prosecutor v. Bockarie*, Case no. SCSL-03-04-I, Warrant of Arrest and Order for Transfer and Detention, 7 March 2003.

[...]

AND FURTHER ORDERS TO THE REGISTRAR OF THE SPECIAL COURT:

1. To address this Warrant of Arrest and Order, Decision Approving the Indictment, the Approved Indictment of the Accused and a Statement of the Rights of the Accused to the national authorities of such States and the International Criminal Police Organisation (INTERPOL) in accordance with Article 3 of the Agreement and Rule 56 of the Rules;

> **Rule 57: Procedure after Arrest**
> *(amended 7 March 2003)*
>
> Upon the arrest of the accused, the State concerned shall detain him, and shall promptly notify the Registrar. The transfer of the accused to the seat of the Special Court, or to such other place as the President may decide, after consultation with the Vice-President, the Prosecutor and the Registrar, shall be arranged by the State authorities concerned, in liaison with the authorities of the host country and the Registrar.

TRIAL CHAMBERS DECISIONS

- **Rule 57: Procedure After Arrest – Order to the Authorities of Sierra Leone**

R57-TC-1

o *Prosecutor v. Sesay*, Case No. SCSL-03-05-I, Warrant of Arrest and Order for Transfer and Detention, 7 March 2003:[65]

HEREBY ORDERS THE REGISTRAR OF THE SPECIAL COURT

[...]

(D) to remand the Accused, into the custody of the Special Court Detention Facility or such other Detention Facility as determined by the President in accordance with Rule 57.

HEREBY ORDERS THE RELEVANT AUTHORITIES OF THE GOVERNMENT OF SIERRA LEONE

(A) Promptly notify the Registrar of the Court of the arrest of the Accused for the purposes of effectuating his transfer to the custody of the Court, and to surrender the Accused to the Court without delay;

(B) To transfer the Accused to the custody of the Special Court without delay, or to such other place as the President may decide. The transfer shall be arranged between with the relevant national authorities of the Government of Sierra Leone and the Registrar of the Special Court;

---

[65] See also *Prosecutor v. Brima*, Case No. SCSL-03-06-I, Warrant of Arrest and Order for Transfer and Detention, 7 March 2003; *Prosecutor v. Kallon*, Case No. SCSL-03-07-I, Warrant of Arrest and Order for Transfer and Detention, 7 March 2003; *Prosecutor v. Norman*, Case No. SCSL-03-08-I, Warrant of Arrest and Order for Transfer and Detention, 7 March 2003.

(C) To assist and facilitate the Office of the Prosecutor of the Special Court, at any location, in the search for and seizure of all evidence related to the crimes alleged to have been committed by the Accused;

DECISIONS OF THE PRESIDENT

- **Rule 57: Procedure After Arrest – Transfer to ICTY/ICTR Detention Facility**

o *Prosecutor v. Koroma*, Case No. SCSL-03-03-I, Under Seal – Decision Modifying Location of Detention, 18 March 2003:

Pursuant to Rule 57 of the Rules of Procedure and Evidence of the Special Court, and after consultations with the Registrar and Judge King, Vice President, and having considered the exchange of letters between the Registrar of the Special Court and the Registrar of the International Criminal Tribunal for the former Yugoslavia;

I hereby direct that **JOHNNY PAUL KOROMA** be transferred to United Nations Detention Facility Detention Unit in The Hague, or alternatively in Arusha.

Rule 58: Transfer to the Special Court from Third States
(amended 29 May 2004)

The Special Court may request third States to arrest and transfer suspects and accused to the Special Court on the basis of an ad hoc arrangement, an agreement with such State or any other appropriate basis.

TRIAL CHAMBERS DECISIONS

- **Rule 58: Transfer to the Special Court from Third States – Request to Third States**

R58-TC-1

o *Prosecutor v. Taylor*, Case No. SCSL-03-01-I, Warrant of Arrest and Order for Transfer and Detention, 7 March 2003:[66]

To: The Governments of all States.

[…]

HEREBY REQUESTS ALL STATES CONCERNED

[…]

(B) to promptly notify the Registrar of the Special Court of the arrest if the Accused in accordance with Rule 57, for the purposes of effectuating his transfer to the custody of the Special Court, or to such other place as the President may decide, and to surrender the Accused to the Special Court without delay. The transfer shall be arranged by the State authorities concerned, in liaison with the authorities of the host country and the Registrar of the Special Court

A Member of the Office of the Prosecutor may be present from the time of arrest.

---

[66] See also *Prosecutor v. Sankoh*, Case No. SCSL-03-02-I, Warrant of Arrest and Order for Transfer and Detention, 7 March 2003; *Prosecutor v. Koroma*, Case No. SCSL-03-03-I, Warrant of Arrest and Order for Transfer and Detention, 7 March 2003; *Prosecutor v. Bockarie*, Case no. SCSL-03-04-I, Warrant of Arrest and Order for Transfer and Detention, 7 March 2003; *Prosecutor v. Koroma*, Case No. SCSL-03-03-I, Warrant of Arrest and Order for Transfer and Detention, 25 November 2003.

- **Rule 58: Transfer to the Special Court from Third States – Third States Have no *Locus Standi***

R58-TC-2

o *Prosecutor v. Taylor*, Case No. SCSL-03-01-I, Order Pursuant to Rule 72(E) Defence Motion to Quash the Indictment and to Declare the Warrant of Arrest and All Other Consequential Orders Null and Void, 19 September 2003:

CONSIDERING that the same Indictment has then been issued against the Accused personally and not against the Government of the Republic of Liberia;

[...]

CONSIDERING, in particular, that the Accused submits that the alleged primacy of the Special Court is limited to the national courts of the Republic of Sierra Leone and lacks the power to assert its primacy over national court of any third States as well as to request the surrender of an accused from any third State;

AND

GIVEN that the Accused, in light of the above, argues that the Indictment, the Warrant of Arrest and all other consequential Orders issued against him by the Special Court are in violation of the criminal immunity of the Head of the Sovereign State of the Republic of Liberia and contrary to the principles of customary international law and the jurisprudence of the International Court of Justice;

GIVEN, furthermore, that the Accused argues that the Indictment, the Warrant of Arrest and all other consequential Orders issued against him by the Special Court are in violation of the principle that a State may not exercise its authority on the territory of another State and the principle of sovereign equality among all Member States of the United Nations as laid down in Article 2, paragraph 1 of the Charter of the United Nations.

[...]

THE CHAMBER

FINDS that the Government of the Republic of Liberia has no *locus standi* to file such a preliminary motion nor to be a party to such a motion;

Rule 59: Failure to Execute a Warrant of Arrest or Transfer Order
(amended 29 May 2004)

(A) Where the Sierra Leone authorities, to whom a warrant of arrest or transfer order has been transmitted, are unable to execute the warrant of arrest or transfer order, they shall report forthwith their inability to the Registrar, and the reasons therefore.

(B) If, within a reasonable time after the warrant of arrest or transfer order has been transmitted to the Sierra Leone authorities, no report is made on action taken, this shall be deemed a failure to execute the warrant of arrest or transfer order and the Registrar may refer to the President to take appropriate action.

TRIAL CHAMBERS DECISIONS

- **Rule 59: Failure to Execute a Warrant of Arrest – Order to the Authorities of Sierra Leone**

R59-TC-1
o *Prosecutor v. Sesay*, Case No. SCSL-03-05-I, Warrant of Arrest and Order for Transfer and Detention, 7 March 2003:[67]

HEREBY ORDERS THE RELEVANT AUTHORITIES OF THE GOVERNMENT OF SIERRA LEONE

[. . .]

(F) if the relevant national authorities of the Government of Sierra Leone are unable to immediately execute the present Warrant of Arrest and Order for Transfer, as requested, the Government of Sierra Leone is requested to indicate the reason for its inability to effect thereto.

---

[67] See also *Prosecutor v. Brima*, Case No. SCSL-03-06-I, Warrant of Arrest and Order for Transfer and Detention, 7 March 2003; *Prosecutor v. Kallon*, Case No. SCSL-03-07-I, Warrant of Arrest and Order for Transfer and Detention, 7 March 2003; *Prosecutor v. Norman*, Case No. SCSL-03-08-I, Warrant of Arrest and Order for Transfer and Detention, 7 March 2003.

> **Rule 60: Trial in the Absence of the Accused**
> *(amended 1 August 2003)*
>
> (A) An accused may not be tried in his absence, unless:
>
> (i) the accused has made his initial appearance, has been afforded the right to appear at his own trial, but refuses so to do; or
>
> (ii) the accused, having made his initial appearance, is at large and refuses to appear in court.
>
> (B) In either case the accused may be represented by counsel of his choice, or as directed by a Judge or Trial Chamber. The matter may be permitted to proceed if the Judge or Trial Chamber is satisfied that the accused has, expressly or impliedly, waived his right to be present.

TRIAL CHAMBERS DECISIONS

- **Rule 60: Trial in Absence of Accused – Refusal to Attend Hearings**

R60-TC-1 o *Prosecutor v. Gbao*, No. SCSL-04-15-T, Ruling on the Issue of the Refusal of the Third Accused, Augustine Gbao, to Attend Hearing of the Special Court for Sierra Leone on 7 July 2004 and Succeeding Days, 12 July 2004, para. 7-11:[68]

> 7. In the Chamber's opinion, Rule 60 provides that, as a matter of law, the right of an accused person to be tried in his or her presence can be derogated from in two clearly-defined circumstances, to wit, (i) where he has made his initial appearance and has been afforded the right to appear at his trial but refuses to do so, or (ii) where, having made his initial appearance, he is at large and refuses to appear in court.
>
> 8. Interestingly, the law also provides that a trial can lawfully be continued in the absence of an accused person whose con-

---

[68] See *Prosecutor v. Norman, Fofana, Kondewa*, No. SCSL-04-14-T, Ruling on the Issue of Non-Appearance of the First Accused Samuel Hinga Norman, the Second Accused Moinina Fofana, and the Third Accused, Allieu Kondewa at the Trial Proceedings, 1st October 2004, para. 14-16; *Prosecutor v. Sesay, Kallon*, Case No. SCSL-05-15-PT, Ruling on the Issue of the Refusal of the Accused Sesay and Kallon to Appear for their Trial, 19 January 2005, para. 12-15.

duct at his trial has been disruptive. To this effect, is Rule 80(B) of our Rules which is in these terms:

> "The Trial Chamber may order the removal of an accused from the proceedings and continue the proceedings in his absence if he has persisted in disruptive conduct following a warning that he may be removed."

The Chamber, therefore, finds that, though in essence trial in the absence of an accused person is an extraordinary mode of trial, yet it is clearly permissible and lawful in very limited circumstances. The Chamber opines that it is a clear indication that it is not the policy of the criminal law to allow the absence of an accused person or his disruptive conduct to impede the administration of justice or frustrate the ends of justice. To allow such an eventuality to prevail is tantamount to judicial abdication of the principle of legality and a capitulation to a frustration of the ends of justice without justification.

9. Consistent with this reasoning, the Chamber also notes that in most national law systems, and especially in the common law jurisdiction, the general rule is that an accused person should be tried in his or her presence, but that exceptionally, courts of justice can have recourse to trial of an accused person in his absence where such an option becomes imperative but in limited circumstances. For example, in Canada it is open to a court to continue to try an accused person in his or her absence where he or she was present at the start of the trial, a situation that is on all fours with the instant situation with which this Chamber is confronted as a result of the Third Accused's refusal to appear for his trial. The Chamber further notes that in civil law systems, the practice is widespread for accused persons to be tried in their absence subject to certain procedural and due process safeguards, for example, proof of service of actual notice to attend.

10. From the Chamber's perspective, it is particularly noteworthy that the international law practice is on two levels: (i) the practice at the European Court of Human Rights ("ECHR") level and (ii) the practice at the International Criminal Tribunal for the former Yugoslavia ("ICTY") and International Criminal Tribunal for Rwanda ("ICTR") level. At the ECHR level, there is nothing in the jurisprudence of that Court to indicate that Articles 6(1) and 6(3)(c) of the European Convention on Human Rights providing basic legal guarantees for a person charged with crime have been construed in a manner suggesting the impermissibility of trial in absentia.[1] At the level of the ICTY and ICTR, the Chamber finds that the statutory provisions of these tribunals on the subject are akin to those of this Court, and that in so far as ICTY is concerned, to date no trial in the absence of an accused has been conducted. However, the ICTR has conducted one trial in the absence of an accused in the case of *Prosecutor v. Jean Bosco Barayagizwa*.[2]

In that case, the Accused boycotted his trial on the grounds that he "challenged the ability of the ICTR to render and [sic] independent and impartial justice due, notably, to the fact that it is so dependent on the dictatorial anti-hutu regime of Kigali"[3] It is perhaps, instructive to note that the similarity here evidences a trend in the sense that the Third Accused herein, Augustine Gbao, is boycotting the Special Court because he does not "recognize the Special Court" and due to, as he alleges "its political nature".

11. It is abundantly clear to the Chamber that the jurisprudence, evolving or past, points to the legal sustainability of trial *in absentia* in certain circumstances. Hence the Chamber's Orders which are based on our significant findings establishing the legal foundation for invoking Rule 60 (A)(i) of the Rules, which we take the liberty of reproducing *in extenso*, here, to wit:

(i) the Third Accused made his initial appearance on the Indictment upon which he is charged before the Court pursuant to Rule 61 of the Rules on 26 April 2003;

(ii) the Third Accused did appear for his trial on 5 and 6 July 2004;

(iii) the Third Accused has been afforded the right to appear at his trial;

(iv) the Third Accused was present in Court on 6 July 2004 when the matter was adjourned to 7 July 2004;

(v) the Third Accused was fully notified on the morning of 7 July 2004 by Johannes Wagenaar that he should attend court for the purpose of his trial but refused to do so;

(vi) the Third Accused appeared to Mr. Wagenaar on the morning of 7 July 2004 to be in good health."

---

[1] See *Ali Maleki v. Italy*, Communication No 699/1996 U.N. doc CCPR/C/667/669/1996 (27 July 1979) of the UN Human Rights Committee and *F. C. B. v. Italy*, European Court of Human Rights, 40/1990/231/297 (26 June 1991).
[2] Decision on Defence Counsel Motion to Withdraw, Case No ICTR-97-19-T, 2 November 2000.
[3] Id. para 5.

R60-TC-2   o *Prosecutor v. Norman, Fofana, Kondewa*, No. SCSL-04-14-T, Ruling on the Issue of Non-Appearance of the First Accused Samuel Hinga Norman, the Second Accused Moinina Fofana, and the Third Accused, Allieu Kondewa at the Trial Proceedings, 1st October 2004, para. 17, 22:

17. The Chamber, accordingly, emphasizes that it is settled law, nationally and internationally, that while an accused person has the right to be tried in his presence, there are circumstances under which a trial in the absence of the accused can be permitted. While due consideration must be given to ensure that all rights to a fair trial are respected, an Accused person charged with serious crimes who refuses to appear in court should not be permitted to obstruct the judicial machinery by preventing the commencement or a continuation of trials by deliberately being absent, after his initial appearance, or refusing to appear in Court after he has been afforded the right to do so, and particularly in circumstances as in this case, where no just cause, such as illness, has been advanced to justify the absence.

[. . .]

22. It is our considered judgment, therefore, that in the absence of any lawful excuse, and we find that there exists no such excuse, it would not be in the interests of justice to allow the Accused's deliberate absence from the courtroom to interrupt the trial. The Trial Chamber considers that any deliberate absence from the trial proceedings will certainly undermine the integrity of the trial and will not be in the interests of justice.

- **Rule 60(B): Trial in Absence of Accused – Withdrawal of Counsel – Interim Representation by Co-Counsel**

R60-TC-3

o *Prosecutor v. Brima, Kamara, Kanu*, Case No. SCSL-04-16-T, Decision on the Confidential Application for Withdrawal by Counsel for Brima and Kamara and on the Request for Further Representation by Counsel for Kanu, 20 May 2005, para. 68-69:

68. We note that Rule 45(E) provides that *"[i]n the event of such withdrawal the Principal Defender **shall assign another Counsel**. . ."* This may or may not cause regrettable delays. Nevertheless, we note that this Court has established a Defence Office for exactly these situations. It is the duty of the Defence Office to support new Counsel and to introduce them to the case.

69. We are of the view that the rights of the Accused – in particular their right to be tried without undue delay as enshrined in Article 17 (4) (c) of the Statute – would best be served by directing Co-Counsel pursuant to Rule 60 (B) to represent the Accused on an interim basis until the respective Defence teams are complete again through the assignment of new Lead Counsel.

APPEALS CHAMBER DECISIONS

- **Rule 60: Trial in Absence of Accused – Refusal to Attend Hearings and to Be Represented**

R60-AC-1

o *Prosecutor v. Gbao*, Case No. SCSL-04-15-AR73, Decision on Appeal Against Decision on Withdrawal of Counsel, 23 November 2004, para. 52, 57–58:[69]

52. Where an accused is present in court but refuses to participate in the proceedings because he does not recognize the court and requests that his counsel do not participate for the same reason, the court should treat the accused as an absent accused and exercise its powers as if Rule 60 applied. Applying that Rule it would be inconsistent with the position taken by such accused to expect the accused to proffer a choice to be represented, in terms of Rule 60(B), "by counsel of his choice". The appropriate thing for the court to do in such circumstances is to ensure that the accused is represented, also in terms of Rule 60(B), as directed by the Trial Chamber. In these circumstances, the Trial Chamber, comprising professional judges, pro-ceeds in the knowledge and awareness that counsel is acting without instructions from the accused when it directs that counsel continue to provide representation whether as 'assigned counsel' or 'court appointed counsel'. While Rule 60(B) could have been drafted to indicate various options open to the Judge or Trial Chamber in terms of the type of representation, this is left to the Judge or Trial Chamber's discretion.

[...]

57. As to the first form of relief, the rights which an accused has in regard to the conduct of his defence in terms of Article 17(4)(d) of the Statute are: (i) to defend himself or herself in person; or (ii) to defend himself or herself through legal assistance of his or her own choosing; and (iii) to have legal assistance assigned to him or her, in any case where the interests of justice so require.

58. The first two are within his choice but not the third. The law does not recognise a right "not to have counsel assigned" to an accused who has refused to exercise the choice available to him under (i) and (ii).

---

[69] See also *Prosecutor v. Brima, Kamara, Kanu*, Case No. SCSL-04-16-T, Decision on the Confidential Application for Withdrawal by Counsel for Brima and Kamara and on the Request for Further Representation by Counsel for Kanu, 20 May 2005, para. 67.

Rule 61: Initial Appearance of Accused and Plea
(amended 1 August 2003)

Upon his transfer to the Special Court, the accused shall be brought before the Designated Judge as soon as practicable, and shall be formally charged. The Designated Judge shall:

(i) Satisfy himself that the right of the accused to counsel is respected, and in so doing, shall question the accused with regard to his means and instruct the Registrar to provide legal assistance to the accused as necessary, unless the accused elects to act as his own counsel or refuses representation;

(ii) Read or have the indictment read to the accused in a language he speaks and understands, and satisfy himself that the accused understands the indictment;

(iii) Call upon the accused to enter a plea of guilty or not guilty on each count; should the accused fail to do so, enter a plea of not guilty on his behalf;

(iv) In case of a plea of not guilty, instruct the Registrar to set a date for trial;

(v) In case of a plea of guilty, shall refer the plea to the Trial Chamber so that it may act in accordance with Rule 62.

TRIAL CHAMBERS DECISIONS

- **Rule 61: Initial Appearance – Accused Fitness to Plead and to Stand Trial**

R61-TC-1
o *Prosecutor v. Sankoh*, Case No. SCSL-03-02-I, Order for Further Physiological and Psychiatric Examination and Detention on Remand, 21 March 2003:

CONSIDERING the Prosecuting Counsel's oral request and submission made to me to enter a plea of 'Not Guilty' on behalf of the Accused;

[...]

NOW THEREFORE: I, Judge Benjamin Mutanga Itoe, considering that the Report recommends, *inter alia*, further examination of the Accused in order to better assess his present physiological and psychiatric condition and, in particular, to evaluate the future development of such condition,

DO HEREBY ORDER:

[...]

2. That the Accused be subjected to a further physiological and psychiatric examination, whose report should be conclusive and shall be subject to non disclosure excepting to Counsels for the Prosecution and the Defence until further Order, with a view to determining if the Accused is fit to plead and eventually to stand trial before the Special Court;

3. That the Prosecutor's submission for a plea of "Not Guilty" to be entered is overruled as it is premature and cannot be considered before a final medical report on the physiological and psychiatric condition of the Accused is made available for analysis by Counsels for the Prosecutions and the Defence;

R61-TC-2

o *Prosecutor v. Sankoh*, Case No. SCSL-03-02-PT, Decision on the Prosecution Motion to Allow Disclosure to the Registry and to Keep Disclosed Materials Under Seal Until Appropriate Protective Measures Are in Place, 17 April 2003, para. 5-7, 10:[70]

5. In its Order for Further Medical Examination of the Accused, following the Medical Report on the Accused and the parties' oral observations at the initial appearance of the Accused of the 21st of March, 2003, the Court ruled that the Accused be submitted to a further and final physiological and psychiatric examination with a view to determine if the Accused is fit to plead and to stand trial.

6. This order clearly suspends *sine die* the continuing of the initial appearance of the Accused. The proceedings will resume as soon as it become feasible to determine the medical status of the Accused and, in particular, to establish his fitness to enter a plea on the charges brought against him on the indictment.

7. This provision is confirmed by the rejection of the Prosecution oral submission at the initial appearance of the Accused on the 21st of March, 2003 for plea of not guilty to be entered on behalf of the Accused contained in the same Order for Further Medical Examination.

[...]

---

[70] See also *Prosecutor v. Sankoh*, Case No. SCSL-03-02-PT, Decision on the Prosecutor's Motion for Immediate Protective Measures for Witnesses and Victims and for Non-Public Disclosure, 23 May 2003, para. 6.

10. The Court therefore hereby confirms that the initial appearance of the Accused has not been concluded, pending fulfilment of the provisions contained in the Order for Further Medical Examination of the Accused and subsequent deliberations. Consequently, the Prosecution's requests contained in the Prosecution Motion for Disclosure are deemed premature and shall not be ruled upon until the initial appearance of the Accused shall have been concluded.

R61-TC-3

o *Prosecutor v. Sankoh*, Case No. SCSL-03-02-PT, Ruling on the Motion for a Stay of Proceedings Filed by the Applicant, 22 July 2003, pages 3-5, 7:

On the 15th of March, 2003, he made his initial appearance as an accused for a plea to be taken during a Pre-trial session of the Special Court for Sierra Leone in Bonthe, and this, in accordance with the provisions of Rules 28 and Rule 61 of the Rules of Evidence and Procedure of the Court.

Curiously enough, he was brought before me in a wheel chair. He looked tired, exhausted, pale feeble. He was apparently and indeed in a pitiful state. In a bid to verify his identity, I asked him if his name, as indicated on the indictment, was Foday Saybana Sankoh, also known as Popay, also known as Papa, also known as Pa. He did not even look up to face me. His face was inclined downwards. Each time he looked like he was trying to make an effort to raise his head as if he wanted to talk to me, he still dropped it downwards and finally never talked to me at all. He kept mute and provided no answer to all the questions I put to him in various forms, all of this intended to confirm his identity as a preliminary to his being called upon to take a plea. In fact, he remained embarrassingly indifferent and irresponsive.

At this stage, Duty Counsel, Barrister Mrs Hadijattou Kah Jallow, who had put in appearance for him, drew my attention to a letter she had addressed to the Court in which she highlighted the poor medical condition of her client and requested a physiological and psychological examination to be conducted on him before he could be called upon to plead. This letter, she said, was a sequel to and the result of the experiences she had had during her Counsel/Client relationship and briefings with the Applicant before his initial appearance.

[...] I accordingly ruled by granting the application and ordering, under the provisions of Section 74 *bis* of Rules of Procedure and Evidence, that the Applicant be subjected to a Physiological and Psychiatric examination. No plea was called or taken for very obvious reasons. [...]

[...] When the pre-trial proceedings resumed on the 21st of March, 2003, the Applicant still appeared before me in a wheel chair. I proceeded again to question him on his identity. This I did twice but he did not respond. I there and then resorted to calling in an interpreter to put these questions to him in Krio. 'Are you Mr. Foday Saybana Sankoh', I asked him. He remained irresponsive. At this stage, I called in the Registrar of the Court, Mr. Robin Vincent, to report on the state of the execution of my Order dated 15th March, 2003, for a medical examination to be carried out on the Applicant. He produced a report to this effect. When questioned on it, Dr. Verkaik stated that the report was inconclusive and that the Applicant needed to undergo a further and more detailed examination. [...]

Mrs Hollis [Counsel for the Prosecution] continued however, and urged me to rule, not only that the Applicant's identity was not in doubt and that a further verification was not necessary, but also and in addition, that a plea of 'Not Guilty' be entered for the Applicant, given the circumstances of the case at that stage.

[...] I upheld the Defence Counsel's objection and issued another Order, still for a further, but this time, a conclusive physiological and psychiatric examination of the Applicant whose results would enable me to determine whether he is fit to plead and to stand trial or not.

[...]

It is indeed my view, that it would be very premature and pretentious for a team of non-medical or paramedical actors in the judicial of scene like the Prosecution and the Defence or least still, the Presiding Judge, to conclude one way or the other at this stage and this, before the results of the medical examination on the Applicant become available. I in fact consider any attempt to conclude the issue at this stage one way or the other, to be a purely speculative exercise.

[...] Since the entry of the plea is a mandatory preliminary to the commencement of these proceedings, it stands to reason that pending the fixing of the date for a continued hearing, the Pre-trial process stands adjourned and suspended until the psychological and physiological condition stands adjourned and suspended until the psychological and physiological condition of the Applicant is verified and certified as either good or bad.

- **Rule 61: Initial Appearance – Role of the Plea**

R61-TC-4

o *Prosecutor v. Sankoh*, Case No. SCSL-03-02-PT, Ruling on the Motion for a Stay of Proceedings Filed by the Applicant, 22 July 2003, pages 5-7:

In taking this stand, I was and am still guided by a reverence to the importance a plea occupies in a criminal trial because it marks, after the filing of the indictment, the actual commencement of criminal proceedings which, in any event, cannot get underway without a plea having been entered.

It is indeed a cardinal principle of criminal law that entering a plea is the exclusive privilege of the accused. This prerogative cannot be delegated to anyone, not even to his Counsel, for, when the trial begins, he and he alone is stigmatised as the culprit. He and he alone holds the secret as to who committed the offence, indeed as to whether he committed the offence or not. He has two options: to plead guilty or not guilty in the full exercise of this fundamental Human Right of his. In so doing, he must fully understand and appreciate the nature and the consequences of the plea he is entering. In this regard, he must be seen to be sane and lucid and must equally be seen, not only to have pleaded, but also to have fully understood the nature and the consequences of the plea he has taken and on which his trial or subsequent proceedings will be based.

LORD READING in the case of *R vs Lee Kun* 11 C.A.R at page 293, had this to say to lend credence to this trend of thought:

'The reason why the accused should be present at the trial is that he may hear the case made against him, and have the opportunity of answering to it; the presence of the accused means not merely that he must be physically present and in attendance but also that he must be capable of understanding the nature of the proceedings',

indeed, I would add, the nature of the charges brought against him.

In fact, the Applicant's presence in Court is ineffective and immaterial in so far as it is least presumed for now, and pending the results of the medical examination, that there is no cause to believe that he is fit to plead. I agree with the Defence Counsel when she submits that the preliminary issue to be determined is whether the Applicant is fit to plead or not. In this regard, the test to guide our practice and relevant in determining issues of this nature and which was enunciated in the case of *R. v. Prichard* (1836) 7 C&P Page 303 is, 'whether the Defendant was of sufficient intellect to comprehend the course of the Proceedings of the trial so as to make a proper Defence, to challenge a juror to whom he might wish to object and to understand the details of the evidence if there was no certain mode of communication to the Defendant, the details of the evidence so that he could clearly understand them and be able to properly make his Defence to the charge against him'.

- **Rule 61: Initial Appearance – Accused Refusal to Enter a Plea**

R61-TC-5

o *Prosecutor v. Sankoh*, Case No. SCSL-03-02-PT, Ruling on the Motion for a Stay of Proceedings Filed by the Applicant, 22 July 2003, pages 7-8:

> Since the entry of the plea is a mandatory preliminary to the commencement of these proceedings, it stands to reason that pending the fixing of the date for a continued hearing, the Pre-trial process stands adjourned and suspended until the psychological and physiological condition stands adjourned and suspended until the psychological and physiological condition of the Applicant is verified and certified as either good or bad.
>
> If the former were to be the case, it could probably be concluded that there is a credible reason to believe that the consistent conduct of irresponsiveness of the Applicant is a design to enable him evade a trial, in which event, a plea of 'Not Guilty' may automatically be entered at that stage in his favour to enable the trial to proceed.

- **Rule 61(iv): Initial Appearance – Date for Trial**

R61-TC-6

o *Prosecution v. Sesay*, Case No. SCSL-03-05-I, Scheduling Order, 22 March 2003:[71]

> **NOW THEREFORE:** I, Judge Benjamin Mutanga Itoe, considering the need to coordinate the Parties and the Registrar for the disposal of all pre-trial issues and formalities with a view to eventually fix a date for the trial of the Accused, pursuant to Rule 61(A)(iv) of the Rules,
>
> **HEREBY INSTRUCT** the Registrar to concert with the Office of the Prosecutor and the Defence Counsels in

---

[71] See also *Prosecution v. Kallon*, Case No. SCSL-03-07-I, Scheduling Order, 22 March 2003.

order to fix dates for the Pre-Trial Conference and eventually for the commencement of the trial of the Accused;

CONSEQUENTLY ADJOURN the matter to dates that would have been so fixed by the Registrar,

ORDER that the dates so fixed be duly communicated to the Court and all the Parties before the hearings.

APPEALS CHAMBER DECISIONS

- **Rule 61: Initial Appearance – Further Appearance – Discretion to Permit if Requested**

R61-AC-1   o *Prosecutor v Norman, Fofana, Kondewa*, Case No. SCSL-04-14-AR73, Decision on Amendment of the Consolidated Indictment, 16 May 2005, para. 73:

73. We should point out, because some submissions seem to misunderstand the position, that a further appearance and plea is simply a formal act by which a count in an Indictment is read to the defendant in open court by the clerk, and he is asked to answer with his plea, normally "guilty" or "not guilty", which is thereupon recorded. It is by no means a "once and for all" process: very often the defendant at a later stage will ask for the Indictment to be "put again" in order to change a plea to "guilty". If he has been properly advised by Counsel, the court will rarely hesitate to grant his request. An application to change a "guilty" plea to "not guilty" will, however, be carefully scrutinised. But there is no reason in principle why a defendant's request to further appear pursuant to Rule 61 on an unamended consolidated Indictment should be refused. It is not required by the Rules but it is a short formality that cannot prejudice the Prosecution and on this basis the Trial Chamber had a discretion to permit further appearance if requested.

Rule 62: Procedure upon Guilty Plea
(amended 29 May 2004)

(A) If an accused pleads guilty in accordance with Rule 61(v), or requests to change his plea to guilty, the Trial Chamber shall satisfy itself that the guilty plea:

  (i) is made freely and voluntarily;
  (ii) is an informed plea;
  (iii) is unequivocal;
  (iv) is based on sufficient facts for the crime and accused's participation in it, either on the basis of independent indicia or of lack of any material disagreement between the parties about the facts of the case.

(B) Thereafter the Trial Chamber may enter a finding of guilt and instruct the Registrar to set a date for the sentencing hearing.

TRIAL CHAMBERS DECISIONS

- **Rule 62: Procedure upon Guilty Plea – Contempt Proceedings**

R62-TC-1

o *Prosecutor v. Brima (Margaret), Jalloh, Kamara (Ester), Kamara (Anifa)*, Case No. SCSL-05-02, Findings and Scheduling Order Pursuant to Rule 62, 27 July 2005:[72]

CONSIDERING that, at the said hearing, the Alleged Contemnors Margaret Fomba Brima, Neneh Binta Ba Jallow and Ester Kamara have informed me that they intended to change their plea of not guilty and enter a guilty plea to the charge against them as contained in the *Order in Lieu of the Indictment*;

CONSIDERING that the Independent Counsel does not oppose to this change of plea;

BEING SATISFIED that the guilty plea entered by each and every one of the Alleged Contemnors has been made freely and voluntarily, has been discussed by each of them with their respective defence counsel, that their guilty plea is unequivocal and based on sufficient facts for the crime and the

---

[72] See also *Prosecutor v. Kamara (Anifa)*, Case No. SCSL-05-03, Findings and Scheduling Order Pursuant to Rule 62, 21 September 2005.

Alleged Contemnors' participation in it, as contained in the *Order in Lieu of the Indictment*;

PURSUANT to Rule 54, 62, 77, and 82 of the Rules;

I DO HEREBY

ENTER A FINDING OF GUILT against Margaret Fomba Brima, Neneh Binta Ba Jallow and Ester Kamara on the charge against them contained in the *Order in Lieu of the Indictment*, and consequently

ORDER that the trial against Margaret Fomba Brima, Neneh Binta Ba Jallow and Ester Kamara shall be adjourned for a sentencing hearing on the 21st of September, 2005 at 2:30 pm;

> **Rule 64: Detention on Remand**
> *(amended 29 May 2004)*
>
> Upon his transfer to the Special Court, the accused shall be detained in the Detention Facility, or facilities otherwise made available pursuant to Rule 8(C). The Registrar, in a case where he considers it necessary, may order special measures of detention of an accused outside the Detention Facility. The order of the Registrar shall be put before the President for endorsement within 48 hours of the order being issued.

TRIAL CHAMBERS DECISIONS

- **Rule 64: Detention on Remand – International Standards of Detention – Verification by the International Committee of the Red Cross**

R64-TC-1

o *Prosecutor v. Norman*, SCSL-04-14-T, Decision on Request by Samuel Hinga Norman for Additional Resources to Prepare His Defence, 23 June 2004, para. 20:

> 20. According to the findings of the Registrar, the standard applied for exercise and food for detainees at the Detention Facility is in conformity with prescribed international standards verified from time to time by the International Committee for the Red Cross. The Trial Chamber accordingly finds no merit in these requests.

- **Rule 64: Detention on Remand – Restrictions and Supervision on Visits to Detainees**

R64-TC-2

o *Prosecutor v. Brima, Kamara, Kanu*, Case No. SCSL-04-16-T, Decision on Joint Defence Motion for General Orders Pursuant to Rule 54, 28 July 2005, para. 24-25, 29-31:

> 24. Under Rule 41 of the Rules of Detention, the Chief of Detention, in consultation with the Registrar, has the power to impose such restrictions and supervision on visits to detainees as he may deem necessary in the interests of the administration of justice or the security and good order of the Detention Facility. All visitors are obliged to comply with the separate requirements of the visiting regime of the Detention Facility, which may include personal searches, and any person who refuses to comply with such requirements shall be refused access.

25. One such requirement is the completion of a Visitors Declaration and Application Form, wherein the visitor provides personal information such as his or her name, address, date and place of birth, the name of the Detainee to be visited, his or her relationship to the Detainee, as well as proof of identity and a declaration as to criminal antecedents. By signing the Form, the visitor authorizes the Special Court to check the information given by the visitor. The visitor also certifies that all information is true and that any omission or false information will result in the immediate denial of the visiting application.

[...]

29. The visitors may not have liked the formalities with which they had to comply, but there is no support for the Defence submission that the rights of the Accused to a fair trial were interfered with.

30. Further, the given facts do not entitle us to find that any potential Defence witness was interfered with or intimidated, or that any security officer of the Special Court misused information given by the visitors or exceeded his or her authority in any way.

31. We note that the Defence did not avail itself of the complaints procedure provided by the Rules of Detention. Under Rule 59, each Detainee or his Counsel may make a complaint to the Chief of Detention or his representative at any time. If not satisfied with the response, the Detainee has the right to make a written complaint, without censorship, to the Registrar, who is obliged to deal with the complaint promptly and to reply without undue delay.

- **Rule 64: Detention on Remand – Detainee's Visit on his Mother's Grave**

R64-TC-3

o *Prosecutor v. Kanu*, Case No. SCSL-04-16-T, Decision on the Defence Motion for the Temporary Provisional Release to Allow the Accused Santigie Borbor Kanu to Visit His Mother's Grave, 18 October 2005, para. 1-2, 12:

1. On 24 June 2005 the Defence approached the Registrar requesting that the Accused Santigie Borbor Kanu be permitted to visit his ailing mother. Although the accused was not granted permission to leave the Detention Unit of the Special Court, the Registrar instead made arrangements for Mr. Kanu's mother to visit her son at the Detention Unit on 26 June 2005. In July 2005 the Defence made a second request to the Registrar for the accused Kanu to visit his mother as her

health was deteriorating and she was no longer able to travel to the Detention Unit to see her son. Mr. Kanu did not get a response to this request. On 2 September 2005 Mr. Kanu's mother passed away and the accused was informed accordingly. Upon receipt of the news, Mr. Kanu requested the Registrar for permission to attend his mother's funeral. The Registrar declined the request on the grounds that "in view of the risk assessment made in respect of the security arrangements which would need to be in place to ensure both his custodial status and his safety, it is not recommended that he be allowed out of the Detention Facility." Accordingly the accused Kanu did not attend his mother's funeral which took place on 2 September 2005.

2. Following his inability to attend his mother's funeral, the Accused Santigie Borbor Kanu filed this Motion requesting for "*temporary provisional release*" from custody to enable him to visit the grave of his late mother in order to pay his last respects as he was unable to attend the funeral.

[. . .]

12. [. . .] We therefore agree with the submissions of the Registrar that the Motion is misconceived and wrongly filed under Rule 65 of the Rules. In reality Mr. Kanu's application is one for an order for special measures of detention outside the Detention Facility under Rule 64 of the Rules. In that regard we also agree that the proper functionary to make such an order is the Registrar with the approval of the President of the Special Court.

DECISIONS OF THE PRESIDENT

- **Rule 64: Detention on Remand – Generalities**

R64-P-1

o *Prosecutor v. Norman*, Case No. SCSL-03-08-PT, Decision on Motion for Modification of the Conditions of Detention, 26 November 2003, para. 3, 6, 13:

3. All indictees arrested in Sierra Leone or transferred there after arrest abroad must initially be detained in the facilities run by the Special Court administration. Rule 64, inherited from the International Criminal Tribunal for Rwanda ("ICTR") under Article 14 of the Statute, originally provided:

Upon his transfer to the Special Court, the accused shall be detained in the facilities of the Special Court, or facilities otherwise made available pursuant to Article 22 of the Statute. The President may, on the application of a party or the Registrar, order special measures of detention of an accused.

This was the rule as it existed when the application was made on 23 July this year. It gave the President the power to order "special measures of detention", i.e. special ways of treating a particular prisoner who was detained within the facility. The prisoner himself, for example, might seek an order for solitary confinement or special medical treatment while the Registrar might make a request for CCTV surveillance of a cell for a "suicide watch" or where there was suspicion of a plan of escape. It was, in my view, a rule which envisaged the ordering of a special regime for a prisoner confined within the detention facility or else (e.g. if being treated in a hospital) being guarded by and remaining in the custody of the Special Court. It did not empower the President to order bail, which is a measure of provisional liberty to be dealt with under Rule 65.

[...]

6. At the second plenary, Rule 64 was amended so that it would best serve a court where the President, who is an Appeals Chamber judge, would not be in full-time office until after the first trial had ended. Except in these very serious matters for which the Rules of Detention provide for Presidential involvement, "special measures" could be approved by any judge – normally by one of the three full-time and resident Trial Chamber judges. Moreover, in keeping with the policy that detention is a matter for administrative rather than judicial decision, any order for such exceptional measures should be made by the Registrar. In order to protect the detainee, if subjected to them without consent, the Registrar is required to seek judicial endorsement within 48 hours of imposing the measure. Rule 64 (Detention on Remand) now reads:

> Upon his transfer to the Special Court, the accused shall be detained in the facilities of the Special Court, or facilities otherwise made available pursuant to Article 22 of the Statute. The Registrar, in a case where he considers it necessary, may order special measures of detention of an accused. Such special measures shall be put before a judge for endorsement within 48 hours.

[...]

13. [...] It will henceforth be right under amended Rule 64 where the Registrar's power to order "special measures" cannot be interpreted as a power to order conditional release or any measure which places a detainee outside the 24 hour control of the Head of Detention. Applications for conditional freedom must proceed under Rule 65, where they will receive the attention of the Chamber that is actually trying the accused, or of a resident Trial Chamber judge. [...]

- **Rule 64: Detention on Remand – Conditions of Detention**

R64-P-2

o *Prosecutor v. Norman*, Case No. SCSL-03-08-PT, Decision on Motion for Modification of the Conditions of Detention, 26 November 2003, para. 5, 7:

5. The actual administration of the conditions of detention must comply with the Rules of Detention,[1] which are designed to provide for a regime of humane treatment for unconvicted prisoners, subject to restrictions and discipline necessary for security, good order, and for the fairness of ongoing trials. They should conform with the provisions of the 1949 Geneva Conventions, suitably updated (the right to smoke cigarettes, for example, regarded as virtually inalienable in 1949, may be qualified because of more recent health concerns about fellow detainees).[2] The Detention Rules give necessary powers to the Head of Detention, subject to direction by the Registrar. Judges have no part in administering or ordering these rules, although in three difficult or urgent situations the President does have a role to order a report into the death in custody of an indictee (Rule 24(c)); to approve any order by the Registrar for cell video surveillance which order lasts longer than 14 days (Rule 26); and to hear appeals by a detainee from any decision to deny him contact with any person (Rule 48). These are serious situations where it is right that the President, as head of the Special Court, should oversee the Registrar. Otherwise, judges are not inolved in administrative detention matters unless they impact significantly upon the right under Article 17(4)(b) of the Statute to adequate preparation of the defence, when they may be raised by motion before the Trial Chamber judges who are best placed to make such a determination.

[...]

7. The prisoner remains in detention under Rule 64 and the Rules of Detention when transferred to holding areas prior to entry into court or outside the prison for medical treatment (even if placed for a lengthy period in hospital) and in the courtroom itself while being tried. [...]

---

[1] Rules governing the detention of persons awaiting trial or appeal before the Special Court for Sierra Leone or otherwise detained on the authority of the Special Court for Sierra Leone, 7 March 2003, as amended 25 September 2003.

[2] See Article 26 of Convention (III) relative to the treatment of prisoners of war, Geneva, 12 August 1949.

- **Rule 64: Detention on Remand – House Arrest**

R64-P-3

o *Prosecutor v. Norman*, Case No. SCSL-03-08-PT, Decision on Motion for Modification of the Conditions of Detention, 26 November 2003, para. 4, 12:

4. A distinction, upon which this application will turn, should be simple to understand and apply, once the ambiguity of the phrase "house arrest" is recognised and removed. Some "house arrests" involve round-the-clock guards from the detaining power, albeit in the more comfortable surrounds of a private house rather than a prison cell. The other form of "house arrest", for example that served in Britain by General Pinochet, requires residence in a private house outside the control of any prison authority, but subject to conditions such as the surrender of passport and reporting to police. It is this second, Pinochet-style form of "house arrest" that the applicant seeks and it is of course (as in Pinochet's case) a form of conditional bail rather than a "special measure of detention". The essential distinction between "house arrest" and conditional bail involving a form of house arrest is the presence or absence of the detaining authority as the power controlling the movements of the detainee. The applicants have not put before me any approval to their desired course from the Head of Detention. His ability to operate a control regime would be essential before I could consider any application under old Rule 64 for a variation in the place and conditions of detention.

[. . .]

12. The applicant justified his "innovative" use of the old Rule 64 on the basis of a decision of Judge Cassese, when President of the International Criminal Tribunal for the Former Yugoslavia (ICTY), to use his powers under that Rule to order that General Blaskic be permitted to reside outside the Court and to spend some nights with his wife and children.[1] Having examined the *Blaskic* case, I do not think that it assists. It is briefly reported, and does not fully describe the regime which is being approved. I am told that it proved impractical in any event. There was some background – the President said that the General's "voluntary surrender deserved some recognition" and that "house arrest is a form of detention"[2] – but as I have pointed out in paragraph 4 above this depends on what is meant by the ambiguous phrase "house arrest". The Pinochet style of house arrest is emphatically not a form of detention; it is a form of conditional bail. The issue turns on whether the indictee remains under the control of the detention unit and that fact is not clear from the *Blaskic* decision. There was a subsequent decision dealing with security arrangements, from which it may be inferred

that the accused was in fact to be guarded whilst at home. This fact would eliminate the case as a precedent for this application which as I have indicated is one for bail with a condition (amongst others) of residence at a particular address. That comparable applications have always been made and dealt with as applications for bail (or for "provisional release" as bail is there described) is apparent from many other ICTY and ICTR cases.[3]

---

[1] *Prosecutor v Tihomir Blaskic*, Case No. IT-95-14-T, Decision of the President on the Defence Motion filed pursuant to Rule 64, 3 April 1996.
[2] Ibid., para. 3(d).
[3] See e.g. *Prosecutor v Bagosora*, Case No. ICTR-98-41-T, Decision on Defence Motion for Release, 12 July 2002; Prosecutor v Brdanin, Case No. IT-99-36-PT, Decision on Motion by Radoslav Brdanin for Provisional Release, 25 July 2000; *Prosecutor v Mrda*, IT-02-59-PT, Decision on Darko Mrda's Request for Provisional Release, 15 April 2002; *Prosecutor v Ademi*, Case No. IT-01-46-PT, Order on Motion for Provisional Release, 20 February 2002; *Prosecutor v Jokic*, Case No. IT-01-42-PT, Order on Miodrag Jokic's Motion for Provisional Release, 20 February 2002; *Prosecutor v Brdanin and Talic*, Case No. IT-99-36-PT, Decision on Motion by Momir Talic for Provisional Release, 28 March 2001.

- **Rule 64: Detention on Remand – Hospitalisation**

  R64-P-4

  o *Prosecutor v. Sankoh*, Case No. SCSL-03-02-I, Order Modifying Condition of Detention, 29 March 2003:

  CONSIDERING that the medical condition of the Accused has deteriorated and now requires urgent medical treatment at a suitable hospital;

  CONSIDERING the Registrar's urgent oral application pursuant to Rule 64 of the Rules for the transfer of the Accused to the United Nations Hospital in Freetown on the ground of medical emergency;

  CONSIDERING that the transfer of the Accused to a hospital will require him, as feasible, to be segregated from other patients of the hospital;

  THANKING the offer of the Deputy Special Representative of the Secretary General for Sierra Leone identifying the United Nations Choithram Hospital in Freetown as a suitable location of the transfer of the Accused;

  NOW THEREFORE, pursuant to Rule 8, Rule 21 and Rule 64 of the Rules and pursuant to Rule 29 and Rule 32 of the Rules Governing the Detention of Persons Awaiting Trial or Appeal before the Special Court for Sierra Leone or Otherwise Detained on the Authority of the Special Court for Sierra Leone,

HEREBY ORDER the immediate transfer of the Accused to segregated quarters of the United Nations Choithram Hospital in Freetown with a view to provide him with all necessary medical treatment;

INSTRUCTS AND EMPOWERS the Registrar to take all the necessary measures for ensuring the medical treatment of the Accused and the necessary security during the period of hospitalization;

- **Rule 64: Detention on Remand – Rule of Detention 47(A) – Prohibition or Conditions on Communications and Visits – Power to Prohibit, Regulate or Set Conditions on Visits and Communications**

R64-P-5

o *Prosecutor v. Norman*, Case No. SCSL-04-14-RD47, Decision on Request to Reverse the Order of the Acting Registrar Under Rule 47(A) of the Rules of Detention of 6 June 2005, 29 June 2005, para. 10, 12, 19-20:

10. The Applicant does not provide for any authority supporting the submission that the power to prohibit, regulate or set conditions on visits and communications shall be exercised only in respect of specified visits or visitors, but not to prohibit visits generally. References in the Rule to "communications" and to "any other person" are, in the opposite, very broad and give support to general interdictions of the kind ordered by the Registrar in the Decision, which was therefore perfectly grounded.

[...]

12. Rule 47(A) of the Rules of Detention provides that the Registrar may prohibit, regulate or set conditions for communications and visits "if there are reasonable grounds for believing" that such a measure is necessary. Paragraph (G) of the same Rule further provides that the Detainee may request the President to reverse the decision of the Registrar. It results from the combination of these two sub-Rules that the "reasonable grounds" supporting a decision to prohibit, regulate or set conditions for visits and communications shall be specified, in order to provide the President with the reasons of the decision for his determination on the request to reverse.

[...]

19. The Decision is consistent with the dispositions of Rule 47(A) of the Rules of Detention as regards the nature of the sanction applicable to the breach, namely the suspension of the right to visits and communication. The *quantum* of the

sanction, namely the next 28 days from the date of the letter, was under the discretion of the Acting Registrar and does not appear to be manifestly disproportionate. The Applicant therefore fails to demonstrate any ground for reversing the Decision on that aspect.

20. [. . .] The Decision clearly states that the threat to the security and good order of the Detention Facility is constituted by the fact that the Applicant is "continuing unauthorised communications". Such unauthorised communications, by breaching the Registrar's regulations under Rule 47(A), undeniably threaten the good order of the Detention Facility, irrespective of their substance. The Decision was therefore grounded on this aspect.

- **Rule 64: Detention on Remand – Rule of Detention 47(C) – Prohibition or Conditions on Communications and Visits – Reasonable Grounds – Notification to the Accused – Presumption of Innocence**

R64-P-6

o *Prosecutor v. Norman*, Case No. SCSL-04-14-RD48, Decision on Motion to Reverse the Order of the Registrar Pursuant to Rule 48(C) of the Rules of Detention, 18 May 2004, para. 7, 10, 12:

7. On a proper construction of the Rule not only must the Prosecutor have 'reasonable grounds for believing that such contact' will result as listed, but the Registrar, or in cases of emergency, the Chief of Detention, must be satisfied that the Prosecutor has reasonable grounds for so believing, before granting the Prosecutor's request. *A fortiori*, the Prosecutor does not have to satisfy either the Registrar or the Chief of Detention (as the case may be) that one or other or all of the situations will result – it is enough if either is satisfied that the situations envisaged in Rule 48(A)(i) to (iv) are *likely* to result.

[. . .]

10. The necessity for swift action does not, however, excuse any failure to inform the Applicant of the Prosecutor's request in accordance with Rule 48(B). Although it is not stated in the Rule that the notification of a request by the Prosecutor must be given to the detainee prior to the notification of the Order of the Registrar, it is implicit in the Rule that the Registrar or Chief of Detention has the duty to inform the detainee of the request. Such notification will give an opportunity to the detainee to ask that the President deny or reverse the request of the Prosecutor. However, having regard to the fact that an

immediate reaction to the contents of the taped conversation was needed, it could not reasonably be said that the detainee's rights under Rule 48(C) were violated. The emergency situation outweighed the right to immediate notification. Furthermore, the Applicant has been provided with rapid notification by the Registrar of both request and order.

[. . .]

12. The Applicant has requested the disclosure of the alleged telephone conversation for transcription by his counsel through the use of independent experts. I refuse this request because it is sufficient that the Applicant has been provided with the transcript relied upon by the Prosecutor and Registrar especially as the restrictions ordered were of a short duration. It is not for the Applicant to prove that the conversation was incorrectly recorded. It is for the Registrar to demonstrate that he had reasonable grounds for believing, on the basis of the transcript before him, that action under Rule 48 was necessary as a matter of urgency. Furthermore as the transcript indicates that one of the Applicant's lawyers, "the female lawyer",[1] is part of the threatened action, the disclosure of the tape would not seem appropriate. The presumption of innocence is unaffected by the imposition of restrictions under Rule 48 which are simply regulatory and precautionary.

[1] Motion, Annex B.

- **Rule 64: Detention on Remand – Rule of Detention 47(G) – Prohibition or Conditions on Communications and Visits – Admissibility of Request and Procedure**

R64-P-7

o *Prosecutor v. Norman*, Case No. SCSL-04-14-RD47, Decision on Request to Reverse the Order of the Acting Registrar Under Rule 47(A) of the Rules of Detention of 6 June 2005, 29 June 2005, para. 7-8:

7. Under Rule 47(G) of the Rules of Detention, the request is admissible, since:

o the challenged decision was rendered by the Acting Registrar under Rule 47 of the Rules of Detention;
o there is no time limit for such a Request;
o the Request comes from the Detainee to whom the impugned decision was addressed.

8. Rule 47(G) of the Rules of Detention does not provide for any particular procedure to follow in the treatment of such request. Nor are applicable the dispositions of Rules 59-60 of

the Rules of Detention, which provide for a right to make complaints to the Chief of Detention and the Registrar. There is therefore no requirement to wait for a formal response from the Registrar on the Request which can be determined on the basis of the sole submissions from the Defence, and the answer sent by the Registrar to Norman's Counsel on 15 June 2005 which are part of the records.

Rule 65: Bail
(amended 7 March 2003)

(A) Once detained, an accused shall not be granted bail except upon an order of a Judge or Trial Chamber.

(B) Bail may be ordered by a Judge or a Trial Chamber after hearing the State to which the accused seeks to be released and only if it is satisfied that the accused will appear for trial and, if released, will not pose a danger to any victim, witness or other person.

(C) An accused may only make one application for bail to the Judge or Trial Chamber unless there has been a material change in circumstances.

(D) The Judge or Trial Chamber may impose such conditions upon the granting of bail to the accused as it may determine appropriate, including the execution of a bail bond and the observance of such conditions as are necessary to ensure the presence of the accused at trial and the protection of others.

(E) Any decision rendered under this Rule shall be subject to appeal in cases where leave is granted by a Single Judge of the Appeals Chamber, upon good cause being shown. Applications for leave to appeal shall be filed within seven days of the impugned decision.

(F) If necessary, the Trial Chamber may issue a warrant of arrest to secure the presence of an accused who has been granted bail or is for any other reason at large. The provisions of Section 2 of Part V shall apply.

(G) The Prosecutor may appeal a decision to grant bail. In the event of such an appeal, the accused shall remain in custody until the appeal is heard and determined.

(H) Appeals from bail decisions shall be heard by a bench of at least three Appeals Chamber Judges.

TRIAL CHAMBERS DECISIONS

- **Rule 65(B): Bail – "Liberty Rule, Detention Exception"**

  R65-TC-1   o *Prosecutor v. Fofana*, Case No. SCSL-04-14-T, Decision on Application for Bail Pursuant to Rule 65, 5 August 2004, para. 87-92, 97:

87. The perception of detention being the Rule and Liberty the exception appears to stem from the former formulation of Rule 65(B) of the Rules of Procedure and Evidence of the ICTY which provided that bail can only be granted "in exceptional circumstances." Following an amendment of the Rule, the phrase "exceptional circumstances" was deleted thereby creating the impression that the move was more towards making liberty the rule and detention the exception.

88. What is interesting however is that the Trial Chamber of the ICTY, even after that important amendment, still rendered a majority decision on the 8th of October 2001 in the case of the *PROSECUTOR VS MOMCILO KRAJISNIK AND BILJANA PLASVIC* to the effect that granting bail is the exception and detention the rule and further adopted the position that even when the Accused fulfils the criteria for granting bail, the Court is not bound to grant it.

89. This very important and interesting case which was decided on the basis of a majority decision or two of the Honourable Learned Judges with a dissenting opinion by His Lordship, Hon. Judge Patrick Robinson. Hon. Judge Robinson, to highlight his reasoning succinctly, is of the opinion that at no time should detention, as his Colleagues decided, be the rule, and liberty the exception. In so holding, he is of the opinion that the majority decision seriously compromises the right to liberty and is, to that extent, in contravention of International Customary Law principles and Conventions, particularly and amongst others, those of Article 9(3) of the International Covenant of Civil and Political Rights, (the ICCPR).

90. In yet another development which went contrary to the *MOMCILO KRAJISNIK* decision, the Trial Chamber of the ICTY in the case of the *PROSECUTOR VS BRANDIN* on provisional release, decided that since the phrase "exceptional circumstances" was deleted from the provisions of Rule 65(B), the presumption is that release will now remain the norm.

91. In the case of ILIJKOV VS BULGARIA, CASE NO 33977196 of the 26th of July, 2001, the European Court of Human Rights held that any system of mandatory detention or remand is per se, incompatible with Article 5(3) of the European Convention on Human Rights ("ECHR") which provides as follows:

> Everyone who is arrested or detained in accordance with the provisions of paragraph 1(c) of this article shall be brought promptly before a judge or other officer authorized by law to exercise judicial power and shall be entitled to trial within a reasonable time or to release pending trial. Release may be conditioned by guarantees to appear for trial.

92. As far as the contention that detention is the rule and liberty the exception is concerned, I am of the opinion that it is contrary to internationally entrenched principles of the presumption of innocence which are enshrined in Article 17(3) of the Statute of the Special Court, and embedded in principles of customary international law, and in particular, the provisions of Article 9(3) of the International Covenant on Civil and Political Rights (ICCPR) which provides as follows:

> It shall not be a general rule that persons awaiting trial shall be detained in custody but release may be subject to guarantees to appear for trial.

[...]

97. [...] [E]ven if it is conceded that the standards required in International Criminal Justice for the exercise of the discretion under Rule 65(B), because of the gravity of the offences and the penalties involved, are understandably placed on a very strict threshold, the liberty of the individual which is a very sacred, longstanding consecrated right is, and should, under either Customary International Law or Municipal law, continue to be and remain the Rule, and Detention, the exception.

- **Rule 65(B): Bail – Burden of Proof**

R65-TC-2 o *Prosecutor v. Brima*, Case No. SCSL-03-06-PT, Ruling on the Application for the Issue of a Writ of *Habeas Corpus* Filed by the Applicant, 22 July 2003:

In this regard, I would like to refer to a very well known principle that was laid down in the case of *Zamir vs the United Kingdom* 40 DR 42 at page 102 where it was decided that the burden of proving the legality of the detention rests on the State.

R65-TC-3 o *Prosecutor v. Kallon*, Case No. SCSL-04-15-PT, Decision on the Motion by Morris Kallon for Bail, 24 February 2004, para. 23, 25-33:[73]

23. The question of the burden of proof is closely linked to that of determining whether pre-trial detention is the rule or the exception in international criminal proceedings. If detention is the rule, thus the burden of establishing that detention is not required rests essentially with the Defence. If detention

---

[73] See also *Prosecutor v. Sesay*, Case No. SCSL-04-15-PT, Decision on Application of Issa Sesay for Provisional Release, 31 March 2004, para. 35-37.

is the exception, the burden of proof would normally belong to the Prosecution.

[...]

25. Bail, or provisional release, has been the subject matter of many decisions before both *ad hoc* International Tribunals and of one decision from the Special Court. Indeed, it has given rise to substantial debate. Traditionally, the position of the ICTY and the ICTR has been that bail is the exception and that, therefore, the burden of proof rests on the Defence. The Rules of Procedure and Evidence of the ICTY and the ICTR both included, at first, reference to "exceptional circumstances" that needed to be shown by the Defence in order for the Accused to be granted bail. This formulation suggests that bail is the exception and pre-trial detention the rule. However, in November 1999, the ICTY Judges amended Rule 65 on Provisional Release, relieving the Defence of the burden of proving "exceptional circumstances".[1] The reason behind this amendment appears to have been to bring the ICTY more in line with international human rights norms. The European Court of Human Rights has repeatedly held that the gravity of the charges cannot by itself serve to justify long periods of detention on remand. It also held that "shifting the burden of proof to the detained person in such matters is tantamount to overturning [...] a provision which makes detention an exceptional departure from the right to liberty".[2] Therefore, it is possible to deem after such amendment that pre-trial detention should not be the rule but, rather, the exception. This would seem to be confirmed by the decisions on bail rendered in December 2001 by Trial Chamber II of the ICTY in the case of *Prosecutor v. Hadžihasanović et al.*, where the Judges held that "*de jure* pre-trial detention should be the exception and not the rule as regard prosecution before International Tribunals".[3]

26. Nonetheless, the change in the ICTY Rule 65 did not result in immediate or even widespread success by accused in bringing motions for provisional release.[4] One of the major concerns of the ICTY Judges, in refusing to grant bail in other cases, has been the Tribunal's inability to execute arrest warrants on persons in the former Yugoslavia were they not to voluntarily appear for trial. In October 2001, for instance, in the case of *Momcilo Krajišnik*,[5] where despite the new reading of Rule 65, provisional release was still held to constitute the exception and the Judges retained discretion to deny bail even if the requirements were fulfilled by the Accused. The decision in this case, however, was not unanimous. Judge Patrick Robinson appended a dissenting opinion to the majority's decision, thereby denouncing what he called a "culture of detention" prevailing at the ICTY, that is "wholly at variance with the customary norm that detention shall not be the general rule".[6]

27. On the contrary, at the ICTR, the Judges at that time declined to amend Rule 65 in line with the amendment introduced by the ICTY. The Defence of several accused argued that because the proof of exceptional circumstances was no longer required before the ICTY, such should also be the case before the ICTR. This argument was not initially accepted by the Judges:

> concerning the argument that the Chamber should apply the Rule [65] as it appears at the ICTY, the Chamber recalls that Article 1 of the Statute establishes the Tribunal as separate and sovereign, with a competence *ratione materiae* and *ratione temporis* distinct from that of the ICTY. The Judges of the Tribunal are bound to apply the ICTR Rules.[7]

28. Despite such an initial approach, the ICTR Judges recently decided to amend the Rules during the 13th Plenary Session of 26-27 May 2003. In conformity with the ICTY provisions, the proof by the Defence of "exceptional circumstances" is now no longer required for bail to be granted.[8]

29. It would appear from the majority of the jurisprudence of both the ICTY and ICTR, however, that through the weighing process of the submissions of both parties, the burden of proof continues to rest on the Defence, and not on the Prosecution.[9] The removal of the "exceptional circumstances" requirement from Rule 65(B) of each set of Rules does not per se make detention the exception and provisional release the rule, but I would say that this was rather intended to lower the burden of proof by the Defence when attempting to establish that an accused should be provisionally released[10] by introducing a two-prong rather than a three-prong test.

30. In the case of *Prosecutor v. Miodrag Jokić* and *Prosecutor v. Rahim Ademi*,[11] the Trial Chamber of the ICTY held that, when dealing with a request for bail, the focus must be on the particular circumstances of each individual case without considering that the eventual outcome is either the rule or the exception. More explicitly, as stated in the *Mrdja* Decision, the Trial Chamber "must interpret Rule 65 of the Rules not *in abstracto* but with regard to the factual basis of the single case and with respect to the concrete situation of the individual applicant".[12] As a general rule, a decision to release an accused should be based on an assessment of whether public interest requirements outweigh the need to ensure respect for an accused's right to liberty,[13] as formulated in the two-prong test found in Rule 65(B).

31. Pursuant to Article 14 of the Statute of the Special Court, the Rules of the ICTR in force at the time of the establishment of the Special Court applied *mutatis mutandis*. However, Rule 65 was amended during the 2nd Plenary Meeting of the Special Court on 7 March 2003, in order to abolish the

requirement of "exceptional circumstances". I do consider that the approach of the two sister International Tribunals previously referred to should be followed in the best interest of both Parties. In support of this position, reference may be made to the recent decision on the Appeals Chamber of the ICTY on a motion for provisional release in the case of *Prosecutor v. Limaj et al.*, rendered on October 2003, in which it was held that:

> It is the Bench's view, contrary to the argument of the Defence, that the Trial Chamber did not err in not imposing the burden on the Prosecution to demonstrate that provisional release was inappropriate. First, Rule 65(B) does not place the burden of proof on the Prosecution. Pursuant to that Rule, the Trial Chamber was required to determine whether it was "satisfied" that [the Accused], if released would appear for trial. After taking into account the information submitted to it by the parties and weighing all the relevant factors, it held that it was not satisfied. There is no basis for holding that, by not placing the burden of proof on the Prosecution, the Trial Chamber erred in its application of Rule 65(B).[14]

32. Although not generally bound by jurisprudence of the other International Tribunals,[15] I concur with this position and, therefore, I find based upon the preceding review and analysis that it is for the Defence to show that further detention of the Accused is neither justified nor justifiable in the circumstances at hand.

33. The Prosecution is not, however, relieved from any obligation in connection with such an application for the bail. After hearing from the State and were the Defence to satisfy the two-prong test of Rule 65(B), i.e. the certainty that the Accused will appear to stand trial and that he will not pose any danger to victims and witnesses or other person, the Prosecution would then be compelled to submit some information or evidence to rebut or challenge as appropriate what has been submitted by the Defence and demonstrate that, indeed in the circumstances, the public interest requirement for pre-trial detention does outweigh the right of the Accused to be released.[16]

---

[1] See ICTY, Rules of Procedure and Evidence, IT/32/REV.17, 17 November 1999. The amendment of Rule 65(B) entered into force on 6 December 1999. Previous version of ICTR Rule 65(B) read as follows:
"Release may be ordered by a Trial Chamber only in exceptional circumstances, after hearing the host country and only if it is satisfied that the accused will appear for trial and, if released, will not pose any danger to any victim, witness or other person."

[2] See, for instance, the case of *Ilijkov v. Bulgaria*, ECHR Appl. 33977/96, 26 July 2001 ("*Ilijkov v. Bulgaria*"), at para. 85.

[3] *Prosecutor v. Hadžihasanović et al.*, IT-01-47-PT, Decision Granting

Provisional Release to Enver Hadžihasanović, 19 December 2001, para 7; *id.*, Decision Granting Provisional Release to Mehmed Alagić, 19 December 2001; *id.*, Decision Granting Provisional Release to Amir Kubura, 19 December 2001. Trial Chamber II of the ICTY reiterated its finding in subsequent decisions in other cases. See *Prosecutor v. Darko Mrdja*, Decision on Darko Mrdja's Request for Provisional Release, 15 April 2002 ("*Mrdja* Decision").[4] Provisional release has not been granted in any case before the ICTR. Motions for provisional release have been denied at the ICTY in numerous cases since the rule was changed. See., e.g., *Prosecutor v. Mile Mrksić*, IT-95-13/1-AR65, Decision on Appeal against Refusal to grant Provisional Release, 8 October 2002; *Prosecutor v. Dragan Obrenović*, IT-02-60-PT, Decision on Dragan Obrenović's Application for Provisional Release, 19 November 2002, upheld on appeal in IT-02-60-AR65.3 & AR.65.4, Decision on Applications by Blagojević and Obrenović for Leave to Appeal, 16 January 2003; *Prosecutor v. Naser Orić*, IT-03-68-PT, Decision on Application for Provisional Release, 25 July 2003; *Prosecutor v. Milan Milutonović et al.*, IT-99-37-PT, Decision on Provisional Release (Milan Milutinović), 3 June 2003 and Decision on General Ojdanić Third Application for Provisional Release, 16 December 2003; and *The Prosecutor v. Pasko Ljubičić*, IT-00-41-PT, Decision on the Defence Motion for Provisional Release of the Accused, 2 August 2002.

In those cases where provisional release has been granted, relevant factors in favour of granting provisional release have included: whether the accused voluntarily surrendered; whether the Prosecution supported the motion; and the nature of the guarantees offered by the State to which the accused will be released, as well as the compliance to date of that State. See, e.g., *The Prosecutor v. Miodrag Jokić*, IT-01-42-PT, Order on Miodrag Jokić's Motion for Provisional Release, 20 February 2002; *Prosecutor v. Sefer Halilović*, IT-01-48-PT, Decision on Request for Pre-Trial Provisional Release, 13 December 2001; *Prosecutor v. Momcilo Krajišnik and Biljana Plavsić*, IT-00-39 & 40-PT, Decision on Biljana Plavsić's Application for Provisional Release, 5 September 2001; *Prosecutor v. Obrenović and Jokić*, IT-02-53-AR65, Decision on Application for Provisional Release, 28 May 2002; and *Prosecutor v. Gruban*, IT-95-4-PT, Decision on Request for Provisional Release, 17 July 2002.

[5] *Prosecutor v. Momcilo Krajišnik and Biljana Plavsić*, IT-00-39 & 40-PT, Decision on Momcilo Krajišnik's Notice of Motion for Provisional Release, 8 October 2001 ("*Krajišnik* Decision").

[6] *Id.*, Dissenting Opinion of Judge Patrick Robinson, para. 22. Judge Robinson held that there must be "cogent reasons" for pre-trial detention, but found that this "does not mean that it is impermissible to impose a burden on an accused person awaiting trial to justify his release," *Id.* para. 7. See generally, paras 6-11 for a discussion on pre-trial detention under customary international law and in light of international human rights standards, and particularly the right to be presumed innocent.

[7] *Prosecutor v. Elie Ndayambaje*, ICTR-98-42-T, Decision on the Defence Motion for the Provisional Release of the Accused, Tr. Ch., 21 October 2001, para. 20; see also: *Innocent Sagahutu v. Prosecutor*, Decision on Leave to Appeal against the Refusal to Grant Provisional Release, App. Ch., 26 March 2003.

[8] ICTR, Rules of Procedure and Evidence, Adopted on 29 June 1995, as amended on 27 May 2003.

[9] See *Krajišnik* Decision, supra note 8, paras 11-12.

[10] See *Prosecutor v. Brdanin et al.*, IT-99-36-PT, Decision on Motion by Momir Talić for Provisional Release, 28 March 2001, para 17; *id.*, Decision on Motion by Radoslav Brdanin for Provisional Release, 25 July 2000, para. 12.

[11] *Prosecutor v. Miodrag Jokić* and *Prosecutor v. Rahim Ademi*, IT-01-42-PT and IT-01-46-PT, Orders on Motions for Provisional Release, Tr. Ch., 20 February 2002.

(12) *Mrdja* Decision, supra note 6, para. 29.
(13) Accordingly, in *Ilijkov v. Bulgaria*, supra note 5, at para 84, the Court reiterated that "continued detention can be justified in a given case only if there are specific indications of a genuine requirement of public interest which, notwithstanding the presumption on innocence, outweighs the rule of respect for individual liberty".
(14) *Prosecutor v. Limaj et al.*, IT-03-66-AR65, Decision on Fatmir Limaj's Request for Provisional Release, App. Ch., 31 October 2003, para 41. The Appeal was brought against the Trial Chamber decision denying the provisional release. See *id.*, IT-03-66-PT, Decision on Provisional Release of Fatmir Limaj, 12 September 2003.
(15) See *Prosecutor v. Issa Hassan Sesay*, SCSL-03-05-PT, *Prosecutor v. Alex Tamba Brima*, SCSL-03-06-PT, *Prosecutor v. Morris Kallon*, SCSL-03-07-PT, *Prosecutor v. Augustine Gbao*, SCSL-03-09PT, *Prosecutor v. Brima Bazzy Kamara*, SCSL-03-10-PT, *Prosecutor v. Santigie Borbor Kanu*, SCSL-03-13-PT, Decision on Prosecution Motions for Joinder, 27 January 2004, para 26.
(16) See also the *Brima* Ruling, supra note 1, pp. 9-10.

R65-TC-4

o *Prosecutor v. Fofana*, Case No. SCSL-04-14-T, Decision on Application for Bail Pursuant to Rule 65, 5 August 2004, para. 95:

95. Even though I contest the rather controversial trend that expressly makes detention the rule and liberty the exception, I think it is compelling to concede that in matters relating to bail, the burden of establishing that the Applicant has fulfilled the conditions laid down in Rule 65(B), lies on him as the person seeking to benefit from the exercise of the Court's discretion in favour of granting those measures in his favour. I am also however, of the opinion and do so hold in this matter, as I did in the Brima Bail Application, that the prosecution has an equally formidable burden of negating the facts advanced by the Defence and to demonstrate that the requisite conditions have neither been met nor would they be fulfilled by the Applicant.

- **Rule 65(B): Bail – Conditions – Generalities**

R65-TC-5

o *Prosecutor v. Kallon*, Case No. SCSL-04-15-PT, Decision on the Motion by Morris Kallon for Bail, 24 February 2004, para. 34-35, 40, 45:[74]

34. Applications for bail require a close review and careful consideration of the requirements of Rule 65 given that they

---

[74] See also *Prosecutor v. Sesay*, Case No. SCSL-04-15-PT, Decision on Application of Issa Sesay for Provisional Release, 31 March 2004, para. 39-40.

entail the risk of affecting the proceedings before the Special Court, as well as the risk of infringement upon the rights of the Accused. However, in so doing one should bear in mind that, in the specific nature of international tribunals, the crimes over which such tribunals have jurisdiction can be categorised as the most serious crimes under international law. Therefore, it can be said that the approach to bail that prevails in national courts of law may be different that that for an international tribunal, such as the Special Court.

35. This interpretation of the provisions of Rule 65 is consistent with that of the President of this Court, Judge Geoffrey Robertson, who, in a recent ruling – albeit one that is not binding on this case – relative to an application seeking modification of the conditions of detention of an Accused into a regime arguably close to that of bail, has stated that "[t]here is no presumption in favour of bail, which is understandable given the very serious nature of the crimes charged".[1]

[...]

40. As discussed above at length, before granting a motion for bail, I must be satisfied, after hearing the State to which the accused seeks to be released, that (a) the accused will appear for trial and (b) if released, the accused will not pose a danger to any victim, witness or other person. I will now, therefore, examine the question of whether the Accused will appear for trial if granted bail and whether the said will pose a danger to any victim, witness or other person if granted bail, basing my findings on the submissions of the Accused, the Prosecution and the Government of Sierra Leone.

[...]

45. Having not been satisfied that the Accused will appear for trial if granted bail, I find it unnecessary to examine in detail the question of whether the Accused will pose a danger to any victim, witness or other person if granted bail.

---

[1] *Prosecutor against Sam Hinga Norman*, SCSL-03-08-PT, Decision on Motion for Modification of Conditions of Detention, 26 November 2003, at para. 8.

R65-TC-6   o *Prosecutor v. Fofana*, Case No. SCSL-04-14-T, Decision on Application for Bail Pursuant to Rule 65, 5 August 2004, para. 61-63:

61. From these provisions, certain key elements that condition the granting of bail are apparent, namely:

(i) The granting of bail is a matter is entirely within either the discretion of the Judge or that of the Trial Chamber so seized of the Application.

(ii) The Judge or the Trial Chamber will grant bail only after hearing the State to which the Accused seeks to be released.
(iii) The Judge or the Trial Chamber in the exercise of that discretion in favour of the Accused, has to do so only if he is satisfied that the Accused will appear for trial. This requires that the Applicant furnishes legal, moral or material guarantees to assure the Judge or the Chamber that he will not escape if released on bail.
(iv) The Judge or the Trial Chamber, before ordering the release on bail, should also be satisfied that the Accused, if released, will not pose a danger to any victim or witness or other person.

62. It stands to reason therefore, that before exercising my discretion to grant this application or not, I must first be satisfied, considering all the circumstances of the case and the submissions and facts presented by the parties, that the Applicant who stands indicted for alleged command and direct responsibility for the offences alleged against him in the indictment, if released on bail will:

(a) appear for trial; and
(b) not pose a danger to any victim, witness or other persons.

63. In the determination of the application, it is prudent, I would observe, for the Judge or the Chamber to apply those criteria on a case to case basis and to ensure a balance between the public interest and the presumption of innocence of the Accused as enshrined in the provisions of Article 17(3) of the Statute. Further- more, in determining whether bail should be granted or not, I am of the opinion that the conditions laid down in Rule 65(B) should be read conjunctively and that if the Applicant fails to satisfy the Court that he meets all the conditions enumerated therein, the application should necessarily be refused.

- **Rule 65(B): Bail – Conditions – Appearance at Trial**

R65-TC-7

o *Prosecutor v. Kallon*, Case No. SCSL-04-15-PT, Decision on the Motion by Morris Kallon for Bail, 24 February 2004, para. 42-43:

42. The Accused puts forth various grounds to support his claim that he will appear for trial if granted bail. The Accused has provided assurances with respect to residence, movement and conduct, as well as financial sureties to a value of $85,000 USD. Such assurances and sureties are indeed indispensable when an accused decides to apply for bail. However, no matter the importance and certainty of the assurances and

sureties secured by the Accused, it is within the purview of the discretionary power of this Court to determine the real value and weight should be given to them.

43. The Accused has submitted several other grounds in his application, as summarized above, none of which, separately or cumulatively, have succeeded in convincing me that in the specific circumstances of the presence of the Special Court in Sierra Leone, particularly in light of the submissions by the Government of Sierra Leone, and the power of either Sierra Leone or the Court to execute arrest warrants,[1] he should be granted provisional release. I believe, however, that the reference by the Defence to the *Brima* Ruling, in this respect, should be addressed. Indeed, when arguing that the Accused's strong community ties in Sierra Leone constitute evidence of his willingness to appear for trial if he were released, the Defence contends that such community ties are among the "factors which are not incompatible with the spirit of the elements in Rule 65(B) and which are linked to the element of a possible flight of the accused".[2] However, after referring to the case of *Neumeister v. Austria* before the European Court of Human Rights,[3] in which it was held that in granting bail, it is relevant to consider the character of the person, his morals, his home, his occupation and his assets, such Ruling held that the Accused "did not exhibit any assets to show to the satisfaction of the Court, his stakes and attachment in the society to which he is seeking to be released".[4] Accordingly, I would like to state that I subscribe to these findings that community ties are indeed of importance when considering whether or not to grant bail, but I nevertheless find that in the present case the community ties alleged by the Defence on behalf of the Accused do not constitute sufficient foundation to meet the prescribed requirements for bail.

---

[1] See Response, paras 7-11.
[2] *Brima* Ruling, supra note n. 1, p. 11.
[3] European Court of Human Rights, *Neumeister v. Austria* 1EHRR 91.
[4] *Brima*, Ruling, supra note n. 1, p. 12.

R65-TC-8 o *Prosecutor v. Fofana*, Case No. SCSL-04-14-T, Decision on Application for Bail Pursuant to Rule 65, 5 August 2004, para. 65-71, 76-77:

65. The vital and more important question to be answered is whether the Accused, if released, will appear for trial.

66. In the case of *NEUMEISTER VS AUSTRIA*, it was stated that it is relevant in granting bail, to consider the character of the person, his home, his occupation and his assets.

67. In the application for bail for Alex Tamba Brima, one of the reasons for refusing it was that he did not exhibit any assets to show to the satisfaction of the Court, his stakes and attachment in the society to which he was seeking to be released. In this case, the Applicant, like Alex Tamba Brima, has failed to advance any proof of ownership of property to show his attachment to the society to which he is seeking to be released. The Defence even admits that he does not own a bank account.

68. I have taken cognisance of the guarantees he has offered in Counsel's submissions to back his application but these, to my mind, do not rise up to the expectation that would convince me to exercise the discretion in his favour.

69. The Trial Chamber of the ICTY in the case of *MOMCILO KRAJISNIK*, had this to say on undertakings like these and I quote:

> As to undertakings given by the Accused himself the Trial Chamber cannot but note that it given by a person who faces a substantial sentence if convicted and therefore has a considerable incentive to abscond.[1]

70. Furthermore, in the case of the *PROSECUTOR VS BLASKIC*,[2] the Trial Chamber of the ICTY observed that guarantees offered by General Blaskic are in no way sufficient to ensure that if released, he would appear before this International Tribunal; that the gravity of the crimes allegedly committed and the sentence which might be handed down justify fears as to the appearance of the Accused.

71. Mr. Fofana, the Applicant in this case who, it should be noted, is indicted for offences for which he could face a substantial term of imprisonment if found guilty, could have a considerable incentive to abscond as the hazards of flight could seem to be a lesser evil than continued imprisonment.

[...]

76. On the risk of flight, the Prosecution argues that the Special Court does not have the means to execute a warrant of arrest issued by it in the event of the flight of the released prisoner and that the local Sierra Leonean Police (assuming the indictee is still within the territory) does not posses sufficient resources and capabilities to re-arrest the fleeing indictee. In the *Brima, Sesay* and *Kallon*[3] motions for bail, this Chamber considered this factor to be very determining in exercising the discretion to grant bail or not, in view of the fragility of infrastructures relating to the maintenance of law and order in Sierra Leone.

77. In the case of the *PROSECUTOR VS BRDJANIN & TALIC*,[4] the Trial Chamber of the ICTY had this to say on this issue:

> ... the absence of any power in the Tribunal to execute its own arrest warrant upon an applicant in the former Yugoslavia in the event that he does not appear for trial, and the said tribunals need to rely upon local authorities within that territory or upon international bodies to effect arrests on its behalf, places a substantial burden upon any applicant for provisional release to satisfy the Trial Chamber the he will indeed appear for trial if released ...

---

[1] Prosecutor v. Krajisnik, Notice of Motion for Provisional Release, 8 October 2001.
[2] Prosecutor v. Blaskic, Decision Rejecting A Request for Provisional Release, 25 April 1996.
[3] *The Prosecutor v Tamba Alex Brima*, SCSL-03-06-PT, Ruling on a Motion applying for Bail or Provisional Release, 22 July 2003 ("*Brima* Ruling"); *Prosecutor v. Sesay, Kallon and Gbao*, SCSL-04-15-PT, Decision on the Motion by Morris Kallon for Bail, 24 February 2004 ("*Kallon* Decision"); *Prosecutor v. Issa Hassan Sesay,* Decision on Application of Issa Sesay for Provisional Release, 31 March 2004 ("*Sesay* Decision").
[4] *Prosecuor v. Brdjanin*, Decision on Motion by Radoslav Brdjanin for Provisional Release, 25 July 2000, para. 18.

- **Rule 65(B): Bail – Conditions – Gravity of the Offence**

R65-TC-9

o *Prosecutor v. Fofana*, Case No. SCSL-04-14-T, Decision on Application for Bail Pursuant to Rule 65, 5 August 2004, para. 72–74:

> 72. Even though it is not expressly provided for in Rule 65 of the Rules, it is discernable, from an examination of this Rule, that since the provision for a release on bail is tied to the condition that the Judge or Trial Chamber should be satisfied that the accused will appear for trial, it necessarily leads to concluding that a release on bail is and should also inextricably be conditioned by factors which are germane to the gravity of the offence for which the applicant is indicted, and the sentence that is likely to be meted out to him if convicted.
>
> 73. This consideration is important because it continuously lingers in the mind of the adjudicating Judge. In fact, even though neither the gravity of the offence nor the severity of the sentence can "in themselves" be used to justify a refusal to grant bail to an applicant who, at that stage, still benefits from the statutory provisions of Article 17(3) of the Statute that guarantee his innocence until he is proven guilty, they remain capital elements that are and should be taken into consideration in the process of examining applications for bail because of their affinity with the primary consideration of the likelihood of flight of the indictee.

74. Indeed, as was decided in the case of *STOGMULLER VS AUSTRIA 1 EHRR 155*, "on the risk that the indictee would fail to appear for trial, bail should be refused where it is certain that the hazards of flight would seem to be a lesser evil than continued imprisonment.

- **Rule 65: Bail – Conditions – Danger to Victims and Witnesses**

R65-TC-10
o *Prosecutor v. Sesay*, Case No. SCSL-04-15-PT, Decision on Application of Issa Sesay for Provisional Release, 31 March 2004, para. 54:

54. [...] The Prosecution in fact submits that the possible threat to victims and witnesses, as well as to other persons, deriving from a release of the Accused might now be further heightened. The fact that the Accused knows the potential evidence against him following the progress of the disclosure process might put him in a position to identify witnesses in support of the Prosecution case, despite the applicable orders for protective measures. As rightfully quoted by the Defence, the mere ability of the Accused to exert pressure upon any witness following disclosure of evidence by the Prosecution cannot alone affect his release on bail, as stated in the *Brdanin* Decision.[1] I concur with such findings. Indeed, the issuance and enforcement of the protective measures as ordered by this Trial Chamber stands explicitly as safeguard of the relevant categories of witnesses and a certain measure of disclosure of any witnesses statement does not per se operate as a further burden on the detention of the Accused. Having so found, it is however, necessary to stress that the need to protect victims and witnesses is also part of the overall additional circumstances that this Chamber must consider to arrive at a proper decision.

[1] *Brdanin* Decision, supra note 12, para. 19.

R65-TC-11
o *Prosecutor v. Fofana*, Case No. SCSL-04-14-T, Decision on Application for Bail Pursuant to Rule 65, 5 August 2004, para. 78, 80:

78. The other condition to fulfil for a release on bail is that if released, the Applicant will not pose any danger to any victims, witnesses, or other persons. As I had indicated, the Confidential Declaration alleges that the Applicant was present at meetings where members of the CDF were threatened not to provide information to the Special Court.

[. . .]

80. I believe the contents of the Chief of Investigations' Confidential Declaration which highlights the threat made to CDF members not to cooperate with the Special Court and do observe that these threats which implicitly include threats that underscored the possibility of reprisals against those who are seen to be cooperating in any capacity, particularly as witnesses or victims, with the Special Court, legally deprive the Applicant of any possibility to be granted bail as this would be in contravention of the provisions of the second arm of Rule 65(B) of the Rules.

- **Rule 65: Bail – Conditions – Public Order Concerns**

R65-TC-12

o *Prosecutor v. Sesay*, Case No. SCSL-04-15-PT, Decision on Application of Issa Sesay for Provisional Release, 31 March 2004, para. 55-57:

55. Contrary to the ICTY and the International criminal Tribunal for Rwanda ("ICTR"), the Special Court for Sierra Leone has its seat in Freetown, Sierra Leone, which makes the issue of bail somewhat different, not with respect to the applicable principles but when assessing the particular circumstances of an application for provisional release. Granting bail to an Accused before the Special Court entails that he will be released in the very country where he is alleged to have committed the crimes for which he has been indicted. In this respect, reference can be more properly made to the ICTR, the judicial history of which, it has to be noted, shows that it has never granted an application for provisional release. I would suggest that it could be argued that the particular situation of the Special Court and its direct presence in the territory of Sierra Leone and more specifically in Freetown, the capital of this Country, makes it an even more important, difficult, critical and sensitive situation than that of the ICTR which sits in Tanzania, a neighbouring country to Rwanda.

56. In my opinion, such a specific context should not be overlooked, and, in this respect, I duly take into consideration the information provided by the Government of Sierra Leone in its written submissions, as well as the situation further described in the Secretary General Report, as to the ability, I would say more accurately the inability, of the Sierra Leonean authorities to assist the Special Court should an application for bail being granted to this Accused.

57. In the present circumstances and, in particular, in consideration of the proximity of the trials, the lack of police enforcement capability by the Government of Sierra Leone

and the potential threat to stability with the associated risk of affecting the public order would lead me to conclude that the public interest requirement in this case outweigh the Accused's right to be released on bail.

R65-TC-13 o *Prosecutor v. Fofana*, Case No. SCSL-04-14-T, Decision on Application for Bail Pursuant to Rule 65, 5 August 2004, para. 83-84:

83. One of the arguments to be factored into the examination of this application is that the Applicant, like the other co-accused, is alleged to be a member of the CDF which has sympathisers on the one hand, as well as many victims of their alleged crimes, on the other. In such a situation, it is normal to envisage a probability where granting a release on bail could provoke unrest and disgruntlement that could be prejudicial to public peace and security amongst supporters and opponents alike.

84. In the case of LETELLIER VS FRANCE, 14 EHRR 83, it was held that if the nature of the alleged crime and the likely public reaction is such that a release of the Applicant may give rise to public disorder, then a temporary detention on remand may be justified.

- **Rule 65: Bail – Conditions – Voluntary Surrender**

R65-TC-14 o *Prosecutor v. Kallon*, Case No. SCSL-04-15-PT, Decision on the Motion by Morris Kallon for Bail, 24 February 2004, para. 41:

41. The Accused was arrested on 10 March 2003, following the unsealing of the indictment against him; he did not know about the existence of the indictment brought against him. Therefore the issue of voluntary surrender, often a factor in decisions on bail, is not applicable to the present case.

R65-TC-15 o *Prosecutor v. Sesay*, Case No. SCSL-04-15-PT, Decision on Application of Issa Sesay for Provisional Release, 31 March 2004, para. 46-48:

46. In this respect, the Accused has indeed provided numerous personal guarantees as well as submitted various pieces of evidence, mainly in the form of witness declarations, with the

intent to demonstrate his general character, trustworthiness and willingness to face his trial before this Court. I note that different witnesses have stated that the Accused is a trustworthy man who actively engaged himself in numerous activities pertaining to the development of the peace process following the end of the conflict in Sierra Leone. It is observed that the Prosecution has not presented evidence in rebuttal of these assertions.

47. To further support his assertion that he intends to appear for his trial, the Accused also submitted that he had previous knowledge of the establishment of the Special Court and, because of the position he occupied as interim leader of the RUF, he knew that he would be the subject of investigations by the Prosecution. However, it has to be noted that the investigative activity against the Accused has been largely conducted confidentially and the indictment and related warrant of arrest were kept confidential until their execution in early March 2003,[1] as remarked by the Prosecution.

48. Upon my review of the evidence, I am not satisfied that the Accused was aware of the existence of any indictment against him or that he would have then surrendered to the Special Court. In addition, and more importantly, the Accused has not satisfied me that prior to his arrest he was informed and aware of the extreme seriousness of the crimes falling within the jurisdiction of the Special Court.

---

[1] The original indictment, now consolidated in pursuance to the joinder of the trials, and the warrant of arrest against the Accused were approved confidentially on 7 March 2003. See *Prosecutor v. Issa Hassan Sesay*, SCSL-2003-05-I, Decision Approving the Indictment and Order for Non-Disclosure, 7 March 2003; and *id.*, Warrant of Arrest and Order for Transfer and Detention, 7 March 2003. Subsequently, their confidentiality has been lifted on 14 March 2003. See *id.*, Order for the Disclosure of the Indictment and the Warrant of Arrest and Order for Transfer and Detention, 14 March 2003.

- **Rule 65(B): Bail – State Submissions**

R65-TC-16   o *Prosecutor v. Kallon*, Case No. SCSL-04-15-PT, Decision on the Motion by Morris Kallon for Bail, 24 February 2004, para. 36-39:[75]

36. One additional issue that needs to be addressed in the present decision is that of the weight that should be afforded to

---

[75] See also *Prosecutor v. Sesay*, Case No. SCSL-04-15-PT, Decision on Application of Issa Sesay for Provisional Release, 31 March 2004, para. 42-43.

the opinion of the Government of Sierra Leone on bail when it files, as in the present case, written submissions on the matter pursuant to Rule 65(B) of the Rules.

37. I deem that the opinion of the Government of Sierra Leone is very useful, and is a matter that must be properly assessed within the parameters of Rule 65(B). I encourage the filing of written submissions on such a sensitive issue as it has already done so in the past for the *Brima* Ruling.[1] However, considering that the Special Court, an independent institution, has been established by means of a bilateral agreement between the United Nations and the Government of Sierra Leone, not only it would not be appropriate but it cannot be bound by the opinion as expressed by the Government of Sierra Leone as the question whether the Accused should be provisionally released or not. This is a matter for the Court and the Court only. Nonetheless, it is important to stress the fact that the present submissions have been given due consideration in so far as they provide very valuable and substantial information on the current situation in Sierra Leone and is, in this respect, an important factor in determining the public interest aspect.

38. The Special Court, contrary to the ICTY and ICTR, has its seat in Freetown, Sierra Leone, which – given the special circumstances – does make the issue of bail somewhat different, not with respect to the applicable principles but when assessing the particular circumstances. Granting bail to an Accused before the Special Court entails that he will be released in the country where he is alleged to have committed the crimes for which he has been indicted. In this respect, reference can be more properly made to the ICTR, the judicial history of which, it has to be noted, has never granted an application for provisional release. I would suggest that it could be argued that the particular situation of the Special Court and its direct presence in the territory of Sierra Leone makes it an even more important, difficult, critical and sensitive situation than that of the ICTR which sits in Tanzania, a neighbouring country of Rwanda.

39. In my opinion, such a specific context should not be overlooked, and I duly take into consideration the information provided by the Government of Sierra Leone in its written submissions as to the ability of the Sierra Leonean authorities to assist the Special Court with the consequences of an order granting bail to the Accused.

---

[1] See *Prosecutor v. Alex Tamba Brima*, SCSL-03-06-PT, Submission of the Government of the Republic of Sierra Leone in Response to Motion for Bail or for Provisional Release, 7 July 2003.

R65-TC-17

o *Prosecutor v. Fofana*, Case No. SCSL-04-14-T, Decision on Application for Bail Pursuant to Rule 65, 5 August 2004, para. 40-41:

40. After due consideration of the arguments advanced by the Defence against hearing the Government of Sierra Leone in applications for bail, I hold that they are misguided because hearing the opinion of the Government of Sierra Leone, in the light of the provisions of Rule 65(B) of the Rules is mandatory, and is a prerequisite for examining the merits of the application and this, notwithstanding the fact that it is a party to the Special Court Agreement.

41. In this regard and as a matter of statutory interpretation, I hold that the words in Rule 65(B) should be given their ordinary meaning[1] rather than importing into them some extraneous interpretations that defeat the meaning, purpose, and necessary intendment of the Rule.

[1] *Bank of England Vs. Vagliano Brothers* [1891] AC 107.

Rule 65: Bail – Right to File a Writ of Habeas Corpus – Same Procedure as Application for Bail

R65-TC-18

o *Prosecutor v. Brima*, Case No. SCSL-03-06-PT, Order for Oral Hearing in the Motion Filed by the Defence for Leave to File a Write of *Habeas Corpus ad Subjidiciendum*, 18 June 2003:

CONSIDERING the Defence Motion for Leave to Issue a Writ of Habeas Corpus [...];

CONSIDERING the nature of this application and its impact on accessing whether the fundamental rights of the Applicant under Article 17 and under International Human Rights law have been violated by his continued detention;

[...]

MINDFUL of the necessity to ensure, in all circumstances, that these fundamental human rights are being and have been respected in this matter;

PURSUANT to Rule 28 and Rule 54 of the Rules and notwithstanding the fact that Habeas Corpus is not provided for in the Rules of Evidence and Procedure;

HEREBY ORDERS:

1) That leave is granted to the Applicant to file his substantive application for the issue of a Writ of Habeas Corpus in his favour.

[...]

3) That this Order and the filed Writ be served on the Honourable and Learned Attorney General and Minister of Justice of the Republic of Sierra Leone for him to file or cause written submissions to be filed in the Registry of the Special Court, and to eventually appear or be represented at the hearing in view of the fact that the consequences of this application may, as in the case of matters relating to bail brought under the provisions of Rule 65(B) of the Rules, eventually result in an Order for the release of the applicant from custody to the Republic of Sierra Leone, 'the State to which the accused seeks to be released', through his application for the issue of a Writ of Habeas Corpus.

4) That the Applicant will continue to remain in custody.

APPEALS CHAMBER DECISIONS

- **Rule 65: Bail – "Liberty Rule, Detention Exception"**

   o *Prosecutor v. Fofana*, Case No. SCSL-04-14-AR65, Appeal Against Decision Refusing Bail, 11 March 2005, para. 38-41:

   38. The appellant, faced with a number of persuasive ICTY decisions which all recognise that the burden of proving bail pre-conditions rests upon the applicant, have chosen to rely on the dissenting judgement in *Krajisnik*, and upon European Court of Human Rights decisions striking down laws that make pre-trial detention mandatory for certain classes of offences – an issue which does not arise here. We consider that the majority decision of Judge May and Judge Fihri in *Krajisnik* reflects the repeated decisions of ICTY panels and the plain meaning of Rule 65(B).[1]

   39. The international instruments cited by the appellant do not have the meaning for which he contends. The International Covenant on Civil and Political Rights, for example, provided by Article 9(3) that those arrested on criminal charges are entitled to release if they cannot be tried within a reasonable time. This refers not to bail but to unconditional release when prolonged delays amount to an abuse of process. The Article further provides:

   'It shall not be the general rule that persons awaiting trial shall be detained in custody, but release may be subject to guarantees to appear for trial, at any other stage of the judicial proceedings, and, should occasion arise, for execution of the judgement.'

Again, this principle strikes at laws which provide for mandatory detention of persons charged with certain classes of offence. But Rule 65(B) does not require mandatory detention, it simply makes release subject to guarantees to appear for trial. A guarantee is only a "guarantee" if the applicant can establish it, at least to the court's satisfaction.

40. Article 5 of the European Convention on Human Rights is of even less assistance to the appellant. It provides merely that detainees *"shall be entitled to trial within a reasonable time or to release pending trial. Release may be conditioned by guarantees to appear for trial."* This gives the somewhat outdated impression that the right to apply for bail only arises when trials cannot be held within a reasonable time. International human rights law has moved on since the Convention, which came into operation in 1953. In any event, Article 5 permits bail to be conditioned by "guarantees", a word which implies that the applicant has produced firm assurances of the matters requiring guarantee.

41. The appellant complains that the Judge in paragraphs 95–97 of his decision articulated opinions that contradicted his allocation of the burden of proof. He stated that the Prosecution does bear "an equally formidable burden of negating the facts advanced by the defence" and that "the liberty of the individual, which is a very sacred, long-standing, consecrated right, is and should continue to be and remain the rule, and detention the exception". However, we do not consider that it can be correct to state that the Prosecution has "an equally formidable burden of negativing the facts advanced by the defence" on an issue on which the legal burden of proof falls squarely on the defence. Nor is it helpful, for reasons we have already explained, to speak of liberty as a "sacred" or "sacrosanct" right which is the rule, as against the exception of pre-trial detention. Each case, as this court explained in *Sesay*, must turn on its own facts and circumstances, with the ultimate question being whether the applicant for bail has produced sufficient (i.e. sufficiently convincing) guarantees for his attendance at trial and for his good conduct while on provisional release. The Judge's comments were over-favourable to the defence.

---

[1] See *Prosecutor v Krajisnik and Plavsic*, Decision on provisional release, 8 October 2001.

- **Rule 65: Bail – Standard of Proof**

  R65-AC-2

  o *Prosecutor v. Fofana*, Case No. SCSL-04-14-AR65, Appeal Against Decision Refusing Bail, 11 March 2005, para. 21:

  21. Any decision to grant or deny bail will involve the most anxious consideration of questions which are not susceptible of proof but rather turn on substantial grounds for belief. Whether there is a real risk that the defendant will flee or intimidate witnesses or commit further offences calls for a calculation of odds based on all the inferences, arguments and evidential materials that the parties can muster. Frequently they will produce hearsay statements, or speculative opinion by persons who know the defendant or are involved with the Prosecution or its witnesses. The weight accorded to such evidential material will vary and will often depend on whether it can be tested by cross-examination or at least by forensic argument. But strict rules of evidence are inherently inappropriate to a court which must decide whether there are substantial grounds for believing something.[1]

  ---

  [1] See *R. E. Moles*, 1981, Crim Law LR 170 and *R v Mansfield Justices Ex Parte Sharkey* (1985) QB613.

- **Rule 65: Bail – Burden of Proof**

  R65-AC-3

  o *Prosecutor v. Fofana*, Case No. SCSL-04-14-AR65, Appeal Against Decision Refusing Bail, 11 March 2005, para. 33:

  33. So far as this court is concerned, the rules of evidence and procedure in relation to bail are set forth in plain language in Rule 65(B), namely

  > Bail may be ordered by a Judge or a Trial Chamber after hearing the state to which the accused seeks to be released and **only** if it is satisfied that the accused will appear for trial and, if released, will not pose a danger to any victim, witness or other person. (emphasis added)

  In other words, it is a precondition to any grant of bail that the applicant must satisfy the court that he will appear for trial and will not endanger witnesses or any other potential victim (including himself). Absent legislation to the contrary, the burden of proving a proposition in a court room rests upon the party obliged to assert it, and the language of Rule 65(B) (note the force of "only") confirms that the burden lies squarely on the applicant. It is, no doubt, a civil rather than a criminal burden, but as Judge David Hunt observed in *Sainovic*:

> 'The more serious the matter asserted or the more serious the consequences flowing from a particular finding, the greater the difficulty there will be in satisfying the relevant tribunal that what is asserted is more probably true than not. That is only commonsense.'[1]

---

[1] *Prosecutor v Nikola Sainovic & Dragoljub Ojdanic*, ICTY Appeals Chamber, Dissenting Opinion of Judge David Hunt on Provisional Release, 30 October 2002, paragraph 29.

- **Rule 65(B): Bail – State Submissions**

R65-AC-4
  o *Prosecutor v. Fofana*, Case No. SCSL-04-14-AR65, Appeal Against Decision Refusing Bail, 11 March 2005, para. 28:

   28. The error was compounded – although not to the appellant's detriment – by excluding for the same reason the written submission of the Sierra Leone government. A hearing (by written or oral submission) must be accorded to the State of Sierra Leone (being the state to which the defendant seeks to be released) under 65(B) before bail can be ordered, and the refusal to admit the Attorney General's submissions had the unintended and unrecognised result that bail could in no circumstances have been ordered, because the rejection of this evidence denied a "hearing" to the State of Sierra Leone. It was open to the judge to invite Mr Kobba to present the State's submission in person: if he required further "authentication" the Judge could have instructed his court clerk to telephone Mr Kobba and establish that the submissions were authentic. It is surprising that the Prosecution did not take this simple step in any event. In consequence, submissions which the court was obliged to consider before it could make any order for bail were held to be inadmissible by reference to a "best evidence rule" which did not apply to them.

- **Rule 65(E): Bail – Leave to Appeal**

R65-AC-5
  o *Prosecutor v. Kallon*, Case No. SCSL-04-15-AR65, Decision on Application for Leave to Appeal Against Refusal of Bail, 23 June 2004, para. 5-9, 11:[76]

---

[76] See also *Prosecution v. Sesay*, Case No. SCSL-04-15-AR65, Decision on Application for Leave to Appeal Against Refusal of Bail, 28 July 2004, para. 9, 12.

5. [...] It must be said *in limine* that what amounts to "good cause" is for the Single Judge of the Appeals Chamber to determine and NOT the Trial Chamber as contended by the Defence.[1]

6. The Appeals Chamber in other international jurisdictions has held that in order to show "good cause" the Defence must show that the Trial Chamber may have erred in making the impugned decision.[2]

7. The test, it seems to me, lies in the answer to the question: From the submissions of the Defence, could it be said that the Trial Chamber or the designated Judge of that Chamber may have erred in making the impugned decision? If the answer is in the affirmative then according to these decisions, "good cause" is shown.

8. With respect, it seems to me that that test, while useful and helpful is unnecessarily restrictive. It gives only one instance of "good cause", i.e. where the Defence makes out a *prima facie* case that an error of law and/or fact has been made by the Trial Chamber or a single Judge of that Chamber, as the case may be.

9. In my judgement the concept of "good cause" ought to be extended to include those instances where the question in relation to which leave to appeal is sought, is one of general principle to be decided for the first time, or a question of public importance upon which further argument and a decision of the Appeals Chamber would be in the interests of justice paying particular regard to the fact that ordinarily the "accused may only make one application for bail to the Judge or Trial Chamber.[3]

[...]

11. Having given the definitive parameters of "good cause", how do I relate it to the instant application? It seems to me that the questions raised by the Defence in its Motion, quite apart from the errors they allege the learned Judge made, are of such importance as to merit further argument and also that a decision of the Appeals Chamber would be in the interests of justice having regard to the circumstances of the application.

---

[1] Ibid.
[2] *Prosecutor v. Brdjanin and Talic*, Case No. IT-99-36/1, "Decision on Application for Leave to Appeal", 7 September 2000; *Sagahutu v. The Prosecutor*, Case No. ICTR-00-56-I, "Decision on Leave to Appeal Against the Refusal to Grant Provisional Release", 26 March 2003, para. 26; *Ndayambaje v. The Prosecutor*, Case No. ICTR-96-A-8, "Decision on Motion to Appeal Against the Provisional Release Decision of Trial Chamber II of 21 October 2002", 10 January 2003, para. 29; and *Prosecutor v. Simic et al.*, Case No. IT-95-9, "Decision on Application for Leave to Appeal", 19 April 2000, para. 11.
[3] Rule 65(c)

R65-AC-6

o *Prosecutor v. Fofana*, Case No. SCSL-04-14-AR65, Decision Application for Leave to Appeal Bail Decision, 5 November 2004, para. 14:

14. The jurisprudence of the ICTY,[1] the International Criminal Tribunal fore Rwanda ("ICTR")[2] and the Special Court[3] states that good cause is shown where the Defence makes out a prima facie case that the Trial Chamber or a single Judge thereof has erred in law and/or in fact in making the impugned decision. According to ICTY jurisprudence, good cause may also be shown if it is demonstrated that the impugned decision is inconsistent with other decisions of the Tribunal on the same issues.[4] Special Court jurisprudence adds that good cause may be shown where the issue raised in the appeal is one of general principle to be decided for the first time, or a question of public importance upon which further argument and a decision of the Appeals Chamber would be in the interests of justice paying particular regard to the fact that ordinarily the accused may only make one application for bail to the Judge or Trial Chamber.[5] In other words, good cause may be shown where a substantial issue is raised. The 'good cause test' defines and limits the judge's discretion to grant leave to appeal.

---

[1] *Prosecutor v. Brdjanin and Talic*, Case No. IT-99-36/1, Decision on Application for Leave to Appeal, 7 September 2000; *Prosecutor v. Simic et al.*, Case No. IT-95-9, Decision on Application for Leave to Appeal, 19 April 2000, para. 11.
[2] *Sagahutu v. The Prosecutor*, Case No. ICTR-00-56-I, Decision on Leave to Appeal Against the Refusal to Grant Provisional Release, 26 March 2003, para. 26; *Ndayambaje v. The Prosecutor*, Case No. ICTR-96-A-8, Decision on Motion to Appeal Against the Provisional Release Decision of Trial Chamber II of 21 October 2002, 10 January 2003, para. 29.
[3] *Prosecutor v. Sesay, Kallon and Gbao*, Case No. SCSL-2004-15-PT, Sesay – Decision on Application for Leave to Appeal Against Refusal of Bail, 28 July 2004.
[4] *Prosecution v. Cermac and Markac*, Case No. IT-03-73-AR65.1, Decision on Joint Motion for Leave to Appeal Decision on Provisional Relase, 13 October 2004, para. 4.
[5] See *Prosecutor v. Sesay, Kallon and Gbao*, Case No. SCSL-2004-15-PT, Kallon – Decision on Application for Leave to Appeal Against Refusal of Bail, 23 June 2004, para. 9.

- **Rule 65(H): Bail – Scope of Appeal**

R65-AC-7

o *Prosecutor v. Fofana*, Case No. SCSL-04-14-AR65, Appeal Against Decision Refusing Bail, 11 March 2005, para. 20, 42:

20. By virtue of Rule 65 it is primarily the function of a Judge or Trial Chamber to grant bail to an accused. It is therefore not appropriate for this court to hear first instance evidence with a view to granting bail to an accused who has been denied bail by a Judge or Trial Chambers. If new facts emerge or changed circumstances justify a fresh exercise of discretion, the application for such exercise of fresh discretion is to the Trial Chamber. Where the Judge or Trial Chamber has exercised his or their discretion to grant or refuse bail the Appeals Chamber will not substitute its own discretion for that of the Judge or Trial Chamber. It is for them to assess submissions from the government of Sierra Leone and to take the primary decision as to whether the bail pre-conditions in that Rule – namely that the defendant will attend at and during trial and will not interfere with witnesses – have been fulfilled. As the ICTY has noted, "[a] Trial Chamber's exercise of discretion will be overturned if the challenged decision was (i) based on an incorrect interpretation of governing law; (ii) based on a patently incorrect conclusion of fact; or (iii) so unfair or unreasonable as to constitute an abuse of the Trial Chamber's discretion."[1] If we are satisfied that there has been such a serious misunderstanding of the facts that the decision must be overturned, the case will still have to be remitted to the Trial Chamber Judge to hear evidence concerning bail conditions and to decide whether they satisfy the Rule 65(B) tests and if so to set and supervise appropriate conditions. In determining whether the Trial Chamber has erred in its appreciation of the facts in bail appeals we do not sit to re-hear the application: we adopt a judicial review standard and will only quash the decision if satisfied that it is logically perverse or evidentially unsustainable.

[...]

42. The role of the Appeals Chamber is to review the Trial Chamber's decision only to the extent of determining whether its discretion was properly exercised. In undertaking this review, the question for the Appeals Chamber is not whether it agrees with the Trial Chamber's conclusion but whether the Trial Chamber correctly exercised its discretion in reaching that decision.[2]

---

[1] *Slobodan Milosevic v Prosecutor*, Decision on Interlocutory Appeal of the Trial Chamber's Decision on the Assignment of Defence Counsel, ICTY, Case No. IT-02-54-AR73.7, 1 November 2004, para. 10.
[2] See the discussion above at paragraph 20.

- **Rule 65: Bail – Conditions – Specific Situation of the Special Court**

R65-AC-8

o *Prosecutor v. Sesay*, Case No. SCSL-04-15-AR65, Decision on Appeal Against Refusal of Bail, 14 December 2004, para. 35-37:

35. The Defence argues that by elevating the public interest and factors outside the control of the Accused to the status of determining factors, the Judge demonstrated that an accused at the Special Court could never be granted bail. In the view of this Chamber, the Judge was right to reflect on the "particular circumstances" of the Special Court, which in contrast to the ICTY and ICTR has its seat in the country where the crimes are alleged to have occurred, but this does not appear to have been treated as anything more than another factor to be weighed in the balance. Pointing to the fact that in contrast to the ICTY, no accused person before the ICTR has been granted provisional release, the Judge stated: "I would suggest that it could be argued that the particular situation of the Special Court and its direct presence in the territory of Sierra Leone and more specifically in Freetown, the capital of this Country, makes it an even more important, difficult, critical and sensitive situation than that of the ICTR which sits in Tanzania, a neighbouring country to Rwanda."[1]

36. In the particular situation of Sierra Leone, public interest factors such as the ability of the authorities to uphold conditions may take on a greater relevance. While in principle a judge could be satisfied that a particular accused would appear for trial notwithstanding any lack of police enforcement capability, at the same time conditions and guarantees need to be meaningful. This Chamber is satisfied that the Judge took into account the "important, difficult, critical and sensitive" situation with which he was faced, as well as the Accused's right to be presumed innocent and to be released on bail.

37. The fact that this situation was taken into account does not detract from the fundamental principle that each individual case must be decided on its merits, and there may well be circumstances where an accused person before the Special Court can be granted bail. In each case all relevant factors will need to be weighed. As the security situation and authoritative structures in Sierra Leone evolve and improve, the public interest factors may weigh less heavily in the balance.

---

[1] Trial Chamber Decision on Bail, para. 55.

- **Rule 65: Bail – Conditions – Personal Guarantees**

R65-AC-9

o *Prosecutor v. Sesay*, Case No. SCSL-04-15-AR65, Decision on Appeal Against Refusal of Bail, 14 December 2004, para. 30:

30. The Judge did not elaborate upon or make a specific finding in relation to the personal guarantees provided by the Accused as to his character, trustworthiness and willingness to take part in his trial, which, notably, were not rebutted by the Prosecution. In this context it is to be recalled that all written submissions filed by both parties and the Government of Sierra Leone in connection with the original application dated 4 February 2004 were filed confidentially and the Judge noted in the Trial Chamber Decision on Bail that the confidentiality of particular submissions or evidence would not be endangered and would be limited to a general reference.[1] Thus, because the confidentiality of the personal guarantees needed to be ensured, the impression may have been created that these guarantees were given less attention in the reasoning than the public interest factors. Whether or not the Judge's failure to elaborate on the personal guarantees was in fact influenced by the need to protect confidentiality, the Appeals Chamber is satisfied that these guarantees were taken into account in the context in which they were presented and weighed against the public interest findings. Moreover, as pointed out by the Prosecution, the Judge was not required to "articulate every step of its reasoning for each particular finding it makes",[2] in order to fulfil his duty to provide a reasoned opinion. While it is desirable for the reasoning to be fully articulate and transparent, and the Judge could have indicated where his reasoning was influenced by the need to protect confidentiality, the Appeals Chamber is unable to discern any error.

---

[1] Trial Chamber Decision on Bail, para. 33.
[2] Prosecution Submissions, para. 27, citing *Prosecutor v Musema*, Case No. ICTR-96-13-A, Judgment, 16 November 2001, para. 18.

- **Rule 65: Bail – Conditions – Voluntary Surrender**

R65-AC-10

o *Prosecutor v. Sesay*, Case No. SCSL-04-15-AR65, Decision on Appeal Against Refusal of Bail, 14 December 2004, para. 31:

31. The Appeals Chamber is unable to discern any error in the manner in which the Judge considered the Accused's personal knowledge of the existence of the Special Court and the

indictment against him, and the likelihood that he would surrender. Ordinarily, where a sealed indictment has been used, the fact that an Accused did not surrender voluntarily is irrelevant to a decision on bail.[1] In the current case, however, specific evidence was adduced to demonstrate that the Accused would have surrendered voluntarily had he known about the indictment. This evidence failed to satisfy the Judge that the Accused would have surrendered and the Appeals Chamber is unable to find any error in the reasoning. The reference to the fact that the indictment was sealed was not inappropriate since it was taken as evidence that the Accused could not have known the precise charges against him or their gravity.

[1] See Decision on Motion by Radoslav Brđanin for Provisional Release, para. 17.

- **Rule 65: Bail – Conditions – Contribution to the Peace Process**

R65-AC-11   o *Prosecutor v. Sesay*, Case No. SCSL-04-15-AR65, Decision on Appeal Against Refusal of Bail, 14 December 2004, para. 32:

32. The Judge referred to the evidence indicating that the Accused participated in the peace process that followed the end of hostilities but concluded that it was not relevant in the circumstances of the bail application. The Appeals Chamber finds that this was a conclusion the Judge was entitled to reach as an exercise of his discretion and finds no error in it.

- **Rule 65: Bail – Conditions – Bail Granted After Commencement of Trial**

R65-AC-12   o *Prosecutor v. Sesay*, Case No. SCSL-04-15-AR65, Decision on Appeal Against Refusal of Bail, 14 December 2004, para. 33-34:

33. The Prosecution argues that bail could not be granted in any event now that the trial of the Accused is ongoing since there is a stronger incentive to flee. Reference is made to the case of *Prosecutor v Ndayambaje* before the International Criminal Tribunal for Rwanda ("ICTR") in which the Appeals Chamber considered "that the Trial Chamber rightly took into account the fact that there is an ongoing trial, which ... needs to be completed in an orderly manner, and found that in these circumstances, provisional release would not be justified."[1]

The Prosecution also distinguishes the ICTY case of *Momir Talic* where provisional release was granted during trial on humanitarian grounds.⁽²⁾

34. The Appeals Chamber is unconvinced by these submissions and does not consider it to be established as a general principle (with exceptions) that bail cannot be granted after the commencement of trial. In its Decision in the *Aleksovski* case, the ICTY Trial Chamber declared the defence motion for provisional release to be admissible (although it was denied on the merits) despite the Prosecution's objections on the basis that the trial had started. The Trial Chamber held:

> the justification for provisional release must be seen as emanating from or as the corollary of the principle of the presumption of innocence. Thus provisional release must accord with the presumption of innocence, and this principle applies until such time as the final decision has been taken. In any case in respect of questions of individual freedom, the Trial Chamber considers that an accused must be able to turn to it at any time. ⁽³⁾

Furthermore, in ICTY jurisprudence provisional release has been granted pending a judgment on appeal against conviction where it could be argued that the incentive to flee is at its strongest. ⁽⁴⁾

⁽¹⁾ *Prosecutor v Ndayambaje*, Case No. ICTR-96-8-A, Decision on Motion to Appeal against the Provisional Release Decision of Trial Chamber II of 21 October 2002, 10 January 2003.
⁽²⁾ *Prosecutor v Brdanin and Talic*, Case No. IT-99-36-T, Decision on the Motion for Provisional Release of the Accused Momir Talic, 20 September 2002.
⁽³⁾ *Prosecutor v Zlatko Aleksovski*, Case No. IT-95-14/1-T, Decision Denying a Request for Provisional Release, 23 January 1998, p. 3.
⁽⁴⁾ *Prosecutor v Miroslav Kvocka et al.*, Case No. IT-98-30/1-A, Decision on Request for Provisional Release of Miroslav Kvocka, 17 December 2003. In that case the fact that the appellant had already served around 80% of the sentence imposed by the Trial Chamber amounted to a special circumstance warranting his release. Notably in the case of *Prosecutor v Dario Kordic and Mario Cerkez*, Case No. IT-95-14/2-A, Decision on Dario Kordic's Request for Provisional Release, 19 April 2003, the Appeals Chamber denied Kordic's request for five days provisional release on compassionate grounds, pointing to the fact that he had been sentenced to 25 years imprisonment which, notwithstanding the guarantees offered by the Republic of Croatia, was found to create a strong incentive to flee. The Appeals Chamber did however remark that in case of exceptional circumstances such as a substantial deterioration of the health conditions of Kordic's mother, the Defence could submit a detailed request for a temporarily controlled visit to his mother.

DECISIONS OF THE PRESIDENT

- **Rule 65: Bail – No Presumption – Discretion**

R65-P-1
o *Prosecutor v. Norman*, SCSL-03-08-PT, Decision on Motion for Modification of the Conditions of Detention, 26 November 2003, para. 8:[77]

8. [...] There is no presumption in favour of bail, which is understandable given the very serious nature of the crimes charged. It may be applied for to a single judge (generally, prior to trial) or to the Trial Chamber once the trial has started and may only be appealed by leave of the pre-hearing judge of the Appeals Chamber, upon good cause being shown. Under Rule 65D any judge or chamber minded to grant liberty has a wide discretion to impose conditions and restrictions. [...]

- **Rule 65: Bail – Conditions – Right to a Fair and Speedy Trial**

R65-P-2
o *Prosecutor v. Norman*, Case No. SCSL-03-08-PT, Decision on Motion for Modification of the Conditions of Detention, 26 November 2003, para. 13-15:

13. [...] Applications for conditional freedom must proceed under Rule 65, where they will receive the attention of the Chamber that is actually trying the accused, or of a resident Trial Chamber judge. In its original ICTY incarnation, Rule 65 limited bail to 'exceptional circumstances'.[(1)] Now, and in this Court, all circumstances must be taken into account: obviously there would need to be convincing guarantees that the accused will not abscond or tamper with witnesses or victims or pose a threat to others. A Rule 65 application also has the right of an appeal, should leave be granted.

14. In ICTY and ICTR practice, bail has not often been granted. In Sierra Leone, when crimes of murder and treason are charged, the terms of Section 79(1) of the Criminal Procedure Act of 1965 (as amended) require any grant of bail to be made by a judge and not a magistrate. The harshness of a bail refusal is tempered where the Court can provide a relatively speedy trial at which the 'presumption of innocence' operates

---

[77] See also *Prosecutor v. Kallon*, Case No. SCSL-04-15-PT, Decision on Motion by Morris Kallon for Bail, 24 February 2004.

to require the Prosecution to prove its case beyond reasonable doubt. I recognise that continued incarceration is particularly burdensome to this accused who was a minister in the Government both at the time of his arrest and at the time of his alleged crimes. The Prosecution accepts that its charges against him arise out of his leadership of forces which acted in defence of the democratically elected government, sometimes at its request, and that it would fail if it could not prove that the degree of force used was unreasonable in all the circumstances. His counsel refer, rightly and repeatedly, to his right to a fair and speedy trial.

15. The importance of this right in the Special Court has already been emphasized by the Appeals Chamber.[2] That prospective delay is a relevant circumstance to be taken into account in bail applications has been confirmed by ICTY and ICTR jurisprudence which rightly warns prosecutors against reliance on early and aberrant decisions of the European Commission of Human Rights excusing very lengthy pre-trial detentions.[3] The very act of bringing an indictment implies that the Prosecution has a case that is almost ready for trial and can be made ready within 6 to 9 months of the date of arrest, a time that is probably the minimum necessary to allow defence preparation. Arguments that concern delay in trial fixtures considerably beyond that time period will be carefully scrutinised to ensure that both parties are genuinely working towards trial at the earliest practicable time.

---

[1] See Rule 65(B) of the ICTY Rules of Procedure and Evidence adopted on 14 March 1994 (as amended 8 January 1996), UN Doc. IT/32/Rev.7 (1996), "Release may be ordered by a Trial Chamber only in exceptional circumstances, after hearing the host country and only if it is satisfied that the accused will appear for trial and, if released, will not pose a danger to any victim, witness or other person."

[2] *Prosecutor v. Norman*, Case No. SCSL-2003-08, *Prosecutor v Kallon*, Case No. SCSL-2003-07, *Prosecutor v Gbao*, Case No. SCSL-2003-09, Decision on the Applications for a Stay of Proceedings and Denial of Right to Appeal, 4 November 2003.

[3] See *Prosecutor v. Brdanin*, Decision on Motion by Brdanin for Provisional Release, in particular at paras 24-28. Note also footnote 62 in which the aberrant European Commission case of *Ventura v. Italy* is discussed. Other such cases are distinguished on the basis that they are applications of the "margin of appreciation" doctrine.

> **Rule 65*bis*: Status Conferences**
> *(amended 1 August 2003)*
>
> A status conference may be convened by the Designated Judge or by the Trial Chamber. The status conference shall:
>
> (i) organize exchanges between the parties so as to ensure expeditious trial proceedings;
> (ii) review the status of his case and to allow the accused the opportunity to raise issues in relation thereto.

TRIAL CHAMBERS DECISIONS

- **Rule 65*bis*: Status Conferences – Reasons for Convening a Status Conference**

R65*bis*-TC-1

○ *Prosecutor v. Norman, Fofana, Kondewa*, Case No. SCSL-04-14-PT, Scheduling Order for Status Conference (Under Rule 65*bis*), 13 February 2004:[78]

CONSIDERING THAT the rights of the Accused will be advanced by convening a Status Conference to organize exchanges between the Parties so as to ensure expeditious trial proceedings, with the aim to set a trial date as soon as practicable;

PURSUANT TO Rule 54 and Rule 65*bis* of the Rules of Procedure and Evidence of the Special Court ("Rules");

HEREBY ORDERS that a Status Conference shall be held on [...]

R65*bis*-TC-2

○ *Prosecutor v. Sesay, Kallon, Gbao*, Case No. SCSL-04-15-PT, Reasons for Order for Closed Session of the Status Conference and Modification of Said Order in Part, 5 March 2004:

CONSIDERING FURTHER THAT the Trial Chamber noted that status conferences are not simply court management matters, but are far more than that;

---

[78] See also *Prosecutor v. Sesay, Kallon, Gbao*, Case No. SCSL-04-15-PT, Scheduling Order for Status Conference (Under Rule 65*bis*), 13 February 2004; *Prosecutor v. Brima, Kamara, Kanu*, Case No. SCSL-04-16-PT, Scheduling Order for Status Conference (Under Rule 65*bis*), 13 February 2004.

Rule 66: Disclosure of Materials by the Prosecutor
(amended 29 May 2004)

(A) Subject to the provisions of Rules 50, 53, 69 and 75, the Prosecutor shall:

   (i) Within 30 days of the initial appearance of an accused, disclose to the Defence copies of the statements of all witnesses whom the Prosecutor intends to call to testify and all evidence to be presented pursuant to Rule 92*bis* at trial.

   (ii) Continuously disclose to the Defence copies of the statements of all additional prosecution witnesses whom the Prosecutor intends to call to testify, but not later than 60 days before the date for trial, or as otherwise ordered by a Judge of the Trial Chamber either before or after the commencement of the trial, upon good clause being shown by the Prosecution. Upon good cause being shown by the Defence, a Judge of the Trial Chamber may order that copies of the statements of additional prosecution witnesses that the Prosecutor does not intend to call be made available to the defence within a prescribed time.

   (iii) At the request of the defence, subject to Sub-Rule (B), permit the defence to inspect any books, documents, photographs and tangible objects in his custody or control, which are material to the preparation of the defence, upon a showing by the defence of categories of, or specific, books, documents, photographs and tangible objects which the defence considers to be material to the preparation of a defence, or to inspect any books, documents, photographs and tangible objects in his custody or control which are intended for use by the Prosecutor as evidence at trial or were obtained from or belonged to the accused.

(B) Where information or materials are in the possession of the Prosecutor, the disclosure of which may prejudice further or ongoing investigations, or for any other reasons may be contrary to the public interest or affect the security interests of any State, the Prosecutor may apply to a Judge designated by the President sitting *ex parte* and *in camera*, but with notice to the Defence, to be relieved from the obligation to disclose pursuant to Sub-Rule (A). When making such an application the Prosecutor shall provide, only to such Judge, the information or materials that are sought to be kept confidential.

TRIAL CHAMBERS DECISIONS

- **Rule 66: Disclosure by the Prosecution – Generalities**

R66-TC-1

o *Prosecutor v. Norman, Fofana, Kondewa*, Case No. SCSL-04-14-T, Decision on Disclosure of Witness Statements and Cross-Examination, 16 July 2004, para. 5-7:[79]

5. As a matter of statutory interpretation, it is the Chamber's opinion that Rule 66 requires, *inter alia*, that the Prosecution disclose to the Defence copies of the statements of all witnesses which it intends to call to testify and all evidence to be presented pursuant to Rule 92bis, within 30 days of the initial appearance of the Accused. In addition, the Prosecution is required to continuously disclose to the Defence, the statements of all additional Prosecution witnesses it intends to call, not later than 60 days before the date of trial, or otherwise ordered by the Trial Chamber, upon good cause being shown by the Prosecution. Rule 67 also requires reciprocal disclosure of evidence, from the Prosecution and the Defence. The Chamber opines that the Prosecution is required to disclose the names of the witnesses that it intends to call as early as reasonably practicable, prior to commencement of trial. The Defence is required to notify the Prosecutor of its intent to enter the

---

[79] See also *Prosecutor v. Sesay*, Case No. SCSL-04-15-T, Ruling on Oral Application for the Exclusion of "Additional" Statement for Witness TF1-060, 23 July 2004, para. 8-9; *Prosecutor v. Norman, Fofana, Kondewa*, Case No. SCSL-04-14-T, Ruling on Disclosure of Witness Statements, 1st October 2004, para. 3; *Prosecutor v. Sesay, Gbao*, Case No. SCSL-04-15-T, Ruling on Oral Application for the Exclusion of Statements of Witness TF1-141 Dated Respectively 9th of October, 2004 19th and 20th of October, 2004, and 10th of January, 2005, 3 February 2005, para. 4, 17-19; *Prosecutor v. Norman, Fofana, Kondewa*, Case No. SCSL-04-14-T, Decision on Prosecution Request for Leave to Call an Additional Expert Witness, 10 June 2005, para. 5; *Prosecutor v. Gbao*, Case No. SCSL-04-15-T, Ruling on the Oral Application for the Exclusion of Part of the Testimony of Witness TF1-199, 26 July 2004, para. 6-7; *Prosecutor v. Kanu*, Case No. SCSL-03-16-PT, Decision on Motion for Exclusion of Prosecution Witness Statements and Stay of Filing of Prosecution Statements, 30 July 2004, para. 20; *Prosecutor v. Brima*, Case No. SCSL-04-16-PT, Decision on Motion for Exclusion of Prosecution Witness Statements and Stay of Filing of Prosecution Statements, 2 August 2004, para. 16, 20; *Prosecutor v. Sesay, Kallon, Gbao*, Case No. SCSL-04-15-T, Ruling on Disclosure Regarding Witness TF1-195, 4 February 2005, para. 6; *Prosecution v. Sesay, Kallon, Gbao*, Case No. SCSL-04-15-T, Ruling on Application for the Exclusion of Certain Supplemental Statements of Witness TF1-361 and Witness TF1-122, 1st June 2005, para. 19-20; *Prosecutor v. Sesay, Kallon, Gbao*, Case No. SCSL-04-15-T, Decision on Prosecution Request for Leave to Call an Additional Expert Witness, 10 June 2005, para. 5; *Prosecutor v. Brima, Kamara, Kanu*, Case No. SCSL-04-16-T, Decision on Joint Defence Motion Pertaining to Objections to the Nature of Testimony in Chief of Witness TF1-150, 16 June 2005, para. 9; *Prosecutor v. Samura* (Case No. SCSL-05-01), *Brima (Margaret), Jalloh, Kamara (Anifa), Kamara (Ester)*(Case No. SCSL-05-02), Written Reasons for the Decision on the Standing of Independent Counsel and on Disclosure Obligations, 23 June 2005, para. 12.

defence of alibi or any special defence. Rule 68 also requires the Prosecutor to disclose exculpatory evidence within 30 days of the initial appearance of the Accused, and thereafter to be under a continuing obligation to disclose exculpatory material.

6. The Chamber finds that these provisions clearly require more disclosure from the Prosecutor, than from the Defence, which is more in line with the civil law system than the common law tradition. The Prosecutor is obliged to continuously disclose evidence under Rule 66, which is limited to new developments in the investigation, and under Rule 68, to further exculpatory material. Rule 67(D) enunciates continuous disclosure obligations and provides as follows:

> If either party discovers additional evidence or information or materials which should have been produced earlier pursuant to the Rules, that party shall promptly notify the other party and the Trial Chamber of the existence of the additional evidence or information or materials.

7. It is evident that the premise underlying the disclosure obligations is that the parties should act bona fides at all times.[1] There is authority from the evolving jurisprudence of the International Criminal Tribunals that any allegation by the Defence as to a violation of the disclosure rules by the Prosecution should be substantiated with prima facie proof of such a violation. This Chamber in recent decisions has indeed ruled that the Defence must "make a prima facie showing of materiality and that the requested evidence is in the custody or control of the Prosecution".[2] It is of course the role of the Trial Chamber to enforce disclosure obligations in the interests of a fair trial, and to ensure that the rights of the Accused, as provided in Article 17(4)(e) of the Statute, to examine or have examined, the witnesses against him or her, are respected and where evidence has not been disclosed or is disclosed so late as to prejudice the fairness of the trial, the Trial Chamber will apply appropriate remedies which may include the exclusion of such evidence.[3]

---

[1] *Prosecutor v. Delalic,* Decision on the Applications Filed by the Defense for the Accused Zejnil Delalic and Esad Landzo, 14 February 1997 and 18 February 1997, 21 February 1997, para 14.
[2] *Prosecutor v. Sesay*, Decision on Defence Motion for Disclosure Pursuant to Rules 66 and 68 of the Rules, Para. 27. See also *Prosecutor v. Kondewa*, Decision on Motion to Compel the Production of Exculpatory Witness Statements, Witness Summaries and materials Pursuant to Rule 68, 8 July 2004.
[3] See *Prosecutor v. Furundzija*, Scheduling Order, 29 April 1998.

R66-TC-2   o *Prosecutor v. Kanu*, Case No. SCSL-03-16-PT, Decision on Motion for Exclusion of Prosecution Witness Statements and Stay of Filing of Prosecution Statements, 30 July 2004, para. 14, 19-24:[80]

14. It is worth noting that Old Rule 66(A) was amended for purposes of clarity and better comprehension at the 5th Plenary Meeting of the Judges of the Special Court that was held between 11 and 14 March 2004, as a result of issues raised about its interpretation during the Status Conference held on 8 March 2004. Even though the amended Rule is more specific and clearly provides for continuous disclosure, it was nevertheless already understood prior to these amendments that the previous version of the Rule did impose upon the Prosecution a continuous disclosure obligation.

[. . .]

19. In considering whether the Defence will suffer any material prejudice should their Motion not be granted, in addition to the finding of the Trial Chamber in its Order to File Disclosure Materials referred to above, further relevant jurisprudence from this Court as well as from the International criminal Tribunal for the former Yugoslavia ("ICTY") and International Criminal tribunal for Rwanda ("ICTR") do provide appropriate guidance on this matter.[(1)]

20. In its *Norman* decision, the Trial Chamber of the Special Court held the following with reference to disclosure:

"It is of course the role of the Trial Chamber to enforce disclosure obligations in the interests of a fair trial, and to ensure that the rights of the Accused, as provided in Article 17(4)(e) of the Statute, to examine or have examined, the witnesses against him or her, are respected and where evidence has not been disclosed or is disclosed so late as to prejudice the fairness of the trial, the Trial Chamber will apply appropriate remedies which may include the exclusion of such evidence."[(2)]

21. In the case of *Prosecutor v. Bagosora*,[(3)] the Trial Chamber of the ICTR held that despite the failure of the Prosecution to strictly comply with its disclosure obligations vis a vis the Defence, it was clearly of the view that the Defence will not be prejudiced in any way since the trial had been postponed and the Defence will consequently have sufficient time to prepare for the trial.

---

[80] See also *Prosecutor v. Brima*, Case No. SCSL-04-16-PT, Decision on Motion for Exclusion of Prosecution Witness Statements and Stay of Filing of Prosecution Statements, 2 August 2004, para. 13, 19-24; *Prosecutor v. Sesay, Kallon, Gbao*, Case No. SCSL-04-15-T, Ruling on Disclosure Regarding Witness TF1-195, 4 February 2005, para. 6.

22. Furthermore, in the case of *Prosecutor v. Furundzija*,[4] while the Trial Chamber of the ICTY noted with grave concern and deplored the Prosecution's failure to comply with its obligation to disclose to the Defence, it did not exclude the Prosecution witness statements,[5] but required the Prosecution to strictly comply with its order to provide full disclosure to the Defence by a particular date.

23. In the instant case, the Defence contention that the Prosecution has failed to comply with its disclosure obligations cannot be legally sustained in that, as demonstrated above, the Defence erred in its interpretation of the applicable provisions of Rule 66(A) either as these provisions existed before the amendment or since the new amendments.

24. In addition, I am of the view that the Defence will not be prejudiced in any way as a consequence of the disclosure practice so far undergone by the Prosecution, as the Motions have failed to show how such disclosure could *in concreto* prejudice the preparation of its case. All the statements whose disclosure is contested by the Defence in either the First Motion or the Additional Motion were disclosed well within the Pre-Trial stage. Indeed, no trial date has yet been set, thusfar in this case. Therefore, I find that the Defence has been provided with adequate notice of the case against the Accused and has sufficient time to adequately prepare for trial.[6]

---

[1] On the applicability of jurisprudence from the ICTY and ICTR, see Decision and Order on Defence Preliminary Motion on defects in the Form of the Indictment, 1 April 2004, paras 19-26.

[2] *Norman* decision, para. 7. see also *Prosecutor v. Sesay et al.*, Case No, SCSL-2004-15-T, Ruling on the Oral Application of the Exclusion of Part of the Testimony of Witness TF1-199, 26 July 2004, para. 7; Ruling on Oral Application for the Exclusion of "Additional" Witness Statements for Witness TF1-060, 23 July 2004, para. 10; Ruling on the Oral Application for the Exclusion of Part of the Testimony of Witness TF1-1999, 26 July 2004, para. 7. See also *Prosecutor v. Furundzija*, Case No. IT-95-17/1, Scheduling Order, 29 April 1998.

[3] *Prosecutor v. Bagosora*, Case No. ICTR-96-7-T, decision on the motion by the Defence Counsel for Disclosure, 27 November 1997. (E)(v).

[4] *Prosecutor v. Furundzija*, Case No. IT-95-17/1, decision on Motion of Defendant Anto Furundzija to Preclude Testimony of Certain Prosecution Witnesses, 29 April 1998.

[5] *Prosecutor v. Furundzija*, Case No. IT-95-17/1, Scheduling Order, 29 April 1998.

[6] Similarly, in the *Sesay* Decision the Trial Chamber found that the Defence in that case had sufficient time to prepare for the commencement of the trial scheduled on 5 July 2004 although it received redacted disclosure for several witness statements as late as 26 April 2004, which coincide with the date of disclosure for several witness statements for this case. See *Sesay* Decision, para. 44. See also *id.*, decision on Defence Motion, 15 July 2004, para. 12.

R66-TC-3

o *Prosecutor v. Brima, Kamara, Kanu*, Case No. SCSL-04-16-T, Decision on Joint defence Motion on Disclosure of All Original Witness Statements, Interview Notes and Investigator's Notes Pursuant to Rule 66 and/or 68, 4 May 2005, para. 16:[81]

16. It is our opinion that the following propositions are correct statements of the law governing disclosure obligations.

o [Rule 66, 67 and 68] impose an obligation of continuous disclosure.[1]

o **What is a Witness Statement**: Any statement or declaration made by a witness in relation to an event he or she witnessed and recorded in any form by an official in the course of an investigation, falls within the meaning of a "witness statement" under Rule 66(A)(i). Accordingly, facts contained in an investigator's interview notes which constitute statements made by the witness in the course of an investigation come within the meaning of "witness statements" under Rule 66(A)(i).[2]

o **What must be disclosed**: Rule 66 requires disclosure of all witness statements in the possession of the Prosecution, regardless of their form or source, save for any material covered by Rule 70 (A). An investigator's notes of statements made by a witness would therefore be disclosable,[3] but only to that extent.

o **What need not be disclosed**: Pursuant to Rule 70(A), any reports, memoranda, or other internal documents prepared by a party, its assistants or representatives in connection with the investigation or preparation of the case, are not subject to disclosure or notification under the aforementioned provisions. It follows that investigator's notes of an internal nature not containing statements made by a witness would not be disclosable.

o **The role of the Trial Chamber**: It is the role of the Trial Chamber to enforce disclosure obligations in the interests of a fair trial, and to ensure that the rights of the Accused, as provided in Article 17(4), to have adequate time and facilities for the preparation of his or her defence and to examine, or have examined, the witnesses against him or her, are respected.[4]

o **Late Disclosure**: Where evidence has not been disclosed or is disclosed so late as to prejudice the fairness of the trial, the Trial Chamber will apply appropriate remedies, which may include the exclusion of such evidence.[5] The specific remedy applied may vary from case to case.

---

[81] See also *Prosecutor v. Brima, Kamara, Kanu*, Case No. SCSL-04-16-T, Decision on Objection to Question Put by the Defence in Cross-Examination of Witness TF1-227, 15 June 2005, para. 37.

o ***Bona Fides of the Parties***: In explaining the rationale behind Rule 66, we adopt the principle enunciated by Trial Chamber 1, which is as follows: "The premise underlying disclosure obligations is that the parties should act bona fides at all times. There is authority from the evolving jurisprudence of the International Criminal Tribunals that any allegation by the Defence as to a violation of the disclosure rules by the Prosecution should be substantiated with prima facie proof of such a violation. This Chamber in recent decisions has indeed ruled that the Defence must "make a prima facie showing of materiality and that the requested evidence is in the custody or control of the Prosecution".[6]

---

[1] See *Prosecutor v. Norman et al.*, Case No. SCSL-2004-14-T, Ruling on disclosure of Witness statements, 1 October 2004, para. 2.
[2] See *Prosecutor v. Norman et al.*, Case No. SCSL-2004-14-PT, Decision on Disclosure of Witness Statements and Cross-examination, 16 July 2004, para. 10.
[3] See *Prosecutor v. Norman et al.*, Case No. SCSL-2004-14-PT, Decision on Disclosure of Witness Statements and Cross-examination, 16 July 2004, para. 7 and 16.
[4] See *Prosecutor v. Furundzija*, Scheduling Order, 29th April 1998; *Prosecutor v. Sam Hinga Norman, Moinina Fofana, Allieu Kondewa*, Decision on Disclosure of Witness Statements and Cross-Examination, 16th July 2004, para. 7
[5] See *Prosecutor v. Sesay et al.*, Case No. SCSL-2004-15-T, Ruling on Oral Application for the Exclusion of Statements of Witness TF1-141 Dated Respectively 9th of October, 2004, 19th and 20th of October, 2004, and 10th of January, 2005, 3 February 2005, para. 20 f.
[6] See *Prosecutor v. Sesay*, Decision on Defence Motion for Disclosure Pursuant to Rules 66 and 68 of the Rules, 9 July 2004, para. 27.

- **Rule 66: Disclosure by the Prosecution – "Witness Statement"**

o *Prosecutor v. Norman, Fofana, Kondewa*, Case No. 04-14-T, Decision on Disclosure of Witness Statements and Cross-Examination, 16 July 2004, para. 8-15, 23-24, 26-27:[82]

8. We note that the Defence raised the issue of what constitutes witness statements within the meaning of Rule 66. The

---

[82] See also *Prosecution v. Sesay, Kallon, Gbao*, Case No. SCSL-04-15-T, Ruling on Application for the Exclusion of Certain Supplemental Statements of Witness TF1-361 and Witness TF1-122, 1st June 2005, para. 16; *Prosecutor v. Sesay, Kallon, Gbao*, Case No. SCSL-04-15-T, Decision on the Gbao and Sesay Joint Application for the Exclusion of the Testimony of Witness TF1-141, 26 October 2005, para. 19; *Prosecutor v. Sesay, Kallon, Gbao*, Case No. SCSL-04-15-T, Decision on the Joint Defence Motion Requesting Conformity of Procedural Practice for Taking Witness Statements, 26 October 2005, para. 25, 29, 35; *Prosecutor v. Sesay, Kallon, Gbao*, Case No. SCSL-04-15-T, Decision on Prosecution Motion Objecting to Defence Submissions of Witness Statements with Inconsistencies Marked, 27 October 2005, para. 1, 19.

Defence has strenuously argued that a statement made or recorded in the third person rather than in the first person cannot properly be classified as a witness statement, and further, that interview notes do not amount to statements within the meaning of Rule 66 of the Rules.

9. In this regard, the Chamber would like to refer to the definition of a statement in Black's Law Dictionary,[1] which defines a statement as:

> 1. *Evidence.* A verbal assertion or non-verbal conduct intended as an assertion. 2. A formal and exact presentation of facts. 3. *Criminal Procedure.* An account of a person's (usu. a suspect's) knowledge of a crime, taken by the police pursuant to their investigation of the offence.

10. Indeed, the Chamber observes that nowhere in the rules is a witness statement defined. It is worth noting that the Appeals Chamber of the ICTY has considered that the usual meaning to be ascribed to a witness statement is "an account of a person's knowledge of a crime, which is <u>recorded through due procedure</u> in the course of an investigation into the crime".[2] (emphasis added) The Tribunals have also considered that transcribed trial testimony,[3] radio interviews,[4] unsigned witness declarations[5] and records of questions put to witnesses and answers given, constitute witness statements.[6]

11. The Trial Chambers of the ICTY have interpreted Rule 66 of the Rules to require disclosure of all witness statements in the possession of the Prosecution, regardless of their form or source. For instance, the Trial Chamber of the ICTY in the *Blaskic* case, stated that:

> The same interpretation of Sub-rule 66(A) leads the Trial Chamber to draw no distinction between the form or forms which these statements may have. Moreover, nothing in the text permits the introduction of the distinctions suggested by the Prosecution between "the official statements taken under oath or signed and recognised by the accused" and the others.[7]

12. In addition, that Trial Chamber decided that all documents in the Prosecution's file should be disclosed, regardless of their source and making an analogy between the criteria for prior statements of the accused person and those in respect of witnesses, observed as follows:

> [t]he principles [...] in support of the interpretation of Sub-rule 66(A) lead the Trial Chamber to the decision that all the previous statements of the accused which appear in the Prosecutor's file, whether collected by the Prosecution or originating from any other source, must be disclosed to the Defence immediately. [...] furthermore, the Trial Chamber considers that the same criteria as

those identified in respect of the accused's previous statements must apply mutatis mutandis to the previous statements of the witnesses also indicated in Sub-rule 66(A).[8] (emphasis added)

13. The ICTY Trial Chamber in the *Kordic*[9] case, considering a motion to compel the compliance of the Prosecution with Rule 66(A) and 68, ruled that:

[a]ny undisclosed prior statements of [co] Accused in the possession of the Prosecution made in any type of judicial proceedings, and whether collected by the Prosecution or originating from any other source, save for any material covered by Rule 70(A) of the Rules which have not been disclosed.

14. In its recent Judgement, the Appeals Chamber of the ICTR in the *Niyitegeka* case, observed that the Prosecution is required to make available to the Defence, the witness statement in the form in which it has been recorded.[10] Setting out the standard for recording interviews with witnesses, the Appeals Chamber, however, stated that the mere fact that a particular witness statement does not correspond to this standard, does not relieve a party from its obligation to disclose it pursuant to Rule 66(A)(ii) of the Rules. The said Chamber stated furthermore, that a statement not fulfilling the ideal standard is not inadmissible as such and that any inconsistency of a witness statement with that standard would be taken into consideration when assessing the probative value of the statement, if necessary.[11]

15. The Trial Chamber of the ICTR in the *Akayesu* case, determined that statements by witnesses that were not made under solemn declaration and not taken by judicial officers were still admissible. However, the probative value attached to them was considerably less than direct sworn testimony before the Chamber. The Chamber approached the issue of inconsistencies and contradictions between these statements and testimony at trial with caution. [12]

[...]

23. In this regard, we are of the opinion and we so hold, that any statement or declaration made by a witness in relation to an event he witnessed and recorded in any form by an official in the course of an investigation, falls within the meaning of a 'witness statement' under Rule 66(A)(i) of the Rules. When confronted with matters of legal characterization, this Chamber must also take cognisance of the socio-cultural dynamics at work in the context of the legal culture in which it functions, for example, the limited language abilities and capabilities of potential prosecution witnesses, and their level of educational literacy. In addition, and in the particular circumstances of this case, the witness who we have on record as an illiterate, certainly depended largely on the investigator

to record all the information that he disclosed to him during his interrogation.

24. We find that the facts contained in the interview notes, which, in the final analysis, are far from being statements of the investigator who is only the recorder, in fact constitute and are indeed, statements made by the witness in the course of an investigation and consequently, come within the purview, context, and meaning, of 'witness statements' under the provisions of Rule 66(A)(i) of the Rules.

[...]

26. Accordingly, the Trial Chamber finds that there is no evidence that the Prosecution has breached Rule 66(A)(i) as regards the disclosure of witness statements. In effect, there is no *prima facie* showing of materiality by the Defence that the allegedly objectionable evidence sought to be suppressed as inadmissible, was in the possession or in control of the Prosecution and that it withheld disclosure of the same.

27. The Trial Chamber recalls that on 26 April 2004, the Prosecution disclosed to the Defence copies of all witness statements for witnesses they intended to call at the trial, that had not already been disclosed. The Prosecution, in keeping with its continuing obligation to disclose additional materials, have continued to disclose such materials prior to and during trial, in some instances up to a day before the witness is due to testify. The Trial Chamber does not have any evidence before it, at this time, that the continued disclosure of witness statements by the Prosecution has violated the disclosure rules. Rule 67(D) provides that if either party discovers additional evidence that should have been produced earlier pursuant to the Rules, that party should notify the other party and the Trial Chamber of the existence of such material. In circumstances where the Prosecution obtains additional evidence from a witness that is subject to disclosure, then the Prosecution is required, pursuant to this Rule, to continuously disclose this material. Should there be evidence, however, that the Prosecution has failed in its duty to prepare and disclose witness statements in accordance with these Rules, the Defence should provide concrete evidence of this violation. As previously stated, there is no material before the Trial Chamber from which it may be concluded that the Prosecution is in breach of its disclosure obligations.

---

[1] Black's Law Dictionary, Seventh Edition, 1999, page 1416.

[2] *Prosecutor v. Blaskic*, Decision on the Appellant's Motion for the Production of Material, Suspension or Extension of the Briefing Schedule, and Additional Filings, 26 September 2000, paras 15-16.

[3] *Prosecutor v. Blaskic*, Decision on the Defence Motion for Sanctions for the Prosecutor's Failure to Comply with Sub-Rule 66(A) of the Rules and the Decision of 27 January 1997 Compelling the Production of All Statements of

the Accused, 15 July 1998; *Prosecutor v. Kupreskic*, Decision on the Prosecutor's Request to Release Testimony Pursuant to Rule 66 of the Rules of Procedure and Evidence Given in Closed Session Under Rule 79 of the Rules, 29 July 1998.
[4] *Prosecutor v. Musema*, Judgment, 27 January 2000, para. 85.
[5] *Prosecutor v. Musema*, Judgment, 27 January 2000, para. 85; *Prosecutor v. Akayesu*, Trial Judgment, 2 September 1998, para. 137.
[6] *Prosecutor v. Niyitegeka*, Appeals Judgment, 9 July 2004, para. 34.
[7] *Prosecutor v. Blaskic*, Decision on the Production of Discovery Materials, 27 January 1997, para. 37.
[8] *Prosecutor v. Blaskic*, Decision on Motion to Compel the Production of Discovery Materials, 27 January 1997, para. 37-38.
[9] *Prosecutor v. Kordic*, Order on Motion to Compel the Compliance by the Prosecutor with Rule 66(A) and 68, 26 February 1999.
[10] *Prosecutor v. Niyitegeka*, Appeals Judgement, 9 July 2004, para. 35.
[11] *Id*, para. 36.
[12] *Prosecutor v. Akayesu*, Trial Judgement, 2 September 1998, para. 137.

R66-TC-5

o *Prosecutor v. Sesay, Kallon, Gbao*, Case No. SCSL-04-15-T, Ruling on the Admission of Command Structure Chart as an Exhibit, 4 February 2005, para. 22:

22. Another Defence submission on the issue is that the Chart is analogous to a statement made by a witness, and that it is in violation of Rule 66, the Prosecution having failed to disclose it. Consistent with our *Decision on Disclosure of Witness Statements and Cross-Examination*,[1] we are of the opinion that the Chart can be considered a witness statement.

[1] *Prosecutor v. Norman et al.*, Case No. SCSL-04-14-T, Decision on Disclosure of Witness Statements and Cross-Examination, 16 July 2004.

R66-TC-6

o *Prosecutor v. Sesay, Kallon, Gbao*, Case No. SCSL-04-14-T, Decision on the Joint Defence Motion Requesting Conformity of Procedural Practice for Taking Witness Statements, 26 October 2005, para. 26-28:

26. We, therefore, reiterate that the Prosecution is required to disclose all witness statements to the Defence in accordance with Rule 66 regardless the form in which they are recorded. The Chamber has found that the Prosecution "witness statements" include interview notes that were not signed by the witness,[1] handwritten interview notes taken by the Prosecution and its investigators,[2] and new evidence elicited during "proofing sessions" with Prosecution counsel.[3] This broad definition of witness statements under Rule 66 affords the Defence the broadest disclosure rights.

27. The Chamber recalls that while highlighting that witness statements were disclosable even if they do not meet this standard, the Appeals Chamber of the ICTR outlined the ideal standard for the taking of witness statements in these terms:

> A record of a witness interview, ideally is composed of all the questions that were put to a witness and of all the answers given by the witness. The time of the beginning and the end of an interview, specific events such as requests for breaks, offering and accepting of cigarettes, coffee and other events that could have an impact on the statement or its assessment should be recorded as well.
>
> Such an interview must be recorded in a language the witness understands. As soon as possible after the interview has been given, the witness must have the chance to read the record or to have it read out to him or her to make the corrections he or she deems necessary and then the witness must sign the record to attest to the truthfulness and correctness of its content to the best of his or her knowledge and belief. A co-signature by the investigator and interpreter, if any, concludes such a record.[4]

28. It is noteworthy, however, that the Appeals Chamber emphasised that "a witness statement which does not correspond to the standard set out above does not necessarily render the proceedings unfair."[5]

---

[1] Id., para. 22-24.
[2] *Prosecutor v. Norman, Fofana, Kondewa*, SCSL-04-14-T, "Ruling on Disclosure of Witness of Witness Statements", 1 October 2004, para. 5-6.
[3] *Prosecutor v. Sesay, Kallon, Gbao*, SCSL-04-15-T, "Decision on the Gbao and Sesay Joint Application for the Exclusion of the Testimony of Witness TF1-141", 26 October 2005, para. 34.
[4] *Prosecutor v. Niyitegeka*, supra [...], para. 31-32.
[5] Id. para 35.

- **Rule 66: Disclosure by the Prosecution – Investigator's Notes**

R66-TC-7

o *Prosecutor v. Brima, Kamara, Kanu*, Case No. SCSL-04-16-T, Decision on Joint Defence Motion on Disclosure of All Original Witness Statements, Interview Notes and Investigator's Notes Pursuant to Rule 66 and/or 68, 4 May 2005, para. 17-19:

17. In the present case, the Prosecution has explained in its Response that during the initial investigation phase investigators' notes were taken in rough form which included statements

of potential witnesses together with information that was relevant only to the internal functioning of the OTP, such as investigative leads. In other words, disclosable and non-disclosable materials were recorded in the same investigator's notes without distinction. All evidentiary material collected in rough form was then transferred to written witness statements (either handwritten or typewritten) and non-disclosable material was transferred to Internal Memoranda. The rough notes were thus rendered superfluous and were destroyed.

18. It seems to us that the procedure adopted by the Prosecution to separate disclosable and non-disclosable material by reducing the disclosable material to the form of a witness statement was reasonable in the circumstances. In our view, the fact that the rough notes containing both disclosable and non-disclosable material were later destroyed does not, by itself, amount to a failure by the Prosecution to fulfil its disclosure obligations.

19. There is nothing before the Trial Chamber which would entitle it to conclude that the Prosecution has concealed or destroyed material which it was obliged to disclose. As stated by the Prosecution, all witness statements within the possession or control of the OTP have been disclosed to the Defence, and there are no longer any original investigators notes in existence. The Defence has not established any reason to refute the assumption that the Prosecution acted in good faith. Further, the Prosecution undertakes that in the future, it will provide handwritten statements as well as typed versions thereof, where such hand written versions exist. The Trial Chamber therefore finds that the Defence has failed to demonstrate or substantiate by prima *facie* proof the allegation of breach by the Prosecution of Rules 66 and 68.

R66-TC-8   o *Prosecutor v. Sesay, Kallon, Gbao*, Case No. SCSL-04-15-T, Decision on the Gbao and Sesay Joint Application for the Exclusion of the Testimony of Witness TF1-141, 26 October 2005, para. 27-28:[83]

27. [...] This Chamber, in its "Ruling on Disclosure of Witness Statements" did not accept this assertion and we found instead that interview notes recorded by the Prosecution, in whatever form, are the witness' statements and were thus disclosable under Rule 66(A)(i) of the Rules.[(1)] [...]

---

[83] See also *Prosecutor v. Sesay, Kallon, Gbao*, Case No. SCSL-04-14-T, Decision on the Joint Defence Motion Requesting Conformity of Procedural Practice for Taking Witness Statements, 26 October 2005, para. 26.

DIGEST OF JURISPRUDENCE OF THE SPECIAL COURT FOR SIERRA LEONE   443

28. The Chamber reiterates its findings of the 1st of October 2004 that investigator's notes, in whatever form they may be, taken during interviews with witnesses constitute witness statements and are thus disclosable. However, this Court recognises that investigators' notes may also contain, in addition to the witness statements, information that should be protected from disclosure pursuant to Rule 70(A) when the information relates solely to matters internal to the investigation or prosecution.

(1) *Prosecutor v. Norman, Fofana and Kondewa*, SCSL-04-14-T, "Ruling on Disclosure of Witness Statements", 1 October 2004, paras. 10 and 16.

- **Rule 66(A)(i): Disclosure by the Prosecution – "Preliminary" and "Subsequent" Disclosures**

R66-TC-9

o *Prosecutor v. Kamara*, SCSL-04-16-PT, Decision and Order on Defence Preliminary Motion on Defects in the Form of the Indictment, 1 April 2004, para. 28:

28. Interestingly, the Prosecution seeks to make a distinction between "Preliminary Disclosure" and "Subsequent Disclosure",(1) a distinction which in the Trial Chamber's view is not supported by Rule 66(A)(i) which stated at the time applicable to this Motion that: [Rule 66(A)(i)]

(1) See Response, para. 1.

- **Rule 66(A)(i): Disclosure by the Prosecution – Protection of Victims and Witnesses**

R66-TC-10

o *Prosecutor v. Norman*, Case No. SCSL-03-08-PT, Decision on the Prosecution Motion to Allow Disclosure to the Registry and to Keep Disclosed Materials Under Seal Until Appropriate Protective Measures Are in Place, 17 April 2003, para. 9-11:[84]

[84] See also *Prosecutor v. Kallon*, Case No. SCSL-03-07-PT, Decision on the Prosecution Motion to Allow Disclosure to the Registry and to Keep Disclosed Material Under Seal Until Appropriate Protective Measures Are in Place, 17 April 2003; *Prosecutor v. Sesay*, Case No. SCSL-03-05-PT, Decision on the Prosecution Motion to Allow Disclosure to the Registry and to Keep Disclosed Material Under Seal Until Appropriate Protective Measures Are in Place, 17 April 2003; *Prosecutor v. Brima*, Case No. SCSL-03-06-PT, Order on Disclosure to the Registry, 17 April 2003; *Prosecutor v. Gbao*, Case No. SCSL-03-09-PT, Scheduling Order and Order on Disclosure to the Registry, 23 May 2003.

9. [...] [T]he Court deems it necessary that disclosures pursuant to Rule 66 (A)(i) and Rule 68 (B) shall be made with a view to ensure appropriate protection of witnesses and victims as well as for the confidentiality of all non-public materials subject to such disclosure;

10. Pending a ruling on the Prosecution Motion for Immediate Protective Measures for Witnesses and Victims and for Non-Public Disclosure, it is therefore necessary to guarantee that the fulfilment of the Prosecution's obligations to disclose shall encompass appropriate interim measures for the protection of witnesses and victims as well as for the confidentiality of all non-public materials subject to disclosure by the Prosecution.

11. Therefore, the Court is of the opinion that the Prosecution should be allowed to comply with its obligations to disclose pursuant to Rule 66 (A)(i) and Rule 68 (B) by making such disclosures to the Registry;

R66-TC-11

o *Prosecutor v. Fofana*, Case No. SCSL-03-11-PT, Interim Order for the Transmission of Disclosure Materials to the Registrar, 30 July 2003, para. 10-14:[85]

10. The Court notes that in the Practice Direction for Disclosure by the Prosecutor, the Registrar directs that disclosure pursuant to Rule 66(A)(i) shall be made to the Defence Counsel, identified either as a Counsel engaged by an accused pursuant to Rule 44 or a Counsel assigned to an accused pursuant to Rule 45, and that the Defence Office is not in a position to receive disclosure of materials.

11. Pending assignment of Counsel in accordance with Rule 45, the Registry shall certify the Prosecution fulfilment of the obligations to disclose and the sealing and dating of the disclosure materials until assignment of Counsel is accomplished.

12. The Court accepts and endorses the provisions set forth in the Practice Direction for Disclosure by the Prosecutor. With a view to ensure the appropriate protection of witnesses and victims as well as the confidentiality of all non-public materials subject to disclosure, the Court nevertheless deems it essential and necessary that disclosures pursuant to Rule 66(A)(i) and Rule 68(B) be made;

---

[85] See also *Prosecutor v. Kamara*, Case No. SCSL-03-10-PT, Interim Order for the Transmission of the Disclosure Materials to the Registrar, 2 July 2003, para. 10-13; *Prosecutor v. Kondewa*, Case No. SCSL-03-12-PT, Interim Order for the Transmission of the Disclosure Materials to the Registrar, 30 July 2003, para. 6-10; *Prosecutor v. Kanu*, Case No. SCSL-03-13-PT, Decision on Urgent Request for Interim Measures Until Appropriate Protective Measures Are in Place, 15 October 2003, para. 5-6.

13. Pending deliberation and ruling on the Motion, it is therefore necessary to guarantee the fulfilment of the Prosecution's obligations to disclose and this shall encompass appropriate interim measures for the protection of witnesses and victims as well as for the confidentiality of all non-public materials subject to disclosure.

14. Considering the aforementioned and relying on a common practical procedure previously adopted by the Special Court, the Prosecution may comply with its disclosure obligations pursuant to Rule 66(A) (i) and Rule 68(B) of the Rules by transmitting the disclosure materials to the Registrar, the Registrar keeping the disclosure materials under seal until deliberation on the Motion is rendered and orders for appropriate protective measures for witnesses, victims and non-public materials have been issued.

- **Rule 66(A)(i): Disclosure by the Prosecution – Material in Support of Joinder**

R66-TC-12   o *Prosecutor v. Sesay* (Case No. SCSL-03-05-PT), *Brima* (Case No. SCSL-03-06-PT), *Kallon* (Case No. SCSL-03-07-PT), *Gbao* (Case No. SCSL-03-09-PT), *Kamara* (Case No. SCSL-03-10-PT), *Kanu* (Case No. SCSL-03-13-PT), Decision and Order on Prosecution Motions for Joinder, 27 January 2004, para. 19:

19. On the prematurity issue, it was also submitted that delayed disclosure of statements of Prosecution witnesses pursuant to Rules 66(A)(i), Rule 69 and Rule 75 of the Rules rendered the Motions premature. Relying on the *Nyiramasuhuko* Decision, the response of the Chamber to this submission is that despite the importance of timely disclosure, it is not an issue at this stage of the proceedings. The Chamber is of the view that even if the Prosecution had not disclosed such material, the rights of the Accused would not have been infringed by the operation of Rule 66(A)(i) of the Rules. It is noteworthy that the said Rule refers to the disclosure of material in support of evidence the Prosecutor intends to present at trial, not disclosure of material in support of a joinder motion.

- **Rule 66(A)(i): Disclosure by the Prosecution – Failure to Disclose – Exclusion of Evidence**

R66-TC-13
o *Prosecution v. Sesay, Kallon, Gbao*, Case No. SCSL-04-15-T, Ruling on Disclosure Regarding Witness TF1-195, 4 February 2005, para. 2-8:[86]

2. After the conclusion of the examination in chief of Witness TF1-195, the Defence raised the objection that certain portions of the evidence pertaining to two specific episodes, firstly the rape of Witness TF1-195 which allegedly took place about two miles from Gandorhun and, secondly an allegation of forced labour, were new. They also contended that they were already in possession of the Prosecution and had not been previously disclosed to the Defence.

3. Consequently, the Defence claimed that the Prosecution had breached its obligations to disclose pursuant to Rule 66 of the Rules and accordingly requested that the Chamber excludes these portions of the evidence from the examination in chief of Witness TF1-195.

4. The Chamber requested that the Defence explain why it had only raised its objection after the conclusion of the examination in chief of the witness rather than at each specific moment when the evidence in question was led by the Prosecution. The Defence submitted that it was not sure whether the evidence of the rape was new or rather whether it referred, with some modifications, to another episode of rape contained in the previously disclosed statement. It was also stated by the Defence that only when evidence on this second episode of rape was led by the Prosecution, at the very end of the examination-in-chief of Witness TF1-195, the Defence became sure of the novelty of the portion of evidence pertaining to the first rape. In addition, the Defence indicated that it deliberately decided not to raise any objection until the end of the examination-in-chief of Witness TF1-195 in order to avoid causing her undue distress during her testimony.

5. In its response to the objection, the Prosecution stated that it would not oppose an application to exclude or rule inadmissible evidence pertaining to the first episode of rape and to the forced labour. Asked by the Chamber whether it was in possession of the evidence of both the first episode of rape of Witness TF1-195 and the forced labour, the Prosecution responded that it had been in possession of this evidence for two days and admitted that it accordingly ought to have been disclosed to the Defence prior to testimony in court.

---

[86] See also *Prosecutor v. Sesay, Kallon, Gbao*, Case No. SCSL-04-15-T, Decision on the Gbao and Sesay Joint Application for the Exclusion of the Testimony of Witness TF1-141, 26 October 2005, para. 36.

6. The Chamber is of the opinion that the aforesaid matters complained of clearly constitute a breach on the part of the Prosecution of their disclosure obligation pursuant to Rule 66 of Rules. The rationale of this rule, as expounded in our recent decisions on the subject,[1] is that both parties must act in good faith at all times in respect of their disclosure obligations.

7. The Chamber acknowledges that, as a general rule, the judicially preferred remedy for a breach of disclosure obligations by the Prosecution is an extension of time to enable the Defence to adequately prepare their case. It is not exclusion of the evidence. However, in the particular circumstances at hand, this Chamber finds that the Prosecution has failed to promptly exercise due diligence that is required in discharging its duty to disclose to the Defence all of the information in its possession in accordance with Rule 66 of the Rules, and given the gravity of the allegations, is satisfied that this is a proper case in which to apply the remedy of exclusion.

8. The Chamber, therefore, **ORDERS** that the aforesaid portions of the testimony of Witness TF1-195 are to be excluded and will not be given any consideration by this Chamber as part of the Prosecution case.

---

[1] See, for example: *Prosecutor v. Sesay et al.*, Case No. SCSL-04-15-T, Ruling on Oral Application for the Exclusion of "Additional" Statement for Witness TF1-060, 23 July 2004; *Prosecutor v. Norman et al.*, Case No SCSL-04-14-T, Decision on Disclosure of Witness Statements and Cross-Examination, 16 July 2004; *Prosecutor v. Brima et al.*, Case No. SCSL-04-16-PT, Kanu – Decision on Motions for Exclusion of Prosecution Witness Statements and Stay of Filing of Prosecution Statements; *Prosecutor v. Sesay et al.*, Case No. SCSL-04-15-T, Sesay – Decision on Defence Motion for Disclosure Pursuant to Rules 66 and 68 of the Rules, 9 July 2004; *Prosecutor v. Sesay et al.*, Case No. SCSL-04-15-T, Ruling on the Oral Application of the Exclusion of Part of the Testimony of Witness TF1-199, 26 July 2004; and *Prosecutor v. Sesay et al.*, Case No. SCSL-04-15-T, Ruling on Disclosure Regarding Witness TF1-015, 28 January 2005.

- **Rule 66(A)(ii): Disclosure by the Prosecution – Scope of Disclosure**

R66-TC-14

o *Prosecutor v. Sesay*, Case No. SCSL-04-15-T, Decision on Defence Motion for Disclosure Pursuant to Rule 66 and 68 of the Rules, 9 July 2004, para. 21-22:[87]

21. From an ordinary and plain reading of Rule 66(A)(ii) of the Rules, it is clear that it imposes a reciprocal obligation;

---

[87] See also *Prosecutor v. Sesay, Kallon, Gbao*, Case No. SCSL-2004-15-T, Ruling on Disclosure Regarding Witness TF1-195, 4 February 2005, para. 6.

one on the Prosecution and the other on the Defence. The first part of the Rule places the onus of showing good cause on the Prosecution, in a case where it intends to call additional witnesses to testify at the trial. There is no contention here, as the Prosecution states that it has made such disclosures and pledged to continue disclosure of supplemental copies to the Defence should the need arise. The second part of the Rule places the burden on the Defence to show good cause why the evidence of witnesses whom the Prosecution does not want to call to testify at trial should be disclosed to the Defence. The Defence acknowledges in its motion that "it is obvious from a reading of Rule 66(A)(ii) of the Rules that the obligation is on the Defence to show good cause", although it asserts that it cannot show such good cause "without knowing what material exists in the possession of the Prosecution." Despite this admission by the Defence, it still seeks to rely on what it describes as guarantee by the Prosecution to allow the Defence access to materials pertaining to Rule 66(A)(ii) of the Rules, which guarantee is contested by the Prosecution.

22. The obligation in Rule 66(A)(ii) of the Rules should be resolved by a clear interpretation of the Rules. The Chamber takes cognisance of the Prosecution's statement that it has disclosed to the Defence the statements of the witnesses it intends to call to testify at trial and observes that the Defence has made some sweeping requests for disclosure by the Prosecution of material under Rule 66(A)(ii) of the Rules, without specifying any evidence that could guide the Chamber in deciding whether or not the Prosecution is in possession of additional witness statements it does not intend to call to testify. Furthermore, the Defence has not adduced any evidence to show good cause why such materials, if they exist, should be disclosed to it.

- **Rule 66(A)(ii): Disclosure by the Prosecution – Time of Disclosure – Additional Statements Containing New allegations**

R66-TC-15   o *Prosecutor v. Sesay*, Case No. SCSL-04-15-T, Ruling on Oral Application for the Exclusion of "Additional" Statement for Witness TF1-060, 23 July 2004, para. 10-13, 15-17:[88]

---

[88] See also *Prosecutor v. Sesay, Kallon, Gbao*, Case No. SCSL-04-15-T, Ruling on Oral Application for the Exclusion of Statements of Witness TF1-141 Dated Respectively 9th of October, 2004 19th and 20th of October, 2004, and 10th of January, 2005, 3 February 2005, para. 5, 19-20, 24-26; *Prosecutor v. Sesay, Kallon, Gbao*, Case No. SCSL-04-15-T, Ruling on Disclosure Regarding Witness TF1-195, 4 February 2005, para. 6; *Prosecution v. Sesay, Kallon, Gbao*, Case No. SCSL-04-15-T, Ruling on Application for the Exclusion of Certain

10. Taking due cognizance of the importance of Article 17(4) of the Statute in ensuring ample protection of the rights of an accused to have time and adequate facilities for the preparation of his case, and also to examine or have examined the witnesses against him, the Trial Chamber emphasized its role to enforce disclosure obligations in the interest of a fair trial "where evidence has not been disclosed or is disclosed so late as to prejudice the fairness of the trial".[1] In this regard, the Chamber indicated that its judicial option in such an eventuality would be "to apply appropri-ate remedies which may include exclusion of such evidence."[2]

11. Consistent with the foregoing exposition of the law, we note that in the case of *Prosecutor v. Bagosora*,[3] the Trial Chamber of the International Criminal Tribunal for Rwanda ("ICTR") reasoned as follows:

   i. that the issue whether the material disclosed is new requires a comparative assessment;
   ii. that such an assessment requires an examination of the allegedly new statement and the original statement of the witness including any reference of the event in question in the Indictment and the Pre-Trial Brief of the Prosecution;
   iii. that such an examination should also include a consideration of notice to the Defence that the particular witness will testify on that event, and the extent to which the evidentiary material alters the incriminating quality of the evidence of which the Defence already had notice.[4]

12. The reasoning of this same Chamber was similar to the above regarding the admissibility on the same grounds of the evidence of another witness in the same case. On that issue, the Chamber had this to say:

> These Rules and the arguments of the parties give rise to three distinct questions. First, is this evidence relevant to the charges in the Indictments, or do they constitute entirely new charges? Second, do the will-say statements merely provide additional details of matters already disclosed in Witness DBQ original witness statement, or in other materials disclosed to the Defence? Third, if this is indeed new evidence, should it be admitted and under what conditions?[5]

Supplemental Statements of Witness TF1-361 and Witness TF1-122, 1st June 2005, para. 21-22; *Prosecutor v. Brima, Kamara, Kanu*, Case No. SCSL-04-16-T, Decision on Objection to Question Put by the Defence in Cross-Examination of Witness TF1-227, 15 June 2005, para. 42; *Prosecutor v. Brima, Kamara, Kanu*, Case No. SCSL-04-16-T, Decision on Joint Defence Motion Pertaining to Objections to the Nature of Testimony in Chief of Witness TF1-150, 16 June 2005, para. 9.

13. Guided by these principles and reasoning, the major question for determination by this Chamber is whether the Defence has demonstrated or substantiated with prima facie proof that the Prosecution is in breach of its disclosure obligations under Rule 66(A)(ii) and in violation of the Article 17(4) of the Statute rights of the Accused persons herein on the alleged grounds of disclosing at this stage a witness statement constituting entirely new allegations from those in the Indictment, and one that is not at all supplemental in character vis-à-vis the original statement of the witness but which amounts to, as it were, an entirely new statement of an entirely new witness.

[...]

15. As a matter of law, the Chamber would like to reiterate what it emphasized in a previous Ruling that Rule 66 does impose upon the Prosecution the obligation to continuously disclose to the Defence copies of statements of all witnesses whom they intend to call which include new developments in the investigation[6] whether in the form of "will-say statements" or interview notes or any other forms obtained from a witness at any time prior to the witness giving evidence in trial.

16. Based on the foregoing considerations and our specific findings, the Chamber is of the opinion that the Defence has not substantiated by a *prima facie* showing the allegations of breach by the Prosecution of Rule 66(A)(ii) of the Rules, Article 17(4) of the Statute, and the Chamber's Order for Disclosure dated 1 April 2004.

17. Accordingly, the application for exclusion or suppression of the supplemental evidence is denied, on the understanding however, that the Defence reserves its right to cross examine this witness on all issues raised including those in the supplemental statement.

---

[1] *Prosecutor v. Norman et al., supra*, para 7.
[2] *Id.*
[3] *Prosecutor v. Bagosora*, Case No. ICTR-98-41-T, Decision on Admissibility of Evidence of Witness DP, 18 November 2003.
[4] *Id.*, para 6.
[5] *Id.*, Decision on Admissibility of Evidence of Witness DBQ, 18 November 2003. See also *Id.*, Decision on Certification of Appeal Concerning Will-Say Statements of Witnesses DBQ, DP and DA, 5 December 2003.
[6] *Prosecutor v. Norman et al., supra*, para 6.

R66-TC-16

o *Prosecutor v. Brima, Kamara, Kanu*, Case No. SCSL-04-16-T, Decision on Objection to Question Put by the Defence in Cross-Examination of Witness TF1-227, 15 June 2005, para. 38-40:

38. We agree with the observation of the ICTR in the case of the *Prosecutor v. Bagosora and others* and do not:

> [b]elieve that there is a serious possibility that the Rules could be interpreted to mean, as argued by the Defence, that any new evidence disclosed or discovered after the start of a trial is categorically inadmissible. In the Chamber's view, this decision involves an exercise of discretion based on an assessment of the factual significance of the evidence, within the framework of clear legal guidelines.⁽¹⁾

39. The Trial Chamber cannot impose one inflexible time limit applicable to the many possible allegations and situations that arise in Trial. We consider the Court would not be acting in the interests of the proper administration of justice or of an expeditious hearing if it imposed a definite period of notice applicable to all and every case.

40. Late notice of further statements which contain new allegations is curable by allowing time to the Defence to properly prepare.

⁽¹⁾ *The Prosecutor v. Bagosora et al.*, Case No. ICTR-98-41-T, Decision on Certification of Appeal Concerning Will-Say Statements of Witnesses DBQ, DP, DA, 5 December 2003, para. 10.

- **Rule 66(A)(ii): Disclosure by the Prosecution – Will-Say Statements Are Not Evidence**

R66-TC-17   o *Prosecutor v. Brima, Kamara, Kanu*, Case No. SCSL-04-16-T, Decision on Joint Defence Motion Pertaining to Objections to the Nature of Testimony in Chief of Witness TF1-150, 16 June 2005, para. 9-13:[89]

9. Witness TF1-150 has not yet given evidence and is only scheduled to testify some time in the near future. As such, it is pre-mature and speculative for anyone to refer to the "Testimony-in-chief" or "oral evidence" of this witness as it does not yet exist. Neither is the Trial Chamber seized with an application by the Prosecution to tender into evidence the impugned Report or any portions thereof pursuant to Rule 92bis. What the

---

[89] See also *Prosecutor v. Brima, Kamara, Kanu*, Case No. SCSL-04-16-T, Decision on Joint Defence Motion on Admissibility of Expert Witness/Expert Evidence and Filing of Notice Pursuant to Rule 94*bis*(B)(i) and (ii), on Re-filed Defence Request for Disclosure, and on the Joint Defence Motion for Exclusion of Medical Information, Statistics and Abstracts Pertaining to Witnesses TF1-081 and TF1-188, 16 June 2005, para. 12.

Prosecution has done however, is to disclose the witness' pre-trial statement of 18 April 2005 together with the impugned report as an attachment thereto, in discharge of their disclosure obligation pursuant to Rule 66 of the Rules. The Prosecution disclosure obligation under Rule 66 as persuasively elaborated by the Special Court in the case of The *Prosecutor v. Norman et al.*[1] and the case of the *Prosecutor v. Sesay et al.*[2] should not be misinterpreted to mean that the disclosed material is automatically evidence. In both these cases the trial Chamber observed that the Prosecution is under an obligation pursuant to Rule 66 to continuously disclose to the defence copies of all statements of all witnesses whom they intend to call, including new developments in the investigation in the form of "will say statements" or interview notes or other forms obtained from a witness at any time prior to the witness giving his testimony in court.

10. The Prosecution in their submissions have made it clear that they do not intend to lead opinion evidence with regard to this witness. Nor does the Prosecution intend to tender the whole of the impugned Report in evidence. The Prosecution intends merely "*to lead oral evidence relating to some of the matters referred to in the report.*" The Trial Chamber is of the view that for it to entertain any objections on what amounts to mere "intentions" by the Prosecution with regard to Witness TF1-150 and not on his oral testimony, would at best be premature and speculative.

11. We note that the impugned Report is annexed to and forms part of the witness' pre-trial statement to the Prosecution, dated 18 April 2005. We further note that both the pre-trial statement and the annexed report are not evidence. They are merely documents disclosed by the Prosecution under Rule 66 in order to put the Defence on notice about the kind of evidence the Prosecution intends to adduce, and to enable the Defence to adequately prepare to cross-examine Witness TF1-150 on any aspect thereof, if the Defence so wishes. The Trial Chamber is further of the view that the disclosure of a witness' pre-trial statement does not automatically transform it into "evidence" in the absence of an application or request to tender by the party wishing to rely upon it. We know of no authority to the contrary.

12. By their Joint Motion, the Defence for the Accused Brima, Kanu and Kamara are in fact asking the Trial Chamber to exclude certain portions of the pre-trial statement of Witness TF1-150 dated 18 April 2005, namely the Report annexed to that statement. The Trial Chamber has no power or authority to order the Prosecution to change or alter the content of a witness' pre-trial statement. The Trial Chamber's power to entertain any objections with regard to "the intended oral evidence" of Witness TF1-150, is only set into motion once the Witness

begins to testify or when the Prosecution has through his testimony applied or requested to tender documentary evidence pursuant to the Rules, but not before.

13. The *Kordic and Cerkez* Case[3] cited by both parties is both instructive and distinguishable. In that case the Office of the Prosecutor applied to tender in evidence the *Tulica* Dossier and Investigator's Report (consisting of maps, video footage, witness statements, court transcripts, exhumation reports, photographs and an investigators report) in response to the Trial Chamber's request to *"expedite proceedings without compromising the right of the accused to a fair trial."* Clearly the Defence objections in the *Tulica* Case were made at an appropriate time after the Prosecution made its application to tender in evidence the Report. In the present Motion, the Prosecution has not yet led any oral evidence in regard to the impugned Report nor has the Prosecution applied to tender in evidence the said report or portions thereof as yet. The Trial Chamber accordingly finds that the Defence objections with regard to the intended testimony of Witness TF1-150 and the report annexed to this witness' pre-trial statement on grounds of lack of foundation, inadmissibility and relevance, are speculative and premature at this stage.

---

[1] *The Prosecutor v. Norman et al.*, Case No. SCSL-04-14-T, Decision on Disclosure of Witness Statements and cross-examination, 16 July 2004, para. 6).
[2] *The Prosecutor v. Sesay et al.*, Case No. SCSL-2004-15-T, Ruling on Oral Application for the Exclusion of "Additional" Statement for Witness TF1-060, 23 July 2004, para. 15.
[3] *The Prosecution v. Kordic and Cerkez* Case No. IT-95-14/2-T, Decision on the Prosecution Application to Admit the Tulica Report and Dossier into Evidence, 29 July 1999

- **Rule 66(A)(iii): Inspection of Books, Documents, Photographs and Tangible Objects**

R66-TC-18

o *Prosecutor v. Sesay*, Case No. SCSL-04-15-T, Decision on Defence Motion for Disclosure Pursuant to Rule 66 and 68 of the Rules, 9 July 2004, para. 26-30:[90]

26. In the *Celibici* case,[1] the Trial Chamber of the ICTY acknowledged that the Rules provide no guidelines regarding

---

[90] See also *Prosecutor v. Sesay, Kallon, Gbao*, Case No. SCSL-04-15-T, Ruling on Disclosure Regarding Witness TF1-195, 4 February 2005, para. 6; *Prosecutor v. Sesay, Kallon, Gbao*, Case No. SCSL-04-15-T, Decision on the Gbao and Sesay Joint Application for the Exclusion of the Testimony of Witness TF1-141, 26 October 2005, para. 24.

the process of determining the materiality of evidence. However, recourse to national jurisdictions has elucidated what parameters should be taken into consideration in determining the materiality of evidence.[2]

27. In this regard, the Chamber finds instructive the reasoning of the U.S. Supreme Court in the case of *United States v. Mandel*, where it was held that as a threshold matter, the Prosecution is initially the party responsible for deciding what evidence it has in its possession that may be material to the preparation of the Defence, by virtue of the simple fact that it is the party with possession of the evidence. If the Defence believes that the Prosecution has withheld evidence material to its preparation, it can challenge the Prosecution by reasserting its rights to the evidence. At that point there are three alternatives for the Prosecution: (i) hand over the requested evidence; (ii) deny that it has the requested evidence in its possession; (iii) admit that it has the evidence but refuse to allow the Defence to inspect it. It is only if there is a dispute as to materiality that the Trial Chamber would become involved and act as a referee between the parties in order to make this determination. We therefore emphasize that when presenting this issue to the Trial Chamber, the Defence should be guided by the above definitions of materiality. The Defence however, may not rely on unspecified and unsubstantiated allegations or a general description of the information, but must make a prima facie showing of materiality and that the requested evidence is in the custody or control of the Prosecution.[3]

28. In this regard, case law from the ICTY and International Criminal Tribunal for Rwanda ("ICTR") has articulated the requirements for disclosure under Rule 66(A)(iii). Instructively, in the *Celibici* Decision, the Trial Chamber of the ICTY concluded with regard to the extent of the Prosecution's disclosure obligations under the ICTY Rules that "Rule 66(B) imposes on the Prosecution the responsibility of making the initial determination of materiality of evidence within its possession and if disputed, requires the Defence to specifically identify evidence material to the preparation of the Defence that is being withheld by the Prosecutor."[4] The same interpretation was adopted in the case of *Prosecutor v. Ndayambaje*,[5] where the Trial Chamber of the ICTR found that the Defence must, prima facie, establish materiality.

29. Consistent with our recent decision in the *Kondewa* case,[6] it is the Chamber's view that the materials requested by the Defence are in general, germane to the conflict that unraveled in Sierra Leone, but not specific to the alleged criminal responsibility of the Accused in particular.

30. The Chamber finds that the Defence has not shown how the evidence it requests, namely the role of ECOWAS in the disarmament of the RUF, AFRC and CDF, pursuant to the

peace agreement; the role played by Charles Taylor in the conflict; the alleged training of the RUF command structure in Libya; clarification of the role played by the Accused in the release of UNAMSIL troops at the time of the conflict, will be material to its case.

---

[1] *Prosecutor v. Delalic et al.*, Case No. IT-96-21, Decision on the Motion by the Accused Zejnil Delalic for the Disclosure of Evidence, 26 September 1996 ("*Celibici* Decision").

[2] *United States v. Jackson*, 850 F. Supp. 1481,1503 (U.S. Dist. Ct. D. Kan. 1994*)* quoting *United States v. Lloyd,* 992 F.2d 348, 351 (U.S. Ct. App. D.C. Cir. 1993), quoted in the *Celibici* Decision, *id*: it was held that the requested evidence must be "significantly helpful to an understanding of important inculpatory or exculpatory evidence"; it is material if there "is a strong indication that ... it will 'play an important role in uncovering admissible evidence, aiding witness preparation, corroborating testimony, or assisting impeachment or rebuttal.'" Significant jurisprudence in the United States Federal courts on the scope of "materiality" demonstrates that it is generally accepted that to be material, the requested information must have "more than an abstract logical relationship to the issues." Jurisprudence from the British system establishes that the test of materiality was adopted by the Court of Appeals in *R v. Keane (99 CR. App.R.1)*, which similarly defines disclosable matter as that which can be seen on a sensible appraisal by the prosecution (1) to be relevant or possibly relevant to an issue in the case; (2) to raise or possibly raise a new issue whose existence is not apparent from the evidence the Prosecution proposes to use; (3) to hold out a real, as opposed to fanciful, prospect of providing a lead on evidence which goes to (1) or (2).

[3] *See United States v. Mandel*, 914 F.2d 1215, 1219 (9th Cir. 1990); quoted in the *Celibici* Decision, *supra*, para. 9.

[4] *Celibici* Decision, *supra*, para. 11.

[5] *Prosecutor v. Ndayambaje*, Case No. ICTR-96-8-T, Decision on the Defence Motion for Disclosure, 25 September 2001, para. 11 ("*Ndayambaje* Decision").

[6] *Kondewa* Decision, *supra*.

Rule 67: Reciprocal Disclosure of Evidence
(amended 7 March 2003)

Subject to the provisions of Rules 53 and 69:

(A) As early as reasonably practicable and in any event prior to the commencement of the trial:

    (i) The Prosecutor shall notify the defence of the names of the witnesses that he intends to call to establish the guilt of the accused and in rebuttal of any defence plea of which the Prosecutor has received notice in accordance with Sub-Rule (ii) below, or any defence pleaded in the Defence Case Statement served under Sub-Rule (C);

    (ii) The defence shall notify the Prosecutor of its intent to enter:

        (a) The defence of alibi; in which case the notification shall specify the place or places at which the accused claims to have been present at the time of the alleged crime and the names and addresses of witnesses and any other evidence upon which the accused intends to rely to establish the alibi;

        (b) Any special defence, including that of diminished or lack of mental responsibility; in which case the notification shall specify the names and addresses of witnesses and any other evidence upon which the accused intends to rely to establish the special defence.

(B) Failure of the defence to provide such notice under this Rule shall not limit the right of the accused to rely on the above defences.

(C) To assist the Prosecutor with its disclosure obligations pursuant to Rule 68, the defence may prior to trial provide the Prosecutor with a Defence Case Statement. The Defence Case Statement shall:

    (i) set out in general terms the nature of the accused's defence;
    (ii) indicate the matters on which he takes issue with the prosecution; and
    (iii) set out, in the case of each such matter, the reason why he takes issue with the prosecution.

(D) If either party discovers additional evidence or information or materials which should have been produced earlier pursuant to the Rules, that party shall promptly notify the other party and the Trial Chamber of the existence of the additional evidence or information or materials.

TRIAL CHAMBERS DECISIONS

- **Rule 67: Reciprocal Disclosure – Mandatory**

R67-TC-1   o *Prosecutor v. Norman, Fofana, Kondewa*, Case No. SCSL-04-14-T, Ruling on Disclosure of Witness Statements, 1st October 2004, para. 2:[91]

2. [. . .] The jurisprudence also reveals that reciprocal disclosure is mandated by Rule 67 of the Rules [. . .].

- **Rule 67(A)(ii)(a): Defence of Alibi – Burden of Proof – Notification**

R67-TC-2   o *Prosecutor v. Kamara*, SCSL-04-16-PT, Decision and Order on Defence Preliminary Motion on Defects in the Form of the Indictment, 1 April 2004, para. 39:

39. [. . .] As a matter of law, the defence of *alibi* does not carry a separate burden of proof; it is for the Prosecution to prove beyond any reasonable doubt that the accused was present and committed the crimes for which he is charged and thereby discredit the defence of *alibi*.[(1)] It is worth observing that even though Rule 66(A)(ii)(a) of the Rules requires the Defence to notify the Prosecution if its intent to enter a defence of *alibi* as early as reasonably practicable, *failure to fulfil that obligation shall not limit the right of the accused to rely on the said defence.* [. . .]

[(1)] See *Prosecutor v. Mitar Vasiljevic*, Case No. IT-98-32-T, Judgement, 29 November 2002, para. 15: "When a 'defence' of alibi is raised by an accused person, the accused bears no onus of establishing that alibi. The onus is on the Prosecution to eliminate any reasonable possibility that the evidence of alibi is true." And footnote 7: "It is not sufficient for the Prosecution merely to establish beyond reasonable doubt that the alibi is false in order to conclude that his guilt has been established beyond reasonable doubt. Acceptance by the Trial Chamber of the falsity of an alibi cannot establish the opposite to what it asserts. "The Prosecution must also establish that the facts alleged in the Indictment are true beyond a reasonable doubt before a finding of guilt can be made against the accused." See also, *Prosecutor v. Musema*, Case No. ICTR-96-13-T, Judgement, 27 January 2000, para. 108.

---

[91] See also *Prosecutor v. Brima, Kamara, Kanu*, Case No. SCSL-04-16-T, Decision on Objection to Question Put by the Defence in Cross-Examination of Witness TF1-227, 15 June 2005, para. 34.

- **Rule 67(D): Disclosure of Additional Evidence**

R67-TC-3

o *Prosecutor v. Brima, Kamara, Kanu*, Case No. SCSL-04-16-T, Decision on Objection to Question Put by the Defence in Cross-Examination of Witness TF1-227, 15 June 2005, para. 35-36:

35. Rule 67(D) imposes a duty on both parties. The time provided for such reciprocal disclosure is provided in Rule 67(A) "as early as reasonably practicable and in any event prior to the commencement of the trial."

36. That time has now expired. The duty of disclosure on the Prosecution is now not under Rule 67(D) but under Rule 66(A)(ii). We consider that Rule 67(D) does not apply. However, the Prosecution is under a continuing duty to disclose exculpatory material throughout the case as provided by Rule 68(B) and as confirmed by the jurisprudence of the Special Court.[1]

---

[1] *The Prosecutor v. Norman et al.*, Case No. SCSL-2004-14-T, Ruling on Disclosure of Witness Statements, 1 October 2004, para. 2.

> **Rule 68: Disclosure of Exculpatory Evidence**
> *(amended 14 March 2004)*
>
> (A) The Prosecutor shall, within 14 days of receipt of the Defence Case Statement, make a statement under this Rule disclosing to the defence the existence of evidence known to the Prosecutor which may be relevant to issues raised in the Defence Case Statement.
>
> (B) The Prosecutor shall, within 30 days of the initial appearance of the accused, make a statement under this Rule disclosing to the defence the existence of evidence known to the Prosecutor which in any way tends to suggest the innocence or mitigate the guilt of the accused or may affect the credibility of prosecution evidence. The Prosecutor shall be under a continuing obligation to disclose any such exculpatory material.

TRIAL CHAMBER DECISIONS

- **Rule 68: Disclosure of Exculpatory Evidence – Generalities**

R68-TC-1
 o *Prosecutor v. Sesay*, Case No. SCSL-04-15-T, Decision on Defence Motion for Disclosure Pursuant to Rule 66 and 68 of the Rules, 9 July 2004, para. 33-34:

> 33. A review of the ICTY and the ICTR jurisprudence elicits that in the case of *Prosecutor v. Bagilishema*,[1] the Trial Chamber found that Rule 68 has two main elements. Firstly, the evidence is known to the Prosecutor, which can be interpreted as the evidence is in the 'custody and control' or 'possession' of the Prosecution; and secondly, it must in some way be exculpatory, suggest the innocence or mitigate the guilt of the Accused. The Trial Chamber held that "the obligation on the Prosecutor to disclose possible exculpatory evidence would be effective only when the Prosecutor is in actual custody, possession, or has control of the said evidence. The Prosecutor cannot disclose that which she does not have."[2] The Trial Chamber of the ICTR in *Prosecutor v. Kajelijeli*,[3] concurred with the above interpretation in the *Bagilishema* Decision, of Rule 68.[4] Furthermore, in the case of *Prosecutor v. Ndayambaje*,[5] the ICTR Trial Chamber held that it is the established jurisprudence of the ICTY and ICTR that pursuant to Rule 68 of the Rules, the Prosecutor is only to disclose any exculpatory material that is in her possession. It is also established that the Defence must justify such request by *prima facie* establishing the exculpatory nature of the material requested.[6]

34. It is evident that pursuant to Rule 26*bis* of the Rules, the proceedings of the Special Court are conducted with full respect for the rights of the Accused and due regard for the protection of victims and witnesses. Accordingly, the Chamber opines that it is incumbent on the Prosecution to disclose all potentially exculpatory evidence. In this view, an established extraction of the said evidence from its context would not, in principle, be conducive to a full understanding of the text nor permit one to measure its full scope.[7]

---

[1] *Prosecutor v. Bagilishema*, Case No. ICTR-95-1A-T Decision on the Request of the Defence for an Order for Disclosure by the Prosecutor of the Admissions of Guilt of Witnesses Y, Z, and AA, 8 June 2000 (*"Bagilishema* Decision").
[2] *Id.*, paras 5-7.
[3] *Prosecutor v. Kajelijeli*, Case No. ICTR-98-44A-T, Decision on Kajelijeli's Urgent Motion and Certification with Appendices in Support of Urgent Motion for Disclosure of Materials Pursuant to Rule 66(B) and Rule 68 of the Rules of Procedure and Evidence, 5 July 2001.
[4] *Id.*, para. 13.
[5] *Ndayambaje* Decision, *supra*, para. 11.
[6] See notably, *Kondewa* Decision, *supra; Prosecutor v. Blaskic*, Case No. IT-95-14-PT, Decision on the Motion to Compel the Production of Discovery Materials, 27 January 1997; *Prosecutor v. Delalic et al.*, Case No. IT-96-21, Decision on the Request by the Accused Hazim Delic Pursuant to Rule 68 for Exculpatory Information, 24 June 1997; *Prosecutor v. Nyiramasuhuko et al.*, Case No. ICTR-97-21, Decision on the Defence Motion for Disclosure of the Declarations of the Prosecutor's Witnesses Detained in Rwanda, and All Other Documents or Information Pertaining to Judicial Proceedings in Their Respect, 18 September 2001.
[7] *Prosecutor v. Blaskic*, Case No. IT-95-14, Decision on the Defence Motion for sanctions for the Prosecutor's Repeated Violations of Rule 68 of the Rules of Procedure and Evidence, 29 April 1998.

R68-TC-2

o *Prosecutor v. Sesay*, Decision on Sesay Motion Seeking Disclosure of the Relationship Between Governmental Agencies of the United States of America and the Office of the Prosecutor, 2 May 2005, para. 35:

35. For the purposes of the instant Motion and guided by the foregoing principles, we again, on this issue reiterate our stand that Rule 68 imposes on the Prosecution, a legal obligation to disclose "within 30 days of the initial appearance of the accused," and continuously thereafter, exculpatory evidence, meaning evidence that in anyway leads to suggest the innocence of the accused, or evidence that in anyway tends to mitigate the guilt of accused or evidence favourable to the accused that may affect the credibility of the prosecution evidence.

- **Rule 68: Disclosure of Exculpatory Evidence – Definition of "Exculpatory Evidence"**

R68-TC-3

o *Prosecutor v. Kondewa*, No. SCSL-04-14-T, Decision on Motion to Compel the Production of Exculpatory Witness Statement, Witness Summaries and Materials Pursuant to Rule 68, 8 July 2004, para. 22, 24:

22. [. . .] [T]he Chamber holds that [. . .] Rule 68 of the Rules imposed on the Prosecution the legal obligation to disclose "as soon as practicable", to the defence evidence of the generic type, to wit, exculpatory evidence, but of any of these three species – (a) exculpatory evidence that in anyway tends to suggest the innocence of the accused, (b) exculpatory evidence that in any way tends to mitigate the guilt of the accused, and (c) exculpatory evidence that may affect the credibility of prosecution evidence.

[. . .]

24. Still guided by the "plain meaning rule" and the doctrine that the law is what it says it is, the Chamber holds the view that under Rule 68 of the Rules, whether in its original form or its twice amended form, exculpatory evidence is simply evidence favourable to the accused [. . .].

- **Rule 68: Disclosure of Exculpatory Evidence – Burden of Proof of the Exculpatory Nature of the Evidence**

R68-TC-4

o *Prosecutor v. Kondewa*, No. SCSL-04-14-T, Decision on Motion to Compel the Production of Exculpatory Witness Statement, Witness Summaries and Materials Pursuant to Rule 68, 8 July 2004, para. 24-27:[92]

24. [. . .] [T]he Chamber holds the view that under Rule 68 of the Rules, whether in its original form or its twice amended form, [. . .] the burden is on the Defence to make a *prima facie* showing of the exculpatory character of the evidence sought from the Prosecution.[(1)] And so, the threshold issue for the Chamber's determination is whether the Defence herein has advanced sufficient proof of a *prima facie* nature to show that the material sought from the Prosecutor is exculpatory in

---

[92] See also *Prosecutor v. Sesay*, Decision on Sesay Motion Seeking Disclosure of the Relationship Between Governmental Agencies of the United States of America and the Office of the Prosecutor, 2 May 2005, para. 59-61, 64.

nature. And in addressing this question, it is necessary for the Chamber to recall here the Rule 66 perspective or context of the Prosecutor's general obligation to disclose evidence in his possession. In the *Blaskic* Decision, the Trial Chamber reasoned that evidence "which is material for the preparation of the Defence" necessarily includes evidence "which in any way tends to suggest the innocence or mitigate the guilt of the accused."[2] On the strength of this reasoning, it stands to reason that material of an exculpatory nature will always be material for the preparation of the Defence.[3] This Chamber adopts this reasoning and takes the view that any request by the Defence for exculpatory material alleged to be in the Prosecutor's possession, custody or control must be specific as to such material.

25. The key question now for this Chamber is – Has the Defence made a *prima facie* showing of the exculpatory material sought from the Prosecution? Further, in resolving this key question, the Chamber must be satisfied that the request by the Defence has been specific as to the targeted material alleged to be in the Prosecutor's possession, control or custody.

26. The Chamber has carefully examined each alleged violation put forward by the Defence in the instant Motion as set out at paragraphs 1-12 of this Motion alongside the Relief or declaration sought or particularised at page 4 of the said Motion. The Chamber finds that nowhere in the said Motion does the request for disclosure of the targeted exculpatory evidence or material clearly specify the material so desired. It leaves a vast penumbra of uncertainty as to which exculpatory material is being sought. It invites the Chamber to speculate on the issue. In such matters, it is not sufficient merely to allege non-compliance, on the part of the Prosecution, with its disclosure obligation or merely to restate the law on the subject in the form of submissions. It is essential to set out with much particularity what the information is about or what precisely it is, and the extent to which it is exculpatory, for example, whether it is material establishing the defence of alibi. It is not sufficient to say that they are "redacted witness statements of an exculpatory nature". The Chamber, therefore, takes the view and rules that "in the absence of specific identification of the material evidence that the Defence alleges the Prosecution has withheld, it is inappropriate for the Trial Chamber to intervene at this time."[4]

27. Finally, the Trial Chamber is convinced that the Defence has failed to indicate with any degree of specificity the targeted exculpatory material in respect of which the Prosecutor bears an obligation to disclose under Rule 68 of the Rules. Therefore, the Defence has failed to satisfy the overriding test in applications of this nature, to wit to establish by *prima facie* showing that the material sought from the Prosecution

under Rule 68 of the Rules is in actual fact exculpatory in character.

(1) *Prosecutor v. Delalic et al.*, IT-96-21, Decision On the Request of the Accused Hazim Delic Pursuant to Rule 68 for Exculpatory Information; 24 June 1997, ("*Delacic* Decision") para. 13; see also *Prosecutor v. Thomir Blaskic*, IT-95-14-PT, Decision on the Production of Discovery Materials, 27 January 1997 ("*Blaskic* Decision"), para. 50, where Trial Chamber I decided that the defence "must submit to the Trial Chamber all *prima facie* proof tendering to make it likely that the evidence is exculpatory and is in the Prosecutor's possession."
(2) *Id.*, para. 50.
(3) *Id.*
(4) *Delalic* Decision, para. 10.

R68-TC-5   o *Prosecutor v. Sesay*, Case No. SCSL-04-15-T, Decision on Defence Motion for Disclosure Pursuant to Rule 66 and 68 of the Rules, 9 July 2004, para. 36-43:[93]

36. With regard to the scope of the Prosecution's obligation to disclose exculpatory evidence to the Defence, the Trial Chamber of the ICTY in the case of *Prosecutor v. Blaskic*[(1)] reasoned:

> If the Prosecution fulfils its above indicated obligations but the Defence considers that evidence other than that disclosed might prove exculpatory for the Accused and was in the possession of the Office of the Prosecution, it must submit to the Trial Chamber all *prima facie* proofs tending to make it likely that the evidence is exculpatory and was in the Prosecutor's possession. Should it not present this *prima facie* proof to the Trial Chamber, the Defence will not be granted authorisation to have the evidence disclosed.

37. The same Trial Chamber of the ICTY in another decision in the case of *Prosecutor v. Blaskic*, held that: all "these considerations lead the Trial Chamber to deem that the Prosecutor's obligation is, in part and of necessity, tinged with subjectivity, which also leads the Chamber to presume that the Prosecutor has acted in good faith."[(2)]

38. The Defence asserts that the jurisprudence from the ICTY and ICTR clearly demonstrate at the very least, the desirability for the Prosecution to identify exculpatory material, pursuant to Rule 68. It asserts that although it is the Special

---

[93] See also *Prosecutor v. Sesay*, Case No. SCSL-04-15-T, Decision on Sesay Motion Seeking Disclosure of the Relationship Between Governmental Agencies of the United States of America and the Office of the Prosecutor, 2 May 2005, para. 62-65.

Court's prerogative whether or not to follow *stare decisis* of other tribunals when the rights of an Accused to a fair trial are under consideration, nothing but inequity results from ignoring lessons learnt elsewhere.[3]

39. In the recent judgement rendered by the Appeals Chamber of the ICTY in the case of *Prosecutor v. Krstic*,[4] the Defence contended that the Prosecution violated its disclosure obligations under Rule 68 by, *inter alia*, by failing to disclose a number of witness statements containing exculpatory materials, and failing to disclose exculpatory materials amongst other evidence without identifying that material as exculpatory, and wanted a re-trial as a result. The Appeals Chamber proceeded to clarify the rules of disclosure under Rule 68 as follows:

> As a general proposition, where the Defence seeks a remedy for the Prosecution's breach of its disclosure obligations under Rule 68, the Defence must show (i) that the Prosecution has acted in violation of its obligations under Rule 68, and (ii) that the Defence's case suffered material prejudice as a result. In other words, if the Defence satisfies the Tribunal that there has been a failure by the Prosecution to comply with Rule 68, the Tribunal in addressing the aspect of appropriate remedies will examine whether or not the Defence has been prejudiced by that failure to comply before considering whether a remedy is appropriate.[5]

40. In the instant case however, the Defence simply claims that it has ascertained through its own investigation that there are several Prosecution witnesses whose evidence is wholly exculpatory of the Accused. The Chamber has taken note of the concession by the Defence that the Prosecution have indeed served exculpatory evidence on the Defence, albeit, contained in statements which are principally incriminatory in their nature.

41. The Appeals Chamber of the ICTY in the *Krstic* Judgement agreed with the Prosecution that "Rule 68 does not require the Prosecution to identify the material being disclosed to the Defence as exculpatory. The jurisprudence of the Tribunal shows that while some Trial Chambers have recognised that it would be fairer for the Prosecution to do so,[6] there is no prima facie requirement, absent an order of the Trial Chamber to that effect."[7]

42. In the case of *Prosecutor v. Jean Paul Akayesu*, the Appeals Chamber of the ICTR held that "an order staying proceedings on the ground of abuse of process[...] should never be made where there were other ways of achieving a fair hearing of the case, still less where there was no evidence of prejudice to the defendant."[8]

43. Relying persuasively on the aforementioned, the Trial Chamber considers that the key question to be answered here is whether the Defence has made a *prima facie* showing of exculpatory material sought from the Prosecution.[9] Furthermore, in resolving this important question, the Chamber must be satisfied that the request by the Defence has been specific as to the targeted material alleged to be in the Prosecutor's possession, control or custody.

---

[1] *Prosecutor v. Blaskic, supra.*
[2] *Prosecutor v. Blakic, supra*, para. 21.
[3] This Chamber has already ascertained this prerogative in its decision in the case of *Prosecutor v. Kamara*, Case No. SCSL-04-16-PT, Decision and Order on Defence Preliminary Motion on Defects in the Form of Indictment, paras 19-25.
[4] *Prosecutor v. Krstic*, IT-98 – 33-A, Appeals Chamber Judgement, 19 April 2004 ("*Krstic* Judgement").
[5] *Id.*, para. 153.
[6] *Prosecutor v. Krajisnik & Plavsic*, Case No. IT-00-39 & 40, Decision on Motion from Momcilo Krajisnik to Compel Disclosure of Exculpatory Evidence Pursuant to Rule 68, p. 2, 19 July 2001:
"as a matter of practice and in order to secure a fair and expeditious trial, the Prosecution should normally indicate which material it is disclosing under the Rule and it is no answer to say that the Defence are in a better position to identify it.";
See also *Prosecutor v. Krnojelac*, Case No. IT-97-25, Decision on Motion by Prosecution to Modify Order for Compliance with Rule 68, 1 November 1999, where Judge David Hunt, sitting as the ICTY Trial Chamber, ordered pursuant to Rule 68 of the Rules that the Prosecution to:
"disclose to the Defence the existence of evidence known to it: (a) which in any way tends to suggest the innocence of, mitigate the guilt of, the Accused, or (b) which may affect the credibility of the prosecution evidence. The expression "evidence" is intended to include any material which may put the Accused on notice that material exists which may assist him in his defence, and it is not limited to material which is itself admissible in evidence."
[7] *Krstic* Judgement, *supra*, para. 190.
[8] *Prosecutor v. Jean Paul Akayesu*, Case No. ICTR-96-4-A, Appeal Judgement, 1 June 2001, para. 340.
[9] *Kondewa* Decision, *supra*, paras 24-25.

R68-TC-6

o *Prosecutor v. Sesay*, Case No. SCSL-04-15-T, Decision on Sesay Motion Seeking Disclosure of the Relationship Between Governmental Agencies of the United States of America and the Office of the Prosecutor, 2 May 2005, para. 36:

36. Having examined the legal nature and scope of the Prosecution's obligation under Rule 68 to disclose exculpatory evidence, we would like to restate here that in order to sustain an allegation by the Defence of a breach by the Prosecution of its disclosure obligations under Rule 68, the Defence must demonstrate, by prima facie proof: (1) that the targeted evidentiary

material is exculpatory in nature, (2) the materiality of the said evidence, (3) that the Prosecution has, in its possession, custody, or control, the targeted exculpatory evidentiary material, and (4) that the Prosecution has, in fact, failed to disclose the targeted exculpatory evidentiary material.

- **Rule 68: Disclosure of Exculpatory Evidence – Specificity of the Request for Disclosure of Exculpatory Evidence**

R68-TC-7
o *Prosecutor v. Sesay*, Case No. SCSL-04-15-T, Decision on Sesay Motion Seeking Disclosure of the Relationship Between Governmental Agencies of the United States of America and the Office of the Prosecutor, 2 May 2005, para. 53-56:

53. In the same vein, a mere speculative assertion without specifying or advancing concrete proof of the nature and content of the exculpatory evidence which the Defence is alleging to be in the possession of the Prosecution of General Tarnue and his family's relocation, to our mind, fails to meet the test required to warrant an Order by the Chamber for the Prosecution to disclose under Rule 68 of the Rules.

54. The Chamber recognizes that disclosure procedures are not only intended to ensure and protect the rights of the accused to a fair trial, but also and more importantly, for him to be informed of the nature and cause of the charge against him, and further, to enable him to have adequate time and facilities for the conduct of his or her defence.

55. We observe however, that where the request to disclose lacks specificity as to the details of facts sought to be disclosed, and proof that those facts are indeed in the possession of the Prosecution, the Chamber cannot, and should not be called upon to grant, a vaguely formulated request particularly so because even if it were conceded that such facts, unknown to the Prosecution, exist with the F.B.I. or the US Government, the Prosecution cannot be compelled to produce information that is in possession of a foreign Independent Agency or in that of the US Government represented by the Department of State.

56. In circumstances such as these where the Prosecution has declared that it has disclosed everything and that it has nothing more to disclose to the Defence under Rule 68, the Defence, in the absence of concrete elements to substantiate its claims, we contend, has the alternative weapon of cross-examination to establish such facts in evidence and thereafter, to base an application of this nature on the facts so established.

- **Rule 68: Disclosure of Exculpatory Evidence – Time of the Disclosure of Exculpatory Evidence**

R68-TC-8

o *Prosecutor v. Kondewa*, No. SCSL-04-14-T, Decision on Motion to Compel the Production of Exculpatory Witness Statement, Witness Summaries and Materials Pursuant to Rule 68, 8 July 2004, para. 23:

> 23. It is absolutely clear from the original version of Rule 68 of the Rules that there was a legal obligation on the Prosecutor to disclose, as soon as was practicable, exculpatory evidence of the kind specified in the Rule. What was a matter of legal controversy was whether the Prosecutor's obligation was of a continuing nature. But the Prosecution has always acknowledged this to be a continuing obligation. Further, applying the golden rule of interpretation to Rule 68 of the Rules as formulated during the second time frame, the Chamber is of the view that the legislative intent behind Rule 68(B) of the Rules was to put the legal obligation on the Prosecutor for disclosure of exculpatory material within a prescribed time frame and distinct from the open-ended "as soon as practicable" time frame of the Rule prior to March 2003. Hence, the limitation period of disclosure of the three (3) species of exculpatory material to that of "within 30 days of the initial appearance of the accused" but this time, evidently, making it clear that the obligation was a continuing one.[1] Hence further, the necessity, in the Chamber's opinion, of the most recent amendment to the rule which clearly puts beyond doubt the issue of the continuing nature of the Prosecutor's obligation to disclose exculpatory material under Rule 68(B) by re-enacting that provision as a qualifying clause to the new sub-rule (B).

---

[1] *Prosecutor v. Norman*, SCSL-03-08-PT, Scheduling Order, 11 April 2003; *id.*, Decision on the Prosecution Motion to Allow Disclosure to the Registry and to Keep Disclosed Materials Under Seal Until Appropriate Protective Measures are in Place, 17 April 2003, paras 5-6 and 11.

- **Rule 68: Disclosure of Exculpatory Evidence – Time of the Motion for Disclosure of Exculpatory Evidence**

R68-TC-9

o *Prosecutor v. Sesay*, Case No. SCSL-04-15-T, Decision on Sesay Motion Seeking Disclosure of the Relationship Between Governmental Agencies of the United States of America and the Office of the Prosecutor, 2 May 2005, para. 57-58:

57. In this regard we observe that General Tarnue was in the witness box for slightly over 8 days, when these and other issues arose and were extensively highlighted, not only during examination – in – chief which lasted 7 hours 12 minutes but also, and even more fully highlighted and explored in the course of the extensive, lengthy, exhaustive cross examination of this witness by Learned Counsel for the 1st Accused, the Applicant in this Motion, Mr. Jordash, which lasted 15 hours 38 minutes, by counsel for 2nd Accused which lasted 4 hours 38 minutes, and by counsel for 3rd Accused which lasted 5 hours 27 minutes.

58. It would, in our opinion, be unfair, after such a lengthy, protracted, and extensive cross-examination, to compel a disclosure of evidence under Rule 68 when the Prosecution avers, and without any concrete evidence proffered by the Defence to contradict this assertion, that it has disclosed all it had to disclose and that it has nothing more to disclose following the vague and speculative application of the Defence for it to fulfil this obligation under Rule 68 of the Rules.

- **Rule 68(B): Disclosure of Exculpatory Evidence – Protection of Victims and Witnesses**

R68-TC-10

o *Prosecutor v. Norman*, Case No. SCSL-03-08-PT, Decision on the Prosecution Motion to Allow Disclosure to the Registry and to Keep Disclosed Materials Under Seal Until Appropriate Protective Measures Are in Place, 17 April 2003, para. 9-10:

9. [. . .] [T]he Court deems it necessary that disclosures pursuant to Rule 66 (A)(i) and Rule 68 (B) shall be made with a view to ensure appropriate protection of witnesses and victims as well as for the confidentiality of all non-public materials subject to such disclosure;

10. Pending a ruling on the Prosecution Motion for Immediate Protective Measures for Witnesses and Victims and for Non-Public Disclosure, it is therefore necessary to guarantee that the fulfilment of the Prosecution's obligations to disclose shall encompass appropriate interim measures for the protection of witnesses and victims as well as for the confidentiality of all non-public materials subject to disclosure by the Prosecution.

Rule 69: Protection of Victims and Witnesses
(amended 29 May 2004)

(A) In exceptional circumstances, either of the parties may apply to a Judge of the Trial Chamber or the Trial Chamber to order the non-disclosure of the identity of a victim or witness who may be in danger or at risk, until the Judge or Chamber decides otherwise.

(B) In the determination of protective measures for victims and witnesses, the Judge or Trial Chamber may consult the Witnesses and Victims Section.

(C) Subject to Rule 75, the identity of the victim or witness shall be disclosed in sufficient time before a witness is to be called to allow adequate time for preparation of the prosecution and the defence.

TRIAL CHAMBERS DECISIONS

- **Rule 69: Protection of Victims and Witnesses – Applicable Criteria for the Determination of Appropriate Protective Measures**

R69-TC-1

o *Prosecutor v. Norman*, Case No. SCSL-03-08-PT, Decision on the Prosecutor's Motion for Immediate Protective Measures for Witnesses and Victims and for Non-Public Disclosure, 23 May 2003, para. 10, 12-15:[94]

10. In determining the appropriateness of the protective measures sought, I have evaluated the security situation affecting concerned witnesses in the context of the available information [...]. Despite some formal defects, generalities and unsubstantiated matters, rightly pointed out by the Defence, in

---

[94] See also *Prosecutor v. Kallon*, Case No. SCSL-03-07-PT, Decision on the Prosecutor's Motion for Immediate Protective Measures for Witnesses and Victims and for Non-Public Disclosure, 23 May 2003, para. 11, 13-16; *Prosecutor v. Sesay*, Case No. SCSL-03-05-PT, Decision on the Prosecutor's Motion for Immediate Protective Measures for Witnesses and Victims and for Non-Public Disclosure, 23 May 2003, para. 10, 12-15; *Prosecutor v. Brima*, Case No. SCSL-03-06-PT, Decision on the Prosecutor's Motion for Immediate Protective Measures for Witnesses and Victims and for Non-Public Disclosure, 23 May 2003, para. 10, 12-15; *Prosecutor v. Kamara*, Case No. 03-10-PT, Decision on the Prosecution Motion for Immediate Protective Measures for Witnesses and Victims and for Non-Public Disclosure, 23 October 2003, para. 17-19; *Prosecutor v. Fofana*, Case No. SCSL-03-11-PT, Decision on the Prosecutor's Motion for Immediate Protective Measures for Witnesses and Victims and for Non-Public Disclosure, 16 October 2003, para. 10, 12-15.

respect of those documents, it is my considered view that, in terms of substance, the combined effect of those affirmations is to demonstrate, within the bounds of reasonable foreseeability and not absolute certainty, the delicate and complex nature of the security situation in the country and the level of threat from several quarters of the ex-combatant population that participated in the conflict to witnesses and potential witnesses. It is significant to note that there was no affidavit in opposition. The irresistible inference, therefore, is that such threats may well pose serious problems to such witnesses and the effectiveness of the Court in the faithful discharge of its international mandate.

[...]

12. Instructive though, from a general jurisprudential viewpoint, some of the decisions of ICTR and ICTY relied upon by both Prosecution and Defence Office on the subject of delayed disclosure and confidentiality of witnesses and victims may be in terms of the principles therein enunciated, the issue is really one of contextual socio-legal perspective. Predicated upon such a perspective, one can reach various equally valid conclusions applying a comparative methodology into: (a) whether the security situation in Sierra Leone can, at this point in time, in relation to Rwanda be objectively characterized as really more or less volatile; (b) whether the security situation in Rwanda during the grant or denial of the protective measures sought in those cases, was more or less volatile than the present security situation in Sierra Leone; or (c) whether there is any logical basis for comparison at all. Indeed, perhaps, Defence Counsel got it absolutely right when he observed at paragraph 8 of his Response that (i) "the question of the security situation in Rwanda is a factual question which has nothing to do with the security situation in Sierra Leone" and that (ii) "the security measures for Sierra Leone are quite independent of what is necessary in Rwanda." Evidently, it takes no stretch of the legal imagination to discover that in such matters speculation can be endless and quite fruitless. It depends on one's analytical or methodological approach. They are not matters that can be determined with any mathematical exactitude.

13. With all due respect to learned Counsel for the Defence, it must be pointed out that the five-fold criteria enunciated by the ICTY in the case of *The Prosecutor vs. Tadic*, IT-4-I-10, Decision on the Prosecutor's Motion Requesting Protective Measures for Victims and Witnesses, 10th August 1995, cannot logically be applied to the instant Motion. In that case, the Trial Chamber was confronted with a request by the Prosecution to provide anonymity for one of its witnesses in testifying by withholding the identity of the witness from the Accused. A majority of the Trial Chamber held that it had to balance

the right of the Accused to a "fair and public trial" against the protection of victims and witnesses. Observing that the right to a "fair trial" was not absolute but was subject to derogation in exceptional circumstances such as a state of emergency and that the situation of on-going conflict in the area where the alleged atrocities took place constituted such exceptional circumstances, the Chamber took a "contextual approach" and held that it was justified in accepting anonymous testimony if: (1) there was real fear for the safety of the witness or his or her family; (2) the testimony of the witness was important to the Prosecution's case; (3) there was no prima facie evidence that the witness is untrustworthy; (4) the measures were strictly necessary (see May and Wierda, *International Criminal Evidence*, 2002 at page 282). It is evident that the situation in *Tadic* concerning that of a witness seeking to testify anonymously and that (as in the instant Motion) of an order for delayed disclosure of identifying data in respect of certain categories of prosecution witnesses *at the pre-trial stage* are clearly distinguishable both as a matter of fact and law.

14. Which principle, then, is applicable here? The answer is that it is the general principle propounded by the ICTY, in the case of *The Prosecutor v. Blaskic*, IT-95-14, Decision on the Application of the Prosecution dated 17th October 1996 Requesting of Protective Measures for Victims and Witnesses, 5th November 1996. It states that:

> The philosophy which imbues the Statute and Rules of the Tribunal appears clear: the Victims and Witnesses merit protection, even from the Accused, during the preliminary proceedings and continuing until a reasonable time before the start of the trial itself; from that time forth, however, the right of the Accused to an equitable trial must take precedence and require that the veil of anonymity be lifted in his favour, even if the veil must continue to obstruct the view of the public and the media.

Applying this general principle to the totality of the affidavit evidence before me, it is my considered view that a reasonable case has been made for the prosecution witnesses herein to be granted at this preliminary stage a measure of anonymity and confidentiality. In addition, in matters of such delicacy and sensitivity, it would be unrealistic to expect either the Prosecution or the Defence, at the pre-trial phase, to carry the undue burden of having each witness narrate in specific terms or document the nature of his or her fears as to the actual or anticipated threats or intimidation. Such an approach would frustrate, if not, (using a familiar legal metaphor) drive a horse and coach through the entire machinery created by the Founding Instruments of the Court and its Rules for protection of witnesses and victims.

15. Further, as designated Judge under Rule 28 of the Rules, my judicial evaluation of the measures requested by the Prosecution pursuant to Articles 16 and 17 of the Statute and Rules 53, 54, and 75 of the Rules, is also predicated upon the reasoning that even though the Court must, in such matters, seek to balance the right of the Accused to a fair and public trial with the interest of the witnesses in being given protection, such a right is subject to derogating exceptional circumstances (Article 17(2) of the Statute) and that the existing context of the security situation in Sierra Leone does justify, at this point in time, delaying the disclosure of the identities of witnesses during the pre-trial phase.

R69-TC-2

o *Prosecutor v. Kanu*, Case No. SCSL-03-13-PT, Decision on the Prosecution Motion for Immediate Protective Measures for Witnesses and Victims, 24 November 2003, para. 25-28:

25. In fact, the fast emerging principle of protection of witnesses and victims which today is deeply rooted in the core dynamics of the International Criminal Justice system and procedures, is founded on the understanding that those "protégés" whose testimony is vital in establishing the case for the Prosecution and to some extent, that of the Defence, deserve a cloud of anonymity around them, at least for some time pending their appearance and testimony in Court.

26. This position is even the more so justified because given the gruesomeness of the nature of crimes for which they might be called upon to the feature as victims and/or witnesses, the circumstances surrounding these offences, and the personality of the perpetrators, coupled with the fear of recriminations on them or on members of their families, this temporary camouflage on their identity, even though it impugns, albeit temporarily, on the rights of the Accused and the proper conduct of his defence, appears plausible after all because it is quite in harmony with the revered objective we are committed to upholding, that is, to safeguard the integrity of the proceedings where some element of secrecy and in-camera procedures form an integral part; this, on the understanding of course, that the veil that would so far have shielded them from the Accused, is lowered at the crucial stage of the trial and in time to permit the Accused to enjoy and fully exercise, amongst others, his statutory right to a fair and public hearing guaranteed to him under Article 17 of the Statute of the Special Court.

27. In the determination therefore of applications on issues relating to the granting of protective measures to victims and witnesses, I think three factors, all of which I consider of public interest, should be borne in mind:

(i) Firstly, acknowledging that the rights of the Accused as defined by the Statute and the Rules must be respected, and this, subject to measures, if any, ordered by the Court for the Protection of victims and witnesses;

(ii) Secondly, taking cognisance of the rights and entitlements of victims and witnesses to some shielding and protection during the pre-trial phase and shortly before the trial commences, given the circumstances surrounding the commission of these offences; and

(iii) Thirdly, recognising, as was observed in the case of *Kayishema and Ruzindana*, 'the need to maintain a perfect balance between, on the one hand, the rights of the Accused to a fair trial, and on the other hand, the right of victims and witnesses as well as the interest of the International Community that justice is done in the most diligent manner possible.'

28. In this regard and in the case of the *Prosecution v. Allieu Kondewa*, Case No. SCSL-2003012-PD of 10th October, 2003, also based on an application for Protective Measures for Victims and Witnesses, I had this to say on a related issue and I quote:

"This balance is very difficult to strike as the very thin line of demarcation separating the fundamental interests of the Accused to protect his entrenched legal and constitutional entitlements to a fair trial as against the statutorily evolving right of a witness or a victim to protection and non disclosure which is an emanation of International Statutes and Rules of practice in ad hoc and exceptional International Criminal jurisdictions, is too slim, or rather, too faint to ensure the equilibrium of the said balance without violating in one way or the other, one's or the other's legal rights".

R69-TC-3

o *Prosecutor v. Norman, Fofana, Kondewa*, Case No. SCSL-04-14-PT, Order to the Prosecution for Renewed Motion for Protective Measures, 2 April 2004:[95]

CONSIDERING the distinction to be drawn between granting protective measures vis-à-vis the public versus granting protective measures that amount to non-disclosure or delayed disclosure to the Accused and the Defence;

---

[95] See also *Prosecutor v. Sesay, Kallon, Gbao*, Case No. SCSL-04-15-PT, Order to the Prosecution for Renewed Motion for Protective Measures, 2 April 2004.

- **Rule 69: Protection of Victims and Witnesses – Criteria – Seat in Sierra Leone**

R69-TC-4

o *Prosecutor v. Gbao*, Case No. SCSL-03-09-PT, Decision on Prosecution Motion for Immediate Protective Measures for Witnesses and Victims and for Non-Public Disclosure, 10 October 2003, para. 21-23, 25, 29:[96]

21. Prior to addressing the legal issues and the legal basis for this Motion, the Special Court finds it essential for a proper determination of the necessity, or not, of the protective measures requested to consider and try to assess the security situation which currently prevails in Sierra Leone. In this respect, and based upon the information provided to the Special Court, it is of importance to first note that the Special Court currently sits in Freetown, Sierra Leone. Indeed, Article 10 of the Agreement between the United Nations and the Government of Sierra Leone on the Establishment of a Special Court for Sierra Leone provides, inter alia, that "the Special Court shall have its seat in Sierra Leone".

22. The physical location of the Special Court, in itself, has a substantial impact on security considerations. In comparison, it should be recalled that the ad hoc Tribunals, namely the ICTY and the ICTR, do not have their seat in the States over which they have jurisdiction.

23. In proceeding with the assessment of the security situation, the Special Court has given much consideration to the situation that now prevails in Sierra Leone, as such is amply described in the materials produced by the Prosecution in support of its Motion. It should also be observed that no contradictory materials, information or evidence have been produced, nor has the nature or content of this information been disputed or challenged by the Defence.

[...]

25. The Special Court, therefore, based upon its examination of the documentation produced and, in particular, of the foregoing, concludes that there exists, at this particular time in Sierra Leone, a very exceptional situation causing a serious threat to the security of potential witnesses and to victims,

---

[96] See also *Prosecutor v. Kamara*, Case No. SCSL-03-10-PT, Decision on the Prosecution Motion for Immediate Protective Measures for Witnesses and Victims and for Non-Public Disclosure, 23 October 2003, para. 15; *Prosecutor v. Norman, Fofana, Kondewa*, Case No. SCSL-04-14-T, Decision on Prosecution Motion for Modification of Protective Measures for Witnesses, 08 June 2004, para. 29; *Prosecutor v. Brima (Margaret), Jalloh, Kamara (Ester)* (Case No. SCSL-05-02) *and Kamara (Anifa)* (Case No. SCSL-05-03), Sentencing Judgement in Contempt Proceedings, 21 September 2005, para. 28.

and accepts the affirmation that, according to the words of Mr. Vahidy, "*in Sierra Leone the protection of witnesses is a far more serious and difficult matter even than in Rwanda*".

[...]

29. Turning now to the legal issues, the Special Court would like to acknowledge the fact that the Defence Response is indeed very well articulated and constitutes an interesting basis for philosophical or doctrinal arguments. However, it seems to ignore in part the realities of the Special Court, which sits in Freetown, Sierra Leone, and the factual issues related to the Prosecution Motion requesting specific measures of protection for witnesses and victims. In the opinion of the Special Court, the Defence cannot simply state, as it does in paragraph 18 of the Motion, without any supporting evidence, that "*the circumstances pertaining in Sierra Leone at the time of the establishment of the Court have not worsened*".

R69-TC-5

o *Prosecutor v. Kondewa*, Case No. SCSL-03-12-PT, Ruling on the Prosecution Motion for Immediate Protective Measures for Witnesses and Victims and for Non-Public Disclosure and Urgent Request for Interim Measures Until Appropriate Protective Measures Are in Place, 10 October 2003, para. 20-28:[97]

20. Indeed, the current doctrine of non-disclosure constitutes a fast developing hide – and-seek legal strategy and gimmick between the Prosecution and the Defence, which, in traditional legal practice, has not enjoyed the predominance it does today in the International Criminal Justice system. In a hitherto and currently dominant adversarial system which is based on the 2 parties enjoying a parity in the privileges to which they are entitled to present their cases and particularly the accused whose right to a guaranteed fair trial with a special reference to acceding to facilities under the due process to defend himself, this situation certainly leads me to categorise the doctrine of disclosure as the rule and non-disclosure which can only be applied if and where the Prosecution, within the context of

---

[97] See also *Prosecutor v. Norman, Fofana, Kondewa*, Case No. SCSL-04-14-T, Decision on Prosecution Motion for Modification of Protective Measures for Witnesses, 08 June 2004, para. 29-30; *Prosecutor v. Norman, Fofana, Kondewa*, Case No. SCSL-04-14-T, Order on Protective Measures for Additional Witnesses, 1st October 2004; *Prosecutor v. Brima (Margaret), Jalloh, Kamara (Ester)* (Case No. SCSL-05-02) *and Kamara (Anifa)* (Case No. SCSL-05-03), Sentencing Judgement in Contempt Proceedings, 21 September 2005, para. 27; *Prosecutor v. Samura*, Case No. SCSL-05-01, Judgment in Contempt Proceedings, 26 October 2005, para. 65.

Rule 69 of the Rules of Evidence and Procedure, demonstrates that exceptional circumstances exist to warrant a non – disclosure, the exception.

21. This said, and as was observed in the case of *Kayishema and Ruzindana* on a motion filed by the Prosecution on the protection of victims and witnesses, November 6th 1996, "the need to maintain a perfect balance between, on the one hand, the rights of the accused to a fair trial, and on the other hand, the rights of victims and witnesses as well as the interest of the International Community that justice is done in the most diligent manner possible."

22. It must be conceded, however, that this balance is very difficult to strike as the very thin line of demarcation separating the fundamental interests of the accused to protect his entrenched legal and Constitutional entitlement to a fair trial as against the statutorily evolving right of a witness or a victim to protection and non-disclosure which is an emanation of International Statutes and Rules of practice in ad hoc and exceptional International Criminal Jurisdictions, is too slim, or rather, too faint to ensure the equilibrium and justice of the said balance without violating in one way or the other, ones or the other's legal rights.

23. In whatever circumstances, the instant matter comes up after the end of a gruesome and cruel civil war that had ravaged and destroyed not only human beings, but also property within the territory of Sierra Leone. The wounds caused by that civil conflict are still healing. The actors, perpetrators, victims and witnesses alike, are living relatively in peace in the same community where there is of course a genuine fear of judicial action looming over the heads of many and sundry. The evidence required will be given here in the Special Court that will sit in Freetown very much unlike the Yugoslavian or Rwandan situations where the Tribunals are operating and sitting in cities other than those of the locus delicti, indeed, the Countries where the crimes were committed.

24. The Republic of Sierra Leone is a relatively small Community where people are bound to and in fact know and identify themselves very easily thereby increasing the danger of risk of a recruitment of hostilities against potential witnesses and victims and their families if they are identified by the indictees or their sympathisers as those whose testimony would incriminate them, or in due course and more still, the indictees who they support out there.

25. One of the goals targeted by the International community is to track down and bring before justice, those who bear the greatest responsibility for a breach of International Humanitarian Law by committing heinous crimes against humanity. In view of the particularly bloody, hostile, and vicious environment in which these gruesome offences were cruelly per-

petrated and the necessity to fulfil the procedural imperatives of an adversarial system of justice governing the Courts by providing witnesses to sustain the charges, a mechanism had to be worked out to achieve the targeted objectives. One of this is certainly to create incentives geared towards encouraging victims and witnesses of those crimes to testify, albeit against those front line perpetrators and one of these measures is to put in place, a protective wall between the victim or witness and the accused so that neither the latter nor his sympathisers would identify the former for possible recriminations and eventual eliminations. It is only to this strategy that International Criminal Justice owes its exceptional survival, for, in the absence of these protected witnesses and victims, there will be no trials and consequently, no end to the criminal impunity that the International Community is endeavouring to contain and to combat through the International Criminal Courts which function virtually on the same basis and on similar rules of procedure and evidence as do the Municipal Criminal Jurisdictions.

26. This accounts for the consistent and constant sympathy of these jurisdictions to impose non disclosure measures not indefinitely though but on a temporary basis, in favour of the prosecution at the pre-trial stages of the proceedings. This said, it must be emphasised however, that the measures so ordained can only be made on a temporary basis so as to avoid violating the statutory rights of the accused to a fair trial.

27. In saying this, I share and concur with the diction of the ICTY in the case of the *Prosecutor vs. Blaskic*, IT-95-14 where Their Lordships had to this to say:

> "The philosophy which imbues the Statute and Rules of the Tribunal appears clear: the victims and witnesses merit protection, even from the accused during preliminary proceedings and until a reasonable time before the start of the trial itself; from that time however, the right of the accused to an equitable trial must take precedence and require that the veil of anonymity be lifted in his favour, even if the veil must continue to obstruct the view of the public and the media."

28. In the light of the foregoing analysis, I am of the opinion that the Applicants, through their factual and legal analysis in the presentation of the Motion brought before me, have sufficiently discharged the burden of establishing "exceptional circumstances" an ingredient that is the gateway to acceding to an Order for non disclosure, just as they have satisfied me, given the security situation in Sierra Leone and the threats to the security and life of the witnesses and victims, that there is merit in, and an imperative necessity to grant their motion seeking to protect all the 3 categories of witnesses solicited coupled with other remedies they have applied for.

- **Rule 69: Protection of Victims and Witnesses – Criteria – Victims of Sexual Violence, Children and Insiders – Post-Traumatic Stress**

R69-TC-6

o *Prosecutor v. Sesay, Kallon, Gbao*, Case No. SCSL-04-15-PT, Decision on Prosecution Motion for Modification of Protective Measures for Witnesses, 5 July 2004, para. 32-35:[98]

32. [. . .] [I]t is trite law that the need for special consideration to victims of sexual violence or children during their testimonials in court has been widely recognised in both domestic laws of states and in international courts.[(1)]

33. Specifically, for Categories A and C (victims of sexual violence and insider witnesses), voice distortion for the public speakers were sought. Regarding Category A, victims of sexual violence, the Prosecution pointed out the risk for re-traumatisation and rejection by the victim's family and community and the possibility to recognise the voice of the witness.[(2)] For insider witnesses in Category C, the Prosecution underlined the particular vulnerability of members of this group and their families to acts of retaliation and potential harm, due to their important testimony implicating directly the Accused. In the opinion of the Trial Chamber, these submissions once more demonstrate convincingly the risks for the security and danger to which both categories of witnesses could be exposed if disclosed and the requirement to grant appropriate measures for their protection.

34. As regards Category B witnesses, child witnesses, the Prosecution seeks the possibility for testimony by way of closed-circuit television. While the witness testifies in a back room in the court building, this would allow the Accused and the Defence, as well as the Trial Chamber and the Prosecution, to see the witness on a television-screen and observe his/her demeanour while the image on the screen for the public at that time would be distorted. As stated by Psychologist An Michels,[(3)] vulnerable witnesses such as children have a high risk of re-traumatisation and the possibility of stigmatisation and rejection is real and high. On this issue the U.S. Supreme Court, whose reasoning we find instructive and persuasive, held in *Maryland v. Craig* that the use of closed circuit television does not violate the constitutional right of an Accused to confrontation if it is necessary in the opinion of the Court to protect a child witness from psychological harm.[(4)]

---

[98] See also *Prosecutor v. Sesay, Kallon, Gbao*, Case No. SCSL-04-15-T, Order on Protective Measures for Additional Witnesses, 24 November 2004.

35. In the light of the above and of the evidence submitted, the Chamber finds that such risks as described would exist and therefore deems it necessary in the interest of justice, for children to be allowed to testify in the way in which the Prosecution has requested, in accordance with Rule 75(B)(i)(a) and to grant such a measure.

[...]

HEREBY grants the Motion and **ORDERS** for all witnesses in Group I (witnesses of fact) as follows:

a. That all witnesses shall be referred to by pseudonyms at all times during the course of proceedings whether during the hearing or in documents, including the transcript of the proceedings;
b. That the names, addresses, whereabouts and any other identifying information of witnesses shall be sealed and not included in any of the public records of the Special Court;
c. That to the extent that the names, addresses, whereabouts or other identifying data concerning witnesses are contained in existing public documents of the Special Court, that information shall be expunged from those documents;
d. That documents of the Special Court identifying witnesses shall not be disclosed to the public or media;
e. That all witnesses testify with the use of a screening device from the public;
f. That photographing, video-recording, sketching and recording or reproducing in any other manner of images of any witness of Group I (witnesses of fact) are prohibited while he or she is in the precincts of the Special Court;

And **FURTHER ORDERS**

a. That the voice of witnesses in Category A (victims of sexual violence) during their testimony in trial be distorted in the speakers for the public;
b. That witnesses in Category B (children) testify with the use of a closed-circuit television; the image appearing on the public's monitors being distorted;
c. That the voice of witnesses in Category C (insider witnesses) during their testimony in trial be distorted in the speakers for the public;
d. The Defence shall refrain from sharing, discussing or revealing, directly or indirectly, any disclosed non-public materials of any sort, or any information contained in any such documents, to any person or entity other than the Defence;
e. The Defence shall maintain a log indicating the name, address and position of each person or entity which receives a copy of, or information from, a witness statement, interview report or summary of expected testimony, or any other non-public material, as well as the date of

disclosure; and that the Defence shall ensure that the person to whom such information was disclosed follows the order of non-disclosure;

f. The Defence shall provide to the Registrar and to the Defence Office a designation of all persons working on the Defence team who, pursuant to paragraph 35(f) above, have access to any information referred to in paragraphs 35(a) through 35(d) above, and requiring the Defence to advise the Registrar and to the Defence Office in writing of any changes in the composition of this Defence team;

g. The Defence shall ensure that any member leaving the Defence team remits to the Defence team all disclosed non-public materials;

h. The Defence shall return to the Registry, at the conclusion of the proceedings in this case, all disclosed materials and copies thereof, which have not become part of the public record;

i. The Defence Counsel shall make a written request to the Trial Chamber or a Judge thereof, for permission to contact any Prosecution witness who is a protected witness or any relative of such person, and such request shall be timely served on the Prosecution. At the direction of the Trial Chamber or a Judge thereof, the Prosecution shall contact the protected person and ask for his or her consent or the parent's or guardian's consent if that person is under the age of 18, to an interview by the Defence, and shall undertake the necessary arrangements to facilitate such contact.

j. That the unredacted witness statements are to be disclosed to the Defence 42 days prior to the testimony at trial of these witnesses.

---

(1) See *Tadic* Decision, supra note 34, para. 47.
(2) See also *Prosecutor v Delalic et al.*, IT-96-21-T, Judgement, para. 495.
(3) Motion, Annex G.
(4) See *Maryland v Craig*, 497 U.S. 836 (1990).

R69-TC-7

o *Prosecutor v. Sesay, Kallon, Gbao*, Case No. SCSL-04-15-T, Ruling on the Oral Application of the Prosecution to Vary Protective Measures of Witness TF1-141, 6 April 2005, para. 6:

In the course of her testimony, Ms. Michels stated that from her observations she has concluded that Witness TF1-141 suffered from post-traumatic stress. She found that the Witness exhibits clearly the three groups of symptoms of post-traumatic stress and that he falls within the category of a witness who is severely traumatised. She also emphasized that he was particularly vulnerable given the level of his mental development due to his young age, the fact that he was a child ex-combatant and the fact that he was confronted with the traumatic events when he was much younger. As a result of these factors, she opined that this particular witness has a higher risk for retraumatisation from testifying. In light of her findings, Ms. Michels recommended that the Witness testify via closed-circuit television as this would create a quieter and less overwhelming environment for him and also prevent a direct confrontation. In addition, she recommended that he testify in the presence of a support person from the Victims and Witness Unit with whom the Witness is familiar in order to increase his comfort level and to control his feelings of fear and depersonalisation.

- **Rule 69: Protection of Victims and Witnesses – Measures of a General Nature – Case by Case Approach (Yes or No)**

R69-TC-8

o *Prosecutor v. Norman*, Case No. SCSL-03-08-PT, Decision on the Prosecutor's Motion for Immediate Protective Measures for Witnesses and Victims and for Non-Public Disclosure, 23 May 2003, para. 9:[99]

9. Pre-eminently mindful of the need to guarantee the utmost protection and respect for the rights of the victims and witnesses, and seeking to balance those rights with the competing interests of the public in the administration of justice, of the international community in ensuring that persons accused of violations of humanitarian law be brought to trial on the one hand, and the paramount due process right of the Accused to a fair trial, on the other, I am enjoined to order any appropriate measures for the protection of the victims and witnesses at the pre-trial stage that will ensure a fair determination of the matter before me, deciding the issue on a case-by case basis consistent with internationally recognised standards of

---

[99] See also *Prosecutor v. Kallon*, Case No. SCSL-03-07-PT, Decision on the Prosecutor's Motion for Immediate Protective Measures for Witnesses and Victims and for Non-Public Disclosure, 23 May 2003, para. 10; *Prosecutor v. Sesay*, Case No. SCSL-03-05-PT, Decision on the Prosecutor's Motion for Immediate Protective Measures for Witnesses and Victims and for Non-Public Disclosure, 23 May 2003, para. 9; *Prosecutor v. Brima*, Case No. SCSL-03-06-PT, Decision on the Prosecutor's Motion for Immediate Protective Measures for Witnesses and Victims and for Non-Public Disclosure, 23 May 2003, para. 9; *Prosecutor v. Kamara*, Case No. SCSL-03-10-PT, Decision on the Prosecution Motion for Immediate Protective Measures for Witnesses and Victims and for Non-Public Disclosure, 23 October 2003, para. 10; *Prosecutor v. Fofana*, Case No. SCSL-03-11-PT, Decision on the Prosecutor's Motion for Immediate Protective Measures for Witnesses and Victims and for Non-Public Disclosure, 16 October 2003, para. 9.

due process. Such orders are to take effect once the particulars and locations of the witnesses have been forwarded to the Victims and Witnesses Support Unit.

o *Prosecutor v. Gbao*, Case No. SCSL-03-09-PT, Decision on Prosecution Motion for Immediate Protective Measures for Witnesses and Victims and for Non-Public Disclosure, 10 October 2003, para. 51-57:

51. The Special Court, with Judge Bankole Thompson ruling, has already had the opportunity to decide on the issue of protective measures in the cases of *The Prosecutor v. Issa Hassan Sesay, The Prosecutor v. Alex Tamba Brima, The Prosecutor v. Morris Kallon* and *The Prosecutor v. Hinga Norman* (Decisions on the Prosecutor's Motions for Immediate Protective Measures for Witnesses and Victims and for Non-Public Disclosure, all four filed on the 23rd day of May 2003).

52. It is useful, first of all, to recall the Decision on the Application of the Prosecution Requesting Protective Measures for Witnesses and Victims, dated the 5th November 1996, rendered in the *Blaskic* case, in which the ICTY states that: *"the philosophy which imbues the Statute and Rules of the Tribunal appears clear: the Victims and Witnesses merit protection, even from the Accused, during the preliminary proceedings and continuing until a reasonable time before the start of the trial itself; from that forth, however, the right of the accused to an equitable trial must take precedence and require that the veil of anonymity be lifted in his favour, even if the veil must continue to obstruct the view of the public and the media"*.

53. After having noted this general principle enunciated by the ICTY, the Special Court now wishes to recall the findings made by Judge Bankole Thompson in the above-mentioned four decisions (paras. 14 and 15): *"Applying this general principle to the totality of the affidavit evidence before me, it is my considered view that a reasonable case has been made for the Prosecution witnesses herein to be granted at this preliminary stage a measure of anonymity and confidentiality. In addition, in matters of such delicacy and sensitivity, it would be unrealistic to expect either the Prosecution or the Defence, at the pre-trial phase, to carry the undue burden of having each witness narrate in specific terms or document the nature of his or her fears as to the actual or anticipated threats or intimidation (...)"*.

54. The Special Court concurs with the findings in the above-cited cases and, therefore, contrary to the arguments submitted by the Defence, does not see any valid reason to order a case by case approach combined with a schedule. Indeed, at

this stage of pre-trial proceedings, the measures sought for in the Motion being merely of a general nature, it would be inappropriate and unrealistic for the Special Court to decide otherwise.

55. Regarding rolling disclosure, Rule 69 (C) of the Rules, as previously quoted, clearly states that the date of testimony is to be used as a starting point for disclosure.

56. In this respect, Judge Bankole Thompson, in the previously described decision, held that "in the context of the security situation in Sierra Leone and in the interest of justice, one judicial option available to me, at this stage, in trying to balance the interests of the victims and witnesses for protection by a grant of anonymity and confidentiality with the pre-eminent interest of effectively protecting the Accused's right to a fair and public trial is to enlarge the time frame for disclosure beyond twenty-one (21) days to forty-two (42) days" (para. 15 and 16).

57. Given the previously reached finding that rolling disclosure is a fair mechanism which is in compliance with the principle of equality of arms, the Special Court, in light of the above comments, equally does not see any justification for departing or deviating from the rolling disclosure practice.

R69-TC-10

o *Prosecutor v. Kanu*, Case No. SCSL-03-13-PT, Decision on the Prosecution Motion for Immediate Protective Measures for Witnesses and Victims, 24 November 2003, para. 32, 36-42:

32. The issue which the Trial Chamber of the Special Court has addressed all along is that the Applicant in cases of this nature, must show that the disclosure to the Accused and his defence team of the identity to the public of a victim or a witness at this stage would put them in danger or at risk. In fact, there must be some objective foundation for the fear that the witness may be in danger or at risk: Archbold's *International Criminal Courts: Practice, Procedure and Evidence* (2003) at Paragraph 8-64c.

[...]

36. In a situation where the Trial Chamber, as at now, is estranged from the scenery and secrecy of the investigations, I cannot in advance, at least not before the commencement of the Pre-Trial Conferences, say, nor do I know, how many witnesses either the Prosecution or the Defence would call to make their cases. It is a question which at this moment, is entirely and only exclusively within the competence of the Prosecutor, and to some extent, the Defence, to provide a response.

37. This said however, I find that the argument based on the mention of "a witness" to exclude other witnesses who are, or may equally be entitled to the measures stipulated under Rule 69(A), cannot stand in view of the provisions of Rule 2(B) of the Rules. Besides, Rule 69 is made pursuant to the provisions of the Statute which is the enabling instrument. In this regard, Article 16(4) of the Statute provides as follows:

> "The Registrar shall set up a Victims and Witnesses Unit within the Registry. This Unit shall provide in consultation with the office of the Prosecutor, protective measures and security arrangements, counselling and other appropriate assistance for witnesses, victims who appear before the Court and others who are at risk on account of testimony given by such witnesses..."

38. Besides, Rule 69(B) of the Rules of stipulates that in the determination of protective measures for victims and witnesses, the Judge or the Trial Chamber may consult the Victims and Witnesses Unit. If the Respondent as he has done, raises the issue of singularity as far as the interpretation of the words 'a witness' in Rule 69(A) is concerned, Rule 69(B) is in plural terms. In any event, Article 16(4) of the Statute talks of Victims and Witnesses (in plural terms) and therefore, impliedly renders, only to the extent of the words 'or witness' in the regulatory text, if it could ever be construed in singular terms, null and void, because the Regulatory Authority (The Plenary), which drafted the Rules of Procedure and Evidence, was not supposed to, and could not of course have allowed itself to act *ultra vires* since it had neither the powers nor the mandate to modify or to limit the scope of the application of Article 16(4) of the Statute, an integral part of the Enabling Act, that is the Agreement dated 16th January, 2002, on the Establishment of the Special Court for Sierra Leone, signed by Two High Contracting Parties, namely, the United Nations Organisation and the Government of Sierra Leone.

39. In order to attempt to get out of the dilemma of a case-by-case examination so strongly canvassed by the Respondent at this stage of the proceedings, it would be interesting to find answers to the following questions. How many witnesses is the Prosecution holding for this trial? How many will they call to prove their case? Which of these witnesses is entitled to protection on a case-by-case basis as argued by the Respondent?

40. I find it difficult to answer any of these questions at the moment without prematurely delving into the trial process of examining the witnesses and their statements even before the trial begins. I indeed decline to encourage such an exercise which to my mind is complex, time consuming, and capable of unnecessarily protracting and complicating the proceedings and the process, in addition to the premature disclosure of even

those witnesses who deserve the protection much more than others. I accordingly have no hesitation therefore in dismissing this argument for want of any remedial merit of fostering the interest of a fair and expeditious trial.

41. From the foregoing, I find that unless exceptional cause to the contrary is shown by a Respondent in cases of this nature to warrant creating an exception, the option of globally protecting witnesses and victims, if chosen, instead of justifying such measures on a case-by-case basis, is legally well-founded and should be the rule, particularly so because as has been pointed out by the Trial Chamber in applications of this nature, it would be unrealistic to expect the Prosecution to carry the undue burden of having each witness narrate in specific terms in a document, the nature of his or her fears as to the actual or anticipated threats or intimidation before the Chamber rules on the substantive application.

42. In the present case, I find as a matter of fact that the Sierra Leonean society is still volatile and fragile as all indications are that it has not quite recovered from the memories, the ravages and the damage done by the devastating civil war. As a result, the witnesses, victims and their families are very vulnerable and should they fail to benefit from protective measures, they would be exposed to all forms of risks and recriminations from the indictees or their sympathisers.

- **Rule 69(A): Protection of Victims and Witnesses – Need for an Application**

R69-TC-11

o *Prosecutor v. Norman, Fofana, Kondewa*, Case No. SCSL-04-14-PT, Order to the Prosecution for Renewed Motion for Protective Measures, 2 April 2004:[100]

FINDING that at this advanced stage of the pre-trial proceedings, it would be in the interests of justice to review the protective measures required in this case, and make any necessary and appropriate variations consistent with the pre-eminent need to balance the interests of the Prosecution and those of the Defence;

[...]

---

[100] See also *Prosecutor v. Sesay, Kallon, Gbao*, Case No. SCSL-04-15-PT, Order to the Prosecution for Renewed Motion for Protective Measures, 2 April 2004.

HEREBY ORDERS that:

1. The Prosecution file a renewed motion for protective measures by 3 May 2004, pursuant to Rules 69 and 75 of the Rules, for each witness who appears on the Prosecution Witness List, which will be filed on 26 April 2004 in accordance with "Order to the Prosecution to File Disclosure Materials and Other Materials in Preparation for the Commencement of Trial," of 1 April 2004. The motion shall specify the form of protection being sought for each witness including delayed disclosure, pseudonym, face distortion or closed session, to the extent that the Prosecution can provide such specification. This motion shall further provide an overview of the reasons for the protective measures sought for witnesses whose names appear on the witness list. In this regard, the Trial Chamber finds that the Prosecution's reference to specific categories of witnesses may facilitate the Prosecution's task; [...]

R69-TC-12
o *Prosecutor v. Norman, Fofana, Kondewa*, Case No. SCSL-04-14-T, Order on Protective Measures for Additional Witnesses, 1st October 2004:

CONSIDERING that it is not the role of the Prosecution to inform the Trial Chamber of its intention to extend protective measures to witnesses, but that it should instead make a request to the Trial Chamber to consider and make a determination on this issue;

- **Rule 69(A): Protection of Victims and Witnesses – Burden of Proof of "Exceptional Circumstances"**

R69-TC-13
o *Prosecutor v. Norman, Fofana, Kondewa*, Case No. SCSL-04-14-T, Decision on Prosecution Motion for Modification of Protective Measures for Witnesses, 8 June 2004, para. 31-36:

31. In order to satisfy the general requirement of exceptional circumstances envisaged in Rule 69(A) of the Rules,[1] the Prosecution has accompanied the Motion with various confidential statements from its witnesses alleging serious threats made to them or their families in different occasions, aiming at discouraging their testimonies against the Accused. Pursuant to Rule 89(C) of the Rules the Chambers accepts this evidence submitted by the Prosecutor.[2]

32. In addition, in a signed declaration dated 3 May 2004, the Prosecution's Chief of Investigation reports of information as

of several threats made against witnesses for the Prosecution in this case as well as various attempts from what is described as CDF hardliners to disrupt the investigative activity of the Prosecution.[3] In particular, the Declaration submits that

> "Potential witnesses have also expressed fear of reprisals from relatives and friends of the accused, associates of the accused, and those who support the causes or faction the accused represents ... Potential witnesses have also expressed fears for their own family members if it became known that the potential witnesses was co-operating with the Special Court ... The fears expressed by potential witnesses and by sources have increased dramatically over the period of time that I have been supervising the investigations ... indeed almost every individual with whom we come into contact to obtain information regarding the activities of the CDF/Kamajors are at first instance terrified at the thought of testifying in public and are fully convinced that doing so will bring reprisal against themselves and their families ... In addition to the fears expressed by sources and potential witnesses, there have been numerous instances of direct threats against such persons."[4]

33. Finally, the Chief of Investigations concludes the Declaration as follows:

> "I firmly believe that witnesses, sources, and/or their family or associates risk their lives on a daily basis through their cooperation with the Special Court. It is essential for the safety and security of these potential witnesses be provided with the greatest possible protection under the law that this Court can provide."[5]

34. This Chamber expresses grave concerns about the seriousness of the increased threats made against the Prosecution witnesses at this stage of the proceedings as such has been described in the evidence adduced by the Prosecution. It emerges also from the review of the evidence in support of this application by the Prosecution that the CDF holds a structure actively organized within the country and still capable of substantial intimidations to witnesses.[6]

35. Furthermore, the Chamber also recalls the contents of the Twenty-First Report of the Secretary General on the United Nations Mission in Sierra Leone, dated 19 March 2004, in which it is stated:

> "Some elements of the former Civil Defence Forces (CDF) who are opposed to the indictment of Sam Hinga Norman, the Former Internal Affairs Minister and National Coordinator of the CDF, could seek to disrupt the work of the [Special] Court through violent activities. Although the group was disarmed, it is believed

that its command and control structures remain intact, especially in the east. For this reason, some observers believe that CDF could be capable of mobilizing a credible force."[7]

36. Based on the overwhelming weight of un-contradicted affidavit evidence before us it is therefore in the considered opinion of this Trial Chamber that a reasonable case has been made for the Prosecution witnesses to be granted, now, at this further stage of the trial of the Accused, a modification to the current measures of rolling disclosure of the Prosecution witness statements [. . .]."

---

[1] *Kondewa* Decision, paras 16-20; *Gbao* Decision, para. 25. See also *Prosecutor v. Musema*, ICTR-96-13-T, Decision on the Prosecution Motion for Witness Protection, 20 November 1998, para. 15-17; *Tadic* Decision, para. 62.
[2] Rule 89(C) of the Rules provides that "A Chamber may admit any relevant evidence".
[3] Motion, Annex 8 ("Declaration"). The contents of the Declaration are corroborated by the Declaration of the Inspector General of the Sierra Leone Police. See also the Declaration from the Chief of the Victims and Witnesses Unit. It is worth to observe that no evidence to rebut the Prosecution's submissions has been produced by the Defence.
[4] Declaration, paras 6-9. See also paras 15, 17 and 20.
[5] *Id.*, para. 39.
[6] *Id.*, paras 16, 20, 22, 24-25, and 30-34. See also Annex 9 to the Motion, paras 4-13.
[7] S/2004/228, Twenty-First Report of the Secretary General on the United Nations Mission in Sierra Leone, 19 March 2004, para. 50.

R69-TC-14

o *Prosecutor v. Norman, Fofana, Kondewa*, Case No. SCSL-04-14-T, Order for Submissions and Interim Order Pursuant to Rule 54 of the Rules, 1st December 2005:

HAVING RECEIVED the "Motion by the Third Accused Allieu Kondewa for Orders of Protective Measures for Defence Witnesses" [. . .]

NOTING that the Motion is unsupported by any documentary or affidavit evidence;[1]

MINDFUL that, when protective measures are sought for witnesses, it must be shown that there is a real fear for the safety of a witness and of his or her family and that there is an objective justification for this fear;[2]

[. . .]

CONSIDERING that the Special Court is located in Sierra Leone where the offences charged against the Accused are alleged to have been committed and that this fact has a substantial impact on the security considerations for victims and witnesses; [3]

CONSIDERING that, to be able to make an objective assessment of the appropriateness of the measures sought by the defence in its Motion, the Trial Chamber needs to be in possession of all the relevant information showing that there is a real fear for the Defence witnesses and their families and that there is an objective justification for such fear;[4]

[...]

THE TRIAL CHAMBER

ORDERS the Defence to provide adequate and appropriate materials in support of the Motion by no later than Monday, the 5th of December, 2005, at 4.00pm;

---

[1] See also the Prosecution response, at paras 3 ff.
[2] See, for instance, *Prosecutor against Kondewa*, Case No. SCSL-03-12-PT, Ruling on the Prosecution Motion for Immediate Protective Measures for Witnesses and Victims and for Non-Public Disclosure and Urgent request for Interim Measures until Appropriate Protective Measures are in Place, 10 October 2003, paras 18-19. See also, *Prosecutor v. Simba*, Case No. ICTR-01-76-I, decision on defence Request for Protection of Witnesses, 25 August 2004, para. 5. See also *Prosecutor v. Samuel Hinga Norman*, SCSL-03-08-PT, decision on the Prosecutor's Motion for Immediate Protective Measures for Witnesses and Victims and for Non-Public Disclosure, 23 May 2003; *Prosecutor v. Moinina Fofana*, SCSL-03-11-PD, Decision on the Prosecutor's Motion for Immediate Protective Measures for Witnesses and Victims and for non-Public Disclosure, 16 October 2003.
[3] *Prosecutor against Norman, Fofana, and Kondewa*, case No, SCSL-04-14-T, Order on Protective Measures for Additional Witnesses, 21 September 2004.
[4] See also *Prosecutor v. Karera*, Case No. ICTR-01-74-R54, Order for submission – Rule 54 of the Rules of Procedure and Evidence, 21 November 2005.

- **Rule 69(A): Protection of Victims and Witnesses – Witness' Fear**

R69-TC-15

o *Prosecutor v. Kondewa*, Case No. SCSL-03-12-PT, Ruling on the Prosecution Motion for Immediate Protective Measures for Witnesses and Victims and for Non-Public Disclosure and Urgent Request for Interim Measures Until Appropriate Protective Measures Are in Place, 10 October 2003, para. 16-19:

16. [...] The test to be applied in matters of this nature is that the Prosecution must show that the disclosure to the accused and this defence team of the identity of a witness at this stage despite the obligation imposed upon the accused and his defence team not to disclose to the public may put the witness in danger or at risk. There must be some objective foundation for the fear that the witness may be in danger or at

risk. *Archbold: International Criminal Courts Practice, Procedure and Evidence*, Para 8-64 c.

17. To highlight these fears and to meet up with the vital ingredient of proving "exceptional circumstances" in order to secure non-disclosure, the Applicants have produced some Sworn Declarations of Mr. Gbekie, an Investigator, Dr. White, the Chief of Investigations, Alan Quee, the Director of Post Conflict Re-integration Initiative for the development and Empowerment, an NGO which deals directly with combatants, Saleem Vahidy, the Chief of the Witness Unit and the former and present Inspector General of Police for Sierra Leone. These Declarations have the common denominator of outlining the fears expressed by the Applicants for the safety of potential witnesses and their families if a non-disclosure order were not made to protect their identities for the time being as real threats of elimination, according to the said Declarations, exist if they are identified as testifying against the indictee, the Respondent in this Motion.

18. In the cases of *The Prosecutor vs. Alfred Musema*, ICTR-96-13-T and *The Prosecutor vs. Tadic*, IT-94-I-T 1995, the Trial Chambers of the ICTR and ICTY, applying the same Rules as our Rules 69 and 75, it was held that for a witness to qualify for the protection of his identity from disclosure to the public and the media, there must be real fear for the safety of the witness or his or her family and there must always be an objective basis to the fear. In the same decisions, it was held that a non-disclosure Order may be based on fears expressed by persons other than the witness as is the case in the matter under adjudication where the Applicants are relying on the declarations of a number of privileged Officials who are closely and very involved in the process of investigation, custody and a follow-up of the actors of this violent and gruesome internal conflict in Sierra Leone.

19. In the case of the *Prosecutor vs. Brdanin*, November 8, 2000, at Paragraph 13, it was held that there must be some objective foundation for the fear that the witness may be in danger and that the fears of a potential witness are not themselves sufficient to establish a real likelihood that the witness may be in danger. Something more than that has to be demonstrated before an interference with the right of the accused to know the witnesses' identity is warranted. Still on another application by the Prosecution for non-disclosure in the *Brdanin* case, July 3, 2003, the Trial Chamber of the ICTY held that in the absence of evidence of risk that particular witnesses will be interfered with, it is logical to conclude that the exceptional circumstance provided for under Rule 69 cannot be justified.

o *Prosecutor v. Norman, Fofana, Kondewa*, Case No. SCSL-04-14-T, Ruling on Motion for Modification of Protective Measures for Witnesses, 18 November 2004, para. 39-40, 47:

39. We, therefore, restate with emphasis the factors to be taken into account in confirming the validity of protective measures. They are: (1) fears expressed by the witnesses in Court; (2) concerns expressed by the VWS and by the investigators of the Office of the Prosecutor; (3) various confidential statements from the witnesses alleging serious threats made to them and their families; (4) declarations from numerous sources on the recent Kamajor activities attempting to disrupt the activities of the Court.

(b) The objective test

40. As indicated above, the subjective feeling of a witness is not in itself conclusive for granting the protective measures, although it is one of the factors to be considered in the protective measures equation. Therefore, the admission by a witness in the course of the trial of lack of fear for disclosure of his or her identity cannot be decisive of the issue. In fact, the Trial Chamber notes that replies of witnesses on this matter should be taken into consideration within the context of their entire testimonies. [...]

[...]

47. We recall our previous rulings denying requests for a *voir dire* assessment of each witness' fears prior to his or her testimony, and accordingly reiterate our observation to the extent that "it would be unrealistic to expect either the Prosecution or the Defence, at the pre-trial phase, to carry the undue burden of having each witness narrate in specific terms or document the nature of his or her fears as to the actual or anticipated threats or intimidation"[1] in the context of the general security situation in Sierra Leone towards the witnesses. The Trial Chamber is satisfied that the Prosecution has clearly established that the security threats and risk of interference are real, generalized and extend to <u>all</u> witnesses and persons who are suspected or perceived to be prepared to testify against the Accused.

---

[1] *Prosecutor v. Samuel Hinga Norman*, Decision on the Prosecutor's Motion for Immediate Protective Measures for Witnesses and Victims and for Non-Public Disclosure, 23 May 2003, para. 14 (emphasis omitted); See also *Prosecutor v. Gbao*, Decision on the Prosecution Motion for Immediate Protective Measures for Witnesses and Victims and for Non-Public Disclosure, 10 October 2003, paras 53-54 and *Prosecutor v. Brima*, Decision on the Prosecutor's Motion on Immediate Protective Measures for Witnesses and Victims and for Non-Public Disclosure, 23 May 2003, para. 14.

- **Rule 69(A): Protection of Victims and Witnesses – Non-Disclosure of Identities**

R69-TC-17   o *Prosecutor v. Norman*, Case No. SCSL-03-08-PT, Decision on the Prosecutor's Motion for Immediate Protective Measures for Witnesses and Victims and for Non-Public Disclosure, 23 May 2003, para. 16:[101]

16. As regards the 21 (twenty-one) day time limit prayed for by the Prosecution in sought Order (a), despite the existence of some instructive ICTY and ICTR decisions supporting the 21 day rule limitation for disclosure, it is my considered view that there is no legal logic or norm compelling an inflexible adherence to this rule. In the context of the security situation in Sierra Leone and in the interest of justice, one judicial option available to me, at this stage, in trying to balance the interest of the victims and witnesses for protection by a grant of anonymity and confidentiality with the pre-eminent interest of effectively protecting the Accused's right to a fair and public trial is to enlarge the time frame for disclosure beyond 21 (twenty-one) days to 42 (forty-two) days. And I so order.

R69-TC-18   o *Prosecutor v. Kanu*, Case No. SCSL-03-13-PT, Decision on the Prosecution Motion for Immediate Protective Measures for Witnesses and Victims, 24 November 2003, para. 29-31:

29. What, however, appears certain in my mind is that the doctrine of anonymity and non-disclosure, even though it might appear contradictory to, is not necessarily inconsistent with the principles of a fair trial that are guaranteed to the

---

[101] See also *Prosecutor v. Kallon*, Case No. SCSL-03-07-PT, Decision on the Prosecutor's Motion for Immediate Protective Measures for Witnesses and Victims and for Non-Public Disclosure, 23 May 2003, para. 11, 13-16; *Prosecutor v. Sesay*, Case No. SCSL-03-05-PT, Decision on the Prosecutor's Motion for Immediate Protective Measures for Witnesses and Victims and for Non-Public Disclosure, 23 May 2003, para. 10, 12-15; *Prosecutor v. Brima*, Case No. SCSL-03-06-PT, Decision on the Prosecutor's Motion for Immediate Protective Measures for Witnesses and Victims and for Non-Public Disclosure, 23 May 2003, para. 16; *Prosecutor v. Gbao*, Case No. SCSL-03-09-PT, Decision on the Prosecution Motion for Immediate Protective Measures for Witnesses and Victims and for Non Public Disclosure, 10 October 2003, para. 58; *Prosecutor v. Kamara*, Case No. 03-10-PT, Decision on the Prosecution Motion for Immediate Protective Measures for Witnesses and Victims and for Non-Public Disclosure, 23 October 2003, para. 20; *Prosecutor v. Fofana*, Case No. SCSL-03-11-PT, Decision on the Prosecutor's Motion for Immediate Protective Measures for Witnesses and Victims and for Non-Public Disclosure, 16 October 2003, para. 17; *Prosecutor v. Sesay, Kallon, Gbao*, Case No. SCSL-04-15-PT, Decision on Prosecution Motion for Modification of Protective Measures for Witnesses, 5 July 2004, para. 23.

Accused under Article 17(2) of the Statute because the lifting of the veil of anonymity before the calling of these shielded witnesses balances the legal claim to a status of and prerogative to protection and anonymity that they might have enjoyed all along with the leave of the Court.

30. Indeed, as Justice Brooking of the Supreme Court of Victoria stated in the case *Jarvie and Another v. The Magistrate's Court of Victoria at Brunswick and Others* [1994] V.R. 84,88, and I quote:

> "The balancing exercise now so familiar in this and other fields of the law must be undertaken. On the other hand, there is public interest that the Defendant should be able to elicit (directly or indirectly) and to establish facts and matters, including those going to the credit, as may assist in securing a favourable outcome to the proceedings. There is also a public interest in the conduct by the Courts of their proceedings in public."

31. What further appears to be palpably certain is that the protection given to these Victims and Witnesses is justified because of the role they are expected to, and are in fact called upon to play in the administration of international criminal justice which is in conformity with what I stated, in the Ruling in the case of the *Prosecutor v. Allieu Kondewa*, cited earlier, and I quote:

> "... One of the goals targeted by the International community is to track down and bring before justice, those who bear the greatest responsibility for a breach of International Humanitarian Law by committing heinous crimes against humanity. In view of the particularly bloody, hostile, and vicious environment in which these gruesome offences were cruelly perpetrated and the necessity to fulfil the procedural imperatives of an adversarial system of justice governing the Courts by providing witnesses to sustain the charges, a mechanism had to be worked out to achieve the targeted objectives. One of this is certainly to create incentives geared towards encouraging victims and witnesses of those crimes to testify, albeit, against those front-line perpetrators and one of these measures is to put in place, a protective wall between the victim or witness and the Accused so that neither the latter nor his sympathisers would identify the former for possible recriminations and eventual eliminations. It is only to this strategy that International Criminal Justice owes its exceptional survival, for, in the absence of these protected witnesses and victims, there will be no trials and consequently, no end to the criminal impunity that the International Community is endeavouring to contain and combat through the International Criminal Courts..."

R69-TC-19

o *Prosecutor v. Norman, Fofana, Kondewa*, Case No. SCSL-04-14-T, Decision on Prosecution Motion for Modification of Protective Measures for Witnesses, 8 June 2004, para. 36:

36. Based on the overwhelming weight of un-contradicted affidavit evidence before us it is therefore in the considered opinion of this Trial Chamber that a reasonable case has been made for the Prosecution witnesses to be granted, now, at this further stage of the trial of the Accused, a modification to the current measures of rolling disclosure of the Prosecution witness statements for the accused Norman and Fofana from a 42 days period to a 21 days period, in line with the same time period provided for in the *Kondewa* Decision. This measure provides now and in these circumstances for a proportionate balance of the interests of the witnesses for protection and the Accused right to a fair trial.

R69-TC-20

o *Prosecutor v. Sesay*, Case No. SCSL-04-15-T, Decision on Defence Motion, 15 July 2004, para. 11-12, 14:

11. The Chamber has taken notice of the fact that the Defence did not raise any of these disclosure issues at the most recent Status Conference held on 23 June 2004.

12. The Chamber further opines that from the day of its Order to the Prosecution to File Disclosure Materials, the Defence had sufficient time to analyse the material disclosed by the Prosecution before 5 July 2004, when the trial commenced and still has the opportunity to challenge it during cross examination.[1]

[...]

14. Furthermore, the Chamber wishes to underline that the 42 day period for the full disclosure of witness statements in an unredatected form, pursuant to the provisions of Rule 69(C) of the Rules and the established jurisprudence of the Special Court on the system of "rolling disclosure", applies to the date of testimony at trial of each witness rather that the date of commencement of the trial.[2]

---

[1] Decision on Defence Motion for Disclosure Pursuant to Rule 66 and 68 of the Rules, 9 July 2004, para. 44.
[2] Decision on Prosecution Motion for Modification of Protective Measures for Witnesses, 5 July 2004, Order p.; see also para. 23; Ruling on Oral Application for Respect of Disclosure Obligations, 9 July 2004, para. 3. In addition, see *Prosecutor v. Issa Hassan Sesay*, SCSL-2003-05-PT, Decision on the Prosecutor's Motion for Immediate Protective Measures for Witnesses and Victims and for Non-public Disclosure, 23 May 2003; *Prosecutor v. Morris Kallon*, SCSL-

2003-07-PT, Decision on the Prosecutor's Motion for Immediate Protective Measures for Witnesses and Victims and for Non-public Disclosure, 23 May 2003; *Prosecutor v. Augustine Gbao*, SCSL-2003-09-PT, Decision on the Prosecutor's Motion for Immediate Protective Measures for Witnesses and Victims and for Non-public Disclosure, 10 October 2003, para. 55.

- **Rule 69(A): Protection of Victims and Witnesses – Non-Disclosure of Identities – Late Disclosure – Postponement of Testimony**

R69-TC-21

o *Prosecutor v. Sesay*, Case No. SCSL-04-15-T, Ruling on the Oral Application for the Postponement of the Testimony of Witness TF1-060, 27 July 2004, para. 2-5:

2. It should be observed, however, that by granting this application this Chamber is not now opening a new avenue for application of such nature in the future. The Court is still deeply concerned about delays and will do its utmost to try to limit any applications that will have as a consequence delays in the proceedings.

3. Applications of this nature will be dealt with on a case by case basis and will have to be duly substantiated. With regard to this particular application, the Chamber is of the view that it would be best to proceed with the complete testimony of this witness when he is called rather than breaking the cross-examination and allow then a postponement of that part of the witness' cross-examination related to his most recent written statement.

4. Although the bulk of the evidence of this witness has been disclosed more that 42 days before he is to testify,[1] the most recent written statement has only been obtained and disclosed to the Defence on 16 July 2004.[2]

5. Furthermore, it would appear that this written statement would for the first time directly implicate the First Accused and consequently the Defence is asking for additional time to investigate this matter further. They have stated that their investigators cannot be contacted at this time and therefore are not able to pursue that part of the investigation prior to proceeding with the cross-examination of Witness TF1-060.

[1] Decision on Prosecution Motion for Modification of Protective Measures for Witnesses, 5 July 2004.
[2] Copy of Witness Statements Produced Pursuant to "Order to Prosecution to Produce Witness List and Witness Summaries", 19 July 2004.

- **Rule 69(A): Protection of Victims and Witnesses – Right to a Public Trial**

R69-TC-22

o *Prosecutor v. Kamara*, Case No. SCSL-03-10-PT, Decision on the Prosecution Motion for Immediate Protective Measures for Witnesses and Victims and for Non-Public Disclosure, 23 October 2003, para. 19:[102]

19. [. . .] [E]ven though the Court must, in such matters, seek to balance the right of the Accused to a fair and public trial with the interest of the witness in being given protection such a right is subject to derogating exceptional circumstances (Article 17(2) of the Statute) [. . .].

R69-TC-23

o *Prosecutor v. Norman, Fofana, Kondewa*, Case No. SCSL-04-14-T, Ruling on Motion for Modification of Protective Measures for Witnesses, 18 November 2004, para. 48-50:

48. [. . .] The Trial Chamber emphasizes that the existing protective measures, i.e. use of a screen from public and use of a pseudonym, do not jeopardize the right of the Accused to a fair and public trial. These protective measures are designed to protect the witnesses' identity from the public. They do not prevent the Accused from exercising freely his rights to a fair trial, i.e. those envisaged in Article 17 (4) of the Statute and specifically in Article 17(4)(b) and 17(4)(e). As for the public nature of the trial, the Trial Chamber concludes that the minimum protective measures in no way prevent the public and the media from attending and following this trial. The Trial Chamber agrees with the Defence submission that through the public trial the people of Sierra Leone have a right to be informed about what happened during the civil war as one step towards reconciliation. But, there is clearly no authority from the jurisprudence to support the theory, as canvassed by learned Counsel for the First Accused, that there is an obligation, in the criminal adjudicative process, on the public to participate in the ascertainment of the truth by bringing forward evidence of a rebutting or exculpatory nature in response to the Prosecution's case.

49. As for the hearing in closed session, the Trial Chamber stresses that a measure of hearing the testimony in closed session is only granted to a certain category of the witnesses and is based on the principle of protection of victims and wit-

---

[102] See also *Prosecutor v. Sesay, Kallon, Gbao*, Case No. SCSL-04-15-T, Order to Hear the Evidence of Witness TF1-235 in Closed Session, 8 November 2004.

nesses where the interests of justice so dictate. We have held on numerous occasions that this is "an extraordinary protective measure that will only be granted where it is shown that there is a real risk to the witness and / or his or her family and that their privacy or security will be threatened."[(1)]

50. We, therefore, opine that the Defence submission that the trial conducted in closed session would prejudice the Accused by denying the possibility of witnesses who hear the testimony coming forward and being able to controvert it, is misconceived and without legal foundation. It is our considered view that though the conception of a fair trial may notionally include that of a public trial, in the circumstances of this application, the Trial Chamber does not agree with the Defence contention that permitting a witness's testimony in closed session in the context of the application of protective measures, with all the necessary judicial guarantees for the protection of the due process rights of the accused persons, necessarily detracts from the fairness of the trial. The Defence position is mistakenly predicated upon some notion of a perfect trial.

[(1)] *See, inter alia, Prosecutor v. Sam Hinga Norman, Moinina Fofana, Allieu Kondewa*, Order on an Application by the Prosecution to Hold a Closed Session Hearing of Witness TF2-223, 27 October 2004.

- **Rule 69(A): Protection of Victims and Witnesses – Evolution**

R69-TC-24

o *Prosecutor v. Norman, Fofana, Kondewa*, Case No. SCSL-04-14-PT, Order to the Prosecution for Renewed Motion for Protective Measures, 2 April 2004:[103]

CONSIDERING that the Decisions for protective measures specified that the protective measures granted were applicable at that stage of the proceedings, namely at the start of the pre-trial phase;[(1)]

FINDING that at this advanced stage of the pre-trial proceedings, it would be in the interests of justice to review the protective measures required in this case, and make any necessary and appropriate variations consistent with the pre-eminent need to balance the interests of the Prosecution and those of the Defence;

[...]

[103] See also *Prosecutor v. Sesay, Kallon, Gbao*, Case No. SCSL-04-15-PT, Order to the Prosecution for Renewed Motion for Protective Measures, 2 April 2004.

HEREBY ORDERS that:

1. The Prosecution file a renewed motion for protective measures by 3 May 2004, pursuant to Rules 69 and 75 of the Rules, for each witness who appears on the Prosecution Witness List, which will be filed on 26 April 2004 in accordance with "Order to the Prosecution to File Disclosure Materials and Other Materials in Preparation for the Commencement of Trial," of 1 April 2004. The motion shall specify the form of protection being sought for each witness including delayed disclosure, pseudonym, face distortion or closed session, to the extent that the Prosecution can provide such specification. This motion shall further provide an overview of the reasons for the protective measures sought for witnesses whose names appear on the witness list. In this regard, the Trial Chamber finds that the Prosecution's reference to specific categories of witnesses may facilitate the Prosecution's task; and

2. The protective measures granted in this case[2] shall remain in force until further notice.

---

[1] See *Norman* Decision, paras 14 and 15 ("a reasonable case has been made for the prosecution witnesses herein to be granted at this preliminary stage a measure of anonymity and confidentiality" and "justify, at this point in time, delaying the disclosure of the identities of the witnesses during the *pre-trial phase*), *Fofana* Decision, para 16 ("justify, at this point in time, delaying the disclosure of the identities of the witnesses during the *pre-trial phase*); *Kondewa* Decision, para 29 ("at this pre-trial stage").
[2] See note 1.

- **Rule 69(A): Protection of Victims and Witnesses – Removal**

R69-TC-25   o *Prosecutor v. Norman, Fofana, Kondewa*, Case No. SCSL-04-14-T, Ruling on Motion for Modification of Protective Measures for Witnesses, 18 November 2004, para. 41-43:

41. We note that while vesting the Court with authority to grant protective measures to victims and witnesses, the Statute and the Rules do not specify the duration of these protective measures or the circumstances when such measures cease to have legal force in the "first proceedings".[1] A reasonable interpretation, in the view of the Trial Chamber, is that once protective measures are granted, they cannot be revoked or varied in the "first proceedings". Therefore, the Trial Chamber must emphasize that, if protective measures granted during the "first proceedings" are to have any efficacy, the Court must guarantee that witnesses who have come forward to testify relying on such a guarantee do in reality enjoy the veil of anonymity from the public. To withdraw such a guarantee *ex*

post-facto would indeed undermine the integrity of the proceedings of the Court. Contrastingly, it is noteworthy that the Rules do confer authority on the Court to rescind, vary or augment in the "second proceedings"[2] protective measures granted during the "first proceedings".

42. Drawing some persuasive guidance from the ICTY decision in *Tadic* on the issue of withdrawal of protective measures for Prosecution witness L in the "first proceedings",[3] it is significant to note that the Trial Chamber in that case indicated that "if a less restrictive measure can satisfy the requested protection, that lesser measure should be applied". The Trial Chamber further observed that "if at any time, [protective] measures are no longer required, they shall cease to apply". In that case, the Trial Chamber did order the withdrawal of the protective measures on the premises of its "preference to limit protective measures to those that are truly necessary, and the fact that the Motion [was] unopposed".[4]

43. Based on the above considerations, this Trial Chamber concludes that where a Party in a case seeks to rescind, vary or augment protective measures granted to the witness, it should present supporting evidence capable of establishing on a preponderance of probabilities that the witness is no longer in need of such protection. The Trial Chamber holds that the Defence have failed to adduce any evidence capable of showing, on a preponderance of probabilities, the dramatically changed circumstance justifying a radical variation of the protective measures. The contention that no retaliation or retribution has occurred to any witnesses whose identity has long been known to the Defence and who has so far testified before this Court does not constitute such changed circumstance. We, therefore, find such a submission both logically and legally unsustainable. On the contrary, there seems to be some plausibility in the Prosecution's contention that it may well be that witnesses have been free from retaliation due to the mechanism of protective measures.

---

[1] As defined in Rule 75 (F) of the Rules.
[2] As defined in Rule 75 (F) (i) of the Rules.
[3] *Prosecutor v. Dusko Tadic a/k/a "Dule"*, Decision on Prosecution Motion to Withdraw Protective Measures for Witness L, 5 December 1996.
[4] *Ibid.*, paras 5-6.

Rule 70: Matters Not Subject to Disclosure
(amended 7 March 2003)

(A) Notwithstanding the provisions of Rules 66 and 67, reports, memoranda, or other internal documents prepared by a party, its assistants or representatives in connection with the investigation or preparation of the case, are not subject to disclosure or notification under the aforementioned provisions.

(B) If the Prosecutor is in possession of information which has been provided to him on a confidential basis and which has been used solely for the purpose of generating new evidence, that initial information and its origin shall not be disclosed by the Prosecutor without the consent of the person or entity providing the initial information and shall in any event not be given in evidence without prior disclosure to the accused.

(C) If, after obtaining the consent of the person or entity providing information under this Rule, the Prosecutor elects to present as evidence any testimony, document or other material so provided, the Trial Chamber may not order either party to produce additional evidence received from the person or entity providing the initial information, nor may the Trial Chamber for the purpose of obtaining such additional evidence itself summon that person or a representative of that entity as a witness or order their attendance. The consent shall be in writing.

(D) If the Prosecutor calls as a witness the person providing or a representative of the entity providing information under this Rule, the Trial Chamber may not compel the witness to answer any question the witness declines to answer on grounds of confidentiality.

(E) The right of the accused to challenge the evidence presented by the Prosecution shall remain unaffected subject only to limitations contained in Sub-Rules (C) and (D).

(F) Nothing in Sub-Rule (C) or (D) above shall affect a Trial Chamber's power to exclude evidence under Rule 95.

DIGEST OF JURISPRUDENCE OF THE SPECIAL COURT FOR SIERRA LEONE 501

TRIAL CHAMBERS DECISIONS

- **Rule 70(A): Matters Not subject to Disclosure – Internal Documents Prepared by the Parties in the Preparation of Their Case**

R70-TC-1

o *Prosecutor v. Sesay, Kallon, Gbao*, Case No. SCSL-04-15-T, Decision on the Gbao and Sesay Joint Application for the Exclusion of the Testimony of Witness TF1-141, 26 October 2005, para. 20-21:

20. It is noteworthy, however, that Rule 70(A) of the Rules provides that "reports, memoranda, or other internal documents prepared by a party, its assistants or representatives in connection with the investigation or preparation of the case" are not subject to disclosure under Rule 66. Thus, internal documents prepared by the Prosecution or the Defence "in connection with an investigation or the preparation of a case"[1] are not disclosable.

21. We held that, in accordance with these provisions, the Prosecution is therefore obligated to disclose all witness statements in its possession, in whatever form they may exist, unless the information contained therein is exempted in whole or in part from disclosure in accordance with Rule 70.

[1] *Prosecutor v. Norman, Fofana and Kondewa*, SCSL-04-14-T, "Ruling on Disclosure of Witness Statements", 1 October 2004, para. 15.

- **Rule 70(A): Matters Not subject to Disclosure – Notes on Proofing Sessions**

R70-TC-2

o *Prosecutor v. Sesay, Kallon, Gbao*, Case No. SCSL-04-15-T, Decision on the Gbao and Sesay Joint Application for the Exclusion of the Testimony of Witness TF1-141, 26 October 2005, para. 29-34:

29. The records show that the original notes that are the object of this Application were taken by counsel with the Office of the Prosecutor, Ms. Sharan Parmar, during "proofing" sessions in October 2004 and January 2005 with Witness TF1-141 and that supplemental statements or proofing notes containing new evidence or amendments to previously disclosed evidence were disclosed to the Defence while the original notes were destroyed.[1]

30. It is instructive to note that the Trial Chamber of the ICTY examined the practice of Prosecution proofing sessions

in the case of *Prosecutor v. Limaj*.[2] It observed that there was a widespread practice of proofing witnesses by both the Prosecution and the Defence in adversary systems. The Chamber then identified a number of advantages that the practice of proofing has for the judicial process in these terms:

> It must be remembered that when a witness is proofed this is directed to identifying fully the facts known to the witness that are relevant to the charges in the actual Indictment ...
>
> ... The process of human recollection is likely to be assisted, in these circumstances, by a detailed canvassing during the pre-trial proofing of the relevant recollection of a witness. Proofing will also properly extend to a detailed examination of deficiencies and differences in recollection when compared with each earlier statement of the witness. In particular, such proofing is likely to enable the more accurate, complete, orderly and efficient presentation of the evidence of a witness in the trial.
>
> Very importantly, proofing enables differences in recollection, especially additional recollections, to be identified and notice of them to be given to the Defence, before the evidence is given, thereby reducing the prospect of the defence being taken entirely by surprise.[3]

31. The Prosecution submitted that notes made by counsel during proofing sessions are lawyer's "work product" not subject to disclosure in accordance with Rule 70(A).

32. The Chamber is mindful of the decision of the Trial Chamber of the ICTY in the case of *Prosecutor v. Blagojevic* where it was stated that:

> Rule 70(A) aims to protect work product from disclosure, as it is in the public interest that information related to the internal preparation of a case, including legal theories, strategies and investigations, shall be privileged and not subject to disclosure to the opposing party.[4]

33. The Chamber finds that proofing witnesses prior to their testimony in court is a legitimate practice that serves the interests of justice. This is especially so given the particular circumstances of many witnesses in this trial who are testifying about traumatic events in an environment that can be entirely foreign and intimidating for them.

34. We consider, however, that notes taken by counsel from the Office of the Prosecutor during these proofing sessions contain a combination of material, some of which is disclosable under Rules 66 and 68 of the Rules and some of which may not be subject to disclosure in accordance with Rule 70(A). It is our view that any new evidence elicited during

these proofing sessions must be disclosed on a continuing basis in accordance with Rules 66 and 68. Furthermore, we hold that those portions of the notes that relate to the internal preparation for the Prosecution case that constitute work product, however, are not disclosable.

(1) Response, para. 15.
(2) *Prosecutor v. Limaj, Bala and Musliu*, IT-03-66-T, "Decision on defence Motion on Prosecution Practice of 'Proofing' Witnesses", 10 December 2004.
(3) *Id.*, p. 2.
(4) *Prosecutor v. Blagojevic and Jokic*, IT-02-60-T, "Decision on Videoje Blagojevic's Expedited Motion to Compel the Prosecution to Disclose its Notes from Plea Discussions with the Accused Nikolic & request for an Expedited Open Session Hearing", 13 June 2003.

- **Rule 70(B): Matters Not Subject to Disclosure – Confidential Information – Communications Between Doctors and Clients**

R70-TC-3

o *Prosecutor v. Brima, Kamara, Kanu,* Case No. SCSL-04-16-T, Decision on Joint Defence Motion on Admissibility of Expert Witness/Expert Evidence and Filing of Notice Pursuant to Rule 94*bis*(B)(i) and (ii), on Re-filed Defence Request for Disclosure, and on the Joint Defence Motion for Exclusion of Medical Information, Statistics and Abstracts Pertaining to Witnesses TF1-081 and TF1-188, 16 June 2005, para. 15-16:

15. We note that the Defence has not disputed the Prosecution submission that it cannot disclose the requested information as it falls into the privilege of confidential communications between doctors and their clients. There is no evidence that the consent of the person or entity providing the initial information has been given. We therefore, conclude that the requested material falls under Rule 70(B) of the Rules, and that the defence is not entitled to receive the requested information.

16. We accept that Prosecution does not have any other documents and therefore the Trial Chamber cannot make any order for disclosure.

- **Rule 70(B): Matters Not Subject to Disclosure – Confidential Information – Privileged Relationship Between Human Rights Officer and Informants**

R70-TC-4

o *Prosecutor v. Brima, Kamara, Kanu*, Case No. SCSL-04-16-T, Decision on the Prosecution's Oral Application for Leave to Be Granted to Witness TF1-150 to Testify Without Being Compelled to Answer Any Questions in Cross-Examination That the Witness Declines to Answer on Grounds of Confidentiality Pursuant to Rule 70(B) and (D) of the Rules, 16 September 2005, para. 19-20:

19. First of all, we are of the view that the provisions of Rule 70 upon which the Prosecution seeks to rely are not applicable to Witness TF1-150 or his testimony. The Rule applies only where the Prosecutor "*is in possession of information which has been provided to him on a confidential basis and which has been used solely for the purpose of generating new evidence...*" That has not been shown to be the case here. We might add that it is that initial information together with its source that may not be disclosed by the Prosecutor without the prior consent of the source. In this case the Prosecution has not shown that they are in possession of that initial information. [...]

20. Secondly, whereas the Trial Chamber recognises the privileged relationship between a Human Rights officer and his informants as well as the public interest that attaches to the work of Human Rights officers gathering confidential information in the field, we do not think that the privilege and/or public interest should outweigh the rights of the accused persons to a fair trial as guaranteed by Article 17 of the Statute. In any event, we are of the view that the protective measures pertaining to a closed session under Rule 79 are more than sufficient to maintain the confidentiality of any information that Witness TF1-150 may divulge in the course of his testimony, without the need for additional measures whose effect is to curtail the statutory rights of the accused. In this regard we agree with the view expressed by the witness's former employer in their letter referred to above. In our opinion it would be prejudicial to the rights of the accused persons if Witness TF1-150 were permitted to disclose certain information and withhold the names of the sources, as the Defence would be handicapped in their attempts to challenge the information disclosed without knowing the name of the source.

- **Rule 70(D): Matters Not Subject to Disclosure – "Person or Representative Providing Initial Information"**

R70-TC-5

o *Prosecutor v. Brima, Kamara, Kanu*, Case No. SCSL-04-16-T, Decision on the Prosecution's Oral Application for Leave to Be Granted to Witness TF1-150 to Testify Without Being Compelled to Answer Any Questions in Cross-Examination That the Witness Declines to Answer on Grounds of Confidentiality Pursuant to Rule 70(B) and (D) of the Rules, 16 September 2005, para. 19:

19. [. . .] Similarly, the Prosecution has not satisfied the criteria envisaged under Rule 70 (D) of the Rules. In our view Rule 70 (D) applies where "*the person or representative of the entity providing the initial information*" (i.e. the informant himself) has been called upon to testify. In this case Witness TF1-150 is not the originator of the initial information nor "*the person or representative of the entity providing the initial information*" but is merely a recipient thereof. As such he cannot rely on the protection offered by Rule 70 (D) of the Rules. Furthermore the ICTY authorities cited by the Prosecution in support of their arguments, including *The Prosecutor v. Slobodan Milosevic*[1] and *The Prosecutor v. Radoslav Brdjanin and Momir Talic*,[2] are persuasive but distinguishable and therefore not pertinent to this case.

[1] *The Prosecutor v. Slobodan Milosevic*, Confidential Decision on Prosecution's Application for a Witness Pursuant to Rule 70 (B), 30 October 2003; *The Prosecutor v. Slobodan Milosevic*, Case No. IT-02-54-AR108bis & AR 73.3, Public Version of the Confidential Decision on the Interpretation and Application of Rule 70, 23 October 2002.
[2] *The Prosecutor v. Radoslav Brdjanin and Momir Talic*, Case No. IT-99-36-AR73.9, Decision on Interlocutory Appeal, 11 December 2002.

Rule 72: Preliminary Motions
(amended 29 May 2004)

(A) Preliminary motions by either party shall be brought within 21 days following disclosure by the Prosecutor to the Defence of all the material envisaged by Rule 66(A)(i).

(B) Preliminary motions by the accused are:
   (i) Objections based on lack of jurisdiction;
   (ii) Objections based on defects in the form of the indictment;
   (iii) Applications for severance of crimes joined in one indictment under Rule 49, or for separate trials under Rule 82(B);
   (iv) Objections based on the denial of request for assignment of counsel; or
   (v) Objections based on abuse of process.

(C) Objections based on lack of jurisdiction or to the form of the indictment, including an amended indictment, shall be raised by a party in one motion only, unless otherwise allowed by the Trial Chamber.

(D) The Trial Chamber shall, except as provided by Sub-Rules (E) and (F) below, dispose of preliminary motions before the trial, and its decisions thereon shall not be subject to interlocutory appeal.

(E) Preliminary motions made in the Trial Chamber prior to the Prosecutor's opening statement which raise a serious issue relating to jurisdiction shall be referred to a bench of at least three Appeals Chamber Judges, where they will proceed to a determination as soon as practicable.

(F) Preliminary motions made in the Trial Chamber prior to the Prosecutor's opening statement which, in the opinion of the Trial Chamber, raise an issue that would significantly affect the fair and expeditious conduct of the proceedings or the outcome of a trial shall be referred to a bench of at least three Appeals Chamber Judges, where they will proceed to a determination as soon as practicable.

(G) Where the Trial Chamber refers a motion to the Appeals Chamber pursuant to Sub-Rules (E) or (F) above, any party wishing to file additional written submissions must seek leave from the Appeals Chamber which will impose time limits for further submissions, responses and replies if leave is granted.

(H) References by the Trial Chamber pursuant to Sub-Rules (E) and (F) above shall not operate as a stay of proceedings. Such references shall not operate as a stay of the trial itself unless the Trial or Appeal Chamber so orders.

(I) This Rule shall be deemed to have entered into force on the 7th of March, 2003.

TRIAL CHAMBERS DECISIONS

- **Rule 72(A): Preliminary Motions – Request for Extension of Time to File (Denied)**

R72-TC-1
o *Prosecutor v. Kallon*, Case No. SCSL-03-07-PT, Decision on the Defence Motion for Extension of Time to File Preliminary Motions, 14 June 2003, para. 10-13:

10. The Chamber has carefully reviewed the authorities from sister international tribunals cited by the Prosecution in their Response, to wit, in *The Prosecutor v. Krajisnik*, IT-00-39 & 40-PT, 31 May 2003 and *The Prosecutor v. Obrenovic, Blagoljevic, Jovic*, IT-01-43-PT, IT-98-33/1-PT, IT-1-44-PT, 4 October 2001 and wish to observe that those authorities do not, understandably, provide any definition as to what constitutes "good cause". The only reasonable inference to draw from those cases is that what constitutes "good cause" depends upon the particular facts and circumstances of each case. The Chamber is of the same mind.

11. The Trial Chamber further notes that the request of the Defence for an extension of time is entirely predicated upon the need to conduct extensive and complex consideration and research on the issue of the jurisdiction and legality of the Court as the first and only "hybrid" international criminal tribunal established by the international community. The Chamber agrees that this is an interesting research theme for the purposes of developing the jurisprudence of the Court. However, the Court does not share the view that this is necessarily a subject that requires such extensive and complex research for the reason that being the first and only "hybrid" international tribunal for adjudicating crimes against international humanitarian law there are no previous institutional paradigms with which to compare the Court and derive insightful legal guidance.

12. The Chamber also notes that the Defence intends to pursue another jurisdictional issue through a preliminary motion,

to wit, "the applicability and effect of the Lomé Agreement on the accused indicted by the Court as well (as) the criteria adopted and applied in determining which persons are alleged to bear the "greatest responsibility for offences in Sierra Leone". Again, the Chamber's findings on these points are that, by parity of reasoning, these are not issues of such great complexity that it would require exhaustive and demanding research beyond the prescribed time limit under Rule 72.

13. The Chamber concludes that having regard to the totality of the circumstances of the instant Motion, no good cause has been shown by the Defence for an extension of time.

R72-TC-2

o *Prosecutor v. Sesay*, SCSL-03-05-PT, Decision no the Defence Motion Requesting the Suspension of delays for Filing Preliminary Motions or New Request for an Extension of Delays, 7 November 2003, para. 22-23, 27:

22. Following its previous jurisprudence,[1] the Chamber is disposed to adopt the "exceptional circumstances or good cause" criteria for determining the merits of a request for an extension of time in the instant Motion.

23. The Chamber notes the difficulty the Defence has experienced difficulties in constructing the Defence team, its perceived lack of contact with the Accused, and the lack of internet access in the six days it took Counsel to travel to Sierra Leone, however, these do not meet the necessary legal standard of "exceptional circumstance or good cause" to warrant an extension of time.

[...]

27. The Chamber agrees with the Prosecution's submission that 'the suspension of all time limits concerning all other preliminary motions is contrary to the principle of finality and other time limits in the Rules as already spelled out in the Confidential Order of the 26th day of June 2003.

---

[1] *The Prosecutor against Morris Kallon*, Case No. SCSL-03-07-PT, Decision on the Defence Motion for an Extension of Time to File Preliminary Motions, Trial Chamber, 14th day of June 2003. See also *The Prosecutor against Alex Tamba Brima*, Case No. SCSL-03-06-PT, Decision on the Application for Extension of Time for Leave to be Granted to File Defence Motion to Appeal against the Decision Refusing an Application for the Issue of the Writ of Habeas Corpus, Trial Chamber, 15th day of October 2003.

- **Rule 72(A): Preliminary Motions – Time Limit – Denial of Request for Assignment of Counsel under Rule 72(B)(iv)**

R72-TC-3
    o *Prosecutor v. Brima*, Case No. SCSL-04-16-PT, Decision on Applicant's Motion Against Denial by the Acting Principal Defender to Enter a Legal Service Contract for the Assignment of Counsel, 6 May 2004, para. 35-38:

    35. We agree with the submission of the 1st Respondent questioning the propriety of the applicant bringing this motion under Rule 72(B)(iv) of the Rules and this, because the provisions of the Directive on the Assignment of Counsel promulgated by the Registrar on the 3rd October, 2003, cannot operate to either replace or to amend the Rules of Procedure and Evidence adopted by the Plenary of Judges of the Special Court.

    36. Article 12(A) of the Directive on which the Applicant is relying to base his motion cannot under these circumstances therefore, apply to sustain it.

    37. In this regard it is our opinion that motions brought under Rule 72(A) and 72(B) can only be brought within 21 days following disclosure to the Defence of all material envisaged by Rule 66(A)(1).

    38. Accordingly, this motion, not having been brought within the time limits of 21 days after the said disclosure, cannot be entertained under Rule 72(B)(iv) as provided for in the Directive for the Assignment of Counsel.

- **Rule 72(B): Preliminary Motions – Matters Requiring a Factual Determination**

R72-TC-4
    o *Prosecutor v. Fofana*, Case No. SCSL-04-14-PT, Decision on the Preliminary Defence Motion on the Lack of Personal Jurisdiction Filed on Behalf of the Accused Fofana, 3 March 2004, para. 44, 46-47:

    44. It should be emphasised that in the ultimate analysis, whether or not in actuality the Accused is one of the persons who bears the greatest responsibility for the alleged violations of international humanitarian law and Sierra Leonean law is an evidentiary matter to be determined at the trial stage. At this procedural stage, the Chamber is essentially concerned with mere allegations.

    [...]

46. The Trial Chamber notes that trial chambers at the ICTY have similarly declined to view matters that have jurisdictional dimensions which require a factual determination as matters to be dealt with by way of preliminary motions. In numerous cases where the defence have challenged charges of grave breaches under Article 2 or violations of the laws and customs of war under Article 3 of the Statue of the ICTY on the basis that such charges require an international armed conflict and no such armed conflict existed, Trial Chambers – while finding that such *charges* fall within the jurisdiction of the ICTY – have consistently held that factual submissions related to the nature of the armed conflict are to be dealt with at trial.[1]

47. Finally, the Trial Chamber would like to recall that while it is satisfied that a sufficient basis exists for bringing an indictment against the Accused, the Trial Chamber has made no findings about the guilt – or innocence – of the Accused. The Accused continues to enjoy the presumption of innocence, and will continue to do so until and unless a finding to the contrary is made at the conclusion of the trial proceedings against him.

---

[1] See, e.g., *Prosecutor v. Blagoje Simić et al.*, Case No. IT-95-9-PT, Decision on the Pre-Trial Motion by the Prosecution Requesting the Trial Chamber to Take Judicial Notice of the International Character of the Conflict in Bosnia-Herzegovina, 25 March 1999; *Prosecutor v. Tihomir Blaskić*, Case No. IT-95-15, Decision Rejecting a Motion of the Defence to Dismiss Counts 4, 7, 10, 14, 16 and 18 based on the Failure to Adequately Plead the Existence of an International Armed Conflict, 4 April 1997, para. 7; and *Prosecutor v. Momčilo Krajičnik*, Case No. IT-00-39 & 40-PT, Decision on Motion Challenging Jurisdiction – with Reasons, 22 September 2000, para. 25.

- **Rule 72(B)(i): Preliminary Motions – Objections on Lack of Jurisdiction Shall be Submitted by Way of Preliminary Motions**

R72-TC-5

o *Prosecutor v. Norman,* Case No. SCSL-04-14-T, Decision on First Accused's Motion on Abuse of Process, 28 April 2005, para. 4-5:

4. The Chamber notes that this Motion contains arguments that relate to the jurisdiction of the Court from its very inception, and in particular, the personal jurisdiction of the Court over the Accused persons.[1] In this regard, Rule 72 of the Rules provides that any submissions on the jurisdictional basis of the Court should be filed by way of a preliminary motion. Preliminary motions, according to this Rule, are to be brought 21 days following the disclosure by the Prosecution to the Defence, of all materials envisaged in Rule 66(A)(i) of the

Rules and it takes place 30 days following the initial appearance of the Accused. This disclosure in fact took place since the 5th of June, 2003.

5. Considering that Rule 72 is the special law governing the filing of motions on jurisdiction, the Chamber is of the opinion that this Motion, in so far as it touches on and raises issues of the jurisdictional competence of the Court, having been filed on the 3rd of February 2004, is time barred because the Prosecution in fact complied with its disclosure obligations under Rule 66 (A)(i) of the Rules as we have indicated above, since the 5th of June, 2003.

[1] See paras 1, 2, 11, 27 and 28 of Motion.

- **Rule 72(B)(v): Preliminary Motions – Abuse of Process**

R72-TC-6

o *Prosecutor v. Kanu*, Case No. SCSL-04-16-PT, Written Reasons for the Trial Chamber's Oral Decision on the Defence Motion on Abuse of Process Due to Infringement of Principles of *Nullum Crimen Sine Lege* and Non-Retroactivity as to Several Accounts, 31 March 2004, para. 18-26, 30:

18. Rule 72(B)(v) was incorporated into the Rules qt the 2nd Plenary meeting in March 2003. It is a provision found in neither the Rules of Procedure and Evidence of the ICTY nor the ICTR. The Rule codifies the practice at other tribunals where Judges exercise their inherent powers to control abuse of process motions as a right deriving from common law precedent. The rationale behind providing for an additional basis for bringing preliminary motions in the Rules of the Special Court is primarily to enhance and further protect the rights of the accused. The Trial Chamber is in accord with the Appeals Chamber, which recently stated: "At the root of the doctrine of abuse of process is fairness. The fairness that is involved is not fairness in the process of adjudication itself but fairness in the use of the machinery of justice."[1]

19. The Rules do not, however, provide guidance as to what constitutes an abuse of process. On this point the Prosecution Response highlights the lack of authorities in the Defence Motion. Some attempt to remedy this was made in the Reply. For the purposes of this Decision, it is imperative to examine the principle of abuse of process as it has been applied in international criminal law and in national systems.

20. According to Black's Law Dictionary, abuse of process is defined as the "improper and tortuous use of legitimately issued court process to obtain a result that is either unlawful or beyond the process's scope."

21. Under the abuse of process doctrine, proceedings that have been lawfully initiated may be terminated after an indictment has been issued if "improper or illegal proceedings" are employed in pursuing an otherwise lawful process.[2]

22. The doctrine operates as a matter of judicial discretion, and will be utilised where proceeding with the trial would contravene the court's sense of justice, due to pre-trial impropriety or misconduct.[3] As the House of Lords made clear in *R v. Latif*,

> proceedings may be stayed in the exercise of the judge's discretion not only where a fair trial is impossible, but also where it would be contrary to the public interest in the integrity of the criminal justice system that a trial should take place.[4]

23. The doctrine's flexibility was also alluded to in *Toronto (City) v. C.U.P.E.*[5] To the same effect is McLachlin J.'s observation in *R. v. Scott*:

> abuse of process may be established where: (1) the proceedings are oppressive or vexatious; and, (2) violate the fundamental principles of justice underlying the community's sense of fair play and decency. The concepts of oppressiveness and vexatiousness underline the interest of the accused in a fair trial. But the doctrine evokes as well the public interest in a fair and just trial process and the proper administration of justice.[6]

24. Although this Chamber does not accept the Defence's unsupported observation that "the doctrine [of abuse of process] has no limitations as to the extent of the legal principles it may apply to", the Trial Chamber acknowledges the breadth and latitude of its discretionary authority in this regard.[7] The categories of such circumstances are indeed not closed. It has, for example, been invoked in extradition proceedings where the prosecuting authority has an obligation of due diligence to make a good faith effort to bring the defendant before the court.[8] It has also been frequently invoked in cases of delay in proceedings caused by the Prosecution,[9] on the grounds that the delay must not be "unconscionable".[10] Another use has been in quashing a conviction based on an unlawful arrest and an illegally obtained confession.[11]

25. The Trial Chamber wishes to emphasise that the operation of judicial discretion involves an assessment of the nature and severity of the crimes with which the accused is charged, weighed against the abuse of process that continuing the prosecution would engender. In this regard, Lord Lowry in the House of Lords case *ex parte Bennett* was of the opinion that there may be situations:

in which the seriousness of the crime is so great relative to the nature of the abuse of process that it would be a proper exercise of judicial discretion to permit a prosecution to proceed or to allow a conviction to stand notwithstanding an abuse of process in relation to the defendant's presence within a jurisdiction. *In each case it is a matter of discretionary balance, to be approached with regard to the particular conduct complained of and the particular offence charged.*[12] (Emphasis added)

26. Evidence of improper motive is not required for a finding of abuse of process. In its decision of 3 November 1999 in the case of *Jean-Bosco Barayagwiza v. The Prosecutor*, the Appeals Chamber of the ICTR emphasised that the finding of specific fault by one section of the court is not required. If the rights of the Accused have been violated, that is sufficient for the Chamber to find that the integrity of the judicial process has been undermined.[13] In the Trial Chamber's opinion the authorities show that any violation of the rights of the accused must reach a certain threshold level to constitute an abuse of process.[14] A finding of impropriety on the part of one party may, however, contribute to the ultimate finding that a violation of the rights of an accused has reached such a threshold as to undermine the integrity of the proceedings. As the Supreme Court of Canada observed in *Toronto (City) v. C.U.P.E.*, the focus is less on the interests of the parties and more on the integrity of judicial decision making as a whole.[15]

[...]

30. This Trial Chamber finds that neither the <u>lawful</u> exercise of the powers of the Prosecutor to bring an Indictment which is based upon the alleged commission of crimes within the jurisdiction of the Special Court for Sierra Leone nor the approval of such an Indictment by a Judge of the Special Court in accordance with the Statute and the Rules would, and indeed could, constitute an abuse of process. The veiled suggestion that the designated Judge may have contributed to the alleged abuse of process is objectionable, particularly when there is no evidence put forward to rebut the presumption of regularity. Counsel is admonished that such submissions, depending on the facts and circumstances, may well border on contempt of court.

---

[1] *Prosecutor v. Morris Kallon*, Case No. SCSL-04-15-AR72(E) & *Prosecutor v. Brima Bazzy Kamara*, Case No. SCSL-04-16-AR72(E), Decision on Challenge to Jurisdiction: Lomé Accord Amnesty, dated 13 March 2004 and filed 15 March 2004, para. 79. see generally, *Id.*, paras 75-85.
[2] See *Jean-Bosco Barayagwiza v. The Prosecutor*, Case No. ICTR-91-19-I, Decision, 3 November 1999 ("*Barayagwiza* Appeals Decision"), para. 74. See also *Hui Chi-ming v. R.* [1992] 1 A.C. 34, 57 in which the Privy Council observed that the doctrine of abuse of process should be applied where there

is, "something so unfair and wrong that the court should not allow a prosecutor to proceed with what is in all other respects a regular proceeding".

[3] See *R. v. Latif* [1996] 2 CR. App. R. 92 [1996] 1 WLR 104 HL, pp. 101 and 112H as per Lord Steyn; *Barayagwiza* Appeals Decision, para. 77; *R. v. Horseferry Road Magistrates Court* ex parte *Bennett* [1994] 1 AC 42.

[4] *R. v. Latif* [1996] 2 CR. App. R. 92 [1996] 1 WLR 104 HL, pp. 101 and 112H as per Lord Steyn.

[5] *Canadian Union of Public Employees, Local 79 v. City of Toronto and Douglas C. Stanley and A-G of Toronto*, 2003 SCC 63, para. 37. See also *House of Srping Gardens Ltd. V. Waite* [1990] 3 W.L.R. 347 at p. 358, [1990] 2 All E.R. 990 (C.A.).

[6] *R. v. Scott* [1990] 3 S.C.R. 979, at p. 1007.

[7] Reply, para 2.

[8] *Smith v. Hooey*, 393 U.S. 374 (1969).

[9] See for example *Bell v. DPP of Jamaica* [1985] 1 AC 937; [1985] 2 All ER 585.

[10] *R. v. Oxford City Justices*, ex parte Smith (D.K.B.)

[11] *The Prosecutor v. Dragan Nikolic*, case No. IT-94-2-PT, Decision on Defence Motion Challenging the Exercise of Jurisdiction by the Tribunal, 9 October 2002 ("*Nikolic* Decision"). See also *R. v. Hartley*, Wellington Court of Appeal, [1978] 2 NZLR 199.

[12] *R. v. Horseferry Road Magistrates Court, ex p. Bennett* [1994] 1 AC 42 at p. 158.

[13] The Appeals Chamber noted, "First and foremost, this analysis focuses on the alleged violations of the Appellant's rights and is not primarily concerned with the entity responsible for the alleged violation(s) . . . even if fault is shared between the three organs of the Tribunal – or the result of the actions of a third party . . . – *it would undermine the integrity of the judicial process to proceed.*" (Emphasis added). *Barayagwiza* Appeals Decision, para. 73.

[14] In the *Nikolic* Decision, the Trial Chamber had to decide whether "such serious factors" were involved in a case of alleged illegal arrest that it would amount to an impediment for the Tribunal to exercise its jurisdiction. *Nikolic* decision, paras 73-74, and the analysis that follows.

[15] *Canadian Union of Public Employees, Local 79 v. City of Toronto and Douglas C. Stanley and A-G of Toronto*, 2003 SCC 63, para. 43.

R72-TC-7

o *Prosecutor v. Norman,* Case No. SCSL-04-14-T, Decision on First Accused's Motion on Abuse of Process, 28 April 2005, para. 18:

18. The Chamber is of the view that a Court may exercise its discretion to order a stay of proceedings on the grounds of an abuse of process but "only in the clearest of cases"[1] and "where there is overwhelming evidence that the proceedings under scrutiny are unfair to the point that they are contrary to the interests of justice".[2]

---

[1] *R. v. Young* [1984] 40 C.R. (3d) 289.
[2] *R. v. Power* [1994] 1 S.C.R. 601, 616.

- **Rule 72(E): Referral to the Appeals Chamber**

R72-TC-8

o *Prosecutor v. Kondewa*, Case No. SCSL-03-12-PT, Order Pursuant to Rule 72(E) – Defence Motion Based on Lack of Jurisdiction – Establishment of Special Court Violates Constitution of Sierra Leone, 04 December 2003:[104]

NOTING FURTHER THAT the Defence filed the Motion as falling within the concepts of both lack of jurisdiction and abuse of process which is not instructive and can lead to confusion. The Trial Chamber, having authority pursuant to Rule 72(D) to dispose of motions based on abuse of process and not motions raising a serious issue relating to jurisdiction which must be referred to the Appeals Chamber. In combining these two motions together the Trial Chamber has therefore no option but to refer the whole motion to the Appeals Chamber for their determination as the issue about jurisdiction is serious one. The process is however depriving the applicant of obtaining a decision by the Trial Chamber on the abuse of process with a possibility of an appeal pursuant to Rule 72(F). This approach is even more with regards to the Defence Preliminary Motion Based on Lack of Jurisdiction: Establishment of the Special court Violates the Constitution of Sierra Leone, also filed on the 7th November 2003 and noted above, the Chamber is of the opinion that it would have been much preferable for the Defence to combine the two motions with the result that all the aspects of lack of jurisdiction are in one motion and all the aspects relating to abuse of process are filed in a separate motion rather than filing multiple motions on the same basis.

- **Rule 72(E): Referral to the Appeals Chamber – "Serious Issue Relating to Jurisdiction"**

R72-TC-9

o *Prosecutor v. Taylor*, Case No. SCSL-03-01-I, Order Pursuant to Rule 72(E) Defence Motion to Quash the Indictment and to Declare the Warrant of Arrest and All Other Consequential Orders Null and Void, 19 September 2003:

CONSIDERING that the Accused submits that the Special Court Agreement, 2002 (Ratification) Act, 2002 and the Rules are

---

[104] See also *Prosecutor v. Kanu*, Case No. SCSL-03-13-PT, Order Pursuant to Rule 72(E) – Defence Motion Challenging the Jurisdiction of the Special Court Raising Serious Issues Relating to Jurisdiction on Various Grounds and Objections Based on Abuse of Process, 22 January 2004.

ipso facto bad in law and in clear breach of customary international law;

CONSIDERING, in particular, that the Accused submits that the alleged primacy of the Special Court is limited to the national courts of the Republic of Sierra Leone and lacks the power to assert its primacy over national court of any third States as well as to request the surrender of an accused from any third State;

AND

GIVEN that the Accused, in light of the above, argues that the Indictment, the Warrant of Arrest and all other consequential Orders issued against him by the Special Court are in violation of the criminal immunity of the Head of the Sovereign State of the Republic of Liberia and contrary to the principles of customary international law and the jurisprudence of the International Court of Justice;

GIVEN, furthermore, that the Accused argues that the Indictment, the Warrant of Arrest and all other consequential Orders issued against him by the Special Court are in violation of the principle that a State may not exercise its authority on the territory of another State and the principle of sovereign equality among all Member States of the United Nations as laid down in Article 2, paragraph 1 of the Charter of the United Nations.

GIVEN that the Accused also argues that the aforementioned grounds are procedural in nature and go to jurisdiction *in limine* of the Special Court;

THE CHAMBER

[...]

AND THEREFORE, PURSUANT TO RULE 72(E) OF THE RULES,

REFERS the Defence 'Motion to Quash the Indictment and to Declare the Warrant of Arrest and All Other Consequential Orders Null and Void', together with the Prosecution Response and the Defence Reply thereto, to the Appeals Chamber of the Special Court for determination;

o *Prosecutor v. Norman*, Case No. SCSL-03-08-PT, Order Pursuant to Rule 72(E) – Defence Preliminary Motion on Lack of Jurisdiction: Judicial Independence, 17 September 2003:

CONSIDERING that the Accused submits that the Special Court lacks of sufficient guarantees of judicial independence as its funding arrangements create a legitimate fear of political interference by economical manipulation;

CONSIDERING, in particular, that the Accused submits that Articles 6 and 7 of the Agreement between the United Nations and the Government of the Republic of Sierra Leone on the Establishment of the Special Court create an opportunity for pressure on all Organs of the Special Court by the donor States who voluntarily contribute to its financial and administrative budget, particularly those States who have representatives on the Management Committee of the Special Court;

CONSIDERING that the Accused also submits that a reasonable observer apprised of the financial and administrative structure of the Special Court, which do not insulate the judiciary from political pressure through financial manipulation, would have legitimate grounds to fear for its independence;

GIVEN that the Accused, in light of the above, argues that the lack of institutional financial independence created by the Special Court system of voluntary contribution adversely and directly affects its jurisdiction to try him for any of the counts contained in the Indictment;

[...]

FINDS that the foregoing submissions raise a serious issue relating to the jurisdiction of the Special Court to try the Accused on all the counts of the Indictment that has been preferred against him;

R72-TC-11

o *Prosecutor v. Norman*, Case No. SCSL-03-08-PT, Order Pursuant to Rule 72(E) – Defence Preliminary Motion on Lack of Jurisdiction: Child Recruitment, 17 September 2003:

CONSIDERING that the Accused submits that Article 4(C) of the Statute violates the principle *nullum crimen sine lege* in that according to him, the crime of child recruitment was not part of customary international law at the time relevant to the indictment;

[...]

FINDS that the foregoing submissions raise a serious issue relating to the jurisdiction of the Special Court to try the Accused on Count 8 of the Indictment that has been preferred against him; [...]

R72-TC-12 o *Prosecutor v. Norman*, Case No. SCSL-03-08-PT, Order Pursuant to Rule 72(E) – Defence Preliminary Motion on Lack of Jurisdiction: Lawfulness of the Court's Establishment, 17 September 2003:

CONSIDERING that the Accused submits that in establishing the Special Court the Government of Sierra Leone acted unlawfully and in contravention of the Constitution of Sierra Leone, 1991;

CONSIDERING, in particular, that the Accused submits that the concurrent jurisdiction and primacy of the Special Court with respect to the national courts of the Republic of Sierra Leone by virtue of Article 8 of the Statute is *ultra vires* the Constitution of Sierra Leone, 1991 and in particular of Sections 122 and 125 thereof;

CONSIDERING, furthermore, that the Accused submits that the Government of Sierra Leone as a party of the Agreement establishing the Special Court acted unconstitutionally;

CONSIDERING that the Accused also submits that in May 2000 the absence of effective control and obedience from the bulk of the population of Sierra Leone have the effect of rendering nugatory the Agreement establishing the Special Court;

[...]

FINDS that the foregoing submissions raise a serious issue relating to the jurisdiction of the Special Court to try the Accused on all the counts of the Indictment that has been preferred against him;

R72-TC-13 o *Prosecutor v. Kallon*, Case No. SCSL-03-07-PT, Order Pursuant to Rule 72(E) – Defence Motion Based on Lack of Jurisdiction – Establishment of Special Court Violates Constitution of Sierra Leone, 17 September 2003:

CONSIDERING that the Accused submits that in establishing the Special Court the Government of Sierra Leone was duty bound to abide by and honour the Constitution of Sierra Leone, 1991;

CONSIDERING that the Accused submits that the creation of the Special Court by the United Nations and the Government of Sierra Leone has the effect of amending fundamental aspects of the Constitution of Sierra Leone, 1991 for which no referendum has been consequently held;

CONSIDERING, in particular, that the Accused submits that in creating the Special Court, the Government of Sierra Leone acted unconstitutionally in relying on Section 40(4) of the Constitution of Sierra Leone, 1991 instead of Section 108;

GIVEN that the Accused, in light if the above, argues that the Special Court is unconstitutional, an illegal and *ultra vires* institution lacking jurisdiction to try him for any of the counts contained in the Indictment;

[...]

FINDS that the foregoing submissions raise a serious issue relating to the jurisdiction of the Special Court to try the Accused on all the counts of the Indictment that has been preferred against him;

R72-TC-14

o *Prosecutor v. Kallon*, Case No. SCSL-03-07-PT, Order Pursuant to Rule 72(E) – Defence Motion Based on Lack of Jurisdiction – Abuse of Process: Amnesty Provided by Lomé Accord, 30 September 2003:

CONSIDERING that the Accused submits that the Government of Sierra Leone is bound to observe the amnesty provisions it has granted in signing the Lomé Accord, as contained in Article 9 thereof, and that the Special Court, as a creation of the United Nations and the Government of sierra Leone, should not include in its subject matter jurisdiction any acts for which the Government of Sierra Leone has already granted an amnesty;

CONSIDERING that the Accused, in light of the above, submits that the Special Court should not, notwithstanding the provisions of Article 10 of the statute, assert its jurisdiction over the alleged crimes committed by him prior to the signing of the Lomé Accord, on the 7th day of July 1999;

CONSIDERING that the Accused further argues that after the granting of an amnesty in the Lomé Accord, it would be an abuse of process of the Special court to try him for the crimes allegedly committed prior to the signing of the Lomé Accord, on the 7th day of July 1999;

[...]

FINDS that the foregoing submissions raise a serious issue relating to the jurisdiction of the Special Court to try the Accused on all the counts of the Indictment that has been preferred against him;

R72-TC-15

o *Prosecutor v. Kamara*, Case No. SCSL-03-10-PT, Order Pursuant to Rule 72 Re: Application by Brima Bazzy Kamara in respect of Jurisdiction and Defects in the Indictment, 9 October 2003:

CONSIDERING that the Accused, in light of the above, contends that the Indictment against the Accused is invalid in so far as the Prosecutor David Crane is not a prosecutor pursuant to *Sierra Leonean law*, the approval of the Indictment was not made in the course of a public hearing and Judge Boutet, who confirmed the said Indictment, was not appointed pursuant to the Constitution of Sierra Leone;

CONSIDERING that the Accused further argues that the crimes defined in Articles 2, 3 and 4 of the Statute, adopted into *Sierra Leonean law* by *the Act of 2002*, offend the Constitution of Sierra Leone in so far as the said *Act of 2002* purports to create liability for punishment prior to its passing and that, therefore, allegations in the Indictment prior to the passing of the *Act of 2002* should be struck out;

CONSIDERING that the Accused also recalls that a general amnesty was granted by Article IX of the Lomé Peace Agreement in respect of crimes committed in Sierra Leone pre-dating the 7th day of July 1999, and argues that the disclaimer by the Special Representative of the United Nations issued upon signing of the said Agreement, according to which no amnesty would be granted in respect of international criminal law, does not create law in so far as it was not adopted by the parties to the said Agreement;

CONSIDERING that, in the light of the above, the Accused concludes that the Government of Sierra Leone cannot ignore its obligations under the Lomé Peace Agreement and that the latter has full force and effect in respect of the Indictment against the Accused, and requests, therefore, the relevant counts in the Indictment to be struck out;

[...]

FINDS that the foregoing submissions raise a serious issue relating to the jurisdiction of the Special Court to try the Accused on all the counts of the Indictment that has been issued against him;

R72-TC-16

o *Prosecutor v. Norman*, Case No. SCSL-03-08-PT, Decision on the Defence Preliminary Motion on Lack of Jurisdiction: Command Responsibility, 15 October 2003, para. 18, 21-22, 24:

18. The Chamber would like to draw the parties' attention to the provisions of Sub-Rule 72(E) above. In particular, this Sub-Rule provides for the reference of the preliminary motions to the Appeals Chamber in cases where the preliminary motion raises a "serious issue of jurisdiction". It is therefore within the inherent power of the Chamber, in order to provide for the reference of a preliminary motion to the Appeals Chamber, to assess whether such preliminary motion objects to lack of jurisdiction and, more particularly, if the substance of such objection is verified, whether such objection could be deemed as "serious".

[...]

21. However, the Chamber views the Defence submissions as solely relying on such possible findings of the Appeals Chamber of the ICTY in the case before it. As correctly submitted by the Prosecution, the Chamber finds that the Defence failed in its Motion to provide the Chamber with any valid or substantial argument or submissions in support of its general allegation of lack of jurisdiction. The Motion also failed to provide the Chamber with authorities or other supportive jurisprudence.

22. The Chamber is of the opinion that the Motion is fundamentally an application to reserve the right to raise an issue at a later stage rather than one which was intending to seriously challenge the jurisdiction of the Special Court with reference to internal armed conflicts.

[...]

24. The doctrine of command responsibility as element of the individual criminal responsibility of the Accused is very important and its application as part of customary international law to an internal armed conflict is undoubtedly an issue that could involve jurisdiction. However, in consideration of the aforementioned, the Chamber concludes that the Motion introduced by the Defence was both in form and substance not an objection to the jurisdiction of the Special Court.

R72-TC-17

o *Prosecutor v. Gbao*, Case No. SCSL-03-09-PT, Order Pursuant to Rule 72(E) – Defence Preliminary Motion on the Invalidity of the Agreement Between the United Nations and the Government of Sierra Leone on the Establishment of the Special Court for Sierra Leone, 03 December 2003:

CONSIDERING that the Defence makes the following objections to the validity of the Agreement between the United Nations and the Government of Sierra Leone establishing the Special Court namely,

1. That the responsibility for the maintenance of international peace and security falls within the primary responsibility of the Security Council of the United Nations. When the latter, through the Secretary-General, concluded a treaty with the Government of Sierra Leone, the Agreement on the Establishment of the Special Court for Sierra Leone ("the Special Court Agreement") to create anew international organisation with a separate legal personality, it unlawfully delegated and transferred the responsibility of the United Nations as guardians of international peace to another body that is not under the direct control of the United Nations. Furthermore, unlike the United Nations or its subsidiaries this new body does not enjoy the blessing of the international community of States as a whole.

2. That in so far as international organisations have the power to create new international organisations by treaties, it is nevertheless clear that such power would not extend to the exercise of criminal jurisdiction which falls within the preserve of the sovereign States unless States have manifested a very clear intention to transfer that power to a particular international organisation.

3. That the prosecution of international crimes is a customary right which can be voluntarily renounced – as was done by Sierra Leone in article IX of the Peace Agreement Between the Government of Sierra Leone and the Revolutionary United Front of Sierra Leone of the 7th July 1999 ("the Lomé Accord"). Sierra Leone thereby lost its capacity to conclude a treaty to exercise this sovereign power which it no longer possessed, and lastly,

4. That according to the law, if a treaty concluded as the result of a fundamental error, either by fraud of one party or where there has been no negligence on the part of the other, then that treaty is invalid. That when the Government of Sierra Leone concluded the Special Court Agreement they failed to give full disclosure to the United Nations that it and the ECOWAS States had continued to represent to the Revolutionary United Front expressly or impliedly that the Lomé Accord continued to apply and its members would not be punished for crimes under international law up until the disarmament of the 14th January 2002. Consequently, had the United Nations known of this deception, they would nit have been party to the Special Court Agreement and therefore the Special Court Agreement was concluded through a fraud against the United Nations or by error for which the United Nations is not responsible. As a result of the foregoing, the Defence contends that the Special Court Agreement is invalid.

[…]

FINDS that the foregoing submissions and the arguments in rebuttal advanced by the Prosecution raise a serious issue relating to the jurisdiction of the Special Court to try the Accused on all the counts of the Indictment that have been issued against him;

R72-TC-18   o *Prosecutor v. Kondewa*, Case No. SCSL-03-12-PT, Order Pursuant to Rule 72(E) – Defence Motion Based on Lack of Jurisdiction – Establishment of Special Court Violates Constitution of Sierra Leone, 04 December 2003:

CONSIDERING that the Defence makes the following submissions in support of its objection that the Special Court lacks jurisdiction over the Accused:

1. In establishing the Special Court the Government of Sierra Leone has acted in contravention of the Constitution of Sierra Leone.

2. The Government of Sierra Leone was bound to respect the Constitution of Sierra Leone ("the Constitution") when it created the Special Court in an Agreement with the United Nations. The Report of the Secretary-General on the Establishment of a Special Court for Sierra Leone[1] stated *inter alia*, that: "Its [the Special Court's] implementation at the national level would require that the agreement is incorporated in the national law of Sierra Leone in accordance with constitutional requirements".

3. Section 108 of the Constitution prescribes that various Sections of the Constitution may not be amended without first having been approved by referendum and the necessary process that must be followed in order for this to be valid. Failure to comply with the Constitution renders the Special Court unconstitutional and thereby lacking the jurisdiction to prosecute persons before it.

4. The creation of the Special Court clearly amends the judicial framework and court structure in Sierra Leone without complying with fundamental aspects of the Constitution of Sierra Leone for which no referendum has been held.

5. Further, the only courts empowered to order deprivation of liberty (as envisaged by Section 17(1) of the Constitution) are those provided for in Section 30(1) of the Constitution. The Defence avers that the Special Court is not one of those courts and subsequently cannot detain persons in accordance with the Constitution. Neither is the Special Court a court as envisaged by Section 30(1) of the Constitution able to determine the charges against someone within the terms of Section 23(1) of the Constitution.

[. . .]

FINDS that the foregoing submissions relate to an objection based on lack of jurisdiction which raises a serious issue relating to the jurisdiction of the Special Court to try the Accused.

---

(1) UN Doc. S/2000/915, 4 October 2000, paragraph 9.

R72-TC-19 o *Prosecutor v. Kondewa*, Case No. SCSL-03-12-PT, Order Pursuant to Rule 72(E) – Defence Motion Based on Lack of Jurisdiction/Abuse of Process: Amnesty Provided by Lomé Accord, 8 December 2003:

CONSIDERING that pursuant to Rule 72(B)(i) and (v) of the Rules the Defence raises preliminary motions on objections on lack of jurisdiction and objections based on abuse of process on the following grounds:

1. The Government of Sierra Leone is duty bound to honour the undertaking made in agreeing to and signing the Peace Agreement Between the Government of Sierra Leone and the Revolutionary United Front of Sierra Leone of the 7th of July 1999 ("the Lomé Accord"), including the amnesty provisions contained in Article IX of the said Accord. Moreover, while the Special Representative of the Secretary-General of the United Nations appended his signature on behalf of the United Nations a disclaimer to the effect that the amnesty provision contained in Article IX would not apply to crimes against humanity, war crimes and other serious violations of international humanitarian law, no such similar reservation was appended by President Kabbah on behalf of the Government of Sierra Leone. Consequently, on the part of the Government of Sierra Leone the amnesty provision was accepted, valid and effective and additionally no steps have been taken by the Government of Sierra Leone to remove legal and/or constitutional provisions referred to in Part X of the Lomé Accord preventing implementation of the Lomé Accord.

2. The Special Court was established pursuant to an Agreement between the United Nations and the Government of Sierra Leone of the 16th day of January 2002. Indeed, the Special Court could only have been established with the agreement of the Government of Sierra Leone and its participation and role was vital and central. As a Government creation, the jurisdiction of the Special Court should not include acts for which the Government has already granted amnesty, all allegations of crimes pre-dating the 7th day of July 1999 should be removed from the Indictment. Moreover, the burden is on the Prosecution and/or Government of Sierra Leone to demonstrate why the amnesty granted in the Lomé Accord should not be respected by the Special Court as it was a creation of the very same Government of Sierra Leone.

AND additionally or in the alternative:

It would be an abuse of process of the Special Court to permit the prosecution of Allieu Kondewa for alleged crimes pre-dating the 7th day of July 1999. After granting an amnesty or undertaking not to prosecute, *inter alia*, members of the Civil Defence Forces ("the CDF") at Lomé, it would be an abuse of process of the Special Court to permit the prosecution of such persons for conduct pre-dating this Agreement. This is particularly true of members of the CDF "who are particulary prejudiced" by prosecution given the "special relationship" of trust between the CDF and the Government of Sierra Leone.

[...]

FINDS that the foregoing submissions relate to an objection based on lack of jurisdiction which raises a serious issue relating to the jurisdiction of the Special Court to try the Accused.

R72-TC-20

o *Prosecutor v. Kanu*, Case No. SCSL-03-13-PT, Order Pursuant to Rule 72(E) – Defence Motion Challenging the Jurisdiction of the Special Court Raising Serious Issues Relating to Jurisdiction on Various Grounds and Objections Based on Abuse of Process, 22 January 2004:

CONSIDERING that the Defence seeks relief pursuant to Rule 72(B) and (E) of the Rules for the flowing reasons:

1. There are defects as to the international legal foundation of the Special Court on the grounds that:

   a. The Agreement between the United Nations and the Republic of Sierra Leone on the Establishment of the Special Court for Sierra Leone ('the Special Court Agreement') of the 16th January 2002 is a bilateral treaty between an international organisation and a State and as such cannot judicially amount to an international instrument which can set aside certain constitutional rights and provision. Consequently, Article IX of the Peace Agreement Between the Government of Sierra Leone and the Revolutionary United Front of Sierra Leone of the 7th of July 1999 ('the Lomé Peace Agreement') ought to be considered taking precedence over, *inter alia*, Article 1 of the Special Court Agreement;

   b. Chapter XII of the Constitution exhaustively enumerates the sources of law in Sierra Leone without mentioning international law as such or bilateral agreements between the Government of Sierra Leone and international organisations. Therefore, without further national legislative measures the Special Court Agreement does not have direct effect within the domestic legal system of Sierra Leone;

c. The entering of a bilateral agreement which established the Special Court may be deemed to be unconstitutional as it infringes the sovereign rights of the people of Sierra Leone bestowed upon them by Article 5(2)(a) of Chapter XII of the Constitution;

d. According to Article 120(2) of Chapter VII, Part I of the Constitution the people of Sierra Leone can, in principle, only be tried by their national courts. Furthermore, any law that is inconsistent with the Constitution shall be void and have no effect pursuant to Article 171(15) of the Constitution. The Special Court Agreement cannot supersede the Constitution as the "Supreme Law" of the land;

e. Pursuant to Article 169(3) of Chapter XI of the Constitution, military courts martial, not the Special Court, have exclusive jurisdiction over Sierra Leonean servicemen such as the Accused;

f. The transfer of nationals is an unconstitutional phenomenon resulting in lack of jurisdiction. The Constitution does not specifically refer to the eligibility of its nationals as to extradition to foreign courts. According to Sierra Leonean domestic law such extradition may be possible presupposed the existence of an extradition treaty. However, the "transfer" of nationals to the Special Court prescribed in Article 17(2)(d) of the Statute is not within the contemplation of "extradition" under the domestic law provisions nor does it comply with the aforesaid Article and, therefore, the "transfer" of the Accused to the Special Court is deemed to be unconstitutional.

2. The amnesty clause in the Lomé Peace Agreement clearly affects the jurisdiction of the Special Court:

a. The Accused is covered by the judicial and factual scope of the amnesty provisions of Article IX of the Lomé Peace Agreement;

b. It is an abuse of process, as enshrined in Rule 72(B)(v) of the Rules, for the Government of Sierra Leone to enter a bilateral agreement to establish the Special Court to prosecute persons to whom the Government has already granted amnesty;

c. The Special Court lacks jurisdiction for the crimes set forth in the Indictment, insofar as these are punishable under the Sierra Leonean domestic laws.

3. The Special Court cannot assume jurisdiction with regard to Superior Responsibility for crimes which were allegedly committed prior to assuming command or allegedly taking the position of a superior and, consequently, the Special Court cannot hear charges committed by the Accused prior to February 1998.

[. . .]

FINDS that the foregoing submissions raise a serious issue relating to the jurisdiction of the Special Court to try the Accused on all the counts of the Indictment that has been issued against him;

APPEALS CHAMBER DECISIONS

- **Rule 72: Preliminary Motions – Requirement for Initial Appearance Before Filing a Preliminary Motion**

R72-AC-1   o *Prosecutor v. Taylor*, Case No. SCSL-03-01-AR72, Decision on Immunity from Jurisdiction, 31 May 2004, para. 23-24, 30, 33:

23. However, both Rules 72 and 73 appear to require an initial appearance. [. . .]

24. By virtue of Rule 72(A), a preliminary motion shall be brought within 21 days following disclosure by the Prosecutor of all material envisaged by Rule 66(A)(i).[1] It is evident from the provision of Rule 72(A) read with Rule 66(A)(i) that the Rules do not permit an accused to bring a preliminary motion until the accused has made an initial appearance. [. . .]

[. . .]

30. Technically, an accused who has not made an initial appearance before this court cannot bring a preliminary motion in terms of Rule 72(A), nor a motion under Rule 73 of the Rules and in a normal case such application may be held premature and accordingly struck out. [. . .]

[. . .]

33. The final aspect of the Prosecution's objection [. . .] is that as a general proposition, an accused does not have standing to file motions before the Special Court until he has been transferred to its custody or appeared before it and that there is no exception where an accused claims immunity since according to the Special Court Statute, an accused has no immunity by reason of his status as acting or former Head of State. [. . .] As we have already found that a) the nature of a claim of immunity constitutes a discretionary exception to the ordinary requirements of an accused first submitting himself to the jurisdiction of the court; and that b) jurisdiction and immunity are closely related, it is not necessary to determine this final objection.

---

[1] Rule 66(A)(i) provides that: "within 30 days of the initial appearance

of an accused the Prosecution shall disclose to the Defence copies of the statement of all witnesses whom the Prosecution intends to call to testify and all evidence to be presented pursuant to Rule 92 *bis at* trial".

- **Rule 72: Preliminary Motions – Competence to Determine on its Own Jurisdiction**

o *Prosecutor v. Kallon, Norman, Kamara*, Case No. SCSL-04-14-AR72, Decision on Constitutionality and Lack of Jurisdiction, 13 March 2004, para. 30-34:[105]

30. In resolving the first question, the Agreement between the UN and the Government of Sierra Leone which may be termed the primordial constitutive document, must necessarily be our starting point, together with the Statute of the Special Court.

31. Article 1 of the Special Court Agreement is captioned "Establishment of the Special Court" and it states:

1. There is hereby established a Special Court for Sierra Leone to prosecute persons who bear the greatest responsibility for serious violations of international humanitarian law and Sierra Leonean law committed in the territory of Sierra Leone since 30 December 1996.

2. The Special Court shall function in accordance with the Statute of the Special Court for Sierra Leone. The Statute is annexed to the Agreement and forms an integral part thereof.

32. The conduct of legal proceedings in the Special Court is governed by Article 14 of the Statute, which empowers the Special Court to apply the Rules of Procedure and Evidence of the ICTR, obtaining at the time of the establishment of the Special Court, the necessary changes to be made (Article 14(1)). Furthermore, the Special Court is mandated to amend the Rules or adopt additional Rules where the applicable Rules do not, or do not adequately, provide for a specific situation (Article 14(2)).

33. A perusal of the Rules reveals that the Appeals Chamber of the Special Court is clothed with the exclusive power to determine, as soon as practicable, issues relating to jurisdiction. In the words of Rule 72(E):

---

[105] See also *Prosecutor v. Kondewa*, Case No. SCSL-04-14-PT, Decision on Preliminary Motion on Lack of Jurisdiction: Establishment of Special Court Violates Constitution of Sierra Leone, 25 May 2004, para. 2.

'Preliminary motions made in the Trial Cham-ber prior to the Prosecutor's opening statement which raise a serious issue relating to jurisdiction shall be referred to the Appeals Chamber, where they will proceed to a determination as soon as practicable.'

34. It is beyond argument, therefore, that the Appeals Chamber of the Special Court has the competence to determine whether or not the Special Court has jurisdiction to decide on the lawfulness and validity of its creation.

R72-AC-3

o *Prosecutor v. Fofana*, Case No. SCSL-04-14-AR72, Decision on Preliminary Motion on Lack of Jurisdiction *Materiae*: Illegal Delegation of Powers by the United Nations, 25 May 2004, para. 13-14, 16-29:[106]

13. To find an answer to the above mentioned questions one has to look first and foremost to the Charter of the United Nations itself and the Agreement between the United Nations and the Government of Sierra Leone on the Establishment of a Special Court for Sierra Leone.

a) Does the Security Council have the power to delegate its powers to the Secretary-General to conclude an agreement between the United Nations and the Government of Sierra Leone?

14. According to Article 24(1) of the Charter the primary responsibility for the maintenance of international peace and security lies with the Security Council.[(1)] In its Resolution 1315, the Security Council stated in accordance with Article 39 of the UN Charter:[(2)] that such a situation, namely a threat to international peace and security, had arisen in Sierra Leone.[(3)]

[...]

16. These articles [Articles 97-100(1) of the U.N. Charter] clearly state that the Secretary-General as head of the Secretariat is an executive organ (Article 97 states that "He shall be the chief administrative officer [...]"; Article 98 states "[...] and shall perform such other functions as are entrusted to him [...]"; Article 100(1) states "[...] shall not seek or receive instructions from any government or from any other authority external to the Organization."). As an executive organ the Secretary-General has to fulfil the orders of the Security

---

[106] See also *Prosecutor v. Gbao*, Case No. SCSL-04-15-AR72, Decision on Preliminary Motion on the Invalidity of the Agreement Between the United Nations and the Government of Sierra Leone on the Establishment of the Special Court, 25 May 2004.

Council and does therefore not need a delegation of power to become active as his mandate consists in executing the orders given by the power-bearer, in this case the Security Council. The question whether the Security Council has the power to delegate its powers to the Secretary-General is thus not in issue.

b) Does the Secretary-General have powers to conclude such an agreement on his own?

17. The question whether the Secretary-General has power on his own to conclude an agreement between the United Nations and the Government of Sierra Leone as mentioned above is also of no consequence, as the Secretary-General acted at the request of the Security Council in his capacity as executive organ.

c) Does the Security-Council have the power to establish an international tribunal such as the Special Court for Sierra Leone through an agreement?

18. The Defence and the Prosecution agree that it is well established that the United Nations can conclude treaties with a government[4] and that it is not necessary to address the issue of the precise legal basis on which the Security Council acted in this regard.[5]

19. It is indeed irrelevant which article of the Charter was the basis for the above-mentioned Agreement as the Charter does not limit the power of the Security Council to find means and measures to end a situation of threat to international peace and security beyond the prohibition of using arms,[6] the mandate of Article 42 of the Charter and the obligation to act within the purposes and principles of the UN Charter.

20. As stated in Article 1(1) of the Charter, the Purposes of the United Nations are:

> To maintain international peace and security, and to that end: to take effective collective measures for the prevention and removal of threats to the peace, and for the suppression of acts of aggression or other breaches of the peace, and to bring about by peaceful means, and in conformity with the principles of justice and international law, adjustment or settlement of international disputes or situations which might lead to a breach of the peace; [...]

21. 'Effective collective measures for [...] removal of threats to the peace' can therefore be taken. Based on the systematic interpretation of the Charter, the establishment of an international court is part of such collective measures. Therefore, there is no reason why the Security Council could not have established an international criminal tribunal in a non-coercive way. The only question remaining to be dealt with is the ques-

tion whether the Special Court as a sui generis organ[7] is under the control of the Security Council and if so, under what conditions.

d) Did the Security Council act *ultra vires* in creating a *sui generis* organ such as the Special Court for Sierra Leone with regard to lack of control?

22. The UN as a party to the Agreement acts under the umbrella of the UN Charter. Under the Charter, the primary responsibility for the maintenance of international peace and security is conferred on the Security Council,[8] which has to act according to the Charter. The Security Council can establish any organ to fulfil duties in exercise of its powers pursuant to Article 39 of the Charter. Therefore, control over the *sui generis* organ should be exercised by analogy to Security Council's control over a subsidiary organ. It follows that a *sui generis* organ created by the UN under the request of the Security Council, must stay within its control. The Defence submitted that subsidiary organs as may be found necessary may be established in accordance with the Charter only if the Security Council "can exercise effective authority and control over the way in which the delegated powers are being exercised".[9] Although the Defence agrees that this does not mean that the Council can interfere with the judicial functions of the tribunal, it argues that the Council must remain empowered to terminate the operation of a tribunal or amend the terms of the statute.[10] The argumentation continues, stating, that such control is not possible due to the bilateral agreement between the United Nations and the Government of Sierra Leone which states under Article 22 and Article 23 that an amendment or termination of the treaty must be agreed upon by the parties.

23. In creating the Special Court for Sierra Leone by a bilateral agreement the Security Council has not abandoned its primary responsibility for the maintenance of international peace and security. The Special Court has been created as a *sui generis* organ, because the Security Council is not a judicial organ and therefore is not able to exercise judicial functions for itself. As a judicial organ (due to its independence) the Court cannot be controlled otherwise than in administrative matters, meaning advice and policy direction.

24. As an example, this control is provided by article 7 of the Agreement.[11] The Management Committee has been established in such a way as to meet all necessary requirements. It provides "advice and policy direction" in non-judicial matters, thus not interfering with the independence of the judiciary, as this Chamber held in its decision in *Norman* on Independence of the Judiciary.[12] The Secretary-General represents the Security Council in the Management Committee, thereby ensuring the internal administrative control of the Security Council over the Court.[13] It follows that the Security Council upholds

its general power to control the performance of a *sui generis* organ established by the Security Council as a consequence of its mandate from the international community.

25. The Prosecution is correct in stating that the Special Court has no responsibility for the maintenance of international peace and security.[14] The Special Court constitutes only one of the measures available to the Security Council in fulfilling this aim. Therefore, the Security Council could not have delegated its power to the Special Court.

26. The question of the sufficiency of control of the Security Council over the Special Court therefore does not arise.

27. The power and responsibility of the Security Council under the Charter to maintain international peace and security is preserved. Entering an agreement which states that the Statute can be amended only by consent does not impact on the primary responsibility of the Security Council to maintain international peace and security. The fact that the Security Council entered into an agreement in order to exercise its power in terms of maintenance of international peace and security does not mean that the Security Council cannot act within its powers under the Charter if it believes that international peace and security are in any way threatened, even if this threat arose as a consequence of the Government of Sierra Leone not consenting to the amendment of the Statute of the Special Court or to the Special Court's termination.

28. On the other hand, at the time when the Agreement was concluded, the Government of Sierra Leone, as member state to the UN must have known the Security Council's mandate in relation to the maintenance of international peace and security. Therefore, a unilateral redress by the Security Council would not constitute a breach of "good faith" in relation to the Agreement. In case of threat to the maintenance of international peace and security, the Security Council would act in the fulfilment of a higher-ranking obligation under the Charter of the United Nations.

29. No agreement can influence the duties of the Security Council within the framework of the Charter of the United Nations. In this regard the Agreement cannot override the mandate of the Security Council as stated in the Charter nor can it bar the Security Council in the fulfilment of the above mentioned duties, as the primary responsibility for maintenance of international peace and security of the Security Council cannot be challenged.

---

[1] U.N. Charter, article 24(1): "In order to ensure prompt and effective action by the United Nations, its Members confer on the Security Council primary responsibility for the maintenance of international peace and security, and agree that in carrying out its duties under this responsibility the Security Council acts on their behalf."

⁽²⁾ U.N. Charter, article 39: "The Security Council shall determine the existence of any threat to the peace, breach of the peace, or act of aggression and shall make recommendations, or decide what measures shall be taken in accordance with Articles 41 and 42, to maintain or restore international peace and security."
⁽³⁾ U.N. Security Council Resolution 1315, 14 August 2000, p. 13.
⁽⁴⁾ Prosecution Response, para. 6; Defence Reply, para. 2.
⁽⁵⁾ Additional Defence Submission Pertaining to the Preliminary Motion Based on Lack of Jurisdiction: Illegal Delegation of Powers by the United Nations, 6 January 2004, para.12; Prosecution Response to the Additional Defence Submission Pertaining to the Preliminary Motion on Lack of Jurisdiction: Illegal Delegation of Powers by the United Nations, 20 January 2004, para. 7.
⁽⁶⁾ Article 41:"The Security Council may decide what measures not involving the use of armed force are to be employed to give effect to its decisions, and it may call upon the Members of the United Nations to apply such measures. These may include complete or partial interruption of economic relations and of rail, sea, air, postal, telegraphic, radio, and other means of communication, and the severance of diplomatic relations."
⁽⁷⁾ Report of the Secretary-General on the establishment of a Special Court for Sierra Leone, para. 9, S/2000/915, 4 October 2000.
⁽⁸⁾ Article 24(1) of the U.N. Charter.
⁽⁹⁾ Preliminary Motion, para. 10, quoting D. Sarooshi, The United Nations and the Deployment of Collective Security, p. 41 and p. 159 (1999).
⁽¹⁰⁾ Preliminary Motion, para. 10.
⁽¹¹⁾ Article 7 "It is the understanding of the Parties that interested States will establish a management committee to assist the Secretary General in obtaining adequate funding, and provide advice and policy direction on all non-judicial aspects of the operation of the Court, including questions of efficiency, and to perform other functions as agreed by interested States. The management committee shall consist of important contributors to the Special Court. The Government of Sierra Leone and the Secretary General will also participate in the management committee."
⁽¹²⁾ *Prosecutor v Sam Hinga Norman*, Case Number SCSL-2004-14-AR72(E), Decision on Preliminary Motion based on Lack of Jurisdiction (Judicial Independence), 13 March 2004.
⁽¹³⁾ *Ibid.*
⁽¹⁴⁾ Prosecution Response, para. 17.

- **Rule 72: Preliminary Motions – Safeguard of Judicial Independence – Pecuniary Bias**

R72-AC-4

o *Prosecutor v. Norman*, Case No. SCSL-04-14-AR72, Decision on Preliminary Motion on Lack of Jurisdiction (Judicial Independence), 13 March 2004, para. 20-28, 36:

20. Safeguard of judicial independence takes several forms. However, since the question raised by the motion falls within a narrow compass it is unnecessary to enter into any lengthy discourse of the concept of judicial independence or of the various mechanisms usually put in place to safeguard judicial independence.

21. One prominent safeguard of judicial independence in a democratic State is the doctrine of separation of powers

which, in regard to the independence of the judiciary, operates to reserve to the judiciary the exercise of judicial powers of the State and protects the judiciary from being so dependent on other arms of Government as to raise a reasonable apprehension of a real likelihood that judicial functions of the judiciary are performed under the influence of another arm of Government or body.

22. In practice, in regard to the judiciary, there are various models of separation of powers. However, in hardly any is the judiciary required or expected to raise revenue by itself to fund its operations so that it could maintain judicial independence. Indeed, as will be seen shortly, were the judiciary to run its operations and pay its judges from moneys generated from its judicial activities the apprehension of likelihood of bias would become more real and reasonable.

23. In some models the executive deals with staffing and administration of the judiciary, sometimes under the umbrella of a Ministry of Justice. In others the executive is excluded from participation in such process. In some models the judiciary is self-accounting, in others the budget of the judiciary is part of the budget of a Ministry of Justice in which the judiciary is treated, at least for budgetary purposes, as a department of the Ministry of Justice.

VI. FUNDING ARRANGEMENT AND INDEPENDENCE

24. Where the allegation is that the funding arrangement of a judiciary raises a real likelihood of bias so that an accused entertains a reasonable apprehension that he cannot have a fair trial, much more is required than merely showing that the court derives its funding from a source which may be displeased by its decisions. There are other considerations, the principal of which is whether such funding arrangement leads to a real likelihood that the court will be influenced by such arrangement to give decisions, not on the merits of the case, but to please the funding body or agency. Such factors as the obligation, moral or legal, of the funding body or agency and the guarantee of payment of judicial remuneration, however the judiciary is funded, are relevant factors.

25. Denial of adequate funding of the judiciary which would emasculate its performance while the payment of judicial remuneration remained protected must be distinguished from denial of funding where judicial remuneration is unprotected and would therefore affect the payment of judicial remuneration. The former is a shirking of responsibility by the state to provide an efficient or any machinery of justice, while the latter may raise a concern of real likelihood of judicial bias. The conclusion seems clear that it is not every inadequacy in funding arrangement that leads to an inability of courts to dispense justice without bias.

26. It has long been acknowledged that judicial independence rests on the twin pillars of security of tenure of the judge and guarantee of judicial remuneration and its protection from the whims and caprices of governments or bodies charged with the responsibility of funding the judiciary.

27. As early as 1701 it was provided by the Act of Settlement that:

> Judges Commission be made *Quamdiu se bene gesserint* [that is, during good behaviour] and their salaries ascertained and established.[1]

Commenting on that English statute, Chief Justice Burgher, delivering the lead opinion of the US Supreme Court in *United States v. Will*,[2] said:

> The English statute is the earliest legislative acknowledgment that control over the tenure and compensation of judges is incompatible with a truly independent judiciary, free of improper influence from other forces within government.[3]

In the same vein as in the Act of Settlement, several modern Constitutions make provision for the security of tenure of judges and for protection of judicial remuneration. Thus, by section 138(1) of the Constitution of Sierra Leone of 1991,[4] it is provided that:

> The salaries, allowances, gratuities and pensions of Judges of the Superior Court of judicature shall be charged upon the Consolidated Fund.

Section 138(3) of the same Constitution provided that:

> The salary, allowances, privileges, right in respect of leave of absence, gratuity or pension and other conditions of service of a Judge of the Superior Court of Judicature shall not be varied to his disadvantage.

A similar but shorter provision to the same effect is contained in section 1 of Article III of the Constitution of the United States[5] which provides that:

> ... The Judges, both of the supreme and inferior courts, shall hold their offices during good behavior, and shall, at stated times, receive for their services, a compensation, which shall not be diminished during their continuance of office.

28. Some would reason that a safeguard of judicial independence is the payment of handsome remuneration to judges. Another view, and this would appear to be the better view, is that the level of remuneration of a judge is an acknowledgment of the high skill he possesses and which he is expected to bring to the discharge of his judicial function in order to

enhance the quality of justice. Be that as it may, of more value in securing judicial independence are the assurance and guarantee of security of tenure and guarantee and protection of the level and payment of judicial remuneration.

[. . .]

36. The position is sufficiently clear to enable it to be stated in the following propositions:

a. A judge is disqualified from adjudication where he has a direct, personal or pecuniary interest in the litigation and, particularly, in criminal trials where pecuniary benefit accrues to him by his convicting.[6]

b. A judge is not disqualified from adjudicating where there is no objective reason to infer on any showing that failure to convict (or acquit) in any case or cases would deprive him of or affect his fixed remuneration.[7]

c. A judge should disqualify himself if a reasonable and informed person would believe that there is a real danger of bias.

d. A reasonable person will not rush to an assumption that a judge will violate his oath and the duties of his office on a remote and speculative belief that his remuneration may be affected in any way by the decision he gives.

---

[1] Act of Settlement, 12 & 13 Will. III, ch. 2, § III, cl. 7 (1701).
[2] *United States v. Will* 449 U.S. 200 (1980).
[3] *Ibid.* at p. 218.
[4] The Constitution of Sierra Leone 1991, 24 September 1991.
[5] U.S. Const. art. III, § 1 (2004).
[6] See *Ward v. Village of Monroeville supra* note 21; See *Tumey v. Ohio, supra* note 19.
[7] *Dugan v. Ohio, supra* note 19.

- **Rule 72: Preliminary Motions – Immunity Is a Jurisdiction Related Issue**

R72-AC-5

o *Prosecutor v. Taylor*, Case No. SCSL-03-01-AR72, Decision on Immunity from Jurisdiction, 31 May 2004, para. 32:

32. The Prosecution contended that the Preliminary Motion did not raise an issue of jurisdiction in terms of Rule 72 because the claim to immunity, rather than raising 'a serious issue relating to jurisdiction', raised an issue of defence. That was a narrow view of jurisdictional immunity of the type claimed by the Applicant. Such immunity connoted immunity from the jurisdiction of the court. Professor Shaw succinctly put it when he wrote that: "the principle of jurisdictional immunity asserts that in particular situations a court is pre-

vented from exercising the jurisdiction that it possesses."[1] In that sense it cannot be rightly said that the question of immunity raised by the Applicant does not raise a serious issue relating to jurisdiction. An objection to the proceedings on the ground that in the particular situation the court is prevented from exercising its jurisdiction raises an issue *relating to jurisdiction*.

[1] Shaw, *International Law*, p. 623.

- **Rule 72 (F): Preliminary Motions – Referral to the Appeals Chamber**

R72-AC-6   o *Prosecutor v. Kallon, Norman, Gbao*, Cases No. SCSL-03-07-A, SCSL-03-08-A, SCSL-03-09-A, Decision on the Applications for a Stay of Proceedings and Denial of Right to Appeal, 4 November 2003, para. 12-14:

12. Rule 72, as inherited by the Special Court from the ICTR permitted certain motions raising jurisdictional questions to be appealed, prior to trial, to the appeals chamber. The judges of the Special Court met in plenary session in March 2003, to consider whether the ICTR machinery was appropriate for the Special Court. They decided that defendants would be given additional rights to take preliminary issues, with leave of the Trial Chamber, to the Appeals Chamber, such as motions which in the Trial Chamber's judgment would "affect the fair and expeditious conduct of proceedings" (72(F)) and certain trial chamber decisions which might otherwise cause irreparable prejudice. To this very considerable extent, the plenary enhanced defence rights. But the judges were aware of the problem of undue delay and the propensity for Rule 72 "preliminary motions" which often involve complicated questions of international law, to contribute many months and even years of delay, if they are first argued out in a Trial Chamber with the arguments repeated, after that Chamber's reserve judgement, in the Appeals Chamber whose judgement, again reserved, must be delivered before the trial itself can begin. Conscious of the duty to secure expeditious justice, the plenary determined to amend Rule 72.

13. The remedy was found in an amendment which would permit the Trial Chamber to "fast-track" a preliminary motion by referring it for a decision to the Appeals Chamber. The power given to the Trial Chamber was discretionary to the extent that the Rule provided that substantial issues relating to jurisdiction "may be referred". However, Trial Chamber judges put on the agenda for the following plenary – in August – a

reconsideration of the Rule, and at this meeting the judges unanimously decided to amend Rule 72 by removing the discretion to refer preliminary motions once the Trial Chamber had determined that they "raise a serious issue relating to jurisdiction". The operative part of Rule 72 now reads as follows:

> (E) Preliminary motions made in the Trial Chamber prior to the Prosecutor's opening statement which raise a serious issue relating to jurisdiction shall be referred to the Appeals Chamber, where they will proceed to a determination as soon as practicable.
>
> (F) Preliminary motions made in the Trial Chamber prior to the Prosecutor's opening statement which, in the opinion of the Trial Chamber, raise an issue that would significantly affect the fair and expeditious conduct of the proceedings or the outcome of a trial shall be referred to the Appeals Chamber, where they will proceed to a determination as soon as practicable.

14. The Rule as amended is not one of automatic referral nor one that (as has been argued) deprives the defendant for all time of a second bite of the legal cherry. It will be for the Trial Chamber to determine, under (E) that the motion raises a serious issue related to jurisdiction, and under (F) whether it would significantly affect the proceedings. The referral requires a judicial determination: the Rule does not turn the Trial Chamber into a post box. More important, if unspecified, is the inherent power of the Appeals Chamber to return the referred motion, in whole or in part, to the Trial Chamber for determination. It may turn out, on closer examination by this Chamber, that the motion is not one of 'pure' law, in that it really does call for a determination of facts, perhaps after hearing evidence, and this Chamber may be persuaded that it is more appropriate to have a Trial Chamber decision. It may be – especially in relation to motions referred under Rule 72(F) – that the issues can, on examination, readily or properly be decided by the Trial Chamber in the course of the trial, and taken up if necessary in a notice of appeal. There may be other grounds which have a particular relevance to a specific motion, in respect of which substantial benefits will derive from having a first-tier determination by the Trial Chamber. We would need to be convinced, in any particular case, that a Trial Chamber pre-determination would be of particular assistance for us to consider before reaching a conclusive determination and we must make crystal clear that any such request for us to remit the matter for Trial Chamber determination must be made as part of the substantive application in the written submissions or at an oral hearing (where such is permitted). We will not consider a remission request other than in the course of the referred application.

Rule 72*bis*: General Provisions on Applicable Law
(adopted 29 May 2004)

The applicable laws of the Special Court include:

(i) the Statute, the Agreement, and the Rules;
(ii) where appropriate, other applicable treaties and the principles and rules of international customary law;
(iii) general principles of law derived from national laws of legal systems of the world including, as appropriate, the national laws of the Republic of Sierra Leone, provided that those principles are not inconsistent with the Statute, the Agreement, and with international customary law and internationally recognized norms and standards.

TRIAL CHAMBERS DECISIONS

- **Rule 72*bis*: Applicable Law – Reference to Former Decisions of the Special Court for Sierra Leone**

R72*bis*-TC-1

o *Prosecutor v. Kondewa*, Case No. SCSL-03-12-PT, Decision and Order on Defence Preliminary Motion for Defects in the Form of the Indictment, 27 November 2003, para. 5-6:

5. In a seminal Decision[1] on objections and challenges to the formal validity of indictment, this Court took the opportunity to expound exhaustively the principles governing the framing of indictments for the purpose of International Criminal Law, predicated upon an analysis of the evolving jurisprudence of sister international criminal tribunals on the subject. The principles applied in that case were also followed, with necessary adaptations and modifications, in the more recent Decision of *The Prosecutor Against Santigie Borbor Kanu*[2] of the Court. Conscious of the need to preserve logical coherence and consistency in developing the Court's jurisprudence, the Chamber now proceeds to examine, as to their merit, the several challenges and objections raised by the Defence to the formal validity of the Indictment herein in the light of the aforesaid principles.

6. In addressing the issue of the formal validity of the Indictment, the Chamber, by way of precedent, must begin with two fundamental principles. [...]

---

[1] *The Prosecutor v. Hassan Issa Sesay*, Case No. 03-05-PT, Decision and Order on Defence Preliminary Motion for defects in the Form of the Indictment, 13 October 2003.

(2) Case No. SCSL-03-13-PT, Decision and Order on Defence Preliminary Motion for Defects in the Form of the Indictment, 19 November 2003.

- **Rule 72*bis*(iii): Applicable Law – General Principles of Law – *Res Judicata* Principle**

R72*bis*-TC-2   o *Prosecutor v. Norman*, Case No. SCSL-04-14-T, Decision on First Accused's Motion on Abuse of Process, 28 April 2005, para. 6-10:

6. In our consideration of the jurisdictional issue, we would like to invoke the well established principle in international law of *Res Judicata*, and to hold that decisions rendered by a Court that is competent to make them are final and that the same issues, except in very exceptional circumstances, may not again be raised or litigated by the parties before that Court.

7. Rule 72*bis* of the Rules sets out the applicable laws of the Special Court that include "general principles of law derived from national laws of legal systems of the world". [...]

8. The principle of *Res Judicata* is one of the general principles of law recognised in national laws of various legal systems. The Appeals Chamber of the ICTR in the *Barayagwiza*[1] case stated as follows:

"The principle of *res judicata* is well settled in international law as being one of those "general principles of law recognized by civilised nations", referred to in Article 38 of the Statute of the Permanent Court of International Justice ... and the International Court of Justice ... As such it is a principle which should be applied by the Tribunal."

9. It is indeed founded on the logical understanding of the need and necessity for expediency and finality in the judicial process, which is that there should, at a certain stage, be an end to litigation in order to prevent parties from relitigating issues that have finally been laid to rest by the Judges.

10. The Permanent Court of International Justice ("ICJ") has applied the doctrine of *Res Judicata*. in the *Case Concerning Arbitral Award Made by the King of Spain on 23 December 1906*, where it found non-justiciable, a claim by Nicaragua to re-examine the substantive issues of a dispute which was decided by the King of Spain in a prior arbitration case.[2] In *The Pious Fund Case*, the ICJ upheld the submission by the

United Sates which contended that Mexico was raising issues that had been decided in a previous legal action.[3]

---

[1] *Prosecutor v. Barayagwiza,* Decision on the Prosecutor's Request for Review or Reconsideration, 31 March 2000, para. 20.
[2] *Case Concerning Arbitral Award made by the King of Spain on 23 December 1906* (Honduras v. Nicaragua), I.C.J. Reports, 1960, 192.
[3] *The Pious Fund Case (U.S. v. Mex.),* 9 R.I.A.A. 1 (May 22, 1902).

Rule 73: Motions
(amended 14 May 2005)

(A) Subject to Rule 72, either party may move before the Designated Judge or a Trial Chamber for appropriate ruling or relief after the initial appearance of the accused. The Designated Judge or the Trial Chamber, or a Judge designated by the Trial Chamber from among its members, shall rule on such motions based solely on the written submissions of the parties, unless it is decided to hear the parties in open Court.

(B) Decisions rendered on such motions are without interlocutory appeal. However, in exceptional circumstances and to avoid irreparable prejudice to a party, the Trial Chamber may give leave to appeal. Such leave should be sought within 3 days of the decision and shall not operate as a stay of proceedings unless the Trial Chamber so orders.

(C) Whenever the Trial Chamber and the Appeals Chamber of the Court are seized of the same Motion raising the same or similar issue or issues, the Trial Chamber shall stay proceedings on the said Motion before it until a final determination of the said Motion by the Appeals Chamber.

(D) Irrespective of any sanctions which may be imposed under Rule 46(A), when a Chamber finds that a motion is frivolous or is an abuse of process, the Registrar shall withhold payment of all or part of the fees associated with the production of that motion and/or costs thereof.

TRIAL CHAMBERS DECISIONS

- **Rule 73(A): Motions – Need for a Proper Application**

R73-TC-1   o *Prosecutor v. Brima*, Case No. SCSL-03-06-PT, Order on Filing, 16 May 2003:

> **CONSIDERING** that the filing of judicial submissions, in form of a motion, in different stages complicates the Special Court's duty to control its judicial proceedings, and that the practice of international criminal tribunals requires that motions shall be filed in one single, substantive and comprehensive document;

CONSIDERING the need to conduct an efficient handling of the Special Court judicial proceeding, entailing, *inter alia*, an unambiguous filing and serving of a party's submission, with a view to allow a regular and timely deliberation on such submission and on the response from its counterpart;

[...]

HEREBY ORDERS the Counsel for the Accused to:

1. consolidate the Notice and the Brief in one comprehensive submission, with all necessary supporting materials attached thereto, to be then considered as the only relevant motion pertaining to this issue; [...]

R73-TC-2
o *Prosecutor v. Sesay, Kallon, Gbao*, Case No. SCSL-04-15-T, Decision on Prosecution's Intention to Extend Protective Measures for Additional Witnesses, 22 October 2004:

CONSIDERING that the Prosecution has just informed the Trial Chamber of its intention to extend protective measures to witnesses;

CONSIDERING therefore that the Trial Chamber is not properly seized of an application for protective measures;

FOR THERE REASONS, THE TRIAL CHAMBER:

DISMISSES the Prosecution's declaration of intent of Protective Measures for Additional Witnesses;

- **Rule 73(A): Motions – Purpose of Motions – Seek Ruling or Relief**

R73-TC-3
o *Prosecutor v. Sesay*, Case No. SCSL-04-15-T, Decision on Defence Motion, 15 July 2004, para. 13:[107]

13. Although the Rules do not provide for a specific form in which a party might bring a motion before the Trial Chamber, Rule 73(A) of the Rules however, clearly provides that motions at this stage of the process are to be entertained for the purpose of seeking a ruling or relief. This provision does not provide for a declaration. The Chamber has noted that the Defence failed to seek any ruling or relief in its Motion but simply provides notice to the parties of potential actions it may undertake before the Trial Chamber.

---

[107] See also *Prosecutor v. Kallon*, Case No. SCSL-04-15-T, Decision on Confidential Motion, 11 October 2004, para. 21.

- **Rule 73(A): Motions – Purpose of Motions – Writ of *Habeas Corpus***

R73-TC-4

o *Prosecutor v. Brima*, Case No. SCSL-03-06-PT, Ruling on the Application for the Issue of a Writ of *Habeas Corpus* Filed by the Applicant, 22 July 2003:

On the preliminary issue of the propriety of the Special Court entertaining an application for '*Habeas Corpus*', a fact which surfaces in the proceedings, albeit subtly, as a preliminary objection by the Respondents to this application, I will like to observe that this historic Common Law Writ is founded basically on the principle that no individual should be subjected to an illegal detention.

Indeed, one of the most regularly and too-often deplored breaches of human rights today is the violation of individual liberties which are guaranteed not only by the provisions of Article 3 of the Universal Declaration of Human Rights but also, by practically all democratically inspired Constitutions of Countries of the world, and particularly, those of Member States of the United Nations Organisation.

It is my opinion that because the right to liberty is too sacred to be violated by whoever, any Court faced with or called upon to rule on applications of this nature, in whatever form they may be brought, should, for reasons based on the universal resolve and determination to uphold by all lawful means, respect by all and sundry and in all circumstances, of this entrenched fundamental human right, should entertain such applications and refrain from dismissing them merely on technical pretexts or niceties, geared at and designed to prevent them from being entertained and examined.

This is the philosophy that has guided me all along in granting the application "*ex-parte*" on the 18th of June 2003, for leave to file the substantive application for the issue of the writ of "*Habeas Corpus*". In so doing, I agree with the submission of the Respondents that the procedure for granting a release through a Writ of "*Habeas Corpus*" features nowhere in the Rules of Procedure and Evidence which are applicable to the Special Court. However, entertaining this Writ is dictated by the imperatives of universally ensuring the respect of human rights and liberties.

Besides, this application can be assimilated to a motion under Section 73 of our Rules of Procedure and Evidence which, like in this case, which, just as a single Judge can handle applications for Writs of "*Habeas Corpus*", confers on a single Judge of the Trial Chamber designated under Rule 28 of the Rules of Procedure, the right to handle issues of this nature, after hearing the parties.

In the case of the ***Prosecutor vs Radoslav Brdanin,*** in the matter of an application for the issue of a writ of *"Habeas Corpus"* in the favour of the Applicant, the Trial Chamber of the International Criminal tribunal for Yugoslavia (ICTY), on the 8th of December, 1999, composed of His Lordship, Judge Antonio Cassese, Presiding, and Their Lordships, Florence Ndepele Mwachande Mumba, and David Hunt, Judges, had this to say:

> "This Tribunal has no power to issue Writs in the name of any Sovereign or other Head of State. But the Tribunal certainly does have both power and the procedure to resolve a challenge to the lawfulness of detainees in detention."

This decision was preceded by that of ***Jean Bosco Barayagwiza vs The Prosecutor***, where the Appeal's Chamber of the International Criminal Tribunal of Rwanda (ICTR) presided by His Lordship Judge Gabrielle Kirk Mc Donald, flanked by Their Lordships, Judges Mohamed Shahabuddeen, Lalchand Vorah, Wang Tieya and Rafael Nieto-Navia, made the following remarks, and I quote:

> "Although neither the Statute nor the Rules specifically addressed Writs of *"Habeas Corpus"* as such, the notion that a detained individual shall have recourse to an independent judicial officer for a review of the detaining authorities' act, is well established by Statute and Rules".

In the light of the above analysis, I hold that the Applicant's Writ of *"Habeas Corpus"* is properly before me, and this, notwithstanding the objection of Learned Counsel for the Respondents, Mr. Browne-Marke, based on the failure of the Applicant to file a proper substantive Writ after he had obtained leave to file same. In this regard, I will like to observe that an examination of the traditional practice in filing Writs of *"Habeas Corpus"* is, as in this case, and as it is indeed permissible, to couple the application for leave with the substantive application and to file and serve them at the same time since the application for leave to file Writs of this nature is hardly refused at that preliminary level.

- **Rule 73(A): Motions – Need to Address One Single Jurisdiction**

R73-TC-5

o *Prosecutor v. Sesay*, Case No. SCSL-03-05-PT, Order on the Defence Application for Reconsideration of and/or Leave to Appeal "Decision on the Prosecutor's Motion on Protective Measures for Witnesses", 16 July 2003:[108]

---

[108] See also *Prosecutor v. Kallon*, Case No. SCSL-03-07-PT, Order on the Defence Application for Reconsideration of and/or Leave to Appeal "Decision on the Prosecutor's Motion on Protective Measures for Witnesses", 16 July 2003.

CONSIDERING that in its Application the Defence addressed the then Designated Judge in order to seek reconsideration of his Decision on Protective Measures and consequently vary his Orders on Protective Measures;

CONSIDERING that in the same Application the Defence also addressed the Trial Chamber in order to request, in the alternative to its request for reconsideration, an order for leave to Appeal the same Decision on Protective Measures;

CONSIDERING that, from a procedural point of view, it is improper and confusing to address two different jurisdictions in one single application;

THE TRIAL CHAMBER FINDS that the Defence erroneously and improperly addressed its Application at two different jurisdictions, i.e. the Designated Judge that rendered the Decision on Protective Measures and the Trial Chamber;

- **Rule 73(A): Motions – Submissions of the Parties – Purpose of Response/Reply – "Counter Motion"**

R73-TC-6

o *Prosecutor v. Sesay, Kallon, Gbao*, Case No. SCSL-04-15-T, Decision on Prosecution Request for Leave to Call Additional Witnesses and Disclose Additional Witness Statements, 11 February 2005, para. 28:

28. The Chamber wishes to express its strong disfavour of the practice of expanding the nature of submissions in response to a motion to the extent of introducing specific, new and separate arguments amounting to, as it has been identified by the Defence in its Response, a "counter motion". The proper course of action in order to avoid confusion with reference to the nature and time limits for subsequent responses and replies is for the Defence to identify and distinguish the new legal issue, and then file a separate and distinct motion. In the context of the instant Motion, the Prosecution had indeed filed a separate response to these Defence submissions and no reply had been filed by the Defence.[1] However, in the interest of justice, the Chamber will on this occasion address the issues raised therein.

---

[1] See Prosecution Response to the Counter Motion of the Accused Kallon for an Order that Witnesses TF1-103, TF1-106, TF1-146, TF1-189, TF1-274, TF1-013 and TF1-302 Be Excluded from the Prosecution Renewed Witness List, 8 December 2004.

R73-TC-7 o *Prosecutor v. Brima, Kamara, Kanu*, Case No. SCSL-04-16-T, Decision on Joint defence Motion on Disclosure of All Original Witness Statements, Interview Notes and Investigator's Notes Pursuant to Rule 66 and/or 68, 4 May 2005, para. 20:[109]

> 20. [. . .] The Trial Chamber notes that, in its Reply, the Defence sought to substantially modify the relief sought. This is a practice that must be discouraged. A Reply is meant to answer matters raised by the other party in its Response, not to claim additional relief to that sought in the Motion. Obviously the other party, having already filed a Response to the Motion, has no way under the Rules to answer the new prayer, except to apply to the Trial Chamber for leave to do so. In future, the Trial Chamber will not hear claims for additional relief contained in a Reply.

R73-TC-8 o *Prosecutor v. Brima, Kamara*, Case No. SCSL-04-16-T, Decision on the Extremely Urgent Confidential Joint Motion for the Re-Appointment of Kevin Metzger and Wilbert Harris as Lead Counsel for Alex Tamba Brima and Brima Bazzy Kamara and Decision on Cross-Motion by Deputy Principal Defender to Trial Chamber II for Clarification of its Oral Order of 12 May 2005, 9 June 2005, para. 53:

> 53. The Deputy Principal Defender has filed a Cross-Motion in response to the Defence Motion. We again repeat, a response or reply should not be used as a vehicle to seek further relief. [. . .]

R73-TC-9 o *Prosecutor v. Brima, Kamara, Kanu*, Case No. SCSL-04-16-T, Decision on Objection to Question Put by Defence in Cross-Examination of Witness TF1-227, 15 June 2005, para. 28:

---

[109] See also *Prosecutor v. Brima, Kamara*, Case No. SCSL-04-16-T, Decision on the Extremely Urgent Confidential Joint Motion for the Re-Appointment of Kevin Metzger and Wilbert Harris as Lead Counsel for Alex Tamba Brima and Brima Bazzy Kamara and Decision on Cross-Motion by Deputy Principal Defender to Trial Chamber II for Clarification of its Oral Order of 12 May 2005, 9 June 2005, para. 20; *Prosecutor v. Brima, Kamara, Kanu*, Case No. SCSL-04-16-T, Decision on Objection to Question Put by Defence in Cross-Examination of Witness TF1-227, 15 June 2005, para. 43.

28. We restate that any replying submission should not be used as a means of seeking other relief. This practice will not be allowed in future.

R73-TC-10

o *Prosecutor v. Brima, Kamara, Kanu*, Case No. SCSL-04-16-T, Decision on Prosecution request for Leave to Call an Additional Witness (Zainab Hawa Bangura) Pursuant to Rule 73*bis*(E), and on Joint Defence Notice to Inform the Trial Chamber of its Position vis-à-vis the Proposed Expert Witness (Mrs Bangura) Pursuant to Rule 94*bis*, 5 August 2005, para. 27:

27. The Trial Chamber wishes to express its strong disfavour for the practice of combining pleadings or submissions for which the Rules prescribe different filing time limits. As the Defence has rightly observed, Rule 7 (C) of the Rules provides that "unless otherwise ordered by the Trial Chamber, a response to a motion shall be filed within ten days while a reply to response shall be filed within five days." We note that in this case the Prosecution's Combined Reply comprises two pleadings, namely the Prosecution Response to the Defence Reply (for which a filing time limit of five days is applicable), and the Prosecution's Reply to the Defence Notice and Request (for which a filing time limit of ten days is applicable). The proper and preferred course of action is for the parties to file the various responses and replies in separate documents in order to avoid confusion over issues as well as time frames. In the present case we observe that the irregularity by the Prosecution has not occasioned a miscarriage of justice as their "Combined Reply" was filed on the 18 May 2005, five days after the filing of the Defence Reply. The Prosecution therefore appears to have complied with both time limits prescribed by Rule 7 (C). The preliminary objection is accordingly overruled.

- **Rule 73(A): Motions – Submissions of the Parties – No Requirement for Oral Hearing**

R73-TC-11

o *Prosecutor v. Kondewa*, Case No. SCSL-03-12-PD, Decision on the Urgent Defence Application for Release from Provisional Detention, 21 November 2003, para. 22:[110]

---

[110] See also *Prosecutor v. Fofana*, SCSL-03-11-PD, Decision on the Urgent Defence Application for Release from Provisional Detention, 21 November 2003.

22. According to Rule 73 (A) of the Rules,[1] the Chamber has no obligation to hear the parties in open court. The case of *The Prosecutor v. Bizimungu* before the ICTR is particularly instructive on this issue. In its Decision on Bizimungu's Motion for Provisional Release Pursuant to Rule 65 of the Rules,[2] the Trial Chamber held that it was not compelled to proceed with an oral hearing and could decide solely on the basis of the written submissions of the parties if it were satisfied that it could make a determination of the said submissions without hearing the parties. In the present matter, the Chamber is indeed satisfied that it can make such a determination on the matter at stake solely on the basis of the written submissions of the Parties, as expressed through a Court Management Section Memorandum issued on the 26th day of June 2003. Furthermore, the Chamber would like to stress the fact that written submissions provide a proper opportunity for both Parties to respond and reply to each other.

---

[1] Rule 73 (A) of "the Rules" reads "(...) the Designated Judge or the Trial Chamber, or a judge designated by the Trial Chamber from among its members, shall rule on (...) motions solely on the written submissions of the parties, unless it is decided to hear the parties in open court".

[2] *The Prosecutor v. Bizimungu*, Decision on Bizimungu's Motion for Provisional Release Pursuant to Rule 65 of the Rules, ICTR-99-50-T, 4 November 2002, para. 23.

R73-TC-12

o *Prosecutor v. Brima, Kamara*, Case No. SCSL-04-16-T, Decision on the Extremely Urgent Confidential Joint Motion for the Re-Appointment of Kevin Metzger and Wilbert Harris as Lead Counsel for Alex Tamba Brima and Brima Bazzy Kamara and Decision on Cross-Motion by Deputy Principal Defender to Trial Chamber II for Clarification of its Oral Order of 12 May 2005, 9 June 2005, para. 25:

25. [...] Furthermore, we observe that there has been no submission to support or explain this application for a public hearing. Counsel refers to "security concerns" but ignores the fact that the Lead Counsel, in their original application to withdraw from the case sought to have the facts under seal and *ex-parte* as well as confidential. In the circumstances, we consider this application vexatious.

- **Rule 73(A): Motions – Submissions of the Parties – No Requirement to Await Responses and Replies**

R73-TC-13
o *Prosecutor v. Brima*, Case No. SCSL-04-16-T, Decision on Renewed Defence Motion for Defects in the Form of the Indictment and Application for Extension of Time, 24 May 2005, para. 12-13:

12. Secondly, Defence Counsel contends that the Trial Chamber has not awaited the complete submissions of the Parties to the first Motion, in particular a response of the Prosecutor and a Defence reply thereto.

13. There is no mandatory obligation on the Trial Chamber to await responses or replies if the Trial Chamber is of the opinion that the law and facts are sufficiently clear to enable it to rule on the motion particularly when a delay could jeopardise the commencement of the trial and cause hardship to the accused.

- **Rule 73(A): Motions – Submissions of the Parties – No Response to a Reply**

R73-TC-14
o *Prosecutor v. Sesay*, Case No. SCSL-03-05-PT, Order on Defence Objection Filed as Reply Evidence in the Prosecution Motion for Immediate Protective Measures for Witnesses and Victims and for Non-Public Disclosure, 21 May 2003:[111]

CONSIDERING that the Defence in its Objection avers, *inter alia*, that new evidence has been submitted in the Reply and that the defence was therefore deprived of the opportunity to address evidence forming part of a moving party's case;

[…]

CONSIDERING that the additional bases of the Prosecution's Reply, in particular the declarations cited above, cannot be considered as fresh evidence, but may only be considered as evidence of a rebutting character, as the declarations only add and strengthen the line of argument in the Motion, and that the additional declarations do not initiate an entire new line of argumentation;

CONSIDERING that the Rules do not provide for a response to a reply;

---

[111] See also *Prosecutor v. Kallon*, Case No. SCSL-03-07-PT, Order on Defence Objection Filed as Reply Evidence in the Prosecution Motion for Immediate Protective Measures for Witnesses and Victims and for Non-Public Disclosure, 21 May 2003.

NOW HEREBY, pursuant to Rule 54 of the Rules,

REJECTS the Request of the Defence in its entirety.

- **Rule 73(A): Motions – Leave to File Supplementary Materials Supporting a Motion**

R73-TC-15
o *Prosecutor v. Norman, Fofana, Kondewa*, Case No. SCSL-04-14-T, Ruling Granting the Prosecution Leave to Submit Supplementary Materials, 9 November 2004:

CONSIDERING that the Prosecution has demonstrated good cause for filing Supplementary Materials, which are relevant for the Trial Chamber's consideration on the 1st Motion;

PURSUANT TO Rule 54 of the Rules of Procedure and Evidence of the Special Court;

HEREBY GRANTS the 2nd Motion.

- **Rule 73(A): Motions – Moot**

R73-TC-16
o *Prosecutor v. Kanu*, Case No. SCSL-04-16-PT, Decision on Kanu's Motion for Dismissal of Counts 15-18 of the Indictment Due to an Alibi Defence and Lack of *Prima Facie* Case and Request for Extension of Time for the Hearing of the Defence Motion, 15 February 2005:

NOTING the Decision of this Trial Chamber granting leave to the Prosecution to amend the Amended Consolidated Indictment by withdrawal of the counts 15, 16, 17, and 18 filed 15 February 2005;

UPHOLDS the objections by the Prosecution to the Defence Application in the Request to present its arguments in written form;

CONSIDERS that both aforementioned Defence applications were filed on the premise that counts 15 to 18 of the Amended Consolidated Indictment would continue to be part of the indictment;

NOTING that the withdrawal of Counts 15, 16, 17, and 18 have rendered it unnecessary to decide either of the defence motions and that any determination thereof would be purely academic and theoretical;

HOLDS that the Motion is now moot and an argument thereon is not called for;

- **Rule 73(A): Motions – Relief Sought – Proportionality Between the Relief and the Breach**

R73-TC-17

o *Prosecutor v. Brima, Kamara, Kanu*, Case No. SCSL-04-16-T, Decision on the Confidential Joint Defence Motion to Declare Null and Void Testimony-in-Chief of Witness TF1-023, 25 May 2005, para. 18-23:

18. [...] Neither Party refers the Trial Chamber to any precedent or authority holding that the doctrine of proportionality applies to remedies for alleged breach of procedure in the International Criminal Tribunals. The doctrine is more commonly applied in argument and decisions relating to enforcement of human or constitutional rights. However, given the continuing development of the jurisprudence of the International Criminal Tribunals we are of the opinion that the Trial Chamber is entitled to ask itself the question whether the expunging of evidence – not challenged by cross-examination or as breach of procedure at the time it was adduced – is a proportionate remedy for an alleged breach of a procedural provision.

19. The concept of proportionality involves a court weighing up the remedy sought to the alleged breach or wrong suffered.

20. Defence say (we assume) that there was a breach of Article 17 of the Statute but do not say which of the several rights enshrined therein was breached or why the only remedy must be expunging of evidence.

21. We consider the Trial Chamber may look at the application and interpretations of international treaties and conventions by other International Courts. The Trial Chamber is entitled to consider the jurisprudence of other jurisdictions, a practice commonly adopted by the International Criminal Tribunals.[1] We note the similarity of the provisions of Article 17 of the Statute to Article 6 of the European Convention of Human Rights (ECHR). We draw a contrast to Article 17(2) of the Statute and Article 6(1) of the ECHR both providing for a "fair and public hearing". Article 17(2) of the Statute is "subject to measures ordered by the Special Court for the protection of victims and witnesses" and Article 6(1) of the ECHR empowers a Court to exclude the press and public for reasons enumerated therein.

22. Cases show that Article 6(1) of the ECHR has to be given a broad and purposive interpretation.[2] Article 6(1) of the ECHR was considered by the English House of Lords in *R. v. A. (No. 2) 2002*, 1 A.C.45. The Court observed that:

> "[...] it is well established that the right to a fair trial in Article 6 is absolute. [...] The only balancing per-

mitted was in respect of what the concept of a fair trial entails; account may be taken of the familiar triangulation of the interests of the accused, the victim and society. In that context proportionality has a role to play."

The criteria for determining the test of proportionality have been analysed in similar terms in the case law of the European Court of Justice and the European Court of Human Rights.

23. We consider that the Trial Chamber may consider if the remedy sought is proportionate to the mischief alleged. In the circumstances of this case, the expunging of evidence for an alleged breach of a procedural rule is disproportionate, particularly as it was not challenged at the time and was cured. Further, we note Rule 5 does not specify what relief the Trial Chamber may grant and we consider such relief must be proportionate to any material prejudice caused. In any case, no material prejudice has been established by the Defence, and thus there are no grounds for granting relief.

---

(1) *The Prosecutor v. Dragoljub Kunarac et al.*, Case No. IT-96-23, Trial Chamber, Judgement, 22 February 2001, para. 454 ff.; *The Prosecutor v. Ferdinand Nahimana et al.*, Case No. ICTR-99-52-T, Trial Chamber, Judgement and Sentence, 3 December 2003, para. 1074 ff.

(2) E.g. *Moreiva de Azvedo v. Portugal*, 13 E.H.R.R. 721, at para. 66.

- **Rule 73(A): Motions – Reconsideration of Interlocutory Decisions – Inherent Jurisdiction**

R73-TC-18 o *Prosecutor v. Norman, Fofana, Kondewa*, Case No. SCSL-04-14-T, Decision on Urgent Motion for Reconsideration of the Orders for Compliance with the Order Concerning the Preparation and Presentation of the Defence Case, 7 December 2005, para. 10-14:

10. In the Chamber opinion, under the adversarial scheme for international criminal adjudication set up by the Special Court system, there is no express statutory authority conferred upon a Trial Chamber of the Special Court to reconsider a previous interlocutory decision once it is *finctus officio*.(1) However, the fact that the Rules are silent as to whether a Chamber can reconsider its decisions is not necessarily inconsistent with a judicial body's inherent jurisdiction to exercise this power in exceptional circumstances.(2)

11. In the absence of an express statutory provision vesting the Trial Chamber with powers to reconsider its previous decision, the instant issue is whether the Chamber can exercise such a power by virtue of its inherent jurisdiction. Indeed, the

Appeals Chamber has previously held that a Chamber has an inherent jurisdiction to reconsider its own decisions in the event of a clear error of reasoning and to avoid injustice or a miscarriage of justice.[3]

12. This Chamber consequently holds that, as a matter of law, it can exercise its power to reconsider a previous decision under its inherent jurisdiction. Whether or not a Chamber does reconsider its own previous decisions is in itself a discretionary decision.[4] However, in the Chamber's opinion, the critical question for preliminary determination is in what circumstances is such a power exercisable?

13. Established jurisprudence of the ICTY and the ICTR confirms that a Chamber has an inherent power to reconsider its own decisions only in exceptional circumstances.[5] In this regard, the Chamber finds persuasive and accordingly adopts, the view taken by Trial Chamber III of the ICTR in its *Decision on Prosecution Motion for Variation, or, in Alternative Reconsideration of the Decision on Protective Measures for Defence Witnesses*.[6] On this issue, the Chamber stated:

> "following the jurisprudence of the Tribunal, a Trial Chamber has an instant power to reconsider its own decision where (i) a clear error of reasoning in the previous decision has been demonstrated and (ii) the decision sought to be reconsidered has led to an injustice."[7]

14. We also adopt, for persuasive reasons, the reasoning of Trial Chamber II of the aforementioned ICTR in its *Decision on Renzaho's Motion to Reconsider the Decision on Protective Measures for Victims and Witnesses to Crimes Alleged in the Indictment*[8] where, alluding to the circumstances, the Chamber observed that such circumstances include but are not limited to the following:

> "(i) where the impugned decision was erroneous in law or an abuse of discretion when decided and for this reason a procedural irregularity has caused a failure of natural justice; or,
>
> (ii) where the new material circumstances have arisen since the decision was issued."[9]

---

[1] See *Prosecutor v. Issa Sesay*, case No. SCSL-03-05-PT, Order on the Defence Application for Reconsideration of and/or Leave to Appeal "Decision on the Prosecutor's Motion for Protective Measures for Witnesses and Victims and for Non-Public Disclosure", 16 July 2003; *Prosecutor against Brima, Kamara, Kanu*, Case No. SCSL-04-16-T, Decision on renewed Motion for Defects in the Form of the Indictment and Application for Extension of Time, 24 May 2005, para. 8.

[2] See also *Prosecutor v. Renzaho*, Case no. ICTR-97-31-I, Decision on Renzaho's Motion to Reconsider the Decision on Protective Measures for Victims and Witnesses to Crimes Alleged in the Indictment, 9 November 2005, para. 20.

(3) *Prosecutor against Norman, Fofana and Kondewa*, Decision on Prosecution Appeal Against the Trial Chamber's Decision of 2 August 2004 Refusing Leave to File and Interlocutory Appeal, 17 January 2005, paras 35 and 40.

(4) *Prosecutor v. Bagosora et al.*, ICTR-98-41-A, Decision on Interlocutory Appeal from Refusal to Reconsider Decisions Relating to Protective Measures and Application for a Declaration of "Lack of Jurisdiction", 2 May 2002, para. 10.

(5) See, for instance, *Prosecutor v. Mucic, Delic and Landzo*, Case No. IT-96-21-A*bis*, Judgment on Sentence, 8 April 2003, para. 49; *Prosecutor v. Semanza*, Case No. ICTR-97-20-A, Decision on Appeal against the Oral Decision Dismissing the Motion to Review, 16 April 2002.

(6) *Prosecutor against Rwamakuba*, Case No. ICTR-98-44C-T, Decision on Prosecutor Motion for Variation, or in the Alternative Reconsideration of the Decision on Protective Measures for Defence Witnesses, 2 November 2005.

(7) *Id.* para. 4.

(8) *Prosecutor v. Renzaho*, Case No. ICTR-97-31-I, decision on Renzaho's Motion to Reconsider the Decision on Protective Measures for Victims and witnesses to Crimes Alleged in the Indictment, 9 November 2005, paras 20-21.

(9) *Id.* para 21. See also *Prosecutor v. Bizimungu, Ndindiliyimana, Nzuwonemeye and Sagahutu*, Case No. ICTR-00-56-T, Decision on Bizimungu's Motion in Opposition to the Admissibility of the Testimonies of Witnesses LMC, BB, GS, CJ/ANL and GFO and for Reconsideration of the Chamber's Decision of 13 May 2005, 24 November 2005, paras. 18-19. See also *Prosecutor v. Karemera, Ngirumpatse and Nzirorera*, Case No. ICTR-98-44-PT, Decision on the Defence Motions for Reconsideration of Protective Measures for Prosecution Witnesses, 29 August 2005, para. 8.

- **Rule 73(B): Motions – Interlocutory Appeal – Purpose of the Requirement for a Leave to Appeal**

R73-TC-19
o *Prosecutor v. Kallon*, Case No. SCSL-03-07-PT, Decision on the Defence Application for Leave to Appeal 'Decision on the Prosecution's Motion for Immediate Protective Measures for Witnesses and Victims and for Non-Public Disclosure, 10 December 2003, para. 36:

36. The Trial chamber observes that the special Court is a jurisdiction with a limited duration of three years and that appeals on interlocutories, unless good reason is shown for a real necessity or legal justification to grant them, should not be allowed to undertake a premature and speculative journey to the Appeals Chamber for adjudication since this option, it should be conceded, is very time consuming and therefore, inconsistent and incompatible with, and also prejudicial to what an expeditious trial is supposed to achieve and which the Applicant wants the Chamber to believe, he is targeting.

R73-TC-20 o *Prosecutor v. Sesay, Kallon, Gbao*, Case No. SCSL-04-15-T, Decision on the Defence Applications for Leave to Appeal Ruling of the 3rd of February, 2005 on the Exclusion of Statements of Witness TF1-141, 28 April 2005, para. 14:

14. The present Applications confront the Chamber once more with the delicate judicial task faced by international criminal tribunals of how to balance the due process rights of the Accused, which include pre-eminently that of a fair and expeditious trial, with the interests of the international community in not having criminal trials bogged down or encumbered by a plethora of interlocutory appeals thereby causing protracted delays in bringing the accused persons to justice.

- **Rule 73(B): Motions – Interlocutory Appeal – Standards for Leave to Appeal Interlocutory Decisions**

R73-TC-21 o *Prosecutor v. Sesay, Kallon, Gbao*, Case No. SCSL-04-15-PT, Decision on Prosecution's Application for Leave to File an Interlocutory Appeal Against the Decision on the Prosecution Motions for Joinder, 13 February 2004, para. 9-15:[112]

---

[112] See also *Prosecutor v. Brima, Kamara, Kanu*, Case No. SCSL-04-16-PT, Decision on Prosecution's Application for Leave to File an Interlocutory Appeal Against the Decision on the Prosecution Motions for Joinder, 13 February 2004, para. 12-18; *Prosecutor v. Sesay, Kallon and Gbao*, Case No. SCSL-04-15-PT, Decision on the Prosecution Application for Leave to File an Interlocutory Appeal Against Decision on Motion for Concurrent Hearing of Evidence Common to Cases SCSL-2004-15-PT and SCSL-2004-16-PT, 1 June 2004, para. 20-21; *Prosecutor v. Brima, Kamara, Kanu*, Case No. SCSL-04-16-PT, Decision on Prosecution Application for Leave to File an Interlocutory Appeal Against Decision on Motion for Concurrent Hearing of Evidence Common to Cases SCSL-2004-15-PT and SCSL-2004-16-PT, 1 June 2004, para. 18-19; *Prosecutor v. Norman, Fofana, Kondewa*, Case No. SCSL-04-14-T, Majority Decision on the Prosecution's Application for Leave to File an Interlocutory Appeal Against the Decision on the Prosecution's Request for Leave to Amend the Indictment Against Samuel Hinga Norman, Moinina Fofana and Allieu Kondewa, 2 August 2004, para. 21-23; *Prosecutor v. Gbao*, Case No. SCSL-04-15-T, Decision on Application for Leave to Appeal Decision on Application to Withdraw Counsel, 4 August 2004, para. 35, 39; *Prosecutor v. Norman, Fofana, Kondewa*, No. SCSL-04-14-T, Decision on Joint Request to Appeal Against Decision on Prosecutor's Motion for Judicial Notice, 19 October 2004, para. 13-14; *Prosecutor v. Kanu*, Case No. SCSL-04-16-PT, Decision on Application for Leave to File an Interlocutory Appeal Against Decision on Motions for Exclusion of Prosecution Witness Statements and Stay on Filing of Prosecution Statements, 4 February 2005; *Prosecutor v. Sesay, Kallon, Gbao*, Case No. SCSL-04-15-T, Decision on the Defence Applications for Leave to Appeal Ruling of the 3rd of February, 2005 on the Exclusion of Statements of Witness TF1-141, 28 April 2005, para. 17-19; *Prosecutor*

9. In addressing the key aspects of Rule 73(B), the Chamber wishes to emphasise at the outset that the first part of Rule 73(B) contains a clear statement of the general position in relation to interlocutory appeals. The second part of that Rule creates an extremely limited exception to this general position.

10. As a general rule, interlocutory decisions are not appealable and consistent with a clear and unambiguous legislative intent, this rule involves a high threshold that must be met before this Chamber can exercise its discretion to grant leave to appeal. The two limbs to the test are clearly conjunctive, not disjunctive; in other words, they must both be satisfied.

11. This interpretation is unavoidable, given the fact that the second limb of Rule 73(B) was added by way of an amendment adopted at the August 2003 Plenary. This is underscored by the fact that prior to that amendment no possibility of interlocutory appeal existed and the amendment was carefully couched in such terms so as only to allow appeals to proceed in very limited and exceptional situations. In effect, it is a restrictive provision.

12. The Chamber also notes that the amendment to Rule 73(B) created a novel test for granting leave to interlocutory appeal, as the requirement of "exceptional circumstances" does not feature in similar provisions in the Rules of the International Criminal Tribunal for the former Yugoslavia ("ICTY") and the International Criminal Tribunal for Rwanda ("ICTR"). The relevant provision in the Rules of those Tribunals states that:

---

v. Kallon, Case No. SCSL-04-15-T, Decision on Application for Leave for Interlocutory Appeal Against the Majority Decision of the Trial Chamber of the 9th December 2004 on the Motion on Issues of Urgent Concern to the Accused Morris Kallon, 2 May 2005, para. 16-17; *Prosecutor v. Norman*, Case No. SCSL-04-14-T, Decision on Request by the First Accused for Leave to Appeal Against the Trial Chamber's Decision on Presentation of Witness Testimony on Moyamba Crime Base, 23 May 2005; *Prosecutor v. Norman*, Case No. SCSL-04-14-T, Decision on Request by the First Accused for Leave to Appeal Against the Trial Chamber's Decision on First Accused's Motion on Abuse of Process, 24 May 2005; *Prosecutor v. Brima, Kamara, Kanu*, Case No. SCSL-04-16-T, Decision on Joint Defence Application to Appeal Against the Ruling of Trial Chamber II of 5 April 2005, 15 June 2005, para. 14; *Prosecutor v. Norman*, Case No. SCSL-04-14-T, Decision on Defence Request for Leave to Appeal Against the Consequential Non-Arraignment Order of Trial Chamber I, 18 May 2005, 25 July 2005; *Prosecutor v. Brima, Kamara, Kanu*, Case No. SCSL-04-16-T, Decision on Joint Defence Application for Leave to Appeal from Decision on Defence Motion to Exclude All Evidence from Witness TF1-277, 2 August 2005, para. 8-9; *Prosecutor v. Brima, Kamara*, Case No. SCSL-04-16-T, Decision on Brima-Kamara Application for Leave to Appeal from Decision on the Re-Appointment of Kevin Metzger and Wilbert Harris as Lead Counsel, 5 August 2005; *Prosecutor v. Brima, Kamara, Kanu*, Case No. SCSL-04-16-T, Decision on Prosecution Application for Leave to Appeal Decision on Oral Application for Witness TF1-150 to Testify Without Being Compelled to Answer Questions on Grounds of Confidentiality, 12 October 2005.

"Decisions on all motions are without interlocutory appeal save with certification by the Trial Chamber, which may grant such certification if the decision involves an issue that would significantly affect the fair and expeditious conduct of the proceedings or the outcome of the trial, and for which, in the opinion of the Trial Chamber, an immediate resolution by the Appeals Chamber may materially advance the proceedings."[1]

This Chamber must apply an entirely new and considerably more restrictive test than the one applied by the ICTR or the ICTY. Furthermore, the only relevant decision of the Special Court to date applied the earlier version of Rule 73(B).[2] There is therefore the need for an authoritative statement by the Chamber on the implication and effect of the amended rule. Nevertheless, this restriction is in line with the trend and our determination to tighten the test for granting leave in respect of interlocutory appeals in the interests of expeditiousness. The further restriction is appropriate and acceptable in the peculiar circumstances of the Special Court whose mandate, we must observe, is limited in its duration.

13. It is clear then from a plain reading of Rule 73(B) that granting leave is an exceptional option. As this is an exclusionary rule, if the two-limb test has been complied with, the Prosecution must demonstrate that there is something to justify the exercise of this discretion by the Chamber in its favour.

14. In the Motion before the Chamber, the Prosecution submissions focus primarily on the question of "irreparable prejudice to a party", which is only the second limb of the test in Rule 73(B) which the Chamber must apply. The Prosecution has failed to make substantive references to "exceptional circumstances", and the Chamber has no basis to conclude that any exceptional circumstances have been established.

15. Based on the foregoing, and having found that no exceptional circumstances have been articulated by the Prosecution to warrant additional comments, it would not be necessary to address the question of irreparable prejudice given that the test is conjunctive. The Chamber, however, notes that the main submissions of the Prosecution on this point relate mostly to questions such as cost and security of witnesses, the order in which the trials commence, and the fairness of the trials if they are heard before a single Trial Chamber. It has been suggested by the Prosecution that there might be some added difficulties in the management of the Prosecution case, some additional work and possibly problems if this application for leave to appeal were turned down, but nothing that has been shown in our view to constitute "irreparable prejudice".

---

[1] ICTY Rules of Procedure and Evidence, adopted 11 February 1994, as amended 17 July 2003 and ICTR Rules of Procedure and Evidence, adopted

29 June 1995, as amended 27 May 2003, common Rule 73 (B) [Other Motions]. This certification procedure was added in 2002 in the ICTY, (prior to which leave applications were decided by a bench of 3 Appeal Chamber judges on the basis of incurable prejudice or "if the issue in the proposal appeal is of general importance to proceedings before the Tribunal or in international law generally"), and in the ICTR in May 2003 (prior to which there was no interlocutory appeal on Motions).
(2) *Prosecutor v. Morris Kallon*, Decision on the Defence Application for Leave to Appeal, 10 Dec. 2003.

R73-TC-22

o *Prosecutor v. Sesay, Kallon and Gbao*, Case No. SCSL-04-15-PT, Decision on the Prosecution Application for Leave to File an Interlocutory Appeal Against Decision on Motion for Concurrent Hearing of Evidence Common to Cases SCSL-2004-15-PT and SCSL-2004-16-PT, 1 June 2004, para. 21-22:[113]

21. [. . .] [T]he overriding legal consideration in respect of an application for leave to file an interlocutory appeal is that the applicant's case must reach a level of exceptional circumstances and irreparable prejudice. Nothing short of that will suffice having regard to the restrictive nature of Rule 73(B) of the Rules and the rationale that criminal trials must not be heavily encumbered and consequently unduly delayed by interlocutory appeals.

22. As we noted in those Decisions, our test for granting leave to file interlocutory appeals is more restrictive in comparison with that applied by International Criminal Tribunal for the former Yugoslavia and the International Criminal Tribunal for Rwanda in the interest of expeditiousness and the peculiar circumstances of this Court's limited mandate. [. . .]

---

[113] See also *Prosecutor v. Brima, Kamara, Kanu*, Case No. SCSL-04-16-PT, Decision on Prosecution Application for Leave to File an Interlocutory Appeal Against Decision on Motion for Concurrent Hearing of Evidence Common to Cases SCSL-2004-15-PT and SCSL-2004-16-PT, 1 June 2004, para. 20; *Prosecutor v. Norman, Fofana, Kondewa*, Case No. SCSL-04-14-T, Majority Decision on the Prosecution's Application for Leave to File an Interlocutory Appeal Against the Decision on the Prosecution's Request for Leave to Amend the Indictment Against Samuel Hinga Norman, Moinina Fofana and Allieu Kondewa, 2 August 2004, para. 24; *Prosecutor v. Gbao*, Case No. SCSL-04-15-T, Decision on Application for Leave to Appeal Decision on Application to Withdraw Counsel, 4 August 2004, para. 38; *Prosecutor v. Norman, Fofana, Kondewa*, Case No. SCSL-04-14-T, Decision on Prosecution Application for Leave to Appeal "Decision on the First Accused's Motion for Service and Arraignment on the Consolidated Indictment", 15 December 2004; *Prosecutor v. Sesay*, Case No. SCSL-04-15-T, Decision on Application for Leave to Appeal the Ruling (2nd May 2005) on Sesay Motion Seeking Disclosure of the Relationship Between Governmental Agencies of the United States of America and the Office of the Prosecutor, 15 June 2005, para. 15.

R73-TC-23

o *Prosecutor v. Norman, Fofana, Kondewa*, Case No. SCSL-04-14-T, Majority Decision on the Prosecution's Application for Leave to File an Interlocutory Appeal Against the Decision on the Prosecution's Request for Leave to Amend the Indictment Against Samuel Hinga Norman, Moinina Fofana and Allieu Kondewa, 2 August 2004, para. 33:

> 33. We would like to re-emphasise that the test applicable by this Tribunal in considering applications for leave to file interlocutory appeals "is more restrictive in comparison with that applied by the International Criminal Tribunal for Rwanda and the International Tribunal for former Yugoslavia and to state that in the interests of expeditiousness and the peculiar circumstances of this Court's limited mandate".[1] [...]

[1] Decision on Concurrent Hearing of Evidence, *supra* note 29, para. 22.

R73-TC-24

o *Prosecutor v. Sesay, Kallon, Gbao*, Case No. SCSL-04-15-T, Decision on the Defence Applications for Leave to Appeal Ruling of the 3rd of February, 2005 on the Exclusion of Statements of Witness TF1-141, 28 April 2005, para. 30:

> 30. Having thus found that no legally sustainable "exceptional circumstances" have been articulated by both Counsel for the First Accused and for the Third Accused to warrant additional analysis, it would be unnecessary to address the issue of "irreparable prejudice" given that the test is conjunctive.[1] It may, however, be pointed out that, as a matter of law, wrongful admission of evidence cannot cause, "irreparable prejudice" to the rights of an Accused person to a fair trial since it can, depending on the particular facts and circumstances of the case and the nature of the evidence, properly be a ground for reversal, in the event of a conviction. It cannot, therefore, be plausibly contended that the wrongful admission of evidence is a matter that "cannot be cured or resolved by final appeal against judgement."[2]

[1] *Prosecutor v. Sesay, Kallon and Gbao*, Case No. SCSL-04-15-PT, and *Prosecutor v. Brima, Kamara and Kanu*, Case No SCSL-2004-16-PT, Decision on Prosecution Application For Leave To File An Interlocutory Appeal Against Decision On Motion For Concurrent Hearing of Evidence Common to Cases SCSL-2004-15-PT and SCSL-2004-16-PT, 1 June 2004, para. 24.
[2] Appeals Chamber Decision, supra note 23.

R73-TC-25

o *Prosecutor v. Kallon*, Case No. SCSL-04-15-T, Decision on Application for Leave for Interlocutory Appeal Against the Majority Decision of the Trial Chamber of the 9th December 2004 on the Motion on Issues of Urgent Concern to the Accused Morris Kallon, 2 May 2005, para. 16-17:[114]

16. In a series of recent Decisions given by this Chamber on the subject of interlocutory appeals, we enunciated the principles of law governing the issue granting leave to file an interlocutory appeals within the jurisdiction of the Special Court for Sierra Leone.

17. The said principles may be summarised as follows:

(i) As a general rule, interlocutory decisions are not appealable;[1]
(ii) Rule 73 (B) involves a high threshold that must be met before the Chamber can exercise its discretion to grant leave to appeal;[2]
(iii) Rule 73 (B) specifically requires that an application for leave to appeal must show "exceptional circumstances" and "irreparable prejudice";
(iv) The two-pronged test prescribed under the aforesaid Rule 73 (B) is conjunctive not disjunctive;[3]
(v) The rationale behind Rule 73 (B) is to avoid international criminal trials becoming encumbered by a multiplicity of interlocutory appeals thereby causing protracted delays in such trials.[4]

---

[1] See, for example, *Prosecutor v. Sesay et al.*, Case No. SCSL-04-15-PT, Decision On Prosecution's Application For Leave To File An Interlocutory Appeal Against the Decision On the Prosecution's Motion For Joinder, 13 February 2004, para. 10.
[2] *Id.*
[3] *Id.*
[4] *Prosecutor v. Sesay et al.*, Case No. SCSL-04-15-T, Applications for Leave to Appeal Rulings of the 3rd of February, 2005, on the Exclusion of Statements of Witness TF1-141, para. 14.

---

[114] See also *Prosecutor v. Sesay*, Case No. SCSL-04-15-T, Decision on Application for Leave to Appeal the Ruling (2nd May 2005) on Sesay Motion Seeking Disclosure of the Relationship Between Governmental Agencies of the United States of America and the Office of the Prosecutor, 15 June 2005, para. 17.

- **Rule 73(B): Motions – Interlocutory Appeal – Standards for Leave to Appeal – "Exceptional Circumstances"**

R73-TC-26

o *Prosecutor v. Sesay, Kallon and Gbao*, Case No. SCSL-04-15-PT, Decision on the Prosecution Application for Leave to File an Interlocutory Appeal Against Decision on Motion for Concurrent Hearing of Evidence Common to Cases SCSL-2004-15-PT and SCSL-2004-16-PT, 1 June 2004, para. 23:[115]

> 23. [...] The Chamber fails to see how the fact that one hundred and fifty witnesses will have to testify in two separate trials in a relatively short period of time to the exact same facts which constitute the most atrocious violations of international criminal law to which they were victims or witnesses, as alleged by the Prosecution, before a court located in the country where the violations, allegedly took place coupled with, as the Prosecution submits, the likelihood of re-traumatization do constitute "exceptional circumstances" for the purposes of Rule 73(B) of the Rules especially in the light of the Chamber's analysis at paragraphs 34-39 of the Decision in question. In what lies the exceptionality, considering the entitlement in law of each accused to a separate trial barring a joinder decision? These contingencies may create some inconveniences and hardships but do not, singly or cumulatively, amount to "exceptional circumstances" in the context of Rule 73(B) of the Rules, taking into account the Orders for witnesses' protective measures[(1)] and the expert services of the Victims and Witnesses Unit of the Special Court including the psychological counselling component of such services. The claim of "exceptional circumstances" by the Prosecution is legally unsustainable, and therefore fails.
>
> _____
>
> [(1)] *Prosecutor v. Issa Hassan Sesay*, SCSL-03-05-PT, Decision on the Prosecutor's Motion for Immediate Protective Measures for Witnesses and Victims and for Non-Public Disclosure, 23 May 2003; *Prosecutor v. Morris Kallon*, SCSL-03-07-PT, Decision on the Prosecutor's Motion for Immediate Protective Measures for Witnesses and Victims and for Non-Public Disclosure, 23 May 2003; *Prosecutor v. Augustine Gbao*, SCSL-03-09-PT, Decision on the Prosecution Motion for Immediate Protective Measures for Witnesses and Victims and for Non-Public Disclosure, 10 October 2003.

_____

[115] See also *Prosecutor v. Brima, Kamara, Kanu*, Case No. SCSL-04-16-PT, Decision on Prosecution Application for Leave to File an Interlocutory Appeal Against Decision on Motion for Concurrent Hearing of Evidence Common to Cases SCSL-2004-15-PT and SCSL-2004-16-PT, 1 June 2004, para. 21.

R73-TC-27 o *Prosecutor v. Norman, Fofana, Kondewa,* Case No. SCSL-04-14-T, Majority Decision on the Prosecution's Application for Leave to File an Interlocutory Appeal Against the Decision on the Prosecution's Request for Leave to Amend the Indictment Against Samuel Hinga Norman, Moinina Fofana and Allieu Kondewa, 2 August 2004, para. 27-29:

27. In this regard, it is submitted by the Prosecution that a strong and articulate dissenting opinion by a member of the Trial Chamber may itself constitute the exceptional circumstance warranting the granting of the application. Although this proposition sounds interesting and novel, the Prosecution has failed to elaborate on it thereby leaving the Chamber with no option but to observe that such a view is neither supported by case-law authority nor is it grounded on any legal foundation.

28. It would, in our opinion, be erroneous to hold that every legal situation or variable which appears to be novel or unique should, for that reason, qualify as "exceptional circumstances" within the meaning of Rule 73(B). We would only want to observe in this regard, that disagreements amongst Judges on some of the multi-faceted legal and factual issues which constitute the core of legal disputes is a normal judicial feature that is inherent in the exercise by the Judges of judicial independence on which the administration of justice is, and will continue to be, based.

29. The second key submission put forward by the Prosecution is that the high profile nature of gender based crimes under international law constitutes an exceptional circumstance given its statutory duty "to prosecute to the full extent of the law and to present before the court all relevant evidence reflecting the totality of crimes committed by the Accused". In the Chamber's view, the fact that the counts sought to be incorporated in the Indictment by the way of the amendment are gender based crimes, cannot be the sole determinant or overriding variable in working out the "exceptional circumstances" equation as to whether or not to grant leave to appeal [. . .].

R73-TC-28 o *Prosecutor v. Sesay, Kallon, Gbao,* Case No. SCSL-04-15-T, Decision on the Defence Applications for Leave to Appeal Ruling of the 3rd of February, 2005 on the Exclusion of Statements of Witness TF1-141, 28 April 2005, para. 25-29:

25. As already noted, the Defence is virtually arguing the substantive merits of the projected appeal and advancing the

argument that the alleged erroneous nature of the Ruling is tantamount to "exceptional circumstances." In this regard, it must be asserted that this Chamber has studiously refrained from embarking on any comprehensive or exhaustive definition of the concept of "exceptional circumstances" primarily because the notion is one that does not lend itself to a fixed meaning. Nor can it be plausibly maintained that the categories of "exceptional circumstances" are closed or fixed. It is, however, appropriate at this stage, to observe that what constitutes "exceptional circumstances" must necessarily depend on, and vary with, the circumstances of each case.[1]

26. "Exceptional circumstances" may exist depending upon the particular facts and circumstances, where, for instance the question in relation to which leave to appeal is sought is one of general principle to be decided for the first time, or is a question of public international law importance upon which further argument or decision at the appellate level would be conducive to the interests of justice, or where the cause of justice might be interfered with, or is one that raises serious issues of fundamental legal importance to the Special Court for Sierra Leone, in particular, or international criminal law, in general,[2] or some novel and substantial aspect of international criminal law for which no guidance can be derived from national criminal law systems.

27. Further, addressing the issue for determination, it is the Chamber's view, therefore, that the critical question for determination, at this stage, is whether, in relation to the first part of the conjunctive test prescribed under Rule 73(B), the Defence has shown "exceptional circumstances" to justify the granting of leave by the Chamber, taking into account the exposition of the law in the foregoing paragraphs. Admittedly, showing "exceptional circumstances" does not automatically entitle the party seeking leave to the order sought. The test, we reiterate, is conjunctive in the sense that there must also be a showing of "irreparable prejudice".

28. Has the Defence, therefore, established "exceptional circumstances" to warrant the granting of leave to appeal against the impugned Decision? The Defence allege that the Trial Chamber erred in law in concluding that the "Defence has failed to demonstrate or substantiate by prima facie proof the allegations of breach of the Prosecution of Rule 66(A)(ii) of the Rules, Article 17(4) of the Statute and the Chamber's Order for Disclosure".[3] It is also contended by the Defence that the Ruling is "a breach of the spirit and purpose (if not letter) of Rule 66 and more fundamentally of the Accused" rights pursuant to Article 17(4)."[4]

29. Based on the foregoing considerations, it is the Chamber's considered view, and we so hold, that no exceptional circumstances have been established. That the probability of an

erroneous ruling on the admissibility of evidence, without more, especially in light of the primacy given to the principle of extensive admissibility of evidence in the practice of international criminal tribunals, as opposed to the doctrine of strict adherence to the technical rules of admissibility applicable in some national law systems, cannot constitute "exceptional circumstances" for the purposes of a Rule 73(B) application. Furthermore, as previously stated, when deciding the admissibility of evidence, leave to appeal has to be the absolute exception, and in our opinion this has certainly not been demonstrated. Needless to mention that it would be premature for the Chamber, at this stage, to determine or speculate upon the issue of the probative value of the evidence whose admissibility is being challenged by the Defence in the projected appeal.[5]

---

[1] See also *Prosecutor v. Norman et al.*, Case No. SCSL-04-14-T, Majority Decision on the Prosecution's Application for Leave to File an Interlocutory Appeal Against the Decision on the Prosecution's Request for Leave to Amend the Indictment Against Samuel Hinga Norman, Moinina Fofana and Allieu Kondewa, 2 August 2004, para. 22. In interpreting the concept of "exceptional circumstances", the European Court of Human Rights stated that it "is capable of being interpreted and applied in a wide variety of ways in the absence of a more precise statutory definition of the circumstances." See *H v. Belgium*, ECHR, 1/1986/99/147, 28 October 1987.

[2] See, for instance, *Prosecutor v. Sesay et al.*, Case No SCSL-04-15-T, Decision on Application for Leave to Appeal Gbao – Decision on Application to Withdraw Counsel, 4 August 2004, para. 55-57; *Prosecution v. Norman et al.*, Case No. SCSL-04-14-T, Decision on Joint Request for Leave to Appeal Against Decision on Prosecution's Motion for Judicial Notice, 19 October 2004, para. 20; See also *id*, Decision on Application by First Accused for Leave to Make Interlocutory Appeal Against the Decision on the First Accused's Motion for Service and Arraignment on the Consolidated Indictment, 16 December 2004. The ECHR found exceptional circumstances in situations where public safety my be affected or where there is a serious risk that the course of justice might be interfered with. See *Clooth v. Belgium*, ECHR, 49/1990/240/311, 27 November 1991 and *The Sunday Times*, ECHR, 29 March 1979.

[3] *Sesay's* Application, para. 2; Gbao's Application, para. 2.

[4] *Sesay's* Application, para. 3.

[5] See also *Nyiramasuhuko* Decision, para. 8:
"... the admission into evidence does not in any way constitute a binding determination as to the authenticity or trustworthiness of the documents sought to be admitted. These are to be assessed by the Trial Chamber at a later stage in the case when assessing the probative weight to be attached to the evidence".

R73-TC-29   o *Prosecutor v. Kallon,* Case No. SCSL-04-15-T, Decision on Application for Leave for Interlocutory Appeal Against the Majority Decision of the Trial Chamber of the 9th December 2004 on the Motion on Issues of Urgent Concern to the Accused Morris Kallon, 2 May 2005, para. 20-21:

20. As to the merit or otherwise of submissions of this nature, the Chamber recently held that (1) a submission that the targeted ruling is erroneous is an invitation to the tribunal to whom the request for leave is addressed to examine preliminarily the substantive merit of the projected appeal, and (2) that the probability of an erroneous ruling by the Trial Chamber does not, of itself, constitute "exceptional circumstances" for the purposes of a Rule 73 (B) application.[1] By parity of reasoning, we see no reason to depart from that holding in the context of the present Motion.

21. The Chamber therefore, holds that the Applicant has failed to establish "exceptional circumstances" to warrant an exercise by the Chamber of its discretion under Rule 73 (B) to grant leave for interlocutory appeal. The application is meretricious.

---

[1] *Prosecutor v. Sesay et al.*, Case No. SCSL-04-15-T, Applications for Leave to Appeal Rulings of the 3rd of February, 2005, on the Exclusion of Statements of Witness TF1-141, paras 15 and 16.

- **Rule 73(B): Motions – Interlocutory Appeal – Standards for Leave to Appeal – "Exceptional Circumstances" – Dissenting Opinions**

R73-TC-30 o *Prosecutor v. Norman, Fofana, Kondewa*, Case No. SCSL-04-14-T, Decision on Prosecution Application for Leave to Appeal "Decision on the First Accused's Motion for Service and Arraignment on the Consolidated Indictment", 15 December 2004:[116]

CONVINCED ALSO of the controversial nature of the specific issues addressed by the Trial Chamber in the Decision which is the subject of the application herein and the diverse legal perspectives from which they can be viewed as evidenced by the Majority Decision, Separate Concurring Opinion, and Dissenting Opinion of the Judges of the Trial Bench; and that it does not conduce to the overall interests of justice and the preservation of the integrity of the proceedings to leave the law on such important issues in international criminal adjudication unsettled and in a state of uncertainty;

---

[116] See also *Prosecutor v. Norman*, Case No. SCSL-04-14-T, Decision on Application by First Accused for Leave to Make Interlocutory Appeal Against the Decision on the First Accused's Motion for Service and Arraignment on the Consolidated Indictment, 16 December 2004.

CONSIDERING that the difference of legal opinion expressed by the Judges on the Decision on Norman's Indictment on issues of such fundamental importance constitute exceptional circumstances;

R73-TC-31

o *Prosecutor v. Norman*, Case No. SCSL-04-14-T, Decision on Request by the First Accused for Leave to Appeal Against the Trial Chamber's Decision on First Accused's Motion on Abuse of Process, 24 May 2005:

CONSIDERING that the fact of existence of differing opinions amongst the Judges of the Trial Chamber on one aspect of the applicable law in the Impugned Decision[1] does not in itself constitute an exceptional circumstance and that the nature and significance of this Decision is relevant to this determination;

---

[1] Motion, para. 7 addressing *functus officio* and *res judicata*.

R73-TC-32

o *Prosecutor v. Sesay*, Case No. SCSL-04-15-T, Decision on Application for Leave to Appeal the Ruling (2nd May 2005) on Sesay Motion Seeking Disclosure of the Relationship Between Governmental Agencies of the United States of America and the Office of the Prosecutor, 15 June 2005, para. 19:

19. As already noted, Counsel for the First Accused submits forcefully that the Partially Dissenting Opinion from the Decision bears a direct relationship to "the criteria of exceptionality which governs the grant of leave to appeal pursuant to Rule 73(B)." The Chamber's response to this submission is threefold. First, that, analytically, the precise legal meaning of this assertion seems incomprehensible. Second, the submission lacks lucidity as to the presumed legal or logical nexus between the notion of "exceptional circumstances" as stated in the Rule and the Partially Dissenting Opinion in terms of its thrust and focus. Third, the Chamber has ruled before that the fact that there is a dissenting opinion on the issue or issues forming the subject matter of the intended appeal does not, of itself, constitute "exceptional circumstances" within the letter and spirit of Rule 73(B). This finding was recently confirmed by the Appeals Chamber.[1]

---

[1] *Prosecutor v. Norman, Fofana and Kondewa*, SCSL-04-14-AR73, Decision on Amendment of the Consolidated Indictment, 16 May 2005, para. 43.

- **Rule 73(B): Motions – Interlocutory Appeal – Standards for Leave to Appeal – "Irreparable Prejudice"**

R73-TC-33

o *Prosecutor v. Norman, Fofana, Kondewa*, No. SCSL-04-14-T, Decision on Joint Request to Appeal Against Decision on Prosecutor's Motion for Judicial Notice, 19 October 2004, para. 21, 23-24:

21. Based on the finding that the application for the Second Accused has met the first arm of the test required by Rule 73(B) of the Rules, the Chamber will now proceed further with the evaluation as to whether the second arm of the said test, namely the irreparable prejudice, has been satisfied.

[...]

23. The second arm of the threshold test contained in Rule 73(B) is indeed a more complex one, requiring that the determination not only may result in a prejudice to the accused but also that such prejudice is irreparable in that it may not be remediable by appropriate means within the final disposition of the trial.

24. Indeed, it is submitted by the Accused that such irreparable prejudice could or would result from the improper application within the Decision of criteria for the determination of facts of common knowledge unless it will be subject of proper remediation through a further decision, as judicial guarantee, by the Appeals Chamber for which leave to appeal against an interlocutory ruling should be granted. Having reviewed the submissions made in this Motion, the Chamber finds that a resolution from the Appeals Chamber at this stage of the contentions in issue is indeed necessary to provide an appropriate judicial guarantee on the state of the contested findings of the Decision and in particular, on the application of the criteria for judicial notice laid down therein.

R73-TC-34

o *Prosecutor v. Gbao*, Case No. SCSL-04-15-T, Decision on Application for Leave to Appeal Decision on Application to Withdraw Counsel, 4 August 2004, para. 58-59:

58. The Defence and the Prosecution have also submitted that irreparable prejudice will occur of leave is not granted to appeal the Gbao decision. Since the Decision was delivered, the Accused Gbao has not attended trial proceedings. He has also chosen not to provide instructions to his counsel who continue to represent him in accordance with the Court's order.

59. This Chamber acknowledges that the conduct of the Accused has placed Defence Counsel in a difficult position since, as they have stated, they would normally be professionally embarrassed by the Accused's refusal to provide instructions which could, *inter alia*, serve in enhancing their cross-examination of Prosecution witnesses and eventually the examination-in-chief and re-examination of Defence witnesses. While the chamber does note that the Accused has chosen not to recognise the Special Court and has accordingly decided neither to attend proceedings nor to instruct Counsel, it accepts that irreparable prejudice may arise in these circumstances if leave to appeal were not granted.

- **Rule 73(B): Motions – Interlocutory Appeal – Standards for Leave to Appeal – "Issue of General Importance"**

R73-TC-35

o *Prosecutor v. Gbao*, Case No. SCSL-04-15-T, Decision on Application for Leave to Appeal Decision on Application to Withdraw Counsel, 4 August 2004, para. 54-55, 57:

54. Both the Defence and Prosecution have submitted that exceptional circumstances exist in this case due to the very nature of the request by an accused to exercise his right to self-representation and, we add, the appointment of standby Counsel by the Court. They also point out that a decision of the Appeals Chamber on the issues of self-representation and withdrawal of counsel could provide useful guidance on very complex and important issues.

55. This Chamber agrees that the right of an accused to represent him or herself is a fundamental right and an essential component of due process. It is also cognisant that there is no appellate case law in international criminal fora that have addressed the important issues of withdrawal of counsel and self-representation of accused persons and that could provide guidance on this matter. Viewed from this perspective, the results of the proposed appeal would be "of general importance ... in international law".[1]

[...]

57. Having regard to the foregoing and in the interests of justice, we find that the issues raised in the submissions are of fundamental nature and constitute exceptional circumstances. Moreover, a decision from our Appeals Chamber would provide useful guidelines for the future in such situations and would contribute to the advancement of the jurisprudence of international criminal law on the very important issues

raised, this time, in total agreement by the rarely concordant choruses of the Prosecution and the Defence.

---

(1) Prior version of Rule 73(B) of the Rules of Procedure and Evidence of the ICTY.

- **Rule 73(B): Motions – Interlocutory Appeal – Standards for Leave to Appeal – Appeal on Protective Measures**

R73-TC-36 o *Prosecutor v. Kallon*, Case No. SCSL-03-07-PT, Decision on the Defence Application for Leave to Appeal 'Decision on the Prosecution's Motion for Immediate Protective Measures for Witnesses and Victims and for Non-Public Disclosure, 10 December 2003, para. 17-18:

17. The Chamber is therefore mindful of the need for the protection of and respect for the rights of the victims and witnesses when considering the interests of the public and of the international community while examining cases of this nature and to ensure that persons accused of violations of international humanitarian law be brought to trial, whilst at the same time, guaranteeing on the other hand, the paramount rights recognised under the principles of due process to which the accused is entitled in the conduct of his defence.

18. Consequently, in deciding on the issue of whether or not to grant leave to appeal on these matters, the Chamber considers matters relating to protective measures, their consequences for the witnesses and victims and the resulting effect on the rights of the Accused, as being equally predominantly important.

- **Rule 73(B): Motions – Leave to Appeal – Irrelevance of Grounds of Appeal in the Application for Leave to Appeal**

R73-TC-37 o *Prosecutor v. Sesay, Kallon, Gbao*, Case No. SCSL-04-15-T, Decision on the Defence Applications for Leave to Appeal Ruling of the 3rd of February, 2005 on the Exclusion of Statements of Witness TF1-141, 28 April 2005, para. 15-16:

15. Both Defence Counsel in their Motions, and the Prosecution in its subsequent Consolidated Response, appear to be attempting or seeking to re-litigate and expand the issues already presented orally before the court and disposed of in the Ruling. In addition, both requests for leave do incorporate

the proposed grounds of appeal which, having regard to the principle of judicial hierarchy, are premature and irrelevant in determining whether the prescribed test in Rule 73(B) for leave to appeal has been met.[1]

16. Unquestionably, the only relevant issue for determination by the Chamber is whether the Defence have met the requirements for leave to appeal as prescribed by Rule 73(B). Any other submissions not germane to that issue are, for the purposes of the present Applications, irrelevant and immaterial.

---

[1] See, for instance, *Sesay's* Application, paras 8-19; *Gbao's* Application, paras 7-8, and 12-14. On the subject of interlocutory appeals, the International Criminal Tribunal for Rwanda has also condemned the practice of the parties of re-litigating the main thrust of submissions on which an impugned decision was rendered within an application for leave for interlocutory appeals, as well as proposing possible grounds of appeal in the same context. See *Prosecutor v. Nyiramasuhuko et al.*, Case No. ICTR-98-42-T, Decision on Prosecutor's Motion for Certification to Appeal the Decision of the Trial Chamber dated 30 November 2004 on the Prosecution Motion for Disclosure of Evidence of the Defence, 4 February 2005, paras 11-12; *Prosecutor v. Bizimungu et al.*, Case No. ICTR-99-50-T, Decision on Bicamumpaka's Request Pursuant to Rule 73 for Certification to Appeal the 1 December 2004 "Decision on the Motion of Bicamumpaka and Mugenzi for Disclosure of Relevant Material", 4 February 2005, para. 28.

- **Rule 73(B): Motions – Leave to Appeal – Time Limit for Filing Interlocutory Appeal – Separate Opinions**

R73-TC-38

o *Prosecutor v. Norman, Fofana, Kondewa*, Case No. SCSL-04-14-T, Decision on Prosecution Application for Leave to Appeal "Decision on the First Accused's Motion for Service and Arraignment on the Consolidated Indictment", 15 December 2004:

CONSIDERING that the Prosecution filed the Application within the time limits prescribed in Rule 73(B) of the Rules and in conformity with Rule 7(A) of the Rules and paragraph 8 of the Practice Direction for Certain Appeals Before the Special Court,[1] and that the time limits for filing of an interlocutory appeal run from the day after the filing of the complete Decision of the Trial Chamber, which includes in this instance, a Separate and Concurring Opinion and a Dissenting Opinion;

---

[1] Adopted on 30 September 2004.

R73-TC-39   o *Prosecutor v. Norman, Fofana, Kondewa*, Case No. SCSL-04-14-T, Decision on Extremely Urgent Prosecution Request for an Extension of Time to Seek Leave to Appeal, 7 June 2005:

CONSIDERING that the two later decisions of the 1st and 2nd of June, 2005, are related to the "Admissibility Decision" of 23rd May, 2005 for which a written reasoned decision and dissenting opinion are still pending, and that the Prosecution cannot consider its position until the awaited reasons are published;

CONSIDERING that the Prosecution has shown good cause to justify the extension of time to file leave to appeal the 1st and 2nd June, 2005 decisions;

HEREBY ORDERS the Prosecution to file their Request for Leave to Appeal within 3 days of the publication of the written reasoned Decision and dissenting opinion to the Admissibility Decision of the Trial Chamber.

- **Rule 73(B): Motions – Leave to Appeal – Application for Leave and for Reconsideration Shall Be Filed Separately**

R73-TC-40   o *Prosecutor v. Norman, Fofana, Kondewa*, Case No. SCSL-04-14-T, Order on Urgent Motion for Reconsideration or, in the Alternative, for Leave to Appeal the Orders for Compliance with the Order Concerning the Preparation and Presentation of the Defence Case, 29 November 2005:

NOTING that the Motion contains, *inter alia*, two separate and distinct applications, namely reconsideration or, alternatively, leave to appeal the Oral Ruling Issued by this Court on the 25th of November, 2005 as well as the Order for Compliance;

CONSIDERING that, due to the particular nature of the applications made, two separate and distinct motions should have been filed;

[...]

THE TRIAL CHAMBER

REJECTS the Defence Motion on the ground that this matter is not properly before the Chamber;

- **Rule 73(B): Motions – Appeal Decision – Application in Other Cases Where No Appeal Was Sought – Impact on Parties Submissions**

R73-TC-41
o *Prosecutor v. Sesay, Kallon, Gbao*, Case No. SCSL-04-15-T, Consequential Order Regarding Decision on Prosecution's Motion for Judicial Notice and Admission of Evidence, 23 May 2005:

CONSIDERING the recent decision of the Appeals Chamber in the proceedings against Sam Hinga Norman, Moinina Fofana and Allieu Kondewa [...];

NOTING that leave was not sought to appeal the Decision on Prosecution's Motion for Judicial Notice and Admission of Evidence in the RUF proceedings;

MINDFUL of the importance of ensuring the consistent application of legal principles in the trial proceedings before this Chamber;

NOTING the powers of the Chamber pursuant to Rule 54 of the Rules of Procedure and Evidence of the Special Court;

RECOGNISING that certain findings of the Chamber in the RUF Decision are identical to those findings made in the CDF Decision that were overturned on appeal by the Appeals Chamber;

ACCORDINGLY FINDS that the Fact D should not have been judicially noticed by the Trial Chamber [...]

R73-TC-42
o *Prosecutor v. Brima, Kamara, Kanu*, Case No. SCSL-04-16-T, Scheduling Order on Judicial Notice Motion, 27 May 2005:

NOTING the recent decision of the Appeals Chamber "*decision on the Appeal Against Decision on the Prosecution's Motion for Judicial Notice and Admission of Evidence*" dated 16 May 2005 in the proceedings against *Moinina Fofana* in Case No SCSL-04-14 before the Special Court;

NOTING that the submissions of the Prosecution predate the Appeals Chamber ruling and that they may reconsider their submissions in light of this recent decision;

- **Rule 73(C): Motions – Appeal – Stay of Proceedings – Amended Indictment**

R73-TC-43

o *Prosecutor v. Norman, Fofana, Kondewa*, Case No. SCSL-04-14-T, Decision on Presentation of Witness Testimony on Moyamba Crime Base, 1st March 2005, para. 11-13, 16-18:

11. In accordance with the Rule 73(C) of the Rules and Evidence of the Special Court ("Rules"), in circumstances where there is an appeal against an Impugned Decision, the proceedings on the Motion against that Decision will be stayed until a final determination by the Appeals Chamber. As a consequence of the appeal against the Impugned Decision, the Trial Chamber has not made a ruling on the Prosecution's request to amend the Indictment, and while the Decision of the Trial Chamber is not suspended, its Order for the Prosecution to seek leave of the Trial chamber to either expunge the identified portions of the Indictment or to amend such portions *in fieri* by virtue of Rule 73(C) of the Rules, which prevents the Trial chamber from making a ruling on this issue until the rendering of the appeals decision on this issue.

12. On this basis the Trial chamber may conclude that the portions of the Consolidated Indictment that the Trial Chamber ruled should be stayed against the First Accused, continue in existence against the Accused, pending a further order by the Trial Chamber to grant leave to amend the Indictment, or decline to do so. As a consequence, the evidence of witnesses who will testify on matters relating to the Moyamba crime base, is relevant to the charges against the First Accused as they exist in the Consolidated Indictment.

13. The Trial Chamber considers that no prejudice will ensue to the Accused if the trial proceeds with the testimony of witnesses who give evidence related to the Moyamba crime base. The Accused has has adequate time and resources to prepare for the cross-examination of these witnesses. Court Appointed Counsel for the First Accused have themselves represented that the First Accused is ready to proceed with the testimony of these witnesses and wishes to proceed with the trial.

[...]

16. In accordance with the Statute and Rules of the special Court, the Trial Chamber considers that it is in the interests of justice and judicial economy to continue the trial and hear the testimony of witnesses who will give evidence on the Moyamba crime base. The Trial Chamber does not consider that any prejudice will ensue for the Accused. The Trial Chamber will competently and fairly consider the relevance of this evidence to the charges contained in the Consolidated

Indictment against the First Accused in conformity with the Decision of the Appeals Chamber when that Decision is rendered on that issue.

17. The Trial Chamber notes that this finding is in accord with the Decisions of the International Tribunal for the Former Yugoslavia ("ICTY") and the International Criminal Tribunal for Rwanda ("ICTR"). In the *Simic* case, the Defence requested the Trial Chamber to refuse to hear particular witness testimony until the Appeals Chamber delivered its Decision on an appeal against the Trial Chamber's Decision granting leave to the Prosecution to amend the Indictment, claiming that this testimony was related to the amended portions of the Indictment. The Trial Chamber ruled that it was entitled to proceed with the witness testimony and that it was satisfied that the proceedings were being followed by the Accused, that they were able to give instructions to their Defence Counsels concerning their Defence and that they were not facing new charges.[1]

18. In the *Kvocka* case the Defence requested a stay of proceedings in relation to all witnesses who were related to an appeal pending before the Appeals Chamber.[2] In opposition, the Prosecution submitted that "[i]f an Appellate Chamber were to determine that the evidence of these new witnesses cannot be considered in reaching a decision in this case, the Trial Judges are presumed to be able to set aside that evidence in reaching your verdict". The Prosecution, furthermore, submitted that "[i]f they then decide the evidence is not admissible, there is a presumption that the judges can set aside that evidence and not consider it in reaching their decision". The Trial Chamber in that case ruled to continue the hearing of witness testimony and advised the Defence that if it felt prejudiced because it had not had time to prepare they should communicate their reasons to the chamber who would make a ruling on pertinent measures so that there would be no prejudice to the Defence.

---

[1] *Prosecutor v. Simic*, Transcript of 14 January 2002, pages 5274-5295.
[2] *Prosecutor v. Kvocka*, Transcript of 25 september 2000, pages 5590-5593.

R73-TC-44

o *Prosecutor v. Norman*, Case No. SCSL-04-14-T, Decision on First Accused's Motion on Abuse of Process, 28 April 2005, para. 13, 16-17:

13. [. . .] In addition, the Decision on the Motion for Service and Arraignment on the Second Indictment is currently on appeal, and in accordance with Rule 73(C) of the Rules, the proceedings on the said Motion are stayed until a final determination by the Appeals Chamber of the issues at stake.

[...]

16. The Chamber, again here, is of the view that these issues are precisely and textually the same as those that were fully presented and canvassed by the Parties in an earlier Motion by this same Applicant and his Learned Counsel on Service and Arraignment on the Second Indictment, whose decision we rendered on the 29th of November, 2004, and against which an Appeal has been filed, not only by this Applicant and his Learned Counsel, but also by the Prosecution.

17. These Appeals, we note, are still pending before the Appeals Chamber and Learned Counsel, knows very well and more than anyone else, that this Chamber, having rendered its Decision on these same issues which he is again now raising before it in this recently filed 'Abuse of Process Motion', is now functus officio as far as those issues are concerned, pending of course, the decision of the Appeals Chamber on the 2 appeals filed by both the Prosecution and Defence against our Decision.

- **Rule 73(D): Motions – Abuse of Process**

R73-TC-45   o *Prosecutor v. Norman*, Case No. SCSL-04-14-T, Decision on First Accused's Motion on Abuse of Process, 28 April 2005, para. 12-13, 20-22:

12. We observe that the issues which Learned Counsel is raising here are glaringly and textually the same as those that were raised during our examination of the Joinder Motion whose decision we rendered on the 29th day of January, 2004, with a partially dissenting opinion that is appended to it. It is pertinent to note in this regard, that no leave to appeal was sought by the Applicant within 3 days of our Decision as provided for by Rule 73(B) of the Rules of Procedure and Evidence. In fact, no leave can now be sought for an appeal to be filed by any party at this stage, as this would not only violate the law but will also and above all, constitute an abuse of process which Learned Counsel for the Applicant is canvassing in this Motion.

13. Furthermore, the Trial Chamber finds that Counsel in this case is, for the time being, estopped from bringing this Motion as the issues raised therein touch on and concern matters that have already been determined by the Chamber in its Joinder Decision and that The Chamber, as far as that Decision is concerned, is now *functus officio*.[1] We observe that no appeal was lodged against that Decision and that the time limit for filing any appeal has expired. [...]

[. . .]

20. We would like to observe here that the language used by Learned Counsel for the Applicant is unprofessional and borders on contempt. In this regard, The Chamber would like to draw Learned Counsel's attention to the provisions of Rule 46(C) of the Rules [. . .].

21. Finally we observe; firstly, that the applicant has again raised in his submissions and reopened arguments on issues that have already been determined by this Chamber and for which it is now *functus officio*; secondly, that notwithstanding the very clear and unambiguous provisions of Rule 73(C) of the Rules, he has submitted for re-litigation, the same issues which have been dealt with by this Chamber and are now pending before the Appeals Chamber; and thirdly, he has raised jurisdictional issues which have been finally litigated in the Appeals Chamber and which are now *Res Judicata*.

22. Having regard to these 3 observations and given the foregoing analysis, we, in conclusion, hold that this Motion is not only frivolous, but also amounts to a gross abuse of process, indeed, even more abusive of the process than what the Applicant and his Learned Counsel are deploring in this "Abuse of Process Motion" which, in our considered opinion, is bereft of any merits.

FOR THE ABOVE REASONS, THE TRIAL CHAMBER FINDS AS FOLLOWS:

THAT THIS Motion which in itself, is misconceived and without any merits constitutes an abuse of process.

IT IS THEREFORE DENIED AND ACCORDINGLY DISMISSED.

---

[1] See in particular, paras 13, 30, 32, 37, 38 of the Indictment Decision and paras 11, 15, 32 and 35 of the Joinder Decision.

- **Rule 73: Motions – Rule Before 1st August 2003 Amendment – Applicable Criterion for Leave to Appeal**

R73-TC-46

o *Prosecutor v. Kallon*, Case No. SCSL-03-07-PT, Decision on the Defence Application for Leave to Appeal 'Decision on the Prosecution's Motion for Immediate Protective Measures for Witnesses and Victims and for Non-Public Disclosure, 10 December 2003, para. 20, 26, 28:

20. In seeking leave to appeal, the Applicant is relying on the provisions of Rule 73(B) of the Rules which, before it was amended, read as follows:

"Decisions rendered on such motions are without interlocutory appeal save where leave is granted by the Trial Chamber on the grounds that a decision would be in the interest of a fair and expeditious trial."

[...]

26. In seeking leave to appeal against this Decision which, as an interlocutory decision, is ordinarily not appealable, the applicant must satisfy the Trial Chamber that a decision on it would be in the interests of a "fair and expeditious trial".

[...]

28. The words "fair and expeditious", we observe, are conjunctively used and should be construed as such. It stands to reason therefore, that the Applicant must demonstrate to our satisfaction that the decision of the Appeals Chamber would not only be in the interest of a fair trial on the one hand, but also, and at the same time, an expeditious trial, on the other hand.

APPEALS CHAMBER DECISIONS

- **Rule 73: Motions – Requirement for Initial Appearance Before Filing a Motion**

R73-AC-1

o *Prosecutor v. Taylor*, Case No. SCSL-03-01-AR72, Decision on Immunity from Jurisdiction, 31 May 2004, para. 23-24, 30, 33:

23. However, both Rules 72 and 73 appear to require an initial appearance. [...]

24. [...] Even if Rule 73(A) were to apply, it is clear that that rule permits either party to move before the designated judge or a Trial Chamber for appropriate ruling or relief after the initial appearance of the accused.

[...]

30. Technically, an accused who has not made an initial appearance before this court cannot bring a preliminary motion in terms of Rule 72(A), nor a motion under Rule 73 of the Rules and in a normal case such application may be held premature and accordingly struck out. [...]

[...]

33. The final aspect of the Prosecution's objection [...] is that as a general proposition, an accused does not have standing to file motions before the Special Court until he has been trans-

ferred to its custody or appeared before it and that there is no exception where an accused claims immunity since according to the Special Court Statute, an accused has no immunity by reason of his status as acting or former Head of State. [...] As we have already found that a) the nature of a claim of immunity constitutes a discretionary exception to the ordinary requirements of an accused first submitting himself to the jurisdiction of the court; and that b) jurisdiction and immunity are closely related, it is not necessary to determine this final objection.

- **Rule 73(A): Motions – Hearing – Discretion of the Trial Chamber**

R73-AC-2

o *Prosecutor v. Brima, Kamara, Kanu*, Case No. SCSL-04-16-AR73, Decision on Brima-Kamara Defence Appeal Motion Against Trial Chamber II Majority Decision on Extremely Urgent Confidential Joint Motion for the Re-Appointment of Kevin Metzger and Wilbert Harris As Lead Counsel for Alex Tamba Brima and Brima Bazzy Kamara, 8 December 2005, para. 106:

106. The Appeals Chamber further finds that Rule 73(A) provides for a discretion of the Trial Chamber to determine on the opportunity of having an hearing, which may not be public if the Chamber decides so pursuant to Rule 79, and that Trial Chamber II did not err in law in deciding to determine the Motion to re-assign without organising such hearing in the Impugned Decision. This decision in no way could jeopardize the Accused right to a fair and public hearing pursuant to Article 17(2) of the Statute.

- **Rule 73(B): Motions – Leave to Appeal and Reconsideration**

R73-AC-3

o *Prosecutor v Norman, Fofana, Kondewa*, Case No. SCSL-04-14-A, Decision on Prosecution Appeal Against the Trial Chamber's Decision of 2 August 2004 Refusing Leave to File an Interlocutory Appeal, 17 January 2005, para. 34-40:[117]

---

[117] See also *Prosecutor v. Norman, Fofana, Kondewa*, Case No. SCSL-04-14-T, Decision on Urgent Motion for Reconsideration of the Orders for Compliance with the Order Concerning the Preparation and Presentation of the Defence Case, 7 December 2005, para. 11.

34. The Prosecution also refers to the ICTY Appeals Chamber's power to **reconsider** its own decisions. The ICTY Judgment on Sentence Appeal in the *Delic* case was referred to as being relevant. The accused in that case argued that according to the 'law of the case' doctrine, a party is entitled to litigate issues which have already been decided when the strict application of the *res judicata* principle would cause 'manifest injustice' to a party. The Appeals Chamber stated:

The Appeals Chamber has an inherent power to reconsider any decision, including a judgment where it is necessary to do so in order to prevent an injustice. The Appeals Chamber has previously held that a Chamber may reconsider a decision, and not only when there has been a change of circumstances, where the Chamber has been persuaded that its previous decision was erroneous and has caused prejudice. Whether or not a Chamber does reconsider its decision is itself a discretionary decision.[1]

35. A power to reconsider would arise in the event of a clear error of reasoning. Judge Shahabuddeen added in a separate opinion that the 'clear error' should be 'something which the court manifestly or obviously overlooked in its reasoning and which is material to the achievement of substantial justice.'[2] However, the Appeals Chamber was clearly referring to the power of a Chamber to reconsider its own decision and not to review the decision of another Chamber.

36. In the *Prosecutor v. Tadic* (Appeal Judgement on Allegation of Contempt against Prior Counsel, Milan Vujin) the appellant – defence counsel – was found guilty of contempt by the Appeals Chamber at first instance pursuant to Rule 77 of the ICTY Rules of Procedure and Evidence and fined. He was treated by the Appeals Chamber as an accused whose right of appeal from conviction is protected by Article 14(5) of the International Covenant on Civil and Political Rights ("the Convention"). The Appeals Chamber having noted that Rule 77 of the ICTY Rules did not expressly provide for the right to appeal a contempt conviction of the Appeals Chamber, reasoned that the Convention provided that "Everyone convicted of a crime shall have the right to his conviction and sentence being reviewed by a higher tribunal according to law"[3] and that article 14 of the Convention reflects an imperative norm of international law to which the Tribunal must adhere. Following from this reasoning, it held that that the procedure established under Rule 77 of the Rules being of a penal nature pursuant to which a person convicted under the Rule faces a potential custodial sentence of up to 7 years imprisonment, a person found guilty of contempt by the Appeals Chamber must have the right to appeal the conviction. It is evident that the Appeals Chamber had recourse to an "imperative norm of international law" rather than inherent jurisdiction to entertain the appeal, because "it is the duty of

the International Tribunal to guarantee and protect the rights of those who appear as accused before it."[4]

37. In *Prosecutor v. Brdjanin and Talic*[5] the appellant was a person who had unsuccessfully applied to the Trial Chamber to have a subpoena issued against him set aside. The Trial Chamber granted him certification for leave to appeal. It was pursuant to that leave that an appeal was brought to the Appeals Chamber. The Appellant in that case did not appeal as a witness but as a person affected by the issue of a subpoena, failure to comply with which would have rendered him liable to be held for contempt.

38. In *Prosecutor v. Milosevic* the *amici curiae* were granted leave to appeal. On the appeal coming before the Appeals Chamber, that Chamber said:

> Not being a party to the proceedings, the *amici* are not entitled to use Rule 73 to bring an interlocutory appeal. The fact that the *amici* were instructed by the Trial Chamber to take all steps they consider appropriate to safeguard a fair trial for the Accused does not alter this conclusion.[6]

39. However, it seemed clear that the Appeals Chamber admitted the appeal because it found an identity of interest between the accused and the *amici*, a consideration of the appeal would not infringe the interest of the Accused and the Prosecution did not oppose consideration of the appeal which would in the case serve the interests of justice. In the event, the Appeals Chamber considered the appeal and dismissed it on the merits. It is instructive that Judge Shahabuddeen was of the opinion that the dismissal of the appeal "should have rested on the more fundamental fact that the interlocutory appeal ha[d] not been brought by a 'party' within the meaning of Rule 73(A) of the Rules of Evidence and Procedure of the Tribunal."[7]

40. It is clear that there is really nothing in these cases that establish a principle that could be of use in these proceedings. Those cases were not illustrative of inherent power being exercised to initiate appellate proceedings before the Appeals Chamber. It appears to be a misreading of the decisions of the ICTY to submit that the jurisprudence of the ICTY and ICTR reflects **a general principle** that any decision that is erroneous and that has led to injustice, and which is not capable of being remedied by other means, must be capable of being corrected by the Appeals Chamber. What can be discerned as emerging from the jurisprudence of the ICTY is that the Appeals Chamber has an inherent jurisdiction to reconsider **its own decision** to avoid injustice or miscarriage of justice.

---

[1] *Prosecutor v Delic et al.*, Case No. IT-96-21-A*bis*, Judgement on Sentence Appeal, Appeals Chamber, 8 April 2003, para. 48.

(2) *Prosecutor v Delic et al.*, Case No. IT-96-21-A*bis*, Judgement on Sentence Appeal, Appeals Chamber, 8 April 2003, Separate Opinion of Judge Shahabuddeen, para. 15.
(3) *Prosecutor v. Tadic,* Case No. IT-94-1-A-AR77, Appeal Judgement on Allegations of Contempt by Prior Counsel, 27 February 2001, p. 2.
(4) *Ibid.*, p. 3.
(5) *Prosecutor v. Brdanin and Talic*, Case No. IT-99-36-AR, Appeals Chamber, Decision on Interlocutory Appeal, 11 December 2002.
(6) *Prosecutor v. Milosevic,* Case No. IT-02-54-AR, Decision on the Interlocutory Appeal by the Amici Curiae against the Trial Chamber Order Concerning the Presentation and Preparation of the Defence Case, 20 January 2004, para. 4.
(7) *Prosecutor v. Milosevic*, Case No. IT-02-54-AR, Decision on the Interlocutory Appeal by the Amici Curiae against the Trial Chamber Order Concerning the Presentation and Preparation of the Defence Case, of 20 January 2004, Separate Opinion of Judge Shahabuddeen, para. 21.

R73-AC-4

o *Prosecutor v. Fofana*, Case No. SCSL-04-14-AR73, Decision on Appeal Against "Decision on Prosecution's Motion for Judicial Notice and Admission of Evidence", 16 May 2005, para. 15:

15. Before addressing the main issue at stake in the present appeal, the Appeals Chamber notes that the Trial Chamber failed to take account of the oral response given by Fofana to the Prosecution Motion for Judicial Notice. The Trial Chamber found in its Decision on Leave to Appeal that "it may not have given proper consideration to the oral Response of the Second Accused".[1] In its oral response, the Defence accepted facts B, P and W as facts of common knowledge and indicated that it might be able to agree to E, Q, F, G, L, U, if the wording were amended somewhat after discussions with the Prosecution. In its response to the Joint Request of the Second and Third Accused for Leave to Appeal against Decision on Prosecutor's motion for Judicial Notice, the Prosecution argued that taking into consideration the oral response of the second Accused at the Pre-trial conference would not have affected the outcome of the Decision, so that the decision could stand.[2] As an Oral Response has to be accepted the same way as a written one, it is the view of the Appeals Chamber that the oral response of the Defence was valid and directly relevant to the issue at stake and that the Trial Chamber erred in not taking it into account. However, the Appeals Chamber has now taken it fully into account, so the granting of leave did repair any miscarriage of justice. We note that the Trial Chamber could simply have reconsidered its decision and taken the oral submissions into account, rather than using its own failure as a reason to give leave to appeal.

[1] Decision on Leave to Appeal, para. 20.
[2] Prosecution Response, 16 June 2004, at para 7.

R73-AC-5   o *Prosecutor v. Brima, Kamara, Kanu*, Case No. SCSL-04-16-AR73, Decision on Brima-Kamara Defence Appeal Motion Against Trial Chamber II Majority Decision on Extremely Urgent Confidential Joint Motion for the Re-Appointment of Kevin Metzger and Wilbert Harris As Lead Counsel for Alex Tamba Brima and Brima Bazzy Kamara, 8 December 2005, para. 124-126:

124. This being said, the Appeals Chamber does not find that the sole fact that the application to re-assign was an attempt to reverse the decision on the application to withdraw makes it necessarily a "frivolous and vexatious" motion. An applicant whose application has been fully granted by a Chamber may have reasons to seek review of the Chamber's decision when the circumstances which led to his or her application have changed. This opportunity to seek review of a decision by the same Chamber which rendered it, which is different from the right to appeal the decision,[1] is admitted in the jurisprudence of both sister International Tribunals. The Appeals Chamber of the International Criminal Tribunal for Rwanda clarified the criteria for review in the following terms:[2]

> [...] it is clear from the Statute and Rules[3] that, in order for a Chamber to carry out a review, it must be satisfied that four criteria have been met. There must be a new fact; this new fact must not have been known by the moving party at the time of the original proceedings; the lack of discovery of the new fact must not have been through the lack of due diligence on the part of the moving party; and it must be shown that the new fact could have been a decisive factor in reaching the original decision.

125. This Appeals Chamber considers that the possibility to seek review of a previous decision when the circumstances have changed is broadly admitted at the international level. Beyond the jurisprudence of the other sister International Tribunals, Article 4, paragraph 2 of Protocol No. 7 to the European Convention for the Protection of Human Rights and Fundamental Freedoms (1950) provides for the reopening of cases if there is *inter alia* "evidence of new or newly discovered facts". [4] Article 14 of the International Covenant on Civil and Political Rights (ICCPR)(1966) refers to the discovery of "newly or newly discovered facts". The International Law Commission has also considered that such a provision was a "necessary guarantee against the possibility of factual error relating to material not available to the accused and therefore not brought to the attention of the Court at the time of the initial trial or of any appeal."[5] Finally, Article 84(1) of the Rome Statute of the

International Criminal Court provides for the revision of judgements on the following grounds:[6]

(a) New evidence has been discovered that:

    a. Was not available at the time of trial, and such unavailability was not wholly or partially attributable to the party making application; and

    b. Is sufficiently important that had it been proved at trial it would have been likely to have resulted in a different verdict;

(b) It has been newly discovered that decisive evidence, taken into account at trial and upon which the conviction depends, was false, forged or falsified;

(c) One or more of the judges who participated in conviction or confirmation of the charges has committed, in that case, an act of serious misconduct or serious breach of duty of sufficient gravity to justify the removal if that judge or those judges from office under Article 46.

The facility to seek review on the ground of a change of circumstances has also been admitted for interlocutory decisions rendered in the course of trials.[7]

---

[1] ICTY, *Prosecutor v. Tadic*, Case No. IT-94-1-A, Decision on Appellant's Motion for Extension of the Time-Limit and Admission of Additional Evidence (AC), 15 October 1998, para. 30.

[2] ICTR, *Prosecutor v. Barayagwiza*, Case No. ICTR-97-19-AR72, Decision (Prosecutor's Request for Review or Reconsideration) (AC), 31 March 2000, para. 41.

[3] Article 25, Rules 120 and 121.

[4] 22 November 1984, 24 ILM 435 at 436.

[5] *Report of the International Law Commission on the work of its 46th session*, Official Records, 49th session, Supplement Number 10 (A/49/10) at page 28.

[6] Article 84(1) of the Rome statute of the International Criminal Court.

[7] ICTR, *Prosecutor v. Barayagwiza*, Case No. ICTR-97-19-AR72, Decision (Prosecutor's Request for Review or Reconsideration) (AC), 31 March 2000, para. 41; ICTR, *Prosecutor v. Ndindiliyimana et al. ("Military II")*, Case No. ICTR-00-56-T, Decision on Bizimungu's Motion for Reconsideration of the Chamber's 19 March 2004 Decision on Disclosure of Prosecution Materials, 3 November 2004, para. 21; *Prosecutor v. Ndindiliyimana et al. ("Military II")*, Case No. ICTR-00-56-T, Decision on Nzuwonemeye's Motion for Reconsideration of the Chamber's Oral Decision of 14 September 2005 on Admissibility of Witness XXO's Testimony in the *Military I* Case in Evidence, 10 October 2005.

- **Rule 73(B): Motions – Leave to Appeal – Rationale of the Requirement of a Leave to Appeal**

R73-AC-6

o *Prosecutor v. Norman, Fofana, Kondewa*, Case No. SCSL-04-14-A, Decision on Prosecution Appeal Against the Trial Chamber's Decision of 2 August 2004 Refusing Leave to File an Interlocutory Appeal, 17 January 2005, para. 26-29:[118]

26. The original Rule 73(B) did not provide for an interlocutory appeal at all. It was an addition of a second limb by an amendment adopted at the August 2003 Plenary that made provision for appeal by leave.

27. The equivalent ICTY/R rule (Rule 73(B)) states:

Decisions on all motions are without interlocutory appeal save with certificate by the Trial Chamber, which may grant such certificate if the decision involves an issue that would significantly affect the fair and expeditious conduct of the proceedings or the outcome of the trial, and for which, in the opinion of the Trial Chamber, an immediate resolution by the Appeals Chamber may materially advance the proceedings.

28. The old ICTY rule provided that decisions were without interlocutory appeal save with the leave of a bench of three judges of the Appeals Chamber which could grant leave if one of the following tests were satisfied.

(1) if the impugned decision would cause such prejudice to the case of the party seeking leave as could not be cured by the final disposal of the trial including post-judgment appeal.

(2) if the issue in the proposed appeal is of general importance to proceedings before the Tribunal or in international law generally.

29. The underlying rationale for permitting such appeals is that certain matters cannot be cured or resolved by final appeal against judgment. However, most interlocutory decisions of a Trial Chamber will be capable of effective remedy in a final appeal where the parties would not be forbidden to challenge the correctness of interlocutory decisions which were not otherwise susceptible to interlocutory appeal in accordance with the Rules.

---

[118] See also *Prosecutor v. Sesay, Kallon, Gbao*, Case No. SCSL-04-15-T, Decision on the Defence Applications for Leave to Appeal Ruling of the 3rd of February, 2005 on the Exclusion of Statements of Witness TF1-141, 28 April 2005, para. 21-22.

- **Rule 73(B): Motions – Leave to Appeal – Standard for Leave to Appeal**

R73-AC-7   o *Prosecutor v. Norman, Kondewa, Fofana*, Case No. SCSL-04-14-AR73, Decision on Amendment of the Consolidated Indictment, 16 May 2005, para. 43:[119]

43. [...] The standard for leave to appeal at an interlocutory stage is set high by Rule 73(B), which restricts such leave to "exceptional cases" where "irreparable prejudice" may otherwise be suffered. That test is not satisfied merely by the fact that there has been a dissenting opinion on the matter in the Trial Chamber, or that the issue strikes the Trial Chamber judges as interesting or important for the development of international criminal law. In this Court, the procedural assumption is that trials will continue to their conclusion without delay or diversion caused by interlocutory appeals on procedural matters, and that any errors which affect the final judgment will be corrected in due course by this Chamber on appeal. The consideration that weighed most relevantly with members of the Trial Chamber in granting leave to these appellants was that the differences between its members over the interpretation of the rules and procedures of the court were fundamental, and required authoritative resolution for the sake of this trial and others, sooner rather than later.

- **Rule 73(B): Motions – Jurisdiction of the Appeals Chamber on Decisions Under Rule 73(B)**

R73-AC-8   o *Prosecutor v. Norman, Fofana, Kondewa*, Case No. SCSL-04-14-A, Decision on Prosecution Appeal Against the Trial Chamber's Decision of 2 August 2004 Refusing Leave to File an Interlocutory Appeal, 17 January 2005, para. 23-24:

23. The threshold question to be decided is not whether the Appeals Chamber can exercise jurisdiction to entertain an appeal from a decision of the Trial Chamber rendered pur-

---

[119] See also *Prosecutor v. Brima, Kamara, Kanu*, Case No. SCSL-04-16-T, Decision on Prosecution Application for Leave to Appeal Decision on Oral Application for Witness TF1-150 to Testify Without Being Compelled to Answer Questions on Grounds of Confidentiality, 12 October 2005; *Prosecutor v. Brima, Kamara, Kanu*, Case No. SCSL-04-16-AR73, Decision on Brima-Kamara Defence Appeal Motion Against Trial Chamber II Majority Decision on Extremely Urgent Confidential Joint Motion for the Re-Appointment of Kevin Metzger and Wilbert Harris As Lead Counsel for Alex Tamba Brima and Brima Bazzy Kamara, 8 December 2005, para. 17.

suant to Rule 73(A) of the Rules, but whether in certain cases it can exercise inherent power to dispense with the need to comply with the provisions of Rule 73(B) in order to admit an appeal from an interlocutory decision of the Trial Chamber refusing leave to appeal to the Appeals Chamber.

24. That question raises an immediate procedural question whether in the situation that has arisen the appellant without first obtaining the leave of the Trial Chamber pursuant to Rule 73(B) can initiate these appeal proceedings, by directly approaching the Appeals Chamber. There is no reason to treat a motion for leave to appeal an interlocutory decision of the Trial Chamber as anything other than a motion under Rule 73(A) of the Rules. But for the need to deal with the issue raised in these proceedings once and for all in order to clear any doubt as to the limits of the Court's inherent jurisdiction, it would have been in order to refuse to entertain the proceedings on the ground that there is no procedural foundation for approaching the Appeals Chamber in matters such as this, touching on a decision of the Trial Chamber rendered in a motion under Rule 73(A), without prior leave of the Trial Chamber. While it is undisputed that the Court has an inherent jurisdiction which it exercises as and when such is appropriate, it is an assumption of the extent of the inherent powers of the Court that goes too far, to assume that the Court also has an inherent jurisdiction to fashion a procedure for originating proceedings before it outside the express provisions of the Rules.

- **Rule 73(B): Motions – Time Limit for Filing Applications for Leave to Appeal – Separate Opinions**

R73-AC-9

o *Prosecutor v. Brima, Kamara, Kanu*, Case No. SCSL-04-16-AR73, Decision on Brima-Kamara Defence Appeal Motion Against Trial Chamber II Majority Decision on Extremely Urgent Confiden-tial Joint Motion for the Re-Appointment of Kevin Metzger and Wilbert Harris As Lead Counsel for Alex Tamba Brima and Brima Bazzy Kamara, 8 December 2005, para. 19, 25-26:

19. Rule 73(B) of the SCSL Rules of Procedure and evidence provides that application for leave to appeal interlocutory decision shall be filed within 3 days of the impugned decision. This Rule does not make any exception as regards the later filing of concurring/dissenting opinions appended to the impugned decision.

[. . .]

25. This being said, the 3-day time limit for filing an application for leave to appeal under Rule 73(B) obviously runs from the date when the decision the applicant wishes to appeal is filed, without any exception on the ground of the later filing of a dissenting/concurring opinion being admissible.

(c) Application to the Current Case

26. In the instant case, the application for leave to appeal was filed more than three days after the appealed Decision was rendered. This application was therefore out of time and should have been dismissed accordingly. However, taking into account the fact that neither of the Respondents have objected to the Applicants' non-compliance with the Rules and the fact that the application for leave to appeal was filed on credence of a wrong precedent established by Trial Chamber I,[1] and in accordance with the practice of the ICTR Appeals Chamber,[2] the Appeals Chamber considers that it is nevertheless properly seized of the Appeal.

---

[1] *Prosecutor v. Norman, Fofana, Kondewa*, Case No. SCSL-2004-14-T, Decision on Prosecution Application for Leave to Appeal "Decision on the First Accused's Motion for Service and Arraignment on the Consolidated Indictment", 15 December 2004.
[2] ICTR, *Prosecutor v. Nyiramasuhuko et al.*, Case No. 98-42-AR73.2, Decision on Pauline Nyiramasuhuko's Appeal on the Admissibility of Evidence, 4 October 2004, para. 4-5.

Rule 73*bis*: Pre-Trial Conference
(amended 29 May 2004)

(A) The Trial Chamber or a Judge designated from among its members shall hold a Pre-Trial Conference prior to the commencement of the trial.

(B) At the Pre-Trial Conference the Trial Chamber or a Judge designated from among its members may order the Prosecutor, within a time limit set by the Trial Chamber or the said Judge, and before the date set for trial, to file the following:

    (i) A pre-trial brief addressing the factual and legal issues;
    (ii) Admissions by the parties and a statement of other matters not in dispute;
    (iii) A statement of contested matters of fact and law;
    (iv) A list of witnesses the Prosecutor intends to call with:

        (a) The name or pseudonym of each witness;
        (b) A summary of the facts on which each witness will testify;
        (c) The points in the indictment on which each witness will testify; and
        (d) The estimated length of time required for each witness;

    (v) A list of exhibits the Prosecutor intends to offer stating, where possible, whether or not the defence has any objection as to authenticity.

The Trial Chamber or the said Judge may order the Prosecutor to provide the Trial Chamber with copies of written statements of each witness whom the Prosecutor intends to call to testify.

(C) The Trial Chamber or a Judge designated from among its members may order the Prosecutor to shorten the examination-in-chief of some witnesses.

(D) The Trial Chamber or a Judge designated from among its members may order the Prosecutor to reduce the number of witnesses, if it considers that an excessive number of witnesses are being called to prove the same facts.

(E) After the commencement of the Trial, the Prosecutor may, if he considers it to be in the interests of justice, move the Trial Chamber for leave to reinstate the list of witnesses or to vary his decision as to which witnesses are to be called.

(F) At the Pre-Trial Conference, the Trial Chamber or a Judge designated from among its members may order the defence to file a statement of admitted facts and law and a pre-trial brief addressing the factual and legal issues, not later than seven days prior to the date set for trial.

TRIAL CHAMBERS DECISIONS

- **Rule 73*bis*(B)(i): Pre-Trial Conference – Prosecutor Pre-Trial Brief – Purpose**

R73*bis*-TC-1 o *Prosecutor v. Sesay, Kallon, Gbao*, Case No. SCSL-04-15-PT, Order to the Prosecution to File a Supplemental Pre-Trial Brief, 30 March 2004:[120]

CONSIDERING the purpose of a pre-trial brief is to provide the opposing party and the Trial Chamber with notice and an overview of the case to be presented at trial, including an indication of the evidence (testimonial and documentary) that will be relied upon in establishing that case;[(1)]

[...]

FINDING FURTHER however, that the Prosecution pre-trial brief does not sufficiently address factual issues;

FINDING ALSO that the Prosecution pre-trial brief does not provide the Defence or the Trial Chamber, with reasonable sufficiency, of notice and an overview of the Prosecution's case against each individual accused, and particularly the nexus between the crimes alleged and the alleged individual criminal responsibility of each individual accused;

FINDING THEREFORE that it will be of assistance to the Defence and the Trial Chamber, and in the interests of conducting a fair and expeditious trial, to receive a supplemental Prosecution pre-trial brief addressing, with reasonable sufficiency, the issues herein before highlighted;

---

[120] See also *Prosecutor v. Norman, Fofana, Kondewa*, Case No. SCSL-04-14-PT, Order to the Prosecution to File a Supplemental Pre-Trial Brief, 1st April 2004; *Prosecutor v. Brima, Kamara, Kanu*, Case No. SCSL-04-16-PT, Order to the Prosecution to File a Supplemental Pre-Trial Brief and Revised Order for Filing Defence Pre-Trial Briefs, 1st April 2004.

HEREBY ORDERS *proprio motu*, that:

1. The Prosecution shall file a Supplemental Pre-Trial Brief on or before 19 April 2004;
2. The Supplemental Pre-Trial Brief shall:

   a. Include references to the evidence, both testimonial and documentary, upon which the Prosecution will rely to establish the factual allegations set out in the Indictment and the Prosecution pre-trial brief of 1 March 2004; [. . .]

---

(1) In this respect, the Trial Chamber highlights the distinct purposes and requirements for an indictment, including that it must plead the <u>material facts</u> underpinning the charges contained therein so as to provide the accused with notice of the case against him, and a pre-trial brief, which should address the specific factual issues underpinning those charges, including an indication of the <u>evidence</u> that will be relied upon to establish those facts.

- **Rule 73*bis*(B)(i): Pre-Trial Conference – Prosecutor Pre-Trial Brief – Time for Filing**

R73*bis*-TC-2

o *Prosecutor v. Norman, Fofana, Kondewa*, Case No. SCSL-04-14-PT, Order for Filing Pre-Trial Briefs (Under Rules 54 and 73*bis*), 13 February 2004:[121]

NOTING Rule 73*bis* of the Rules of Procedure and Evidence of the special Court ("Rules"), which provides for the filing of a pre-trial brief by the Office of the Prosecutor ("Prosecution") addressing the factual and legal issues in the case at a time after the Pre-Trial Conference has been held, and further provides for the filing of a pre-trial brief by the Defence addressing the factual and legal issues not later than seven days prior to the date set for trial;

NOTING the "Practice Direction on Filing Documents Before the Special Court for Sierra Leone", issued by the Registrar on 27 February 2003, and specifically Article 9 thereof,

CONSIDERING THAT the right of the Accused to a fair and expeditious trial will be advanced by the filing of the pre-trial briefs at an earlier stage in the pre-trial process than after the Pre-Trial Conference;

---

[121] See also *Prosecutor v. Sesay, Kallon, Gbao*, Case No. SCSL-04-15-PT, Order for Filing Pre-Trial Briefs (Under Rules 54 and 73*bis*), 13 February 2004; *Prosecutor v. Brima, Kamara, Kanu*, Case No. SCSL-04-16-PT, Order for Filing Pre-Trial Briefs (Under Rules 54 and 73*bis*), 13 February 2004.

- **Rule 73*bis*(B)(iv): Pre-Trial Conference – List of Witnesses – Rationale of the Obligation to File a List of Witnesses**

R73*bis*-TC-3

o *Prosecutor v. Sesay, Kallon, Gbao*, Case No. SCSL-04-15-T, Order to Prosecution to Produce Witness List and Witness Summaries, 7 July 2004:

CONSIDERING the determination of the Trial Chamber to ensure that the trial is fair and expeditious and that the proceedings before the Special Court are conducted in accordance with the Rules of Procedure and Evidence of the Special Court ("Rules"), with full respect for the rights of the accused and due regard for the protection of victims and witnesses;

CONSIDERING the provisions of Article 17(4)(b) of the Statute of the Special Court for Sierra Leone, that stipulate, *inter alia*, that the Defence shall be entitled to have adequate time and facilities for the preparation of its defence;

CONSIDERING that it is in the interests of justice for the Prosecution to disclose to the Defence and the Court a modified witness list that identifies clearly which witnesses the Prosecution has identified as its "core" witnesses and which witnesses are meant to be used only as "back-up" witnesses if some of the "core" witnesses are not available to testify;

CONSIDERING that the Trial Chamber would benefit from having access to witness statements in advance of each witness testifying at trial, for the purpose of promoting comprehension of the issues and for the effective management of the trial;

[…]

PURSUANT TO Rules 54 and Rule 73*bis* of the Rules;

HEREBY ORDERS the Prosecution:

(1) To produce a list of the "core" witnesses that the Prosecution is intending to call to testify at trial;

(2) To produce a list of the "back-up" witnesses that the Prosecution intends to call only if it is later deemed necessary at trial; […]

R73*bis*-TC-4

o *Prosecutor v. Brima, Kamara, Kanu*, Case No. SCSL-04-16-T, Decision on Prosecution request for Leave to Call an Additional Witness (Zainab Hawa Bangura) Pursuant to Rule 73*bis*(E), and on Joint Defence Notice to Inform the Trial Chamber of its Position vis-à-vis the Proposed Expert Witness (Mrs Bangura) Pursuant to Rule 94*bis*, 5 August 2005, para. 19:

19. The provisions of Rule 73*bis*(B) of the Rules requiring the Prosecution to file before the commencement of the trial certain documents (specified in Rule 73*bis*(B)) including a list of witnesses that the Prosecution intends to call in order to prove its case, are amongst others intended to put the Defence and the Trial Chamber on notice as to the number of witnesses the Prosecution intends to call and the substance of their evidence in relation to the indictment. This is in addition to the Prosecution's disclosure obligations pursuant to Rules 66, 67 and 68 of the Rules. The overall rationale for such early disclosure is to afford the Defence sufficient time to prepare their defence as well as to ensure an orderly and expeditious trial.[1] Accordingly, once the trial has commenced the Prosecution is obligated to abide by their witness list and statements as filed and may only vary the witness list in accordance with the provisions of Rule 73*bis*(E) of the Rules [. . .].

---

[1] Under Article 17(4) of the Statute of the Special Court, an accused person is entitled inter alia, to adequate time to prepare as well as to be tried without undue delay.

- **Rule 73*bis*(B)(ii): Pre-Trial Conference – List of Witnesses – Continuous Disclosure of the Order of Witnesses to Be Called**

R73*bis*-TC-5

o *Prosecutor v. Sesay, Kallon, Gbao*, Case No. SCSL-04-15-T, Order to Prosecution to Provide Order of Witnesses, 15 September 2004:

CONSIDERING that it is in the interests of justice for the Prosecution to disclose to the Defence and the Trial Chamber the order of testimony of the witnesses it intends to call, with sufficient time available for case preparation and investigation and for the effective management of the trial;

PURSUANT TO Rule 54 and Rule 73*bis* of the Rules;

HEREBY ORDERS the Prosecution to each Defence Team and the Trial Chamber with a list of the order it intends to call its witnesses to testify at trial during each trial session, 14 days prior to each future trial session; and

FURTHER ORDERS the Prosecution to provide a column in this list that identifies the particular protective measures to be applied for the testimony of each of these witnesses in accordance with the Decision on Prosecution Motion for Modification of Protective Measures for Witnesses of 5 July 2004;

R73*bis*-TC-6 o *Prosecutor v. Norman, Fofana, Kondewa*, Case No. SCSL-04-14-PT, Order to Prosecution to Provide Order of Witnesses and Witness Statements, 28 May 2004:[122]

CONSIDERING that it is in the interests of justice for the Prosecution to disclose to the Defence the order of witnesses it intends to call, with sufficient time available for case preparation and investigation;

[...]

PURSUANT TO Rule 54 and Rule 73*bis* of the Rules;

HEREBY ORDERS the Prosecution:

For the first trial session that runs from 3 June to 22 June 2004:

(1) [...] for the remaining witnesses called in the first trial session, to provide each defence Team and the Trial Chamber with a list of the order it intends to call witnesses to testify, 14 days in advance of their testimony;

- **Rule 73*bis*(B)(ii): Pre-Trial Conference – List of Witnesses – Limits of the Obligations Binding on the Prosecution**

R73*bis*-TC-7 o *Prosecutor v. Norman, Fofana, Kondewa*, Case No. SCSL-04-14-T, Decision on Request for Stayed Witness Indexing, 28 April 2005:

SEIZED of the *Defence Request for "Stayed" Witness Indexing* ("Request"), filed by Court Appointed Counsel for the First Accused on the 7th of March, 2005, where the Defence sought an order from the Chamber to the Prosecution to provide a comprehensive list of all Prosecution witnesses who have given testimony and those who the Prosecution will call to testify, in respect of the "stayed" portions of the Consolidated Indictment, in addition to providing trifurcated indexing of the "stayed" portions according to the categories of (a) new geographic locations, (b) extended time-scales or temporal jurisdictions and (c) new substantive elements of charges;

---

[122] See also *Prosecutor v. Norman, Fofana, Kondewa*, Case No. SCSL-04-14-T, Order to Prosecution to Provide Order of Witnesses and Witness Statements, 29 July 2004; *Prosecutor v. Norman, Fofana, Kondewa*, Case No. SCSL-04-14-T, Order to Prosecution to Provide Order of Witnesses and Witness Statements, 26 January 2005; *Prosecution v. Brima, Kamara, Kanu*, Case No. SCSL-04-16-PT, Order to Prosecution to Provide Order of Witnesses and Witness Statements, 9 February 2005.

[…]

NOTING that the Prosecution submitted two tables listing 100 "core" witnesses, who they intend to call to testify at trial and 58 "back-up" witnesses, who they intend to call "only if it is later deemed necessary at trial" by its filing on the 8th of October, 2004,[1] and that the Prosecution filed a "Revised List of Prosecution Witnesses", on the 3rd of February, 2005, reducing the number of witnesses on the "core" list to 82 by moving 18 witnesses to the "back-up" list ("Revised Witness List");

CONSIDERING that the Prosecution have provided the Defence with the Revised Witness List of all witnesses to be called at trial, together with a summary of their expected testimony and a chart on the testimonial and documentary evidence upon which the Prosecution will rely to establish the allegations contained in the Consolidated Indictment;

CONSIDERING that the Prosecution have already put the Defence on notice as to the witnesses it intends to call and the evidence that it seeks to elicit from them with reference to each Count of the Indictment;

CONSIDERING that the Request of Court Appointed Counsel for the First Accused does not raise a fundamental issue about the fairness of the trial;

CONSIDERING that it would not be in the interests of justice for the Chamber to order the Prosecution to perform an administrative function that falls within the domain of the Defence and its own trial preparations;

---

[1] Revised List of Prosecution Witnesses, para. 3.

R73bis-TC-8

o *Prosecutor v. Sesay, Kallon, Gbao*, Case No. SCSL-04-15-T, Consequential Order to the Decision on Further Renewed Witness List, 14 April 2005:

RECOGNIZING the Prosecution's continuous efforts in reducing the total number of its witnesses;

[…]

FINDING that the rights of the Accused in this case would be enhanced by requiring the Prosecution to update the materials already provided to the Defence and to the Trial Chamber […]

PURSUANT to the provisions of Article 17 of the Statute of the Special Court ("Statute") and Rules 26*bis*, 54, 66(A)(ii), 67, 68, 69 and 75 of the Rules of Procedure and Evidence ("Rules");

HEREBY ORDERS the Prosecution, for both its current "core" and "back-up" witness list, to file by no later than Thursday, the 5th of May 2005 the following:

1. An <u>Updated Witness List</u> with the name or the pseudonym of each witness, the relevant category for protective measures, the summary of the witness testimony, the indication of the exact paragraph and/or count in the Amended Consolidated Indictment of the witness testimony for which the witness is being called, as well as, if applicable, an estimated length of time required for the examination-in-chief of each witness;

2. An <u>Updated Compliance Report</u> indicating the date of each witness statement, the date upon which each statement was disclosed to each of the accused and the total number of pages of each statement;

3. An <u>Updated Proofing Chart</u> which indicates, for each paragraph in the Amended Consolidated Indictment, the testimonial evidence upon which the Prosecution will rely to establish the allegations contained therein.

- **Rule 73*bis*(E): Pre-Trial Conference – Leave to Call Additional Witnesses – Need for an Application**

R73*bis*-TC-9
o *Prosecutor v. Sesay, Kallon, Gbao*, Case No. SCSL-04-15-T, Order to Prosecution Concerning Renewed Witness List, 3 December 2004:

CONSIDERING the determination of the Trial Chamber to ensure that the trial is fair and expeditious and that the proceedings before the Special Court are conducted in accordance with the Statute and Rules of Procedure and Evidence of the Special Court ("Rules"), with full respect for the rights of the accused and due regard for the protection of victims and witnesses;

CONSIDERING that this Chamber has repeatedly encouraged the Prosecution to attempt to reduce the number of Prosecution witnesses and that it would like to recognise of the Prosecution's efforts in substantially reducing the total number of "core" Prosecution witnesses;

REAFFIRMS that the Prosecution is required to seek leave and demonstrate good cause in order to add witnesses to its witness list;

- **Rule 73*bis*(E): Pre-Trial Conference – Leave to Call Additional Witnesses – Applicable Standards**

R73*bis*-TC-10

o *Prosecutor v. Norman, Fofana, Kondewa*, Case No. SCSL-04-14-T, Decision on Prosecution Request for Leave to Call Additional Witnesses, 29 July 2004, para. 15-19, 24, 28, 32:[123]

15. Rule 73*bis*(E) becomes applicable after the commencement of the trial, and where it is in the interests of justice. It serves as an instrument to vary the list of witnesses disclosed prior to trial, pursuant to Rule 67 of the Rules. With respect to the disclosure of witness statements after the commencement of trial, Rule 66(A)(ii), stipulates that where copies have not been submitted within 60 days before the date for trial, or as otherwise ordered by the Judge, or Trial Chamber, the Prosecution must show good cause to disclose the witness statements.

16. Rule 73*bis*(E) is similar in formulation to the corresponding ICTR Rule. The Chamber notes that when interpreting this Rule, together with Rule 66(A)(ii), and the circumstances that give rise to a showing of "good cause" and the "interests of justice", Trial Chambers of the ICTR have taken into account a number of factors that include, the complexity of the case, the materiality of the testimony, and any prejudice caused to the Defence.[(1)] For instance, the Trial Chamber of the International Criminal Tribunal for Rwanda ("ICTR") in the *Nahimana* case,[(2)] noted that:

---

[123] See also *Prosecutor v. Sesay, Kallon, Gbao*, Case No. SCSL-04-15-T, Decision on Prosecution Request for Leave to Call Additional Witnesses, 29 July 2004, para. 28-32; *Prosecutor v. Sesay, Kallon, Gbao*, Case No. SCSL-04-15-T, Decision on Prosecution Request for Leave to Call Additional Witnesses and Disclose Additional Witness Statements, 11 February 2005, para. 25-27; *Prosecutor v. Sesay, Kallon, Gbao*, Case No. SCSL-05-15-T, Decision Regarding the Prosecutor's Further Renewed Witness List, 5 April 2005, para. 15-19; *Prosecutor v. Norman, Fofana, Kondewa*, Case No. SCSL-05-14-T, Decision on Prosecution Request for Leave to Call an Additional Expert Witness, 10 June 2005, para. 8; *Prosecutor v. Sesay, Kallon, Gbao*, Case No. SCSL-04-15-T, Decision on Prosecution request for Leave to Call an Additional Expert Witness, 10 June 2005, para. 8; *Prosecutor v. Norman, Fofana, Kondewa*, Case No. SCSL-04-14-T, Decision on Prosecution Request for Leave to Call Additional Witnesses and for Orders for Protective Measures, 21 June 2005; *Prosecutor v. Brima, Kamara, Kanu*, Case No. SCSL-04-16-T, Decision on Prosecution Request for Leave to Call an Additional Witness (Zainab Hawa Bangura) Pursuant to Rule 73*bis*(E), and on Joint Defence Notice to Inform the Trial Chamber of its Position vis-à-vis the Proposed Expert Witness (Mrs Bangura) Pursuant to Rule 94*bis*, 5 August 2005, para. 21-22; *Prosecutor v. Brima, Kamara, Kanu*, Case No. SCSL-04-16-T, Decision on Prosecution Request for Leave to Call an Additional Witness Pursuant to Rule 73*bis*(E), 5 August 2005, para. 19.

In assessing the "interests of justice" and "good cause" Chambers have taken into account such considerations as the materiality of the testimony, the complexity of the case, prejudice to the Defence, including elements of surprise, on-going investigations, replacements and corroboration of evidence. The Prosecution's duty under the Statute to present the best available evidence to prove its case has to be balanced against the right of the Accused to have adequate time and facilities to prepare his Defence and his right to be tried without undue delay.

17. We note that additional factors that Trial Chambers have taken into account when considering the circumstances giving rise to "good cause" and the "interests of justice", include the sufficiency and time of disclosure of the witness information to the Defence, and the probative value of the proposed testimony. The Trial Chamber of the ICTR in the *Bagosora*[3] case, went further to expand on the factors identified in the *Nahimana* decision and observed that:

> These considerations [under Rule 73*bis*(E)] require a close analysis of each witness, including the sufficiency and time of disclosure of witness information to the Defence; the probative value of the proposed testimony in relation to existing witnesses and allegations in the indictments; the ability of the Defence to make an effective cross-examination of the proposed testimony, given its novelty or other factors; and the justification offered by the Prosecution for the addition of the witness.

18. This Trial Chamber acknowledges its important role in ensuring a fair and expeditious trial when weighing the abovementioned factors consistent with Rule 26*bis* of the Rules and the rights of Accused persons to adequate time and facilities for the preparation of their defence, as set forth in Article 17(4)(b) of the Statute. The Prosecution should not be allowed to surprise the Defence with additional witnesses, who were accessible to it prior to the commencement of trial. As we noted in our recent Decision on Disclosure of Witness Statements and Cross-Examination, we emphasize that the Prosecution is required to fulfil in good faith its disclosure obligations.[4]

19. Taking our judicial cue from the reasoning of the ICTY in the Delalic case, where it stated that it will "[u]tilise all its powers to facilitate the truth finding persons in the impartial adjudication of the matter between the parties",[5] this Chamber will approach the determination of this issue with due regard for the doctrine of "equality of arms".

[...]

24. The Trial Chamber considers that the proposed evidence of this witness appears relevant and could have probative value in relation to the allegations in paragraphs 20, 23, 24,

25, 26 and 28 of the Indictment. The Chamber also notes that the proposed evidence purports to be direct evidence of the individual criminal responsibility of the 1st and 2nd Accused and is distinguishable from corroborative or cumulative evidence. The Chamber, having weighed the timing of the application and disclosure of the witness statement on 19 May 2004 against the materiality of the evidence, considers that good cause has been shown and it is in the interests of justice to add this witness to the Modified Witness List. Given that the trial of the Accused persons commenced on 3 June 2004, and the representation by the Prosecution that it would not be calling this witness until a much later stage in the trial, the Trial Chamber does not consider that the Defence would suffer any prejudice to its case. The Trial Chamber is of the opinion that the Defence will have adequate time and resources to investigate and prepare for the cross-examination of this witness.

[...]

28. The Trial Chamber considers that the proposed evidence of this witness appears relevant and could have probative value in relation to the allegations in paragraphs 20, 24, 25, 26 and 28 of the Indictment. The Chamber also notes that the proposed evidence purports to be direct evidence of the individual criminal responsibility of all three Accused. The Chamber, having weighed the timing of the application and disclosure of the witness statement on 18 May 2004 against the materiality of the evidence, considers that good cause has been shown and it is in the interests of justice to add this witness to the Modified Witness List. Given that the trial of the Accused persons commenced on 3 June 2004, and the representation by the Prosecution that it would not be calling this witness until a much later stage in the trial, the Trial Chamber is not convinced that the Defence would suffer any prejudice to its case. The Trial Chamber is of the opinion that the Defence will have adequate time and resources to investigate and prepare for the cross-examination of this witness.

[...]

32. The Trial Chamber is of the opinion that the proposed evidence of this witness appears relevant and could have probative value in relation to the allegations in paragraphs 20, 23, 24, 25, 26 and 28 of the Indictment. The Chamber also notes that the proposed evidence purports to be direct evidence of the individual criminal responsibility of the 1st Accused, and to the involvement of all three Accused in the attacks on Kenema, Zimmi and the Black December Operation. The Chamber, having weighed the lateness of the application and disclosure of the witness statement on 20 May 2004 against the materiality of the evidence, finds that good cause has been shown and it is in the interests of justice to add this witness to the

Modified Witness List. Given that the trial of the Accused persons commenced on 3 June 2004, and the representation by the Prosecution that it would not be calling this witness until a much later stage in the trial, the Trial Chamber does not consider that the Defence would suffer any prejudice to its case. The Trial Chamber is of the opinion that the Defence will have adequate time and resources to investigate and prepare for the cross-examination of this witness.

---

(1) *Prosecutor v. Nahimana*, Decision on the Prosecutor's Oral Motion for Leave to Amend the List of Selected Witnesses, 26 June 2001, para. 20; *Prosecutor v. Nahimana*, Decision on the Prosecutor's Application to Add Witness X to its List of Witnesses and for Protective Measures, 14 September 2001, para. 5; *Prosecutor v. Bagosora*, Decision on Prosecutor's Motion for Leave to Vary the Witness List Pursuant to Rule 73*bis*(E), para. 8.
(2) *Prosecutor v. Nahimana*, Decision on the Prosecutor's Oral Motion for Leave to Amend the List of Selected Witnesses, 26 June 2001, para. 20.
(3) *Prosecutor v. Bagosora*, Decision on Prosecution Motion for Addition of Witnesses Pursuant to Rule 73*bis*(E), 26 June 2003, para. 14.
(4) *Prosecutor v. Sam Hinga Norman, Moinina Fofana, Allieu Kondewa*, 16 July 2004, para. 9.
(5) *Prosecutor v. Delalic*, Decision on Confidential Motion to Seek Leave to Call Additional Witnesses, 4 September 1997, para. 7.

R73*bis*-TC-11

o *Prosecutor v. Norman, Fofana, Kondewa*, No. SCSL-04-14-T, Decision on Prosecution Request for Leave to Call Additional Expert Witness Dr William Haglund, 1st October 2004, para. 13-16, 19, 21-22:[124]

13. The Chamber notes that Rule 73bis(E) is similar in formulation to the corresponding Rule of the ICTR, which provides as follows:

> (E) After commencement of Trial, the Prosecutor, if he considers it to be in the interests of justice, may move the Trial Chamber for leave to reinstate the list of witnesses or to vary his decision as to which witnesses are to be called.

The Chamber further notes that when interpreting Rule 73*bis*(E) as to the applicable criteria of showing "good cause" and the "interest of justice", Trial Chambers of the ICTR have articulated certain factors in their exposition of law.(1) In the *Nahimana* case, for instance,(2) the Trial Chamber observed as follows:

---

[124] See also *Prosecutor v. Sesay, Kallon, Gbao*, Case No. SCSL-04-15-T, Decision on Prosecution Request for Leave to Call an Additional Expert Witness, 10 June 2005, para. 13.

"In assessing the "interests of justice" and "good cause" Chambers have taken into account such considerations as the materiality of the testimony, the complexity of the case, prejudice to the Defence, including elements of surprise, on-going investigations, replacements and corroboration of evidence. The Prosecution's duty under the Statute to present the best available evidence to prove its case has to be balanced against the right of the Accused to have adequate time and facilities to prepare his Defence and his right to be tried without undue delay."

14. The Trial Chamber further notes that additional factors, taken into account by Trial Chambers of the ICTR when considering the circumstances giving rise to "good cause" and the "interests of justice", include the time of disclosure of the witness information to the Defence and the probative value of the proposed testimony.

15. While acknowledging the importance of its role to ensure a fair and expeditious trial when considering the abovementioned factors as provided for in Rule 26*bis* of the Rules and the rights of accused persons to adequate time and facilities for the preparation of their defence, as stipulated in Article 17(4)(b) of the Statute, we reassert the principle that the Prosecution should not be allowed to surprise the Defence with additional witnesses and should fulfil in good faith its disclosure obligations.

16. In deciding on similar issues, The Trial Chamber of the ICTY in the *Delalic* case,[3] stated that it will "[u]tilise all its powers to facilitate the truth finding process in the impartial adjudication of the matter between the parties". This Chamber will, in the determination of this issue, have due regard for the doctrine of "equality of arms".

[...]

19. The evidence sought to be added by the Prosecution appears not to be a duplication of the evidence of other witnesses on the Modified Witness List. Since it is statement of facts, Dr Haglund's testimony is additional and supplemental to oral witness testimonies and, therefore, appears to be relevant in relation to existing witnesses, and their testimony.

[...]

21. In particular, the Chamber finds that there is no element of surprise resulting in detriment to the Defence, since the events covered by the expert testimony are already mentioned in the statements of witnesses TF2-030 and TF2-156, disclosed to the Defence by the Prosecution in November 2002 and November 2003. On the contrary, it is our opinion that the Defence will have adequate time to investigate and prepare for the cross-examination of this Expert Witness.

22. In such circumstances, the Chamber must draw a balance between the Statutory right of the accused persons, as the Defence contends, to a fair and expeditious trial and the equally important and very challenging right of the Prosecution for access to evidence and all material that would contribute not only to discharging the onerous legal burden that it bears to prove the guilt of the accused beyond all reasonable doubt, but also to furnish the Court with evidence that would contribute to fulfilling its mission of ensuring that justice is done to all parties.

---

(1) *Prosecutor v. Nahimana*, Decision on the Prosecutor's Oral Motion for Leave to Amend the List of Selected Witnesses, 26 June 2001, para. 20; *Prosecutor v. Nahimana*, Decision on the Prosecutor's Application to Add Witness X to its List of Witnesses and for Protective Measures, 14 September 2001, para. 5; *Prosecutor v. Bagosora*, Decision on Prosecutor's Motion for Leave to Vary the Witness List Pursuant to Rule 73*bis*(E), para. 8.
(2) *Prosecutor v. Nahimana*, Decision on the Prosecutor's Oral Motion for Leave to Amend the List of Selected Witnesses, 26 June 2001, para. 20.
(3) *Prosecutor v. Delalic*, Decision on Confidential Motion to Seek Leave to Call Additional Witnesses, 4 September 1997, para. 7.

R73*bis*-TC-12

o *Prosecutor v. Sesay, Kallon, Gbao*, Case No. SCSL-04-15-T, Decision on Prosecution Request for Leave to Call Additional Witnesses and Disclose Additional Witness Statements, 11 February 2005, para. 34-35:[125]

34. In our opinion and in this context, the criterion "upon good cause being shown", by the Prosecution, means and connotes a responsibility on the part of the Prosecution to advance a credible reason, reasons or justification, for failing to either meet up with or to fulfil, within the time limits imposed by Rule 66(A)(ii) of the Rules, the obligation of disclosing to the Defence, the existence of these witnesses and more importantly, the statements on which their viva voce testimony will be based.

35. To discharge this obligation, the Prosecution, in our view, must satisfy the Chamber:

---

[125] See also *Prosecutor v. Sesay, Kallon, Gbao*, Case No. SCSL-05-15-T, Decision Regarding the Prosecutor's Further Renewed Witness List, 5 April 2005, para. 15-19; *Prosecutor v. Norman, Fofana, Kondewa*, Case No. SCSL-05-14-T, Decision on Prosecution Request for Leave to Call an Additional Expert Witness, 10 June 2005, para. 9; *Prosecutor v. Sesay, Kallon, Gbao*, Case No. SCSL-04-15-T, Decision on Prosecution Request for Leave to Call an Additional Expert Witness, 10 June 2005, para. 9; *Prosecutor v. Brima, Kamara, Kanu*, Case No. SCSL-04-16-T, Decision on Prosecution Request for Leave to Call an Additional Witness (Zainab Hawa Bangura) Pursuant to Rule 73*bis*(E), and on Joint Defence Notice to Inform the Trial Chamber of its Position vis-à-vis the Proposed Expert Witness (Mrs Bangura) Pursuant to Rule 94*bis*, 5 August 2005, para. 28.

o That the circumstances surrounding these reasons or explanations as advanced by the Prosecution are directly related, and are material to the facts in issue;

o That the facts to be provided by these witnesses in their statements and eventually in their testimony, are relevant to determining the issues at stake and would contribute to serving and fostering the overall interest of the law and justice;

o That granting, at this stage, leave to call new witnesses and the disclosure of new statements, will not unfairly prejudice the right of the accused to a fair and expeditious trial as guaranteed by Article 17(4)(a) and 17(4)(b) of the Statute as well as by the provisions of Rules 26bis of the Rules;

o That the evidence the Prosecution is now seeking to call, could not have been discovered or made available at a point earlier in time notwithstanding the exercise of due diligence on their part.

- **Rule 73*bis*(E): Pre-Trial Conference – Leave to Call Additional Witnesses – Witness Reluctance**

R73*bis*-TC-13

o *Prosecutor v. Sesay, Kallon, Gbao*, Case No. SCSL-04-15-T, Decision on Prosecution Request for Leave to Call Additional Witnesses and Disclose Additional Witness Statements, 11 February 2005, para. 36-37:

36. The Chamber, in these circumstances, given the explanations furnished by the Prosecution, recognises that in trials of this magnitude and complexity, it would not be unusual for some key witnesses to manifest, for diverse reasons, a reluctance and a lukewarmness to cooperate with investigators and the Prosecution in their attempt to get them to volunteer statements and to eventually testify on matters relevant to the issues for determination.

37. In the light of the above, The Chamber is satisfied that the explanation provided by the Prosecution in this regard and particularly in relation to the difficulties they encountered in securing the cooperation of these 3 new witnesses is credible.

- **Rule 73*bis*(E): Pre-Trial Conference – Leave to Call Additional Witnesses – Corroborative Evidence**

R73*bis*-TC-14

o *Prosecutor v. Sesay, Kallon, Gbao*, Case No. SCSL-04-15-T, Decision on Prosecution Request for Leave to Call Additional Witnesses and Disclose Additional Witness Statements, 11 February 2005, para. 30-33:

30. We have noted that the objection by the Defence to the granting of this application is based on the argument that each of the testimonies of the three new witnesses will be merely repetitive or corroborative of evidence already adduced by the Prosecution and that it is not as new or as unique as the Prosecution professes, nor will it have any further impact on the case for the Prosecution.

31. In our opinion, the Prosecution in this regard, enjoys a prosecutorial latitude in the domain of the strategies it puts in place to establish its case particularly in the light and within the context of the provisions of Article 15(1) of the Statute which confers on the Prosecutor, of course, within the limits and confines of the Law and the applicable Rules and the doctrine of equality of arms, the competence to act independently as a separate Organ of the Special Court.

32. In this context, we would like to observe that even if it were conceded, as the Defence contends, that the testimony of these three witnesses may be merely corroborative of the testimony that is already available on record, The Chamber is not prepared to impose on the Prosecution, at this stage, a limit on the number of witnesses it considers necessary to prove or to corroborate a particular fact or facts. This contention by the Defence is therefore, in our opinion, without merit.

33. Furthermore, The Chamber cannot be certain as to whether the information provided by these witnesses may give rise to new facts or details which are relevant to the issues at stake.

- **Rule 73*bis*(E): Pre-Trial Conference – Leave to Call Additional Witness – Reduction in the Total Number of Witnesses**

R73*bis*-TC-15   o *Prosecutor v. Sesay, Kallon, Gbao*, Case No. SCSL-04-15-T, Decision on Prosecution Request for Leave to Call Additional Witnesses and Disclose Additional Witness Statements, 11 February 2005, para. 40:

40. In the light of the above and given the significant reduction in the total number of the Prosecution witness from 266 to 102 as contained in its Renewed Witness List and the representation by the Prosecution that it would not be calling these witnesses until a much later stage in the trial, the Trial Chamber is of the view that the provisions of Article 17(4)(b) of the Statute would not be violated as the Defence would not suffer any unfair prejudice if the Prosecution's application were granted.

- **Rule 73*bis*(E): Pre-Trial Conference – Leave to Call Additional Witnesses – Move from the List of "Back-up Witnesses" to the List of "Core Witnesses"**

R73*bis*-TC-16

o *Prosecutor v. Sesay, Kallon, Gbao*, Case no. SCSL-05-15-T, Decision Regarding the Prosecutor's Further Renewed Witness List, 5 April 2005, para. 26-31:

26. This Chamber opines that while the Prosecution has been ordered to distinguish between "core" witnesses and "back-up" witnesses in order to facilitate the work of the Defence and the Court, this does not change the fact that the Prosecution is still relying on the same witness list that was filed on the 26th of April 2004. Moreover, as noted above, our Order envisaged that these lists were not static since the "back-up" witnesses were meant to replace "core" witnesses who were not available to testify.

27. This Chamber recently recognised in its Decision on Prosecution Request for Leave to Call Additional Witnesses and Disclose Additional Witness Statements that:

[I]n trials of this magnitude and complexity, it would not be unusual for some key witnesses to manifest, for diverse reasons, a reluctance and a lukewarmness to cooperate with investigators and the Prosecution in their attempt to get them to volunteer statements and to eventually testify on matters relevant to the issues for determination.[1]

28. Although Counsel for Kallon suggested that these changes to the "core" and "back-up" lists demonstrate "inconsistency and caprice on the part of the Prosecution", this Chamber finds that no grounds have been established by the Defence as a basis for this assertion. The Chamber notes that this is the first occasion on which the Prosecution has sought to move witnesses from the "back-up" list to the "core" list.

29. The Chamber finds that the Defence has been provided with disclosure pursuant to Rules 66 and 68 of the Rules with regard to all of the witnesses on both the "core" and "back-up" witness lists. Moreover, the trial was commenced on the basis that all of these 266 witnesses could be called at trial.

30. This Chamber concludes that the Prosecution may, from time to time, substitute witnesses from the "back-up" list for witnesses from the "core" list who are not able to testify. In particular, the Chamber is satisfied that the Prosecutor may add witnesses TF1-029 and TF1-122 to its "core" witness list to replace witnesses TF1-085 and TF1-126.

31. The Chamber is cognisant of the critical importance of the right of the Accused under Article 17(4)(b) of the Statute of the Special Court for Sierra Leone to have "adequate time and facilities for the preparation of his or her defence". Thus, this Chamber notes that the Defence may, in the appropriate circumstances, seek the remedy of an adjournment of testimony in order to allow adequate preparation. In relation to the two witnesses at bar, the Chamber is satisfied that the Prosecution has indicated that it intends to call witness TF1-122 towards the end of the April-May 2005 trial session and that witness TF1-029 will be called at a later trial session.

---

[1] *Prosecutor v. Sesay et al.*, *supra*, Decision of the 29th of July 2004, para. 36.

- **Rule 73bis(F): Pre-Trial Conference – Statements of Agreed Points of Fact and Law**

R73*bis*-TC-17

o *Prosecutor v. Kondewa*, Case No. SCSL-04-14-PT, Order Rejecting the Filing of the Defence Objection to Prosecution's Motion for Judicial Notice and Admission of Facts, 05 May 2004:

NOTING that Counsel for the Accused may file any statements of admissions or matters not in dispute at any time and that such approach is encouraged by the Trial Chamber;

R73*bis*-TC-18

o *Prosecutor v. Norman, Fofana, Kondewa*, Case No. SCSL-04-14-T, Decision on Co-operation Between the Parties, 26 May 2004:

NOTING that at the Pre-Trial Conference held on 28 April 2004, the parties were encouraged to continue to meet to seek agreement on points of fact and law;

CONSIDERING that points of agreement between the parties would help to expedite the trial and be in the interests of justice;

CONSIDERING that the filing of the Prosecution Supplemental Pre-Trial Brief and the disclosure by the Prosecution of materials listed above, provides a basis for the parties to agree at this time, where possible, on a number of factual and legal matters that are not in dispute, and that the parties will have the opportunity to continue to meet and agree to points of fact and law throughout the trial;

PURSUANT TO Rules 54 and 73*bis* of the Rules of Procedure and Evidence of the Special Court;

ORDERS as follows:

The parties to submit a joint statement, signed by both parties, no later than 1 June 2004, stating all the agreed points of fact and law reached by them;

The parties intensify their efforts to identify further points of agreement and to submit a report on the progress made every fifteen (15) days from the date of this decision, until further notice by the Trial Chamber.

R73*bis*-TC-19   o *Prosecutor v. Sesay, Kallon, Gbao*, Case No. SCSL-04-15-PT, Decision on Co-operation Between the Parties, 16 June 2004:

CONSIDERING that points of agreement between the parties would help to expedite the trial and be in the interests of justice;

CONSIDERING that the filing of the Prosecution Supplemental Pre-Trial Brief and the disclosure by the Prosecution of materials listed above, provides a basis for the parties to agree at this time, where possible, on a number of factual and legal matters that are not in dispute, and that the parties will have the opportunity to continue to meet and agree to points of fact and law throughout the trial;

PURSUANT TO Rules 54 and 73*bis* of the Rules of Procedure and Evidence of the Special Court;

ORDERS as follows:

a. The parties to submit a joint statement, signed by both parties, no later than 1 July 2004, stating all the agreed points of fact and law reached by them;
b. The parties to intensify their efforts to identify further points of agreement and to submit a report on the progress made every fifteen (15) days from the date of this decision, until further notice by the Trial Chamber.

R73*bis*-TC-20   o *Prosecutor v. Norman, Fofana, Kondewa*, Case No. SCSL-04-14-T, Order on Co-operation Between the Parties, 03 November 2004:

NOTING that pursuant to this Decision the Parties have been filing their Status Reports every fifteen (15 days) and that so far nine (9) Status Reports were filed by the Parties, the last being filed on the 15th of October, 2004;

CONSIDERING the continuous lack of progress by the Parties to identify further points of agreement in points of law and fact, which would otherwise help to expedite the trial and be in the interests of justice;

CONSIDERING that at the Status Conference held on the 1st of November, 2004, the Parties did not object to the proposal by the Trial Chamber to file their Status Reports only once every session or at the end of each session;[1]

PURSUANT TO Rules 54 and 73*bis*(F) of the Rules of Procedure and Evidence of the Special Court;

ORDERS as follows:

The Parties to submit a Status Report to the Trial Chamber on the progress made on the last day of every trial session instead of every fifteen (15) days, until further notice by the Trial Chamber.

---

[1] Transcript of the 1st of November, 2004, pages 35-36.

R73*bis*-TC-21 o *Prosecutor v. Sesay, Kallon, Gbao*, Case No. SCSL-04-15-T, Order on Co-operation Between the Parties, 9 November 2004:

RECALLING the Trial Chamber's *Decision on Co-operation Between the Parties*, of the 16th of June, 2004 ("Decision"), [...]

NOTING that pursuant to the Decision four (4) Status Reports were filed by the Parties, the last being filed on the 16th of September, 2004;

CONSIDERING the continuous lack of progress to identify further points of agreement in points of law and fact expressed by the Parties in their Status Reports;

CONSIDERING that at the Status Conference held on the 1st of October, 2004, the Parties informed that co-operation between them was continuing and even increasing but that they would prefer to be able to meet on an informal and ad hoc basis without the formal obligation to report to the Chamber on a regular basis; [...]

BEING SATISFIED from the proceedings during the various sessions of the trial that the Parties have markedly increased their informal co-operation, contributing to the expedition of the trial and the interests of justice;

PURSUANT TO Rules 54 and 73*bis*(F) of the Rules of Procedure and Evidence of the Special Court;

ORDERS AS FOLLOWS:

1. That the Parties shall no longer be required to submit on a regular basis a Status Report to the Chamber;

2. That the Parties should continue to co-operate on a regular basis and, in case they wish to do so, to promptly report to the Chamber any agreed points of fact and law.

- **Rule 73*bis*(F): Pre-Trial Conference – Purpose of the Defence Pre-Trial Brief**

R73*bis*-TC-22 o *Prosecutor v. Norman, Fofana, Kondewa*, Case No. SCSL-04-14-PT, Decision on Request for Extension of Time to File Pre-Trial Brief, 26 May 2004:

CONSIDERING that Rule 73*bis* of the Rules of Procedure and Evidence of the Special Court ("Rules"), provides for the filing of a pre-trial brief by the Defence, addressing the factual and legal issues not later than seven days prior to the date set for trial;

CONSIDERING that the Defence Pre-Trial Brief is principally intended to provide a response to the case presented in the Prosecution's Pre-Trial Brief and to address factual and legal issues, setting forth a framework for the commencement of trial;

- **Rule 73*bis*(F): Pre-Trial Conference – Time of the Defence Pre-Trial Brief**

R73*bis*-TC-23 o *Prosecutor v. Norman, Fofana, Kondewa*, Case No. SCSL-04-14-PT, Revised Order for the Filing of defence Pre-Trial Briefs, 22 March 2004:[126]

CONSIDERING that defence counsel for Sam Hinga Norman requested that the date for filing its pre-trial brief be suspended until after full disclosure or otherwise until after the order on Protective Measures is lifted;

CONSIDERING that each party is to address factual and legal issues in its pre-trial brief for the purposes of, *inter alia*, assisting the Trial Chamber in determining contested issues of fact and law;

---

[126] See also *Prosecutor v. Kondewa*, Case No. SCSL-04-14-PT, Additional Revised Order for Filing Defence Pre-Trial Brief, 22 April 2004.

CONSIDERING that the Trial Chamber, and indeed opposing counsel, will be more greatly assisted by a well-prepared, detailed pre-trial brief than by a pre-trial brief dated without the benefit of extensive disclosure and sufficient pre-trial preparation; [grants the Motion]

R73*bis*-TC-24

o *Prosecutor v. Norman, Fofana, Kondewa*, Case No. SCSL-04-14-PT, Decision on Request for Extension of Time to File Pre-Trial Brief, 4 June 2004:

CONSIDERING that the Pre-Trial Brief was not filed in time, and that the Request for an extension of time to file the Pre-Trial Brief was filed after the date ordered by the Trial Chamber in the Revised Order, and that the Defence team did not advise the Trial Chamber of any foreseen difficulties in preparing and filing the Pre-Trial Brief, prior to expiry of the time for filing the Pre-Trial Brief;

[...]

FINDING that it is in the interest of justice to receive the Defence Pre-Trial Brief as validly filed;

Rule 73*ter*: Pre-Defence Conference
(amended 29 May 2004)

(A) The Trial Chamber or a Judge designated from among its members may hold a Conference prior to the commencement by the defence of its case.

(B) At that Conference, the Trial Chamber or a Judge designated from among its members may order that the defence, before the commencement of its case but after the close of the case for the prosecution, file the following:

   (i) Admissions by the parties and a statement of other matters which are not in dispute;
   (ii) A statement of contested matters of fact and law;
   (iii) A list of witnesses the defence intends to call with:

      (a) The name or pseudonym of each witness;
      (b) A summary of the facts on which each witness will testify;
      (c) The points in the indictment as to which each witness will testify; and
      (d) The estimated length of time required for each witness;

   (iv) A list of exhibits the defence intends to offer in its case, stating where possible whether or not the Prosecutor has any objection as to authenticity.

The Trial Chamber or the said Judge may order the Defence to provide the Trial Chamber and the Prosecutor with copies of the written statements of each witness whom the Defence intends to call to testify.

(C) The Trial Chamber or a Judge designated from among its members may order the defence to shorten the estimated length of the examination-in-chief for some witnesses.

(D) The Trial Chamber or a Judge designated from among its members may order the defence to reduce the number of witnesses, if it considers that an excessive number of witnesses are being called to prove the same facts.

(E) After the commencement of the defence case, the defence may, if it considers it to be in the interests of justice, move the Trial Chamber for leave to reinstate the list of witnesses or to vary its decision as to which witnesses are to be called.

TRIAL CHAMBERS DECISIONS

- **Rule 73*ter*(B)(i): Pre-Defence Conference – Preparation of the Defence Case**

R73*ter*-TC-1   o *Prosecutor v. Norman, Fofana, Kondewa*, Case No. SCSL-04-14-T, Order for the Preparation and the Presentation of the Defence Case, 21 October 2005:[127]

MINDFUL of Rule 73*ter* of the Rules which provides for a Pre-Defence Conference to be held prior to commencement of the Defence Case;

CONSIDERING that Article 17(4)(b) of the Statute of the Special Court for Sierra Leone ("Statute") provides that the Accused shall be entitled to have "adequate time and facilities for the preparation of his defence";

CONSIDERING that Article 17(4)(c) of the Statute provides that the Accused shall be entitled "to be tried without undue delay";

THE CHAMBER, THEREFORE, ORDERS:

1. That a Status Conference be held with the parties on the 27th of October, 2005 at 9:30 a.m. in Court Room 1, for the purpose of considering the preparation and presentation of the Defence Case. At the Status Conference, the Chamber will require the Defence to present the particulars for their preparation of the Defence Case, that may include the following:

   a) the number of Defence witnesses that will be called for each Defence Team;
   b) whether joint witnesses will be called by the Defence Teams;
   c) whether expert witnesses will be called, and if so, the nature of such witnesses;
   d) whether the Accused will testify at trial;
   e) whether protective measures are necessary for Defence witnesses;
   f) the anticipated length of the Defence case;
   g) whether opening statements will be made by the Accused;

2. That the Defence file the following materials, no later than the 17th of November, 2005:

---

[127] See also *Prosecutor v. Norman, Fofana, Kondewa*, Case No. SCSL-04-14-T, Consequential Order for Compliance with the Order Concerning the Preparation and Presentation of the Defence Case, 28 November 2005.

a) A list of witnesses that each Defence Team intends to call, including:
   (i) the name of each witness;
   (ii) a summary of their respective testimony;
   (iii) the points of the Indictment to which each witness will testify;
   (iv) the estimated length of time for each witness to testify;
   (v) an indication of whether the witness will testify in person or pursuant to Rule 92*bis*;
b) A list of expert witnesses with an indication of when their report will be ready and made available to the Prosecution;
c) A list of exhibits the Defence intends to offer in its case, containing a brief description of their respective nature and contents, and stating where possible whether or not the Prosecution has any objection to their authenticity;
d) A chart which indicates, for each paragraph in the Indictment, the testimonial evidence and documentary evidence upon which the Defence will rely to defend the Accused against the allegations contained therein;

3. That a Pre-Defence Conference will be held on the 11th of January, 2006, for the following purpose:

a) to consider the compliance of the Defence with the Chamber's Order on Filings;
b) to review the Defence witness lists and to set the number of witnesses each Defence Team will be entitled to call;
c) to determine the time which will be available to each Defence Team to present their case;
d) for the parties to submit a statement of agreed facts and matters which are not in dispute, if available, and in accordance with the Chamber's *Order on Cooperation Between the Parties*, of 3 November 2004, continue to submit such Status Reports to the Chamber on the last day of every trial session;
e) to deal with any other matters that the Chamber considers appropriate for the purposes of facilitating the presentation of each Defence case;

4. The Defence case shall commence on the 17th of January, 2006, subject to any further Order by the Chamber.

> **Rule 74: Amicus Curiae**
> *(amended 7 March 2003)*
>
> A Chamber may, if it considers it desirable for the proper determination of the case, invite or grant leave to any State, organization or person to make submissions on any issue specified by the Chamber.

TRIAL CHAMBERS DECISIONS

- **Rule 74:** *Amicus Curiae* – **Criterion for Leave to Call**

R74-TC-1
o *Prosecutor v. Kallon*, Case No. SCSL-03-07-PT, Decision on the Application for Leave to Submit *Amicus Curiae* Briefs, 17 July 2003, para. 8-10:

8. The Chamber notes that the above provision, in clear and unambiguous language, confers on the special court a discretionary authority to invite or grant leave to any state, organization or person to make submissions on any issue specified by "any Chamber of the Special court. From the plain language of the said Rule, such a discretionary power is not intended to be exercised lightly. Hence the qualification that its exercise must be predicated upon a prior judicial determination that the *amicus curiae* submissions contemplated are "desirable for the proper determination of the case". This is the governing criterion.

9. Upon a careful consideration of the jurisprudence of other sister international criminal tribunals, particularly the ICTR, the Chamber's finding is that leave to appear as *amicus curiae* has been granted mainly on the following grounds:

  (a) that one has strong interests in or views on the subject matter before the Court (see *Prosecutor v. Bagosora*, Case No. ICTR-96-7-T, Decision on the Amicus Curiae Application by the Government of the Kingdom of Belgium, 6 June 1998);
  (b) that it is desirable to enlighten the Tribunal on the events that took place (see *Prosecutor v. Akayesu*, Case No. ICTR-96-4-T, Order Granting Leave for Amicus Curiae to Appear, 12 February 1998);
  (c) that it may be useful to gather additional legal views with respect to the legal principles involved, not with respect to the particular circumstances of this or any other case (see *Prosecutor v. Semanza*, Case No. ICTR-97-20-T, Decision on the Kingdom of Belgium's

Application to File and Amicus Curiae and on the Defence Application to strike out the Observation of the Kingdom of Belgium Concerning the Preliminary Response by the Defence, 9 February 2001);

10. Instructively, the aforementioned grounds do follow logically from, and can be subsumed under the broad criterion of *"for the proper determination of the case"* as provided in rule 74. [...]

In the context of the instant Motion, however, the Chamber recalls that the Defence Office seeks leave to make *amicus curiae* submissions on the three main grounds: (a) that, as in *Milosevic* case, "it retains the right and duty to make submissions to assist the proper determination of the case," (b) that it is "desirable for the proper determination of the case that the Chamber should have benefit" of such submissions; and (c) that because of its "historical significance as the first 'public defender's office' to be established in an international court or tribunal, that it is in the interests of justice" for leave to be granted.

- **Rule 74: Amicus Curiae – Amicus Counsel**

R74-TC-2   o *Prosecutor v. Brima, Kamara, Kanu*, Case No. SCSL-04-16-T, Decision on the Confidential Application for Withdrawal by Counsel for Brima and Kamara and on the Request for Further Representation by Counsel for Kanu, 20 May 2005, para. 63:

63. We reject the suggestion by the Principal Defender that Lead Counsel be re-designated as "Amicus Counsel". An "Amicus Counsel" is not recognised by the Rules, although Rule 74 makes provision for Amicus Curiae. Amicus Curiae is not, of course, a party to the case. We therefore find that the suggestion is totally inappropriate and would involve the Trial Chamber's participation in a sham in which the Amicus Curiae were really the Counsel for the Accused.

APPEALS CHAMBER DECISIONS

- **Rule 74:** *Amicus Curiae* – **Role and Appointment**

R74-AC-1

o *Prosecutor v. Kallon*, Case No. SCSL-03-07-AR72, Decision on Application by the Redress Trust, Lawyers Committee for Human Rights and the International Commission of Jurists For Leave to File *Amicus Curiae* Brief and Present Oral Submissions, 1 November 2003, para. 3-11:[128]

> 3. The kinds of intervention envisaged by Rule 74 are by no means novel in common law jurisdictions. Appeal Courts, in particular, when confronted with new or complex points of law, have an inherent power to permit or invite submissions from an *amicus* – a "friend of the court". The Latin translation is not always apt, because such submissions are made without any warrant that the Court will be predisposed or indeed disposed to accept them. Counsel invited under Rule 74 by the Court or its presiding judge, usually because of his or her expertise in the legal subject under question, will be expected to present all relevant material and if appropriate to express a view on the law: counsel for the parties should feel no inhibition in examining or challenging that view.
>
> 4. More recently, the highest courts in the UK and Australia have been willing to grant leave to interested parties, such as corporations or NGOs, to make submissions on points of law arising in cases before them – a practice that has long been adopted by the US Supreme Court. The intervening parties may have a direct interest, insofar as this decision will be likely to create a precedent affecting them in the future. The intervener's interest may be indirect, in the sense that a State or NGO or campaigning group may wish to have the law clarified or declared or developed in a particular way. An example of a grant of leave to intervene in a similar matter to this is provided by the House of Lords in the Pinochet cases,[(1)] where Amnesty International was permitted to file submissions and develop them in oral argument, whilst other organizations such as Human Rights Watch (an NGO allied to the Lawyers Committee) were allowed to file written submissions. NGOs and law professors and even States have been permitted to intervene, usually to address points of law, at the International Criminal Tribunal for the Former Yugoslavia ("ICTY") and International Criminal Tribunal for Rwanda ("ICTR").

---

[128] See also *Prosecutor v. Norman*, Case No. SCSL-03-08-AR72(E), Decision on Application by the University of Toronto International Human Rights Clinic for Leave to File *Amicus Curiae* Brief, 01 November 2003, para. 2; *Prosecutor v. Taylor*, Case No. SCSL-03-01-AR72(E), Decision on Application by the African Bar Association for Leave to File *Amicus Curiae* Brief, 20 November 2003.

5. Our Rule 74, adopted without amendment from the equivalent ICTR Rule, does not discriminate between the different interests of parties seeking to intervene: it focuses on the potential assistance they can provide to the Court. The "proper determination" of the case refers, quite simply, to the Court reaching the decision which most accords with the end of justice – i.e. that gets the law right. Sitting as we do in Freetown, albeit with the benefit of the Internet and of capable resident lawyers, we can nevertheless be assisted by outside counsel provided at its own expense by an organization with a legitimate interest in the subject matter of our hearings. The issue is whether it is <u>desirable</u> to receive such assistance, and "desirable" does not mean "essential" (which would be over-restrictive) nor does it have an over-permissive meaning such as "convenient" or "interesting". The discretion will be exercised in favour of an application where there is a real reason to believe that written submissions, or such submissions supplemented by oral argument, will help the Court to reach the right decision on the issue before it.

6. The Rule may, however, be approached differently in the Trial Chamber as distinct from the Appeals Chamber. What is desirable in the latter may be most undesirable in the former where the equality of arms principle may require that the parties engage in an adversarial exercise untrammelled by interventions from third parties, however well-intentioned. The overriding need to get on with the trial, without disruption and fairly both to prosecution and defence, may well make it undesirable to grant leave to any "State or organisation or person" to make submissions on facts, or even on law, in the course of the trial. Any third party which is in possession of material it wishes the Trial Chamber to notice should properly convey it to the Prosecution or the Defence – preferably, to both. It will then be up to these parties in litigation to decide whether or to what extent to deploy it at the trial. At an appellate level, however, different considerations will apply and it may be possible for a more generous view to be taken as to the grant of leave.

7. The applicants are not mere busybodies: they are distinguished international organizations with long experience of dealing with issues relating to torture, international law and war crimes. We do not consider that they seek leave to intervene for any ulterior motive, for example to provide a publicity platform for themselves, or to use the Court's privileges and immunities to put declarations on the record or to promote some hidden agenda. They offer legal submissions on an issue that has difficulties and complications, pre-sented through competent counsel. It may be, as the Prosecution protest, that these submissions will go wider than the issues before the Court, but if so, such inappropriate breadth will be ignored and will not be examined in the course of the short oral hearing they will be allocated. In any event, the Prosecution will

have every opportunity to refute or confound their arguments as of course will the defence. There is a real likelihood that these submissions will assist – the Rule requires no more – in the judicial determination of the Kallon Application.

8. This decision accords with two ICTR Trial Chamber decisions which have been cited to us: *Akayesu*,[2] where the Secretary General of the United Nations was granted leave to make submissions on the scope of the immunity of a UN Commander (General Dallaire) that he was prepared to lift in the interests of making the Commander's evidence available to the defence, and *Semanza*, where the Belgian government, over defence objection, was given leave to make submissions as to international law and the interpretation of the Geneva Conventions "but not with respect to the particular circumstances of this or any other case".[3] This last qualification is important: leave to intervene will be granted much more readily if what is offered is legal argument – all facts should normally be proved or presented by the parties themselves.

9. Our attention has been drawn by the Prosecution to a Decision of the Trial Chamber of the Special Court on an application by the Defence Office to submit an amicus brief on this and other motions by Morris Kallon.[4] This application was filed prematurely in the Trial Chamber before both Kallon motions were referred to the Appeals Chamber. It would have been more appropriate, in retrospect, for the decision to have been taken in the Appeals Chamber, since the discretion to permit an amicus can only sensibly reside in the chamber (or the representative judge thereof) which is to hear the substantive motion in question. The actual decision to deny leave turned, quite unexceptionally, upon the fact that all interested defendants were at that time represented by counsel, whom the Defence Office could instruct to present its arguments without the need for any separate appearance. But we should caution against reading paragraph 9 of the Decision as the Prosecution reads it, i.e. as "setting forth the criteria which should govern" the grant of leave. The Trial Chamber was merely summarising three grounds (by no means exhaustive) upon which ICTR decisions on the subject had turned. The first was that the intervener "has strong interest in or views on the subject matter before the Court" although this cannot determine whether it is desirable that such views should be expressed. The second ground was "that it is desirable to enlighten the Tribunal on the events that took place" but it will seldom be appropriate, as we have explained, for third parties to "enlighten the Tribunal" by giving evidence of fact. The third ground – which counsels against giving leave for submissions on facts as distinct from legal issues – derives from *Semanza* as described in paragraph 8 above.

10. As with all our rules, Rule 74 should not be construed narrowly or technically. The issue on which leave is sought may be specified by the Chamber directly, or simply be an issue specified in the substantive motion. The potential intervener is widely defined as 'any State, organisation or person' and notwithstanding the doubts of the Trial Chamber on this point, we think that definition is broad enough to include, for example, the Defence Office. That Office has a duty to provide assistance to indigent defendants, and there may be occasions when it will be appropriate for it to seek to intervene to protect the interests of those indictees who are as yet unrepresented but who have a real interest in the outcome of another defendant's application. Whether it would be given leave, however, will depend, as with all other such applications, on the Court's assessment of the value of the assistance it is likely to render; an assessment easier for us to make the more the Court is told about the proposed submission.

11. It is necessary to avoid the procedural confusion that can occur if applications to intervene in the Appeals Chamber are filed in and determined by the Trial Chamber (or *vice versa*). Generally, such applications should be made on or after referral to the Appeals Chamber, in writing to the Legal Officer of this Chamber. He or she will consult with the pre-hearing judge and with the President and normally it should be possible for leave to be granted (for written submissions and in some cases for oral argument) in good time for those submissions to be filed at least a week before the hearing. It would assist if the application is accompanied by a description of the submissions which the potential intervener wishes to make. In the event that leave is granted for oral argument, the time allocated will normally be no more than one hour. It must clearly be understood that although the Court's Registry and the Chamber's legal officers will provide working facilities and suchlike assistance to intervening lawyers, those 'States, organisations and persons' who are granted leave to intervene must do so at their own expense in terms of travel, accommodation and counsel's fees."

---

[1] [1998] 3 WLR 1456; [1999] 2 WLR 827.
[2] *Prosecutor v. Jean-Paul Akayesu*, Case No. ICTR-96-4-T, "Order Granting Leave for Amicus Curiae to Appear", 12 February 1998.
[3] *Prosecutor v. Laurent Semanza*, Case No. ICTR-97-20-T, "Decision on the Kingdom of Belgium's Application to File an Amicus Curiae Brief and on the Defence Application to Strike Out the Observations of the Kingdom of Belgium Concerning the Preliminary Response by the Defence", 9 February 2001, para. 10.
[4] *Prosecutor v. Morris Kallon*, "Decision on the Application for Leave to Submit Amicus Curiae Briefs", 17 July 2003.

- **Rule 74: *Amicus Curiae* – Invitation by a Chamber**

R74-AC-2
o *Prosecutor v. Norman*, Case No. SCSL-03-08-AR72, Order on the Appointment of *Amicus Curiae*, 12 December 2003:[129]

NOTING that the United Nations Children's Fund ("UNICEF") was invited by the Chamber to submit an *amicus curiae* brief on the issues raised by the Preliminary Motion and accepted this invitation;

CONSIDERING that there is a real reason to believe that an *amicus curiae* brief by UNICEF and other interested organisations that may be approached by UNICEF providing material that is not already before the Appeals Chamber will assist it in reaching its decision on the issues raised by the Preliminary Motion;

---

[129] *Prosecutor v. Brima, Kamara, Kanu*, Case No. SCSL-04-16-AR73, Order on the Appointment of *Amicus Curiae*, 24 November 2005; *Prosecutor v. Brima, Kamara, Kanu*, Case No. SCSL-04-16-AR73, Order on the Appointment of *Amicus Curiae*, 28 November 2005; *Prosecutor v. Brima, Kamara, Kanu*, Case No. SCSL-04-16-AR73, Order on the Appointment of *Amicus Curiae*, 2 December 2005.

Rule 74*bis*: Medical Examination of the Accused
(amended 1 August 2003)

(A) A Judge or Trial Chamber may, on its own motion, or at the request of a party, order a medical, psychiatric or psychological examination of the accused.

(B) The Registrar shall keep a list of approved experts for the purpose of examinations under Sub-Rule (A) above.

(C) Where the Trial Chamber is satisfied that the accused is unfit to stand trial, it shall order that the trial be adjourned. The Trial Chamber may, on its own motion or at the request of the Prosecutor or the Defence, review the case of the accused. In any event, the case shall be reviewed every ninety days unless there are reasons to do otherwise. If necessary, the Trial Chamber may order further examinations of the accused. When the Trial Chamber is satisfied that the accused has become fit to stand trial, it shall proceed.

TRIAL CHAMBERS DECISIONS

- **Rule 74*bis*: Medical Examination of the Accused – Fitness to Plead and Stand Trial**

R74*bis*-TC-1

o *Prosecutor v. Sankoh*, Case No. SCSL-03-02-I, Order for Physiological and Psychiatric Examination and Detention on Remand, 15 March 2003:

CONSIDERING the request of the Duty Counsel for the adjournment of the Initial Appearance of the Accused in order to undertake full his physiological and psychiatric examination;

CONSIDERING the favourable opinion expressed by the Prosecutor for such examination of the Accused and, consequently, for the adjournment of his Initial Appearance;

CONSIDERING the Order for Adjournment of the Initial Appearance of the Accused to 20 March 2003;

PURSUANT to Rule 54 and Rule 74*bis* of the Rules,

HEREBY ORDERS, the physiological and psychiatric examination of the Accused;

DISPENSES the Accused of any further attendance in court until further order;

DIRECTS the Registrar to undertake, after consultation with the Defence Office and the Office of the Prosecutor, all necessary measures for the execution of this order;

ORDERS the detention on remand of the Accused until further order of the Special Court.

R74*bis*-TC-2

o *Prosecutor v. Sankoh*, Case No. SCSL-03-02-I, Order for Further Physiological and Psychiatric Examination and Detention on Remand, 21 March 2003:

CONSIDERING the Report of the 20th of March, 2003 on the Physiological and Psychiatric Examination of the Accused ("the Report") [...]

[...]

CONSIDERING the observations of both Counsels for the Prosecution and the Defence that a further examination on the physiological and psychiatric condition of the Accused is necessary;

CONSIDERING the necessity to carry out a further and conclusive medical examination on the physiological and psychiatric condition of the Accused and the establishment of a final medical report in this regard;

NOW THEREFORE: I, Judge Benjamin Mutanga Itoe, considering that the Report recommends, *inter alia*, further examination of the Accused in order to better assess his present physiological and psychiatric condition and, in particular, to evaluate the future development of such condition,

DO HEREBY ORDER:

1. That the Report be served on Counsels for the Prosecution and for the Defence;

2. That the Accused be subjected to a further physiological and psychiatric examination, whose report should be conclusive and shall be subject to non disclosure excepting to Counsels for the Prosecution and the Defence until further Order, with a view to determining if the Accused is fit to plead and eventually to stand trial before the Special Court;

- **Rule 74*bis*(C): Medical Examination of the Accused – Initial Appearance – Situation Where the Accused Is Unfit to Trial and Plea – Inhumane and Degrading Treatment**

R74*bis*-TC-3

o *Prosecutor v. Sankoh*, Case No. SCSL-03-02-PT, Ruling on the Motion for a Stay of Proceedings Filed by the Applicant, 22 July 2003, pages 7-12:

Since the entry of the plea is a mandatory preliminary to the commencement of these proceedings, it stands to reason that pending the fixing of the date for a continued hearing, the Pre-trial process stands adjourned and suspended until the psychological and physiological condition stands adjourned and suspended until the psychological and physiological condition of the Applicant is verified and certified as either good or bad.

[. . .] If the latter finding were however the credible thesis of his condition, he may be subjected to other judicial measures but will certainly be entitled to neither a discharge, nor, least still, an acquittal, and this indeed, within the practice underlying the principles which were well established in the historic MacNaughten Rules 10CL & FIN 200 (1843).

In the present proceedings, the Applicant allegedly remains, following the indictment approved by His Lordship, the Judge, Bankole Thompson, criminally answerable for the offences for which he today is being called upon to defend himself, and particularly so because it is so far, neither contended nor is it alleged on his behalf that he, at the material time he is alleged to have committed those offences which are particularised in the indictment, was in the physical state in which he is today, nor was he or is he mentally deranged.

Indeed, the determination of the application before me calls for answers to three questions: Firstly, it is clearly established that the process of commencing a trial against the applicant or pursuing it if it became necessary, on an indictment which accuses him of having allegedly committed or facilitated the commission of grave and serious crimes against humanity, without more, amount to or fall within the purview of the definition of what the law considers as inhuman and degrading treatment? In other words, what does it take to complain of inhuman and degrading treatment? Secondly, what would be the consequences of putting on hold, the on-going and pending pre-trial process? Indeed, should the remedy sought by the applicant be granted and the pre-trial process put on hold? Thirdly, should, or can this application for a stay of proceedings be granted in these circumstances particularly given the reasons for the adjournment of the applicant's proceedings, merely on the grounds that a continuation of the process would tantamount to, as it is alleged in his favour, subjecting him to inhuman and degrading treatment?

As far as the first question is concerned, it is my considered opinion that for a treatment to be termed inhuman or degrading, it should be established that the said treatment, intended or not, and which at times could be spiced by a deprivation of liberty, be it lawful or otherwise, is such as causes or inflicts anguish, human suffering, hardship, and humiliation on the victim. In other words, it should amount to a violation of the human integrity of the individual subjected to it.

In fact, even though the provisions of Article 5 of the Universal Declaration of Human Rights enshrine the key elements of torture, degrading and inhuman treatment as does Article 5 of the African Charter of Human Rights and People's Liberty, it is observed that a treatment which amounts to inhuman and degrading treatment might not necessarily fulfil the ingredients of what constitutes the element of torture, but torture could encompass those acts that individually or collectively, constitute what is considered as being inhuman and degrading.

Does this application in favour of Mr. Foday Saybana Sankoh, allege or canvass facts or acts which sustain the contention that he has been or is being, or indeed, would be subjected to inhuman and degrading treatment.

From the fact before me so far, the applicant has been accorded the type of rare care and delicate attention that certainly is completely the contrary of anything that is considered cruel, inhuman or degrading. It is on record, from what the Expert, Dr Verkaik who examined him said, that he is receiving very delicate and special attention from his attendants. Dr Verkaik's medical report states that the Applicant could not feed himself; he could not walk or put himself in an upright position; he was incontinent for urine and faeces, which is the reason why he wears diapers. This denotes that his diapers are regularly changed, a fact which again highlights what is referred to as the delicate treatment which the applicant is receiving and which can certainly not be assimilated to what could, by any stretch of the imagination, be likened to degrading and inhuman treatment.

As far as his medical condition is concerned, I have indicated my desire to verify his physiological and psychiatric state before holding any further proceedings. This Order was reinforced by a similar Order dated the 7th of April, 2003, by His Lordship, Honourable Judge Bankole Thompson. When soon thereafter it was reported that the applicant's health was deteriorating, His Lordship, Honourable Judge Gelaga King, in an Order dated the 29th of March, 2003, ordered his immediate transfer to a segregated quarter of the United Nations Choithram Hospital in Freetown, with a view to providing him with all necessary medical treatment. On the same day, that is the 29th of March, 2003, following a further deterioration of his situation, His Lordship, Honourable Judge George Gelaga King, again issued another Order authorising his transfer to a Military Hospital in a neighbouring Country. This followed a medical report to the effect that the Applicant has suffered a paralysis on his left arm and leg, a heart arethemea and a reduced level of consciousness.

In my judgment, given the delicate and personal care accorded to the Applicant in custody, the medical treatment he receives, coupled with the concern this Court has expressed in by issuing a Order in favour of medical evacuation, is very far from what could be termed 'inhuman and degrading treatment'.

I am comforted in this view by an examination of certain judicial decisions whose facts savoured of acts of inhuman and degrading treatment such as that of Ireland vs. the U.K. (1978) 2 EHRR 25, where it were held that interrogation techniques such as sleep deprivation and a denial of adequate food was considered to be inhuman and degrading treatment just as treatment is considered inhuman if it causes intense physical or mental suffering. In the case of **Cyprus vs. Turkey** (1976) 4 EHRR 482, it was held that physical assault can amount to inhuman treatment, particularly where weapons or other instruments have been used, and so also are sexual assaults. In **Ribitch vs. Austria (1995) 21 EHRR 573** it was considered an infringement of the protection of the individuals right against inhuman and degrading treatment where the person is deprived of his liberty and there is any recourse to physical force which has not been necessitated by his own conduct, and which act, diminishes human dignity.

In the application before me for consideration, there is no proof that the applicant was, is being, or would be subjected to any of the aforementioned analysed situations. On the contrary, there is proof that he was and is still being treated humanely, delicately, and kindly. In the absence therefore of any proof by counsel that the continued judicial proceedings against his client have amounted to, do or would amount to inhuman and degrading treatment, Counsel's arguments on this point cannot stand.

On the second question as to what effect a halt in judicial proceedings would have, I would like to observe that this would be very counter productive. It will indeed occasion a clog in the wheel of the judicial machinery because is a stay were to be ordered as canvassed by Counsel for the Applicant, this will erode the whole foundation on which further judicial orders, pronouncements or proceedings would be based when the medical report on his physiological and psychological examination becomes available. The stay of proceedings would even affect the Applicant more adversely than it would any other party because, the Defence, through a myriad of judicial due processes, is expected to remain very much in the scene as a watch dog to challenge all possible illegalities that may affect his client. In so doing, he ensures the protection of his client and the right to a fair hearing which the rule of law guarantees to him.

It therefore stands to reason, as a reply to the third question, that the application to stay proceedings in this matter and the reasons advanced to sustain it, from the fore-going analysis, [are] unwarranted and without substance. It is accordingly dismissed.

I do order that the proceedings related thereto which, for reasons of a continued medical evaluation of the applicant were adjourned, remain adjourned for the time being and to resume as soon as the Order on the medical examinations to be conducted on him is executed and a report on it, made available to warrant a resumption of the proceedings.

The Applicant will continue to remain in custody within the territory of the Republic of Sierra Leone until a further Order to the contrary.

Rule 75: Measures for the Protection of Victims and Witnesses
(amended 14 May 2005)

(A) A Judge or a Chamber may, on its own motion, or at the request of either party, or of the victim or witness concerned, or of the Witnesses and Victims Section, order appropriate measures to safeguard the privacy and security of victims and witnesses, provided that the measures are consistent with the rights of the accused.

(B) A Judge or a Chamber may hold an *in camera* proceeding to determine whether to order:

  (i) Measures to prevent disclosure to the public or the media of the identity or whereabouts of a victim or a witness, or of persons related to or associated with him by such means as:

   (a) Expunging names and identifying information from the Special Court's public records;
   (b) Non-disclosure to the public of any records identifying the victim or witness;
   (c) Giving of testimony through image – or voice – altering devices or closed circuit television, video link or other similar technologies; and
   (d) Assignment of a pseudonym;

  (ii) Closed sessions, in accordance with Rule 79;
  (iii) Appropriate measures to facilitate the testimony of vulnerable victims and witnesses, such as one-way closed circuit television.

(C) A Judge or a Chamber shall control the manner of questioning to avoid any harassment or intimidation.

(D) The Witnesses and Victims Section shall ensure that the witness has been informed before giving evidence that his or her testimony and his or her identity may be disclosed at a later date in another case, pursuant to Rule 75(F).

(E) When making an order under Sub-Rule (A) above, a Judge or Chamber shall wherever appropriate state in the order whether the transcript of those proceedings relating to the evidence of the witness to whom the measures relate shall be made available for use in other proceedings before the Special Court.

(F) Once protective measures have been ordered in respect of a witness or victim in any proceedings before the Special Court (the "first proceedings"), such protective measures:

(i) shall continue to have effect *mutatis mutandis* in any other proceedings before the Special Court (the "second proceedings") unless and until they are rescinded, varied or augmented in accordance with the procedure set out in this Rule; but;

(ii) shall not prevent the Prosecutor from discharging any disclosure obligation under the Rules in the second proceedings, provided that the Prosecutor notifies the Defence to whom the disclosure is being made of the nature of the protective measures ordered in the first proceedings.

(G) A party to the second proceedings seeking to rescind, vary or augment protective measures ordered in the first proceedings shall apply to the Chamber seized of the second proceedings.

(H) Before determining an application under Sub-Rule (G) above, if the effect of the change serves to decrease the protective measures granted to the victim or witness by the Chamber in the first proceedings, the Chamber seized of the second proceedings shall obtain all relevant information from the first proceedings, and may consult with any Judge who ordered the protective measures in the first proceedings, or the relevant Chamber.

(I) An application to a Chamber to rescind, vary or augment protective measures in respect of a victim or witness may be dealt with either by the Chamber or by a Judge of that Chamber, and any reference in this Rule to "a Chamber" shall include a reference to "a Judge of that Chamber".

(J) If the Chamber seized of the second proceedings rescinds, varies or augments the protective measures ordered in the first proceedings, these changes shall apply only with regard to the second proceedings.

TRIAL CHAMBERS DECISIONS

- **Rule 75(A): Protective Measures for Witnesses – Discretion of the Court**

R75-TC-1 o *Prosecutor v. Sesay, Kallon, Gbao*, Case No. SCSL-04-15-T, Decision on Prosecution's Intention to Extend Protective Measures for Additional Witnesses, 22 October 2004:

CONSIDERING that decisions about protective measures are solely within the discretion of the Court;

- **Rule 75(A): Protective Measures for Witnesses – Binding Authority**

R75-TC-2   o *Prosecutor v. Norman, Fofana, Kondewa*, Case No. SCSL-04-14-T, Oral Ruling on Motion for Modification of Protective Measures for Witnesses, 2 November 2004:

FINDS that the Defence have violated their obligation under the Trial Chamber's Decision on Protective Measures by identifying data of a protected witness and information provided in closed session and **ORDERS** that the Defence comply with Decision on Protective Measures and refrain from disclosing any information that discloses the identities of protected witnesses; and

ORDERS that both Parties should comply with their respective obligations under the Trial Chamber's Decision on Protective Measures and all Orders of the Trial Chamber regarding protective measures for witnesses and closed sessions.

- **Rule 75(B): Protective Measures for Witnesses – Screen from Public and Prohibition of Photography**

R75-TC-3   o *Prosecutor v. Norman, Fofana, Kondewa*, Case No. SCSL-04-14-T, Decision on Prosecution Motion for Modification of Protective Measures for Witnesses, 8 June 2004, para. 37-42:[130]

37. The Prosecution seeks additional measures for the protection of all witnesses residing in Sierra Leone who have not waived their right to protection. They request that all these witnesses be allowed to testify with the use of screening from the public. Moreover, it is requested that the public and the media shall not be allowed to photograph, video-record, sketch or in any other manner record or reproduce images of any witness while he or she is in the precincts of the Special Court.

38. Article 17(2) of the Statute entitles the Accused to a right "to a <u>fair</u> and <u>public</u> hearing, subject to measures ordered by

---

[130] See also *Prosecutor v. Sesay, Kallon, Gbao*, Case No. SCSL-04-15-PT, Decision on Prosecution Motion for Modification of Protective Measures for Witnesses, 5 July 2004, para. 24-29.

the Special Court for the protection of victims and witnesses" (emphasis added). As has been clarified in the Prosecution Reply, the use of a screen during the testimony of a witness is intended to protect witnesses' identity <u>from the public</u> and not from the Accused.[1] Thus, the "veil of anonymity" is lifted in favour of the Accused, and the right of the Accused to a fair hearing is not infringed.

39. A screen to protect the identity of the witness from the public does – to a minor extent – negatively affect the public nature of the trial and the possibility of the public to fully follow the proceedings, and, consequently the right of the Accused to a public hearing. It is established by jurisprudence of other international criminal tribunals and courts[2] that, generally, preference should be given to a public hearing to avoid the impression of "*in camera*" justice for the Accused, as well as to give the public the possibility to follow the trial. However, it is also established that "this preference has to be balanced with other mandated interests",[3] among them protective measures for victims and witnesses, as laid down in Article 17(2) of the Statute.

40. As stated above, the location of the Special Court in the very country where the crimes were allegedly committed increases considerably the risks to witnesses. Based upon the information provided and the statements submitted, the Prosecution has demonstrated that there exist legitimate fears on the side of the witnesses, making it necessary to give considerable weight to security risks that could be encountered.

41. Concluding, it is our opinion that the use of a screen to protect all witnesses in court, who have not waived their right to protection, is a reasonable, appropriate and sensible way of a balancing the right of the Accused to a public hearing and the right of the public to be properly informed about the proceedings before the Special Court on the one side, with the security interests of the witnesses on the other.

42. The Defence did not raise any objection regarding the measure sought by the Prosecution not to allowing photographs, video-recording, sketching or in any other manner recording or reproducing images of any witness while he or she is in the precincts of the Special Court. We would like to observe that, in the case against *Andre Rwamakuba*, the ICTR found that such a measure was a "normal" protective measure which does "not affect the rights of the Accused."[4]

---

[1] Consolidated Reply, para. 9.
[2] See *Tadic* Decision, para. 32.
[3] *Id.* para. 33.
[4] *Prosecutor v Andre Rwamakuba*, ICTR-98-44-T, Decision on the Prosecutor's Motion for Protective Measures for Witnesses, 22 September 2000, para. 14.

- **Rule 75(B): Protective Measures for Witnesses – Voice Distortion and Closed Circuit Television**

R75-TC-4

o *Prosecutor v. Norman, Fofana, Kondewa*, Case No. SCSL-04-14-T, Decision on Prosecution Motion for Modification of Protective Measures for Witnesses, 8 June 2004, para. 43-48:[131]

43. The Prosecution also seeks additional protective measures for certain groups of witnesses:

(i) Voice distortion for the public for witnesses in Sub-Category A and C, namely victims of sexual violence and insider witnesses; and
(ii) closed circuit television for child witnesses in Sub-Category B, while the image appearing on the public's monitors is distorted.

It is noted that the Fofana Defence did not oppose these additional measures in its Response.

44. Contrary to the understanding of Counsel for the Accused Norman of the Prosecution Motion these protective measures sought apply only <u>with regards to the public</u>. Thus, these measures will not preclude an accused to see and observe the demeanour of these witnesses.

45. The arguments used to demonstrate the necessity of a balancing of public hearing and witness security also apply to these additional measures. Moreover, the need for special consideration to victims of sexual violence or children during their testimonials in court has been widely recognised in both domestic laws of states and in international courts.[(1)]

46. Specifically, for Sub-Categories A and C, (victims of sexual violence and insider witnesses) voice distortion for the public speakers were sought. Regarding Sub-Category A, victims of sexual violence, the Prosecution pointed out the risk for re-traumatisation and rejection by the victim's family and community and the possibility to recognise the voice of the witness. For insider witnesses in Category C, the Prosecution underlined the vulnerability of this group to acts of retaliation and potential harm, given the strict laws of the Kamajors not to share information with outsiders. In the opinion of the Trial Chamber these submissions demonstrate convincingly again the risks for the security of witnesses of both categories.

---

[131] See also *Prosecutor v. Sesay, Kallon, Gbao*, Case No. SCSL-04-15-PT, Decision on Prosecution Motion for Modification of Protective Measures for Witnesses, 5 July 2004, para. 30-35.

47. For Sub-Category B, child witnesses, the Prosecution seeks the possibility for testimony by way of closed-circuit-television. While the witness testifies in a back room in the court building, this would allow the Accused and the Defence, as well as the Trial Chamber and the Prosecution, to see the witness on a television-screen and observe his/her demeanour. The image on the screen for the public at that time would be distorted. As stated by Psychologist An Michels, especially children[2] are vulnerable witnesses, the risk of re-traumatisation and the possibility of stigmatisation and rejection is real and high. On this issue the U.S. Supreme Court held in *Maryland v. Craig* held that the use of closed circuit television does not violate the constitutional right of an Accused to confrontation if it is necessary in the opinion of the Court to protect a child witness from psychological harm.[3]

48. Based upon these information and the evidence submitted the Chamber finds that such risks as described would exist, and, therefore, deems it necessary in the interest of justice for children to be allowed to testify in the way the Prosecution asks for, in accordance with Rule 75(B)(i)(a).

---

[1] See *Tadic* Decision, para. 47.
[2] Motion, Annex 11.
[3] See *Maryland v. Craig, 497 U.S. 836 (1990)*.

- **Rule 75(F): Protective Measures for Witnesses – Application in Other Cases**

R75-TC-5 o *Prosecutor v. Brima, Kamara, Kanu*, Case No. SCSL-04-16-PT, Oral Decision on Prosecution's Motion for Protective Measures Pursuant to Order to the Prosecution for Renewed Motion for Protective Measures Dated 2 April 2004, 3 February 2005, para. 4-5:

4. I consider that once protective measures have been ordered in respect of a witness or a victim in any proceedings, such protective measures continue to have effect *mutatis mutandis* in cases where a witness will testify in different proceedings before the Special Court and unless and until they are rescinded, varied, or augmented by the Court making them. I would add that such measures, however, cannot be used as an excuse to prevent the Prosecutor from discharging any disclosure obligation under the Rules in other proceedings provided that the Prosecutor notifies the Defence to whom the disclosure is being made of the nature of the protective measures ordered in the first proceedings where the witness appeared.

5. I therefore hold that this application before me today is redundant in respect of all witnesses contained in the list in the Updated Compliance Report filed by the Prosecution on 11 May 2004. I therefore invite the Prosecution to withdraw this application in relation to all witnesses. Before doing so, I would note that this ruling confirms that the order of the Court in the matter of the *Prosecutor v. Sesay, Kallon, Gbao*, Case No. SCSL-2004-15 in its Decision on Prosecution Motion for Modification of Protective Measures for Witnesses of 5 July 2004, as varied from time to time, extends to all witnesses in this case, that is, the case of *Prosecutor v. Brima, Kamara, and Kanu*. The Court further notes that references to the Defence in the Order are deemed to include the Accused Brima, Kamara and Kanu and their Defence teams for the purposes of this case.

- **Rule 75(G): Protective Measures for Witnesses – Applicability of the Rule**

R75-TC-6

o *Prosecutor v. Brima, Kamara, Kanu*, Case No. SCSL-04-16-T, Decision on the Confidential Joint Defence Motion to Declare Null and Void Testimony-in-Chief of Witness TF1-023, 25 May 2005, para. 15-16:

15. Further, the Defence submitted that the Trial Chamber had no authority to order a closed session, as such authority was with Trial Chamber I pursuant to Rule 75(G)(i) of the Rules and further Rule 75(H) did not apply. We consider there is no validity in this argument, and to hold otherwise could lead to cumbersome delays in the proper running of both Trial Chambers of the Special Court.

16. The provisions for closed sessions are contained in Rule 75(B)(ii) and Rule 79. Rule 75(A) deals with the provisions for the protection of witnesses and allows a Trial Chamber to order a closed session as one of several protective measures to "prevent disclosure to the public or the media of the identity or whereabouts of a victim or witness". Variations of protective measures are provided in Rule 75(G) and applications must be made to the Chamber "remaining seized of the first proceeding". The decision to order protection of a witness by way of a closed session must be implemented in accordance with Rule 79. The powers to order a closed session in Rule 79 are independent of Rule 75. Rule 79 vests powers in "[T]he Trial Chamber" – that is the Trial Chamber hearing a case – to order the exclusion of the press and the public. It is distinguished from "any Chamber, however constituted, remaining seized of the first proceedings" as provided for in Rule 75(G).

- **Rule 75(I): Protective Measures for Witnesses – Modification of Protective Measures – Change in Circumstances**

R75-TC-7

o *Prosecutor v. Sesay, Kallon, Gbao*, Case No. SCSL-04-15-PT, Decision on Prosecution Motion for Modification of Protective Measures for Witnesses, 5 July 2004, para. 21:

21. From the convincing and uncontradicted statements, attached to the Prosecutions' Motion, the Chamber concludes that there exists no substantial change in the circumstances regarding the security of witnesses that would justify any modification to the protective measures decisions that were previously issued at the pre-trial phase save and except those changes required to make the necessary adjustments for the trial phase. Accordingly, the Chamber finds that there exist no requirement or circumstances that would justify reconsidering them.

APPEALS CHAMBER DECISIONS

- **Rule 75: Protective Measures for Witnesses – Balance with the Rights of the Defence**

R75-AC-1

o *Prosecutor v. Brima, Kamara, Kanu*, Case No. SCSL-04-16-AR77, Decision on Defence Appeal Motion Pursuant to Rule 77 (J) on Both the Imposition of Interim Measures and an Order Pursuant to Rule 77(C)(iii), 23 June 2005, para. 3:

3. It goes without saying that a war crimes court, sitting in a country which for ten years was riven by a war which affected all its people, must be astute to protect its witnesses, especially victims of that war who come forward to give evidence against defendants alleged to have occupied command positions in factions that may still have support. The Court must use its powers to safeguard them from any risk of reprisal. At the same time, it must uphold the rights of defendants to a fair trial – not any arguable 'rights', but those basic rights that are enshrined in Article 17 of the Court's Statute. This exercise is mandated by Rule 75 whenever the Court orders that a particular witness be "protected" from having his or her name disclosed to members of the public. [. . .] This principle – and it is not a balancing act, but rather an injunction to ensure that witness protection measures do not breach those fair trial rights in Article 17 – must be kept in mind in all decisions relating to protected witnesses.

- **Rule 75: Protective Measures for Witnesses – Reinforcement of Pre-Existing Interim Measures and Right to Appeal**

R75-AC-2

o *Prosecutor v. Brima, Kamara, Kanu*, Decision on Defence Appeal Motion Pursuant to Rule 77(J) on Both the Imposition of Interim Measures and an Order Pursuant to Rule 77(C)(iii), 23 June 2005, para. 31-32:

31. [. . .] The Appeals Chamber considers they were in reality Rule 75 "measures for the protection of Victims and Witnesses." As such, they were ancillary to the protective orders designed to preserve the anonymity of Witness TF1-023 and of prosecution witnesses yet to come. They were an 'augmentation' of existing measures, as provided by Rule 75(I). That sub-rule specifically allows applications to "rescind, vary or augment protective measures" to be made to the Trial Chamber. It should not normally be necessary, therefore, to seek alteration by way of appeal. But if the defence – or the prosecution – wishes to appeal a decision made under Rule 75, or Rule 54, then it must seek leave from the Trial Chamber pursuant to Rule 73B.

32. The Trial Chamber, although it made no explicit reference to Rule 75 as such, stated that it was imposing the interim measures because "the duty of the court is to ensure that its orders for protected witnesses are upheld and to ensure that allegations against persons associated with the reference are properly heard and ruled on."[1] The protective measures had already been ordered in relation to Witness TFI-023 and Rule 75 I provides for orders which re-inforce existing protections. It is apt for use to prevent further violations, and was so used by the ICTY Trial Chamber in Simic.[2] There is no basis, therefore, for disputing the Trial Chamber's jurisdiction to make the "interim measures" order. But since that interlocutory order was not made pursuant to the Rule 77 contempt jurisdiction, but in a case to which the appellants were parties, it follows that they have a right to appeal subject to the Rule 73(B) leave requirement.

[1] *Ibid.*, p. 15, lines 16-19.
[2] ICTY, Prosecutor v. Simic *et al.*, IT-95-9-T, 30 September 1999.

Rule 77: Contempt of the Special Court
(amended 14 May 2005)

(A) The Special Court, in the exercise of its inherent power, may punish for contempt any person who knowingly and wilfully interferes with its administration of justice, including any person who:

   (i) being a witness before a Chamber, subject to Rule 90(E) refuses or fails to answer a question;
   (ii) discloses information relating to proceedings in knowing violation of an order of a Chamber;
   (iii) without just excuse fails to comply with an order to attend before or produce documents before a Chamber;
   (iv) threatens, intimidates, causes any injury or offers a bribe to, or otherwise interferes with, a witness who is giving, has given, or is about to give evidence in proceedings before a Chamber, or a potential witness;
   (v) threatens, intimidates, offers a bribe to, or otherwise seeks to coerce any other person, with the intention of preventing that other person from complying with an obligation under an order of a Judge or Chamber; or
   (vi) knowingly assists an accused person to evade the jurisdiction of the Special Court.

(B) Any incitement or attempt to commit any of the acts punishable under Sub-Rule (A) is punishable as contempt of the Special Court with the same penalties.

(C) When a Judge or Trial Chamber has reason to believe that a person may be in contempt of the Special Court, it may:

   (i) deal with the matter summarily itself;
   (ii) refer the matter to the appropriate authorities of Sierra Leone; or
   (iii) direct the Registrar to appoint an experienced independent counsel to investigate the matter and report back to the Chamber as to whether there are sufficient grounds for instigating contempt proceedings. If the Chamber considers that there are sufficient grounds to proceed against a person for contempt, the Chamber may issue an order in lieu of an indictment and direct the independent counsel to prosecute the matter.

(D) Proceedings under Sub-Rule (C)(iii) above may be assigned to be heard by a single judge of any Trial Chamber or a Trial Chamber.

(E) The rules of procedure and evidence in Parts IV to VIII shall apply, as appropriate, to proceedings under this Rule.

(F) Any person indicted for or charged with contempt shall, if that person satisfies the criteria for determination of indigence established by the Registrar, be entitled to legal assistance in accordance with Rule 45.

(G) The maximum penalty that may be imposed on a person found to be in contempt of the Special Court pursuant to Sub-Rule (C)(i) shall be a term of imprisonment not exceeding six months, or a fine not exceeding 2 million Leones, or both; and the maximum penalty pursuant to Sub-Rule (C)(iii) shall be a term of imprisonment for seven years or a fine not exceeding 2 million leones, or both.

(H) Payment of a fine shall be made to the Registrar to be held in a separate account.

(I) If a counsel is found guilty of contempt of the Special Court pursuant to this Rule, the Chamber making such finding may also determine that counsel is no longer eligible to appear before the Special Court or that such conduct amounts to misconduct of counsel pursuant to Rule 46, or both.

(J) Any conviction rendered under this Rule shall be subject to appeal.

(K) Appeals pursuant to this Rule shall be heard by a bench of at least three Judges of the Appeals Chamber. In accordance with Rule 117 such appeals may be determined entirely on the basis of written submissions.

(L) In the event of contempt occurring during proceedings before the Appeals Chamber or a Judge of the Appeals Chamber, the matter may be dealt with summarily from which there shall be no right of appeal or referred to a Trial Chamber for proceedings in accordance with Sub-Rules (C) to (I) above.

TRIAL CHAMBERS DECISIONS

- **Rule 77: Contempt of Court – Legal Basis for Contempt Proceedings – Inherent Power of the Court**

R77-TC-1

o *Prosecutor v. Brima (Margaret), Jalloh, Kamara (Ester)* (Case No. SCSL-05-02), *and Kamara (Anifa)* (Case No. SCSL-05-03), Sentencing Judgement in Contempt Proceedings, 21 September 2005, para. 11-12:

11. As this provision notes, the basis for this Rule is the inherent power of the Special Court to deal with cases of contempt before it. Indeed, it is well-established that courts have an inherent jurisdiction to ensure that its administration of justice is not obstructed, prejudiced or abused.[1] The Appeals Chamber of the International Tribunal for the Former Yugoslavia ("ICTY") stated in the *Tadic* case:

> A power in the Tribunal to punish conduct which tends to obstruct, prejudice or abuse its administration of justice is a necessity in order to ensure that its exercise of jurisdiction which is expressly given to it by its Statute is not frustrated and that its basic judicial functions are safeguarded. Thus the power to deal with contempt is clearly within its inherent jurisdiction.[2]

12. As a result, Rule 77 does not, and was not intended to, limit the Special Court's inherent contempt of court powers.

---

[1] The subsistence and the nature of this power in International Tribunals have been previously recognized by various decisions of the ICTY and the ICTR. In addition to *Tadic* below, see also, for instance *Prosecutor v. Aleksovski*, IT-95-14/1-AR77, Judgment on Appeal by Anto Nobilo Against Finding of Contempt, May 30, 2001; *Prosecutor v. Blaskic*, IT-95-14-AR108*bis*, Judgment on the Request of the Republic of Croatia for Review of the Decision of Trial Chamber II of 18 July 1997, 29 October 1997; See, more recently, *Prosecutor v. Kamuhanda*, Case No. ICTR-99-54A-A, Oral Decision (Rule 115 and Contempt of False Testimony), 19 May 2005. See also M. Bohlander, "International Criminal Tribunals and Their Power to Punish Contempt and False Testimony", *Criminal Law Forum*, 2001, pp. 91-118.

[2] *Prosecutor v. Tadic*, IT-94-1, Judgment on Allegations of Contempt Against Prior Counsel, Milan Vujin, 31 January 2000, para. 18.

R77-TC-2

o *Prosecutor v. Samura*, Case No. SCSL-05-01, Judgment in Contempt Proceedings, 26 October 2005, para. 13-16:

13. The specific provisions in the Rules related to contempt of court are contained in Rule 77 which sets out in the fol-

lowing terms the regime to be followed in cases of contempt of court before the Special Court [. . .].

14. The basis for this Rule is the inherent power of the Special Court, in the exercise and discharge of its judicial function, to allow the court to deal with cases of contempt before it. As the Appeals Chamber of the Special Court recently held:

> All court must possess the powers necessary to enable them to administer and deliver justice fairly and efficiently.[1]

15. It is well-established that courts have an inherent jurisdiction to ensure that its administration of justice is not obstructed, prejudiced or abused.[2] The Appeals Chamber of the International Tribunal for the Former Yugoslavia ("ICTY") in the *Tadic* case had this to say in this respect:

> A power in the Tribunal to punish conduct which tends to obstruct, prejudice or abuse its administration of justice is a necessity in order to ensure that its exercise of jurisdiction which is expressly given to it by its Statute is not frustrated and that its basic judicial functions are safeguarded. Thus the power to deal with contempt is clearly within its inherent jurisdiction.[3]

16. As I previously held in a recent Judgment, this inherent power subsists independently of the specific terms of Rule 77 of the Rules. Therefore, Rule 77 must be read in that context and therefore I am of the opinion that Rule 77 does not, and was not intended to, limit the Special Court's inherent contempt of court powers.[4] As such, Rule 77(A) identifies and describes certain conducts relating to the offence of contempt of court throughout a defined, though non-exhaustive,[5] list of acts.

---

[1] *Prosecutor v. Brima et al.*, Case No. SCSL-04-16-AR77, Decision on Defence Appeal Motion pursuant to Rule 77(J) on Both the Imposition of Interim Measures and an Order pursuant to Rule 77(C)(iii), 23 June 2005, para. 2. For a description of the specific provisions of Rule 77, see also *id.*, para. 26.
[2] The subsistence and the nature of this power in International Tribunals have been previously recognized by various decisions of the ICTY and the ICTR. In addition to *Tadic* below, see also, for instance *Prosecutor v. Aleksovski*, IT-95-14/1-AR77, Judgment on Appeal by Anto Nobilo Against Finding of Contempt, May 30, 2001; *Prosecutor v. Blaskic*, IT-95-14-AR108*bis*, Judgment on the Request of the Republic of Croatia for Review of the Decision of Trial Chamber II of 18 July 1997, 29 October 1997; See, more recently, *Prosecutor v. Kamuhanda*, Case No. ICTR-99-54A-A, Oral Decision (Rule 115 and Contempt of False Testimony), 19 May 2005; *Prosecutor v. Beqaj*, Case No. IT-03-66T-R77, Judgment on Contempt Allegations, 27 May 2005. For general reference, see also M. Bohlander, "International Criminal Tribunals and Their Power to Punish Contempt and False Testimony", *Criminal Law Forum*, 2001, pp. 91-118. Another author describes contempt as "the most powerful device in the legal conceptual armoury of

the courts designed to preserve the dignity and integrity of the judicial process." See B. Thompson, *The Criminal Law of Sierra Leone*, American University Press Inc., 1999, at page 219.

(3) *Prosecutor v. Tadic*, IT-94-1, Judgment on Allegations of Contempt Against Prior Counsel, Milan Vujin, 31 January 2000, para. 18. See also para. 13.

(4) See *Independent Counsel v. Margaret Fomba Brima et al.*, Case No. SCSL-2005-02 and *Independent Counsel v. Anifa Kamara*, Case No. SCSL-2005-03, Sentencing Judgement in Contempt Proceedings, 21 September 2005, para. 12. See also *Tadic*, supra [...], para. 28.

(5) *Prosecutor v. Brima et al.*, Case No. SCSL-04-16-AR77, Decision on Defence Appeal Motion pursuant to Rule 77(J) on Both the Imposition of Interim Measures and an Order pursuant to Rule 77(C)(iii), 23 June 2005, supra [...], para. 26. See also *Prosecutor v. Marijacic and Rebic*, Case No. IT-95-14-R77.2, Decision on Prosecution Motions to Amend the Indictment, 7 October 2005, para. 31.

- **Rule 77(A): Contempt of Court – *Mens Rea***

R77-TC-3

o *Prosecutor v. Samura*, Case No. SCSL-05-01, Judgment in Contempt Proceedings, 26 October 2005, para. 18-27:

18. Rule 77(A) provides specifically that any person may be punished for contempt for knowingly and wilfully interfering with the administration of justice. I am of the view that the *mens rea* requirement of "knowingly and wilfully" does apply to those various types of conduct listed under Rule 77 and forms part of the specific intent for the contempt alleged in this case to be a knowing violation of an order of a Chamber.

19. A review and analysis of the jurisprudence of the International *ad hoc* Tribunals provides some guidance as to the specific circumstances related the disclosure of the identity of a protected witness in violation of an order. In the *Brdjanin* Case, the Trial Chamber of the ICTY held that there are differences in the states of mind required for each of the various types of conduct envisaged in Rule 77. That Trial Chamber also stated that the *mens rea* had to be established on a case by case basis in relation to the conducts referred to in Rule 77(A). It also held that "for each criminal contempt, it has to be established that an accused acted with a specific intent to interfere with the administration of justice."[(1)] I accept the holding of the Trial Chamber in the *Brdjanin* Case as being of application in this case where it is alleged to have been a violation of an order.

20. In the case before me, Trial Chamber II of the Special Court, upon an investigation undergone pursuant to Rule 77(C)(iii), issued an *Order In Lieu of Indictment* against Brima Samura and directed an Independent Counsel to prosecute the matter pursuant to Rule 77(C)(iii). In particular, Brima Samura, the alleged contemnor, is charged with con-

tempt of the Special Court, in violation of Rule 77(A)(ii) for knowingly and wilfully interfering "with the Special Court's administration of justice by disclosing information relating to proceedings ... in knowing violation of an order of a Trial Chamber."[2]

21. In particular, in the *Brdjanin* Case it was held that it must be established that:

a) an accused disclosed the identity of a witness to a member of the public
b) the disclosure was in violation of an order of a Chamber; and
c) the violation was knowingly and wilfully committed.[3]

22. It also ruled that in further determining whether a specific order of a Chamber has been violated, reference must be made to the exact content of the relevant order which is the subject to the allegation of contempt of court.[4]

23. In *Aleksovski*, the Trial Chamber of the ICTY held that a knowing violation "means not only a deliberate violation, but also a deliberate failure to ascertain the circumstances under which a witness testified."[5] Subsequently, at the appeal stage, having considered whether "knowing" implied that actual knowledge was required before a finding of contempt could be made, the Appeals Chambers then concluded that the knowledge requirement could be met by actual knowledge or wilful blindness (also known as deliberate ignorance), but not by negligence:

> Mere negligence in failing to ascertain whether an order had been made granting protective measures to a particular witness could never amount to such conduct. It is unnecessary in this appeal to determine whether any greater degree of negligence could constitute contempt. Negligent conduct could be dealt with sufficiently, and more appropriately, by way of disciplinary action, but it could never justify imprisonment or a substantial fine even though the unintended consequence of such negligence was an interference with the Tribunal's administration of justice. At the other end of the spectrum, wilful blindness to the existence of the order in the sense defined is, in the opinion of the Appeals Chamber, sufficiently culpable conduct to be more appropriately dealt with as contempt.[6]

24. More specifically on wilful blindness, proof of knowledge of the existence of the relevant fact or, in the circumstances, of a specific order is accepted where it is established that the alleged contemnor suspected that the fact or order existed, or was aware that its existence was highly probable, but refrained from finding out whether it did exist, so as to be able to deny knowledge of it.[7]

25. However, reckless indifference as to whether a specific conduct was in violation of an order as been deemed to be sufficient to warrant punishment for contempt. Indeed, with reference to the specific intent to violate or disregard an order, the Appeals Chamber in *Aleksovski* held as follows:

> In most cases where it has been established that the alleged contemnor had knowledge of the existence of the order (either actual knowledge or a wilful blindness of its existence), a finding that he intended to violate it would almost necessarily follow. There may, however, be cases where such an alleged contemnor acted with reckless indifference as to whether his act was in violation of the order. In the opinion of the Appeals Chamber, such conduct is sufficiently culpable to warrant punishment as contempt, even though it does not establish a specific intention to violate the order.[8]

26. On the issue of compliance with an order of the court, in *Milosevic*, the ICTY Trial Chamber held that "it is an obvious consequence of refusing to comply with an order of the Chamber that the administration of justice is interfered with".[9]

27. I find the aforementioned decisions persuasive and therefore consider that, within the meaning of Rule 77, the requirement of *mens rea* includes both actual knowledge or wilful blindness, but not mere negligence. This *mens rea* will apply not only to the general elements of contempt, but also to the specific intent to interfere with the administration of justice required by the particular form of commission provided for by Rule 77(A)(ii).

---

[1] *Prosecutor v. Brdjanin*, Case No. IT-99-36-R77, Concerning Allegations against Milka Maglov, Decision on Motion for Acquittal Pursuant to Rule 98bis, 19 March 2004, para. 16. See also *Aleksovski*, supra [. . .], para. 40 and 42.
[2] See Order in Lieu of the Indictment, The Particulars, contained as Annex A in the Trial Chamber II Decision, supra [. . .].
[3] *Prosecutor v. Brdjanin*, Case No. IT-99-36-R77, Concerning Allegations against Milka Maglov, Decision on Motion for Acquittal Pursuant to Rule 98bis, 19 March 2004, supra [. . .], paras 36-41.
[4] *Id.*
[5] This finding by the Trial Chamber was so reported in the subsequent judgment by the Appeals Chamber. See *Aleksovski*, supra [. . .].
[6] *Id.*, para. 45.
[7] *Brdjanin*, supra [. . .]. *Aleksovski*, supra [. . .].
[8] *Aleksovski*, supra [. . .].
[9] *Prosecutor v. Milosevic*, Case No. IT-02-54-R77.4, Contempt Proceedings against Kosta Bulatovic, Decision on Contempt of the Tribunal, 13 May 2005, para. 17.

- **Rule 77(A): Contempt of Court – Violation of Witness Protection – No Sanction**

R77-TC-4

o *Prosecutor v. Brima, Kamara, Kanu*, Case No. SCSL-04-16-PT, Order Regarding the Disclosure of a Protected Witness TF1-081, 8 March 2005:

FINDS that the Defence Request for Disclosure filed by Defence Counsel Kevin Metzger and Glenna Thompson does reveal the identity of TF1-081, a protected witness for the Prosecution, in clear violation of the Orders of this Chamber regarding protective measures;

REMINDS all Counsel for the Defence and Prosecution that identifying protected witnesses is in violation of the Court Orders and could amount to a contempt of court, punishable in accordance with Rule 77 of the Rules;

ORDERS that the Defence Request for Disclosure be removed from all public records of the Court Management Section of the Special Court.

- **Rule 77(A): Contempt of Court – Public Comments on Pending Issues**

R77-TC-5

o *Prosecutor v. Norman*, Case No. SCSL-04-14-PT, Decision on *Inter Partes* Motion by Prosecution to Freeze the Account of the Accused Sam Hinga Norman at Union Trust Bank (SL) Limited or at Any Other Bank in Sierra Leone, 9 April 2004, para. 17:

17. By way of a strong caution embodied as a footnote to this Decision addressed to Counsel who practise before the Special Court, I take this opportunity as Designated Judge in this matter to remind all Counsel that matters pending before courts of justice are subject to the doctrine of ***sub judice*** until final disposition. Accordingly, public comments and press interviews given while litigation is pending may well border on contempt of court, having regard to how such comments are framed. Specifically, my attention was directed to some immoderate comments on the Interim Order in this matter by Defence Counsel during a radio interview. I say, with all judicial forthrightness, that it is expected that learned Counsel of seniority and standing at the Bar should appreciate the difference between their obligations, as Officers of the Court, and the alluring attractions of populism and ideological posturing so as to ensure the harmonious co-operation and mutual respect that

have always characterised the relationship between the Bench and the Bar in the administration of justice.

- **Rule 77(A): Contempt of Court – Unfounded Suggestion of Abuse of Process**

R77-TC-6

o *Prosecutor v. Kanu*, Case No. SCSL-04-16-PT, Written Reasons for the Trial Chamber's Oral Decision on the Defence Motion on Abuse of Process Due to Infringement of Principles of *Nullum Crimen Sine Lege* and Non-Retroactivity as to Several Accounts, 31 March 2004, para. 30-32:

30. This Trial Chamber finds that neither the lawful exercise of the powers of the Prosecutor to bring an Indictment which is based upon the alleged commission of crimes within the jurisdiction of the Special Court for Sierra Leone nor the approval of such an Indictment by a Judge of the Special Court in accordance with the Statute and the Rules would, and indeed could, constitute an abuse of process. The veiled suggestion that the designated Judge may have contributed to the alleged abuse of process is objectionable, particularly when there is no evidence put forward to rebut the presumption of regularity. Counsel is admonished that such submissions, depending on the facts and circumstances, may well border on contempt of court.

31. On this finding alone, the Trial Chamber deems it to be sufficient to dismiss the motion in its entirety.

32. In order to prevent the defence in this case, or for that matter defence in other cases, from bringing a similar Motion in which the alleged violations are re-characterised as errors of law in defining the competence or jurisdiction of the Special Court, the Trial Chamber will briefly address this issue.

- **Rule 77(C)(iii): Contempt of Court – Disclosure of the Report of the Independent Counsel**

R77-TC-7

o *Prosecutor v. Brima, Kamara, Kanu*, Case No. SCSL-04-16-T, Decision on Joint Defence Application to Appeal Against the Ruling of Trial Chamber II of 5 April 2005, 15 June 2005, para. 17:

17. [. . .] The investigation of events in which Brima Samura was allegedly involved is the subject of a report by an Independent Counsel. Rule 77(C)(iii) provides that the investigator informs the Chamber. There is no obligation on the Independent Coun-

sel to report to any other persons and in particular no right or obligation to inform persons who are not subject to the investigation or allegation.

R77-TC-8

o *Prosecutor v. Brima, Kamara, Kanu*, Case No. SCSL-04-16-T, Decision on Confidential Defence Request for Disclosure of Independent Investigator's Report on Contempt of Court Proceedings and Request for Stay of Proceedings, 30 June 2005:

CONSIDERING that the Trial Chamber in its Decision on The Report of The Independent Counsel Pursuant to Rules 77(C)(iii) and 77(D) of the Rules delivered and published on 29 April 2005[1] did not institute contempt proceedings against any of the Accused Alex Tamba Brima, Brima Bazzy Kamara and Santigie Borbor Kanu;

NOTING the Order Assigning Cases To A Trial Chamber issued by the President of the Special Court on 2 May 2005[2] in which Justice Emmanuel Ayoola assigned the conduct of the Contempt of Court Proceedings to Trial Chamber I or a single Judge thereof;

NOTING that Counsel for the Accused Alex Tamba Brima, Brima Bazzy Kamara and Santigie Borbor Kanu do not in their Request for Disclosure of the Report of The Independent Counsel claim to be acting on behalf of the alleged contemnors in the Contempt of Court Proceedings;

CONSIDERING that the Defence for the Accused Alex Tamba Brima, Brima Bazzy Kamara and Santigie Borbor Kanu has not persuasively argued how the non-disclosure by the Trial Chamber of the Report of The Independent Counsel is likely to prejudice the Defence case or the conduct of a fair trial in the case of *the Prosecutor v. Alex Tamba Brima et al.*;

CONSIDERING further that for the same reasons the Defence for the Accused Alex Tamba Brima, Brima Bazzy Kamara and Santigie Borbor Kanu has not persuasively argued how a stay of proceedings pending the disclosure of the Report of the Independent Counsel is an appropriate relief in the circumstances;

---

[1] *Prosecutor v. Alex Tamba Brima et al.*, Decision on the Report of the Independent Counsel Pursuant to Rules 77(C)(iii) and 77(D) of the Rules of Procedure and Evidence, 29 April 2005, Document No. SCSL-2004-16-T-237.
[2] *The Prosecutor v. Brima Samura*: Case No. SCSL-2005-1 and *the Prosecutor v. Margaret Fomba Brima, Neneh Binta Bah Jalloh, Anifa Kamara and Ester Kamara*: Case No. SCSL – 2005-2, Order Assigning Cases To A Trial Chamber of 2 May 2005.

- **Rule 77(C)(iii): Contempt of Court – Independent Proceedings – Counsel Testimony**

R77-TC-9

o *Prosecutor v. Brima, Kamara, Kanu,* Case No. SCSL-04-16-T, Decision on the Confidential Application for Withdrawal by Counsel for Brima and Kamara and on the Request for Further Representation by Counsel for Kanu, 20 May 2005, para. 40-42:

40. Another factor claimed by Lead Counsel to be creating difficulties in the relationship with their clients is the possibility that they will be called as witnesses in the two contempt proceedings involving a Defence investigator and the wives of the Accused respectively. In this regard, we note the Principal Defender's claim that Counsel for Kamara will not be called as a witness in such proceedings. The first of the contempt proceedings was concluded before Trial Chamber I on 9 May 2005, and neither Counsel was required to give evidence. The second contempt proceedings will resume on 27 June 2005, and whether either Lead Counsel will be called to give evidence in that case remains to be seen. In any event, Lead Counsels' claim is that they are concerned "about the potential difficulties surrounding the position of Counsel who, on any view, are likely to be called as witnesses in the pending Contempt Proceedings. This singular fact did not assist in strengthening the relationship between the Accused and their Legal Representatives."

41. In addition, during the course of the proceedings, Lead Counsel foreshadowed a potential conflict of interest arising should they have to give evidence. However, what this conflict would be and why it would arise has not been made clear to us, particularly when it is considered that the present trial and the contempt proceedings before Trial Chamber I are two separate, independent proceedings. It may even prove the case that Counsel will not be required to give evidence at all, and, in any event, there is certainly no indication that they would be required to give evidence for the Prosecution.

42. We can understand Lead Counsels' concerns that the anticipated testimony has affected their relationship with their clients. However, they have not established any reason why the anticipated testimony would affect their capacity to act as Counsel in the present trial. [. . .]

- **Rule 77(C)(iii): Contempt of Court – Proceedings – Functions of the Independent Counsel**

R77-TC-10

o *Prosecutor v. Samura* (Case No. SCSL-05-01), *Brima (Margaret), Jalloh, Kamara (Anifa), Kamara (Ester)* (Case No. SCSL-05-02), Written Reasons for the Decision on the standing of Independent Counsel and on Disclosure Obligations, 23 June 2005, para. 13-16:[132]

13. I have considered the submission of the Principal Defender and that of the Independent Counsel regarding the interpretation of Rule 77(C)(iii). The Principal Defender has essentially submitted that considering the specific wording of this provision, with the use of the world "the", it requires that the Independent Counsel who conducted the investigation should now be the same prosecuting the contempt matter.

14. Looking as some of the information background,[(1)] I note that the Registrar appointed Mr. Louis Tumwesige as the first Independent Counsel exclusively to conduct the investigation into the contempt allegations and to report back to Trial Chamber II "whether there are sufficient grounds to instigate contempt proceedings".[(2)] This Independent Counsel fulfilled his mandate, reported back to Trial Chamber II and the said Chamber found that the Alleged Contemnors should be prosecuted for contempt. Due to the unavailability of Mr. Tumwesige, the Registrar has now appointed a different Independent Counsel in the name of Mrs. Adelaide Whest to conduct the prosecution of the Contempt Proceedings.

15. In my opinion, interpreting Rule 77(C)(iii) in the narrow way suggested by the Principal Defender in her Preliminary Objection would be to frustrate the purpose of the Statute to have fair and expeditious contempt proceedings if the appointed Independent Counsel was for any reason unable to carry out his or her duties. To apply such reasoning, in my opinion, would defeat the real purpose of the Statute in this respect.

16. Reiterating the reasoning of a Decision of this Trial Chamber, no rule, however formulated, should be applied in a way that contradicts its purpose. [. . .]

17. Thus, with reference to Rule 77(C)(iii), I find that this provision must be understood to allow the Registrar to appoint any Independent Counsel in order to investigate and/or prosecute contempt matters. Provided that, on the one hand, the criteria of independence, experience and impartiality of an

---

[132] The numbering of Paragraphs mistakenly goes up to 16 and then back to 15. This quotation should have normally run from Paragraph 13 to Paragraph 18.

Independent Counsel are fulfilled and, on the other hand, that the paramount rights of an alleged contemnor to a fair and expeditious trial are ensured at any stage of the proceedings, the Registrar enjoys the latitude to appoint any Independent Counsel that might be required according to the specific circumstances of each contempt case.

18. Moreover, I am not convinced that these Alleged Contemnors will suffer any prejudice from having now an Independent Counsel to prosecute the contempt proceedings different from the first Independent Counsel that conducted the initial investigation. In my view, this practice, justified in the circumstances by the unavailability of the first Independent Counsel, will serve to ensure the complete independence of the appointed Independent Counsel conducting the prosecution of the Alleged Contemnors and is in the overall interest of justice.

---

(1) Letter of Appointment of Experienced Independent Counsel Under Rule 77 of the Rules of Procedure and Evidence of the Special Court for Sierra Leone, 11 March 2005, supra [. . .].
(2) *Id.*

- **Rule 77(D): Contempt of Court – Proceedings – Assignment to a Single Judge**

R77-TC-11   o *Prosecutor v. Samura* (Case No. SCSL-05-01), *Brima (Margaret), Jalloh and Kamara (Ester)* (Case No. SCSL-05-02), and *Kamara (Anifa)* (Case No. SCSL-05-03), Order Designating a Judge for Contempt Proceedings, 2 May 2005:

I, HON. JUSTICE BENJAMIN MUTANGA ITOE, Presiding Judge of Trial Chamber I;

[. . .]

NOTING the *Order Assigning Cases to a Trial Chamber* filed by the President of the Special Court on the 2nd of May, 2005 ("Order of the President");

[. . .]

NOTING that the Order of the President confirms the assignment of the Contempt Proceeding to Trial Chamber I or to a single Judge thereof;

PURSUANT to Rules 27 and 77 of the Rules;

DO HEREBY

DESIGNATE Hon. Justice Pierre Boutet to deal as necessary with the contempt proceedings against Brima Samura, Case

No. SCSL-05-01, and Margaret Fomba Brima, Neneh Binta Bah Jalloh, Anifa Kamara and Ester Kamara, Case No. SCSL-05-02;

• **Rule 77(E): Contempt of Court – Proceedings –** *Locus Standi*

R77-TC-12 o *Prosecutor v. Samura* (Case No. SCSL-05-01), *Brima (Margaret), Jalloh and Kamara (Ester)* (Case No. SCSL-05-02), and *Kamara (Anifa)* (Case No. SCSL-05-03), Decision on Defence Motion on Stay of the Contempt Proceedings, 21 September 2005:

NOTING that Decisions were recently rendered by both Trial Chamber II and the Appeals Chamber on the pending motions and the appeals referred to by the Defence in support of the Motion,[1] and that all these Decisions reiterate and confirm the position that the present Contempt Proceedings have no bearing on the AFRC Case nor on any of the Accused therein;[2]

CONSIDERING that a professional or personal nexus between the Accused in the AFRC Case and all the alleged contemnors in these Contempt Proceedings in not of itself a sufficient basis to characterize these proceedings as being part of the proceedings in the AFRC Case;

[. . .]

PURSUANT to Rules 2, 73, 74 and 77 of the Rules;

I FIND as follows:

1. that the Contempt Proceedings constitutes Proceedings that are distinct and different from the proceedings in the AFRC Case; and

2. that the Defence for the Accused in the AFRC Case does not possess the necessary *locus standi* to file the Motion;

---

[1] *Prosecutor v. Brima et al.*, Case No. SCSL-04-16-T, Decision on Joint Defence Application for Leave to Appeal against the Ruling of Trial Chamber II of 5 April 2005, 15 June 2005; Id., Decision on Confidential Defence Request for Disclosure of Independent Investigator's Report on Contempt of Court Proceedings and Request for Stay of Proceedings, 30 June 2005; Id., Case No. SCSL-04-16-AR77, Decision on Defence Appeal Motion pursuant to Rule 77(J) on Both the Imposition of Interim Measures and an Order Pursuant to Rule 77(C)(iii), 23 June 2005; and Id., Decision on Joint Defence Appeal Against the Decision on the Report of the Independent Counsel Pursuant to Rule 77(C)(iii) and 77(D), 17 August 2005. No stay of the AFRC proceedings, it has to be noted, has been previously ordered by either Trial Chamber II or the Appeals Chamber for any of these pending motions and appeals.

[2] See Id., Case No. SCSL-04-16-T, Decision on Joint Defence Application

for Leave to Appeal against the Ruling of Trial Chamber II of 5 April 2005, 15 June 2005, para. 16, in these terms:
"We re-state our view that the possible contempt proceedings have no bearing on this trial. None of the accused has been the subject of investigation for alleged contempt."
See also Id., Case No. SCSL-04-16-AR77, Decision on Defence Appeal Motion pursuant to Rule 77(J) on Both the Imposition of Interim Measures and an Order Pursuant to Rule 77(C)(iii), 23 June 2005, para. 33.

- **Rule 77(E): Contempt of Court – Proceedings – Applicability of the Rules of Procedure and Evidence to Contempt Proceedings**

R77-TC-13 o *Prosecutor v. Samura* (Case No. SCSL-05-01), *Brima (Margaret), Jalloh, Kamara (Anifa), Kamara (Ester)* (Case No. SCSL-05-02), Written Reasons for the Decision on the standing of Independent Counsel and on Disclosure Obligations, 23 June 2005, para. 17-19:[133]

17. The Principal Defender submitted that pursuant to Rule 77 of the Rules, the provision of Rule 66 of the Rules shall apply, as appropriate, to the contempt proceedings. Conversely, the Independent Counsel submitted that due to the very nature of the case, no disclosure of materials to the Defence is *per se* necessary.

18. In the present circumstances, I find that the Independent Counsel is under an obligation to disclose the materials in her possession to the Defence. Pursuant to the provisions of Rule 77(E), Rule 66 of the Rules shall apply, as appropriate, to the proceedings. The purpose of these provisions is indeed to ensure that proceedings involving allegations of contempt before this Court are subjected to the same judicial guarantees and procedures, as they might become appropriate due to the ancillary nature of contempt proceeding, set for the crimes falling within the statutory competence of the Special Court. In particular, I would like to state that persons prosecuted pursuant to such Rule are guaranteed the same safeguards and are entitled to the full respect of their fundamental rights.

19. No particular redaction of such materials prior to their disclosure to the Defence will be necessary. As noted by the Principal Defender, all Defence Counsel of the Contempt Proceedings are reminded, however, of their duty and obligation to abide by this Court provisions and orders concerning the protection of victims and witnesses applies before these

---

[133] *Prosecutor v. Samura*, Case No. SCSL-05-01, Judgment in Contempt Proceedings, 26 October 2005, para. 17.

proceedings and the Defence shall not disclose these materials to third parties. [1]

---

[1] For the specific instance of the identifying information on the particular protected witness involved in the Contempt Proceedings, namely Witness TF1-023, see *Prosecutor v. Sesay et al.*, Case No. SCSL-04-15-T, Decision on Prosecution Motion for Modification of Protective Measures for Witnesses, 5 July 2004. See also Decision of 29 April 2005, supra [. . .], para. 5.

- **Rule 77(E): Contempt of Court – Proceedings – Standards of Proof**

R77-TC-14

o *Prosecutor v. Samura*, Case No. SCSL-05-01, Judgment in Contempt Proceedings, 26 October 2005, para. 28-29, 55, 71-76:

28. The standard of proof required to establish the commission of an offence of contempt of court is that of proof beyond reasonable doubt. Rule 77(E) provides that Part IV to VIII of the Rules are applicable, as appropriate, to contempt proceedings and Rule 87, contained in Part VI of the Rules, provides that a finding of guilty may be reached only when the Court is satisfied that guilty has been proved beyond reasonable doubt.

29. The conduct of the accused must be such in the circumstances that it constituted beyond reasonable doubt a contempt of the court as defined in Rule 77. All subjective and objective essential elements of the allegations contained in the charge as particularized must therefore be proved to that standard.[1]

[. . .]

55. Considering these specific allegations made in the case against the Accused and the required *mens rea* for such a violation, for the Accused to be found guilty of this charge, the evidence must establish beyond reasonable doubt that:

a) Brima Samura did disclose the identity of a protected witness to members of the public, more specifically the identity of Witness TF1-023;

b) the said disclosure by Brima Samura was in knowing violation of an order of the *Decision on Prosecution Motion for Modification of Protective Measures for Witnesses* dated the 5th of July 2004; and

c) the violation of the order was knowingly and wilfully committed.

[. . .]

71. The specific charge proffered against Brima Samura requires the Independent Counsel to show that the disclosure of the identity of the protected Witness was knowingly done in violation of an order, presumably, I have to say, the *Decision on Prosecution Motion for Modification of Protective Measures for Witnesses*, as this is what appears to be suggested by the Independent Counsel although the evidence does not support such submission. Therefore, in reaching a decision, with respect to the specific charge against this accused, I have to be satisfied that this *Decision on Prosecution Motion for Modification of Protective Measures for Witnesses* was applicable to Brima Samura and that the disclosure of the identity of the protected witness by Brima Samura was done in specific violation of an order of a Trial Chamber.

72. No evidence has been adduced at trial by the Independent Counsel to prove that Brima Samura, due to his association and the specific nature of his work within the Defence Team for the Accused Alex Tamba Brima, knew of the *Decision on Prosecution Motion for Modification of Protective Measures for Witnesses* or of any other such decision nor that any specific provision of protective measures ordered by the Court has been knowingly violated by his conduct.

73. The Independent Counsel, in her closing arguments, did not address the issue of actual knowledge of an order nor did she refer to any evidence to support the intent by the Accused of knowingly and wilfully violate an order. Instead, she submitted that it is not necessary to prove this actual knowledge in order to establish the guilt of the alleged contemnor as Brima Samura is automatically bound by the protective measures solely by that fact that he is a member of the Defence Team and that he might have well obtained the identifying information of that witness elsewhere. However, pursuant to Rule 77(A)(ii), one element of the specific offence contained in the charge is that the alleged disclosure must be in knowing violation of an order. Indeed, although it is widely accepted that the different forms of commission of the offence of contempt articulated in Rule 77(A)(i) to (iv) do not constitute an exclusive list, for the specific circumstances of the case the Independent Counsel is called by the *Order in Lieu of the Indictment*, in its current formulation, to prove that there is evidence of a specific conduct under Rule 77(A)(ii), namely the knowing violation of an order of the Court by the Accused.

74. Although I have found and concluded that Brima Samura disclosed the identity of a protected witness to members of the public, namely Margaret Fomba Brima and Neneh Binta Bah Jallow, I am not satisfied that there is evidence beyond reasonable doubt that such disclosure was willingly done and was in violation of any of the orders contained in the *Decision on Prosecution Motion for Modification of Protective*

Measures for Witnesses dated the 5th of July 2004 issued by Trial Chamber I or any other decision about protective measures.

75. I have concluded that there is absolutely no evidence in this trial to establish which order, if any, was violated by the Accused person.

C) Was the violation knowingly and wilfully committed?

76. Considering that the Independent Counsel failed to prove that Brima Samura acted in violation of an order, it will not be necessary to further debate whether he acted with the specific *mens rea* required pursuant to Rule 77(A)(ii).

---

[1] See, for instance, *Prosecutor v. Simic*, Case No. IT-95-9, Trial Chamber, Judgment in the Matter of Contempt Allegations against the Accused and His Counsel, 30 June 2000, para. 99. See also *Beqaj*, supra [. . .], para. 56-57.

- **Rule 77(G): Contempt of Court – Sentence – Applicable Criteria**

R77-TC-15   o *Prosecutor v. Brima (Margaret), Jalloh, Kamara (Ester)* (Case No. SCSL-05-02), *and Kamara (Anifa)* (Case No. SCSL-05-03), Sentencing Judgement in Contempt Proceedings, 21 September 2005, para. 9-19:

14. Paragraph (G) of Rule 77 sets out the "maximum penalty that may be imposed on a person found to be in contempt of the Special Court . . . pursuant to Sub-Rule (C)(iii) shall be a term of imprisonment for seven years or a fine not exceeding 2 million leones, or both."

15. With regard to sentencing principles that are to be applied by the Trial Chamber, Article 19(2) of the Statute states:

> In imposing the sentences, the Trial Chamber should take into account such factors as the gravity of the offence and the individual circumstances of the convicted person.

16. Rule 101(B), which is applicable to contempt proceedings as appropriate in accordance with Rule 77(E), further elaborates that:

> (B) In determining the sentence, the Trial Chamber shall take into account the factors mentioned in Article 19(2) of the Statute, as well as such factors as:
>
> (i) Any aggravating circumstances;
> (ii) Any mitigating circumstances including the substantial cooperation with the Prosecutor by the convicted person before or after conviction;

(iii) The extent to which any penalty imposed by a court of any State on the convicted person for the same act has already been served, as referred to in Article 9(3) of the Statute.

17. As I have noted, the Rules are silent regarding the minimum penalty that may be imposed on a person who either pleads guilty or is found guilty after trial of contempt of court under Rule 77(C)(iii). I therefore find that I may exercise my inherent power with regard to contempt cases to determine the appropriate sentence for the Contemnors in this case in light of all the considerations outlined above.

18. I am mindful that the ICTY has, on occasion, imposed sentences that are variations on those sentences specifically described in Rule 77. In that respect, the Trial Chamber in the *Aleksovski* case suspended the payment of a portion of the fine for one year on the condition that Mr. Nobilo not be found in contempt of the Tribunal again within that period.[1] The Appeals Chamber in *Tadic* stated that it would provide a direction to "the Registrar to consider striking the Respondent off the list [of assigned counsel] and reporting his conduct as found by the Appeals Chamber to the professional body to which he belongs." Since it found that the Registrar would necessarily do this "in the reasonable exercise of her power", the Appeals Chamber took this into account when determining the appropriate sentence and ordered a fine.[2]

19. I consider in light of the above that the Rules provide that certain punishments may be imposed by setting out a maximum penalty without however prescribing any minimum punishment. Therefore, I find that I have the inherent power to impose a sentence other than a fine or imprisonment and that, consequently, a sentence such as a conditional discharge could be imposed subject to the particular circumstances of the case.

---

[1] *Prosecutor v. Alekovski*, IT-95-14/1-AR77, Judgment on Appeal by Anto Nobilo Against Finding of Contempt, 30 May 2001, para. 22. The finding of guilt was overturned on appeal.
[2] *Prosecutor v. Tadic, supra* note [. . .] para. 172.

- **Rule 77(G): Contempt of Court – Sentence – Criminal Discharge**

R77-TC-16   o *Prosecutor v. Brima (Margaret), Jalloh, Kamara (Ester)* (Case No. SCSL-05-02), *and Kamara (Anifa)* (Case No. SCSL-05-03), Sentencing Judgement in Contempt Proceedings, 21 September 2005, para. 35-40:

35. In light of all of the above factors, I have come to the conclusion that the appropriate sentence for all of the Contem-

nors in this case would carry a sentence that is neither a fine nor imprisonment, but rather another form of sentence. I am satisfied, as I have stated earlier, that I have the inherent power to impose a conditional discharge as suggested and recommended by all of the Parties in this matter given that the Rules define only the maximum sentence that may be imposed and do not preclude the imposition of such a sentence by a Trial Chamber.

36. I should add for a better and complete understanding that the conditional discharge will be deemed not to constitute a criminal conviction for the offence of contempt of court. The Contemnors will be required to fully respect all of the conditions, set out below, for their probation which will be for a duration of one year from today's date. If any of the Contemnors fail to respect these conditions, her discharge will be converted automatically to a criminal conviction and the Special Court may then impose any other sentence that could have been imposed if the Contemnor had been convicted at the time of the imposition of the conditional discharge.

I THEREFORE ORDER AS FOLLOWS:

37. Having accepted the guilty plea from the Contemnors, Margaret Fomba Brima, Neneh Binta Bah Jalloh, Ester Kamara and Anifa Kamara, and having found these contemnors guilty of the charge that had been laid against them, I hereby sentence the said Contemnors, Margaret Fomba Brima, Neneh Binta Bah Jalloh, Ester Kamara and Anifa Kamara, to a conditional discharge, and considering that in all the aforesaid circumstances, a conditional discharge as described would be an appropriate sentence, I impose the following conditions;

38. The Contemnors shall serve a period of probation to commence on today's date, the 21st of September 2005, and to end in one year on the 20th of September 2006;

39. During their period of probation, the Contemnors, Margaret Fomba Brima, Neneh Binta Bah Jallow, Ester Kamara and Anifa Kamara, shall respect the following conditions:

1. To keep the peace and be of good behaviour;
2. Not to reveal the identity of Prosecution Witness TF1-023 to any persons whatsoever;
3. Not to seek to obtain the identity or location of any Prosecution witness before the Special Court for Sierra Leone;
4. Not to communicate, directly or indirectly, with any Prosecution witness before the Special Court for Sierra Leone;
5. Not to take part in any action that threatens either directly or indirectly a witness before the Special Court for Sierra Leone;
6. To respect all conditions imposed by the Special Court for Sierra Leone in the public gallery of the Court; and

7. To respect all conditions imposed by the Detention Services Unit of the Special Court for Sierra Leone.

40. I further order that any failure by any of the said Contemnors to comply with these conditions is to operate as a suspension of the probation and a revocation of the conditional discharge.

APPEALS CHAMBER DECISIONS

- **Rule 77: Contempt of Court – Generalities**

R77-AC-1

o *Prosecutor v. Brima, Kamara, Kanu*, Case No. SCSL-04-16-AR77, Decision on Defence Appeal Motion Pursuant to Rule 77 (J) on Both the Imposition of Interim Measures and an Order Pursuant to Rule 77(C)(iii), 23 June 2005, para. 2, 26-27:

2. All courts must possess the powers necessary to enable them to administer and deliver justice fairly and efficiently. These powers are not vouchsafed to bolster the self-regard of judges, officials or counsel, who must in the discharge of their duties put up with criticisms, however wrong-headed, of their actions. The power to investigate and punish what is generically (and somewhat misleading) described as "contempt of court" can only be used against those whose actions are calculated to obstruct the court's task of getting at the truth – in the terms laid down by Rule 77A, "any person who knowingly and wilfully interferes with its administration of justice." That sub-rule gives six, non-exhaustive, ways in which contempt of court may be committed, e.g. by disclosing information relating to proceedings in knowing violation of an order (ii) and by threatening or intimidating a witness (iv). It should be obvious that witnesses must never be put under any pressure in their choice to give evidence for one party or another or as to what evidence they should give, and must be rigorously protected thereafter from any reprisals. Where the court, because there is a real danger of such reprisals, has taken the exceptional step of ordering that the name and any identifying details of a witness should not be disclosed to the public, a credible allegation of breach of that order by a person subject to it must be investigated without delay.

[...]

26. Rule 77(A) defines the crime – knowing and unlawful interference with the administration of justice – which the court has inherent power to punish, and identifies five ways in which it may be committed (e.g. by disclosing information in

violation of an order and intimidating a witness). Sub-rule B extends the power to enable punishment of incitement or attempt. Sub-rule C sets out the test ('reason to believe') which entitles the court to proceed and chose between the three process options – summary trial, reference to Sierra Leone authorities, or appointment of independent counsel. Sub-rule D provides that any prosecution by independent counsel may be heard by a single Judge of that Trial Chamber or another Trial Chamber. Sub-rule E applies the Rules of Procedure and Evidence to those proceedings, i.e. to the trial of the contempt case brought by the independent prosecutor pursuant to a decision to take option 77(C)(iii). Sub-rule F provides legal aid to poor persons facing such a trial. Sub-rule G provides for maximum penalties on conviction, both after summary trial or trial prosecuted by the independent counsel. Moving on to the stage after conviction, Sub-rule H provides for payment of any fine to the Registrar, and Sub-rule I gives the Court power to order an additional professional penalty if the convicted defendant is of counsel. Sub-rule J moves us forwards to the Appeal stage. It says: "Any decision rendered by a Single Judge or Trial Chamber under this Rule shall be subject to appeal." Sub-rule K provides that "appeals pursuant to this rule" – i.e. by a convicted defendant, or by a dissatisfied prosecutor – shall be heard by three Judges of the Chamber, and Sub-rule L provides for the unhappy if unlikely circumstance of a contempt committed during appeal proceedings.

27. Rule 77 has only to be read – or set forth as above – to recognise that it is a coherent and chronological code, setting out the procedure at every stage from the time the allegation is made to the final appeal against conviction or acquittal. Sub-rule J comes into play _after_ the final decision of conviction or acquittal (under Sub-rules D, E & F) and _after_ sentencing as provided for by sub-rules G, H & I. By simple and self-evident alphabetical declension, Sub-Rule J is next in time. It opens the door to a direct appeal (without leave) to a three Judge appeal court. It is directly _before_ the constitution of the appeal bench triggered by an appeal (K), and it is before provision is made for dealing with contempts at hearing: Sub-Rule (L). It is, therefore, not a Rule that should come into play (even with leave) before a final decision is made by the Trial Judge. And in its context, it is a Rule that only allows an appeal by the parties involved in the trial – i.e. the alleged contemnor (if convicted) and the prosecutor (if there has been an acquittal). It cannot be activated at any stage by a defendant in another trial who may have a connection with the contemnor, and it cannot be activated at all prior to the result of the contempt trial.

- **Rule 77: Contempt of Court – Proceedings –** *Locus Standi*

R77-AC-2
o *Prosecutor v. Brima, Kamara, Kanu*, Case No. SCSL-04-16-AR77, Decision on Defence Appeal Motion Pursuant to Rule 77(J) on Both the Imposition of Interim Measures and an Order Pursuant to Rule 77(C)(iii), 23 June 2005, para. 33:

33. This appeal is brought without leave by the three defendants in the AFRC trial. None are subject to the contempt investigation ordered by the Trial Chamber. Their counsel have not been assigned to represent any of the five alleged contemnors nor do they purport to have been instructed to represent them. It follows that they have no standing, in any event, to prosecute an appeal against the two decisions taken by the Trial Chamber in relation 1) to its reason to believe that a contempt had been committed by others or 2) to its direction for an independent investigation of that alleged contempt.

R77-AC-3
o *Prosecutor v. Brima, Kamara, Kanu*, Case No. SCSL-04-16-AR77, Decision on Joint Defence Appeal Against the Decision on the Report of the Independent Counsel Pursuant to Rule 77(C)(iii) and 77(D), 17 August 2005, para. 16:

16. The arguments developed by the Defence in its Reply to the Prosecution Response on the issue of standing do not provide anything which might cause a change to the ruling of the Appeals Chamber in its Decision in the First Appeal on Contempt. In particular, the Appeals Chamber is not convinced by the submissions of the Defence that the outcome of the contempt proceedings will affect the fairness of the case against the Accused in the AFRC trial and that they therefore have a reasonable interest to a participation in these proceedings. The contempt proceedings are parallel to the Case against the Accused and their outcome shall have no effect on the Trial against them, as none of the Accused is indicted for having had a part in the alleged contempt. Therefore, it is the view of the Appeals Chamber that the Appellants have no *locus standi* in the current Appeal.

- **Rule 77(C): Contempt of Court – Procedure**

R77-AC-4

o *Prosecutor v. Brima, Kamara, Kanu*, Case No. SCSL-04-16-AR77, Decision on Defence Appeal Motion Pursuant to Rule 77(J) on Both the Imposition of Interim Measures and an Order Pursuant to Rule 77(C)(iii), 23 June 2005, para. 9, 11-13, 16-19, 30:

9. It is clear from the terms of Rule 77(C) that the situation required the court to take three decisions. In the first place, it had to decide whether, on the material placed before it, there was reason to believe that a contempt may have been committed. If so, it had to decide whether: i) to proceed to summary trial, or ii) to refer the matter to the authorities of Sierra Leone or iii) to direct the Registrar to appoint independent counsel to investigate and report back to the Chamber as to whether there were sufficient grounds to proceed for contempt. Thirdly, it had to decide, under its inherent jurisdiction or pursuant to its Rule 54 power to make orders or its Rule 75 power to protect witnesses, whether any or all of the interim measures urged by the prosecutor should be put in place.

[...]

11. [...][T]he Defence counsel were entitled, if they chose, to present argument that the material submitted by the prosecution did not give any cause for reasonable belief that a contempt might have been committed. Obviously the court could not allow itself at this stage to be drawn into a summary trial, or a trial before a trial. But if the Defence could provide evidence that entirely refuted the allegation – e.g. if it could prove that the investigator was in another country at the material time, or that there had been an obvious misunderstanding or misidentification, then it should be permitted to produce it. It is much better that a demonstrably mistaken allegation should be exposed at once, before unnecessary contempt proceedings or investigations are commenced. [...]

12. If the Chamber decides that there may have been a contempt, then it must next decide whether to try the matter summarily (with a maximum sentence of six months) or to pass it to the Sierra Leone authorities or to direct the Registrar to appoint an independent Counsel to investigate: a procedure for serious cases which could result eventually in a seven years jail sentence. This is essentially a question for the Trial Chamber, but it might be assisted by submissions from counsel.

13. On the third decision – the interim orders – the right of the defence to be heard is self evident. The court must be told the extent to which the proposed order will impact on the

course of the trial or hinder defence preparation or cause distress to a defendant, and it must hear argument as to whether any draconian order sought by the prosecution is really proportionate to deal with the apprehended risk.

[...]

16. [...] [T]he evidential hurdle is low, and was satisfied by the testimony on oath of Witness TF1-023, the report from the head of the Witness Protection Unit and the witness statements from the two guards. True it is that these two statements included hearsay, were not on oath and cried out for cross-examination, but at this initiating stage the court is not concerned with their veracity – that will be tested by a trial, if the essential material submitted by the Prosecution gives 'reason to believe' that contempt 'may' have been committed.

17. [...] [T]he standard is not that of a *prima facie* case, which is the standard for committal for trial. It is the different and lower standard of "reason to believe" that an offence <u>may</u> have been committed, which is the pre-condition for ordering an independent investigation. [...]

18. The decision to proceed by way of 77(C)(iii), i.e. by appointing an independent counsel, rather than by way of summary trial, was essentially a matter for the Trial Chamber. Summary Trial is preferable if the parties are before the Court and the matter is not overly serious and can be determined speedily and with minimum disruption. It may be inappropriate if the alleged contempt is very serious or will require counsel to give evidence. It will be inappropriate if the Judges of the Chamber feel personally involved: any cases of contempt by the media should for that reason be dealt with by another Chamber. [...]

19. [...] Sub-Rule (C)(iii) does not permit the Court to direct an independent counsel to prosecute at this initiating stage. An independent counsel is appointed in circumstances where it is inappropriate for the Special Court's own prosecutor to act: he serves as an independent officer, reaching his own independent decision as to whether there are sufficient grounds for a prosecution. Only if he comes to that conclusion in his report to the Chamber, and if the Chamber agrees with that conclusion, may it direct him to commence a prosecution.

[...]

30. [...] [A]pplication of 73(B) to a decision taken under 77(C)(iii) would be inappropriate. That is a decision to appoint an independent counsel to collect and consider evidence: such decisions, routinely made by law enforcement agencies, are not normally susceptible to appeal or to judicial review. Moreover, as this case in particular demonstrates, contempt proceedings are apt to disrupt trials and it is of great

importance that they should be concluded as quickly as possible – and that means, without interlocutory appeal.

• Rule 77(J): Contempt of Court – Appeal

R77-AC-5

o *Prosecutor v. Brima, Kamara, Kanu*, Case No. SCSL-04-16-AR77, Decision on Defence Appeal Motion Pursuant to Rule 77(J) on Both the Imposition of Interim Measures and an Order Pursuant to Rule 77(C)(iii), 23 June 2005, para. 29:

29. [. . .] 'Any decision' means in context 'any final decision' and not "any decision taken by the Court at any time in the course of investigating or processing a contempt allegation." So this appeal is incompetent in so far as it relates to the two decisions taken by the trial chamber under sub-rule C.

DECISIONS OF THE PRESIDENT

• Rule 77(D): Contempt of Court – Proceedings – Assignment of Contempt Cases to a Trial Chamber or to a Single Judge – Power of the President

R77-P-1

o *Prosecutor v. Samura* (Case No. SCSL-05-01), *Brima (Margaret), Jalloh and Kamara (Ester)* (Case No. SCSL-05-02), and *Kamara (Anifa)* (Case No. SCSL-05-03), Order Assigning Cases to a Trial Chamber, 2 May 2005:

I, JUSTICE EMMANUEL AYOOLA, President of the Special Court for Sierra Leone ("Special Court");

CONSIDERING Rule 19(A) of the Rules of Procedure and Evidence of the Special Court ("Rules"), which authorizes the President to coordinate the work of the Chambers;

NOTING the Decision on the Report of the Independent Counsel pursuant to Rules 77(C)(iii) and 77(D) of the Rules of Procedure and Evidence issued by Trial Chamber II on 29 April 2005 ("the Decision") and the Corrigendum thereto dated 2 May 2005, which issued orders in lieu of indictments against BRIMA SAMURA, MARGARET FOMBA BRIMA, NENEH BINTA BAH JALLOH, ANIFA KAMARA, ESTER KAMARA, which were annexed to the Decision ("the contempt proceedings");

NOTING that pursuant to Rule 77(D) of the Rules the Decision assigned the contempt proceedings to Trial Chamber I or a single judge thereof,

HEREBY confirm the assignment of Case No. SCSL – 05-1, *Prosecutor v. Brima Samura* and Case No SCSL – 05-2, *Prosecutor v. Margaret Fomba Brima, Neneh Binta Bah Jalloh, Anifa Kamara, Ester Kamara* to Trial Chamber I or a single judge thereof.

Rule 78: Open Sessions

All proceedings before a Trial Chamber, other than deliberations of the Chamber, shall be held in public, unless otherwise provided.

TRIAL CHAMBERS DECISIONS

- **Rule 78: Open Sessions – Publicity – Submissions and Decisions**

R78-TC-1

o *Prosecutor v. Kallon*, Case No. SCSL-04-15-PT, Decision on the Motion by Morris Kallon for Bail, 24 February 2004, para. 19-20:[134]

19. All written submissions filed by both parties and the Government of Sierra Leone in connection with the Motion were marked as confidential and, accordingly, have not been disclosed to the public. I would like to reiterate that as a matter of general principle, all documents filed before the Special Court should be public, unless a cogent reason is offered to the contrary. Consistent with this approach, as stated above, a short part of the hearing of the Motion was held in closed session and the remainder was open in accordance with Rules 78 and 79 of the Rules.[(1)]

20. In reviewing this matter and in rendering this Decision on the Motion, I have come to the conclusion that there is no reason why this decision should not be made public. Although the justified confidentiality of particular submissions will not be endangered, herein being only limited to a general reference, the public nature of this Decision will better serve the fundamental rights of the Accused, and in particular his right to a fair and public hearing, as well as the right for the public to be properly informed of the nature of such Motion and

---

[134] See also *Prosecutor v. Sesay*, Case No. SCSL-04-15-PT, Decision on Application of Issa Sesay for Provisional Release, 31 March 2004, para. 32-33; *Prosecutor v. Sesay*, Case No. SCSL-04-15-T, Decision on Defence Motion, 15 July 2004, para. 9; *Prosecutor v. Kallon*, Case No. SCSL-04-15-T, Decision on Confidential Motion, 11 October 2004, para. 16; *Prosecutor v. Brima, Kamara, Kanu* Case No. SCSL-04-16-T, Decision on the Confidential Application for Withdrawal by Counsel for Brima and Kamara and on the Request for Further Representation by Counsel for Kanu, 20 May 2005, para. 22; *Prosecution v. Sesay, Kallon, Gbao*, Case No. SCSL-04-15-T, Ruling on Application for the Exclusion of Certain Supplemental Statements of Witness TF1-361 and Witness TF1-122, 1st June 2005, para. 15; *Prosecutor v. Brima, Kamara, Kanu*, Case No. SCSL-04-16-T, Decision on Confidential Joint Defence Request to Inspect *Locus in Quo* Concerning Evidence of Witness TF1-024, 15 June 2005, para. 4.

of the Decision thereto, and of all matters forming part of the trial of an accused.

(1) Rule 78 of the Rules, in particular, provides for the following: "All proceedings before a Trial Chamber, other than the deliberations of the Chamber, shall be held in public, unless otherwise provided."

R78-TC-2

o *Prosecutor v. Norman, Fofana, Kondewa*, Case No. SCSL-04-14-T, Order to the Prosecution on Filing, 20 September 2005:

NOTING that all three Defence Motions have been filed publicly;

CONSIDERING that Article 17(2) of the Statute of the Special Court provides that "[t]he accused shall be entitled to a fair and public hearing, subject to measures ordered by the Special Court for the protection of victims and witnesses";

[...]

CONSIDERING that the three Responses have been filed confidentially with an explanation in the Court Management Form that the "Response contains transcript quotes and other references to testimony from closed court session. Such sessions were closed to protect the identity of witnesses "in accordance with the Witness Protection Order. A public filing of this document could potentially identify the names of the protected witnesses..;

CONSIDERING that generally hearings should be conducted publicly but "this preference has to be balanced with other mandated interests", among them protective measures for victims and witnesses";(1)

CONSIDERING therefore, that for the interests of conducting a public hearing the Prosecution must file a redacted public version of their Responses, in addition to the confidential Responses already filed;

CONSIDERING that it is the practice of the other International criminal tribunals that in those cases where witness protection issues arise, both confidential and public motions and responses may be filed;(2)

THE CHAMBER ORDERS the Prosecution to file a public version of each of the three Responses filed on the 18th August 2005 with redactions as necessary to protect the identity of the witnesses;

(1) *Prosecutor v. Sam Hinga Norman, Moinina Fofana, Allieu Kondewa*, Decision

on Prosecution Motion for Modification of Protective Measures for Witnesses, dated the 8th of June, 2004, para. 39 (footnotes omitted).
(2) E.g. *Prosecutor v. Brdjanin*, Case No. IT-99-36-T, decision on Motion for Acquittal Pursuant to Rule 98*bis*, 28 November 2003, para. 1.

> **Rule 79: Closed Sessions**
> *(amended 14 May 2005)*
>
> (A) The Trial Chamber may order that the press and the public be excluded from all or part of the proceedings for reasons of:
>
>   (i) national security; or
>   (ii) protecting the privacy, security or non-disclosure of the identity of a victim or witness as provided in Rule 75; or
>   (iii) protecting the interest of justice.
>
> (B) The Trial Chamber shall make public the reasons for its order.
>
> (C) In the event that it is necessary to exclude the public, the Trial Chamber should if appropriate permit representatives of monitoring agencies to remain. Such representatives should, if appropriate, have access to the transcripts of closed sessions.

TRIAL CHAMBERS DECISIONS

- **Rule 79: Closed Sessions – Authority of the Trial Chamber to Order**

R79-TC-1

o *Prosecutor v. Brima, Kamara, Kanu*, Case No. SCSL-04-16-T, Decision on the Confidential Joint Defence Motion to Declare Null and Void Testimony-in-Chief of Witness TF1-023, 25 May 2005, para. 15-16:

> 15. Further, the Defence submitted that the Trial Chamber had no authority to order a closed session, as such authority was with Trial Chamber I pursuant to Rule 75(G)(i) of the Rules and further Rule 75(H) did not apply. We consider there is no validity in this argument, and to hold otherwise could lead to cumbersome delays in the proper running of both Trial Chambers of the Special Court.
>
> 16. The provisions for closed sessions are contained in Rule 75(B)(ii) and Rule 79. Rule 75(A) deals with the provisions for the protection of witnesses and allows a Trial Chamber to order a closed session as one of several protective measures to "prevent disclosure to the public or the media of the identity or whereabouts of a victim or witness". Variations of protective measures are provided in Rule 75(G) and applications must be made to the Chamber "remaining seized of the first proceeding". The decision to order protection of a witness by

way of a closed session must be implemented in accordance with Rule 79. The powers to order a closed session in Rule 79 are independent of Rule 75. Rule 79 vests powers in "[T]he Trial Chamber" – that is the Trial Chamber hearing a case – to order the exclusion of the press and the public. It is distinguished from "any Chamber, however constituted, remaining seized of the first proceedings" as provided for in Rule 75(G).

- **Rule 79: Closed Sessions – Applicable Standards**

R79-TC-2   o *Prosecutor v. Norman*, Case No. SCSL-03-08-PT, Reasons for Ordering a Closed Session, 15 March 2003:

PURSUANT to Rule 79(B) of the Rules, which provides that the Court shall make public the reasons for ordering a closed session;

HEREBY orders that the Initial Appearance of the Accused be held in closed session, excluding the press and public from the proceedings for reasons, as provided in Rule 79(A)(iii), that publicity would prejudice the interests of justice.

R79-TC-3   o *Prosecutor v. Sesay, Kallon, Gbao*, Case No. SCSL-04-15-PT, Reasons for Order for Closed Session of the Status Conference and Modification of Said Order in Part, 5 March 2004:

RECALLING THAT the Office of the Prosecutor ("Prosecution") and the Acting Principal Defender of the Defence Office of the Special Court ("Defence Office") submitted a letter to the Presiding Judge of the Trial Chamber on 17 February 2004 in which it was jointly recommended that the Status Conference be held *in camera* before a designated Judge of the Trial Chamber in order to "facilitate the frank and open exchange of views between the parties," particularly as many of the issues on the proposed agenda for the Status Conference are "still at a preliminary stage and may well change before trial," thereby creating confusion at this stage if disclosed to the public;

RECALLING THAT the Trial Chamber convened a meeting with the Parties before the commencement of the Status Conference to hear their submission on whether to hold the Status Conference in open session or closed session;

CONSIDERING THAT the Prosecution submitted that the Status Conference may be more productive if held in closed session, as closed session would promote an open and frank dialogue between the Parties, and that if the Trial Chamber held that the Status Conference were to be conducted in open session, that it would request to go into closed session for discussion of matters pertaining to witness protection;

CONSIDERING FURTHER THAT the Prosecution expressed concern that preliminary indications it would provide in relation to the trial proceedings at the Status Conference may not be put, if made public, in their proper procedural and technical context;

CONSIDERING THAT the Defence for Accused Issa Sesay submitted that issues concerning case management could be dealt with in a neutral way and would not require closed session, with closed session remaining an option for those issues that may arise which could require it;

CONSIDERING THAT the Defence for Accused Augustine Gbao submitted that the Status Conference should be held in open session to promote transparency of the proceedings, and that closed session could be requested on a case-by-case basis as required;

CONSIDERING THAT the Accused Morris Kallon was represented at the Status Conference by Duty Counsel from the Defence Office pursuant to Rule 45 of the Rules, and that Duty Counsel submitted that the proceedings should only be held in closed session with good reason being shown;

CONSIDERING THAT after hearing the parties, the Trial Chamber, pursuant to Rule 79(iii) of the Rules, held that the Status Conference would be conducted in open session for four agenda items, namely appearances of the parties, issues related to the Accused, general housekeeping matters, and the trial schedule, and that the remainder of the agenda, comprising the issues of pending motions, disclosure, witnesses, protective measures, points of agreement, and judicial notice, would be held in closed session;

CONSIDERING THAT the Trial Chamber based its decision to hold certain sections of the Status Conference in closed session out of an abundance of caution for the following reasons:

(i) The closed sessions on the items of the agenda so designated will be more conducive to candid and more open views between the parties.
(ii) Unlike the actual trials, status conferences are in essence informal meetings of the parties the objective of which is to identify and resolve mostly the procedural and technical aspects of a trial.
(iii) Since most of the factual and legal issues to be deliberated upon at status conferences are still at a prelim-

inary stage, there is a potential that by the premature disclosure of such factual and legal issues the interests of justice and the integrity of the proceedings may be jeopardised;

R79-TC-4

o *Prosecutor v. Norman, Fofana Kondewa*, Case No. SCSL-04-14-T, Order on an Application by the Prosecution to Hold a Closed Session Hearing of Witnesses TF2-082 and TF2-032, 13 September 2004:[135]

CONSIDERING the rights of the Accused to a fair and public hearing must be balanced with the need to guarantee the utmost protection and respect for the rights of victims and witnesses;

CONSIDERING that provision is made in Rule 75 of the Rules for the Trial Chamber to order appropriate measures to safeguard the privacy and security of victims and witnesses and that when read together with Rule 79 and in conformity with Article 17(2) of the Statute of the Special Court, Rule 79 reflects the affirmative obligation of the Court to afford protection to victims and witnesses where their privacy or security may be threatened;

CONSIDERING the special feature of the Special Court is that it is located in Sierra Leone where the crimes being tried are alleged to have been committed and that this fact has a substantial impact on the security considerations for victims and witnesses;

CONSIDERING that the Special Court has already established a precedent of permitting the testimony of witnesses to be elicited during closed session based upon the principle of protection of victims and witnesses where the interests of justice so dictate as was the case in the RUF trial;[(1)]

CONSIDERING that permissibility of closed session testimony is an extraordinary protective measure that will only be granted where it is shown that there is a very real risk to the witness and/or his or her family that their privacy or security will be threatened;

CONSIDERING that the Trial Chamber has already granted Witness TF2-082 the protective measures of testifying under a

---

[135] See also *Prosecutor v. Norman, Fofana, Kondewa*, Case No. SCSL-04-14-T, Order on an Application by the Prosecution to Hold a Closed Session Hearing of Witness TF2-151, 24 September 2004; *Prosecutor v. Norman, Fofana, Kondewa*, Case No. SCSL-04-14-T, Order on an Application by the Prosecution to Hold a Closed Session Hearing of Witness TF2-223, 27 October 2004.

pseudonym and with voice distortion, and granted Witness TF2-032 the protective measures of testifying under a pseudonym;[2]

CONSIDERING that additional protective measures are required for Witness TF2-082 and Witness TF2-032 because of the positions that they held in their respective communities, and that if any of this evidence is heard publicly it would lead to the identification of these witnesses;

CONSIDERING that it is in the interests of justice that these two witnesses be allowed to testify with the protection of appropriate measures, where the full testimony of Witness TF2-082 and those above-mentioned portions of the testimony of Witness TF2-032 be given in closed session;

---

[1] Witness TF1-235, RUF Trial Transcript, 29 July 2004.
[2] Decision on Prosecution's Motion for Modification of Protective Measures for Witnesses, 8 June 2004.

R79-TC-5

o *Prosecutor v. Sesay, Kallon, Gbao*, Case No. SCSL-04-15-T, Order to Hear the Evidence of Witness TF1-071 in Closed Session, 19 January 2005:

NOTING that the Trial Chamber on the 18th of January, 2005 delivered an oral Ruling ordering that the testimony of Witness TF1-071 would be heard in closed session;

[...]

Mindful of Article 17(2) of the Statute which provides that the "accused shall be entitled to a fair and public hearing, subject to measures ordered by the Special Court for the protection of victims and witnesses", and pursuant to Rules 75 and 79 of the Rules, the Trial Chamber rules that considering the information disclosed to the Court in support of the application, the portions of the testimony of witness TF1-071 as indicated by the Prosecution will be heard in closed session.

This exceptional procedure is required because, as submitted by the Prosecution, if the portions of his testimony so indicated are heard in public his identity will thereby be revealed with a high potential of exposing him and his family to threats and retaliation. Furthermore, and significantly, he is someone who had held key positions in the RUF leadership during the relevant period of time.

It is, accordingly, the considered opinion of the Trial Chamber that if the said portions of his testimony are heard in public, it would lead to his identification and would jeopardise his safety and security, and that of his family, a matter over which he has directly expressed grave concern.

- **Rule 79: Closed Sessions – Privilege and Immunities of Witness**

R79-TC-6

o *Prosecutor v. Norman, Fofana, Kondewa*, Case No. SCSL-04-14-T, Decision on Prosecution Application for Closed Session for Witness TF2-218, 15 June 2005:

CONSIDERING that witness TF2-218 is a former employee of an international organization, and continues to enjoy privileges and immunities, including immunity from legal process in respect of all words spoken or written and all acts performed by him in the course of the performance of his official functions;

CONSIDERING that the evidence which witness TF2-218 is called to give includes sensitive and confidential information which he allegedly obtained in the course of the performance of his official functions;

CONSIDERING that his former employer has waived witness TF2-218's immunity from legal process on the condition that he be allowed to testify in closed session in view of the nature of his evidence;

CONSIDERING that testifying on relevant, sensitive and confidential information in a closed session, would, in this case, not prejudice the interests of the Accused or the conduct of the trial as a whole;

R79-TC-7

o *Prosecutor v. Brima, Kamara, Kanu*, Case No. SCSL-04-16-T, Decision on the Prosecution's Oral Application for Leave to Be Granted to Witness TF1-150 to Testify Without Being Compelled to Answer Any Questions in Cross-Examination That the Witness Declines to Answer on Grounds of Confidentiality Pursuant to Rule 70(B) and (D) of the Rules, 16 September 2005, para. 1-3, 14-17:

1. Prosecution Witness TF1-150 is a foreign national who served in Sierra Leone during the period May 1998 to 2001 as a Human Rights advisor to an international organisation ("the former employer"). By virtue of his employment, Witness TF1-150 obtained information relating to the conflict situation in Sierra Leone during the said period, some of which information he obtained on a confidential basis. In the interest of the former employer, Witness TF1-150 enjoyed and continues to enjoy by virtue of his employment, certain privileges and immunities in respect of all words spoken or written and all acts performed by him in the performance of his duties, including immunity from legal process. That means

that he cannot testify before a court of law regarding his work except with the express permission of his former employer.

2. By a letter dated 23 May 2005 addressed to the Prosecutor, SCSL, the former employer waived part of that immunity and granted Witness TF1-150 permission to testify before the Special Court in a number of cases including *the Prosecutor v. Alex Tamba Brima et al.* However, due to the sensitive and confidential nature of some of the information that the witness might divulge, the waiver of immunity is conditional upon certain conditions, one of which is that the witness must testify in closed session. In compliance with the request of the former employer, the Trial Chamber on 13 September 2005 ordered pursuant to Rule 79(A)(iii) of the Rules that in the interests of justice Witness TF1-15 – do testify in closed session.

3. In addition to the closed session, the Prosecution now seeks an order from the Trial Chamber guaranteeing before Witness TF1-150 is called to testify, that he will not be compelled to answer any questions in cross-examination, relating to the names of his informants or sources of information, on the grounds that he obtained information from these sources on conditions of confidentiality.

[...]

14. Witness TF1-150 worked as a Human Rights monitor for an international organisation in Sierra Leone during a period relevant to the indictment in the case of *The Prosecutor v. Alex Tamba Brima et al.*[1] By virtue of his employment in the organisation he enjoyed and continues to enjoy certain privileges and immunities including immunity from legal process. In other words he cannot be compelled to appear and testify in a court of law relating to his employment without the express permission of his former employer.

15. The Prosecution tendered to the court a letter dated 23 May 2005 in which the former employer of Witness TF1-150 did in fact waive part of that immunity and granted him permission to appear before the Special Court in the AFRC Case and to "*testify freely as to the existence or otherwise of any of the elements of any of the crimes set out in the Statute of the Special Court or other matters which, in the opinion of the Court, are relevant to the individual criminal responsibility of an accused person or of any circumstance of an exculpatory or mitigatory nature, as well as to be asked and to answer questions which seek to establish the existence of any such element or circumstance.*"

16. However, the former employer observes in the said letter that in view of the "*sensitive and confidential information*" that the witness is likely to divulge, his testimony should only be given on that following conditions, namely that he

"*testifies in closed session; that transcripts and recordings of his testimony be restricted to the trial Chambers and their staff, to the Prosecution and their staff and to the accused and their counsel and expert advisers; and that the Prosecution and their staff as well as accused and their counsel and expert advisers be prohibited from divulging the contents of such testimony to the media or to any other third part.*" The waiver does not extend to the release confidential documents of the former employer unless prior permission in this regard is sought and obtained.

17. Based upon the contents of this letter the Trial Chamber on 13 September 2005 granted leave to Witness TF1-150 to testify in closed session pursuant to Rule 79(A)(iii) of the Rules. [...]

(1) Case No. SCSL-04-16-T

- **Rule 79: Closed Sessions – Attendance by Investigators**

R79-TC-8

o *Prosecutor v. Norman, Fofana, Kondewa*, Case No. SCSL-04-14-T, Decision on the Joint Motion by Sam Hinga Norman, Moinina Fofana and Allieu Kondewa Seeking Permission for Defence Investigators to Sit in Court During Closed Sessions, 28 February 2005, para. 10-11, 14-19:[136]

10. The Defence argue that investigators should be considered as part of the "Defence Team" and not part of the press or public that are excluded from attending closed session hearings within the meaning of Rule 79(A) of the Rules. Article 1 of the Directive on the Assignment of Counsel, adopted on the 1st of October 2003, defines a "Defence Team" as composed of those individuals providing services to a Suspect or Accused in accordance with a Provisional Assignment Agreement or Legal Services Contract described in Article 16 of the Directive.

11. Given the plain and ordinary meaning of Article 1 of the said Directive, the Trial Chamber holds that where investigators conduct investigations or provide services to the Accused for the preparation of the Defence of the Accused, they should be considered part of a Defence team for that Accused person. The Chamber further holds that investigators, by the very nature of their work, may provide immediate and invaluable information to assist in the preparation and conduct of the Defence of the Accused [...].

---

[136] See also *Prosecutor v. Samura*, Case No. SCSL-05-01, Judgment in Contempt Proceedings, 26 October 2005, para. 67.

[...]

14. We conclude, therefore, that the presence of defence investigators in the Court Room during closed session hearings of witness testimony would be consistent with the rights of the Accused to have adequate time and facilities available for the preparation of the Defence of the Accused, and for the Accused to be given the full opportunity to examine or have examined, the witnesses against him or her as enshrined respectively in Articles 17(4)(b) and (e) of the Statute.

15. We also note that in accordance with the Trial Chamber's Decision on Protective Measures, Defence investigators, as part of the defence Team may be provided with the unredacted statements of witnesses and that the defence is required to "maintain a log indicating the name, address and position of each person or entity which receives a copy of, information from, a witness statement, interview report or summary of expected testimony, or any other non-public material, as well as the date of disclosure; and that the Defence shall ensure that the person to whom such information was disclosed follows the order of non-public disclosure".[1]

16. Emphasising that the practice at International Criminal Tribunal for the Former Yugoslavia ("ICTY") has been to allow investigators to be present in Court during trial proceedings,[2] we here recall that the Trial Chamber of the ICTY, presided over by Judge May, in the case of *Kordic and Cerkez* granted permission for investigators to be present in Court during closed session hearings.[3]

17. We have carefully balanced the rights of the Accused to a fair and public hearing with the need to guarantee adequate protection and respect for the rights of victims and witnesses, and conclude that it is permissible for Defence investigators to be present in Court during the testimony of witnesses in closed session. In addition, we hold that defence investigators, as members of the Defence Team, are required to comply with the Trial Chamber's Decisions on Protective Measures for Witnesses [...].

18. Furthermore, the Chamber directs that Court Appointed Counsel for the Accused, responsible for leading the Defence Team of the Accused person, will be held accountable to it for ensuring the full compliance of all members of the Defence Team with the existing Decisions on Protective Measures delivered by the Trial Chamber and with future Decisions of this nature, and in particular, for ensuring that Defence investigators that comprise members of the Defence Team and who may be present during closed sessions hearings, do not disclose the identity of protected witnesses or the evidence given during those closed sessions to anybody outside the Defence Team.

19. In conclusion, the Trial Chamber is of the opinion that it is in the interests of justice and in conformity with the doctrine of equality of arms for investigators that comprise members of both the Defence and Prosecution Teams to be allowed access in the Court Room during the testimony of witnesses in closed session, and that Senior Counsel in the Prosecution Teams, in the same terms as Leading Counsel in the Defence Teams, shall ensure the compliance of all members of the Prosecution Team with the Decisions delivered by the Trial Chamber in relation to this Decision and others of a similar nature.

---

(1) Order 2(g).
(2) *Prosecution v. Naletilic and Martinovic*, Decision on Prosecutor's Motion to Permit Investigators to Follow the Proceedings, 31 April 2001; *Prosecution v. Mrksic, Radic, Sljivancanin and Dokmanovic*, Order Permitting Investigators to Follow Proceedings, 23 April 1998.
(3) Oral Ruling, later confirmed in writing: *Prosecutor v. Kordic and Cerkez*, Order Permitting Investigators to Follow Proceedings, 19 April 1999.

- **Rule 79(B): Closed Sessions – Obligation to Make Public the Reasons for Ordering a Closed Session**

R79-TC-9

o *Prosecutor v. Brima, Kamara, Kanu*, Case No. SCSL-04-16-T, Decision on the Confidential Joint Defence Motion to Declare Null and Void Testimony-in-Chief of Witness TF1-023, 25 May 2005, para. 6-8:

6. Rule 79(B) imposes a mandatory obligation on the Trial Chamber to make public the reasons for its order, that is to make the reasons known. In contract to Rule 79(A), the obligation is not to make the reasons known to "the press and the public". The obligation under 79(B) is wide, ot obliges the Trial Chamber "make public the reasons" *viz* to have a reason made on record and publicly available.

7. Further, if there is a defect, it can be cured by compliance with Rule 79(B) by the Trial Chamber publicising its reason.

8. The Trial Chamber notes that no exception was taken by Defence Counsel at the time the Trial Chamber ordered a closed session. In fact, Defence Counsel permitted the witness to be examined in chief without objection. At the end of examination in chief, all Defence Counsel evinced an intention to cross-examine but not at that time. They indicated that leave of the Court would be sought at a later date to recall the witness. This Trial Chamber considers and holds that the clear decision on the part of Defence Counsel to permit examination-in-chief to continue and indicate that they would

seek leave to cross-examine at a later date knowing they would later apply to have the evidence adduced in closed session declared null and void is not in keeping with the professional standards this Court expects of Counsel in their duty to the Court.

- **Rule 79(C): Closed Sessions – Attendance by Court Monitors**

  o *Prosecutor v. Norman, Fofana, Kondewa*, Case No. SCSL-2004-14-T, Order on Trial Monitoring During Closed Session, 27 October 2004:[137]

  PURSUANT TO the provisions of Rule 79 and particularly those of Rule 79(C) of the Rules of Procedure and Evidence of the Special Court;

  ORDERS AS FOLLOWS:

  [. . .]

  2. That the following national monitors from the Coalition for Justice and Accountability and the International Center for Transitional Justice are authorised to be present in the Courtroom during trial proceedings when the Court is sitting in closed session: [. . .]

  3. That the following international monitors from the War Crimes Studies Center, University of California at Berkeley, are authorised to be present in the Courtroom during trial proceedings when the Court is sitting in closed session [. . .]

  4. That the monitors listed in paragraphs 1 and 2 of this Order are required to sign a declaration at the Office of the Registrar stating that they will not disclose any of the evidence elicited by witnesses during closed session and that they will report only on the practice and procedure of the Court during closed session;

  5. That at any given time not more than two authorised monitors, one international and one national, from those listed in paragraphs 1 and 2 of this Order are allowed to be present during the court proceedings conducted in closed sessions;

---

[137] See also *Prosecutor v. Sesay, Kallon, Gbao*, Case No. SCSL-04-15-T, Order on Trial Monitoring During Closed Session, 27 October 2004; *Prosecutor v. Norman, Fofana, Kondewa*, Case No. SCSL-04-14-T, Order on Trial Monitoring During Closed Session, 5 November 2004; *Prosecutor v. Sesay, Kallon, Gbao*, Case No. SCSL-04-15-T, Order on Trial Monitoring During Closed Session, 5 November 2004; *Prosecutor v. Sesay, Kallon, Gbao*, Case No. SCSL-04-15-T, Order on Trial Monitoring During Closed Session, 9 November 2005.

6. That the monitors shall seek the approval of the Registrar of the material on the practice and procedure of the Court during closed session before such material is reported upon or published by the said monitors;

7. That the monitors may share such material with other international and national organizations with the approval of the Registrar;

8. That the monitors must comply with all Orders of the Court regarding protective measures for witnesses and closed sessions.

Rule 81: Records of Proceedings and Preservation of Evidence

(A) The Registrar shall cause to be made and preserve a full and accurate record of all proceedings, including audio recordings, transcripts and, when deemed necessary by the Trial Chamber, video recordings.

(B) The Trial Chamber may order the disclosure of all or part of the record of closed proceedings when the reasons for ordering the non disclosure no longer exist.

(C) The Registrar shall retain and preserve all physical evidence offered during the proceedings.

(D) Photography, video-recording or audio-recording of the trial, otherwise than by the Registry, may be authorised at the discretion of the Trial Chamber.

TRIAL CHAMBERS DECISIONS

- **Rule 81(B): Records of Proceedings – Exclusion from Records**

R81-TC-1

o *Prosecutor v. Brima, Kamara, Kanu*, Case No. SCSL-04-16-PT, Order Regarding the Disclosure of a Protected Witness TF1-081, 8 March 2005:

FINDS that the Defence Request for Disclosure filed by Defence Counsel Kevin Metzger and Glenna Thompson does reveal the identity of TF1-081, a protected witness for the Prosecution, in clear violation of the Orders of this Chamber regarding protective measures;

[…]

ORDERS that the Defence Request for Disclosure be removed from all public records of the Court Management Section of the Special Court.

R81-TC-2

o *Prosecutor v. Brima, Kamara, Kanu*, Case No. SCSL-04-16-PT, Order on Filing of Document, 9 June 2005:

NOTING the document entitled "Prosecution Response to Urgent Joint Defence Motion on Stay of the Contempt Proceedings", filed on 12 May 2005 ("Document") before Trial Chamber II;

NOTING that this Document does not form part of the pleadings in the Case of Alex Tamba Brima, Brima Buzzy Kamara and Santigie Borbor Kanu (Case No. SCSL-2004-16-T) and therefore should not have been filed before Trial Chamber II;

HEREBY ORDERS Court Management to delete the Document "Prosecution Response to Urgent Joint Defence Motion on Stay of the Contempt Proceedings" from the Court Records in Case No. SCSL-2004-16-T.

- **Rule 81(B): Records of Proceedings – Public Decision on Confidential Submissions**

R81-TC-3
o *Prosecutor v. Kallon*, Case No. SCSL-04-15-T, Decision on Confidential Motion, 11 October 2004, para. 16-17:

16. This Chamber would like to reiterate that as a matter of general principle, all documents filed before the Special Court should be public, unless a cogent reason is offered to the contrary.[1] In reviewing this matter and in rendering this Decision on the Motion, the Chamber however concludes now that there is no reason why such a decision should not be made in public.

17. The Chamber will dispose of the confidential submissions pertaining to the Motion in accordance with Rule 81(B) of the Rules. [. . .]

---

[1] See also *Prosecutor v. Kallon*, SCSL-03-07-PT, Decision on the Motion by Morris Kallon for Bail, 23 February 2004, paras 19-20.

- **Rule 81(D): Records of Proceedings – Photography, Video- and Audio-Recording – Authorization**

R81-TC-4
o *Prosecutor v. Sankoh,* Case No. SCSL-03-02-I, Order to Permit Photography, Video-Recording or Audio-Recording, 14 March 2003:[138]

---

[138] See also *Prosecutor v. Sesay*, Case No. SCSL-03-05-I, Order to Permit Photography, Video-Recording or Audio-Recording, 14 March 2003; *Prosecutor v. Brima*, Case No. SCSL-03-06-I, Order to Permit Photography, Video-Recording or Audio-Recording, 14 March 2003; *Prosecutor v. Kallon*, Case No. SCSL-03-07-I, Order to Permit Photography, Video-Recording or Audio-Recording, 14 March 2003; *Prosecutor v. Gbao*, Case No. SCSL-03-09-PT, Order to Permit Photography, Video-Recording or Audio-Recording, 24 April 2003.

HAVING CONSIDERED the requests of certain officials of the press for attending the initial appearance of Morris Kallon ("the Accused") on 15 March 2003;

PURSUANT TO Rule 28 and Rule 81(D) of the Rules;

HEREBY ORDERS that any taking of still photograph, video recording or audio-recording of the initial appearance of the Accused from any member of the press otherwise than by the Registry shall not be permitted.

DIRECTS the Chief of Security of the Special Court to take all necessary measures for the enforcement of this Order.

o *Prosecutor v. Norman, Fofana, Kondewa, Sesay Kallon, Gbao*, Case No. SCSL-2004-14-PT & SCSL-2004-15-PT, Urgent Order to Permit Photography at the Opening of the Trials, 02 June 2004:[139]

PURSUANT TO Rule 81 (D) of the Rules of Procedure and Evidence,

ORDERS AS FOLLOWS:

- o That Mr. Ben Curtis is authorised to be present in the Court Room on the 3rd of June 2004. [...]
- o That he is granted permission to photograph within the Court Room from the beginning of the Court Session up to the duration of the Prosecutor's Opening Statement.
- o That when the Statement of the Prosecutor is concluded, he must cease all photography within the Court Room.
- o That he may also photograph the accused persons, provided that the rights guaranteed to them under Article 17 of the Statute of the Special Court are respected and the administration of justice is not brought into disrepute.
- o That as the only photographer that will have access into the courtroom, he agrees to make available the photographs so taken to the national and international press.
- o That he supplies the Press and Public Affairs Office of the Special Court with a selection of pictures so taken for internal use.
- o That these Orders be carried out.

---

[139] See also *Prosecutor v. Norman, Fofana, Kondewa*, Case No. SCSL-04-14-PT, Urgent Order to Permit Filming of the Public Gallery, 18 June 2004; *Prosecutor v. Norman, Fofana, Kondewa*, Case No. SCSL-04-14-T, Order to Permit Filming in the Court Room, 04 October 2004.

R81-TC-6

o *Prosecutor v. Norman, Fofana, Kondewa, Sesay Kallon, Gbao*, Case No. SCSL-04-14-PT & SCSL-04-15-PT, Urgent Order to Permit Filming of the Public Gallery, 18 June 2004:[140]

ORDERS AS FOLLOWS:

[...]

o That he is granted to film within the public gallery during Court proceedings.
o That he may not, under any circumstances, film any of the witnesses before the Court [...]

R81-TC-7

o *Prosecutor v. Sesay, Kallon, Gbao*, Case No. SCSL-04-15-T, Order to Permit Filming in the Court Room, 04 October 2004:

ORDERS AS FOLLOWS:

- That the representatives of the Press and Public Affairs Office of the Special Court are authorised to film in the Courtroom during Trial proceedings except when Court is sitting in closed session.
- That the said Press and Public Affairs Office must advise the Presiding Judge at least 2 days before access is required in the Courtroom.
- Unless specifically authorised, they may not, under any circumstances, film any of the witnesses before the Court and must comply with all orders of the Court regarding protective measures for witnesses and closed sessions.
- That the use of the images and any commentary related thereto, should not, in any circumstances, be used in any way that could compromise or impair the fairness of the proceedings.

R81-TC-8

o *Prosecutor v. Sesay, Kallon, Gbao*, Case No. SCSL-04-15-T, Order to Permit Filming in the Courtroom, 18 November 2005:

---

[140] See also *Prosecutor v. Norman, Fofana, Kondewa*, Case No. SCSL-04-14-T, Order to Permit Filming in the Court Room, 04 October 2004; *Prosecutor v. Norman, Fofana, Kondewa*, Case No. SCSL-04-14-T, Order to Permit Filming in the Court Room, 26 November 2004; *Prosecutor v. Norman, Fofana, Kondewa*, Case No. SCSL-04-14-T, Order to Permit Photography in Court Room, 14 February 2005; *Prosecutor v. Norman, Fofana, Kondewa*, Case No. SCSL-04-14-T, Order to Filming in the Court Gallery, 2 June 2005 (2 Orders).

ORDERS AS FOLLOWS:

[...]

2. That, unless specifically authorised, they may not film any of the witnesses before the Court or be present in the Courtroom during closed sessions, and must comply with all orders of the Court regarding protective measures for witnesses.

[...]

4. That a representative of the Press and Public Affairs Office of the Special Court shall accompany them at any time during their filming in the Public Gallery of Courtroom I.

- **Rule 81(D): Records of Proceedings – Photography, Video- and Audio-Recording – Disclosure of Video and Audio Records of the Accused**

R81-TC-9

o *Prosecutor v. Brima, Kamara, Kanu*, Case No. SCSL-04-16-PT, Decision on Defence Applications Not to Disclose Photography, Video and Audio Recordings of the Trial to the Public and/or Third Parties, 28 February 2005:

CONSIDERING FURTHER that the proper time for the Trial Chamber to assess the reliability of witnesses is when they give evidence at the trial. If it is contended by an Accused that the credibility of a witness has been adversely affected by his or her exposure to images or audio recordings of the Accused prior to testifying, then that is a matter which can be raised in cross-examination.

This was the view taken by the ICTY in the case of *Prosecutor v. Dusko Tadic*,[1] in which it held that: "In all trials, the potential impact of pre-trial media coverage is a factor that must be taken into account in considering the reliability of witnesses, and where this aspect was raised in cross-examination of witnesses, it has been taken into account in the evaluation of their testimony."

The ICTY applied the same principle in *Prosecutor v. Zelko Mejakic & Others*: Decision on Motion to Remove Photographs of Accused from ICTY Website,[2] in which it held that "the potential impact of pre-trial media coverage is a factor to be taken into account in considering the reliability of witnesses in all trials before the International Tribunal and is therefore a matter for consideration at trial and not a matter for determination by the Trial Chamber at this stage of the proceedings".

In a later case,[3] the ICTY dealt with an application which sought (inter alia) orders identical to those sought in the present Motions, i.e. (1) to prohibit photography, video and audio recording of the accused by third persons and (2) directing the Registry not to publish or disclose photographs, video and audio records of the accused to the media. In dismissing the motion, the ICTY again held that" *"the potential impact of pre-trial media coverage is a factor that must be taken into account at trial and not a matter for determination at this stage of the proceedings"*;

HOLDING that, notwithstanding the Accused having appeared before the Trial Chamber on many previous occasions on which the proceedings were recorded by the Registry by means of photography, video and audio recordings, their submissions regarding the potential impact of such recordings on witnesses at the trial remain purely speculative and do not support any material prejudice that would warrant the orders sought;

HOLDING FURTHER that at present there is no application before the Trial Chamber by any "third" or other person seeking authorisation for photography, video-recording or audio-recording of the trial, and that it would not be appropriate for the Trial Chamber to consider exercising its discretion under Rule 81(D) until such an application were made,

HEREBY DISMISSES the Motions.

---

[1] *Prosecutor v. Dusko Tadic*, Case No. IT-94-1, Opinion and Judgment, 7 May 1997, para. 542-544.
[2] *Prosecutor v. Zelko Mejakic and Others*, Case No. IT-02-65-PT, Decision on Motion to Remove Photographs of Accused from ICTY Website, 20 April 2004.
[3] *Prosecutor v. Zelko Mejakic and Others*, Case No. IT-02-65-PT, Decision on Dusko Knezevic's Request Pursuant to Rule 81(D), 28 July 2004.

> **Rule 82: Joint and Separate Trials**
>
> (A) In joint trials, each accused shall be accorded the same rights as if he were being tried separately.
>
> (B) The Trial Chamber may order that persons accused jointly under Rule 48 be tried separately if it considers it necessary in order to avoid a conflict of interests that might cause serious prejudice to an accused, or to protect the interests of justice.

TRIAL CHAMBERS DECISIONS

- **Rule 82(A): Joint Trial – Rights of the Accused**

R82-TC-1

o *Prosecutor v. Sesay, Kallon, Gbao*, Case No. SCSL-04-15-PT, Order to the Prosecution to File a Supplemental Pre-Trial Brief, 30 March 2004:[141]

CONSIDERING the right of all accused, including accused who are jointly indicted and tried, to be informed of the nature and cause of the charges against him <u>individually</u>, and to have adequate time and facilities to prepare his defence;

[...]

FINDING ALSO that the Prosecution pre-trial brief does not provide the Defence or the Trial Chamber, with reasonable sufficiency, of notice and an overview of the Prosecution's case against each individual accused, and particularly the nexus between the crimes alleged and the alleged individual criminal responsibility of each individual accused;

[...]

HEREBY ORDERS *proprio motu*, that:

1. The Prosecution shall file a Supplemental Pre-Trial Brief on or before 19 April 2004;

2. The Supplemental Pre-Trial Brief shall:

[...]

b. Elaborate on the specific case against each individual accused, with particular attention given to the alleged nexus between each accused and the alleged crimes.

---

[141] See also *Prosecutor v. Norman, Fofana, Kondewa*, Case No. SCSL-04-14-PT, Order to the Prosecution to File a Supplemental Pre-Trial Brief, 1st April 2004.

R82-TC-2

o *Prosecutor v. Norman*, Case No. SCSL-04-14-T, Decision on the First Accused's Motion for Service and Arraignment on the Consolidated Indictment, 29 November 2004, para. 30:[142]

30. [. . .] In joint trials each Accused shall be accorded the same rights as if he or she were being tried separately.[1] The rights of the Accused as enshrined in Articles 9 and 14 of the ICCPR and Article 7 of the ACHPR, and as outlined in Rule 26*bis* of the Rules, including the right to a fair and expeditious trial, and in Article 17 of the Statute, which include the right "to be informed promptly and in detail in a language which he or she understands of the nature and cause of the charge against him or her,"[2] and "to have adequate time and facilities for the preparation of his or her defence,"[3] apply equally to an Accused person tried separately on a single indictment as to an Accused person tried jointly on a consolidated indictment.[4] In either instance, where new changes are sought to be added to an Indictment against an Accused person, whether in a separate or joint trial, the Prosecution is obligated pursuant to Rule 50 of the Rules, to seek leave of the Trial Chamber to amend the Indictment.[5]

---

[1] See Rule 82(A) of Rules.
[2] Para. 4(a).
[3] Para. 4(b).
[4] See *The Prosecutor v. Sam Hinga Norman, Moinina Fofana, Allieu Kondewa*, Decision and Order on Prosecution Motions for Joinder, 27 January 2004, para. 4.
[5] Rule 50 of the Rules.

---

[142] See also *Prosecutor v. Fofana*, Case No. SCSL-04-14-T, Decision on the Second Accused's Motion for Service and Arraignment on the Consolidated Indictment, 6 December 2004, para. 31.

Rule 85: Presentation of Evidence
(amended 14 May 2005)

(A) Each party is entitled to call witnesses and present evidence. Unless otherwise directed by the Trial Chamber in the interests of justice, evidence at the trial shall be presented in the following sequence:

    (i) Evidence for the prosecution;
    (ii) Evidence for the defence;
    (iii) Prosecution evidence in rebuttal, with leave of the Trial Chamber;
    (iv) Evidence ordered by the Trial Chamber.

(B) Examination-in-chief, cross-examination and re-examination shall be allowed in each case. It shall be for the party calling a witness to examine him in chief, but a Judge may at any stage put any question to the witness.

(C) The accused may, if he so desires, appear as a witness in his own defence. If he chooses to do so, he shall give his evidence under oath or affirmation and, as the case may be, thereafter call his witnesses.

(D) Evidence may be given directly in court, or via such communications media, including video, closed-circuit television, as the Trial Chamber may order.

TRIAL CHAMBERS DECISIONS

- **Rule 85(A): Presentation of Evidence – Evidence Ordered by the Trial Chamber**

R85-TC-1
    o *Prosecutor v. Norman, Fofana, Kondewa*, Case No. SCSL-04-14-T, Order on Prosecution Map Exhibits, 27 October 2004:[143]

        CONSIDERING that it would benefit the trial proceedings if the Prosecution would highlight on this map all locations referred to in the Indictment, that include districts and towns within the territory of Sierra Leone;

---

[143] See also *Prosecutor v. Sesay, Kallon, Gbao*, Case No. SCSL-2004-15-T, Order on Prosecution Map Exhibits, 28 October 2004.

PURSUANT TO Rule 54 of the Rules of Procedure of the Special Court;

ORDERS AS FOLLOWS:

1. That the Prosecution highlight on the map, to a readable scale, all locations referred to in the Consolidated Indictment [...] and submit this copy to the Trial Chamber and to the Defence; and

2. That the Prosecution submit additional maps to the Trial Chamber and the Defence Teams that highlight all locations referred to in each specific count of the consolidated Indictment [...]

3. That the Prosecution submit all highlighted maps to the Trial Chamber and the parties by Tuesday the 2nd November, 2004 and seek to have these maps admitted into evidence as exhibits;

4. That the Defence file their responses, if any, on the issue of admissibility of the maps by the 9th of November, 2004.

R85-TC-2

o *Prosecutor v. Sesay, Kallon, Gbao*, Case No. SCSL-04-15-T, Ruling on Disclosure Regarding Witness TF1-015, 28 January 2005, para. 2-3:

2. The Chamber is of the opinion that in relation to the matters complained of by the defence regarding the circumstances of the alleged arrest and mistreatment of this witness by Captain Banya, there has been a breach of Rule 66 of the Rules of the Court.

3. In these circumstances, we **ORDER** that the Prosecution disclose fully by the latest the end of this 28th day of January 2005 all information on the aforesaid matters and any undisclosed related information provided by this witness to the Office of the Prosecutor.

R85-TC-3

o *Prosecutor v. Norman, Fofana, Kondewa*, Case No. SCSL-04-14-T, Ruling on Defence Oral Application to Call an OTP Investigator Who Took a Written Statement from Prosecution Witness TF2-022, 1st March 2005, para. 6-8:

6. The Chamber reaffirms that it has the statutory authority to call a witness *proprio motu* at any stage of the trial proceedings. Consistent with its obligation to ensure that the trial is fair and expeditious and that "the proceedings before the Special

Court are conducted in accordance with the Agreement, the Statute and the Rules, with full respect for the rights of the accused and due regard for the protection of victims and witnesses".[1]

7. In keeping with this obligation, Rule 54 of the Rules states that the Trial Chamber may issue "[a]ny orders, summonses, subpoenas, warrants and transfer orders as may be necessary for the purposes of an investigation or for the preparation or conduct of the trial". Rule 90(F) of the Rules provides that the Trial Chamber shall exercise control over the mode and order of interrogation of witnesses and the presentation of evidence.

8. In this Trial Chamber's opinion, unquestionably the above-mentioned Rules provide it with the authority to exercise control over the conduct of the trial, and in particular, to call witnesses before it. The Trial Chamber endorses the following comments of the Trial Chamber of the ICTY in the *Delalic* case where it held that the Chamber has power to call witnesses and to control the nature of the testimony, stating that:

> 26. There is no doubt that the Trial Chamber is vested with powers as defined in the Statute and the Rules for regulating the proceedings before it. This power involves control of the witnesses before it, and their testimony. If properly construed, it extends to the calling of witnesses. If properly construed, it extends to the calling of witnesses. Article 20(1) of the Statute states the general powers vested in the Trial Chambers "to ensure that a trial is fair and expeditious and that proceedings are conducted in accordance with the rules of procedure and evidence, with full respect for the rights of the accused . . .". This provision summarises and includes the protection of the rights of the accused, without spelling them out *in extenso* as in Article 21. A fair trial involves all the protection for the accused as stated in Article 21. It will be fair to describe it as a pithy epitome of what constitutes "a fair administration of justice". In addition, Rule 54 provides another general rule under which "at the request of either party or *proprio motu*, a Judge or Trial Chamber may issue such orders, summonses etc., as may be necessary for the purposes of an investigation or for the preparation or conduct of the trial". Although this rule has been applied to orders, summonses, safe conduct, arrest warrants deemed necessary for the purposes of investigation or conduct of the trial, it is also applicable to measures for the control of proceedings necessary for the conduct of the trial.
>
> [. . .]
>
> 28. There [are] therefore ample statutory provisions enabling the Trial Chamber to determine whether a par-

ticular witness could be called and to control the nature of the testimony.⁽²⁾

⁽¹⁾ Rule 26*bis*.
⁽²⁾ *Prosecutor v. Delalic et al.*, Case No. IT-96-21-T, Decision on the Motion of the Joint Request of the Accused Persons Regarding the Presentation of Evidence, Dated 24 May 1998, 12ᵗʰ of June, 1998.

- **Rule 85(B): Presentation of Evidence – Examination-in-Chief – Prohibition of Leading Questions**

R85-TC-4

o *Prosecutor v. Sesay, Kallon, Gbao*, Case No. SCSL-04-15-T, Ruling on the Admission of Command Structure Chart as an Exhibit, 4 February 2005, para. 10-18:

10. Recalling that the Prosecution sought leave to produce the Chart as an exhibit in the course of the examination-in-chief of witness TF1-071, and that the Chamber's Oral Ruling refusing admission of the said Chart, at that stage, was predicated upon the sole ground that its reception in evidence then would violate the prohibition against leading questions asked in the course of examination-in-chief, the Chamber takes this opportunity to restate, in clear and explicit terms, its appreciation of the existing state of the law nationally and in the practice of international criminal tribunals.

11. Any such restatement of the law must begin with a definition of a "leading question." In *Black's Law Dictionary*, a leading question is defined in these terms:

> A question that suggests the answer to the person being interrogated: especially, a question that may be answered by a mere "yes" or "no"...⁽¹⁾

12. It has long been settled that leading questions are generally prohibited in examination-in-chief or re-examination. *Phipson on Evidence* states the rule in these terms:

> Generally a party may not, either in direct or re-examination, elicit the facts of his case by means of leading questions – i.e. questions which suggest the desired answer, or which put disputed matters to the witness in a form permitting of a simple reply of "yes" or "no."⁽²⁾

13. *Cross on Evidence* observes that while it is often said that a leading question is one to which the response will be a "yes" or a "no", this is not necessarily true in all circumstances and it must always be considered if such a question either suggests a response or assumes the existence of disputed facts.⁽³⁾

14. Judge May notes that the "adversarial nature of international criminal trials is most pronounced in rules of presentation of evidence."[4] In this way, it is trite law that international criminal practice has adopted the common law restrictions regarding leading questions as have been outlined above.[5]

15. The Chamber wishes to emphasise that the rationale behind the exclusionary rule as to leading questions is clearly the presumption that a witness is "favourable to the party calling him, who, knowing exactly what the former can prove, might prompt him to give only the advantageous answers."[6] The effect of such evidence, the Chamber notes, is that it "would be open to suspicion as being rather the prearranged version of the party then the spontaneous narration of the witness."[7]

16. The Chamber however notes that, like almost every general principle of law this rule of prohibition has never been inflexible. In the context of some national criminal law systems and the international criminal law system, exceptionally leading questions are permissible in, at least, five clearly-defined circumstances. Firstly, in respect of introductory matters. Secondly, as regards undisputed or non-contentious matters. Thirdly, in relation to identification of persons or objects. Fourthly, in assisting memory recollection. Fifthly, where a witness is called to contradict another as to expressions used by the latter.[8]

17. The Chart that the Prosecution has sought to enter into evidence details the alleged command structure of the RUF during the period of April to December 1998 in Kailahun, identifying the names and positions of alleged high-ranking members of the RUF. While some of the individuals and positions identified in the Chart had been referred to by the Witness during his examination-in-chief, the Witness had neither been asked nor provided specific, detailed information concerning the command structure of the RUF in that time and place.

18. Guided by the foregoing principles and after careful review of the contents of the Chart sought to be admitted in evidence as an exhibit by the Prosecution, the Chamber is satisfied that were the Prosecution to be allowed to introduce the Chart in evidence as an exhibit this would be both, in fact and in law, permitting the Prosecution to ask leading questions of the witness herein on disputed and contentious issues.

---

[1] *Black's Law Dictionary*, 7th ed., Bryan A. Garner, Ed., (St. Paul: West Group, 1999) at p. 897.
[2] *Phipson on Evidence*, (London: Sweet & Maxwell, 1963) at p. 1522.
[3] D.M. Byrne, Q.C. and J.D. Heydon, *Cross on Evidence*, 3rd Australian Edition, (Melbourne: Butterworths Pty Ltd, 1986) at p. 387.
[4] Judge R. May and M. Wierda, *International Criminal Evidence*, (New York: Transnational Publishers, 2002) at pp. 143-144.

(5) *Id.*, at p. 147. See also: *Prosecutor v. Galic*, International Criminal Tribunal for the Former Yugoslavia, IT-98-29-T, Transcripts of 1 November 2002, at pp. 14872-14874.
(6) *Phipson on Evidence, supra* note 3 at para. 1523.
(7) *Id.*
(8) *Id.*, paras 1523 and 1524.

- **Rule 85(B): Presentation of Evidence – Cross-Examination – Inconsistent Statements**

R85-TC-5

o *Prosecutor v. Norman, Fofana, Kondewa*, Case No. SCSL-04-14-T, Decision on Disclosure of Witness Statements and Cross-Examination, 16 July 2004, para. 16-21, 25:[144]

16. Black's Law Dictionary defines a prior inconsistent statement as:

A witness's earlier statement that conflicts with the witness's testimony at trial. In federal practice, extrinsic evidence of an unsworn prior inconsistent statement is admissible – if the witness is given an opportunity to explain or deny the statement for impeachment purposes only.[(1)]

17. The adversarial criminal system requires certain safeguards to be met before a witness can be cross-examined on a prior inconsistent statement or have that statement admitted into evidence.[(2)] This is a feature of the common law tradition and the practice of the International Criminal Tribunals. A cursory review of the applicable legislation in the United Kingdom,[(3)] Canada,[(4)] Australia,[(5)] and Sierra Leone,[(6)] reveals that in all of these systems a certain standard and procedure is followed when dealing with prior inconsistent statements. Generally, a witness may be asked whether he or she made a statement and be cross-examined upon the general nature of the statement's contents without being shown the statement. However, if the prior statement is made in writing, the witness will be shown this statement before he can be asked about any alleged inconsistency, and if the statement is proved, the statement is admitted into the record as evidence. This requirement is consistent with the ruling in *The Queen's Case*[(7)] that a witness is not compelled to answer any questions on a statement until the statement is shown to him or her and is tendered. Such documents must therefore be capable of being admitted into evidence.

---

[144] See also *Prosecutor v. Gbao*, Case No. SCSL-04-15-T, Ruling on the Oral Application for the Exclusion of Part of the Testimony of Witness TF1-199, 26 July 2004, para. 8.

18. In the opinion of the Chamber, prior inconsistent statements are generally admissible in international criminal trials, as a means to impeach the credibility of a witness.[8] In the *Akayesu*[9] case, the ICTR Trial Chamber was confronted with a similar problem of alleged inconsistencies between the oral testimonies of witnesses and pre-trial statements that were composed of interview notes not made in English and had to be translated from the indigenous language spoken by the witness. The Chamber decided that the issue was one of probative value and not of admissibility. As far as admissibility of evidence is concerned, due to its *sui generis* mixture of common and civil law procedural and evidentiary rules, this Court does not necessarily conform to any specific legal system or tradition. Indeed, as enshrined in Rule 89(B) of the Rules, it will be guided by the will to "favour a fair determination of the matter before it".

19. The ICTR Trial Chamber in the *Ruzindana*,[10] case ruled that whenever Counsel for the Prosecution or the Defence perceives that there is a contradiction between the written and oral statement of a witness, they should raise this issue formally by:

> [p]utting to the witness the exact portion in issue to enable the witness to explain the discrepancy, inconsistency or contradictions, if any, before the Tribunal. Counsels should then mark the relevant portion of such a written statement and formally exhibit it so as to form part of the record of the Tribunal.

20. During the *Kunarac* trial, the ICTY Trial Chamber ruled that a prior statement may be tendered in evidence as an exhibit, after an inconsistency with the trial testimony has been established.[11]

21. Considering this analysis and the applicable jurisprudence, this Trial Chamber, as a matter of law, is of the opinion, and rules accordingly, that:

(i) A witness may be cross-examined as to previous statements made by him or her in writing, or reduced into writing, or recorded on audio tape, or video tape or otherwise, relative to the subject matter of the case, in circumstances where an inconsistency has emerged during the course of viva voce testimony, between a prior statement and this testimony;

(ii) In conducting cross-examination on inconsistencies between viva voce testimony and a previous statement, the witness should first be asked whether or not he or she made the statement being referred to. The circumstances of the making of the statement, sufficient to designate the situation, must be put to the witness when asking this question;

(iii) Should the witness disclaim making the statement, evidence may be provided in support of the allegation that he or she did in fact make it;

(iv) That a witness may be cross-examined as to previous statements made by him or her, relative to the subject matter of the case, without the statement being shown to him or her. However, where it is intended to contradict such witness with the statement, his or her attention must, before the contradictory proof can be given, be directed to those parts of the statement alleged to be contradictory;

(v) That the Trial Chamber may direct that the portion of the witness statement that is the subject of cross-examination and alleged contradiction with the viva voce testimony, be admitted into the Court record and marked as an exhibit.

[. . .]

25. The contention that Witness TF2-198 testified at trial about matters not included in his witness statement does not find support from the evolving jurisprudence as invalidating his oral testimony. The Defence argument is that the witness testified about burning plastic being placed on his back and to suffering serious burns, evidence which was not part of his witness statement disclosed prior to trial. The fact that burns to the witness' shoulders were not in the brief interview notes, does not amount to a breach by the Prosecution of its Rule 66 disclosure obligations. The Trial Chamber considers that it may not be possible to include every matter that a witness will testify about at trial in a witness statement. The Special Court adheres to the principle of orality, whereby witnesses shall, in principle, be heard directly by the Court. While there is a duty for the Prosecution to diligently disclose witness statements that identify matters that witnesses will testify about at trial, thereby providing the Defence with essential information for the preparation of its case, it is foreseeable that witnesses, by the very nature of oral testimony, will expand on matters mentioned in their witness statements, and respond more comprehensively to questions asked at trial. The Trial Chamber notes that where a witness has testified to matters not expressly contained in his or her witness statement, the cross-examining party may wish to highlight this discrepancy and further examine on this point.

---

[1] *Black's Law Dictionary*, Seventh Edition, 1999, page 1416,
[2] An important Rule of Common Law practice is that known in *Browne v. Dunn* (1984) 6 R 67 (HL), where Hunt J stated:
   It has in my experience always been a rule of professional practice that, unless notice has already clearly been given of the cross-examiner's intention to rely upon such matters, it is necessary to put to an opponent's

witness in cross-examination the nature of the case upon which it is proposed to rely in contradiction of his evidence, particularly where that case relies upon inferences to be drawn from other evidence in the proceedings. Such a rule of practice is necessary both to give the witness the opportunity to deal with that other evidence, or the inferences to be drawn from it, and to allow the other party the opportunity to call evidence either to corroborate that explanation or to contradict the inference sought to be drawn.

(3) Sections 4 and 5 of the United Kingdom Criminal Procedure Act 1865, cited in Peter Murphy, Murphy on Evidence (2000) Blackstone Press Limited, 524.

(4) Sections 10 and 11, Canada Evidence Act, Revised Statutes of Canada, 1985, as amended in 1994.

(5) Section 36, Evidence Act 1958, Victoria, Australia.

(6) Sierra Leone Criminal Procedure Act 1965 (as amended).

(7) *The Queen's Case*, 4 Wigmore, para. 1259.

(8) See *Prosecutor v. Musema*, Judgement and Sentence, 27 January 2000, para. 86; *Prosecutor v. Akayesu*, Judgment, 2 September 1998, para. 137; *Prosecutor v. Tadic*, Decision on Prosecutor's Motion for Production of Defense Witness Statements (Separate Opinion of Judge McDonald), 27 November 1996, para. 46.

(9) *Prosecutor v. Akayesu*, Judgment, 2 September 1998, para. 137.

(10) *Prosecutor v. Ruzindana*, Order on the Probative Value of Alleged Contradiction Between the Oral and Written Statement of a Witness During Examination, 17 April 1997.

(11) *Prosecutor v. Kunarac*, Transcript, 24 July 2000, T.5189-5190. See also *Prosecutor v. Kayishema*, Decision on the Prosecution Motion Request to Rule Inadmissible the Evidence of Defence Expert Witness, Dr. Pouget, 29 June 1998.

R85-TC-6

o *Prosecutor v. Gbao*, Case No. SCSL-04-15-T, Ruling on the Oral Application for the Exclusion of Part of the Testimony of Witness TF1-199, 26 July 2004, para. 9, 11:

9. Further, an assessment of whether material disclosed or evidence adduced orally in court is new requires a comparative assessment of the allegedly new evidence, the original witness statement as well as the Indictment and the Pre-Trial Brief, combined with the period of notice to the Defence that the particular witness will testify on that event and the extent to which the alleged new evidence alters the evidence the Defence has already notice of. If the evidence is not new, but merely supplements evidence which has previously been disclosed in accordance with the Rules, it is then admissible.[1]

[...]

11. In light of the foregoing considerations and our specific findings, the Chamber is of the unanimous opinion that the Defence has not substantiated by a *prima facie* showing the allegations of negligence or lack of diligence by the Prosecution. Furthermore, we also find that the Defence has been sufficiently put on notice and given adequate time to prepare

on the allegations concerning the kidnapping of UNAMSIL personnel in Makeni from both the Indictment and the Pre-Trial Briefs and, in the instant case, from the disclosed written statement of Witness TF1-199.

(1) Ruling of 23 July 2004, para. 11. See also *Prosecutor v. Bagosora et al.*, Decision on Admissibility of Evidence of Witness DP, 18 November 2003, para. 6.

- **Rule 85(B): Presentation of Evidence – Order to Re-Open Cross-Examination**

R85-TC-7

o *Prosecutor v. Sesay, Kallon, Gbao*, Case No. SCSL-04-15-T, Ruling on Request to Re-Open the Cross-Examination of Witness TF1-012, 6 April 2005, para. 5-9:

5. In *Kupreskic*, the Trial Chamber of the International Criminal Tribunal for the Former Yugoslavia ("ICTY") remarked that:

> [I]t is incumbent upon the Tribunal to ensure a fair and expeditious trial and to conduct orderly proceedings, and that these interests are best served by the aforementioned order of presentation of evidence.(1)

6. Adopting this observation, the Chamber is of the view that it possesses discretion to vary the order of the presentation of evidence in order to ensure the fairness of the trial proceedings. However, it should be emphasised that in our opinion such a discretionary power should only be exercised in exceptional circumstances to meet the justice of the case, for example, when new material is introduced warranting rebuttal by the opposing party as was held by the ICTY in the *Delalic* decision. There, the Tribunal noted that:

> [W]here during re-examination new material is introduced, the opposing party is entitled to further cross-examine the witness on such new material. Similarly, where questions put to a witness by the Trial Chamber after cross-examination raise entirely new matters, the opponent is entitled to further cross-examine the witness on such new matters. The rationale is clear in the sense that further cross-examination is to re-examination what cross-examination is to examination-in-chief. Hence to deny further cross-examination when new material is raised in re-examination is tantamount to a denial of the right to cross-examination on such new material.(2)

7. In this case, Mr. Jordash, Counsel for the Accused Sesay, requested that he be allowed to re-open his cross-examination

after the cross-examination of Counsel for the Second and Third Accused and before the Prosecution began its re-examination.

8. The Chamber wishes to emphasise that the questions that Counsel was seeking to ask did not arise from any new information elicited through either re-examination by the Prosecution[3] or examination-in-chief by the Court. Regarding the list of persons who had lived with the Witness in Tombodu, the Witness had stated during cross-examination by Counsel for the Accused Sesay that he could not remember who they were. During cross-examination by Counsel for the Accused Gbao, the Witness stated that he could remember their names, but did not want to specifically name them for security reasons. At that point, the Court invited Counsel to go into closed session but Counsel refused, noting that he did not intend to adduce any such names.[4] As already noted, Counsel for the Accused Sesay admitted that he had not thought of asking for the names of the miners in 2000 during his cross-examination due to an oversight.

9. Of much significance in the opinion of this Chamber is the fact that Counsel for all three Accused were provided with the ample and unlimited opportunity to cross-examine Witness TF1-012, despite its standing injunction against lengthy and repetitious cross-examination. While recognising that it has the discretion to allow counsel to re-open cross-examination where the interests of justice and the fairness of trial proceedings so require, the Chamber finds that Counsel has failed to show any exceptional circumstances justifying the exercise of its discretion in the present situation.

FOR ALL THE ABOVE-STATED REASONS,

DENIES the request of Counsel for the Accused Sesay to re-open his cross-examination of Witness TF1-012.

---

[1] *Prosecutor v. Kupreskic et al.*, Case No. IT-95-16, Decision on Order of Presentation of Evidence, 21 January 1999.
[2] *Prosecutor v. Delalic et al.*, Case No. IT-96-21-T, Decision on the Motion on Presentation of Evidence by the Accused, Esad Landzo, 1 May 1997 at para. 30.
[3] In fact, because Defence objections to the questions asked by the Prosecution during re-examination were sustained, no evidence was elicited during re-examination.
[4] Transcripts of Trial Proceedings, 4 February 2005 at pp. 42-43.

Rule 89: General Provisions
(amended 7 March 2003)

(A) The rules of evidence set forth in this Section shall govern the proceedings before the Chambers. The Chambers shall not be bound by national rules of evidence.

(B) In cases not otherwise provided for in this Section, a Chamber shall apply rules of evidence which will best favour a fair determination of the matter before it and are consonant with the spirit of the Statute and the general principles of law.

(C) A Chamber may admit any relevant evidence.

TRIAL CHAMBERS DECISIONS

- **Rule 89: Evidence – Assessment of Evidence**

R89-TC-1
o *Prosecutor v. Brima, Kamara, Kanu*, Case No. SCSL-04-16-T, Decision on Prosecution Tender for Admission into Evidence of Information Contained in Notice Pursuant to Rule 92*bis*, 18 November 2005:

CONSIDERING that the reliability of the evidence is something to be considered by the Trial Chamber at the end of the trial when weighing and evaluating the evidence as a whole, in light of the context and nature of the evidence itself, including the credibility and reliability of the relevant evidence.

CONFIRMING HOWEVER that when the Trial Chamber comes to consider the reliability of the present evidence it will disregard opinion evidence and any evidence which goes to the ultimate issue, or which draws any conclusions or inferences which the Trial Chamber will have to draw, or which makes any judgments which the Trial Chamber will have to make;

- **Rule 89(B): Evidence – "Best Evidence" Rule**

R89-TC-2
o *Prosecutor v. Sesay, Kallon, Gbao*, Case No. SCSL-04-15-T, Ruling on the Admission of Command Structure Chart as an Exhibit, 4 February 2005, para. 20:

20. Counsel for all three Accused persons relied upon the doctrine of the best evidence rule. They submitted that the Chart did not provide the best evidence in the case for the purpose for which it was sought to be tendered. The Chamber sees no merit in this submission for the reason that, generally, the best evidence rule, originating from the traditional common law, does "not formally apply to exclude evidence in international criminal trials."[1]

---

[1] Judge R. May and M. Wierda, *supra* note 5, p. 242.

- **Rule 89(B): Evidence – Balance Between Probative Value and Prejudicial Effect**

R89-TC-3   o *Prosecutor v. Sesay, Kallon, Gbao*, Case No. SCSL-04-15-T, Ruling on the Admission of Command Structure Chart as an Exhibit, 4 February 2005, para. 21:[145]

21. It was also submitted by the Defence that, if admitted in evidence, the prejudicial effect of the Chart would outweigh its probative value. As evidence seeking to incriminate the Accused persons (which is essentially and always the object of Prosecution evidence adduced against persons charged with criminal offences), the Chamber is not satisfied that its prejudicial effect outweighs its probative value. In our own appreciation, in no way does the evidence contained in the Chart alter in a prejudicial way, the incriminating quality of the evidence against the Accused persons.

- **Rule 89(B): Evidence – Self-Serving Evidence – Circumstances of Obtaining**

R89-TC-4   o *Prosecutor v. Sesay, Kallon, Gbao*, Case No. SCSL-04-15-T, Ruling on the Admission of Command Structure Chart as an Exhibit, 4 February 2005, para. 23:

23. Counsel for the Defence also submitted that the Chart is self-serving and had not been obtained in transparent circumstances.[1] This contention could not be sustained on the grounds that the notion of a document being self-serving and not having been obtained in transparent circumstances, as a

---

[145] *Prosecutor v. Sesay, Kallon, Gbao,* Case No. SCSL-04-15-T, Ruling on Gbao Application to Exclude Evidence of Prosecution Witness Mr. Koker, 23 May 2005, para. 8.

ground of inadmissibility, given the existing state of the law, is nebulous.

(1) Transcript, *supra* note 1 at pp. 79-80.

- **Rule 89(C): Evidence – Chamber's Discretion on Admissibility – Difference Admissibility / Reliability**

R89-TC-5

o *Prosecutor v. Sesay, Kallon, Gbao*, Case No. SCSL-04-15-T, Ruling on Gbao Application to Exclude Evidence of Prosecution Witness Mr. Koker, 23 May 2005, para. 4-7:[146]

4. Thus, as has often been noted by this Court, the Rules favour a flexible approach to the issue of admissibility of evidence, leaving the issue of weight to be determined when assessing probative value of the totality of the evidence.[1]

5. This view of the law is reinforced by the observation of the Trial Chamber of the International Criminal Tribunal for the Former Yugoslavia that:

> The principle ... is one of extensive admissibility of evidence – questions of credibility or authenticity being determined according to the weight given to each of the materials by the judges at the appropriate time.[2]

6. To this effect is Rule 89(c) of our Rules whose object and purpose, gathered from its plain and ordinary meaning, is to vest the Trial Chamber with discretionary power to admit any relevant evidence and to exclude evidence that is not relevant.

7. By parity of reasoning, under Rule 95, the Trial Chamber can exclude evidence where its admission would bring the administration of justice into disrepute. Thus, the Chamber may exercise its discretion under this Rule and under its inherent jurisdiction to exclude evidence where its probative value is manifestly outweighed by its prejudicial effect.

(1) See, for example, *Prosecutor v. Norman et al.*, SCSL-04-14-AR65, *Fofana – Appeal Against Decision Refusing Bail*, 11 March 2005 at paras 22-24.
(2) *Prosecutor v. Blaskic*, IT-95-14-T, *Judgement*, 3 March 2000 at para. 34.

---

[146] See also *Prosecution v. Sesay, Kallon, Gbao*, Case No. SCSL-04-15-T, Ruling on Application for the Exclusion of Certain Supplemental Statements of Witness TF1-361 and Witness TF1-122, 1st June 2005, para. 18; *Prosecutor v. Sesay, Kallon, Gbao*, Case No. SCSL-04-15-T, Ruling on the Identification of Signature by Witness TF1-360, 14 October 2005, para. 4-5; *Prosecutor v. Sesay, Kallon, Gbao*, Case No. SCSL-04-15-T, Decision on the Joint Defence Motion Requesting Conformity of Procedural Practice for Taking Witness Statements, 26 October 2005, para. 32.

R89-TC-6

o *Prosecutor v. Brima, Kamara, Kanu*, Case No. SCSL-04-16-T, Decision on Joint Defence Application for Leave to Appeal from Decision on Defence Motion to Exclude All Evidence from Witness TF1-277, 2 August 2005, para. 6:[147]

> 6. As stated in the impugned decision, "[T]he probative value of hearsay evidence is something to be considered by the Trial Chamber at the end of the trial when weighing and evaluating the evidence as a whole, in light of the context and nature of the evidence itself, including the credibility and reliability of the relevant witness."[(1)] In other words, evidence may be excluded because it is unreliable, but it is not necessary to demonstrate the reliability of the evidence before it is admitted. [...]

[(1)] Para. 15 of the impugned Decision.

R89-TC-7

o *Prosecutor v. Sesay, Kallon, Gbao*, Case No. SCSL-04-15-T, Ruling on the Identification of Signature by Witness TF1-360, 14 October 2005, para. 8:

> 8. [...] While the Defence have questioned the reliability of this evidence, the Chamber is satisfied that this determination will be made at a later stage and is not relevant in terms of assessment of the admissibility of the evidence. The Defence will have the opportunity to fully explore the foundation for the witness' opinion that the signatures are those of Sam Bockarie and Issa Sesay.

R89-TC-8

o *Prosecutor v. Sesay, Kallon, Gbao*, Case No. SCSL-04-15-T, Decision on the Joint Defence Motion Requesting Conformity of Procedural Practice for Taking Witness Statements, 26 October 2005, para. 37-38:

> 37. After setting out the ideal standard for a witness statement as noted above, the Appeals Chamber of the ICTR had this to say:
>
>> Also, a statement not fulfilling the ideal standard set out above is not inadmissible as such. Pursuant to Rule 89(C) of the Rules, a Chamber may admit any relevant

---

[147] See also *Prosecutor v. Brima, Kamara, Kanu*, Case No. SCSL-04-16-T, Decision on Prosecution Tender for Admission into Evidence of Information Contained in Notice Pursuant to Rule 92*bis*, 18 November 2005.

evidence which it deems to have probative value. However, any inconsistency of a witness statement with the standard set out above may be taken into consideration when assessing the probative value of the statement, if necessary.[1]

38. We, nevertheless, emphasise that the Trial Chamber may choose to admit for the truth of their contents witness statements with formal or procedural irregularities into evidence under Rule 92*bis* or Rule 89(C) of the Rules, the impact of these on the weight to be given to the witness statement, if any, can only be properly determined in light of the totality of the evidence before the Chamber, taking into account all the relevant factors and indicia of reliability.

---

[1] *Prosecutor v. Niyitegeka*, supra [. . .], para. 36.

- **Rule 89(C): Evidence – Relevance**

R89-TC-9

o *Prosecutor v. Norman, Fofana, Kondewa*, Case No. SCSL-04-14-T, Reasoned Majority Decision on Prosecution Motion for a Ruling on the Admissibility of Evidence, 24 May 2005, para. 19:

19. [. . .] [T]he Chamber finds significantly as follows:

[. . .]

(iv) that it would gravely undermine the procedural due process rights of accused persons and thereby bring the administration of justice into disrepute if, at every stage during the conduct of their trial, they are confronted with new pieces of evidence designed to prove factual allegations not specifically pleaded in the Indictment, under the guise of a prosecutorial latitude to broaden the definitional scope of the statutory categories of offences chargeable, the effect of which is to bring about an alignment between such expanded category of criminality and evidence in respect of which no factual allegations have been specifically pleaded, on the grounds of a prosecutorial imperative to prosecute the entire range or spectrum of alleged culpable criminal acts;

[. . .]

(vi) that the Chamber finds plausible the Defence submission that the Motion is "an attempt to back door the Trial Chamber prior ruling that the indictment could not be amended to include sex crimes";

(vii) that it is a legal misconception that once a determination is made that evidence sought to

be adduced is relevant and of probative value, such a finding automatically triggers off its reception in evidence, even though the Indictment may not contain any specific factual allegations underlying that evidence;

(viii) that admitting the disputed evidence, at this very late and crucial stage of the trial, when the Prosecution is about to close its case is not only not fair to the Accused persons but does derogate significantly from their Article 17 due process rights especially, the Article 17(4) (a) which guarantees every Accused person the right to be informed promptly and in detail in a language which he or she understands of the nature and cause of the charge against him or her.

- **Rule 89(C): Evidence – Hearsay Evidence**

R89-TC-10   o *Prosecutor v. Brima, Kamara, Kanu*, Case No. SCSL-04-16-T, Decision on Joint Defence Motion to Exclude All Evidence from Witness TF1-277 Pursuant to Rule 89(C) and/or Rule 95, 24 May 2005, para. 13, 15, 24:

13. Rule 89(C), under which evidence need only be relevant to be admissible, is in broader terms than the equivalent provisions of the ICTY and ICTR Rules, which require that evidence be both relevant and probative.

[...]

15. It is clear that the admission of hearsay evidence is not indicative of a finding as to its probative value. In the *Akayesu Appeal Judgement* the Appeals Chamber of the ICTR held that the admission of hearsay evidence does not automatically carry any particular finding as to its assessment.[1] The fact that a Trial Chamber admits hearsay does not imply that it accepts it as reliable and probative. The probative value of hearsay evidence is something to be considered by the Trial Chamber at the end of the trial when weighing and evaluating the evidence as a whole, in light of the context and nature of the evidence itself, including the credibility and reliability of the relevant witness.[2] This principle was also followed by the Appeals Chamber of this Court in *Fofana*, in which it held that:

"Evidence is admissible once it is shown to be relevant: the question of its reliability is determined thereafter, and is not a condition for its admission."[3]

[...]

DIGEST OF JURISPRUDENCE OF THE SPECIAL COURT FOR SIERRA LEONE 703

24. We hold that the hearsay evidence given by the Witness is relevant evidence and is therefore admissible evidence under Rule 89(C). We find that the Defence has not made out a case for the exclusion of that evidence, let alone for the exclusion of the Witness's evidence in its entirety. Nor has anything been put before us which would justify the conclusion that the admission of the evidence would bring the administration of justice into serious disrepute pursuant to Rule 95. On the contrary, the evidence in our view is so clearly relevant that the judicial process would be brought into disrepute by excluding it.[4]

---

(1) *Prosecutor v. Jean-Paul Akayesu*, Case No. ICTR-96-4-A, Appeals Chamber, Judgment, 1 June 2001, para. 292.
(2) John R.W.D. Jones & Steven Powles, *International Criminal Practice* (Third Edition), Oxford University Press 2003, para. 8.5.654.
(3) *Prosecutor v. Sam Hinga Norman et al.*, Case No. SCSL-04-14-AR65, Fofana – Appeal against Decision Refusing Bail, 11 March 2005, para. 24
(4) *Prosecutor v. Sam Hinga Norman et al.*, Case No. SCSL-04-14-AR65, Fofana – Appeal against Decision Refusing Bail, 11 March 2005, para. 27.

R89-TC-11   o *Prosecutor v. Brima, Kamara, Kanu*, Case No. SCSL-04-16-T, Decision on the Prosecution Motion for Judicial Notice and Admission of Evidence, 25 October 2005, para. 22:

22. [...] We agree with the view expressed by Robertson J. in *Fofana* that since the rule against hearsay does not apply to the Special Court there is no reason to treat authoritative sources as "pieces of documentary evidence received by way of exception to the hearsay rule". The preferable view is for courts to "look at such sources simply in order to equip themselves to take judicial notice." A party seeking judicial notice of a particular fact "must direct the court's attention to the range of authoritative sources which taken together demonstrate that the fact is indisputable."[1]

---

(1) *Fofana*, Separate Opinion of Justice Robertson, para. 7.

- **Rule 89(C): Evidence – Reliability of Unauthenticated Documents**

R89-TC-12   o *Prosecutor v. Fofana*, Case No. SCSL-04-14-T, Decision on Application for Bail Pursuant to Rule 65, 5 August 2004, para. 50-58:

50. Section 89(C) of the Rules provides, as follows:

"A Chamber may admit any relevant evidence."

It stands to reason that for such evidence to be admissible, it must be relevant. On this issue and as was decided in the *CELEBICI CASE* by the Trial Chamber of the ICTY in its "Decision On the Motion of the Prosecution for the Admissibility of Evidence", 19th of January, 1998, such evidence is admissible "as long as it is relevant" and furthermore "is deemed to have probative value."

51. The contents of both the unsigned submissions of the Government of Sierra Leone and the unsigned Defence Declaration are relevant but what is to be determined is whether they are, in the circumstances, admissible under the provisions of Rule 89(C). As these circumstances would invariably vary from one situation to the other, it is necessary to consider decisions to be taken under Rule 89(C) on a case to case basis.

52. In the case of ALEKSOVSKI, the Appeals Chamber of the ICTY held that "Trial Chambers have a broad discretion under Rule 89(C) to admit relevant hearsay evidence." The Appeals Chamber went further to hold that "Since such evidence is admitted to prove the truth of its contents, a Trial Chamber must be satisfied that it is reliable for that purpose..."[1]

53. In a "Directive on Guidelines on the Standards Governing the Admission of Evidence" issued by the Trial Chamber 1 of the ICTY on the 23rd of April, 2003, in the case of THE PROSECUTOR VS BLAGOJEVIC AND THREE OTHERS[2], it was laid down as a rule that "THE BEST EVIDENCE RULE" will be applied in the determination of matters before this Trial Chamber; this means that the Trial Chamber will rely on the best evidence available in the circumstances of the case. What is the best evidence will depend on the particular circumstances, attached to each document..."

54. In the application under consideration, the unsigned Document containing the submissions of the Government of Sierra Leone on one hand, is certainly not the best evidence available in the circumstances particularly where a representative of the said Government could alternatively have appeared to be heard during the oral hearing by the Chamber on the opinion and reservations expressed in the submissions.

55. On the other hand, the unsigned Defence Declaration is equally not the "best evidence" to attest to an issue as fundamental as establishing the good character of the Applicant for purposes of securing his bail, particularly in circumstances where the Court had ordered that a sworn affidavit be filed and an adjournment granted for this purpose in order to also give the Prosecution, the opportunity to exercise a right of reply on the facts that were to be sworn to in the affidavit.

56. Besides and more importantly, a sworn affidavit has more probative value than an ordinary Declaration particularly where it touches on and concerns threshold issues that are canvassed for purposes of fulfilling the conditions laid down by Rule 65(B) of the Rules, the reason being that the facts which are deposed to on oath and which legally engage the personal responsibility of the deponent in the event of a perjury, have a more convincing probative value which the ordinary Declaration does not have.

57. Indeed, I would say that even though Rule 89(C) enlarges the scope of admissibility of evidence which, under the rigid conventional evidentiary rules would ordinarily not be admissible, this door of a liberalised concept of admissibility which has been thrown so widely open in International Criminal Tribunals should be left open but at varying degrees and with a lot of caution and scrutinous control of all incoming facts so as to avoid admitting in evidence, facts and documents which, *prima facie*, are clearly inadmissible and which, if admitted, could lead to abuse and a violation of established judicial norms, principles and processes, thereby inevitably bringing the administration of justice and the entire judicial process into disrepute.

58. In light of the above, I am not minded to favourably invoke the provisions of Rule 89(C) to accept these two documents which are unauthenticated and therefore unreliable. I accordingly exclude them from impacting on the substantive determination of this matter.

---

[1] *Prosecutor v. Aleksovski*, Decision on Prosecutor's Appeal on Admissibility of Evidence, 16 February 1999, para. 15.
[2] *Prosecutor v. Blagojevic*, Decision on Prosecution's Motion for Clarification of Oral Decision Regarding Admissibility of Accused's Statement, 18 September 2003, para. 15.

- **Rule 89(C): Evidence – Site Visit**

R89-TC-13   o *Prosecutor v. Brima, Kamara, Kanu*, Case No. SCSL-04-16-T, Decision on Confidential Joint Defence Request to Inspect Locus in Quo Concerning Evidence of Witness TF1-024, 15 June 2005, para. 6-9:

6. We agree with recent ICTR decisions that the need for a site visit has to be assessed in view of the particular circumstances of each trial.[1] The present trial is still at an early stage. It may well be that as more evidence is received the need for a site inspection will be made redundant.

7. As stated in the cited ICTR decisions:

> *[I]n view of the logistics and costs involved, a decision to carry out a site visit should preferably be made when the visit will be instrumental in the discovery of the truth and determination of the matter before the Chamber.*

8. We would not expect the logistics and costs of a site visit to be prohibitive in the present case. However, after considering the relevant circumstances in this case, we find that a site visit would not be instrumental in the discovering the truth or in determining the case, at least at this stage of the trial.

9. However, we do not exclude that a site visit may be feasible at a later stage. The Defence is at liberty to renew its request.

---

(1) *The Prosecutor v. Simba*, Case No. ICTR-01-76-T, Decision on the Defence Request for Site Visits in Rwanda, 31 January 2005, para. 2; *The Prosecutor v. Bagosora et al.*, Case No. ICTR-98-41-T, Decision on Prosecutor's Motion for Site Visits in the Republic of Rwanda, para. 4.

R89-TC-14

o *Prosecutor v. Brima, Kamara, Kanu*, Case No. SCSL-04-16-T, Decision on Prosecution Motion for a Locus in Quo Visit to Karina, Bombali District, The Republic of Sierra Leone, 25 October 2005, para. 14-23:

14. The Rules do not specifically provide for site inspections. However, Rule 54 of the Rules generally empowers the Trial Chamber:

> *At the request of either party or on its own motion, to issue such orders, summonses, subpoenas, warrants and transfer orders as may be necessary for the purposes of an investigation or for the preparation or conduct of the trial.*

15. Rule 89(B) of the Rules enjoins the Trial Chamber to "*apply rules of evidence that will best favour a fair determination of the matter before it, and are consonant with the spirit of the Statute and the general principles of law*"; while Rule 89(C) of the Rules permits the Trial Chamber to admit "*any relevant evidence*".

16. The Trial Chamber is of the opinion therefore that it generally has power pursuant to the above Rules, to order site inspections where necessary. Article 10 of the Agreement Between the United Nations and the Government of Sierra Leone on the Establishment of a Special Court for Sierra Leone provides that the Special Court shall have its seat in Sierra Leone. Consequently, Rule 4 of the Rules which permits the Trial Chamber to "*exercise their functions away from the Seat of the Special Court if so authorised by the President*" is inapplicable in the

circumstances since Karina Town, the site of the proposed visit, is in Sierra Leone.

17. This Trial Chamber has previously ruled that whilst "*the need for a site inspection has to be assessed in view of the particular circumstances of each trial*", the Chamber will not undertake a site inspection unless it is shown that the inspection would be "*instrumental in the discovery of the truth and the determination of the matter before the Trial Chamber.*"[1]

18. The Trial Chamber also finds jurisprudence from other international tribunals in this regard quite instructive. For example the International Criminal Tribunal for Rwanda (ICTR), whose Rules are similar to those cited above, has ruled that it would not undertake a site inspection which "*though informative, would not be instrumental in the discovery of the truth and the determination of the matter before it*".[2] In another instance the ICTR declined to undertake a site inspection where it was considered financially and logistically unfeasible to do so.[3] In other instances the ICTR has ruled that the most appropriate time for a site inspection is "*at the end of the presentation of both the Prosecution and Defence cases*".[4]

19. The International Criminal Tribunal for the Former Yugoslavia (ICTY) took the view that a site inspection should only take place in the presence of the accused unless the accused has waived his right to be present. The Tribunal then went on to decline a proposed site inspection on the grounds that

> the presence of the Accused in Sarajevo during a visit by the Trial Chamber would pose a considerable security risk for the Parties and accompanying staff, [and] that it would be virtually impossible to guarantee the safety of the Accused during the visit, considering the charges brought against him, his former position in the VRS and the locations to be visited.[5]

In addition the Trial Chamber observed that although the proposed site visit was intended to acquaint the Trial Chamber with certain locations in Sarajevo and its surroundings, the Trial Chamber found that those places were described by witnesses, that photographs and maps of the locations were exhibited, that videos were played during the trial and that "*such visualisation was of substantial assistance to the Trial Chamber in its process of adopting an image of the terrain*".[6] The Trial Chamber also considered that denying the Prosecution Motion would not affect the rights of the accused to a fair and expeditious trial, nor would it adversely affect the Trial Chamber's ability to try the case.

20. Applying the above guidelines to the present case, we note that while the Prosecution would on the one hand, like the proposed site inspection of Karina conducted at the close

of their case, the Defence would on the other, prefer that such an inspection be conducted at the conclusion of both the Prosecution and Defence cases. We also note that neither of the parties has referred to the presence of the Accused persons during such a site visit. The right of an accused person to be tried in his presence is guaranteed by Article 17(4)(d) of the Statute. Accordingly, the Trial Chamber is of the view that a site inspection should only take place in the presence of each of the Accused persons unless the Accused have expressly waived their right to be present, which is not the case here.

21. We also note the Registrar's undertaking that adequate logistical arrangements are available in order to enable the Trial Chamber to complete the proposed site inspection to Karina within one day. We are concerned however, that the presence of the Accused in Karina during such a visit, is likely to pose a considerable security risk for the parties and accompanying staff and that the security arrangements available may not adequately guarantee the safety and security of the Accused persons during such a visit.

22. In addition we note that although the proposed site visit is intended to acquaint the Trial Chamber of "*the environs, spatial configuration, and physical character of the locations within Karina Town and its environs*", a number of Prosecution witnesses have already given graphic testimony describing scenes and locations at Karina and its environs, and maps have been exhibited to assist the Trial Chamber in visualising the scene or scenes of the alleged crimes.

23. In the premises we are of the view that a site inspection while perhaps informative, would not be instrumental in the discovery of the truth and the determination of the matter before us.

---

[1] *Prosecutor v. Brima, Kamara, Kanu*, Case No. SCSL-2004-16-T, Decision on Confidential Joint Defence Request to Inspect Locus in Quo Concerning Evidence of Witness TF1-024, 16 June 2005, para. 6, 7.
[2] *Prosecutor v. Akayesu*, Case No. ICTR-96-4-T, Decision on the Defence Motion Requesting an Inspection of the Site and the Conduct of a Forensic Analysis, 17 February 1998, para. 8.
[3] *Prosecutor v. Simba*, Case No. ICTR-01-76-T, Decision on the Defence Request for Site Visits in Rwanda, 31 January 2005, para. 3.
[4] *Prosecutor v. Ndayambaje et al.*, Case No. ICTR-98-42-T, Decision on Prosecutor's Motion for Site Visits in the Republic of Rwanda under Rules 4 and 73 of the Rules of Procedure and Evidence, 23 September 2004, para. 14-15; *Prosecutor v. Bagosora et al.*, Case No. ICTR-98-41-T, Decision on Prosecutor's Motion for Site Visits in the Republic of Rwanda, 29 September 2004, para. 3.
[5] *Prosecutor v. Galic*, Case No. IT-98-29-T, Trial Chamber Judgment, 5 December 2003, para. 774.
[6] Ibid.

DIGEST OF JURISPRUDENCE OF THE SPECIAL COURT FOR SIERRA LEONE   709

- **Rule 89(C): Evidence – Maps**

R89-TC-15
o *Prosecutor v. Norman, Fofana*, Kondewa, Case No. SCSL-04-14-T, Order on Prosecution Map Exhibits, 27 October 2004:[148]

CONSIDERING that it would benefit the trial proceedings if the Prosecution would highlight on this map all locations referred to in the Indictment, that include districts and towns within the territory of Sierra Leone;

PURSUANT TO Rule 54 of the Rules of Procedure of the Special Court;

ORDERS AS FOLLOWS:

5. That the Prosecution highlight on the map, to a readable scale, all locations referred to in the Consolidated Indictment [...] and submit this copy to the Trial Chamber and to the Defence; and

6. That the Prosecution submit additional maps to the Trial Chamber and the Defence Teams that highlight all locations referred to in each specific count of the consolidated Indictment [...]

7. That the Prosecution submit all highlighted maps to the Trial Chamber and the parties by Tuesday the 2nd November, 2004 and seek to have these maps admitted into evidence as exhibits;

8. That the Defence file their responses, if any, on the issue of admissibility of the maps by the 9th of November, 2004.

- **Rule 89(C): Evidence – Identification of Signature – Lay Witness**

R89-TC-16
o *Prosecutor v. Sesay, Kallon, Gbao*, Case No. SCSL-04-15-T, Ruling on the Identification of Signature by Witness TF1-360, 14 October 2005, para. 7-8:

7. At common law, the opinion evidence of a lay person identifying handwriting has always been admissible in those cases "where the witness had seen the person write and those where the witness had acquired some previous familiarity with the person's handwriting in another way."[(1)] Expert evidence is often used in order to conduct a comparison between a

---

[148] See also *Prosecutor v. Sesay, Kallon, Gbao*, Case No. SCSL-04-15-T, Order on Prosecution Map Exhibits, 28 October 2004.

disputed writing and a writing considered to be genuine,[2] but even here, courts have permitted lay persons or the trier of fact to compare disputed handwriting with admitted evidence and draw inferences thereon without the benefit of expert testimony.[3]

8. The evidence of TF1-360 relating to the identification of the signatures of Sam Bockarie and Issa Sesay may be relevant and is therefore admissible in accordance with Rule 89(C) of the Rules. [...]

---

[1] *Lockheed-Arabia v. Owen* [1993] QB 806 (Court of Appeal), para. 7. See also, *Doe d. Mudd v. Suckermore* (1837) 4 Ad. & E. 703 and *R. v. Wright* [1980] VR 593 (Supreme Court of Victoria).
[2] See, for example, *Prosecutor v. Stakic*, IT-97-24, Order Pursuant to Rule 98 to Appoint a Forensic Handwriting Examiner, 28 June 2002.
[3] See, for example, *R. v. Abdi*, (1997) 116 C.C.C. (3d) 384 (Ontario Court of Appeal), paras 16 and 21-22.

- **Rule 89(C): Evidence – Assessment of Reliability – Witness Statements**

R89-TC-17

o *Prosecutor v. Sesay, Kallon, Gbao*, Case No. SCSL-04-15-T, Decision on the Joint Defence Motion Requesting Conformity of Procedural Practice for Taking Witness Statements, 26 October 2005, para. 39-49:

39. The present application, however, concerns the impact of defects in the procedure and form of witness statements taken by the Prosecution on the weight to be given to the statement when the Defence uses a written statement in order to impeach the credibility of Prosecution witnesses.

40. It is of interest to note that this issue came up before the Trial Chamber of the ICTR in the case of *Prosecutor v. Akayesu*. The said Chamber addressed specifically the issue if the impact of the circumstances surrounding the taking of pre-trial statements on their probative value. The Chamber reasoned thus:

> During the trial, the Prosecutor and the Defence relied on pre-trial statements from witnesses for the purpose of cross-examination. The Chamber ordered that any such statements to which reference was made in the proceedings be submitted in evidence for consideration. In many instances, the Defence has alleged inconsistencies and contradictions between the pre-trial statements of witnesses and their evidence at trial. The Chamber notes that these pre-trial statements were composed following

interviews with witnesses by investigators of the Office of the Prosecution. These interviews were mostly conducted in Kinyarwanda, and the Chamber did not have access to transcripts of the interviews, but only translations thereof. It was therefore unable to consider the nature and form of the questions put to the witnesses, or the accuracy of interpretation at the time. The Chamber has considered inconsistencies and contradictions between these statements and testimony at trial with caution for these reasons, and in light of the time lapse between the statements and the presentation of evidence at trial, the difficulties of recollecting precise details several years after the occurrence of the events, the difficulties of translation, and the fact that several witnesses were illiterate and stated that they had not read their written statements. Moreover, the statements were not made under solemn declaration and were not taken by judicial officers. In the circumstances, the probative value attached to the statements is, in the Chamber's view, considerably less than direct sworn testimony before the Chamber, the truth if which has been subjected to the test of cross-examination.[1]

41. Noting that it was open to the Trial Chamber to make the finding which it made in light of the particular circumstances of the case,[2] the Appeals Chamber of the ICTR underscored its opinion on the pre-eminence of the principle of orality in these terms:

[T]he general principle is that Trial Chambers of the Tribunal shall hear live, direct testimony. In the opinion of the Appeals Chamber prior statements of witnesses who appear in court are as a rule relevant only insofar as they are necessary to a Trial Chamber in its assessment of the credibility of a witness. It is not the case ... that they should or could generally in and of themselves constitute evidence that the content thereof is truthful. For this reason, live testimony is primarily accepted as being the most persuasive evidence before a court.[3]

42. The Defence argue that they are prejudiced if the Prosecution does not ask a witness to read through his or her statement and sign to attest as to the truth of its contents since the Court will accord less weight to an unsigned statement thereby diminishing their ability to highlight prior inconsistencies and the Court will not be able to control false testimony under Rule 91.

43. On this issue, the Chamber notes that in the case of *Prosecutor v. Rwamakuba* before the ICTR, the Defence brought a motion seeking that the Prosecution be required to have will-say statements read to and signed by the witnesses.

There, the Trial Chamber characterised will-say statements as communications from one party to the other "anticipating that a witness will testify about matters that were not mentioned in previously disclosed witness statements"[4] that were disclosable under Rule 67(D) of the Rules and noted that they were distinguishable from written and signed witness statements that were disclosed pursuant to Rule 66.[5] In that case, the Chamber denied the defence Motion and held:

> In the Chamber's view, the fact that the will-say statement is not signed does not limit the right of the Accused to cross-examine the Witness and show inconsistencies with his testimony at trial. The weight to be attached to such related evidence will be addressed at a later stage by the Chamber in light of the circumstances including the manner in which the interview was recorded and on a case-by-case basis.[6]

44. In the application before us, the Defence have emphasised that they are seeking that those statements that the witness "knows, or has reason to know, may be used in evidence in proceedings before the Special Court" be signed by the witness and not will-say statements.[7] As already noted, it is clear from our jurisprudence that all witness statements, in whatever form they are recorded, are disclosable under Rule 66 of the Rules.

45. We take the view that the findings of the Trial Chamber of the ICTR in *Rwamakuba* are applicable to all forms of witness statements. We accordingly restate our position that the Defence have the right to cross-examine witnesses on unsigned statements and to demonstrate that there are inconsistencies between these statements and oral testimony. We also observe that they have, in fact, full exercised this right throughout the trial proceedings. The weight to be attached to this evidence will be assessed by the Chamber having regard to the particular circumstances surrounding the making of the statement and testimony in question on a case-by-case basis.

46. The Chamber would like to emphasise that a signature at the end of a statement is neither the conclusive nor the sole factor in determining a statement's reliability. It is merely one of a number of factors to be considered in the final assessment and determination of the weight to be given to each witness' evidence before the Court.

47. In the Chamber's view, the presence of a signature is even less important when the witness is subjected to cross-examination. The witness can be asked whether or not he or she actually made the statement. If the witness admits to making the statement, then, as the Defence admitted in oral submissions, it is not relevant whether or not the statement was signed. If the witness denies ever having made the statement, then other

evidence can be called by the Defence to refute this assertion. Once it has been established that a witness has made a statement, the issue of any inaccuracies in the statement can also be addressed through cross-examination and will be considered and weighed by the Chamber on a case-by-case basis in light of the totality of the evidence before the Chamber.

48. This Chamber has already noted that it is good practice to have witness statements read back to the witness and to have the witness then sign the statement as to the truth of its contents and agrees with the comments of the Appeals Chamber of the ICTR in the *Niyitegeka* [decision] as to what would constitute an "ideal" standard for taking witness statements. However, the Chamber does recognize the peculiarity of the circumstances existing in this case of testifying in a hostile environment and under conditions similar to those outlined in the *Akayesu* Judgment.[8]

49. Based on the foregoing considerations, the Chamber is of the view that it would not be in the interests of justice to depart from the current practice and order the Prosecution to comply with any particular practice or to promulgate a practice direction on the issue of the signing of witness statements. Each situation and each statement will be assessed on the basis of its own circumstances and a proper determination of the weight and reliability to be attached to it will be proceeded with in due course.

---

[1] *Prosecutor v. Akayesu*, Trial Judgment, *supra* [. . .], para. 137.
[2] *Prosecutor v. Akayesu*, Appeals Judgment, *supra* [. . .], para. 133.
[3] *Id.*, para. 134.
[4] *Prosecutor v. Simba*, ICTR-01-76-T, "Decision on the Admissibility of Evidence of Witness KDD", 1 November 2004, para. 9.
[5] *Prosecutor v. Rwamakuba*, ICTR-98-44C-T, "Decision on the Defence Motion Regarding Will-Say Statements", 14 July 2005, paras 3-4.
[6] *Id.*, para. 5.
[7] Transcripts of trial proceedings, 27 July 2005, p. 2-4.
[8] *Prosecutor v. Akayesu*, Trial Judgment, *supra* [. . .], para. 137.

APPEALS CHAMBER DECISIONS

- **Rule 89: Evidence – Provisions of Rule 89 Are Not Restrictive**

R89-AC-1   o *Prosecutor v. Fofana*, Case No. SCSL-04-14-AR65, Appeal Against Decision Refusing Bail, 11 March 2005, para. 22:[149]

---

[149] See also *Prosecutor v. Brima, Kamara, Kanu*, Case No. SCSL-04-16-T, Decision on Joint Defence Motion to Exclude All Evidence from Witness TF1-277 Pursuant to Rule 89(C) and/or Rule 95, 24 May 2005, para. 12.

22. Rule 89 of the Rules, which is not restrictive in its provisions, is applicable in an application for bail as it is in a trial by the Trial Chamber. [...]

- **Rule 89: Evidence – Non Disputed Facts**

R89-AC-2   o *Prosecutor v. Fofana*, Case No. SCSL-04-14-AR73, Decision on Appeal Against "Decision on Prosecution's Motion for Judicial Notice and Admission of Evidence", 16 May 2005, para. 38:

38. In addition, the appellant in this case has already approached this Chamber on a previous occasion, arguing that there was an international armed conflict in Sierra Leone, thus acknowledging the existence of an armed conflict as such and challenging the jurisdiction of the Court to proceed.[(1)] [...]

[(1)] *Prosecutor v. Fofana*, Case No. SCSL-2004-14-AR72(E), Decision on Preliminary Motion on Lack of Jurisdiction – Nature of the Armed Conflict, 25 May 2004. The existence of an armed conflict was acknowledged in that Motion.

- **Rule 89: Evidence – Reliability of Unauthenticated Documents**

R89-AC-3   o *Prosecutor v. Fofana*, Case No. SCSL-04-14-AR65, Appeal Against Decision Refusing Bail, 11 March 2005, para. 25-27:[150]

25. It follows that the Judge made an error of law in refusing to admit the statement of Ms Fortune, who had attended court to give evidence on the previous hearing but had been unable to sign her statement because she was overseas. [...]

The fact that a statement is unauthenticated does not make it necessarily unreliable – especially where the identity of its maker and the fact that she made it are not in dispute. The fact that both documents were relevant meant that they should both have been admitted, for what they were worth when their probative value could be assessed in the context of all the other evidential material.

---

[150] See also *Prosecutor v. Brima, Kamara, Kanu*, Case No. SCSL-04-16-T, Decision on Joint Defence Motion to Exclude All Evidence from Witness TF1-277 Pursuant to Rule 89(C) and/or Rule 95, 24 May 2005, para. 14, 24.

26. Rule 89(C) ensures that the administration of justice will not be brought into disrepute by artificial or technical rules, often devised for jury trial, which prevent judges from having access to information which is relevant. Judges sitting alone can be trusted to give second hand evidence appropriate weight, in the context of the evidence as a whole and according to well-understood forensic standards. The Rule is designed to avoid sterile legal debate over admissibility so the court can concentrate on the pragmatic issue of whether there is a real risk that the defendant will not attend the trial or will harm others.

27. [...] Relevant evidence is not "clearly inadmissible". By virtue of Rule 89(C), it is clearly admissible. There is no judicial norm violated in admitting for curial consideration of a bail application information that is relevant: the judicial process would be brought into disrepute by excluding it. In any event, it is inappropriate to release into the community pending or during trial a defendant facing charges of this gravity merely on the strength of a written witness statement, whether or not made on affidavit: sureties for his attendance and good behaviour must attend court and be examined, and the court must at the end of the day be satisfied that they fully understand the heavy obligations which they undertake.

- **Rule 89(C): Evidence – Difference Admissibility/Reliability**

R89-AC-4   o *Prosecutor v. Fofana*, Case No. SCSL-04-14-AR65, Appeal Against Decision Refusing Bail, 11 March 2005, para. 24, 29:[151]

24. The so-called "best evidence rule" is an anachronism. It was developed in a pre-industrial age when copying was done by hand and, given the risk of transcription errors, the courts required to see the handwritten originals. The rule has no modern application other than to require a party in possession of the original document to produce it.[(1)] If the original is unavailable then copies may be relied upon – the rule has no

---

[151] See also *Prosecutor v. Sesay, Kallon, Gbao*, Case No. SCSL-04-15-T, Ruling on Gbao Application to Exclude Evidence of Prosecution Witness Mr. Koker, 23 May 2005, para. 4; *Prosecutor v. Brima, Kamara, Kanu*, Case No. SCSL-04-16-T, Decision on Joint Defence Motion to Exclude All Evidence from Witness TF1-277 Pursuant to Rule 89(C) and/or Rule 95, 24 May 2005, para. 15; *Prosecution v. Sesay, Kallon, Gbao*, Case No. SCSL-04-15-T, Ruling on Application for the Exclusion of Certain Supplemental Statements of Witness TF1-361 and Witness TF1-122, 1st June 2005, para. 18; *Prosecutor v. Sesay, Kallon, Gbao*, Case No. SCSL-04-15-T, Decision on the Joint Defence Motion Requesting Conformity of Procedural Practice for Taking Witness Statements, 26 October 2005, para. 33, 36.

bearing at all on the question of whether an unsigned statement or submission is admissible. If relevant, then under Rule 89(C) they may (and in bail applications, should) be admitted, with their weight to be determined thereafter. There is no rule that requires, as a precondition for admissibility, that relevant statements or submissions must be signed. That may be good practice, but it is not a rule about admissibility of evidence. Evidence is admissible once it is shown to be relevant: the question of its reliability is determined thereafter, and is not a condition for its admission.[2]

[...]

29. The Judge was correct to admit under Rule 89(C) the declaration of the Chief of Investigations, having found it relevant. Once admitted, the weight to be attached was a matter for him. The appellant's objections, that the declaration was both partisan and hearsay, are not objections to admissibility – they go to weight. There is no bar on a party adducing evidence in support of its position from its own employees and there is no bar on hearsay evidence. Questions of partiality and reliability go to the assessment of the weight of evidence that has been admitted. It was open to the defence to ask Mr White to be called and to cross-examine him or to controvert his evidence by calling their own witnesses or by arguing that it was speculative or rumour-based, in order to undermine its weight.

---

[1] See Richard May, *Criminal Evidence*, 3rd Edition (1995), p. 24; *Garton v. Hunter* 1969 (2QB 37); Sapinka et al., *The Law of Evidence in Canada*, 2nd Edition (Butterworths 1999), Chapter 18.6.

[2] See *Prosecutor v. Zejnil Delalic, Zdravko Mucic et al.*, Decision on the Motion of the Prosecutor for the Admissibility of Evidence, International Criminal Tribunal for Yugoslavia (ICTY), para. 19: "it is neither necessary or desirable to add to the provisions of sub-Rule 89(C) a condition of admissibility which is not expressly prescribed by that provision."

Rule 90: Testimony of Witnesses
(amended 7 March 2003)

(A) Witnesses may give evidence directly, or as described in Rules 71 and 85(D).

(B) Every adult witness shall, before giving evidence, make one of the following solemn declarations:

"I solemnly declare that I will speak the truth, the whole truth and nothing but the truth."

Or

"I solemnly swear on the [insert holy book] that I will speak the truth, the whole truth and nothing but the truth."

(C) A child shall, be permitted to testify if the Chamber is of the opinion that he is sufficiently mature to be able to report the facts of which he had knowledge, that he understands the duty to tell the truth, and is not subject to undue influence. However, he shall not be compelled to testify by solemn declaration.

(D) A witness, other than an expert, who has not yet testified may not be present without leave of the Trial Chamber when the testimony of another witness is given. However, a witness who has heard the testimony of another witness shall not for that reason alone be disqualified from testifying.

(E) A witness may refuse to make any statement which might tend to incriminate him. The Chamber may, however, compel the witness to answer the question. Testimony compelled in this way shall not be used as evidence in a subsequent prosecution against the witness for any offence other than false testimony under solemn declaration.

(F) The Trial Chamber shall exercise control over the mode and order of interrogating witnesses and presenting evidence so as to:

   (i) Make the interrogation and presentation effective for the ascertainment of the truth; and
   (ii) Avoid the wasting of time.

TRIAL CHAMBERS DECISIONS

- **Rule 90: Testimony of Witnesses – Assessment of Credibility – Material Inconsistencies With Written Statements**

R90-TC-1

o *Prosecutor v. Brima, Kamara, Kanu*, Case No. SCSL-04-16-T, Decision on Joint Defence Motion to Exclude All Evidence from Witness TF1-277 Pursuant to Rule 89(C) and/or Rule 95, 24 May 2005, para. 20:

20. The Defence has made reference to material inconsistencies between the Witness's prior written statement and his sworn evidence. This, in our view, would not affect the admissibility of either the sworn evidence or the prior written statement. In the *Akayesu* case, the ICTR Trial Chamber was confronted with the problem of alleged inconsistencies between the oral testimonies of witnesses and pre-trial statements that were composed of interview notes not made in English which had to be translated from the indigenous language of the witness.[1] The Trial Chamber decided that the issue was one of probative value and not of admissibility.

[1] *Prosecutor v. Jean Paul Akayesu*, Case No. ICTR-96-4-. Trial Chamber, Judgment, 2 September 1998, para. 137.

- **Rule 90(C): Testimony of Witnesses – Child Witnesses – Special Protective Measures**

R90-TC-2

o *Prosecutor v. Norman, Fofana, Kondewa*, Case No. SCSL-04-14-T, Decision on Prosecution Motion for Modification of Protective Measures for Witnesses, 8 June 2004, para. 47-48:

47. For Sub-Category B, child witnesses, the Prosecution seeks the possibility for testimony by way of closed-circuit-television. While the witness testifies in a back room in the court building, this would allow the Accused and the Defence, as well as the Trial Chamber and the Prosecution, to see the witness on a television-screen and observe his/her demeanour. The image on the screen for the public at that time would be distorted. As stated by Psychologist An Michels, especially children[1] are vulnerable witnesses, the risk of re-traumatisation and the possibility of stigmatisation and rejection is real and high. On this issue the U.S. Supreme Court held in *Maryland v. Craig* held that the use of closed circuit televi-

sion does not violate the constitutional right of an Accused to confrontation if it is necessary in the opinion of the Court to protect a child witness from psychological harm.[2]

48. Based upon these information and the evidence submitted the Chamber finds that such risks as described would exist, and, therefore, deems it necessary in the interest of justice for children to be allowed to testify in the way the Prosecution asks for, in accordance with Rule 75(B)(i)(a).

---

[1] Motion, Annex 11.
[2] See *Maryland v Craig*, 497 U.S. 836 (1990).

R90-TC-3

o *Prosecutor v. Norman, Fofana, Kondewa*, Case No. SCSL-04-14-T, Order on Disclosure and Characterisation of the Age of Witness TF2-080, 14 April 2005:

MINDFUL OF Article 1 of the United Nations Convention on the Rights of the Child, which entered into force on the 2nd of September 1990 and Article 2 of the African Charter on the Rights and Welfare of the Child, which entered into force on the 29th of November 1999, which defines a child as "every human being below the age of 18 years";

NOTING that the Decision on Prosecution Motion for Modification of Protective Measures for Witnesses ("Protective Measures Decision"), rendered by the Trial Chamber on the 8th of June, 2004, which granted Child Witnesses listed in Category B of Annex 38 of the underlying Prosecution Motion, the protective measure of testifying by closed-circuit television;

[...]

CONSIDERING that it is necessary in the interests of justice to ascertain the age of the witness by independent and objective assessment;

CONSIDERING that it is important to protect vulnerable witnesses and child witnesses from psychological harm and that protective measures may be granted for this purpose;

PURSUANT TO Rules 54 and 66(A)(ii) of the Rules of Procedure and Evidence of the Special Court ("Rules");

FOR THE ABOVE REASONS, THE TRIAL CHAMBER

FINDS that Witness TF2-080 is a vulnerable witness and is considered to be a Category B witness who will testify by closed-circuit television, pursuant to the Trial Chamber's Decision on Protective Measures;

ORDERS the Prosecution to disclose immediately to all Defence Teams the statements and briefing notes relating to Witness TF2-080 that are in their possession, and any information they may have in relation to the age of this witness; and

ORDERS the Prosecution to ascertain the age of Witness TF2-080 by independent and objective assessment and disclose this assessment to the Defence Teams and the Trial Chamber by the 2nd of May, 2005.

- **Rule 90(D): Testimony of Witnesses – Former Exposure to Images or Audio Recordings**

R90-TC-4   o *Prosecutor v. Brima, Kamara, Kanu*, Case No. SCSL-04-16-PT, Decision on Defence Applications Not to Disclose Photography, Video and Audio Recordings of the Trial to the Public and/or Third Parties, 28 February 2005:

CONSIDERING FURTHER that the proper time for the Trial Chamber to assess the reliability of witnesses is when they give evidence at the trial. If it is contended by an Accused that the credibility of a witness has been adversely affected by his or her exposure to images or audio recordings of the Accused prior to testifying, then that is a matter which can be raised in cross-examination.

- **Rule 90(D): Testimony of Witnesses – Contact Between Witnesses During Testimony**

R90-TC-5   o *Prosecutor v. Brima, Kamara, Kanu*, Case No. SCSL-04-16-T, Decision on Confidential Urgent Joint Defence Motion to Exclude Evidence Given by Witness TF1-157 and Evidence to Be Given by Witness TF1-158 Based on Lack of Authenticity and Violation of Rule 95, 10 October 2005, para. 1, 16-17, 19-22:

1. During the cross-examination of Witness TFI-157 on 25 July 2005 it emerged that he was a close family member of Witness TFI-158, who was due to testify next, and that they lived in the same room, even during the period that Witness TFI-157 was giving evidence. [...]

[...]

16. Thus there is nothing to show that the two witnesses had ever discussed with each other the evidence they gave in

Court. All the Defence can point to is a "potential contamination of evidence". Despite this, we are urged by the Defence to exclude their testimony in its entirety, solely because they are closely related and shared the same room during the time that one of them was in the process of giving evidence in Court. In our view, it would be wrong to conclude that, as a general principle of law, witnesses in such situations are deemed to be inherently unreliable. We agree with what was said in *Tadic* that "[t]*he reliability of witnesses, including any motive they may have to give false testimony, is an estimation that must be made in the case of each individual witness.*" The court in that case held that a conclusion that a witness is deemed to be inherently unreliable can only be made "*in the light of the circumstances of each individual witness, his individual testimony, and such concerns as the Defence may substantiate either in cross-examination or through its own evidence-in-chief.*"[1]

17. The Defence draws an analogy between the present case and the ICTY case of *Prosecutor v. Kupreskic et al.*[2] We do not think that that case assists the Defence. In *Kupreskic*, the person who spoke to the witness after commencement of the witness's testimony was one of the parties; it was not a case of witnesses speaking together. We do not agree with the reasoning of the Defence that the risk of two closely-related witnesses influencing each other's testimony is a more serious risk than the risk of a witness being influenced by a party. Unlike a witness, a party has a definite cause to pursue and therefore a motive to influence the testimony of a witness. That, in our view, is a risk of much more intensity than any which may arise from two witnesses communicating. Even then, the court in *Kupreskic* did not hold that the evidence of the witness in question ought to be excluded.

[...]

19. In the absence of express provisions, the spirit of the Rules in regard to witnesses who hear the testimony of other witnesses can be ascertained from Rule 90(D), which states:

> "A witness, other than an expert, who has not yet testified may not be present without leave of the Trial Chamber when the testimony of another witness is given. However, a witness who has heard the testimony of another witness shall not for that reason alone be disqualified from testifying."

Under Rule 90(D) a witness who has heard the testimony of another witness by sitting in court while that other witness gives evidence cannot thereby be disqualified from testifying. It seems to us to be wrong and grossly inconsistent with the spirit of this provision to say that the testimony of a witness who may or may not have heard the evidence of another witness, not from sitting in court, but from the other witness himself, should attract the draconian measure of exclusion or preclusion in its entirety.

20. It is trite law that the way to test the credibility of witnesses is by cross-examination, which can be used to determine whether witnesses have colluded or exchanged information on their testimony.[3] The Defence has not referred us to any authority which would support the proposition that exclusion of evidence is the appropriate remedy in circumstances such as those in this case. In fact, although the Defence relies on *Jones & Powles* in support of its argument on the "potential contamination of evidence", we note that the learned authors themselves endorse cross-examination as the correct remedy to determine whether witnesses have spoken to each other about their testimony.[4] Moreover, in the *Prosecutor v. Nyiramasuhuko*,[5] the Trial Chamber held that where a number of witnesses are transferred at the same time to the Detention Unit, the right to cross-examine on credibility provides sufficient protection against the possibility of communication between those witnesses. Nevertheless, a Trial Chamber should take all reasonable measures to ensure that such communication does not take place.[6]

21. It is the practice of this Trial Chamber to caution every witness not to discuss either the case or his or her evidence with any person during the trial. The Trial Chamber also ensures that every witness understands the meaning of this caution. This was done with respect to Witness TFI-157 when the case was adjourned on 25 July 2005 with his cross-examination incomplete. Not only was he given the usual caution, but it was in even stronger terms.[7] In addition, when he was allowed to go home later that day, the Witness's Unit was requested by the Prosecution to reinforce the caution given by the Trial Chamber.[8] We consider that those were reasonable measures and that, in the circumstances, additional measures were neither practical nor necessary. Moreover, the testimonies of the two witnesses were not identical and there was no indication that the caution had been contravened.

22. We find the evidence of Witness TFI-157 and Witness TFI-158 to be admissible. [. . .]

---

[1] *Prosecutor v. Tadic*, Case No. IT-94-I-T Opinion and Judgment, 7 May 1997, para. 541.
[2] *Prosecutor v. Kupreskic et al.*, Case No. IT-95-16-T, Decision on Communications Between the Parties and Their Witnesses, Decision of 21 September 1998.
[3] See Jones & Powles, *International Criminal Practice*, Oxford University Press, 3rd Edition, paras. 8.5.698, 8.5.713.
[4] See Jones & Powles, *International Criminal Practice*, Oxford University Press, 3rd Edition, paras. 8.5.698, 8.5.713.
[5] *Prosecutor v. Nyiramasuhuko et al.*, Case No. ICTR-99-21-T, Decision on

the Prosecutor's Motions for Leave to Call Additional Witnesses and For the Transfer of Detained Witnesses, 24 July 2001.
(6) Jones & Powles, *International Criminal Practice*, Oxford University Press, 3rd Edition, para. 8.5.698.
(7) Transcript 25 July 2005, page 76, lines 22, 23, page 77, lines 10 to 18, page 78, lines 2 to 4.
(8) Transcript 26 July 2005, page 99, lines 19 to 23.

- **Rule 90(F): Testimony of Witnesses – Chamber's Control on Witness Examination – Service of Witness Statements to the Chamber Prior to their Appearance**

R90-TC-6   o *Prosecutor v. Norman, Fofana, Kondewa*, Case No. SCSL-04-14-PT, Scheduling Order, 27 May 2004:[152]

CONSIDERING that the Trial Chamber would benefit from having access to witness statements in advance of each witness testifying at trial, for the purpose of promoting comprehension of the issues and for the effective management of the trial;

CONSIDERING that previous Trial Chambers of the International Criminal Tribunal for the former Yugoslavia and the International Criminal Tribunal for Rwanda, have in some instances ordered that the Prosecutor should submit all available written witness statements to the Trial Chamber.(1)

PURSUANT TO Rules 54 and Rule 73*bis* of the Rules;

HEREBY ORDERS the Prosecution to:

(1) List the witnesses it intends to call two weeks in advance of each trial session; and

(2) Provide the Trial Chamber with a copy of the statement of each witness who will testify, no later than one week before their testimony.

---

(1) *Prosecutor. v. Jean-Paul Akayesu*, ICTR-96-4-T, Decision by the Tribunal on its Request to the Prosecutor to Submit the Written Witness Statements, 28 January 1997; *Prosecutor v. Darko Kordic and Mario Cerkez*, Case No. IT-95-14/2-PT, *Order for Disclosure of Documents and Extension of Protective Measures*, 27 November 1998; *Prosecutor v. Dokmanovic*, IT-95-13a-PT, Order, 28 November. 1997, p. 2; See *Prosecutor v. Vidoje Blagojevic, Dragan Jokic, Momir Nikolic*, Decision in the Appeals Chamber, 8 April 2003.

---

[152] See also *Prosecutor v. Norman, Fofana, Kondewa*, Case No. SCSL-04-14-PT, Order to Prosecution to Provide Order of Witnesses and Witness Statements, 28 May 2004; *Prosecutor v. Norman, Fofana, Kondewa*, Case No. SCSL-04-14-T, Order to Prosecution to Provide Order of Witnesses and Witness Statements, 29 July 2004.

- **Rule 90(F): Testimony of Witnesses – Chamber's Control on Witness Examination – Scope of Cross-Examination – Rule 90(H) of the ICTR Rules**

R90-TC-7

o *Prosecutor v. Brima, Kamara, Kanu*, Case No. SCSL-04-16-T, Decision on Objection to Question Put by Defence in Cross-Examination of Witness TF1-227, 15 June 2005, para. 15-26:

15. It is common ground between the parties that there is no precise rule in our Rules of Procedure and Evidence equivalent to Rule 90(H) of the ICTR. The powers and duties of the Special Court are contained in Rule 90(F) [. . .].

16. The Trial Chamber has a duty to both ascertain the truth and avoid wasting time on matters of evidence where there is no other specific provision. Rule 89(B) imposes a duty on the Trial Chamber to

[. . .] apply rules of evidence which will best favour a fair determination of the matter before it consonant with the spirit of the Statute and the General principles of law

17. The Trial Chamber also has to bear in mind the primary duty to ensure a fair trial. To quote Archbold International Courts Practice, Procedure and Evidence paragraph 8-48(a):

The concept of a fair trial is the cornerstone of the work of the ad hoc International Tribunals. The overriding consideration in all proceedings before international criminal courts is the fairness of the proceedings, as provided for in Articles 20(1) and 19(1) of the ICTY and ICTR Statutes respectively, "The Trial Chambers shall ensure that a trial is fair". As was held in Prosecutor v. Tadic, Judgement, ICTY Appeals Chamber, July 15, 1999, para. 43: "This provision mirrors the corresponding guarantee provided for in international and regional human rights instruments: the International Covenant on Civil and Political Rights (1966) (ICCPR), the European Convention on Human Rights(1950), and the American Convention on Human Rights (1969). The right to a fair trial is central to the rule of law: it upholds the due process of law".

[. . .] A fair trial demands that certain minimum requirements are met to protect the rights of the accused, as set out in Articles 20 and 21 of the ICTR and ICTY Statues respectively.

The rights of victims must also be taken into consideration, but "the Tribunal's Statute makes the rights of the

> *accused the first consideration, and the need to protect victims and witnesses the secondary consideration" (Prosecutor v. Brdanin, Decision on third motion by Prosecution for protective measures, November 8, 2000, para. 13; also see, Prosecutor v Tadic, Decision on the Prosecution's motion requesting protective measures for witness R, July 31, 1996 at 4).*
>
> *The principle of a fair trial must not result in there being an excessive infringement on the rights of the Prosecution, for example, to conduct effective cross-examination of the Defence witnesses (see, Prosecutor v. Blaskic, Decision on the defence motion for protective measures for witnesses D/H and D/I, September 25, 1998).*
>
> *[. . .] The Statute and Rules must be read to include the rights of parties to be heard in accordance with the judicial character of the Trial Chambers. See, Prosecutor v Jelisic, Judgement, Appeals Chamber, July 5, 2001, para 27.*

18. With that general duty imposed upon this Trial Chamber, we are of the opinion that the Trial Chamber should not ignore its duty of upholding the general principles of fairness in the proceedings incumbent upon it by holding that the absence of an equivalent Rule 90 (H) precludes the Trial Chamber limiting cross-examination.

19. We cite with approval the juxtaposition posed by Hon. Judge Jorda in *The Prosecutor v. Blaskic*.[1] He drew a parallel to a defence Counsel being asked "what exactly happened in your relationship between the witness that you are offering and yourself", to the Defence cross-examining a Prosecution witness "to see what happened within the confidential relationship between the Prosecutor and the witness". His Honour held that such line of questioning was "not appropriate" (ex tempore ruling).

20. We consider the Trial Chamber may follow the principles enunciated in the *Bizimungu* Decision. Unless there are specific and substantiated allegations of misconduct on the part of Counsel,

> "[t]he Chamber concludes that questions relating to pre-testimony meetings between the Prosecutor and witnesses, while permissible, must in the absence of any substantiated allegation of misconduct be limited to the number of such meetings, the dates of the meetings, and their duration."[2]

21. We note that use of the word "Counsel" in the decision and Defence Counsel's submission that not all Prosecution interviewers who speak to witnesses are bound by the ethics of a Bar.

22. The Rules define "Prosecutor" as "The Prosecutor appointed pursuant to Art. 3 of the Agreement between the United Nations and the Government of Sierra Leone".

23. Article 3(3) of the Agreement between the United Nations and the Government of Sierra Leone on the Establishment of the Special Court provides *inter alia*:

> *The Prosecutor and the Deputy Prosecutor shall be of high moral character and possess the highest level of professional competence and extensive experience in the conduct of investigations and prosecutions of criminal cases.*

24. The highest level of professional competence and experience brings with it an awareness that those under their control must act in a professional, competent and ethical manner. It carries a duty to supervise and ensure conformity with such standards.

25. Unless the contrary is shown by way of a specific allegation of misconduct on the part of Prosecution staff any questions relating to pre-testimony meetings between Prosecution staff and witnesses are similarly restricted as ruled above.

26. For the foregoing reasons we answer the objections as follows:

(1) We uphold the objection and find the question goes beyond the scope permissible in cross-examination.

(2) Unless the contrary is shown by way of a specific allegation of misconduct on the part of Prosecution staff any questions relating to pre-testimony meetings between Prosecution staff and witnesses are similarly restricted as ruled above.

---

(1) *The Prosecutor v. Blaskic*, Case No. IT-95-14-T, Transcripts, 21 August 1997, pp. 1812-1813.
(2) *Bizimungu* Decision, para. 37.

- **Rule 90(F): Testimony of Witnesses – Scope of Cross-Examination – Calling Investigators Who Took Down Witness Statements**

R90-TC-8 o *Prosecutor v. Norman, Fofana, Kondewa*, SCSL-04-14-T, Ruling on Defence Oral Application to Call OTP Investigators Who Took Down in Writing Statements of Prosecution Witness TF2-021, 7 December 2004, para. 13-23:[153]

---

[153] See also *Prosecutor v. Norman, Fofana, Kondewa*, Case No. SCSL-04-14-T, Ruling on Defence Oral Application to Call OTP Investigators Who Took in Writing Statements of

13. The key issue for determination by the Chamber in this application is whether, in the light of the repudiation by Witness TF2-021 of significant and highly contentious portions of Exhibits 19A and 19B, statements taken down in writing by OTP investigators Virginia Chitanda and Tamba Gbeki on 4th February 2003 and 13th January 2003 respectively, the Chamber will, at the appropriate phase of this trial proceeding, be able, without more, to adequately, fairly, and effectively evaluate the probative value of the testimony of this witness. The Defence submits that the Court will not be able to do so without the testimonies of the investigators. The Prosecution also submits that it is a futile and time-wasting exercise and that there is no dispute that the investigators did take down Exhibits 19A and 19B in writing and that the accepted procedure for taking such statements was regularly followed.

14. We do emphasize that in the sphere of the criminal law the doctrine of *Omnia praesumuntur rite esse acta*, has a limited application. It generally applies to the diverse aspects of judicial administration covering the service of legal processes, production of official documents from lawful custody, and the exercise of supervisory roles in the context of judicial administration. It does not, we maintain, apply to matters of proof in the domain of criminal adjudication in respect of the very factual and legal issues, directly or indirectly, in controversy before the Court. In the context of the instant application, the presumption of regularity cannot legitimately apply to the specific and contentious issues (factual and legal) forming the substratum of the Defence Application.

15. In effect, in our considered view, this Chamber finds no legal basis for presuming that an investigator who took down a witness's statement in writing did comply with every rule, requirement or practice governing the recording of witness statements. There is no judicial warrant to apply such a presumption in criminal trials.

16. Given, therefore, the state of the portions of the testimony of TF2-021 on those significant and highly contentious issues between the parties herein, coupled with the equally significant repudiations of what the witness allegedly told or did not tell the investigators, we find it extremely difficult, at this stage, to come to the conclusion that we do have before us all the necessary and relevant evidence upon which to evaluate adequately and effectively the probative value of the witness's testimony.

Prosecution Witness TF2-021, 2 February 2005, para. 13-23; *Prosecutor v. Norman, Fofana, Kondewa*, Case No. SCSL-04-14-T, Ruling on Defence Oral Application to Call an OTP Investigator Who Took a Written Statement from Prosecution Witness TF2-022, 1st March 2005, para. 10-13.

17. It is the Chamber's view that to adopt the approach canvassed by the Prosecution is tantamount to acknowledging a novel principle in international criminal law whereby the Courts are precluded from looking into the investigator's record of the statement in the absence of an irregularity *ex facie*, implying that to probe beyond the pale of the investigator's record of the witness' statement is not a proper matter for judicial inquiry. Such a position flies in the face of the doctrine that the persuasive burden of proof which it must discharge beyond reasonable doubt rests on the Prosecution. The Chamber is of the opinion that we can properly look behind the scenes and inquire whether a statement taken by investigators from witnesses was properly taken down in writing and is an accurate portrayal of the facts as stated.

18. A related issue that needs to be disposed of at this point is on whom the burden of producing the investigators as witnesses rest? Our considered reply to this question is that it is on the Prosecution. To suggest that it is on the Defence or the Bench is to shift some of the burden for establishing the guilt of the Accused persons on to the Defence or to the Bench.

19. It is noteworthy, as a matter of law, that the Prosecution is right in its citation of page 166 of May and Wierda *International Criminal Evidence* in support of the proposition that inconsistencies need not be fatal to the testimony of a witness, provided that they are not material. However, it is also the law that one of the key factors in assessing credibility is *consideration of other witness accounts or other evidence submitted in the case and not only that of "strength under cross-examination"*.[1]

20. Significantly, this Chamber recognises that one operative doctrine on this subject is the doctrine of collaterality. The essence of the principle is that questions in cross-examination designed ***solely*** at discrediting a witness or impeaching the witness' credibility are essentially collateral in nature if they do not touch on an issue which the Court is necessarily required to determine such as an element of the offence. The typical legal situation calling for the application of the so-called collateral-fact rule is where an effort is made to discredit a witness in a manner unrelated to the subject-matter of the offence. The law is that under cross-examination, in the context of the application of the collateral-fact rule, there is, generally, no opportunity to call evidence to refute answers which have been given by a witness, after asking further questions. Exceptionally, the Defence may be afforded the opportunity, where proper foundation has been laid, to call evidence where a prior inconsistent statement is alleged to contradict a witness's testimony.[2]

21. In this regard, whether an issue in a trial is collateral or central is not determined by reference to some judicial crystal

ball. It depends upon the nature of the charges, the factual allegations in support, the definition of the issues in controversy, and the totality of the circumstances of the case. It is, therefore, the considered opinion of the Chamber that some clarifications from the OTP investigators will provide an evidentiary basis upon which TF2-021 can be judged on the grounds that TF2-021's credibility is central to the proof of the Prosecution's case in respect of the matters to which he has testified. Having regard to the nature of his testimony, some explanation as to why he has repudiated significant portions of his out-of-court statements may assist the Court in accurately evaluating his credibility. It is certainly within the realm of probability that the OTP investigator's evidence might remove any doubt that might be cast on the witness' credibility, and emanating from his unequivocal repudiation in court of certain significant portions of the said out-of-court statements to them.

22. In *R. v. Krause*, the Court laid down this guiding principle:

"In the cross-examination of witnesses essentially the same principles apply. Crown counsel in cross-examining an accused are not limited to subjects which are strictly relevant to the essential issues in case. Counsel are accorded a wide freedom in cross-examination which enable them to test and question the testimony of the witnesses and their **credibility**. Where something new emerges in cross-examination, which is new in the sense that the Crown had no chance to deal with it in its case-in-chief (i.e., there was no reason for the Crown to anticipate that the matter would arise), and where the matter is concerned with the merits of the case (i.e. it concerns an issue essential for the determination of the case) then the Crown may be allowed to call evidence in rebuttal. Where, however, the new matter is **collateral**, that is, not determinative of an issue arising in the pleadings or indictment or not relevant to matters which must be proved for the determination of the case, no rebuttal will be allowed."

Continuing, the Court observed that:

"An early expression of this proposition is to be found in *Attorney-General v. Hitchcock*, [1847] 1 Ex. 91, 154 E.R. 38, and examples of the application of the principle may be found in *R. v. Cargill*, [1913] 2 K.B. 271 (Ct. Crim. App.); *R. v. Hrechuk* (1951), 58 Man. R. 489 (C.A); *R. v. Rafael*, [1972] 3 O.R. 238 (Ont. C.A.); and *Latour v. The Queen*, [1978)]1 S.C.R. 361. This is known as the rule against rebuttal on **collateral** issues."[3]

23. In the light of the foregoing considerations, The Chamber has no alternative option, given the state of the evidence of

TF2-021 and the repudiations of significant portions of those statements, but to grant the said application. We must emphasize, however, that in granting the order sought, we do not suggest that every application of this nature will be granted as a matter of course. This Chamber will exercise its discretion on a case-by-case basis and will examine each application according to its merits having regard to the nature of the crimes, the nature of the pleadings, the definition of the issues, and the particular facts and circumstances of the case. It is important to mention that in this peculiar and almost extreme case we are confronted with the testimony and out-of-court statements of a prosecution witness, a child witness, who, without equivocation or hesitation, repudiated significant and highly contentious portions of his statements to the investigators, bearing in mind of course, that the testimonies of this category of witnesses should, either as a matter of law or practice, be examined with some degree of judicial vigilance in view of their particular susceptibilities.

---

[1] May and Wierda, *International Criminal Evidence*, New York: Transnational Publishers Inc., 2002 p. 167.
[2] See an instructive article on the subject of collaterality by Peter M. Brauti, *40 Criminal Law Quarterly*, (1997), pages 69-105, at pages 96-98. See also, *R.v.R. (D)* (1996) 2 S.C.R 291, *James Epley Jr, Appellant v. The State of Texas*, *Appellie* 704 S.W.2d 502 (1986), *People v. Frazier* 95 Mich App. 570 (1980).
[3] See *R. v. Krause* (1986) 2 S.C.R 466.

R90-TC-9

o *Prosecutor v. Norman, Fofana, Kondewa*, Case No. SCSL-04-14-T, Ruling on Defence Oral Application to Call an OTP Investigator Who Took a Written Statement from Prosecution Witness TF2-022, 1st March 2005, para. 14:

14. In our considered opinion, therefore, the current application before the Trial Chamber concerns a prior statement of Witness TF2-022 regarding the organizations that were in "control" of Tongo at a particular time, which is alleged to be at variance with his oral testimony in Court. It is noteworthy that the period of time testified to by this witness both in Court and in his prior statement concerns a timeframe that is not included within the specific factual allegations underpinning counts in the Indictment. We observe that while this evidence may be relevant to the Indictment, it is collateral and is unrelated to the subject-matter of the offences as charged in the Consolidated Indictment. The Defence in making this application is effectively requesting the Court to subpoena an investigator to respond to one alleged inconsistency between the witness' oral testimony and written statement of the 27th of January, 2004, which inconsistency does not appear to us to be material

or highly contentious and certainly not of such a nature that it could not have been properly canvassed and dealt with by appropriate cross-examination. As a matter of law, even if it were material, the question of whether its materiality goes to the issue of the probative value of the witness' testimony is a matter for judicial determination at the appropriate stage.

- **Rule 90(F): Testimony of Witnesses – Motion to Recall Witness – Defence Counsel Failure to Cross-Examine (granted)**

R90-TC-10   o *Prosecutor v. Brima, Kamara, Kanu*, Case No. SCSL-04-16-T, Decision on Joint Defence Motion for Leave to Recall Witness TF1-023, 25 October 2003, para. 13-19(27):[154]

13. The Prosecution rely on *Prosecutor v. Bagosora* and the citation quoted above and submit:

it is incumbent upon the Trial Chamber to consider whether or not each accused has individually demonstrated good cause, as each Defence Counsel made a choice on behalf of his client to decline to cross examine the witness.[(1)]

14. The ICTR decision shows that a party must demonstrate "a substantial reason amounting in law to a legal excuse for failing to perform a required act."[(2)]

15. A Chamber must consider:

  a. the purpose of the proposed testimony;
  b. the party's justification for not offering the evidence (in the instant case for not cross-examining) when the witness originally testified;
  c. the right of the accused to be tried without undue delay;
  d. judicial economy.

16. We agree with the proposition in *Prosecutor v. Bagosora* that leave should only be granted in the most compelling circumstances.[(3)]

17. It is clear from Defence submissions that the purpose of recalling the witness is to challenge identification evidence and we agree with the Prosecution that the Defence were aware that identification of the accused was an issue both during examination-in-chief of witness TF1-023 and at the pre-trial brief stage.

---

[154] There is a mistake in the numbering of paragraphs of the decision, which goes up to 24 and then restart for the last three paragraphs from 17 to 19. The paragraph referred here is the second Paragraph 19, which should be Paragraph 27.

18. The Defence justify their decision not to cross-examine the witness stating that they first needed to verify and cross-check the information provided to them by their investigator. However, this applies only to the first accused and, to a lesser extent the second accused, but not the third accused. We consider that the defence argument that they needed to verify and cross-check information is a weak one particularly when seen in the lapse of some seven months since they formed the view that such verification was necessary.

19. As Defence is making this application, it must be taken to have accepted any delay that could result from such an application. However, such an acceptance does not relieve the Trial Chamber from its duty to ensure that the Trial is conducted without undue delay and with judicial economy.

20. We consider there is merit in the Prosecution submission that the Defence has failed to show good cause and that Counsel erred when they refused to cross-examine the witness when they were accorded an opportunity to do so, in accordance with Rule 85(B) at the end of examination-in-chief.

21. However, we consider that there is a further aspect that arises from Counsel's decision not to cross-examine the witness. We ask ourselves if the decision and failure to cross-examine prevents the accused from having a fair trial.

22. The attitude of Courts to errors by Counsel has varied. In cases such as *Boodran v. the State* the Privy Council spoke of *"failure of so fundamental a nature"* that the trial was not fair.[4]

23. In the European Court of Human Rights Case *Daud v. Portugal*, the test applied was whether failure of Counsel was such that it prevented the accused from having a fair trial. In the that case the ECHR went further imposing a duty upon courts to *"[inquire] into the manner in which the lawyer was fulfilling his duty..."*, when alerted to possible deficiencies, and stated that *"the Court should not have remained passive."*[5]

[...]

17. We are of the opinion that Counsels' failure to cross-examine the witness has prejudiced the rights of the accused enshrined in these provisions.

18. We are also mindful of the duty imposed on the Trial chamber by Rule 26*bis* to conduct the hearing with full respect for the rights of the accused and due regard for the protection of victims and witnesses.

19. For this restricted reason, and taking into account the exceptional circumstances that led to Counsel's failure to cross-examine, we grant the motion.

---

[1] *Prosecutor v. Bagasora et al.*, ICTR-98-41-T, Decision on the Prosecution Motion to recall Witness Nyanjwa, 29 September 2004.

(2) *Ibid.*, para. 6.
(3) Ibid.
(4) *Boodram v. The State*, Privy Council, 1 Cr. App. R. 12, 10 April 2001.
(5) *Daud v. Portugal*, 11/1997/795/997, Judgment, 21 April 1998.

> **Rule 92*bis*: Alternative Proof of Facts**
> *(amended 14 March 2004)*
>
> (A) A Chamber may admit as evidence, in whole or in part, information in lieu of oral testimony.
> (B) The information submitted may be received in evidence if, in the view of the Trial Chamber, it is relevant to the purpose for which it is submitted and if its reliability is susceptible of confirmation.
> (C) A party wishing to submit information as evidence shall give 10 days notice to the opposing party. Objections, if any, must be submitted within 5 days.

TRIAL CHAMBERS DECISIONS

- **Rule 92*bis*: Alternative Proof of Facts – Protecting Interests of Victims and Witnesses**

R92*bis*-TC-1   o *Prosecution v. Sesay, Kallon, Gbao*, Case No. SCSL-04-15-PT, Decision on the Prosecution Motion for Concurrent Hearing of Evidence Common to Cases SCSL-2004-15-PT and SCSL-2004-16-PT, 11 May 2004, para. 36:[155]

> 36. [...] [T]he Chamber wishes to observe that it is one of the harsh realities of the functioning of the criminal law, as a social control mechanism, that witnesses called to testify as to the commission of crimes of international gravity and dimension will experience some measure of inconvenience and hardship. *In the instant situation, such inconvenience and hardship could be reduced by prosecutorial creativity and foresight, given the provision of 'back-up witnesses' as was stated by learned Counsel for the Prosecution during the Pre-Trial Conferences.* Furthermore, the interests of victims and witnesses will remain protected in accordance with Article 16 of the Statute of the Special Court through the Victims and Witnesses Unit and by the judicious use of Rule 92*bis* of the Rules.

---

[155] See also *Prosecutor v. Brima, Kamara, Kanu*, Case No. SCSL-04-16-PT, Decision on the Prosecution Motion for Concurring Hearing of Evidence Common to Cases SCSL-2004-15-PT and SCSL-2004-16-PT, 11 May 2004, para. 36.

- **Rule 92*bis*: Alternative Proof of Facts – Admissibility of Evidence – Applicable Criteria**

R92*bis*-TC-2

o *Prosecutor v. Norman, Fofana, Kondewa*, Case No. SCSL-04-14-T, Decision on Prosecution's Request to Admit into Evidence Certain Documents Pursuant to Rule 92*bis* and 89(C), 14 July 2005:[156]

CONSIDERING that the standard for admitting evidence under Rule 92*bis* of the Rules is more flexible as it prescribes that for the evidence to be "relevant to the purpose for which it is submitted", its "reliability" should be "susceptible of confirmation", which is a standard quite different from Rule 92*bis* standard in ICTY and ICTR Rules of Procedure and Evidence;[(1)]

NOTING that the Rules favour a flexible approach to the issue of admissibility of evidence, leaving the issue of weight to be determined at the end of the trial when assessing probative value of the totality of the evidence;[(2)]

CONSIDERING however, that this "flexibility" should not lead the Chamber to admit "evidence where its probative value is manifestly outweighed by its prejudicial effect";[(3)]

NOTING the interpretation of Rule 92*bis* of the Rules, given by the Appeals Chamber, which provides guidance to the Chamber's interpretation of this Rule:

> SCSL Rule 92*bis* is different to the equivalent Rule in the ICTY and ICTR and deliberately so. The judges of this Court, at one of their first plenary meetings, recognised a need to amend ICTR Rule 92*bis* in order to simplify this provision for a court operating in what was hoped would be a short time-span in the country where the crimes had been committed and where a Truth and Reconciliation Commission and other authoritative bodies were generating testimony and other information about the recently concluded hostilities. The effect of the SCSL Rule is to permit the reception of "information" – assertions of fact (but not opinion) made in documents or electronic communications – if such facts are relevant and their reliability is "susceptible of confirmation". This phraseology was chosen to make clear that proof of reliability is not a condition of admission: all that is required is that the information should be capable of corroboration in due course.[(4)]

---

[156] See also *Prosecutor v. Sesay, Kallon, Gbao*, Case No. SCSL-04-15-T, Decision on the Prosecution Confidential Notice Under 92*bis* to Admit the Transcripts of Testimony of TF1-023, TF1-104 and TF1-169, 9 November 2005; *Prosecutor v. Sesay, Kallon, Gbao*, Case No. SCSL-04-15-T, Decision on the Joint Defence Motion Requesting Conformity of Procedural Practice for Taking Witness Statements, 26 October 2005, para. 31.

CONSIDERING that proof of reliability is not a condition for admitting "information" under Rule 92bis and that a requirement under this Rule of such information being capable of corroboration in due course leaves open the possibility for the Chamber to determine the reliability issue at the end of the trial in light of all evidence presented in the case and decide whether the information is indeed corroborated by other evidence presented at trial,[5] and what weight, if any, should the Chamber attach to it;

CONSIDERING therefore, that what is required of the Chamber at this stage in deciding to admit or reject highlighted portions of the documents tendered by the Prosecution, is to determine whether they are relevant, posses sufficient indicia of reliability and whether their admission would not prejudice unfairly the Defence;

CONSIDERING that the Accused will be unfairly prejudiced if documents pertaining to their acts and conduct are admitted into evidence without giving the Defence the opportunity of cross-examination and noting in this regard view of *May and Wierda* that:

> [. . .] [A]s a matter of practice, Trial Chambers still prefer to hear evidence on the acts and conduct of the accused from live witnesses who can be cross-examined. [. . .] The trend which may, therefore, be discerned is for a preference for live testimony on matters pertaining directly to the guilt or innocence of the accused. This practice allows the accused to examine witnesses *against him* [. . .].[6]

NOTING that in defining what constitutes the evidence which goes to prove acts and conduct of the accused, the Chamber takes guidance from the case-law of the ICTY, where it was held that "the phrase, 'acts and conduct of the accused' is a plain expression and should be given its ordinary meaning: deeds and behaviour of the accused"[7] and that the fact of the conduct being that of co-perpetrators or subordinates is relevant in determining if cross-examination should be allowed and not in deciding if a document should be admitted;

CONSIDERING that the international tribunals admit documentary evidence in various forms, when such evidence is: "(a) 'crime-base' evidence; (b) whether there was a widespread and systematic attack on a civilian population; (c) issues of command structure (leaving aside, however, whether a particular accused exercised the role of a commander); and (d) whether crimes occurred in the context of an international armed conflict";[8]

CONSIDERING that in the jurisprudence of the international tribunals "newspaper articles generally are not considered a reliable source of evidence and are often excluded for lack of probative value";[9]

CONSIDERING that admissibility of books, journals and newspapers "will depend on the circumstances of the particular occasion and the significance of the evidence" and such evidence will not be admitted "if it [is] related to some crucial issue in the case" but more likely will be admitted "if it deals with matters by way of background";[10]

CONSIDERING that in its Decision on Judicial Notice, the Chamber has taken judicial notice of the "existence and authenticity" of the Reports of the UN Secretary General and other UN reports, which are enumerated in Annex II part I to that Decision, but not of their "contents";

[...]

CONSIDERING that although the Prosecution represented at the outset of trial that there were no 92*bis* documents that it would seek to introduce, it did disclose all exhibits that it intended to offer, which include all the documentary evidence it now seeks to tender through Rule 92*bis* of the Rules, and that the Prosecution failure to "ear-mark" documents as Rule 92*bis*, pursuant to Rule 66(A)(i) of the Rules, does not result in any prejudice to the Defence;

---

[1] ICTY and ICTR Rule 92*bis* is designed for admission of a written statement of a witness and/or a transcript from a witness' previous testimony before the Tribunal in lieu of the oral testimony.
[2] See e.g. *Prosecutor v. Norman, Fofana, Kondewa*, SCSL-04-14-AR65, Fofana – Appeal Against Decision Refusing Bail, 11 March 2005 at paras. 22-24.
[3] See e.g. *Prosecutor v. Sesay, Kallon, Gbao*, SCSL-04-15-T, Ruling on Gbao Application to Exclude Evidence of Prosecution Witness Mr. Koker, 23 May 2005, paras. 7 and 8.
[4] Appeals Decision on Judicial Notice, para. 26.
[5] For example, in the *Kovacevic* case, the ICTY Trial Chamber admitted the report from a member of the Commission of Experts, including analysis, but the Chamber explicitly stated that there was no question of the defendant being convicted on any count based on this evidence alone, Prosecutor v. *Kovacevic*, transcript 6 July 1998, p. 71.
[6] *May and Wierda*, International Criminal Evidence, 2002, para. 10.54, pp. 343-344.
[7] *Prosecutor v. Milosevic*, Decision on Prosecution Request to Have Written Statements Admitted under Rule 92*bis*, 21 March 2002, para. 22.
[8] *May and Wierda*, para. 10.59, p. 346.
[9] *May and Wierda*, para. 7.105, p. 248; *see also Prosecutor v. Kvocka et al.*, Decision on Zoran Zigic's Motion for Rescinding Confidentiality of Schedules Attached to the Indictment Decision on Exhibits, 19 July 2001.
[10] *May and Wierda*, para. 10.59, p. 346.

- **Rule 92*bis*: Alternative Proof of Facts – Admissibility of Documents – Identification of Relevant Information**

R92*bis*-TC-3   o *Prosecutor v. Brima, Kamara, Kanu*, Case No. SCSL-04-16-T, Decision on the Prosecution Motion for Judicial Notice and Admission of Evidence, 25 October 2005, para. 71-75:

> 71. Annex B contains no less than 94 documents, ranging from UN Security Council Resolutions, Reports of the Secretary General, Reports of the UN Observer Mission in Sierra Leone (UNOMSIL), Reports of the UN Office for the Coordination of Humanitarian Affairs, Miscellaneous UN Reports, Reports of Non-Governmental Organizations, Sierra Leone Official Documents, other Public Documents, Maps, Peace Agreements, Treaties, and Reports of other Governments. We do not think that we are required by Rule 92*bis* to wade through this mountain of material trying to separate relevant facts from what are irrelevancies, opinions, and legal findings, in order to admit into evidence only the information that satisfies the Rule. Instead, the Prosecution should have clearly indicated on each document the passages that we are being asked to consider on the question of relevance.
>
> 72. We agree with the comments of Robertson J. in Fofana (which apply to facts in documents, whether sought to be judicially noticed or admitted under Rule 92*bis*) that: "This mass of undigested paperwork should not be imposed upon the Trial Chamber and the Defence in such an undisciplined fashion" and that "[i]t must not become a practice in this Court."[1]
>
> 73. Robertson J. also emphasised that there is a duty that rests upon a party seeking to introduce documents: "All relevant material is admissible, but that is not an invitation to parties to deluge the court with thousands of pages of NGO and UN reports. The wider admissibility provisions in the SCSL carry a concomitant duty on the parties to narrow the documentary material they seek to introduce and to identify only those passages which are of direct relevance to the case, however interesting or insightful other aspects of the report may be."[2]
>
> 74. Since the Prosecution has not indicated on any of the 94 documents listed in Annex B the passages it claims to be relevant, we are unable to make any finding as to whether the facts sought to be put into evidence (whatever they may be) satisfy the requirements of Rule 92*bis*. We therefore rule that the information contained in the said documents is, at present, not in an admissible form.

75. Robertson J. in *Fofana*[3] prescribed the following simple procedure, which we think the Prosecution should have followed: "Any party, whether prosecution or defence, that seeks to introduce a lengthy document must indicate in the margin the passages they claim to be relevant and indeed, if judicial notice under Rule 94(A) is sought, they must identify and set out as a proposition the fact which they want judicially noticed and direct the court's attention to the assertion of that fact in any document that they present in pursuance of their application." (The requirements of this procedure which relate to judicial notice do not, of course, apply to the issue with which we are presently concerned.)

---

[1] *Fofana*, Separate Opinion of Justice Robertson, at para. 30.
[2] *Fofana*, Separate Opinion of Justice Robertson, at para. 31.
[3] *Fofana*, Separate Opinion of Justice Robertson, para. 30.

- **Rule 92*bis*: Alternative Proof of Facts – Admissibility of Documents – Legibility of Documents**

R92*bis*-TC-4
- *Prosecutor v. Brima, Kamara, Kanu*, Case No. SCSL-04-16-T, Consequential Order to the Decision on Prosecution Tender for Admission into Evidence of Information Contained in Notice Pursuant to Rule 92*bis*, 23 November 2005:

  NOTING the Prosecution's explanation that they do not have a more legible copy of Document 81;

  NOTING that Document 81 is an abstract of data held at the Office of the Deputy Registrar of Births and Deaths and that the original is retained and available for inspection upon request at his office;

  NOTING further that the hard copy filed with the Court Management Services of the Special Court is legible and accessible to the Defence;

  HEREBY CONFIRMS that Document 81 is admitted as Exhibit P 72;

- **Rule 92*bis*: Alternative Proof of Facts – Admissibility of Transcripts of Previous Testimony in Place of Examination-in-Chief**

R92*bis*-TC-5
- *Prosecutor v. Sesay, Kallon, Gbao*, Case No. SCSL-04-15-T, Decision on the Prosecution Confidential Notice Under 92*bis* to Admit the Transcripts of Testimony of TF1-023, TF1-104 and TF1-169, 9 November 2005:

PURSUANT to Rule 92*bis* of the Rules;

HEREBY GRANTS the Prosecution's Application to admit the transcripts and exhibits from the AFRC trial for the Prosecution Witnesses TF1-023, TF1-104 and TF1-169; and

ORDERS that the Prosecution file in this trial the following transcripts and exhibits from the AFRC trial: [. . .]

ORDERS that those transcripts of closed sessions in the AFRC trial be sealed and that those exhibits that were sealed in the AFRC trial be sealed;

AND ORDERS that the Defence Counsel may cross-examine all of the Witnesses and the Prosecution may re-examine the Witnesses relating to matters raised in any cross-examination by Defence Counsel.

APPEALS CHAMBER DECISIONS

- **Rule 92*bis*: Alternative Proof of Facts – Admissibility of Evidence – Comparison with Rule 94**

R92*bis*-AC-1   o *Prosecutor v. Fofana*, Case No. SCSL-04-14-AR73, Decision on Appeal Against "Decision on Prosecution's Motion for Judicial Notice and Admission of Evidence", 16 May 2005, para. 25-27:[157]

25. Judicial notice under Rule 94 must be distinguished from the court's reception of information under Rule 92*bis*, which the prosecution relies upon as an alternative mode of proof. [. . .]

26. SCSL Rule 92*bis* is different to the equivalent Rule in the ICTY and ICTR and deliberately so. The judges of this Court, at one of their first plenary meetings, recognised a need to amend ICTR Rule 92*bis* in order to simplify this provision for a court operating in what was hoped would be a short timespan in the country where the crimes had been committed and where a Truth and Reconciliation Commission and other authoritative bodies were generating testimony and other information about the recently concluded hostilities.[(1)] The effect of the SCSL Rule is to permit the reception of "infor-

---

[157] See also *Prosecutor v. Brima, Kamara, Kanu*, Case No. SCSL-04-16-T, Decision on the Prosecution Motion for Judicial Notice and Admission of Evidence, 25 October 2005, paras 69-70; *Prosecutor v. Brima, Kamara, Kanu*, Case No. SCSL-04-16-T, Decision on Prosecution Tender for Admission into Evidence of Information Contained in Notice Pursuant to Rule 92*bis*, 18 November 2005.

mation" – assertions of fact (but not opinion) made in documents or electronic communications – if such facts are relevant and their reliability is "susceptible of confirmation". This phraseology was chosen to make clear that proof of reliability is not a condition of admission: all that is required is that the information should be *capable* of corroboration in due course. It is for the trial chamber to decide whether the information comes in a form, or is of a kind, that is "susceptible to confirmation". It follows, of course, from the fact that its reliability is "susceptible of confirmation", that it is also susceptible of being disproved, or so seriously called into question that the court will place no reliance upon it.

27. Rule 92*bis* permits facts that are not beyond dispute to be presented to the court in a written or visual form that will require evaluation in due course. A party which fails in an application to have a fact judicially noticed under Rule 94(A) may nonetheless be able to introduce into evidence the sources upon which it has relied under 92*bis* and at the end of the trial the court may well conclude that the fact has been proved beyond reasonable doubt. The weight and reliability of such "information" admitted via Rule 92*bis* will have to be assessed in light of all the evidence in the case.

---

[1] The amendment was adopted on 7 March 2003.

> **Rule 94: Judicial Notice**
> *(amended 1 August 2003)*
>
> (A) A Chamber shall not require proof of facts of common knowledge but shall take judicial notice thereof.
>
> (B) At the request of a party or of its own motion, a Chamber, after hearing the parties, may decide to take judicial notice of adjudicated facts or documentary evidence from other proceedings of the Special Court relating to the matter at issue in the current proceedings.

TRIAL CHAMBER DECISIONS

- **Rule 94: Judicial Notice – General Principles**

R94-TC-1

o *Prosecutor v. Norman, Fofana, Kondewa*, No. SCSL-04-14-PT, Decision on Prosecution's Motion for Judicial Notice and Admission of Evidence, 2 June 2004, para. 15, 18-20:[158]

> 15. This Motion invokes the jurisdiction of this Court with respect to the application of one of the law's oldest doctrines, namely the doctrine of judicial notice. To underscore the universality of the doctrine, it is important to note that though the doctrine, as is understood today, can be traced back to its common law origins, yet it has received recognition in some civil law jurisdictions but not in others.[(1)] It is imperative, therefore, preliminarily, for the court to expound on the nature and scope of the doctrine nationally and internationally as a basis for examining the merits of the Motion.
>
> [...]
>
> 18. Judicial notice is "the means by which a court may take as proven certain facts without hearing evidence.[(2)] The principle underlying the doctrine of judicial notice has been variously stated. It was clearly articulated by the English Court of Appeal in the recent case of *Mullen v. Hackney London Borough Council*[(3)] in these terms:
>
>> "It is well established that the courts may take judicial notice of various matters when they are notorious or clearly established, or susceptible of demonstration by reference

---

[158] See *Prosecutor v. Sesay, Kallon, Gbao*, Case No. SCSL-04-15-PT, Decision on Prosecution's Motion for Judicial Notice and Admission of Evidence, 24 June 2004, para. 26, 29-32.

to a readily obtainable and authoritative source that evidence of their existence is unnecessary (see Phipson on Evidence, 14th edn., 1990 CL 2/06)."

Continuing, the Court noted:

"Generally, matters directed by statute, or which have been so noticed by the well-established practice or precedents of the Court, must be recognized by the judges; but beyond this, they have a wide discretion and may notice much which they cannot be required to notice. The matters noticeable may include facts which are in issue or relevant to the issue; and the notice is in some cases conclusive and in others merely prima facie and rebuttable (see Phipson Ch2/07)."

Concluding, the Court remarked:

"Moreover, a judge may rely on his own local knowledge where he does so properly and within reasonable limits". This judicial function appears to be acceptable where "the type of knowledge is of a quite general character and is not liable to be barred by specific individual characteristics of the individual case." This test allows a judge to use what might be called "special" (or local) general knowledge (see Phipson Ch. 1/09)."

19. As to its scope in English law, courts are enjoined to be cautious in treating a factual conclusion as obvious, even though the man in the street would unhesitatingly hold it to be so.[4] It is also the law that judges and juries may, in arriving at their decisions, use their general information and that knowledge of the common affairs of life which men of ordinary intelligence possess, they may not act on their own private knowledge or belief regarding the facts of the particular case.[5]

20. By way of comparison, the American version of the doctrine bears significant juridical affinity to the English model. At the federal level, judicial notice is covered by either Rule 44.1 of the **Federal Rules of Civil Procedure** or Rule 26.1 of the **Federal Rules of Criminal Procedure**. Under these provisions, an American court can take judicial notice of a fact if it is "not subject to reasonable dispute" and falls within one of two categories: (a) if it is "generally known within the territorial jurisdiction of the trial court" or (b) if it is "capable of accurate and ready determination by resort to sources whose accuracy cannot reasonably be questioned". Federal Rule 201 cover is limited in scope and governs only "adjudicative facts".

---

[1] See an instructive article on the subject entitled: "Judicial Notice in International Criminal Law: A Reconciliation of Potential, Peril and Precedent" by

James G. Stewart in *International Criminal Law Review* 3, 2003, pp. 245-274. See also a Paper entitled *"Presumptions and Judicial Notice"* by Michael A. Patterson and Edward J. Walters Jr., Baton Rouge Bar Association, 1998 Bench Bar Conference, Alabama. One example of a civil law system adoption of the doctrine is Section 244(3) of the **German Criminal Procedural Code** which promulgates thus: *"An application to take evidence shall be rejected if the taking of such evidence is inadmissible. In all other cases, an application to take evidence may be rejected only if the taking of such evidence is superfluous because the matter is common knowledge, if the fact to be proved is irrelevant to the decision or has already been proved..."*. Article 90 of the recently adopted **Russian Penal Code** also deals with the theme of previously adjudicated facts. By contrast, the **Austrian Penal Code 1975**, does not embody any provision recognising the doctrine of judicial notice presumably due to the existence of the inquisitorial system which envisages a strong role for the judge in the process of gathering evidence, especially the investigative judge in pre-trial proceedings, which do not allow the parties to request that judicial notice be taken of facts (See Federal Law Gazette, no 631/1975 as amended by the Federal Law Gazette 15/2004). Also the **Slovenian Criminal Procedure** Act does not recognise the doctrine of judicial notice (See Zakon o Kazenskem Postopku, Ur.1 RS st 116/2003).
(2) The Concise Oxford Dictionary of Law, 2nd ed. 1992 at 223; see also Black's Law Dictionary, 7th ed. 1999 at 851.
(3) *Mullen v. Hackney London Borough Council*, [1997] 1WLR 1103.
(4) *Carter v. Eastbourne*, B.C. 164 J.P. 233 DC.
(5) *R. v. Sutton* (1816) 4 M. & S. 532.

- **Rule 94: Judicial Notice – Purpose**

R94-TC-2

o *Prosecutor v. Norman, Fofana, Kondewa*, No. SCSL-04-14-PT, Decision on Prosecution's Motion for Judicial Notice and Admission of Evidence, 2 June 2004, para. 21:[159]

21. In the context of international criminal law, it has been observed that the doctrine "has had a significant but unhappy existence".[1] Despite this profile of the doctrine in international criminal law, its importance in the field is unequivocally acknowledged to be that of significantly expediting trials.[2] One such viewpoint is that "the failure to exercise [judicial notice] tends to smother trials with technicality and monstrously lengthens them out".[3]

(1) See Stewart, supra note 17, p. 245.
(2) *Id.*, p. 245.
(3) See Thayer, I, *Preliminary Treatise on Evidence*, 809 (1898) cited in Stewart, supra note 17.

[159] See *Prosecutor v. Sesay, Kallon, Gbao*, Case No. SCSL-04-15-PT, Decision on Prosecution's Motion for Judicial Notice and Admission of Evidence, 24 June 2004, para. 33.

- **Rule 94: Judicial Notice – Judicially Noticeable Facts**

R94-TC-3
o *Prosecutor v. Norman, Fofana, Kondewa*, No. SCSL-04-14-PT, Decision on Prosecution's Motion for Judicial Notice and Admission of Evidence, 2 June 2004, para. 24:[160]

> 24. As to its scope, the Chamber takes the view that, from a plain and literal construction of Rule 94 of the Rules, the said Rule authorises either the Trial or Appeals Chamber to take judicial notice of three (3) categories of facts: (i) facts of common knowledge, (ii) adjudicated facts from other proceedings before the Court, and (iii) documentary evidence from other proceedings before the Court. The obligation is mandatory. As was stated in the *Semanza* Decision which this Court applies persuasively as being logical and consistent with the plain meaning and intendment of the Rule, the rationale behind the doctrine is twofold: (i) to expedite the trial by dispensing with the need to submit formally proof on issues that are patently indisputable, and (ii) to foster consistency and uniformity of decisions on factual issues where diversity in factual findings would be unfair.[(1)]
>
> ---
>
> [(1)] *Semanza* Decision, supra note 4, para. 20. See also *Prosecutor v. Simic et al.*, Decision on the pre-trial motion by the Prosecution requesting the Trial Chamber to take judicial notice of the international character of the conflict in Bosnia-Herzegovina, 25 March 1999, p. 3: "The purpose of judicial notice under Rule 94 is judicial economy . . . and . . . a balance should be struck between judicial economy and the right of the accused to a fair trial".

- **Rule 94: Judicial Notice – "Facts of Common Knowledge"**

R94-TC-4
o *Prosecutor v. Norman, Fofana, Kondewa*, No. SCSL-04-14-PT, Decision on Prosecution's Motion for Judicial Notice and Admission of Evidence, 2 June 2004, para. 25-29:[161]

> 25. Evidently, in the Chamber's opinion, Rule 94(A) of the Rules does require judicial cognisance of only facts which rise to a threshold level of "common knowledge", which interpretation of the rule is clearly supported by case-law authorities from ICTY and ICTR, two such decisions being rendered in the cases of *Prosecutor v. Tadic*[(1)] and *Prosecutor v. Ntagerura*

---

[160] See *Prosecutor v. Sesay, Kallon, Gbao*, Case No. SCSL-04-15-PT, Decision on Prosecution's Motion for Judicial Notice and Admission of Evidence, 24 June 2004, para. 36.

[161] See *Prosecutor v. Sesay, Kallon, Gbao*, Case No. SCSL-04-15-PT, Decision on Prosecution's Motion for Judicial Notice and Admission of Evidence, 24 June 2004, paras. 37-41.

et al.,[2] which this Chamber finds to be logical and consistent with the plain and literal meaning of the rule and its purpose, and will therefore apply persuasively.

26. As a matter of statutory significance, the Chamber finds that the expression "common knowledge" has been, and continues to be, the subject of subtle legal interpretation. Instructively, in the *Semanza* Decision,[3] the Trial Chamber took the view that the phrase includes facts ". . . so notorious, or clearly established or susceptible to determination by reference to readily obtainable and authoritative sources that evidence of their existence is unnecessary." Professor Bassiouni and Manikas have also suggested that the interpretation of "facts of common knowledge" does cover and extend to all "those facts which are not subject to reasonable dispute, including common or universally known facts, such as general facts of history, generally known geographical facts and the laws of nature."[4]

27. The Chamber further notes that despite the exacting requirement that facts must rise to a level of "common knowledge" to be judicially noticed, yet there is authority for the proposition that "a proposition need not to be universally accepted in order to qualify as common knowledge",[5] implying that courts may take judicial notice of facts that are not scientifically provable or beyond all dispute under Rule 94(A) of the Rules.[6]

28. In the Chamber's view, another key principle for which the *Semanza* Decision is authority as to the scope of Rule 94(A) of the Rules relates to the issue of to whom a fact or proposition must commonly be known to qualify for judicial cognisance. On this issue, the Court had this to say:

> ". . . 'common knowledge' encompasses those facts that are generally known within a tribunal's jurisdiction or capable of accurate and ready determination by resort to sources whose accuracy cannot be called in question."[7]

29. By logical deduction, in the Chamber's estimation as a matter of statutory construction, commonly known but inaccurate facts cannot be judicially noticed within the meaning and intendment of Rule 94(A) of the Rules. Therefore, based on the reasoning in the *Semanza* Decision, once a Court makes a preliminary determination that a fact is one of common knowledge within a court's jurisdiction, it must then proceed to a judicial evaluation of whether the fact merits the characterization of one that is "reasonably indisputable".

---

[1] I-94-1-AR72, Transcripts of Hearing on Interlocutory Appeal on Jurisdictional Challenge, 7 September 1995 at p. 108: "the Tribunal *must* in the interests of fairness take judicial notice of notorious facts".

[2] ICTR-99-46-T, 4 July 2002, Oral Decision, p. 9: Accordingly the Chamber must, pursuant to the provisions of Rules 94(A), take judicial notice of this fact of common knowledge."

(3) *Semanza* Decision, supra note 4, para. 25.
(4) *The Law of International Criminal Tribunal for the former Yugoslavia*, New York: Transnational Publishers Inc, 1996 (cited with approval in the *Semanza* Decision).
(5) *Semanza* Decision, supra note 4, para. 31.
(6) Stewart, supra note 17, p. 249.
(7) *Semanza* Decision, supra note 4, para. 23.

APPEALS CHAMBER DECISIONS

- **Rule 94: Judicial Notice – Purpose**

R94-AC-1

o *Prosecutor v. Fofana*, Case No. SCSL-04-14-AR73, Decision on Appeal Against "Decision on Prosecution's Motion for Judicial Notice and Admission of Evidence", 16 May 2005, para. 22-24:

22. The doctrine of judicial notice has been said to serve two main purposes:[1]

a) to expedite the trial by dispensing with the need to submit formal proof on issues that are patently indisputable; and

b) to foster consistency and uniformity of decisions on factual issues where diversity in factual findings would be unfair.

23. It was stated in *Semanza* that:

'It is appropriate to apply the doctrine of judicial notice in the context of this case in some of the instances requested by the Prosecutor because to do so will ensure the Accused a fair trial without undue delay rather than one unnecessarily drawn out by the introduction of evidence on matters which are patently of common knowledge in the territorial area of the Tribunal and reasonably indisputable.'[2]

It has also been stated by an ICTY Trial Chamber that: 'The purpose of judicial notice under Rule 94 is judicial economy ... and ... a balance should be struck between judicial economy and the right of the accused to a fair trial'.[3]

24. The Charter of the International Military Tribunal at Nuremberg as well contained a provision on judicial notice in Article 21 which reads as follows:

Article 21: The Tribunal shall not require proof of facts of common knowledge but shall take judicial notice thereof. It shall also take judicial notice of official governmental documents and reports of the United Nations, including the acts and documents of the committees set up in the various allied countries for the investigation of war crimes, and of records and findings of military or other Tribunals of any of the United Nations.

⁽¹⁾ *Semanza* Decision, para. 20.
⁽²⁾ *Semanza* Decision, para. 46.
⁽³⁾ *Prosecutor v. Simic et al.*, Case No IT-95-9-PT, Decision on the Pre-trial Motion by the Prosecution Requesting the Trial Chamber to take judicial notice of the international character of the conflict in Bosnia-Herzegovina, 25 March 1999, p. 3.

- **Rule 94: Judicial Notice – "Facts of Common Knowledge"**

R94-AC-2

o *Prosecutor v. Fofana*, Case No. SCSL-04-14-AR73, Decision on Appeal Against "Decision on Prosecution's Motion for Judicial Notice and Admission of Evidence", 16 May 2005, para. 20-21, 35-36:[162]

20. In order to establish the meaning of "facts of common knowledge", the Trial Chamber relied on the ICTR decision in *Semanza*, which dealt extensively with facts of common knowledge following a Prosecution request that the Trial Chamber take judicial notice of:

'a panoply of facts, which collectively may fairly be characterized as socio-political historical background facts relating to the existence of 'genocide', 'armed conflict', and 'widespread and systematic attacks' against the Tutsi civilian population in Rwanda during the months of April through July, 1994.'[(1)]

21. In the *Semanza* Decision, relied upon by both Prosecution and Defence in this Appeal, 'facts of common knowledge' were interpreted to mean 'those facts which are not subject to reasonable dispute including, common or universally known facts, such as general facts of history, generally known geographical facts and the law of nature'.[(2)] The Trial Chamber also held that common knowledge encompassed "those facts that are generally known within a tribunal's territorial jurisdiction".[(3)] Therefore, '[u]nder the rubric of matters of common knowledge, a court may generally take judicial notice of matters so notorious, or clearly established or susceptible to determination by reference to readily obtainable and authoritative sources that evidence of their existence is unnecessary.'[(4)]

[...]

---

[162] See also *Prosecutor v. Brima, Kamara, Kanu*, Case No. SCSL-04-16-T, Decision on the Prosecution Motion for Judicial Notice and Admission of Evidence, 25 October 2005, para. 14, 18, 23, 30.

35. The existence of an armed conflict is an important factual or contextual element in all war crimes by definition. This is reflected in the wording of Articles 3 and 4 of the Statute, as it is in the equivalent provisions in the Statutes of the ICTY and ICTR. In the *Simic* case, the Trial Chamber found that Rule 94 was intended to cover facts and not legal consequences inferred from them so that the trial chamber could take only judicial notice of factual findings and not of a legal characterisation as such.[5]

36. The relevant test therefore comes back first to the question of whether these facts are beyond reasonable dispute and can be described as facts of common knowledge. According to principle, this requires an examination of whether the fact is generally known within the territorial jurisdiction of this Court or whether it is capable of accurate and ready determination by resort to sources whose accuracy cannot reasonably be called into question.[6] A judge may rely on his own local knowledge, which is the case here, especially, as the SCSL is located in Sierra Leone.[7] The fact that there was an armed conflict in Sierra Leone is a 'notorious fact of history'. Furthermore, in the context of Sierra Leone these facts cannot be subject to *reasonable* dispute taking into consideration the general knowledge of the population. A multitude of victims with mutilations which cannot stem from anything other than an armed conflict allows for an accurate and ready determination of this fact by immediately obtainable evidence. To contest the fact that there was an armed conflict is frivolous. The armed conflict even provided the context in which the Special Court was created to try those who bear the greatest responsibility for crimes committed.

---

[1] *Prosecutor v. Semanza*, Case No. ICTR-97-20-T, Decision on the Prosecutor's Motion for Judicial Notice and Presumption of Facts Pursuant to Rules 94 and 54, 3 November 2000, para. 4 ("*Semanza* Decision").
[2] *Semanza* Decision, para. 23.
[3] *Semanza* Decision.
[4] *Semanza* Decision, para. 25.
[5] *Prosecutor v. Simic*, Case No. IT-95-9-PT, Decision on Pre-Trial Motion by the Prosecution Requesting the Trial Chamber to take Judicial Notice of the International Character of the Conflict in Bosnia-Herzegovina, 25 March 1999, p. 5.
[6] *Semanza* Decision, para. 24.
[7] *Mullen v. Hackney Borough Council*, [1997] 2 All ER 906.

- **Rule 94: Judicial Notice – Facts of Common Knowledge Cannot Be Challenged**

R94-AC-3

o *Prosecutor v. Fofana*, Case No. SCSL-04-14-AR73, Decision on Appeal Against "Decision on Prosecution's Motion for Judicial Notice and Admission of Evidence", 16 May 2005, para. 30-32:[163]

> 30. It is helpful at this point to examine the legal implications of judicial notice. The ICTR Trial Chamber in *Semanza* stated that judicially noticed facts serve as conclusive proof of those facts and the taking of judicial notice "ends the evidentiary inquiry." The Chamber went on to say that:
>
>> To permit the Defence to submit evidence in rebuttal of the judicially noticed facts would undermine the very nature of the doctrine which is aimed at dispensing with formal proofs for matters that are of common knowledge and are reasonably indisputable.[(1)]
>
> As a result, the Chamber held that it did not need to determine the question of whether it would accept presumptions of the same facts, which had been pleaded as an alternative by the Prosecution in that case.
>
> 31. The Appeals Chamber notes that ICTY trial chambers have taken two approaches. The first is that once a fact has been judicially noticed this ends the evidentiary inquiry and the fact is taken as conclusively proven. The second is that taking judicial notice of a fact means that the moving party does not have to present formal proof of that fact at trial, and shifts the burden of proof to the opposing party to disprove the fact. The 'burden shifting approach' has been adopted specifically in relation to Rule 94(B) as opposed to Rule 94(A). Indeed, it does not seem to be compatible with the concept that facts capable of being judicially noticed are beyond reasonable dispute. If the possibility of a reasonable dispute exists then the fact should not be judicially noticed. In the *Krajisnik* decision, the Trial Chamber stated that judicial notice of "*facts of common knowledge*" under Rule 94(A) normally implies that such facts *cannot* be challenged during trial.[(2)]

---

[163] See also *Prosecutor v. Brima, Kamara, Kanu*, Case No. SCSL-04-16-T, Decision on the Prosecution Motion for Judicial Notice and Admission of Evidence, 25 October 2005, para. 20.

32. This Chamber comes to the conclusion that facts of common knowledge under Rule 94(A) cannot be challenged during trial and that legal conclusions as well as facts which constitute legal findings cannot be judicially noticed.

(1) *Semanza* para. 41.
(2) *Krajisnik* Decision, para. 16.

- **Rule 94: Judicial Notice – Official Documents**

R94-AC-4
o *Prosecutor v. Fofana*, Decision on Appeal Against "Decision on Prosecution's Motion for Judicial Notice and Admission of Evidence", 16 May 2005, para. 49:

49. Whether or not the source of a document is a political body, and more particularly whether that body was party to the establishment of the Special Court, is of no relevance. There is no legal reason for any difference in applying the same test to all documents. It must be up to the Trial Chamber to determine whether the content satisfies the test of "beyond reasonable dispute". It therefore might be possible that some factual assertions in a UN Security Council Resolution can be judicially noticed and others cannot. The question of whether a fact stated in a Security Council resolution is to be judicially noticed will ultimately depend on whether it is capable of reasonable dispute. It follows that there is no point in judicially noticing the contents of a document as such. Facts asserted within Security Council Resolutions, Secretary General Reports and other reports by reputable organizations may be the subject of judicial notice. However, this cannot be achieved by noticing the contents of the whole resolution or report, which may contain hundreds of factual assertions, mostly irrelevant. The proper procedure would be to extract from the resolutions or reports the factual propositions which a party wants the Court to notice. It will then be for the Trial Chamber, after considering any defence material, to decide whether the extracted proposition really is incontrovertible.

Rule 94*bis*: Testimony of Expert Witnesses
(amended 7 March 2003)

(A) Notwithstanding the provisions of Rule 66(A), Rule 73*bis*(B)(iv)(b) and Rule 73*ter*(B)(iii)(b) of the present Rules, the full statement of any expert witness called by a party shall be disclosed to the opposing party as early as possible and shall be filed with the Trial Chamber not less than twenty-one days prior to the date on which the expert is expected to testify.

(B) Within fourteen days of filing of the statement of the expert witness, the opposing party shall file a notice to the Trial Chamber indicating whether:

   (i) It accepts the expert witness statement; or
   (ii) It wishes to cross-examine the expert witness.

(C) If the opposing party accepts the statement of the expert witness, the statement may be admitted into evidence by the Trial Chamber without calling the witness to testify in person.

TRIAL CHAMBERS DECISIONS

- **Rule 94*bis*: Expert Witnesses – Definition**

R94*bis*-TC-1

o *Prosecutor v. Norman, Fofana, Kondewa*, Case No. SCSL-04-14-T, Decision on Prosecution Request for Leave to Call Additional Witnesses and for Orders for Protective Measures, 21 June 2005:

> **CONSIDERING** that as Rule 94*bis* of the Rules does not provide a definition of an expert witness, the Chamber accepts the definition of an "expert" as more fully described in the case law of the ICTY to mean:
>
>> A person whom by virtue of some specialised knowledge, skill or training can assist the trier of fact to understand or determine an issue in dispute.[1]
>
> [...]
>
> **CONSIDERING** that Colonel Iron can be properly characterised as an expert, since his specialised military education and 25 years of professional military experience, including his field experience, as documented in his CV, have provided him with

sufficient training and specialised knowledge to qualify him as a military expert;

(1) *Prosecutor v. Stanislav Galic*, IT-98-29-T, Decision Concerning the Expert Witnesses Ewa Tabeau and Richard Philipps, 3 July 2002, p. 2.

R94*bis*-TC-2

o *Prosecutor v. Brima, Kamara, Kanu*, Case No. SCSL-04-16-T, Decision on Prosecution Request for Leave to Call an Additional Witness (Zainab Hawa Bangura) Pursuant to Rule 73*bis*(E), and on Joint Defence Notice to Inform the Trial Chamber of its Position vis-à-vis the Proposed Expert Witness (Mrs. Bangura) Pursuant to Rule 94*bis*, 5 August 2005, para. 23, 25, 31:

23. On the issue of Mrs. Bangura's qualification as an expert on the subject of forced marriage during the Sierra Leonean conflict, neither the Statute of the Special Court nor the Rules contain a definition of the term "expert". However, Article 1 (f) of the Headquarters Agreement Between the Republic of Sierra Leone and the Special Court for Sierra Leone contains the following definition:

"(f) 'Expert' means a person referred to as such in Article 15 of the Agreement establishing the Special Court and appearing at the instance of the Special Court, a suspect or an accused to present testimony based on special knowledge, skills, experience or training."

[...]

25. The purpose of this Rule (which is identical to Rule 94*bis* of the ICTR Rules of Procedure and Evidence) is to expedite trial proceedings by arranging for early exchange of expert reports to facilitate identification of the issues in dispute and to identify the need or otherwise to call the expert witnesses to testify in person.(1) Although the Rule does not contain a definition of "*an expert*" or what qualifies as "*expert evidence or opinion*" international tribunals have had occasion to interpret and apply similar provisions, thereby greatly contributing to the jurisprudence in this area. The International Criminal Tribunal for the Former Republic of Yugoslavia (ICTY) has defined an expert as "*a person whom by virtue of some specialised knowledge, skill or training, can assist the court to understand or determine an issue in dispute.*"(2) Similarly the International Criminal Tribunal for Rwanda (ICTR) has observed that "*the role of an expert is to assist the Chamber in understanding the context in which the events took place. The expert must possess a relevant specialised knowledge acquired*

through education, experience or training in his proposed field of expertise."[3] The ICTY has further held that *"an expert witness is expected to give his or her expert opinion in full transparency of the established or assumed facts he or she relies upon and of the methods used when applying his or her knowledge, experience or skills to form his or her opinion."*[4] Lastly the ICTY has held that *"the admission of evidence should clearly be distinguished from the weight and probative value that will eventually be given to each piece of evidence. The weight to be attributed to an expert witness statement will be appreciated by the Trial Chamber at the end of the trial and in light of all the evidence adduced."*[5]

[...]

31. Regarding Mrs. Bangura's qualifications as "an expert" or lack thereof, we adopt the accepted qualitative definition that "an expert must possess relevant specialised knowledge acquired through education, experience or training in the proposed field of expertise" and the defined role of an expert as being "to assist the Chamber to understand or determine an issue in dispute and the context in which the events took place." We note and accept the Prosecution submissions that despite Mrs. Bangura's educational background being in the field of insurance, her extensive experience is a material factor that qualifies her as an expert with relevant specialised knowledge on the issue of forced marriage during the Sierra Leone conflict. We note from Mrs. Bangura's curriculum vitae (Annex A) that as Coordinator and co-founder of the organisation known as "Campaign for Good Governance" (CGG) she has extensive experience in monitoring human rights abuses across Sierra Leone including police stations, rebel-controlled areas, and refugee camps for returning women and internally displaced persons. She also has experience in documentation of human rights violations across Sierra Leone for over five years and in providing care and support to victims of domestic and sexual violence, which experience the Prosecution submits is a relevant factor in determining her expertise on the subject of "forced marriages during the Sierra Leone conflict". We also note the acknowledgment in paragraph 1.1 of Mrs. Bangura's report that "her testimony is based on her experience as a campaigner for women's and civil rights in Sierra Leone, upon personal experience in dealing with women victims of forced marriages and also upon extensive secondary and primary data." More importantly, we note and accept the Prosecution submissions that Mrs. Bangura's testimony will "assist the Chamber to understand or determine the issues of sexual violence and forced marriages during the conflict in Sierra Leone and the context in which the events took place". In the premises we find no merit in the Defence objection to Mrs. Bangura's qualifications and hold that she possesses relevant experience and that the Prosecution is entitled to call her as an

expert witness and to disclose her report to the Defence pursuant to the provisions of Rule 94*bis* of the Rules.

---

(1) *International Criminal Practice* by Jones and Powles, 3rd Edition, para. 8.5.736.
(2) *The Prosecutor v. Stanislav Galic*, IT-98-29-T, Decision Concerning the Expert Witness Ewa Tabeau and Richard Philips, 3 July 2002; and *The Prosecutor v. Stanislav Galic*, IT-98-29-T, Decision on the Expert Witness Statements Submitted by the Defence, 27 January 2003.
(3) *The Prosecutor v. Casimir Bizimungu, et al.*, Case No. ICTR-99-50-T, Oral Decision on Qualification of Prosecution Expert Sebahire Deo Mbonyikebe, 2 May 2005; and *The Prosecutor v. Aloys Simba*, Case No. ICTR-01-76-I, Decision on Defence Motion to Disqualify Expert Witness Alison Des Forges, and to Exclude Her Report, 14 July 2004.
(4) *The Prosecutor v. Galic*, IT-98-29-T, Decision Concerning the Expert Witness Ewa Tabeau and Richard Philips, 3 July 2002.
(5) *The Prosecutor v. Stanislav Galic*, IT-98-29-T, Decision on the Expert Witness Statements Submitted by the Defence, 27 January 2003.

- **Rule 94*bis*: Expert Witness – Scope of Testimony**

R94*bis*-TC-3 o *Prosecutor v. Norman, Fofana, Kondewa*, Case No. SCSL-2004-14-T, Decision on Prosecution Request for Leave to Call Additional Witnesses and for Orders for Protective Measures, 21 June 2005:

NOTING further with approval the comment of the ICTR Trial Chamber in *Akayesu* case, where the Chamber stated that an expert's testimony is "testimony intended to enlighten the Judges on specific issues of a technical nature, requiring special knowledge in a specific field"[1] and as stated in *May and Wierda*:

> The purpose of expert evidence is to provide a court with information that is outside its ordinary experience and knowledge. Indeed, a Trial Chamber should refrain from acting as its own expert in cases where expert evidence is appropriate.[2]

[...]

CONSIDERING that as a military expert, Colonel Iron is likely to assist the Chamber in understanding and determining the issues relating to the structure of the CDF, its military organization, the chain of command and control of the CDF;

CONSIDERING that Colonel Iron will not give testimony on the criminal liability of the Accused[3] and in this respect, the Chamber concurs with the finding of the ICTY Trial Chamber in *Hadzihasanovic* case, where it was held that:

[...] an expert witness may not be authorised to offer his opinion on the criminal liability of the accused, a matter which falls within the sole jurisdiction of the Chamber at the close of the trial [...]

[...]

[...] an expert may provide the judges with any information useful to an evaluation of the facts, particularly, for a military expert, as regards the military structures, chain of command and disciplinary procedures of an army, and the military responsibility deriving from such provisions [...][4]

---

[1] *Prosecutor v. Akayesu*, ICTR-96-4-T, Decision on a Defence Motion for the Appearance of an Accused as an Expert Witness, 9 March 1998; *see also* Richard May and Marieke Wierda, *International Criminal Evidence*: Transnational 2002, ("*May and Wierda*"), p. 202, para. 6.88 (footnotes omitted).
[2] *May and Wierda*, p. 199, para. 6.83.
[3] *See* Response, para. 17.
[4] *Prosecutor v. Hadzihasanovic and Kubura*, IT-01-47-T, Decision on Report of Prosecution Expert Klaus Reinhardt, 11 February 2004, paras. 11 and 13 (footnotes omitted).

- **Rule 94*bis*: Expert Witness – Protective Measures**

R94*bis*-TC-4   o *Prosecutor v. Norman, Fofana, Kondewa*, Case No. SCSL-04-14-T, Decision on Prosecution Request for Leave to Call Additional Witnesses and for Orders for Protective Measures, 21 June 2005:

MINDFUL OF the Chamber's previous ruling in this case that "the process of granting protection to witnesses entails in each specific circumstance a balance between the 'full respect' for the rights of the Accused and 'due regard' for the protection of victims and witnesses";[1]

CONSIDERING that the nature of Child Soldier Witness' current employment and the fact that both the witness herself and her current employer expressed strong concerns that if she and her testimony were exposed to the public, it would give rise to a significant threat to her personal safety;[2]

CONSIDERING further that both Child Soldier Witness' previous and current employers have made her anonymity a condition to the release of her testimony and that her previous employer stipulated that another condition for the release of her testimony would be to hold a closed session for this witness;[3]

CONSIDERING that exceptional circumstances do exist in this case for granting protective measures for the Child Soldier Witness and that "a measure of hearing the testimony in closed session is only granted to a certain category of the witnesses and is based on the principle of protection of victims and witnesses where the interests of justice so dictate"[4] and that it is "an extraordinary protective measure that will only be granted where it is shown that there is a real risk to the witness and/or his or her family and that their privacy or security will be threatened";[5]

PURSUANT TO Rules 54, 66(A)(ii), 69(A) and (C), 73*bis*(E), 75(A) and (B) and 94*bis* of the Rules;

THE CHAMBER GRANTS THE MOTION.

---

[1] Decision on Prosecution Motion for Modification of Protective Measures for Witnesses, dated the 8th of June, 2004, para. 27.
[2] Annex A.
[3] Annex A, para. 6.
[4] Ruling on Motion for Modification of Protective Measures for Witnesses, dated the 18th of November, 2004, para. 49.
[5] *See, inter alia, Prosecutor v. Sam Hinga Norman, Moinina Fofana, Allieu Kondewa*, Order on an Application by the Prosecution to Hold a Closed Session Hearing of Witness TF2-223, 27 October 2004.

- **Rule 94*bis*(A): Expert Witness – Timely Disclosure of Statement**

R94*bis*-TC-5

o *Prosecutor v. Norman, Fofana, Kondewa*, Case No. SCSL-04-14-T, Decision on Prosecution Request for Leave to Call Additional Witnesses and for Orders for Protective Measures, 21 June 2005:

NOTING that the Defence were aware, at least since the 1st of November, 2004, of the Prosecution' intention to call additional experts[1] and therefore, the element of surprise or prejudice in this instance cannot be entertained;

CONSIDERING that due diligence was exercised by the Prosecution in complying with their disclosure obligations, as the name of the military expert and a summary of his professional background, have been disclosed to the Defence since the 7th of June, 2004,[2] and Colonel Iron's expert report was filed on the 24th of May, 2005;

CONSIDERING that, although the Prosecution did not disclose to the Defence the name of the Child Soldier Witness until the 8th of February, 2005, for which they provided satisfactory explanation,[3] the Prosecution exercised due diligence in fulfilling their disclosure obligations and filed her expert report on the 24th of May, 2005;

NOTING that various Trial Chambers of the ICTR have adopted "a liberal approach" to the admission of expert testimony[(4)] and concluded that "[t]here is no exact deadline for disclosure" of an expert report;[(5)]

[(1)] At the Status Conference held on the 1st of November, 2004, the Chamber urged the Prosecution to disclose the identity of additional expert witnesses as soon as possible to avoid any prejudice to the Defence case; Transcript of the Status Conference of the 1st of November, 2004, pages 28-31.
[(2)] Second Annex A, Reply.
[(3)] As elaborated in the Second Annex A, Reply.
[(4)] *The Prosecutor v. Bagosora et al.*, ICTR-98-41-T, Decision on Motion for Exclusion of Expert Witness Statement of Filip Reyntjens, 28 September 2004, para. 8.
[(5)] *The Prosecutor v. Semanza*, ICTR-97-20-T, Decision on Defence Extremely Urgent Motion for Extension of Time and for an Order of Cooperation of the Government of Rwanda, 13 December 2001, para. 4.

- **Rule 94*bis*(A): Expert Witness – Disclosure of the Expert's Curriculum Vitae**

o *Prosecutor v. Norman, Fofana, Kondewa*, Case No. SCSL-2004-14-T, Order for Compliance of the Prosecution with Rule 94*bis*, 16 July 2004:[164]

CONSIDERING FURTHER that the Prosecution should provide the Trial Chamber and the Defence with the curriculum vitae of the expert witness, that includes his credentials, that qualify him as an expert, his specific field of expertise, and the purpose of his report, for the Defence to make a an informed response and for the Trial Chamber to consider the admissibility of the expert report;

- **Rule 94*bis*(B): Expert Witness – Purpose of the Notice**

o *Prosecutor v. Brima, Kamara, Kanu*, Case No. SCSL-2004-16-T, Decision on Prosecution Request for Leave to Call an Additional Witness (Zainab Hawa Bangura) Pursuant to Rule 73*bis*(E), and on Joint Defence Notice to Inform the Trial Chamber of its Position vis-à-vis the Proposed Expert Witness (Mrs Bangura) Pursuant to Rule 94*bis*, 5 August 2005, para. 30:

---

[164] See also *Prosecutor v. Norman, Fofana, Kondewa*, Case No. SCSL-04-14-T, Order to Prosecution to File Military Experts Curriculum Vitae, 24 February 2005; *Prosecutor v. Sesay, Kallon, Gbao*, Case No. SCSL-04-15-T, Order for Compliance of Prosecution with Rule 94*bis*, 9 March 2005.

30. We note that under the provisions of Rule 94*bis*(B) of the Rules a party opposing the filing of the statement of an expert witness has two options, namely (a) to notify the Trial Chamber that it accepts the expert witness statement, in which case the Trial Chamber may admit the statement without necessarily calling the witness to testify; or (b) to notify the Trial Chamber that it wishes to cross-examine the expert witness, in which case the witness will necessarily appear in court for purposes of cross-examination. There is no third option under the Rule whereby the Trial Chamber is permitted, at the request of the opposing party, to exclude or lock out an expert witness or her evidence, much less at this early stage when the witness has not yet testified. We note the Defence submissions that in their opinion, since Mrs. Bangura's educational background is not in sociology, anthropology, psychology, medicine or other related field but rather is in insurance, she is not qualified to give expert opinion on the subject of forced marriages. [. . .] It is our considered view that all the above concerns are matters that go to the weight and not admissibility of the evidence, and that can adequately be tested during cross-examination. The weight to be attributed to expert evidence will be determined by the Trial Chamber not at this stage but rather at the end of the trial and in light of all the evidence adduced. We also note that in the interests of justice and a fair trial, the Defence are themselves entitled not only to cross-examine Mrs. Bangura but also to submit expert findings to the contrary and to call their own expert witness or witnesses in their defence.

> **Rule 95: Exclusion of Evidence**
> *(amended 7 March 2003)*
>
> No evidence shall be admitted if its admission would bring the administration of justice into serious disrepute.

TRIAL CHAMBERS DECISIONS

- **Rule 95: Exclusion of Evidence – Hearsay Evidence**

R95-TC-1

o *Prosecutor v. Brima, Kamara, Kanu*, Case No. SCSL-04-16-T, Decision on Joint Defence Motion to Exclude All Evidence from Witness TF1-277 Pursuant to Rule 89(C) and/or Rule 95, 24 May 2005, para. 24:

> 24. We hold that the hearsay evidence given by the Witness is relevant evidence and is therefore admissible evidence under Rule 89(C). We find that the Defence has not made out a case for the exclusion of that evidence, let alone for the exclusion of the Witness's evidence in its entirety. Nor has anything been put before us which would justify the conclusion that the admission of the evidence would bring the administration of justice into serious disrepute pursuant to Rule 95. On the contrary, the evidence in our view is so clearly relevant that the judicial process would be brought into disrepute by excluding it.[1]

---

[1] *Prosecutor v. Sam Hinga Norman et al.*, Case No. SCSL-04-14-AR65, Fofana – Appeal against Decision Refusing Bail, 11 March 2005, para. 27.

> **Rule 98: Motion for Judgment of Acquittal**
> *(amended 14 May 2005)*
>
> If, after the close of the case for the prosecution, there is no evidence capable of supporting a conviction on one or more counts of the indictment, the Trial Chamber shall enter a judgment of acquittal on those counts.

TRIAL CHAMBERS DECISIONS

- **Rule 98: Motion for Judgment of Acquittal – Applicable Standard**

R98-TC-1
o *Prosecutor v. Norman, Fofana, Kondewa*, Case No. SCSL-04-14-T, Decision on Motions for Judgment of Acquittal Pursuant to Rule 98, 21 October 2005, para. 34-51, 53, 131:

A. APPLICABLE STANDARD UNDER RULE 98 OF THE RULES OF PROCEDURE AND EVIDENCE OF THE SPECIAL COURT

34. In our considered opinion, Rule 98 defines the standard for determining the merits or otherwise of a Motion for Judgment of Acquittal. Guided by the contextual approach to the rule, we do emphasize that in its plain and ordinary meaning, it is limited in scope in the sense that it does not envisage a judicial pronouncement on the guilt or the innocence of the Accused at this stage. What the Rule envisages as an appropriate legal standard, we do observe, is one that limits and restricts a tribunal only to a determination as to whether the evidence adduced by the Prosecution at the close of its case, is such as is legally capable of supporting a conviction on one or more of the counts in the Indictment.

35. In fact, in interpreting this new version of a simply drafted Rule and giving it its natural and ordinary meaning, the Chamber is of the opinion that the evidence adduced by the Prosecution does not, within its present context, need to attain the threshold of the required "proof beyond reasonable doubt" but rather, should only be such as is "capable of supporting a conviction." We stress here, and are of the opinion that the standard is not whether the evidence is such as "should" support a conviction, but rather, such as "could" support a conviction.

B. RULE 98 AND THE "PROOF BEYOND REASONABLE DOUBT" THRESHOLD

36. On the submission by Counsel for Kondewa that the standard of proof the Prosecution is supposed to meet and satisfy at this stage is that of "proof beyond reasonable doubt" as canvassed in the *Jelisic* case[1] which was referred to in the *Strugar* case, we are of the opinion that the proof beyond reasonable doubt standard can and should only be addressed at a later stage of the proceedings.

37. We say this because we are of the opinion, and do take the view, that in our quest at this stage to arrive at a determination as to whether the evidence so far adduced by the Prosecution is capable of supporting a conviction or not, we should not, at this stage, delve into examining factors that are considered as the real basis for justifying a finding of 'proof beyond reasonable doubt' such as an exhaustive analysis or examination of the quality and reliability of the evidence so far available in the records and even the credibility of the witnesses.

38. Indeed, although our decision to uphold or to dismiss the Motions for Judgment of Acquittal is necessarily based on our preliminary appreciation of the evidence so far available for purposes of determining whether such evidence is capable of supporting a conviction or not, we consider that the evaluation of the evidence, its reliability, as well as the credibility of the witnesses, should be kept in abeyance for a later stage, depending on the finding and particularly, on the attitude of the Defence, in the event of a dismissal of the Motion. It is only at the end of the case that we consider it appropriate to determine whether the Prosecution's case against the Accused has been established to the required standard, and this, of "proof beyond reasonable doubt", in order to justify a finding of guilt or a finding of not guilty, should the contrary be the case.

39. As stated in the *Kordic* case, when examining the purpose of Rule 98, it becomes clear that this procedure, at this stage of the Trial, is not to determine the guilt of the accused, which should be made at the end of the case, but instead, to rule on "whether the Prosecution has put forward a case sufficient to warrant the defence being called upon to answer it".[2]

40. Indeed, as was reiterated in the case of *Strugar*, and we quote:

> [...] A decision on Motion pursuant to Rule 98*bis* involves no evaluation of the guilt of the accused in the light of all the evidence in the case at that stage, nor any evaluation of the respective credit of witnesses or the strengths and weaknesses of contradictory or different

evidence, whether oral or documentary which is then before the Chamber.[3]

41. We would therefore, within the context of our Rule 98, reserve making at this stage, our finding on whether the "Proof Beyond Reasonable Doubt" threshold has indeed been attained. We consider that it is only at the close of the case for the Defence if we were ever to get to that stage, or alternatively, if the Defence, should we find that there is evidence capable of supporting a conviction on one or more of the counts, decide to exercise their legal rights to rest their case on that of the Prosecution.

42. Should any of these eventualities occur, it would then become necessary for us to proceed to the final stage of assessing the totality of the evidence so far adduced by the Prosecution in relation to the quality and reliability of the evidence, as well as the credibility of the Prosecution Witnesses, in order to determine whether it rises up to the standard threshold of having proved the guilt of the Accused "beyond reasonable doubt" to enable us to enter a verdict of guilty or to acquit on any or on all the counts, if the contrary turns out to be the case.

43. As the Appeals Chamber of the ICTY stated in the *Milosevic* case on this issue:

> Thus if, following a ruling that there is sufficient evidence to sustain a conviction on a particular charge, the Accused calls no evidence, it is perfectly possible for the Trial Chamber to acquit the Accused of that charge if, at the end of the case, it is not satisfied of his guilt beyond a reasonable doubt.[4]

44. In his oral submissions, Counsel for Kondewa, Mr. Charles Margai, as a new addition to his written submissions, argued that the Prosecution's evidence must, at that stage, attain the threshold of "proof beyond reasonable doubt" and that a failure of the evidence to attain that standard must necessarily give rise to the acquittal of his client on all the counts.

45. We are indeed of the opinion that for a Motion for Judgment of Acquittal to be upheld, the evidence led by the Prosecution at that stage of the proceedings, must be such that it could not be concluded, if that evidence is accepted, that the Accused has committed the offence or offences for which he is charged. This implies that from the totality of the evidence adduced by the Prosecution, there is, at that stage, no legal basis that warrants his being put to his defence on one or more of the offences for which he has been indicted even though, we would like to reiterate here, that this is not necessarily conclusive of the fact that he would, at the close of the case for the Defence, be convicted of any of those offences.

46. Put succinctly, as was stated by Trial Chamber II of the ICTY in the *Strugar* case:

> [. . .] The issue is often shortly stated as NOT being whether, on the evidence as it stands the accused *should* be convicted, but whether the accused *could* be convicted.[5]

47. We recall here that this decision was based on the provisions of Rule 98*bis* of the Rules of Procedure and Evidence of the ICTY adopted on the 19th of November 1999. It stipulated that the Trial Chamber shall order the entry of a judgment of acquittal "if it finds that the evidence is insufficient to sustain a conviction" on that or those charges. In fact, "insufficiency of evidence" to sustain a conviction as provided for in the ICTY Rules, is not different in context from there being "no evidence capable of supporting a conviction" as provided for in the Rules of the Special Court for Sierra Leone.

48. Applying the standard of "insufficiency of evidence" as provided for in the Rules of Procedure and Evidence of the ICTR, Trial Chamber III of that Tribunal, in their Decision in the case of *Kamuhanda*,[6] held that it was not satisfied that "the evidence is sufficient to sustain a conviction" on Count 1 which indicted the Accused for conspiracy to commit genocide. The Chamber, on the other hand, found "that the Prosecution has adduced sufficient evidence to sustain" a conviction on count 6 which alleged Crimes Against Humanity (Rape).

49. In the *Milosevic* Case, the Appeals Chamber of the ICTY had this to say on this issue of sufficiency and the test to be applied to make a determination as whether a Motion for Judgment of Acquittal pursuant to Rule 98 should be granted:

> The test whether there is evidence if, accepted, on which a Trial Chamber could convict, will be applied on the following bases:
>
> (1) Where there is evidence to sustain a charge, the Motion is to be allowed. Although Rule 98*bis* speaks of the sufficiency of evidence to sustain a conviction on a charge, the Trial Chamber has, in accordance with the practice of the Tribunal, considered the sufficiency of the evidence as it pertains to elements of a charge, whether set out in separate paragraphs or schedule items;
>
> (2) Where there is some evidence, but it is such that, taken at its highest, a Trial Chamber could not convict on it, the Motion is to be allowed. [. . .][7]

50. Consistent with the standard enunciated in the foregoing case law authorities, to the extent that they reinforce our view on the plain meaning of our Rule 98, we note that the key feature of the test is conceptually grounded on the idea of a judicial assessment of the capability of the evidence to support a conviction which would of course eventually entail a

concise evaluation of the counts in the indictment with a view to ascertaining whether there is patently no evidence in respect of any of them upon which a reasonable tribunal of fact could convict the Accused.

51. It follows therefore, that if the evidence available at the close of the case for the Prosecution, is not such as it "could" support a conviction in respect of one or more counts, a Decision of Acquittal should be entered on that or on those counts.

[...]

53. In view of the fact that the standard of proof, as we have held, for entering a Decision of Acquittal under Rule 98 is that there is no evidence capable of supporting a conviction on one or more counts, we would, in examining these details, consider very succinctly, the sufficiency of the evidence as it relates to each separate paragraph as charged in the various counts of the Indictment.

[...]

131. The Chamber is of the opinion that a determination of the Accused liability depends to a degree on the issues of fact and weight to be attached to the evidence, which require an assessment of the credibility and reliability of that evidence. These issues, however, do not arise for determination at this stage. The Chamber has, however, reviewed the evidence as it is relevant to the modes of participation of each Accused in the alleged crimes, and finds, for the purposes of the Rule 98 standard, that the Accused participated in each of the crimes charged in Counts 1 to 8 of the Indictment. The Chamber, therefore, is not in a position at this stage to dismiss any of the modes of liability as alleged in the Indictment and accordingly rejects the Defence Motions in this regard.

---

[1] *Prosecutor v. Jelisic*, Judgment, 5 July 2001, Appeals Chamber, para. 37.
[2] *Prosecutor v. Kordic*, Decision on Defence Motions for Judgement of Acquittal, 6 April 2000, Trial Chamber, para. 11.
[3] *Prosecutor v. Strugar*, Decision on Defence Motion Requesting Judgement of Acquittal Pursuant to Rule 98*bis*, 21 June 2004, Trial Chamber, para. 10.
[4] *Prosecutor v. Milosevic*, Decision on Motion for Judgement of Acquittal, 16 June 2004, Trial Chamber, para. 13 (6).
[5] *Prosecutor v. Strugar*, Decision on Defence Motion Requesting Judgement of Acquittal Pursuant to Rule 98*bis*, 21 June 2004, Trial Chamber, para. 11.
[6] *Prosecutor v. Kamuhanda*, ICTR-99-54A-T, 20 August 2002.
[7] *Prosecutor v. Milosevic*, Decision on Motion for Judgement of Acquittal, 16 June 2004, Trial Chamber, para. 13 (1)-(2).

- **Rule 98: Motion for Judgment of Acquittal – Procedure – Filing of Submissions**

R98-TC-2

o *Prosecutor v. Norman, Fofana, Kondewa*, Case No. SCSL-04-14-T, Scheduling Order on Filing Submissions by the Parties Should a Motion for Judgement of Acquittal Be Filed by Defence, 2 June 2005:

CONSIDERING that it is in the interests of justice and in keeping with the conduct of a fair and expeditious trial, for the Trial Chamber to issue guidelines for the filing of a Motion for Judgement of Acquittal at this time;

PURSUANT TO Rule 26*bis*, 54 and 98 of the Rules of Procedure and Evidence of the Special Court;

HEREBY ORDERS:

1. That the Defence Teams notify The Chamber and the Prosecution at the conclusion of the Prosecution case, whether they intend to submit a Motion for Acquittal;

2. In the event that any Defence Team intends to submit such a motion, they should file it in writing within three weeks from the date that the Prosecution case closes;

3. That the length of each defence motion shall not exceed fifty (50) pages in length;

4. That the Prosecution may file a response to any such motion within three weeks from the date of filing each Defence motion;

5. That the length of the Prosecution response to each Defence motion shall not exceed 50 pages in length;

6. That all filings by the parties should comply with the requirements of the Practice Direction;

7. That The Chamber will hear oral submissions and responses on the said motion on the 16th of September, 2005;

8. That the time allocated for the oral submissions to each Defence Team shall not exceed 30 minutes in length, and that the Prosecution accordingly should not exceed 30 minutes to make an oral response for each Accused.

R98-TC-3

o *Prosecution v. Brima, Kamara, Kanu*, Case No. SCSL-04-16-T, Scheduling Order on Filing of a Motion for Judgement of Acquittal, 30 September 2005:

CONSIDERING that it is in the interests of justice and in keeping with the conduct of a fair and expeditious trial, for the Trial Chamber to issue guidelines for the filing of a Motion for Judgement of Acquittal at this time;

PURSUANT TO Rules 26*bis*, 54 and 98 of the Rules;

HEREBY ORDERS:

1. Any Motion for a Judgment of Acquittal shall be filed by the Defence in writing within three weeks from the date that the Prosecution case closes;

2. That the length of any Joint Defence Motion relating to legal issues shall not exceed thirty (30) pages in length;

3. That the length of any additional submissions on facts on behalf of each individual Accused shall not exceed 30 pages.

4. That the Prosecution may file a Response to any Defence Motion within three weeks from the date of filing of such Defence Motion;

5. That the length of the Prosecution Response to any Defence Motion shall not exceed 30 pages in length and should the Prosecution choose to file a single Response to all Defence Motions it shall not exceed 120 pages;

6. That any Defence Reply to the Prosecution Response shall be filed within 5 days of the filing of the Prosecution Response and shall not exceed 10 pages in respect of each Accused;

7. That Article 6(C) of the Practice Direction shall not apply to any motion or response or reply herein.

Rule 104: Forfeiture of Property
(amended 7 March 2003)

(A) After a judgement of conviction containing a specific finding as provided in Rule 88(B) the Trial Chamber, at the request of the Prosecutor or at its own initiative, may hold a special hearing to determine the matter of property forfeiture, including the proceeds thereof, and may in the meantime order such provisional measures for the preservation and protection of the property or proceeds as it considers appropriate.

(B) The determination may extend to such property or proceeds, even in the hands of third parties not otherwise connected with the crime, for which the convicted person has been found guilty. Such third parties shall be entitled to appear at the hearing.

(C) The Trial Chamber may order the forfeiture of any property, proceeds and any assets it finds has been acquired unlawfully or by criminal conduct, and order its return to the rightful owner, or its transfer to the State of Sierra Leone, as circumstances may require.

TRIAL CHAMBERS DECISIONS

- **Rule 104(C): Forfeiture of Property – Freeze of Assets During Arrest – Order to the Authorities of Sierra Leone**

R104-TC-1

o *Prosecutor v. Sesay*, Case No. SCSL-03-05-I, Warrant of Arrest and Order for Transfer and Detention, 7 March 2003:[165]

HEREBY ORDERS THE RELEVANT AUTHORITIES OF THE GOVERNMENT OF SIERRA LEONE

[...]

(D) to identify and locate assets owned by the Accused located within the territory of any State and adopt provisional measures to freeze such assets without prejudice to the rights of third parties;

---

[165] See also *Prosecutor v. Brima*, Case No. SCSL-03-06-I, Warrant of Arrest and Order for Transfer and Detention, 7 March 2003; *Prosecutor v. Kallon*, Case No. SCSL-03-07-I, Warrant of Arrest and Order for Transfer and Detention, 7 March 2003; *Prosecutor v. Norman*, Case No. SCSL-03-08-I, Warrant of Arrest and Order for Transfer and Detention, 7 March 2003.

- **Rule 104(C): Forfeiture of Property – Freeze of Assets During Arrest – Request to Third States**

R104-TC-2 o *Prosecutor v. Taylor*, Case No. SCSL-03-01-I, Warrant of Arrest and Order for Transfer and Detention, 7 March 2003:[166]

HEREBY REQUESTS ALL STATES CONCERNED

[. . .]

(C) to identify and locate assets owned by the Accused located within the territory of any State and adopt provisional measures to freeze such assets without prejudice to the rights of third parties;

- **Rule 104(C): Forfeiture of Property – Order to Freeze of Assets – Applicable Criteria**

R104-TC-3 o *Prosecutor v. Norman*, Case No. SCSL-04-14-PT, Decision on *Inter Partes* Motion by Prosecution to Freeze the Account of the Accused Sam Hinga Norman at Union Trust Bank (SL) Limited or at Any Other Bank in Sierra Leone, 19 April 2004, para. 4-14:

4. This Motion confronts the Special Court with the tremendous task entrusted by the international community to international criminal tribunals to determine where the freedom of persons charged with international crimes ends and where the coercive authority of the international community and the state begins. In ascertaining the regime of legal doctrines and principles applicable in addressing this task, a court, in my considered judgement, is duty bound to be mindful of the cardinal principle that runs throughout the entire web of the criminal law, as a social control mechanism, namely, the presumption that every person accused of crime is innocent until proven guilty. What is at stake here is the need to balance the competing interest of the legal right of the international community and individual states to interfere with the assets of a citizen accused of crime, before any conviction has been recorded

---

[166] See also *Prosecutor v. Sankoh*, Case No. SCSL-03-02-I, Warrant of Arrest and Order for Transfer and Detention, 7 March 2003; *Prosecutor v. Koroma*, Case No. SCSL-03-03-I, Warrant of Arrest and Order for Transfer and Detention, 7 March 2003; *Prosecutor v. Bockarie*, Case No. SCSL-03-04-I, Warrant of Arrest and Order for Transfer and Detention, 7 March 2003.

against him and his right to be presumed innocent until proven guilty.

5. In the specific context of this Motion, the Court is called upon to demarcate that delicate boundary line between the Accused's freedom to own and enjoy property guaranteed both under national laws[1] and international law,[2] as a fundamental human right and the authority of the international community and the state of Sierra Leone to deprive him of the same in certain defined circumstances. It is noteworthy that the courts have always considered it their exclusive prerogative to define such circumstances. In traversing this extremely complex and sensitive terrain of the law governing the freezing of the assets of persons accused of crime who are awaiting trial and presumed innocent until proven guilty, it is necessary to begin by ascertaining the precise state of the law on the issue. The judicial decisions and academic commentaries show that the contemporary jurisprudence, national and international, on the subject is disparate, incoherent, and unclear.

6. This Court, therefore, seizes the opportunity to shed some light on this rather arcane area of the law, predicating its analysis on first principles and interpretations of relevant statutory provisions, case-law authorities from national law systems, and international criminal jurisprudence. In undertaking this exercise, the first question for me to address, as Designated Judge, is whether there exists a law enforcement power, nationally, to obtain a court order to freeze the bank account of a person accused of crime who is awaiting trial, being an unconvicted accused. One scholarly view is that such a power seems justified on the basis of common sense. Another is that such a power, even if it exists, has been "constructed on dubious legal foundation."[3] The law, in its present form, seems to be that of judicial recognition of the existence of such a power, a sort of pragmatic response to the new and complex operational dynamics of contemporary criminal justice systems in the prevention and detection of crime.[4]

English Case-Law Perspectives

7. *Consistent with this judicial pragmatism, the general trend in most national courts in adjudicating on the issue has been to recognise the existence of a common law or statutory right in this regard, but not to grant such applications in the absence of legal justification.* Instructively, in the English case of *Chief Constable of Hampshire v. A and Others*,[5] the defendants had purchased properties by means of substantial bank loans. The loans had been repaid out of the proceeds of fraudulent trading, the properties sold, and the proceeds paid into a bank account. The defendants had been charged with conspiracy to defraud. The Court acknowledged the existence of the power of the police to seek an injunction to freeze the bank account but refused to grant the application

on the grounds that even if the trading receipts contained substantial proceeds of the fraudulent transactions, the receipts themselves were not "specific" identifiable sums of money. On appeal, affirming the lower court, the Court of Appeal clearly restricted the power to only those assets which the court could identify as either being or representing stolen property or which were otherwise unlawfully obtained.

ICTY and ICTR Jurisprudence

8. In the international criminal law sphere, there is a dearth of judicial authorities on the subject. For example, in the sister jurisdictions of ICTY and the International Criminal Tribunal for Rwanda ("ICTR") there are only statutory provisions at this point in time from which guidance may be sought. Article 19(2) of the Statute of ICTY provides as follows:

> "Upon confirmation of an indictment, the judge may, at the request of the Prosecutor, issue such orders and warrants for the arrest, detention, surrender or transfer of persons, *and any other orders as may be required for the conduct of the trial.*" (emphasis added)

Further, Rule 47(H)(i) of the Rules of Procedure and Evidence of ICTY states that:

> "The Judge may issue an arrest warrant, in accordance with Sub-Rule 55(A), *and any orders provided in Article 19 of the Statute*" (emphasis added)

Rule 54 of the said Rules provides as follows:

> "At the request of either party or *proprio motu*, a Judge or a Trial Chamber may issue such orders, summonses, subpoenas, warrants and transfer orders as may be necessary for the purposes of an investigation or for the preparation of the trial."

Rule 61(D) states that:

> "The Trial Chamber shall also issue an international arrest warrant in respect of the accused which shall be transmitted to all States. Upon request by the Prosecutor or *proprio motu*, after having heard the Prosecutor, *the Trial Chamber may order a State or States to adopt provisional measures to freeze the assets of the accused, without prejudice to the rights of third parties.*" (emphasis added)

In addition, Rule 98*ter* states:

> "(B) If the Trial Chamber finds the accused guilty of a crime and concludes from the evidence that unlawful taking of property by the accused was associated with it, it shall make a specific finding to that effect in its judgement. The Trial Chamber may order restitution as provided in Rule 105." (emphasis added)

The ICTR provisions on this issue are almost identical to those of the ICTY.

9. In both ICTY and ICTR, apart from statutory provisions and rules relating to the post-conviction setting no express authority is granted to law enforcement to seek a judicial order for the freezing of bank accounts of persons accused of crime pending trial. An examination of the jurisprudence of the said tribunals reveals one ICTY decision so far on the issue, to wit, *Prosecutor v. Milosevic et al.*[(6)] There, the Court reasoned as follows:

> "The application was initially based solely upon Rule 54, which gives power to a judge (as well as to a Trial Chamber) to issue such orders as may be necessary for the preparation or conduct of the trial . . . Freezing the assets of the accused, the Prosecutor submitted, may be done for two distinct purposes – for the purpose of granting restitution of property or payment from its proceeds (which may be ordered by a Trial Chamber pursuant to rule 105 after conviction, subject to appropriate findings having been made in the judgement pursuant to Rule 98*ter*) and also for the purpose of preventing an accused . . . from taking steps to disguise his assets or putting them beyond the reach of the Tribunal."

SCSL Jurisprudence: Applicable Test

10. By parity of reasoning, under the statutory mechanism established by the founding instruments of the Special Court for Sierra Leone for the prosecution of persons who are alleged to bear the greatest responsibility for the violation of international humanitarian law and specified laws of Sierra Leone, ***nowhere is it expressly provided that there is a law enforcement power to seek an order from a court to freeze the assets of an indicted person pending trial.*** Article 19(3) of the Court's Statute authorises the Court to freeze or forfeit assets of accused persons in a post-conviction rather than a pre-conviction setting in these terms:

> "In addition to imprisonment, the Trial Chamber may order the forfeiture of the property, proceeds and any assets ***acquired unlawfully or by criminal conduct***, and their return to their rightful owner or to the State of Sierra Leone." (emphasis added)

To a like effect, are Rules 88 and 104 of the Rules. Rule 88(B) states that:

> "If the Trial Chamber finds the accused guilty of a crime, the Trial Chamber may order the forfeiture of the property, proceeds ***and any assets acquired unlawfully or by criminal conduct*** as provided in Rule 104." (emphasis added)

According to Rule 104(C):

> "The Trial Chamber may order the forfeiture of any property, proceeds and any assets it finds has been *acquired unlawfully or by criminal conduct*, and order its return to the rightful owner, or its transfer to the state of Sierra Leone, as circumstances may require." (emphasis added)

Rule 105 provides a machinery for compensation to victims in a post-conviction setting.

11. *It is of the utmost significance that the common thread that runs throughout the foregoing provisions, even in a post-conviction context, is the requirement that the targeted property must either have been acquired unlawfully or as a result of criminal conduct.*

12. By way of further elucidation, it is significant to note that the power is effectuated in the Warrant of Arrest ordered by a Judge who approves an indictment pursuant to Rule 47 of the Rules of Procedure and Evidence of the Court, by way of a consequential order subject to a major limitation to wit, *with-out prejudice to the rights of third parties*. In the instant case it was so ordered when the indictment was approved, *ex parte*, by me on 7 March 2003. However, as already noted, the existing state of the law is that there is judicial recognition of such law enforcement power. As Designated Judge, I do not propose in this Decision to revisit the issue of the soundness or otherwise of the legal foundation for the power. My immediate task is twofold: (1) to articulate a test to be applied in determining whether to grant an application of this nature or not; and (2) whether the instant Motion satisfies the requirements of that test.

13. What, then, should be the applicable test? *In my considered view, the proper test to be applied in determining whether or not to grant an application by the police or the Prosecution to freeze assets in the bank account of a person charged with crime pending trial is whether there is clear and convincing evidence that the targeted assets have a nexus with criminal conduct or were otherwise illegally acquired. What is 'clear and convincing evidence' depends on the particular facts and circumstances of each case. The targeted property must be specifically identifiable as a product of criminality or illegality. Neither probable cause nor mere suspicion or speculation will suffice.*

14. As Designated Judge, I also deem it my judicial obligation to emphasise that an application of this nature with far-reaching implications for a constitutionally guaranteed and internationally recognised right, to wit, an individual's right to own property cannot be granted as a matter of course and without sound legal justification especially in a context where the presumption of innocence is a competing, if not

compelling, juridical imperative. For this reason, I do not consider myself bound by some doctrine of judicial estoppel as regards the original order of 7 March 2003 made consequentially during the *ex parte* review of the Indictment for approval under Rule 47.

---

[1] The Constitutions of nearly all states, and in the specific context of Sierra Leone, the Sierra Leone Constitution 1991, (Act No. 6 of 1991) section 22.
[2] The Universal Declaration of Human Rights, 1948, Article 17 of which provides thus:
   Everyone has the right to own property, alone as well as in association with others.
   No one shall be arbitrarily deprived of his property.
   and the African Charter of Human and Peoples' Rights, 1981, Article 14 of which states that:
   The Right to property shall be guaranteed. It may only be encroached upon in the interest of public need or in the general interest of the community and in accordance with the provisions of appropriate laws.
[3] See a useful article by Suzanne Bailey entitled "Freezing the Assets of the Accused: Recommendations of the Hodgson Report" in the *New Law Journal*, September 28, 1984 pp. 829-830.
[4] Id.
[5] (1984) *Times*, March 3. See also the English case of *West Mercia Constabulary v. Wagener* (1982) 1 WLR 127 where the Judge, reasoning by analogy, recognized the existence of the power in this way: that if magistrates could grant a search warrant authorising the police to seize a suitcase filled with stolen money stored at a bank, then why should the High Court not grant the power to freeze the same money if it was deposited in a bank account? By parity of reasoning, in *Chief Constable of Kent v. A and Another*, (another English decision), the Court held that the Chief Constable had an interest, or common law right, on behalf of the public to seize the stolen goods, detain them pending trial and eventually restore them to the rightful owner.
[6] Case Number IT-02-54, Decision on Review of Indictment and Application for Consequential Orders, 24 May 1999, before Judge David Hunt, at para. 27.

Rule 108: Notice of Appeal
(amended 1 August 2003)

(A) Subject to Sub-Rule(B), a party seeking to appeal a judgement or sentence shall, not more than 14 days from the receipt of the full judgement and sentence, file with the Registrar and serve upon the other parties a written notice of appeal, setting forth the grounds.

(B) In appeals pursuant to Rules 77 and 91, the notice and grounds of appeal shall be filed within seven days of the receipt of the decision.

(C) In appeals pursuant to Rules 46, 65 and 73(B), the notice and grounds of appeal shall be filed within 7 days of the receipt of the decision to grant leave.

APPEALS CHAMBER DECISIONS

- **Rule 108: Notice of Appeal – Time Limits for Filing**

R108-AC-1

o *Prosecutor v. Kallon*, Case No. SCSL-04-15-AR65, Decision on Appeal Against the Decision of the Trial Chamber Refusing Application for Bail by Morris Kallon, 17 September 2004, para. 11-14:

> 11. Leaving aside the question of the nature of the document filed by the defence, there was a blatant failure to file anything at all within the time limit laid down in Rule 108(C). The Defence has provided no explanation or excuse for this failure to comply with the time limit under Rule 108 beyond a casual remark by defence Counsel in their Reply to the Prosecution Objection that they did not "avert their minds" to the relevant Rule. In particular, Article 12 of the Practice Direction on Filing Documents and Rule 116 of the rules were completely ignored.
>
> 12. The Special Court has a limited time to complete its judicial activities, hence the time scale for filing documents should be strictly adhered to. A Judge's or Chamber's discretion to extend the time available can only be exercised where reasonable grounds for a late filing have been demonstrated and where a refusal to extend time would occasion a miscarriage of justice.
>
> 13. An applicant who files a document outside the time limits and framework of the Rules and Practice Directions does so

at his peril. It is within the discretion of the Judge or Chamber to decide whether or not to accept a document despite its late filing and there are procedures that need to be followed in order to bring a late filing to the attention of a Judge or Chamber. In the instant case, the failure to provide reasons for the late filing has deprived the Chamber of any material on which it could have based an exercise of discretion.

14. The Appeals Chamber finds itself unable to accept the Appeal in the absence of application for an extension of time or explanation for the delay beyond the casual statement by counsel that the applicable Rule was overlooked.

o *Prosecutor v. Norman, Fofana, Kondewa*, Case No. SCSL-04-14-AR73, Decision on Amendment of the Consolidated Indictment, 16 May 2005, para. 47:

47. [...] One further matter to deal with at the outset is whether we should even consider the Defence appeal in Norman's case, which was filed, in contravention of the Rules, four days out of time.[1] Similarly, we would be entitled to consider the Prosecution appeal without looking at the Defence response, which was filed, again in contravention of the Rules, five days out of time.[2] It is ironic that an appeal which claims that it is an abuse of process for the Prosecution to fail in literal and rigid compliance with the Rules should itself fail to comply with a rule that lays down strict time limits. We have carefully considered whether we should disallow both the Defence appeal and the Defence response to the Prosecution appeal, but in the end we have decided to treat them as procedural errors by the Defence occurring in the course of a case which has included a number of procedural errors by the Prosecution and by the Trial Chamber itself. This indulgence must not be regarded as a precedent for any other parties which fail to comply with time limits for submissions to this court. The relevant time limits are clearly set out in both the Rules and the Practice Direction on Certain Appeals before the Special Court of 30 September 2004 and will henceforth be strictly enforced unless leave is sought for an extension in accordance with the Rules.

---

[1] Rule 108(c) specifies that the notice and grounds of appeal shall be filed within 7 days of the receipt of the decision to grant leave. The final date for filing was 13 January 2005 but the appeal was not filed until 17 January 2005.
[2] Pursuant to paragraph 12 of the Practice Direction for Certain Appeals before the Special Court of 30 September 2004, a response should be filed within 7 days of the filing of the appeal. The response was due on 21 January 2005. It was not filed until 26 January 2005.

R108-AC-3

o *Prosecutor v. Brima, Kamara, Kanu*, Case No. SCSL-04-16-AR73, Decision on Brima-Kamara Defence Appeal Motion Against Trial Chamber II Majority Decision on Extremely Urgent Confidential Joint Motion for the Re-Appointment of Kevin Metzger and Wilbert Harris As Lead Counsel for Alex Tamba Brima and Brima Bazzy Kamara, 8 December 2005, para. 30-35, 38:

30. Rule 108(C) provides that "[i]n appeals pursuant to Rules 46, 65 and 73(B), the notice and grounds of appeal shall be filed within 7 days of the receipt of the decision to grant leave." This Rule is implemented by Article 11 of the Practice Direction for Certain Appeals before the Special Court (the "Practice Direction for Certain Appeals")[1] which provides that "[t]he appellant's submissions based on the grounds of appeal shall be filed on the same day as the Notice of Appeal...."

31. Article 12 of the Practice Direction on Certain Appeals, which also applies to leave conditioned appeals, further provides that "[t]he opposite party shall file a response within seven days of the filing of the appeal. This response shall clearly state whether or not the appeal is opposed, the grounds therefore, and the submissions in support of those grounds."

32. Those time limits shall be computed in accordance with Rule 7(A) and (B), which provide as follows:

(A) Unless otherwise ordered by a Chamber or by a Designated Judge, or otherwise provided by the Rules, where the time prescribed by or under the Rules for the doing of any act shall run from the day after the notice of the occurrence of the event has been received in the normal course of transmission by the Registry, counsel for the Accused or the Prosecutor as the case may be.

(B) Where a time limit is expressed in days, only ordinary calendar days shall be counted. Weekdays, Saturdays, Sundays and Public Holiday shall be counted as days. However, should the time limit expire on a Saturday, Sunday or Public Holiday, the time limit shall automatically be extended to the subsequent working day.

33. On computation of time, Article 18 of the Practice Direction for Certain Appeals before the Special Court adds:

In accordance with the Rules, the time-limits prescribed under this Practice Direction shall run from, but shall not include, the day upon which the relevant document is filed. Should the last day of time prescribed fall upon a non-working day of the Special Court it shall be considered as falling on the first working day thereafter.

34. The Practice Direction on Filing Documents before the Special Court for Sierra Leone (the "Practice Direction on Filing of Documents")[2] regulates the format and contents of documents. Its Article 9 – Method of Filing Documents – provides:

(B) The official filing hours are from 9:00 to 17:00 hours every weekday, excluding official holidays. However, documents filed after 16:00 hours shall be served the next working day. Documents shall not be accepted for filing after 17:00 hours except as provided under Article 10 of this Practice Direction.[3]

(C) The date of filing is the date that the document was received by the Court Management Section. The Court Management Section shall stamp the document legibly with the date of its receipt, subject to the provisions of Articles 4 to 8 of this Practice Direction [...]

(c) Application to the Current Case

35. Since leave to appeal was granted by the Trial Chamber on Friday 5 August 2005 and the Summer Recess froze all time-limits for filing submissions from Monday 8 August 2005 until Sunday 28 August 2005,[4] Rule 108(C) 7-days time-limit ended on Friday 2 September 2005. According to Article 9(B) of the Practice Direction on Filing of Documents, the Notice and grounds of Appeal were to be filed at the latest on 5.00 p.m. The stamp on the Notice of Appeal shows that it was received by the Court Management Section of the Special Court at 5.13 p.m., in violation of Article 9(B) of the Practice Direction.

[...]

38. For the foregoing reason, the Appeals Chamber finds that the Court Management Section erred by accepting the filing of the Defence Notice of Appeal after the 5.00 p.m. time limit provided by Article 9(B) of the Practice Direction on Filing of Documents. The Appeals Chamber finds consequently that the Defence Notice of Appeal was filed out-of-time pursuant to Rule 108(C) and Article 9(B) of the Practice Direction on Filing of Documents. However, taking into account the fact that neither of the Respondents have objected to the Applicants' non-compliance with the Rules and Practice Directions on that ground and the fact that part of the responsibility for the mistake visibly bears on the Court Management Section of the Special Court which was not strict enough as regards the respect of time limits, the Appeals Chamber considers that it is nonetheless properly seized of the Appeal.

---

[1] Practice Direction for Certain Appeals Before the Special Court, 30 September 2004.

(2) Practice Direction on Filing Documents Before the Special Court for Sierra Leone, 27 February 2003, Amended on 1 June 2004.
(3) Article 10 deals with urgent measures.
(4) *See* Order Designating Judicial Recess, 23 June 2005.

- **Rules 108(C): Notice of Appeal – Grounds of Appeal Are to Be Clearly Formulated**

R108-AC-3

o *Prosecutor v. Kallon*, Case No. SCSL-04-15-AR65, Decision on Appeal Against the Decision of the Trial Chamber Refusing Application for Bail by Morris Kallon, 17 September 2004, para. 10:

10. [...] The question arises, however, whether the Appeal filed by the Defence can in fact be regarded as "notice and grounds of appeal" under Rule 108(C) in view of the absence of any itemized grounds of appeal. It is not the function of the Chamber and the opposite party to formulate grounds of appeal from the arguments of the Defence. The Defence would be expected to separate out its notice of appeal, grounds of appeal and submissions based on those grounds even under the limited guidance provided by Rule 108. The Chamber is compelled to conclude that there is really no notice of appeal in this case.

R108-AC-4

o *Prosecutor v. Sesay*, Case No. SCSL-04-15-AR65, Decision on Appeal Against Refusal of Bail, 14 December 2004, para. 24-25:

24. The key issue is the interpretation of Rule 108(C) of the Special Court Rules in the absence of any additional guidance in the form of a Practice Direction. The Appeal was filed within the time limit under Rule 108(C) and therefore 'notice of appeal' was provided in due time even though the form of this 'notice' lacked clarity. In particular, confusion is caused by the fact that the Sesay Appeal does not separate grounds of appeal from submissions and in fact has the heading "submissions" only. The Defence might have been expected to set out clearly their grounds of appeal under Rule 108(C) even if their submissions were included in the same document or combined with the grounds of appeal as an elaboration of them. It is not for the Appeals Chamber to pick out the grounds of appeal from the detailed submissions. Thus, the document presented by Sesay as an Appeal would appear to be deficient though the Rules applicable at the time of its filing may be said to have provided inadequate guidance.

25. Nonetheless, the Chamber finds that to reject the Appeal on the basis of this technicality might be unfair to the Defence especially since it was unclear what was expected under Rule 108(C) in the absence of a Practice Direction. Moreover, even though the submissions seem somewhat confused, full arguments have been presented, and despite objection, the Prosecution has responded to these arguments in full. The Chamber will therefore proceed to a determination of the merits of the Appeal.

Rule 110: Record on Appeal
(amended 7 March 2003)

The record on appeal shall consist of the parts of the trial record as designated by the Pre-Hearing Judge, as certified by the Registrar.

APPEALS CHAMBER DECISIONS

- **Rule 110: Record on Appeal – Contents – Compilation by the Registrar**

R110-AC-1
o *Prosecutor v. Gbao*, Case No. SCSL-04-15-AR73, Order on Time Limits, 8 September 2004, para. 4:

> 4. The record on appeal shall consist of the Decision of the Trial Chamber and all documents in the proceedings before Trial Chamber necessary to the decision in appeal. The Defence shall indicate to the Appeals Chamber and to the Prosecution in an index the documents believed to be necessary for the decision in the appeal. The Prosecution shall in its Response be at liberty to request an amendment to the index with reasons therefore. Any such request shall be decided upon by the Presiding Judge of the Appeals Chamber. The Registrar shall within seven days of receipt of the final index on appeal compile the record on appeal for distribution to the Appeals Chamber.

> **Rule 113: Submissions in Reply**
> *(amended 7 March 2003)*
>
> (A) An Appellant may file submissions in reply within five days after the filing of the Respondent's submissions.
>
> (B) No further submissions may be filed except with leave of the Appeals Chamber.

APPEALS CHAMBER DECISIONS

- **Rule 113: Submissions in Reply – No Right for Further Submissions**

R113-AC-1   o *Prosecutor v. Brima, Kamara, Kanu*, Case No. SCSL-04-16-AR73, Decision on Brima-Kamara Defence Appeal Motion Against Trial Chamber II Majority Decision on Extremely Urgent Confidential Joint Motion for the Re-Appointment of Kevin Metzger and Wilbert Harris As Lead Counsel for Alex Tamba Brima and Brima Bazzy Kamara, 8 December 2005, para. 61-64:

> 61. The Registrar's Additional Motion requests the Appeals Chamber not to consider the "Additional Grounds and Arguments" raised by the Defence Office in its Response, or, in the alternative, that the Appeals Chamber leaves the Registrar respond them. The Appeals Chamber will address these two alternative requests separately.
>
> 62. As regards the request for the Appeals Chamber not to consider the "Additional Grounds and Arguments" raised by the Defence Office in its Response to the Appeal, Rule 113(B) specifically provides that no further submissions, but the appellant's submissions in appeal[(1)] and reply[(2)] and the respondent's response[(3)] may be filed, except with leave of the Appeals Chamber. In particular, the Statute and the Rules nowhere provide for a right of a respondent to reply/rejoin another respondent's response. It is therefore the view of the Appeals Chamber that the proper way to address the new grounds and arguments raised in the Defence Office's Response was for the Registrar to address them in his own Response and that the request not to consider the Defence Office's "Additional Grounds and Arguments" was anyway to be filed within the time-limit for filing the Registrar's Response pursuant to Paragraph 12 of the Practice Direction for Certain Appeals. In the current case, and for the reasons set out earlier,[(4)] the

time-limit for filing responses to the Appeal expired on 12 September 2005. Since the Registrar's Additional Motion was filed on 13 September 2005 and no application for extension of time under Rule 116 was filed by the Registrar, the Appeals Chamber finds that the Registrar's request not to consider the Defence Office's "Additional Grounds and Arguments" was out-of-time. The Registrar's Additional Motion is therefore dismissed on this aspect.

63. The second request mentioned above seeks leave to respond the Defence Office's "Additional Grounds and Arguments". Such response to grounds and arguments brought in another Respondent's response can only be made, pursuant to Rule 113(B), with the Appeals Chamber's express leave. Rule 113(B) does not specify the criteria to be satisfied for such leave, but it is obvious that such leaves shall remain very exceptional and be granted only where the respect of the adversarial character of the proceedings strongly requires so. Since the Appeals Chamber has already decided that the additional ground raised in the Defence Office's Response was inadmissible, there is no need for the Registrar to respond it. Leave to do so under Rule 113(B) is accordingly denied. As regards the application for leave to respond the Defence Office's additional arguments, the Appeals Chamber is of the view that these arguments were properly made in the Defence Office's Response, that the Registrar has already been given full opportunity to respond the Appeal Motion and that he did so, that the Statute and Rules do not provide for a right of a respondent to reply/rejoin another respondent's response and that there is consequently no reason for leaving the Registrar to file further submissions in relation to these arguments.

64. The Registrar's Additional Motion is therefore denied in its entirety. This finding does not vary, however, the Appeals Chamber's earlier finding on the admissibility of the Defence Office's "Additional Grounds and Arguments".[5]

---

[1] Rule 111 of the Rules of Procedure and Evidence.
[2] Rule 113(A) of the Rules of Procedure and Evidence.
[3] Rule 112 of the Rules of Procedure and Evidence.
[4] *Supra*, Second Preliminary Issue.
[5] *Supra*, Third Preliminary Issue.

> **Rule 115: Additional Evidence**

(A) A party may apply by motion to present before the Appeals Chamber additional evidence which was not available to it at the trial. Such motion must be served on the other party and filed with the Registrar not less than fifteen days before the date of the hearing.

(B) The Appeals Chamber shall authorize the presentation of such evidence if it considers that the interests of justice so require.

APPEALS CHAMBER DECISIONS

- **Rule 115: Additional Evidence – New Relief Sought for the First Time in Appeal – Admission in Certain Circumstances**

R115-AC-1 o *Prosecutor v. Brima, Kamara, Kanu*, Case No. SCSL-04-16-AR73, Decision on Brima-Kamara Defence Appeal Motion Against Trial Chamber II Majority Decision on Extremely Urgent Confidential Joint Motion for the Re-Appointment of Kevin Metzger and Wilbert Harris As Lead Counsel for Alex Tamba Brima and Brima Bazzy Kamara, 8 December 2005, para. 134:

> 134. Now the Applicants seek for the first time in this pending appeal a judicial review of the Registrar's decision by the Appeals Chamber. It may be argued that such a new relief cannot be sought for the first time in appeal and shall therefore be denied. But the Appeals Chamber notes that the Parties did not raise any objection as regards this new request, that the Appellants had no knowledge, when they filed their Motion to re-assign before the Trial Chamber, of that decision of the Registrar which was taken while the matter was pending before the Trial Chamber, and that they tried to challenge this decision before the Trial Chamber in a public hearing on the Motion, which was refused by the Trial Chamber. The Appeals Chamber therefore accepts to consider this new request.

> **Rule 116: Extension of Time Limits**
>
> The Appeals Chamber may grant a motion to extend a time limit upon a showing of good cause.

APPEALS CHAMBER DECISIONS

- **Rule 116: Extension of Time Limit – "Good Cause"**

R116-AC-1   o *Prosecution v. Kallon*, Case No. SCSL-04-15-PT, Decision on Defence Motion for Extension of Time for Filing Application for Leave to Appeal Against Refusal of Bail, 19 April 2004:

CONSIDERING that the interests of justice require adequate representation for the protection of the rights of the Accused in accordance with Article 17 of the Statute of the Special Court;

CONSIDERING that Rule 116 of the Rules demands "a showing of good cause";

CONSIDERING that the withdrawal of Counsel and assignment of a new Counsel in this case satisfies the test under Rule 116 of the Rules;

CONSIDERING that the newly assigned Counsel will need time for preparation;

PURSUANT TO Rule 116 of the Rules;

HEREBY GRANTS an extension of the time limit for an additional fourteen days from the date of this Decision for the filing of an application for leave to appeal.

Rule 117: Expedited Procedure
(amended 29 May 2004)

(A) A reference under Rule 72(E) or (F), or any appeal under Rules 46, 65, 73(B), 77 or 91 shall be heard expeditiously by a bench of at least three Appeals Chamber Judges and may be determined entirely on the basis of written submissions.

(B) All time limits and other procedural requirements not otherwise provided for in these Rules shall be fixed by a practice direction issued by the Presiding Judge.

(C) Unless as otherwise ordered, Rules 109 to 114 and 118(D) shall not apply to such procedures.

APPEALS CHAMBER DECISIONS

- **Rule 117: Expedited Procedure – Time Limits**

R117-AC-1
o *Prosecution v. Kanu*, Case No. SCSL-03-13-AR72(E), Order on Expedited Filing of Additional Submissions, 27 January 2004:

NOTING that a meeting of the Judges of the Appeals Chamber is due to commence on 30 January 2004;

CONSIDERING that a fair and expeditious consideration of the Preliminary Motion at the forthcoming meeting necessitates the imposition of an expedited timetable for additional submissions before the Appeals Chamber;

PURSUANT to Rule 7 of the Rules;

HEREBY ORDERS that additional submissions be filed as follows:

1. Any Defence additional submissions by 30 January 2004;
2. Any Prosecution Response to those additional submissions by 2 February 2004;
3. Any Defence Reply to that Response by 4 February 2004.

- **Rule 117: Expedited Procedure – Reasons to Order Full Bench**

 R117-AC-2

o *Prosecutor v. Brima, Kamara, Kanu*, Case No. SCSL-04-16-AR77, Order for Full Bench under Rule 117(A), 18 May 2005:

CONSIDERING that it is in the interests of justice for the Appeal to be determined by a full bench of the Appeals Chamber;

LIST OF REVIEWED DECISIONS

Decisions of the Appeals Chamber have their title followed by "(AC)". Decisions of the President have their title followed by "(P)".

QRN in **Bold** refer to the abstracts reproduced in the *Digest*. QRN in *Italics* refer to the decision mentioned in the author's footnotes under the abstracts.

Prosecutor v. Charles Taylor, Case No. SCSL-03-01

1. Decision Approving the Indictment and Order for Non-Disclosure, 7 March 2003: **R47-TC-15**
2. Warrant of Arrest and Order for Transfer and Detention, 7 March 2003: **R52-TC-1, R53-TC-2, R56-TC-1, R56-TC-2, R58-TC-1, R104-TC-2**
3. Decision on Immunity from Jurisdiction (AC), 31 May 2004: **S1-AC-2, S6-AC-1, S6-AC-2, S6-AC-3, R72-AC-1, R72-AC-5, R73-AC-1**
4. Order for the Disclosure of the Indictment, the Warrant of Arrest and Order for Transfer and Detention and the Decision Approving the Indictment and Order for Non-Disclosure, 12 June 2003: **R53-TC-5**
5. Order Pursuant to Rule 72(E) Defence Motion to Quash the Indictment and to Declare the Warrant of Arrest and All Other Consequential Orders Null and Void, 19 September 2003: **R58-TC-2, R72-TC-9**
6. Decision on Application by the African Bar Association for Leave to File *Amicus Curiae* Brief, 20 November 2003: *R74-AC-1*

Prosecutor v. Foday Saybana Sankoh, Case No. SCSL-03-02

1. Decision Approving the Indictment and Order for Non-Disclosure, 7 March 2003: *R47-TC-15*
2. Warrant of Arrest and Order for Transfer and Detention, 7 March 2003: *R52-TC-1, R53-TC-2, R56-TC-1, R56-TC-2, R58-TC-1, R104-TC-2*
3. Order for Disclosure of Indictment, Warrant of Arrest and Order for Transfer and Detention, 14 March 2003: **R53-TC-3**
4. Order to Permit Photography, Video-Recording or Audio-Recording, 14 March 2003: **R81-TC-4**
5. Order for Physiological and Psychiatric Examination and Detention on Remand, 15 March 2003: **R74*bis*-TC-1**
6. Order for Further Physiological and Psychiatric Examination and Detention on Remand, 21 March 2003: **R61-TC-1, R74*bis*-TC-2**
7. Order Modifying Condition of Detention (P), 29 March 2003: **R21-P-1, R64-P-4**

DIGEST OF JURISPRUDENCE OF THE SPECIAL COURT FOR SIERRA LEONE   789

8. Decision on the Prosecution Motion to Allow Disclosure to the Registry and to Keep Disclosed Materials Under Seal Until Appropriate Protective Measures Are in Place, 17 April 2003: **R61-TC-2**
9. Decision on the Prosecutor's Motion for Immediate Protective Measures for Witnesses and Victims and for Non-Public Disclosure, 23 May 2003: *R61-TC-2*
10. Ruling on the Motion for a Stay of Proceedings Filed by the Applicant, 22 July 2003: **S2-TC-2, S2-TC-6, S3-TC-6, R61-TC-3, R61-TC-4, R61-TC-5, R74bis-TC-3**
11. Withdrawal of Indictment, 8 December 2003: **R51-TC-1**

Prosecutor v. Johnny Paul Koroma, Case No. SCSL-03-03

1. Decision Approving the Indictment and Order for Non-Disclosure, 7 March 2003: *R47-TC-15*
2. Warrant of Arrest and Order for Transfer and Detention, 7 March 2003: *R52-TC-1, R53-TC-2, R56-TC-1, R56-TC-2, R58-TC-1, R104-TC-2*
3. Under Seal – Decision Modifying Location of Detention (P), 18 March 2003: **R57-P-1**
4. Warrant of Arrest and Order for Transfer and Detention, 25 November 2003: *R52-TC-1*, **R56-TC-3**, *R58-TC-1*
5. Order for the Disclosure of the Indictment, 28 March 2003: **R53-TC-4**

Prosecutor v. Sam Bockarie, Case No. SCSL-03-04

1. Decision Approving the Indictment and Order for Non-Disclosure, 7 March 2003: *R47-TC-15*
2. Warrant of Arrest and Order for Transfer and Detention, 7 March 2003: *R52-TC-1, R53-TC-2, R56-TC-1, R56-TC-2, R58-TC-1, R104-TC-2*
3. Decision Modifying Location of Detention (P), 10 March 2003
4. Order for the Disclosure of the Indictment, 28 March 2003
5. Withdrawal of Indictment, 8 December 2003: *R51-TC-1*

Prosecutor v. Issa Hassan Sesay, Case No. SCSL-03-05

1. Decision Approving Indictment and Order for Non-Disclosure, 7 March 2003: *R47-TC-15*
2. Warrant of Arrest and Order for Transfer and Detention, 7 March 2003: *R52-TC-1*, **R53-TC-1, R55-TC-1, R57-TC-1, R59-TC-1, R104-TC-1**

3. Order to Permit Photography, Video-Recording or Audio-Recording, 14 March 2003: *R81-TC-4*
4. Order for the Disclosure of the Indictment and the Warrant of Arrest and Order for transfer and Detention, 14 March 2003
5. Order for Legal Assistance and Detention on Remand, 15 March 2003
6. Scheduling Order, 22 March 2003: **R61-TC-6**
7. Scheduling Order, 10 April 2003
8. Decision on the Prosecution Motion to Allow Disclosure to the Registry and to Keep Disclosed Material Under Seal Until Appropriate Protective Measures Are in Place, 17 April 2003: *R66-TC-10*
9. Order on Defence Objection Filed as Reply Evidence in the Prosecution Motion for Immediate Protective Measures for Witnesses and Victims and for Non-Public Disclosure, 21 May 2003: **R73-TC-14**
10. Decision on the Prosecutor's Motion for Immediate Protective Measures for Witnesses and Victims and for Non-Public Disclosure, 23 May 2003: *R69-TC-1, R69-TC-8, R69-TC-17*
11. Order on the Defence Application for Reconsideration of and/or Leave to Appeal "Decision on the Prosecutor's Motion on Protective Measures for Witnesses", 16 July 2003: **R73-TC-5**
12. Decision and Order on Defence Preliminary Motion for Defects in the Form of the Indictment, 13 October 2003: **S6-TC-4, R47-TC-1, R47-TC-3, R47-TC-8, R47-TC-9**
13. Decision on the Defence Motion Requesting the Suspension of Delays for Filing Preliminary Motions or New Request for an Extension of Delays, 7 November 2003: *R7bis-TC-1*, **R72-TC-2**
14. Order on the Defence Motion Requesting that the Time Limit to Respond to the Motion Filed by the Prosecution for a Joinder to Commence Upon Receipt of the Modified or Particularised Indictment(s) or on a Date Set by the Trial Chamber, 12 November 2003: **R7*bis*-TC-6, R48-TC-8**
15. Decision and Order on Prosecution Motions for Joinder, 27 January 2004: **S6-TC-2, S20-TC-6, R48-TC-1, R48-TC-2, R48-TC-3, R48-TC-4, R48-TC-5, R48-TC-6, R66-TC-12**

Prosecutor v. Alex Tamba Brima, Case No. SCSL-03-06

1. Decision Approving Indictment and Order for Non-Disclosure, 7 March 2003: *R47-TC-15*
2. Warrant of Arrest and Order for Transfer and Detention, 7 March 2003: *R52-TC-1, R53-TC-1, R55-TC-1, R57-TC-1, R59-TC-1, R104-TC-1*

3. Order to Permit Photography, Video-Recording or Audio-Recording, 14 March 2003: *R81-TC-4*
4. Order for the Disclosure of the Indictment and the Warrant of Arrest and Order for Transfer and Detention, 14 March 2003
5. Adjournment of the Initial Appearance and Detention on Remand, 15 March 2003
6. Order for Legal Assistance, 19 March 2003
7. Scheduling Order, 22 March 2003
8. Scheduling Order, 10 April 2003
9. Order on the Decision of the Registrar to Provisionally Assign Counsel for the Accused, 16 April 2003
10. Order on Disclosure to the Registry, 17 April 2003: *R66-TC-10*
11. Order on Filing, 16 May 2003: **R73-TC-1**
12. Decision on the Prosecutor's Motion for Immediate Protective Measures for Witnesses and Victims and for Non-Public Disclosure, 23 May 2003: *R69-TC-1, R69-TC-8, R69-TC-17*
13. Order for Oral Hearing in the Motion Filed by the Defence for Leave to File a Write of *Habeas Corpus ad Subjidiciendum*, 18 June 2003: **R65-TC-18**
14. Ruling on the Application for the Issue of a Writ of *Habeas Corpus* Filed by the Applicant, 22 July 2003: **S8-TC-1, R28-TC-1, R47-TC-17, R55-TC-2, R65-TC-2, R73-TC-4**
15. Ruling on a Motion Applying for Bail or for Provisional Release Filed by the Applicant, 22 July 2003
16. Decision on the Application for Extension of Time for Leave to Be Granted to File Defence Motion to Appeal Against the Decision Refusing an Application for the Issue of the Writ of *Habeas Corpus*, 16 October 2003: **R7*bis*-TC-12, R7*bis*-TC-14**
17. Decision and Order on Prosecution Motions for Joinder, 27 January 2004: **S6-TC-2, S20-TC-6, R48-TC-1, R48-TC-2, R48-TC-3, R48-TC-4, R48-TC-5, R48-TC-6, R66-TC-12**

Prosecutor v. Morris Kallon, Case No. SCSL-03-07

1. Decision Approving the Indictment and Order for Non-Disclosure, 7 March 2003: *R47-TC-15*
2. Warrant of Arrest and Order for Transfer and Detention, 7 March 2003: *R52-TC-1, R53-TC-1, R55-TC-1, R57-TC-1, R59-TC-1, R104-TC-1*
3. Order to Permit Photography, Video-Recording or Audio-Recording, 14 March 2003: *R81-TC-4*
4. Order for the Disclosure of the Indictment and the Warrant of Arrest and Order for Transfer and Detention, 14 March 2003

5. Order for Legal Assistance, 19 March 2003: **R45*bis*-TC-1**
6. Scheduling Order, 22 March 2003: *R61-TC-6*
7. Scheduling Order, 10 April 2003
8. Decision on the Prosecution Motion to Allow Disclosure to the Registry and to Keep Disclosed Material Under Seal Until Appropriate Protective Measures Are in Place, 17 April 2003: *R66-TC-10*
9. Order on Defence Objection Filed as Reply Evidence in the Prosecution Motion for Immediate Protective Measures for Witnesses and Victims and for Non-Public Disclosure, 21 May 2003: *R73-TC-14*
10. Decision on the Prosecutor's Motion for Immediate Protective Measures for Witnesses and Victims and for Non-Public Disclosure, 23 May 2003: *R69-TC-1, R69-TC-8, R69-TC-17*
11. Decision on the Defence Motion for Extension of Time to File Preliminary Motions, 14 June 2003: **R7*bis*-TC-1, R72-TC-1**
12. Order on the Defence Application for Extension of Time to File Reply to Prosecution Response to Preliminary Motion, 24 June 2003: *R7bis-TC-1*
13. Order on Time Limits to File Reply to the Prosecution Response to the Preliminary Motions, 27 June 2003
14. Order on the Defence Further Application for Extension of Time to File Preliminary Motions, 8 July 2003: *R7bis-TC-14*
15. Decision on the Defence Application for Extension of Time to File Reply to Prosecution Response to the First Defence Preliminary Motion (Lomé Agreement), 16 July 2003: **R7*bis*-TC-3**
16. Order on the Defence Application for Reconsideration of and/or Leave to Appeal "Decision on the Prosecutor's Motion on Protective Measures for Witnesses", 16 July 2003: *R73-TC-5*
17. Decision on the Application for Leave to Submit *Amicus Curiae* Briefs, 17 July 2003: **R45-TC-2, R74-TC-1**
18. Order Pursuant to Rule 72(E) – Defence Motion Based on Lack of Jurisdiction – Establishment of Special Court Violates Constitution of Sierra Leone, 17 September 2003: **R72-TC-13**
19. Order on the Defence Request for *Subpoena Duces Tecum*, 24 September 2003
20. Decision on the Motion for Leave to Appeal Order on the Defence Application for Extension of Time to File Reply to Prosecution Response to the First Preliminary motion (Lomé Agreement), 29 September 2003: **R6-TC-2**
21. Order Pursuant to Rule 72(E) – Defence Motion Based on Lack of Jurisdiction – Abuse of Process: Amnesty Provided by Lomé Accord, 30 September 2003: *S13-TC-1*, **R72-TC-14**
22. Order on the Application by the Redress Trust and Lawyers Committee for Human Rights for Leave to File an *Amicus Curiae* Brief, 2 October 2003

23. Order on the Application by the Redress Trust and Lawyers Committee for Human Rights for Leave to File an *Amicus Curiae* Brief (AC), 14 October 2003
24. Decision on Application by the Redress Trust, Lawyers Committee for Human Rights and the International Commission of Jurists For Leave to File *Amicus Curiae* Brief and Present Oral Submissions (AC), 1 November 2003: **R74-AC-1**
25. Decision on the Applications for a Stay of Proceedings and Denial of Right to Appeal (AC), 4 November 2003: **S14-AC-1, S14-AC-2, S17-AC-6, S20-AC-2, S20-AC-3, R72-AC-6**
26. Decision on Defence Application on the Denial of Right to Appeal, 7 November 2003
27. Decision on the Defence Application for Leave to Appeal 'Decision on the Prosecution's Motion for Immediate Protective Measures for Witnesses and Victims and for Non-Public Disclosure, 10 December 2003: **S17-TC-6, S17-TC-11, R6-TC-3, R73-TC-19, R73-TC-36, R73-TC-46**
28. Decision and Order on Prosecution Motions for Joinder, 27 January 2004: **S6-TC-2, S20-TC-6, R48-TC-1, R48-TC-2, R48-TC-3, R48-TC-4, R48-TC-5, R48-TC-6, R66-TC-12**

Prosecutor v. Sam Hinga Norman, Case No. SCSL-03-08

1. Decision Approving the Indictment and Order for Non-Disclosure, 7 March 2003: *R47-TC-15*
2. Warrant of Arrest and Order for Transfer and Detention, 7 March 2003: *R52-TC-1, R53-TC-1, R55-TC-1, R57-TC-1, R59-TC-1, R104-TC-1*
3. Reasons for Ordering a Closed Session, 15 March 2003: **R79-TC-2**
4. Order for the Disclosure of the Indictment and the Warrant of Arrest and Order for Transfer and Detention, 15 March 2003
5. Order for Disclosure of any Information Inherent to the Initial Appearance of the Accused, 11 April 2003
6. Decision on the Prosecution Motion to Allow Disclosure to the Registry and to Keep Disclosed Materials Under Seal Until Appropriate Protective Measures Are in Place, 17 April 2003: **R66-TC-10, R68-TC-10**
7. Decision on the Prosecutor's Motion for Immediate Protective Measures for Witnesses and Victims and for Non-Public Disclosure, 23 May 2003: **S20-TC-1, R69-TC-1, R69-TC-8, R69-TC-17**
8. Order on the Prosecution Application for an Extension of Time to Respond to Four Defence Motions as to Jurisdiction, 03 July 2003: *R7bis-TC-1*
9. Order on Defence Request for Extension of Time Within Which to

File Reply to the Prosecution Response to Defence Preliminary Motion, 17 September 2003: **R7*bis*-TC-9**
10. Order Pursuant to Rule 72(E) – Defence Preliminary Motion on Lack of Jurisdiction: Judicial Independence, 17 September 2003: **R72-TC-10**
11. Order Pursuant to Rule 72(E) – Defence Preliminary Motion on Lack of Jurisdiction: Child Recruitment, 17 September 2003: **R72-TC-11**
12. Order Pursuant to Rule 72(E) – Defence Preliminary Motion on Lack of Jurisdiction: Lawfulness of the Court's Establishment, 17 September 2003: **R72-TC-12**
13. Decision on the Defence Preliminary Motion on Lack of Jurisdiction: Command Responsibility, 15 October 2003: **S6-TC-5, S20-TC-3, R72-TC-16**
14. Decision on the Request by the Truth and Reconciliation Commission of Sierra Leone to Conduct a Public Hearing with Samuel Hinga Norman, 29 October 2003: **S1-TC-5, S17-TC-1, S17-TC-7**
15. Decision on Application by the University of Toronto International Human Rights Clinic for Leave to File *Amicus Curiae* Brief (AC), 01 November 2003: *R74-AC-1*
16. Decision on the Applications for a Stay of Proceedings and Denial of Right to Appeal (AC), 4 November 2003: **S14-AC-1, S14-AC-2, S17-AC-6, S20-AC-2, S20-AC-3, R72-AC-6**
17. Decision on Motion for Modification of the Conditions of Detention (P), 26 November 2003: **R64-P-1, R64-P-2, R64-P-3, R65-P-1**
18. Decision on Appeal by the Truth and Reconciliation Commission for Sierra Leone ("TRC" or "the Commission") and Chief Samuel Hinga Norman JP Against the Decision of His Lordship, Mr Justice Bankole Thompson Delivered on 30 October 2003 to Deny the TRC's Request to Hold a Public Hearing With Chief Samuel Hinga Norman JP (AC), 28 November 2003: **S1-AC-9, S17-AC-3, S17-AC-5**
19. Decision on Defence Motion on Denial of Right of Appeal, 4 December 2003
20. Order on the Appointment of *Amicus Curiae* (AC), 12 December 2003: **R74-AC-2**
21. Decision and Order on Prosecution Motions for Joinder, 27 January 2004: *S6-TC-2, S20-TC-6, R48-TC-3, R48-TC-4, R48-TC-5, R48-TC-6*

Prosecutor v. Augustine Gbao, Case No. SCSL-03-09

1. Order for Transfer and Provisional Detention Pursuant to Rule 40*bis*, 18 March 2003: **R40*bis*-TC-1**
2. Decision Approving the Indictment, 16 April 2003: *R47-TC-15*

3. Order Confirming Prior Arrest and Ordering Continued Detention, 16 April 2003
4. Order to Permit Photography, Video-Recording or Audio-Recording, 24 April 2003: *R81-TC-4*
5. Order for Detention on Remand, 25 April 2003
6. Order on the Urgent Request for Direction on the Time to Respond to and/or an Extension of Time for the Filing of a Response to the Prosecution Motions and the Suspension of Any Ruling on the Issue of Protective Measures That May Be Pending Before Other Proceedings Before the Special Court as a Result of Similar Motions Filed to Those that Have Been Filed by the Prosecution in this Case, 16 May 2003: **R7*bis*-TC-13, R26*bis*-TC-1**
7. Scheduling Order and Order on Disclosure to the Registry, 23 May 2003: *R66-TC-10*
8. Decision on the Prosecution Motion for Immediate Protective Measures for Witnesses and Victims and for Non-Public Disclosure, 10 October 2003: **S17-TC-2, S17-TC-4, S20-TC-2, R26*bis*-TC-2, R33-TC-4, R44-TC-6, R69-TC-4, R69-TC-9,** *R69-TC-17*
9. Decision on the Request by the TRC of Sierra Leone to Conduct a Public Hearing with the Accused, 3 November 2003: *S1-TC-5*, **S1-TC-6, S17-TC-18**
10. Decision on the Applications for a Stay of Proceedings and Denial of Right to Appeal (AC), 4 November 2003: **S14-AC-1, S14-AC-2, S17-AC-6, S20-AC-2, S20-AC-3, R72-AC-6**
11. Order Pursuant to Rule 72(E) – Defence Preliminary Motion on the Invalidity of the Agreement Between the United Nations and the Government of Sierra Leone on the Establishment of the Special Court for Sierra Leone, 3 December 2003: **R72-TC-17**
12. Decision and Order on Prosecution Motions for Joinder, 27 January 2004: **S6-TC-2, S20-TC-6, R48-TC-1, R48-TC-2, R48-TC-3, R48-TC-4, R48-TC-5, R48-TC-6, R66-TC-12**

Prosecutor v. Brima Bazzy Kamara, Case No. SCSL-03-10

1. Decision Approving the Indictment, the Warrant of Arrest and Order for Non-Public Disclosure, 28 May 2003: *R47-TC-16*
2. Warrant of Arrest and Order for Transfer and Detention, 28 May 2003
3. Order for the Disclosure of the Indictment and the Warrant of Arrest and Order for Transfer and Detention, 3 June 2003
4. Order on the Request by the Defence Office for Suspension of Consideration of Prosecution's Motion for Protective Measures Until Counsel Is Assigned, 26 June 2003: **R7*bis*-TC-2, R7*bis*-TC-5, R45-TC-1**

5. Interim Order for the Transmission of the Disclosure Materials to the Registrar, 2 July 2003: *R66-TC-11*
6. Order Pursuant to Rule 72 Re: Application by Brima Bazzy Kamara in Respect of Jurisdiction and Defects in the Indictment, 9 October 2003: **R72-TC-15**
7. Decision on the Prosecution Motion for Immediate Protective Measures for Witnesses and Victims and for Non-Public Disclosure, 23 October 2003: **S20-TC-4,** *R69-TC-1, R69-TC-4, R69-TC-8, R69-TC-17,* **R69-TC-22**
8. Decision on the Defence Motion for Extension of Time to File Response to Prosecution Motion for Joinder and for Adjournment of Hearing, 1 December 2003: **R7-TC-1**
9. Decision and Order on Prosecution Motions for Joinder, 27 January 2004: **S6-TC-2, S20-TC-6, R48-TC-1, R48-TC-2, R48-TC-3, R48-TC-4, R48-TC-5, R48-TC-6, R66-TC-12**

Prosecutor v. Moinina Fofana, Case No. SCSL-03-11

1. Order for Transfer and Provisional Detention Pursuant to Rule 40*bis*, 28 May 2003
2. Decision Approving the Indictment and Order for the Continued Detention of the Accused, 26 June 2003: *R47-TC-16*
3. Order on the Defence Office Application for Extension of Time to Respond to Prosecution Motion for Immediate Protective Measures for Victims and Witnesses, 10 July 2003
4. Interim Order for the Transmission of Disclosure Materials to the Registrar, 30 July 2003: **R66-TC-11**
5. Decision on the Prosecutor's Motion for Immediate Protective Measures for Witnesses and Victims and for Non-Public Disclosure, 16 October 2003: *R69-TC-1, R69-TC-8, R69-TC-17*
6. Order on the Defence Request for an Extension of Time for the Filing of a Response to the Prosecution Motion for Joinder, 12 November 2003: **R48-TC-7**
7. Decision on the Urgent Defence Application for Release from Provisional Detention, 21 November 2003: *R7bis-TC-10, R40bis-TC-2, R40bis-TC-3, R40bis-TC-4, R73-TC-11*
8. Decision and Order on Prosecution Motions for Joinder, 27 January 2004: *S6-TC-2, S20-TC-6, R48-TC-3, R48-TC-4, R48-TC-5, R48-TC-6*

Prosecutor v. Allieu Kondewa, Case No. SCSL-03-12

1. Order for Transfer and Provisional Detention Pursuant to Rule 40*bis*, 28 May 2003
2. Decision Approving the Indictment and Order for the Continued Detention of the Accused, 26 June 2003: **R47-TC-16**
3. Order on the Defence Office Application for Extension of Time to Respond to Prosecution Motion for Immediate Protective Measures for Victims and Witnesses, 10 July 2003
4. Interim Order for the Transmission of the Disclosure Materials to the Registrar, 30 July 2003: *R66-TC-11*
5. Ruling on the Prosecution Motion for Immediate Protective Measures for Witnesses and Victims and for Non-Public Disclosure and Urgent Request for Interim Measures Until Appropriate Protective Measures Are in Place, 10 October 2003: **R69-TC-5, R69-TC-15**
6. Decision on the Urgent Defence Application for Release from Provisional Detention, 21 November 2003: **S1-TC-1, R7*bis*-TC-10, R40*bis*-TC-2, R40*bis*-TC-3, R40*bis*-TC-4, R73-TC-11**
7. Decision and Order on Defence Preliminary Motion for Defects in the Form of the Indictment, 27 November 2003: **S6-TC-1**, *R47-TC-1*, **R47-TC-5, R72*bis*-TC-1**
8. Order Pursuant to Rule 72(E) – Defence Motion Based on Lack of Jurisdiction – Establishment of Special Court Violates Constitution of Sierra Leone, 04 December 2003: **R72-TC-8, R72-TC-18**
9. Order Pursuant to Rule 72(E) – Defence Motion Based on Lack of Jurisdiction/Abuse of Process: Amnesty Provided by Lomé Accord, 8 December 2003: **S13-TC-1, R72-TC-19**
10. Decision and Order on Prosecution Motions for Joinder, 27 January 2004: *S6-TC-2, S20-TC-6, R48-TC-3, R48-TC-4, R48-TC-5, R48-TC-6*

Prosecutor v. Santigie Borbor Kanu, Case No. SCSL-03-13

1. Decision Approving the Indictment, the Warrant of Arrest, and Order for Transfer and Detention, and Order for Non-Public Disclosure, 16 September 2003: *R47-TC-16*
2. Warrant of Arrest and Order for Transfer and Detention, 16 September 2003
3. Order for Disclosure of Warrant of Arrest and Order for Transfer and Detention, 19 September 2003
4. Decision on Urgent Request for Interim Measures Until Appropriate Protective Measures Are in Place, 15 October 2003: *R66-TC-11*
5. Decision and Order on the Defence Preliminary Motion for Defects in

the Form of the Indictment, 19 November 2003: *R47-TC-1, R47-TC-3*, **R47-TC-4, R47-TC-10, R47-TC-12**
6. Decision on the Prosecution Motion for Immediate Protective Measures for Witnesses and Victims, 24 November 2003: **S20-TC-5, R69-TC-2, R69-TC-10, R69-TC-18**
7. Order Pursuant to Rule 72(E) – Defence Motion Challenging the Jurisdiction of the Special Court Raising Serious Issues Relating to Jurisdiction on Various Grounds and Objections Based on Abuse of Process, 22 January 2004: *R72-TC-8,* **R72-TC-20**
8. Decision and Order on Prosecution Motions for Joinder, 27 January 2004: **S6-TC-2, S20-TC-6, R48-TC-1, R48-TC-2, R48-TC-3, R48-TC-4, R48-TC-5, R48-TC-6, R66-TC-12**
9. Order on Expedited Filing of Additional Submissions, 27 January 2004: **R117-AC-1**

Prosecutor v. Norman, Fofana, Kondewa ("C.D.F. Case"),
Case No. SCSL-04-14

1. Scheduling Order for Status Conference (Under Rule 65*bis*), 13 February 2004: **R65*bis*-TC-1**
2. Order for Filing Pre-Trial Briefs (Under Rules 54 and 73*bis*), 13 February 2004: **R73*bis*-TC-2**
3. Order under Rule 65(B) on the Submissions from the Government of Sierra Leone, 13 February 2004
4. Order for Filing a Consolidated Reply, 23 February 2004
5. Order to Submit Indication of Specific Changes to Indictments, 26 February 2004: **R50-TC-1**
6. Decision on the Preliminary Defence Motion on the Lack of Personal Jurisdiction Filed on Behalf of the Accused Fofana, 3 March 2004: **S1-TC-2, R47-TC-13, R47-TC-14, R72-TC-4**
7. Decision on Constitutionality and Lack of Jurisdiction (AC), 13 March 2004: **S1-AC-1, S1-AC-4, S1-AC-6, S8-AC-1, R72-AC-2**
8. Decision on Preliminary Motion on Lack of Jurisdiction (Judicial Independence) (AC), 13 March 2004: **S13-AC-1, R72-AC-4**
9. Revised Order for the Filing of Defence Pre-Trial Briefs, 22 March 2004: **R73*bis*-TC-23**
10. Order to the Prosecution to File Disclosure Materials and Other Materials in Preparation of the Commencement of Trial, 1st April 2004: **R6-TC-1**
11. Order to the Prosecution to File a Supplemental Pre-Trial Brief, 1st April 2004: *R73bis-TC-1, R82-TC-1*
12. Interim Order and Scheduling Order, 2 April 2004: **R7-TC-4**

13. Order to the Prosecution for Renewed Motion for Protective Measures, 2 April 2004: **R69-TC-3, R69-TC-24**
14. Order for a Pre-Trial Conference (Under Rule 73*bis*), 2 April 2004
15. Revised Scheduling Order, 6 April 2004
16. Decision on *Inter Partes* Motion by Prosecution to Freeze the Account of the Accused Sam Hinga Norman at Union Trust Bank (SL) Limited or at Any Other Bank in Sierra Leone, 19 April 2004: **R8-TC-1, R54-TC-2, R77-TC-5**
17. Additional Revised Order for Filing Defence Pre-Trial Brief, 22 April 2004: *R73*bis-*TC-23*
18. Decision on Defence Motion Requesting an Extension of Time Within Which to Respond to Prosecution's Motion for Judicial Notice and Admission of Evidence, 30 April 2004: **R7*bis*-TC-4**
19. Order Rejecting the Filing of the Defence Objection to Prosecution's Motion for Judicial Notice and Admission of Facts, 05 May 2004: **R7-TC-2, R73*bis*-TC-17**
20. Order for Commencement of Trial, 11 May 2004
21. Order for Filing of a Consolidated Reply, 13 May 2004: **R7-TC-5**
22. Decision on Motion to Reverse the Order of the Registrar Pursuant to Rule 48(C) of the Rules of Detention (P), 18 May 2004: **R64-P-6**
23. Decision on Prosecution Request for Leave to Amend the Indictment, 20 May 2004: **R50-TC-3, R50-TC-6**
24. Decision on Preliminary Motion on Lack of Jurisdiction *Materiae*: Nature of the Armed Conflict (AC), 25 May 2004: **S3-AC-1, S3-AC-2, S4-AC-1, S20-AC-1**
25. Decision on Preliminary Motion on Lack of Jurisdiction: Establishment of Special Court Violates Constitution of Sierra Leone (AC), 25 May 2004: *S8-AC-1, R72-AC-2*
26. Decision on Preliminary Motion on Lack of Jurisdiction *Materiae*: Illegal Delegation of Powers by the United Nations (AC), 25 May 2004: **R72-AC-3**
27. Decision on Preliminary Motion on Lack of Jurisdiction – Illegal Delegation of Jurisdiction by Sierra Leone (AC), 25 May 2004
28. Decision on Lack of Jurisdiction/Abuse of Process: Amnesty Provided by the Lomé Accord (AC), 25 May 2004
29. Decision on Co-operation Between the Parties, 26 May 2004: **R73*bis*-TC-18**
30. Decision on Request for Extension of Time to File Pre-Trial Brief, 26 May 2004: **R73*bis*-TC-22**
31. Scheduling Order, 27 May 2004: **R90-TC-6**
32. Decision on the Motion to Recuse Judge Winter from the Deliberation in the Preliminary Motion on the Recruitment of Child Soldiers (AC), 28 May 2004: **R15-AC-2**

33. Order to Prosecution to Provide Order of Witnesses and Witness Statements, 28 May 2004: **R73*bis*-TC-6,** *R90-TC-6*
34. Decision on Preliminary Motion Based on Lack of Jurisdiction (Child Recruitment)(AC), 31 May 2004: **S1-AC-5, S4-AC-2, S4-AC-3, S4-AC-5**
35. Urgent Order to Permit Photography at the Opening of the Trials, 02 June 2004: **R81-TC-5**
36. Decision on Prosecution's Motion for Judicial Notice and Admission of Evidence, 2 June 2004: **R94-TC-1, R94-TC-2, R94-TC-3, R94-TC-4**
37. Decision on Request for Extension of Time to File Pre-Trial Brief, 4 June 2004: **R73*bis*-TC-24**
38. Decision on the Application of Samuel Hinga Norman for Self-Representation Under Article 17(4)(d) of the Statute of the Special Court, 8 June 2004: **S17-TC-12, S17-TC-13, R44-TC-1**
39. Decision on Prosecution Motion for Modification of Protective Measures for Witnesses, 08 June 2004: *R69-TC-4, R69-TC-5,* **R69-TC-13, R69-TC-19, R75-TC-3, R75-TC-4, R90-TC-2**
40. Consequential Order on Assignment and Role of Standby Counsel, 14 June 2004: *S17-TC-12,* **S17-TC-15, R44-TC-5**
41. Urgent Order to Permit Filming of the Public Gallery, 18 June 2004: *R81-TC-5,* **R81-TC-6**
42. Decision on Request by Samuel Hinga Norman for Additional Resources to Prepare His Defence, 23 June 2004: **S17-TC-9, R64-TC-1**
43. Decision on Motion to Compel the Production of Exculpatory Witness Statement, Witness Summaries and Materials Pursuant to Rule 68, 8 July 2004: **S14-TC-2, R68-TC-3, R68-TC-4, R68-TC-8**
44. Decision on Disclosure of Witness Statements and Cross-Examination, 16 July 2004: **R66-TC-1, R66-TC-4, R85-TC-5**
45. Order for Compliance of the Prosecution with Rule 94*bis*, 16 July 2004: **R94*bis*-TC-6**
46. Order to Prosecution to Provide Order of Witnesses and Witness Statements, 29 July 2004: *R73bis-TC-6, R90-TC-6*
47. Decision on Prosecution Request for Leave to Call Additional Witnesses, 29 July 2004: **R73*bis*-TC-10**
48. Scheduling Order for Status Conference (Under Rule 65*bis*), 29 July 2004
49. Order for Prosecution to Supplement Request, 30 July 2004
50. Majority Decision on the Prosecution's Application for Leave to File an Interlocutory Appeal Against the Decision on the Prosecution's Request for Leave to Amend the Indictment Against Samuel Hinga Norman, Moinina Fofana and Allieu Kondewa, 2 August 2004: **S1-TC-7, S15-TC-2, R50-TC-7,** *R73-TC-21, R73-TC-22,* **R73-TC-23, R73-TC-27**

51. Decision on Application for Bail Pursuant to Rule 65, 5 August 2004: **R65-TC-1, R65-TC-4, R65-TC-6, R65-TC-8, R65-TC-9, R65-TC-11, R65-TC-13, R65-TC-17, R89-TC-12**
52. Order Appointing Rule 65(E) Judge (AC), 7 September 2004
53. Order on Time Limits, 10 September 2004
54. Order on an Application by the Prosecution to Hold a Closed Session Hearing of Witnesses TF2-082 and TF2-032, 13 September 2004: **S14-TC-3, R79-TC-4**
55. Order on Filing, 23 September 2004
56. Order on an Application by the Prosecution to Hold a Closed Session Hearing of Witness TF2-151, 24 September 2004: *S14-TC-3, R79-TC-4*
57. Ruling on the Issue of Non-Appearance of the First Accused Samuel Hinga Norman, the Second Accused Moinina Fofana, and the Third Accused, Allieu Kondewa at the Trial Proceedings, 1 October 2004: **S17-TC-14,** *R60-TC-1,* **R60-TC-2**
58. Consequential Order on the Role of Court Appointed Counsel, 1 October 2004: **R44-TC-3**
59. Ruling on Disclosure of Witness Statements, 1st October 2004: *R66-TC-1,* **R67-TC-1**
60. Order on Protective Measures for Additional Witnesses, 1st October 2004: **R69-TC-5, R69-TC-12**
61. Decision on Prosecution Request for Leave to Call Additional Expert Witness Dr William Haglund, 1st October 2004: **R73*bis*-TC-11**
62. Consequential Order to Decision on Prosecution Request for Leave to Call Additional Expert Witness, 1st October 2004
63. Ruling on Defence Request for Disclosure of the Identity of a Possible Prosecution Expert Witness, 1st October 2004
64. Order to Permit Filming in the Court Room, 04 October 2004: **R81-TC-5,** *R81-TC-6*
65. Decision on Joint Request to Appeal Against Decision on Prosecutor's Motion for Judicial Notice, 19 October 2004: *R73-TC-21*, **R73-TC-33**
66. Order on an Application by the Prosecution to Hold a Closed Session Hearing of Witness TF2-223, 27 October 2004: *S14-TC-3, R79-TC-4*
67. Order Revoking Additional resources Provided to Sam Hinga Norman for the Preparation of His Self Defence, 27 October 2004: **S17-TC-10**
68. Order on Trial Monitoring During Closed Session, 27 October 2004: **R79-TC-10**
69. Order on Prosecution Map Exhibits, 27 October 2004: **R85-TC-1, R89-TC-15**
70. Oral Ruling on Motion for Modification of Protective Measures for Witnesses, 2 November 2004: **R75-TC-2**
71. Order on Co-operation Between the Parties, 3 November 2004: **R73*bis*-TC-20**

72. Order to Prosecution to Re-File Motion and Seek Leave to Submit Supplementary Materials, 3 November 2004
73. Decision Application for Leave to Appeal Bail Decision (AC), 5 November 2004: **R65-AC-6**
74. Order on Trial Monitoring During Closed Session, 5 November 2004: *R79-TC-10*
75. Ruling Granting the Prosecution Leave to Submit Supplementary Materials, 9 November 2004: **R73-TC-15**
76. Decision and Order on Prosecution Request for an Extension of Time (AC), 12 November 2004: **R7*bis*-AC-1**
77. Ruling on Motion for Modification of Protective Measures for Witnesses, 18 November 2004: **R69-TC-16, R69-TC-23, R69-TC-25**
78. Consequential Order on the Withdrawal of Ms. Quincy Whitaker as Court Appointed Counsel for the First Accused, 19 November 2004: **S17-TC-3, R44-TC-9**
79. Decision on Motion to Correct the Record Concerning the Decision for Modification of the Conditions of Detention (AC), 25 November 2004
80. Order to Permit Filming in the Court Room, 26 November 2004: *R81-TC-6*
81. Order under Rule 65(H), 26 November 2004
82. Decision on the First Accused's Motion for Service and Arraignment on the Consolidated Indictment, 29 November 2004: **S9-TC-2, R47-TC-6, R50-TC-8, R50-TC-10, R50-TC-12, R52-TC-2, R82-TC-2**
83. Consequential Order to the Decision on the First Accused's Motion for Service and Arraignment on the Consolidated Indictment, 30 November 2004
84. Decision on Motion Requesting Reasons for Decision Ordering Witness TF2-201 to Testify in Closed Session, 2 December 2004
85. Decision on Protective Measures for Witness TF2-067, 2 December 2004
86. Decision on Request of the First Accused for Leave to Cross-Examine Expert Witness Out of Time, 2 December 2004
87. Decision on the Second Accused's Motion for Service and Arraignment on the Consolidated Indictment, 6 December 2004: *R47-TC-6*, **R50-TC-11**, *R52-TC-2, R82-TC-2*
88. Ruling on Defence Oral Application to Call OTP Investigators Who Took Down in Writing Statements of Prosecution Witness TF2-021, 7 December 2004: **R90-TC-8**
89. Decision on the Third Accused's Motion for Service and Arraignment on the Consolidated Indictment, 8 December 2004: *R50-TC-11, R50-TC-12, R52-TC-2*
90. Decision on Prosecution Application for Leave to Appeal "Decision on

the First Accused's Motion for Service and Arraignment on the Consolidated Indictment", 15 December 2004: *R73-TC-22,* **R73-TC-30, R73-TC-38**
91. Decision on Application by First Accused for Leave to Make Interlocutory Appeal Against the decision on the First Accused's Motion for Service and Arraignment on the Consolidated Indictment, 16 December 2004: *R73-TC-30*
92. Decision on Prosecution Appeal Against the Trial Chamber's Decision of 2 August 2004 Refusing Leave to File an Interlocutory Appeal (AC), 17 January 2005: **S1-AC-7, R73-AC-3, R73-AC-6, R73-AC-8**
93. Order to Prosecution to Provide Order of Witnesses and Witness Statements, 26 January 2005: *R73bis-TC-6*
94. Scheduling Order for Status Conference (Under Rule 65*bis*), 26 January 2005
95. Ruling on Defence Oral Application to Call OTP Investigators Who Took in Writing Statements of Prosecution Witness TF2-021, 2 February 2005: *R90-TC-8*
96. Order on Filing, 7 February 2005: **R33-TC-5**
97. Order to Permit Photography in Court Room, 14 February 2005: *R81-TC-6*
98. Order to Prosecution to File Military Experts Curriculum Vitae, 24 February 2005: *R94bis-TC-6*
99. Decision on the Joint Motion by Sam Hinga Norman, Moinina Fofana and Allieu Kondewa Seeking Permission for Defence Investigators to Sit in Court During Closed Sessions, 28 February 2005: **R79-TC-8**
100. Ruling on Request for Withdrawal of Mr. Tim Owen QC, as Court Appointed Counsel for the First Accused, 1 March 2005: **R44-TC-10**
101. Decision on Presentation of Witness Testimony on Moyamba Crime Base, 1 March 2005: **R73-TC-43**
102. Ruling on Defence Oral Application to Call an OTP Investigator Who Took a Written Statement from Prosecution Witness TF2-022, 1st March 2005: **R85-TC-3,** *R90-TC-8,* **R90-TC-9**
103. Appeal Against Decision Refusing Bail (AC), 11 March 2005: **R65-AC-1, R65-AC-2, R65-AC-3, R65-AC-4, R65-AC-7, R89-AC-1, R89-AC-3, R89-AC-4**
104. Order for Full Bench (AC), 18 March 2005
105. Order on Disclosure and Characterisation of the Age of Witness TF2-080, 14 April 2005: **R90-TC-3**
106. Decision on First Accused's Motion on Abuse of Process, 28 April 2005: **R46-TC-1, R72-TC-5, R72-TC-7, R72*bis*-TC-2, R73-TC-44, R73-TC-45**

107. Decision on Request for Stayed Witness Indexing, 28 April 2005: **R73*bis*-TC-7**
108. Decision on Amendment of the Consolidated Indictment (AC), 16 May 2005: **S14-AC-3, S14-AC-4, S20-AC-7, S20-AC-9, R3-AC-1, R5-AC-1, R45*bis*-AC-2, R47-AC-1, R47-AC-2, R47-AC-3, R48-AC-1, R50-AC-1, R50-AC-2, R50-AC-3, R50-AC-4, R50-AC-5, R52-AC-1, R61-AC-1, R73-AC-7, R108-AC-2**
109. Decision on Appeal Against "Decision on Prosecution's Motion for Judicial Notice and Admission of Evidence" (AC), 16 May 2005: **S3-AC-3, R73-AC-4, R89-AC-2, R92*bis*-AC-1, R94-AC-1, R94-AC-2, R94-AC-3, R94-AC-4**
110. Decision on Request by the First Accused for Leave to Appeal Against the Trial Chamber's Decision on Presentation of Witness Testimony on Moyamba Crime Base, 23 May 2005: *R73-TC-21*
111. Decision on the Urgent Prosecution Motion Filed on the 15th of February 2005 for a Ruling on the Admissibility of Evidence, 23 May 2005
112. Decision on Request by the First Accused for Leave to Appeal Against the Trial Chamber's Decision on First Accused's Motion on Abuse of Process, 24 May 2005: **R3-TC-1, R46-TC-2**, *R73-TC-21, R73-TC-31*
113. Reasoned Majority Decision on Prosecution Motion for a Ruling on the Admissibility of Evidence, 24 May 2005: **S2-TC-3, R47-TC-2, R89-TC-9**
114. Decision on Prosecution Request for Leave to Call Additional Witnesses and for Orders for Protective Measures, 24 May 2005
115. Consequential Order on Amendment of the Consolidated Indictment, 25 May 2005
116. Order to Filming in the Court Gallery, 2 June 2005 (2 Orders): *R81-TC-6*
117. Scheduling Order on Filing Submissions by the Parties Should a Motion for Judgement of Acquittal Be Filed by Defence, 2 June 2005: **R98-TC-2**
118. Decision on Extremely Urgent Prosecution Request for an Extension of Time to Seek Leave to Appeal, 7 June 2005: **R73-TC-39**
119. Decision on Prosecution Request for Leave to Call an Additional Expert Witness, 10 June 2005: *R66-TC-1, R73bis-TC-10, R73bis-TC-12*
120. Decision on Prosecution Application for Closed Session for Witness TF2-218, 15 June 2005: **R79-TC-6**
121. Decision on Prosecution Request for Leave to Call Additional Witnesses and for Orders for Protective Measures, 21 June 2005: *R73bis-TC-10*, **R94*bis*-TC-1, R94*bis*-TC-4**

122. Decision on Request to Reverse the Order of the Acting Registrar Under Rule 47(A) of the Rules of Detention of 6 June 2005 (P), 29 June 2005: **S18-P-1, R64-P-5, R64-P-7**
123. Decision on Prosecution's Request to Admit into Evidence Certain Documents Pursuant to Rule 92*bis* and 89(C), 14 July 2005: **R92*bis*-TC-2**
124. Decision on Norman Counsel's Request for Leave to Appeal under Rule 46(H), 25 July 2005: **R46-TC-3, R46-TC-4**
125. Decision on Defence Request for Leave to Appeal Against the Consequential Non-Arraignment Order of Trial Chamber I, 18 May 2005, 25 July 2005: *R73-TC-21*
126. Order to the Prosecution on Filing, 20 September 2005: **R78-TC-2**
127. Decision on Motions for Judgement of Acquittal Pursuant to Rule 98, 21 October 2005: **S2-TC-1, S3-TC-1, S3-TC-2, S3-TC-3, S3-TC-4, S3-TC-5, S3-TC-7, S4-TC-1, S6-TC-3, S20-TC-8, R98-TC-1**
128. Order for the Preparation and the Presentation of the Defence Case, 21 October 2005: **R73*ter*-TC-1**
129. Scheduling Order for Status Conference, 18 November 2005
130. Order Re-Scheduling Status Conference and Order for Submissions by the Prosecution, 21 November 2005
131. Order Detailing Judicial Calendar, 25 November 2005
132. Consequential Order for Compliance with the Order Concerning the Preparation and Presentation of the Defence Case, 28 November 2005: *R73*ter-TC-1*
133. Order on Urgent Motion for Reconsideration or, in the Alternative, for Leave to Appeal the Orders for Compliance with the Order Concerning the Preparation and Presentation of the Defence Case, 29 November 2005: **R73-TC-40**
134. Order for Submissions and Interim Order Pursuant to Rule 54 of the Rules, 1st December 2005: **R69-TC-14**
135. Order for Expedited Filing, 1st December 2005
136. Decision on Urgent Motion for Reconsideration of the Orders for Compliance with the Order Concerning the Preparation and Presentation of the Defence Case, 7 December 2005: **R5-TC-2, R73-TC-18**, *R73-AC-3*
137. Order on the Appointment of Additional Counsel for the Norman Defence Team, 8 December 2005
138. Decision on Fofana Motion for Adjustment of Status of Counsel, 9 December 2005

Prosecutor v. Sesay, Kallon, Gbao ("R.U.F. Case"),
Case No. SCSL-04-15

1. Decision for the Assignment of a New Case Number, 3 February 2004
2. Order for Expedited Filing, 4 February 2004: **R7-TC-3**
3. Scheduling Order for Status Conference (Under Rule 65*bis*), 13 February 2004: *R65*bis*-TC-1*
4. Decision on Prosecution's Application for Leave to File an Interlocutory Appeal Against the Decision on the Prosecution Motions for Joinder, 13 February 2004: **R73-TC-21**
5. Order for Filing Pre-Trial Briefs (Under Rules 54 and 73*bis*), 13 February 2004: *R73*bis*-TC-2*
6. Order for Filing a Consolidated Reply, 23 February 2004
7. Decision on the Motion by Morris Kallon for Bail, 24 February 2004: **R65-TC-3, R65-TC-5, R65-TC-7, R65-TC-14, R65-TC-16,** *R65-P-1,* **R78-TC-1**
8. Order to Submit Indication of Specific Changes to Indictments, 26 February 2004: *R50-TC-1*
9. Reasons for Order for Closed Session of the Status Conference and Modification of Said Order in Part, 5 March 2004: **R65*bis*-TC-2, R79-TC-3**
10. Order for the Suspension of the Time Limit for Filing of Application for Leave to Appeal Against Refusal of Bail (AC), 5 March 2004
11. Decision on Constitutionality and Lack of Jurisdiction (AC), 13 March 2004: **S1-AC-1, S1-AC-4, S1-AC-6, S8-AC-1**
12. Decision on Challenge to Jurisdiction: Lomé Accord Amnesty (AC), 13 March 2004: **S4-AC-4, S8-AC-2, S10-AC-1, S10-AC-2, S17-AC-2**
13. Decision on Defence Motion Seeking the Disqualification of Justice Robertson from the Appeals Chamber (AC), 13 March 2004: **R15-AC-1, R23-AC-1**
14. Decision on the Defence Motion for Extension of Time to File Reply to "Prosecution Response to Defence Motion for Quashing Consolidated Indictment", 19 March 2004: **R45-TC-9**
15. Order to the Prosecution to File a Supplemental Pre-Trial Brief, 30 March 2004: **R73*bis*-TC-1, R82-TC-1**
16. Decision on Application of Issa Sesay for Provisional Release, 31 March 2004: **S19-TC-5,** *R65-TC-3, R65-TC-5,* **R65-TC-10, R65-TC-12, R65-TC-15,** *R65-TC-16, R78-TC-1*
17. Order to the Prosecution to File Disclosure Materials and Other Materials in Preparation of the Commencement of Trial, 1st April 2004: *R6-TC-1*
18. Order to Extend the Time for Filing of the Prosecution Supplemental Pre-Trial Brief, 2 April 2004: **R26*bis*-TC-5**

19. Order to the Prosecution for Renewed Motion for Protective Measures, 2 April 2004: *R69-TC-3, R69-TC-11, R69-TC-24*
20. Order for a Pre-Trial Conference (Under Rule 73*bis*), 2 April 2004
21. Defence Motion for Extension of Time for Filing Application for Leave to Appeal Against Refusal of Bail, 19 April 2004: **R116-AC-1**
22. Decision on Motion for Quashing of Consolidated Indictment, 21 April 2004
23. Scheduling Order for *In Camera* Hearing, 23 April 2004: *R7-TC-4*
24. Decision on the Defence Motion for Extension of Time to File Response to the Prosecution Motion for Judicial Notice and Admission of Evidence, 26 April 2004: **R7*bis*-TC-7**
25. Order for Expedited Filing, 30 April 2004: *R7-TC-4*
26. Order to File Outstanding Documents in Support of the Judicial Notice Motion, 4 May 2004
27. Decision on Defence Urgent Request for Extension of Time to Respond the Prosecution's Motion to Hear Evidence Concurrently, 5 May 2004: **R7*bis*-TC-8**
28. Decision on Prosecution request for Leave to Amend the Indictment, 6 May 2004: **S2-TC-4, S15-TC-1, S17-TC-5, S17-TC-8, R50-TC-2, R50-TC-5**
29. Decision on Appeal by the Truth and Reconciliation Commission ("TRC") and Accused Against the Decision of Judge Bankole Thompson on 3 November 2003 to Deny the TRC's Request to Hold a Public Hearing with Augustine Gbao (AC), 7 May 2004: *S1-AC-9*
30. Order Appointing Rule 65(E) Judge (AC), 10 June 2004
31. Decision on the Prosecution Motion for Concurrent Hearing of Evidence Common to Cases SCSL-2004-15-PT and SCSL-2004-16-PT, 11 May 2004: **R26*bis*-TC-3, R26*bis*-TC-4, R48-TC-9, R92*bis*-TC-1**
32. Scheduling Order, 11 May 2004
33. Order for Commencement of Trial, 11 May 2004
34. Consequential Order and Corrigendum to the Decision on Prosecution Request for Leave to Amend the Indictment, 12 May 2004
35. Scheduling Order for the Further Appearance of the Accused on the Amended Consolidated Indictment, 12 May 2004
36. Order for Filing of a Consolidated Reply, 13 May 2004: *R7-TC-5*
37. Order on Extension of Time for the Principal Defender to File Report, 14 May 2004
38. Order for Expedited Filing, 17 May 2004: *R7-TC-3*
39. Order for Rescheduling (AC), 17 May 2004
40. Decision on Preliminary Motion on the Invalidity of the Agreement Between the United Nations and the Government of Sierra Leone on the Establishment of the Special Court (AC), 25 May 2004: *S1-AC-1, S10-AC-1, R72-AC-3*

41. Decision on Defence Motion Seeking Clarification of the Decision on the Disqualification of Justice Robertson from the Appeals Chamber, 25 May 2004
42. Order Detailing Judicial Calendar for the Upcoming Trial Sessions, 26 May 2004
43. Decision on the Prosecution Application for Leave to File an Interlocutory Appeal Against Decision on Motion for Concurrent Hearing of Evidence Common to Cases SCSL-2004-15-PT and SCSL-2004-16-PT, 1 June 2004: *R73-TC-21,* **R73-TC-22,** *R73-TC-26*
44. Urgent Order to Permit Photography at the Opening of the Trials, 2 June 2004: **R81-TC-5**
45. Order for Call Over, 2 June 2004
46. Scheduling Order for Status Conference (Under Rule 65*bis*), 15 June 2004
47. Decision on Co-operation Between the Parties, 16 June 2004: **R73*bis*-TC-19**
48. Urgent Order to Permit Filming of the Public Gallery, 18 June 2004: *R81-TC-5*, **R81-TC-6**
49. Scheduling Order (AC), 18 June 2004
50. Revised Scheduling Order (AC), 21 June 2004
51. Decision on Application for Leave to Appeal Against Refusal of Bail (AC), 23 June 2004: **S20-AC-8, S65-AC-5**
52. Decision on Prosecution's Motion for Judicial Notice and Admission of Evidence, 24 June 2004: *R94-TC-1, R94-TC-2, R94-TC-3, R94-TC-4*
53. Decision on Prosecution Motion for Modification of Protective Measures for Witnesses, 5 July 2004: *R44-TC-6*, **R69-TC-6**, *R69-TC-17, R75-TC-3, R75-TC-4*, **R75-TC-7**
54. Decision on Application to Withdraw Counsel, 7 July 2004: **R44-TC-2, R45-TC-11**
55. Order to Prosecution to Produce Witness List and Witness Summaries, 7 July 2004: **R73*bis*-TC-3**
56. Decision on Defence Motion for Disclosure Pursuant to Rule 66 and 68 of the Rules, 9 July 2004: *S14-TC-2*, **R66-TC-14, R66-TC-18, R68-TC-1, R68-TC-5**
57. Ruling on Oral Application for Respect of Disclosure Obligations, 9 July 2004
58. Ruling on the Issue of the Refusal of the Third Accused, Augustine Gbao, to Attend Hearing of the Special Court for Sierra Leone on 7 July 2004 and Succeeding Days, 12 July 2004: **R60-TC-1**
59. Order for Expedited Filing, 13 July 2004: *R7-TC-3*
60. Decision on Defence Motion, 15 July 2004: **R69-TC-20, R73-TC-3,** *R78-TC-1*
61. Ruling on Oral Application for the Exclusion of "Additional" Statement for Witness TF1-060, 23 July 2004: *R66-TC-1*, **R66-TC-15**

62. Ruling on the Oral Application for the Exclusion of Part of the Testimony of Witness TF1-199, 26 July 2004: *R66-TC-1, R85-TC-4,* **R85-TC-6**
63. Scheduling Order (AC), 26 July 2004
64. Ruling on the Oral Application for the Postponement of the Testimony of Witness TF1-060, 27 July 2004: **R69-TC-21**
65. Scheduling Order (AC), 27 July 2004
66. Decision on Confidential Motion Seeking Disclosure of Documentation Relating to the Motion on the Recruitment of Child Soldiers (AC), 28 July 2004
67. Decision on Application for Leave to Appeal Against Refusal of Bail (AC), 28 July 2004: *S20-AC-8, R65-AC-5*
68. Decision on Prosecution Request for Leave to Call Additional Witnesses, 29 July 2004: *R73bis-TC-10*
69. Scheduling Order for Status Conference (Under Rule 65*bis*), 2 August 2004
70. Decision on Application for Leave to Appeal Decision on Application to Withdraw Counsel, 4 August 2004: *S17-TC-13, R73-TC-21, R73-TC-22,* **R73-TC-34, R73-TC-35**
71. Order on Time Limit (AC), 30 August 2004
72. Order Under Rule 65(H) (AC), 30 August 2004
73. Order on Time Limits (AC), 8 September 2004: **R110-AC-1**
74. Order to Prosecution to Provide Order of Witnesses, 15 September 2004: **R73*bis*-TC-5**
75. Decision on Appeal Against the Decision of the Trial Chamber Refusing Application for Bail by Morris Kallon (AC), 17 September 2004: **R108-AC-1, R108-AC-4**
76. Order Under Rule 65(H) (AC), 20 September 2004
77. Order to Permit Filming in the Court Room, 04 October 2004: **R81-TC-7**
78. Order for Expedited Filing, 4 October 2004
79. Order Detailing Judicial Calendar, 8 October 2004
80. Decision on Confidential Motion, 11 October 2004: *R73-TC-3, R78-TC-1*
81. Decision on Application to Withdraw Motion Seeking the Disqualification of Justice Robertson from all Judicial Functions Regarding the RUF (AC), 15 October 2004
82. Decision on Prosecution's Intention to Extend Protective Measures for Additional Witnesses, 22 October 2004: **R73-TC-2, R75-TC-1**
83. Order on Trial Monitoring During Closed Session, 27 October 2004: *R79-TC-10*
84. Order on Prosecution Map Exhibits, 28 October 2004: *R85-TC-1, R89-TC-15*

85. Scheduling Order for Status Conference, 1 November 2004
86. Order on Trial Monitoring During Closed Session, 5 November 2004: *R79-TC-10*
87. Order to Hear the Evidence of Witness TF1-235 in Closed Session, 8 November 2004: *R69-TC-22*
88. Order on Co-operation Between the Parties, 9 November 2004: **R73*bis*-TC-21**
89. Decision on Appeal Against Decision on Withdrawal of Counsel (AC), 23 November 2004: **R45-AC-3, R45*bis*-AC-1, R60-AC-1**
90. Order on Protective Measures for Additional Witnesses, 24 November 2004: *R69-TC-6*
91. Order to Prosecution Concerning Renewed Witness List, 3 December 2004: **R73*bis*-TC-9**
92. Decision on Motion on Issues of Urgent Concern to the Accused Morris Kallon, 9 December 2004: **R50-TC-9, R52-TC-3**
93. Decision on Appeal Against Refusal of Bail (AC), 14 December 2004: **S20-AC-4, R65-AC-8, R65-AC-9, R65-AC-10, R65-AC-11, R65-AC-12, R108-AC-5**
94. Ruling on the Issue of the Refusal of the Accused Sesay and Kallon to Appear for their Trial, 19 January 2005: *R60-TC-1*
95. Order to Hear the Evidence of Witness TF1-071 in Closed Session, 19 January 2005: **R79-TC-5**
96. Ruling on Disclosure Regarding Witness TF1-015, 28 January 2005: **R85-TC-2**
97. Ruling on Oral Application for the Exclusion of Statements of Witness TF1-141 Dated Respectively 9th of October, 2004 19th and 20th of October, 2004, and 10th of January, 2005, 3 February 2005: *R66-TC-1, R66-TC-15*
98. Ruling on Disclosure Regarding Witness TF1-195, 4 February 2005: *R66-TC-1, R66-TC-2,* **R66-TC-13**, *R66-TC-14, R66-TC-15, R66-TC-18*
99. Ruling on the Admission of Command Structure Chart as an Exhibit, 4 February 2005: **R66-TC-5, R85-TC-4, R89-TC-2, R89-TC-3, R89-TC-4**
100. Scheduling Order for Status Conference in the Trial of the RUF Group of Indictees (Under Rules 65*bis*), 07 February 2005
101. Decision on Prosecution Request for Leave to Call Additional Witnesses and Disclose Additional Witness Statements, 11 February 2005: **R73-TC-6,** *R73*bis*-TC-10,* **R73*bis*-TC-12, R73*bis*-TC-13, R73*bis*-TC-14, R73*bis*-TC-15**
102. Order for Compliance of Prosecution with Rule 94*bis*, 9 March 2005: *R94*bis*-TC-6*
103. Decision Regarding the Prosecutor's Further Renewed Witness List, 5 April 2005: *R73*bis*-TC-10, R73*bis*-TC-12,* **R73*bis*-TC-16**

104. Ruling on the Oral Application of the Prosecution to Vary Protective Measures of Witness TF1-141, 6 April 2005: **R69-TC-7**
105. Ruling on Request to Re-Open the Cross-Examination of Witness TF1-012, 6 April 2005: **R85-TC-7**
106. Consequential Order to the Decision on Further Renewed Witness List, 14 April 2005: **R73*bis*-TC-8**
107. Order Detailing Amendments to Judicial Calendar, 18 April 2005
108. Decision on the Defence Applications for Leave to Appeal Ruling of the 3rd of February, 2005 on the Exclusion of Statements of Witness TF1-141, 28 April 2005: **R73-TC-20,** *R73-TC-21*, **R73-TC-24, R73-TC-28, R73-TC-37,** *R73-AC-6*
109. Decision on Sesay Motion Seeking Disclosure of the Relationship Between Governmental Agencies of the United States of America and the Office of the Prosecutor, 2 May 2005: *S14-TC-1, S14-TC-2*, **S15-TC-3, R39-TC-1, R68-TC-2,** *R68-TC-4, R68-TC-5*, **R68-TC-6, R68-TC-7, R68-TC-9**
110. Decision on Application for Leave for Interlocutory Appeal Against the Majority Decision of the Trial Chamber of the 9th December 2004 on the Motion on Issues of Urgent Concern to the Accused Morris Kallon, 2 May 2005: *R73-TC-21*, **R73-TC-25, R73-TC-29**
111. Order on Urgent Application for Extension of Time, 2 May 2005
112. Decision on the Urgent and Confidential Prosecution Application to Vary Protective Measures Regarding Witnesses TF1-104 and TF1-081, 11 May 2005
113. Ruling on the Prosecution's Application for Portions of the Testimony of Witness TF1-060 to Be Heard in Closed Session, 11 May 2005
114. Ruling on the Prosecution's Application for the Entire Testimony of Witness TF1-362 to Be Heard in Closed Session, 11 May 2005
115. Ruling on the Prosecution's Application for the Entire Testimony of Witness TF1-129 to Be Heard in Closed Session, 11 May 2005
116. Ruling on the First Accused's Application for Portions of the Testimony of Witness TF1-125 to Be Heard in Closed Session, 16 May 2005
117. Order Detailing Amendment to Judicial Calendar and Scheduling Order for Status Conference, 20 May 2005
118. Consequential Order Regarding Decision on Prosecution's Motion for Judicial Notice and Admission of Evidence, 23 May 2005: **R73-TC-41**
119. Ruling on Gbao Application to Exclude Evidence of Prosecution Witness Mr. Koker, 23 May 2005: *R89-TC-3*, **R89-TC-5**, *R89-AC-4*
120. Order Permitting the Temporary Transfer of Certain Exhibits, 31 May 2005: **R48-TC-10**
121. Ruling on Application for the Exclusion of Certain Supplemental Statements of Witness TF1-361 and Witness TF1-122, 1st June 2005: *R66-TC-1, R66-TC-4, R66-TC-15, R78-TC-1, R89-TC-5, R89-AC-4*

122. Order Detailing Judicial Calendar, 2 June 2005
123. Decision on Prosecution request for Leave to Call an Additional Expert Witness, 10 June 2005: *R66-TC-1, R73bis-TC-10, R73bis-TC-11, R73bis-TC-12*
124. Decision on Application for Leave to Appeal the Ruling (2nd May 2005) on Sesay Motion Seeking Disclosure of the Relationship Between Governmental Agencies of the United States of America and the Office of the Prosecutor, 15 June 2005: *R73-TC-22, R73-TC-25,* **R73-TC-32**
125. Ruling on the Identification of Signatures by Witness TF1-360, 14 October 2005: *R89-TC-5*, **R89-TC-7, R89-TC-16**
126. Decision on the Gbao and Sesay Joint Application for the Exclusion of the Testimony of Witness TF1-141, 26 October 2005: *R66-TC-4*, **R66-TC-8**, *R66-TC-13, R66-TC-18*, **R70-TC-1, R70-TC-2**
127. Decision on the Joint Defence Motion Requesting Conformity of Procedural Practice for Taking Witness Statements, 26 October 2005: *R66-TC-4*, **R66-TC-6**, *R66-TC-8, R89-TC-5*, **R89-TC-8**, *R89-AC-4*, **R89-TC-17**, *R92bis-TC-2*
128. Order for Extension of Time to Respond the Prosecution Confidential Notice Under 92*bis* to Admit Transcripts of Testimony of TF1-023, TF1-104 and TF1-169, 27 October 2005: **R7*bis*-TC-15**
129. Decision on Prosecution Motion Objecting to Defence Submissions of Witness Statements with Inconsistencies Marked, 27 October 2005: *R66-TC-4*
130. Decision on the Prosecution Confidential Notice Under 92*bis* to Admit the Transcripts of Testimony of TF1-023, TF1-104 and TF1-169, 9 November 2005: *R92bis-TC-2*, **R92*bis*-TC-5**
131. Order on Trial Monitoring During Closed Session, 9 November 2005: *R79-TC-10*
132. Order to Permit Filming in the Courtroom, 18 November 2005: **R81-TC-8**

Prosecutor v. Brima, Kamara, Kanu ("A.F.R.C. Case"),
Case No. SCSL-04-16

1. Decision for the Assignment of a New Case Number, 3 February 2004
2. Order for Expedited Filing, 4 February 2004: *R7-TC-3*
3. Order for Interim Measures in Relation to Assignment of Counsel for Accused Brima, 12 February 2004
4. Scheduling Order for Status Conference (Under Rule 65*bis*), 13 February 2004: *R65bis-TC-1*

5. Decision on Prosecution's Application for Leave to File an Interlocutory Appeal Against the Decision on the Prosecution Motions for Joinder, 13 February 2004: *R73-TC-21*
6. Order for Filing Pre-Trial Briefs (Under Rules 54 and 73*bis*), 13 February 2004: *R73bis-TC-2*
7. Order to Submit Indication of Specific Changes to Indictments, 26 February 2004: *R50-TC-1*
8. Decision on Constitutionality and Lack of Jurisdiction (AC), 13 March 2004: **S1-AC-1, S1-AC-4, S1-AC-6, S8-AC-1**
9. Decision on Challenge to Jurisdiction: Lomé Accord Amnesty (AC), 13 March 2004: **S4-AC-4, S8-AC-2, S10-AC-1, S10-AC-2, S17-AC-2**
10. Written Reasons for the Trial Chamber's Oral Decision on the Defence Motion on Abuse of Process Due to Infringement of Principles of *Nullum Crimen Sine Lege* and Non-Retroactivity as to Several Accounts, 31 March 2004: **S1-TC-3**, *S8-TC-1*, **S9- TC-1, R72-TC-6, R77-TC-6**
11. Decision and Order on Defence Preliminary Motion on Defects in the Form of the Indictment, 1 April 2004: *S6-TC-1*, **S20-TC-7**, *R47-TC-1, R47-TC-3, R47-TC-5*, **R47-TC-7**, *R47-TC-8*, **R47-TC-11, R55-TC-3, R66-TC-9, R67-TC-2**
12. Order to the Prosecution to File Disclosure Materials and Other Materials in Preparation of the Commencement of Trial, 1st April 2004: *R6-TC-1*
13. Order to the Prosecution to File a Supplemental Pre-Trial Brief and Revised Order for Filing Defence Pre-Trial Briefs, 1st April 2004: *R73bis-TC-1*
14. Order to the Prosecution for Renewed Motion for Protective Measures, 2 April 2004
15. Order for a Pre-Trial Conference (Under Rule 73*bis*), 2 April 2004
16. Scheduling Order Setting a New Date for the Pre-Trial Conference, 28 April 2004
17. Order for Expedited Filing, 30 April 2004
18. Order to File Outstanding Documents in Support of the Judicial Notice Motion, 4 May 2004
19. Decision on Prosecution Request for Leave to Amend the Indictment, 6 May 2004: *S2-TC-4, S15-TC-1, S17-TC-5, S17-TC-8*
20. Decision on Applicant's Motion Against Denial by the Acting Principal Defender to Enter a Legal Service Contract for the Assignment of Counsel, 6 May 2004: **S1-TC-4, S14-TC-1, S17-TC-16, R31-TC-1, R33-TC-1, R44-TC-7, R45-TC-4, R45-TC-5, R45-TC-6, R45-TC-10,** *R50-TC-2, R50-TC-5,* **R72-TC-3**
21. Decision on the Prosecution Motion for Concurring Hearing of Evidence Common to Cases SCSL-04-15-PT and SCSL-04-16-PT, 11 May 2004: *R26bis-TC-3, R26bis-TC-4, R48-TC-9, R92bis-TC-1*

22. Scheduling Order, 11 May 2004
23. Consequential Order and Corrigendum to the Decision on Prosecution Request for Leave to Amend the Indictment, 12 May 2004
24. Scheduling Order for the Further Appearance of the Accused on the Amended Consolidated Indictment, 12 May 2004
25. Order for Expedited Filing, 17 May 2004
26. Decision on Motion Challenging Jurisdiction and Raising Objections Based on Abuse of Process (AC), 25 May 2004: **S1-AC-3**
27. Decision on Defence Motion in Respect of Santigie Borbor Kanu for an Order under Rule 54 with Respect to Release of Exculpatory Evidence, 1 June 2004: **R8-TC-2, R54-TC-2**
28. Decision on Prosecution Application for Leave to File an Interlocutory Appeal Against Decision on Motion for Concurrent Hearing of Evidence Common to Cases SCSL-2004-15-PT and SCSL-2004-16-PT, 1 June 2004: *R73-TC-21, R73-TC-22, R73-TC-26*
29. Decision on Motion for Exclusion of Prosecution Witness Statements and Stay of Filing of Prosecution Statements, 30 July 2004: *S20-TC-7*, **R6-TC-4,** *R66-TC-1*, **R66-TC-2**
30. Decision on Motion for Exclusion of Prosecution Witness Statements and Stay of Filing of Prosecution Statements, 2 August 2004: *R6-TC-4, R66-TC-1, R66-TC-2*
31. Order Assigning a Case to a Trial Chamber (P), 17 January 2005: **R19-P-1**
32. Order for Commencement of Trial and Scheduling Order, 20 January 2005
33. Interim Order on Modification of Protective Measures for Witnesses, 20 January 2005
34. Scheduling Order, 28 January 2005
35. Decision on Prosecution's Motion for Protective Measures Pursuant to Order to the Prosecution for Renewed Motion for Protective Measures Dated 2 April 2004, 3 February 2005: **R75-TC-5**
36. Decision on Application for Leave to File an Interlocutory Appeal Against Decision on Motions for Exclusion of Prosecution Witness Statements and Stay on Filing of Prosecution Statements, 4 February 2005: *R73-TC-21*
37. Order for Expedited Filing and Scheduling Order, 7 February 2005
38. Order to Prosecution to Provide Order of Witnesses and Witness Statements, 9 February 2005: *R73*bis-*TC-6*
39. Decision on the Prosecution Application to Further Amend the Amended Consolidated Indictment by Withdrawing Counts 15-18, 15 February 2005: **R50-TC-4**
40. Decision on Kanu's Motion for Dismissal of Counts 15-18 of the Indictment Due to an Alibi Defence and Lack of *Prima Facie* Case

and Request for Extension of Time for the Hearing of the Defence Motion, 15 February 2005: **R73-TC-16**
41. Decision on Defence Applications Not to Disclose Photography, Video and Audio Recordings of the Trial to the Public and/or Third Parties, 28 February 2005: **R81-TC-9, R90-TC-4**
42. Decision on the Defence Motion for Defects in the Form of the Indictment, 2 March 2005
43. Order Regarding the Disclosure of a Protected Witness TF1-081, 8 March 2005: **R77-TC-4, R81-TC-1**
44. Decision on Kanu Motion to Disclose Prosecution Material and/ or Other Information Pertaining to Rewards to Prosecution Trial Witnesses and Brima's Motion in Support, 16 March 2005
45. Order Under Rule 117(A) (AC), 6 April 2005
46. Decision on Confidential Prosecution Motion for Protective Measures for Witness TF1-272, 15 April 2005
47. Decision on the Report of the Independent Counsel Pursuant to Rules 77(C)(iii) and 77(D) of the Rules of Procedure and Evidence, 29 April 2005
48. Scheduling Order Detailing Amendments to the Judicial Calendar, 3 May 2005
49. Decision on Joint Defence Motion on Disclosure of All Original Witness Statements, Interview Notes and Investigator's Notes Pursuant to Rule 66 and/or 68, 4 May 2005: **R66-TC-3, R66-TC-7, R73-TC-7**
50. Order to Show Cause and Scheduling Order, 5 May 2005
51. Decision on the Urgent and Confidential Prosecution Application to Vary Protective Measures Regarding Witnesses TF1-104 and TF1-081, 11 May 2005
52. Consequential Order on the Role of Court Appointed Counsel, 13 May 2005: **R44-TC-4**
53. Order for Full Bench under Rule 117(A) (AC), 18 May 2005: **R117-AC-2**
54. Decision on the Confidential Application for Withdrawal by Counsel for Brima and Kamara and on the Request for Further Representation by Counsel for Kanu, 20 May 2005: **R44-TC-8, R45-TC-12, R45-TC-14, R60-TC-3,** *R60-AC-1*, **R74-TC-2, R77-TC-9,** *R78-TC-1*
55. Decision on Renewed Defence Motion for Defects in the Form of the Indictment and Application for Extension of Time, 24 May 2005: **R4-TC-1, R7*bis*-TC-11, R73-TC-13**
56. Decision on Joint Defence Motion to Exclude All Evidence from Witness TF1-277 Pursuant to Rule 89(C) and/or Rule 95, 24 May 2005: **R89-TC-10,** *R89-AC-1, R89-AC-3, R89-AC-4*, **R90-TC-1, R95-TC-1**
57. Decision on the Confidential Joint Defence Motion to Declare Null

and Void Testimony-in-Chief of Witness TF1-023, 25 May 2005: **R5-TC-1, R73-TC-17, R75-TC-6, R79-TC-1, R79-TC-9**
58. Scheduling Order on Judicial Notice Motion, 27 May 2005: **R73-TC-42**
59. Decision on the Extremely Urgent Confidential Joint Motion for the Re-Appointment of Kevin Metzger and Wilbert Harris as Lead Counsel for Alex Tamba Brima and Brima Bazzy Kamara and Decision on Cross-Motion by Deputy Principal Defender to Trial Chamber II for Clarification of its Oral Order of 12 May 2005, 9 June 2005: **S17-TC-17, R45-TC-3, R45-TC-8, R45-TC-13,** *R73-TC-7*, **R73-TC-8, R73-TC-12**
60. Order on Filing of Document, 9 June 2005: **R81-TC-2**
61. Decision on Objection to Question Put by Defence in Cross-Examination of Witness TF1-227, 15 June 2005: **R33-TC-6, R37-TC-1,** *R66-TC-3, R66-TC-15,* **R66-TC-16,** *R67-TC-1,* **R67-TC-3,** *R73-TC-7,* **R73-TC-9, R90-TC-7**
62. Decision on Joint Defence Application to Appeal Against the Ruling of Trial Chamber II of 5 April 2005, 15 June 2005: *R73-TC-21,* **R77-TC-7**
63. Decision on Confidential Joint Defence Request to Inspect *Locus in Quo* Concerning Evidence of Witness TF1-024, 15 June 2005: *R78-TC-1,* **R89-TC-13**
64. Decision on Joint Defence Motion Pertaining to Objections to the Nature of Testimony in Chief of Witness TF1-150, 16 June 2005: *R66-TC-1, R66-TC-15,* **R66-TC-17**
65. Decision on Joint Defence Motion on Admissibility of Expert Witness/Expert Evidence and Filing of Notice Pursuant to Rule 94*bis*(B)(i) and (ii), on Refiled Defence Request for Disclosure, and on the Joint Defence Motion for Exclusion of Medical Information, Statistics and Abstracts Pertaining to Witnesses TF1-081 and TF1-188, 16 June 2005: *R66-TC-17,* **R70-TC-3**
66. Order for a Written Representation from the Registrar Pursuant to Rule 33, 21 June 2005: **R33-TC-3**
67. Decision on Defence Appeal Motion Pursuant to Rule 77 (J) on Both the Imposition of Interim Measures and an Order Pursuant to Rule 77(C)(iii) (AC), 23 June 2005: **S14-AC-5, R75-AC-1, R75-AC-2, R77-AC-1, R77-AC-2, R77-AC-4, R77-AC-5**
68. Decision on Confidential Defence Request for Disclosure of Independent Investigator's Report on Contempt of Court Proceedings and Request for Stay of Proceedings, 30 June 2005: **R77-TC-8**
69. Order Under Rule 16 to Continue Trial in Absence of a Judge, 5 July 2005: **R16-TC-1**
70. Scheduling Order, 26 July 2005
71. Decision on Joint Defence Motion for General Orders Pursuant to Rule 54, 28 July 2005: **R54-TC-1, R64-TC-2**

72. Decision on Joint Defence Application for Leave to Appeal from Decision on Defence Motion to Exclude All Evidence from Witness TF1-277, 2 August 2005: *R73-TC-21*, **R89-TC-6**
73. Decision on Prosecution request for Leave to Call an Additional Witness (Zainab Hawa Bangura) Pursuant to Rule 73*bis*(E), and on Joint Defence Notice to Inform the Trial Chamber of its Position vis-à-vis the Proposed Expert Witness (Mrs Bangura) Pursuant to Rule 94*bis*, 5 August 2005: **S2-TC-5, S15-TC-4, R73-TC-10, R73*bis*-TC-4,** *R73*bis*-TC-10, R73*bis*-TC-12,* **R94*bis*-TC-2, R94*bis*-TC-7**
74. Decision on Brima-Kamara Application for Leave to Appeal from Decision on the Re-Appointment of Kevin Metzger and Wilbert Harris as Lead Counsel, 5 August 2005: *R73-TC-21*
75. Decision on Prosecution Request for Leave to Call an Additional Witness Pursuant to Rule 73*bis*(E), 5 August 2005: *R73bis-TC-10*
76. Decision on Joint Defence Appeal Against the Decision on the Report of the Independent Counsel Pursuant to Rule 77(C)(iii) and 77(D) (AC), 17 August 2005: **R77-AC-3**
77. Decision on the Prosecution's Oral Application for Leave to Be Granted to Witness TF1-150 to Testify Without Being Compelled to Answer Any Questions in Cross-Examination That the Witness Declines to Answer on Grounds of Confidentiality Pursuant to Rule 70(B) and (D) of the Rules, 16 September 2005: **R70-TC-4, R70-TC-5, R79-TC-7**
78. Order for a Written Representation of the Registrar Pursuant to Rule 33 on Security Measures for a Potential Temporary release of the Accused Kanu, 22 September 2005: *R33-TC-3*
79. Scheduling Order on Filing of a Motion for Judgement of Acquittal, 30 September 2005: **R98-TC-3**
80. Order for a Written Representation from the Registrar Pursuant to Rule 33 on Security Measures for a Site Visit to Karina Town in the Bombali District of Sierra Leone, 10 October 2005: *R33-TC-3*
81. Decision on Confidential Urgent Joint Defence Motion to Exclude Evidence Given by Witness TF1-157 and Evidence to Be Given by Witness TF1-158 Based on Lack of Authenticity and Violation of Rule 95, 10 October 2005: **R90-TC-5**
82. Order Under Rule 16 to Continue Trial in Absence of a Judge, 11 October 2005: *R16-TC-1*, **R17-TC-1**
83. Decision on Prosecution Application for Leave to Appeal Decision on Oral Application for Witness TF1-150 to Testify Without Being Compelled to Answer Questions on Grounds of Confidentiality, 12 October 2005: *R73-TC-21, R73-AC-7*
84. Decision on Defence Submission Providing Evidentiary Proof of Registry's Repeated Dissemination of Confidential Documents to the

Press and Public Affairs Office, 18 October 2005: **R19-TC-1, R27-TC-1, R33-TC-2**
85. Decision on the Defence Motion for the Temporary Provisional Release to Allow the Accused Santigie Borbor Kanu to Visit His Mother's Grave, 18 October 2005: **R27-TC-2, R64-TC-3**
86. Order for Full Bench (AC), 18 October 2005
87. Decision on the Prosecution Motion for Judicial Notice and Admission of Evidence, 25 October 2005: **R89-TC-11, R92*bis*-TC-3**, *R92*bis-*AC-1, R94-AC-2, R94-AC-3*
88. Decision on Prosecution Motion for a *Locus in Quo* Visit to Karina, Bombali District, The Republic of Sierra Leone, 25 October 2005: **R89-TC-14**
89. Decision on Joint Defence Motion for Leave to Recall Witness TF1-023, 25 October 2005: **R90-TC-10**
90. Decision on Prosecution Tender for Admission into Evidence of Information Contained in Notice Pursuant to Rule 92*bis*, 18 November 2005: **R89-TC-1,** *R89-TC-6, R92*bis-*AC-1*
91. Consequential Order to the Decision on Prosecution Tender for Admission into Evidence of Information Contained in Notice Pursuant to Rule 92*bis*, 23 November 2005: **R92*bis*-TC-4**
92. Order on the Appointment of *Amicus Curiae* (AC), 24 November 2005: *R74-AC-2*
93. Order on the Appointment of *Amicus Curiae* (AC), 28 November 2005: *R74-AC-2*
94. Order on the Appointment of *Amicus Curiae* (AC), 2 December 2005: *R74-AC-2*
95. Decision on Brima-Kamara Defence Appeal Motion Against Trial Chamber II Majority Decision on Extremely Urgent Confidential Joint Motion for the Re-Appointment of Kevin Metzger and Wilbert Harris As Lead Counsel for Alex Tamba Brima and Brima Bazzy Kamara (AC), 8 December 2005: *S1-AC-7*, **S1-AC-8, S17-AC-1, S17-AC-4, S17-AC-7, S18-AC-1, S20-AC-5, S20-AC-6, R31-AC-1, R33-AC-1, R45-AC-1, R45-AC-2, R45-AC-4, R45-AC-5, R73-AC-2, R73-AC-5,** *R73-AC-7,* **R73-AC-9, R108-AC-3, R113-AC-1, R115-AC-1**

Prosecutor v. Brima Samura (Contempt Proceeding),
Case No. SCSL-05-01

1. Order Assigning Cases to a Trial Chamber (P), 2 May 2005: **R19-P-2, R77-P-1**
2. Order Designating a Judge for Contempt Proceedings, 2 May 2005: **R27-TC-3, R77-TC-11**

3. Scheduling Order on Contempt Proceedings, 2 May 2005
4. Order on Filing, 10 June 2005
5. Written Reasons for the Decision on the standing of Independent Counsel and on Disclosure Obligations, 23 June 2005: *S14-AC-4, R66-TC-1*, **R77-TC-10, R77-TC-13**
6. Decision on Defence Motion on Stay of the Contempt Proceedings, 21 September 2005: **R77-TC-12**
7. Judgment in Contempt Proceedings, 26 October 2005: **R44-TC-11**, *R69-TC-5*, **R77-TC-2, R77-TC-3**, *R77-TC-13*, **R77-TC-14**, *R79-TC-8*

Prosecutor v. Margaret Fomba Brima, Neneh Binta Bah Jalloh and Ester Kamara (Contempt Proceeding), Case No. SCSL-05-02

1. Order Assigning Cases to a Trial Chamber (P), 2 May 2005: **R19-P-2, R77-P-1**
2. Order Designating a Judge for Contempt Proceedings, 2 May 2005: **R27-TC-3, R77-TC-11**
3. Scheduling Order on Contempt Proceedings, 2 May 2005
4. Order on Filing, 10 June 2005
5. Order Designating a Judge for Initial Appearance, 22 June 2005
6. Written Reasons for the Decision on the Standing of Independent Counsel and on Disclosure Obligations, 23 June 2005: *S14-AC-4, R66-TC-1*, **R77-TC-10, R77-TC-13**
7. Findings and Scheduling Order Pursuant to Rule 62, 27 July 2005: **R62-TC-1**
8. Order for Severance and Scheduling Order, 27 July 2005
9. Sentencing Judgement in Contempt Proceedings, 21 September 2005: **S19-TC-1, S19-TC-2, S19-TC-3, S19-TC-4**, *R69-TC-4, R69-TC-5*, **R77-TC-1, R77-TC-15, R77-TC-16**
10. Decision on Defence Motion on Stay of the Contempt Proceedings, 21 September 2005: **R77-TC-12**

Prosecutor v. Anifa Kamara (Contempr Proceeding),
Case No. SCSL-05-03

1. Order Assigning Cases to a Trial Chamber (P), 2 May 2005: **R19-P-2, R77-P-1**
2. Order Designating a judge for Contempt Proceedings, 2 May 2005: **R27-TC-3, R77-TC-11**
3. Scheduling Order on Contempt Proceedings, 2 May 2005
4. Order on Filing, 10 June 2005

5. Order Designating a Judge for Initial Appearance, 22 June 2005
6. Written Reasons for the Decision on the Standing of Independent Counsel and on Disclosure Obligations, 23 June 2005: *S14-AC-4, R66-TC-1*, **R77-TC-10, R77-TC-13**
7. Findings and Scheduling Order Pursuant to Rule 62, 27 July 2005: **R62-TC-1**
8. Order for Severance and Scheduling Order, 27 July 2005
9. Findings and Scheduling Order Pursuant to Rule 62, 21 September 2005: *R62-TC-1*
10. Sentencing Judgement in Contempt Proceedings, 21 September 2005: **S19-TC-1, S19-TC-2, S19-TC-3, S19-TC-4,** *R69-TC-4, R69-TC-5,* **R77-TC-1, R77-TC-15, R77-TC-16**
11. Decision on Defence Motion on Stay of the Contempt Proceedings, 21 September 2005: **R77-TC-12**

CONTENTS

Foreword by Honorable Justice Raja Fernando	xi
Foreword by Mr. Lovemore Munlo, SC	xiii
Introduction	xv

Part I – STATUTE OF THE SPECIAL COURT	1
Article 1 – Competence of the Special Court	1
TRIAL CHAMBERS DECISIONS	1
Article 1: Competence of the SCSL – Nature of the Special Court	1
S1-TC-1	1
Article 1: Competence of the SCSL – "Persons Who Bear the Greatest Responsibility"	2
S1-TC-2	2
Article 1: Competence of the SCSL – Principle of Legality	5
S1-TC-3	5
Article 1: Competence of the SCSL – Inherent Jurisdiction	6
S1-TC-4	6
Article 1: Competence of the SCSL – The Special Court and the Truth and Reconciliation Commission (TRC)	8
S1-TC-5	8
S1-TC-6	10
Article 1: Competence of the SCSL – History	12
S1-TC-7	12
APPEALS CHAMBER DECISIONS	13
Article 1: Competence of the SCSL – Nature of the SCSL – Application of International Law	13
S1-AC-1	13
S1-AC-2	13
S1-AC-3	16
Article 1: Competence of the SCSL – Principle of Legality	17
S1-AC-4	17
S1-AC-5	17
Article 1: Competence of the SCSL – *Ratione Loci* Jurisdiction	19
S1-AC-6	19

Article 1: Competence of the SCSL – Inherent Jurisdiction –
  Absence of Express Statutory Provision 19
  S1-AC-7 19
  S1-AC-8 20
Article 1: Competence of the SCSL – The Special Court and
  the TRC 23
  S1-AC-9 23
Article 2 – Crimes against humanity 26

TRIAL CHAMBERS DECISIONS 26

Article 2: Crimes Against Humanity – Elements of Crimes 26
  S2-TC-1 26
Article 2(f): Crimes Against Humanity – "Torture" –
  Difference with Inhuman and Degrading Treatment 28
  S2-TC-2 28
Article 2(i): Crimes Against Humanity – "Others Inhumane
  Acts" – Exclusion of Sexual Violence 29
  S2-TC-3 29
Article 2(i): Crimes Against Humanity – "Others Inhumane
  Acts" – Forced Marriage 30
  S2-TC-4 30
  S2-TC-5 31
Article 2(i): Crimes Against Humanity – "Others Inhumane
  Acts" – Inhuman and Degrading Treatment 31
  S2-TC-6 31
Article 3 – Violations of Article 3 common to the Geneva
  Conventions and of Additional Protocol II 33

TRIAL CHAMBERS DECISIONS 33

Article 3: Violations of Article 3 Common and Protocol II –
  Elements of Crimes 33
  S3-TC-1 33
Article 3(a): Violations of Article 3 Common and Protocol II –
  "Murder" 34
  S3-TC-2 34
Article 3(a): Violations of Article 3 Common and Protocol II –
  "Cruel Treatment" 35
  S3-TC-3 35
Article 3(b): Violations of Article 3 Common and Protocoll II –
  "Collective Punishment" 36
  S3-TC-4 36

Article 3(d): Violations of Article 3 Common and Protocol II –
"Acts of Terrorism" 37
    S3-TC-5 37
Article 3(e): Violations of Article 3 Common and Protocol II –
"Outrages Upon Personal Dignity" – Inhuman and
Degrading Treatment 39
    S3-TC-6 39
Article 3(f): Violations of Article 3 Common and Protocol II –
"Pillage" 40
    S3-TC-7 40

APPEALS CHAMBER DECISIONS 40

Article 3: Violations of Article 3 Common and Protocol II –
Applicability and Jurisdiction 40
    S3-AC-1 40
Article 3: Violations of Article 3 Common and Protocol II –
Nature of the Conflict 45
    S3-AC-2 45
Article 3: Violations of Article 3 Common and Protocol II –
Existence of an Armed Conflict Admitted by Way of
Judicial Notice 45
    S3-AC-3: 45
Article 4 – Other Serious Violations of International
Humanitarian Law 47

TRIAL CHAMBERS DECISIONS 47

Article 4(c): Other Serious Violations – "Enlisting Children
Under the Age of 15 Years into Armed Forces" 47
    S4-TC-1 47

APPEALS CHAMBER DECISIONS 48

Article 4: Other Serious Violations – Applicability and
Jurisdiction – Not Limited to Internal Armed Conflicts 48
    S4-AC-1 48
Article 4: Other Serious Violations – Additional Protocol II
and Convention on the Rights of Children Form Part of
Customary International Law 49
    S4-AC-2 49
Article 4: Other Serious Violations – All Parties Bound by
International Humanitarian Law 50

S4-AC-3	50
S4-AC-4	51
Article 4: Other Serious Violations – Individual Responsibility for Child Recruitment	52
S4-AC-5	52
Article 6 – Individual Criminal Responsibility	63
TRIAL CHAMBERS DECISIONS	63
Article 6(1): Individual Criminal Responsibility – Generalities	63
S6-TC-1	63
S6-TC-2	64
S6-TC-3	65
Article 6(1)/6(3): Individual Criminal Responsibility – Charges Under 6(1) and 6(3) Are Cumulative	65
S6-TC-4	65
Article 6(3): Individual Criminal Responsibility – Command Responsibility – Guidance from Other International Tribunals	67
S6-TC-5	67
APPEALS CHAMBER DECISIONS	68
Article 6(2): Individual Criminal Responsibility – Immunity of Jurisdiction Before the Special Court	68
S6-AC-1	68
Article 6(2): Individual Criminal Responsibility – Immunity of Jurisdiction (Cessation)	71
S6-AC-2	71
Article 6(2): Individual Criminal Responsibility – Immunity of Arrest	71
S6-AC-3	71
Article 8 – Concurrent Jurisdiction	73
TRIAL CHAMBERS DECISIONS	73
Article 8: Concurrent Jurisdiction – Primacy on Sierra Leonean Tribunals	73
S8-TC-1	73
APPEALS CHAMBER DECISIONS	76
Article 8(2): Concurrent Jurisdiction – Primacy on SL Tribunals	76

S8-AC-1	76
S8-AC-2	77
Article 9 – Non Bis in Idem	79

TRIAL CHAMBERS DECISIONS 79

Article 9: *Non Bis In Idem* – Attempt to Relitigate Matters Determined in Another Case – *Stare decisis* 79
S9-TC-1 79
Article 9(1): *Non Bis In Idem* – Initial and Consolidated Indictments 80
S9-TC-2 80
Article 10 – Amnesty 82

APPEALS CHAMBER DECISIONS 82

Article 10: Amnesty – Status of the Lomé Agreement 82
S10-AC-1 82
Article 10: Amnesty – Effects of the Amnesty 84
S10-AC-2 84
Article 13 – Qualification and Appointment of judges 89

TRIAL CHAMBERS DECISIONS 89

Article 13(1): Qualification and Appointment of Judges – Impartiality – Assertions of Partiality to Be Supported by Evidence 89
S13-TC-1 89

APPEALS CHAMBER DECISIONS 90

Article 13(1): Qualification and Appointment of Judges – Judicial Independence – Funding of the Special Court for Sierra Leone 90
S13-AC-1 90
Article 14 Rules of Procedure and Evidence 99

TRIAL CHAMBERS DECISIONS 99

Article 14: Rules of Procedure and Evidence – Interpretation of Statutory Instruments – Ordinary and Natural 99
S14-TC-1 99
Article 14: Rules of Procedure and Evidence – Purposive Interpretation 100

S14-TC-2	110
S14-TC-3	101

APPEALS CHAMBER DECISIONS ... 101

Article 14: Rules of Procedure and Evidence – Amendment ... 101
S14-AC-1 ... 101
Article 14: Rules of Procedure and Evidence – Amendment – Sierra Leonean Law Guidance ... 102
S14-AC-2 ... 102
S14-AC-3 ... 103
Article 14: Rules of Procedure and Evidence – Purposive Interpretation of the Rules of Procedure and Evidence ... 103
S14-AC-4 ... 103
S14-AC-5 ... 104
Article 15 The Prosecutor ... 105

TRIAL CHAMBERS DECISIONS ... 106

Article 15(1): Discretionary Power to Prosecute ... 106
S15-TC-1 ... 106
S15-TC-2 ... 107
Article 15(1): Independence of the Prosecutor ... 108
S15-TC-3 ... 108
Article 15(1): Prosecutorial Latitude to Call the Witnesses of His Choice ... 110
S15-TC-4 ... 110
Article 17 Rights of the Accused ... 111

TRIAL CHAMBERS DECISIONS ... 112

Article 17: Rights of the Accused – Generalities ... 112
S17-TC-1 ... 112
Article 17(2): Rights of the Accused – Right to a Fair Trial ... 112
S17-TC-2 ... 112
S17-TC-3 ... 115
Article 17(2): Rights of the Accused – Equality of Arms ... 116
S17-TC-4 ... 116
S17-TC-5 ... 119
Article 17(2): Rights of the Accused – Measures for Protection of Victims and Witnesses ... 119
S17-TC-6 ... 119

Article 17(3): Rights of the Accused – Presumption of Innocence 120
S17-TC-7 120
Article 17(3): Rights of the Accused – Presumption of Innocence – Burden of Proof 120
S17-TC-8 120
Article 17(4)(b): Rights of the Accused – Adequate Time and Facilities to Prepare His Defence 121
S17-TC-9 121
S17-TC-10 123
Article 17(4)(c): Rights of the Accused – Right to Be Triad Without Undue Delay 124
S17-TC-11 124
Article 17(4)(d): Rights of the Accused – Right to Self-Representation 124
S17-TC-12 124
Article 17(4)(d): Rights of the Accused – Right to Self-Representation – "Interests of Justice" 129
S17-TC-13 129
Article 17(4)(d): Rights of the Accused – Right to Self-Representation and Refusal to Attend Proceedings 130
S17-TC-14 130
Article 17(4)(d): Rights of the Accused – Right to Self-Representation – Standby Counsel 130
S17-TC-15 130
Article 17(4)(d): Rights of the Accused – Right to Representation of the Accused Choosing 131
S17-TC-16 131
S17-TC-17 131
Article 17(4)(g): Rights of the Accused – Right Not to Be Compelled to Testify Against Himself or to Confess Guilt 132
S17-TC-18 132

APPEALS CHAMBER DECISIONS 133

Article 17: Rights of the Accused – Shared Responsibility for the Implementation of the Rights of the Accused 133
S17-AC-1 133
Article 17: Rights of the Accused – Abuse of Process 134
S17-AC-2 134
Article 17: Rights of the Accused – Freedom of Speech 135
S17-AC-3 135

Article 17(2): Rights of the Accused – Right to a Fair and
Public Hearing – Difference Between Publicity and Orality 136
    S17-AC-4 136
Article 17(3): Rights of the Accused – Presumption of
Innocence 138
    S17-AC-5 138
Article 17(4)(c): Rights of the Accused – Expeditious Trial 139
    S17-AC-6 139
Article 17(4)(d): Rights of the Accused – Legal Assistance of
the Accused Choosing 140
    S17-AC-7 140
Article 18 Judgement 142

APPEALS CHAMBER DECISIONS 142

Article 18: Judgement – Separate Opinions Shall Be Filed
Together With the Majority Decision 142
    S18-AC-1 142

DECISIONS OF THE PRESIDENT 143

Article 18: Judgement – Reasons of Decisions 143
    S18-P-1 143
Article 19 Penalties 145

TRIAL CHAMBERS DECISIONS 145

Article 19(2): Penalties – Determination of Sentence –
Applicable Factors – Gravity of the Offence – Contempt
Proceedings 145
    S19-TC-1 145
Article 19(2): Penalties – Determination of Sentence –
Applicable Factors – Individual Circumstances –
No Forethought – No Criminal Record – Contempt
Proceedings 146
    S19-TC-2 146
Article 19(2): Penalties – Determination of Sentence –
Applicable Factors – Individual Circumstances – Guilty
Plea – Contempt Proceedings 147
    S19-TC-3 147
Article 19(2): Penalties – Determination of Sentence –
Applicable Factors – Individual Circumstances – Remorse –
Contempt Proceedings 147
    S19-TC-4 147

Article 19(2): Penalties – Determination of Sentence – Applicable Factors – Mitigating Factors – Participation in the Peace Process 148
   S19-TC-5 148
Article 20 Appellate Proceedings 149

TRIAL CHAMBERS DECISIONS 149

Article 20(3): Appellate Proceedings – Guidance by other International Tribunals Decisions 149
   S20-TC-1 149
   S20-TC-2 150
   S20-TC-3 150
   S20-TC-4 150
   S20-TC-5 151
   S20-TC-6 152
   S20-TC-7 152
   S20-TC-8 155

APPEALS CHAMBER DECISIONS 155

Article 20: Appellate Proceedings – Need for an Oral Hearing 155
   S20-AC-1 155
Article 20: Appellate Proceedings – Right to Appeal 156
   S20-AC-2 156
Article 20: Appellate Proceedings – Scope of Appeal 159
   S20-AC-3 159
Article 20: Appellate Proceedings – No Interference With Trial Chamber's Discretion 160
   S20-AC-4 160
Article 20(1): Appellate Proceedings – "Grounds" – "Requests" – Submissions in Response or Reply 161
   S20-AC-5 161
Article 20(1)(c): Appellate Proceedings – Error of Fact 165
   S20-AC-6 165
Article 20(2): Appellate Proceedings – Power of the AC to Affirm, Reverse or Revise 166
   S20-AC-7 166
Article 20(3): Appellate Proceedings – Guidance by other International Tribunals Decisions 167
   S20-AC-8 167
   S20-AC-9 167

PART II – RULES OF PROCEDURE AND EVIDENCE 168

Rule 3: Working Language 168

TRIAL CHAMBERS DECISIONS 168

Rule 3(A): Working Language – Comprehensibility 168
R3-TC-1 168

APPEALS CHAMBER DECISIONS 169

Rule 3(A): Working Language – Comprehensibility 169
R3-AC-1 169
Rule 4: Sittings Away from the Seat of the Special Court 170

TRIAL CHAMBER DECISIONS 170

Rule 4: Sittings Away from the Seat of the Special Court – Decisions Rendered Away from the Seat of the Special Court 170
R4-TC-1 170
Rule 5: Non-Compliance with the Rules 171

TRIAL CHAMBERS DECISIONS 171

Rule 5: Non-Compliance with the Rules – Objections to Be Raised "at the Earliest Opportunity" 171
R5-TC-1 171
R5-TC-2 172

APPEALS CHAMBER DECISIONS 173

Rule 5: Failure to Raise an Objection "At the Earliest Opportunity" 173
R5-AC-1 173
Rule 6: Amendment of the Rules 175

TRIAL CHAMBERS DECISIONS 175

Rule 6: Amendment of the Rules – Rights of the Accused 175
R6-TC-1 175
Rule 6(D): Amendment of the Rules – Entry on Force – Opposability 176

R6-TC-2	176
R6-TC-3	176
R6-TC-4	176
Rule 7: Time Limits	178

TRIAL CHAMBERS DECISIONS 178

Rule 7: Time Limits – Notification – Duty to Ensure Ability to Receive Documents 178
R7-TC-1 178
Rule 7(C): Time Limits – Filing a Response – Inadmissibility of Further "Objections" 179
R7-TC-2 179
Rule 7(C): Time Limits – Expeditions Consideration of Motion 180
R7-TC-3 181
R7-TC-4 181
R7-TC-5 181
Rule 7*bis*: Motions for extension of time 183

TRIAL CHAMBERS DECISIONS 183

Rule 7*bis*: Motions for Extension of Time – Applicable Criteria 183
R7*bis*-TC-1 183
R7*bis*-TC-2 183
R7*bis*-TC-3 184
R7*bis*-TC-4 184
Rule 7*bis*: Motions for Extension of Time – "Good Cause" Criterion 184
R7*bis*-TC-5 184
R7*bis*-TC-6 185
R7*bis*-TC-7 185
R7*bis*-TC-8 186
Rule 7*bis*: Motions for Extension of Time – Time of the Application 187
R7*bis*-TC-9 187
R7*bis*-TC-10 188
Rule 7*bis*: Motions for Extension of Time – Lack of Legal Basis 188
R7*bis*-TC-11 188
Rule 7*bis*: Motions for Extension of Time – Appeal – "Exceptional Circumstances or Good Cause" 189
R7*bis*-TC-12 189

Rule 7*bis*: Motions for Extension of Time – Materiality of the
Subject 189
    R7*bis*-TC-13 189
Rule 7*bis*: Motions for Extension of Time – Repetitive
Applications 190
    R7*bis*-TC-14 190
Rule 7*bis*: Motions for Extension of Time – Time Limit to
Raise Objections under Rule 92*bis* 190
    R7*bis*-TC-15 190

APPEALS CHAMBER DECISIONS 191

Rule 7*bis*: Motions for Extension of Time – Time Limits for
Filing – Reasons of Delay 191
    R7*bis*-AC-1 191
Rule 8: Requests and Orders 193

TRIAL CHAMBERS DECISIONS 193

Rule 8(A): Requests and Orders – Assistance Between the
Government of Sierra Leone and the Special Court 193
    R8-TC-1 193
    R8-TC-2 194
Rule 15: Disqualification of Judges 196

APPEALS CHAMBER DECISIONS 197

Rule 15(B): Disqualification of Judges – Apprehension of Bias 197
    R15-AC-1 197
    R15-AC-2 200
Rule 16: Absence and Resignation 204

TRIAL CHAMBERS DECISIONS 204

Rule 16(A): Absence and Resignation – Inability to Sit for a
Short Duration 204
    R16-TC-1 204
Rule 17: Precedence 206

TRIAL CHAMBER DECISIONS 206

Rule 17(A): Precedence – Temporary Replacement of Presiding
Judge 206
    R17-TC-1 206

Rule 19: Functions of the President 207

TRIAL CHAMBERS DECISIONS 207

Rule 19(A): Functions of the President – Authority on the Registrar 207
R19-TC-1 207

DECISIONS OF THE PRESIDENT 208

Rule 19(A): Functions of the President – Coordination of the Work of Chambers 208
R19-P-1 208
Rule 19(A): Functions of the President – Coordination of the Work of Chambers – Contempt Proceedings 208
R19-P-2 208
Rule 21: Functions of the Vice-President 209

DECISIONS OF THE PRESIDENT 209

Rule 21: Functions of the Vice-President – Absence of the President 209
R21-P-1 209
Rule 23: The Council of Judges 210

APPEALS CHAMBER DECISIONS 210

Rule 23(B): Council of Judges – Major Questions Relating to the Functioning of the Special Court – Disqualification of Judges 210
R23-AC-1 210
Rule 26bis: The Chambers 211

TRIAL CHAMBERS DECISIONS 211

Rule 26bis: The Chambers – Role of the Judge 211
R26bis-TC-1 211
R26bis-TC-2 211
R26bis-TC-3 212
Rule 26bis: The Chambers – "Judicial Economy", "Consistency in Jurisprudence", "Credibility of Judicial Process" 213
R26bis-TC-4 213

Rule 26*bis*: The Chambers – Correspondences to the Trial
Chamber to Be Filed *Inter Partes* 215
    R26*bis*-TC-5 215
Rule 27: The Trial Chambers 216

TRIAL CHAMBERS DECISIONS 216

Rule 27(B): Trial Chambers – Functions of the Presiding
Judge – Competitive Authority with the President on
Registrar's Decisions 216
    R27-TC-1 216
    R27-TC-2 217
Rule 27(B): Trial Chambers – Functions of the Presiding
Judge – Contempt Proceedings 218
    R27-TC-3 218
Rule 28: Designated Judges 219

TRIAL CHAMBERS DECISIONS 219

Rule 28: Designated Judges – Limit of Competence 219
    R28-TC-1 219
Rule 31: Appointment of the Deputy Registrar and Registry
Staff 220

TRIAL CHAMBERS DECISIONS 220

Rule 31: Appointment of the Deputy Registrar and Registry
Staff – Acting Officials 220
    R31-TC-1 220

APPEALS CHAMBER DECISIONS 223

Rule 31: Appointment of the Deputy Registrar and Registry
Staff – Acting Officials 223
    R31-AC-1 223
Rule 33: Functions of the Registrar 225

TRIAL CHAMBERS DECISIONS 225

Rule 33: Functions of the Registrar – Discretionary Powers 225
    R33-TC-1 225
Rule 33(A): Functions of the Registrar – Authority of the
President 227
    R33-TC-2 227

Rule 33(B): Functions of the Registrar – Representations to Chambers	227
R33-TC-3	227
Rule 33(D): Functions of the Registrar – Practice Directions – Binding Authority	228
R33-TC-4	228
R33-TC-5	228
R33-TC-6	229

APPEALS CHAMBER DECISIONS 229

Rule 33(B): Functions of the Registrar – Representations to Chambers – Notice to the Parties	229
R33-AC-1	229
Rule 37: Functions of the Prosecutor	231

TRIAL CHAMBERS DECISIONS 231

Rule 37: Functions of the Prosecutor – Qualifications	231
R37-TC-1	231
Rule 39: Conduct of Investigations	232

TRIAL CHAMBERS DECISIONS 232

Rule 39(iii): Conduct of Investigations – Cooperation of States	232
R39-TC-1	232
Rule 40*bis*: Transfer and Provisional Detention of Suspects	235

TRIAL CHAMBERS DECISIONS 236

Rule 40*bis*(B): Transfer and Provisional Detention of Suspects – Decision of the Designated Judge	236
R40*bis*-TC-1	236
R40*bis*-TC-2	237
Rule 40*bis*(B): Transfer and Provisional Detention of Suspects – Necessity of the Detention – Proportionality Test	238
R40*bis*-TC-3	238
Rule 40*bis*(K): Transfer and Provisional Detention of Suspects – Applications – Procedure	240
R40*bis*-TC-4	240
Rule 44: Appointment and Qualifications of Counsel	241

TRIAL CHAMBERS DECISIONS ... 241

Rule 44(B): Appointment and Qualifications of Counsel – Role of the Defence Counsel ... 241
- R44-TC-1 ... 241
- R44-TC-2 ... 242
- R44-TC-3 ... 242
- R44-TC-4 ... 242

Rule 44(B): Appointment and Qualifications of Counsel – Role of the Standby Counsel ... 243
- R44-TC-5 ... 243

Rule 44(B): Appointment and Qualifications of Counsel – Composition of the Defence Team – Information to the Registry ... 245
- R44-TC-6 ... 245

Rule 44(B): Appointment and Qualifications of Counsel – Authority of the Directive on the Assignment of Defence Counsel ... 246
- R44-TC-7 ... 246

Rule 44(B): Appointment and Qualifications of Counsel – Contradiction Between the Code of Conduct of Counsel and the Bar Code of Counsel ... 246
- R44-TC-8 ... 246

Rule 44(B): Appointment and Qualifications of Counsel – Appointed Counsel – Applicable Rules – Withdrawal ... 247
- R44-TC-9 ... 247
- R44-TC-10 ... 248

Rule 44(B): Appointment and Qualifications of Counsel – Defence Team – Investigators ... 249
- R44-TC-11 ... 249

Rule 45: Defence Office ... 251

TRIAL CHAMBERS DECISIONS ... 252

Rule 45: Defence Office – Role of the Defence Office ... 252
- R45-TC-1 ... 252
- R45-TC-2 ... 253

Rule 45: Defence Office – Duty of the Registrar to Maintain a Defence Office – Powers of the Registrar ... 254
- R45-TC-3 ... 254

Rule 45: Defence Office – Decisions of the Principal Defender – Power of the Trial Chamber to Judicially Review ... 255
- R45-TC-4 ... 255

Rule 45(C): Defence Office – Choice of Counsel 257
    R45-TC-5 257
Rule 45(C)(iv): Defence Office – Criteria of Eligibility of Counsel – Full Time Availability – Illness 258
    R45-TC-6 258
Rule 45(C): Defence Office – Criteria of Eligibility of Counsel – Full Time Availability – Counsel Representing More Than One Accused – Article 14(C) of the Directive 260
    R45-TC-7 260
Rule 45(D): Defence Office – Replacement of Counsel – Exceptional Circumstances – Attempt to Delay the Proceedings 261
    R45-TC-8 261
Rule 45(E): Defence Office – Term of Representation 262
    R45-TC-9 262
Rule 45(E): Defence Office – Withdrawal of Counsel – Withdrawal by the Defence Office 262
    R45-TC-10 262
Rule 45(E): Defence Office – Withdrawal of Counsel – Application to Withdraw – Exceptional Circumstances 264
    R45-TC-11 264
    R45-TC-12 265
Rule 45(E): Defence Office – Withdrawal of Counsel – Appointment of "Another Counsel" 269
    R45-TC-13 269
Rule 45(F): Defence Office – Withdrawal of Counsel – Interim Representation by Co-Counsel 269
    R45-TC-14 269

APPEALS CHAMBER DECISIONS 271

Rule 45: Defence Office – Repartition of Powers Between the Defence Office and the Registry 271
    R45-AC-1 271
Rule 45(C): Defence Office – List of Qualified Counsel – Jurisdiction to Review Decision to Withdraw Counsel from the List 274
    R45-AC-2 274
Rule 45(E): Defence Office – Withdrawal of Counsel – Exceptional Circumstances – Accused Refusal to Be Represented 275
    R45-AC-3 275

Rule 45(E): Defence Office – Withdrawal of Counsel – Impossibility of re-Assignment of the Withdrawn Counsel 276
R45-AC-4 276
Rule 45(E): Defence Office – Assignment of Counsel – Power to Review Decision Refusing Assignment of Counsel 276
R45-AC-5 276
Rule 45(E): Defence Office – Assignment of Counsel – Legal Services Contracts 280
R45-AC-6 280
Rule 45*bis*: Declaration of Means by the Accused 281

TRIAL CHAMBERS DECISIONS 281

Rule 45*bis*(A): Declaration of Means by the Accused – Request for Legal Assistance 281
R45*bis*-TC-1 281

APPEALS CHAMBER DECISIONS 281

Rule 45*bis*(B): Declaration of Means by the Accused – Request for Self-Representation 281
R45*bis*-AC-1 281
Rule 45*bis*(B): Declaration of Means by the Accused – Self-Defence Creating Estoppel 282
R45*bis*-AC-2 282
Rule 46: Misconduct of Counsel 283

TRIAL CHAMBERS DECISIONS 284

Rule 46(C): Misconduct of Counsel – Frivolous Motions and Abuse of Process – Sanction (Or Not) 284
R46-TC-1 284
R46-TC-2 284
R46-TC-3 285
Rule 46(H): Misconduct of Counsel – Frivolous Motions and Abuse of Process – Leave to Appeal Sanctions 285
R46-TC-4 285
Rule 47: Review of Indictment 287

TRIAL CHAMBERS DECISIONS 288

Rule 47(C): Review of Indictment – Formal Validity of the Indictment 288

R47-TC-1	288
R47-TC-2	290
Rule 47(C): Review of Indictment – Vagueness of Indictment – Generalities	291
R47-TC-3	291
R47-TC-4	293
R47-TC-5	294
R47-TC-6	295
R47-TC-7	298
Rule 47(C): Review of Indictment – Vagueness of Indictment – Article 6(3) Charges	299
R47-TC-8	299
Rule 47(C): Review of Indictment – Vagueness of Indictment – Joint Criminal Enterprise	300
R47-TC-9	300
R47-TC-10	301
R47-TC-11	302
Rule 47(C): Review of Indictment – Form of Indictment – Cumulative Charging	303
R47-TC-12	303
Rule 47(E): Review of Indictment – Discretion of the Reviewing Judge	303
R47-TC-13	303
Rule 47(E): Review of Indictment – Scope of Review	304
R47-TC-14	304
Rule 47(E): Review of Indictment – Criteria of Review	306
R47-TC-15	306
R47-TC-16	306
R47-TC-17	307

APPEALS CHAMBER DECISIONS 307

Rule 47: Review of Indictment – No Requirement for a *Prima Facie* Case	307
R47-AC-1	307
Rule 47(C): Review of Indictment – Information to Be Included in the Indictment	308
R47-AC-2	308
Rule 47(C): Review of Indictment – Vagueness of Indictment	310
R47-AC-3	310
Rule 48: Joinder of Accused or Trials	311

TRIAL CHAMBERS DECISIONS ... 311

Rule 48: Joinder – Purpose of the Joinder – "Collective Criminal Responsibility" ... 311
R48-TC-1 ... 311
Rule 48: Joinder – Chamber's Discretion ... 312
R48-TC-2 ... 312
Rule 48: Joinder – Applicable Principles ... 312
R48-TC-3 ... 312
Rule 48: Joinder – The Test for Joinder ... 316
R48-TC-4 ... 316
Rule 48: Joinder – Interest of Justice ... 317
R48-TC-5 ... 317
Rule 48: Joinder – Procedure – No Requirement for Expected Consolidated Indictment at the Stage of the Motion for Joinder ... 319
R48-TC-6 ... 319
Rule 48: Joinder – Procedure – Requirement for Complete Disclosure of Supporting Materials Attached to the Initial Indictments at the Stage of the Motion for Joinder ... 320
R48-TC-7 ... 320
R48-TC-8 ... 320
Rule 48(C): Joinder – Concurrent Hearing of Evidence ... 321
R48-TC-9 ... 321
R48-TC-10 ... 324

APPEALS CHAMBER DECISIONS ... 325

Rule 48: Joinder – No Requirement for Consolidation of Individual Indictments ... 325
R48-AC-1 ... 325
Rule 50: Amendment of Indictment ... 326

TRIAL CHAMBERS DECISIONS ... 326

Rule 50: Amendment of Indictment – Procedure – Order to Submit Indication of Specific Changes ... 326
R50-TC-1 ... 326
Rule 50(A): Amendment of Indictment – Discretion of the Trial Chamber ... 327
R50-TC-2 ... 327
R50-TC-3 ... 327
R50-TC-4 ... 328

Rule 50(A): Amendment of Indictment – Time of the
Application for Leave to Amend 328
   R50-TC-5 328
   R50-TC-6 332
   R50-TC-7 335
Rule 50(A): Amendment of the Indictment – Initial and
Amended Indictments 335
   R50-TC-8 335
   R50-TC-9 336
Rule 50(B): Amendment of Indictment – Need for a
Further Appearance 336
   R50-TC-10 336
   R50-TC-11 338
Rule 50(B): Amendment of Indictment – *Proprio Motu*
Review of the Amended Indictment 339
   R50-TC-12 339

APPEALS CHAMBER DECISIONS 340

Rule 50: Amendment of Indictment – Criteria – Late
Amendment 340
   R50-AC-1 340
Rule 50: Amendment of Indictment – Criteria – Less Serious
Allegation 342
   R50-AC-2 342
Rule 50: Amendment of Indictment – Reference to Rule 47(G)
and Rule 52 342
   R50-AC-3 342
Rule 50: Amendment of Indictment – Previous Indictment(s)
"Not to Be Proceeded With" 343
   R50-AC-4 343
Rule 50(B): Amendment of Indictment – Requirement for
Further Appearance 344
   R50-AC-5 344
Rule 51: Withdrawal of Indictment 345

TRIAL CHAMBERS DECISIONS 345

Rule 51: Withdrawal of Indictment – Death of the Accused 345
   R51-TC-1 345
Rule 52: Service of Indictment 347

TRIAL CHAMBERS DECISIONS ... 347

Rule 52: Service of Indictment – Order to Serve the Indictment ... 347
R52-TC-1 ... 347
Rule 52: Service of Indictment – Service on Counsel ... 348
R52-TC-2 ... 348
R52-TC-3 ... 349

APPEALS CHAMBER DECISIONS ... 351

Rule 52: Service of Indictment – Service on Counsel ... 351
R52-AC-1 ... 351
Rule 53: Non-disclosure ... 352

TRIAL CHAMBERS DECISIONS ... 352

Rule 53: Non-Disclosure – Order to the Authorities of Sierra Leone ... 352
R53-TC-1 ... 352
Rule 53: Non-Disclosure – Request to Third States ... 353
R53-TC-2 ... 353
Rule 53: Non-Disclosure – Order for Disclosure ... 353
R53-TC-3 ... 353
R53-TC-4 ... 354
R53-TC-5 ... 354
Rule 54: General Provision ... 355

TRIAL CHAMBERS DECISIONS ... 355

Rule 54: Orders – Necessity of the Order ... 355
R54-TC-1 ... 355
Rule 54: Order – *Subpoena Duces Tecum* – State Cooperation ... 355
R54-TC-2 ... 355
Rule 55: Execution of Arrest Warrants ... 361

TRIAL CHAMBERS DECISIONS ... 361

Rule 55: Execution of Warrant of Arrest – Transmission to the Authority of Sierra Leone ... 361
R55-TC-1 ... 361
Rule 55: Execution of Warrant of Arrest – Format ... 362
R55-TC-2 ... 362

Rule 55(C): Execution of Warrant of Arrest – Obligation to Serve the Accused with a Case Summary 362
    R55-TC-3 362
Rule 56: Warrant of Arrest to Third States 364

TRIAL CHAMBERS DECISIONS 364

Rule 56: Warrant of Arrest to Third States – Cooperation of Third States – *Ad Hoc* **Arrangements** 364
    R56-TC-1 364
Rule 56: Warrant of Arrest to Third States – All States and INTERPOL 365
    R56-TC-2 365
    R56-TC-3 365
Rule 57: Procedure after Arrest 367

TRIAL CHAMBERS DECISIONS 367

Rule 57: Procedure After Arrest – Order to the Authorities of Sierra Leone 367
    R57-TC-1 367

DECISIONS OF THE PRESIDENT 368

Rule 57: Procedure After Arrest – Transfer to ICTY/ICTR Detention Facility 368
    R57-P-1 368
Rule 58: Transfer to the Special Court from Third States 368

TRIAL CHAMBERS DECISIONS 369

Rule 58: Transfer to the Special Court from Third States – Request to Third States 369
    R58-TC-1 369
Rule 58: Transfer to the Special Court from Third States – Third States Have no *Locus Standi* 370
    R58-TC-2 370
Rule 59: Failure to Execute a Warrant of Arrest or Transfer Order 371

TRIAL CHAMBERS DECISIONS 371

Rule 59: Failure to Execute a Warrant of Arrest – Order to the Authorities of Sierra Leone 371
R59-TC-1 371
Rule 60: Trial in the Absence of the Accused 372

TRIAL CHAMBERS DECISIONS 372

Rule 60: Trial in Absence of Accused – Refusal to Attend Hearings 372
R60-TC-1 372
R60-TC-2 374
Rule 60(B): Trial in Absence of Accused – Withdrawal of Counsel – Interim Representation by Co-Counsel 375
R60-TC-3 375

APPEALS CHAMBER DECISIONS 376

Rule 60: Trial in Absence of Accused – Refusal to Attend Hearings and to Be Represented 376
R60-AC-1 376
Rule 61: Initial Appearance of Accused and Plea 377

TRIAL CHAMBERS DECISIONS 377

Rule 61: Initial Appearance – Accused Fitness to Plead and to Stand Trial 377
R61-TC-1 377
R61-TC-2 378
R61-TC-3 379
Rule 61: Initial Appearance – Role of the Plea 381
R61-TC-4 381
Rule 61: Initial Appearance – Accused Refusal to Enter a Plea 382
R61-TC-5 382
Rule 61(iv): Initial Appearance – Date for Trial 382
R61-TC-6 382

APPEALS CHAMBER DECISIONS 383

Rule 61: Initial Appearance – Further Appearance – Discretion to Permit if Requested 383
R61-AC-1 383

Rule 62: Procedure upon Guilty Plea	384

TRIAL CHAMBERS DECISIONS 384

Rule 62: Procedure upon Guilty Plea – Contempt Proceedings	384
R62-TC-1	384
Rule 64: Detention on Remand	386

TRIAL CHAMBERS DECISIONS 386

Rule 64: Detention on Remand – International Standards of Detention – Verification by the International Committee of the Red Cross	386
R64-TC-1	386
Rule 64: Detention on Remand – Restrictions and Supervision on Visits to Detainees	386
R64-TC-2	386
Rule 64: Detention on Remand – Detainee's Visit on his Mother's Grave	387
R64-TC-3	387

DECISIONS OF THE PRESIDENT 388

Rule 64: Detention on Remand – Generalities	388
R64-P-1	388
Rule 64: Detention on Remand – Conditions of Detention	390
R64-P-2	390
Rule 64: Detention on Remand – House Arrest	391
R64-P-3	391
Rule 64: Detention on Remand – Hospitalisation	392
R64-P-4	392
Rule 64: Detention on Remand – Rule of Detention 47(A) – Prohibition or Conditions on Communications and Visits – Power to Prohibit, Regulate or Set Conditions on Visits and Communications	393
R64-P-5	393
Rule 64: Detention on Remand – Rule of Detention 47(C) – Prohibition or Conditions on Communications and Visits – Reasonable Grounds – Notification to the Accused – Presumption of Innocence	394
R64-P-6	396

Rule 64: Detention on Remand – Rule of Detention 47(G) – Prohibition or Conditions on Communications and Visits – Admissibility of Request and Procedure 395
    R64-P-7 395
Rule 65: Bail 397

TRIAL CHAMBERS DECISIONS 397

Rule 65(B): Bail – "Liberty Rule, Detention Exception" 397
    R65-TC-1 397
Rule 65(B): Bail – Burden of Proof 399
    R65-TC-2 399
    R65-TC-3 399
    R65-TC-4 404
Rule 65(B): Bail – Conditions – Generalities 404
    R65-TC-5 404
    R65-TC-6 405
Rule 65(B): Bail – Conditions – Appearance at Trial 406
    R65-TC-7 406
    R65-TC-8 407
Rule 65(B): Bail – Conditions – Gravity of the Offence 409
    R65-TC-9 409
Rule 65: Bail – Conditions – Danger to Victims and Witnesses 410
    R65-TC-10 410
    R65-TC-11 410
Rule 65: Bail – Conditions – Public Order Concerns 411
    R65-TC-12 411
    R65-TC-13 412
Rule 65: Bail – Conditions – Voluntary Surrender 412
    R65-TC-14 412
    R65-TC-15 412
Rule 65(B): Bail – State Submissions 413
    R65-TC-16 413
    R65-TC-17 415
Rule 65: Bail – Right to File a Writ of *Habeas Corpus* – Same Procedure as Application for Bail 415
    R65-TC-18 415

APPEALS CHAMBER DECISIONS 416

Rule 65: Bail – "Liberty Rule, Detention Exception" 416
    R65-AC-1 416

Rule 65: Bail – Standard of Proof 418
   R65-AC-2 418
Rule 65: Bail – Burden of Proof 419
   R65-AC-3 419
Rule 65(B): Bail – State Submissions 419
   R65-AC-4 419
Rule 65(E): Bail – Leave to Appeal 421
   R65-AC-5 421
   R65-AC-6 421
Rule 65(H): Bail – Scope of Appeal 421
   R65-AC-7 421
Rule 65: Bail – Conditions – Specific Situation of the Special Court 423
   R65-AC-8 423
Rule 65: Bail – Conditions – Personal Guarantees 424
   R65-AC-9 424
Rule 65: Bail – Conditions – Voluntary Surrender 424
   R65-AC-10 424
Rule 65: Bail – Conditions – Contribution to the Peace Process 425
   R65-AC-11 425
Rule 65: Bail – Conditions – Bail Granted After Commencement of Trial 425
   R65-AC-12 425

DECISIONS OF THE PRESIDENT 425

Rule 65: Bail – No Presumption – Discretion 427
   R65-P-1 427
Rule 65: Bail – Conditions – Right to a Fair and Speedy Trial 427
   R65-P-2 429
Rule 65*bis*: Status Conferences 429

TRIAL CHAMBERS DECISIONS 429

Rule 65*bis*: Status Conferences – Reasons for Convening a Status Conference 429
   R65*bis*-TC-1 429
   R65*bis*-TC-2 429
Rule 66: Disclosure of materials by the Prosecutor 430

TRIAL CHAMBERS DECISIONS ... 431

Rule 66: Disclosure by the Prosecution – Generalities ... 431
  R66-TC-1 ... 431
  R66-TC-2 ... 433
  R66-TC-3 ... 435

Rule 66: Disclosure by the Prosecution – "Witness Statement" ... 436
  R66-TC-4 ... 436
  R66-TC-5 ... 440
  R66-TC-6 ... 440

Rule 66: Disclosure by the Prosecution – Investigator's Notes ... 441
  R66-TC-7 ... 441
  R66-TC-8 ... 442

Rule 66(A)(i): Disclosure by the Prosecution – "Preliminary" and "Subsequent" Disclosures ... 443
  R66-TC-9 ... 443

Rule 66(A)(i): Disclosure by the Prosecution – Protection of Victims and Witnesses ... 443
  R66-TC-10 ... 443
  R66-TC-11 ... 444

Rule 66(A)(i): Disclosure by the Prosecution – Material in Support of Joinder ... 445
  R66-TC-12 ... 445

Rule 66(A)(i): Disclosure by the Prosecution – Failure to Disclose – Exclusion of Evidence ... 446
  R66-TC-13 ... 446

Rule 66(A)(ii): Disclosure by the Prosecution – Scope of Disclosure ... 447
  R66-TC-14 ... 447

Rule 66(A)(ii): Disclosure by the Prosecution – Time of Disclosure – Additional Statements Containing New allegations ... 448
  R66-TC-15 ... 448
  R66-TC-16 ... 450

Rule 66(A)(ii): Disclosure by the Prosecution – Will-Say Statements Are Not Evidence ... 451
  R66-TC-17 ... 451

Rule 66(A)(iii): Inspection of Books, Documents, Photographs and Tangible Objects – Materiality to the Case ... 453
  R66-TC-18 ... 453

Rule 67: Reciprocal Disclosure of Evidence ... 456

TRIAL CHAMBERS DECISIONS	457
Rule 67: Reciprocal Disclosure – Mandatory	457
R67-TC-1	457
Rule 67(A)(ii)(a): Defence of Alibi – Burden of Proof – Notification	457
R67-TC-2	457
Rule 67(D): Disclosure of Additional Evidence	458
R67-TC-3	458
Rule 68: Disclosure of Exculpatory Evidence	459
TRIAL CHAMBERS DECISIONS	459
Rule 68: Disclosure of Exculpatory Evidence – Generalities	459
R68-TC-1	459
R68-TC-2	460
Rule 68: Disclosure of Exculpatory Evidence – Definition of "Exculpatory Evidence"	461
R68-TC-3	461
Rule 68: Disclosure of Exculpatory Evidence – Burden of Proof of the Exculpatory Nature of the Evidence	461
R68-TC-4	461
R68-TC-5	463
R68-TC-6	465
Rule 68: Disclosure of Exculpatory Evidence – Specificity of the Request for Disclosure of Exculpatory Evidence	466
R68-TC-7	466
Rule 68: Disclosure of Exculpatory Evidence – Time of the Disclosure of Exculpatory Evidence	467
R68-TC-8	467
Rule 68: Disclosure of Exculpatory Evidence – Time of the Motion for Disclosure of Exculpatory Evidence	467
R68-TC-9	467
Rule 68(B): Disclosure of Exculpatory Evidence – Protection of Victims and Witnesses	468
R68-TC-10	468
Rule 69: Protection of Victims and Witnesses	469
TRIAL CHAMBER DECISIONS	469
Rule 69: Protection of Victims and Witnesses – Applicable Criteria for the Determination of Appropriate Protective Measures	469
R69-TC-1	469

R69-TC-2	472
R69-TC-3	473
Rule 69: Protection of Victims and Witnesses – Criteria – Seat in Sierra Leone	474
R69-TC-4	474
R69-TC-5	475
Rule 69: Protection of Victims and Witnesses – Criteria – Victims of Sexual Violence, Children and Insiders – Post-Traumatic Stress	478
R69-TC-6	478
R69-TC-7	480
Rule 69: Protection of Victims and Witnesses – Measures of a General Nature – Case by Case Approach (Yes or No)	481
R69-TC-8	481
R69-TC-9	482
R69-TC-10	483
Rule 69(A): Protection of Victims and Witnesses – Need for an Application	485
R69-TC-11	485
R69-TC-12	486
Rule 69(A): Protection of Victims and Witnesses – Burden of Proof of "Exceptional Circumstances"	486
R69-TC-13	486
R69-TC-14	488
Rule 69(A): Protection of Victims and Witnesses – Witness' Fear	489
R69-TC-15	489
R69-TC-16	491
Rule 69(A): Protection of Victims and Witnesses – Non-Disclosure of Identities	492
R69-TC-17	492
R69-TC-18	492
R69-TC-19	494
R69-TC-20	494
Rule 69(A): Protection of Victims and Witnesses – Non-Disclosure of Identities – Late Disclosure – Postponement of Testimony	495
R69-TC-21	495
Rule 69(A): Protection of Victims and Witnesses – Right to a Public Trial	496
R69-TC-22	496
R69-TC-23	496
Rule 69(A): Protection of Victims and Witnesses – Evolution	497
R69-TC-24	497

Rule 69(A): Protection of Victims and Witnesses –Removal 498
    R69-TC-25 498
Rule 70: Matters Not Subject to Disclosure 500

TRIAL CHAMBERS DECISIONS 501

Rule 70(A): Matters Not subject to Disclosure – Internal Documents Prepared by the Parties in the Preparation of Their Case 501
    R70-TC-1 501
Rule 70(A): Matters Not subject to Disclosure – Notes on Proofing Sessions 501
    R70-TC-2 501
Rule 70(B): Matters Not Subject to Disclosure – Confidential Information – Communications Between Doctors and Clients 503
    R70-TC-3 503
Rule 70(B): Matters Not Subject to Disclosure – Confidential Information – Privileged Relationship Between Human Rights Officer and Informants 504
    R70-TC-4 504
Rule 70(D): Matters Not Subject to Disclosure – "Person or Representative Providing Initial Information" 505
    R70-TC-5 505
Rule 72: Preliminary Motions 506

TRIAL CHAMBERS DECISIONS 507

Rule 72(A): Preliminary Motions – Request for Extension of Time to File (Denied) 507
    R72-TC-1 507
    R72-TC-2 508
Rule 72(A): Preliminary Motions – Time Limit – Denial of Request for Assignment of Counsel under Rule 72(B)(iv) 509
    R72-TC-3 509
Rule 72(B): Preliminary Motions – Matters Requiring a Factual Determination 509
    R72-TC-4 509
Rule 72(B)(i): Preliminary Motions – Objections on Lack of Jurisdiction Shall be Submitted by Way of Preliminary Motions 510
    R72-TC-5 510
Rule 72(B)(v): Preliminary Motions – Abuse of Process 511

R72-TC-6	511
R72-TC-7	514
Rule 72(E): Referral to the Appeals Chamber	**515**
R72-TC-8	515
Rule 72(E): Referral to the Appeals Chamber – "Serious Issue Relating to Jurisdiction"	**515**
R72-TC-9	515
R72-TC-10	516
R72-TC-11	517
R72-TC-12	518
R72-TC-13	518
R72-TC-14	519
R72-TC-15	520
R72-TC-16	520
R72-TC-17	521
R72-TC-18	523
R72-TC-19	524
R72-TC-20	525
APPEALS CHAMBER DECISIONS	**527**
Rule 72: Preliminary Motions – Requirement for Initial Appearance Before Filing a Preliminary Motion	**527**
R72-AC-1	527
Rule 72: Preliminary Motions – Competence to Determine on its Own Jurisdiction	**528**
R72-AC-2	528
R72-AC-3	529
Rule 72: Preliminary Motions – Safeguard of Judicial Independence – Pecuniary Bias	**533**
R72-AC-4	533
Rule 72: Preliminary Motions – Immunity is a Jurisdiction Related Issue	**536**
R72-AC-5	536
Rule 72 (F): Preliminary Motions – Referral to the Appeals Chamber	**537**
R72-AC-6	537
Rule 72*bis*: General Provisions on Applicable Law	**539**
TRIAL CHAMBERS DECISIONS	**539**
Rule 72*bis*: Applicable Law – Reference to Former Decisions of the Special Court for Sierra Leone	**539**
R72*bis*-TC-1	539

Rule 72*bis*(iii): Applicable Law – General Principles of Law – *Res Judicata* Principle	540
R72*bis*-TC-2	540
Rule 73: Motions	542
TRIAL CHAMBERS DECISIONS	542
Rule 73(A): Motions – Need for a Proper Application	542
R73-TC-1	542
R73-TC-2	543
Rule 73(A): Motions – Purpose of Motions – Seek Ruling or Relief	543
R73-TC-3	543
Rule 73(A): Motions – Purpose of Motions – Writ of *Habeas Corpus*	544
R73-TC-4	544
Rule 73(A): Motions – Need to Address One Single Jurisdiction	545
R73-TC-5	545
Rule 73(A): Motions – Submissions of the Parties – Purpose of Response/Reply – "Counter Motion"	546
R73-TC-6	546
R73-TC-7	547
R73-TC-8	547
R73-TC-9	547
R73-TC-10	548
Rule 73(A): Motions – Submissions of the Parties – No Requirement for Oral Hearing	548
R73-TC-11	548
R73-TC-12	549
Rule 73(A): Motions – Submissions of the Parties – No Requirement to Await Responses and Replies	550
R73-TC-13	550
Rule 73(A): Motions – Submissions of the Parties – No Response to a Reply	550
R73-TC-14	550
Rule 73(A): Motions – Leave to File Supplementary Materials Supporting a Motion	551
R73-TC-15	551
Rule 73(A): Motions – Moot	551
R73-TC-16	551
Rule 73(A): Motions – Relief Sought – Proportionality Between the Relief and the Breach	552
R73-TC-17	552

Rule 73(A): Motions – Reconsideration of Interlocutory Decisions – Inherent Jurisdiction 553
R73-TC-18 553
Rule 73(B): Motions – Interlocutory Appeal – Purpose of the Requirement for a Leave to Appeal 555
R73-TC-19 555
R73-TC-20 556
Rule 73(B): Motions – Interlocutory Appeal – Standards for Leave to Appeal Interlocutory Decisions 556
R73-TC-21 556
R73-TC-22 559
R73-TC-23 560
R73-TC-24 560
R73-TC-25 561
Rule 73(B): Motions – Interlocutory Appeal – Standards for Leave to Appeal – "Exceptional Circumstances" 562
R73-TC-26 562
R73-TC-27 563
R73-TC-28 563
R73-TC-29 565
Rule 73(B): Motions – Interlocutory Appeal – Standards for Leave to Appeal – "Exceptional Circumstances" – Dissenting Opinions 566
R73-TC-30 566
R73-TC-31 567
R73-TC-32 567
Rule 73(B): Motions – Interlocutory Appeal – Standards for Leave to Appeal – "Irreparable Prejudice" 568
R73-TC-33 568
R73-TC-34 568
Rule 73(B): Motions – Interlocutory Appeal – Standards for Leave to Appeal – "Issue of General Importance" 569
R73-TC-35 569
Rule 73(B): Motions – Interlocutory Appeal – Standards for Leave to Appeal – Appeal on Protective Measures 570
R73-TC-36 570
Rule 73(B): Motions – Leave to Appeal – Irrelevance of Grounds of Appeal in the Application for Leave to Appeal 570
R73-TC-37 570
Rule 73(B): Motions – Leave to Appeal – Time Limit for Filing Interlocutory Appeal – Separate Opinions 571
R73-TC-38 571
R73-TC-39 572

Rule 73(B): Motions – Leave to Appeal – Application for Leave and for Reconsideration Shall Be Filed Separately 572
    R73-TC-40 572
Rule 73(B): Motions – Appeal Decision – Application in Other Cases Where No Appeal Was Sought – Impact on Parties Submissions 573
    R73-TC-41 573
    R73-TC-42 573
Rule 73(C): Motions – Appeal – Stay of Proceedings – Amended Indictment 574
    R73-TC-43 574
    R73-TC-44 575
Rule 73(D): Motions – Abuse of Process 576
    R73-TC-45 576
Rule 73: Motions – Rule Before 1st August 2003 Amendment – Applicable Criterion for Leave to Appeal 577
    R73-TC-46 577

APPEALS CHAMBER DECISIONS 578

Rule 73: Motions – Requirement for Initial Appearance Before Filing a Motion 578
    R73-AC-1 578
Rule 73(A): Motions – Hearing – Discretion of the Trial Chamber 579
    R73-AC-2 579
Rule 73(B): Motions – Leave to Appeal and Reconsideration 579
    R73-AC-3 579
    R73-AC-4 582
    R73-AC-5 583
Rule 73(B): Motions – Leave to Appeal – Rationale of the Requirement of a Leave 585
    R73-AC-6 585
Rule 73(B): Motions – Leave to Appeal – Standard for Leave to Appeal 586
    R73-AC-7 586
Rule 73(B): Motions – Jurisdiction of the Appeals Chamber on Decisions Under Rule 73(B) 586
    R73-AC-8 586
Rule 73(B): Motions – Time Limit for Filing Applications for Leave to Appeal – Separate Opinions 587
    R73-AC-9 587
Rule 73*bis*: Pre-Trial Conference 589

TRIAL CHAMBERS DECISIONS 590

Rule 73*bis*(B)(i): Pre-Trial Conference – Prosecutor Pre-Trial Brief – Purpose 590
R73*bis*-TC-1 590
Rule 73*bis*(B)(i): Pre-Trial Conference – Prosecutor Pre-Trial Brief – Time for Filing 591
R73*bis*-TC-2 591
Rule 73*bis*(B)(iv): Pre-Trial Conference – List of Witnesses – Rationale of the Obligation to File a List of Witnesses 592
R73*bis*-TC-3 592
R73*bis*-TC-4 592
Rule 73*bis*(B)(ii): Pre-Trial Conference – List of Witnesses – Continuous Disclosure of the Order of Witnesses to Be Called 593
R73*bis*-TC-5 593
R73*bis*-TC-6 594
Rule 73*bis*(B)(ii): Pre-Trial Conference – List of Witnesses – Limits of the Obligations Binding on the Prosecution 594
R73*bis*-TC-7 594
R73*bis*-TC-8 595
Rule 73*bis*(E): Pre-Trial Conference – Leave to Call Additional Witnesses – Need for an Application 596
R73*bis*-TC-9 596
Rule 73*bis*(E): Pre-Trial Conference – Leave to Call Additional Witnesses – Applicable Standards 597
R73*bis*-TC-10 597
R73*bis*-TC-11 600
R73*bis*-TC-12 602
Rule 73*bis*(E): Pre-Trial Conference – Leave to Call Additional Witnesses – Witness Reluctance 603
R73*bis*-TC-13 603
Rule 73*bis*(E): Pre-Trial Conference – Leave to Call Additional Witnesses – Corroborative Evidence 603
R73*bis*-TC-14 603
Rule 73*bis*(E): Pre-Trial Conference – Leave to Call Additional Witness – Reduction in the Total Number of Witnesses 604
R73*bis*-TC-15 604
Rule 73*bis*(E): Pre-Trial Conference – Leave to Call Additional Witnesses – Move from the List of "Back-up Witnesses" to the List of "Core Witnesses" 605
R73*bis*-TC-16 605

Rule 73*bis*(F): Pre-Trial Conference – Statements of Agreed Points of Fact and Law 606
   R73*bis*-TC-17 606
   R73*bis*-TC-18 606
   R73*bis*-TC-19 607
   R73*bis*-TC-20 607
   R73*bis*-TC-21 608
Rule 73*bis*(F): Pre-Trial Conference – Purpose of the Defence Pre-Trial Brief 609
   R73*bis*-TC-22 609
Rule 73*bis*(F): Pre-Trial Conference – Time of the Defence Pre-Trial Brief 609
   R73*bis*-TC-23 609
   R73*bis*-TC-24 610
Rule 73*ter*: Pre-Defence Conference 611

TRIAL CHAMBERS DECISIONS 612

Rule 73*ter*(B)(i): Pre-Defence Conference – Preparation of the Defence Case 612
   R73*ter*-TC-1 612
Rule 74: Amicus Curiae 614

TRIAL CHAMBERS DECISIONS 614

Rule 74: *Amicus Curiae* – Criterion for Leave to Call 614
   R74-TC-1 614
Rule 74: *Amicus Curiae* – Amicus Counsel 615
   R74-TC-2 615

APPEALS CHAMBER DECISIONS 616

Rule 74: *Amicus Curiae* – Role and Appointment 616
   R74-AC-1 616
Rule 74: *Amicus Curiae* – Invitation by a Chamber 620
   R74-AC-2 620
Rule 74*bis*: Medical Examination of the Accused 621

TRIAL CHAMBER DECISIONS 621

Rule 74*bis*: Medical Examination of the Accused – Fitness to Plead and Stand Trial 621

R74*bis*-TC-1	621
R74*bis*-TC-2	622
Rule 74*bis*(C): Medical Examination of the Accused – Initial Appearance – Situation Where the Accused Is Unfit to Trial and Plea – Inhumane and Degrading Treatment	623
R74*bis*-TC-3	623
Rule 75: Measures for the Protection of Victims and Witnesses	627

TRIAL CHAMBERS DECISIONS 628

Rule 75(A): Protective Measures for Witnesses – Discretion of the Court	628
R75-TC-1	629
Rule 75(A): Protective Measures for Witnesses – Binding Authority	629
R75-TC-2	629
Rule 75(B): Protective Measures for Witnesses – Screen from Public and Prohibition of Photography	629
R75-TC-3	629
Rule 75(B): Protective Measures for Witnesses – Voice Distortion and Closed Circuit Television	631
R75-TC-4	631
Rule 75(F): Protective Measures for Witnesses – Application in Other Cases	632
R75-TC-5	632
Rule 75(G): Protective Measures for Witnesses – Applicability of the Rule	633
R75-TC-6	633
Rule 75(I): Protective Measures for Witnesses – Modification of Protective Measures – Change in Circumstances	634
R75-TC-7	634

APPEALS CHAMBER DECISIONS 634

Rule 75: Protective Measures for Witnesses – Balance with the Rights of the Defence	634
R75-AC-1	634
Rule 75: Protective Measures for Witnesses – Reinforcement of Pre-Existing Interim Measures and Right to Appeal	635
R75-AC-2	635
Rule 77: Contempt of the Special Court	636

CONTENTS

TRIAL CHAMBERS DECISIONS 638

**Rule 77: Contempt of Court – Legal Basis for Contempt
Proceedings – Inherent Power of the Court** 638
R77-TC-1 638
R77-TC-2 638
Rule 77(A): Contempt of Court – *Mens Rea* 640
R77-TC-3 640
**Rule 77(A): Contempt of Court – Violation of Witness
Protection – No Sanction** 643
R77-TC-4 643
**Rule 77(A): Contempt of Court – Public Comments on
Pending Issues** 643
R77-TC-5 643
**Rule 77(A): Contempt of Court – Unfounded Suggestion of
Abuse of Process** 644
R77-TC-6 644
**Rule 77(C)(iii): Contempt of Court – Disclosure of the Report
of the Independent Counsel** 644
R77-TC-7 644
R77-TC-8 645
**Rule 77(C)(iii): Contempt of Court – Independent
Proceedings – Counsel Testimony** 646
R77-TC-9 646
**Rule 77(C)(iii): Contempt of Court – Proceedings – Functions
of the Independent Counsel** 647
R77-TC-10 647
**Rule 77(D): Contempt of Court – Proceedings – Assignment to
a Single Judge** 648
R77-TC-11 648
Rule 77(E): Contempt of Court – Proceedings – *Locus Standi* 649
R77-TC-12 649
**Rule 77(E): Contempt of Court – Proceedings – Applicability
of the Rules of Procedure and Evidence to Contempt
Proceedings** 650
R77-TC-13 650
**Rule 77(E): Contempt of Court – Proceedings – Standards of
Proof** 651
R77-TC-14 651
**Rule 77(G): Contempt of Court – Sentence – Applicable
Criteria** 653
R77-TC-15 653

Rule 77(G): Contempt of Court – Sentence – Criminal Discharge 654
R77-TC-16 654

APPEALS CHAMBER DECISIONS 656

Rule 77: Contempt of Court – Generalities 656
R77-AC-1 656
Rule 77: Contempt of Court – Proceedings – *Locus Standi* 658
R77-AC-2 658
R77-AC-3 658
Rule 77(C): Contempt of Court – Procedure 659
R77-AC-4 659
Rule 77(J): Contempt of Court – Appeal 661
R77-AC-5 661

DECISIONS OF THE PRESIDENT 661

Rule 77(D): Contempt of Court – Proceedings – Assignment of Contempt Cases to a Trial Chamber or to a Single Judge – Power of the President 661
R77-AC-6 661
Rule 78: Open Sessions 663

TRIAL CHAMBERS DECISIONS 663

Rule 78: Open Sessions – Publicity – Submissions and Decisions 663
R78-TC-1 664
R78-TC-2 666
Rule 79: Closed Sessions 666

TRIAL CHAMBERS DECISIONS 666

Rule 79: Closed Sessions – Authority of the Trial Chamber to Order 666
R79-TC-1 666
Rule 79: Closed Sessions – Applicable Standards 667
R79-TC-2 667
R79-TC-3 667
R79-TC-4 669
R79-TC-5 670

Rule 79: Closed Sessions – Privilege and Immunities of Witness 671
   R79-TC-6 671
   R79-TC-7 671
Rule 79: Closed Sessions – Attendance by Investigators 673
   R79-TC-8 673
Rule 79(B): Closed Sessions – Obligation to Make Public the Reasons for Ordering a Closed Session 675
   R79-TC-9 675
Rule 79(C): Closed Sessions – Attendance by Court Monitors 676
   R79-TC-10 676
Rule 81: Records of Proceedings and Preservation of Evidence 678

TRIAL CHAMBER DECISIONS 678

Rule 81(B): Records of Proceedings – Exclusion from Records 678
   R81-TC-1 678
   R81-TC-2 678
Rule 81(B): Records of Proceedings – Public Decision on Confidential Submissions 679
   R81-TC-3 679
Rule 81(D): Records of Proceedings – Photography, Video – and Audio-Recording – Authorization 679
   R81-TC-4 679
   R81-TC-5 680
   R81-TC-6 681
   R81-TC-7 681
   R81-TC-8 681
Rule 81(D): Records of Proceedings – Photography, Video – and Audio-Recording – Disclosure of Video and Audio Records of the Accused 682
   R81-TC-9 682
Rule 82: Joint and Separate Trials 684

TRIAL CHAMBERS DECISIONS 684

Rule 82(A): Joint Trial – Rights of the Accused 684
   R82-TC-1 684
   R82-TC-2 685
Rule 85: Presentation of Evidence 686

TRIAL CHAMBER DECISIONS 686

Rule 85(A): Presentation of Evidence – Evidence Ordered by the Trial Chamber 686
   R85-TC-1 686
   R85-TC-2 687
   R85-TC-3 687
Rule 85(B): Presentation of Evidence – Examination-in-Chief – Prohibition of Leading Questions 689
   R85-TC-4 689
Rule 85(B): Presentation of Evidence – Cross-Examination – Inconsistent Statements 691
   R85-TC-5 691
   R85-TC-6 694
Rule 85(B): Presentation of Evidence – Order to Re-Open Cross-Examination 695
   R85-TC-7 695
Rule 89: General Provisions 697

TRIAL CHAMBERS DECISIONS 697

Rule 89: Evidence – Assessment of Evidence 697
   R89-TC-1 697
Rule 89(B): Evidence – "Best Evidence" Rule 697
   R89-TC-2 697
Rule 89(B): Evidence – Balance Between Probative Value and Prejudicial Effect 698
   R89-TC-3 698
Rule 89(B): Evidence – Self-Serving Evidence – Circumstances of Obtaining 698
   R89-TC-4 698
Rule 89(C): Evidence – Chamber's Discretion on Admissibility – Difference Admissibility / Reliability 699
   R89-TC-5 699
   R89-TC-6 700
   R89-TC-7 700
   R89-TC-8 700
Rule 89(C): Evidence – Relevance 701
   R89-TC-9 701
Rule 89(C): Evidence – Hearsay Evidence 702
   R89-TC-10 702
   R89-TC-11 703

Rule 89(C): Evidence – Reliability of Unauthenticated Documents 703
    R89-TC-12 703
Rule 89(C): Evidence – Site Visit 705
    R89-TC-13 705
    R89-TC-14 706
Rule 89(C): Evidence – Maps 709
    R89-TC-15 709
R89(C): Evidence – Identification of Signature – Lay Witness 709
    R89-TC-16 709
Rule 89(C): Evidence – Assessment of Reliability – Witness Statements 710
    R89-TC-17 710

APPEALS CHAMBER DECISIONS 713

Rule 89: Evidence – Provisions of Rule 89 Are Not Restrictive 713
    R89-AC-1 713
Rule 89: Evidence – Non Disputed Facts 714
    R89-AC-2 714
Rule 89: Evidence – Reliability of Unauthenticated Documents 714
    R89-AC-3 714
Rule 89(C): Evidence – Difference Admissibility/Reliability 715
    R89-AC-4 715
Rule 90: Testimony of Witnesses 717

TRIAL CHAMBERS DECISIONS 718

Rule 90: Testimony of Witnesses – Assessment of Credibility – Material Inconsistencies With Written Statements 718
    R90-TC-1 718
Rule 90(C): Testimony of Witnesses – Child Witnesses – Special Protective Measures 718
    R90-TC-2 718
    R90-TC-3 719
Rule 90(D): Testimony of Witnesses – Former Exposure to Images or Audio Recordings 720
    R90-TC-4 720
Rule 90(D): Testimony of Witnesses – Contact Between Witnesses During Testimony 720
    R90-TC-5 720

Rule 90(F): Testimony of Witnesses – Chamber's Control on
Witness Examination – Service of Witness Statements to the
Chamber Prior to their Appearance 723
    R90-TC-6 723
Rule 90(F): Testimony of Witnesses – Chamber's Control on
Witness Examination – Scope of Cross-Examination –
Rule 90(H) of the ICTR Rules 724
    R90-TC-7 724
Rule 90(F): Testimony of Witnesses – Scope of Cross-
Examination – Calling Investigators Who Took Down
Witness Statements 726
    R90-TC-8 726
    R90-TC-9 730
Rule 90(F): Testimony of Witnesses – Motion to Recall
Witness – Defence Counsel Failure to Cross-Examine
(granted) 731
    R90-TC-10 731
Rule 92*bis*: Alternative Proof of Facts 734

TRIAL CHAMBERS DECISIONS 734

Rule 92*bis*: Alternative Proof of Facts – Protecting Interests
of Victims and Witnesses 734
    R92*bis*-TC-1 734
Rule 92*bis*: Alternative Proof of Facts – Admissibility of
Evidence – Applicable Criteria 735
    R92*bis*-TC-2 735
Rule 92*bis*: Alternative Proof of Facts – Admissibility of
Documents – Identification of Relevant Information 738
    R92*bis*-TC-3 738
Rule 92*bis*: Alternative Proof of Facts – Admissibility of
Documents – Legibility of Documents 739
    R92*bis*-TC-4 739
Rule 92*bis*: Alternative Proof of Facts – Admissibility of
Transcripts of Previous Testimony in Place of Examination-
in-Chief 739
    R92*bis*-TC-5 739

APPEALS CHAMBER DECISIONS 740

Rule 92*bis*: Alternative Proof of Facts – Admissibility of
Evidence – Comparison with Rule 94 740
    R92*bis*-AC-1 740
Rule 94: Judicial Notice 742

CONTENTS

TRIAL CHAMBERS DECISIONS 742

Rule 94: Judicial Notice – General Principles 742
R94-TC-1 742
Rule 94: Judicial Notice – Purpose 744
R94-TC-2 744
Rule 94: Judicial Notice – Judicially Noticeable Facts 745
R94-TC-3 745
Rule 94: Judicial Notice – "Facts of Common Knowledge" 745
R94-TC-4 745

APPEALS CHAMBER DECISIONS 747

Rule 94: Judicial Notice – Purpose 747
R94-AC-1 747
Rule 94: Judicial Notice – "Facts of Common Knowledge" 748
R94-AC-2 748
Rule 94: Judicial Notice – Facts of Common Knowledge Cannot Be Challenged 750
R94-AC-3 750
Rule 94: Judicial Notice – Official Documents 751
R94-AC-4 751
Rule 94*bis*: Testimony of Expert Witnesses 752

TRIAL CHAMBERS DECISIONS 752

Rule 94*bis*: Expert Witnesses – Definition 752
R94*bis*-TC-1 752
R94*bis*-TC-2 753
Rule 94*bis*: Expert Witness – Scope of Testimony 755
R94*bis*-TC-3 755
Rule 94*bis*: Expert Witness – Protective Measures 756
R94*bis*-TC-4 756
Rule 94*bis*(A): Expert Witness – Timely Disclosure of Statement 757
R94*bis*-TC-5 757
Rule 94*bis*(A): Expert Witness – Disclosure of the Expert's Curriculum Vitae 758
R94*bis*-TC-6 758
Rule 94*bis*(B): Expert Witness – Purpose of the Notice 758
R94*bis*-TC-7 758
Rule 95: Exclusion of Evidence 760

TRIAL CHAMBERS DECISIONS ... 760

Rule 95: Exclusion of Evidence – Hearsay Evidence ... 760
R95-TC-1 ... 760
Rule 98: Motion for Judgment of Acquittal ... 761

TRIAL CHAMBERS DECISIONS ... 761

Rule 98: Motion for Judgment of Acquittal – Applicable Standard ... 761
R98-TC-1 ... 761
Rule 98: Motion for Judgment of Acquittal – Procedure – Filing of Submissions ... 766
R98-TC-2 ... 766
R98-TC-3 ... 766
Rule 104: Forfeiture of Property ... 768

TRIAL CHAMBERS DECISIONS ... 768

Rule 104(C): Forfeiture of Property – Freeze of Assets During Arrest – Order to the Authorities of Sierra Leone ... 768
R104-TC-1 ... 768
Rule 104(C): Forfeiture of Property – Freeze of Assets During Arrest – Request to Third States ... 769
R104-TC-2 ... 769
Rule 104(C): Forfeiture of Property – Order to Freeze of Assets – Applicable Criteria ... 769
R104-TC-3 ... 769
Rule 108: Notice of Appeal ... 775

APPEALS CHAMBER DECISIONS ... 775

Rule 108: Notice of Appeal – Time Limits for Filing ... 775
R108-AC-1 ... 775
R108-AC-2 ... 776
R108-AC-3 ... 777
Rules 108(C): Notice of Appeal – Grounds of Appeal Are to Be Clearly Formulated ... 779
R108-AC-3 ... 779
R108-AC-4 ... 779
Rule 110: Record on Appeal ... 781

APPEALS CHAMBER DECISIONS 781

Rule 110: Record on Appeal – Contents – Compilation by the
 Registrar 781
 R110-AC-1 781
Rule 113: Submissions in Reply 782

APPEALS CHAMBER DECISIONS 782

Rule 113: Submissions in Reply – No Right for Further
 Submissions 782
 R113-AC-1 782
Rule 115: Additional Evidence 784

APPEALS CHAMBER DECISIONS 784

Rule 115: Additional Evidence – New Relief Sought for the
 First Time in Appeal – Admission in Certain
 Circumstances 784
 R115-AC-1 784
Rule 116: Extension of Time Limits 785

APPEALS CHAMBER DECISIONS 785

Rule 116: Extension of Time Limit – "Good Cause" 785
 R116-AC-1 785
Rule 117: Expedited Procedure 786

APPEALS CHAMBER DECISIONS 786

Rule 117: Expedited Procedure – Time Limits 786
 R117-AC-1 786
Rule 117: Expedited Procedure – Reasons to Order Full
 Bench 787
 R117-AC-2 787

INDEX

The present Index refers to QRN of the abstracts.

Acquittal (Motion for Judgement of -):
R98-TC-1 to R98-TC-3   761, 766
African Charter of Human Rights:
S2-TC-2, S2-TC-6, S3-TC-6   28, 31, 39
Alibi: R67-TC-1   457
Amicus Curiae: R74-TC-1, R74-AC-1,
R74-AC-2   614, 616, 620
Amnesty: S1-AC-9, S8-AC-2, S10-AC-1,
S10-AC-2   23, 77, 82, 84
Appeal
  Appellate Proceedings: S20-AC-1,
  S20-AC-5, R108-AC-1 to R108-AC-2,
  R110-AC-1, R113-AC-1, R115-AC-1,
  R116-AC-1, R117-AC-1, R117-AC-2
  155, 161, 775, 776, 781, 782, 784,
  785, 786, 787
  Error of Fact: S20-AC-6   165
  Grounds of -: S20-AC-3, S20-AC-5,
  R73-TC-37, R108-AC-3, R108-AC-4
  159, 161, 570, 777, 779
  Powers of the Appeals Chamber:
  S20-AC-3, S20-AC-4, S20-AC-6,
  S20-AC-7, R65-AC-7   159-160,
  165, 166, 421
  Right to -: S20-AC-2, R46-TC-4,
  R65-AC-5, R65-AC-6, R73-TC-18 to
  R73-TC-46, R73-AC-3 to R73-AC-9,
  R75-AC-2, R77-AC-5   156, 285, 419,
  421, 553-577, 579-587, 635, 661
Armed Conflict: S2-AC-3, S3-TC-1,
S3-TC-5, S3-AC-1, S4-AC-1, S4-AC-2,
S4-AC-4, S4-AC-5, S72-TC-4,
R89-AC-2, R94-AC-2   45, 33, 37,
40, 48, 49, 51, 52, 509, 714, 748

Bail: R65-TC-1 to R65-TC-18, R65-AC-1
to R65-AC-12, R65-P-1, R65-P-2,
R89-AC-1   397-415, 416-425, 427, 713
Burden of Proof: S13-AC-1, S17-TC-7,
S17-TC-8, R50-TC-5, R65-TC-2 to
R65-TC-4, R65-AC-3, R67-TC-2,
R68-TC-4 to R68-TC-6, R69-TC-13,
R69-TC-14, R90-TC-8, R94-AC-3   90,
120, 328, 399-404, 418, 457, 461-465,
486, 488, 726, 750

Child Soldiers: S1-AC-6, S4-TC-1,
S4-AC-1 to S4-AC-3, S4-AC-5,
R50-AC-2, R69-TC-7   19, 47-50, 52,
342, 480
Closed Sessions: R75-TC-6, R79-TC-1 to
R79-TC-10   633, 666-676
Collective Punishment: S3-TC-4,
R47-TC-12   36, 303
Command Responsibility: S6-TC-4,
S6-TC-5, S20-TC-3, R47-TC-3,
R47-TC-6, R47-TC-8, R50-AC-1,
R72-TC-16   65, 67, 150, 291, 295, 299,
340, 520
Contempt: S19-TC-1 to S19-TC-5,
R19-P-2, R27-TC-3, R77-TC-1 to
R77-TC-16, R77-AC-1 to R77-AC-5,
R77-P-1   145-148, 208, 218, 638-654,
656-661
Counsel
  Assignment: R44-TC-1, R44-TC-2,
  R45-TC-14, R45-AC-5, R45-AC-6
  241, 242, 269, 276, 280
  Code of Conduct for -: R44-TC-8
  246
  **Directive on the Assignment of
  Defence -:** S1-AC-8, R44-TC-7   20,
  246
  Duty Counsel: R44-TC-3, R44-TC-4
  242
  Eligibility: R45-TC-5 to R45-TC-7,
  R45-AC-1, R45-AC-2   257-260, 271,
  274
  Misconduct: R46-TC-1 to R46-TC-4
  284-285
  Reassignment: S1-AC-8, R45-TC-13,
  R45-AC-1, R45-AC-4, R74-TC-2   20,
  269, 271, 276, 615
  Replacement: R45-TC-8   261
  Standby -: R44-TC-5   243
  Withdrawal: R44-TC-9, R44-TC-10,
  R45-TC-9 to R45-TC-14, R45-AC-3,
  R60-TC-3   247, 248, 267-269, 275,
  375
Creation of the Special Court:
S1-TC-1, S1-TC-2, S1-AC-2, S8-TC-1,
S8-AC-1, S17-AC-6   1, 2, 13, 73, 76,
139
Crimes against Humanity: S2-TC-1,
S2-TC-3 to S2-TC-6   26, 29-31
Cruel Treatment: S3-TC-3   35

870 INDEX

Death of the Accused: R51-TC-1   345
Defence Office: S17-AC-1, R31-TC-1, R31-AC-1, R44-TC-6, R45-TC-1 to R45-TC-8, R45-TC-10, R45-AC-1, R45-AC-2, R45-AC-5   133, 220, 223, 245, 252-261, 262, 271, 274, 276
Defence Team: R44-TC-6, R44-TC-11, R79-TC-8   245, 249, 673
Detention
  Conditions: R64-TC-1 to R64-TC-1, R64-P-2 to R64-P-7   386-387, 390-395
  - on Remand: R40bis-TC-3, R40bis-TC-4, R57-P-1, R64-TC-3, R64-P-1, R64-P-4   238, 240, 368, 387, 388, 392
  Rules of -: R64-P-5 to R64-P-7   393-395
Disclosure: R48-TC-7, R48-TC-8, R53-TC-3 to R53-TC-5, R66-TC-1 to R66-TC-18, R67-TC-1 to R67-TC-3, R69-TC-3, R69-TC-17 to R69-TC-21, R70-TC-1 to R70-TC-5   320, 353-354, 431-453, 457-458, 473, 492-495, 501-505
  Exculpatory Evidence: R66-TC-1, R67-TC-3, R68-TC-1 to R68-TC-10   431, 458, 459-468

Earliest Opportunity: R5-TC-1, R5-TC-2, R5-AC-1   171, 172, 173
Equality of Arms: S15-TC-4, S17-TC-4, S17-TC-5, R50-TC-5, R50-TC-6, R69-TC-9, R73bis-TC-10, R73bis-TC-11, R73bis-TC-14, R74-AC-1, R79-TC-8   110, 116, 807, 328, 332, 482, 597, 600, 603, 616, 667
Estoppel: R45bis-AC-2, R48-TC-9, R104-TC-3   282, 321, 769
Evidence
  Admissibility: R66-TC-17, R89-TC-4 to R89-TC-12, R89-AC-4, R92bis-TC-1 to R92bis-TC-5, R92bis-AC-1   451, 698-703, 715, 734-739, 740
  Documentary -: R66-TC-18, R85-TC-1, R89-TC-15, R89-TC-16, R89-AC-3, R92bis-TC-2 to R92bis-TC-5   453, 686, 709, 709, 714, 735-739
  Exclusion: R95-TC-1   760
  Hearsay -: R65-AC-2, R77-AC-4, R89-TC-6, R89-TC-10 to R89-TC-12, R89-AC-4, R95-TC-1   418, 659, 700, 702-703, 715, 760
  Presentation: R85-TC-1 to R85-TC-7, R90-TC-6 to R90-TC-10   686-695, 723-731
  Reliability: R85-TC-5, R85-TC-6, R89-TC-1 to R89-TC-12, R89-TC-17,

   R89-AC-3, R89-AC-4, R90-TC-1, R90-TC-4, R90-TC-5   691, 694, 697-703, 710, 714, 715, 718, 720, 720
  Site Visit: R89-TC-13, R89-TC-14   705, 706
  Testimonial -: S15-TC-4, R66-TC-4, R73bis-TC-14, R85-TC-3, R90-TC-1, R90-TC-4 to R90-TC-10   110, 436, 603, 687, 718, 720-731
Exceptional Circumstances / Good Cause: R7bis-TC-2 to R7bis-TC-6, R7bis-TC-8, R7bis-TC-12, R44-TC-8, R44-TC-10, R45-TC-8, R45-TC-11, R45-TC-12, R45-AC-3, R48-TC-8, R65-TC-1, R65-P-2, R66-TC-1, R69-TC-1, R69-TC-5, R69-TC-13, R69-TC-14, R69-TC-22, R72-TC-1, R72-TC-2, R72bis-TC-2, R73-TC-18, R73-TC-21 to R73-TC-32, R73-TC-35, R73bis-TC-10 to R73bis-TC-13, R85-TC-7, R90-TC-10, R94bis-TC-4, R116-AC-1   183-185, 186, 189, 246, 248, 261, 264, 265, 275, 320, 397, 427, 431, 469, 475, 486, 488, 496, 507, 508, 540, 553, 556-567, 569, 597-603, 695, 731, 756, 785

Forced Marriage: S2-TC-4, S2-TC-5, R50-TC-5, R94bis-TC-2   30, 31, 328, 753

Guidance from Other International Tribunals: S6-TC-5, S20-TC-1 to S20-TC-8, S20-AC-8, S20-AC-9   67, 149-155, 167, 167
Guilty Plea: S1-TC-5, S17-AC-3, S19-TC-1, S19-TC-3, R61-AC-1, R62-TC-1, R77-TC-16   8, 135, 145, 147, 383, 384, 654

Habeas Corpus: R65-TC-18, R73-TC-4   415, 544

Immunity: S1-AC-2, S6-AC-1 to S6-AC-3, S17-TC-4, R45-TC-4, R72-AC-1, R72-AC-5, R73-AC-1, R74-AC-1, R79-TC-6, R79-TC-7   13, 68, 71, 116, 255, 527, 536, 578, 618, 671
Indictment
  Amendment: S9-TC-2, R47-TC-6, R48-TC-6, R48-AC-1, R50-TC-1 to R50-TC-12, R50-AC-1 to R50-AC-5, R73-TC-43, R73-TC-44   80, 295, 319, 325, 326-339, 340-344, 574, 575
  Form: R47-TC-1, R47-TC-12, R47-AC-2   288, 303, 308

Review: R47-TC-1, R47-TC-13 to R47-TC-17, R47-AC-1, R50-TC-12, R50-AC-3   288, 303-307, 307, 339, 343
Vagueness: R47-TC-2 to R47-TC-11, R47-AC-3   290-302, 310
Inhumane and Degrading Treatment: S2-TC-2, S2-TC-6, S3-TC-6, R74*bis*-TC-3   28, 31, 30, 623
Initial Appearance: R61-TC-1 to R61-TC-6, R72-AC-1, R73-AC-1, R74*bis*-TC-1 to R74*bis*-TC-3   377-382, 527, 578, 621-623
   Further Appearance: R50-TC-10, R50-TC-11, R50-AC-5, R61-AC-1   336, 338, 344, 383
Individual Responsibility: S4-AC-5, S6-TC-1 to S6-TC-4, R47-TC-6, R48-TC-1   52, 63-65, 295, 311
Interests of Justice: S17-TC-13, S17-TC-15, R44-TC-1, R44-TC-2, R44-TC-5, R48-TC-2 to R48-TC-5, R50-TC-2, R50-TC-5, R50-TC-6, R50-AC-1, R73-TC-43, R73*bis*-TC-10 to R73*bis*-TC-13   129, 130, 241, 242, 243, 312-317, 327, 328, 332, 340, 574, 597-603
International Criminal Court (ICC): S1-TC-3, S1-AC-2, S4-TC-1, S4-AC-5, S6-AC-1, S6-AC-3, S17-TC-2, S17-TC-4, S20-TC-7, R73-AC-5   4, 13, 47, 52, 68, 71, 112, 116, 152, 583
International Committee of the Red Cross (ICRC): S3-TC-4, S3-TC-5, R64-TC-1   36, 37, 386

Joinder: R48-TC-1 to R48-TC-10, R48-AC-1, R66-TC-12, R82-TC-1, R82-TC-2   311-324, 325, 445, 684, 685
Joint Criminal Enterprise: S6-TC-3, R47-TC-6, R47-TC-9 to R47-TC-11, R48-TC-1, R48-TC-3, R48-TC-4   65, 295, 300-302, 311, 312, 316
Judge
   Designated -: R28-TC-1, R40*bis*-TC-1, R40*bis*-TC-2   219, 236, 237
   Disqualification: R15-AC-1, R15-AC-2, R23-AC-1   197, 200, 210
   Impartiality: S13-TC-1, R15-AC-1, R15-AC-2   89, 197, 200
   Independence: S13-AC-1, R26*bis*-TC-1 to R26*bis*-TC-3, R72-AC-4   90, 211-212, 533
Judicial Economy: R26*bis*-TC-4, R48-TC-3, R48-TC-5, R73-TC-43, R90-TC-10, R94-TC-3, R94-AC-1   213, 312, 317, 574, 731, 745, 747

Judicial Notice: S2-AC-3, R94-TC-1 to R94-TC-4, R94-AC-1 to R94-AC-4   45, 742-745, 747-751
Jurisdiction: R72-TC-9 to R72-TC-20, R72-AC-2, R72-AC-3, R72-AC-5   515-525, 528, 529, 536
   Inherent -: S1-TC-4, S1-AC-7, S1-AC-8, R45-TC-4, R73-TC-18, R73-AC-8, R77-TC-1, R77-TC-2   5, 19, 20, 255, 553, 586, 638, 638
   Ratione Loci: S1-AC-6   19
   Ratione Materiae: S3-AC-1, S3-AC-2, S4-AC-1, S4-AC-2, S4-AC-5, S10-AC-2   40, 45, 48, 49, 52, 84
   Ratione Personae: S6-AC-1, S6-AC-2   68, 71

Locus Standi: R58-TC-2, R77-TC-12, R77-AC-2, R77-AC-3   370, 649, 658
Lomé Agreement: S4-AC-4, S8-AC-2, S10-AC-1, S10-AC-2   51, 77, 82, 84

Motions: R73-TC-1 to R73-TC-18, R73-AC-1   542-553, 578
Murder: S3-TC-2   34

Non Bis in Idem: S9-TC-1, S9-TC-2   79, 80
Nullum Crimen: S1-TC-3, S1-AC-4, S1-AC-5, S4-AC-5, S20-TC-7, R47-TC-1   4, 17, 52, 152, 288

Opinions (Concurring/Dissenting): S18-AC-1, R73-TC-30 to R73-TC-32, R73-TC-38, R73-TC-39, R73-AC-9   142, 566-567, 571, 572, 587
Outrages upon Personal Dignity: S3-TC-6   39

Pillage: S3-TC-7   40
Practice Directions: R33-TC-4 to R33-TC-6   228-229
Preliminary Motions: R72-TC-1 to R72-TC-20, R72-AC-1 to R72-AC-6   507-525, 527-537
President of the Special Court: S1-AC-8, R19-TC-1, R19-P-1, R19-P-2, R21-P-1, R27-TC-1, R27-TC-2, R33-TC-2, R45-AC-5, R64-P-5, R77-P-1   20, 207, 208, 209, 216, 217, 227, 276, 393, 661
Pre-Trial / Pre-Defence Conference: R73*bis*-TC-1 to R73*bis*-TC-24, R73*ter*-TC-1   590-610, 612
Primacy: S1-TC-5, S8-TC-1, S8-AC-1, S8-AC-2, R58-TC-2   8, 73, 76, 77, 370
Property of the Accused: R104-TC-1 to R104-TC-3   768-769

Prosecution: S15-TC-1 to S15-TC-3 106-108
Prosecutor: R37-TC-1   231
Purposive Interpretation: S14-TC-2, S14-TC-3, S14-AC-4, S14-AC-5, R50-AC-3, R73-TC-17   100, 101, 103, 104, 343, 552

Reasons of Decisions: S18-P-1, R65bis-TC-1, R65bis-TC-1   143, 429
Reconsideration: R73-TC-5, R73-TC-18, R73-TC-40, R73-AC-3 to R73-AC-5   545, 553, 572, 579-582
Registrar: S17-AC-1, R19-TC-1, R27-TC-1, R27-TC-2, R31-AC-1, R33-TC-1 to R33-TC-6, R33-AC-1, R45-TC-3, R45-TC-4, R45-AC-1, R64-TC-2, R64-P-1, R64-P-2, R64-P-4 to R64-P-7   133, 207, 216, 217, 223-229, 229, 254, 255, 271, 386, 388, 390, 392-395
Res Judicata: R7-TC-2, R72bis-TC-2, R73-TC-45, R73-AC-3   179, 540, 576, 579
Rights of the Accused (Generalities): S17-TC-1, S17-AC-1, S17-AC-3, R6-TC-1, R75-AC-1   112, 133, 135, 175, 634
  Abuse of Process: S17-AC-2, R72-TC-6, R72-TC-7, R73-TC-45, R77-TC-6   134, 511, 514, 576, 644
  Fair Trial: S1-TC-6, S1-AC-9, S17-TC-2, S17-TC-3, S17-TC-6, R26bis-TC-4, R48-TC-3, R48-TC-4, R50-TC-3, R50-TC-4, R50-TC-12, R65-P-2, R66-TC-1 to R66-TC-3, R69-TC-2, R70-TC-4, R73-TC-17   10, 23, 112, 115, 119, 213, 312, 316, 327, 328, 339, 427, 431-435, 472, 504, 552
  Legal Assistance: S17-TC-15 to S17-TC-17, S17-AC-7, R45bis-TC-1   130-131, 140, 281
  Presumption of Innocence: S1-TC-5, S17-TC-7, S17-TC-8, S17-TC-18, S17-AC-5, R64-P-6, R65-TC-1, R65-TC-6, R65-TC-9   8, 120, 120, 132, 138, 394, 397, 405, 409
  Public Hearing: S17-AC-4, R69-TC-22, R69-TC-23, R78-TC-1, R78-TC-2   136, 496, 496, 663, 664
  Self-Representation: S17-TC-12 to S17-TC-16, R45bis-AC-1, R45bis-AC-2   124-131, 281, 282
  Time and Facilities for the Preparation of the Defence: S17-TC-9, S17-TC-10, R73bis-TC-3, R73bis-TC-4, R82-TC-1, R82-TC-2   121, 123, 592, 592, 684, 685

Trial Without Undue Delay: S17-TC-11, S17-AC-6, R7-TC-3 to R7-TC-5, R26bis-TC-1, R26bis-TC-4, R65-P-2   124, 139, 180-181, 211, 213, 427

Sentencing Practice (Generalities): S19-TC-1, R77-TC-15, R77-TC-16   145, 653, 654
  Individual Circumstances: S19-TC-2 to S19-TC-4   146-147
  Mitigating Circumstances: S19-TC-5, R77-TC-15   148, 653
Sexual Violence: S2-TC-3 to S2-TC-6, R50-TC-5, R69-TC-6, R75-TC-4   29-31, 328, 478, 631
Sierra Leonean Law: S1-TC-1, S1-TC-5, S1-AC-3, S1-AC-9, S8-TC-1, S8-AC-1, S14-AC-2, S14-AC-3, S20-AC-2, R8-TC-1, R54-TC-2, R65-P-2   1, 8, 16, 23, 73, 76, 102, 103, 156, 193, 355, 427
State Cooperation: R8-TC-1, R8-TC-2, R39-TC-1, R53-TC-1, R53-TC-2, R54-TC-2, R55-TC-1, R56-TC-1 to R56-TC-3, R57-TC-1, R58-TC-1, R58-TC-2, R59-TC-1, R65-TC-16, R65-TC-17, R65-AC-4   193-194, 232, 352-353, 355, 361, 364, 365, 367, 369, 370, 371, 413, 415, 419
Stay of Proceedings: R72-TC-7, R73-TC-43, R73-TC-44, R74bis-TC-3, R77-TC-8   514, 574, 575, 623, 645
Submissions: S20-AC-5, R3-TC-1, R3-AC-1, R26bis-TC-5, R73-TC-6 to R73-TC-15, R73-TC-41, R73-TC-42, R73-AC-2, R108-AC-3, R108-AC-4, R110-AC-1, R113-AC-1   161, 168-169, 215, 546-551, 573, 573, 579, 777, 779, 781, 782

Terrorism: S3-TC-5   37
Time
  Computation: R7-TC-1, R73-AC-9, R108-AC-3   178, 587, 777
  Extension of Time: R7bis-TC-1 to R7bis-TC-15, R116-AC-1   183, 190, 785
Torture: S2-TC-2, S2-TC-6, S3-TC-3, S3-TC-6, S17-TC-2, R74bis-TC-3   28, 31, 35, 39, 112, 623
Transfer: R40bis-TC-1, R40bis-TC-2, R57-P-1   236, 237, 268
Trial in the Absence of the Accused: R60-TC-1 to R60-TC-3, R60-AC-1, R61-TC-4   372, 375, 376, 381
Truth and Reconciliation Commission (TRC): S1-TC-5, S1-TC-6, S1-AC-9, S17-AC-3   8, 10, 23, 135

UN Charter: S1-AC-2, S8-AC-1, S10-AC-1   13, 76, 82

Victims and Witnesses (Protection)
  Child Witness: R90-TC-2, R90-TC-3, R94*bis*-TC-4   718, 719, 756
  Criteria: S17-TC-6, R69-TC-1 to R69-TC-25, R73-TC-36, R75-TC-1, R75-TC-7, R75-AC-1, R75-AC-2   119, 469, 475, 570, 628, 634, 634, 635
  Expert Witness: R94*bis*-TC-1 to R94*bis*-TC-7   752-758
  Other Cases: R75-TC-5   632

Protective Measures: R65-TC-10, R65-TC-11, R66-TC-10, R66-TC-11, R68-TC-10, R75-TC-3, R75-TC-4, R79-TC-4 to R79-TC-7, R81-TC-1, R81-TC-9, R92*bis*-TC-1   410, 410, 443, 444, 468, 629, 631, 669, 671, 678, 682, 734

Removal of Protective Measures: R69-TC-25, R75-TC-7   498, 634

Violations of Article 3 Common and Additional Protocol II: S3-TC-1 to S3-TC-7, S3-AC-1 to S3-AC-3, S4-AC-3 to S4-AC-5   33-40, 40-45, 50-52